Handbook of
The Sociology of Morality

Handbooks of Sociology and Social Research

Series Editor:
Howard B. Kaplan, *Texas A & M University, College Station, Texas*

HANDBOOK OF COMMUNITY MOVEMENTS AND LOCAL ORGANIZATIONS
Edited by Ram A. Cnaan and Carl Milofsky

HANDBOOK OF DISASTER RESEARCH
Edited by Havidán Rodríguez, Enrico L. Quarantelli, and Russell Dynes

HANDBOOK OF DRUG ABUSE PREVENTION
Theory, Science and Prevention
Edited by Zili Sloboda and William J. Bukoski

HANDBOOK OF THE LIFE COURSE
Edited by Jeylan T. Mortimer and Michael J. Shanahan

HANDBOOK OF POPULATION
Edited by Dudley L. Poston and Michael Micklin

HANDBOOK OF RELIGION AND SOCIAL INSTITUTIONS
Edited by Helen Rose Ebaugh

HANDBOOK OF SOCIAL PSYCHOLOGY
Edited by John Delamater

HANDBOOK OF SOCIOLOGICAL THEORY
Edited by Jonathan H. Turner

HANDBOOK OF THE SOCIOLOGY OF EDUCATION
Edited by Maureen T. Hallinan

HANDBOOK OF THE SOCIOLOGY OF EMOTIONS
Edited by Jan E. Stets and Jonathan H. Turner

HANDBOOK OF THE SOCIOLOGY OF GENDER
Edited by Janet Saltzman Chafetz

HANDBOOK OF THE SOCIOLOGY OF MENTAL HEALTH
Edited by Carol S. Aneshensel and Jo C. Phelan

HANDBOOK OF THE SOCIOLOGY OF THE MILITARY
Edited by Giuseppe Caforio

HANDBOOK OF SOCIAL MOVEMENTS ACROSS DISCIPLINES
Edited by Bert Klandermans and Conny Roggeband

HANDBOOK OF THE SOCIOLOGY OF RACIAL AND ETHNIC RELATIONS
Edited by Hernán Vera and Joseph R. Feagin

For more information about books in this series, please visit: www.springer.com/series/6055

Handbook of
The Sociology of Morality

Edited by

Steven Hitlin
University of Iowa
Department of Sociology
Iowa City, IA, USA

Stephen Vaisey
University of California, Berkeley
Department of Sociology
Berkeley, CA, USA

 Springer

Editors
Dr. Steven Hitlin
Department of Sociology
University of Iowa
W140 Seashore Hall
Iowa City, IA 52242-1401, USA
steven-hitlin@uiowa.edu

Dr. Stephen Vaisey
Department of Sociology
University of California
410 Barrows Hall #1980
Berkeley, CA 94720-1980, USA
vaisey@berkeley.edu

ISSN 1389-6903
ISBN 978-1-4419-6894-4 (hardcover)   ISBN 978-1-4419-6896-8 (eBook)
ISBN 978-1-4419-6895-1 (softcover)
DOI 10.1007/978-1-4419-6896-8
Springer New York Heidelberg Dordrecht London

Library of Congress Control Number: 2010934569

Springer is part of Springer Science+Business Media (www.springer.com)

Introduction: The Return of the Moral

In assembling the very first *Handbook of the Sociology of Morality*, Steven Hitlin and Stephen Vaisey have not only demonstrated remarkable intellectual vision, but also rendered a great service to the social sciences and to all those interested in broader normative and empirical thinking about morality and the state of societies. Here is why:

(1) The educated public has always been eager to learn about and reflect upon the moral fabric of their communities. Readers have often turned to the interpretive social sciences to inform their thinking – witness the popularity of books such as *The Lonely Crowd* and *Habits of the Heart*, two of the sociological best sellers of the last 50 years. They are now increasingly turning to popular books from psychology and philosophy to reflect on broad moral issues. These books often consider how individuals respond to ethical problems that are abstracted from their social context – e.g., the famous "trolley" dilemma. The sociological voice has been less present in these conversations than desirable. More than establishing disciplinary presence is at stake. Indeed, the various fields offer different ways of framing questions – a focus on an ahistorical human nature, boot strapping and individual will power, or on institutions and cultural repertoires (bolstering greater security and recognition). These frames have huge consequences for the thinking of policy makers and the general public about how to address social problems. Sociologists need to be at the table in order to shape conversations about how to create more successful societies – including more moral (fairer, less exploitative, more inclusive) ones.

(2) Hitlin and Vaisey recognized the need to orchestrate a broader substantive conversation within our discipline among experts of morality. Thus they had the foresight to create a much needed "shared context of recognition," with the goal of facilitating disciplinary exchange. They have brought together a wide range of scholars who vary in their theoretical approach to the study of morality (favoring the phenomenological, functionalist, rational choice, etc), their preferred method (as they are inspired by grounded theory, inductive or deductive approaches, idiographic or nomothetic ones, and so forth), the research techniques they favor (experimental, interview or survey based, ethnographic, historical, etc.), the analytical level they privilege (micro, meso, macro), and the disciplines and subfields with which they are in conversation (social psychology, criminology, philosophy, cultural sociology, religion, etc.). But this pluralism of approach goes even further: contributors belong to various academic generations. While some came of "academic age" at a time when Harvard's

Department of Social Relations remained an important point of reference in the social sciences at large (e.g., Teriakyian), many received their PhD only recently and are generally energizing (not to mention energetic) voices in the sociological study of morality. Because of this generational diversity, the new *Handbook for the Sociology of Morality* offers a window into current scholarship which reflects changes in taste and fashion over several decades, as well as a more or less implicit intergenerational dialogue.

But one might ponder: What does sociology bring to the table when it comes to the study of morality?

The centrality of morality to the sociological agenda is not debatable and remains remarkably strong, as this volume demonstrates. Not only was it a concern of our sociological forefathers – most predominantly Durkheim – but it continues to attract considerable interest, as various waves of neo-Durkheimians succeed one another, as exemplified by the work of Mary Douglas, Robert Bellah, Robert Wuthnow, Jeffrey Alexander, John Evans, Gabriel Abend, Mary Blair Loy, Paul Lichterman, and many others. Concern for morality is also central to scholarship inspired by research on small-group study as well as the phenomenological and the symbolic interaction traditions (witness the lasting influence of Berger and Luckman, the work of Anne Rawls, Gary Alan Fine, Robert Jackall, Boltanski and Thevenot, and others). Finally, the literature on morality continues to refract the influence of communitarian thinking and other conversations inspired by philosophy (e.g., in the work of Alan Wolfe and Craig Calhoun, among others).

Although psychologists have more often considered moral universalism (but see signal contributions in cultural psychology such as those of Hazel Markus and Richard Shweder), sociologists have made crucial contributions to the study of the diversity of morality across segments of various populations. They have documented moral visions shared by co-nationals, but also as it is instantiated in working class cultures, in variously gendered cultures, in religious cultures, and so forth. They have shown that individuals draw on available cultural repertoires to develop lives that they consider meaningful, to consider whether they are treating their partners, children, and coworkers fairly, as well as broader societal issues having to do with bioethics, abortion, homosexuality, bank bailouts, unemployment, and diversity – to consider what we owe to ourselves and others. We have also considered the implications of boundary work for understanding the causes for poverty, the culture of the poor, and attitudes toward the poor, including views concerning our responsibilities toward them.

But equally importantly, the sociology of morality has been central to our understanding of fundamental social processes, such as that of identity and group formation. We cannot understand deviance, scape goating, and group hierarchies without factoring in the cultural and often moral meanings on which they are predicated. The study of social movements generally requires a consideration of the moral causes to which they are committed, as does the study of politics, conflict, and self-formation. Moreover, morality is also central to the study of collective memory, reputations, group boundaries, and valuation processes, as exemplified in the work of Ezra Zuckerman, Bruce Carruthers, Wendy Espeland, Carol Heimer, Kieran Healy, Marion Fourcade, Mitchell Stevens, Viviana Zelizer, and others. As such, the study of morality remains at the very center of the sociological enterprise. And there is no sign of its importance diminishing.

Cultural sociology has had a particularly important role in identifying an intermediary analytical plane between traditional social psychology and the more structural dimensions of social life. To mention only a few examples, the work of Sharon Hays alerts gender researchers that available cultural repertoires form a crucial dimension for understanding gender inequality. Indeed, an understanding of cultural repertoires is an essential complement to labor market research on gender inequality, to symbolic interaction-derived work a la Arlie Hochschild, and to more social psychological work on biases, stereotypes and implicit association. The task of disentangling these analytical levels is far from complete, and much remains to be done in terms of raising awareness of the centrality of cultural repertoires as intermediary analytical levels essential, yet absent, in many causal models.

A complementary research agenda, also tied to the growth of cultural sociology and spreading rapidly, is the study of alternative and competing concepts of worth. Boundary work generated by intra and inter-individual conversations feeds into wider social and symbolic boundaries, into the boundaries drawn toward (for instance) the poor and immigrants, and has implications for policies aimed at dealing with poverty or other social issues, as illustrated in this volume by the paper by Steensland and others. Thus normativity and politics are deeply intertwined; the task of untangling these relationships and of understanding role of meaning making (and morality in particular) in political transformation and reproduction falls to us.

Against the background of such a proliferation of approaches and empirical research, it is clear that we stand to benefit enormously from the timely publication of this *Handbook*. By offering such a broad umbrella, Hitlin and Vaisey are sure to facilitate intellectual exchanges in very palpable ways and to contribute in defining an important research frontier ahead. May this *Handbook* find the readers it deserves.

Michèle Lamont

Contributors

Gabriel Abend, New York University, New York, NY, USA

Christopher D. Bader, Baylor University, Waco, TX, USA

Wayne Baker, University of Michigan, Ann Arbor, MI, USA

Mary Blair-Loy, Department of Sociology, University of California, CA, San Diego, USA

Raymond Boudon, Académie des sciences morales et politiques, Institut de France, Paris, France

Jeffrey S. Dill, Sociology Department, University of Virginia, Charlottesville, VA, USA

Matthew Feinberg, University of California, Berkeley, CA, USA

Roger Finke, Pennsylvania State University, University Park, PA, USA

Rengin Firat, University of Iowa, Iowa, IA, USA

Sabine Frerichs, Centre of Excellence, Foundations of European Law and Polity, University of Helsinki, Helsinki, Finland

Karen A. Hegtvedt, Emory University, Atlanta, GA, USA

Carol A. Heimer, American Bar Foundation, Northwestern University, Evanston, IL, USA

Steven Hitlin, Department of Sociology, University of Iowa, Iowa City, IA, USA

James Davison Hunter, Sociology Department, University of Virgina, Charlottesville, VA, USA

Gabriel Ignatow, Department of Sociology, University of North Texas, Denton, TX, USA

Kyle Irwin, Baylor University, Waco, TX, USA

Robert Jackall, Department of Antropology & Sociology, Williams College, Williamstown, MA, USA

Donald N. Levine, The University of Chicago, Chicago, IL, USA

Brian M. Lowe, Department of Sociology, State Univeristy of New York College at Oneonta, New York, NY, USA

Steven Lukes, Department of Sociology, New York University, New York, NY, USA

Rebekah P. Massengill, Princeton University, Princeton, NJ, USA

Douglas W. Maynard, University of Wisconsin-Madison, Madison, WI, USA

Chad Michael McPherson, University of Iowa, Iowa, IA, USA

Jal Mehta, Harvard University, Cambridge, MA, USA

Richard Münch, University of Bamberg, Bamberg, Germany

Christopher Powell, Department of Sociology, University of Manitoba, Winnipeg, Manitoba, Canada

Anne Warfield Rawls, Department of Sociology, Bentley University, Waltham, MA, USA

Amy Reynolds, Wheaton College, Wheaton, IL, USA

Leslie T. Roth, Department of Sociology, Duke University, Durham, NC, USA

Andrew Sayer, Department of Sociology, Lancaster University, Lancaster, United Kingdom

Heather L. Scheuerman, Emory University, Atlanta, GA, USA

Michael Schultz, University of California, Berkeley, CA, USA

Brent Simpson, University of South Carolina, Columbia, SC, USA

Brian Steensland, Department of Sociology, Indiana University, Bloomington, IN, USA

Jan E. Stets, Department of Sociology, University of California, Riverside, CA, USA

Edward A. Tiryakian, Duke University, Durham, NC, USA

Jonathan H. Turner, Department of Sociology, University of California, Riverside, CA, USA

Jason J. Turowetz, University of Wisconsin-Madison, Madison, WI, USA

Stephen Vaisey, Deparment of Sociology, University of California, Berkeley, CA, USA

Frederick F. Wherry, University of Michigan, Ann Arbor, MI, USA

Per-Olof H. Wikström, University of Cambridge, Cambridge, UK

Robb Willer, Department of Sociology, University of California, Berkeley, CA, USA

Christopher Winship, Harvard University, Cambridge, MA, USA

Table of Contents

Part I
Sociological Perspectives on Morality
("What Is It"?)

CHAPTER 1

Back to the Future

Reviving the Sociology of Morality

STEVEN HITLIN AND STEPHEN VAISEY

If we could travel back in time and speak with Emile Durkheim or Max Weber, they might be puzzled by this handbook, with its goal to renew "the sociology of morality." "Can there be," we imagine them asking, "a sociology that is *not* a sociology of morality?" Durkheim, after all, once claimed that

> [i]f there is one fact that history has irrefutably demonstrated, it is that the morality of each people is directly related to the social structure of the people practicing it...The connection is so intimate that, given the general character of the morality observed in a given society ... one can infer the nature of that society, the elements of its structure and the way it is organized (1961 [1925]:87)

Weber, from a different angle, also saw moral ("value-rational") action as a vital force in social life and argued that the analysis of such action was an integral part of the sociological method (1978:24–26). He described his most famous work, *The Protestant Ethic and the Spirit of Capitalism*, as a study of "the motives of moral action" (Weber 2003:231; see also Campbell 2006). For all their differences, Durkheim and Weber – along with many other classical theorists – would have considered the separation of the moral from the social unthinkable.

From our perch in the 21st century, however, it is clear that sociologists are capable of neglecting morality. Indeed, our discipline has successfully neglected it for some time (see Calhoun 1991, Campbell 2006, Lukes 1973, Smith 2003, Stivers 1996). This realization might be troubling under any circumstances, but it is especially disconcerting given the explosion of interest in morality happening in law (e.g., Sunstein 2004), neuroscience (e.g., Greene et al. 2004), philosophy (e.g., Knobe and Leiter 2007), and psychology (e.g., Haidt 2001, Hauser 2006). Researchers in these fields have even started to recognize that they need to think more deeply about the social dimensions of morality (e.g., Haidt and Graham 2009, Turiel 2002). Unfortunately, after neglecting morality for decades, we have too little systematic guidance in sociology to provide our peers.

How did sociology – a discipline in which cutting-edge research must begin by tipping its hat to the "founding fathers" – let one of its most important intellectual inheritances fall into such disrepair (see chapters in this volume by Boudon, Levine, Powell, and Tiryakian)? Sociology's gradual disengagement from morality is likely due to a wide range of factors,

S. Hitlin, S. Vaisey (eds.), *Handbook of the Sociology of Morality*,
Handbooks of Sociology and Social Research, DOI 10.1007/978-1-4419-6896-8_1,
© Springer Science+Business Media, LLC 2010

including political apprehension (Patterson 2002, Lamont and Small 2008), intellectual fashion (Campbell 1996) and methodological suspicion (Spates 1983, Vaisey 2009). Perhaps a future intellectual history of the discipline will address this question more thoroughly. But although we touch briefly on the past to provide necessary context, our goal for this chapter is to focus on the present and future of the sociology of morality. We have methodological and theoretical tools at our disposal today that Weber and Durkheim did not, and we hope to help stimulate their application to the oldest of questions about the human experience.

PERSISTENT OBSTACLES TO A SOCIOLOGY OF MORALITY

In this section, we summarize several ongoing challenges that can help explain why contemporary sociologists have not figured more centrally in the past decade's "morality renaissance". There are undoubtedly more reasons than what we consider here, but we outline what we see as key institutional and intellectual barriers to a fuller sociological engagement with the study of morality. As the existence of this handbook attests, sociologists are beginning to overcome these barriers, but a clearer and more accessible development of these ideas must continue if we are to influence this rapidly growing interdisciplinary conversation. Although we have learned – and continue to learn – a great deal about morality from the cognitive and behavioral sciences, many scholars are now beginning to realize that we cannot learn everything we want to know about morality using fMRI machines. Without due consideration of the social and cultural dimensions of human morality, our collective understanding of the subject will remain exceedingly limited.

Disciplinary Fragmentation

Classical sociology's broad focus on the complex interplay between social structures, historical shifts, moral codes, and value-rational action eventually yielded to a system of subdisciplinary specialization that made such intellectual breadth difficult to maintain. Rich – but vague – notions like "moral order" were necessarily subdivided into terms more tractable for empirical research. Though these divisions have deep historical and institutional origins, our primary concern is with their contemporary consequences. Today, those who study norms (e.g., Willer et al. 2009), values (e.g., Hitlin and Piliavin 2004, Baker 2005), codes (e.g., Lamont 1992), and "interaction orders" (Rawls 1987, Fine and Fields 2008) find themselves located far from one another in sociological research networks. Subdisciplines inevitably developed their own – occasionally parallel – approaches to particular dimensions of moral life. For example, many scholars now focus on the development of values, but they work in different domains, including (among others) the intergenerational transmission of attitudes (e.g., Glass et al. 1986), the shaping of religious values (e.g., Starks and Robinson 2007), cultural notions of specific values (e.g., Finke and Adamczyk 2008), or institutional influences on values (e.g., Jackall 1988). Although some big-picture, morally relevant concepts managed to retain their names, they eventually came to mean different things to different subfields. For example, depending on one's specialty, "identity" might refer to anything from an individual's role set (Stryker and Burke 2000) to a domain of postmodern politicking in which groups "struggle to self-name, self-characterize, and claim social prerogative" (Cerulo 1997:393).

As a result of this disciplinary fragmentation and the sheer cognitive difficulty (and lack of institutional rewards) for ranging too far from one's "home" area of research, most scholars rarely build connections to other lines of research even if doing so would greatly enrich their own work. Students of value development in children, for instance, rarely reference those who focus on the existence of conflicting cultural codes. Those who investigate cross-national variation in moral worldviews rarely engage with theorists exploring the role of moral emotions in maintaining social order. Scholars of the self too seldom consider vast literatures about contextual influences on moral behavior. And those who delve into the nuances of various "moral repertoires" hardly ever draw on relevant social psychological research on emotion, justice, or cooperation. What has been missing is a sense of common cause among scholars who appear on the surface to be studying vastly different phenomena but whose specialties are actually "cousins" with a high degree of common intellectual ancestry. Unlike psychologists and philosophers, who maintain some shared reference points via the institutionalized subfields of moral psychology and moral philosophy, sociologists who are interested in morality have few places to congregate that are explicitly defined by that interest. Taken together, the breadth of the moral domain coupled with the eclectic character of sociology points toward the possibility of a rich and varied empirical engagement. But without a shared context of recognition, our attempts at synthesis must remain hopelessly fractured and underappreciated. This handbook is one step toward developing mutual recognition. But much more institutional work remains to be done.

Incompatible Definitions of Morality

Even when sociologists in diverse subfields *have* recognized their common concern with morality, they have not always understood the term in the same way. This continues to lead to misunderstandings. The adjective "moral" seems to have two main definitions applicable to academic research:

> (1) "relating to human character or behaviour considered as good or bad ... [or] the distinction between right and wrong, or good and evil, in relation to the actions, desires, or character of responsible human beings"; and
> (2) "good, virtuous; conforming to standards of morality" ("Moral," *Oxford English Dictionary*, http://dictionary.oed.com)

"Moral" is thus used both to denote a domain where concepts like good and bad, right and wrong are relevant, and to evaluate the status of a particular action or practice in that domain. For example, since some groups hold female genital mutilation to be an integral part of the "good life" while others see it as a horrible violation of rights, one might reasonably refer to it as a "moral" practice using the first definition's sense of "morally relevant" (see e.g., Shweder 2003, chapter 4). On the other hand, those who condemn the act claim that the practice is *immoral* (consistent with the second definition) because it violates "standards of morality," usually meaning Kantian standards about harm, rights, and fair treatment (see e.g., Turiel 2002).

Airtight distinctions are impossible, but cultural and historical sociologists tend to gravitate toward the first definition, exploring temporal and social variation in the understandings of obligation, value, and worth (Baker 2005, Calhoun 1991, Inglehart and Baker 2000, Lamont 1992, Lamont et al. 1996, Rawls 1987) while social psychologists generally follow the second definition, using "moral" as a synonym for "altruistic" or "prosocial" (Piliavin and Charng 1990, Schwalbe 1991, Stets and Carter 2006, Simpson and Willer 2008). This parallels the divide in moral psychology between methodological relativists like Richard Shweder and Jon Haidt, for whom moral variation is *qualitative* (i.e., reflects different standards) and neo-Kantians like Lawrence Kohlberg and Eliot Turiel, for whom moral variation is *quantitative* (i.e., corresponds more or less well to substantive or procedural standards of ethical conduct). Of course, this terminological confusion also causes difficulties for moral psychology, including – but not limited to – various iterations of the moral/conventional debate (e.g., Kelley et al. 2003, Nado et al. 2009, Turiel 2002, 2006). In sociology, however, the absence of "centripetal" institutional forces makes it vital for would-be sociologists of morality to address definitional issues in a satisfactory fashion. For our purposes, the interesting questions seem less about the truth of any particular moral code and more about (a) determining the proper relationship between innate moral capacities and the moral variation observed within and between societies (e.g., Hauser 2006, Turner this volume); (b) empirically analyzing the contours of moral variation within and between societies; and (c) uncovering the social antecedents of particular moral frameworks and their social and behavioral consequences.

An Ambivalent Relationship to the Normative

Although social psychologists and sociologists of religion routinely use terms like norms and values in their work, most cultural sociologists strongly reject them (Smith 2003, Vaisey 2009, 2010). This is not the place for the full story of cultural sociology's repudiation of formerly central terms, but the view that relying on norms and values to explain behavior is "dated and simplistic" is widespread among today's cultural sociologists (Small 2002:5–6, see also Swidler 2001, Harding 2007, Lamont and Small 2008, Wilson 2009). The new approach does not regard culture as a normative force, but rather as a cognitive "toolkit" or "repertoire" made up of "rule-like structures" that serve as "resources that can be put to strategic use" (DiMaggio 1997:265). Some scholars have offered intellectual justifications for this shift away from the normative (e.g., Collins 1981, Swidler 1986, 2001, Lamont and Small 2008), although others have argued that it can be explained at least partially by cultural sociologists' reluctance to "blame the victim," as some were accused of doing in the political backlash against "culture of poverty" researchers in the late 1960s (Patterson 2002, Vaisey 2010). Whatever the reason may be, most cultural sociologists now scrupulously segregate the "normative" from the "cognitive," neglecting the former and focusing exclusively on the latter (see Small 2002:30, Young 2004:19, Harding 2007:352–353, Lamont and Small 2008:80, Wilson 2009:17).

    Because cultural sociologists possess conceptual and methodological expertise vital to the sociological study of moral life, their abdication of the normative has been – and continues to be – a significant stumbling block for a nascent sociology of morality. Fortunately, there is evidence – in this volume and elsewhere – that cultural sociologists are relearning that "what is" and "what ought to be" cannot really be separated when it comes to understanding the role that culture plays in people's judgments (e.g., Boudon, this volume, Martin and Desmond 2010, Vaisey 2010, see also Geertz 1957:437, Shweder 1992). If this trend continues, it will help contribute to a more robust sociology of morality. There is much to be gained by building bridges between moral psychologists, who use laboratory research to hone detailed models of the interplay between cognition, emotion, and situations, and cultural sociologists, who specialize in decoding the "real world" patterns of shared meaning that comprise the content of so much "individual" cognition. We explicate this in the next section.

Wariness of Biology and Psychology

The final obstacle we suggest here is the "Durkheimian" tendency for sociologists to be wary of biology and psychology.[1] Given the ubiquity of "personality" and "genes" as folk explanations in Western culture, sociologists might be forgiven for their tendency to react with "minimization and denial" to biological and psychological accounts of social phenomena (Freese 2008:S5). However understandable such reactions may be, aversion to research in these fields has made it less likely that sociologists would be influenced by the developments in the cognitive and neurosciences that have been at the heart of morality's resurgence as a focus of inquiry (e.g., Sinnott-Armstrong 2008). Unfortunately, many sociologists exaggerate the "individualism" of psychological work that incorporates biological factors, when in fact, exemplars of this tradition go to great extent to discuss the interplay of genetic predispositions and environments (e.g., Caspi et al. 1998, Moffitt et al. 2002). The widespread suspicion of the biological and cognitive sciences helps explain sociology's lack of engagement with interdisciplinary dialogue about morality, runs the risk of suggesting "oversocialized" models of human development (e.g., Wrong 1961), and leaves the discussion of environmental factors in the hands of scholars less suited to describe, theorize, and measure them. Regardless of one's particular position on the proper role of biology and cognition in the study of morality, the fact is that – rightly or wrongly – this is where much of the recent action is. There is therefore little to be gained by facile denials (destined in any case for "domestic consumption") and much to be gained by a sustained – and critical – empirical engagement with biologically informed research on morality.

Fortunately, there are signs that this hostility is fading. While many sociologists are too quick to resist models of morality that are informed by biology and psychology, contemporary work at the boundaries of social, behavioral, and biological sciences is becoming more nuanced. Researchers are growing more and more interested in the interplay between biological potentialities, individual differences, and micro and macrodynamics of the social environment (e.g., Shanahan and Hofer 2005, Freese 2008, Adkins and Vaisey 2009, Turkheimer et al. 2003). More specifically, many biologically and cognitively influenced models of morality are not hostile to social factors but are explicitly designed to incorporate them (e.g., Haidt and Graham 2009, Oishi et al. 2009). As we mentioned above, researchers from other fields lack the training and experience needed to theorize and measure social factors effectively. Though we acknowledge a diversity of views on this subject, we believe that sociological contributions in this area have primarily been held back by sociologists themselves. Overcoming

---

[1] Weber, by contrast, was "in general positive toward psychology and interested in its findings" and regarded "psychophysical" characteristics as potential elements of which "account must be taken" even though they were not the focus of sociological inquiry per se (Swedberg 2005:217).

our in-group prejudice against biological and psychological factors will not lead to a rampant reductionism and the demise of our discipline, but will contribute to a more realistic integration of social, psychological, and biological explanations of moral phenomena. Not only will such bridging lead to the development of more realistic models, but it may also help us to export sociological insights more effectively to our disciplinary cousins. But this can only happen to the extent we demonstrate that we have substantive contributions to make and are willing to listen and learn. No one wants to talk with someone who continually insists on changing the subject

TOWARD A "SOCIOLOGICAL PERSPECTIVE" ON MORALITY

This handbook is an attempt to address these obstacles, though it is necessarily more successful with some than others. Its main purpose is to bring together a wide range of sociological work on morality in the hope of surmounting some of the effects of disciplinary fragmentation; in one volume we bring together empirical social psychologists, macrosociological theorists, and experts in a wide range of substantive sociological subfields. If we are successful, it will be one step toward establishing a stronger collective identity. We hope to create a mini-movement that will inspire taking a step beyond one's typical self-identification and becoming part of the sociology of morality. We also hope that the proximity of so many varied scholars and topics stimulates easy – but substantive – engagement with topics outside of readers' typical purview. This collection demonstrates the wide reach – methodically, topically, and theoretically – of the discipline of sociology. Perhaps this collection serves as a useful starting point for morality scholars from other disciplines, as well, to enter into interdisciplinary dialogue.

The other issues we identified – definitional confusion, ambivalence about the normative, and our unwarranted wariness of biology and psychology – receive a more uneven treatment as these issues remain to be worked out by the members of our discipline. Some chapters address one or more of these issues, and it is only through continual collisions between scholars and research programs that we might approach any sort of consensus, if such a consensus is possible. It may be that the moral aspects of institutions are qualitatively different from the moral concerns surrounding nation-states, the polity, or individual behavior. (Or, more pragmatically, it may simply not be *useful* to treat these concerns as essentially unified.) But even though sociology cannot provide a unified corrective to the limitations of psychological or other research on morality, this volume offers a number of possibilities for future interdisciplinary research.

Although the bridge-building we envision is in its initial stages, we can draw on the contributions to this handbook to provide a preliminary answer to the question, "What is a *sociological* approach to morality?" Does this handbook lead to a better sense of our discipline's *distinctive* contribution to the science of the moral? If we wanted to evade the question, we might say that a sociological approach to morality is neither more nor less than the sum of the approaches taken by the individual papers in this volume. Given the disparate treatments, approaches, theoretical traditions, and empirical concerns, allowing scholars to develop and utilize their own terminology, presuppositions, and analyses, and simply calling it all "the sociology of morality" might be the safest way to go. But we prefer to take up the challenge of characterizing a nascent sociological approach to morality in more general terms. At the risk of losing some of the nuances of each contribution, we highlight three themes that cross-cut the papers in this volume: (1) attention to social structures, resources, and power; (2) a focus on historically and socially patterned complexes of meaning; and (3) an emphasis on studying moral judgment, action, and discourse in ecologically valid contexts.

With the possible exceptions of those in the concluding section by Abend, Frerichs, and Munch and Lukes, few of the chapters in this handbook treat all of these themes simultaneously; nevertheless, they represent three key aspects of the emerging "sociology of morality." These analytic emphases are certainly compatible with the psychological, biological, and economic approaches to morality that have recently drawn so much attention. And they can help rectify the simplistic treatments – or omissions – of the "social" that characterize these approaches. As should be evident by now, we find much of value in the research on morality conducted in other fields. Nevertheless, it is worth recalling these widely noted findings – that brains that are wired to draw moral distinctions, to weigh costs and benefits, and to process the cognitions and emotions that influence moral judgment and behavior – do not exist in and did not develop in a vacuum. Humans are fundamentally social creatures and human interaction is fundamentally shaped by moral concerns (see Turowetz and Maynard, and Rawls, this volume). Our development as members of primary groups and larger collectivities inevitably shapes our reasoning and reactions, our judgments and embodied senses of "proper" and "taboo." Religion, education, language, social movements, and public policy all set the backdrop for the formation of a human person as they go about their lives. As our contributors point out, this inextricably social element of human life affect evolutionary pressures on our brains and fundamental interactional properties, and shape the "self-evidently true" moral codes that guide social action across a series of substantive life-domains. We briefly consider the three themes we have identified and discuss their importance for the interdisciplinary study of morality.

Social Structures, Resources, and Power

Social structure refers to enduring patterns of relationships among members of a society, including the formal and informal mechanisms through which people's needs are addressed (e.g., education, health, reproduction). Within a given society, individuals are embedded in social structures that organize their lives, ranging from religious communities, educational systems, government, medical systems, family structures, and (more abstractly) social classes. These patterns of resource possession, access, and usage locate members in various in-groups and out-groups and situate them on a number of horizontal and vertical axes of distinction. Human development occurs simultaneously across all of these structures, each of which has the capacity to influence moral thinking in a variety of ways.

At the micro level, differential access to resources is a crucial dimension of moral formation because it creates the bounds within which people come to imagine what a "good life" looks like and to understand their relationship to members of other groups in pursuing that life (Sayer 2005 and this volume). A person is not simply a "decider," doing his or her best to make isolated moral choices according to reasonable rules or idiosyncratic intuitions; each person is also a member of many groups and a player of many roles. One's position in social space provides a vantage point from which allies and rivals, role models and cautionary tales, all play a role in shaping the salience of particular kinds of moral judgment over others (e.g., Lamont 1992).

At the macro level, not all groups or actors possess the same degree of power to pro-mote their version of "good life" or "good society." Though sociologists differ in how much influence they attribute to powerful actors, they agree that historical shifts, government action, social movement advocacy, and other forms of contested collective action influence percep-tions about right and wrong, good and bad. Part 2 of this handbook is largely focused on these sorts of patterned influence, though certainly many more chapters necessarily offer hints about these processes (see the chapters by Sayer, Heimer, Jackall, Wikstrom, Bader and Finke, Baker, Steensland, Roth, and Massengill and Reynolds.)

Complexes of Moral Meanings

"Culture" – a term usually used as a synonym for "society" or "nation" in psychology (Cohen 2009) – has a more specific meaning in sociology. The term is generally used to refer to a "complex of meaning" (Weber 1978:9) that may or may not be identified with membership in a well defined group. Complexes of meaning, though stored and processed in individual bodies, are not primarily about individual cognition. Like knowledge of one's native language (which is also "stored" within individuals), culture is composed of durable patterns of mean-ing that emerge socially and are acquired experientially. The chapters by Baker and Dill and Hunter in this volume show, for example, that "progressivist" and "orthodox" moral cultures – though neither monolithic nor perfectly coherent – serve to structure beliefs and attitudes in disparate domains like law, education, religion, science, and aesthetics. This cultural dimen-sion of morality means that people's judgments in one domain are at least loosely coupled to judgments in other domains, providing any particular position a degree of moral-cultural "baggage" that can spill over into other areas of life.

Because moral judgments cohere to some extent into cultural meaning complexes, they play at least three roles in structuring moral life that are not typically addressed in more bio-logical or psychological accounts. First, shared moral meanings can serve as a basis for group solidarity, bringing people together in ways that can lead to collective action and identification (see Winship and Mehta, this volume). Second, moral meanings can also serve as a mecha-nism of exclusion when the negative side of a complex of moral meaning is used to condemn out-groups (e.g., Lamont 1992). Finally, moral meanings are used to create narrative coher-ence around an *individual's* life, such that seemingly discrete decisions can sometimes take on larger significance because of their implications about what kind of person one is becoming (see Smith 2003, Vaisey 2008a, b). Studying these complexes of meaning across one or more societies and across time is more challenging and "messy" than treating moral judgments and decisions one by one. Nevertheless, such investigations are central to the sociological approach to morality and, we suggest, should be part of any science of morality that seeks to understand real-life moral concerns.

Ecological Validity

The final aspect of sociology's distinctive contribution is that it involves a higher degree of attention to ecological validity than is typical of related work in psychology, philosophy, or neuroscience. Certainly, psychological and neurological literatures are replete with improvements in measurement of moral functioning, reasoning, emotion, and (to some extent) behavior (see Firat and McPherson's chapter for an introduction and Ignatow's chapter for a sociological version). But the exciting and rigorous work that occurs in psychological laboratories isolates processes that sociologists have often attempted to study in more realistic contexts. Even laboratory work can be improved by distinctively sociological approaches to experimentation that capture more aspects of "real" social relationships and interactions (see the chapters by Stets, Hegdvedt and Scheuerman, and Willer and colleagues).

Sociology's main contribution in this vein is the determination to investigate moral phenomena "in the wild" as far as possible. Focusing on a single individual's moral mind isolated from context, networks, interaction partners, history, social location, and self-understandings, is indeed the study of something – perhaps even something important – but it cannot claim to be the study of morality. Sociological theories of morality and supporting research suggest that moral judgments are rarely dependent on abstract understandings about the nature of right and wrong, but rather on one's own standpoint in the social world (Taylor 1989, Smith 2003) and on the ways these standpoints are implicated in particular situations. What is "right" at home might not be "right" at work. Moral commitments and standards are not solely personal but exist within the context of recurrent situations, identities, and relationships one has developed (e.g., Hitlin 2008). Much of the psychological work on moral development implicates the famous Trolley Problem, but many of the moral dilemmas people face in their real lives are not about the life or death of imagined others (see Blair-Loy this volume for one important example). Life involves real conflicts and trade-offs that have moral elements but that rarely involve the extremes of immediate physical or psychological harm. This does not mean that we advocate closing down lines of inquiry where they remain productive, but an ecologically valid sociology of morality can contribute much to understanding how moral phenomena work in day-to-day life.

LOOKING TO THE FUTURE

The goal of this handbook is to provide an institutional resource and a focus for the development of a common identity that we hope will contribute to the revival of the "sociology of morality." More generally, our objective is to aid sociology's contribution to the growing interdisciplinary dialogue around moral phenomena. This is not, however, merely because we want to avoid being left out, but rather because we believe we have something vital to add to the conversation.

We trust that readers both inside and outside sociology will take us at our word and not consider this an attempt at the discipline's final word on "the sociology of morality," much less on morality in general. Reviving and revising our intellectual inheritance in the domain of morality will take time and effort well beyond what any single book or collection of papers could achieve. This handbook's need is only to provide a rallying point for other sociologists who will join us in going well beyond what we have accomplished here. Though we are confident that the papers in this handbook provide an adequate "down payment" on sociology's potential contribution to the study of morality – including attention to resources and power, consideration of cultural meanings, and a commitment to ecological validity – future work that overcomes more fully the obstacles outlined above will have an even greater impact. More than anything, we simply need to roll up our sleeves and engage with our colleagues from other fields, challenging, confirming, and complementing their models as warranted by research not yet conducted.

We cannot, of course, go back in time and discover exactly what Durkheim, Weber, or other classical theorists might have said about our attempt to revive the sociology of morality. However, we do know that morality was once central to sociology and that somehow over the past half-century we have, as Calhoun puts it, become "unmusical" in this domain (Calhoun 1991:232). We hope that this collection of papers will be the start of a much needed tuning up; if so, perhaps the sociology of morality will once again become something worth listening to.

REFERENCES

Adkins, D. E., and S. Vaisey. 2009. "Toward a Unified Stratification Theory: Structure, Genome, and Status Across Human Societies." *Sociological Theory* 27:99–121.

Baker, W. E. 2005. *America's Crisis of Values: Reality and Perception*. Princeton, NJ: Princeton University Press.

Calhoun, C. 1991. "Morality, Identity, and Historical Explanation: Charles Taylor on the Sources of the Self." *Sociological Theory* 9:232–263.

Campbell, C. 1996. *The Myth of Social Action*. New York, NY: Cambridge University Press.

Campbell, C. 2006. "Do Today's Sociologists Really Appreciate Weber's Essay The Protestant Ethic and the Spirit of Capitalism?" *Sociological Review* 54(2):207–223.

Caspi, A., B. R. E. Wright, T. E. Moffitt, and Silva Phil A. 1998. "Early Failure in the Labor Market: Childhood and Adolscent Predictors of Unemployment in the Transition to Adulthood," *American Sociological Review* 63(3):424–451.

Cerulo, K. A. 1997. "Identity Construction: New Issues, New Directions." *Annual Review of Sociology* 23:385–409.

Cohen, A. B. 2009. "Many Forms of Culture." *American Psychologist* 64:194–204.

Collins, R. 1981. "On the Microfoundations of Macrosociology." *The American Journal of Sociology* 86:984–1014.

DiMaggio, P. 1997. "Culture and Cognition," *Annual Review of Sociology* 23:263–287.

Durkheim, E. 1961[1925]. *Moral Education*. Glencoe, IL: Free Press.

Fine, G. A., and C. D. Fields. 2008. "Culture and Microsociology: The Anthill and the Veldt." *The Annals of the American Academy of Political and Social Science* 619:130–148.

Finke, R., and A. Adamczyk. 2008. "Cross-National Moral Beliefs: The Influence of National Religious Context," *Sociological Quarterly* 49:617–652.

Freese, J. 2008. "Genetics and the Social Science Explanation of Individual Outcomes." *American Journal of Sociology* 114:S1–S35.

Geertz, C. 1957. "Ethos, World-View and the Analysis of Sacred Symbols." *The Antioch Review* 17:421–437.

Glass, J., V. L. Bengtson, and C. C. Dunham. 1986. "Attitude Similarity in Three-Generation Families: Socialization, Status Inheritance or Reciprocal Influence?" *American Sociological Review* 51(5):685–698.

Greene, J. D., L. E. Nystrom, A. D. Engell, J. M. Darley, and J. D. Cohen. 2004. "The Neural Bases of Cognitive Conflict and Control in Moral Judgement," *Neuron* 44:389–400.

Haidt, J. 2001. "The Emotional Dog and Its Rational Tail: A Social Intuitionist Approach to Moral Judgement," *Psychological Review* 108(4):814–834.

Haidt, J., and J. Graham. 2009. "Planet of the Durkheimians, Where Community, Authority, and Sacredness Are Foundations of Morality." PP. 371–402 in *Social and Psychological Bases of Ideology and System Justification*, edited by J. T. Jost, A. C. Kay, and H. Thorisdottir. New York: Oxford University Press.

Harding, D. J. 2007. "Cultural Content, Sexual Behavior, and Romantic Relationships in Disadvantaged Neighborhoods." *American Sociological Review* 72:341–364.

Hauser, M. D. 2006. *Moral Minds: How Nature Designed Our Universal Sense of Right and Wrong*. New York, NY: HarperCollins Publishers.

Hitlin, S. 2008. *Moral Selves, Evil Selves: The Social Psychology of Conscience*. New York: Palgrave Macmillan.

Hitlin, S., and J. A. Piliavin. 2004. "Values: Reviving a Dormant Concept." *Annual Review of Sociology* 30: 359–393.

Inglehart, R., and W. E. Baker. 2000. "Modernization, Cultural Change, and the Persistence of Traditional Values." *American Sociological Review* 65:19–51.

Jackall, R. 1988. *Moral Mazes: The World of Corporate Managers*. New York, NY: Oxford University Press.

Kelley, H. H., J. G. Holmes, N. L. Kerr, H. T. Reis, C. E. Rusbult, and P. A. M. Van Lange. 2003. *An Atlas of Interpersonal Situations*. New York, NY: Cambridge.

Knobe, J., and B. Leiter. 2007. "The Case for Nietzschean Moral Psychology," PP. 83–109 in *Nietzsche and Morality*, edited by B. Leiter and N. Sinhabubu. New York, NY: Oxford University Press.

Lamont, M. 1992. *Money, Morals, and Manners: The Culture of the French and the American Upper-Middle Class*. Chicago: University of Chicago Press.

Lamont, M., J. Schmalzbauer, M. Waller, and D. Weber. 1996. "Cultural and Moral Boundaries in the United States: Structural Position, Geographic Location, and Lifestyle Explanations." *Poetics* 24:31–56.

Lamont, M., and M. L. Small. 2008. "How Culture Matters: Enriching Our Understanding of Poverty." PP. 76–102 in *The Colors of Poverty: Why Racial and Ethic Disparities Persist*, edited by A. C. Lin and D. R. Harris. New York: Russell Sage Foundation.

Lukes, S. 1973. *Individualism*. New York: Harper and Row.

Martin, J. L., and M. Desmond. 2010. "The Effects of Ideology on Descriptive and Prescriptive Reasoning," *Sociological Forum* 25(1):1–26.

Moffitt, T. E., A. Caspi, H. Harrington, and B. J. Milne. 2002. "Males on the Life-Course-Persistent and Adolescence-Limited Antisocial Pathways: Follow Up at Age 26 Years," *Development and Psychopathology* 14(1):179–207.

Nado, J., D. Kelly, and S. Stich. 2009. "Moral Judgment," PP. 621–633 in *Companion to the Philosophy of Psychology*, edited by J. Symons and P. Calvo. New York, NY: Routledge.

Oishi, S., S. Kesebir, and B. H. Snyder. 2009. "Sociology: A Lost Connection in Social Psychology." *Personality and Social Psychology Review* 13:334–353.

Patterson, O. 2002. "Taking Culture Seriously: A Framework and an Afro-American Illustration." PP. 202–218 in *Culture Matters: How Values Shape Human Progress*, edited by L. E. Harrison and S. P. Huntington. New York: Basic Books.

Piliavin, J. A., and H.-W. Charng. 1990. "Altruism: A Review of Recent Theory and Research," *Annual Review of Sociology* 16:27–65.

Rawls, A. W. 1987. "The Interaction Order Sui Generis: Goffman's Contribution to Social Theory." *Sociological Theory* 5:136–149.

Sayer, A. 2005. *The Moral Significance of Class*. Cambridge: Cambridge University Press.

Schwalbe, M. L. 1991. "The Autogenesis of the Self," *Journal for the Theory of Social Behaviour* 21(3):269–295.

Shanahan, M. J., and S. M. Hofer. 2005. "Social Context in Gene-Environment Interactions: Retrospect and Prospect." *The Journals of Gerontology, Series B, Psychological Sciences and Social Sciences* 60:65–76.

Shweder, R. A. 1992. "Ghost Busters in Anthropology." PP. 45–58 in *Human Motives and Cultural Models*. New York: Cambridge University Press.

Shweder, R. A. 2003. *Why Do Men Barbecue? Recipes for Cultural Psychology*. Cambridge, MA: Harvard University Press.

Simpson, B., and R. Willer. 2008. "Altruism and Indirect Reciprocity: The Interaction of Person and Situation in Prosocial Behavior," *Social Psychology Quarterly* 71(1):37–52.

Sinnott-Armstrong, W. 2008. "Introduction." PP. xiii–xix in *The Evolution of Morality: Adaptations and Innateness*, vol. 1, *Moral Psychology*, edited by W. Sinnott-Armstrong. Cambridge, MA: MIT Press.

Small, M. L. 2002. "Culture, Cohorts, and Social Organization Theory: Understanding Local Participation in a Latino Housing Project." *The American Journal of Sociology* 108:1–54.

Smith, C. 2003. *Moral, Believing Animals: Human Personhood and Culture*. New York: Oxford University Press.

Spates, J. L. 1983. "The Sociology of Values," *Annual Review of Sociology* 9:27–49.

Starks, B., and R. V. Robinson. 2007. "Moral Cosmology, Relgion, and Adult Values for Children," *Journal for the Scientific Study of Religion* 46(1):17–35.

Stets, J. E., and M. J. Carter. 2006. "The Moral Identity: A Principle Level Identity," *Purpose, Meaning, and Action: Control System Theories in Sociology*, edited by K. McClelland and T. J. Fararo. New York, NY: Palgrave Macmillan.

Stivers, R. 1996. "Towards a Sociology of Morality," *The International Journal of Sociology and Social Policy* 16(1/2):1–14.

Stryker, S., and P. J. Burke. 2000. "The Past, Present, and Future of an Identity Theory." *Social Psychology Quarterly* 63:284–297.

Sunstein, C. R. 2004. "Moral Heuristics and Moral Framing," *Minnesota Law Review* 88:1556–1597.

Swedberg, R. 2005. *The Max Weber Dictionary: Key Words and Central Concepts*. Stanford, CA: Stanford Social Sciences.

Swidler, A. 1986. "Culture in Action: Symbols and Strategies." *American Sociological Review* 51:273–286.

Swidler, A. 2001. *Talk of Love: How Culture Matters*. Chicago: University of Chicago Press.

Taylor, C. 1989. *Sources of the Self: The Making of the Modern Identity*. Cambridge, MA: Harvard University Press.

Turiel, E. 2002. *The Culture of Morality: Social Development, Context, and Conflict*. New York: Cambridge University Press.

Turiel, E. 2006. "Thought, Emotions, and Social Interactional Processes in Moral Development," PP. 7–36 in *Handbook of Moral Development*, edited by M. Killen and J. Smetana. Mahwah, NJ: Lawrence Erlbaum Associates.

Turkheimer, E., A. Haley, M. Waldron, B. D'Onofrio, and I. I. Gottesman. 2003. "Socioeconomic Status Modifies Heritability of IQ in Young Children." *Psychological Science* 14:623–628.

Vaisey, S. 2008a. "Reply to Ann Swidler." *Sociological Forum* 23:619–622.

Vaisey, S. 2008b. "Socrates, Skinner, and Aristotle: Three Ways of Thinking About Culture in Action." *Sociological Forum* 23:603–613.

Vaisey, S. 2009. "Motivation and Justification: A Dual-Process Model of Culture in Action." *American Journal of Sociology* 114:1675–1715.

Vaisey, S. 2010. "What People Want: Poverty, Aspirations, and Educational Attainment," *Annals of the American Academy of Political and Social Sciences* 629:75–101.

Weber, M. 1978. *Economy and Society*. Berkeley, CA: University of California Press.

Weber, M. 2003. *The Protestant Ethic and the Spirit of Capitalism*. Translated by T. Parsons. Mineola, NY: Dover Publications.

Willer, R., K. Kuwabara, and M. W. Macy. 2009. "The False Enforcement of Unpopular Norms." *American Journal of Sociology* 115:451–490.

Wilson, W. J. 2009. *More than Just Race: Being Black and Poor in the Inner City*. New York: W.W. Norton & Co.

Wrong, D. 1961. "The Oversocialized Conception of Man in Modern Sociology," *American Sociological Review* 26:183–193.

Young, A. A. 2004. *The Minds of Marginalized Black Men: Making Sense of Mobility, Opportunity, and Future Life Chances*. Princeton, NJ: Princeton University Press.

CHAPTER 2

The Cognitive Approach to Morality

RAYMOND BOUDON

Many contemporary social scientists tend to reduce rationality to its instrumental form and ignore or even disqualify the notion coined by Max Weber of *Wertrationalität*. In this chapter, I propose a formal definition and defense of the notion of *value rationality* or *axiological rationality*, as I prefer to translate the notion of *Wertrationalität*. Axiological rationality may be defined as the type of rationality grounding value statements and value feelings, and their species, moral and prescriptive statements and feelings. But what does *axiological rationality* mean? I will claim that this notion can be given a clear analytical definition, that it labels and encapsulates a powerful theory that explains many sociological data on morality and more generally on axiological feelings and also that it was more or less implicitly used, not only by Max Weber in his empirical analyses, but also by many other sociologists before and after him. In a word, starting from Weber's notion, I will try to show that many powerful sociological analyses of moral feelings use more or less implicitly a *cognitive approach.*

SOCIOLOGY AND PHILOSOPHY ON MORAL FEELINGS

Moral, normative and generally axiological feelings—i.e., the feelings that *X is good, legitimate*, etc.—are one of the most important social phenomena and of the least mastered scientifically. The unsatisfactory state of the social scientific art on this topic is partly due to the fact that the available theories of axiological feelings produced by philosophy are highly influential among social scientists, though as a result of the division of labor in the human sciences they often fail to see it. Now, while these philosophical theories are grounded on powerful ideas, they cannot be accepted literally by sociologists. Major examples illustrate this point.

1. Kant's *theory of practical reason* maintains that an action is good if it rests on maxims that all would accept, as *never do something that you would not like to be done to you.* From his theory Kant drew controversial consequences, as that lying is always bad. This statement is contradicted by many observations though, as the fact that most people would normally consider that it is good for a war prisoner to lie when an investigation officer asks him to deliver the names of his companions of arms. Benjamin Constant, the French political theorist of the 19th century, already raised this objection. But the main sociological objection to Kant's theory is that it fails to explain

S. Hitlin, S. Vaisey (eds.), *Handbook of the Sociology of Morality*,
Handbooks of Sociology and Social Research, DOI 10.1007/978-1-4419-6896-8_2,
© Springer Science+Business Media, LLC 2010

many *ought-feelings*, as the fact that people accept inequalities in some circumstances and not in others or the consensus on the point that some occupations should receive higher salaries than others.

2. *The utilitarian theory* developed from Bentham and earlier La Rochefoucauld to modern writers as Harsanyi (1955) maintains that individuals are guided by the principle of maximizing the differences between positive and negative outcomes, to them, of their actions. This theory is contradicted by the fact that people can behave altruistically, as shown by plain observation as well as by the findings from experiments as the *ultimatum game*. The latter shows that in situations where people could impose an unequal sharing of an amount of money to their own advantage many of them opt for an equitable sharing. The shortcomings of the utilitarian approach to morality led social scientists as Sen (2002) to propose to correct it by taking the Kantian approach into consideration.

3. Rawls' (1971) *theory of justice as fairness* has a more limited scope but has attracted a great deal of attention. It maintains notably that we have the feeling that some institution or state of affairs is good if it has the effect of making the situation of the worse-off in a society as good as possible. Thus, the level of inequality between salaries in a firm is good if it can be shown that making it lower would affect negatively the activity of the firm and hence threaten the worse paid. This theory is contradicted by the fact that the people appear as Rawlsian only under specific cognitive circumstances.

4. Habermas' (1981) *communication theory* states that a collective decision is good if it can be considered as deriving from individual opinions expressed in a context of free discussion between equals. This *procedural* theory is confronted with the objection that discussions among scientists are the closest approximation of the ideal situation of free and perfect communication. Pareto qualified rightly though the history of science as *a churchyard of false theories*. Why would then *communicative rationality* be immunized against wrong answers as far as normative or axiological questions are concerned, while it is obviously not as far as scientific questions are concerned?

5. The *relativistic theory* according to which axiological feelings would always be context-bound and without other ground than the strength of tradition and socialization has also to face serious objections: "truth on this side of the Pyrenean mountains, error beyond" (*vérité en deça des Pyrénées, erreur au-delà*, wrote Pascal (1954 [1670]). The relativistic theory is contradicted by the existence of axiological universals: stealing is held everywhere as bad in principle. Killing intentionally a human being is universally considered as more serious than killing him unintentionally. Corruption is treated in principle as bad by all cultures. Above all, the relativistic theory oversees that contextual variations in the *customs* can hide non-contextual *values*. Respecting the other man is a value in all societies. It inspires norms that are expressed by symbols highly variable from one context to another.

All these theories include important intuitions, but none of them can be literally borrowed by social scientists, for the reason that, though they explain some observational data on moral feelings, they appear also as incompatible with or as unable to explain other data. A good sociological theory should provide a grid from which sociologists could draw a convincing explanation of the moral, prescriptive and axiological feelings they observe on given issues in given contexts. A great achievement of Weber and Durkheim is that they use such a grid.

Sociologists do not always recognize it for two reasons: (a) it remains implicit in their work and (b) the conventional history of sociology tends to insist on the differences between Durkheim and Weber and to disregard their similarities.

I will try here to make analytical Weber's notion of *axiological rationality*. My thesis is that axiological rationality should be considered as a variant of *cognitive rationality*.

In a nutshell, Weber's notion of axiological rationality owes its importance to the fact that it implies that instrumental rationality cannot be considered as the exclusive or even the main dimension of rationality. Social action is always grounded on a combination of axiological and instrumental rationality. Most people prefer obviously to serve rather than hurt their own interests and preferences, but they also prefer that their actions are positively evaluated by others, more precisely by the anonymous other as they see him: the other G.H. Mead christened the *generalized Other*. Weber's notion overcomes the opposition between individual instrumentality and a collective sense of moral justice and generally of values. It also overcomes another shortcoming of the instrumental conception of rationality: while instrumental rationality can explain the means used by social actors to satisfy their goals or preferences, axiological rationality provides a guideline to explain their values and hence their preferences.

WEBER'S NOTION OF AXIOLOGICAL RATIONALITY

Max Weber's notion of *axiological rationality* (Weber 1922) contains in a highly condensed fashion an idea that, once developed, generates a theory with a more general scope than the Kantian, the utilitarian, the procedural or the relativistic ones.

Many interpretations have been given of Weber's notion. Many writers hold it as controversial. Lukes (1967:259–60) goes as far as to contend that it is meaningless. Sukale (1995:43), one of the most knowledgeable contemporary commentators of Weber, qualifies the concept as misleading (*irreführend*): "Weber's distinction between axiological and instrumental rationality, as though there would be two types of rational action, is extremely misleading." (*Damit ist Webers Einteilung des rationalen Handelns in zweckrationales und wertrationales, als gäbe es zwei verschiedene Arten rationalen Handelns, äußerst irreführend.*) Why this brutal rejection? My guess is that, to Sukale, as to Lukes, rationality means *instrumental rationality*. So, their rejection of *axiological rationality* as a genuine form of rationality is probably the outcome of the influence on them of the dominant contemporary definition of rationality. They endorse the widespread idea that the notion of rationality can exclusively be applied to the relation between means and ends. This idea is frequently considered as axiomatic notably in the English-speaking world under the influence of the followers of pragmatism and of major thinkers as Bertrand Russell or Herbert Simon. Thus, to Russell (1954), "Reason has a perfectly clear and precise meaning. It signifies the choice of the right means to an end that you wish to achieve. It has nothing whatever to do with the choice of ends". To Simon (1983), "Reason is fully instrumental. It cannot tell us where to go; at best it can tell us how to get there".

The skeptical interpretation of Weber's *axiological rationality* was presumably also reinforced by the fact that Weber is often described as supporting a *decisionist* theory of values, i.e., a theory according to which the ultimate values cannot be grounded. It is true that, if ultimate values could be grounded, they would not be ultimate. But Weber (1995[1919]:41) makes the point that physics itself can build reliable theories although they rest on undemonstrated principles: "every science rests on principles" (*keine Wissenschaft ist voraussetzungslos*). Axiological statements can in the same way be valid, although they rest on undemonstrated principles. Moreover, if values were endorsed without being grounded in the minds of social actors, how could Weber insist on the crucial importance of his notion of *Verstehen* in sociology, i.e., on the idea that the ultimate causes of social action lie in the reasons and motivations of people? Finally, Weber (1995[1919]:38) states clearly that the goals and values involved in social action can be rationally discussed.

But what does *axiological rationality* mean? *Rationality* is widely used as a major concept by two disciplines: economics and philosophy of science. To economists, rationality means generally instrumental rationality, in other words: congruence between means and ends. As to the ends, they hold them as rational if they are compatible with one another, but they reject the idea that ends as such could be treated as rational or not. To historians and philosophers of science, rationality has a different meaning: to them, a scientist is rational if, to the best of his knowledge, he prefers a stronger to a weaker theory. Thus, it became irrational to believe that the earth is flat once the proofs that it is round had accumulated. I propose to qualify this form of rationality as *cognitive*.

COGNITIVE RATIONALITY

Cognitive rationality can be defined in the following fashion. Let us assume that we can draw some conclusion from a set of statements and that this conclusion explains some phenomenon. To take an example, the two statements: "the air has a given weight" and "the air is heavier at the bottom than at the top of a mountain" lead to the conclusion that the quicksilver in the barometer should be higher at the bottom of a mountain. Now, this is precisely what we observe. So, the two statements explain the behavior of the barometer. Still in the 16th century, an alternative theory was available: the Aristotelian theory according to which the quicksilver rises in an empty tube because nature would abhor emptiness. It does not explain why the barometer is higher at the bottom of a mountain and it introduces a conjectural anthropomorphic statement on nature, while these two shortcomings are eliminated in the alternative theory independently devised by Torricelli and Pascal. This well-known example suggests that it is cognitively rational to endorse a given explanation of a phenomenon, if the explanation is made of acceptable and mutually compatible statements and if the competing available theories are weaker in one way or another.

Radnitzky (1987) has proposed to build a bridge between the two basic meanings of the notion of *rationality*. He uses an example to illustrate his point: it became irrational to believe that the earth is flat from the moment when it became more *costly*, he contends, to defend this theory than to accept its competitor. But the costs of defending a theory are higher than the costs of defending an alternative theory if and only if the latter explains more *easily* the observed phenomena than the former. Without knowing and understanding the arguments used by the alternative theories to explain, say, why the sails of a ship disappear at the horizon after the hull or why the moon has the form of a crescent, I cannot evaluate the costs of endorsing the theory that the earth is flat or the theory that it is round. So, the reduction proposed by Radnitzky of cognitive to instrumental rationality is artificial. The important point is: the theory that the earth is round explains more convincingly a number of phenomena than the theory that the earth is flat.

My claim is that Weber had in mind the distinction between *instrumental* and *cognitive rationality* when he coined the expression *axiological rationality*. In other words, I interpret this notion as indicating that cognitive rationality can be applied, not only to descriptive or representative but also to prescriptive, moral or axiological questions.

I will leave aside the question as to whether my interpretation describes what Weber had actually in mind and say only that, if it is true that Weber never clearly stated what he meant by *axiological rationality*, he implicitly uses it in most of his empirical analyses. I have made elsewhere the point that his analyses in the sociology of morals and religion amount at disentangling the cognitive reasons responsible for the collective beliefs he explores, of their change over time and of their contextual variations and that, as Weber, Durkheim explains long-term change in moral feelings and variations of religious beliefs as the outcome of cognitive rationality (Boudon 2008, chapters 4 and 5). But my aim here is rather to develop the theory of axiological feelings that can be drawn from Weber's notion of axiological rationality and to show its powerfulness for the explanation of moral, prescriptive and generally axiological feelings. The Weber scholars who would feel embarrassed by my interpretation of Weber's intuitions could very well forget about this point and consider the cognitive theory of morality and axiological feelings I develop below as mine, if they prefer, although on my side I find hard to forget the process through which I came to this theory.

THE COGNITIVE THEORY OF MORAL, PRESCRIPTIVE, AND AXIOLOGICAL FEELINGS

This cognitive theory of moral, prescriptive and axiological feelings I propose rests upon the four following postulates.

1. Theories can be built on moral, prescriptive and axiological as well as on descriptive questions; moreover, moral, prescriptive or axiological theories can be in many cases unambiguously characterized, as descriptive ones, as stronger or weaker when they are compared to one another.
2. People tend to endorse the theory they see as stronger.
3. They tend to endorse a moral, prescriptive or value statement and to experience the feeling that *X is good, bad, legitimate, fair, etc.* when it appears to them—more or less vaguely depending on the circumstances—as grounded on valid reasons.
4. These reasons can be context-dependent but also context-free.

The Weberian–Durkheimian sociological tradition recognizes fully the validity of the distinction introduced by postulate 4. Scientific beliefs aim at being context-free. In the same way, a belief such as the belief that a democratic regime is more likely than an authoritarian one to respect the dignity of people is commonly considered as context-free. Clearly, the citizens of democratic societies do not feel that being democratic is better than dictatorial regimes simply because they have been socialized to think so, but because they perceive their feeling as right. In the same way, I think that Pythagoras' theorem is right, not simply because I have been socialized to think so. As representational beliefs, moral beliefs can also be context-dependent. The belief that rain rituals are efficient is context-bound, as is the moral belief that death penalty is a legitimate form of punishment.

My claim is that the cognitive approach to morality is useful to explain moral, prescriptive and axiological feelings, as they are observed by empirical research, that it can explain the phenomena of consensus which can be observed in societies on many issues and that it can explain the change of moral feelings over time and generally of collective axiological feelings.

At this point, it is necessary to mention an almost inescapable objection. As no *ought*-statement can be drawn from *is*-statements, it is often contended that normative and generally axiological theories are by their very nature basically different from representational ones. This is true to some extent. Still, as *is*-statements, *ought*-statements can be weaker or stronger. Thus, to take a trivial example, under general conditions, people prefer riding a car smoothly in the city traffic because, as moving is, to them, a means rather than an end, they want normally the means to be as little unpleasant as possible. For this reason, they consider traffic lights as a *good*—though unpleasant—thing. The value statement *traffic lights are a good thing* is the conclusion of a valid argument grounded on the empirical indubitable statement that traffic is more fluid with traffic lights than without. Though elementary, this example is typical of many normative arguments. It shows that a normative argument can be as convincing as a descriptive one. This is the case when the argument involves empirical statements that can be checked and axiological statements on which all would agree, as *traffic jam is a bad thing*. The example also shows that an *ought*-statement can be derived from *is*-statements, provided the set of statements concluding to the *ought*-statement includes at least one *ought*-statement.

Max Weber has well seen, however, the point of utmost importance that, by difference with the example of the evaluation of traffic lights, axiological statements cannot always be considered as the conclusion of *instrumental* arguments. By creating his notion of *axiological rationality*, he wanted possibly to insist on the point that people may have in some circumstances subjectively strong and objectively valid reasons to believe that *X is good or bad, legitimate or illegitimate, fair or unfair*, etc. without these reasons belonging to the instrumental category. He introduced by so doing a powerful idea, crucial with regard to our understanding of axiological feelings and of moral and normative feelings in particular. It provides an indispensable tool to explain the social processes whereby moral evaluations are constructed.

Once properly elaborated, the notion is also indispensable, as I will suggest below, to explain the change of moral feelings over time: why do we consider, for instance, as illegitimate types of punishment that were considered earlier as normal and legitimate? Why is death penalty abolished in a growing number of countries?

AXIOLOGICAL RATIONALITY

As I have earlier defined *cognitive rationality* formally, I would define *axiological rationality* in the following way. Let us assume (1) that a set of statements leads to a given normative or axiological conclusion, (2) that the set of statements is made of acceptable and mutually compatible empirical and axiological statements, then, if no alternative set of acceptable and mutually compatible statements leading to a different or opposite normative or axiological conclusion is available, it will be *axiologically rational* to assume that the given normative or axiological conclusion is good.

To summarize, I would define a feeling or a statement as *axiologically rational* if people would consider it as derived from acceptable and mutually compatible arguments which can be—but are not necessarily—of the *instrumental* type, and if no set of arguments is available that would be as strong and would lead to a different conclusion. I propose in other words to define axiological rationality as a form of cognitive rationality characterized by the fact that it deals with arguments where at least one statement is axiological, since an *ought*-statement cannot be derived from statements that would *all* be *is*-statements.

By making *axiological rationality* a variant of *cognitive rationality*, I introduce a strong thesis. For this reason it is important to stress a trivial point: *cognitive rationality* is in many cases unable to provide a solution to the questions we raise. We have no answer to a considerable number of scientific questions. We really do not know whether stress is a cause of stomach ulcers or whether bees actually have a language. In the same way, we have no answer to numerous moral and generally axiological questions. Thus, there is presently no universal consensus on the question as to whether and under which conditions a woman can rent her belly for the purpose of procreation. But the *search* for a valid answer always follows the rules of *cognitive rationality*. This is true of axiological as well as representational questions.

AN ILLUSTRATION OF AXIOLOGICAL RATIONALITY

My thesis associating *axiological rationality* and *cognitive rationality* is actually an old one. My own contribution is to express it in analytical terms and to show that it is implicitly present in many illuminating sociological works. While Weber was probably the first author who proposed to conceptualize the notion of *axiological rationality*, he is not the first one who has used it practically, as an example drawn from Adam Smith among other possible examples can illustrate. This example shows that *axiological rationality* is a much more concrete and hence much more useful notion to the social sciences than Kant's general maxims of *practical reason.*

In his *Wealth of Nations*, Smith (1793) wonders why his fellowmen have strong collective feelings on the fairness of salaries. Thus, a strong collective feeling among 18th century Englishmen is that miners should be paid more than soldiers. What are the causes of this consensus? Adam Smith's answer consists in showing that this feeling is grounded on subjectively strong and objectively valid reasons, which can be reconstructed in the following fashion: (1) A salary is the reward of a contribution. 2) Equal rewards should correspond to equal contributions. 3) Several components enter in the value of a contribution, as the investment required in order to generate the type of competence needed to produce the contribution and the risks involved in the realization of the contribution. (4) The investment is comparable in the case of the miner and of the soldier. It takes about as much time and effort to train a soldier as a miner. The two jobs are characterized by similar risks. The two include above all a high risk of being wounded or killed. (5) Nonetheless, there are important differences between the two. The soldier serves a function that is central in any society. He contributes preserving the very existence of the nation. The miner fulfils by contrast an economic activity among others. (6) This difference has the consequence that the death of the two men has a different social meaning. The miner's death will be commonly identified as an *accident*; the death of the soldier on the battlefield as a *sacrifice*. (7) Because of this difference in the social meaning of their activities, the soldier is entitled to symbolic rewards, in terms of moral prestige, symbolic distinctions, glory notably when he has won a battle, or funeral honors in the case of death on the battlefield. (8) For symmetric reasons, the miner is not entitled to the same symbolic rewards. (9) As the contributions of the two categories in terms notably of risk and investment are the same, the salaries of the miners should be higher; otherwise, an unjustifiable disequilibrium between the contributions and the rewards of the two categories would appear. (10) Conclusion: This system of reasons is responsible for the strong feeling of most people, Adam Smith states, that miners should be paid more than soldiers. QED.

Two remarks can be introduced at this point. First remark: the set of reasons appears as entirely convincing, *given the context*. In a utopian other context where technical progress would make possible that miners exploit the mine from the floor, instructing robots with the help of computers, the validity of the system of reasons would clearly collapse: the minors would no more run a deadly risk, but they would have to have a high level of competence and hence a long training. Second remark: the reasons grounding moral feelings are generally *metaconscious* in the mind of people—they are there, but in many cases become really conscious only from the moment when an individual asks himself or is asked by others why he thinks so. The reasons Socrates extracts from the mind of the people he interviews in Plato's early *Dialogues* are typically *metaconscious*.

These two points are of utmost importance for the construction of our own moral feelings and the understanding of the moral feelings we register in contexts to which we do not belong. Why do we normally consider the rainmaking practices in use in some traditional societies as *strange* and the fire-making practices as *normal*? Because we know the laws of transformation of energy, while the members of these societies ignore them. They consider their fire-making and rainmaking practices as equally *magical*: as recipes likely to bring magical forces into action. If we ignore the parameterization of the cognitive reasons by the context, we fail to understand the reasons as to why people in other contexts do what they do and we tend to treat them as *irrational*, if not as *primitive*, as the anthropologists and sociologists of the 19th century did. The cognitive approach to morality provides a useful explanation of prejudices as well as a tool to fight them.

LESSONS FROM SMITH'S EXAMPLE

Several lessons can be drawn from Smith's example. Systems of reasons on the salaries of miners and soldiers different from Smith's could be devised. One could argue for instance that soldiers are taken from their families and thus deserve more financial compensation. The argument may have been present in some minds. Would have it been sufficient by itself to create a widely shared consensus? Given that an empirical confirmation is in the case of this example practically impossible, it can only be stated that the reasons proposed by Smith are all straightforward, easily acceptable by anybody and compatible with one another, so that the consensus crystallized plausibly because this ideal–typical system of reasons appears as particularly convincing. In other cases, it can be easier to opt unambiguously for one of the plausible systems of reasons, as when people can be asked why they think on an issue as they do and generally when additional empirical data are available.

The philosopher and sociologist Scheler (1954) disagreed deeply with Adam Smith, since he developed himself an intuitionist theory of values. But he saw in full clarity that Smith's theory was of utmost importance for the explanation of moral and other values and he identified it correctly as *judicatory* (*urteilsartig*). He saw well that cognitive rationality was the core of Smith's theory of moral sentiments: that it proposes to analyze them as the consequence of systems of arguments that the members of a group perceive more or less implicitly as valid.

It can also be noted that, while contemporary sociologists seldom consider Adam Smith as a founding father of their discipline, Parsons et al. (1961) fully and rightly recognized his importance for sociology. Though Smith's *Wealth of Nations* is a main source of the so-called instrumental *Rational Choice Theory*, it contains at the same time in many passages as the one I am referring to here a powerful criticism of the limits of instrumental rationality and a proposal to overcome these limits by deriving normative and axiological feelings and judgments from processes guided by *cognitive rationality*.

The approach used by Smith can easily be illustrated by examples taken from modern writers. A contemporary theorist of ethics, Walzer (1993), proposes several analyses of our moral sentiments following the same line as Smith's analysis. To take an example close to Smith's: Why do we spontaneously consider, e.g., conscription as a legitimate recruitment method in the case of soldiers but not of miners, he asks? The answer is again that the function of the former is vital to the country, while the latter is an economic activity among others. If conscription could be applied to mining, it could be applied to any and eventually to all kinds of activities, so that it would lead to a political regime incompatible with the principles of democracy.

I would add in the same vein that we accept easily that soldiers are used as garbage collectors to meet situations of emergency, as when a lasting strike of garbage collectors threatens the public health. But it would be considered illegitimate to use soldiers to fulfill such tasks in normal situations. Strong reasons likely to be widely shared are here too responsible for a collective moral feeling.

In these examples, as in Smith's example, the collective moral feelings are grounded on subjectively strong and objectively valid reasons. These reasons can be qualified as *trans-subjective*, since most people would likely consider them as strong. Using Adam Smith's vocabulary, the *impartial spectator* would accept them. Thus, people who are not directly concerned in their interests because they are neither miners nor soldiers themselves and have no miners or soldiers among their parents and friends are in the position of the *impartial spectator*. They would consider as evident that miners should be paid more than soldiers.

So, Smith's analysis proposes implicitly a general theory of axiological feelings. It suggests that axiological feelings are grounded on reasons and that these reasons are not necessarily instrumental. Smith offers here a *cognitively rational* explanation of the collective feeling he accounts for. The feeling that *miners should be paid more than soldiers* is *collective* and strong because it is grounded on strong reasons in *individual* minds. The collective *feeling* in question is not a feeling in the personal idiosyncratic sense of the word. It illustrates rather a type of feeling a social actor cannot experience without having at the same time the impression that the *Generalized other* would *feel* like him. Though *affective*, this feeling is associated with a system of reasons present in individual minds, though in a half-articulated intuitive fashion. So, the *judicatory*—or cognitive—theory of axiological feelings illustrated by Adam Smith's example has the important property that it overcomes the rigid binary distinction between affectivity and rationality: I have the strong *feeling* that some state of affairs is fair or unfair, legitimate or not, because I have strong *reasons* to believe so. The theory suggests also that the moral states of mind of the *self* depend on the way he perceives the states of mind of the *other*: I cannot experience a reason as valid without having the feeling that the other man would share my view.

This cognitive approach to moral and generally axiological feelings offers moreover an analytical answer to Durkheim's question as to why any human being perceives his moral feelings as *constraining*. It is easily checked that the individual statements used in Smith's argument as I reconstruct it have in common to be *subjectively strong*—and in Durkheim's sense *constraining*—because they are *objectively valid*. Some of these statements are empirical. For instance: it takes as long to train a soldier as a miner; both occupations are exposed to deadly risks. These statements are indubitable. Uncontroversial too is the statement that reinforcing the security of a nation is a central social function, while mining is a particular economic function. Some of the statements derive from the most familiar sociological theory: thus, exchange theory states rightly that people expect the reward they get to reflect the contribution they provide. Some statements express familiar sociological observations: that death is not perceived as having the same meaning when it is the effect of self-sacrifice rather than of an accident; or that symbolic rewards can be used to reward the former but not to compensate the latter. These statements can also be easily accepted. On the whole, all individual statements used in Smith's argument are acceptable. For this reason, most people perceived its conclusion as strong.

Moreover, it should be noted that the *social effects* of paying miners more than soldiers are not evoked in Smith's analysis. For the reasons grounding the statement that minors should be paid more than soldiers are not instrumental but cognitive: it is rational to pay miners more, not because of the eventual social *effects* resulting from paying them more, but because paying them more is congruent with strong *principles*, as the principle of proportionality between contribution and reward: *cognitive axiological* rather than *instrumental* rationality is at work there.

Habermas has suggested, fair communication can *facilitate* the production in people's minds of the reasons justifying a normative conclusion. But communication cannot by itself make the reasons valid. On this point, Durkheim (1979[1912]:624) was more clear-sighted: "in a first stage we believe in a notion because it is collective, then it becomes collective because it is true: we check its credentials before we endorse it" (*Le concept qui, primitivement, est tenu pour vrai parce qu'il est collectif tend à ne devenir collectif qu'à condition d'être tenu pour vrai: nous lui demandons ses titres avant de lui accorder notre créance*). In plain words: consensus is the product of truth, rather than truth the product of consensus regarding moral, prescriptive and axiological as well as representational beliefs. I mean here by *truth*: conclusions grounded on systems of reasons stronger than alternative available systems leading to different or opposite conclusions. Durkheim would certainly have rejected the conventionalist conception of moral, prescriptive or axiological judgments and feelings Habermas' *communicative rationality* unavoidably implies.

CONTEXT-FREE VERSUS CONTEXT-BOUND REASONS

While Durkheim recognizes fully, as Weber does, the parameterization of the reasons by the social context, he also stresses, as Weber, that systems of reasons can be context-free. Nobody doubts that Lavoisier's theory of the composition of the air is better than Priestley's even though one can understand why Priestley was confident in his theory. In the same fashion, nobody doubts that Montesquieu's theory arguing that the separation of powers is a *good* institution, since it makes political power both more efficient and more acceptable, dominates Bodin's or Beccaria's theory according to which political power cannot be efficient without being concentrated. The negative feelings of the citizens of democratic countries against authoritarian or totalitarian regimes or the moral protest that can be observed when they feel that the separation of powers is violated in their country derive from the fact that they have in mind in a more or less conscious fashion the system of reasons elaborated by Montesquieu.

Other illustrations of the distinction context-free/context-bound can easily be mentioned: the value of the respect due to the dead is context-free since it is a consequence of the principle of the dignity of all human beings, while the symbolic norms expressing this value are context-bound; politeness is context-free, but is expressed in context-bound ways.

Durkheim (1960 [1893]:146) has answered the question as to why moral feelings can be context-free: "Individualism and freethinking were born neither with the French Revolution, nor with the Reformation, nor with the Greek and Roman antiquity, nor with the fall of the Oriental Empires; they belong to all times" (*L'individualisme, la libre-pensée ne datent ni de la révolution, ni de la réforme, ni de l'antiquité gréco-romaine, ni de la chute des empires orientaux; ils sont de tous les temps*). Durkheim means here by *individualism*: the sense individuals have for their dignity and basic needs; by *freethinking*, he means: their capacity to evaluate critically notably institutions. In other words, the dignity of human beings is a basic context-free value. This value can of course be deeply hurt in situations of war, when some categories of men are qualified as *enemies*, or in societies introducing the category of *second-class* citizens. But, even then, the value remains alive in many people's minds.

Context-bound moral beliefs can, as representational beliefs, be compared and evaluated. I can understand that in some contexts people believe in the efficiency of rain rituals. But I do not need to believe it myself. I can understand that female genital mutilation is practiced in some societies because it is the consequence of a traditional system of beliefs. I need not seeing this practice as acceptable and I have reasons to think that the reasons prevailing on this issue in modern societies are stronger. I can understand that in an emergent society many people prefer an authoritarian to a democratic political organization. But I feel I have strong reasons to prefer democracy. I can *understand* that in some societies thieves run the risk of having their hand cut. But even radical relativists would find this practice inacceptable. I feel in other words I am entitled do *judge* the practices in use in other contexts. Moral over time change would be entirely unintelligible if the systems of reasons prevailing in various contexts could not be compared to one another.

The next major point of this chapter is that the cognitive approach to morality offers a bridge between theory and empirical sociological studies on axiological feelings.

EQUALITY VERSUS EQUITY

To begin with, I will illustrate this point by considering briefly the issue of the relations between equality and equity. There is a vast sociological and psychological literature on this important issue. I will simply mention that the general conclusion to be drawn from this literature is that the public considers a given type of inequalities equitable or not on the basis of reasons likely to be accepted by the *impartial spectator*, to use again Smith's concept: on the basis of reasons an ideal–typical individual would accept, under the assumption he would be in position to judge the inequalities in question with the sole help of his good sense and not of his passions, interests or prejudices. This cognitive approach explains some puzzling though empirically well-documented facts. I will restrict myself to two of them.

– People tend to perceive the income of the stars of the showbiz or of the most popular sports as *excessive*, but not as *unfair* or inequitable, while the income of big business leaders tends to shock them. This can be explained by the fact that the *impartial spectator* is reluctant to perceive as unfair inequalities resulting from free individual choices from the part of fans or supporters, while he rejects the idea that people could be entitled to decide by themselves or through their associates of the importance of their contribution to society.

– According to some illuminating but rare observations, people do not consider the reduction of the overall income distribution as a major political objective. This results probably from the fact that an overall income distribution is the product of functional inequalities, of inequalities that are not functional but reflect, say, differences in the dynamism of the socio-economic context, and of inequalities of which it is impossible to say whether they are functional or not. Consequently, the *impartial spectator* feels unable to judge whether the global level of inequality is fair or not. A moral negative reaction tends to appear though when the gap between high and low incomes is so great that it makes a functional justification unlikely. People take the standard deviation of overall income distributions into consideration essentially in this case (Forsé and Parodi 2004).

On the whole, once the observations made by the social sciences are synthesized on the issue of the relation between inequality and equity, they show that the *impartial spectator* or, in Weber's vocabulary, *axiological rationality* governs the attitudes and feelings of people on this issue as on all moral issues.

BOUNDED AXIOLOGICAL RATIONALITY

A study by Frohlich and Oppenheimer (1992) illustrates an important point: that the axiological rationality of the *impartial spectator* should be considered as *bounded*. It is bounded notably by the information available to him. Herbert Simon has made popular the idea that instrumental rationality is *bounded* in the sense that it is parameterized by the information available to the decision-maker. The same point can be introduced regarding axiological rationality. I will concentrate my discussion on the parameterization of rationality by the available *information* and disregard the well-known point that rationality is bounded by other social factors.

The study aimed at determining whether current theories of equity are able to reproduce the actual feelings of people as to whether some distribution of goods is fair or not. In this study, a number of groups were asked to choose a fictitious income distribution among a set of distributions. I need not describe the ingenious experimental procedure used by the authors. It suffices to say that the set of distributions was built in such a fashion that the choice of a given distribution among those that were proposed to the respondents allowed according to the authors of the study inferring which one of four principles of justice the subjects had likely in mind. The relations between the principles and the choices were the following.

Those who had in mind the principle drawn from *utilitarian* theory were supposed to choose the distribution with the highest *mean*.

Those who had in mind the *difference principle* drawn from Rawls's theory of justice—inequality should not be decreased to the point where the worse-off would be still worse—were supposed to select a distribution with a high *floor* and a moderate *standard deviation*.

Those who had in mind the principle that may be qualified as *pragmatic* were supposed to select a distribution with a good *mean* and an acceptable *floor*.

Those who had in mind the principle that may be called *functional* were supposed to select a distribution with a good *mean* and a moderate *standard deviation*.

The study has been conducted on samples of Americans and of Poles. First important finding is that one of the principles dominates strongly the others. The by far most frequent choice of the respondents was the *pragmatic* one (77.3%). The *utilitarian* principle comes next, but far behind (12.8%). The *functional* principle is still more seldom retained (8.64%). As to Rawls' *difference principle* of justice, it ranks last (1.23%). Another important finding from the study is that the same structure of answers characterizes the American and the Polish samples. In the two cases, the *pragmatic* choice is by far much more frequent than the three others. So, on the whole a strong majority (1) is concerned with the average income being as high as possible, (2) wants a decent floor, (3) cares little about the standard deviation.

When, as here, the distribution of answers appears as highly structured and context-free, in the sense that the answers of the Polish and the American respondents were similar, one can suppose that strong reasons are responsible for the distribution. The study proposed to the respondents a very abstract decision situation. They had to select the fairest distribution, but had no information as to where the income inequalities came from. The discussions that were conducted with the respondents suggest that they had the feeling that they could not answer the question as to whether the inequalities reflected in the income distributions were fair or not. So, given the *bounded* informational conditions created by the experiment, an attractive answer was to opt for a good mean and to pay little attention to the standard deviation. On the other hand, the respondents considered that it is a good thing to introduce a constraint on the floor, since some protection against the hazards of life is normally expected from a government. These reasons explain that the solution most frequently chosen was: good mean, income higher than some floor, little attention paid to standard deviation. The same reasons explain that actual democratic governments make more or less generally though implicitly the same choice as the respondents in the study. As the present conjuncture illustrates, a government cares about the standard deviation only in the case where the discrepancy between the highest and the lowest incomes is clearly not *functional*.

The system of reasons at work in the answers would have plausibly been different if the experimental conditions had been different. Thus, if the distributions proposed to the respondents would have been presented as reflecting, not fictitious global societies, but the distributions of salaries in some organization, they would probably have considered the standard deviation and tried to see whether it reflected functional inequalities. For, while it is impossible to determine what the fair standard deviation should be as far as a global society is concerned, this is not impossible in the case of an organization.

Other experiments (e.g., Mitchell et al. 1993) confirm the importance of these contextual *informational* effects. It consisted again in the presentation to respondents of fictitious income distributions. But in this case, the respondents were explicitly told whether the fictitious societies where *highly*, *moderately* or *weakly* meritocratic. In the latter case, the respondents tended to choose the Rawlsian solution.

MACROSOCIOLOGICAL MORAL FEELINGS EXPLAINED
BY THE COGNITIVE APPROACH TO MORALITY

The cognitively rational theory of axiological feelings is indispensable to explain macrosociological moral phenomena. The example of the wide consensus observable in modern democratic societies on the legitimacy of a moderately progressive income tax will provide a first illustration of this point.

The democratic societies have during a long period struggled on the question as to whether and in which form an income tax should be introduced. Once the idea was accepted after long political conflicts, the income tax was defined as proportional (*flat tax*). Then a consensus emerged on the principles: (1) that the idea of an income tax is good, (2) that it should be progressive, (3) but *moderately* progressive. The three principles describe the situation currently prevailing in most democratic countries, because the three principles can easily be legitimated by reasons likely to be widely accepted (Ringen 2007).

Sketchily presented, these reasons are the following. Modern societies are roughly composed, as already stated by Alexis de Tocqueville, of three social classes that have relations of cooperation and conflict with one another: (1) the rich, who have at their disposal a significant surplus which can be converted into political or social power; (2) the middle class, which enjoys a more or less important surplus, though insufficient to be converted into political or social power; (3) the poor.

Social cohesion, social peace and the principle of the dignity of all require that the poor benefit from a subvention, from the middle class in the first place, because of its numerical importance. But the middle class would not accept to assume its share if the rich would not accept to bear the load of the subvention to the poor to a greater extent than the middle class, in application of elementary principles of justice. It can be concluded from these reasons that the income tax should be progressive. On the other hand, it must be moderately progressive, since the efficiency principle would be violated if the tax were too brutally progressive, for the rich would then be incited to transfer their resources abroad, generating a loss for the national community.

On the whole, one can legitimately conclude that the consensus which we can observe on this issue results from a sequence of convincing reasons, accepted by most people in democratic societies because of their validity. Once he is sufficiently informed, any citizen, belonging to any of the social classes, would accept the idea that a moderately progressive income tax is a *good* thing. The validity of the argument is responsible for the consensus and for its stability through time. Some citizens are hostile to the idea, under the effect of their interests, prejudices, presuppositions or passions. Some economists recommend substituting a proportional tax (*flat tax*) to a progressive income tax. A few of them go as far as to propose to exclude any income tax. But they are isolated. They oversee the fact that the question has two dimensions: an instrumental and an axiological one and neglect the latter. And there are also Nietzscheans who would prefer to give all to the rich. Few people would follow them though.

Ringen's explanation of the general consensus that crystallized on a progressive income tax rests on a system of simple, obvious and mutually compatible reasons of which it can plausibly be assumed that many people have them in mind in a more or less conscious fashion. Systems of reasons different from the one he proposes could be produced. But, as in Smith's example on miners and soldiers, the challenge would be to show that they are more likely to ground the consensus. Interviews in a Socratic spirit—*focused interviews* in Merton's vocabulary—would of course increase the strength of the theory. When such interviews are not available or not possible though, as when sociologists deal with historical data, an ideal–typical system of simple, valid and compatible reasons is the only way open to them.

LONG-TERM TRENDS IN MORAL FEELINGS EXPLAINED BY THE COGNITIVE APPROACH TO MORALITY

The cognitive theory of axiological feelings makes also possible to explain middle and long-term trends in the institutions or mores, as already more or less explicitly seen by the greatest classical sociologists.

Durkheim (1960[1893]) observes that several secular trends characterize the change of the penalties applied in Western societies: an increasing number of categories of delinquent acts are treated by civil rather than penal courts. An increasing number of acts are prosecuted before courts of lower level. The penalties tend to become softer. These long-term trends are associated to short-term ups and downs that should not lead to ignore the existence of the long-term trends.

These long-term trends come from several factors, but mainly from a process of *rationalization*. The trend of the penalties becoming softer derives from the following mechanism: when a new type of penalty appears as equally effective in terms of dissuasion as a formerly used penalty and also as better from the point of view of some other criteria, the new type of penalty tends to be selected. In other words, a basic two-stage mechanism is at work in this type of processes: (1) innovation, (2) rational selection or rejection of the innovation. As the selection of a new political idea or institution is made, not in a classroom or laboratory, but in the political arena, it can take a long time and be more or less violent, but the new penalty has a chance to be selected as soon as there are subjectively strong and objectively valid reasons to prefer it to the older one. As Durkheim has shown, the increase in the demographic density, its effect on the division of labor and the influence of the latter on the diffusion and social recognition of individualistic values created a context that turned out to be favorable to the rationalization process.

The same analysis can be applied to our modern world. The death penalty tends to disappear from modern democratic societies notably because it has been repeatedly shown that its dissuasive power is questionable. Moreover, it makes judiciary errors irreparable. The progress in the methods of investigation has made that judiciary errors are more easily and have been more frequently identified in the recent years. This circumstance has contributed making judiciary errors a salient issue. These reasons tend to lead a continuously increasing number of people to prefer other types of penalties, as life sentencing.

This change explains why the fact that death penalty is applied in some states of the US is perceived as a moral stain on the American democracy by the Western public opinion as well as by large fractions of the public opinion in the US. Some groups justify the death penalty by religious reasons: by its supposed redemptory value. But the principle of the freedom of opinion implies that no sanction can be considered as acceptable if it is grounded on religious principles. This conclusion derives itself from the fact that a religion cannot be demonstrated true: a point the Catholic Church notably officially accepts since the Council Vatican II. Generally, all religions agree that believing in their dogmas is a matter of *faith*. Consequently, their principles cannot be imposed without hurting the principle of the freedom of opinion, a principle considered as basic in all democracies, since it derives itself from the principle of the dignity of all human beings. This set of strong reasons leads to the prediction that death penalty will probably be abolished in the US in a more or less remote future. The cognitive theory of morality can have a predictive beside its explanatory power.

The process, by which new political ideas or institutions are selected, though rational in the long-term, can of course be thwarted in the short term by unfavorable conjunctures. Max Weber stresses that *historical forces* threaten constantly rationalization (*Rationalisierung*). These unfavorable conjunctures can make, e.g., that the public opinion wants that the death penalty be reintroduced. As surveys have shown, this happens when barbarous crimes have been committed. Thus, in Belgium some years ago, a criminal was tried because he had locked up, raped and killed two young girls. A majority of Belgians appeared in surveys as in favor of reintroducing death penalty. But the political actors have refrained from taking any step in this direction, in many cases because of their personal convictions. But also because their convictions were consolidated by the fact that they were more or less clearly aware that the strong reasons which had led to the abolition of death penalty in all European countries would reappear on the political stage once the public emotion would have passed away and would disown them, since the abolition of death penalty is grounded on subjectively strong and objectively valid reasons.

MIDDLE-TERM CHANGES IN MORAL FEELINGS EXPLAINED BY THE COGNITIVE APPROACH TO MORALITY

The cognitive theory of axiological feelings can also explain middle-term changes in moral feelings. A number of observers have interpreted the trend toward more liberalism on moral issues that can be observed in the last decades in Western societies as an effect of the social movements of the 1960s. These movements should rather be interpreted as the expression of a long-term trend toward a *rationalization* of people's answers to moral, social, political and religious issues. As to the main agent of this rationalization process, it is the two-step *innovation-selection mechanism* evoked in the previous section.

This process of rationalization can be directly observed in the middle-term thanks to the survey on the *World values* led by Inglehart et al. (1998). It has inspired a host of analyses. For my part, I wondered whether the data corroborated the hypothesis of the existence of trends in moral feelings. To this effect, I grounded my reanalysis on a systematic comparison of the answers of the age and educational level groups in eight Western countries (Boudon 2008, Chapter 6).

The questions dealing with authority show that from the group of the older to the younger, from the less to the more educated a trend can be observed toward the disqualification of the *traditional* and *charismatic* forms of authority and an exclusive recognition of the *rational* form of authority. The social, moral and political importance of authority is well recognized by the younger and more educated respondents. But they want authority to be justified. They are ready to follow, but they want to be able to judge whether the goals and means proposed by the social actors invested with authority are legitimate.

The questions dealing with religious issues reveal also a trend toward rationalization in the sense that, from the older to the younger and from the less to the more educated, the attitudes toward religious issues seem to be more clearly led by three principles: (1) Nothing prevents people from worrying about questions dealing with the meaning of life or death. (2) Religions propose answers to this type of questions, but as they themselves recognize, their answers are a matter of faith. (3) Hence once should respect all religions, in agreement with the principle of the respect of all. It follows that the principle of the separation between the spiritual and the temporal authorities is a valid one. The sociological surveys show effectively that the younger and the more educated recognize more easily the importance of this latter principle in today's Western societies.

The questions dealing with moral issues in the narrow sense display the same trend toward rationalization. From the older to the younger and from the less to the more educated, a unique moral principle tends to prevail: the respect of other people. Consequently, the younger and the more educated respondents tend to accept as a fundamental moral principle the idea that, if some action or behavior has no negative effects on other people, it should be permitted. Following this trend, when an act or a type of behavior is forbidden and when it is impossible to show that it is detrimental to other people, the moral interdict tends to be seen as a *taboo*. The taboo against homosexuality weakened in the last decades as an outcome of this rationalization process.

Most respondents, young and old, more and less educated, believe in the distinction between good and evil. But, from the older to the younger and from the less to the more educated, the respondents think less frequently that the distinction would derive from a mechanical application of general principles. They want more frequently to know the reasons that make a state of affairs, an act or behavior good or evil. In most cases, the statistical effect of the variable *age* appears to a non-negligible extent as reflecting the overall increase in the level of education. This indicates that formal education is an important vector of the process of *rationalization* on moral issues.

To summarize, the moral trends in moral feelings that can be observed in Western societies in the last decades are rather the effect of a process of rationalization than the symptom of a *value crisis*.

SOCIOLOGICAL AND SOCIAL RELEVANCE OF THE COGNITIVE THEORY OF MORALITY

On the whole, the theory most likely to federate our growing body of knowledge on moral, prescriptive and generally axiological feelings is the cognitive theory according to which these feelings are the product of more or less coherent systems of reasons people perceive as valid. In a word, the processes generating convictions on moral, prescriptive and generally axiological issues are of the same nature as the processes generating convictions on descriptive issues. The systematization of ideas contained in an implicit and unelaborated fashion in Adam Smith's, Durkheim's, Max Weber's and other writings lead to a powerful theoretical tool. It can be used to explain the various types of data used by sociologists: data drawn from experimental research, survey data, qualitative data or official statistical data. It has also a predictive power, as the example of the death penalty shows.

Moreover, the cognitive approach to morality overcomes the difficulties raised by philosophical theories because it pays attention to the cognitive context individuals are embedded in and sees *axiological rationality* as bounded, in the sense where H. Simon described *instrumental rationality* as bounded.

As to the objection of *intellectualism* occasionally raised against the theory that *reasons* can be the main *causes* of moral feelings and beliefs, it ignores the phenomenon of intuition. I react negatively under the effect of emotion rather than deliberation when a strong young man attacks and steals an old lady. But my reaction is not merely affective. It is also intellectual: I am immediately able to *conceptualize* my reaction as a reaction of indignation and not, say, of fear. My reaction is furthermore *rational* in the sense that I know that it is grounded on subjectively strong and objectively valid reasons, even though I feel them in an *intuitive* fashion. In many cases we have to rely on intuition, on moral as well as representational issues. As the young slave in Plato's *Menon* is able to reconstruct Pythagoras' theorem under Socrates' guidance, people are often able to tell the reasons that ground their moral beliefs once they reflect about it or are guided by questions.

The cognitive theory is able to account for the contextual variations through time and space of axiological feelings, as illustrated by the example where, according to the available information, the respondents judge a given income distribution as fair or not, or by the example of the variations over time of the moral feelings on authority, interdicts, religion or death penalty. The cognitive theory can also explain the variations in moral feelings observed in cross-cultural studies. Thus, Gintis et al. (2003) have observed that the answers to the *ultimatum game* appear as to a limited extent variable with the cultural context. While respondents give the *fair* 50/50 answer in most cases, in countries where the social relations between neighbors are mainly competitive, as in South American rural contexts, respondents more often propose unfair sharing to their own advantage. Given the context, they have *reasons* to prefer instrumental to axiological reasons. But the contextual variation of reasons does not legitimate radical relativism. On many issues, the system of reasons prevailing in a context can be considered as better or worse than the system prevailing in other contexts. The sociological tradition derived from Weber or Durkheim—this is one of its great achievements—overcomes the dualism between contextualism and universalism.

The cognitive theory of morality has also a social and political relevance. Understanding the reasons as to why the rain rituals are practiced in some traditional societies protects against easy explanations of the type *they have a primitive mentality* and is a weapon against prejudice. Understanding the reasons as to why death penalty has been cancelled in a growing number of countries helps taking a position on its legitimacy. Furthermore, the cognitive theory gives sociology a predictive power. One can predict that death penalty is doomed to be abolished in all democracies in a more or less remote future since the dissuasive power of death penalty is controversial, since it makes impossible the correction of judiciary errors, since it can only be grounded on religious reasons and since religious reasons cannot be imposed to all without contradiction with the principle of the freedom of opinion, a principle grounded itself on the principle of the moral dignity of all.

One should not draw the conclusion that there would not be other approaches of morality beside the cognitive sociological approach I have advocated here. The neurological cognitive sciences show that the stimulation or the lesion of some well-identified parts of the brain can affect moral feelings and behavior (Damasio 1994). When some well-identified part of the brain of subjects playing the ultimatum game is stimulated, they accept an unfair proposal although they recognize it as unfair, while the subjects whose brain is not stimulated reject it (Henderson 2006). The cognitive-rational and the cognitive-neurological approaches both follow without doubt the scientific *ethos* and have both an uncontroversial explanatory power. Whether they will merge is an open question, as is the question of the future of sociobiology— another approach illustrated notably by Wilson (1993)—regarding the explanation of moral phenomena.

I doubt that these approaches can be easily integrated though, since the latter deal with the biological or neurological, the former with the cognitively rational dimension of human beings. According to Weber (1920:252), "Ideas are the main immediate causes of human action" (*Ideen beherrschen unmittelbar das Handeln des Menschen*).

REFERENCES

Boudon, R. 2008. *Essais sur la théorie générale de la rationalité: Action sociale et sens commun.* Paris: Presses Universitaires de France. English translation forthcoming 2010: *A Defense of Common Sense, Toward A General Theory Of Rationality.* Oxford: The Bardwell Press.

Damasio, A. 1994. *Descartes' Error: Emotion, Reason and the Human Brain.* London: Vintage Books.

Durkheim, E. 1960 [1893]. *De la division du travail social.* Paris: Presses Universitaires de France.

Durkheim, E. 1979[1912]. *Les Formes élémentaires de la vie religieuse.* Paris: Presses Universitaires de France.

Forsé, M., and M. Parodi. 2004. *La priorité du juste, éléments pour une sociologie des choix moraux.* Paris: Presses Universitaires de France.

Frohlich, N., and J. A. Oppenheimer. 1992. *Choosing Justice, An Experimental Approach to Ethical Theory.* Oxford: University of California Press.

Gintis, H. et al. 2003. "Explaining Altruistic Behaviour in Humans." *Evolution and Human Behavior* 24(3):153–172.

Habermas, J. 1981. *Theorie des Kommunikativen Handelns.* Frankfurt: Suhrkamp.

Harsanyi, J. C. 1955. "Cardinal Welfare, Individualistic Ethics, and Interpersonal Comparisons of Utility." *The Journal of Political Economy*, 63(4):309–321.

Henderson, M. 2006. "Why Say No to Free Money?" *Times Online*, 7 October.

Inglehart, R. et al. 1998. *Human Values and Beliefs – A Cross-Cultural Sourcebook: Political, Religious, Sexual, and Economic Norms in 43 Societies. Findings From the 1990–1993 World Values Survey.* Ann Arbor: University of Michigan Press.

Lukes, S. 1967. "Some Problems About Rationality." *Archives Européennes de Sociologie* 8(2):247–264.

Mitchell, G., P. E. Tetlock, B. A. Mellers, and L. D. Ordonez. 1993. "Judgements of Social Justice: Compromise Between Equality and Efficiency." *Journal of Personality and Social Psychology* 65(4): 629–639.

Parsons, T. et al. 1961. *Theories of Society.* Glencoe, IL: The Free Press.

Pascal, B. 1954 (1670). *Pensées.* Paris: Gallimard.

Radnitzky, G. 1987. "La Perspective économique sur le Progrès Scientifique: Application en philosophie des Sciences de L'analyse Coût-Bénéfice." *Archives de philosophie* 50:177–198.

Rawls, J. 1971. *A Theory of Justice.* Cambridge: The Belknap Press of Harvard University Press.

Ringen, S. 2007. *What Democracy is For?* Princeton: Princeton University Press.

Russell, B. 1954. *Human Society in Ethics and Politics.* London: Allen & Unwin.

Scheler, M. 1954. *Der Formalismus in der Ethik und die materiale Wertethik, in: Gesammelte Werke*, vol. 2. Bern/Munich: Francke.

Sen, A. 2002. *Rationality and Freedom.* Cambridge: The Belknap Press of Harvard University Press.

Simon, H. et al. 1983. *Economics, Bounded Rationality and the Cognitive Revolution.* Aldershot (UK): Edward Elgar.

Smith, A. 1793. *An Inquiry Into the Nature and Causes of the Wealth of Nations*, 7th ed. London: Strahan & Cadell, Ch. X, 151–209. Reproduced in Parsons et al. (1961), I, 518–529.

Sukale, M. 1995. "Introduction to: Max Weber." *Schriften zur Soziologie.* Stuttgart: Philipp Reclam.

Walzer, M. 1993. *Spheres of Justice. A Defense of Pluralism and Equality.* Oxford: Martin Robertson.

Weber, M. 1920. *Gesammelte Aufsätze zur Religionssoziologie.* Tübingen: Mohr.

Weber, M. 1922. *Wirtschaft und Gesellschaft: Grundriss der Sozialökonomik.* Tübingen: Mohr.

Weber, M. 1995(1919) *Wissenschaft als Beruf.* Stuttgart: Philipp Reclam.

Wilson, J. 1993. *The Moral Sense.* New York, Macmillan: The Free Press.

.

CHAPTER 3

Four Concepts of Morality

Differing Epistemic Strategies in the Classical Tradition

CHRISTOPHER POWELL

What is morality? Where does it come from? What are its forms and its dynamics? Each of the thinkers at the core of the classical sociological canon provided differing answers to these questions. Weber, Simmel, Durkheim, and Marx all viewed morality as a social phenomenon, accessible to empirical sociological or historical investigation; however, each conceived of the social in fundamentally different terms, and so each had a different object in view when they set out to investigate moral phenomena, and took different methodological routes into that investigation. This is more than a question of having differing moral priorities or taking differing positions on moral questions. The substantive answer to a specific moral question implicitly assumes a conception of what morality is and how it works. Different theoretical conceptualizations frame the stakes and the options of moral decision in incommensurate ways. Such differences make the sociology of morality a complex field, characterized by competing and, to some extent, mutually incompatible projects. This complexity is evident as much in the classical tradition as in more contemporary work. In this chapter I use the work of Weber, Simmel, Durkheim, and Marx to illustrate four different 'epistemic strategies' in sociology. These strategies are situated on a continuum from methodological individualism, represented by Weber's work, to holism, represented by Durkheim's, with Simmel's and Marx's projects at differing points in between. A fifth distinct strategy, epistemologically less holist than Marx's but more so than Simmel's, is absent from the classical tradition but important to contemporary sociology; I touch briefly on it and its implications at the end of my main discussion.

EPISTEMIC STRATEGIES

One convenient way of commensurating the different sociological conceptions of morality taken by the classical thinkers is provided by Kontopoulos's (1993) notion of "epistemic strategies." Epistemic strategies are types of methodological frameworks characterized by the way in which they refer to *emergent* phenomena. Emergence, loosely speaking, is the quality of "the whole being greater than the sum of its parts," or "much coming from little" (Holland 1998:2); more rigorously, it is "the arising of novel and coherent structures, patterns, and properties during the process of self-organization in complex systems" (Goldstein 1999:49). Emergence can

S. Hitlin, S. Vaisey (eds.), *Handbook of the Sociology of Morality*,
Handbooks of Sociology and Social Research, DOI 10.1007/978-1-4419-6896-8_3,
© Springer Science+Business Media, LLC 2010

be viewed ontologically – as in Durkheim's famous dictum that social facts should be treated as things (Durkheim 1982:60) – or epistemologically, in terms of levels of analysis that cannot be broken down into their constituent phenomena without a loss of explanatory power. One way or the other, emergent phenomena feature in much sociological explanation, whether these are called structures, systems, figurations, relations, discourses, signs, or something else.

Disputes about emergence of social structure have often taken on an all-or-nothing quality (Kontopoulos 1993:75)[1], making the number of epistemic strategies only two: individualism or holism. However, the use of emergence is more fruitfully understood in terms of a continuum, along which Kontopoulos distinguishes at least five general positions.[2] At one end is methodological individualism, which allows no emergent phenomena by insisting that all explanations in terms of collectivities or structures must in principle be reducible to explanation in terms of individual action. This position can be found in Weber's work, and in behaviorism and rational choice theory. Next on the scale is compositionism, which admits of supra-individual phenomena (such as forms, relations, or institutions), but does not propose that these phenomena combine further to constitute systems or organic wholes. This second position is represented in the classical tradition by Simmel. Skipping to the opposite end of the scale, we find holism: not only do social structures exist beyond individuals and exert a constraining effect on individual action; structures act directly on each other to form an integrated, organically unified system – that is, a system so effectively integrated that all of its parts are mutually complementary, with the exception only of some more or less severe pathologies. This position is taken by Durkheim, for whom the term 'society' refers to just such an organically integrated system. One step away from holism is the strategy of explaining social life in terms of systems whose subcomponents are irreducibly at odds with one another, through tensions and contradictions generated by the system itself. Marx's account of capitalism exemplifies this strategy, which Kontopoulos calls "modular hierarchy." Finally, at the middle of the spectrum lie the heterarchical projects: those that explain social life in terms of multiple, mutually irreducible social systems, each with their own relations and institutions, each tending (unsuccessfully) toward the totalization of social life. The heterarchical strategy is not represented in the classical tradition, but it is a feature of contemporary theory, and is exemplified in the work of Pierre Bourdieu. It is the most complex position, and raises interesting questions when applied to morality.

---

[1] As Margolis (1978) points out, this polarization reflects efforts by logical empiricists and other analytic philosophers, such as Dray, O'Neill, Popper, Suppe, and Watkins, to label as "collectivist" all positions other than strict methodological individualism. In this discourse, methodological collectivism was supposed to have an affinity with political collectivism, and methodological individualism with political individualism, so that the debate over emergence in sociological explanation carried resonances of the contest between Soviet communism and American liberalism.

[2] As an aside, I believe that Kontopoulos's five-part levels-of-emergence classification is a more robust way of framing differences among theoretical projects than the scheme presented by Collins (1994) which has become dominant among introductory textbooks, which divides sociology into three main traditions: functionalism, conflict theory, and interactionism. For instance, Kontopoulos's scheme recognizes, as Collins's does not, the fundamental differences between Marx and Weber, given that "'conflict' and 'contradiction' are not, after all, synonyms" (Ramp 2008:149), and recognizes the ways in which Marx's theorizing is more similar to Durkheim's than to that of methodologically individualistic conflict theories.

	Epistemic strategy	Distinguishing explanatory features	Characteristic theorist
5	Holism	Organically unified systems	Durkheim, Parsons
4	Modular hierarchy	Internally contradictory systems	Marx
3	Heterarchy	Multiple, internally contradictory, non-modular systems	Bourdieu, Foucault, Giddens (Not represented in the classical tradition)
2	Compositionism	Structures, but no systems	Simmel
1	Methodological individualism	Individual social action	Weber

FIGURE 3.1.   Five epistemic strategies.

WEBER'S METHODOLOGICAL INDIVIDUALISM AND MORALITY

In methodological individualism, emergent social phenomena do not appear. Social structures are theorized only as patterns in individual action, and are ultimately explained entirely in terms of the meaningful and motivated actions of individuals. Weber states this position explicitly in his methodological comments at the opening of *Economy and Society*[3]. Sociology "is a science concerning itself with the interpretive understanding of social action and thereby with a causal explanation of its course and consequences" (Weber 1978a:4). A social relationship is "the behaviour of a plurality of actors insofar as, in its meaningful content, the action of each takes account takes account of that of the others and is oriented in these terms"; it "thus consists entirely and exclusively in the existence of a probability that there will be a meaningful course of action" irrespective of the basis of that probability (Weber 1978a:26–27). Power is "the probability that one actor within a social relationship will be in a position to carry out his [sic] own will despite resistance, regardless of the basis on which this probability rests", domination is "the probability that a command with a given specific content will be obeyed by a given group of persons," and legitimacy is the "probability that action will actually be so governed" by "belief in the existence of a legitimate order" (Weber 1978a:53, 31). What we could call social structures (Weber does not give the term 'structure' a central place in his conceptual vocabulary) exist only as *clouds of probability* generated by the causal effects of subjectively meaningful motives on the actions of individuals; structures have no independent existence of their own.

In Weber's view, the common-sense way of speaking that says, for example, "the U.S. sent more troops to Iraq this week," or "the North abolished slavery," express a conceptual

---

[3] Weber's methodological statements in this text may not do justice to the full range of his methodological practice. Weber is, famously, interested in the unintended consequences of intentional action. This comes across vividly in *Protestant Asceticism and the Spirit of Capitalism*, in his analysis of how the meaning and consequences of Protestant concern for material success from a "light cape" to an "iron cloak," from a means of spiritual salvation to conformity with capitalist imperatives to produce and consume. A social dynamic informed by 'unintended consequences' is at least weakly emergent, so in practice Weber supplements his individualism with compositionism. Kontopoulos observes that there are degrees of methodological individualism (Kontopoulos 1993:85); Weber admits some emergent phenomena for pragmatic reasons but insists that the task of science in principle is to reduce these to individual action.

mistake: that of treating the combined actions of many people as if they were the single action of a single person. This is not pernicious in all contexts, but it has no place in sociology:

> For still other cognitive purposes – for instance, juristic ones – or for practical ones, it may on the other hand be convenient or even indispensable to treat social collectivities, such as states, associations, business corporations, foundations, as if they were individual persons. ... But for the subjective interpretation of action in sociological work these collectivities must be treated as *solely* the resultants and modes of organization of the particular acts of individual persons, since these alone can be treated as agents in a course of subjectively understandable actions. ... When reference is made in a sociological context to a state, a nation, a corporation, a family, or an army corps, or to similar collectivities, what is meant is, on the contrary, *only* a certain kind of development of actual or possible social actions of individual persons (Weber 1978a:13–14, emphasis in original).

As far as terms like 'Microsoft' or 'the Roman Catholic Church' or 'the state of Alabama' are concerned, Weber insists that:

> Though extremely pedantic and cumbersome, it would be possible, if purposes of sociological terminology alone were concerned, to eliminate such terms entirely, and substitute newly-coined words (Weber 1978a:14).

For Weber, all explanations of social life that make recourse to notions of institutions or collectivities must be reducible to explanations in terms of individual action.[4]

This rigorous methodological individualism accounts for Weber's conviction that sociology cannot answer moral questions.

> I am emphatically opposed to the view that a 'realistic' science of morality, in the sense of a demonstration of the factual influences exercised on the ethical convictions which prevail at any given time in a group of human beings by their other conditions of life and in turn by the ethical convictions on the conditions of life, would produce an 'ethics' which could ever say anything about what *ought* to be the case. [...] The one and only result which can ever be achieved by empirical psychological and historical investigation of a particular value-system, as influenced by the individual, social and historical causes, is its *interpretive explanation*. That is no small achievement (Weber 1978c:80).

Weber's position on this question is rather complex because his view "is certainly not that value-judgments are to be withdrawn from scientific discussion in general simply because in the last analysis they rest on certain ideals and are therefore 'subjective' in origin" (Weber 1949:52). In Weber's analysis, science can address questions of value in several ways: as technical criticism, by making clear the causal sequence of actions necessary to reach a given

---

[4] This principled insistence on thoroughgoing reductionism carries over into Weber's distinctive methodological concept, the ideal type. Weber characterizes the concept of "ideal type" in this way:

"For example, the same historical phenomenon may be in one aspect feudal, in another patrimonial, in another bureaucratic, and in still another charismatic. In order to give a precise meaning to these terms, it is necessary for the sociologist to formulate pure ideal types of the corresponding forms of action which in each case involve the highest possible degree of logical integration by virtue of their complete adequacy on the level of meaning. But precisely because this is true, it is probably seldom if ever that a real phenomenon can be found which corresponds exactly to one of these ideally constructed pure types" (Weber 1978a:20).

Elsewhere, he describes ideal types as "constructed concepts endowed with a degree of consistency seldom found in actual history" (Weber 2002:55).

end and, thereby, the practical cost of achieving that end; hermeneutically, by drawing out an empirically accurate and logically consistent account of the ideas that inform a given end and make it valuable; and critically, by testing the internal consistency of a desired end in light of the content and implications of the axiomatic principles from which the end is purportedly derived (Weber 1949:52–54). However, empirical science cannot go further than these tasks, which amount to clarifying what a person involves themselves in when they take on one or another value-commitment. Specifically, science cannot judge the validity of cultural values (Weber 1949:55, 57).

The normative scope of science is bounded by the dependence of science itself on subjectively generated cultural values:

> The *objective* validity of all empirical knowledge rests exclusively upon the ordering of the given reality according to categories which are *subjective* in a specific sense, namely, that they present the *presuppositions* of our knowledge and are based on the presupposition of the *value* of those *truths* which empirical knowledge alone is able to give us. … It should be remembered that belief in the value of scientific truth is the product of certain cultures and is not a product of man's original nature (Weber 1949:110).

And furthermore:

> The 'objectivity' of the social sciences depends rather on the fact that the empirical data are always related to those evaluative ideas which alone make them worth knowing and the significance of the empirical data is derived from these evaluative ideas. But these data can never become the foundation for the empirically impossible proof of the validity of the evaluative ideas (Weber 1946:111).

Empirically speaking, in Weber's view, all ultimate values, including both moral values and epistemic values, exist objectively within individual subjectivities, and as such are purely the property of individuals. Every individual carries inside herself or himself an ensemble of beliefs about right and wrong; these beliefs cause people to be likely to act in certain ways and not others. Weber affirms that science can study the internal meaning and coherence of moral beliefs, their logical implications for action, and their probable social effects (Weber 1978c:85, 86). However, from an individualistic view it follows that these *beliefs* do not refer to any external, objective reality that is empirically accessible, and so science cannot pronounce moral beliefs correct or incorrect. It's not that all moral views are equally correct or incorrect, but that the notion of 'correctness' does not apply *scientifically* to morals, any more than it applies to the destination of a journey: while one individual may judge another individual's ultimate moral values correct or incorrect on the basis of their *own* ultimate values, to a scientist the differing moral convictions of individuals are merely empirical phenomena to be explained causally.

Thus we can read Weber's "polytheism of values" (Gerth and Mills 1946:70; Weber 1946:147–148) as one expression of his epistemic strategy. Any methodologically individualist sociology of morality will imply a similar polytheism unless it makes recourse one of two additional elements: either a theory of human nature capable of showing certain values to be determined by that nature; or a metaphysical essentialism, such as a Kantian a priori, that sanctions particular values through a mechanism not accessible to a purely naturalistic science. Whatever his private beliefs, Weber did not include either of these in the foundational statements of his scientific method.[5] However, this did not preclude him from taking moral stands, nor from putting science at the service of deeply ethical ends.

Consider again the critical function of science capable of showing the necessary causal preconditions, the full hermeneutic ramifications, and the unintended consequences attendant on any given 'value-rational' course of action. Weber's science is still a *sociology* of action, and as such, it examines a universe in which human beings act, not in isolation, but in relation to each other (indeed, orientation to the actions of another is one of the defining features of social action as such). Any social actor, with her own values and motives, encounters others *as* others with *their* own values and motives, upon which the success of one's own actions depends. Nor is this an equal world; society is fundamentally stratified by various forms of class, by status, and by power and domination. It is amidst such constraints, and not in any transcendental domain, that actors must form their values and make moral choices. We cannot create our values *in practice* through sheer force of will. Moreover, even the most successful actions have causal ramifications that exceed the knowledge, and hence the control, of those who perform them. (*The Protestant Ethic and the Spirit of Capitalism*, for instance, may perhaps be read more fruitfully as a case study in how a social project exceeded its originators' intentions than as an argument about the origins of capitalism.) By conceptualizing the social realm in terms of the play of *causality*, Weber situated subjectivity amidst objective forces that radically exceed the will of the intending subject. Sociology illuminates the dynamics of these causal forces, reveals the conditions and the consequences of action. In this way, sociology extends the ability of subjects to act 'as they intend' – but not infinitely, since the causal dynamics of social interaction are themselves objective forces. Values, too, change in response to sociological knowledge, as we discover that some intentions will necessarily produce outcomes contrary to our desires.

Weber's science is thus a struggle for the freedom to make moral choices against the unknown and unintended constraints of social life. His personal ethics express this struggle. Values, he writes, are most valid when worked out in "those innermost elements of the 'personality'" and "developed in the struggle against the difficulties which life presents" (Weber 1949:55). The political actor he celebrates is the one who can join together passionate commitment to deeply felt personal values with an ethic of responsibility based on the ability to judge the objective constraints to subjectively motivated action. "Politics," Weber writes, "is a matter of boring down strongly and slowly through hard boards" (Weber 1978b:225). Science sharpens the drill.

SIMMEL'S EPISTEMIC STRATEGY: COMPOSITIONISM

If Weber is not a moralizing sociologist, Simmel is even less of one. Indeed, an overt examination of moral values appears at only a few points in Simmel's works. What he does say about morality seems, at first glance, even more explicitly subjectivistic than Weber's position.

---

[5] Or not explicitly. Boudon, in this volume, argues that a cognitive theory of values is implicit in Weber's theorization of value-rationality.

> [L]aw is best limited to the indispensable presuppositions of group life: what the group *can* unconditionally require of the individual is only what is *must* require unconditionally. By contrast, the free morality of the individual knows no other law than that which he autonomously gives himself. In practice, therefore, its jurisdiction has accidental and fluid borderlines that change from case to case, although in principle it extends to the totality of action (Simmel 1950:100).

This fluidity is limited, however, by social value of morality as an instrument of control over individuals.

> Individual morality is important to society and is bred by it only insofar as it guarantees as much as possible that the individual act in a socially efficient manner. [. . .] In its tendency to obtain its prerequisites as cheaply as possible, society also makes use of "good conscience" (Simmel 1950:101)

In practice, then, morality is determined both by individual *and* collective forces. Moreover, these forces are not actually distinct in Simmel's conceptual scheme. Moral conscience results from social forces operating *within* individual subjectivity, as a synthesis of social interaction and cognitive disposition:

> Morality develops in the individual through a second subject that confronts him in himself. By means of the same split through which the ego says to itself "I am" – confronting itself, as a knowing subject, with itself as a known object – it also says to itself "I ought to". The relation of two subjects that appears as an imperative is repeated within the individual himself by virtue of the fundamental capacity of our mind to place itself in contrast to itself, and to view and treat itself as if it were somebody else (Simmel 1950:99).

If we read Simmel in terms of a strict subject-object dualism, his position seems to waver uncertainly between individualist and holist conceptual terms. In the terms of a continuum of epistemic strategies, Simmel's theory reads coherently as a type of theory that is neither individualist nor holist, but compositionist.

Weber's insistence that all sociological concepts must in principle reduce to accounts of individual action means that supra-individual social forces have no autonomous theoretical status. Social relations, institutions, and legitimate orders all reduce to clouds of probabilities of individuals acting towards each other. Georg Simmel frames his sociological inquiry in decisively different terms:

> Let us grant for the moment that only individuals "really" exist. Even then, only a false conception of science could infer from this "fact" that any knowledge which somehow aims at synthesizing these individuals deal with merely speculative abstractions and unrealities. Quite on the contrary, human thought always and everywhere synthesizes the given into units that serve as subject matters for the sciences (Simmel 1950:4–5).

By accepting the epistemological value of synthetic abstractions, Simmel allows collective phenomena to appear as theoretical concepts:

> The stubborn assertion that after all there exist nothing but individuals which alone, therefore, are the concrete objects of science, cannot prevent us from speaking of the histories of Catholicism and Social Democracy, of cities, and of political territories, of the feminist movement, of the conditions of craftsmen, and of thousands of other synthetic events and collective phenomena – and, therefore, of society in general (Simmel 1950:6).

In other words, "out of the sum total of individual elements which constitute it [society], a new entity emerges" (Simmel in Frisby 1990:47).

Admitting emergent phenomena into his sociology allows Simmel to attribute those phenomena with properties and dynamics not present in the minds of individuals. Thus, the mysterious ability of social relations to take forms not anticipated, and even not desired, by the actors who participate in them becomes accessible to direct inquiry:

> The large systems and the super-individual organizations that customarily come to mind when we think of society, are nothing but immediate interactions that occur among men (sic) constantly, every minute, but that have become crystallized as permanent fields, as autonomous phenomena. As they crystallize, they attain their own existence and their own laws, and may even confront or oppose spontaneous interaction itself (Simmel 1950:10).

"At the same time," however, "society, as its life is constantly being realized, always signifies that individuals are connected by mutual influence and determination" (Simmel 1950:10). The social forms postulated by Simmel are always only one level of emergence away from individuals' interactions, from "sociation." Society "certainly is not a 'substance,' nothing concrete, but an *event*: it is the function of receiving and effecting the fate and development of one individual by the other" (Simmel 1950:11). Therefore Simmel does not, as Durkheim does, further synthesize the particular emergent phenomena in society into a whole and proceed to study how the properties of the whole determine those of the parts. His position is rather that "only when we have fully examined all the forms of sociation [...] can we answer the question 'What is society?]'" (Frisby 1990:46). What is theoretically proposed is a field of emergent social forms; the total structure of society is to appear as the outcome of empirical investigation of these forms, and is not theoretically presupposed.

These two features – the admission of emergent social phenomenon, and the refusal of overarching social systems – define the type of epistemic strategy that Kontopoulos labels "compositionist" (1993:12, 20–24, 102ff.).[6] Simmel's unit of analysis for studying the composite structure of society is "sociation," a term that refers to the synthesis of interactions into a relationship (Simmel 1950:9–10)[7]. Society itself is simply the field of all sociation:

---

[6] Although "methodological individualism" and "holism" are widely recognized terms for the epistemic strategies they connote, there is no established terminology for differentiating the positions in between these two poles. Kontopoulos actually uses the terms "constructionist" and "compositionist" interchangeably to refer to strategies, like Simmel's, that posit emergent structures without positing the synthesis of those structures into further emergent systems. However, the term "constructionism" can also refer to a more specific project within sociology (Berger and Luckmann 1966) or to a range of positions in philosophical thought (Hacking 1999). I have chosen to use only 'compositionism', because it lacks these overlapping or extraneous connotations, and because its root suggests an apt image: of society formed as the composite of many particular structures, each of which nevertheless retains its distinctiveness and relative autonomy.

[7] It refers, at the same time, to the existence of a relationship as concrete interactions. Simmel sometimes characterizes sociation in what seem like strikingly different terms – such as "the life of groups as units" (Simmel 1950:26). Expressions like these cohere with the conception of sociation as social relations because Simmel constantly stresses that his synthetic concepts go both ways: the individual derives their social existence from groups, but groups derive their existence from the interactions of individuals.

> Here, "society", properly speaking, is that being with one another, for one another, against one another which, through the vehicle of drives or purposes, forms and develops material or individual contents and interest. The forms in which this process results gain their own life (Simmel 1950:43).

Simmel makes the investigation of these forms the central activity of his sociology, producing formal analyses of sociability, superordination and subordination, secrecy, city life (Simmel 1950), space, fashion, religion (Frisby and Featherstone 1997), money (Simmel 1990), femininity, gender, flirtation, love (Simmel 1984), and "social types," such as "the poor," "the adventurer," and – most famously – "the stranger" (Simmel 1971). His work analyzes the significance of number for social relationships, parsing the different dynamics that are possible for isolated individuals, dyads, triads, and larger groups (Simmel 1950, 1971). In all of these investigations, Simmel puts the emergent properties of social forms at the center of his investigation and analyzes their distinctive dynamics. Although he diligently includes consideration of individuals' motivations and psychological states, and the imperatives of group life on a large scale, social forms do not reduce to individuals' actions and are not subsumed into the functional life of some social body.

Morality receives the same treatment. Morality is a form whose contents are highly variable:

> We deal here with *forms* of the intrinsic and extrinsic relation of the individual to his (sic) social group. For, the same contents of this relation has historically been clothed in different motivations or forms. What at one time or place was a custom, elsewhere or later has been a law of the state or has been left to private morality. What was under the coercion of law, has become mere good custom. What was the matter of individual conscience, later has often enough been legally enforced by the state, etc. The poles of this continuum are law and morality, and between them stands custom, out of which both have developed (Simmel 1950:100).

In this respect, morality is typical of the tendency of the contents of sociation to become detached from their original objects and to "play freely in themselves and for their own sake" (Simmel 1950:41). This autonomization produces a special kind of objectivity. Justice, for instance, develops from "a matter of social expedience or of social impulses" to "an objective relationship which follows necessarily from the intrinsic significance of sin and pain, good deed and happiness, offer and response," something that "must be realized for its own sake" (Simmel 1950:259–260). Morality, similarly, develops from "the devotion of the 'I' to the 'thou'" into philosophical doctrines in which "an absolutely objective Ought is separated from the question of 'I' and 'thou'" (Simmel 1950:260). In both cases, "subordination under society" becomes, over time, through the autonomization of the social contents of normativity, "subordination under objectivity" (Simmel 1950:258).

Simmel's theorization of society as a source of objectivity thus echoes Marx's analysis of commodity fetishism (Marx 1990:58) and foreshadows Berger and Luckmann's discussion of reification (1966:106–109). As Simmel writes, "the concept of society has liberated us" from supposing that "a cultural value either must spring from an individual or must be bestowed upon mankind by an objective power" (Simmel 1950:257). However, the objectivity of society for Simmel is different from that of physical nature. Where nature is concerned, objectivity "denotes the irrelevance of the question of whether or not the subject spiritually participates in nature; whether he has a correct, a false, or no conception of it" (Simmel 1950:257). The objectivity of society, on the other hand, includes and depends upon the involvement of the subjectivity of individuals. Even "harsh indifference towards the individual is also an interest", the result of a particular social formation that needs individual subjectivity without needing any one particular individual. The objectivity of morality, in Simmel's analysis, not only is socially produced, but is so by historically particular social conditions.

Simmel's move away from methodological individualism, toward the middle of the individualism-holism spectrum, accentuates the relativizing tendency of sociological analysis. Simmel himself acknowledges this, writing:

> ... the basic tendency of modern science is no longer to comprehend phenomena through or as specific substances, but as motions, the bearers of which are increasingly divested of any specific qualities; and it expresses the qualities of things in quantitative, i.e. relative, terms. Science posits, instead of the absolute stability of organic, psychic, ethical and social forms, a ceaseless development in which each element has a restricted place determined by the relationship to its own past and future. It has abandoned the search for the essence of things and is reconciled to stating the relationships that exist between objects and the human mind from the viewpoint of the human mind (Simmel 1990:103).[8]

Simmel qualifies this relativism by invoking the absolute preconditions imposed on human perception by cognition itself. That is, he invokes the *a priori* features of individual human subjectivity as a fixed point to which social contingency is anchored. However, Simmel's compositionist epistemic strategy puts his sociology at one further remove from this anchorage point than Weber's methodological individualism, and so it is perhaps not surprising that Simmel expresses skepticism about his own Kantian presuppositions:

> What did this man not inflict upon the world when he explained it as an idea! When will the genius appear who will emancipate us from the spell of the subject in the same way that Kant liberated us from the constraint of the object? And what will this third category be? (Simmel 1980:4).

As we shall also see when comparing Marx to Durkheim, a move away from the poles of the individualism-holism spectrum makes recourse to absolute or universalistic conceptions of morality increasingly untenable.[9]

DURKHEIM'S EPISTEMIC STRATEGY: HOLISM

The conception of social structure that Durkheim lays out in his *Rules of Sociological Method*[10] occupies the opposite pole to the conception that Weber prescribes in *Economy*

---

[8] For an example of this relativizing tendency in Simmel's own work, see his discussion of value in *The Philosophy of Money* (Simmel 1990).

[9] In this regard, Simmel's work foreshadows the stance of postmodernists (e.g. Rosenau 1992) who treat subjectivity as determined by emergent social forces that themselves are undetermined by any overarching systemic logic. The implications of this view for normative questions, and by extension for moral questions in particular, are declared by Lyotard (1984) in his famous analysis of the condition of scientific knowledge in a world without metanarratives.

[10] It is important to be text-specific on this point because the methodology that Durkheim used in his actual studies is more complex than the one laid out in the *Rules*. For example, in the *Rules* Durkheim states that one should

It may be of academic interest to consider the nature & aetiology of morality: Weber's method. indiv. as a property of the indiv (E e S); Durkheim as a sound fact, extent constraint (Rules); B Russell not given by God but emerged in struggle for existence; Schw. beyond about theorising to its practical effects.

3.   **Four Concepts of Morality**   45

and Society. Durkheim affirms that social structures exists as "things" (Durkheim 1982:60), emergent from social action, which he calls *social facts*, which constitute the distinctive and proper object of study for sociology as a science.

> Sociological method as we practice it rests wholly on the basic principle that social facts must be studied as things, that is, as realities external to the individual. ...if no reality exists outside of the individual consciousness, [sociology] wholly lacks any material of its own (Durkheim 1979:37–38).

A social fact is "any way of acting, fixed or not, capable of exerting over the individual an external constraint" (Durkheim 1982:59). Without having the specific concept of emergence at his disposal, Durkheim heralds it by stating that society has a reality *sui generis* (literally, a reality "of its own kind"), and illustrating this reality by analogy to the difference between a living organism and the chemical substances of which it is composed. Echoing Spencer (1971), Durkheim observes that

> Whenever elements of any kind combine, by virtue of this combination they give rise to new phenomena. One is therefore forced to conceive of these phenomena as residing, not in the elements, but in the entity formed by the union of these elements. The living cell contains nothing save chemical particles, just as society is made up of nothing except individuals. Yet it is very clearly impossible for the characteristic phenomena of life to reside in atoms of hydrogen, oxygen, carbon and nitrogen. [. . .] Life cannot be split up in this fashion. It is one, and consequently cannot be located save in the living substance in its entirety. It is in the whole and not in the parts (Durkheim 1982:39).

And, says Durkheim, so too with society, which exists as a whole and not in its parts. Social facts have an existence "independent of their individual manifestations" (Durkheim 1982:59); they "must therefore be considered in themselves, detached from the conscious beings who form their own mental representations of them. They must be studied from the outside, as external things" (Durkheim 1982:70). And in particular, "the determining cause of a social fact must be sought among antecedent social facts and not among the states of individual consciousness" (Durkheim 1982:134). According to the uncompromising precepts of the *Rules of Sociological Method*, causation runs downward and not upward: social facts constrain individuals, but individuals do not constrain social facts through the exercise of their own agency. At times in his other writings, Durkheim even celebrates the insignificance of the individual in the face of the godlike immensity and determining force of society (Durkheim 1995:208–209).

The particular social facts in a society combine to form an integrated whole, which is society. Like Spencer before and Parsons (1951, 1966) after him, Durkheim treated the parts of society as interdependent and complimentary in the manner of the organs of a living body. Although Durkheim's distinction between mechanical and organic solidarity (Durkheim 1984:129–132) might seem to imply that only modern societies with a complex division of

---

always characterize social facts by their "external" characteristics (Durkheim 1982:75), and one should never seek to explain social facts in terms of psychological mechanisms but only explain them in terms of the operation of other social facts (Durkheim 1982:134). However, practice Durkheim often does incorporate subjective perceptions and motivations into his sociology (Durkheim 1979, Durkheim 1995). To borrow a phrase from Friedland and Alford (1991), subjectivity and individual action are "recognized empirically" but "disappear theoretically" in Durkheim's work.

labor are organic, this distinction is situated within a generally functionalist conception of society and an evolutionary model, similar to Spencer's, in which differing "species" of social organism evolve from lower to higher orders of complex functional differentiation. So, for instance, Durkheim asks what "function" is served by the division of labor itself (Durkheim 1984:11). Elsewhere he argues that "the State is the very organ of social thought" and "the organ of moral discipline," the proper function of which is to "persevere in calling the individual to a moral way of life" (Durkheim 1992:51, 72, 69). And in conceptualizing the difference between "normal" and "pathological," Durkheim firstly makes clear that these terms refer to the health and morbidity of societies, as distinct from that of individuals,[11] and secondly asserts that different "species" of societies, like different species of biological organisms, have different functional needs, so that what is normal for one "species" of society might be pathological for another, and vice versa. By opposing "normal" to "pathological," Durkheim equates normal with healthy, and he affirms that the task of sociology is precisely to diagnose ills in the social body and prescribe remedies for them (Durkheim 1982:104).

This brings us to Durkheim's conception of morality. In contrast to Weber, who claimed that there could be no scientific answers to moral questions, Durkheim strongly affirmed that there could:

> Yet because what we propose to study is above all reality, it does not follow that we should give up the idea of improving it. We would esteem our research not worth the labour of a single hour if its interest were merely speculative. [...] [A] state of moral health exists that science alone can competently determine and, as it is nowhere wholly attained, it is already an ideal to strive towards it (Durkheim 1984:xxvi).

The possibility of answering moral questions scientifically ensues from Durkheim's conception of morality as a social fact. In *Rules of the Sociological Method*, he defines as moral any precept whose violation is condemned by public opinion or by widespread, repressive sanction, saying that

> [w]henever we are confronted with a fact that presents this characteristic we have no right to deny its moral character, for this is proof that it is of the same nature as other moral facts (Durkheim 1982:80–81).

In *Professional Ethics and Civic Morals* he reaffirms this formalism by defining moral facts as "rules of conduct that have sanction" (Durkheim 1992:2). In *Moral Education* he characterizes morality in terms of rules that are *customary*, hence socially instituted, but that are *authoritative*, that individuals do not feel free to alter according to their own interests or tastes (Durkheim 2002:23–24, 29–31). The authority of morality comes from outside of individuals, but not from outside the natural universe; rather, it comes from society as a supra-individual entity existing within the natural universe (Durkheim 2002:85–86). And in *The Division of Labour in Society*, Durkheim argues that the ultimate function of morality is social solidarity:

---

[11] So, famously, crime is normal, even though (and precisely because) it is everywhere forbidden (Durkheim 1982:97–104). The existence of crime expresses the presence of (a) communal distinctions between allowed and prohibited conduct and (b) the existence of varying dispositions among the members of the community, both of which Durkheim claims are necessary to social life as such. Therefore, too little crime is equally a symptom of social pathology as too much.

> We must say that which is moral is everything that is a source of solidarity, everything that forces man [sic] to take account of other people, to regulate his actions by something other than the promptings of his own egoism, and the more numerous and strong these ties are, the more solid is the morality (Durkheim 1984:331).

Or again:

> Moral goals, then, are those the object of which is society. To act morally is to act in terms of the collective interest. ..... Above and beyond me as a conscious being, above and beyond those sentient beings who are other individual human beings, there is nothing else save that sentient being that is society. By this I mean anything that is a human group, the family as well as the nation, and humanity, at least to the extent that they constitute societies (Durkheim 2002:59–60).

Morality, for Durkheim, is not any specific set of values or rules but a *type* of rule; moral facts are recognizable by their form, not their content. This allows us to investigate actual moral practices in a non-ethnocentric way. Whenever we encounter a social fact that has the form of morality, we must study it as such, even if its content seems abhorrent to us.

Durkheim's conception of morality is socially relative in an entirely different way than Weber's. For Weber there are scientific answers to the question "what do social actors consider morally right and wrong?", but not to the question "what *should* social actors consider morally right and wrong?", because morality is relative to individual subjectively meaningful action. For Durkheim there *are* scientific answers to this latter question, but they vary from one 'species' of society to the next. This is because they are relative to the objective determinants of solidarity in each social organism – the factors that, in their objective consequences, promote or detract from the integration of the interdependent social facts that make up that society. "Every people has its moral code that is determined by the conditions under which it is living" (Durkheim 1984:184). Moral questions can have objective scientific answers, but these answers will be culture-bound.

However, this relativistic tendency is mitigated by the teleological quality of Durkheim's conception of evolution. Saint-Simon (1975:130–136) postulated that the evolution of societies was linear, from the simple, local, and small-scale units of family and tribe, through the present condition of nation-state societies, to an eventual global society, the outlines of which he believed he could already discern in European internationalism. Durkheim's linear arrangement of types of solidarity, from the 'horde' to mechanical and then to organic solidarity, follows a similar arc (Durkheim 1984), and echoed Saint-Simon in arguing that contemporary national patriotism served as an evolutionary stepping stone to a more 'universal' "human patriotism" (Durkheim 1992:75) proper to a world-society. This teleological evolutionary organicism implies a future-oriented moral universalism, in which the moral norms or different species of society can be judged to be closer to or further away from the culmination of social evolution in a universal human solidarity.

Against this backdrop we can understand the debate over Durkheim's allegedly conservative or progressive tendencies. In the context of his own society Durkheim was in many ways a progressive: secularist, cosmopolitan, a *Dreyfusard*. His progressive stances cohere with his sociological conviction that moral and political individualism ("the cult of the individual") is itself a social fact, produced by the increasingly complex division of labor in society. If individuals perceive themselves as independent agents and act accordingly, a social fact makes this possible. As for rights,

> [t]he reason why [the individual] has more or fewer rights, certain rights and not others,
> is not that he is constituted in a particular way; it is because society attributes this or
> that importance to him and attaches a higher or a lower value to what concerns him
> (Durkheim 1992:67).

Durkheim favored rights because, and to the extent that, the increasing division of labor, and
the demands of organic solidarity, make respect for the freedom and dignity of individuals
appropriate and necessary to the normal functioning of modern society.

On the other hand, Durkheim's criteria of normalcy and pathology have an implicit conservative tendency in their tendency to valorize the status quo. Durkheim proposes that a social
fact *must* be recognized as normal, either if it is common to all members of the species of
social organism in which it is found, or, alternatively and equivalently, if it is grounded in the
nature of that organism (Durkheim 1982:102–107; see also Powell 2011). By this criteria, the
genocidal massacre that was a routine feature of Spanish colonization in the Americas in the
early seventeenth century, or the depredations of the transatlantic slave trade in the late eigh-
teenth century, might well qualify as normal – and the activism of figures like Bartolomé de
las Casas and Olaudah Equiano as pathological. Likewise, if contemporary Chinese society is
taken as belonging a different species of social organism than Western liberal democracies, the
Tiannmen Square protests of 1989 might well count as pathological, for that society. When a
given practice is normalized and an integral part of the order of things, a Durkheimian sociological justification for dissent requires showing that the organic constitution of society is
changing so as to make existing functional structures obsolete, and oppositional activity the
first forms of a new order in the making. This is a higher burden of proof than the converse.[12]

Does this mean that Durkheim morally approves of *any* social order capable of establishing solidarity among its members? Does his work express no preference between, for instance,
the American and the Chinese solutions to the challenges of modernization? The answer is yes
and no. Durkheim's own progressive commitments on the one hand and his formal prescription for the science of morality fit hand in glove as long as it remains empirically plausible
that an advancing division of labor necessarily makes moral individualism the optimum basis
for social solidarity. They part ways if we suppose that moral solidarity may take a variety of
forms within the same economic structure. Between multiple alternative models for the future
development of society, each of which succeeds in establishing its own organic integration,
Durkheim's sociology provides us with no means of adjudicating.

This sort of indeterminacy, however, would be out of place within Durkheim's holist epistemic strategy. For the whole to explain the parts reliably, one must assume that the interaction
of the parts tends automatically to one particular outcome, in which the properties of the parts
are aligned with the needs of the whole. Durkheim assumed that human nature was highly
socially malleable. On the one hand, individuals are incapable of limiting their own desires
without externally imposed social constraints; without these constraints, individuals cannot
satisfy their desires and therefore cannot be happy (Durkheim 2002:38–46). On the other hand,

---

[12] This high burden of proof might help to explain why Durkheim failed to incorporate feminist thought into his analysis of moral individualism (Kandal 1988, Lehman 1995, Pedersen 2001, Sydie 1987). That is, perhaps Durkheim
was unable to perceive women's struggles for emancipation as having the sort of critical mass indicative of a transformation grounded in the very nature of modern society, and so felt justified in ignoring it as a pathological symptom
of anomie.

individuals experience happiness relative to the constraints and opportunities of their society, so that "the savages are as content with their lot as we can be with our own" (Durkheim 1984:189). Therefore, in a healthy society, human happiness is adapted to the moral duties made necessary by the social organism.

A holist theory like Durkheim's can criticize society for not having effective moral norms adequate to the practical interdependency fostered by its division of labor. It cannot criticize society on the grounds that the very principle of its integration is somehow pathological. For this criticism to be possible, one must be able to imagine an irreconcilable contradiction between the demands of society and the fulfillment of human happiness. Such a contradiction could be argued on the basis of a pre-social human nature which goes unfulfilled in the current form of society. However, arguments from human nature are difficult even to entertain if one accepts the strong claims of emergence found in holist epistemic strategies. More troubling to a sociologist of the Durkheimian persuasion is the contention that the social order contradicts *itself*, that it systematically imbues its members with imperatives which it ensures they cannot fulfill. Just this sort of contradiction is at the heart of Marx's sociology and his hierarchical epistemic strategy.

MARX'S EPISTEMIC STRATEGY: HIERARCHY

Although Marx's theoretical project has been read in the terms of holist (Althusser 1971), compositionalist (e.g., Thompson 1963) or even individualist terms (e.g., Elster 1985, 1986), his theoretical concern with structure *and* agency, with how "men make their own history, but they do not make it as they please" (Marx 1979:103), is most coherent in the terms of a hierarchical epistemic strategy (Kontopoulos 1993:192–193). Hierarchical epistemologies conceptualize society as a partially integrated, partially self-contradictory system. It is integrated inasmuch as all actions, relations, and institutions combine to generate, and are inexorably constrained by, a single overarching systemic logic. In Marxian theory this is the logic of class, embodied in the mode of production. Within the mode of production, however, social forces are organized into mutually interdependent *and antagonistic* tendencies, which Kontopoulos calls 'modules'. The most important modules in Marxian theory are the opposed forces of capital and labor, whose interdependence and antagonism are generated by the logic of the mode of production (Marx 1975). All other antagonisms are theoretically subordinate to the class struggle, so that sex/gender, for instance, is conceived of as generating its divisions *within* the divisions of class (Engels 1972, Marx and Engels 1976). Theoretically speaking, these divisions are "nested" within class divisions. Open a box to find inside it many smaller boxes, each of which itself contains many smaller boxes, and so on: this is a rough image of a nested modular hierarchy.[13]

Marx's theorization in terms of a modular and nested hierarchy distinguishes his analysis fundamentally *both* from Durkheim's functionalism *and* from Weber's pluralist conflict theory.

---

[13] This is an oversimplified image, however, because it leaves out the lateral relations among modular subsystems at the same level of emergence.

In the first, case modularity means that there can be contradictions between different structures, and that these contradictions can be an intrinsic feature of the overall organization of the system. In first case, although both Marx and Durkheim employ strongly emergentist and systemic concepts (social relations constituting a mode of production; social facts constituting a social organism), their emergentisms differ fundamentally on the question of integration. For Durkheim, society forms or tends to form an organically interdependent whole, such that severe antagonisms which destabilize the social order are conceptualized as pathological exceptions to the systemic logic. Specifically, the conflicts between workers and owners are not radically irreconcilable within capitalism, but are the contingent pathologies of a system in transition (Durkheim 1984). In Marx's analysis, on the other hand, the relationship between labor and capital cannot *by any means* be transformed into one of functional interdependence and complimentarity. For Marx, exploitation is not some exceptional or pathological state of affairs, but a necessary, ubiquitous, and constitutive feature of capitalism: the appropriation of surplus value from workers by capitalists, from which all profit derives (Marx 1990:326). Exploitation is implicit in the "general formula for capital", M–C–M (Marx 1990:256–257), and as such is part of the genetic code of capitalist society, distributed throughout the social body and conditioning its operation on the most fundamental level. Because of exploitation, "the worker becomes poorer the richer is his [sic] production" (Marx 2000a:86): exploitation turns the productive forces of workers against them: "Just as he turns his production into his own loss of reality and punishment and his own product into a loss, a product that does not belong to him, so he creates the domination of the man who does not produce over the production and the product. (Marx 2000a:92).

In the second case, although both Marx and Weber make conflict central to their sociologies, they conceptualize it in substantially opposed ways. Weber's theory assumes that conflict arises from the *separateness* of individuals: their being separate and relatively autonomous units of action accounts for why individuals should compete for class, status, and power. In Marxian theory, on the other hand, it is the very *connections* between individuals and their *integration* into class relations that generates class struggle. Labor and capital do not exist separately from one another and come into conflict only through a historical process; they are not even, primarily, groups of people with common attributes. Rather, labor and capital are the two ends of the same relationship; "capitals presupposes wage labor; wage labor presupposes capital. They reciprocally condition the existence of each other; they reciprocally bring forth each other" (Marx 2000b:283). Or, again, "wages and private property are identical."

> The relationship of the worker to his labour creates the relationship to it of the capitalist, or whatever else one wishes to call the master of the labour. Private property is thus the product, result, and necessary consequence of externalized labour, of the exterior relationship of the worker to nature and to himself (Marx 2000a:93).

Because certain fundamental social conflicts[14] result, not from any existential condition, but precisely from the manner in which people are joined together socially – that is, class relations – and because class relations generate, through their normal operation, tensions that cannot be resolved without the abolition of class, capitalism as a system of relations produces the

---

[14] Marx never suggests that all social conflicts result from the contradictions of the class relation, or that a communist revolution would create a society without conflict.

forces that move towards its own supercedure or, as Marx and Engels put it, produces its own "grave-diggers" (Marx and Engels 2000:255).

In Weber's sociology, morality is relative to subjective social action; in Durkheim's, it is relative to the objective functional needs of societies; and in Marx's, morality is relative to class. So the first implication of Marx's hierarchical conception of society is that there can be no socially absolute morality in a class society, since 'the good' is different and opposed for labor and for capital. This class-relativity is captured starkly in the title of Léon Trotsky's *Their Morals and Ours* (Trotsky et al. 1973). Beliefs in the present existence of a socially absolute morality, or even in a socially relative cross-class organic solidarity of the kind advocated by Durkheim, are, for Marx, mere fictions that serve the interests of capital. This is why Marx refuses ethics or morality as justifications for revolutionary struggle:

> The theoretical conclusions of the Communists are in no way based on ideas or princi-
> ples that have been invented, or discovered, by this or that would-be universal reformer.
> They merely express, in general terms, actual relations springing from an existing class
> struggle, from a historical movement going on under our very eyes (Marx and Engels
> 2000:256).

As Foucault puts it,

> the proletariat doesn't wage war against the ruling class because it considers such a war
> to be just. The proletariat makes war with the ruling class because, for the first time in
> history, it wants to take power. And because it will overthrow the power of the ruling
> class it considers such a war to be just (Chomsky and Foucault 1997:136).

Under these conditions, genuine social solidarity (solidarity based on an accurate perception of one's real relations) can exist only within classes. So, synchronically speaking, class solidarity is the highest possible morality, as much for the capitalists as for workers.[15]

There does exist a basis for reciprocal social obligations capable of including all human beings. In a classless society, contradiction (not conflict) would be abolished, making a general human solidarity genuinely possible. For Marx, this classless society exists as a real potentiality, implicit the structure of class societies as the condition towards which they tend inexorably. The achievement of classless society would abolish alienation for capitalists as well as for workers, enabling for the first time in history the realization of a general human good. In this sense, action that works to realize the class revolution constitutes a kind of socially absolute normative value.[16] However, it is important to stress that this is not normative in the sense of

---

[15] For all the criticism that Marx heaps on capitalism and capitalists, as a class and individually, it is important to note that he also praises them as a revolutionary force in human history. The most conspicuous example of this occurs in the *Manifesto* (Marx and Engels 2000:486–489). A passage in the *Critique of the Gotha Program* gives a sense of the quality of what we could very advisedly call Marx's moral judgments: "The bourgeoisie is here conceived as a revolutionary class – as a bearer of large-scale industry – relatively to the feudal lords and middle estates, who desire to maintain all social positions that are the creation of obsolete modes of production. [...] On the other hand, the proletariat is revolutionary relative to the bourgeoisie because, having itself grown up on the basis of large-scale industry, it strives to strip off from production the capitalist character that the bourgeoisie seeks to perpetuate" (Marx 2009:29). The class solidarity of capitalists is revolutionary as long as it works to dissolve the "fixed, fast-frozen relations" of the feudal order, and reactionary whenever it stands in the way of proletarian revolution.

[16] The disjuncture between the, as it were, synchronic and diachronic aspects of Marx's theorization of normativity explain the difficulty, noted by Ollman (1976) of reconciling Marx's principled critique of moralism with his abundant use of moralistic-sounding praise and blame in discussing not only concrete social conditions but also competing

instantiating a universal moral principle located in human nature, in a Kantian a priori, or in any other sense. Marx is scathing about humanistic socialists, like Karl Heinzen, who believe "that entire classes, which are based upon economic conditions independent of their will, and are set by these conditions in a relation of mutual antagonism, can break away from their real relations, by the quality of 'humanity' which is inherent in all men" (Marx 2000:234). Throughout his work, and prominently in the *Manifesto*, he attacks "Utopian" socialist who justify revolution in the name of some ideal. As Ollman points out, if "ethics" refers to justification in terms of a principle that is held to stand outside the concrete situations in which people act, then the phrase "'Marxian ethics' is clearly a misnomer"(Ollman 1976:43). The movement towards revolution is not justified by ethics, or by anything else; it is simply that which working people must do, that which they are driven to do, by the force of class contradiction.

Moreover, every indication suggests that the moral life of a classless society is not, for Marx, something that can be predicted in advance from our knowledge of the morality of class societies. The closest that Marx comes to describing a world after the proletarian revolution is his *Critique of the Gotha Program*, and even this description is mostly limited to the practices that would exist immediately after a revolution, "as it *emerges* from capitalist society; which is thus in every respect, economically, morally and intellectually, still stamped with the birthmarks of the old society" (Marx 2009:24). Only some time after the abolition of capitalism,

> after the enslaving subordination of individuals under division of labour, and therewith also the antithesis between mental and physical labour, has vanished; after labour has ceased to be a means of life and has become itself the primary necessity of life; after the productive forces have also increased with the all-round development of the individual, and all the springs of cooperative wealth flow more abundantly – only then can the narrow horizon of bourgeois right be fully left behind and society inscribe on its banners: from each according to his ability, to each according to his needs (Marx 2009:26–27).

The paucity of Marx's description of what communist society will look like is consistent with his insistence that mental life grows out of material social relations. "Right can never be higher than the economic structure of society and its cultural development thereby determined" (Marx 2009:26). Marx expects that the intellectual and moral forms of classless society will be developed by persons who stand in a radically different relationship to each other than we do; to speculate on the choices they will make is fruitless and misleading.

One important problem for a Marxian sociology of morality is the propensity of working-class actors to believe themselves bound by ties of moral solidarity that cross class lines, to believe in precisely the society-wide solidarity that Durkheim believed essential to social life. Why bourgeois should take themselves for universal human subjects and propagate a universalizing morality which naturalizes their social standpoint is no great mystery; why the workers should take that morality for their own is a serious puzzle. The inquiries of Western Marxists into hegemony and ideology, inaugurated by Gramsci (1971) and Lucács (1971), can be read as an indirect sociology of morality.

---

social-scientific accounts of society. That which is practically mistaken or self-defeating, for a movement to supercede capitalism, is by the same gesture a kind of moral failing. Abolishing the distinction between practical success and moral virtue cuts both ways.

HETERARCHICAL THEORY AND REFLEXIVE MORALITIES

Differing epistemic strategies frame sociological inquiry in fundamentally differing terms, leading to differing substantive accounts of morality. These differences are on display in the work of the classical sociological theorists. In this way, the statements of Weber, Simmel, Durkheim, and Marx illustrate four very different ways of instantiating the general premise that morality can be examined as an empirical social phenomenon amenable to sociological analysis and explanation. If the phrase "socially constructed" has become almost terminally amorphous and vague (Hacking 1999), examining these authors' positions serves as a corrective: saying that morality is socially constructed can lead us to five very different basic positions.

Of these five positions, I have examined only four, the four that are represented in the classical tradition. All four of these relativize morality at least partly – that is, by conceptualizing, investigating, and explaining morality without recourse to transcendental essences, they tend to do away with these absolute foundations. The diversity of the classical tradition shows that sociological relativism about morals can take many forms. For Weber, moral phenomena are relative to the subjective life of individuals; for Simmel, to emergent social forms; for Durkheim, to the functional needs of differing species of social organism; for Marx, to the imperatives of material production and the contradictions of class. At either end of the spectrum of epistemic strategies, morality may plausibly be anchored to forces external to all social action: at the individualist end, to innate human nature; at the holist end, to the teleological imperatives of social development. As we move away from the ends of the spectrum, however, the theoretical link between the play of social forces and these extra-social fixed points becomes more tenuous. The fifth epistemic strategy, heterarchy, occupies the vantage point from which, for a naturalistic social science, any notion of absolute constraints on moral phenomena appears most implausible. This strategy, not represented in the classical tradition, is increasingly characteristic of contemporary theoretical projects, and so its implications for the sociology of morality are worth considering at least briefly.

In heterarchical sociologies, individual actions are synthesized into emergent forms structures, and these emergent structures are further synthesized into dynamic systems, but the dynamic systems running through social life do not combine to form an organically integrated whole, or even an agonistic whole dominated by a single overarching contradiction. Rather, social life is shot through by multiple competing systemic logics, each with its own contradictions, each with striving to totalize the social universe without ever being able to do so (Kontopoulos 1993:6, 20–23, 55–72, 211ff.). Overlapping or intersecting systems may reinforce each other, producing standard overdetermination, or undermine each other, producing a kind of underdetermination by overdetermination in which individual agents can innovate new forms of social practice. This type of conceptualization of society is evident in the work of Bourdieu (1977, 1992), Giddens (1984, 1993), Foucault (1990), in critical theories of sex and sexuality (Fausto-Sterling 2000), in accounts of intersectionality or the 'matrix of domination' (Collins 2000), in institutional analysis (Boltanski and Thévenot 2006, Friedland and Alford 1991), in cultural sociology (Fuchs 2001), and in sociology of knowledge (Pickering 1995). In such theories, the absolutes of individual nature or of meta-organic teleology appear remotely if at all; the complex interplay of social factors suffices to explain both constraint and freedom.[17] Instead of absolutes, heterarchical theories tend to stress *reflexivity*: the involvement of knowing subject in the constitution of the social forces that constrain her.

A heterarchical sociology would therefore ask how moralities are produced and transformed by the intersecting operation of multiple contradictory social systems, and how an awareness of the social conditions that produce moral norms informs agents' moral choices. It also asks how sociology is implicated in the production of normativity, and what social conditions have made possible a reflexive sociology of morality. How will this nexus of sociology of morality and moralizing sociology continue to develop in the future? This reflexive question for today has its roots in the varying projects of the classical tradition.

REFERENCES

Althusser, L. 1971. "Ideology and Ideological State Apparatuses." In *Lenin and Philosophy and Other Essays*. New York: Monthly Review Press.
Berger, P. L., and T. Luckmann. 1966. *The Social Construction of Reality*. Garden City, NY: Anchor Books.
Boltanski, L., and L. Thévenot. 2006. *On Justification: Economies of Worth*. Princeton: Princeton University Press.
Bourdieu, P. 1977. *Outline of a Theory of Practice*. Cambridge: Cambridge University Press.
Bourdieu, P., and L. J. D. Wacquant. 1992. *An Invitation to Reflexive Sociology*. Chicago: University of Chicago Press.
Chomsky, N., and M. Foucault. 1997. "Human Nature: Justice Versus Power." PP. 107–145 in *Foucault and His Interlocutors*, edited by A. I. Davidson. Chicago: University of Chicago Press.
Collins, R. 1994. *Four Sociological Traditions*. New York: Oxford University Press.
Collins, P. H. 2000. *Black Feminist Thought: Knowledge, Consciousenss and the Politics of Empowerment*. London: Routledge.
Durkheim, E. 1979. *Suicide*. Translated by J. A. Spaulding and G. Simpson. New York: The Free Press.
Durkheim, E. 1982. "The Rules of Sociological Method." In *Durkheim: The Rules of Sociological Method and Selected Texts on Sociology and Its Method*, edited by S. Lukes. New York: The Free Press.
Durkheim, E. 1984. *The Division of Labour in Society*. New York: The Free Press.
Durkheim, E. 1992. *Professional Ethics and Civic Morals*. London: Routledge.
Durkheim, E. 1995. *The Elementary Forms of Religious Life*. Translated by K. E. Fields. New York: The Free Press.
Durkheim, E. 2002. *Moral Education*. Translated by E. K. Wilson and H. Schnurer. Mineola, NY: Dover Publications.
Elster, J. 1985. *Making Sense of Marx*. Cambridge: Cambridge University Press.
Elster, J. 1986. "Marxism, Functionalism, and Game Theory." In *Analytic Marxism*, edited by J. Roemer. Cambridge: Cambridge University Press.
Engels, F. 1972. *The Origin of the Family, Private Property, and the State, In Light of the Researches of Lewis H. Morgan*. New York: International Publishers.
Fausto-Sterling, A. 2000. *Sexing the Body: Gender Politics and the Construction of Sexuality*, Basic Books: New York.
Foucault, M. 1990. *The History of Sexuality, Volume 1: An Introduction*. Translated by R. Hurley. New York: Vintage Books.

---

[17] This is not to say that biological and cognitive factors play no role in heterarchical theories. Indeed, they may appear quite prominently. However, their significance is changed. As long as the individual subject was thought of as a bounded, coherent whole, then evidence for the causal importance of bodily mechanisms counted as evidence for the determining effect of the individual's biological nature *as opposed* to their social environment. In heterarchical theories, this 'nature vs. nurture' opposition need no longer obtain. Instead, cognitive, organic, and even genetic factors can appear as factors in social systems, albeit not as simple one-way sources of determination, but as factors whose operation and consequences are themselves affected by systems of social interaction. Fausto-Sterling's (2000) discussion of the complex relationship between genetic sex and embodied sex exemplifies a heterarchical approach to the subject.

Friedland, R., and R. R. Alford. 1991. "Bringing Society Back in: Symbols, Practices, and Institutional Contradictions." PP. 232–263 in *The New Institutionalism in Organizational Analysis*, edited by W. W. Powell and P. J. DiMaggio. Chicago: The University of Chicago Press.

Frisby, D. P. 1990. "Georg Simmel's Concept of Society." PP. 39–55 in *Georg Simmel and Contemporary Sociology*, edited by M. Kaern, B. S. Phillips, and R. S. Cohen. Dordrecht: Kluwer Academic Publishers.

Frisby, D., and M. Featherstone. 1997. *Simmel on Culture: Selected Writings*. London: Sage Publications.

Fuchs, S. 2001. *Against Essentialim: A Theory of Culture and Society*. Princeton, NJ: Harvard University Press.

Gerth, H. H., and C. Wright Mills. 1946. "Introduction: The Man and His Work." PP. 3–74 in *From Max Weber: Essays in Sociology*, edited by H. H. Gerth and C. W. Mills. New York: Oxford University Press.

Giddens, A. 1984. *The Constitution of Society: Outline of a Theory of Structuration*. Berkeley: University of California Press.

Giddens, A. 1993. *New Rules of Sociological Method*. Stanford, CA: Stanford University Press.

Goldstein, J. 1999. "Emergence as a Construct: History and Issues." *Emergence: A Journal of Complexity Issues in Organizations and Management* 1:49–72.

Gramsci, A. 1971. *Selections from the Prison Notebooks*, Edited and translated by Q. Hoare and G. N. Smith. New York: International Publishers.

Hacking, I. 1999. *The Social Construction of What?* Cambridge, MA: Harvard University Press.

Holland, J. H. 1998. *Emergence: From Chaos to Order*. Reading, MA: Addison-Wesley.

Kandal, T. 1988. "Emile Durkheim: *Suicide* and the War Between the Sexes." PP. 79–88 in *The Woman Question in Classical Sociological Theory*. Miami: Florida International University Press.

Kontopoulos, K. M. 1993. *The Logics of Social Structure*, edited by M. Granovetter. New York: Cambridge University Press.

Lehman, J. 1995. "Durkheim's Theories of Deviance and Suicide: A Feminist Reconsideration." *American Journal of Sociology* 100:904–930.

Lukács, G. 1971. *History and Class Consciousness*. Cambridge, MA: MIT Press.

Lyotard, J.-F. 1984. *The Postmodern Condition: A Report on Knowledge*. Translated by G. Bennington and B. Massumi. Minneapolis: University of Minnesota Press.

Margolis, J. 1978. *Persons and Minds: The Prospects of Nonreductive Materialism*. Dordrecht: Reidel.

Marx, K. 1975. "Estranged Labour." PP. 270–282 in *Karl Marx Frederick Engels Collected Works*, vol. 3. New York: International Publishers.

Marx, K. 1979. "The 18th Brumaire of Louis Bonaparte." PP. 99–197 in *Karl Marx, Frederick Engels: Collected Works, Volume 11, Marx and Engels: 1851–1853*. Moscow: Progress Publishers.

Marx, K. 1990. *Capital: A Critique of Political Economy, Volume I*. Translated by B. Fowkes. Toronto: Penguin Books Canada Ltd.

Marx, K. 2000a. "Economic and Philosophical Manuscripts." PP. 83–121 in *Karl Marx: Selected Writings*, edited by D. McLellan. Oxford: Oxford University Press.

Marx, K. 2000b. "Moralizing Criticisms and Critical Morality." PP. 234–236 in *Karl Marx: Selected Writings*, edited by D. McLellan. Oxford: Oxford University Press.

Marx, K. 2000c. "Wage-Labour and Capital." PP. 273–294 in *Karl Marx: Selected Writings*, edited by D. McLellan. Oxford: Oxford University Press.

Marx, K. 2009. *Critique of the Gotha Program*. LaVergne, TN: Wildside Press.

Marx, K., and F. Engels. 1976. "The German Ideology." In *Karl Marx, Frederick Engels: Collected Works, Volume 5, Marx and Engels: 1845–1847*. Moscow: Progress Publishers.

Marx, K., and F. Engels. 2000. "The Communist Manifesto." In *Karl Marx: Selected Writings*, edited by D. McLellan. Oxford: Oxford University Press.

Ollman, B. 1976. *Alienation: Marx's Conception of Man in Capitalist Society*. Cambridge: Cambridge University Press.

Parsons, T. 1951. *The Social System*. New York: The Free Press.

Parsons, T. 1966. *Societies: Evolutionary and Comparative Perspectives*. Englewood Cliffs: Prentice-Hall, Inc.

Pedersen, J. E. 2001. "Sexual Politics in Comte and Durkheim: Feminism, History, and the French Sociological Tradition." *Signs: Journal of Women in Culture and Society* 27:229–263.

Pickering, A. 1995. *The Mangle of Practice: Time, Agency, and Science*. Chicago: University of Chicago.

Powell, C. 2011. "Genocidal Moralities: A Critique." In *New Directions in Genocide Research*, edited by A. Jones. London: Routledge.

Ramp, W. 2008. "Durkheim *Redux*." *Journal of Classical Sociology* 8:147–157.

Rosenau, P. M. 1992. *Post-Modernism and the Social Sciences*. Princeton: Princeton University Press.

Saint-Simon, H. 1975. "The Reorganization of European Society." PP. 130–136 in *Henri Saint-Simon: Selected Writings on Science, Industry and Social Organization*, edited by K. Taylor. New York: Holmes and Meier Publishers Inc.

Simmel, G. 1950. *The Sociology of Georg Simmel*, Edited and translated by K. H. Wolff. New York: The Free Press.

Simmel, G. 1971. *On Individuality and Social Forms: Selected Writings*, Edited by D. N. Levine. Chicago: University of Chicago Press.

Simmel, G. 1980. *Essays on Interpretation in Social Science*, Edited by G. Oakes. Totowa, NJ: Rowman and Littlefield.

Simmel, G. 1984. *Georg Simmel: On Women, Sexuality, and Love*, Edited by D. Frisby and M. Featherstone. Translated by G. Oakes. New Haven: Yale University Press.

Simmel, G. 1990. *The Philosophy of Money*. Translated by T. Bottomore, D. Frisby, and K. Mengelberg. London: Routledge.

Spencer, H. 1971. "A Society is an Organism." PP. 108–120 in *Herbert Spencer: Structure, Function, and Evolution*, edited by S. Andreski. London: Michael Joseph.

Sydie, R. 1987. *Natural Women, Cultured Men*. Toronto: Methuen.

Thompson, E. P. 1963. *The Making of the English Working Class*. New York: Vintage.

Trotsky, L., J. Dewey, and G. E. Novack. 1973. *Their Morals and Ours: Marxist vs. Liberal Views on Morality*. New York: Pathfinder Press.

Weber, M. 1946. "Science as a Vocation." PP. 129–156 in *From Max Weber: Essays in Sociology*, edited by H. H. Gerth and C. W. Mills. New York: Oxford University Press.

Weber, M. 1949. ""Objectivity" in Social Science and Social Science Policy." PP. 50–112 in *The Methodology of the Social Sciences*, edited by E. A. Shils and H. A. Finch. Glencoe, IL: The Free Press.

Weber, M. 1978a. *Economy and Society*, Vol. 1. Berkeley: University of California Press.

Weber, M. 1978b. "Politics as a Vocation." in *Weber: Selections in translation*, edited by W. G. Runciman. Cambridge: Cambridge University Press.

Weber, M. 1978c. "Value-judgments in Social Science." PP. 69–98 in *Weber: Selections in translation*, edited by E. Matthews. Cambridge: Cambridge University Press.

Weber, M. 2002. *The Protestant Ethic and the Spirit of Capitalism*. Translated by S. Kalberg. Los Angeles: Roxbury Publishing Company.

CHAPTER 4

Adumbrations of a Sociology of Morality in the Work of Parsons, Simmel, and Merton

DONALD N. LEVINE

Although a subfield called sociology of morality – of "moral phenomena," more aptly – may seem a new departure for sociologists, the topic has in fact been central to sociological inquiry since its pre-disciplinary days. From that genial precursor of sociology, Adam Smith, and the discipline's official baptizer, August Comte, through virtually all the movers and shakers of the discipline until the ascendance of rational-choice thinking since the 1970s, sociologists have pursued a wide array of questions regarding the forms, contents, genesis, functions, and changes of moral phenomena.

To some extent, this pursuit can be seen embedded in the drive to establish the very discipline of sociology, which included determined efforts to transcend 'economism', a position expressing the abstractions of atomic naturalism and marginal utility theory. With a large eye to the founding figures of Pareto, Durkheim and Weber, this case was made famous in 1937 by Talcott Parsons in *The Structure of Social Action*. The same was true no less in work by earlier figures such as Auguste Comte, John Stuart Mill, John Dewey, W.I. Thomas, Robert Park, and William Graham Sumner – figures with whom Parsons was largely unconversant at the time of writing *Structure*.

Broadly speaking, critiques of economistic thinking proceed from four directions. One emphasizes the hold of traditional habits and routines that preclude the utilitarian calculus so central to economistic thoughtways. This emphasis characterizes, for example, the work of John Dewey, for whom most human conduct is guided by ingrained, habitual response, and by Max Weber, who writes of "the great bulk of everyday action to which people have become habitually accustomed" (Weber 1968:25). In countless instances, tradition and habit have disposed humans to pursue lines of action that most definitely fail to satisfy their needs for their survival and well-being.

Another line of thought questions the rationality postulate of economism by noting the reservoir of unconscious motives and emotional impulses that derail calculations of interest. Diverse formulations of this critique appear in much moral philosophy – the passions were at one time more prominent in moral discourse than were 'interests' (Hirschman 1977) – and figures like Hume and Schopenhauer delved into them deeply. These ideas found dramatic elaboration in the work of Sigmund Freud and Carl Jung and their followers.

S. Hitlin, S. Vaisey (eds.), *Handbook of the Sociology of Morality*,
Handbooks of Sociology and Social Research, DOI 10.1007/978-1-4419-6896-8_4,
© Springer Science+Business Media, LLC 2010

A third line of criticism stems from those who reject the abstractness of analyzing separate individuals instead of considering the myriad ways in which individual conduct is shaped and organized by collective structures. This type of critique was voiced loudly by Auguste Comte's critique of Smith in his *Cours de philosophie positive*, and taken up grandly and extended by Emile Durkheim. Following Montesquieu's attack on Hobbes, both of them disparaged economists for thinking that individuals by themselves were able to organize their decisions and actions (Levine 1995, chapter 8).

The fourth – and perhaps the most charged critique of economism – has taken the form of emphasizing the moral dimension of human action. This concern was shared by nearly all the figures mentioned above. For all that, little has been done to analyze the universe of social theory with an eye to elucidating this dimension of human conduct – to construct what we may call, for reasons to be elucidated below, the moral-evaluative complex.

When we look for originary sociologists whose treatments of morality were most differentiated and best developed philosophically, the names of Georg Simmel and Talcott Parsons come quickly to mind. Both Simmel and Parsons had productive careers in which the topos of morality stood out frequently. Following and to varying degrees influenced by them, Robert K. Merton further enriched the discourse by playing a role complementary to both. All that said it must not be assumed that the thoughtways of either Parsons or Simmel contained a single consistent way of treating morality. Indeed, ideas about morality changed so much in the course of their respective careers that one can only get a fair grasp of what they thought by tracing the evolution of their ideas. To that challenging task, I now turn.

TALCOTT PARSONS: FROM VOLUNTARISM
TO MULTIDIMENSIONAL DETERMINISM

It is common to divide the Parsonian oeuvre into four phases. For the present analysis, I subdivide each of those in two in Figure 4.1.

This figure presents what I regard as the most differentiated paradigm to date for sociology of moral phenomena.

Of motives that promoted young Talcott Parsons to publish his first major opus, *The Structure of Social Action* (1937), a dominant inspiration was patently the wish to demonstrate the crucial constitutive role of moral considerations in human action.[1] This motif was prefigured in a paper published two years before *Structure*, "The Place of Ultimate Values in Sociological Theory" (1935). The use of "ultimate" in the title represented a Weberian concern (*letzte Werte*) about ways in which fundamental convictions mediated by religious traditions affect the most mundane details of daily action. The paper leads right out with a proclamation of what would become an animating assumption of *Structure*: "The positivistic reaction against philosophy has, in its effect on the social sciences, manifested a strong tendency to

---

[1] Although *Structure* has often been thought to mark the starting point of Parsons's publishing career, it actually followed a substantial series of significant published papers (Camic ed. 1997).

Period	Germinal work	Key constructs	Precipitate for paradigm of moral phenomena
I. Early: values in action	I.a. "Place of Ultimate Values" (1935)	Ultimate values Voluntarism	Existential reality
	I.b. *The Structure of Social Action* (1937)	Normative elements: values; norms Typology of norms: efficiency, legitimacy, aesthetic	Forms contents
II. Middle: systemic functions	II.a *The Social System* (1951)	Pattern variables Conformity and deviance Mechanisms of social control	Contents microdynamics
	II.b. *Economy & Society* (1956)	Functional subsystems AGIL; cybernetic hierarchy	Functions
III. Mature: evolution	III.a *Societies: Evolutionary and Comparative Perspectives* (1966)	Societal evolution; Media of interchange Differentiation, adaptive upgrading, generalization, specification	Historical development
	III.b. *The System of Modern Societies* (1971)	Modernity	Modern manifestations
IV. Late: theoretic syntheses	IV.a. *The American University* (1973)	Cognitive Complex	Theoretic paradigm
	IV.b. Paradigm of the Human Condition (1979)	Human condition	Place in worldview

FIGURE 4.1. Modalities of morality in Parsons's oeuvre.

obscure the fact that man is essentially an active, creative, evaluating creature" ([1935]).[2] In support of that claim, the paper makes four points.

(1) Understanding human conduct requires that objective accounts of actions be complemented by accounts of the subjective dimensions.
(2) The preeminent mode of capturing the subjective dimensions involves attending to mean-ends calculation.[3]
(3) Scientific knowledge can be called on to explain the choice of means, but not that of ends; the latter entails a 'voluntaristic' dimension.

---

[2] As must not be forgotten, the ways that Parsons used the concepts of positivism (and utilitarianism) reflect historical misunderstandings that have produced confusions based on semantic conflations. The term positivism, as Comte and is followers have defined it, designates only a methodological principle, not a particular view of human action (and indeed, Comte's view of motivation included the elements of valuation, sentiment, and altruism–another term he coined–as well as instrumental rationality). See Levine (1980:xii–xv).

[3] The epigraph to this volume consists of a quotation from Max Weber: "Jede denkende Besinnung auf die letzten Elemente sinnvollen menschlichen Handelns ist zunächst gebunden an die Kategorien 'Zweck' und 'Mittel'" (Any thoughtful reflection on the ultimate elements of meaningful human action is initially bound to the categories of "ends" and "means.")

(4) Both the ultimate justification of empirical ends and the substance of trans-empirical ends require some kind of transcendent notions, notions that positivism cannot accommodate due to its insistence on empirical justifications for all truth-claims.

By the time *Structure* was published, this thought had been refined. *Structure* incorporates the normative factor into an explicit model of action. Moreover, it distinguishes that model from a number of competing alternatives, and it moves to a sharper conception of norms. This includes distinguishing between objective accounts of norms as facts in a situation and subjective accounts in which norms figure as ideal elements that stand as ideals to be realized through active effort.

The book's argument opens with a diagram that illustrates the point: all action is driven by interests *but also* regulated by normative elements. The schema with which Parsons portrayed diverse theories of action turned heavily on the latter variable. He signified it by the letter *i*, defined as "normative or ideal elements." A major part of the book's argument was contained in the nine chapters of Part II, devoted to showing how the work of three of the four main figures in his account (Marshall, Pareto, and Durkheim) felt constrained to supplement the economistic model of action – consisting solely of a situation, conditions, means, knowledge, and ends – with a normative component. The fourth main author treated, Max Weber, was shown to have repudiated economistic assumptions pointedly ab initio.

To be sure, Parsons's notion of voluntarism received almost no direct attention in the work that sought to establish it as the touchstone for all future social theory. It was draped casually over his lengthy arguments about the place of normativity in action. No matter how loudly he proclaimed his allegiance to the notion of voluntarism or felt that he was rescuing the principle of human agency, Parsons failed to give it serious attention in *Structure*. In contrast to the fastidious manner in which he treated other core concepts, such as action, positivism, and utilitarianism, he never defines the term explicitly and treats it in a vague and at time contradictory manner. As a result, "commentators have been divided over whether Parsons's 'voluntarism' stands for choice, freedom of choice, freedom, free will, purposiveness, subjective decision making, subjectivity, activity and creativity in conduct, autonomy from material conditions, or antideterminism" (Camic 1989:89). What is more, once *Structure* was published, the notion of voluntarism never again appeared in any of Parsons's publications. Parsons signaled his intent in this regard: at the conclusion of the treatise he indicated that since he had now clinched his argument about action, the notion of voluntarism had become superfluous and could be dropped (Parsons 1937:762, n.1; Levine 2005).

Instead, from the very year after *Structure* onwards, Parsons came to treat morality as instantiated in what he came to call institutionalized norms. Analysis of professions in general and the medical profession in particular comprised his watershed work here. Thus, he used the variable of distinct institutionalized norms to account for differences in the orientations of businessmen and medical doctors, not difference in the motives of those who choose to enter those vocations (Parsons [1939] 1949).

Parsons's work on the professions led to a generalized theoretic framework whose central concept became *boundary-maintaining social systems organized about sets of normative role-expectations*. This work culminated in his first substantive synthesis, *The Social System* (1951). In perhaps no major sociological work since Sumner's *Folkways* had the phenomena of moral norms figured so centrally in sociological analysis. In place of defensive rhetoric about the rightful place of moral considerations deployed in *Structure*, this target composition takes the significance of norms as a given and situates them as one of three constitutive elements in all action, along with psychological need-dispositions and cultural symbols. TSS proceeds to make that element the centerpiece of analysis – treating systems of norms as the equivalent of social structure, analyzing diverse types of norms and, in a searching exposition that has barely been improved on in general theory to this time, laying out a schematic analysis of how norms are complied with, sanctioned, deviated from, altered, and overthrown. This phase of work includes the effort to integrate the models of Freud and Durkheim regarding the formation of conscience.

Perhaps the best-known precipitate of this period was the schema of pattern variables, set forth to offer a comprehensive listing of alternative patterns of value-orientation. Although Parsons gamely uses the language of choice when delineating these alternatives, he means it only in the sense that social structures can embody one or the other of each pair of values. In Parsons's third phase, when he developed the notions of double interchange, the AGIL paradigm, the cybernetic hierarchy, and the media of interchange, the shift from voluntarism to a sort of structural determinism comes full swing: the view of morality as orientational and structurally constitutive becomes subordinate to identifying the functions of moral evaluative systems and their relations to other functional subsystems of action. The systemic functions of adaptation, goal-attainment, integration, and pattern maintenance come to drive the establishment of institutionalized norms rather than the vagaries of random cultural choices.

Yet barely had that node been formed when Parsons embarked on another departure, the model of societal evolution. This phase anchored the normative structures of societies in a process of systemic differentiation across world history. Although Parsons himself had dismissed the idea of social evolution forcefully in his first major work in 1937 – an idea which remains anathema to most social anthropologists – he sought three decades later to reclaim it in ways that avoided the objectionable features of the earlier view: unilinearity, uniformity, and the valorization of evolutionary progress.[4] In his reformulation of evolutionary theory, Parsons emphasized the importance of different 'stages' of evolutionary development, stating that "we do not conceive societal evolution to be either a continuous or a simple linear process, but we can distinguish among broad levels of advancement without overlooking the considerable variability found in each" (Parsons 1966:26). Broadly speaking, he distinguished three evolutionary levels – primitive, intermediate, and modern – identified by the scope of their 'generalized adaptive capacity'. By implication, he held that each evolutionary stage harbored a distinctive set of normative structures, a kind of claim most resonant with Durkheim.

In the final phase of Parsons's work, two innovations pertinent to sociology of morality stand out. The first appeared in the effort, with George Platt, to analyze the American university, an effort that offered a paradigm to identify and connect manifestations at all four levels of the universe of action to a single action modality. This, they designated as the Cognitive Complex (Figure 4.2). For present purposes, the relevance of this schema consists

---

[4] Since some readers may be inclined to dismiss this exposition on grounds that employs the notion of societal evolution is necessarily suspect if not illegitimate, the author emphasizes the importance of those revisions. In making them, Parsons was aided substantially by a seminal paper of Robert Bellah, "Religious Evolution" (1964) – and in fleshing out his evolving conception, by the assistance of Victor Lidz. Bellah's forthcoming volume on Religious Evolution will provide the most comprehensive realization of this conception to date.

in its offering a model for the normative sphere, which might as well be designated as the Moral-Evaluative Complex.

The other is his testamentary model of the Human Condition. This model presented the most complex and inclusive synthesis of all components not only of action, but also of its environments. Incorporating what Parsons had long called the cybernetic hierarchy, the Human Condition paradigm located the entire complex of moral phenomena is a cosmic context, indicated the diverse ways and points where normative elements figured in the total scheme of things.

This concise overview may suggest many points of departure to further inquiry, both into the Parsonian legacy and into an evolving sociology of morals. Two long-term trends stand out. One is the progression from a vague notion of the moral dimension of action to a complex, differentiated analytic scheme. The other marks a journey in which an initial emphasis on agency and voluntarism recedes progressively in favor of an increasingly complex objective analytic framework. That journey, we shall see, appears precisely the opposite of that traversed by Simmel.

GEORG SIMMEL: FROM MULTIDIMENSIONAL DETERMINISM TO EXISTENTIAL VOLUNTARISM

Notably, Parsons excluded Simmel from the short list of European authors treated in *Structure*, an omission that has prompted investigation and debate. The reasons for that omission need not concern us here.[5] What does concern us is the fact that Parsons began his lifelong journey

Period	Germinal Work	Key Constructs	Precipitate for analytic paradigm
I. Objective analysis of norms	*Einleitung in die Moral- wissenschaft* (1892–1893) *Uber soziale Differenzierung* (1890)	Disambiguation of terms into an emerging positive science of ethics: The Ought; Egoism/ Altruism; Happiness; etc. Social origins of morality Levels of moral responsibility	Logics of normativity Sources of normativity
II. Norms within social interaction	*Soziologie* (1896–1908) "Sociability"(1910)	Morality as located within diverse forms of social interaction	"Structural" locations
III. Ideals within the life process	*Lebensanschauung* ([1913] 1918)	"More-than-life" Law of the Individual	Normative creativity

FIGURE 4.2. Modalities of morality in Simmel's oeuvre.

[5] The question has been discussed in a number of publications, including Levine (1980, 1991, 1994), Lidz (1993), and Alexander (1993).

into the normative dimensions of action with a call for a 'voluntaristic theory of action'. To a certain extent, this emphasis appears to be the opposite of Georg Simmel, who began with an emphasis on natural forces as the source of morality, and capped his career by locating the source of binding morality in the tumultuous creativity of the individual will. Simmel's work on this subject is divided into three phases.

The first and only full-scale treatment of morality by Simmel appears in his early two-volume monograph, *Einleitung in die Moralwissenschaft* (1892–1893) (*Introduction to the Scientific Study of Morals*). Described by contemporary reviewers as "acute, ingenious, subtle, suggestive, and almost uniformly interesting" and "one of the least dogmatic treatments of ethics in existence" (Sidgwick 1892:434; Thilly 1893:637), the work is so lengthy and dense that only a sample of its insights and suggestions can be included here.[6]

The *Einleitung* opens with a comment on the current state of the field of ethics. Like Durkheim's first major publication, *De la division du travail social,* and in the very same year (1893), Simmel's text claims that the contemporary study of morality requires the formation of a new discipline. Durkheim starts his tract by announcing that it will be "above all an attempt to treat the facts of moral life according to the method of the positive sciences" ([1893] 1984:xxv); this requires a discipline that eschews both metaphysical methodology and the work of positive sciences that attend to other orders of phenomena. Similarly, Simmel begins by asserting that the "plethora of moral principles and the contradictions within them and in their representations shows immediately that ethics has not yet found the certainty of methods which in other disciplines produces a harmonious juxtaposition and increasing accumulation of achievements", and thus it seems ready to move beyond the stage of abstract generalities, moral preachings, and wisdom literature to that of proper empirical treatment ([1892] 1989:10).

Accordingly, what Simmel proposes is a complex field of ethics composed of three sub-disciplines, formed to investigate moral phenomena by means of: (a) a psychological analysis of phenomena of strivings, feelings, and attitudes that can be counted as moral or immoral; (b) the social scientific analysis of the forms and contents of communal life that relate to individual morality as causes or effects; and (c) the historical analysis of how these moral phenomena developed from primitive to evolved forms.

As propaedeutic to such an emerging discipline, the *Einleitung* seeks to criticize the apparently simple basic concepts (*scheinbar einfachen Grundbegriffe*) with which ethics commonly works. It proposes to do so by revealing (1) their complex and multivocal character; (2) how the abstractions generated from them have turned into potent psychological forces; (3) how they can be linked with opposed principles that possess equal credibility; and (4) how they are entangled with psychological preconditions and social consequences ([1892] 1989:11). In any case, Simmel adds, such work of positive ethics cannot be used for the purpose of providing practical moral guidance.

In executing this task, Simmel analyzes the following concepts: (i) The Ought (*das Sollen*); (ii) Egoism and Altruism; (iii) Moral Merit and Moral Guilt; (iv) Happiness; (v) The Categorical Imperative; and (vi) Freedom. His intricate analysis of the notion of obligation concludes that no particular content of The Ought can be derived from an intrinsic analysis

---

[6] For a translation of its Table of Contents, see Appendix.

of the idea of obligation. Already here, however, Simmel does more than confine himself to disambiguating a complicated moral notion. At numerous points, he inserts trains of thought that adumbrate directions for the psychological, sociological, and historical accounts he advocates. Thus, he discusses the psychological preconditions of feeling a sense of obligation, and the psychological consequences of adhering to such an ultimately unwarrantable belief. He notes the social consequences of conformity to and deviation from to obligatory norms. In addition, he presents an evolutionary account of the origin of the immediately given feeling of obligation: designated as obligatory, he writes, stems originally from society's enforcement of directives that promote its preservation, a thought akin to William Graham Sumner's idea of the mores. Over time, the content of these enforced commands transform into a sense that one is obliged to enact them. The necessary (*das Müssen*) becomes the Ought (*das Sollen*).

In treating both Egoism-Altruism and Happiness, the *Einleitung* dissects a number of common simplistic philosophic notions of the concepts. The views he demolishes include: egoism is more "natural" than altruism; the order in which egoistic and altruistic impulses originated has anything to do with their respective moral valence; these concepts have fixed referents, since what is altruism on behalf of one group may be egoistic when compared to a more encompassing group; the fact that an act is accompanied by pleasure by no means warrants the claim that the act was undertaken for the sake of pleasure; and that there is an inherent connection between happiness and virtue.

The chapter on Merit and Culpability disambiguates or dissolves a number of commonplace notions. It distinguishes the merit of inner disposition from merit of acts it leads to. It criticizes essentializing concepts, such as concept of character, which Simmel claims, simply amounts to a sum of life elements, and offers nothing but a name for something wholly unknown. The concept of Character, he argues, exhibits three common logical failings: (1) it confounds a problem with its solution; (2) it considers something explained when it resembles many other things, akin to the Platonic error of explaining some phenomenon through its "Idea," which is only a summing of similar phenomena; and (3) it considers as character simply that which does not vary. Thereby, it constitutes an illusory term, not useful for denoting phenomena that grasps empirically. Other fused concepts in need of differentiation include merit and duty, since not every fulfillment of duty is meritorious, and the validity of the will, since where the will originates and what its goal have separate normative weightings. What is more, other notions associated with the dichotomy of merit and guilt run the risk of arbitrarily sundering a unified phenomenon. Merit and guilt are not independently variable phenomena but are reciprocally determined. The same is true of supposed conceptual opposites like egoism and altruism, sacrifice and value, the moral and the immoral, and moral depravity and moral elevation.

This chapter concludes with a brief comment on freedom, which is treated in its own right in Chapter 6. What Simmel points out here is that freedom entails a notion of some constraint, which one escapes. Since moral choices involve a conflict between moral and immoral impulses, the victory of either one over the other is liberating. Philosophers from Kant on have erred by restricting freedom to the moral side. Freedom is thus not prior to merit and guilt, but ensues from eliminating one or the other impulse. New lines of thought get opened in the chapter on Freedom. There, we find Simmel noting that contemporary ethics tends to bypass the problem of freedom altogether, a neglect that may indeed be warranted for prescriptive ethics, which needs only to enunciate norms and ideals, but that cannot be condoned for a new empirical science of morality. That discipline would need to raise such questions as the origins

of the notion of freedom, which seems to guide so much human action,[7] and concerning the
sentiments and presuppositions that notion of embodies.

In a stunning final chapter, entitled "Unity and Opposition of Ends," Simmel elevates
his occasional insights into paradoxes and contradictions into a general heuristic principle. He
claims that the entire field of ethics is subject to a number of counterintuitive critical postulates: that every moral position requires elements from its opposite; that there is a greater
coherence among instances of immorality than of morality; and that insofar as moral phenomena can claim some sort of unity, it cannot be located in their subserving a common ethical
goal but only in performing a similar psychological function. This exposition also proposes
a general evolutionary formula for the evolution of moral principles. Further, if we go back
in historic development, the narrower the circle we investigate, the more we find the appel-
lation of morals restricted to narrowly circumscribed ranges of actions identified on the basis
of concrete content. Evolution proceeds by extending the moral concepts thus instantiated to
actions that evince them in some extended, weakened, or deviant form. Thus, if morality is
first equated with negating the individual's interest on behalf of the clan, the concept is broadened when one views the pursuit of self-interest as also serving the general interest. Once the
concept is broadened in this way, its more recent components can be emphasized in their own
right, to the neglect or even dismissal of the original concept. The developmental pattern in
question is represented graphically as follows: (1) $a = A$; (2) $a = M = (A + B)$; (3) $a = B$;
(4) $a = N = (B + C)$; etc. This process of extension and mixing can lead to contents that have
nothing at all to do with the original one. Even so, the (vain) efforts to find a concrete similarity
among the disparate components of morality and therewith an absolute moral principle have
produced valuable relative truths regarding the ethical life; a science of ethics must include the
detailed treatment of such efforts. ([1893] 1991:293).

Just as Parsons broaches the topos of voluntarism in *Structure* with éclat only to ignore the
theme ever after, Simmel presents his searching "Critique of Fundamental Ethical Concepts"
(as the work subtitled) in the *Einleitung* only to forget about that method and its results thereafter. Indeed, when issuing an unaltered reprint of the work in 1904, he observes simply that
the work was composed at a younger age and had been superseded by his later thinking,
although he did not deny that the book continued to have merit. Even so, many of the distinctions, themes, and modes of logic forwarded in the *Einleitung* recur in Simmel's later work up
to the time of his testamentary work, *The View of Life*.[8]

What is more, in addition to the semantic project of unpacking and clarifying the meanings of each of these commonplace terms, along the way, we saw, Simmel connects these moral
principles to sociological observations that he will retrieve and develop later on. The moral
sense, he claims, originates from ideas instilled by society. Already in the early monograph
Uber sociale Differenzierung ([1890] 1989), he had drawn on this assumption in analyzing
diverse customs related to collective responsibility. The trend of moral evolution goes from
lodging moral culpability in the collectivity to making individual persons the subjects of moral
codes.

When considering the social determinations of norms during the succeeding decade, however, Simmel departs from a blanket notion of "societal" determination of norms and the sense

---

[7] For an important pioneering treatise in this vein, see Patterson (1991).

[8] The first English translation of this work is to be published by the University of Chicago Press in Autumn 2010.

of obligation to the more differentiated representation of the social that he began to pursue in 1894 with his seminal programmatic essay, "The Problem of Sociology." In carrying out the specific task of sociology outlined in that essay, Simmel locates the matrix of moral norms in diverse sociological formations. As presented in his compendium of such studies, *Soziologie: Untersuchungen über die Formen der Vergesellschaftungen* (*Sociology: Investigations of the Forms of Association* ([1908] 1991), these appear in the chapters on conflict (Chapter 4), super- and subordination (Chapter 3), the persistence of social groups (Chapter 8), and the significance of numbers for social life (Chapter 2). In a presentation to the first meeting of the German Sociological Association two years later, the essay on sociability (1910), Simmel set forth his final original analysis of a social form and its grounding of norms.

Countering the common perception of conflict as a process that occurs at the expense of unity among conflicting parties, Simmel argues that conflict – both internal and external – is an element essential in promoting the cohesiveness of groups. In order to fight meaningfully, parties must agree on sets of norms that regulate the conflict. Beyond that, Simmel offers the intriguing suggestion that "the intermingling of harmonious and hostile relations presents a case where the sociological and the ethical series coincide. It begins with A's action for B's benefit, moves on to A's own benefit by means of B without benefiting B but also without damaging him, and finally becomes A's egoistic action at B's cost" [1908 (1992), 1971:81, 297].

In the context of analyzing diverse forms of domination and subordination, Simmel offers a typology consisting of three forms: subordination under an individual, under a plurality, and under a principle. The last of these usually takes the form of law, and represents a later feature of evolutionary development. For Simmel, as for Weber and others, the difference between obedience based on devotion to a person and obedience to an objective principle represents a transformation with far-reaching consequences. In this typology, Simmel treats principles much as Parsons would talk about cultural objects, and how they become internalized much as Freud and Durkheim describe conscience.

A third venue for discovering ways that particular social forms engender norms may be found in Simmel's late essay on sociability ([1910] 1971).[9] By its very definition, interaction just for the sake of associating with others entails the expectation that extraneous interests, which constitute the basis for nearly all other interactions, are not to be engaged. This amounts to an aesthetic norm, as it were: it would not be appropriate to intrude instrumental motives into a purely sociable gathering. The case of sociability suggests that investigation of other interactional forms with an eye to discerning norms immanent to them may open up fruitful lines of inquiry.

The foregoing examples show ways that particular associational forms can engender moral directives, often of a specific sort. In "The Persistence of Social Groups," which may be glossed as a purely functional analysis – perhaps the only such that Simmel ever composed– modalities of morality are treated explicitly with regard to their role in enabling groups to survive and persist over time. Building on the general notion of normative constraints from custom, represented in his first period, Simmel goes on here to identify morality, honor, and

---

[9] Late in the sense that it was the last of Simmel's original treatments of forms of association, and reprinted in his 1917 reprise of the sociological enterprise.

law as distinct types of norms, where the demands of law encompass the narrowest range, those of morality the widest; and where law supports external ends through external means, morality internal ends through internal means and honor external ends through inner means ([1898] 1992:330–332). (Simmel touches on the moral imperative of honor in a number of contexts, allusions which readers of his time could be assumed to appreciate). A comparable trichotomy appears in the essay on the significance of numbers for group properties, which offers a structural analysis that presents group custom as a mid-term, out of which morality and law become differentiated.

Simmel's final years were devoted to analyzing cultural forms rather than social forms, and to a number of philosophical inquiries. These culminated in his final work *Lebensanschauung*, which is said to represent a third major stage in his treatment of morality. This set of "four metaphysical chapters" concludes with an essay that represents his final effort to come to terms with Kant's notion of the Categorical Imperative, an effort he had already undertaken in Chapter 6 of the *Einleitung* and revisited in his 1906 lectures on Kant. Although full critical appropriation of this conception belongs to the domains of psychology and philosophy, one can readily connect the very availability of this model of autonomous individuated ethics with Simmel's wide-ranging analyses of the historic conditions that animate the quest for normative authentic individuality, conditions that include the emancipatory potential of the widespread use of currency and the personal freedoms promoted by what Louis Wirth, following Simmel, would gloss as urbanism as a way of life.

The foregoing barely indicates how Simmel's diverse writings stand to yield an abundance of ideas for an encompassing sociology of morality.

ROBERT K. MERTON: FROM ANOMIE TO NORMATIVE AMBIVALENCE

Although Robert Merton may be the only student of Parsons for whom Simmel offered a cornucopia of seminal ideas,[10] his forays into the sociology of morality was stimulated initially more by Durkheim than anyone else. In the later work, however, Merton came to develop a perspective that increasingly resembled Simmel's. Here, how I would chart his development in this area is shown in Figure 4.3.

The title of one of the Merton's earliest publications featured a central concept of Durkheim's sociology of morality, *anomie*. Although in Durkheim's usage, the concept harbored a raft of ambiguities, ambiguities that were exacerbated in Merton's varied appropriations of the term (Levine 1985:55–72), "Social Structure and Anomie" directed the attention of sociologists to the potent influence of normative structures on human action and invited them to a productive research program that made use of current scientific methodologies. To be sure, much of the research inspired by that seminal paper had more to do with differential material opportunities in the situation of action, but it led as well to projects in which Merton applied the notion of normative structure to the professions and thereby spotlighted

---

[10] Besides Merton, who acknowledged his deep indebtedness to Simmel, one may include work by two of his prominent students, Coser (1956) and Caplow (1968). For a full account of Simmel's influence, see Levine et al. (1976).

Period	Germinal work	Key constructs	Precipitate for analytic paradigm
I	"Social Structure and Anomie"(1937)	Relation of goals/norms Anomie	Sources and logics of normativity
II	"Normative Structure of Science"(1942) "Priorities in Scientific Discovery"(1957)	Normative systems Role sets Dysfunctional normative orders	Structural contradictions
III	"Sociological Ambivalence"(1976)	Sociological ambivalence	Moral ambivalence

FIGURE 4.3. Modalities of morality in the work of Merton.

certain moral tensions under which professional live. Exemplars of these departures include "The Normative Structure of Sciences" ([1942] 1979), which afforded a now classic paradigm of the complex of norms that govern the professional scientists–communalism, universalism, disinterestedness, skepticism, and – a later addition – originality.

From an initial commitment to revealing the moral structure behind institutions, an interest sparked by his tutelage under Parsons in the mid-1930s when Parsons was himself was starting to explore the normative structure of professions, Merton paid increasing attention to internal contradictions that problematize conformity to norms, in line with the central syndrome of "social structure and anomie." His conceptualization of the "status-set" and the "role-set" (1957:113–122) highlighted contradictions among diverse normative expectations that may not be readily visible. More pointed contradictions came to the fore in papers such as "Priorities in Scientific Discovery" (1957), which illuminates the conflict between normative goals and social rewards for conformity to them. The Priorities paper examines how the norm of originality evokes strivings that result in actions that contravene the established norms of science such as openness and communalism. Similar tensions appear in phenomena such as priority disputes among scientists, and ways that famous scientists receive disproportionate credit for their contributions while lesser-known scientists receive less credit than their contributions merit – a phenomenon that Merton dubbed the Matthew Effect.

This attention to contradictory outcomes in normative culminated in Marton's late conceptualization of "sociological ambivalence." This notion enabled him to conceptualize patterns of action in terms of socially structured alternatives presented in the form of binary oppositions. For example, he argued that scientists feel obliged (both) to publish quickly *and* to avoid rushing into print, to value humility *as well as* take pride in originality; physicians are socialized (both) to show sympathy as well as detachment; business leaders are expected (both) to project a sharply defined vision of their firm's future *and* to avoid narrow commitments which distance their subordinates, to provide special facilitates so departments can perform well, *and* to subordinate departmental goals to those of the whole organization (Levine 1978:1278).

For Merton, then, this meant that social roles should no longer be analyzed as coherent sets of normative expectations, but as clusters of norms and counternorms that alternatively govern role-behavior. To be sure, the notion of socially structured alternatives appears in

Parsons's conception of the pattern variables and elsewhere. However, Parsons wants to characterize social relations in terms of the dominant pattern alternative they embody. Merton stresses the significance of continuously operative counternorms that alternate with dominant norms in defining social roles. This slight difference is big with theoretical implications. It means that opposition to a dominant norm need not be construed as deviant behavior, expressing some sort of alienative disposition, but rather as normatively valorized conduct. It thereby normalizes ostensible deviance. It intensifies the compulsivity of behavior that veers to one of the normative poles. It produces more openings for the identification of social conflict. It more readily leverages tendencies toward social change.

1. Place of Moral Phenomena in the Universe of Human Action
    a. The sense of moral obligations as a World-shaping form (Simmel 1892)
    b. Ultimate values as a crucial part of existential reality (Parsons 1935)
    c. Placing morality in a general theoretic framework (Parsons 1960)
    d. Situating morality in a view of the human condition (Parsons 1978)
2. Constitution of the moral components of action
    a. Typologies of forms of moral phenomena
      1) morality, honor, and law (Simmel)
      2) values and norms (Parsons)
      3) goals and means (Merton)
    b. Typologies of contents
      1) areas where norms apply (Parsons 1937, Merton 19)
      2) pattern variables (Parsons 1951)
      3) pertaining to functional imperatives (Parsons 1956–1960)
    c. Embodied in potent yet problematic symbols
      1) which need to be disambiguated (Simmel 1892–1893)
      2) which afflict actors with cross-cutting injunctions (Merton 1937, 1968)
3. Sources of moral norms
    a. societal needs and pressures (Simmel 1890)
    b. effects of particular interaction structures (Simmel 1908–1910)
    c. functional requisites (Merton; Parsons 1960)
    d. imperatives of modernity (Parsons 1960)
    e. personal creativity (Simmel 1918)
4. Changes in moral directives
    a. microdynamics of normative change (Merton, Parsons)
    b. historical evolution (Parsons 1963)

FIGURE 4.4. Toward a paradigm of the moral-evaluative complex.

Toward integration

The foregoing purports to indicate that efforts to systematize foundations for sociology of morality would benefit from close attention to the work of the three thinkers examined here. My summary of some of their contributions, which conjoins items from the right-hand columns of the above figures, provides openings for evolving a paradigm for the field. The time may be ripe for constructing a Moral-Evaluative Complex cognate with what Parsons designated as the Cognitive Complex. At the very least, this chapter may serve to codify an array of plausible claims and suggestions yielded by their seminal forays (Figure 4.4).

REFERENCES

Alexander, J. 1993. "'Formal Sociology' is not Multidimensional: Breaking the 'Code' in Parsons' Fragment on Simmel." *Teoria Sociologica* 1/3:101–114.

Bellah, R. 1964. "Religious Evolution." *American Sociological Review* 29(3):358–374

Camic, C. 1989b. "Structure after 50 Years: The Anatomy of a Charter." *American Journal of Sociology* 95:38–107.

Camic, C., ed. 1997. *Reclaiming the Sociological Classics: The State of the Scholarship.* Malden, MA: Blackwell Publishers.

Durkheim, E. 1984 (1893). *The Division of Labor in Society.* New York: The Free Press.

Frisby, D., ed. 1994. *Georg Simmel: Critical Assessments.* 3 vols. New York: Routledge.

Hirschman, A. O. 1977. *The Passions and the Interests.* Princeton: Princeton University Press.

Levine, D. N. 1980. *Simmel and Parsons: Two Approaches to the Study of Society.* With a new Introduction. NY: Arno Press.

Levine, D. N. 1991. "Simmel and Parsons Reconsidered." *American Journal of Sociology* 96(5):1097–1116.

Levine, D. N. 1994a. "Simmel e Parsons riconsiderate/Simmel und Parsons neu betrachtet." *Annali di Sociologia/Soziologisches Jahrbuch* 10. (Translations of 1991.)

Levine, D. N. 1994b. "Further Comments Regarding Parsons's Chapter on Simmel and Tönnies: A Response to *Teoria Sociologica* 1/93, 13–156." *Teoria Sociologica* 2/94: 360–374.

Levine, D. N. 1995. *Visions of the Sociological Tradition.* Chicago: University of Chicago Press.

Levine, D. N. 2005. "Putting Voluntarism back into a Voluntaristic Theory of Action." In *Die Ordnung der Gesellschaft: Festschrift Geburtstag von Richard Münch*, edited by H.-J. Aretz and C. Lahusen. Frankfurt am Main: Peter Lang.

Levine, D. N. 2006. "Merton's Ambivalence Towards Autonomous Theory – and Ours." *Canadian Journal of Sociology* 31(2):235–243.

Lidz, V. 1993. "Parsons and Simmel: Convergence, Difference, and Missed Opportunity." *Teoria Sociologica* 1/3: 130–142.

Merton, R. K. 1968 (1938). "Social Structure and Anomie." Reprinted in *Social Theory and Social Structure.* New York: Free Press.

Merton, R. K. 1973 (1942). "The Normative Structure of Science." In *The Sociology of Science*," edited by N. Storer. Chicago: University of Chicago Press.

Merton, R. K. 1973 (1957). "Priorities in Scientific Discovery." In *The Sociology of Science*," edited by N. Storer. Chicago: University of Chicago Press.

Merton, R. K. 1976. *Sociological Ambivalence.* New York: Free Press.

Parsons, T. 1935. "The Place of Ultimate Values in Sociological Theory". *International Journal of Ethics* 45:282–300. Reprinted in Camic, ed.

Parsons, T. 1949 (1939). "The Professions and Social Structure." In *Essays in Sociological Theory.* New York: Free Press.

Parsons, T. 1951. *The Social System.* New York: Free Press.

Parsons, T. 1966. *Societies: Evolutionary and Comparative Perspectives.* Englewood Cliffs: Prentice-Hall.

Parsons, T. 1971. *The System of Modern Societies.* Englewood Cliffs: Prentice-Hall.

Parsons, T. 1968 (1937). *The Structure of Social Action.* 2 vols. New York: Free Press.

Parsons, T., and N. Smelser. 1956. *Economy and Society.* New York: Free Press.

Parsons, T., with G. M. Platt, and N. J. Smelser. 1973. *The American University.* MA: Harvard University Press.

Patterson, O. 1991. *Freedom in the Making of Western Culture.* NY: Basic Books.

Sidgwick, H. 1892. Review of Simmel, *Einleitung in die Moralwissenschaft.* Mind 1:434. Reprinted in David Frisby, ed. 1994. *George Simmel: Critical Assessments,* Vol. 1. London: Routledge.

Simmel, G. 1971 (1910). "Sociabiility." In *Georg Simmel: On Individuality and Social Forms,* Edited by D. N. Levine. Chicago: University of Chicago Press: 1971. Translation of "Soziologie der Geselligkeit." GSG 12.

Simmel, G. 1989 (1890). "Uber sociale Differenzierung." *Georg Simmel Gesamtausgabe [GSG] 2.* Frankfurt am Main: Suhrkamp.

Simmel, G. 1991 (1892–1893). *Einleitung in die Moralwissenschaft,* 2 vols. GSG 3. Frankfurt am Main: Suhrkamp.

Simmel, G. 1992 (1898). "Die Selbserhaltung der Socialen Gruppe." GSG 5. Frankfurt am Main: Suhrkamp. English version in Wolff 1950.

Thilly, F. 1893. Review of Simmel, *Einleitung in die Moralwissenschaft.* Philosophical Review 3: 637–640. Reprinted in David Frisby, ed. 1994. *George Simmel: Critical Assessments*, Vol. 1. London: Routledge.

Weber, M. 1968. *Economy and Society,* edited by G. Roth and C. Wittich. 3 vols. New York: Bedminster Press.

CHAPTER 5

The (Im)morality of War

Some Sociological Considerations

EDWARD A. TIRYAKIAN

Though long a subject of consideration by historians, philosophers, and political scientists, the topic of war has only recently become of theoretical concern to sociological analysis. Treating war as a complex interaction process, this essay analyzes three dimensions of war and its bearing to modernity. It first considers the moral and cultural aspects of war which provide legitimation for collective mobilization and commitment to war, despite modernity's emphasis on interstate peace and cooperation. The essay then considers the immorality of war in the modern period as manifested in the dehumanization of the "other" and in overcoming normative prohibitions against killing. Third, moral clarity in modern warfare is rendered ambiguous in the treatment of "civilians," protected by the Geneva Conventions yet often disregarded by combatants, even those from democratic societies. This ambiguity is highlighted in the discussion of two contemporary facets of war: terrorism and heroism.

INTRODUCTION

Some 10 years ago, a provocative lead article by Joas, "The Modernity of War" (1999a), intended as a critique of modernization theory for its neglect of war,[1] appeared in the official organ of the International Sociological Association, *International Sociology*. The article was followed in the same issue by two rebuttals (Tiryakian 1999, Roxborough 1999), and a parting riposte by Joas (1999b). As a set, this issue may in retrospect be viewed as a sociological opening for a serious consideration of a theme of the human condition, war.[2]

War itself has long been a multidimensional stimulus prodding reams of writings from the historical consciousness of Thucydides' account of the Peloponnesian War 25 centuries ago to recent anti-war consciousness of peace movements (Collins 2008, Robbins 2008, Woehrle et al. 2008). It has been the focus of penetrating and influential treatises on strategic thinking, from Sun Tzu's ancient classic *The Art of War* to von Clausewitz's *On War*. And of course the

---

[1] Hans Joas, "The Modernity of War," *International Sociology*, 14,4 (1999:457–472). This was later expanded into a book, *War and Modernity*. Cambridge (UK): Polity and Malden, MA: Blackwell. 2003.

[2] Philip Smith has recently (2005) applied a cultural sociology inspired by Durkheim to the study of modern war.

S. Hitlin, S. Vaisey (eds.), *Handbook of the Sociology of Morality*,
Handbooks of Sociology and Social Research, DOI 10.1007/978-1-4419-6896-8_5,
© Springer Science+Business Media, LLC 2010

stark realities of war in the modern period have prodded the artistic creativity and anguish in all the popular media (novels, plays, movies, television).

The title of Joas's essay highlights the problematic relation of war to modernity, particularly if we take as a chrysalis of modernity the Enlightenment and post-Enlightenment period. Its leadings thinkers formulated a paradigm of progress, climaxed in Kant's last great essay on the conditions necessary for an "Eternal Peace" (Friedrich 1948) – published in 1795 on the eve of the Napoleonic Wars. That "war" should be seen as an "enigma" as well as an abomination of modernity – and yet embedded in modernity – has led to important varied reflections and analyses (Wittrock 2001, Gat 2006). While lagging in dealing with war, some recent sociological attempts do have broadened the field of severe violence toward others, to a field like "ethnic cleansing" (Mann 2005) and varieties of violence at the micro level (Collins 2008).

While awaiting the follow-up volume of Collins pertaining to macro level violence, in which he intends to cover war, the present essay offers some considerations of war as a sociological field that links at various levels the micro, the meso and the macro interactional levels. The key focus stems from Joas' parting observation regarding the shortcoming of modernization theory in dealing with war. It is not, he emphasizes, the lack of a normative tradition in modernization analysis he objects to:

> . . . on the contrary! Exactly because I am interested in the continuation of this *normative tradition*, it is important to detect and overcome empirical gaps and flaws. . .(1999:503, emphasis mine).

This essay is not intended to be yet another rejoinder upholding a passé version of modernization; rather, like Joas, my concern is with the normative. More specifically, I wish to prod our theoretical understanding of the moral dimension of modern war as generative of a complex interaction process having unintended consequences. This topic in sociology has taken a back seat to more standard normatively framed topics and fields like race, gender, inequality, and so on . . . despite the fact that the United States has been at war the length of the past decade, since the Declaration of War by President Bush on September 20, 2001. It is a very peculiar war, to be sure, since it is not a war against another nation-state but a total war against "Terrorism," which may be fought anywhere, without time limit:

> We will direct every resource at our command. . . to the disruption and to the defeat of the global terror network. . .our response involves far more than instant retaliation and isolated strikes. . . And we will pursue nations that provide aid or safe haven to terrorism. Every nation, in every region, now has a decision to make. Either you are with us, or you are with the terrorists.[3]

The moral fervor underlying this declaration echoes President Woodrow Wilson's "War Message" to Congress on April 2, 1917 declaring war on Germany for its submarine warfare. The sinking of an American merchant ship 84 years earlier generated then the same moral outrage as the 9/11 Al Qaeda attack:

---

[3] George W. Bush, Declaration of War, address to the Joint Session of Congress, September 20, 2001, http://www.britannica.com/presidents/article-9398253 The symmetry of this post-modern war is that for its alleged major architect, Osama bin Laden, there is no boundary to the war, in time or space.

> Our object... is to vindicate the principle of peace and justice in the life of the
> world... Neutrality is no longer feasible or desirable where the peace of the world is
> involved...we fight without rancour and without selfish object, seeking nothing for our-
> selves but what we shall wish to share with all free peoples... It will be all the easier for
> us to conduct ourselves as belligerents in a high spirit of right and fairness because we
> act without animus... only in armed opposition to an irresponsible government which
> has thrown aside all considerations of humanity.[4]

Also in the preceding century of *pax Americana*, the United States began the 20th Century
with a little colonial war against the Philippines and its Tagalog Republic and was a major
participant in World War I, World War II, the Korean War, and the Vietnam War, ending with
providing NATO-led military intervention in 1999 in the Kosovo War. War, thus, is certainly a
recurrent condition that relates modern American polity and society to the rest of the world.

Standard sociological approaches, functionalist, Marxist, or post-modernist, from introductory textbooks to advanced primers on sociological theory, all tend to have a benign neglect
of war in favor of quotidian aspects of the social order. Severe disruptions of the social order
are, of course, part of our sociological patrimony which is most typically mentioned in connection with "revolutions," "anomie," and an occasional "collective effervescence," such as
in covering social movements or "collective behavior." But wars are instances of primary
disruptions of the social order, whether the war is fought "here" or "there."

How is it that the weight of a social order and social organization geared to the production
and reproduction of an ongoing social order becomes thrown aside in a state going to war
against "the other"? What happens to the internal organization of the social order so that the
typical social behavior and codes of conduct (including sexual behavior) operative in a given
state between various actors undergoes transformation from "peacetime" to "wartime"? By
further extension, how is it that behavior toward "others" and the codes of conduct toward
"others" become transformed, so that the destruction of "others" changes from being seen as
"homicides" to justified "killings"? At another level, if states and collectivities in the quotidian
life of "peace time" seek to act rationally in fiscal expenditures (or pretend they do), once at
war, material and human costs lose practically all their constraints.[5] What accounts for the
"fiscal exuberance" of states in war expenditures, which may be viewed as an instance of a
"moral holiday," to draw from Collins (2008:243)?[6] To try to answer these "hard" questions
is a daunting challenge.

---

[4] http://wwi.lib.byu.edu/index.php/Wilson's_War_Message_to_Congress.

[5] So for example, a 2005 report indicated that three years into the Iraq War, the bill for the United States was
already over 204 billion dollars, a rate of spending of 5.6 billions monthly, excluding long-term costs of health
care and disability payments to Iraq War veterans, and certainly exclusive of costs to the Iraqi civilians and their
shattered economy (Jim Lobe, "Iraq War Costs Now Exceed Vietnam's," Inter Press Service, September 1, 2005
(http://www.commondreams.org/headlines05/0901-02.htm). Even that figure probably underreports considerably the
true costs of the Iraq War. See the more recent analysis of Nobel prize winner Joseph Stiglitz pointing to the Iraq War
having total expenses (especially if care for the psychologically and physiologically wounded veterans are included)
of three trillion dollars (Stiglitz and Bilmes 2008), or three times the amount which figure in the acrimonious debates
over the government costs of health care reforms. It should be borne in mind that their detailed analysis did not foresee
the new (2009) military engagement in Afghanistan under taken by the United States and its allies.

[6] Collins applies this concept in dealing with violence to collective breakdown in normal social controls. I will return
to his usage in a later section, but here I think it is also apt to cover breakdown of fiscal restraints.

To begin to tackle what is a vast set of questions germane for sociological inquiry regarding war and modernity, we will look at dual aspects of the normative frame of war contained in the title of this essay.

The first section will focus on how war in an advanced modern society such as the United States comes to be structured and presented as a moral phenomenon. The United States is imbued with the ideals of the Enlightenment including world trade and commerce replacing the need for war, is a signatory to the Kellogg-Briand Peace Act of 1928, and host to the United Nations dedicated to the ideals of world peace. Yet, America has since the founding of the United Nations 65 years ago engaged in wars and military excursions in multiple Third World theaters. How, then, is war constructed as a moral phenomenon in this contradiction? The second part of this essay is the reciprocal of the first: how or in what actions is war an immoral phenomenon? Taken together, we seek to make a contribution that will be heuristic for a vast field of sociological inquiry, one that in an age of war-prone advanced modernity and global interdependence requires increasing concern.

THE MORALITY OF WAR

Initially it would seem greatly difficult in the modern age not only to mobilize a population to go to war, but also that this should be undertaken and viewed by the civilian population as morally justifiable. How is it not seen as a regressive undertaking?

The "paradigm of progress" having its initial frame in the Enlightenment focused on economic, scientific, and cultural aspects of modernity, with internal variations, was widely shared by liberals, conservatives, and radicals. Alongside individualism seeking the empowerment of individuals in civil society, collectivism, expressed in movements seeking regime changes in the ballot box or in the barricades, sought in various countries the empowerment of groups (classes and ethnic groups, mainly).

The Napoleonic era had tired Western countries of wars against each other, and the new era of modernity after 1815 was intended to be void of war between nation-states, with scientific and economic growth providing the matrix of long-term progressive change.[7] That hands-off war against other nation-states did not prevent countries competing in other ways to establish "spheres of influence," enter into cabals with others in secret alliances in case of war, and engage in "colonial wars" outside the space of the "civilized world" is besides the point. For nearly 100 years, Europe was mostly free of wars between nation-states, with exceptions such as the Franco-Prussian War of 1870, or its preceding Austrian-Prussian War, and the Crimean War (1853–1856). Certainly for the generation born in the second half of the 19th Century, the paradigm of progress held sway, until the momentous assassination at Sarajevo of an Austrian Archduke in 1914 swept aside national boundaries and restraints against war.

Four years later, the West was again exhausted by a war that had now become global in scope and been the bloodiest in human history. Peace barricades sprang up, such as the

---

[7] Even Marx and his followers did not espouse war as the use of force. From that radical perspective, war was devalorized as the pitting of one capitalistic system against another, or one capitalistic system plundering a pre-capitalistic one for its resources. And later in the twentieth century with the proliferation of communist regimes holding different allegiances, the derided political observation that "democracies don't fight each other" could be equally applied to including "communist regimes don't fight each other."

League of Nations, and anti-war novels and films held sway. Even if President Wilson could not persuade a recalcitrant Congress to endorse his plans for peace, his moral commitment to peace and the mechanisms he sought to put in place at Versailles captured the imagination and desire of the world. Yet again, another cycle of war renunciation ending abruptly: massive wars between states and their satellites followed, with the equally horrific World War II that ended with the unconditional surrender and annihilation of Germany and Japan, both of which were laid to waste with weapons of mass destruction: fire bombing and the actual use of nuclear weapons. Still another cycle of anti-war sentiments emerged in 1945 with the United Nations coming into being, then followed in less than 10 years with the United States military engagement in Asia, first in Korea, then after a respite, in IndoChina/Vietnam.

The heralded "new social order" in the wake of the implosion of the Soviet empire at the end of the 1980s indicated a new era for American peaceful leadership in the age of globalization, but this *pax Americana* quickly vanished with violent turmoil in ex-Yugoslavia and the rise of Islamic fundamentalism fueled by breakdown of the peace process involving Israel and Palestine. Timorous in intervening in Middle East conflicts for most of the 1990s, the United States did militarily intervene in the Kosovo War in 1999, ostensibly to put a halt to Serbian "ethnic cleansing" of a Muslim minority.[8] And now, ironically, the United States in the new century has entered into a prolonged conflict and war in the Middle East, involving at least two Islamic countries, Iraq and Afghanistan, with a real possibility that in the new decade some bellicose action might be taken against another Islamic country (Iran) and increasing engagement in yet another (Pakistan).

How is it, then, that the United States, a country both at the vanguard of modernity in political, economic, technological and cultural domains, and which sees itself as a peace-loving democracy, can so readily be drawn into or accept willingly to go to war far outside its borders?

As I shall shortly discuss, "Going to war" is a moral collective act, involving the mobilization not of specific interest groups but of the whole "societal community".[9] For it to take place, there is an important cultural conditioning which modernity has prepared. It is very much involved with national identity as that is imparted in the socialization process and its continuous reproduction in the deployment of patriotism.

That a pre-adult conditioning for accepting war is readily available is shown in the December 2009 release of the newest Nintendo game, "Marines: Modern Urban Combat." Its packaging has as prospectus, "Get ready for the most intense, realistic military shooter on Wii. Grab the Wii Remote and lead your squad into battle with tactics and strategies used by the real U.S. Marine Corps." And as Features:

- "Lead your four-man quad through the deadly streets of Beirut.
- Both your squad and your enemies feature deadly AI unlike anything you've ever seen before."

---

[8] Edward Tiryakian, "Der Kosovo-Krieg und die Rolle der Vereingten Staaten," *Berliner Journal für Soziologie*, 11, 2 (2001): 201–216.

[9] "Mobilization" in the rich sociological literature around it, particularly under the influence of Charles Tilly's historical studies (*From Mobilization to Revolution*, 1978), has tended to be viewed as a popular collective movement *against* the state. Here I treat it as a popular movement *for* the state (and perhaps overtly if not covertly organized *by* the state).

One hundred years ago, Nintendo did not exist. But the appeal of war and the military undoubtedly had a powerful lure for teenagers either in play or coming into proximity of military uniforms. Consider the vivid account by a World War I British veteran who lived to be a centenarian and provided his biographer a detailed narrative of his life before and during the Great War. He recounted that as a schoolboy in 1911 living near an Army camp,

> This was really very thrilling to watch... Bugles were blowing, bands were practicing, the horse lines were formed... it was lovely to see... their officers in their smart uniforms...it made a fourteen year old boy long to be a soldier," (van Emden 2002:31–33).

Learning the history of the country in school will reinforce the image that the country showed its strength and virtue – its virility one might almost say—by entering and winning wars, especially against foes who were tyrants, or oppressors of weak populations, or had sought harm on one's own country. Students will also note the sad events and pages of the country's history when foes attacked the country, and the country's "braves" died but whose death in valor is memorialized as "Remember the Alamo," "Custer's Last Stand," and "Pearl Harbor." They will also learn the meaning of moral fortitude in refusal to surrender, as exemplified by General McAuliffe's epic "Nuts" reply to German demands for surrender at Bastogne in December 1944, for which he won a place in America's Valhalla at Arlington National Cemetery, along with 300,000 others from all foreign wars since the Civil War.

Monuments testifying to the courage and bravery of the military abound throughout modernity, evoking national pride. In the 19th Century, the greatest composers like Beethoven and Tchaikovsky composed orchestral works commemorating Napoleon's defeat, as the French have kept Napoleon's own commissioned Arc of Triumph and Parisians daily use subway stations (Austerlitz, Jena, Solferino) that testify to the military victories of Napoleon I and Napoleon III . Londoners, on the other hand, can see everyday the victories of Nelson and Wellington at Trafalgar Square and Waterloo Station, while Japanese can pay their respect at Yasukuni Shrine to the war dead who fought for the Emperor.[10] There is across the entire period of modernity not only a profusion of monuments to historical great military leaders, but also, monuments at various levels of the societal community, from the national to the communal, which have the names of those killed (as in the Vietnam War Memorial in Washington). Lastly, recognition is also given in a residual sense to the "anonymous" killed, the "unknown soldier" whose remains are unidentified, but recalled in a symbolic "Tomb of the Unknown Soldier" or the cenotaph that one can find in countless countries, whether in Arlington, or Westminster Abbey, Ottawa, Manila, etc.[11]

Additional cultural conditioning for the acceptance of war comes in quotidian rituals of collective saluting of the flag and the singing of the national anthem. The two form an important anchor of national identity, found in a variety of settings, from Boy Scouts' den meetings, athletic stadiums, commencement exercises, and the like. Sousa's "Stars and Stripes Forever" as the National March of the United States has almost the same iconic status, proclaiming both

---

[10] Visits by Japanese Prime ministers to this shrine have raised controversy by both liberal Japanese and by those outside of Japan who recall the wartime conduct of the Japanese in China and elsewhere. What a military burial place signifies to whom has much collective emotional significance, which merits a separate treatment.

[11] For a general listing of sites, see http://en.wikipedia.org/wiki/Tomb_of_the_Unknown_Soldier

the unity of the country in a martial air and by the same token, its defiance of enemies of freedom. The collective rituals of observing these in unison function both to reaffirm the "societal community" and at a more latent level, to show a readiness to come to the defense of the nation if harm's way threatens it. This is an application of what Michael Billig has analyzed in his detailed *Banal Nationalism*(1995).

The morality of war has a very tangible sociological aspect in generating a solidarity of an exceptional quality. Emile Durkheim made solidarity a lodestone of his empirical studies, but he had not foreseen that his pregnant concept of "collective effervescence" would become actualized in France in July 1914 when the left and the right, in the face of Germany's war declarations would reach in embrace across the parliamentary aisle (Tiryakian 2005). The scenario was practically repeated in the United States in the immediate aftermath of 9/11, uniting (for a short while) liberal Democrats and conservative Republicans. Coming together against a common foe, whose action against the collectivity is perceived as vile and immoral, goes beyond Simmel's functional analysis of a group uniting in the face of an external opponent. It unites the wider community (or Parsons' "societal community") in the defense of its core values which take on a moral dimension, of what is the good that we share together.

Even devoid of an explicit religious reference, the sphere of the sacred permeates social relationships during a war and, for those who have participated in it, afterwards until the very last combatant who remembers his fallen comrades (Van Emden 2002, 2006). The extreme situations of combat where the lives of each may well depend upon the action of others, and the altruistic conduct of risking – and frequently losing – one's life to rescue or protect the life of the other are generative of feelings of attachment to the "companion-in-arms" and to the group.[12]

Durkheim's seminal study of religion, *The Elementary Forms of the Religious Life*, gave signal attention to *sacrifice*, as a fundamental aspect of the "sacred."[13] Certainly "sacrifice" is evoked as a price paid for being at war in a moral cause. It is a collective "sacrifice," at the micro level (for the family of the one killed) and at the macro level (the nation). This dimension of war, the giving of life to something greater than the collective self for the sake of a moral cause that makes war meaningful rather than absurd or meaningless, is a very powerful symbolism. It was clearly expressed at the conclusion of Wilson's "War Message" to Congress:

> ...the day has come when America is privileged to spend her blood and her might for the principles that gave birth and happiness and the peace which she has treasured. God is helping her, she can do no other.[14]

To this writer's knowledge, Parsons and two of his associates have come closest in sociological analysis to dealing with this symbolism of the giving of life (Parsons 1978), and even so their brilliant essay does not deal with death as a military combat event but as "gift-giving," particularly in cases of organ transplant.

---

[12] This is perhaps duplicated in quotidian life by groups charged with public safety, like some police units and firefighters (Desmond 2007).

[13] Durkheim amplified the discussion of his associates Henri Hubert and Marcel Mauss, *Sacrifice: Its Nature and Function*. Chicago: University of Chicago Press, 1964 (1899).

[14] Wilson's War Message to Congress, *ibid.*

In the secular ethos of advanced modernity, the moral justification of war and the killing of the enemies as "God's will" – found in the Old Testament and in the great theologian of the Middle Ages, Thomas Aquinas – seems to have outlived this legitimation. But residues of this which permeated discussions of a "just war" in pre-Enlightenment Europe have persisted. Thus, the US Conference of Catholic Bishops set out in 1983 a *Pastoral Letter on War and Peace* which articulated seven conditions for a just war. These included: a "just cause" (such as protection of innocent life and securing basic human rights), comparative justice (do the rights and values involved justify killing?), and proportionality (are the costs and damage of the war proportionate to the good expected?).[15] The most recent instance of the moral element of war was the Nobel Peace Prize acceptance speech of President Barack Obama in Oslo in December 2009, where he invoked "the venerable moral tradition and doctrine of just war", the same month as calling for an increase in the American military forces in Afghanistan.[16]

In brief, then, there is a vast historical and cultural matrix providing grounds for viewing as moral the interaction process of war as a process for killing others – a process which in the "ordinary" setting of the social order is subject to severe punitive sanctions. War is from this perspective an interaction which is sanctioned violence. Participating in war on the side of righteousness is an indication of civic engagement, of accepting the responsibilities of citizenship, while objecting to war or seeking neutrality, whether at the state level or at the individual level, is likely to be viewed as unpatriotic, amoral, if not cowardly.

THE IMMORALITY OF WAR

Thou Shall Kill ! is the unstated first commandment of war, which however unpleasant to the ears of civilized cosmopolitans is nevertheless the message learned by active agents of the military. It is also *de facto* the first commandment of the paramilitary forces that have proliferated in modernity's warfare, and of course, it is the underlying guiding principle of sophisticated makers of advanced weaponry systems.[17]

That commandment is obviously the obverse of a basic moral principle of social interaction: *not* killing (or murdering) the other. That latter moral principle is internalized in the mainstream socialization process and institutionalized in the criminal code, with varying degrees of sanction levied on its violation. The state of war, once declared, tends to change or simplify the web of social relationships, dividing the population at war into a sharp polarity of "us" and "them."

The "modern" period of war may be said to have begun 200 years ago with Napoleon's embrace of the French Revolution in having the entire nation "at arms" with mass compulsory conscription and exporting the Revolutionary ideology with military might. Although, the first modern war may well have been the French–English 100 Years War (1337–1453), it is the

---

[15] http://www.americancatholic.org/Newsletters/CU/ac0883.asp

[16] "Obama, Afghanistan, and the 'just war',"*Crosscut,* December 14,2009. http://crosscut.com/2009/12/14/rights-ethics/19440.

[17] To be sure, the defense industry also seeks a complementary endeavor: to develop systems that avoid *our* side getting killed.

Napoleonic age of warfare which gets recognition for seeking the total annihilation of the foe (McKeogh 2002:124). For the next 200 years (and the process is still continuing in 2010) the underlying aim of modern warfare in most countries boasting of advanced modernity has been to have continued technological progress in the ability to destroy and kill those who are perceived as "the other."

What is the moral involvement of modern war that comes to prevail over the morality of quotidian social interaction? Nietzsche had prophesied a "transvaluation of values" coming at the end of European civilization and its bourgeois values he regarded as derivative of a "slave morality." He need not have gone far to find in 20th Century warfare such a "transvaluation" in conflicting states accepting – with some difficulty because of the inertia of the traditional Judeo-Christian moral envelope – a very different moral code of conduct.

Killing on a very large scale has been a characteristic of warfare between states in the 20th Century – the two World Wars combining for well over 80 million estimated military and civilian deaths.[18] To be sure, mass killing has not been confined to wars. It has also been a feature of domestic murderous "ethnic cleansing" from one end of the 20th century to the other, as Mann amply documents in examining "the dark side of democracy" (2005) with case studies of massacres of Armenians in 1915, Jews in Nazi Germany, Bosniaks and Tutsis in the 1990s. Whether externally or internally, murderous violence and killing are not just skeletons in the closet of various civilizations but are very much contemporary ornaments. They entail desensitizing the religious ethic of military recruits.[19] What is an "inconvenient truth" is that the morality of war requires democratic populations – such as those of the United States, Great Britain, France, Israel, and India, to name some of the commonly accepted democracies – to believe in the morality of their democracy in order to punish violently "others." More broadly, mass killing as Mann sadly observes, connects in the modern world good and evil:

> Evil does not arrive from outside of our civilization, from a separate realm we are tempted to call 'primitive'. Evil is generated by civilization itself (Mann 2005:ix).

Since war involves killing others, it might seem that providing recruits to the military with weapons and incentives to kill the other in combat would suffice. However, the "moral envelope" of civil society, the respect for the other as a human person, which Durkheim saw as modernity's emergent sacred belief,[20] has to be opened for military efficacy. This is a psychological and moral operation put in place by "the system".[21] Although "system" connotes

---

[18] Casualty estimates vary greatly and civilian deaths due to war related causes are often underreported or omitted. For reasonable estimates of World War I and World War II in the aggregate and by countries, see http://en.wikipedia.org/wiki/World_War_I_casualties and http://en.wikipedia.org/wiki/World_War_II_casualties

[19] From the sack of Orthodox Constantinople by Christian crusaders in 1203 AD to the Protestant-Catholic wars of the 16th Century, to the Yugoslav Civil War in the 1990s pitting Orthodox Serbs against Catholic Croats, and to the internal deadly contemporary violence in Iraq between Shia and Sunni, general adherence in a common faith has not stood up as a restraint to killing.

[20] "Individualism and the Intellectuals," pp. 43–57 in Robert N. Bellah, ed., *Emile Durkheim on Morality and Society.* Chicago: University of Chicago Press, 1973 (1898).

[21] I use "system" here following the usage of Lankford (2009) in his comparative analysis of four settings of extreme violence which turned ordinary beings into "killing machines".

impersonality, the violence a system perpetrates on others requires individual agents who, except for psychopaths and sadists, believe in the morality of the system. Belief in the morality of the system is generated before war is declared in the conditioning for war by the cultural matrix discussed in the first part of this essay. With the declaration of war, this is accentuated by the moral denunciation of the "other" as both a deadly menace to the existence of the country and the upholder of an abhorrent moral code.

Even so, the intersubjective nexus relating the agent of the system to the "other" may be sufficient to restrain shooting and killing the other. This was documented in a landmark oft-cited study of combat veterans of World War II (Marshall (1978) that found over 75% of soldiers refusing to fire at the enemy "even in combat when their lives were in great peril" (Lankford 2009:117, Collins 2008:370). Marshall's surprising findings stimulated the military to modernize its training of recruits, putting to good use the method of Skinner's "operant conditioning" and other tactical means. The aggregate result was to sharply decrease during the Vietnam War the infantry troops never firing in combat to around 10% and to 45% those who virtually always fired (Collins 2008:370, Grossman 1996:35). The new training succeeded admirably in its objective of going beyond motivating soldiers to be brave and fight well but equally shooting to kill, such that Vietnam War data indicated 95% of soldiers consistently doing so (Lankford 2009:117).

However informative, statistics do not tell the whole story concerning the dynamics of the morality of killing the other(s), at both the micro level of the individual agent and at the macro level of the system.

To account for the transformation in the perception on the other that leads to viewing the "other" as a suitable target for killing, one can invoke the anthropological tradition of *liminality* (Turner 1995) to indicate how recruits from civilian life are weaned from one moral system to another: in the transition process, they come to accept imposing extreme violence on "the other." Lankford (2009) has provided a useful set of strategies that seek the systematic indoctrination of new recruits into acceptance of such morality.

Following the initial recruitment appealing to the need to protect one's country (family, way of life, etc.) from a dangerous foe, the modern training program increases recruits' willingness to perform violence, the latter sanctioned by complementary forms of *authorization*. One entails an emphasis on the intended ends or outcomes of the violence rather than the destructive means to be deployed ("victory of the just over the unjust" or just simple "total victory"). The second, "mundane authorization", is invoked to portray violence on "the other" as a normal, expected aspect of the agent's overall service to the system. Being a component of the system's bureaucratic *instrumental rationality* facilitates engaging in violence insofar as the agent occupies formal roles that function to attain the objectives of the system.[22]

Two other strategies may be noted. As in rituals of liminality, recruits are physically isolated and stripped of characteristics of the larger society, including of the everyday moral

---

[22] Being a member of a bureaucratic system that sanctions doing extreme violence to "the other" is a two-edged sword. If that system loses a war, occupants of positions in the bureaucracy, high or low, are subject to dire punishment for violence the system has committed, witness Adolf Eichmann at one end of the Nazi bureaucracy and John Demjanjuk at the other end.

code of that society.[23] Such *isolation* allows the "system" to exaggerate or manufacture external threats, and to magnify the danger to the system of the others' agents. Lastly, systematic indoctrination employs *dehumanization* on twin targets: the others, and also the system's own recruits, to get both insulated from moral concerns regarding harming others, even violently (Lankin 2009:25).

Our focus here is to see at the system level how dehumanization has been put in play in modern warfare of the past 100 years, with an emphasis on the most recent instance: its notorious application in "intensive interrogation," i.e, torture of terrorist suspects.[24]

First there is need to consider moral obstacles to dehumanization, assuming that the greater extent the "other" is seen as a fellow human being, the less likely will extreme violence and killing occur. Without exhausting a wider array of obstacles (cultural, political, economic), let us invoke two different sorts: first, the moral obstacle of *guilt*, and second, the category of *civilians*. These two are in their way powerful traditional restraints of killing others in warfare, and both obstacles are subject to being cast aside by the immorality of war as a code of conduct.

Guilt as a Moral Restraint

Beyond Lankin's set, one other component of the process may be recognized, what I will call *secondary identification*. As a variation of the captive falling in love with the captor (the "Stockholm syndrome"), the identification of the military subject with his superior as a beloved figure can provide the motivation to kill the other, from a very different perspective than the Oedipal one. The testimony of an American soldier reflecting on shooting in the back an Iraqi soldier who had caught on fire and running for shelter is a poignant illustration:

> Sergeant Z, my platoon sergeant, wasn't just my tank commander and platoon sergeant.
> In some ways he was almost a father figure... I wanted to do the right thing. I wanted
> to do what would make Sergeant Z proud of me. That's why I killed. I think because I
> didn't have what it took to feel good about myself. I needed someone else's approval. I
> needed Sergeant Z to think of me as a man, and not as the scared little kid I really was
> (Sheehan-Miles 2008:84).

Of course, it is not only with the platoon sergeant or the commanding officer that secondary identification establishes a personal link with (and simultaneously, against) others. As earlier indicated in the introduction, the situation of war also promotes in military and civilian populations alike "altered states" of mind marked by emotional intensity and intensive solidarity approximating Durkheim's analysis of the genesis of the sacred in *The Elementary Forms of the Religious Life*. For recruits and battle-tested combatants, beyond instrumental rewards (decorations, promotions, booty) are the special friendships of having lived and died in extreme at-risk situations. From the liminal state emerges the bonding after the primary group of childhood into a new community, giving the sense of *communitas* that one very seldom finds in

---

[23] Much of the ritual process involved in institutional isolation is discussed in Goffman's insightful, *Asylums* (1962).

[24] If we put the accent on the past 100 years, dehumanization has a much older history, going back no further than the British setting up concentration camps in the Boer War and Sherman's "scorched earth" policy in the Civil War.

"ordinary times." In the present context, this means that the immorality of killing is transvalued, as necessary to save and protect the lives of both one's primary and one's secondary group of identification.

And yet, despite identification with the immediate leader, despite the exhortations of the head of state and military chiefs, despite bonding with one's fellow combatant, there is an irreducible moral or judgmental aspect of the self which after killing experiences a very personal *guilt*. The citation of the American soldier noted above motivated to kill a fleeing Iraqi needs to be completed:

> After my initial exhilaration, however, what came next was horror and shame. . .Shame at myself, for my reaction, for that instant of bloodlust and elation at killing another man. . .twelve years later, I can see his face. I wonder if his family knows what happened to him?. somewhere his mother grieves, (Sheehan-Miles, *ibid.*)

The modernity of war has made us progressively aware that the casualties of war are not limited to a body count but also need include the damages to the psyche. Some awareness of symptoms that take their tolls on combat veterans physiologically and socially on their victims has taken form in common usage labels like "combat fatigue" and "post-traumatic syndrome disorder" (PTSD). Much of the psychic damage has been underreported by those exposed to combat for fear that showing strong emotions goes against a "macho" image of fortitude, typified in popular advertisements by a Marine in dress uniform.

As telltale evidence of internal disruptions of the psyche, Grossman, himself highly qualified as a participant-observer in combat and killing, indicates in a study of 6,810 randomly selected veterans of high-intensity combat that these showed far higher incidence of divorce, marital problems, tranquilizer use, alcoholism, joblessness, heart diseases, and high blood pressure (Grossman 1996:283). And the experience of combat left a telling long-term legacy: estimates of PTSD, besides interference with holding a job in civilian life, run as high as 1.5 million of Viet War veterans, with hundred of thousands of broken marriages that can lead to maladjustments in the offsprings.

Grossman indicates additionally the lethal psychiatric toll of being involved in war-time killing. In World War II, half a million in the American military had psychiatric collapse, and those with continuous combat had a high probability of psychiatric collapse (98% after 60 days). Guilt is ultimately involved:

> Fear, combined with exhaustion, hate, horror, and the irreconcilable task of balancing those with the need to kill, eventually drives the soldier so deeply into a mire of guilt and horror that he tips over . . . into that region we call insanity (*ibid*. 54).

What compounded the psychological damage to military veterans of Vietnam was that unlike previous wars of the United States, veterans returning home the late 1960s found not a welcome from a grateful populace but, if anything, derision and hostility. The moral distance which the combatant is trained to establish between himself and "the other" turned against the returning serviceman, whether or not he had killed, much less been involved. Rather than providing support and praise, as the war progressed (or regressed) in the 1960s, the print and visual media increasingly highlighted the "dark side" of the American presence in Vietnam, with wide publicity given to in incidents such as the 1968 My Lai massacre of innocent villagers. Hence, Grossman noted:

> The Vietnam vet, the average vet who did no killing, is suffering an agony of guilt and torment caused by society's condemnation. During an immediately after Vietnam our society judged and condemned millions of returning veterans as accessories to murder (*ibid*:289).

That the immorality of war generates incapacitating long-term guilt in individuals is one aspect of the dark side of killing the other – the extreme violence returning on the self. But at the macro level, the immorality is compounded by the system being unable, if not unwilling, to deal with the guilt feelings of the combatants. Here Grossman observes that the psychological profession seems poorly prepared to address the guilt caused by the extreme situation of combat and its moral issues:

> The Veterans Administration psychologists are seldom willing to deal with problems of guilt, indeed, they do not even raise the issue of what the soldier did in war. (*ibid*: 96).[25]

The bureaucratic system's immorality is compounded by providing inadequate facilities for those suffering from PTSD (as well as severe physical harm), such as the deplorable over-crowded and understaffed conditions of Walter Reed that prevailed until a public outcry led to the dismissal of its supervisor in 2007.[26] And who is to say that a trained psychiatrist listening to hundreds of stories of brutality and killings from returning combatants might himself not succumb to deeply internal guilt feelings pushing him, as well as his patients, over the brink? This might well have been operative in the horrendous shooting at Ford Hood, Texas, on November 5, 2009 by an Army psychiatrist assigned not only to attend combatants from Iraq but also to rehabilitate them for another round of duty in Iraq; that in its self might make a sensitive person feel like an accomplice to a premeditated homicide/suicide. Since the psychiatrist in question was Muslim, one might see an extra layer of guilt stemming from hearing personal accounts of killings of civilian Muslims by one's soldiers.

It is this and many other instances of actual and potential "role conflicts" that are generated by the immorality of war, without satisfactory resolutions of this ambiguity: an extreme form of such role conflict might well produce as an outcome homicide or suicide.[27] Overall, the bureaucratic apparatus of the system may, if there is a public outcry over immoral actions, find responsibility for the actions in individuals, but usually this is far down the chain of command, as we shall note later in discussing the treatment of prisoners at Abu Ghraib, among other infamous sites.

Collectivities involved in war are less subject to guilt experienced by their collective actions against "others". Such "structural guilt", that is, acknowledging the immorality of actions done on others is a reflection of the moral structures of the collectivity, is more likely to be voiced by those who have lost a war than those who are the "winners." Penitentiary rites of atonement, while having a place in traditional rituals such as "the Day of Atonement" in

---

[25] The "classical" torture experiments of Milgram at Yale (1974) and Zimbardo at Stanford (2007), aside from their ethical ambiguity, do not discuss short-term and long-term guilt effects on subjects.

[26] "The Wider Shame of Walter Reed," *New York Times* editorial, March 7, 2007.

[27] In January 2010 the Veterans Affairs Department released figures showing in the two-year period 2005–2007 a 26% increase in the suicide rate of 18–29-year-old men who have left the military, along with a record increase in suicide in the military. The army suicide rate is now higher than that of the general American population for the first time since the highpoint of the Vietnam War.

Judaism or the confessional in Catholicism, are not institutionalized in modernity's warfare, despite the most immoral actions in the form of crimes against humanity by collectivities. Germany with the process of "Vergangenheitsbewältigung" ("coming to terms with the past") is exceptional in seeking to acknowledge fully guilt and redeem the past wrongs of its previous regime. Its defeated WWII partner, Japan, has been highly reluctant to accept guilt for its wartime treatment of countries its army had overrun (the infamous "Rape of Nanjing" in 1937 and the forced use of "comfort women"), while neutral Turkey, a parliamentary democracy in the Middle East, has been resistant to engage in public discussions of miscreant deeds of an anterior regime during World War I.

It is not only state "losers" that may have difficulty indicating guilt and remorse by saying "sorry" (Lind 2008). It is also "winners" who engage in immoral actions in wartime, and who either expunge these from the collective memory or rationalize these actions as having saved lives, provided added security for the home population, shortened the conflict considerably, etc. We can bring this to light in discussing the second obstacle, that of *civilians*.

Civilians as a Moral Restraint

Wars are not just fought between armies on a neutral, unoccupied space. Ultimately they draw in non-combatants as direct or indirect assistants and at varying distances from combat zones, and their sympathy with the combatants may not be obvious. How they shall be viewed and treated by combatants is subject to varying interpretations as to their involvement. At various points in history, considerations of war and its normative regulations have turned as much on non-combatants as combatants. What, then, are aspects of the status and treatment of this large class called *civilians*?

The major points to be made are that on the one hand, the category "civilian" evokes in the mentality of modernity a protective blanket or an aura of "innocence," suggesting an avoidance of the brutal violence of warfare and concern for non-combatant immunity (McKeogh 2002). That is the normative dimension. On the other hand, the actual, behavioral treatment of civilians in various historical settings, ours included, demonstrates how easily the moral restraint is cast aside, especially by modern democracies: to paraphrase Gilbert and Sullivan, in a broad historical and comparative perspective, "a civilian's lot is not a happy one."

In the evolving moral framework that views civilians as deserving protection from the ravages of combat, the Christian tradition of minimizing war and seeking peace has played an important, albeit frequently ineffective role, in curbing martial appetites. As the moral system of a post-Roman social order, Christian theology gradually established its moral authority well beyond matters of faith and into what may be viewed as social relations. It went counter to the more prevalent norms of warfare that favored spreading fear and chaos in civilian populations by invaders of territories, and stripping civilians of their property, which was a core aspect of booty used to pay or reward military forces (Slim 2008).

One step in formulating moral restraints to warfare and the aggressor's treatment of others came with extended initial discussions of "a just war," first in theological circles, later in the medieval period, and into the modern period. The influential patristic theologian Augustine had earlier justified limited state warfare if the enemy acted in an "unjust" cause which was legally and morally wrong, and hence subject to being killed. Specific recognition that civilians should have immunity did not come about until the Thirteenth Century when Pope Gregory IX drew a list of eight groups of people to be protected in warfare: priests, monks, other religious, pilgrims, merchants, peasants cultivating their lands, and the "naturally weak": women, children, widows, and orphans . These are essentially harmless and not capable of harming: they are the *innocens* (Slim 2008:12).

The theory of a just war (and its related emphases on who – and what treatment to accord combatants and non-combatants, respectively) continued to develop as an important adjunct of international law, even as the original Christian normative frame became secularized . For our purpose, an influential section of international law that arose from the reflections of scholars such as Suarez, Gentili, Grotius, and von Pufendorf, and which continues to draw attention today, is known as *jus in bello,* with its focus on the humane treatment of soldiers and non-combatants. Civilians should not be subject to bombing in their residential areas having no military target, and reprisals should not be taken against civilians. Further, the conduct of war should observe *proportionality:* an attack on a military objective cannot be undertaken if civilian casualties would be clearly excessive in relation to the military objective, and the harm caused to civilian property must be proportional and not excessive to the direct military advantage anticipated.[28] In American history, the Civil War played a part in the frame of the Lieber Code (1863) covering martial law in occupied territory. On the one hand it proscribed crimes that may be punished by execution: wanton violence, pillage, rape and murder of defenseless civilians. On the other, starvation or forced movement of unarmed population is acceptable as a strategy, while "military necessity may trump civilian protection of lives and property," (Slim 2008:18).

As Slim notes, on the question of civilians, this Code was an important forerunner to the Geneva Conventions and reflected enduring moral tensions between protecting civilians and the urgency of winning. If we consider the Geneva Conventions as the core of international humanitarian law, it is the fourth Geneva Convention adopted in 1949 (entering into force in 1950), and reflecting the horrendous experiences of World War II, which turned the world's attention explicitly to civilians. Two additional protocols adopted in 1977 relate to the Protection of Victims of International Armed Conflicts. Among other provisions, it seeks the general protection of populations against "certain consequences of war" and seeks to protect foreigners on the territory of one of the parties and civilians in occupied territory; further, there are detailed provisions on humanitarian relief for populations in occupied territory.[29]

The Geneva Conventions and its provisions (which deal with a wide range of lowering the toll of military devastation, and not just protection of civilian victims) are in some respect the pinnacle of modernity's humanitarian concerns, or, as McKeogh cogently phrases it,

> The Principle of non-combatant immunity (PNCI) has become central to the Western justification and waging of war (2002:2). In this vein, Article 48, "Basic Rule" of the 1977 protocols makes an explicit

differentiation of civilians and combatants, seeking the protection of the former:

---

[28] "Just War," http://en.wikipedia.org/wiki/Just_War.

[29] http://www.icrc.org/web/Eng/siteengO.nsf/html/genevaconventions.

...the Parties to the conflict shall at all times distinguish between civilian population and combatants and between civilian objects and military objectives and accordingly shall direct their operations only against military objectives.[30]

So one can take the PNCI as not only a moral principle but as, in principle, a sort of humanistic beta-blocker of the emotional, martial intensity unleashed by war, a restraint on the altered state of a "moral holiday" with its primacy on extreme violence and killing as many of the enemy as possible.

But, as the historical record shows, when push comes to shove, it is the military expediency which wins out, often at a terrible cost of civilian life.[31] Throughout the 20th century and into our present one, the actual blurring of the normative distinction between combatant and civilian has tragically become widespread in destructive behavior. This has been publicized in various Third World settings where guerilla, military, and paramilitary forces forcibly engage in sexual abuse and "draft" civilians, including young children, to their side (Slim, *op.cit*:231).

Less recognized is the immoral behavior of the most advanced modern democratic societies that have taken to the air to engage in killing, either small targets marked for assassinations or as took place in World War II, with the sanction of civilian leaders (notably Prime Minister Churchill and President Truman) as heads of states, large targets of civilians. Implicitly and explicitly the objective was to demoralize the enemy since the targets predominantly had no strategic value. Thus, in 1943 the British RAF firebombed the German cities of Marburg and Hamburg, with incendiary bombs heating the air to 800°C, killing civilians in underground air shelters. Less than 2 years later, American and British bombers kindled a firestorm in Dresden, killing over 50,000 civilians, many of whom had sought refuge from the Soviet army; similar firebombing was done over Tokyo killing 225,000, climaxed by the atomic bomb dropped on Hiroshima (McKeogh, *ibid*:126; Grossman, *ibid*.:98). The mass killing of civilians, in an impersonal manner such as bombing a large distance away from the victims, may thus be seen as an instance of "instrumental rationality," given the end of severely weakening enemy resistance.

To emphasize the point, aerial killing of civilians has blurred the distinction between military and non-military targets, and despite the moral constraints that the Geneva Conventions have erected, democracies are as prone to immoral conduct in warfare as "rogue" states. The use of napalm bombs, incendiary weapons, and herbicidal warfare (as in Agent Orange) on civilian targets (particularly in Third World countries) has not been done by "rogue states" but by ostensibly civilized countries allegedly fighting to protect their home-based democracies. A further blurring of the distinction between military and civilian has seeped in with the theatre of war in the past two decades being across and within national boundaries. Particular attention needs to be given in closing this section to (im)moral aspects of the war on terrorism, which has and will continue to cast its shadow in the new decade .

---

[30] Michael Bothe, Karl Josef Partsch, Waldemar A. Solf, with the collaboration of Martin Eaton. *New Rules for Victims of Armed Conflicts: commentary on the two 1977 protocols additional to the Geneva Conventions of 1949* (The Hague, Boston: Martinus Nijhoff Publishers, 1982), p. 280. Cited in James A. Stroble, 1996, *The Ethics of War and the Uses of War*, http://www.aloha.net/~stroble/Noncombatant.html.

[31] "When war fever takes its grip, people's instincts are to de-humanize the enemy and distance them from all moral norms," Slim (*op.cit*:277).

THE NEW (IM)MORALITY AFTER SEPTEMBER 11

The terrorist strike on the United States on September 11, 2001 and President Bush's declaration of war nine days later not only on al-Qaeda but also on "every terrorist group of global reach" officially launched a new chapter in globalization, in warfare, and in the (im)morality of combatants. Replacing the bi-polar Long War of the 20th Century between the Western alliance and the Soviet world, the new Long War did not originate "terrorism" of course. However, it has made it such a diffuse quagmire that it is hard to see the criteria for an objective determination of what is "terrorist action," including whether reactions to terrorism are justified by international codes or simply to be accepted for the sake of the security of the system at risk from terrorist organizations.

To detail all the features of the new Long War would be a separate chapter, but some aspects related to the present essay are worth noting.

First, the perception of what is a terrorist action and who are the terrorists has greater ambiguity than what is commonly acknowledged. In the West, it has been taken as a given that the twin attack on the United States on September 11, 2001 was an unprovoked act of terrorism claiming the lives of innocent civilians. Terrorism for the US Department of State is clearly

> … premeditated, politically motivated violence perpetrated against non-combatant targets (civilians) by subnational groups or clandestine agents (Bobbitt 2008:353).

As an extension, the governments of the United States and Israel jointly recognize Hamas in Palestine and Hezbollah in Lebanon as illicit organizations partaking of terrorist activity in sympathy with the perpetrators of attacks on American and Israeli innocent civilians.

In contradistinction, from the perspective of al-Qaeda as the militant organization of Osama bin Laden, *9/11* was part of a continuing operation to recover Islamic lands from Western occupation led by the United States and Israel and to establish the religious law of *sharia* prescribed by the Quran in place of decadent Western-influenced mores (alcoholism, sexual promiscuity, etc.).[32]

Bobbitt's coverage of public opinion worldwide shows divergence between the attitudes in the United States and Israel, and within the Arab countries of Jordan, Syria, Lebanon, Palestine, and Egypt, as to what are "terrorist attacks". The attack on the World Trade Center was most perceived as such in Lebanon (73%), a country that has experienced political assassinations and civil war, but least in Jordan (35%). Hezbollah operations against Israel was only perceived as terrorist in 10% in Jordan, 16% in Lebanon, and 7% in Egypt; on the other hand, assassinations by Israel of Palestinian figures was perceived by 84% in Jordan, 80% in Lebanon, and 87% in Egypt (Bobbitt 2008:354). This suggestive exploratory study of cross-country public opinion needs broadening to permit a better comparative perspective on what are viewed as "terrorist attacks" by various parties.

The theater in which terrorist activity takes place and the targets of attacks also partake of *ambiguity*. Some murderous violence may be claimed by al-Qaeda in any place in the world against both civilian targets (subway and train stations in Europe, resort hotels in Africa and

---

[32] For a readily available discussion of background materials, see "Osama bin Laden", http://en.wikipedia.org/wiki/Osama_bin_Laden, last modified January 5, 2010.

Southeast Asia) or military targets (American and British soldiers). It may be done imperson-ally by remote control (roadside bombing) or by a personal agent willing to sacrifice his or her life as a price for killing "the other" (as in "suicide bombing"). Terrorist combatants engage in insurgency against states or state protected regional governments (as in Chechnya, Kashmir, and elsewhere). Attempts at modeling targets of collective violence, including terrorist activity, are still at a rudimentary albeit promising level and of much vital interest to security services as well as to sociologists (Martin et al. 2009). Is, for example, an attack on a shopping mall in Baghdad or against a mosque in Fallujah an internal event or part of the tactics of a terrorist organization from outside like al-Qaeda or even from another state in the Middle East?

For the time being, it is almost anyone's guess who, when, and where the new "Long War" will find a target, and the impersonality of the terrorist attack is echoed in the impersonality of weapons of counterterrorism: unmanned aerial vehicles (UAV) like the US MQ-9 Reaper having an operational ceiling of 50,000ft (significantly higher than commercial planes) are capable of laser killing targets, but have been prone in Iraq and in Afghanistan, among other theaters, of killing non-combatant civilians who had the misfortune being in the proximity of insurgents. The absence of military uniforms, the evasive tactics of insurgents and their rapid deployment across imaginary boundaries compounds the ambiguity of the new, "post-modern" warfare. Not only is "the enemy" aggressor today not a state (though the enemy views *its* enemy as invading states), but the moral high ground of past wars of fighting for the good against the aggression of "evil" was dealt a severe blow in world opinion as a result of the US–British prefabricated war on Hussein's Iraq, ostensibly for having Weapons of Mass Destruction which did not exist. As part of the immorality of the second Iraq War may be listed: the wanton destruction of the country, the loss of civilian lives, the large number of refugees, including the substantial emigration of highly trained professionals, the severe disruption of the economy and social services, and the existential insecurity of living in a world where school buses, hospitals, and mosques may be tomorrow new targets of violence. Further, the media, as upholders of the cherished freedom of the press, have been as sadly negligent of showing the American and British public what the ugly face of war looks like in the second Iraq War as they failed to do so in the first Gulf War (Zinn 2008).

Of various components of the moral ambiguity of war activated by the War on Terrorism, perhaps the single most important defining moment has been the treatment of captured alleged terrorists at Guantanamo Bay and Abu Ghraib. The latter was the Baghdad Central Prison used by Sadam Hussein during his reign of terror, which turned into a second one a few years later with the American occupation The treatment of prisoners at Abu Ghraib in particular, far in violations of the Geneva Conventions, especially their enforced humiliation in multiple modes, has received sufficient attention in recent years that the specifics of abuses such as water boarding and being photographed in the nude are well documented elsewhere and need no further detailing here (see Greenberg and Dratel 2005, Zimbardo 2007, Gourevitch and Morris 2008, Lankford 2009).

What needs attention, however, is the general (im)moral frame of the handling of alleged terrorists, not just under a military command of the Military Police but also a civilian command reaching to the rallying point of the war on terror after *9/11,* the top of the executive branch of the American government. The White House, in the aftermath of the attack on prime symbols of American primacy in the world (Wall Street and the Pentagon), viewed American protec-tion from further attacks as the top priority above all others, including human rights embodied in the Geneva Conventions. Accordingly, "dark" methods in intelligence gathering that might otherwise be seen as morally questionable were to be put in the service of homeland security: the defeat of the "dark forces" of terrorism and the protection of the homeland were complementary goals that justified whatever means were needed to achieve them (Lankford 2009:120). Among these means would be the "extraction of information" from detainees – the means being justified by the ends sought, including a variety of means that in effect dehumanized the detainees so as to demoralize them. In the process, the captors themselves became dehumanized (Lankford 2009:128, Zimbardo 2007:328).

While the means used contained many immoral actions prohibited by the Geneva Conventions, perhaps another layer of immorality needs to be uncovered. First, the trampling of domestic and international legal and moral constraints by the Attorney General's office to excuse the use of torture in interrogation (Greenberg and Dratel 2005:81, Mayer 2008). Second, the "system's" bureaucratic operation of convicting and disciplining, for prisoner abuse of interrogation tantamount to torture, only low-ranking enlisted officers and enlisted soldiers, leaving untouched those at the top of the bureaucratic hierarchy – military and civilian – who bore the real responsibility.[33]

And "real responsibility" might arguably be taken to be not only for authorizing information gathering by any means, but also for having launched an "unjust war" against a country that had neither WMD nor at the time any known ties to a terrorist organization based in another country. Yet, the top of the "system" has so far publicly experienced neither guilt nor sanctions.

CONCLUSION

To do adequate justice to the relation of war to modernity from a sociological perspective would take far more than covered in these pages. As noted at the onset, the normative aspects of war bearing on social conduct in a situation of large-scale disruption of the social order has been the underlying focus here. Future work is needed to deepen our understanding of the social short-term and long-term consequences of war and its astronomical aggregate costs, even beyond the huge "trillion dollar" estimate of Stiglitz for the Iraq War (2008).[34] While many trails can issue from a sociological consideration of war, I would like to add another moral dimension which might in some respect balance the very "dark side" of the violence inherent in war.

The moral clarity and moral coating cast aside by various strategies, tactics, and actions in modern warfare has had a redeeming aspect in the immediately preceding decade. Alongside the heroism of combat troops engaged in hostile terrain overseas, is the heroism of those at home who have spoken out against the war in the hostile terrain of a mediated patriotism. Cindy Sheehan, Military Families Speak Out (MFSO) and other individuals and organizations

---

[33] As Major General Taguba placed in charge of investigating the Abu Ghraib reported afterwards, he only had access to lowly MPs, not those above: "I was legally prevented from further investigation into higher authority," (Mayer 2008:334).

[34] For example, how does one quantify the world wide loss of trust in the government of the United States and its British ally in the last decade? How does one quantify civilians and military exposed for the rest of their lives to PTSD?

who live, despite ridicule, the "banality of heroism" (Zimbardo 2007:xiv) have shown the way as challenges to the system's "monopolization of patriotism". Many of these activists are wives and mothers at the forefront of the antiwar movement (Robbins 2008, Collins 2008). They have experienced fully the (im)morality of war and deserve recognition as role models for those concerned with reconstructing modern patriotism (Woehrle et al. 2008) and rethinking public sociology (Jeffries 2009) in terms of peace processes.

REFERENCES

Bar-Tal, D. 1997. "The Monopolization of Patriotism," PP. 246–270 in *Patriotism in the Lives of Individuals and Nations*, edited by D. Bar-Tal, and E. Staub. Chicago: Nelson-Hall.

Billig, M. 1995. *Banal Nationalism.* London: Sage.

Bobbitt, P. 2008. *Terror and Consent. The Just Wars for the Twenty-First Century.* New York: Alfred Knopf.

Collins, J. 2008. *For Love of a Soldier. Interviews with Military Families Taking Action Against the Iraq War.* Lanham, MD: Lexington/ Rowman& Littlefield.

Collins, R. 2008. *Violence. A Micro-Sociological Theory.* Princeton and Oxford: Princeton University Press.

Desmond, M. 2007. *On the Fireline: Living and Dying with Wildland Firefighters.* Chicago: University of Chicago Press.

Friedrich, C. J. 1948. *Inevitable Peace.* Cambridge, MA: Harvard University Press.

Gat, A. 2006. *War in Human Civilization.* New York: Oxford University Press.

Greenberg, K. J., and J. L. Dratel, eds., Introduction by Anthony Lewis. 2005. *The Torture Papers. The Road to Abu Ghraib.* Cambridge and New York: Cambridge University Press. 1249 pages

Grossman, D. 1996. *On Killing. The Psychological Cost of Learning to Kill in War and Society.* Boston: Little Brown.

Jeffries, V., ed. 2009. *Handbook of Public Sociology.* Lanham, MD: Rowman & Littlefield.

Joas, H. 1999. "The Modernity of War: Modernization Theory and the Problem of Violence," *International Sociology* 14(4):457–472.

Lankford, A. 2009. *Human Killing Machines. Systematic Indoctrination in Iran, Nazi German, Al Qaeda, and Abu Ghraib.* Lanham, MD: Lexington/Rowman & Littlefield.

Lind, J. 2008. *Sorry States. Apologies in International Politics.* Ithaca and London: Cornell University Press.

Mann, M. 2005. *The Dark Side of Democracy. Explaining Ethnic Cleansing.*Cambridge and New York: Cambridge University Press.

Marshall, S. L. A. 1978 (1947). *Men Against Fire: the Problem of Battle Command in Future War.* Gloucester, MA: Peter Smith.

Martin, A. W., J. D. McCarthy, and C. McPhail, 2009. "Collective Violence: Why Targets Matter," *American Sociological Review* 74(5) (October):821–841.

Mayer, J. 2008. *The Dark Side. The Inside Story of How the War on Terror Turned Into a War on American Ideals.* New York: Doubleday.

McKeogh, C. 2002. *Innocent Civilians. The Morality of Killing in War.* Houndmills, Hampshire (UK) and New York: Palgrave.

Meehan, S. P., with Roger Thompson. 2009. *Beyond Duty. Life on the Frontline in Iraq.* Cambridge and Malden, MA: Polity Press.

Milgram, S. 1974. *Obedience to Authority: An Experimental View.* New York: Harper Collins.

Parsons, T., with Renée Fox and Victor Lidz. 1978. "'The Gift of Life' and Its Reciprocation," PP. 264–299 in *Action Theory and the Human Condition,* edited by T. Parsons. New York: Free Press/Macmillan.

Robbins, M. S., ed. 2008. *Peace not Terror. Leaders of the Antiwar Movement Speak Out Against U.S. Foreign Policy Post 9/11.* Lanham, MD: Lexington/Rowman & Littlefield.

Sheehan-Miles, C. 2008. "What It Feels to Kill." pp. 70–86 in Mary Susannah Robbins, *Peace not Terror, op. cit.*

Slim, H. 2008.*Killing Civilians. Method, Madness and Morality in War.* New York: Columbia University Press.

Smith, P. 2005. *Why War? The Cutlural Logic of Iraq, the Gulf War, and Suez.* Chicago:The University of Chicago Press.

Stiglitz, J., and L. J. Bilmes. 2008.*The Three Trillion Dollar War: The True Cost of the Iraq Conflict.* New York: W.W. Norton.

Tiryakian, E. A. 1999. "War: The Covered Side of Modernity." *International Sociology* 14(4):473–489.

Tiryakian, E. A. 2005. "September 11 and the Actuality of Durkheim." pp. 305–321 in *Cambridge Companion of Durkheim,* edited by J. Alexander, and P. Smith. Cambridge and New York: Cambridge University Press.

Turner, V. W. 1995 (1966). *The Ritual Process: Structure and Anti-Structure.* New York: Aldine de Gruyter.

Van Emden, R. 2002. *Last Man Standing. Norman Collins, The Memoirs of a Seaforth Highlander During the Great War.* Barnsley, South Yorkshire (UK): Leo Cooper.

Van Emden, R. 2006. *Britain's Last Tommies. Final Memories from Soldiers of the 1914–1918 War in Their Own Words.* Barnsley, South Yorkshire (UK): Pen & Sword Military/Pen and Sword Books.

Woehrle, L., P. G. Coy, and G. M. Maney, 2008. *Contesting Patriotism. Culture, Power, and Strategy in the Peace Movement.* Lanham, MD: Rowman & Littlefield.

Zimbardo, P. 2007. *The Lucifer Effect. How Good People Turn Evil.* London: Rider.

Zinn, H. 2008. "What War Looks Like." PP. 51–54 in *Peace not Terror,* edited by M. S. Robbins. *op.cit.*

CHAPTER 6

Social Order as Moral Order

ANNE WARFIELD RAWLS

OPENING REMARKS

The idea that social interaction can be a constitutive order that provides the basis for achieving social self and mutual intelligibility – as emergent features of social order not dependent on social institutions – makes possible a conception of the relationship between morality and society quite different from the conventional view that treats all social orders as produced by some relationship between individuals and social institutions: the agency versus structure dilemma. If constitutive social orders constitute a dimension of reciprocity independent of social institutions – on which both mutual intelligibility and self depend – and if that reciprocity is egalitarian and protects ends of universal moral value (social personhood and mutual intelligibility), then such orders can be characterized as moral in a non-relative sense. In other words, constitutive orders of interaction can provide a foundation for thinking about Ethics.

This conception of social order as a moral order is allied with various arguments (by Wittgenstein, Grice, Searle, Habermas, Garfinkel, Goffman, and Sacks) that talk (language) and/or self (identity) require reciprocity and a working agreement as to the form of practice in order for sense and/or self to be constituted. But, the argument being made here is different from the first four in denying that such orders are social institutions and goes farther in arguing that the constitutive order constraints on self and meaning must be real and not hypothetical, that they are not merely pragmatic, and that they constitute a social contract agreement that makes studies of ordinary interaction relevant to Ethics. I use the word "moral" to refer to social institutionally relative norms and values and Ethics and/or Justice to refer to those transcendent moral principles that I argue are associated with constitutive orders. I make the strong argument that when the constitutive agreement is not kept constitutive orders of meaning and self fail. Institutional orders are not fragile in this way. This makes all the difference.[1]

---

[1] My research has focused on this boundary between institutional and constitutive interaction order (see especially Rawls 1987, 1990, 2009 for theoretical discussions). Whereas most scholars treat problematic interactions between groups as arising because of institutional and cultural differences that interfere, I find interaction between persons self-identified with different racial/cultural groups can go along just fine until some failure of reciprocity (which may

S. Hitlin, S. Vaisey (eds.), *Handbook of the Sociology of Morality*,
Handbooks of Sociology and Social Research, DOI 10.1007/978-1-4419-6896-8_6,
© Springer Science+Business Media, LLC 2010

Confusing constitutive orders with institutional orders has produced important misconceptions. Sociology has often embraced the idea that any particular society's institutionalized beliefs and values are "morals". The problem with this approach is that societies have different and often conflicting beliefs. Furthermore, such beliefs, or norms, often support inequitable social systems that no one would want to call Ethical. So, there is a problem with identifying morality in such a fashion. When constitutive interactional practices are mistakenly identified as social institutions, then they also appear to have the same problems with relativity that institutions have. This appearance of contingency is one reason why philosophers interested in both meaning and Ethics have resisted being dragged into the domain of the social, and why those who have entertained the social, have eschewed the relevance of actual empirical social processes in favor of hypothetical examples and conceptual types.

Debates in theory and methods have also sometimes centered on the question of whether or not methodological approaches could, or should, be something referred to as "value free." But, if the relevant facts are "social" facts, and not "natural" facts, then the possibility that any position could be value free vanishes because the facts themselves have become part of the "moral" universe.

Clearly then, how the relationship between morality and society is viewed will depend to a large extent on the approach taken toward social facts. If social facts are treated as constituted by social institutions and the effects of institutional constraint on individual action, as is typically the case, then the resulting patterns of behavior will seem to bear a "normative" relationship to restrictive and arbitrary institutional constraints. On this view, each society's own peculiar social institutions are taken to define a "morality" specific to that society and relative to the peculiarities of the society and its social institutions. Morality, understood in this way, is both relative and normative.

If however, one treats at least some essential social facts as constituted in and through order properties of interaction (that are not themselves properties of institutions), based on a mutual commitment among participants to do so (which also has nothing to do with social institutions), then the crucial patterns of behavior in question and the social facts they generate are not constituted by social institutions or by an individual orientation toward goals and values. They are constituted, rather by their relationship to the mutual commitment of participants to the practice, which includes a commitment to reciprocate with one another to protect both self and interaction from damage should problems develop. In this case what is moral is also "Just," involving not the relative peculiarities of different societies, but rather the underlying reciprocal commitment that participants make to one another. Many of the "details" of the practices enacted will also be oriented toward this requirement. This means that the details are not merely arbitrary or routinized "patterns" of prior behavior, as they are generally characterized, but are oriented in principle toward reciprocities (which is what gives

---

or may not be category relevant) occurs. In collaborative research with Gary David on interaction between Black and Arab identified persons in convenience stores instances of interaction that began in the ordinary way with displays of mutual reciprocity and then quickly deteriorated into yelling categories at one another post a reciprocity failure were documented (Rawls and David 2006). Rawls (2000) explores similar issues with Black/White identified interaction. In this case the argument is that oppression over time affects the form of reciprocity relations in such significant ways that they may not be recognizable across groups. My earlier work focused on master/slave interaction as a limiting case. More recent research tracks the effects of different theoretical/ontological commitments on the ability of system design engineers to make sense together. Institutional differences in belief result in mismatched turnpairs, misunderstanding, anger and the imputing of motives.

them consistency). While specific elements of practice may vary from one type of situation to another, the underlying mutual commitment participants must make to one another in order for practices to succeed remains essentially the same and even the empirical forms of practice, and their rules, incorporate transcendent moral elements.[2] As this commitment must constantly be displayed, the empirical details will exhibit the logic of this orientation in each individual case.

Because the relevant facts with regard to morality tend to be social facts of both kinds (institutional and constitutive) and the two types of social order often co-exist, sociology as a discipline has a special relationship to moral questions of both the contingent (moral) and the non-contingent (Ethical) kind: a relationship that is generally overlooked. The oversight is serious not only because the relevance of sociology to questions of Ethics and morality is lost, but also because social theorists, both classical and contemporary, have had a great deal to say about this issue. Missing the point has led to a serious misreading of essential classical and contemporary texts. Durkheim for instance opened the first edition of *The Division of Labor in Society* (1893) with an introduction (removed in 1902) which argued that Ethics should properly be a branch of sociology. Social objects and identities however "real" are not natural objects, and hence the moral issues they raise are different from those raised when objects and identities (individuals) are treated as natural objects. This was the basis of Durkheim's charge that a philosophy beginning with individualism (such as utilitarianism, or pragmatism) could not deal properly with Ethics (because it treats the individual as a natural object).[3]

It has been my position that the continuing popularity of individualism and a conception of the social as contingent are the result of positing social order as constituted through and by social institutions. This has created the perception of a separation between agency and structure, highlighting merely contingent aspects of social orders, and reifying the *processes* through which actor and order are constituted, rendering this most important level of social cooperation invisible. The appearance that both actor and order stand alone and before inter-action is a consequence. A sociology focused on aggregated orders (based on probabilities) of individual action viewed as constrained by (or oriented toward) social institutions, and a corresponding philosophy that leads away from the essential insights (of Wittgenstein and others) related to constitutive orders, focusing instead on "instituted" phenomena of language and action build on this consequence (Rawls 2009).

Recognizing the constitutive character of essential social facts changes the understanding of the relationship between morality and society (and between "individual" and "institution"). There is a type of social fact forged through social interaction that is very fragile and requires constant cooperation and mutual displays of that cooperation to achieve. It does not depend on social institutions. The regularities involved can be specified by something like rules that people are "using" to create the witnessable regularities of order. But, these rules are not written or specifiable as institutional rules are. They are not arbitrary and they are not "followed." There is no referee to which participants can appeal, and consequently, constitutive orders do not generate accounts and justifications. They do bear a fundamental principled relationship

---

[2] See Doug Maynard's (2003) discussion of the moral properties of Bad and Good News, and my own discussion of the Ethical properties of preference orders and orders of turn-taking (Rawls 1977, 1987, 1989, 1990).

[3] Because Durkheim was challenging the philosophical approach to the question he used the words "la moralité" and "justice" to refer to transcendent morality in place of the word "ethics" which is associated with philosophy. See Durkheim's "homo-duplex" article for an elaboration of this argument.

to underlying needs of interaction and its participant (or member) selves. What the needs are the rules specify. This produces a consistency that is not arbitrary, conventional, or habitual.

It is this second understanding of social facts, not as "instituted" but as constituted through local "Interaction Order" (Goffman 1983) practices, and a "constitutive foundation of 'Trust' requirements" (Garfinkel 1963) and why it has been misinterpreted and overlooked on which this chapter will focus. The idea that the fundamental requirements of self and mutual intelligibility make consistent demands on constitutive orders of practice that can be *specified empirically* is critical to this approach. It is on the basis of this understanding that I refer to the social order of interaction as a moral order of relevance to Ethics. Instead of depending on the arbitrary character of specific sets of social institutions, morality in the transcendent sense depends on more general and enduring needs of selves presenting to and with others and communicating in interaction, hoping and needing to achieve mutual understanding. It is quite clear that social order conceived of institutionally cannot be described as moral even though we refer to its rules as "morals", "norms," and "values". They consist in almost all cases of rules for maintaining inequalities and are not moral in any general sense at all.

The idea of a constitutive interaction order sui generis, a constitutive social order that is in essential ways independent of and resistant to social institutions and based on a working consensus between participants that acts as a social contract, recasts the understanding of social facts and moral relations (Rawls 1987, 1990). It demands reconsideration of the idea that social institutions define (or constitute) social order, social objects, and meaning, and redirects focus toward constitutive orders of practice in their stead. It also suggests that there has been a serious and systematic misreading of classic texts. In an era in which most theories advise that increased risk, anomie, and chaos characterize modern life because social institutions, values, and beliefs have lost their ability to produce order, the constitutive interaction order perspective offers the possibility that a heightened mutuality and collectivity at the interpersonal level – at the level of practice – and a new security grounded in shared practice can come into play when institutions lose their ability to produce social/moral solidarity.

In elaborating this argument I will first clarify the distinction between institutions and constitutive social orders and consider the relevance of the distinction to the reading of social theory. Then, I will discuss a number of assumptions and misconceptions that have made it difficult to achieve a general understanding of what the argument is. This will involve a discussion of some misconceptions about the relationship between sociology and positivism, an articulation of the idea of institutional accountability as distinct from constitutive interaction orders, and a consideration of how the distinction between institutional order and constitutive order would impact on the current practice of treating all social orders as institutions. Finally, the argument that the working consensus is similar to the philosophical notion of social contract and elaborates it as an actual foundation for mutually intelligible orders of social action, object, and identity will be made.

I hope to convince the reader that a constitutive interaction order approach does not fit within the scope of earlier theories: that in spite of important precursors, like Durkheim, a recognition that the order involved is not institutional changes the way the theoretical problems and questions need to be understood to such a significant degree, giving prominence to constitutive orders, constitutive social objects, and the tacit reciprocal agreements securing them, in place of institutional orders, "instituted" objects, and identities, and replacing independent individuals with interactionally constituted selves – that the whole theoretical landscape needs to be seen quite differently. Otherwise, the idea of constitutive interaction orders will remain misunderstood, and the promise of sociology to essential philosophical questions undelivered.

WHAT IS THE DIFFERENCE BETWEEN SOCIAL INSTITUTIONS AND CONSTITUTIVE ORDER?

First I will elaborate the distinction I am drawing between social institutions and constitutive social orders and then consider where the idea that all social facts should be considered as constituted by social institutions came from. Both social institutions and interaction orders are constitutive of the sense of social facts within them. The essential difference is the dependence of the process on a mutual reciprocity that is not mediated, in which participants are responsible to one another, and which does not involve an appeal to (accountability to) hierarchy. This difference results in a domain of fragile-enacted objects on the one hand, whose empirical characteristics are specifiable by rules (and essential to their mutual intelligibility), and a domain of conceptual and merely accountable objects on the other, whose empirical details are not recoverable from or essential to their accountable adequacy.

The entities I am calling social institutions (1) have formal sets of rules, usually written down somewhere, but specifiable by members of the institution in any case. (2) Those who belong to (or work for) the institution are accountable to those formal rules. But, the rules are not adequate to specify how they should be followed. As a consequence (3) a vocabulary of motives (accounts/justifications) about the relationship between actions and the rule set develops. (4) People who happen to be "in" the institution, but not "of" the institution are not accountable to these rules, although they may be accountable by institutional workers to one another in institutional terms. If they are habitually "in" but not "of" the institution (like prison inmates) they may also develop their own vocabulary of accounts about their relationship to the institution. Weider's (1974) elaboration of the "inmate code" is an empirical illustration of this phenomenon. (5) There is usually a referee of some sort – that is, someone "higher up" in the institutional hierarchy with the authority to arbitrate disputes over accounts and accountable matters. Participants in social institutions are not all equal.[4]

Constitutive interaction orders, by contrast with social institutions, (1) do not have written rules. If you ask people who engage in them they usually cannot specify the rules and will often say that they are not "following" rules. But, there are rules nevertheless. (2) Sometimes constitutive practices are done so often that (like greetings) they seem to have become little routines or rituals. But, there are many ways to do these and their form, content, and context are not often specified as in rituals. Where they are so specified (as in ritual greetings of heads of state) they are institutional orders and not constitutive interaction orders. (3) Whereas rituals and institutions have designated presiders – or referees – and performers are accountable both to

---

[4] Games might appear to escape this distinction. But, I think it is clear that we acknowledge two sorts of play – even within the same game. Professional sports for instance have clear hierarchies (coaches, umpires/referees, owners, managers, etc.) and rule books. But, we still refer to the *spirit of the game* and *sportsmanship* as issues embodying an egalitarian reciprocity that we treat as standing at the heart of what we think of as what the game is really about. We admire most those players who express this sense of *fairplay* in their play in spite of the heavy institutional overlay. In some fundamental sense their achievement is what we collectively aspire to in everyday interaction.

the specifications of the ritual (or institution) they are engaged in and to the referee for the adequacy of their performance, in constitutive orders participants are responsible directly to one another and are expected to repair troubles quickly as and when they occur, using constitutive sequential orders to do so. Accounts are not a preferred way of dealing with such troubles.

If troubles occur and are not quickly resolved sequentially it can be taken as evidence of either a participant's incompetence or lack of commitment. (4) Therefore, constitutive interaction orders do not develop a vocabulary of motive/account. (a) This is partly because there is no referee to which such an account would appeal. The primary persons to whom participants are responsible are the ones with whom they are directly engaged.[5] (b) But, it is also because interaction is organized around the probability that difficulties will continually arise in the production of a mutually sustainable order and need constant attending to. Trying to repair these via accounts would involve a continual infinite regress. The "rules" orient this need. Because of this there are many ways at every point in a conversation of repairing troubles without needing to resort to giving an account. (5) So, needing to give an account in an ordinary conversation (unless there is some institutionally mandated relevance at issue) is already evidence of a failure. All the account could do is name a causal factor that interfered with their normal attention to the practice "I couldn't hear over the noise" or "I didn't see you" and these kinds of problems can be more efficiently achieved sequentially ("huh" or a "question repeat"). These accounts have the character of naming interferences with the practice in question and thus are not like an institutional vocabulary of motives in any case.

One of the problems in sorting out the two types of social order is that they are typically both present. For instance, when people who are working in a formal institutional setting do their work they must make use of constitutive orders of practice to get that work done. But, they are also held accountable at the same time for doing that work in institutionally accountable terms. The differences between the two sorts of order make contradictions inevitable. In most cases work requires adherence to constitutive practices that nevertheless must be accounted for in institutional terms. Even in casual conversations institutionally relevant identities sometimes intrude, and in such cases an institutional vocabulary of accounts may become relevant. This overlay of the two types of order has obscured their distinctiveness (Rawls 1987). But, the fact that they are often found together should not be allowed to obscure the differences.

WHERE DID THE IDEA THAT ALL SOCIAL FACTS ARE INSTITUTIONAL COME FROM?

Durkheim was one of the first to point out that unless a set of rules for understanding how a set of actions were to be interpreted existed before the action was undertaken and were known to all of the parties involved, social action could not be mutually meaningful. He referred to actions that accorded with such pre-existing sets of rules as *social institutions*. He called the

---

[5] Speakers will sometimes turn to persons nearby who may have overheard their conversation and apologize (for swearing, or loudness, etc.) But, these accounts display attentiveness to matters of institutionalized social convention – to matters of culture and shared belief – not to the reciprocal demands of constitutive interaction orders. Similarly, people may in their ordinary talk produce accounts for institutional matters. The appearance of such accounts in ordinary talk does not mean that they are accounts for constitutive action.

mutual intelligibilities that they made possible *social facts* and argued that a new discipline of sociology was required to study these social facts.

So, we might say that the insistence that all social facts must be the result of some relationship to social institutions is Durkheim's contribution to sociology. But, it is also the case that Durkheim made an important distinction between types of social facts. And, this is where an essential misreading of Durkheim has played an important role in obscuring the distinction he made between two kinds of social order that is relevant to the distinction between social institutions and constitutive orders of interaction. The point of the *Division of Labor in Society* was to elaborate this distinction between two social orders (and their respective social facts) and its relevance for a sociological study of morality. In traditional societies, according to Durkheim, in which all members of the group could be constrained by kinship and religious ties to believe in the same things; social facts of even an ordinary everyday kind could be constituted in relation to social institutions. Evans Pritchard's (1944) study of what he characterized as "circular" thinking among the Azande is an illustration of this phenomenon. Anything that occurs can be given a mutually intelligible meaning among a group who share the same religious or cultural orientation (assuming it is sufficiently well elaborated).

In more highly differentiated modern societies, however, in which the division of labor puts diverse groups of people into constant contact, such traditional ways of constituting mutual intelligibility – by convention – would no longer work. In such societies, Durkheim argued, some new way of achieving both mutual intelligibility and social solidarity would be required. This new form of solidarity would need to be free from institutional constraint and would require reciprocity and equal exchange to work: something that could be characterized as Justice would become necessary. This was the focus of Durkheim's much misunderstood Book III of the division of labor on "Abnormal Forms." On this view, modernity could be seen as ushering in a new era in which justice and equality are a requirement for mutual understanding and self (beginning with the shared practices of occupational groups). Durkheim characterized this new order as constitutive and anomie in modern society as a constitutive lack. Unfortunately, Durkheim has been interpreted as having argued that collective representations based on ritual and shared belief are necessary in both traditional and modern social forms and that social solidarity in modern society has been weakened because we no longer share such collective representations. His argument was much more complicated. Toward the end of the text Durkheim emphasized the point that while collective sentiments and representations that are based on "likeness" do become impotent as the division of labor increases, this is *not* a problem and does not leave society without moral solidarity. "What gives unity to organized societies," he argues (1893: 360), "as to all organisms, is the spontaneous consensus of parts. Such is the internal solidarity which not only is as indispensible as the regulative action of higher centers, but which also is their necessary condition, for they do no more than translate it into another language and, so to speak, consecrate it."

Solidarity in the division of labor, according to Durkheim, is a spontaneous process that cannot be produced by constraint. Forms of solidarity based on spontaneous reciprocities of practice (like modern science) and the rules that "translate" them will take the place of constraint. Because these forms of solidarity are just as *collective* as the form of social solidarity based on constraint that they replace, it has been a mistake to see modernity as the domain of individualism (1893: 366):

> Because they misunderstood this aspect of the phenomena, certain moralists have claimed that the division of labor does not produce true solidarity. They have seen in

> it only particular exchanges, ephemeral combinations, without past or future, in which
> the individual is thrown to his own resources. They have not perceived the slow work
> of consolidation, the network of links which little by little have been woven and which
> makes something permanent of organic solidarity.

These new social forms are coordinated by networks of rules and reciprocities that ensure consistency in practices. They develop from the bottom up and are only "translated" by regulation from above. The problem of modernity is that of inhabiting a transition phase in which formal regulations do not adequately translate the constitutive orders of practice that have developed: still trying instead to constrain them. The misinterpretation of this argument is prevalent and problematic. It has led among other things to the misconception that Durkheim argued that a lack of formal institutional (or legal) constraint in modern society leads to anomy. It has led also to interpreting the social problems characterizing the transition to modernity as arising from a lack of social solidarity and a rise of individualism and attributing that position to Durkheim. Whereas Durkheim argued that these problems are evidence that the transition is not complete. A great nostalgia for lost "community" characterizes theories of modernity. But, collective representations were not the "truth" and few of us would want to return to the unjust and unfree social arrangements of the past. The possibility of a conception of "truth" in any modern sense (as not determined by culture or institution) requires the replacement of collective representations and institutional constraint with spontaneous and constitutive self-organizing practices that are unconstrained by particular institutional beliefs and values.[6] This was Durkheim's point.

Contemporary research supporting the claim that constitutive interactional orders provide a foundation for human identity and sensemaking give this argument a new set of teeth. The idea of constitutive interaction orders of practice promises not only to transform the understanding of social order, but also to facilitate a long overdue rapprochement between sociology and philosophy on matters of the social construction of personhood and mutual understanding, the relationship between "truth" and social practices, and their relevance to Ethics.

A rapprochement between a sociology of constitutive interaction order and philosophers interested in language and Ethics would return sociology to its original purpose: Durkheim's original warrant for sociology as a discipline being its relevance as moral philosophy. While sociology was intended to take up such questions, the years between Durkheim and Garfinkel/Goffman offer little evidence of such concern. A great deal has been written about values, norms and beliefs: But, with the exception of a few sociologists of constitutive order, only as contingent matters of culture and usually with a focus on those inequitable power relations that social institutions seem inevitably to support. Little attention has been paid to the idea that equality and freedom are also social productions (depending on constitutive social commitment); or that a sociological analysis of the logics of constitutive orders and an examination of their dependence on working consensus reciprocities could shed light on the essential questions of what equality and freedom (justice) might look like and how they could be achieved.

---

[6] See Durkheim's Lectures on pragmatism (1913–1914) for a longer discussion of this problem than appears in the *Division of Labor*. See also Rawls (1997) for a discussion of those lectures.

TREATING SOCIAL OBJECTS AS CONCEPTS: THE FALLACY OF MISPLACED ABSTRACTION

Social objects are those objects, like "marriages," "greetings," "Presidents," "questions," and "soccer goals," that exist only as and how they are enacted through social processes.[7] Natural objects, even though they have a substance of their own and obey laws of their own, can only be "understood" by rendering them in conceptual terms because we cannot "see" them as they "are." While this idea was elaborated by Kant in the 1760s, the point took on new meaning in the early 20th century in the face of a strong tendency at the time to treat the social understanding of natural objects as the real objects. Alfred North Whitehead coined the phrase "the fallacy of misplaced concreteness," in the late 1920s to refer to the positivist practice of treating concepts and abstractions as though they accurately represented the concreteness of things. The human experience of objects, he pointed out, is fundamentally limited by concepts, and thus, the limits of human knowledge are also conceptual.

In coming to terms with the challenges of positivism both sociology and philosophy accepted the idea that persons only encounter natural objects in their socially defined iterations, as concepts. This position places limits on the validity of "empirical" evidence of all kinds, and sociology, along with other disciplines with an empirical focus, began to rely on conceptual clarity over empirical detail as a solution to positivism. Any approach, like ethnography that relies on "empirical" observation, became subject to the criticism that it was either positivist or subjectivist. The complaint *involves a misconception.*

While the rejection of naïve positivism marked an important moment of progress for disciplines that focus on natural objects, or social objects that are artifactual (like texts), social objects that require constant reciprocal constitutive work for their existence are not subject to the same limitations. Such social objects are differently constituted. They are not just "out" there. They require collaborative work to bring them into being and to maintain that being. Because they are entirely social creations, dependent on the moments of interaction that create them, and the details (and rules) of that social creation are essential to "seeing" them as objects of particular sorts, the constitutive social process of their creation is relevant to their status as social facts. Thus, the limits of the reality of social facts are not conceptual but rather processual: their reality is equivalent to the practices that constitute them. They exist as "empirical" objects in our understanding in a different way than natural objects. They are constituted through practices and the mutual commitment that undergirds them. The details of these practices, as movements and sounds, composed to accord with shared rules and expectations, are constitutive of their status as social objects. When the details of their constitution are reduced to concepts, or treated as an effect of individual action and/or institutional constraint, social objects are lost.

Unfortunately, with regard to the domain of constitutive practices and the fragile social facts they constitute, treating concepts as the basic reality has been a fallacy in the opposite direction, which I call "the fallacy of misplaced abstraction." It has led to a sociology focused

---

[7] Marriages and presidents are institutional social facts, greetings and questions are facts of constitutive orders (except in ritual settings).

on methods for measuring conceptual realities and has generated a faith in statistical counts of these. This has ironically eliminated most social facts and practices from the sociological domain altogether. Social practices which are, unlike natural events, essentially concrete and witnessable – produced by, for, and in the presence of others – and having essential constitutive characteristics have for many decades been reduced to conceptual abstractions, as if those abstractions were not only an inherent characteristic of the social, but defined its publicly recognizable character. *They do not*. It is impossible to recover from the concept "crime," "greeting," "deviance," or "question" the constitutive details which comprise the recognizability of the social object (one reason for the difficulty in specifying conditions of use for such objects conceived conceptually). The working consensus commitment required to constitute them which has important moral implications has been almost entirely overlooked.

THE MICRO/MACRO DISTINCTION AS A MISCONCEPTION OF CONSTITUTIVE SOCIOLOGY

Not only do adherents of the "fallacy of misplaced abstraction" essentially ignore social process in favor of concepts and elevate social *institutions* over social *practices*, they treat the individual as a natural object and elevate the *individual* and individual experience over social objects and identities. Adherents of the "Macro" position refer to studies of constitutive practice as "Micro." But, these studies focus on collective processes not individual action. It is "Macro" sociologists who study the individual orientation toward institutionally constrained norms and goals, carefully mapping out patterns of individual behavior and referring to their correlations as measures of "constraint": a truly micro and individualist approach.

This is an ironic reversal of classical sociological arguments. Durkheim and Marx shared a deep appreciation for the collaborative work required to build the ordered sequences of practice that the existence of social objects require (Marx 1944 MS; Durkheim 1912, Rawls 2004). Progress was made in the 19th and early 20th centuries toward treating socially meaningful objects and persons as socially constituted. The classical position was that because they were socially constituted objects, and, thus different from natural objects, both ontologically and epistemologically, social facts required their own special mode of study.

Durkheim urged that attention be paid to the emergence of a new spontaneous form of social solidarity that would not require external constraint. This type of new self-regulating practice would become particularly prominent in the context of modern professions and sciences. A great undertaking to document social practices got underway under Durkheim's direction in Paris. This progress was interrupted, first by World War I, which decimated the population of young French scholars, and then again by the debate against positivism. A sociology that was not positivist was condemned as though it were. The fact that Durkheim had called his sociology "positivist" (following Comte's use) did not help in this regard. As a consequence, the study of practices under the direction of Levi-Strauss, and later Pierre Bourdieu and others, returned to a treatment of practices as conceptual.

Almost alone among social thinkers Garfinkel and Goffman began quite independently in the 1940s a project of rescuing constitutive practices from this conceptual reduction and returning sociology to a focus on the details of social objects: Garfinkel focusing on the intelligibility of objects and information – and Goffman on the social constitution of selves. That both have been consistently classified as micro sociologists is an unfortunate misunderstanding.[8] Individualism is the original problem responsible making social facts appear to be contingent in the first place. Constitutive sociologies are committed to the idea that only by treating social facts, including the social self, as social productions collaboratively achieved by groups of mutually committed reciprocating social selves, can that problem be overcome.[9]

In spite of these efforts, however, the classics are still read in terms of their success or failure to incorporate an individual perspective (Coleman 1992, Rawls 1994). Goffman and Garfinkel are interpreted in ways that support the dichotomy between individual and struc-ture that they argued so hard against. Theoretical innovations such as *Structuration Theory* (Giddens 1982), which purport to build on the insights of Goffman and Garfinkel, merely posit interaction as a domain of sedimented activity standing between individuals and structures as a sort of bridging device (Rawls 1987).

These tendencies misconceive constitutive interaction order, Garfinkel, Goffman and Sacks, and also the classic arguments, ignoring the most important aspects of social practices. Constitutive practices must accord with known and recognized principles (or rules) of order and these principles orient toward preserving self and meaning. They can only be enacted in assembled groups (technical forms of distance communication can count as "assembled") in the form of a witnessably reproduced regularity of sounds and movements (Rawls 1996, 1998, 2004); they require being enacted again each next time; even concepts cannot be shared unless they take some recognizable empirical form; this, in turn, requires some *agreement* about the form practices will take (Durkheim 1893, Goffman 1959, 1981, Garfinkel [1952]2008). This *constitutive agreement* with regard to practice has been variously referred to as a "working consensus" (Goffman 1959), "listening and hearing obligations" (Sacks 1964), the "Trust con-ditions for concerted action" (Garfinkel [1948] 2006, 1963),[10] and the order involved referred to as an interaction order (Goffman 1983), a "local" or "situated" order (Garfinkel), or a constitutive social order (Rawls 1987, 2009).

The lived experience of social practices consists of an elaborate kaleidoscope of con-crete empirical detail oriented toward this constitutive *agreement*. It is the agreement (and its principled relationship to constant ends: self and mutual intelligibility) that provides for consistency across cases and binds participants together as a collectivity (not a statistically significant aggregation of individual action). The agreement is a working agreement and must be adequate to the details, not to concepts. How the agreement is adequate, and how the details

---

[8] See Rawls (1989) for an extended early discussion of this misunderstanding.

[9] Marx, like Durkheim, does not distinguish between institutional order and interaction order. But, in extensive pas-sages a focus on interactional processes suggests that he recognized the importance of direct mutual face to face relations. In the analysis of money and labor, for instance, in the *1844 Manuscripts*, one of the main arguments is that money becomes a third party, a buffer, in relationships between subjects preventing the direct mutuality and sense of honor that was possible in unmediated exchanges.

[10] The word "Trust" is important and Garfinkel's atypical use has led to confusion. Trust in Garfinkel's sense is not a state of mind or a feeling. It does not indicate an attitude toward a person. Rather, it is a state of mutual commitment to a practice. Participants stand toward one another in a state of mutual trust regardless of any uneasy feelings they may have about one another unless or until the mutual intelligibility of the practice fails. Because of the importance of the idea I have suggested that the word not be translated. The French translation of "trust" as "confiance" for instance does not convey the idea.

are handled in each case, is not irrelevant, or contingent as Garfinkel has shown (small differences can lead to failures of practice); and as Goffman pointed out, the details are closely inspected by participants, not only for coherence, with regard to particular constitutive aspects of the agreement, but also for evidence of any participant's *commitment* to the principle of the working agreement as a whole: the assessment of their moral character. Commitment is essential and closely monitored by all. For Goffman these details related mainly to self. But, as Garfinkel, Sacks, and others have shown, the agreement is also required to support the details of sequences as they relate to communication, information, objects, and other practices of work, etc.

The constitutive agreement, or working consensus, the need for the agreement, and the mutual commitment to the detailed social practices required to sustain it are essential to understanding social order. They explain the consistency of the interaction order. Social institutions by contrast are not based on constitutive agreements. They are an entirely different form of social order, working backward rather than forward, and consequently relying heavily on accounts and justifications for an appearance of consistency.

ACCOUNTABLE INSTITUTIONAL ORDERS VERSUS CONSTITUTIVE INTERACTION ORDERS

At the beginning of this second decade of the 21st century, sociology and philosophy stand at a critical juncture with regard to one another. Philosophers, particularly those who are elaborating insights from philosophy of language, rejuvenating Pragmatism, or working out ideas inspired by Habermas' theory of communicative action, have incorporated notions of the social: social facts, social institutions, the performative character of self, use conditions of speech acts, etc., into their work (Baynes, Brandom, Korsgard). Essential questions in philosophy have entered the social domain. But, that domain as philosophers approach it defines meaning and action in accord with pre-existing rules or practices as *institutional* in character.

Sociologists, while also exploring the dynamics of language and practice, have documented a distinction between more than one kind of social fact, or social order (one institutional one not) that has serious implications for any conception of the social. Why should the understanding that meaningful actions are meaningful because they accord with rules lead to the conclusion that all bodies of such rules are essentially of the same character and can therefore all be called "social institutions" without contradiction? The idea that there are two different orders of rule, and that one type of rule should not be treated as a social institution, changes this equation. Goffman spent much of his career documenting the tensions between interaction within social institutions and interaction in various "public places" without institutional contexts. He argued that interaction orders make demands on their own behalf which are quite different from and capable of resisting institutional constraints. Garfinkel explored the context of accounts that characterize institutions and the way they alter what one would expect of institutional work. He also focused on the domain of ordinary action as one in which accounts do not play the same role. Distinctions have been documented between talk and action occurring within institutional contexts and the sequential order of "ordinary" conversation. The famous "Turn-Taking Paper" (Sacks et al. 1974) treats this distinction (between institutional and ordinary) as foundational to the study of conversation.

The dynamics of order found in the two domains are quite different and these differences are relevant to some of the essential philosophical arguments of the day. Intelligible actions or practices in institutional contexts are ordered according to different principles than intelligible actions in situated constitutive orders. Most immediately relevant to the current discussion of Ethics and morality, justifications and accounts in formal institutional settings have different moral and order properties than accounts in ordinary talk (Mills 1940, Garfinkel 1967, Weider 1974, Pomerantz 1989, Rawls 1987, 1990, Maynard 1999).[11] Given the focus on accounts and justifications in both sociology and philosophy, as a way of approaching moral issues, this is significant (Brandom 2008). One domain of social order is constitutive – the other is accountable. The accounts and/or justifications that characterize institutional domains are inherently different from the mutual obligations, mutual attention, and shared practices required for intelligible action and self in constitutive orders.

That institutions work by justification and not by rule has been understood by some sociologists since at least 1940, when C. Wright Mills published his article on "Vocabularies of Motive". Mills' argument parallels Wittgenstein's in some essential respects. Rules cannot be followed. They work only backward: in retrospect. This order by account is a fact of institutional social order which has caused endless problems for formal organizations, particularly legal and other accountable systems, driven by "Rule of Law." Legal scholars in particular have documented this point. Law, embedded in social institutions, like any other formal rule, has little to say about how it is applied. That is left to the vocabulary of motives and the context of accounts.

Garfinkel (1967) took up this issue in his "Good Reasons for Bad Clinic Records". His point being that the rules of bureaucratic procedure (completing intake forms in this case) can conflict with both the accountability and the work requirements of an organization. He found that the requirements of accountability and work practices took precedence over institutional rules. This means that in the interests of getting all the information required for accountability purposes, gaps would appear in other parts of the records. The intake forms would have the information that the clinic worker actually needed to do their work and the information needed for accountability to monitoring agencies. But, other information asked for on the form would routinely be missing. There are serious implications for the generation of the institutional records on which most statistics are based. Garfinkel's point was that organizational workers were oriented toward what the work of the clinic required and the information they were accountable for producing. Things that were not required they did not do with any regularity. A bureaucratic rule saying they *should* do these things would not change their actions unless the work and accountability requirements themselves changed. In such a case *the way they*

---

[11] Institutions were described by Mills (1940) as comprising "vocabularies of motive" or "accounts." Persons acting within institutional settings are constrained to choose institutionally acceptable accounts or justifications for their actions. Both the practice of asking for accounts and the practice of giving accounts are different in ordinary interactional settings. Furthermore, the preference orders (discussed later in this chapter) work to make it unnecessary to either ask for or give an account in ordinary interaction. There is no such avoidance mechanism available to formal institutional orders. Thus, in ordinary talk, when a person is asked to provide a justification, the occasion for the justification is a failure to adequately anticipate the demand: that is, a failure of either mutual attention or interactional competence (Rawls 1977 unpublished). Because of this, treating justifications as moral reasoning is somewhat problematic.

produced accounts of the work could be expected to change while the *work itself remained essentially the same.*

In bureaucracies such matters are typically treated as non-compliance or as resisting change. But, a constitutive order position treats them as surface manifestations of a much deeper issue. Institutional rules and interactional work practices have little to do with each other. Improvements in the formal rules are rarely meaningful. It is the interactional work practices that are efficacious, not the institutional rules. Therefore, work practices (a constitutive order) *must* take precedence over formal institutional rules, otherwise nothing works. Garfinkel's study of clinic records was the first study of how work done in institutions has little to do with the rules of the institution. Weider's (1974) study "Telling the Convict Code" is another striking example. It not only shows that formal institutional rules have little to do with what occurs within the institution, but that an institutional vocabulary of motive can develop which is very much at odds with what is specified by the formal rules. Inmates name the "code" as the reason they cannot voluntarily comply with requests made by guards. The convict vocabulary of motives had only to be named (or told) as a justification. More recent studies of work by Christian Heath, Paul Luff, Lucy Suchman, Mike Lunch and others, document the increasing importance of this phenomenon in high tech human work sites.

Institutional rules and interaction order expectations and commitments inhabit entirely different domains of social order. One difference is that institutions have an official rule book, and "referees" to whom participants are accountable and to whom their justifications appeal. In constitutive interaction orders participants are directly responsible to one another. As Marx might point out there is no "mediator" to nullify the importance of "honor." Another difference is that the social order to which participants are accountable in an institutional setting is not fragile and does not change moment by moment.[12] Because it is defined in advance, participants can use those definitions, and play against them, in constructing their actual meanings, identities, and accounts. They cannot do this in a constitutive interaction order because they are busy achieving "it" moment by moment. Ironically, it is the stability of an institutional form over time that contributes to this effect. It is the fragility of constitutive orders that requires constant commitment and attention. There are a limited number of "games" defined by an institution, and the identities of the players are also defined by the institution. When a particular game is appropriate is set by institutional norms and values, and the moral orientation that the participants are supposed to take toward one another is also pre-specified; all of these become resources for actors within the institutional setting. But, because they are not constitutive orders (where everything is actually at risk moment by moment), none of this is required.

It is only with regard to interactional demands of the work practices, embedded within institutional contexts that constitutive orders come into play. In order to actually get anything done, institutional members must engage in interactional practices and what these require will necessarily take precedence over institutional rules. During this process, institutional personnel make of institutional rules something that better fits their own sense of their work. To see this as a failing of the individuals, as current practice does, overlooks the fact that it must happen in all social institutions. Underneath the formal veneer of social institutions participants must constantly accomplish a constitutive interaction order if they are to make any real sense

---

[12] The interaction order in an institutional context does change. But, the institutional framework itself stays the same.

together. They must do this because institutional orders cannot provide for the accomplishment of sensemaking, or identity, any more than theoretical accounts based on institutional models can adequately explain them. What individuals do to adapt the rules to their work is in any case often demonstrably an improvement. The problem is with the formal structure itself. It has no way of enforcing its definitions. It generally misconceives its effects, and, its formal definitions are not adequate to achieving that purpose in any case. The apparent functional adequacy and stability of social institutions is a reification undergirded at all points by combination of constitutive interaction orders and institutional vocabularies of motive and account.

It has become popular to refer to this difference between institutional orders and constitutive orders of work practices as a distinction between "formal" and "informal" orders of social institutions. But, this way of referring to the difference further obscures the real distinction. The so-called "informal" orders are actually more, not less "tight" as orders. The problem is that the distinction still assumes that stable social orders are all institutions, but that some are just more informal than others. This is a misconception. Constitutive orders are not institutional orders that are just more informal than others. Constitutive orders are another kind of order altogether that give institutions the appearance that their rules are effective and this reified appearance renders constitutive orders invisible (Rawls 1987, 2009).

Changing formal institutional rules, or accountability requirements, currently the primary means of "controlling" and monitoring institutions, changes accounting procedures and produces subtleties in the work to make it accountable in whatever the new terms are. But, it does not usually change the underlying work practices in meaningful ways.[13] The result of overlooking the role played by constitutive orders within formal institutions is that aspects of constitutive orders of practice that are essential to both human sensemaking and justice, and which can resist the contingencies of arbitrary social institutions, have not been considered central to the process of either maintaining order or justice. Consequently important issues of justice and inequality have been rendered invisible and entirely misconceived.

THE IDEA OF CONSTITUTIVE INTERACTION ORDER

The idea of a constitutive interaction order introduces something important and new into modern social thought.[14] Garfinkel and Goffman elaborated the idea with regard to self and

---

[13] In fact, studies show that when changes do occur they often result in the opposite of what the "reform" was intended to achieve. For example, mandatory gun control laws resulted in lower arrest rates, not because of a drop in gun use, but because police were unwilling to subject the largely middle class, white, married and employed offenders to long mandatory jail terms. When Massachusetts and Oregon first passed such laws, arrests for guns dropped to almost nothing while there was a correspondingly huge increase in arrests for other more minor offences. Research showed that police were exercising other options involving more minor charges. The same thing occurred with mandatory sentences for drink driving (DUI). They justified this in terms of their own moral conviction that a mandatory year in jail was not a just sentence for these men. Meanwhile politicians claimed that passing the law had gotten rid of guns and were re-elected.

[14] Garfinkel wrote out an argument regarding constitutive orders of interaction in his 1948 manuscript, now published as *Seeing Sociologically*, 2006. Goffman had read this manuscript and urged Garfinkel to publish, but he would not; a lifelong problem that will be familiar to those close to Garfinkel over the years. So it was left to Goffman to first introduce the argument that there is a separate order of interaction. My own early work dating from 1974 also made

mutual intelligibility. The extension of this idea to the social production of meaning in talk and language was accomplished by Harvey Sacks (in conjunction with Garfinkel) and formalized by Sacks working with Emmanuel Schegloff, Gail Jefferson, and Anita Pomerantz in the famous Turn-Taking paper (1974) and other work. Together they introduced a focus on constitutive orders of action as they relate to the social constitution of self and mutual intelligibility, an approach that intersects with Wittgenstein in essential respects (Coulter 2009, Rawls 2009). While it is important to recognize that these arguments build on classical insights, particularly those of Durkheim and Parsons, it is at least equally important to recognize that they break entirely new ground. For instance, while some of Goffman's arguments can be seen as elaborations on what Marx and Durkheim might have meant by the claim that the individual is the result of social relations and does not exist unless and until a particular sort of social relation (such as an advanced division of labor) develops, or what Everett Hughes meant by focusing on the details of actual work, the earlier thinkers built on the idea that *social institutions* set the parameters for everything social. Institutions were posited as setting the beliefs and rules; assuming that these order social life, constraining individuals to orient toward them, more or less. This reliance on institutions is evident even in Durkheim, who was the first to use the term "constitutive" in arguing for the rising importance of self-regulating practices in modern society.

This general confusion of all social order, including constitutive social order, with "institutional" and/or aggregated orders is one reason why the social tends to be mistakenly identified as contingent. Aggregate orders *are* contingent (Rawls 2009). This also explains the popularity of the "fallacy of misplaced abstraction." To the extent that social orders are seen as aggregate orders, the social facts involved are contingent, institutional, aggregate, and conceptual. Because there are no constitutive practices in such orders, only conceptual aggregates of individual actions oriented toward institutional norms, accounts, and justifications, there is little constitutive concreteness in the social objects to misplace.

Social "institutions" are conceptual representations of contingent patterns of behavior, described as ordered by rules or customs that develop at a particular time and place, because of a combination of local, historical, and individual conditions. While institutions do frame the intelligible character of some of the actions and objects within them (particularly accounts and justifications), conceived of in this way, like "language", or "common law," institutions are the "routinized" result of the aggregated actions of a great number of individual people acting over time. They are like bell curves. Most of the identities and objects "within" social institutions, however, are not constituted as social objects by those institutions. They are constituted as social objects by constitutive orders of practice that go on within the "walls" of social institutions, but which are not defined by those institutions and in fact resist them. Much of the

---

use of the term Interaction order. Goffman's approach to making this argument through a focus on the presentation of self alone is however distinctive and original in spite of the similarities. Garfinkel and I both placed a greater emphasis on mutual intelligibility. It was only in 2002, when early documents from Garfinkel's archive came into my possession and I was able to talk with Garfinkel about them that I realized the degree of collaboration which had actually occurred between the two beginning in the early 1950s and understood the extent to which Garfinkel's earlier unpublished work, which Goffman had read and discussed with him, also outlined a general sociology based on studies of interaction.

intersubjective character of action and objects within institutional contexts is constituted by mutual engagement at the level of interaction order.

It is a defining characteristic of the idea of institutional, or aggregate orders, that they could be otherwise. Individuals are taken to exist in some sense independently from social institutions, and social institutions are taken in turn to make demands on individual behavior that can be resisted. This has implications for freedom and creativity and for moral relativity. These demands may take the form of beliefs, traditions, ways of speaking or acting, and rules of action. In all cases however it is the defining characteristic of social institutions that these demands are not binding: that people can and do resist and violate these demands.

Because social institutions do not actively constitute the social objects within them, enforcement of institutional constraints is a problem that all societies have to deal with. Vocabularies of motive and justification develop within institutional contexts to frame the relationship between actions taken and institutional rules (Mills 1940). Each institutional context generates its own particular set and within that set each constitutes "morality." By contrast, constitutive orders can enforce commitment to themselves because social objects and identities depend on them. This is what it means to say that they are self-regulating. Social institutions cannot self-regulate, because objects and mutual intelligibility do not depend on them in the same way. It is good that they cannot, as social institutions are notoriously inequitable and their norms are contingent.[15] By contrast, freedom, creativity, and justice, which are often associated with *resisting* institutional constraints, are made possible by constitutive orders.

This relationship between institutions and the vocabularies of justification that develop within them is particularly relevant to the contemporary discussion of morality since philosophers are currently building on an analysis of "justifications" as a way of approaching Ethics (Brandom 2008, Baynes 2004). Justifications belong to social institutions and not to constitutive orders. Actions in constitutive orders do not have justifications. Asking for or making a justification interrupts the practice. The only account that remains within the constitutive interaction order is either to name the practice or a cause that interferes with its performance ("I can't see"). Furthermore, the working consensus asks people to refrain from asking for justifications. The preference orders work to effect repair without needing to make it explicit. Imagine the question "Why did you say hello to me?" It will likely be heard as a challenge or insult, not a request for a justification. Competent people do not do it – except in exceptional circumstances. The answer might be "don't worry I will not do it again" or "Are you kidding" but not the immediate production of a justification. A competent person might respond to a "Hello" from an unrecognized person "Do I know you?" But, this is still not polite. Ordinarily people just say "Hello" back.

When the work of constituting mutually intelligible objects and talk in a constitutive order fails, it is not a failure to comply with norms and therefore cannot be repaired by recourse to naming a justification. It is a failure of competence or commitment and will reflect on the competence and moral character of the person who did it and possibly of all involved in the encounter if it is not repaired quickly. The repair work that must be done to manage

---

[15] Durkheim's argument focused on this problem of inequality. In traditional societies it was ritual forms and shared beliefs that maintained social solidarity. There is a limit to the inequities that will support such systems over time. In modern societies the social forms are more fragile and the requirements of equity much greater. But, the short-term tolerance of inequality by social institutions is also almost without limit.

the mutual constitution of recognizable objects cannot be accomplished through accounts or justifications. As Paul Grice (1974) pointed out, that approach would involve an infinite regress (each clarification requiring a subsequent clarification). What the constitutive interaction order must achieve to make possible the mutual intelligibility of selves and meanings is an evident order that is constantly mutually confirmed by public displays. This requires a high degree of reciprocity and mutual exchange.

THE NEED FOR AN AGREEMENT – A WORKING CONSENSUS

Running through the various iterations of interaction orders, constitutive orders, constitutive background expectancies, working consensus, and "Trust" conditions is the idea that constitutive order is based on an underlying *agreement* between participants that constitutes the meaning of their actions. Jean Jacques Rousseau was the first to argue (in *The Origins of Inequality*) that the state of being we call human, and the moral issues associated with that state of being, only come into existence at the point of social contract. Durkheim considered Rousseau to be a sociologist on this score and built his approach to sociology on the premise that both human reason and morality are the result of social order.[16] Marx did so as well – which was the basis of his critique of economics. This being the case, human reason and morality also constitute the purpose of social order – giving both social order and religion their raison *d'être*, a moral purpose, in Durkheim's view, but one which is grossly distorted by inequality.

However, while Marx and Durkheim both make direct references to this argument (erroneously citing Rousseau's *Social Contract* as the source), and Max Weber (*Economy and Society* pages 8-20) and George Herbert Mead make use of the idea of a reciprocity of position based on a consensus of some sort, in explaining shared meaning and self-reflection, the idea of an agreement remains undeveloped in their work. When it does appear, the emphasis tends to be on institutions and shared beliefs: on institutional constraint rather than mutual agreement. Sartre, who treated the idea of social contract as central to social order, treated it as an ultimate achievement, not as a foundation (Rawls 1984). In spite of the insight regarding the constitutive relationship between an agreement and the constitution of human reason and morality, social objects (and selves) were still often treated by classical theorists as natural objects in ways that take for granted aspects of the same individualism that they criticized.

With the publication of Goffman's *Presentation of Self,* and Garfinkel's argument with regard to "Trust" conditions an articulation of *an actual social agreement* – a "working consensus" – was offered for the first time as the constitutive basis for the coherence of everyday social objects (and selves). Garfinkel's "Trust" argument, which significantly broadened the scope of the agreement as Goffman drew it, was published within a few years in 1963.[17] Both offer the working agreement as an *actual* necessity and not as a hypothetical, or ideal (such as

---

[16] See Durkheim on Rousseau in *Montesquieu and Rousseau* (1960), the first of his two required theses for the doctorate at the Sorbonne.

[17] Garfinkel's "Trust" argument was actually the earlier of the two arguments, dating from at least as early as 1948. But, like most of his work, it was published later.

Habermas' conditions for communicative action). The argument that the agreement is necessary rests on Goffman's particular conception of the self and Garfinkel's conception of mutual intelligibility as a constitutive matter of interaction. Therefore, it is important to understand just exactly what qualities of self and mutual intelligibility make the agreement necessary.

Making any changes to the self, or interaction/communication, that would give them more *resilience,* a built in *stability* over time, or make them depend *less* on interaction will render the working agreement optional. Treating the stable features of interaction order as if they were social institutions has the same effect. Garfinkel's argument is stronger in this regard, making it clearer that all social identities and objects are at risk. Mutual intelligibility, in his view, is almost entirely constituted through sequential orders of action oriented toward "Trust" conditions, which are very like Goffman's working consensus.

It has become popular to argue that since independent individuals obviously exist as bodies with consciousness there must be a "core" self that is resilient, and this has been one of the difficulties. This is especially the case since Goffman resisted the stronger version of the argument that the meaning of social objects and language are also at risk in interaction that was made by Garfinkel and Sacks. If selves and social objects can exist independently of constitutive interaction orders, then a constitutive agreement is not required for either self or sensemaking. The working consensus in that case would not be required. Individuals could be posited as possessing core identities which persist naturally over time and, as somehow having access to reason, or language, as a body of concepts that can be assembled in various logical ways to convey meaning to others. This is the conventional view.

It was the project of Garfinkel and Goffman to challenge this view. Their approach treats the self as almost entirely dependent on constitutive action for its existence. This gives the working consensus a force and a self-correcting character that is missing in earlier sociological treatments of self.

Both the self and its capacity to communicate are very fragile matters.

It is this *fragility* that explains *everything* and on which the constitutive interaction order argument needs to be built. Only if self and meaning must be constituted in and through interaction, will something be required that could make this birthing, maintaining and dying of selves possible: some consistency in the way sounds and gestures are orchestrated that makes them recognizable as "moves" of a particular sort to other participants will be a fundamental requirement. Such a recognizability of moves in turn requires an *agreement*. This makes the empirical research by conversation analysis and ethnomethodology essential to the theoretical argument. Only if the argument can be established empirically does it hold.

It is only because all interaction involves risk, and what is at risk is of enormous consequence, that the agreement holds. There is a risk that others will not ratify the self; a risk that one's view of things will be at fault and damage others, the situation, or oneself; a risk that something that one does will damage someone else; a risk that the essential sociality on which everything else, including *individual self-interest,* depends could be damaged by actions that destroy the mutual understanding of the particular constitutive order we happen to be involved in at the moment. And, so on.

It is essential to the argument to establish that constitutive practices, whose ordered details are constitutive of their meaning, work only in so far as some working agreement about how particulars can be constituted using such practices is actually maintained. The agreement cannot be hypothetical, or work merely as a guide. The agreement must be *actual*, and not only committed to by all participants, but constant displays of that commitment and the ongoing interpretation of sequences must also be performed. The displays of the agreement must be adequate to the details the participants will need to manage. The agreement also needs to provide for how the practices can be extended and amended. Garfinkel's much mis-understood elaboration of the "etcetera clause," "ad hocing," "instruction," and "praxelogical validity" handles these issues by distinguishing "rules" from working expectations about their application.

In theory the constitutive interaction order is something like a game with rules, but with unspecified and incomplete rules, incomplete information, and not one but many games that can change rapidly. This social arena is inhabited by acting selves whose identities orient the "game" in question, and whose ability to make sense of the practice of the moment is made possible only by their orientation to multiple layers of practice, background expectations, and a moral agreement between participants. The analogy would be to many games that follow one after the other, moment by moment; the job of participants being to constantly display the game they are in and their commitment to it; to follow the displays of *others* as they make moves and/or change games, and to display their own interpretations of those moves, in order to both keep track of practices and game changes moving forward, and also to achieve a public display of this reciprocal work that is available to all parties. Thus, as a practical matter, there is no need to deal with concepts in heads. The picture that results is of interaction in public as a challenging and satisfying mutual test of skill. But, one in which everything required for mutual intelligibility is on the table at all times by mutual agreement.

The back and forth mutually confirming character of interaction that results is a solution to the problem of interpretation. What is being proposed is that social life is something like a collection of many games with rules: A collection of many constitutive orders of practice.[18] Some constitutive orders belong to specified places. Others can be enacted anywhere. Some are conducted within an overarching context of institutional rules, norms and values to which their results are accountable, but which do not constitute them. Others are entirely self-organizing. Social life is only "something like" a collection of many games, because the game analogy is too simple to capture what is going on in ordinary constitutive interaction for a number of reasons: (1) rules cannot prescribe how they are to be followed. So they cannot explain the resulting order properties of constitutive interaction order; (2) selves, or actors, in ordi-nary constitutive interaction never have perfect information, or perfect reason, and therefore mutual understanding always depends on a level of interpretation; and (3) since the rational and socially identified character of selves are acquired over the course of play and consist of skills related to that play, reason and logic cannot be used independently to explain the play (as they are in game theory).

In speaking, participants will sometimes tell stories, they will sometimes issue invitations, or ask questions. These "turn-types" each have characteristic markers, and impose obligations that are particular to them (although all are responsive to the working consensus). But, they also have a relative position in an ongoing sequence that will have significance for the work that must be done to make the transition from one constitutive order to another recognizable to other participants.

---

[18] I owe this particular framing of the problem to Peter Manning whose early unpublished manuscript "society as a game of games" I hope someday to see in print.

In building sequential meaning, position can override "type" criteria. Identity issues can override as well. Therefore, while there are some characteristic markers and sequence forms that can be associated with each of these turn-types, the criteria for their recognition cannot be pre-specified. Participants need to build from one "type" to the next, working with sequence sensitivities, identity issues, and maintaining and displaying mutual attention and reciprocity, and doing so while at all times maintaining the working consensus. These considerations, none of which can be pre-specified, are definitional of what any particular act of speech (turn at talk) can be seen to have been doing.

Conversation analysis has documented orders of preference which orient the practices for handling such changes and any troubles that come up in talk.[19] Moves, or turns, are also oriented toward these orders of preference, which hold across forms of talk. Goffman's working consensus could similarly be described as consisting of a number of preferences: The "benefit of the doubt" preference elaborated by Goffman being another expression of a "do no harm" obligation implied by the working consensus. The preference orders that emerge from Conversational analysis give detail to this obligation, although Goffman himself did not fully appreciate this point and criticized Sacks and Schegloff in *Forms of Talk* for employing a kind of formalist empiricism that did not really characterize their work. Sacks in particular had spent a great deal of time with Garfinkel and was more seriously oriented toward documenting empirical details than Goffman (whose method has been characterized as "literary"). But, as students of Goffman, both Sacks and Schegloff were oriented toward interaction order issues in elaborating their ideas about the "turn-taking system" in conversation. The preferences for self-correction, mitigated disagreement, and positive assessments that are specified in the "Turn-Taking Paper" by Sacks et al. (1974), by Alene Terasaki in her work on Pre-turns (1984) and by Anita Pomerantz in her work on assessments (PhD dissertation 1984) are all consistent with Goffman's initial elaboration of a "benefit of the doubt" obligation.

Reciprocity of position is another condition of the agreement – a version of "do unto others" – with an added proviso that one should display to others one's interpretation of what the other has done. It does not, or at least it should not, support inequalities. Goffman worried a great deal because he knew that it sometimes did. One problem is the degree to which institutional orders impinge on interaction orders to produce such inequalities. This is something Goffman explored repeatedly. Because reciprocity is a requirement of constitutive order there should be a limit to the amount of inequality that interaction will tolerate and this should create difficulties in institutional settings in which inequality is extreme. Goffman's first publication, on the social functions of embarrassment (1956), explored this problem. Many of Goffman's subsequent works, *Asylums* in particular, continued to explore the *limiting conditions* of reciprocity on institutional orders; just how far inequality (whether imposed by social institutions or individuals) can go before interaction and selves break down (see also Rawls 1990). He

---

[19] Evans (2009) has recently published an article in which he elaborates a synthesis of speech act theory, Wittgenstein and Garfinkel. In that paper he draws an evocative analogy between dance and talk. He cites a dancer who described the act of walking as "falling while walking". Meaning that a person with their foot in the air is in some sense falling and then catching themselves again when they put their foot down. He pointed out that it could be useful to view communication as being something like this. Making a move that involves putting a foot out there – a move that does not achieve mutual intelligibility until it receives a mutually ratified interpretation. Mutual intelligibility is an achievement that requires work. It is not given in an institution called language that people can master, or concepts that they can learn.

found that there are always limits imposed on an institution by the fragility of self and argued that an orientation toward preserving the social objects that people claim to be, and avoiding damage to both persons and the situation is a requirement that explains those limitations.[20]

Garfinkel's "Trust" conditions extend the idea of an agreement to specifiable sequential procedures that confirm and display reciprocity, while at the same time constituting the recognizability of social objects and meanings. This idea was first elaborated by Garfinkel in the 1948 manuscript (2006) and then in the "Trust" paper (1963). The Trust requirement makes it clearer what the required reciprocity consists of. All participants in a situation must assume that the others are working with the same set of expectations that they are and that they are competent to enact them. They must also assume that the others assume the same things of them. They must also display this orientation with each next move.

This agreement cannot just stand as an assumption. Both competence and commitment must be continually displayed or self and sensemaking fail. At each and every next turn the mutual orientation toward the joint commitment must be displayed: must be made public. Grice (1974) had argued that it is not possible to clarify talk through interpretation because that would involve an infinite regress. But, Garfinkel shows how it is possible. CA has further documented that the interaction order of talk provides for interpretation to be efficiently displayed turn by turn without engaging in any such infinite regress. Participants are required to make constant displays to one another. Furthermore, not knowing which position they will stand in next requires all participants to protect all positions.[21] Thus, maintaining a constant potential reciprocity of position is a limiting condition of the working consensus. Talk *can* be clear without this reciprocal work. But, then, as Sacks points out, there will be fewer resources when problems arise and, because mutual intelligibility is less at risk, the working consensus would be in doubt. Sacks argued that to the extent that talk can be rendered indexical and put at risk in the same way that the self is at risk in interaction, the resulting risk will bind communicants to reciprocity and benefit of the doubt conditions (listening and hearing obligations in Sacks' terms) more forcefully. If only self is at risk people can still make sense without fulfilling involvement obligations. But, if all sensemaking is at risk then damage to either selves, or the order properties of turns and sequences, will damage all the sociality they have together.

It has been my suggestion that the reciprocal commitments involved in the working consensus are an existing and working template for equality, fair distribution and justice: a golden rule in action on which we could profitably build (Rawls 1989). This is how I have interpreted Durkheim's recommendation that constitutive and spontaneous self-regulating practices in modern societies could, because they require justice, become an adequate and satisfying form of social solidarity that does not rest on institutional constraint. As societies have changed and social institutions and their shared norms and values no longer form the basis for social solidarity, a new form of social order based on justice and a fair distribution of opportunities within occupational practices will need to take its place. If it does not, mutual intelligibility and social

---

[20] My own early papers explored this idea that the interaction order places limits on institutional inequality. My later work on race inequality is documentation of that argument and supports the claim that where inequality is severe, sensemaking becomes difficult to impossible.

[21] This is one reason why an institutional context that limits the interchangeability of positions introduces the possibility of greater inequality. It also makes sense of Durkheim's argument that self-regulating practices are not compatible with institutional constraint because they only work under conditions of justice.

personhood will fail. This interpretation is consistent with the misunderstood argument of *The Division of Labor* (1895).[22]

The way we talk, how much indexicality we produce, the extent to which we rest meaning on grammar and syntax, all effect the degree to which meaning is fragile, and thus the moral tone of interaction and the degree to which the working consensus is a requirement.[23] When reciprocity is achieved and all essential goods: persons and intelligibility, are at risk, the required working agreement has serious Ethical overtones. Moral in this case does not mean normative. It means something more like justice, or Kant's categorical imperative, the principles of which will equally distribute across all persons and all of the interaction order forms that are at risk in this way. Kant's logical argument for non-contradiction of practice holds. The moral order of interaction orders supports ends of absolute moral value: human reason and mutual intelligibility. One cannot conceive of violating them without realizing that the violation contradicts the practice on which one is depending. By contrast, because social institutions are static and arbitrary, and the sense of actions within them (even when they are "just") is not at risk in the same way, any morality in social institutions would be strictly contingent and "normative."

The agreement required by a constitutive interaction order is reminiscent of Kant's "Kingdom of Ends" and as such is a domain of both equal opportunity and total necessity. The characteristic of protecting all positions also involves something like a "veil of ignorance" (Rawls 1971). Within a constitutive order persons must assume that all positions could in the near future be their own, and therefore they must treat all positions with the same care and respect in order to preserve their own self-interest (Rawls 1989).

A FEW CLOSING REMARKS

The accepted idea seems to be that as institutional orders (of shared belief, value, culture, and religion) break down under the pressures of modernity, chaos, increased risk and ambiguity, anomie, etc., all inevitably increase unless new institutionalized forms of social relationship replace them. This is how Durkheim is often interpreted, although it is not what he argued. It is both the warning and the promise for a modernity in which persons can become increasingly free from institutional constraint: but free to confront increasing chaos and alienation.

The argument that both self and meaning are grounded in constitutive interaction orders that require a strong working commitment to principles of reciprocity offers a quite different picture of what modernity might have to offer. What would a conception of democratic institutions modeled on this foundation look like? If we accept that institutions are not actually constituting the order of action that occurs within them – but only acting as a sort of referee –

---

[22] For some reason my argument in this regard is often interpreted to mean that there is no morality in modern society. The problem turns on the mistaken equation of norms and values with morality. Attempts to rescue Durkheim from my interpretation that take this view tend to treat his argument with regard to traditional society as if it applied to modern society. Durkheim did not argue that morality erodes in modern society. He argued that some form of morality is always necessary. But, the required morality can no longer be supplied by shared norms and values in a modern differentiated society. Therefore it must have some other basis. Durkheim argued that the new basis of morality is self-regulating practices and they require not just morality, but something more universal that we call justice.

[23] This may explain why "talking proper" is sometimes made as a complaint about members of closely knit groups.

could we structure institutions differently to serve our purposes better? Could we alter the processes of accountability such that they actually changed the play in ways that make it more fair? Could we make formal institutional structures more compatible with the constitutive interaction orders that support and underlie modern social life?

The idea of a constitutive interaction order offers a new way of understanding what this might mean. More importantly, the idea of constitutive interaction order and of self and sensemaking resting on a working consensus offer a new way of understanding social order, social facts, social persons, and their relationship to social institutions in modern differentiated societies that hope to be democratic.

If meaningful and fulfilling social life in modern differentiated societies requires a democratic form of underlying constitutive interaction order to support both mutual intelligibility and self, then to the extent that institutional or structural factors interfere with this process they undermine the possibility of democracy. While it is true that constitutive interaction orders resist institutional constraint, it is also true that selves will retreat from interactional contexts in which their integrity is threatened. This can result in a kind of segmentation in modern society in which selves tend to cluster together with those who share their condition of either oppression or privilege (sometimes mistaken for a "cultural" alignment). To the extent that this does happen the broad foundation of overlapping constitutive interaction orders required for democratic life will not materialize and Durkheim's warning that anomie could result from the lack of justice in such an abnormal social form could come to pass.

This anomie, however, is caused, not by a failure of social institutions, or a failure of individuals to attend institutional order, but a failure of constitutive interaction order. A simple instance: Goffman and Garfinkel both argue that the process by which a self is achieved involves an actor choosing to perform an identified self while other participants either ratify the performance or not. When I explored this idea with ethnically identified students in the US (international, Spanish, Swedish – not just Arab and Black) they responded that in most public encounters with those not in their category (as "other") they are not given a chance to "choose" their own presentation of self. The word "choose" is of course a problem here – as no one really has the experience of choosing an authentic self. But, what they describe is having thrust upon themselves a characterization of self that makes it impossible for them to act "normally." White students do not recognize this distinction. It does not happen to them. Only ethnically identified and international students feel they have been – type-cast on sight – and given no benefit of the doubt. They recognize that in the interaction whatever they do will be seen light of the stereotype – the working consensus is not extended to them in these interactions – however polite the interactions appear to be.

Whatever we make of the idea of choice, this is not the experience that most people have of walking up to a group of similar persons (a student walking up to talk to a group of students on the same campus). Most of us do this quite "normally thoughtlessly" and without the experience of being "pidgeonholed" on the instant. It may happen sometimes – and just because it is so rare it is memorable and upsetting. Ethnically identified and international students say it is what they come to expect as "normal" whenever they communicate with those who are not also "outsiders".[24]

---

[24] That some minorities who are consistently discriminated against refuse to acknowledge such othering constructions of self is a phenomenon in its own right. It is courageous. But renders them functional non-persons to the general public. Waverly Duck and I explore this idea in an unpublished paper "Fractured Reflections in the Looking Glass."

To the extent this is the case it means that there are large numbers of persons in modern democratic society who are being denied access to the constitutive interaction order processes of achieving self that are required for democratic life. An understanding of this as an interaction order problem is a pressing concern with serious consequences for a world in which the presence of "others" is dramatically on the increase.

It is my argument that an unworkable notion of social institutions and a still too static view of language and self pose problems for contemporary approaches to morality. The current focus on *justification* and the treatment of social facts as institutional phenomena creates inconsistencies. There is no way to distinguish those constitutive social orders that involve deep moral commitments from institutional orders which establish social inequalities and lend themselves to instrumental manipulation. The responsibility for dispensing and maintaining justice might best be overseen by the former rather than the latter. The problem with the idea of Justice, from this perspective, is not with persons and their inconsistencies, as Amartya Sen (2009) has recently suggested, but with the identification of social order with institutions rather than with constitutive orders of action. It is in constitutive orders that reciprocities lie and where moral alignment and mutual attention are functional requirements. Importing what has been learned about the differences between formal contexts of accountability (social institutions) and constitutive orders of interaction into questions of Ethics and morality could make a difference.

Acknowledgments I would like to thank Albert Ogien, Louis Quere, L'Ecole des Hautes Etudes en Sciences Sociale, the Marcel Mauss Institute, and the City of Paris International Scholars Program for supporting my work on this chapter through a Senior Scholar "Laureate" appointment 2009–2010. The interest of Louis Quere, Albert Ogien, Michel de Fornel and Bernard Conein in matters of constitutive order over some 40 years has been crucial to the development of studies of constitutive order in France. I thank Albert Ogien and Sandra Laugier for invitations to speak and for facilitating translations and publications. Lorenza Mondada was indispensible on my first trip to Paris in 2003. There have been many earlier versions of this argument over the years and I am indebted in particular to Randy Collins, Norbert Wiley, David Maines, Norman Denzin, and Peter Manning for early support and encouragement. Fran Waksler introduced me to Harold Garfinkel who has been a sustaining critic and touchstone over many years. In a serious way it all began with his insights and their intersection with Goffman. Jeff Coulter introduced me to the philosophical debate on the issues. Alisdair MacIntyre, John Findlay, Tom McCarthy, Erazhim Kohak, Kurt Wolff, and Bernard Elevitch taught me philosophy. From Tom I learned about Habermas. Doug Maynard read and commented on early versions when I was at the University of Wisconsin–Madison in the 1980s and has been a friend and colleague for many years. Anthony Giddens during a visit to Boston in the early 1980s challenged me to demonstrate that in constitutive orders mutual intelligibility does indeed fail when interactional reciprocities (equalities) fail. I hope that I have taken up this challenge. As always my debt to Peter Manning is incalculable.

BIBLIOGRAPHY

Alexander, F., and D. Levine (Joint or separate?). 1988. *Sociological Theory*.

Austin, J. L. 1955. *How to do Things with Words*. Oxford: Oxford University Press.

Austin, J. 1961. *Philosophical Papers*. Oxford: Oxford University Press.

Baynes, K. 2004. The Transcendental Turn: Habermas's "Kantian Pragmatism". In *The Cambridge Companion to Critical Theory*, edited by F. Rush. Cambridge: Cambridge University Press.

Brandom, R. 1994. *Making it Explicit*. Cambridge: Harvard University Press.

Brandom, R. 2008. *Between Saying and Doing*. Oxford: Oxford University Press.

Bourdieu, P. 1972. *Esquisse d'une théorie de la pratique, précédé de trois études d'ethnologie kabyle*, (English. *Outline of a Theory of Practice* Cambridge University Press 1977).

Coulter, J. 2009. "Rule-Following, Rule-Governance and Rule-Accord." 9(4):1–15.

David, G. 2005. "Price Humor in Arab-Owned Convenience Stores: Using Potentially Sensitive Topics to Transform Intergroup Relations." Biograf 36:25–54. Humor page 46 and?

Durkheim, É. 1933 (1893). *The Division of Labor in Society*, trans. George Simpson. Chicago: Free Press.

Durkheim, E. 1912. *The Elementary Forms of the Religious Life*. Chicago: Free Press.

Evans, R. 2009. "The Logical Form of Status-Function Declarations," *Etica and Politica/Ethics and Politics*, XI(1):203–259.

Garfinkel. 1963. "A conception of and experiments with 'trust' as a condition of stable concerted actions" in *Motivation and Social Interaction*. O. J. Harvey (ed.), 187–238. New York: Ronald Press.

Garfinkel, H. 2006 (1948). *Seeing Sociologically*. Boulder: Paradigm Publishers.

Garfinkel, H. 1941. 'Color Trouble'. In *Best Short Stories of 1941: Yearbook of the American Short Story*, edited by E. J. O'Brien. Boston: Houghton Mifflin.

Garfinkel, H. 1949. "Research Note on Inter- and Intra-Racial Homicide." *Social Forces* 27:370–81. (Orig. pub. 1942.)

Garfinkel, H. 2002. *Ethnomethodology's Program: Working Out Durkheim's Aphorism*. Boulder, CO: Rowman & Littlefield.

Garfinkel, H. 2008 (1952). *Toward a Sociological Theory of Information*. Boulder, CO: Paradigm. (Orig. pub. 1952.)

Gellner, E. 1959. *Words and Things: A Critical Account of Linguistic Philosophy and a Study in Ideology*. London: Gollancz.

Giddens, A. 1982. *The Constitution of Society: Outline of the Theory of Structuration*. Cambridge: Polity.

Grice, H. P. 1975. "Logic and Conversation." PP. 41–58 in *Syntax and Semantics*. Vol. 3, *Speech Acts*, edited by P. Cole, and J. L. Morgan. New York: Academic Press.

Grice, P. 1989. *Studies in the Way of Words*. Cambridge, MA: Harvard University Press.

Goffman. 1956. "Embarrassment and Social Organization." *The American Journal of Sociology* 62(3) (Nov., 1956):264–271.

Goffman, E. 1959. *The Presentation of Self in Everyday Life*. Chicago: The Free Press.

Goffman, E. 1961. *Asylums*. Doubleday Anchor: New York.

Goffman, E. 1981. *Forms of Talk*. Philadelphia: University of Pennsylvania Press.

Goffman, E. 1983. "Felicity's Condition." *American Journal of Sociology* 89:1(1983), pp. 1–53.

Habermas, J. 1981. *A Theory of Communicative Action*. London: Beacon Press.

Heath, C., and P. Luff. 2000. *Technology in Action*. Cambridge: Cambridge University Press.

Kant. *Groundwork of the Metaphysic of Morals*. Harper and Row: New York.

Luff, P., J. Hindmarsh, and C. Heath. 2000. *Workplace Studies: Recovering Work Practice and Informing System Design*. Cambridge: Cambridge University Press.

Maynard, D. W. 2003. *Bad News, Good News: Conversational Order in Everyday Talk and Clinical Setting*. Chicago: University of Chicago Press.

Mead, G. H. 1924. *Mind, Self and Society*. Chicago: Free Press.

Mill, J. S. 1866. *Auguste Comte and Positivism*. Philadelphia: J.B. Lippincott.

Mills, C. W. 1940. "Situated Action and the Vocabulary of Motives.'" *American Journal of Sociology* 5:904–13.

Parsons, T. 1937. *The Structure of Social Action*. Chicago: Free Press.

Pomerantz, 1989. "Can You Give me the Time?," in *Interactional Order: New Directions in the Study of Social Order*. (eds.) Helm, Anderson, Meehan and Rawls. Irvington Press: New York.

Rawls, A. W. 1977. "Back-Packaging: A New Plea for the Interactional Relevance of Excuses." Unpublished.

Rawls, A. 1987. "The Interaction Order Sui Generis: Goffman's Contribution to Social Theory." *Sociological Theory* 5(2):136–149.

Rawls, A. 1989. "An Ethnomethodological Perspective on Social Theory," in *Interaction Order: New Directions in the Study of Social Order*, (eds.) Helm, Anderson, Meehan and Rawls. Irvington press: New York.

Rawls, A. 1990. "Emergent Sociality: A Dialectic of Commitment and Order." *Symbolic Interaction*. 13(1): 63–82.

Rawls, A. 1989. "Language, Self, and Social Order: a Re-evaluation of Goffman and Sacks." *Human Studies*. 12(1):147–172.

Rawls, A. 1992. "Can Rational Choice be a Foundation for Social Theory?" *Theory and Society*. Volume 21(2) April: 219–241.

Rawls A. 1996. "Durkheim's Epistemology: The Neglected Argument." *American Journal of Sociology*. 102(2): 430–482.

Rawls, A. W. 1997. "Durkheim and Pragmatism." *Sociological Theory* 15(1):5–29.

Rawls, A. 2000. "Race as an Interaction Order Phenomena: W.E.B. Du Bois Double Consciousness" Thesis Revisited", *Sociological Theory* 18(2):239–272.

Rawls, A. 2001. "Durkheim's Treatment of Practice: Concrete Practice vs Representations as the Foundation for Reason." *The Journal of Classical Sociology*. Vol 1(1).

Rawls, A. 2004. *Epistemology and Practice: Durkheim's The Elementary Forms of Religious Life*. Cambridge: Cambridge University Press.

Rawls, A. "Reciprocity and Practice: Trust in a Context of Globalization." and AJS 1996 translation. Enquete. EHESS Paris.

Rawls, A. 2008. "Harold Garfinkel, Ethnomethodology and Workplace Studies." *Organization Studies* 29(5):701–732.

Rawls, A. W. 2009. "An Essay on Two Conceptions of Social Order: Constitutive Orders of Action, Objects and Identities vs Aggregated Orders of Individual Action." *The Journal of Classical Sociology*.

Rawls, A., D. Mann, A. Garcia, G. David, and M. Burton. 2009. "Semplici enumerazioni: L'etnometodologia e gli Information Assurance Data Standards del MITRE" (English: 'Simple Enumerations: Ethnomethodology and MITRE Information Assurance Data Standards'). *Etnografia e Ricerca Qualitativa* 1:77–106.

Rawls, A., and G. David. 2006. "Accountably Other: Trust, Reciprocity and Exclusion in a Context of Situated Practice." *Human Studies* 28(4):469–497.

Rawls, J. 1955. "Two Concepts of Rules." *The Philosophical Review* 64(1):3–32.

Rawls, J. 1971. *Theory of Justice*. Cambridge: Harvard University Press.

Rousseau, J. J. *Discourse on the Origins of Inequality*. Oxford University Press: Oxford.

Sacks, S.H., E. Schegloff and G. Jefferson. 1974. "A Simplest Systematics for the Organization of Turn-taking in Conversation." Language 50:696–735.

Scarpetta, F., and A. Spagnolli. 2009. "The Interactional Context of Humor in Stand-Up Comedy". *Research on Language and Social Interaction*, 42(3): 210–230(21).

Searle, J. 1969. *Speech Acts*. University of California Press: Berkeley.

Turner, S. 1994. *The Social Theory of Practices*. University of Chicago Press: Chicago.

Uschanov, T. P. 2000–2001. The Strange Death of Ordinary Language Philosophy (www.Helsinki.fi/tuschano/writings/strange).

Uschanov, T. P. 2002. "Ernest Gellner's Criticisms of Wittgenstein and Ordinary Language Philosophy." PP. 23–46 in *Marx and Wittgenstein: Knowledge Morality and Politics,* edited by G. Kitching, and H. Pleasants. London: Routledge.

Weider, L. 1974. Language and Social Reality: The Case of Telling the Convict Code. Rowman and Littlefield: Boulder Colorado.

Wittgenstein, L. 1953. *Philosophical Investigations*, trans. G.E.M. Anscombe. Oxford: Basil Blackwell.

Part II
Sociological Contexts
("Where Does It Come From?")

CHAPTER 7

Natural Selection and the Evolution of Morality in Human Societies

JONATHAN H. TURNER

Humans are the only species of animals to have ever organized themselves by cultural symbols. Most species have general bioprogrammers that direct the behaviors of conspecifics, but only humans have relatively few innate programmers and, as I will argue, the bioprogrammers that humans have inherited from the primate line have often worked against fitness-enhancing patterns of social organization. Yet, there has been rather intense selection on hominin and human phenotypes and underlying genotypes to use systems of cultural symbols to increase the level of social organization among weak-tie primates; and in particular, the charging of these systems of symbols with "morality" has been essential to making culture effective in social control and in forging patterns of solidarity among evolved apes who do not have direct bioprogrammers for organizing around tight-knit groups structures.

Indeed, the bioprogrammers inherited from the ape clade are more suited to macrostructural patterns of organization. There have been relatively few macro societies ever created in the animal world, with the social insects being the most obvious example. As Machaleck (1992) has documented, macro societies are a rare form of social organization, for a variety of reasons, including constraints from habitats, body design, and costs of supporting large numbers and divisions of labor. Moreover, macro societies must have individuals capable of impersonal cooperation, divisions of labor, and modes of integrating these divisions of labor. The fact that humans have been able to organize on such a macro scale is, to a large extent, a byproduct of their capacity form weak-tie networks and to be directed by morality as a force of social control. As I will argue, the evolution of morality among hunter-gathering hominids or hominins and humans not only allowed for organization at the micro level for low-sociality apes, but also, this behavioral for moral regulation of conduct represented a critical preadaptation for macro societies.

THE PROPERTIES OF MORALITY

What, then, is morality? There are no definitive answers to this question, but from my perspective, morality consists of several related elements: (1) highly abstract and general cultural codes specifying what is right–wrong, good–bad, and appropriate–inappropriate; (2) intense emotional valences attached to these codes; (3) feelings of satisfaction and, at times, more

S. Hitlin, S. Vaisey (eds.), *Handbook of the Sociology of Morality*,
Handbooks of Sociology and Social Research, DOI 10.1007/978-1-4419-6896-8_7,
© Springer Science+Business Media, LLC 2010

intense feelings of happiness when self and others have met the proscriptions and prescriptions of these culturing codes; (4) feelings of guilt and shame among individuals who have not lived up to the dictates of these emotionally valenced cultural codes; and (5) arousal of negative emotions revolving around variants and elaborations of anger against those who have failed to behave in terms of these moral codes. These five dimensions of morality are all variable; that is, they can vary by degree, and hence, social situations and the sociocultural formations in which these situations are embedded can be more or less moral. High levels of morality involve high values for each of these variables, while lower levels of morality exist when these variables reveal low values.

Morality exists at different levels of social structure and culture. At the most macro level can be found abstract *value premises* about right–wrong, good–bad, and appropriate–inappropriate that apply to all situations. These highly generalized codes are given specificity by *ideologies* that specify how they are to be realized within the institutional domains of a society – e.g., economy, kinship, polity, law, religion, and other domains that have emerged during societal evolution. These ideologies are, I believe, collated into *meta-ideologies* that selectively combine the ideologies of each domain into a more general set of evaluative codes. These codes will be biased by the dominant institutional domains in a society. For example, if religion is dominant or at least prominent, the meta-ideology will be biased toward moral codes emphasizing the commandments of supernatural forces, whereas if a market-driven economy is dominant, the codes will be biased toward considerations of money, income, and wealth as worthy goals. The ideologies of institutional domains are built from *generalized symbolic media* that are the means by which actors communicate, exchange resources, conduct discourse, develop themes or orientations within a domain, and eventually, construct an ideology specifying what is moral for actors in a domain (Simmel 1978 [1907], Parsons 1963a, b, Luhmann 1982). For instance, if *sacredness/piety* (from the religious domain) is the medium for religious communication, exchange of valued resources, discourse, thematization (Luhmann 1982), and ideological formation will emphasize conformity to proscriptions and prescriptions from the supernatural; or if *love/loyalty* (from kinship) is the medium, moral codes will stress the importance of sustaining kin ties and honoring kindred, and exchanges within kinship will involve giving love/loyalty in order to receive love/loyalty from others, and exchange with actors in other domains, such as religion, will involved giving loyalty and perhaps love (to the supernatural) in exchange for the good will of forces in the sacred realm that comes from being considered pious.

Value premises emerge and change with shifts in the meta-ideologies of a society as different institutional domains evolve and as their relative dominance changes. As these domains change in their relative dominance, so does morality in values, ideologies, and meta-ideologies. In turn, normative systems at different levels of social – from an entire institutional domain to meso-level corporate units to micro-level encounters of face-to-face interaction within a domain – will be variously infused with moral content from the more inclusive domain in which corporate units and encounters in groups are embedded. Moreover, as inequalities increase with societal growth and differentiation, ideologies and meta-ideologies legitimate the system of stratification, making inequality and class formation moral and, as a result, differentially evaluating individuals with different shares of valued resources. Like all moral codes, those legitimating stratification can be described by what I see as the basic properties of morality – that is, proscriptive and prescriptive statements denoting right–wrong, good–bad, and appropriate–inappropriate for individuals; high intensity of emotions attached to these statements; positive emotions for conformity; feelings of guilt or shame when cultural codes are violated; and negative emotional reactions to others who are seen as violating these moral codes.

As is evident, emotions are at the core of morality. While it is possible to explore the structure of the moral codes, per se, my goal in this chapter is to ask what may seem like an obvious question: Why does the power of moral codes depend upon emotional arousal? Since no other animal that we know about uses complex emotional states to generate commitments to, and to sanction violations of, cultural codes, this is not a trivial question because it takes us back to the evolution of the hominin line (on or close to the human clade) and addresses the issue of why humans became so emotional.

Most sociological analysis remains impressed with the size of the human neocortex, assuming that this fact alone explains language, culture, and moral coding. Yet, we know that chimpanzees with brains less than one-third the modal size of the human brain can be trained to use (non-verbal) language at about the level of a human three year old and that much less intelligent monkeys can pass on (non-symbolic) cultural traditions (Savage-Rumbaugh 1988, 1993, 1994). Thus, while no primate can come close to human capacities for culture and language, these capacities are not wholly unique to humans. Similarly, all mammals can experience and emit the basic primary emotions of satisfaction–happiness, aversion–fear, assertion–anger, disappointment sadness, but only humans reveal variants and combinations of these primary emotions at a wide range of intensity. Emotions are generated in the subcortical regions of the brain and, hence, represent older adaptations of both reptiles and mammals to a wide variety of habitats. Long before the large neocortex evolved, natural selection was working on expanding the range of hominin and human emotionality, which, as I will argue, represented a solution to organizing weak-tie primates and, at the same time, a preadaptation for morality. Without the ability to tag moral codes with emotions, morality could not exist; cultural codes would be like dry instruction manuals because they would have no emotional teeth.

Because emotions seem to be central to any conceptualization of morality, an answer to why humans became so emotional compared to other mammals can help explain why and how humans became so moral. Culture and emotions are, therefore, inextricably interwoven in the neurology of the human brain; and by explaining how the brain became wired, first, for emotions and, only later, for symbolically mediated culture, we can increase understanding about the dynamics of morality (Turner 2000). Morality, then, is not possible without emotions; moreover, the first language of hominins or hominids was built from the emotional phonemes and syntax, which served as a preadaptation for morality. Morality could not have ever evolved along the hominin line without prior evolution of dramatically enhanced emotional capacities.

THE EVOLUTION OF PRIMATES

Adaptation to Niches in the Arboreal Habitat

Around 64 million years ago, a small, rodent-like mammal managed to work its way into the forests of Africa to initiate the primate line. Living in an arboreal habitat is very different than adapting to a terrestrial habitat; and the transformations to the body and brain of what became primates is, ultimately, what enabled a particular primate – humans – to become so moral. In many places, I have outlined this story of primate evolution (see, for example, Maryanski and

Turner 1992, Turner 2000, 2002, Turner and Maryanski 2005, 2008). The details of this story are less important than the effects of mammals trying to adapt to the arboreal habitat.

One of the early and most critical transformations of these new arboreal primates came with the shift in their sense modalities from olfactory to visual dominance. All animals must have a dominant sense modality in order to avoid sensory conflict among smell (olfactory), touch (haptic), vision, and hearing (auditory) sensory inputs. Most mammals are olfactory dominant, with all other sense subordinated to the sense of smell. In contrast, primates are visually dominant because smelling one's way about the trees is far less adaptive than seeing branches, estimating their strength and distances, and moving in a three-dimensional world where one false step means death by gravity. The evolution of depth perception by repositioning the eyes so that their fields of vision overlap and the concurrent evolution of color vision further enhanced the ability to judge distance, texture, and strength of branches, thereby facilitating adaptation to the arboreal habitat.

As natural selection changed primates from olfactory to visual dominance, the brain was rewired in critical ways. One of these fundamental changes in the wiring of the brain was the formation of new association cortices around the inferior parietal lobe where the parietal (haptic), occipital (vision), and temporal (auditory) lobes meet. These new association cortices allow for the integration of the senses under visual dominance and, thereby, enable humans to avoid sensory conflict. Thus, when humans hear or touch something, they immediate look in the direction of the sources of these sensory inputs and subordinate information from the parietal (haptic senses) and temporal (auditory) lobes to the occipital (visual). Only the sense of smell remains out of direct control of this area of association cortices, but this sense is dramatically attenuated in the great apes as well as humans and hence does not pose sensory conflicts, and indeed, a strong olfactory input will immediately send a primate looking for the source of this smell. This rewiring of the brain for visual dominance generated a *pre-adaptation* for language (Geschwind 1965a, b, c, Geschwind and Damasio 1984), and it is for this reason that the great apes (orangutans, gorillas, and chimpanzees) can all communicate through hand signs or through pictograms on keyboards (they cannot "speak" because they simply do not have the necessary muscles and anatomical structures in lips, tongue, and larynx for articulated speech production). Unless raised in a human environment, apes do not use this capacity to its fullest extent because they do not need it to adapt to their niches in arboreal habitats, although all apes appear to use some kind of visual signaling (of face and body) to communicate emotional and instrumental dispositions and plans of action (Menzel 1971).

Yet, not all primates have language capacities. Monkeys and prosimians cannot communicate linguistically the way the great apes can. Thus, because the great apes have larger brains than monkeys and prosimians (as well as the small Asian apes, gibbons, and siamangs), it appears that the association cortices around the inferior parietal lobe, *plus* some threshold of intelligence, are essential to generate linguistic potential among the great apes. But, this potential was just that – only a potential – but it is critical that this pre-adaptation was in place since, if language was eventually had fitness-enhancing consequences for apes, it was necessary for natural selection to have an existing capacity on which to select (otherwise, selection would have to wait for large mutations that would are almost always harmful, and especially so for neurological systems). My story on the evolution of emotions will make the point that this pre-adaptation was subject to selection long before the neocortex of apes moved much beyond that of contemporary chimpanzees; indeed, the language of emotions evolved in the hominin line long before speech in humans (see Turner 2000, for the details of this argument).

Other changes in the anatomy of primates, beyond the shift to visual dominance, reflect adaptation to the arboreal habitat: sensitive and strong fingers, hands, and wrists; flexible shoulder joints and, among apes, shoulders capable of allowing brachiation (complete, 360° rotation of the arm in the shoulder joint); generalized body plans with four limbs (and tails for monkeys) for moving about branches; and dietary preferences suitable for finding food in the trees.

Another critical change among primates was the growing differentiation between monkeys and apes, which began around twenty-three million years ago. This differentiation is reflected in anatomical structures: apes have larger brains and, hence, are smarter than monkeys; they can brachiate and thus swing from branch to branch (like children on "monkey bars" which should be termed "ape bars"); and they have stronger and more sensitive fingers and hands, and much stronger arms and shoulder joints. These differences reflect the fact that apes and monkeys occupied different niches in the arboreal habitat. For reasons that are not entirely clear (perhaps, the fact that monkeys can eat unripe fruit, whereas apes cannot), monkeys gained the upper hand in competition for space in the arboreal habitat and were able to command the core and more verdant niches in the trees, whereas as apes were pushed to the terminal feeding areas high in the trees and out to the ends of branches where there is less space and food (Maryanski and Turner 1992, Turner and Maryanski 2008). Ape anatomy evolved because apes must hang, swing, and hold onto branches in the terminal feeding areas, whereas monkey anatomy evolved because monkeys can walk on the tops of limbs in the core areas of trees where branches are stronger and where many more individuals can be supported. Having to live in the more marginal niches of the arboreal habitat led to the evolution of larger brains in apes because the terminal feeding areas are more hazardous; and the body plan of apes with stronger, more flexible, and more sensitive fingers and hands, coupled with stronger appendages, all indicate that apes were adapting to niches where they moved by brachiation and where a great deal of hanging onto branches had to occur. Even the last remaining species of apes cannot scamper across the tops of branches the way monkeys can.

In being forced to the terminal feeding areas of the arboreal habitat, another critical adaptation was necessary, and the evolution of morality is very much connect to this adaptation. The marginal niches of the arboreal habitat could not support larger numbers of individuals, with the result that apes developed a unique pattern of social organization to limit the number of individuals at any given place. If groupings of apes became too large or permanent, the food supply would soon be exhausted, and thus the changes in behavioral propensity and social structures began to diverge from those evident among all monkeys. Monkeys held the more verdant niches and hence could support larger numbers of individuals; and the result was for monkeys to forge stable group structures built around generations of female matrilines and hierarchies of male dominance. Monkey societies are thus highly organized, with females living out their lives in their natal groups and with males leaving their natal groups and entering in competitions for dominance in other groups. Thus, the backbone of monkey social structures revolves around the intergenerational and collateral ties among related females and a formation of dominance hierarchy among males who have migrated into the group. This combination of male hierarchy and female matrilines proved highly adaptive not only in the arboreal habitat but also for species of monkeys who migrated to extreme niches with colder climates or who were forced to survive in a more terrestrial environment such as open-country African savanna.

Indeed, of all species of primates, monkeys represent two-thirds of the total, while all species of apes represent less than ten percent and the five species of great apes (including humans) represent just over two percent of all species of apes. Monkeys, then, are the most fit of the primates. The reason for this fitness resides in their social structure. On the African savanna, their tight-knit structure could be used to coordinate procurement of food and to fend off predators. In contrast to monkeys, apes are not well organized at the local group level because sustaining cohesive and stable groups in marginal niches of the arboreal habitat was impossible. The result was for natural selection to shift both the behavioral propensities and resulting structural arrangements of apes toward a pattern that is almost the exact opposite to that evident among monkeys.

At puberty, all female apes leave not only their natal group but also their larger community or home range forever, transferring to another community. Except for male chimpanzees, males also leave their community and migrate to a new community. The result is that, with female transfer to another community, the possibility for developing the female matrilines evident for monkeys is lost. Furthermore, females in a community are strangers to each other because they have transferred into a community from diverse natal communities. Female chimpanzees tolerate each other, often sitting in proximity when their offspring are at play, but they do not form strong ties; indeed, they often do not form any ties at all. The same is often true for males who, except for chimpanzees, are also migrants from other communities. The result of these transfer patterns is that organization at the level of groups is very weak, fluid, and transitory. Males may form weaker hierarchies than monkeys, and at times, there are some tendencies for group formation among some species of apes. Gorillas, for example, will form forging troops, with the lead silverback male trying to control (unsuccessfully) access of other males to "his" harem of females, and this lead male may form a more permanent bond with a female and her offspring but this tie breaks down once offspring transfer at puberty from the group (indeed, the tie between the lead silverback and females favors the female who uses the lead male as a babysitter while she wonders outside the group, often to have sexual relations with other males; in fact, except for gibbons/siamangs, all apes are highly promiscuous, with chimpanzees the most promiscuous of all). Unlike all other apes, male chimpanzees do not leave their natal community at puberty, as is the case of all other apes. They remain in their community and maintain a strong ties with their mothers, but these ties do not revolve group formation. Males will visit their mothers but then move about their home range alone or join for a short time other foraging parties. Males often develop strong ties with their brothers and with special friends; and they will at times compete for dominance in temporary groups. Thus, chimpanzees and all of the great apes do not have behavioral propensities to forge strong ties. Instead, the most salient structure for apes is their community or home range which can be as large as ten miles square, with individuals wondering alone or in temporary parties that form and reform. There is no stability of social structure at the group level; stability resides in the larger community, which male chimpanzees (and probably gorillas as well, although the data are not clear on this point) will defend against any incursion by males from other community (Goodhall 1986). They will often kill any male who enters their home range, although females are obviously welcomed because the females who were born in the community have left and need to be replaced by migrant females from other communities (thus assuring diversity in the genome of apes).

This lack of stability in the group structure of apes has been brought home with Alexandra Marynanski's cladistic analysis of ape social ties (Maryanski 1986, 1987, 1993, 1995). Cladistic analysis involves comparing the traits of all members of a superfamily – in her analysis, the superfamily of Hominoidea (apes and humans) and the constituent families of

Hylobatidae (gibbons and siamangs), and *Pongidae* (the great apes, or orangutans (*pongo*), chimpanzees (*pan*), and gorillas (*gorilla*). The goal of cladistic analysis is to reconstruct the behavioral propensities and, in Maryanski's analysis, the resultant network structures of apes, with an eye to reconstructing the social structures of the last common ancestor to all of the extant apes. Cladistic analysis assumes that if all species of a given family or superfamily reveal the same characteristics, these characteristics were likely present among the last common ancestor of this family or superfamily. Otherwise, one would have to assume that they evolve independently among multiple species of apes in somewhat different niches. The details of her analysis can be found in a number of sources (e.g., Maryanski and Turner 1992, Turner and Maryanski 2005, 2008), and so I will not outline these here. The critical insight is that by doing cladistic analysis, it becomes evident that the last common ancestor of all present-day apes revealed virtually *no strong ties* – save for those between females and her offspring (a common pattern among all mammals that were then broken at puberty). In fact, present-day orangutans, who are virtually solitary except for mating purposes (which might last several weeks, at most), are probably very close in behavioral and structural arrangements to the last common ancestor of all apes. For this ancestor, males and females left their community forever at puberty; and thus, the only strong tie – mother bonding with her offspring – was broken at puberty, thereby destroying any possibility for group formation. All other ties were weak. Males wondered alone or perhaps in temporary foraging parties, males and females were highly promiscuous in mating, with paternity never to be known (as is the case today with all apes except the monogamous gibbons and siamangs who are very far off the human line). The only stable structure was probably a sense of a larger community or home range; otherwise, all adult ties were non-existent or weak, and mostly temporary. This kind of weak-tie social structure and the behavioral propensities that created and sustained it were highly adaptive for species that evolved at the terminal feeding areas of the arboreal habitat which could not support larger or permanent groups. Over millions of years, natural selection pushed the ape genome toward this kind of weak-tie system, with the only stable social structure being the home range that could encompass many square.

Since humans share 99% of their genes with the common chimpanzee (slightly less with bonobo or "pigmy" chimpanzees), the patterns of behavior and emergent social structures are a reasonable "distant mirror" in which to see the last common ancestor of humans and chimpanzees. Since chimpanzees have been adapted to pretty much the same niche – forests on the edge of the open-country African savanna – for millions of years, natural selection has not changed their genome drastically, with the result that understanding chimpanzee ties does indeed give us a relatively clear view of what our distant hominid ancestors were like. Among common chimpanzees, the home range is the only stable structure; females bond with their offspring until puberty when females leave their home range and when males begin their nomadic ways within the home range; adult males and females form no permanent bonds, but are highly promiscuous in sexual relations (with paternity never known); males maintain contact with their mothers and often forge bonds with brothers and friends (visiting each other but rarely forming permanent groups); females form no permanent bonds and remain strangers to each other, revealing tolerance but no permanent bonds.

This structural pattern has proven viable for many millions of years, as long as chimpanzees can occupy arboreal niches at the edge of the African savanna where they can venture out but rapidly retreat to the trees when danger is present. No present-day ape can live on the savanna, whereas species of monkeys have relatively little trouble doing so because of their tight organization into groups composed of male hierarchy and female matrilines. Since apes do not form stable or cohesive groups structures, they obviously are at a disadvantage in open country savanna habitats where group structures would be fitness enhancing. Indeed, the only present-day ape that can live on the savanna is *Homo sapien sapiens*. The explanation for why humans are so emotional and moral resides in how humans' hominid ancestors beat the odds and found a way to forge more cohesive groups structures that would enable them to survive on the African savanna.

Adaptation to Terrestrial Niches on the African Savanna

About ten million years ago, the forests in Africa began to recede with climate change, forcing many species of apes and monkeys to adapt to open grasslands where predators abounded (to a much greater extent than is the case today). The savanna was, and still is, a dangerous place for a primate for a number of reasons. First, primates are not built for speed but for moving about in the trees; hence, they can easily be run down by predators. Second, primates' sense of smell is attenuated and without a powerful olfactory bulb, they cannot detect predators as can all other mammals that have been able to survive on the savanna. Indeed, primates with their visual dominance will have trouble seeing danger lurking behind tall grasses or other obstructions; and so, the acute vision of primates is much less useful than a strong sense of smell that can pick up airborne chemical emissions from hiding predators. Third, the great apes are emotional in the sense that they do not have much neo-cortical control of their emotions (easily "going postal"), with the result that they will become loud and thereby attract additional predators when they experience danger and fear. Fourth, and perhaps most important, apes are not well organized at the group level and, hence, are not likely to be able to organize defense in the face of danger or to coordinate food gathering. The result of these handicaps doomed most species of apes to extinction; indeed, over the last 10 million years, most species of apes are went extinct with just a handful of species (13 subspecies) still able to survive in the forests of African and Asia. Indeed, because of human population growth and the destruction of the few habitats where apes can barely survive, it is very likely that all other apes except humans will no longer live in their natural habitats.

In contrast, monkeys living on the savanna have little difficulty surviving because they are organized at the group rather than community level. Their matrilines and male hierarchies lead a troop to march across the savanna with military-like precision – with larger males at the front, rear, and flanks, with smaller females and offspring in the center. Males will attack all preda-tors who generally avoid a confrontation with such a well organized phalanx. Apes, however, present a different picture. With no strong ties beyond mother–offspring, with a propensity to be overly loud and emotional when confronting danger, with no stable groups structures, and with the handicaps of all primates on the savanna (e.g., lack of speed, poor sense of smell), it is not surprising that apes were doomed to extinction. Natural selection increased the body size of some apes, resulting in primates as large as nine feet tall (*Gigantopithecus*) who lived until about 1.5 millions years ago and was thus one of the more successful adaptations of evolved apes; another route taken by natural selection may have been to enhanced hierarchy among males but, without the female matrilines to keep females in the group, this strategy was, no doubt, a failure. Somehow, the hominid or hominin ancestors of humans beat the odds by becoming better organized for food forging and defense in the open county. How, then, did natural selection produce this result and, in the process, generate preadaptations for morality once the neo-cortext began to approach the human measure some 1.0–2.0 million years ago with *Homo erectus*? The answer resides in the rewiring of the subcortical portions of the hominin brain to become ever-more emotional.

THE EVOLUTION OF EMOTIONALITY AMONG HOMININS OR HOMINIDS

Natural selection appears to have hit upon a solution to the low sociality and lack of group structure evident among all apes, and certainly prevalent among those apes forced onto the savanna from their arboreal niches some ten million years ago. Most apes, of course, went extinct in the ensuing millennia, but natural selection began to enhance the range of emotions among the hominin ancestors of humans. And, over the course of several million years, hominins and then humans became ever-more emotional. The evidence for this path of evolution can be found in measurements of key structures in primate brains. Table 7.1 presents the relevant data from a series of measurements of primate brains. In this table, I only summarize those measurements for apes and humans. The methodology in these measurements involves taking a very simple mammal – in this case *Tenrecinae* – a species very much like the original small mammal that initiated the primate line over 60 million years ago – and using it as a base of "1." All numbers in the table denote how many times greater than the corresponding structures in *Tenrecinae* (or "1") various brain structures in apes and humans are. These numbers also control for body size, which is roughly correlated with brain size. As can be seen, the neo-cortex (the home of culture and language for humans) is 196 times larger than the neo-cortex of *Tenrecinae*, while the neo-cortex of the great apes (*pongids*) is almost 62 times larger, making the human neo-cortex a bit over three times as large as that among the great apes. There is, of course, no real news here since sociologists generally assume that brain size, per se, accounts for culture, thereby eliminating the need to explore the biology of humans any further. With language and culture, humans construct their reality, which is certainly true, but they do so within the constrains of their neuroanatomy as it evolved over millions of years along the hominin clade.

TABLE 7.1. Relative Size of Brain Components of Apes and Humans, Compared to *Tenrecinae*

Brain component	Apes (Pongids)	Humans (Homo)
Neocortex	61.88	196.41
Diencephalon	8.57	14.76
thalamus		
hypothalamus		
Amygdala	1.85	4.48
centromedial	1.06	2.52
basolateral	2.45	6.02
Septum	2.16	5.45
Hippocampus	2.99	4.87
Transition cortices	2.38	4.43

Source: Data from Stephan 1983, Stephan and Andy 1969, 1977, and Eccles 1989.

Note: Numbers represent how many times larger than Tenrecinae each area of the brain is, with *Tenrecinae* representing a base of 1.

Much more interesting are the measurements of the subcortical areas of the brains for great apes and humans. By reading down the columns, it is clear that human centers for emotions are, on average, twice as large as the same areas in great apes. Moreover, the actual wiring accounting for these differences in size is rather revealing. The diencephalon, especially the thalamus portion, is responsible for routing all sensory inputs to the relevant neo-cortical lobe *and* the emotions centers of the brain. Why would this structure need to be so much larger in humans than apes, controlling for body size? Clearly, the routing sensory inputs to activate emotions enhanced fitness. The amygdala is the center for both fear and anger (in different portions of this structure) and is a holdover from reptiles because without fear of danger and the capacity for defensive aggression, an animal soon goes extinct at the hands of predators. A good portion of the size difference between the ape and the human amygdala is the result of additional areas on the basloateral portions for happiness. Why would happiness be added to the center for fear and anger? Moreover, other portions of the amygdala are also used for routing signals between emotions centers in all subcortical areas to the prefrontal cortex where rational thought and long-term memory operate – another interesting neurological difference between apes and humans. The septum, which is responsible for the pleasure associated with sex (and hence the source of sex drives), is over twice as big in humans as in apes. Why would an area already devoted to pleasure and an area making apes highly promiscuous need to double in size for humans? The hippocampus is an area where shorter term memories are stored (for about two years in humans); and if this memory is reactivated and the emotions associated with it fire off again (thus giving the memory the same "feeling" as when the actual experience occurred), it will eventually be shipped as a memory up to the prefrontal cortex for long-term storage. Among humans, unconscious memories and the emotional valences associated with these memories are stored in the hippocampus; and perhaps this is the neurological source of repressed memories. But, why is this structure so much larger in humans than apes?

All of the structures listed are responsible for emotional arousal in some way; and while these are not the only structures, the pattern in these and other subcortical areas of the brain is clear: they are larger and, equally significant, they look like they were wired up in a punctuated process of very rapid selection. It appears as if natural selection was grabbing onto any area of the brain responsible for emotional production, experience, and memory in order to increase the emotionality of hominins on the human line. Since the subcortical areas of the brain are older in an evolutionary sense and since the neo-cortex only began to grow substantially with *Homo habilis* 2.5 million years ago (to 500 cc or 125 cc larger than that evident among chimpanzees and, in all likelihood, humans and chimpanzee's common ancestor) and reach the very bottom of the smallest human brains some 1.8–20 million years ago with *Homo erectus*, the growth of the neo-cortex is a rather late evolutionary adaptation. Long before the big jump in brain size to the human measure (some 1,200 cc), the subcortical areas of the brain appear to have been under selection for millions of years longer than the neo-cortex. Why should this be so? What did enhanced emotionality provide? The short answer is the capacity to forge emotionally charged social bonds that could increase *group-level* solidarity. Whatever bioprogrammers for group formation that had existed some 24 million years ago had been selected against as apes were forced to adapt to terminal feeding areas of the arboreal habitat where group formation would be maladaptive. There was no going back to being more like a monkey, as was probably the case twenty-four million years earlier; 15 million years of selection *away from* the monkey pattern had occurred, with the consequence that there would be little for natural selection to select on. For movement back to the bioprogrammers driving monkey group formation, natural selection would have to wait for mutations, and as the forest receded, there was simply no time to re-install such complicated bioprogrammers for female matrilines. Natural selection would have to reverse the entire direction of selection on apes as they diverged from monkeys, beginning some 23–24 million years ago. An alternative was found for humans' hominin ancestors; the rest of the terrestrial apes – certainly hundreds if not thousands of species – could not get sufficiently organized at the group level to survive the vicissitudes of the African savanna.

How did selection rewire the hominin brain to make our ancestors more emotional? Probably the first breakthrough was to give hominins more neo-cortical control over emotions so that they would not become loud on the savanna when excited because a loud primate is on the savanna is soon a deal one. Indeed, some species of monkeys on the savanna march across open territory in virtual silence, indicating that this is a fitness enhancing capacity to control loud emotional outbursts that might attract predators or cause panic that would separate individuals from the group. Some of the wiring that makes the amygdala a conduit between the subcortical emotion centers and the prefrontal cortex – the brain structure from which control must come – may have this function of gaining control of emotional outbursts. Once this wiring was in place, the emotion centers could grow without increasing the loudness of emotional reactions to danger. With a wider array of emotions, it became possible to forge more nuanced bonds which would increase attachments to group structures and thus make apes more fit on the savanna.

There was, however, one major obstacle to using emotions to forge social bonds. Three of the four primary emotions are negative (sadness, anger, and fear) and only one (satisfaction–happiness) is positive. Other candidates for primary emotions – that is emotions that are hard wired and universal among primates and indeed all mammals – are also negative (for a lists of hypothesized primary emotions see Turner 2000:68–69, 2007:4–5, Turner and Stets 2005:14–15). Negative emotions work against solidarity. Anger invites counter-anger; sadness distances individuals rather than bringing them together; and fear makes individuals wary of each other. These are not the emotions of bonding; anger can be used to sanction but negative sanctions alone do not promote solidarity. Solidarity is built from the flow of positive emotions and from positive sanctions that generate such emotions, not from negative emotions. How, then, did natural selection get around the fact that most primary emotions from which all other emotions are built (Plutchik 1980, Turner 2000) are negative?

Overcoming this obstacle accounts, ultimately, for the evolution of morality. Morality depends upon experience two key emotions: (1) *guilt* for having violated moral proscription and prescriptions and (2) *shame* for having not behaved competently and in accordance with expectations in situations. Guilt is always moral, whereas shame can occur for any set of expectations, moral or not. My speculative hypothesis, which is just that – speculative – is that natural selection eventually wired the brain to experience the three negative primary emotions simultaneously in different orders of intensity (the neurological mechanisms involved are not clear at present). Table 7.2 outlines what I see as the structure of guilt and shame. Both emotions are mostly sadness with, in order of magnitude, lesser amounts of anger and fear. It is the relative order of magnitude of anger and fear that makes for the difference between guilt and shame. In descending valence, guilt is composed of sadness (about violation moral codes), fear about the consequences to self at having done so, and anger at self for the violation. Shame is sadness about behaving incompetently, anger at self for having done so, and fear about the consequences to self.

TABLE 7.2. The Structure of Second-Order Emotions: Shame, Guilt, and Alienation

Emotion	Rank-ordering of Constituent Primary Emotions		
	1	2	3
Shame	Disappointment- Sadness (at self)	Assertion-Anger (at self)	Aversion-Fear (at consequences for self)
Guilt	Disappointment- Sadness (at self)	Aversion-Fear (at consequences for self)	Assertion-Anger (at self)
Alienation	Disappointment- Sadness (at self, others, situation)	Assertion-Anger (at others, situation)	Aversion-fear (at consequences for self)

Morality cannot exist without guilt and, to a lesser extent, shame. Moreover, guilt and shame are powerful mechanisms of social control, in several ways. First, shame and guilt are very painful, shame more than guilt, to self and motivate individuals to behave morally and competently to avoid experiencing these emotions. They are motivated to become re-integrated in social structure and culture. Second, shame and guilt also cause individuals to monitor and sanction self for either conformity to, or deviation from, moral codes and morally charged situational expectations. The burden of monitoring and sanctioning thus shifts from external others to internal monologues with self. Shame and guilt can only exist in situations where values, ideologies, institutional norms, and situational expectations are emotionally charged, with conformity to moral codes generating other critical emotions such as pride, satisfaction, happiness, and even joy on the positive side and shame and guilt on the negative side. Thus, while shame and guilt are the outcome of natural selection working around the negative bias of primary emotions – creating new emotions that are painful to self and yet cause individuals to mobilize to avoid these emotions through self-sanctioning and self-monitoring – other kinds of emotions must also emerge to create and sustain morality.

Shame and guilt are what I term second-order elaborations because they involve a double combining of primary emotions, initially sadness (the least volatile of the negative primary emotions) with either anger or fear, and then a second combining of sadness–fear or sadness–anger with the remaining third negative primary emotions. There are other emotions that have this second-order quality, the most prominent being alienation which reveals the same profile as shame but the anger component is directed less at self than to the situation. I see these second-order elaborations as the last stage of emotional evolution directed by natural selection, not the beginning point of this evolution.

I would hypothesize that after initial cortical control over emotions, this neurological base would then allow for elaborations of variations of each primary emotion. This would be the easiest route for selection to take and would dramatically increase the variety of emotions that individuals could experience and use in communication with others. This initial expansion of the range of emotional states for each primary emotion probably began to evolve some five million years ago, and once it allowed for more nuanced emotions to forge bonds among hominins. Table 7.3 illustrates the range of emotions that humans now use with variations of each primary emotion from its low intensity end through a middle level and then to a high-intensity end. As is evident, these emotions allow individuals to mutually communicate their internal states and likely courses of action. Moreover, many of these variants can serve as effective sanctions for those who violate moral codes and/or do not behave competently or fail to meet expectations. The more moral the codes and expectations violated, the more intense (are) the negative emotion(s) experienced by others and the more powerful their negative sanctions.

TABLE 7.3. Variants of Primary Emotions

	Low intensity	Moderate intensity	High intensity
Satisfaction–happiness	content	cheerful	joy
	sanguine	buoyant	bliss
	serenity	friendly	rapture
	gratified	amiable	jubilant
		enjoyment	gaiety
			elation
			delight
			thrilled
			exhilarated
Aversion–fear	concern	misgivings	terror
	hesitant	trepidation	horror
	reluctance	anxiety	high anxiety
	shyness	scared	
		alarmed	
		unnerved	
		panic	
Assertion–anger	annoyed	displeased	dislike
	agitated	frustrated	loathing
	irritated	belligerent	disgust
	vexed	contentious	hate
	perturbed	hostility	despise
	nettled	ire	detest
	rankled	animosity	hatred
	piqued	offended	seething
		consternation	wrath
			furious
			inflamed
			incensed
			outrage
Disappointment–sadness	discouraged	dismayed	sorrow
	downcast	disheartened	heartsick
	dispirited	glum	despondent
		resigned	anguished
		gloomy	crestfallen
		woeful	
		pained	
		dejected	

Source: Data from Turner (2007)

From this base, natural selection appears to have rewired the hominin and human brain to generate first-order elaborations, or combinations of two primary emotions, which involves a greater amount of one primary emotions "mixed" (in some unknown way) with a lesser amount of another. The effect of this combining was to overcome the negative bias of the four primary emotions and, at the same time, to increase the range of emotions that individuals could use to form more nuanced social relations and to sanction conformity to moral expectations. By combining happiness with each of the negative primary emotions, many more associative emotions are generated, as is evident by reading the emotions in Table 7.4. For example, satisfaction–happiness combined with a lesser amount of fear generates emotions like *wonder*, *awe*, *pride*, and *gratitude*. Satisfaction–happiness combined with anger generates

TABLE 7.4. **First-Order Elaborations of Primary Emotions**

Satisfaction–happiness		
Satisfaction–happiness + *aversion–fear*	*produces* →	wonder, hopeful, relief, gratitude, pride, reverence
Satisfaction–happiness + *assertion–anger*	*produces* →	vengeance, appeased, calmed, soothed, relish, triumphant, bemused
Satisfaction–happiness + *disappointment–sadness*	*produces* →	nostalgia, yearning, hope
Aversion–fear		
Aversion–fear + *satisfaction–happiness*	*produces* →	awe, reverence, veneration
Aversion–fear + *assertion–anger*	*produces* →	revulsed, repulsed, antagonism, dislike, envy
Aversion–fear + *disappointment–sadness*	*produces* →	dread, wariness
Assertion–anger		
Assertion–anger + *satisfaction–happiness*	*produces* →	condescension, mollified, rudeness, placated, righteousness
Assertion–anger + *aversion–fear*	*produces* →	abhorrence, jealousy, suspiciousness
Assertion–anger + *disappointment–sadness*	*produces* →	bitterness, depression, betrayed
Disappointment–sadness		
Disappointment–sadness + *satisfaction–happiness*	*produces* →	acceptance, moroseness, solace, melancholy
Disappointment–sadness + *aversion–fear*	*produces* →	regret, forlornness, remorseful, misery
Disappointment–sadness + *assertion–anger*	*produces* →	aggrieved, discontent, dissatisfied, unfulfilled, boredom, grief, envy, sullenness

highly negative emotions like *vengeance* but other emotions, such as *appeased, calmed, soothed, triumphant, bemused,* and *relish* that can serve as sanctions, as acceptances of ritual apologies from others violating moral codes, or as means for communicating more complex mental states that can produce more nuanced social bonds. Satisfaction–happiness combined with disappointment–sadness generates emotions that reduce the power of sadness alone, while producing emotions like nostalgia, yearning, and hopefulness that are more associative than pure sadness. Reversing the dominant emotion, fear combined with a lesser amount of happiness produces *reverence*, and *veneration*, which are essential to conformity to moral codes, especially codes expressing the proscriptions and prescriptions of religious forces in the sacred and supernatural realm. Anger mixed with a lesser amount of happiness produces emotions that can serve as effective sanctions – emotions like *snubbing, mollified, placated,* and *righteousness* that make negative sanctions against those who violate moral codes and expectations effective, but without the same tendency of anger alone to arouse counter-anger in those sanctioned. Thus, by reading across the list of emotional states generated by first-order elaborations, a larger set of emotions for orienting individuals to moral codes and for sanctioning their actions as appropriate is generated. Moreover, these emotions also add subtly, nuance, and variety to the ways that individuals can emotionally relate to one another.

Over millions of years, as these subcortical areas of the brain were rewired produce more varieties of primary emotions, then first-order elaborations, and finally second-order elaborations like shame and guilt, hominins and then humans could become increasingly moral. Shame and guilt were the last of the emotions critical to morality to evolve, and it appears that only humans experience these two emotions. Chimpanzees, our closest primate relative, do not appear to experience either (Boehm, n.d.), or if they do, they experience them with much less intensity than humans. Moreover, shame and guilt are even more effective when moral codes that can be articulated in speech acts; and it now appears that fully articulated speech is uniquely human, with the critical alterations those alleles affecting the structures necessary for fine-grained articulated speech being under selection for only 200,000 years (Enard et al. 2002a, b) – the date when humans first appear on earth.

There are several other pre-adaptations that made the expansion of hominins' and humans' emotional repertoire fitness enhancing. One preadaptation is visual dominance. Emotions are read visually and in configurations, with the result that a great deal of information can be communicated rapidly when processed through the visual sense modality. Compared with articulated speech, which is sequential and rather slow, a large repertoire of emotional states allows for robust communication of dispositional states that can facilitate coordinated action while also increasing the potential for attachments to group structures. Without visual dominance, elaborating emotions could not have produced an effective communication system, nor could emotions have ever served as the underpinnings of morality. I have argued (Turner 2000) that the evolution of the association cortices necessary for language (Geschwind 1954a, 1965b, c, Geschwind and Damasio 1984) were another preadaptation that did not wait millions of years for the evolution of the capacity for articulated speech. Instead, as the emotional repertoire was expanded and used for communication of affective states encouraging bonding among weak-tie hominins, these association cortices were subject to selection and produced the "language of emotions" or as is often termed "body language." There are gestures of face and body that are the equivalent of phonemes and these are strung together by syntax to produce an emotional language. Emotions are ordered sequentially by a grammar, some of which is universal (for the primary emotions) because it is lodged in ancient emotion centers, and other portions of are cultural, in much the same way that the phonemes and grammar of spoken or auditory language varies cross-culturally. We tend to think of body language as an adjunct to spoken language but just the opposite is the case; auditory or spoken language is an adjunct to the vision-based language of emotions. When we really want to know what a person is feeling and even thinking, we look at face and body; and when we want to know if a person is really shamed or guilty, we do the same thing. Words are under much more neocortical control and can be employed in deceptive presentations of self, whereas emotions are under much less control and usually provide a gateway to the inner self of another. Thus, the capacity to make emotions a true language – using phonemes organized by a grammar to produce "meanings" in animals without culture and even more elaborate meanings in animals like humans with culture – dramatically increased the effects of emotions in forging more complex social bonds and, eventually, in providing the "teeth" of moral codes.

Another preadaptation is the capacity of the great apes to see themselves in their environments. As the mirror tests have documented, most highly intelligent mammals such as cats and dogs cannot recognize that the reflection they see in a mirror is a reflection of their bodies (Gallup 1970, 1979, 1982, Gallup et al. 1995). They are likely to nudge the mirror or look behind it to determine what they are seeing. Only a few high mammals can recognize self in the mirror test: humans (who preen self in front of a mirror), dolphins, elephants, and great apes. The capacity to see self as an object is an important preadaptation for morality and for sociality mediated by emotions. As the emotional repertoire expanded among hominins, they would increasingly see the evaluations of others in the mirror or "looking glass self" (Cooley 1964 [1902]), experience a judgment of others (that, over millions of years became ever-more moral, even without articulated speech), and form a self-evaluation. Morality is only effective if it has a target; and there are two basic targets: self and others. People make self evaluations and, indeed, some have argued that they have a moral self in which moral codes are internalized and provide standards to behavioral outputs and self appraisals; and in may cases, this moral self (Stets and Carter 2006, Carter 2006, Turner and Stets 2006) is an emotional construct that sometimes may defy articulation in speech. And the reason for this, I believe, is that less elaborate moral selves where evident in hominins but couched in the language of emotions. As hominins communicated with the language of emotions, the gestures were directed at self and all hominins with a brain the size of a chimpanzee would understand that these gestures were indeed directed toward them. As the brain grew with *Homo habilis* and then *Homo erectus*, these emotional communications would lead to an evaluation of self by the non-verbal but still powerful morality inherent in all emotional communication among increasingly intelligent hominins. To behave in ways that would arouse negative emotions would produce, at some point in hominin evolution, the first feelings that would eventually evolve into shame and guilt. Morality has no relevance for animals that cannot evaluate themselves from emotionally valenced codes; and so, without the preadaptation for the capacity to recognize self in a mirror (and hence in the environment), morality as a basis for social organization and social control could never have evolved, no matter how complex the emotions an animal could generate. And once morality became essential to group formation and social control, selection would not only work on expanding the repertoire of emotions but also the capacity of individuals to experience self as an object and to form identities of various kinds.

EMOTIONS, COGNITIONS, AND THE EVOLUTON OF MORALITY

The evolution of the hominin line was directional, once selection began to push hominins toward enhanced emotionality and greater intelligence (Gould 2002), with natural selection working on preadaptations contained in ape neuroanatomy to produce a more social animal. This sociality was accomplished by increasing variations in each of the primary emotions and mixing (in some unknown neurological way) these variants of primary emotions into first-order and second-order combinations. The evidence is clear that natural selection was grabbing onto subcortical areas of the brain where emotions are generated, increasing their size and rewiring their connections to each other and, over time, to neo-cortical areas of the brain, especially the prefrontal cortex. My belief is that these transformations occurred before the neo-cortex began to approach human proportions (Turner 2000). For millions of years, a few hominids survived in open country savanna by virtue of new kinds of emotional ties to each other. Given preadaptations for language and for self-recognition, a language of emotions emerged, as the association cortices were usurped by natural selection to generate a language built around the visual reading of face and body for its emotional content, and as this language evolved, it was increasingly used for self evaluations as selection worked on the neo-cortex and subcortical emotion centers responsible for such evaluations. Only a relatively small increase in the size of the neo-cortex – say to the size of *Homo habilis* at 500 cc – could make self-evaluations a powerful source of social control. Over time, hominins could read the gestural syntax of emotion phonemes given off by conspecifics for clues about their intentions; and as Cooley (1964 [1902]) recognized, this reading also created the "looking glass self" in which emotionally charged evaluative signals about self from others make members of hominin species more self-aware and more likely to engage in self-evaluations. From this point on, I hypothesize, natural selection continued on this path of enhancing the range of emotions that hominins could experience and interpret from face and body, increasing the sense of self among these hominins, and then attaching the emotional reactions of others to this sense of self. All of this could be accomplished without auditory language and without a neo-cortex in the human measure.

Yet, once natural selection went down this path for making hominins more social and for using emotions and self-evaluations as mechanisms of social control, it would continue to select on the tails of the bell curve on which neurological structures generating capacities for emotionality, language production, and self-evaluations were distributed, thereby pushing hominins to be more emotional, to organize emotional phonemes with a syntax, and to see self as an object of evaluation in response to the emotional responses of others. With further growth in the brain, the cognitive capacities of hominins continued to grow as *Homo habalis* gave way to larger-brained *Homo erectus*, with brains in the 750–900 cc range. This increase in brain size set the stage for full-blown morality because, with an upper range of a brain that was close to the lower range for humans, emotions tagged more complex cognitions, emotional syntax may have increasingly been supplemented by other gestural syntaxes – voice calls and hand signals like those of American sign language for some deaf persons – to communicate more purely cognitive content that was, no doubt, emotionally valenced. Even without spoken language in the human measure, it would have been possible to formulate and communicate codes and rules of proper conduct; and as these rules were emotionally valenced and sanctioned, morality as a cultural phenomenon began to emerge. We now have a species capable of formulating rules, even with crude verbal or even completely non-verbal syntax, able to tag cognitions with emotional valences, willing to evaluate self and derive self feelings on the basis of conformity to these codes and rules, and willing and able to use both positive and negative sanctions to assure conformity to moral codes.

With *Homo sapien sapiens*, the only critical step was the emergence of auditory language to articulate moral codes and to supplement face and body gestures in forging social ties and sanctioning conformity to moral codes. Moreover, self would be that much more salient to larger-brained apes so that articulated moral codes would have more power to direct the behaviors of the first humans in hunting and gathering bands. Morality was not the only mechanisms of bonding, but if we use Durkheim's (1912), Goffman's (1958, 1967), and Collins'(1975, 2005) related models of interaction, the mechanisms contained in their interpersonal theories all emphasize co-presence, rituals, emotional arousal, totemization of the group with symbols, and righteous anger at violations of group codes. Each and every interaction ritual, then, is to some degree a moral drama – sometimes very weak and at other times very intense.

I might add at this point some mention of additional preadaptations that make such rituals possible. One is so obvious that we might ignore it; apes can stand and present full face and body to others, and they can use arms, hands, and fingers to communicate emotions, thereby providing multiple channels for others to read emotions and to become attuned to these emotions (Scheff 1988). Another is that apes have the capacity to signal very subtly through face and body gestures plans for instrumental activities such as coordinating the kill of a baboon (in fact, these non-verbal gestures are so subtle that field researchers cannot observe them; see Menzel 1971). This capacity would be subject to selection as the language of emotions was added to this already in-place ability to use non-verbal gestures of great subtly to coordinate actions. Another preadaptation is that chimpanzees and, no doubt, their common ancestor to humans engage in what is often referred to as "carnival" by field researchers (Reynolds 1965); much like Durkheim's secondary accounts of Arunta aborigines, chimpanzees becomes "effervescent" when they come together in larger numbers, becoming highly emotional. To the degree that this kind of activity is part of interaction rituals, these rituals are simply the outcome of natural selection working on an existing preadaptation that could be enhanced for all interactions, as Goffman (1967) was the first to conceptualize in a robust manner and as Collins (2004) has further developed over the last 2 decades.

What is remarkable to me is the fact that no new major mutations may have been required for the evolution of emotions, morality, self, and use of rituals to forge social bonds. Given enough time, and in the case of hominins the time scale is rather short or punctuated, natural selection could work on the tail ends of distribution of traits to push hominins along this line of evolution, once it enhanced fitness of weak-tie apes who desperately needed to get better organized.

THE PRIMATE LEGACY, MORALITY, AND THE FORMATION OF MACROSTRUCTURES

Let me end with one further speculation mentioned at the very outset. If humans had been the descendents of monkeys, survival on the African savanna would not have been problematic. Indeed, our ancestors may never have left the trees since they would have been more like monkeys and controlled the best niches. And, in fact, perhaps Tarzan would not seem so awkward and strange in the trees because his ancestors would not have left the trees in the first place and adapted to a terrestrial habitat. He might have walked more gracefully on tops of limbs and probably would not have swung around so much since he would be an evolved monkey rather than an evolved ape. Moreover, he would not have needed morality to become better organized. But most relevant, macro societies composed many millions of people would never have evolved because monkeys are, in essence, group oriented. Females stay in their matrilines, and males compete for dominance *in the local group*; they are not empire builders or guardians of large-scale social structures. Their world is micro, focused on the foraging troop, even when they are no longer confined by the arboreal habitat and can live on the ground.

In contrast, groups are not natural for apes. Think of how much work people must perform in rituals and animated conversation to keep group solidarity going. Yet, humans have virtually no trouble identifying and feeling solidarity with those in their community. This is the natural unit for an ape, and it represented a preadaptation for macro society, when coupled with the capacity for morality. Durkheim recognized that mechanical solidarity had to give way to organic solidarity as the size of the population to be organized grew. This was not, as so many early sociological theorists felt, a difficult transitions for an evolved ape. Why should this be so? First, apes orient to larger social structures with less effort than they evidence when participating in micro structures; and as evolved apes, humans are no different. Second, as Durkheim understood, the collective conscience had to become more abstract if it was to be relevant to individuals located at different points in the division of labor in organic systems. With morality, this is not a difficult transition because, once all individuals cannot interact face-to-face for solidarity (since there are simple too many) and do not have bioprogrammers for playing genetically regulated roles, they need the behavioral capacity to develop commitments to common symbols, often totemized as objects for ritual and worship. As morality developed to resolve problems of social control and group-level solidarity, it ironically represented a sociocultural preadaptation for macro societies. Humans can construct complex divisions of labor because they can achieve some degree of solidarity by orienting to common symbols; and this mode of orientation is only a few small steps, mediated by the enhancement of emotions and the ability to articulate moral codes for judging self, from the orientation to communities or the home range of chimpanzees and perhaps the other great apes as well (although the data on not clear on this point). Macro society is only possible when individuals can tolerate differences that come with differentiation along many parameters, but it is not possible to organize millions and, perhaps some day, billions of diverse people without the ability to articulate emotionally valenced moral codes for regulating conduct, for sanctioning others, and for evaluating self. So, it is perhaps an odd irony that descendants of species of apes that could barely get organized on the African savanna could construct societal and inter-societal formations that span the globe and make us worthy competitors with social insects; and to be able to do so with such large bodies is doubly amazing.

CONCLUSION

There is little more to say than this: morality is embedded in human biology; it is not wholly a social constructed, or at least it is a construction that is not possible without the necessary wiring in the human brain. And, this wiring is the outcome of natural selection as it decisively moved the primate genome toward a species that was highly emotional, that could tag all cognitions with complex emotional valences, that could evaluate self as an object and arouse self-related emotions like shame, guilt, satisfaction, and pride when deviating form, or conforming to moral codes, and that did not have a wide variety of emotional reactions and sanctioning options in assessing the moral behaviors of others. Humans as evolved apes had two periods of near extinction; indeed, the human genome reveals less variability of any primate because we all come from a very small number of individuals – hundreds and certainly no more than a few thousand members in our ancestral breeding population. Because we eventually created macro societies housing billions of large-bodied primates, it is often assumed that we are very well adapted. But a species that uses emotions in formulating moral codes and in sanctioning conformity to these codes can easily destroy itself, as the history of warfare and genocide document. We must recognize that emotions as our basic tool of survival over the last 200,000 years (not very long at all in evolutionary time scales) are a double-edged sword. They allow us to be moral, but they allow for potential violence when definitions of morality vary. Righteous anger and needs for vengeance can rip societies apart; and as species armed with weapons of incredible power can become emotionally aroused in ways that cause great destruction. This is why insects are likely to outlive us all, despite our grand social structures.

REFERENCES

Boehm, C. n.d. "The Biosocial Evolution of Social Control and Conscience." unpublished paper.

Collins, R. 1975. *Conflict Sociology. Toward an Explanatory Science*. New York:Academic Press.

Collins, R. 2004. *Interaction Ritual Chains*. Princeton, NJ: Princeton University Press.

Eccles, J. 1989. *Evolution of the Brain: Creation of Self*. London: Routledge.

Enard, W. M., et. al. 2002a. "Molecular Evoution of TOXP2, A Gene Involve in Speech and Language." *Nature* 418:869–872.

Enard, W. M., et al. 2002b. "Intra- and Interspecific Variation in Primate Gene Expression Patterns." *Science* 296: 340–342.

Gallup, Jr. G. G. 1970. "Chimpanzees: Self-Recognition." *Science* 167:88–87.

Gallup, Jr. G. G. 1979. *Self-Recognition in Chimpanzees and Man: A Developmental and Comparative Perspective*. New York: Plenum.

Gallup, Jr. G. G. 1982. "Self-Awareness and the Emergence of Mind in Primates." *American Journal of Primatology* 2:237–248.

Gallup, Jr., et al. 1995. "Further Reflections on Self-Recognition in Primates." *Animal Behaviour* 50:1525–1532.

Cooley, C. H. 1964 (1902). *Human Nature and the Social Order*. New York: Schoken.

Geschwind, N. 1965a. "Disconnection Syndromes in Animals and Man, Part I." *Brain* 88:237–294.

Geschwind, N. 1965b. "Disconnection Syndromes in Animals and Man, Part II." *Brain* 88:585–644.

Geschwind, N., and A. Damasio. 1984. "The Neural Basis of Language." *Annual Review of Neuroscience* 7:127–147.

Goffman, E. 1959. *The Presentation of Self in Everyday Life*. Garden City, NY: Anchor.

Goffman, E. 1967. *Interaction Ritual*. Garden City, NY: Anchor.

Gould, S. J. 2002. *The Structure of Evolutionary Theory*. Cambridge, MA: Belknap Imprint of Harvard University Press.

Luhmann, N. 1982. *The Differentiation of Society*. Trans. S. Holmes and C. Larmore. New York: Columbia University Press.

Machalek, R. 1992. "Why Are Large Societies So Rare?" *Advances in Human Ecology* 1:33–64.

Maryanski, A. 1986. "African Ape Social Structure: A Comparative Analysis." Ph.D. dissertation, University of California at Irvine.

Maryanski, A. 1987. "African Ape Social Structure: Is There Strength in Weak Ties?" *Social Networks* 9:191–215.

Maryanski, A. 1993. "The Elementary Forms of the First Proto-Human Society: An Ecological/Social Network Approach." *Advances in Human Ecology* 2:215–241.

Maryanski, A. 1995. "African Ape Social Networks: A Blueprint for Reconstructing Early Hominid Social Structure." In *Archaelogy of Human Ancestry*, edited by J. Steele, and S. Shennan. London: Routledge.

Maryanski, A., and J. H. Turner. 1992. *The Social Cage: Human Nature and The Evolution of Society*. Stanford, CA: Stanford University Press.

Menzel. E. W. 1971. "Communication about the Environment in a Group of Young Chimpanzees." *Folia Primatologica* 15:220–232.

Parsons, T. 1963a. "On The Concept of Political Power." *Proceedings of the American Philosophical Society* 107: 232–262

Parsons, T. 1963b. "On The Concept of Influence." *Public Opinion Quarterly* 27:37–62.

Plutchik, R. 1980. *Emotion: A Psychoevolutionary Synthesis*. New York: Harper and Row.

Scheff, T. J. 1988. "Shame and Conformity: The Deference-Emotion System." *American Sociological Review* 53: 395–406.

Simmel, G. 1978 (1907). *The Philosophy of Money*. Trans. T. Bottomore and D. Frisby. Boston: Routledge.

Savage-Rumbaugh, S., R. Seveik, and W. Hopkins. 1988. "Symbolic Cross-Modal Transfer in Two Species." *Child Development* 59:617–625.

Savage-Rumbaugh, S., J. Murphy, J. Seveik, K. Brakke, S. L. Williams, and D. Rumbaugh. 1993. "Language Comprehension in the Ape and Child." *Monographs of the Society for Research in Child Development*, 58. Chicago, IL: University of Chicago Press.

Savage-Rumbaugh, S., S. Lewin, and R. Lewin. 1994. *Kanzi: The Ape at the Brink of the Human Mind.* New York: Wiley.

Stephen, H. 1985. "Evolutionary Trends in Limbic Structures." *Neuroscience and Biobehavioral Review* 7:367–374.

Stephan, H., and O. J. Andy. 1969. "Quantitative Comparative Neuroanatomy of Primates." *Annals of the New York Academy of Science* 167:370–387.

Stets, J. E., and M. Carter. 2006. "The Moral Identity: A Principle Level Identity. In *Purpose, Meaning and Action: Control Theories in Sociology*, edited by K. McClelland, and T. J. Fararo. New York: Palgrave Macmillan.

Turner, J. H. 2000. On *The Origin of Human Emotions: A Sociological Inquiry into The Evolution of Human Affect.* Stanford, CA: Stanford University Press.

Turner, J. H. 2002. *Face-to-Face: Toward a Sociological Theory of Interpersonal Processes.* Stanford, CA: Stanford University Press.

Turner, J. H. 2007. *Human Emotions: A Sociological Theory.* New York: Routledge.

Turner, J. H., and J. E. Stets. 2005. *The Sociology of Emotions.* New York: Cambridge University Press.

Turner, J. H., and A. Maryanski. 2005. *Incest: Origins of the Taboo.* Boulder, CO: Paradigm Press.

Turner, J. H., and J. E. Stets. 2006. "Moral Emotions." In *Handbook of The Sociology of Emotions*, edited by J. E. Stets, and J. H. Turner. New York: Springer.

Turner, J. H., and A. Maryanski. 2008. *On The Origin of Societies by Natural Selection.* Boulder, CO: Paradigm Press.

CHAPTER 8

The Sacred and the Profane in the Marketplace

FREDERICK F. WHERRY

This chapter examines how moral order is revivified through interaction rituals in the market-place. By modifying Randall Collins' interaction ritual chains theory, the chapter identifies what guides individuals to evaluate objects and each other in the marketplace through a moral lens and what the consequences of such evaluations are for action. If we apply Emile Durkheim's analysis from *The Elementary Forms of Religious Life* to rituals in the market-place, we see that the market is similar to religion in that it is "a system of ideas by means of which individuals imagine the society of which they are members and the obscure yet intimate relations they have with it" (Durkheim [1912] 1995:227). Collective beliefs enter into and become organized within the minds of individuals during focused market gatherings. In marketplace assemblies, socially inculcated impulses are "amplified each time [they are] echoed, like an avalanche that grows as it goes along" (Durkheim [1912] 1995:212). In addi-tion, these impulses enable individuals to distinguish between the sacred and the profane as morality is performed, contested, and regenerated. Moral codes become embodied in routine interactions and actors become aware of these codes in seemingly nonroutine situations. In the marketplace, "we speak a language we did not create; we use instruments [for calcula-tion, negotiation, and distribution] we did not invent; we claim rights we did not establish; each generation inherits a treasure of knowledge it did not itself amass" (Durkheim [1912] 1995:214).

Take the example of a 'typical' marketplace encounter. At the end of the encounter, one imagines the following interaction.

"How much is it with the discount?"

"$250."

"Do you take credit cards?"

Such an interaction differs dramatically from one in which aesthetic or social values are at stake. In those instances, a number of different scenarios are imaginable: (1) the object or service is not for sale; (2) the object or service can only be sold under conditions that "preserve" its moral character; or (3) the conditions under which the object or service may be sold remain highly contested, generating social actors outside the economic transaction to intervene through public protests or political lobbying. This chapter focuses on the first two of these scenarios because they highlight how the ritual interactions in the secular market possess a moral character, influencing the course of the interaction and the evaluation of the transaction

S. Hitlin, S. Vaisey (eds.), *Handbook of the Sociology of Morality*,
Handbooks of Sociology and Social Research, DOI 10.1007/978-1-4419-6896-8_8,
© Springer Science+Business Media, LLC 2010

as "good" or "bad" (Goffman 1959, 1967). The interactions themselves generate emotions and symbols that bolster and refine moral evaluations that then fed into other interactions (Collins 2004, Summers-Effler 2006). This chain of interactions and the varying moral evaluations they generate become inculcated in market actors who can take for granted from where their moral evaluations come.

Imagine that you are in Chiang Mai, Thailand and that you have driven to a village outside the city known for its woodcarvings. Just outside the village, you encounter a small factory employing no more than, say, 30 people but using a wide network of village artisans to produce furniture and other home décor items. The factory owner gives you a tour of the production facility and then takes you to his showroom. Upstairs, by his office where he entertains special guests, there is a spirit house on the balcony. He has had a group of monks come by the engage in the proper rituals for the spirit house and everyday he or his office manager come upstairs to burn joss sticks at the base of the spirit house and to leave food offerings for the gods inhabiting it. Now imagine that wealthy Western buyers see this spirit house and want to sell it as a highly priced birdcage. The factory owner refuses to put real spirit houses into commercial circulation and discussions ensue over what is sacred and what is profane (Wherry 2008). Morality first blocks then highly mediates the commercial transaction, as fake spirit houses are then produced for the marketplace and 'real ones' are decommissioned by the monks in a special ceremony (and at a higher price) as a limited edition collector's item.

This example from my fieldwork shows how morality emerges in commercial transactions and in actual market places. In Thailand and Costa Rica, where I studied artisans crafting wooden furniture, home décor items, and ceramics, individuals distinguished between the sacred and the profane as they negotiated how crafts would be categorized, what the appropriate terms of exchange would be, and what restrictions would be put on the use of their creations. Some potentially lucrative transactions were blocked or sharply mediated on moral grounds, and even the processes of production were constrained by interaction rituals and the morality that the chain of those ritual events creates.

I found that buyers and sellers depend on their evaluative memories and on their immediate affective (emotional) reactions when making judgments in the marketplace. Randall Collins describes the formation of these affective and evaluative memories as the consequence of interaction ritual chains. The four ritual ingredients of the interaction manifest themselves as follows. The buyer and seller are interacting physically with one another and with the commodity in question ([1] "*group assembly with bodily co-presence*") (emphasis added, 2004b:48). In some cases, the products cannot easily be reproduced or their mass reproduction seems an anathema to the buyer. In other cases, the language and culture of the site of production are far away (geographically and/or symbolically) from the site where the goods are displayed and purchased. These conditions constitute [2] *barriers to outsiders*. The buyers have to seek out clues from the sellers and the environment about the object's qualities. The buyers sometime engage with 'folk experts' or with companions to assess what the objects are and what the object's description really signifies ([3] *mutual focus of attention*). This mutual focus of attention generates a shared mood of contemplation about how to assess who the producers are, what their works signify, and what message the buyer will convey to socially relevant others by making such a purchase ([4] *shared mood*).

These ritual ingredients lead to a set of outcomes that generate the emotional energy and moral constraints on the interaction. The buyers become acutely aware that the producers and their canon of goods belong to a particular cultural tradition. In fact, the buyers are often aware of the cultural tradition before initiating contact with the seller and it is this awareness that brings them into interaction. While interaction ritual theory does not explain what attracts individuals to join a particular interaction, the theory is helpful to understand how the emotional intensity of the interaction advances (or not). The goods' symbols begin to resonate as belonging to a group and standards emerge for how the objects and their symbols should (and should not) be used. Although, these standards usually exist, even if fuzzily in the minds of the buyers and sellers, they must be accomplished anew with each interaction. The standards crystallize because there is a focused interaction and a submergence of most distractions. The buyers and sellers are caught up in a predictable pattern of negotiation over the values/qualities of the object with some questions rendered inappropriate (even taboo) or not germane to the situation. The buyers and the sellers obtain emotional energy from the rhythmic entrainment of negotiation that evokes memories from the buyer's past and requires refinements of those memories along with contestations over how prior experiences apply to the current assessments being made. Finally, the buyers and the sellers express righteous indignation for prices deemed too high or too low given the social significance of the goods.

Following Collins, I note that the morality of one's behavior in different market situations emerges from a series of ritual-like activities that give rise to emotional energy – "a strong steady emotion, lasting over a period of time. . .. [that] gives the ability to act with initiative and resolve, to set the direction of social situations rather than to be dominated by others in the micro-details of interaction. . .. [and] to be self-directed when alone" (Collins 2004:134) – and to social solidarities that create and sustain moral standards for a collectivity. While each market situation regenerates *normative* principles, the concatenation of these normative principles gives rise to trans-situational *values*. Norms manifest themselves in situations where the individual feels she ought to behave in a certain way towards a certain object (Hitlin and Piliavin 2004). An individual might feel social pressure to behave in a manner acceptable to others who are present during a market negotiation and thereby choose a normative path of action; however, that same individual might choose to act differently when alone or when in situations lacking that normative pressure. When an individual lacking normative pressure from peers nonetheless feels motivated to pursue a particular course of action in the marketplace. Although, her failure to do so might not elicit social sanctions (disapproving looks or comments) because she is alone, she is appealing to her values – "enduring beliefs that a specific mode of conduct is personally or socially preferable to an opposite or converse mode of conduct or end-state of existence" (Rokeach 1973:5).

Schwartz and Bilsky's (1987:551) summarize how values are usually defined; similarly, this chapter refers to moral values in the marketplace as "(a) concepts or beliefs [about aesthetics and economic justice], (b) about desirable end states and behaviors, (c) that transcend specific situations, (d) guide selection or evaluation of behavior and events, and (3) are ordered by relative importance." This chapter specifies how patterned interactions generate emotional energy that is transmitted from one interaction to the next. Over time, this emotional energy and the categorical ideals of right and wrong, sacred and profane, authentic and inauthentic, just and unjust emerge, strengthen, and travel across situations as values that guide and give meaning to market interactions.

A cultural approach to morality represents the flipside of Schwartz (1993) and Schwartz and Bilsky (1987) who emphasize individual logics and human nature rather than cultural structures for understanding the generation of values. Transforming Schwartz and Bilsky's framework into a cultural one, I recognize three features of moral judgments in the marketplace, namely (1) moral distinctions in the marketplace result from a human-based need to distinguish culturally between the sacred and the profane; (2) the social interactions typical of ritual interactions reaffirm social solidarities and symbols of group membership as well as the emotional energy that gets transferred to subsequent interactions, as Collins argues; and (3) that moral judgments transcend the situations in which they are revived (Collins suggests in his historical accounts of interaction rituals that moral judgments transcend the situation, but he does not specify how it happens). These ritual interactions thereby provide a patterning structure for selecting and evaluating behavior, objects, and situations. In other words, moral values result from a dynamic, relational process (Zelizer 1985).

One observes these dynamics in the second-order recreation of symbols and their third-order recirculation through conversations. The first-order creation of symbols is in the distant past, and the further away in time one imagines this first-order creation to be, the more valuable the symbols created. These symbols become associated with moral categories of thought, but these moral categories do not depend solely on social morphology (as explained by Durkheim) but rather as a result of intense interaction rituals, their second-order recreations, and their third-order recirculations. In this way, moral understandings about what is happening in the marketplace is inculcated in individuals who embody a sense of right and wrong as they engage in particular rituals. The interaction rituals themselves make these embodied moral properties seem salient as behaviors that run counter to the ritual triggering a sense of righteous indignation. While Collins recognizes the differences between the first- and second-order creation/recirculation of symbols, he focuses on micro level interactions within situations and does not specify how some (macro level) latent values come into existence in the first instance before being brought to the fore through interaction rituals.

This embodiment of moral constraints means that the individual acts when alone as if she is being observed by others; moreover, the conversations that the individual has during a price negotiation functions itself as an interaction ritual that conjures past conversations and that animates its current internal dialogue. These thoughts usually flow towards the stock of symbols generating the most positive emotional energy (EE) and away from other symbols that lead to costly losses in positive EE and in material resources. For Collins, it is essentially a utility-maximizing framework. But my ethnographic intuition tells me that other logics can "intrude" into the marketplace and can gravitate towards costly losses in positive EE and in material resources, especially in transactions requiring a ritual sacrifice to the gods of the marketplace, punishing potential perpetrators of the profane with the expectation of a future, otherworldly benefit. Rather than thinking about the interaction ritual chains and action as instrumentally rational, one can think about the *habitus* in which these rituals are enacted, "without presupposing a conscious aiming at ends" (Bourdieu 1990:53).

WHAT ARE PEOPLE THINKING?

In the marketplace, it is possible to ask buyers and sellers why they have made the decisions they have. Buyers and sellers can talk about their conscious intentions but they are not aware of the actions they have taken due to deeply held beliefs in the unconscious. Rather than propose that social scientists employ psychoanalytic techniques to capture a glimpse of what beliefs are held in the unconscious mind, Randall Collins observes the "external chain of social situations" in which the thoughts of the unconscious mind are made manifest and from whence those thoughts come. (Of course, a number of other options exist for capturing the beliefs of the unconscious mind (Vaisey 2009), including fixed-response survey choices, as well as priming and other experiments).

In the case of intentional action, individuals sometimes think aloud, expressing the moral constraints on their action or they externalize their thoughts through role-play. In contrast to the written speech delivered at a formal ceremony, the role played speech is made in preparation for formal business interactions and for informal, social gatherings. For the business interactions, one can imagine a person rehearsing how to ask for more favorable terms of trade and trying out their response to a buyer's objections about price, the time frame for production, or the final form that an object will take. These role-plays become especially important in global market situations where the buyer's native tongue is English, French, or Japanese (for example) but the seller's native tongue is a tonal Asian language, such as Thai. While the seller may rehearse a business negotiation for the conscious reasons of overcoming a language barrier and trying to pick upon and respond appropriately to foreign cultural cues, the seller also makes manifest the ritualistic character of business negotiations. In addition, through hesitation, a pregnant pause, or an involuntary surge of energy and an increase in the pace of a conversation, the seller may reveal how emotional energy triggered at particular points of the interaction and what the moral codes are embedded in different moments of the interactions.

These moral codes are inculcated in buyers and sellers from a very early age. Collins notes that analyses of moral codes are circular when they ignore the ritual interactions that make those codes resonant. Therefore, one has to pay attention to the external conversations, local interactions, and interaction styles that children observe and sometimes consciously replicate. Take the example of children who play the role of adult artisans selling their ceramics to English-speaking tourists:

> In villages such as Guaitil, one sees the artisans' children setting up small kiosks on the edge of the village plaza in view of their parents' kiosks. The children reproduce the working world of their parents in their afternoon games, much as children in the US families setup lemonade stands in the neighborhood to earn spending money. The children chat eagerly with the tourists and explain how the older sister molded the drinking vessel from clay and how the younger brother made the paints from natural sources. For the visitor, the children's games unfailingly attest to the fact that the villagers are born into their craft, that they carry these special skills "in their blood." The tourists who purchase goods from these children do so under the watchful eye of an adult. The children seldom have small currency denominations to make change and speak very little English. Mimicking English-speaking television personalities, the children welcome guests with "Hello!" (Wherry 2008:127)

The children are replicating the role that they have seen their parents take. As they engage in a childhood ritual, they are able to comfortably engage in interactions with the foreign tourists and are able to intuit what is most sacred in the interaction, namely, the natural sources of the paints (some coming from crushed volcanic stone) and indicating what is "made by hand." The children do not yet have the English facility to talk more about their traditions with tourists, but their embodied engagement in the ritual leads the tourists to remark that the children carry these arts "in their blood." Collins notes that in cases such as this one, "the voice will [eventually] become completely internal and silent, and develop into a form of self-control" (Collins 2004:186). For Collins, this means that the internalized voice helps the individual avoid social sanctions by precluding the need for third-party correction. My observations suggest that this process also internalizes moral codes.

Collins observes that there is a continuum of ritual types, which run from the highly scripted formal ritual to its opposite pole of the unscheduled and unscripted informal ritual. Categorical imperatives for moral behavior are reflected in the formal rituals, whereas pragmatic, situational moral fixes are made in the course of informal rituals (Collins 2004:272). At the most informal end of the spectrum are "open public situations" in which buyers and sellers stumble upon one another. There is no sense of occasion; one party shops while the other sells. Neither there is an attempt to match them according to a schedule, nor is there a ceremony to celebrate these matches or to laud the most innovative sellers among them. By contrast, trade fairs offer official, scheduled, publicized events in which design awards are announced and elected officials (sources of authority) are sometimes physically present. Those designers blessed with talent are given a special place of honor and even the layout of the trade fair formalizes the identities of the types of products and the status of the sellers at the fair. For example, take some observations from Bangkok's International Gifts (BIG) Fair:

> The April 2007 OTOP BIG Fair is happening in competition with the Milan show, and this has affected which principals among the sellers have come as well as which buyers have managed to show up. Yesterday, I learned this from a buyer who explained that she decided to forgo the Milan show because she was looking for a particular Thai designer whose work she's been following the last two years. She wanted to see if they had persevered (remained faithful) to the trade show. I met two other buyers last night while having drinks in the Soi 4 area of Silom. they confirmed that the real action was happening in Milan but they always come to Thailand, because it is one of the few times in the year when they are able to meet up with one another as buyers engaged in the same activities (sourcing home décor items) but living in different parts of the world.

> The physical layout of the fair leaves no doubt that there is a "charity" display of the One Tambon One Product (OTOP) goods beside the food court and there is the high-end display with the award winning designs at the polar opposite of the hall away from the food court. At the heart of the hall is the officially sanctioned art where the placards provide the categorical identities for Thai art forms.

> Just behind the Bangkok International Housewares (BIH) exhibit is the 13th National Ceramics Exhibition. The national ceramics competition is the official cultural institution with non-monetary motives and it is juxtaposed with a display of the top house-wares in a museum like arrangement. But, placards on the museum exhibit are in Thai whereas those for the BIH showcase are in English. This may create greater distance, barriers to entry for outsiders who are the English speakers. This increases the authority of the cultural certifying institution's display, perhaps [Fieldnotes April 20, 2007, Impact Center, Thailand].

The hall where the products are being displayed is physically stratified according to the status of the producers and their goods. A seller's placement at the fair reminds her of the status to which she belongs. As potential buyers walk through the hall, they begin to identify different types of sellers and products as high or low culture by virtue of the physical distance these sellers have from the food court. Status group boundaries were emplaced.

From the interactions, one has in structured places, one bolsters a sense of self (ego) and other (alter). How these places come to be structured in these ways are questions often left to the history of intergroup struggles, accidents, and luck. Design is socially constructed and design templates vary from one society to another, but once a template becomes dominant because of the other sources of power within a society or group to proclaim their template as one of the best, other audiences either mimic the winning template or reference it explicitly or implicitly when designing a market display, for example.

In the marketplace, people act "as if" they are minimizing costs and maximizing benefits. These "as if" assumptions go further in ritual theory, according to Erika Summers-Effler, because sometimes people come into conflict as one person does not act "as if" she is following the appropriate logic for the socially defined transaction. The violation sparks emotional energy as the individuals in question are pushed to reflect on why the "as if" assumptions have failed. Summer-Effler writes: "Small variations will bring about subtle modifications of existing 'as if' loops, whereas substantial conflict between what was expected and what ensues requires the dismissal of old loops and the formation of new. ... Situations that call on competing or conflict 'as if' loops also generate conscious thought" (Summers-Effler 2006:145). Over time, modifications of existing "as if" loops can build to have significant, unanticipated consequences. A seller could form new "loops" while using these other transactions as a way to buffer the deviant buyer's behavior or as a way to teach the deviant a lesson. The seller could also form new loops while rejecting the buyer outright or the seller could alter her own assumptions (however subtly) about how the buyer ought to behave in the socially defined transaction. It is difficult to predict what will happen when an "as if" assumption fails because these predictions should be based on repeated observations of such failures and because individuals respond to spikes in emotional energy during such disagreements in different ways.

Emotional energy is theorized as being carried from one set of rituals into the next, and over time, it presents a challenge for the researchers trying to capture how much emotional energy there is from one type of interaction to the next and what types of emotional energy matter for the operations of different ritual chains. A researcher cannot be present at all these steps in the chain, and the research subjects may not be cognizant of the various details that are unfolding from one ritualized interaction to the next. This is especially the case when emotional energy is high. Someone caught up with passion or feeling a sentiment intensely may not be fully cognizant of it after the fact; moreover, these emotions are part of the interactions and are therefore taken for granted.

Collins' discussion of emotional energy is similar to Sheldon Stryker's discussion of "affective commitment" (Stryker 2004) in that it recognizes the capacity of emotional intensity to make identities, group boundaries, and collectively held (sacred) symbols more salient for individuals (Stets 2006). The moral sense of outrage that flows from the violation of the sacred would be less easy to read and less compelling if, it had not been for the interaction rituals that generated the emotional energy in the first place.

DAILY SPIRITUAL RITUALS

As we saw in the discussion of the Thai spirit house at the beginning of the chapter, religious rituals and strong religious beliefs influence how individual sellers approach lucrative business ventures. The relevant links in the interaction ritual chain include private and public religious practices that stretch back in time and are not observed by the social analyst for each individual at all the relevant points in time. The missing observations can be imputed because of the preponderance of evidence indicating that people perform the ritual in roughly the same way and that the ritual has remained more-or-less the same over time.

A moral logic of reparations for past wrongs undergrids the ritual of the spirit house. The sacred houses function as a compensation to displaced spirits who inhabited a specific area of land before human beings arrived and chopped down the inhabited trees where a thick forest once stood, humankind has erected residential and commercial properties. The spirits displaced by constructions cannot be compensated with money. They require new housing, reverence, and daily ritual offerings. Their new housing is the spirit house, ranging in size from about one by one by one and a half feet to a much larger structure that could be three feet in height or more, depending upon the ages and the types of trees removed. The youngest trees have less formidable spirits to placate relative the oldest trees where people have razed older, more revered trees, they have also constructed larger, more elaborate spirit houses.

The daily ritual honors the spirits residing in the spirit house. In return, those occupying the land can expect peace and tranquility versus the chaos wrought by bad kharma and angry ghosts. Each day someone from the home or business sets out offerings to the spirits and whispers prayers while holding lit joss sticks. The offering often includes fermented rice wrapped in a banana leaf, a garland of flowers, lit candles, and red joss sticks (Anuman Rajadhon, 1988). The whispered prayer recognizes the uncertainties of life – people die or become ill, and markets fail – as well as the need to appeal to the supernatural for protection.

The significance of the spirit house provides narratives of peace, protection, and spiritual balance that sellers extra and repackage in the West for profane purposes. Because the ritual significance of the spirit house remains strong, Western sellers cannot appropriate it in any way that they please, and in their negotiations with producers the moral significance of the spirit house as well as the sources of its significance were made manifested. The act of defining what the spirit house is, what its market (monetary) value will be, and what restrictions will be placed on its production and circulation trigger the individuals in these markets to distinguish between the sacred and the profane. Some things are "real" in both their materiality and their symbolic import. The Thai name for a spirit house literally means "the house in which the spirits are invited." Buddhist monks lead the ritual of invitation, and it is only through a religious ritual led by these authorities can the spirits be asked to leave the spirit house for a new home. The public rituals that are well known and widely experienced by Thai people enable the sacred meanings of the spirit house to resonate.

One of my informants in Thailand described a situation in which a Western buyer approached him to source some spirit houses because the buyer had customers willing to pay as much as $1,000 for the old, teak ones. The course of the negotiation was spirited because of the informant's concerns that the sacred not been taken as being similar to something profane. This concern became more urgent when the informant heard that some of the customers wanted to use the spirit houses as birdcages. Negotiations ensue, not about the final price but rather about how the real spirit houses would need to be decommissioned properly in a ritual led by the monks before they could be sold and how "fake" spirit houses could be build and made to look old for larger batches of production. The buyer can purchase a sacred object only after honoring the object's sacred, ritual character (Cf. Goffman 1961:73).

By applying the theory of interaction ritual chains to the case, one can see how the selling of the spirit house might be permitted if some of the ritual ingredients of the interaction are absent. In other words, it is not enough to think that the seller believes that using sacred objects is wrong and that spirits from the other world will punish him (a great cost for a modest benefit). The capacity of this belief to guide action depends on the ritual ingredients that interaction ritual chain-theory identifies. In this way, the theory helps us understand how the transaction might have had other (opposite) outcomes.

A RITUAL DEMONSTRATION

Halfway around the world, less scripted rituals in highly sociable situations also generate situational norms and moral distinctions that might not obtain outside the ritual interaction. To illustrate this, I turn to the demonstration of how pottery is made in Guaitil, Costa Rica. The pottery making tradition is a ritual that stretches back 4,000 years to the pre-Columbian artisanal traditions of the Chorotega. Grand Circle Travel conducted the tour I about to describe in 2003 and their promotional materials for the tour describe the indigenous Chorotega as descendents of the Mayans who were once dominated by the Olmec. These descriptions signal that the cultural lineage of the group is long and that the processes the tourists are about to witness are scripted pass along through oral history and through embodied practices.

The tour bus will make two stops. At its first stop, about twenty-four people disembark for two artisans' workshops about a kilometer short of the center of Guaitil at 10:30a.m. Gustavo and Edwin are the local men whose families own the workshops. They are in the twenties and serve as the guides to lead these tourists into "the other world" – distant and difficult to reach, metaphorically speaking, from the world these tourists usually inhabit. Gustavo and Edwin split the group of twenty-four in half, while the others remaining on the bus are transported to the center of Guaitil where other guides await.

The preparations for the ritual have made. The area around the metaphorical alter of production resembles an outdoor garage with white cement walls rising three feet, intersected by five feet of steel bars. The wooden planks stack onto an A-frame, overlaid by a tin roof. The family elder sits behind the bars, shining a pot in his lap with a smooth quartz stone. Age clearly matches the ritual functions of production. Shining the pot is the final act. The young accomplish acts required at the beginning of the process: a twenty-some-year-old man rolls cylindrical logs and rings them atop his spinning wheel. A teenage boy paints half-man-half-animal figures onto the bodies of the waiting pots. The interactions are repetitive, and the meanings of each phase of production are well known among the artisans on display.

The audience sits in a semicircle on improvised furniture. There are three plastic lawn chairs, four kitchen-table chairs, two logs upturned to function as stools, three metal and plastic-cushioned rocking chairs. The artisans have setup their demonstration table with the instruments of production: a quartz stone the size of a man's palm, a spoon made from the hull of the calabash plant, a small strip of leather, a corn cob, a small piece of sponge, a cutting file, an etching nail, three paint brushes, a base mould; a small mound of clay; three cups filled with white, red, and black paints, three small saucers with a white porous rock, a red terracotta stone, and a volcanic black rock; a small saucer of grey iguana sand; and finally the nonmotorized spinning wheel. The kiln is situated about 15 m past the demonstration table is a kiln - a white cement dome on a rectangular base of roughly hewn stone.

The scene indicates that the individuals remain subordinate to the ritual act. Edwin does not wear a garment marking his role in the ritual. Instead, he dons a T-shirt, nylon shorts, and sandals. The space of the ritual demonstration allows chickens to stray through it, and even the fall of ripe mango seems to contribute to the ethos of the space of interaction. As the demonstration begins, more than the tourists are drawn to it. A teenage boy arrives on his bicycle, carrying fruit bowls to be sold at the end of the demonstration.

Edwin explains that the production process they are about to witness differs significantly, from what the masses do. Whereas individuals involved in mass production (profane) can purchase paints, the individuals involved in traditional (sacred) production must make their own paints by crushing colored stones. Whereas the spinning wheels in a 'regular' pottery factor will use electricity, the spinning wheels in this village are improvised from whatever materials they have on hand (such as a bicycle wheel) and no electricity is required.

Edwin passes around a pot with half of its surface unfinished and the other half newly shined with quartz stone. The tourists rub the smooth and stroke the rough, the contrast high-lighting the ritual transformation and the object's cultural biography (Kopytoff 1986). The tourists has witnessed a ritual process from a pre-mechanized era and seen how the raw becomes refined. At the same time, what is usually a backstage performance for individu-als shopping at a store has now come to the front stage (Goffman 1961). The reactions of awe indicate heightened levels of emotional energy (EE), which is to be expected with so many barriers being erected between the raw and the finished, the rough and the smooth, the pre-mechanized and the mechanized (these latent categories exist prior to interaction). The ritual ingredient (barriers to entry) and the ritual outcome (heightened EE) enable the embodiment of moral regard for the production process and its objects.

Edwin further emphasizes the barriers to entry into authentic cultural production by issu-ing a warning: "Because we use these stones to make our paints, we cannot make the color green. Red, white, and black do not make green. Therefore, when you see a pot painted bright green, it is not from here. It is not of the Chorotega tradition." The colors signal whether the pot belongs to the Chorotega tradition and offers a way to detect false prophets.

At the end of the demonstration, the morality generated by these ritual interactions becomes apparent. The tourists make judgments of what is fair versus unfair and what is appropriate versus offensive in their discussions with the sellers. A married couple has a spir-ited discussion of market morals after her husband dares to ask how many the artisans make *per hour*. The wife's responds to her husband by asking, "How can you ask such a question! This is not manual work. It takes special skills." Had they both not witnessed the demonstra-tion of what it takes to produce these goods and had they both not been exposed to the sense of the sacred, she might not have protested her husband's profane question. She expresses her righteous anger and punishes her mate with her disdainful tone. The different reaction that this couple has to the ritual highlights the fact that people are not automatons. They both experi-enced a successful ritual, but the husband, who is a trained economist by his own admission, still asked a question that embarrassed his wife. She seems to really think that the artisan has special skill, but I cannot rule out the possibility that she is attempting to repair a possible breach of cultural market etiquette caused by her husband's social ineptness. Although, he does not seem to be angry at himself and has not internalized the sense that his question is out of bounds, he has learned that he will be reprimanded by others if he fails to act "as if" he ought to be offended by his own question.

These moral evaluations of the market just further examples of the limits to transforming objects into commodities. In the demonstration in Costa Rica, these tourists will not see the sellers again and could bargain for the lowest price without suffering negative nonsocial con-sequences. However, the buyers do orient their behaviors to the audience of other buyers and to their own internal audience. The natural rhythms of village life inflect the ritual performance.

The demonstration constitutes a multi-focused gathering in which "persons ostensibly engaged in one encounter can simultaneously sustain an additional 'subordinated' one. In the last instance the "subordinated" encounter is sustained through covert expressions or by deferential restriction of the second encounter so that it does not get in the way of the officially dominating one" (Goffman 1961:18–19). Such is the state of marketplace interactions with more than one negotiation and more than one set of encounters happening in the same place, but in the case of the demonstration, these subplots cohere around the central display.

What is most striking is the fact that the reactions that different groups of tourists have to the same demonstration are remarkably similar. While the norms of the negotiation emerge in the ritual interaction, being accomplished anew with each tour group, those norms belong to an overarching moral understanding about how the tourists and their hosts ought to behave. This stable set of expectations and the sense that some actions are right while others wrong provide a moral basis for action in contrast to a dyadic exchange of strangers without any moral compass to indicate what ought to be done and why it ought to be done in a particular way (e.g., Portes 1995). Even among people who know each other well, there are situations in which they coordinate action and have shared expectations, but their actions do not push moral boundaries. In other words, they do not need to contemplate the rightness or wrongness of their action because their behaviors are routine and the emotional energy sustaining them is low.

BACKSTAGE ROUNDS

The author returned at 9:30 the next morning to begin the backstage rounds. In contrast to seeing the work-in-progress, the author left his role as a member of the audience and became an informal inspector of the stage props, producers, stagehands, and of the stage itself. The author was being invited to meet his uncle, cousins, and friends who were situated nearby but out of sight. Mr. Nui and the author spent nearly 2 hours on the rounds. First, he took the author to the neighboring shop that his older sister manages. In the back of the shop, she was painting and applying black resin to a pot. To her left nearly out of sight was an old man carving a mystical animal into a piece of wood about three and a half feet long. He was in no hurry, because the work required great care to detail, but he could not lose too much time because the patience of the customer is not, he realizes, unlimited. Mister Nui and the author walked away from his uncle into a slightly wooded area, where we found a small workstation: a rectangular board nailed to trees to create a roof, no walls, wooden planks assembled into benches, and enough space on the dirt floor for four men to sit comfortably. A calendar with a topless Thai woman and an old television and cassette player were set against a pole where an electrical outlet offered the only source of electricity. In the center of the workstation, there was a person carving. Along the benches, three men watched, another was in a hammock resting, and another was lying flat on his back along a bench, sleeping. The person carving was working on the face of a Buddha. Beside his foot was a glossy picture from a magazine of the Buddha face designed in the Sukhothai style, with the Buddha's hair represented by symmetric rows of small knots. There were several rough-hewn pieces of wood with the outlines of a head, lying about the floor, waiting to be transformed into the faces of Buddha.

Our inspection done and introductory remarks made, Mr. Nui and the author jumped a small ravine and approached a house. At home in his kitchen, a man sat on the floor working on a flat piece of wood. It was probably five feet long and two and a half feet wide. He was carving a face into it - another Buddha! He used one tool to carve the motif along marks already made by a black magic marker with more subtle marks made in pencil for the artistic etch. We left him after a few minutes for another outdoor shop nearby where a man was carving scenes from Thai folklore onto a large panel of wood. Overwhelmed by how similar and different all the scenes were, the author breathed a sigh of relief when Mr. Nui asked the author whether he was hungry.

Over lunch and over the course of the next five months, the author learned that the backstage rounds were not common for prized buyers expected to purchase in bulk or for high status buyers who are well-known designers or some other type of public figure. The rounds reconfirmed their interest in the lives of the artisans and the ongoing integrity of the performance: the diligence of artisans supervised only by no one; the use of electricity for entertainment rather than production; the integration of craftwork into the rhythms of the household; all these elements became part of the object's identity.

AWKWARD INTERACTIONS

In less scripted situations, the interactions are less ritual and more awkward. By awkward, the author meant that the individuals hesitate because they are second-guessing their own moves and having trouble anticipating the moves of their interlocutors. The definitions of the situation they accomplish are not as tightly linked to prior interaction rituals as we saw in this chapter's previous examples. As a result, the actors cannot rely on an overarching, highly resonant set or expectations to guide them through the interaction. There is, nonetheless, a sense of how to perform a moral 'skit' that governs the outer boundaries of the transaction.

In the author's field notes from Thailand, he describes an encounter at the Small and Medium Enterprise (SME) Day Fair at Chiang Mai University. The author met Mark Narongsak of King's Collection for the third time in a year. They were both attending the fashion show held in the great hall where the trade show was underway. Mark was at the display booth for King's Collection and seemed to be rehearsing the interactions he intended to have with Western buyers. After the usual, ceremonial hello, how are you, followed by small talk about the goods and display and the usual question about what the author likes, Mark beckoned one of his business managers to come and to bring him a business card.

The business card was meant to spark a conversation and to set King's Collection apart as being innovative and culturally rich, but there was a problem. The author lacked the prior set of interactions that would allow him to make sense of what the business card lacked and he relied instead on a set of other business interactions he experienced in Thailand to interpret what was happening and how he (perhaps) should respond to it. When Mark's business manager handed the author their card, he noticed that the second 'c' in the world 'Collection' from the company's name was missing. Mark then asked the author what was missing, and the author did not know what to say. Would it be appropriate for the author to say that the business cards had a misprint that should have been corrected before the trade show or was there something in the design of the card that he wanted to highlight.

The author felt embarrassed because he was unsure how he should behave. He wanted an obvious set of protocols to rely on so that he would not have to make sense of this interaction without any context or with the 'wrong' context. The author hesitated a little longer.

"What's missing?" Mark asked, pointing to his associate's card, insisting on an answer. With unease, the author responded, "C".

"The C that is lost is <u>Culture</u>". I became immediately aware of and uncomfortable with the assumptions I had made in an instant. Had I, a politically liberal and multi-cultural omnivore, taken a patronizing attitude toward Mark? Had I seen him as an "equal," I would have lost no time in telling him that there was a minor mistake on his business card. As soon as he flipped over the card, my mood changed. I felt immediately relieved that I had been played a fool in the service of a good cause (With too much reflection, I feared the return of my patronizing attitude and ignored it. After all, the joke was on me). Mark continued his explanation which I remembered especially well because it coincided with a moment of personal discomfort. He reminded me that the lost C of authentic culture alluded to the forgotten history of the Lanna Kingdom, which Mark hoped to revive by playing up local traditions under the Lanna brand name (Thailand, interview with author, October 12, 2002). By disarming the potential buyer through staging an awkward situation, Mark had created a hybrid forum for the exploration of several noncommercial concerns. In short, He had connected other concerns in my life with my current market interaction.

The awkward and smooth social interactions are responsible for the creation of markets. It is well known among economic sociologists that markets do not create sociability; instead, sociability creates markets (Abolafia 1996, Bourdieu 2005, DiMaggio 1990, Fligstein and Dauter 2007, Fourcade and Healy 2007, Granovetter 2002, Guillén et al. 2002, Portes 1995, Swedberg 2003, Zelizer 1985). In order for financial transactions to obtain, the buyer and seller feign some kind of intimacy in order to begin the transaction. This intimacy, however affected, depends on the practices and understandings well known in other areas of social life. Georg Simmel likens economic transactions to romantic exchanges:

> Competition compels the wooer who has a co-wooer, and often in this way alone comes to be a wooer properly speaking, to go out to the wooed, come close to him, establish ties with him, find his strengths and weaknesses and adjust to them, find all bridges, or cast new ones, which might connect the competitor's own being and doing with his. (Simmel 1955:61)

Buyers and sellers do not necessarily learn to intuit the predilections of their customers as a result of market participation but rather as a spillover from their participation in intimate (noneconomic) relationships (Zelizer 2005). Sellers must learn how to sell their products within different expectation sets for behavior. Participation in a whole range of social institutions provides individuals with the tacit knowledge they need for understanding these expectation sets. Often, these expectations are breached, highlighting the tacit knowledge required to engage successfully in market transactions as actors discern how the interaction should be accomplished.

CONCLUSION

It is only fitting that the sociology of morality engages Emile Durkheim's concern with the sacred and the profane by way of ritual. Although, Durkheim theorized the clear separation of the sacred from the profane and thought about the machinations of the market as profane, Durkheim's analysis of religious ritual can usefully be applied to such nonreligious realms as the marketplace. White (1981) reminds us to pay attention to the stories that sellers and buyers tell to those in their own respective role (seller-to-sellers and buyer-to-buyers) and to those in the role of their interlocutors (buyer-to-seller), making the morality of the market simply a part of the story-sets that people carry into the marketplace. Because the sociologists of religion are not thinking about routine economic interactions as reflections of the sacred and because economic sociologists have largely bracketed questions of the sacred and the profane (except for an emergent group led by Viviana Zelizer and Randall Collins), Durkheim's analyses of ritual have not been studied in dynamic, linked cases of market interactions where morality shapes its contours but where also morality is made and re-made through the course of linked interaction-orders. This chapter has only begun to meet this more dynamic, morally infused agenda for analyzing morals and markets.

REFERENCES

Abolafia, M. Y. 1996. *Making Markets: Opportunism and Restraint on Wall Street*. Cambridge, MA: Harvard University Press.

Anuman Rajadhon, P. 1988. *Essays on Thai folklore*. Bangkok: Thai Inter-Religious Commission for Development and Santhirakoses Nagapradipa Foundation.

Bourdieu, P. 1990. *The Logic of Practice*. Cambridge: Polity Press.

Bourdieu, P. 2005. *The Social Structures of the Economy*. Malden, MA: Polity.

Collins, R. 2004. *Interaction Ritual Chains*. Princeton, NJ: Princeton University Press.

DiMaggio, P. 1990. "Cultural Aspects of Economic Action and Organization." PP. 113–136 in *Beyond the Marketplace: Rethinking Economy and Society*, edited by R. Friedland, and A. F. Robertson. New York: Aldine de Gruyter.

Durkheim, E. 1995 (1912). *The Elementary Forms of Religious Life*. Translated by K. E. Fields. New York: The Free Press.

Fligstein, N., and L. Dauter. 2007. "The Sociology of Markets." *Annual Review of Sociology* 33:105–128.

Fourcade, M., and K. Healy. 2007. "Moral Views of Market Society." *Annual Review of Sociology* 33:385–311.

Goffman, E. 1959. *The Presentation of Self in Everyday Life*. Garden City, NY: Doubleday.

Goffman, E. 1961. *Encounters: Two Studies in the Sociology of Interaction*. Indianapolis, IN: Bobbs-Merrill.

Goffman, E. 1967. *Interaction Ritual*. New York: Vintage.

Granovetter, M. 2002. "A Theoretical Agenda for Economic Sociology." PP. 35–60 in *The New Economic Sociology: Developments in an Emerging Field*, edited by M. F. Guillén, R. Collins, P. England, and M. Meyer. New York: Russell Sage Foundation.

Guillén, M. F., R. Collins, P. England, and M. Meyer. 2002. "The Revival of Economic Sociology." PP. 1–32 in *The New Economic Sociology: Developments in an Emerging Field*, edited by M. F. Guillén, R. Collins, P. England, and M. Meyer. New York: Russell Sage Foundation.

Hitlin, S., and J. A. Piliavin. 2004. "Current Research, Methods, and Theory of Values." *Annual Review of Sociology* 30:359–393.

Kopytoff, I. 1986. "The cultural Biography of Things: Commoditization as Process." PP. 64–91 in *The Social Life of Things: Commodities in Cultural Perspective*, edited by A. Appadurai. Cambridge: Cambridge University Press.

Portes, A. 1995. "Economic Sociology and the Sociology of Immigration: A Conceptual Overview." PP. 1–41 in *The Economic Sociology of Immigration: Essays on Networks, Ethnicity, and Entrepreneurship*, edited by A. Portes. New York: The Russell Sage Foundation.

Rokeach, M. 1973. *The Nature of Human Values*. New York: The Free Press.

Schwartz, B. 1993. "On the Creation and Destruction of Value." in *The Origin of Value*, edited by L. N. M. Hechter, and R. E. Michod. New York: De Gruyter.

Schwartz, S. H., and W. Bilsky. 1987. "Toward a Universal Psychological Structure of Human Values." *Journal of Personality and SOcial Psychology* 53:550–562.

Simmel, G. 1955. *Conflict: The Web of Group-Affiliations*. Glencoe, IL: Free Press.

Stets, J. E. 2006. "Identity Theory and Emotions." PP. 203–223 in *Jonathan H. Turner*, edited by J. E. Stets. New York: Springer.

Stryker, S. 2004. "Integrating Emotion Into Identity Theory." *Advances in Group Processes* 21:1–23.

Summers-Effler, E. 2006. "Ritual Theory." PP. 135–154 in *The Handbook of the Sociology of Emotions*, edited by J. E. Stets, and J. H. Turner. New York: Springer.

Swedberg, R. 2003. *The Principles of Economic Sociology*. Princeton: Princeton University Press.

Vaisey, S. 2009. "Motivation and Justification: A Dual-Process Model of Culture in Action." *American Journal of Sociology* 114:1675–1715.

Wherry, F. F. 2008. *Global Markets and Local Crafts: Thailand and Costa Rica Compared*. Baltimore: Johns Hopkins University Press.

White, H. C. 1981. "Where Do Markets Come From?" *American Journal of Sociology* 87:517–547.

Zelizer, V. 1985. *Pricing the Priceless Child: The Changing Social Value of Children*. New York: Basic Books.

Zelizer, V. A. 2005. *The Purchase of Intimacy*. Princeton: Princeton University Press.

There is no ref. to me in this edited collection, which is surprising in a book on sociology of morality. Not in subject index.

This chapter by Wherry, based on ethnog. field work in Thailand & Costa Rica, advances the view that 'morality emerges in commercial transactions and in actual market places'; secular markets have a moral character; but nothing about global capitalism since the 1980s, which he describes blacks tied of ex relations.

CHAPTER 9

Class and Morality

ANDREW SAYER

"class is not an innocent term but a loaded moral signifier"[1]

Class is a matter of enormous moral significance, though this is unevenly registered in lay understanding. The lottery of birth class has a profound effect on our subsequent lives, shaping the kind of people we become, and what we have and do. Like it or not, class raises issues of the perceived relative worth of individuals, and about the relation between how people are valued economically, and how they and their actions are valued ethically. The ethical status of class itself is therefore highly contested. For some, class itself is a form of injustice, and hence fundamentally unethical; for others it is a reflection of their relative worth in a supposedly meritocratic social order; and for some it is accepted fatalistically as a fact or hardly registered at all.[2] Accounts of the struggle for respect and self-respect, the desire for recognition of moral worth, and feelings of inferiority or superiority are common themes in ethnographies of class (Bartky 1990, Lamont 1992, 2000, Kefalas 2003, Sennett and Cobb 1973, Sennett 2003, Reay 1998a, b, Skeggs 1997, Charlesworth 2000). However, the moral dimension of these feelings tends to be left implicit; rarely is it dealt with analytically (Sayer 2005).[3] People's concerns about class go much deeper than the matters of distribution of resources – of how much income and wealth they have – to matters of recognition. How they stand in the eyes of others is often even more important to them than their wealth, for their sense of self-worth depends heavily on how others value them. Because of unequal distribution and unequal recognition, class affects us deeply, influencing our values and moral outlook.[4]

Yet despite all this, the "ethical profile" of class is much lower than that of other axes of inequality today (hooks 1982). In many countries, racism has come to be seen as wrong in official discourse, so that racist abuse is proscribed as unethical; yet snobbery or class contempt,

---

[1] This observation was made by sociologists Mike Savage, Gaynor Bagnall and Brian Longhurst in their study of class identities in North West England, in response to the defensiveness and sense of unease shown by their interviewees in talking about class (Savage et al. 2001).

[2] As Beverley Skeggs notes, it tends to be ignored or not seen by those who have the privilege to ignore it (Skeggs 1997).

[3] I have attempted an analytical treatment in my book *The Moral Significance of Class* (Sayer 2005). This article partly summarizes of some of its main arguments.

[4] Unlike Nancy Fraser, I see recognition not as centred on cultural identity, but as also intimately associated with class (Fraser 1995).

S. Hitlin, S. Vaisey (eds.), *Handbook of the Sociology of Morality*,
Handbooks of Sociology and Social Research, DOI 10.1007/978-1-4419-6896-8_9,
© Springer Science+Business Media, LLC 2010

explicit in terms such as "white trash" or "trailer trash" in the USA, and "chavs" in the UK, are still seen as acceptable, and perhaps a source of amusement. bell hooks notes how class has become an "uncool" subject in the USA becoming ever more unequal (hooks 1982:1). As a black woman living in Greenwich village, local people often assume her to be a nanny or shop assistant. Mostly, her white neighbours "are social liberals and fiscal conservatives. They may believe in recognising multiculturalism and celebrating diversity (our neighbourhood is full of white gay men and straight white people who have at least one black, Asian or Hispanic friend), but when it comes to money and class they want to protect what they have, to perpetuate and reproduce it - they want more. The fact that they have so much while others have so little does not cause moral anguish, for they see their good fortune as a sign they are chosen, special and deserving" (hooks :3).

The moral salience of class has its own sociology, with people's different responses to class reflecting their own class position and experience, interpreted through the cultural and political discourses regarding class that characterise their own society. The neglect of the moral dimension of class is partly a consequence of sociology's tendency to adopt either subjectivist or conventionalist views of morality, that is, as either a matter of subjective beliefs that are beyond the scope of reason and not susceptible to argument or evidence, or merely a matter of convention or norms (Sayer 2005, 2011). These fail to address the seriousness of moral issues and their relation to people's wellbeing, and thereby obscure the moral significance of particular issues like class.

In this chapter, I want to address three issues: (i) class itself as an object of moral concern in society; (ii) the general relation between class and morality, in terms of the harmony or dissonance between the two, and (iii) the ways in which class affects, and is affected by, moral ideas, feelings and judgements. In view of the shortcomings of the sociology of morality and sociology's treatment of the moral dimension of class, it will first be necessary to sketch how we might usefully approach morality and class.

MORALITY AND ETHICS

For the purposes of this chapter, I shall use the terms morality and ethics interchangeably to refer to all that those terms sometimes identify separately. Broadly, they refer to ideas and feelings regarding how people should behave, particularly with respect to others, in relation to their well-being. I suggest that it is best to use a broad definition that includes ideas of justice, and of the good, as philosophers call it, that is, ideas concerning what is a good way of life. Although, some philosophers and social theories might want to separate morality from these, they tend not to be separated out in everyday thought. If we are to understand the moral dimension of class, we have to acknowledge that the boundary between moral evaluations and nonmoral evaluations is often extremely fuzzy; thus people's valuations of their own or others' worth are likely to be a composite of judgements of their competence and intelligence, their economic standing and their moral qualities.

It is important to avoid a reductionist and demeaning view of lay morality as primarily a matter of norm-following, as if people merely internalise or are injected with norms and then follow them; this fails to do justice to the intelligence and seriousness of lay morality. Lay morality is a product of several elements:

(i) *Moral sentiments or emotions* like compassion, benevolence, gratitude, guilt, shame and sense of justice, and injustice. Of course, there are also immoral sentiments too, such as arrogance, callousness, contempt and jealousy. Moral sentiments should not be seen as opposed to reason, but are forms of emotional reason; they are fallible but often intelligent and discriminating responses to events that bear upon individuals' concerns (Archer 2000, Smith 1759). For example, the feeling of guilt indicates that I have harmed someone; in addition to giving me some idea of what has happened, it makes me feel bad and want to do something about it. Emotions thus have cognitive, affective and motivating ("emotive") properties (Oakley 1993, Nussbaum 2001). Without the intelligence of emotions, life would be more difficult and hazardous than it is. Insofar as people's emotions reflect their experiences, we might expect there to be differences in emotions, including moral emotions, across the class spectrum. In turn, class inequalities themselves can prompt sentiments of pride, shame, resentment, envy, compassion, fear and contempt.

(ii) *Fellow-feeling* or the ability to understand others, via not only discourse, but also expressions and body language, is a precondition of everyday moral conduct. Though clearly limited and fallible, it is crucial for social interaction. Through having experienced certain good or bad events ourselves, we have some degree of insight into others' experiences, although they are never identical to our own. Those who lack this ability – for example, through autism – find social interaction difficult (Smith 1759, Nichols 2004).

(iii) *Dispositions* to behave in particular ways (virtues or vices). Individuals acquire particular virtues or vices through repeated practice; for example, a teacher who puts on an authoritarian manner in order to keep discipline in school gradually becomes authoritarian. When an individual instantly goes to the aid of someone who has had a bad fall, without first reflecting on whether she should, she does so because she has acquired the dispositions (virtues) of compassion and benevolence. As both Bourdieu and Aristotle emphasised, these dispositions are flexible so that within a certain range they can respond quickly to variations in circumstances; this is because they are acquired through practical experience in dealing with different situations. They can be intelligently responsive; that someone might instantly help someone who has had bad fall shows recognition that they may have hurt themselves and need help. Bourdieu and Aristotle also argued that the particular bundles of virtues and vices that people acquire are strongly shaped by their social context, and particularly their upbringing: for example, a hostile, competitive environment is not conducive to generosity but encourages dispositions of distrust and aggression (Bourdieu 2000, Aristotle 1980). (Im)moral dispositions should therefore be considered part of the habitus (Reay 1998a, b, Skeggs 1997, 2004). This connection between virtues or vices and social context again suggests that class position is likely to make a difference to moral conduct.

(iv) *Norms* regarding what is or is not acceptable conduct are important, though less so than much sociology assumes. As Bourdieu argues, while norms influence the acquisition of dispositions they are to some extent formalisations of them, though as such they lack the flexibility and responsiveness of dispositions (Bourdieu 2000). *Moral* norms are distinguished from other norms in terms of the *seriousness* of the implications for well-being (Midgley 1972). We believe the Holocaust was unethical not because it transgressed norms, but because of the extraordinary suffering that it caused. Morality is not merely conventional but *eudaimonistic,* that is, related to the pursuit of flourishing and the avoidance of suffering. Studies of young children show they can distinguish those norms which are merely conventional from those which also prohibit harm and promote flourishing or well-being (Nichols 2004). Morality is not merely a set of norms regarding what is acceptable; it is about something independent of itself - namely, how people as inherently social beings who can both harm and be harmed, flourish and suffer, can live together in ways that have regard for their well-being. What constitutes well-being is a difficult issue but it is not merely a matter of collective wishful thinking; we do not imagine that violence, abuse, or humiliation would cease to be problems merely by declaring that they are not.

(v) *Discourses: moral stories, symbols and exemplary individuals.* These provide diverse, complex and often conflicting sources of moral ideas. Their implications for class are likely to be complex and diverse; for example, small numbers of rags-to-riches stories may be used to illustrate class inequalities but also to imply that class does not matter. The discourse of class is itself morally inflected, most obviously in derogatory terms like "trailer trash," which associate a low class position with moral and cognitive inferiority, and in distinctions between the deserving and undeserving poor. As Bourdieu notes, the very meaning of "class" is itself a stake in the struggle among classes. The euphemistic terminology of "working" and "middle" class allows those in subordinate positions a source of value in their productive contribution and avoids the demeaning category of "lower class," while the disappearance of the category of "upper class" allows the dominant to hide in the middle.[5] Discourses relating to class, which need not of course actually mention the word, are worthy objects of sociological and discourse analysis.

(vi) *Individual reflexivity and moral reasoning.* This ranges from concentrated deliberation on major ethical decisions, like whether to divorce, through to more fleeting and fragmented evaluations as part of the stream of consciousness (Archer 2007, Murdoch 1970). Through "the work of attention," as Murdoch calls it, we continually note – albeit sometimes subconsciously - how we and the things we care about are faring; how people are treating us and reacting to our own actions is of particular importance. Individuals' moral and other valuations of persons and actions tend to accumulate based on this ongoing experience, perhaps more than because of concentrated deliberation. As Adam Smith emphasised, the more important the decision, the more people are likely to ask themselves how it would be viewed by others, whether recipients or spectators (Smith 1759). Part of this work of attention involves comparison with others: as deeply social beings, our sense of self is relational, so that we interpret and evaluate ourselves in relation to what we observe in others and how they respond to us. This is particularly important with respect to ideas of justice and injustice. Everyday moral reasoning also has a generalising character.

---

[5] Managers and professionals also sometimes disingenuously deny their class privilege by calling themselves working class on the grounds that they work.

Having experienced unfair or vicious treatment in one case, perhaps directed against ourselves, we come to recognise it as unjust and painful in other cases too, and may apply a similar judgement to them (Alexander 1995). Further, because morality involves relations between people, it is continually negotiated; again, it is not merely a matter of following internalised norms. As Jarrett Zigon puts it:

> "morality is better thought of as a continuous dialogical process during which a person is in constant interaction with their world and the persons in that world, rather than as a set category of beliefs from which one picks appropriate responses to particular situations." (Zigon 2009:155)

Any adequate sociology of morality needs to consider not only these elements, but also the interactions among them. (i) and (ii) are particularly well analysed in Adam Smith's *Theory of Moral Sentiments* – a book which deserves to be treated as foundational for the sociology of morality (Smith 1759; see also Nussbaum 2001, Archer 2000). (iii) – virtues and vices - are implicit in Bourdieu's sociology, and explicit in Aristotle's ethics (Bourdieu 2000, Aristotle 1980).

The sociology of morality is ill-served by the discipline's three main ancestors: Marx's famous scepticism about morality (despite his own moral outrage at capitalism) is problematic, though more complex views of morality can be discerned in his work, particularly his early writings on alienation which in effect deal with the nature of human flourishing and its denial (Kain 1991); Weber's view of values as irrational renders moral reasoning opaque; Durkheim's tendency to represent morality as merely conventional, and his sociologically imperialist refusal of psychological explanations, obscures its relation to human flourishing and suffering. Weber's subjectivist view of values, Durkheim's leaning towards conventionalist views of values and morality, and Marx's suspicion of morality, mean that sociology often fails to grasp how moral and ethical values are not only about how people should behave, but also about how they should behave with respect to their well-being. Of course, different cultures provide different conceptions of the good life, of what it is to be a good person, what is acceptable behaviour, and indeed of what is well-being. However, though it is culturally construed in various ways, well-being is not merely a matter of collective wishful-thinking; the Taliban may try to pass off the subordination of women as good for their well-being but it does not follow that they succeed in making it so and convince the women they dominate that it is so. When sociologists are harmed by someone, they do not say "look, subjectively, I just don't happen to like that," or "please don't do that because it's culturally constructed as bad round here"; rather, like the rest of us, they object to the harm that has been done. This shows the untenability of subjectivist and purely conventionalist views of morality, though of course our judgements of harm are fallible.

Class

To understand the relationship between morality and class, we have to take an inclusive view of the meaning of "class" that covers not only economic inequalities but also differences in cultural and social capital. In addition, not only theoretical concepts of class positions and relations, but also folk understandings of class inequalities as they are lived, as these influence how people interpret and value themselves and others. Different concepts of class identify different characteristics and they are not necessarily mutually exclusive: Erik Olin Wright provides an analytical overview of different class concepts and their possible interrelations (Wright 2004). Bourdieu's analysis of class, incorporating his concepts of capitals, habitus and social field, is especially useful for getting beyond the traditional class-plus-status formulations of mainstream sociology. Individuals' class position is based on the amount and composition of different capitals – primarily economic, cultural and social. From living within particular locations within the social field, they develop a structure of dispositions (habitus) that is attuned to that context, and which tends to shape their values and attitudes. They gradually gain a "feel for the game" in familiar parts of the social field, and equally a lack of such know-how in unfamiliar parts (Bourdieu 1984, 1987). Unlike approaches that use income or occupational classifications to operationalise the concept of class, this approach offers a multidimensional conceptualisation: thus, it acknowledges that people with the same volume of economic capital will differ in class position if they have different amounts of cultural capital. It also makes it unnecessary to draw sharp boundaries between classes; instead, there are gradients of different volumes and mixes of capitals, and the value of these capitals is continually subject to shifts in individuals' valuations of them, according to their material and symbolic power. However, although Bourdieu exhaustively analysed differences in aesthetic values, differences in moral dispositions were left largely implicit.

Further, it has to be remembered that in concrete cases, the difference that class makes mediates and is mediated by other axes of inequality like gender, race and ethnicity, which also have their own moral inflections in terms of dispositions and visual and discursive representations. The net outcomes of these forms of intersectionality are nonlinear and complex (Walby 2009).

It is not only inequalities in the distribution of resources, including ownership of productive resources, that are significant in influencing how people value themselves and others, but also inequalities in terms of what it is possible for people to do or *contribute*. A division of labour that segregates good quality work (skilled/interesting/pleasant) and bad quality work (unskilled/boring/unpleasant) into different jobs means that paid work – so important for shaping who we become – makes us unequal. Under such an arrangement, at any time, only a minority can get high quality work. An unequal division of labour therefore makes competition for good quality employment and the cultural capital that tends to go with it a zero-sum game at any point in time (Gomberg 2007, Murphy 1993). Even if income were equalised across all occupations in such a division of labour, inequality of contribution would remain.

A key ideological effect of class is the illusion that the unequal division of labour is simply a reflection of differences in intelligence and skill, when as Adam Smith claimed, and Bourdieu's work explains, the reverse is more true (Smith 1776:1976, Bourdieu 1996, Bourdieu and Passeron 1990).[6] Roughly speaking, the intergenerational transmission via the

---

[6] Research by Leon Feinstein on children's cognitive capacities shows that these develop more slowly in low social class children than high social class children, so that by 120 months, the brightest of low social class children at 22 months are overtaken by the weakest of high social class children at 22 months (Feinstein 2003). The score at 22 months predicts educational qualifications at age 26 and is related to family background. Feinstein found no evidence that entry into schooling reverses this pattern.

habitus of economic, cultural and social capital tends to endow young people with dispositions and orientations that relate to their parents' position in the unequal division of labour, though differences in individual ability, personality, experience and reflexivity may make a difference too and allow some social mobility. The child of middle class, educated parents is not only well resourced economically relative to other children, but also inherits their cultural capital, through becoming familiar with their cultural goods, and through socialising with others in similar positions in the social field (Lareau 2003, Walkerdine and Lucey 1989, Walkerdine et al. 2001). As Bourdieu shows, the education system functions as a mechanism for enabling such children to convert their *inherited* cultural capital into the consecrated, legitimate and *merited* form of educational capital (qualifications) (Bourdieu 1996, Bourdieu and Passeron 1990). Though it is easier for a child with inherited cultural capital to pass her exams and admitted into dominant positions, these transitions are not automatic and therefore if she do pass, her fortunes may seem wholly deserved, at least to those who are unaware of the importance of the inheritance of capital. Unless people have some awareness of the power of socialisation according to birth class and embodiment of class position in the habitus, they are likely to think simply that those who do well in the educational and labour markets are more deserving, and those who do not, are not. From this lack of awareness flows the belief that modern society is meritocratic, so that adult class position is seen as a product of merit plus effort, and the dominant classes are seen as entitled to their advantages.

I now turn to three key aspects of the relationship between class and morality.

Class as an Object of Moral Concern in Society

Consider two newborn babies in a hospital, one born into an affluent family, the other into a low-income family; they are equally needy and equally deserving, but their life chances are radically unequal because they are born into different positions within the class structure. Since the most important years of socialisation are the early "formative" years, it is not surprising that relative social mobility among classes is low in all modern societies (Aldridge 2004, Erikson and Goldthorpe 1993). Class is morally significant first in that it profoundly and arbitrarily affects what people get to become, to do, and to have.

Therefore, we might first consider class as a form of *injustice*, as an unjust social structure in the sense that it makes people who are in relevant respects equal to one another – that is, similar in needs or deservingness or ability – unequal, whether exploited or able to exploit others, dominant or dominated, included or excluded, celebrated or despised, and hence having unequal life chances and unequal recognition, including recognition of their moral worth. Therefore, class is itself an object of moral concern, though of course some may not see it as such. Some sociologists may feel that whether class is unjust is a matter for political and moral philosophy rather than sociology. However, such parochial thinking is likely to rebound on sociology, for we can hardly expect to understand how people deal with and respond to class – or indeed any other form of inequality and domination – if we refuse to address its arbitrary and unjust character. Why would class, or indeed race and gender, be so contested if they were not forms of social organisation which caused harm to certain groups while benefiting others? To acknowledge that this is what they do is to make an evaluative judgement about what actually happens – a judgement that involves what philosophers call "thick ethical concepts" which defy a positive-normative distinction. One of the reasons why morality is so poorly understood in sociology is precisely the kind of disciplinary parochialism which assumes that normative – or rather, evaluative - matters need not be addressed when trying to explain social processes, and which equates objectivity with avoidance of evaluative judgements (Sayer 2005, 2011; see also Putnam 2002, Taylor 1967, Williams 1985). Sometimes even to describe we have to judge; if we are not told whether a certain kind of situation is empowering or oppressive, then it has not been *described* adequately.

How does the Morality of a Class Society Relate to its Structure and Distribution of Power?

"The moral world and the social world are more or less coherent, but they are never more than more or less coherent." "Morality is always potentially subversive of class and power." (Walzer, *Interpretation and Social Criticism* 1989:22).

Is morality primarily a reflection of, or relative to, the structure of society, including its class structure, or is it significantly independent of social structure? Does it serve the interests of the dominant or provide a source of resistance to them?

The idea sometimes attributed to Marx, that morality is relative to particular societies and has an apologetic function in legitimising structures of domination, has some plausibility, but only some. Hierarchical societies tend to have discourses which legitimise hierarchy as deserved and fair, and hence that inequalities and deference towards the dominant are right and proper. However, moral criteria also refer to situations which do not involve class differences; children may acquire ideas of fairness through their interactions with siblings and friends. The evaluations and norms learned in such contexts are easily generalisable to others. Where the legitimations appeal to special qualities or merit supposedly monopolised by the dominant, such claims are vulnerable to questioning: *are* the dominant any different from others?; *what* have they done to deserve what they have? *Why* should they be allowed to have power over us? The extent to which people may think of such things and feel able to voice them may vary considerably according to the kind of society, but they are always a possibility. There are plenty of legitimations of class – and indeed forms of denial of class - in modern class societies, but they are always vulnerable to scepticism, indeed especially so given the valuation of equality in terms of equal treatment of people who are in relevant respects equal. Why, if equality is the norm in some social settings, is it not the norm in others? Michael Walzer's comments on the relation of the social and morality therefore seem correct. Morality is a source of both discipline, conformity and order *and* resistance and conflict. For example, the moral emotion of shame can produce either effect. We may try to atone for having acted in ways which we and others believe are wrong, and hence conform, but we may also feel shame sometimes if we fail to resist; the antiracist who fails to challenge people who make racist comments is likely to feel shame, and may decide to avoid that painful moral emotion by being more courageous in future.

It is clear from Bourdieu's work on the sociology of taste that aesthetic judgements vary fairly clearly according to people's economic, cultural and social capital, but he makes few explicit comments on how their ethical judgements vary (Bourdieu 1984). While Adam Smith was well aware of the way in which class differences affected moral judgement (see below), he thought it varied less across the social field than does aesthetic taste. One reason for this is that morality cannot be considered simply a private matter, for it is precisely about how our actions affect others. I don't care much what music, clothes and décor others like; such matters do not impact strongly on my well-being. I care much more about how they *treat* me and others. Therefore, morality has a multilateral, dialogical quality that reduces variety within groups (Zigon 2009). Although, people's lives in modern class societies differ radically, everyone is likely to experience both ethical and unethical treatment at some time in their lives, and hence to know something about what benevolence, compassion, cruelty, selfishness, contempt, injustice, disrespect and violence are like. The capacities for fellow-feeling and reflection make it likely that we can have some understanding of what these things are like for others, though as we noted above, the adequacy of this understanding is often quite limited. While the mix of sentiments like pride, shame, guilt, compassion, gratitude, sense of justice and injustice, contempt, envy and resentment that people experience in their lives is likely to vary according to their social position, everyone is likely to experience them at some time in their lives. Despite the radical differences in people's lives, and despite the common processes of snobbery or class contempt, fellow feeling and moral sentiments can cut across differences of class, gender, "race", culture, etc. Hence, there can be middle class egalitarians who react critically to class inequalities as unjust, and men who are sympathetic to feminism who want to reduce male power.

Having noted this general dialectical relation of interdependence and tension between class and morality, I now turn to some more specific effects of the relationship.

How Class Affects, and is Affected by, Moral Ideas, Feelings and Judgements

How does individuals' class position affect what we might call the moral texture of their lives? To what extent do their moral sentiments and judgements vary according to their class position? How are their views on the legitimacy or otherwise of class affected by their own class position? Do they see their own class position as deserved or undeserved, fair or unfair, or as simply a matter of fate? How do their views on other ethical matters vary according to class? Again, this is not merely a matter of social position but available discourses, particularly in terms of the extent to which class is acknowledged and politicised. Michèle Lamont's comparative studies of French and US workers show the former to be significantly more politicised in their view of class and society; the US workers tend to accept class inequalities as natural, and blame themselves for their low position (Lamont 2000). The structure of class positions, along with race and gender, profoundly shapes the social field of relations, and it influences how people respond to their situation and that of others, and what they value. However, while it influences it does not dictate: as we shall see, particular class positions frequently offer quite opposed responses: for example, working class pride and working class deference, and middle class sense of entitlement and superiority and middle class guilt. People's capacity for reflection, drawing upon their cultural and political discourse and history, can always subvert demeaning, deterministic accounts of their behaviour.

The objective differences in what people become, do and have because of their class position affects the kind and degree of recognition they get. As recent theories of recognition argue, people's well-being and life chances are profoundly affected not only by what they get in terms of resources, but also in terms of recognition. Given the relational nature of the self, it is hard for individuals to have self-respect if no one else respects them. Individuals are evaluated in comparison with others. Therefore, class sets up a competition for respect and esteem on a sloping playing field (Sennett and Cobb 1973). Those who occupy positions with economic capital and power, including skilled, interesting work, achieve goods (skills, commodities and lifestyles) that many others aspire to, and tend to get recognition accordingly, and of course, the reverse is true for those occupying low positions. Insofar, as recognition is given for achievement, the former appear to deserve recognition and the latter not; and therefore it appears that the judgements are fair. Compensatory judgements involving positive discrimination, in which the extent to which achievements are the product of inherited economic and cultural capital is taken into account in evaluating them, tend to be the exception.[7]

Structural inequalities such as those of class mean that people have unequal chances to *achieve* the things they value. This in turn tends to make them value things, including character and behaviour, differently. Therefore, the upper middle class French men studied by Michèle Lamont valued people who were highly educated and articulate, and had considerable cultural capital, and tended not to see integrity and fairness as important (Lamont 1992). The US working class men she studied, however, valued above all self-discipline, hard work, commitment to family, trustworthiness and moral integrity, and they saw managers as untrustworthy and manipulative (Lamont 2000). Being unable to gain economic security and wealth, the workers sought compensatory sources of moral worth. Note, however, that to explain their behaviour in this way is not of course to endorse the evaluations of goods made by the dominant; for example, the rich may falsely imagine that ever-increasing wealth will bring them ever-greater happiness.

The competitions or struggles of the social field that Bourdieu analysed thus have a moral dimension. Those in low positions tend to be pulled in two directions. On the one hand, they tend to aspire to the goods (again, in the broad sense) monopolised by the dominant (not least, because they are indeed often better: who would prefer cramped, damp housing to spacious, comfortable housing)? However, the more they want the unattainable, the more deficient they may feel. On the other hand, they may be tempted to dismiss the unattainable as not worth having – and "refuse what they are refused". The risk of the latter strategy is that in so doing, they confirm the prejudices of the dominant that they do not even want to "better themselves". The working class valuation of hard work and self-discipline is one way of negotiating this tension; it is a compensatory and consolatory strategy for achieving recognition and sense of self-worth (Lamont 2000, Kefalas 2003).

Those members of subordinate classes who aspire to the goods (again in the broad sense) monopolised by the dominant and the recognition which goes with having those goods, may attach great importance to *being respectable* (Skeggs 1997). However, the pursuit of respectability is a deferential one; it seeks acceptance and recognition on the terms of the dominant. It is a shame response. By contrast, the more assertive demand for *respect* made by more politicised members of subordinate classes, for example, black UK youth and Afro-Americans, call for recognition more on their own terms (hooks 1982).

The struggle for respect can produce complex, unintended effects. Those who are in low positions and hence tend not to win much respect, but may try to compensate and defend

---

[7] While equal opportunities and affirmative action policies generally attempt to address inequalities of race, gender, ethnicity, sexuality and disability, class inequalities are often overlooked. Although organisations might possibly try to extend equal opportunities and affirmative action policies to countering class differences when recruiting staff to new posts, they themselves actively reproduce class inequalities simply by setting up unequal divisions of labour with unequal pay, which means that the posts for which people compete are already classed.

their self-respect by striving harder than others to conduct themselves with dignity in the face of adversity; we might say they do "dignity work" (Sayer 2007). If they succeed in winning some respect for their fortitude and dignified, self-disciplined conduct, that may have the effect of giving others the impression that there is nothing seriously wrong with their disadvantaged position; they apparently can still live a life of dignity. If, on the other hand, they do not do this compensatory dignity work and hence fail to win the respect of others, then that allows others to assume that they deserve their low position: they are the undeserving poor. Similarly, working class pride may seem defiant in the face of class inequalities, but the strong positive self-evaluation invites the dominant to conclude (disingenuously) that class inequalities do not cause any harm; they are proud of what they are, so why should they need any more?

However, on top of the objective inequalities of class and its effects on people's lives and the unequal responses that they produce in recognition, class also distorts the judgements that people make of others, so that in effect, they apply double standards to them. In other words, class works on both sides of the relationship; in influencing the object of valuation (what people actually do or achieve), and the subjects of evaluation (people making those judgements), so that for any given behaviour, the valuations of it are likely to be influenced by the class position (and gender and race, etc.) of the valuers. On the way in which class inequalities affect moral judgement, Adam Smith commented:

> "This disposition to admire, and almost to worship, the rich and the powerful, and to despise, or at least, to neglect, persons of poor and mean condition, . . . is the great and most universal cause of the corruption of our moral sentiments." (Smith 1759:61).

Like sexism, racism, ageism and homophobia, class contempt and deference act as modifiers of aesthetic, performative and moral judgements of people and their actions, so that the same or similar actions are judged differently according to who does them; a working class drunk is judged more harshly than a middle class drunk. The judgements vary not only in relation to the behaviour itself, but also according to who makes the judgements and of whom they are made. Middle classness is seen not only as a matter of economic advantage, but also of moral superiority; the working class are repeatedly represented as deficient relative to the middle class (Skeggs 2004). To some extent, people, practices and institutions are evaluated simply in relation to their position in the social field. In UK English the pronunciation of the word "class" varies by class; the sound of the vowel functions immediately as a marker of the speaker's social class. Although, there is no good reason why a long *a* should be any better or more correct than a short *a,* the dominant classes claim that the former is "correct" or "received pronunciation"; they attempt to pass off the "posh" – that which is associated with high social class – as necessarily good, and the "common" – that which is associated with the working class – as necessarily inferior. Accents are therefore a medium of symbolic domination, determining who is valued and taken seriously and who is not. In a multitude of ways, the worth of people is taken to be not only a function of what they do or their character, but also of their position in the social field. Yet precisely because this involves double standards, it is vulnerable to questioning.

The distorting effects of structural inequalities on people's judgements can be found in the responses of those who are judged as well. A middle class egalitarian who expresses compassion for the poor risks being interpreted as condescending, for charitable sentiments do not remedy injustice; the poor are likely to want justice, not charity or pity. The latter reproduce and moralise the inequality: the charitable, compassionate dominant person is generous and benevolent, and the recipient is passive, dependent and expected to be grateful. The social field is therefore not just a space of relations and of struggles among the unequals, but a "force field" in which, as Bourdieu argued, the behaviour of each is affected by the force relations bearing upon them in their particular location.

A common feature of class relations is moral boundary drawing, or "othering". This is a process through which groups create a positive identity and sense of self-worth by distinguishing themselves from others onto whom they project qualities they despise or fear – in effect, saying "we are virtuous, they are bad". Maria Kefalas' study of a white working class community in Chicago shows how they valued self-discipline, honesty, patriotism, hard work and pride in home, garden and community. Lacking economic security and fearing slipping into poverty, they defined themselves in contrast to the blacks and poor whites of the inner city, who belonged to what they saw as a dangerous world of disorder, dereliction, fecklessness, ill-discipline, graffiti, filth, drugs and gangs – a world which supposedly posed a constant threat to their lives and their property values. Moral boundary drawing on class and race lines helped them create a reassuring world of moral simplicities. This made "...it difficult for [Beltway] dwellers to reconcile themselves to the existence of *white* teenage mothers, *white* homeless, *white* drug addicts, *white* gangbangers, *white* single mothers, and poor *whites*." (Kefalas 2003:155).[8] When two local teenager girls were murdered, it was immediately presumed that the killers were from the inner city; the trauma of the event was increased by the discovery that they were not, and in fact were local boys, and members of a local gang. This undermined the community's moral self-image. Moral boundary drawing is thus vulnerable to falsification.

Insofar, as people recognise the injustice of birth class and its longer-term effects, they may feel mixtures of guilt, resentment and defensiveness, and the balance of these feelings and the ways of handling them are likely to vary according to class position. Nevertheless, despite the major role of luck, individuals' subsequent fortunes might also be influenced by their own efforts and merits, and so, unsurprisingly, the better off and the upwardly mobile are likely to appeal to these as a defence against any (usually unspoken) feelings that they have merely been lucky in the lottery of birth class. Characteristically, the defensiveness takes the form of individuals making exceptions for themselves, acknowledging that while parental class position is a matter of luck, in their own case, and perhaps that of other similar people, their current adult position is a consequence of hard work and talent, and hence justifiable because deserved. These strategies are seen in some of the middle class people interviewed by Mike Savage, Gaynor Bagnall and Brian Longhurst in their study of class identities in northwest England (Savage et al. 2001). It is nevertheless only a partial defence of class inequalities, as it does not discount that luck is still *also* an influence on class and life chances, and does not deny altogether that these last into adulthood. Therefore, it is hardly surprising that many of the respondents were reluctant to identify their own class position and reacted ambivalently and defensively to questions about class. Insofar, as they evidently sense that luck and injustice characterise class, they find themselves wanting both to acknowledge its unfairness as a social structure and wanting to exempt themselves from complicity in it or from having gained unfair advantage because of it, indeed to claim credit for having apparently overcome it. Hence, in

---

[8] This is an example of intersectionality in terms of an interaction and mutual constitution between race and class. However, othering can occur without racialised divisions, simply on the basis of class differences (see, for example, Southerton 2002).

this case, their reluctance to class themselves is *not* coupled with a denial of the existence of class or of its arbitrariness with respect to the fortunes of others. They did not seem to suggest that they are good people because they are middle class, but that they have made it into the middle class (or stayed within it) because they are worthy people, even though not all middle class people are, and even though making it into the middle classes is not only the possible fate of the meritorious and worthy. In either case, there seems to be an implicit recognition that class is problematic. They are resisting not so much the fact of class as its propriety.

Not all reactions to class inequalities are so generous. The anger and contempt of the better off (including the more secure working class) for those who are dependent on state welfare is not only a reaction to having to pay taxes towards their upkeep, perceived as supporting those "unwilling to work", but also directed at their dependency, for this is seen as evidence of lack of self-discipline and dignity (Gilens 1999). While birth class is a matter of luck, the poor are typically expected to attempt to strive to escape from their unfortunate position. The upwardly mobile may on the one hand be admired for having overcome the disadvantages of a low class position, and on the other hand treated as evidence that class does not matter. In the ideology of meritocracy, the latter strategy is commonly coupled with a fallacy of composition, according to which, what is possible for a few individuals must therefore be possible for everyone simultaneously.

Moral concern in class societies tends to be directed mainly downwards, unless, that is, there is a more politicised sense of the unfairness of class itself. Affluent people who inherit their wealth and/or live off the labour of others are rarely seen as undeserving; the category "unearned income" (i.e., income based upon ownership of existing assets such as land, rather than production of goods and services) is seldom encountered today, having been replaced by the oxymoron "independently wealthy". Resentment of excessive wealth is not absent – witness contemporary antipathy towards "bankers bonuses" and CEO salaries - but it tends to be seen as an aberration or product of greed rather than a product of class power. In the UK, New Labour re-labelled the rich the "successful" – it being of course hard to object to success.[9]

One of the common false assumptions that lies behind many lay reactions to class and a common feature of lay morality is "the belief in a just world" (Lerner 1980). That is, a belief in the moral well-orderedness of the world, so that good intentions straightforwardly produce good actions with good effects, which in turn proportionately reward the actor, "giving them their due". Hence, the extent to which individuals' lives go well or badly is believed to be a simple reflection of their virtues and vices. The American Dream is an example of this belief. As a form of wishful thinking, it is understandable: who would not want a world in which virtue was rewarded and evil was penalised? However, it refuses to acknowledge the contingency and moral luck that disrupt such relations arbitrarily; more particularly it ignores the largely unintended effects of class and other axes of structural inequality. These structures add to the lack of moral well-orderedness in the world, and not only randomly, but

---

[9] Asked to clarify earlier comments that seemed to suggest that he thought economic inequalities were unimportant, Tony Blair, Britain's former Prime Minister replied: "What I meant by that was not that I don't care about the gap, so much as I don't care if there are people who earn a lot of money. They're not my concern. I do care about people who are without opportunity, disadvantaged and poor. We've got to lift those people but we don't necessarily do that by hammering the people who are successful." 'Blair does mind the wealth gap' *Guardian*, 24.3.2005 http://www.guardian.co.uk/politics/2005/mar/24/uk.election2005

also systematically and recurrently, so that the goods and bads tend to fall repeatedly on the same people. Therefore, there is a great deal of path dependence and cumulative causation in the reproduction of class and geographical inequalities (Fielding 1995). In explaining these persistent inequalities, the Right tends to appeal to random contingency as the main cause, while the Left appeals to structural causes.

Social surveys of moral values and attitudes show that most people in advanced capitalist countries think there is too much inequality, and this despite a common tendency to underestimate just how unequal society is (Osberg and Smeeding 2005, BSA 2008, Orton and Rawlingson 2007). However, they are not strongly egalitarian: in the UK, although most would favour an equal society, there is little (and falling) support for redistributive policies (BSA 2008). Manual workers tend to have more leftist views about economic distribution than the middle classes do, though the differences are smaller in the USA than in countries like Sweden where class and income redistribution have historically been prominent political issues (Svallfors 2006:166). In the British Social Attitudes Survey, when asked for their explanation of poverty, more said it was "an inevitable reality of modern life" than either those blaming individual failings or social injustice. Svallfors' comparative study of attitudes in Sweden, the UK, the USA and Germany found little difference in the attitudes of members of different classes towards market related inequalities, and surprisingly little working class opposition to private health care and education. However, working class attitudes to equality between men and women were less positive than were those of the so-called service class. The working class are more conservative about moral issues and less open to difference than are more educated people.

While many such results are unexpected, they are difficult to interpret, not least because people often appear to hold inconsistent beliefs, as in the case of believing that there should be less inequality but being against redistributive policies. What people say in answer to an abstract question might bear little connection to how they feel and think in the flow of everyday life. Qualitative research and ethnographies can reveal more of the complexities of people's views on such matters. For example, even though someone with low income and status might regard class as natural and unavoidable they might still feel uncomfortable and resentful about the way they are treated in particular situations where that treatment is a function of their class position. Although the ethnographic studies that reveal such complexities are inevitably selective, compared to surveys, they tell us much more about class and morality in terms of the moral texture of everyday life. Insofar, as people do wonder about the legitimacy and fairness of class and of their own class position, then they are likely to find conflicting sources of ideas to draw upon, from the socialist to the conservative. They may also feel the conflicting pulls of acknowledging the arbitrariness of class, and justifying the legitimacy of their own position. Resentment at injustice may feel painful and be looked upon unfavourably as a rationalisation of personal failure. By contrast, a person with a low income who willingly expresses acceptance of high incomes may appear generous. Through such pressures, politico-ethical challenges to basic class can be depoliticised and presented as matters of individual moral responses, taking class as natural and legitimate.

CONCLUSION

I have attempted to summarise a complex topic very briefly. There are further complexities that I have tried to deal with in my book, *The Moral Significance of Class* (Sayer 2005). The relationship between class and morality is structured but nevertheless complex, involving moral responses that both legitimise and resist class inequalities. If we are to understand them, we have to get beyond the demeaning subjectivist and conventionalist understandings of morality that have dominated sociology, and engage with everyday morality's responsiveness to the social world and how it affects well-being. We also have to resist the decline in the acknowledgement of class in public life and political discourse, and in social science itself. Like other axes of inequality with which it frequently intersects, and which recently have gained more acknowledgement, it is a form of injustice in that it results in people who in relevant respects are equal being treated unequally and having arbitrarily unequal life chances. It harms people's ability to flourish, and tends to distort their judgements of self and others and what is good or worthwhile.

Such evaluative judgements are not only subjective opinions, but also claims about what happens. To be sure they are fallible, but so too are more standard factual claims, so the objection that they are fallible "cancels all the way through". The fact-value distinction breaks down when we consider things like needs, well-being, suffering and flourishing – precisely the things that matter to us most. If we are to develop a better understanding of this, we therefore have to challenge the modernist attempt also to separate off evaluative from positive (descriptive, explanatory) understanding, a divorce which is institutionalised in the modern academic division of labour between moral and political philosophy or theory and sociology and other social sciences. Normative, or rather evaluative, thought, including moral or ethical matters, is not only a matter of convention or arbitrary opinion, but also a form of reasoning, which we have to take seriously, both to understand others' behaviour, and to decide how to behave ourselves. I have described some different ways in which people respond to class, particularly with regard to ethical matters. There is nothing deterministic about this and the issue of who thinks and responds in these and other ways is an empirical question still requiring much more research. In addition, even when such empirical questions are answered we still will have to *assess* people's responses: are they deluded about class?; are their responses primarily defensive or justifiable? However, class is also a normative concern for all of us.

REFERENCES

Aldridge, S. 2004. *Life Chances and Social Mobility: An Overview of the Evidence.* Prime Minister's Strategy Unit, Cabinet Office, London. Available at: http://www.number10.gov.uk/files/pdf/lifechances_socialmobility.pdf.

Alexander, J. C. 1995. *Fin de Siecle Social Theory.* London: Verso.

Archer, M. S. 2000. *Being Human.* Cambridge: Cambridge University Press.

Archer, M. S. 2007. *Making Our Way Through the World.* Cambridge: Cambridge University Press

Aristotle. 1980. *The Nicomachean Ethics.* Oxford: Oxford University Press.

Bourdieu, P. 1984. *Distinction: A Social Critique of the Judgement of Taste.* London: Routledge.

Bourdieu, P. 1987. "What Makes a Class?: On the Theoretical and Practical Existence of Groups." *Berkeley Journal of Sociology* 32:1–17.

Bourdieu, P. 2000. *Pascalian Meditations.* Cambridge: Polity.

Bourdieu, P. 1996. *The State Nobility.* Cambridge : Polity.

Bourdieu, P., and J.-C. Passeron. 1990. *Reproduction in Education, Society and Culture.* London: Sage.

British Social Attitudes Survey (BSA). 2008. *British Social Attitudes.* London: Sage.

Charlesworth, S. 2000. *A Phenomenology of Working Class Experience.* Cambridge: Cambridge University Press.

Erikson, R., and J. Goldthorpe. 1993. *The Constant Flux: A Study of Class Mobility in Industrial Societies.* Oxford: Clarendon Press.

Feinstein, L. 2003. Inequality in the Early Cognitive Development of British Children in the 1970 Cohort. *Economica* 70:73–97.

Fielding, A. J. 1995. Inter-regional migration and intra-generational social class mobility 1971–1991. In *Social Change and the Middle Classes,* edited by Savage M., and T. Butler. London: University College London Press.

Fraser, N. 1995. "From Redistribution to Recognition? Dilemmas of Justice in a 'Postsocialist' Age," *New Left Review*, no. 212, pp. 68–93.

Gilens, M. 1999. *Why Americans Hate Welfare: Race, Media and the Politics of Antipoverty Policy*. Chicago: Chicago University Press.

Gomberg, P. 2007. *How to Make Opportunity Equal*. Malden MA: Blackwell.

hooks, b. 1982. *Ain't I a woman?: black women and feminism*. London: Pluto.

Kain, P. J. 1991. *Marx and Ethics*. Oxford: Clarendon Press.

Kefalas, M. 2003, *Working-Class Heroes: Protecting Home, Community and Nation in a Chicago Neighbourhood*. CA: University of California Press.

Lareau, A. 2003. *Unequal Childhoods: Class, Race and Family Life*. CA: University of California Press.

Lamont, M. 1992. *Money, Morals and Manners: The Culture of the French and American Upper-Middle Class*. Chicago: Chicago University Press.

Lamont, M. 2000. *The Dignity of Working Men: Morality and the Boundaries of Race, Class and Imagination*. NY: Russell Sage Foundation and Harvard University Press.

Lerner, M. 1980. *The Belief in a Just World*. New York: Plenum Press.

Midgley, M. 1972. "Is 'Moral' a Dirty Word?". *Philosophy*, XLVII, 181:206–228.

Murdoch, I. 1970. *The Sovereignty of Good*. London: Routledge.

Murphy, J. B. 1993. *The Moral Economy of Labor*. New Haven: Yale University Press.

Nichols, S. 2004. *Sentimental Rules: On the Natural Foundations of Moral Judgment*. Oxford: Oxford University Press.

Nussbaum, M. C. 2001. *Upheavals of Thought: The Intelligence of Emotions*. Cambridge: Cambridge University Press.

Oakley, J. 1993. *Morality and the Emotions*. London: Routledge.

Orton, M., and K. Rawlingson. 2007. *Public Attitudes to Inequality*, Joseph Rowntree Foundation http://www. docstoc.com/docs/13435359/Public-attitudes-to-economic-inequality.

Osberg, L., and T. Smeeding, 2005. *"Fair" Inequality? An International Comparison of Attitudes to Pay Differentials*, Russell Sage Foundation Working Papers http://www.russellsage.org/programs/main/inequality/workingpapers/051025.267178 / Accessed 14.10.09.

Putnam, H. 2002. *The Collapse of the Fact-Value Dichotomy*. Cambridge, MA: Harvard University Press.

Reay, D. 1998a. "Re-Thinking Social Class: Qualitative Perspectives on Class and Gender." *Sociology* 32(2):259–275.

Reay, D. 1998b. *Class Work: Mothers' Involvement in Their Children's Primary Schooling*. London: University College London.

Savage, M., G. Bagnall, and B. Longhurst. 2001. "Ordinary, Ambivalent and Defensive: Class Identities in the Northwest of England." *Sociology* 35:875–892.

Sayer, A. 2005. *The Moral Significance of Class*. Cambridge: Cambridge University Press.

Sayer, A. 2007. "Dignity at work: broadening the agenda," *Organization*, 14(4):565–581.

Sayer, A. 2011. *Why Things Matter to People: Social Science, Values and Ethical Life*. Cambridge: Cambridge University Press.

Sennett, R. 2003. *Respect: The Formation of Character in a World of Inequalities*. New York: Alfred K. Knopf.

Sennett, R., and J. Cobb. 1973. *The Hidden Injuries of Class*. Cambridge: Cambridge University Press.

Skeggs, B. 1997. *Formations of Class and Gender: Becoming Respectable*. London: Sage.

Skeggs, B. 2004. *Class, Self, Culture*. London: Routledge.

Smith, A. 1759:1984. *The Theory of Moral Sentiments*. Indianapolis: Liberty Fund.

Smith, A. 1776:1976. *An Inquiry into the Nature and Causes of the Wealth of Nations*, edited by E. Cannan. Chicago: University of Chicago Press.

Southerton, D. K. 2002. "Boundaries of 'Us' and 'Them': Class, mobility and identification in a new town." *Sociology* 36(1) 171–193.

Svallfors, S. 2006. *The Moral Economy of Class*. Stanford, CA: Stanford University Press.

Taylor, C. 1967. Neutrality and political science. PP. 139–170 In *The Philosophy of Social Explanation*, edited by A. Ryan 1973. Oxford: Oxford University Press.

Walby, S. 2009. *Globalization and Inequalities*. London: Routledge.

Walkerdine, V., and H. Lucey. 1989. *Democracy in the Kitchen*. London: Virago.

Walkerdine, V., H. Lucey, and J. Melody. 2001. *Growing Up Girl: Psychosocial Explorations of Gender and Class*. Basingstoke: Palgrave.

Walzer, M. 1989. *Interpretation and Social Criticism*, Cambridge, MA: Harvard University Press.

Williams, B. 1985. *Ethics and the Limits of Philosophy*. Oxford: Oxford University Press.

Wright, E. O. 2004. *Class Counts*. Cambridge: Cambridge University Press.

Zigon, J. 2009. Morality: An Anthropological Perspective. Oxford: Berg.

CHAPTER 10

The Unstable Alliance of Law and Morality

Carol A. Heimer

INTRODUCTION: THREE POSSIBLE RELATIONS BETWEEN LAW AND MORALITY

Many big moral issues are simultaneously legal issues. Is abortion moral? Should abortion be legal? Can physicians be required to perform abortions even when they have religious objections to the procedure? Can states restrict young women's rights to have otherwise legal abortions by requiring parental notification? If abortion is legally restricted to protect the lives of fetuses, should women be held legally accountable for harming fetuses if they engage in risky but ordinarily legal behavior such as drinking or smoking or refusing medical treatment? We generally recognize the rights of adults to follow the dictates of their own consciences in such matters as refusing blood transfusions (which are forbidden by the Jehovah's Witnesses), but do parents have the right to refuse such treatments for their children? What if doctors believe that the child will die without treatment? Do terminally ill people have a moral right to choose to hasten their own deaths? Should physician-assisted suicide be legal? Is torture immoral? Should torture be illegal? Are marriages between people of the same sex moral? Should marriage be legally restricted to unions between men and women?

The relationship between morality and law can be decomposed into three separate but overlapping topics that are the subject of this essay: morality *and* law, the morality *of* law, and morality *or* law. First, some discussions are about morality *and* law. Although law is a very special kind of normative system, it nevertheless must co-exist with other normative systems. These overlapping normative systems sometimes support or reinforce each other but at other times are in fierce competition. When we think of law as one normative system among many, morality is one of the main languages people use to settle the competition. Fetuses are human beings and have a moral right to have their young lives protected, some believe, so the teaching of the Church is more morally correct than American law. Or, women have a right to make decisions about their own bodies, others believe, so Roe v. Wade is morally right and the Catholic Church is morally wrong. Although people may sometimes decide to follow laws that they regard as immoral, nevertheless a claim that is a law is immoral is one of the few legitimate justifications for deciding not to follow the law. In this way of thinking, then,

S. Hitlin, S. Vaisey (eds.), *Handbook of the Sociology of Morality*, Handbooks of Sociology and Social Research, DOI 10.1007/978-1-4419-6896-8_10, © Springer Science+Business Media, LLC 2010

morality operates on a different plane than other normative systems. Most normative systems prescribe courses of action, but use the language of morality to justify their prescriptions. In deciding which course of action is appropriate, people weigh the competing claims of law and other normative systems about morality.

But what then makes a legal system itself seem moral or immoral? What about the morality *of* law? Although some legal theorists have argued that morality is an inherent part of legal systems – that is, that a legal system is not really a legal system if it is immoral – others have disagreed, arguing that morality and law need to be kept separate. These ongoing debates have not kept social scientists from thinking about how lay judgments of the morality of legal systems are shaped by people's experiences with the law and legal actors. Do people believe it unethical and immoral to conduct a capital trial without ensuring that the defendant has a (competent) lawyer? Does felon disenfranchisement make a legal system seem less moral when we know that our legal system is so biased (in how the laws are written and applied) that a very high proportion of African American males spend some portion of their adult life in prison or jail? These are the kinds of questions about systemic fairness that can lead people to conclude that a whole legal system is fundamentally immoral.

Finally, whether or not people think that the law is moral, they may nevertheless feel considerable pressure to follow the law. Often these decisions are mediated by other entities such as people's employers, who instruct them on organizational policy, often reinforcing these prescriptions with blanket assertions that the law requires the organizationally prescribed course of action. They may in effect choose morality *or* law. Keeping a baby on a ventilator even though he is in a persistent vegetative state is legally required, staff members in an infant intensive unit may be told, as they were in the Linares case.[1] Over time, staff learn to ask what is legal rather than meditating on what is moral. Under some circumstances, people may feel that there is little point in thinking about what is moral because their behavior is so constrained by rules and regulations. In such cases, law seems to have displaced other normative systems and people may feel that they must choose law rather than morality or ethics.

When we think about the competition between law and other normative systems ("law *and* morality") and argue that morality is the standard adopted to adjudicate between law and other normative systems, we will suggest that law sometimes loses out because of its insistence on going by the book when other systems of norms can be more flexible. When we consider the morality *of* law, we will point out that law especially fails when an otherwise admirable standard of autonomy simply perpetuates an unfair system. And in thinking about the substitution of law for morality ("law *or* morality"), we will argue that law triumphs by allowing particular kinds of actors – mainly collective ones – to reduce costs by routinizing their responses, a problematic impulse when a nimble moral response to new problems or highly variable circumstances is needed.

Before moving on, let me be a little clearer about what I mean to include in "morality." Morality is about what people feel they ought to do; it is about distinguishing what people feel

---

[1] In this case the hospital legal counsel got the law wrong. See Fost (1989), Goldman et al. (1989), Gostin (1989), and Heimer (1999).

is right from what seems to them wrong.[2] People's sense of what is right comes from a variety of sources, including tradition, religion, professional codes of ethics, and even law (however, much this last assertion might distress legal philosophers). The words "morality" and "ethics" are often accompanied by adjectives naming normative systems to which they are linked – e.g., Buddhist morality or medical ethics. The linking of adjective and noun is essentially a rhetorical strategy, a claim made by representatives of normative systems attempting to shape people's moral judgments and decisions about how to act. As will become clear in my discussion of the relationship between law, normative systems, and morality, I take "normative" to be a broader term than "moral" (as does Smith 2003:8n1). And, as will also become apparent below, not only are we not talking simply about routines and habits, but we are also not talking only about the kind of reflexivity in which the second-order concepts of normative systems are used to reflect on and evaluate first-order reactions (Smith 2003:9, Hitlin 2008:36). Rather – or in addition – we are talking about the judgments that ultimately flow from competitions among the second-order evaluations derived from legal and moral codes. Thus, in this essay morality is conceived as a second-order concept or perhaps even a third-order concept.

MORALITY *AND* LAW

According to the lawyer, Karen Quinlan's parents "believe[d] that the earthly phase of Karen's life ha[d] drawn to a close" and that she should "be allowed to return to God with grace and dignity" (Lepore 2009:64). In April 1975, after returning from a party where she had several drinks and took some valium, Karen Quinlan had been helped to bed by friends, who found that she was not breathing when they returned to check on her a few minutes later. Despite resuscitation attempts, she never regained consciousness. As devout Catholics, the Quinlans accepted Pope Pius XI's teaching that Catholics should extend life only by ordinary means and in July they asked doctors to remove the ventilator. When the doctors (at St. Clare's, a Catholic hospital in Denville, NJ) refused, the Quinlans anticipated that they would need only to talk to the clerk and the judge to settle the dispute. Instead, Judge Muir appointed a guardian for Karen Quinlan. The case went to trial in October. Nine lawyers were present at the trial, including the parents' attorney, Karen Quinlan's court-appointed lawyer, the Attorney General for the State of New Jersey, and an attorney retained by the doctors. Although Karen's mother, her sister, and a close friend testified, most of those asked to offer their views were doctors. And when Judge Muir rendered his decision in November, he clearly signaled his view on who had the right to decide: "This is a medical decision, not a judicial one ... there is no constitutional right to die." Apparently, in his view, it was also neither a religious decision nor a familial one.

But competitions over the right to decide and the grounds for decision are not so easily closed off. The Quinlans appealed and, in March 1976, the Justices of the New Jersey Supreme Court reversed the lower court decision. They agreed that Karen's right to refuse medical

---

[2] My loose definition here is rather similar to that of Smith (2003:8, drawing on Taylor 1989), for whom morality entails "an orientation toward understandings about what is right and wrong, good and bad, worthy and unworthy, just and unjust, that are not established by our own actual desires, decisions, or preferences, but instead believed to exist apart from them, providing standards by which our desires, decisions, and preferences can themselves be judged."

treatment (and her parents' right to refuse it on her behalf) was constitutionally protected. But withdrawal of life-support was only acceptable if there was "no reasonable possibility" that Karen would emerge from her coma and return to a "cognitive, sapient state." The Justices assigned the job of assessing those odds to the hospital ethics committee.[3]

At one point or another in this sad story, the parents, the doctors, legal actors, and (indirectly) religious authorities each presumed that they could decide what to do. Yet in the view of the New Jersey Supreme Court, a morally convincing decision ultimately required contributions from all of these actors. And it required a discussion among them. As I will argue below, morality emerges from the competitions and collaborations of normative systems, including law. In such contestation, law plays two roles. Law is sometimes one of the competing normative systems. In the Quinlan case, a constitutionally protected right to privacy was offered as justification for parents to make decisions about their daughter's treatment. Simultaneously, legal actors function as arbiters in disputes over which normative system should prevail – here supporting the parents but assigning a role to the hospital ethics committee.

Legal Pluralism and Competition Among Normative Systems

In a famous debate with H.L.A. Hart over the relationship between law and morality, Lon Fuller (1958:635) charged Hart with adopting his predecessors' sloppy distinction between law and morality: "[T]he word 'morality' stands indiscriminately for almost every conceivable standard by which human conduct may be judged that is not itself law. The inner voice of conscience, notions of right and wrong based on religious belief, common conceptions of decency and fair play, culturally conditioned prejudices – all of these are grouped together under the heading of 'morality' and are excluded from the domain of law." For Hart, Fuller (1958:635) continued, morality seemed to be "all sorts of extra-legal notions about 'what ought to be,' regardless of their sources, pretensions, or intrinsic worth." Although Fuller was surely right that legal philosophers were (and are) more inclined to be precise about law than morality, one could argue that sloppy definitions of morality are appropriate because morality is in fact sloppy in the empirical world.

Ironically, though, it is far from clear that law can be defined any more precisely than morality. Boundaries that seemed clear to previous generations of sociolegal scholars, have become less rather than more distinct with new research. Legal pluralists – a group that has grown to include anthropologists, political scientists, the social norms theorists of behavioral law and economics, and now scholars of global legal pluralism (Berman 2009) – began initially by noting that multiple legal systems governed social life in colonial societies. Imposing colonial law in some spheres, colonialists were willing to leave other matters, such as family life, to be governed by indigenous law. Yet scholars soon noted that this layering of legal systems typically characterized advanced industrial societies as well as colonial societies. Moreover, the relations among legal systems were complicated in ways that sociolegal scholars had not initially understood. Plural systems are not always hierarchical, for instance. Rather than one

---

[3] Karen's doctors did not "pull the plug" but instead gradually weaned her from the ventilator. She was subsequently moved to a nursing home, where, fed through a tube, she lived for nine more years. Her parents visited daily.

legal system dominating the other, semi-autonomous legal systems sometime existed along-side one another. Rather than state or colonial law penetrating and altering indigenous law, scholars began to see the mutual influence of co-existing systems.

Especially important for this paper, scholars became interested in non-official normative orderings, sometimes even labeling these as non-state law. Griffiths (1986) suggests that only legal centralists, with their focus on formal law, any longer think that "law" can be distin-guished very easily from "non-law." Griffiths' own view is that law should be thought of as a continuous variable – that is, "all social control is *more* or *less* 'legal'" (1986:39).[4] Arguing that courts should be seen as only "one component of a complex system of disputing and reg-ulation" in which they are "not the only source of normative messages," Galanter (1981:17) urges that we "examine courts in the context of their rivals and companions." This, he contin-ues would require that we "put aside our habitual perspective of 'legal centralism,' a picture in which state agencies occupy the center of legal life and stand in a relation of hierarchic control to other, lesser normative orderings such as the family, the corporation, or the business network" (1981:17; reference and footnote omitted). Norms can be created by a variety of entities, working at different levels (they are therefore multi-scalar), serving a variety of pur-poses, and having can quite varying relations with state law. Of course something may get lost if we make no distinctions between law and other normative systems. As Merry (1988:878) asks, "Where do we stop speaking of law and find ourselves simply describing social life?"

Yet those arguing for an abandonment of legal centralism continue to recognize either explicitly or implicitly that state law has special power. It usually has more capacity to enforce decisions and it typically also has considerable cachet. Defining non-official normative order-ings as "forms of social regulation that draw on the symbols of the law to a greater or lesser extent, but that operate in its shadows, its parking lots, and even down the street in mediation offices," Merry (1988:874) emphasizes the connection between non-official forms of regu-lation and official state law. Along the same lines, Michaels (2009) suggests that we might instead ask "what people treat as law." He points out that for lawyers (and others, surely), "a distinction between law and other orders is crucial ... as long as the law treats legal and other norms differently" (2009:250, citing von Benda-Beckmann 2002). Although we would of course be interested in how lay people treat those norms that they believe to be law, it is also crucial that for official state law, designated categories of people who work with law – lawyers and judges – treat official law as different from non-official regulatory forms. The greater deference they accord to official norms makes law more "real" and more august and other norms less reputable and less authoritative. Characterizing judges as "jurispathic," for instance, Cover argues that "judges characteristically do not create law, but kill it" (1983:53). They are particularly inclined to "crush competing legal conceptions pushed by alternative nor-mative communities" (Berman 2009:230, summarizing Cover). Using the tools established by legal systems, legal actors thus have some substantial capacity to defang competitive sources of norms and decisions.

But these tools are not always sufficient to settle competitions among systems of norms. Sometimes when jurisdiction is shared, state law may not have any clear role to play.

---

[4] More recently, Griffiths (2006:63–64) suggests abandoning both the concepts of law and legal pluralism as a way of ending definitional wrangling.

Sometimes when other normative systems have representatives on the ground, there are no front-line legal actors. Sometimes the tools of law simply are not particularly useful or persuasive. The boundary between law and other normative systems is not nearly the bright line that scholars initially imagined. This presents no particular problem when systems of governance do not share jurisdiction, either because only one system is in fact present or because jurisdiction is clearly divided in some way, for instance by subject matter, personnel, or scale. But more often jurisdiction is either shared, and perhaps even shared with multiple legal systems, or not clearly divided. It is in these cases, I argue, that morality is especially likely to be the language in which the normative systems compete and through which "jurisdictional disputes" are settled.

Clusters (bunches, masses, knots, constellations) of normative orders are used as repertoires or tool kits to resolve moral questions. Because these interpenetrating normative systems frequently prescribe somewhat different courses of action, people often feel that being a moral person requires making some independent judgment about how to balance competing prescriptions. Morality is thus especially about the competition among the normative systems that come together in the families, religious bodies, professions, organizations, and states where people live their lives. The competition among normative systems does not work out the same way everywhere, though. Law is especially influential in some arenas and religion in others. Non-state law making is more important in some fields, formal legislation in others.

Normative systems are not all of a piece. Some of them claim jurisdiction over particular categories of people, others over specific geographical spaces; still others claim to regulate particular subject matters. They also vary in their claims about whether and how normative systems should share jurisdiction, some willingly conceding limits on their jurisdiction, others being more reluctant to make such concessions. Although legal systems do recognize that there are arenas in which they have little to say – systems of "liberties," for example – they do also tend to insist that when they speak, they are to be regarded as authoritative. If we conceive morality as especially concerned about the competition among normative systems, then we will be very interested in the boundaries between law, which tends to regard itself as hegemonic, and other normative systems and what happens in areas of overlapping jurisdiction.

The approach outlined above is not the one usually adopted by legal scholars. Instead, legal scholars have more commonly asked whether morality and law were essentially separate ways of thinking about what people should do or whether instead they were to some degree fused because proper law depended on an embedded morality (as is discussed below in the section on the morality of law). The answer offered here is that neither of these is quite right because morality is necessarily interstitial – not a normative system itself but a set of decisions produced and justified as a result of overlapping jurisdictions.

Taking this perspective – that concerns with morality come to the fore when a variety of normative systems share jurisdiction – leads us to look at that these jurisdictional issues from a variety of perspectives. I ask, first, where jurisdictional conflicts are especially likely to occur, and therefore where questions about the morality of law are especially likely to arise. In addition to law (and those who work with law) claiming jurisdiction, people sometimes come to law for answers and solutions, in effect creating conflicts that might otherwise not have been there. This can occur, for instance, because people think the law has something to say even when it does not, because they believe (often correctly) that the law can be enforced when other normative systems have fewer ways of making their prescriptions stick. Then I ask how these questions about conflicts between law and other normative systems tend to be resolved and what makes the resolution seems satisfactory or disturbing to people. I return to these questions about what makes legal solutions satisfactory in the section on the morality of law.

Moral Conundrums and Competing Normative Systems

A big moral issue is almost by definition one on which several groups disagree. It is often also one on which the state has taken a stand although, because the state is by no means a unified actor, the state may speak with an uncertain voice and a variable message. Contending groups often seek state support as a means to an end; having the backing of the law means being able to follow the dictates of one's conscience and even being able to force others to go along a larger share of the time because of the costs they would incur in breaking the law. Yet there are other times when the law is not just a means but an end in itself because the law carries moral authority.[5]

These collaborations and competitions between law and other normative systems over who can or should make the big moral decisions, including life and death decisions, are anything but rare. As death and birth moved from homes to hospitals, medical care providers inevitably became involved in decision making. The last half century's remarkable innovations in medical science have brought us dialysis, organ transplantation, improvements in care for trauma patients, good treatments for some cancers, and help with infertility and premature birth, to name but a few items on a long list. But as Bosk notes, "a technologically muscular medical science possesses on its own no wisdom about when and how it should be deployed" (1999:48). Someone needs to think about who should get replacement organs when they are in short supply, whether we really know enough about the long-term effects on women of the hormonal treatments associated with assisted reproduction, and whether infant intensive care units simply prolong dying for some babies. It was this gap that the hospital ethics committee was probably intended to fill in the Quinlan case, given that Supreme Court rejected Judge Muir's argument that the decision was essentially only a medical one. With dialysis came the Seattle "God Committee," charged with deciding who would receive this costly and scarce medical intervention (Alexander 1962, Fox and Swazey 2008). With early liberalization on abortion came committees to decide whether women met the limited criteria for legal abortions. And around the same time we got ethics committees and bioethicists, although, according to Gaines and Juengst (2008), it is unclear from the "creation myths" whether bioethics was born as a reaction to technical advances in biomedicine, as a proactive social movement within healthcare, or (more likely) both. Whether for good or ill, there is also "no shortage of procedures or moral experts able to speak to the questions on which science is silent" (Bosk 1999:48).

We understand that multiple legal systems (legal pluralism) are especially likely to exist under colonial conditions or their aftermath or where religious law co-exists with secular law. Those designing legal systems often attempt to work out a division of labor between multiple systems of rules, for instance relegating family disputes to indigenous courts or distinguishing

---

[5] States can also squander the moral authority of law. This is especially likely to happen in areas of heated disagreement when legislators misestimate the public sentiment or allow themselves to be captured by a particularly vocal minority. See the discussion below of the Baby Doe Laws.

between marriage (a religious matter) and civil unions (a legal matter). In practice, though, the division of labor between co-existing or competing systems of law tends to be tense and unstable. In the past, family law may have been relegated to indigenous courts, but feminists in countries like Uganda and South Africa, where polygyny is still common, look for legislative and even constitutional support for gender equality.

Legal pluralism is also by no means confined to colonial or post-colonial societies. Overlapping jurisdictions are surely the norm rather than the exception. They occur in ethnically and religiously plural societies, in societies with layered or partially layered legal systems, in societies with private systems of governance developed by organizations and associations, in situations where rules have to be formulated to cover new technologies and new social forms, and in trans-national systems (both public and private) where laws, rules, regulations, and standard operating procedures are created in one place and exported to quite different locales.

When law extends into new settings, new rules may be superimposed on existing rules or may displace them, but rarely is the transformation complete or the fit comfortable. Innovations in infant intensive care created new moral dilemmas, not easily addressed by existing law, religious doctrine, professional ethics, or family norms (Heimer and Staffen 1998, Heimer 1999). The Baby Doe Laws (prohibiting discrimination against handicapped infants) and the Child Abuse Amendments (prohibiting medical neglect of handicapped infants) were intended to fill the perceived legal vacuum and to correct alleged immoral practices of families and physicians. Yet these laws had little effect because the abuses they were intended to correct were in fact extremely rare. That kind of misunderstanding can occur when those crafting laws know little of the organizational rules and the professional norms of the setting in which the new laws are to be deployed. In contrast, the extension of law into new territories may have a greater effect when more versatile legal tools are adopted by local actors familiar with local problems and practices. In infant intensive care units, for instance, although the Baby Doe Laws had little effect, laws on child abuse and neglect had much more effect. With the help of hospital legal departments, physicians routinely use these legal tools to take temporary custody of infants to give life-saving treatments opposed by parents. In this contested moral terrain, doctors tend to prevail over religious bodies such as the Jehovah's Witnesses (who oppose the use of blood products) and even over parents. Over time, doctors and hospital legal staffs have developed a strong working relationship with courts. Professional ethics, organizational routines, and law have become intertwined; law has adapted to the timetables of medical emergencies and court is sometimes convened in the hospital. Doctors have become very skilled in using law to support their view of what is moral.

Blurred and contested boundaries between multiple systems of laws and norms create opportunities for moral, legal, and ethical entrepreneurs and for new professions dedicated to settling these disputes. New technologies made it possible for Karen Quinlan to survive for years, first with ventilatory support and then subsequently with only a feeding tube. Not everyone agreed that the early decisions of doctors were morally correct, but neither Karen's parents nor her doctors were able to make their moral vision stick without several prolonged discussions mediated by legal actors. One would like to think that these messy spaces of contestation and ferment create the possibility for dissent and for moral agency. If many authorities purport to govern some piece of the social terrain, then one important possibility is that no one controls it completely. Whether meaningful moral agency flourishes probably depends on where disputes occur. Spaces controlled by governments (e.g., prisons, government bureaucracies) or organizations (workplaces, hospitals) are surely less fertile ground for effective dissent. They may, however, be exactly the right soil for the new moral experts.

THE MORALITY *OF* LAW

According to Peter Mugyenyi, an internationally prominent Ugandan AIDS doctor and researcher, there have been "gross human rights violations against the poor simply because they were poor"; the world has "stood by and left people to die by the millions" of AIDS (personal interview, 2002). Generally legal scholars argue that the extension of the rule of law is an important antidote to human rights violations. Yet in healthcare, paradoxically, law has not always been an effective remedy. Rather than calling for the extension of law, Mugyenyi, for instance, felt compelled to break the law prohibiting import of cheap generics and joked that "My patients who take Cipla drugs don't know they are breaking the law" (Waldholz 2002:D6). In the view of many AIDS patients and the organizations that work with them, the law has all too often been on the wrong side. Although courts have sometimes decided against pharmaceutical companies and the World Trade Organization (WTO), people like Dr. Mugyenyi or Zackie Achmat (a South African AIDS activist) and the organizations with which they work (Doctors without Borders, Treatment Action Campaign, AIDS Law Project, etc.) clearly believe that the "gross human rights violations" that Mugyenyi mentioned were facil-itated rather than inhibited by the extension of law into new arenas. In Mugyenyi's view, the Ugandan court's offer to let him import drugs solely for his patients only compounded the immorality. The rules favored rich-country pharmaceutical companies and the poor-country patients typically had no way to bring their concerns before the WTO or even before the local courts or their National Drug Authority. The organizations that created and administered the rules were almost completely able to ignore the moral implications and very human effects – HIV deaths – that followed from just following the rules. Only when a powerful national actor (Mugyenyi) refused to go along, saying he would go to jail rather than accept the ruling, did anyone pay attention. With an eminent champion for poor-country patients, Ugandan patent law was reworked to be more even-handed.

The complaints of Mugyenyi, Achmat, and others boil down to a charge that the interna-tional legal system – here the treaty law of the World Trade Organization – is itself immoral because it represents itself as even-handed while systematically advantaging the rich and pow-erful. We turn now to what exactly people are doing when they put the legal system itself on trial and ask what makes law itself moral or immoral.

Legal Theory: Is Morality a Source for Law, an Element of Law, or Separate from Law?

It may be only in the imagination that "normative system" makes sense as a singular noun. Because religious bodies, professional groups, states, and peer groups are unlikely to speak with one voice on all moral questions, people struggle to reconcile the perspectives of the various groups to whom they feel some loyalty, who have jurisdiction, or who have some reason to weigh in. In infant intensive care units, as mentioned above, religious groups, families, medical professions, and the state all claim some right to participate in key decisions and sometimes disagree on such questions as whether "everything should be done" to save the life of a badly damaged child. In schools, education professionals replace medical workers, but otherwise the cast remains much the same, with the similar struggles over who gets to decide what children need. We could multiply examples ad nauseum, but the point is simply this: in whatever setting people confront moral dilemmas and puzzle over what course of action is morally correct, they are essentially certain to encounter multiple views, with some claims of moral authority likely grounded in religion and law. As sources of moral authority, religion and law are especially likely to insist on the primacy of the answers they offer. They are also often reluctant to accept the distinctions between morality and religion or morality and law that social scientists might advance.

Legal philosophers and legal theorists have written much about the relationship between law and morality. And although neither legal theory nor moral philosophy tells us much about how these differences are resolved, it is useful quickly to review these debates because questions about how much legality and morality overlap reappear in day-to-day discussions of moral matters.

The chicken-and-egg problem seems to pervade thinking about law and morality. On the one hand, morality is seen as the source for law – at least when it is "settled" morality. In such a vision, judges draw on a community's moral experience, extracting nuggets of wisdom and systematizing moral thinking. This, more or less, is the common law vision (Cotterrell 2000). Law remains grounded in the particularities of community life, generalized only as much as necessary. Morality, and thus law, is "empirical and historical" (Cotterrell 2000:12). The tie between morality and law is continually crafted and re-crafted by the judge in the daily practice of law. This is the vision of Durkheim as well, although he was writing in a civil law country. Durkheim (e.g., in *Division of Labor*) ([1833] 1984) argued that one might examine law to learn something about the moral precepts of a society. If the common law vision is that law distils the moral precepts of a community, the civil law vision, in contrast, sees law as a more consistent, deductive system in which legislators (more than judges) lay down a set of rules. In this vision, there is no necessary relation between law and morality, although law might function as a system that mediates between the disparate moral systems of communities that are all part of the polity governed by a particular system of law.

Alongside and analytically separate from the differences between civil law and common law legal systems are philosophies of law and jurisprudence such as legal positivism (e.g., Bentham, Austin) and legal realism (e.g., Holmes or Llewelyn), which make the case for what the relation between law and morality ought to be. Although legal positivists (including legal formalists) and legal realists agree that law is made by humans (so it's not "naturally" occurring), they differ especially on the determinacy of law and on the instrumental use of law, with legal realists arguing that the results of legal disputes are not fully determined by the law on the books (but depend on many other social factors) and that law should be an instrument to achieve desired social purposes. The 1958 debate between H.L.A. Hart (the positivist) and Lon Fuller (the realist) over the question of whether Nazi law, immoral as it was, could actually be considered law illustrates these different perspectives. Insisting that Nazi law was valid as law, Hart urged that the fact that it was law did not supply the answer about whether it should be obeyed: "Law is not morality; do not let it supplant morality" (1958:618). Fuller replied with an argument about the internal morality of law: "a dictatorship which clothes itself with a tinsel of legal form can so far depart from the morality of order, from the inner morality of law itself, that it ceases to be a legal system" (1958:660).

This debate over the morality of law continues into the present, as Fish (2009) points out in a *New York Times* editorial discussing President Obama's (realist) criterion that judges should be empathetic. Obama explains his views this way: "I view the quality of empathy, of understanding and identifying with people's hopes and struggles, as an essential ingredient for arriving at just decisions and outcomes." But as Fish points out, "just" and "legal" do not always go hand-in-hand: "A decision is just when it reflects an overarching vision of what is owed is to each man and woman. A decision is legal when it can be said to follow from established rules, statutes, precedents." Decisions that seem substantively just – moral, in short – are not always legally correct and vice versa. Obama is essentially adopting Fuller's view – that morality is (and should be) internal to law. Or perhaps his point is that the justices of Supreme Court should concern themselves with reconciling law and justice. When law and justice seem not to coincide, they, of all people, should try to do something to bring the two into alignment. Yet Hart's plea that law should not supplant morality (because they are really separate matters) seems equally urgent in an era when the reach of law has increased and legal ways of thinking have diffused to new areas. When medical students and medical caregivers seem especially inclined to ask "What is legal?", one wishes that Hart were there to remind them that they also must ask "What is moral?"

Fairness and the Autonomy of Law

Whether or not one accepts the view of Hart and others that morality and law are separate matters, questions about the morality of law itself are not going away. Even if we agree that an external moral compass remains important, we can nevertheless consider when legal systems are more likely to be morally acceptable to citizens, or in Obama's terms, when legal actors more likely to arrive at "just decisions and outcomes."

One might expect that fairness would be a prerequisite if people were to think that the law had any moral relevance as an impartial arbiter for settling disputes among people or resolving disagreements between competing normative systems. The independence of the legal system from other parts of the political system – legal autonomy – is a particular focus of those worrying about the morality and legitimacy of law. It is autonomy that creates the space for legal actors to listen to people and consider the merits of their cases without being swayed by the political power, social status, or economic clout of participants. But where should we look for fairness in a legal system? What does legal autonomy mean in practice?

Of course people are happier when legal decisions favor them, but fairness cannot be just about favorable outcomes. For a legal system to function, people have to be willing to accept judgments that go against them. According to social psychologists, people are in fact willing to accept negative decisions as long as they feel that the procedures were fair (Lind and Tyler 1988). And even when a legal system is not generally held in high regard, people continue to care about fair procedures. Assuming that Israeli courts would never find in their favor, Palestinians wanted at least a chance to be heard, Shamir (1991) finds. In otherwise unfair situations, a basic moral foundation of respect for human dignity and a willingness to listen to both sides of the story continued to matter. While the evidence suggests that people do care about procedural fairness, this does not mean that procedural fairness is the only thing that matters. Procedural justice apparently creates only a limited acceptance of unfavorable outcomes. Although it remains consequential, the effect of procedural fairness is smaller when people do not believe the law itself is legitimate (Murphy et al. 2009).[6] Judicial autonomy is a key part of the autonomy of the legal system, then, but it is by no means all of it. A legal system with considerable judicial independence may nevertheless lack legitimacy if people feel that the laws are biased in favor of one group or another.

Whether law and morality seem to have anything to do with each other probably depends partly on whether legal tools are selectively available to the rich and powerful or accessible by citizens from many social groups (a question raised by scholars interested in access to law), what exactly people see others doing with the law (Ewick and Silbey 1998), and whether the law helps address the questions that seem most morally pressing (Merry 1990). When law is seen as a tool by which the rich oppress the poor (as in Dr. Mugyenyi's comments cited above), when people see others treating the law as a game, or when people find that their concerns are not addressed by law, then law and morality are likely to seem like quite separate matters.

In *Invitation to Law and Social Science*, Lempert and Sanders (1986, esp. 401–475) look systematically at what makes a legal system fair. Conceiving legal autonomy as a variable, they acknowledge the complexity of law and the organizational and institutional settings in which it is created and deployed. We care, first, about the process of creating laws – for instance about whether citizens have more or less equal opportunities to participate in law creation and to shape the resulting laws. We might, for instance, have moral qualms about a legal system in which only propertied white men were able to participate in creating laws since we would not expect them to fairly represent the needs and interests of women and racial and ethnic minorities.

We also care about whether the laws generally treat groups more or less equally rather than favoring one group over others. That is, we care whether the laws are status-neutral. Depending on what kinds of assumptions they make, status-neutral laws can seem quite fair or quite unfair. For instance if they require similar actions (e.g., payment of a poll tax) from people with very different capacities to carry out those actions, status-neutral laws can exacerbate existing inequalities.[7] Likewise, distributively oriented laws often solidify existing inequalities (think of the laws of slavery) or redress imbalances (think of a progressive tax system).

Taken together, difference in capacities to participate in or influence the legislative process and variations in the tilt of the laws themselves create the set of legal endowments that are already in place when most people encounter the law. As a historical matter, unequal systems of participation and distributively oriented laws have tended to solidify the advantages of men over women (e.g., in the laws of coverture in which women lost many legal rights at marriage), white people over non-whites (e.g., black people were property to be bought and sold), and the upper over the lower classes (e.g., laws about imprisoning debtors). As Minow (1991) suggests in *Making All the Difference*, whether law and morality seem pretty much the

---

[6] This finding is based on three Australian studies, two on regulation (taxation and welfare fraud) and one on people's recent experiences with law enforcement. Given the substantive areas of these studies, it remains unclear how legitimacy modifies willingness to comply in substantive areas in which social movements spearhead programs of principled opposition and resistance.

[7] Perhaps the most elegant formulation of this point is France's (1984): "The law, in its majestic equality, forbids the rich as well as the poor to sleep under bridges, to beg in the streets, and to steal bread."

same depends partly on who the legislators had in mind when they were crafting the law. The less a social group is represented among legislators, the more likely it is that members of that group will feel that the law fits their circumstances so badly that violating the law is the only moral course.

When citizens finally arrive in the courtroom, they will already have encountered a legal system that can be stacked against them in several different ways. Under these circumstances, what is fair? In the abstract, a formalistic judicial stance is usually considered fairer than one that attends to substantive outcomes, and this is what the social psychological research (cited above) suggests. But impartial judicial decisions would do little to redress inequalities, for instance, if legal endowments (in either the law creation process or in the bias of the law or both) systematically favored one group over others. Would we then think it was fairer and more moral to even-handedly apply a law that favored one group or fairer to compensate for systematic biases in the law itself? Even if there were some provisions to ensure that such laws were applied fairly, we would probably not think such a system legitimate – at least not if the biases were pervasive. When a system is designed to favor one group over others, it helps only a little if the judges do not magnify the injustices by applying the rules so as to favor the already advantaged group even more.

In real legal systems, a variety of moral elements thus compete: even-handed treatment by judges, redress of inequalities, consistency and predictability, and so forth. People's moral judgments are surely simultaneously attentive to who gets to design the laws, whether the laws are designed to favor some groups over others, and how the laws are administered. Fairness in even one of these elements is surely better than fairness in none. But because the elements only rarely line up completely, moral evaluations of law are almost certainly about shades of gray rather than black and white. An external moral compass thus reminds citizens to keep prodding for fairness in each of these core elements. And most importantly, an external compass is crucial when the elements do align but align to create the "gross human rights violations" that Dr. Mugyenyi condemned.

MORALITY *OR* LAW

In some instances, there is strong pressure to ignore moral compasses. People are pressured (by employers, for instance) to adhere to the routines that are already in place and just get the job done without reflecting on the larger implications of their actions.

According to sociologist Robert Dingwall, the reuse of single-use surgical and anesthetic devices causes something like seven deaths a year in the UK and many more post-operative infections. The National Health Service [NHS] Patient Safety Research Programme commissioned Dingwall and his colleague Emma Rowley to figure out why this strictly prohibited practice persists. They designed "an online survey, using well-established techniques from criminology to encourage self-reporting of deviant behaviour, so that relevant staff in about 350 hospitals could complete the forms without us ever needing to leave Nottingham," Dingwall explains. But then things went awry because "a change in NHS ethical regulation meant that we needed approval from each site, potentially generating about 1600 signatures and 9000 pages of documentation. Although we never planned to set foot in any site, it would also have required my colleague to undergo around 300 occupational health examinations and criminal record checks. As a result, we were unable to carry out the study as commissioned and delivered a more limited piece of work" (2008:9). Dingwall grimly concludes that "[t]he ethical cost of the NHS [ethics regulation] system can be measured by the lives that will not be saved because our study could not investigate the problems of compliance as thoroughly as it was originally designed to" (2008:10).

However much we might wish to dismiss this case as anomalous, it is not. Two more examples illustrate the wide dispersion of ritualistic applications of rules. In the 1980s and early 1990s, American nursing homes quite commonly restrained residents, apparently believing they were protecting residents from harm and the nursing home from tort risk.[8] They also seemed to believe that it was easier and cheaper to care for restrained residents. Yet physically restrained residents actually require more care[9] and restraint raises rates of injury, causes (expensive to treat) pressure sores and increases incontinence, muscle atrophy, psychiatric disorders, and so forth. Only with the "Untie the Elderly Campaign" did restraint rates begin to drop from the late-1980s figure of 42% restrained (Braithwaite et al. 2007:85; the figure is 4% now). The contrasting visions of staff and residents could not be more striking. "Postural support" is the caring term used in official documents to describe restraint. Yet one 84-year-old woman, describing the pain and indignity, said she had been "tied down like Jesus on the cross" (Braithwaite et al. 2007:84). But the main point is that for staff and QA managers, this was all a matter of routine: "better safe than sorry, better to do too much than too little . . . best to train the aides with a simple standard rule" (Braithwaite et al. 2007:85).

Blood donation has long had moral overtones and organizations collecting and storing blood products treat both donors and their blood with considerable respect (Titmuss 1971, Healy 2006). FDA rules prohibit "overbleeding" plasma donors. But although taking too much blood or taking it too frequently can harm donors' health, it does not affect the quality of blood plasma. Yet in one stunning example cited by Bardach and Kagan (2002:83), the FDA rules could hardly have done a better job of offending moral sensibilities. When the FDA discovered that one plasma collection facility had overbled its donors, it closed down the facility and placed an embargo on its blood. As a result of a series of mistakes or accidents by several different organizations, 1000 units of embargoed blood were shipped to a pharmaceutical company where they were mixed with 2000 other units. The FDA then embargoed all 3000 units and fined the pharmaceutical company. Although the plasma facility seems to have been at fault for overbleeding donors, the subsequent shipment (by the plasma center) and mixing of the plasma (by the pharmaceutical company) seem to have been honest mistakes. The director of regulatory affairs at the pharmaceutical company was generally supportive of safety regulations, but not of this particular decision, which seemed to him in "characteristic of the FDA's 'increasingly bureaucratic attitude' of rule for rule's sake" (Bardach and Kagan 2002:83). Such waste of donors' "precious" contributions seems particularly foolish in the moralized economy of blood donation.

Following the rules in these three cases led to the wrong result – no vulnerable research subjects were protected, but a strong research design was weakened; elderly nursing home residents were harmed physically and psychologically; good blood products were wasted and an unfortunate signal sent about husbanding scarce resources. Even when rules have the most

---

[8] The material on restraint of nursing home residents is drawn from Braithwaite et al. (2007:82–87).

[9] This is with the appropriate statistical controls for level of impairment and so forth.

admirable purposes, they hardly ever fit all of the cases to which they are applied. A competition with other norms often leads to more moral outcomes because assumptions and motives are challenged, evidence is examined, and mismatches are brought to light. But, as I argue below, competitions among norms may be especially unlikely to occur when organizations seek to avoid legal accountability by insisting that workers rigidly follow the rules.

Organizations as Moral Actors

Typically what people think about when they consider the effect of law on morality is its influence on moral judgments. But it is surely fair to say that law's influence on other parts of the "stuff" of morality is equally or perhaps even more profound because we are less aware of it. Abend (2010) argues that moral stuff is more than just judgments of the sort that neuroscience investigates. In particular, because morality is about "thick" rather than "thin" judgments it is not really possible to separate the descriptive elements from the evaluations that are fused together in thick ethical concepts.[10] Thus ethics cannot be unvarying across social and cultural contexts because the "descriptions" that are part and parcel of core ethical concepts will necessarily vary. But, in any case, we are not just interested in the moral judgments that people make but in how they act on those judgments. And those actions are deeply shaped by the organizational and institutional contexts in which moral judgments are formulated, encoded in norms and rules, acted upon, assessed, justified, reconsidered, and recorded and disseminated.

These observations are particularly important, I argue, because the relationship between law and morality varies from one organizational and institutional context to another. Since Durkheim, it has been a commonplace among sociologists that morality is rooted in collective life. But if our collective lives are now more shaped by and lived in organizations than they were in the past (Coleman 1974, 1990), then we need to ask whether there is some reason to expect that the relationship between law and morality would be different in organizations than in other parts of the social landscape.

Two lines of research suggest that organizations might indeed draw more heavily on the law or legal reasoning than on other moral authorities in resolving moral dilemmas. First, rules resolve uncertainties and allow organizations to make and implement plans. And, even though they may take their sweet time about it, legal systems are more able than other moral codes to resolve uncertainties definitively (Stinchcombe 2001), perhaps partly because their decisions apply to entire societies and so span boundaries between disparate entities including religious groups, families, occupational and professional groups, organizations and industries, and even municipalities and states. Although the evidence suggests that there has not actually been any increase in litigiousness, people seem to believe that litigiousness has increased and are willing to go to a lot of effort to avoid costly legal battles (Haltom and McCann 2004, Baker 2005). In such a climate, being morally right seems less important than being legally right, and organizational routines are built around practices that are legally defensible, whether they are morally defensible or not.

---

[10] Abend (2010) contrasts such thick ethical concepts as integrity, piety, cruelty, rudeness, exploitation, and fanaticism with thin ones such as right and wrong.

Organizational analysts also suggest, secondly, that in recent decades organizations have become more "legalized" (Meyer 1983, papers in Sitkin and Bies 1994, Sutton et al. 1994, Heimer et al. 2005). Although regulation by states is an important element of this legalization, legalization also changes the way organizations define themselves and others and shapes the procedures they adopt for getting things done.[11] At the most basic level, the law plays an important part in the social construction of actors. By giving legal recognition to corporations, cooperatives, partnerships, and categorizing natural persons by such things as citizenship, age, marital status, or membership in an occupation, the law endows actors with rights and shapes the way they interact. But the legalization of organizational life has extended the reach and influence of law deep into the interior of organizations as they adopt legalistic reasoning, procedures, forms, and structures. In the institutionalists' view, this adoption of legal forms and structures may not be explicable by the instrumental advantages it brings. Instead, it is a more political project, mainly bringing the legitimacy that comes with doing what others expect you to do. As Meyer notes, the introduction of these legalistic procedures is often not an especially orderly process. Instead, it "violate[s] the routinized order and chain of command" and "introduce[s] new rules without their integration into the established set" (Meyer 1983:218–219).

The legalization of organizations has thus muted the voices of other normative orders, perhaps because they offer less certainty, perhaps because they confer less legitimacy. If Meyer is right that legalization is not really about integrating rule systems, then law may speak with a louder voice simply because it has silenced or displaced other voices, not because people are persuaded that it gives better answers than those rendered by other moral authorities.

Even in heavily legalized organizations, though, some people are more subject to rules than others. As a general matter, people who are higher up in organizations make the rules – and are more able to bend them. They sit on ethics panels that reflect on abstract principles; they can debate and disagree; they can sometimes choose between competing courses of action. People who are lower in organizational hierarchies usually must follow the rules even if that means doing something that they believe to be wrong – and if they do find ways around especially cumbersome or dysfunctional rules, they are careful not to advertise this fact. They do not usually get to choose among courses of action, but instead do what their bosses tell them to do. They face serious moral issues, but without the autonomy to make any choices. "Powerful people," Chambliss observes, "have ethical dilemmas; the rest of us have ethical problems" (1996:118).

But this is really only a first cut on how morality is transformed when it is filtered through organizations. Moral questions are first transformed into ethical questions – matters on which professions and other collectivities legitimately reflect and speak rather than matters for the (alleged) individual conscience. But as we know, although professional codes of ethics may codify the moral principles of a professional group, they also serve to burnish a profession's image and protect its reputation for altruism. Organizational rules add another layer of codification, and employees are expected to abide by organizational codes of ethics and organizational policy. This does not mean that people cease to have their own moral reactions, but

---

[11] Scott (1994) refers to these as the definitional and interactional environments, in contrast to the more commonly discussed regulatory environment.

only that there is little role for individual morality in most organizations. This also does not mean that people are not troubled by moral and ethical questions or that they always agree with organizational policy, but rather that their responses are made essentially irrelevant by the obligation to follow the rules. Responsibility for moral action is shifted from individuals to groups ("the staff . . .") and abstract rules ("it's organizational policy that . . ."). Although the organization becomes the effective moral actor, as Chambliss (1996) notes, it remains an odd kind of moral actor. Irresponsibility is "organized into" the complex divisions of labor of "seemingly remote organizations" (Mills 1951:111) because those who are able to see the moral consequences of organizational policy are usually not the ones empowered to make or revise the rules. Organizational ethics displaces individual morality and organizational ethics tends to be highly legalized and defensively oriented to avoiding litigation.

Regulation of Research Ethics

To see in more detail what happens when heavy-handed systems of regulation displace other normative systems, we turn to the example of institutional review boards (IRBs) and the regulation of research ethics.[12] Until fairly recently, research on human subjects was been governed primarily by the ethical codes of professional associations (in medicine and in various social sciences). After the Second World War, governments began to play a larger role in the regulation of human subjects' research. This increased government oversight is usually explained as an attempt to compensate for the failures of unofficial regulatory systems, with a series of scandals offered as evidence of previous regulatory failure. Undoubtedly there were some lapses – the Nazi medical experiments being the most obvious and heinous instance of research abuse. Yet a close investigation shows that the historical record has been mischaracterized. Harms to research subjects were (and are) rare and typically modest; harms attributable to researcher misconduct were (and are) even rarer (Levine 1988, Hamburger 2004, Burris and Moss 2006, Dingwall 2006, Bledsoe et al. 2007).[13] The moral and regulatory traditions of clinical researchers were often quite robust and had been in place for some time (Lederer 1995, Halpern 2004). And some research projects characterized in hindsight as abusive did not seem morally wrong to either researchers or research subjects at the time (see, e.g., Shweder 2004 on the Tuskegee syphilis study). It is also far from obvious that more stringent regulation would

---

[12] This section draws on Heimer and Petty (2010).

[13] Although the point is stated in simple summary form here, we should acknowledge that research is not all of a piece. Some kinds of research are more dangerous and others less. For instance, phase 1 clinical trials (testing the safety of new drugs) are probably riskier than phase 3 trials (to assess the effectiveness of drugs) but phase 1 studies involve small numbers of subjects and phase 3 trials are often large multi-center studies, thus the overall risks may balance out. There are more bad outcomes in research on people who are desperately ill, but of course that is partly because of the illness. Observational research is essentially risk-free because it involves no interventions. Social science research typically carries no physical risk whatever. Misconceptions about the dangers of research probably arise partly from the availability effect (our tendency to remember the most vivid cases) associated with press reports of injuries and abuses and partly from our failure to think about the full panoply of human subjects research when we make quick assessments of danger. To reinforce the general point, we note that even the Office of the Inspector General did "not claim that there are widespread abuses of human subjects" (Office of the Inspector General 1998:iii).

have prevented the worst abuses. The concentration camp experiments occurred despite pre-war German regulations, which were "as strict and comprehensive as the post-war Nuremberg Codes" (Grodin 1990:4) and with the support of the Nazi government.

Moreover, what evidence there is suggests that costs of the current regulatory system are very high indeed.[14] Some of these costs are general administrative costs, including the expenses of staffing the departments that write policy, develop tracking and training programs, provide staff support for review panels, and interface with other parts of the university and with federal agencies. Other administrative costs accrue to research projects: the salaries and time of people who prepare documents, track submission dates, and file forms for periodic review, for updates associated with changes in protocols, or (much less commonly) about adverse events. To this must be added the very substantial and recurring costs of documentation. On top of this we should remember the costs of ethics education for research project staff members and the increasingly common additional layer of certifications and accreditations for university and research center ethics review staff and programs.[15] Beyond these administrative costs, there are the additional costs of participating in the consent process for the subjects and the staff. We tend to think of these as minor, but in some instances the forms are lengthy or the procedures complicated (e.g., because research subjects are not literate). It is not uncommon to have special visits just to get through consent procedures.

And now finally we arrive at the really serious costs: research delayed, derailed, refor-mulated, or shut off even before it is fully conceived (Bledsoe et al. 2007, Hamburger 2007, Johnson 2008). But let us be clear here: the problem is not just the inconvenience to scholars or the costs to their careers. Rather, the cost is in students not trained to do research (because the impediments imposed by IRB are too formidable to navigate in the space of a class), questions not investigated (because the topics are deemed too sensitive by IRBs or the research sub-jects are categorized as vulnerable), registries not created, comparisons and sites dropped, and research findings delayed or not produced at all. Because research on human subjects is how we produce the innovations that improve health, reduce morbidity and mortality, and alleviate human suffering, preventing or delaying research results in vastly more suffering and death than occurs from researchers' ethical lapses. The litany of complaints by outraged researchers is long (for some examples, see Hiller et al. 2005, Burris and Moss 2006, Clark et al. 2006, Green et al. 2006, Coe 2007, Dyrbye et al. 2007, Gawande 2007). To say that the cost in human life is substantial is no exaggeration. Even after the 1993 moratorium on resuscitation research (in response to concerns about informed consent) was lifted and parallel regulations on consent procedures were put in place, US research remained at low levels compared to the European Union. As Hiller et al. (2005:1095) explain, the sharp decrease in clinical cardiac arrest research conducted in the US meant delays in the introduction of new therapies and

---

[14] The literature on this is extensive, though mostly it documents one or another of the elements. For examples, see: Burris (2008) and Zywicki (2007), who summarize other research; Green et al. (2006) who comment on a multi-site observational study.

[15] See the recommendations of the National Bioethics Advisory Commission (2001:vii) urging the development of education, certification, and accreditation systems. IRB professionals can now be certified as CIPs (Certified IRB Professionals) or CIMs (Certified IRB Managers). One organization that offers such certifications is Public Responsibility in Medicine and Research (PRIM&R). The Association for the Accreditation of Human Subjects Protection Programs, Inc. (AAHRPP) accredits programs themselves. Undoubtedly there are or will shortly be other accrediting bodies in this rapidly growing field.

"...a one-year delay of a new therapy that improves survival by 1% may cost approximately 3,000 lives." There were also costs to life and health when OHRP shut down the use of the checklists to combat catheter-related infections in intensive care units on the grounds that data were being collected as part of the program[16] and when IRBs delayed the creation of a national fatal asthma registry (Clark et al 2006).

The objective in this discussion of the regulation of research ethics is to show what happens when organizations shift from considering what is morally right – weighing the pre-scriptions of one normative system against those of another – to uncritically adopting what they believe is legally required. The argument here is that when legal systems refuse to compete with other normative systems, they leave no space for careful weighing of risks, poten-tial harms, and potential benefits. Rather than being elevated, moral discourse is degraded. Ritualistic legally based regulation of research ethics makes research less ethical. The biggest ethical lapse in American regulation of human subjects' research is the death and suffering that has resulted from slowing the pace and altering the focus of research and squandering research funds.

The main regulatory apparatus that has been put in place in the US is the institutional review board (IRB). Although there is a statutory basis for the regulatory system and a gov-ernment body responsible for overseeing the work of IRBs,[17] most of the day-to-day regulatory work is carried out by the IRBs of universities and research centers. IRBs operate under guide-lines issued by the Office of Human Research Protections (OHRP), which is housed in US Department of Health and Human Services. Although they are given some substantial latitude in crafting policies at the local level, in fact most IRBs are exceedingly attentive to signals from OHRP. OHRP has given mixed signals about the independence of IRBs. During some periods, it has urged IRBs to use their discretion and even chided them for being over-zealous. At other times, though, OHRP has conducted random audits and scolded IRBs for being lax (Halpern 2009).

Universities are research institutions; it is not news that they care about research produc-tivity and about funds to support research. But research has become increasingly expensive and universities have become increasingly dependent on federal research dollars to support their research programs and research training (Bledsoe et al. 2007). It is a truism of organi-zational sociology that organizations orient to the parts of their environments on which they are dependent (Pfeffer and Salancik 1978, Scott and Davis 2007). Research universities work hard to garner government research funds (as well as funds from private sources), investing in research infrastructure and administrative units that help secure and manage grants. Because OHRP has the capacity to shut down a university's research if it finds violations, universities

---

[16] Pronovost et al. (2006) present the first research results from the study; Gawande (2007) discusses OHRP's decision to shut down the program; and OHRP (2008) responds to Gawande's editorial.

[17] In 1974, the National Research Act (Pub. L. 93–348) created the National Commission for the Protection of Human Subjects of Biomedical and Behavioral Research [of the Department of Health and Human Services (DHHS)], which issued the Belmont Report in 1978. The guidelines and statements of principle contained in the Belmont Report gradually acquired the force of law in the US in the late 1970s and early 1980s when 45 CFR 46 subparts A–D were adopted, requiring ethics review of all human subjects research funded by the US government and creating the IRB system to carry out those reviews. In 1991, 14 other federal agencies and departments joined DHHS in adopting a uniform set of rules (Subpart A of 45 CFR 46, the Common Rule) to govern research on human subjects; in 1995, an executive order required that the CIA also comply with these rules. Eventually research funded by the US government but conducted outside the US was also brought under the same body of rules.

bend over backwards to signal compliance with ethics rules. That there have been only a few instances of such suspensions of university research programs seems not to matter much. Risk management practices often misestimate the magnitude of risk.[18] Risk management necessarily traffics in uncertainties and unknowns. It often contains a hefty dose of fantasy, as Clarke (1999) has demonstrated, although sometimes it is the risks that are fantasies (e.g., in human subjects research) and sometimes it is the solutions that are fantasies (e.g., programs to deal with oil spills or to evacuate urban areas in the event of nuclear accidents or nuclear war).

The cornerstone of research ethics is informed consent. Most biomedical and social scientists would argue that in any long-term research project, informing participants about the research and securing their consent are ongoing processes. Yet IRBs focuses attention on the informed consent document rather than on the process. Ethical research thus gets operationalized as research in which research subjects have signed documents that conform to the increasingly rigid specifications of OHRP. Modifications of informed consent forms are the most common revision requested by IRBs, although it is not clear that the revisions improve readability (Gray et al 1978, Bell et al. 1998, Hammerschmidt and Keane 1992, Paasche-Orlow et al. 2003). No one checks whether research subjects understand the research and have freely agreed to participate or what their reasons are for wishing to participate. Apparently research subjects treat informed consent as yet another bureaucratic routine, not so much part of decision-making as part of implementing a decision already made (Zussman 1997; Fisher 2009, especially 178). Oversight focuses on the forms themselves, documentation, failures to file forms on time, and so forth (Burris and Welsh 2007, Gunsalus 2004). When researchers get into trouble it is not over the principles of beneficence, autonomy, and justice that undergird OHRP regulations. Rather, the "determination letters" that signal trouble are especially likely to be about documentation because "counting is replacing substantive ethical review" (Gunsalus 2004:372), a phenomenon that Power (1997) would surely recognize.

We are by now several layers removed from anything of direct relevance to the spirit of research ethics. With the professionalization of research ethics administration and the development of training programs and programs to accredit the ethics programs of universities and research centers, IRBs have shifted from concern with risks to research subjects to concern with risks to universities and their funding streams. If anything, formal ethics review provides "such a distraction from the real difficulties that we face and from the real ethical dilemmas that confront us that we may not recognize and discuss the serious and elemental because we are so busy with the procedural and bureaucratic" (Bosk and De Vries 2004:260). And because for a university or research center, the focus is on keeping the machinery of research running, "Is it legal?" matters much more than "Is it moral?"

CONCLUSION: MORAL AGENCY

The moral landscape described above is considerably more complex than that envisaged by moral philosophers. Rather than being populated by individuals or small groups who brood over moral questions, it now includes a variety of collective actors. Of course there is still room

---

[18] See, for instance, Douglas and Wildavsky's (1982) analysis of why differently constructed groups pay attention to different kinds of risk and Baker's (2005) evidence that doctors and healthcare organizations vastly over-estimate the number of medical malpractice suits and so over-protect themselves with malpractice insurance.

for moral agency but moral agency now often requires a sophisticated crafting of responses to options reshaped by organizations and institutions.

Morality is a social accomplishment. We teach it to our children, we demand that people account for their actions in the light of prevailing moral standards, we consider whether moral standards are appropriate and how the moral standards of one group compare with those of another. But, contrary to the impression one gets from many discussion of the topic, morality these days is often an organizational and institutional accomplishment as much as an individual one. Many of the goals we pursue and actions we take are filtered through organizations and institutions, and they help assemble the toolkits that we employ in pursuing moral purposes. Among the most important of the tools in the organizational-institutional moral toolkit is law, although of course it, like other tools, can be used for both moral and immoral purposes.

As people contemplate moral questions, they often draw on the language and thinking offered by religious groups, legal systems, their families or ethnic groups, and professions or workgroups with which they are affiliated. In this, the participants in the dilemmas featured in this essay – the Quinlans, Dr. Mugyenyi, the nursing home workers and residents, biomedical and social scientists, plasma donors and collection facilities, parents and staff in infant intensive care units – were probably quite typical. Morality, for these people, was not exactly the prescriptions of religious bodies, the rules of their employers, or the requirements of law. In fact, those norms, rules, and laws could be immoral and could stifle moral thinking and prevent people from acting morally. Here I have tried to show how morality, a second-order phenomenon, grows from the encounter between law and other normative systems. When systems of rules clash, morality is the best we can do.

Acknowledgment I am grateful to Arthur Stinchcombe and Steve Hitlin for their timely and very helpful comments.

REFERENCES

Abend, G. 2010. "What's New and What's Old About the New Sociology of Morality?" (this volume).

Alexander, S. 1962. "They Decide Who Lives, Who Dies: Medical Miracle Puts a Moral Burden on a Small Community." *Life* 53(November 9):102 ff.

Baker, T. 2005. *The Medical Malpractice Myth*. Chicago: University of Chicago Press.

Bledsoe, C. H., B. Sherin, A. G. Galinsky, N. M. Headley, C. A. Heimer, E. Kjeldgaard, J. Lindgren, J. D. Miller, M. E. Roloff, and D. H. Uttal. 2007. "Regulating Creativity: Research and Survival in the IRB Iron Cage." *Northwestern University Law Review* 101:593–641.

Bardach, E., and R. A. Kagan. 2002 (1982). *Going by the Book: The Problem of Regulatory Unreasonableness*. New Brunswick, NJ: Transaction Publishers.

Bell, J., J. Whiton, and S. Connelly. 1998. *Evaluation of NIH Implementation of Section 491 of the Public Health Service Act, Mandating a Program of Protection for Research Subjects*. Final report prepared for the Office of Extramural Research National Institutes of Health. Arlington, VA: James Bell Associates.

Berman, P. S. 2009. "The New Legal Pluralism." *Annual Review of Law and Social Science* 5:225–242.

Bosk, C. L. 1999. "Professional Ethicist Available: Logical, Secular, Friendly." *Daedalus* 128:47–68.

Bosk C. L., and R. G. De Vries. 2004. "Bureaucracies of Mass Deception: Institutional Review Boards and the Ethics of Ethnographic Research." *Annals of the American Academy of Political and Social Science* 595(September):249–263.

Braithwaite, J., T. Makkai, and V. Braithwaite. 2007. *Regulating Aged Care: Ritualism and the New Pyramid*. Cheltenham, UK: Edward Elgar Publishing.

Burris S. 2008. "Regulatory Innovation in the Governance of Human Subjects Research: A Cautionary Tale and Some Modest Proposals." *Regulation and Governance* 2:65–84.

Burris, S., and K. Moss. 2006. "United States Health Researchers Review Their Ethics Review Boards: A Qualitative Study." *Journal of Empirical Research on Human Research Ethics* 1(2):39–58.

Burris S., and J. Welsh. 2007. "Regulatory Paradox: A Review of Enforcement Letters Issued by the Office for Human Research Protection." *Northwestern University Law Review* 101:643–685.

Chambliss, D. F. 1996. *Beyond Caring: Hospital, Nurses, and the Social Organization of Ethics*. Chicago, IL: University of Chicago Press.

Clark, S., A. J. Pelletier, B. E. Brenner, D. M. Lang, R. C. Strunk, and C. A. Camargo. 2006. "Feasibility of a National Fatal Asthma Registry: More Evidence of IRB Variation in Evaluation of a Standard Protocol." *Journal of Asthma* 43(1):19–23.

Clarke, L. 1999. *Mission Improbable: Using Fantasy Documents to Tame Disaster*. Chicago: University of Chicago Press.

Coe, F. L. 2007. "The Costs and Benefits of a Well-Intended Parasite: A Witness and Reporter on the IRB Phenomenon." *Northwestern University Law Review*. 101:723–733.

Coleman, J. S. 1974. *Power and the Structure of Society*. New York, NY: W.W. Norton.

Coleman, J. S. 1990. *Foundations of Social Theory*. Cambridge, MA: Harvard University Press.

Cotterrell, R. 2000. "Common Law Approaches to the Relationship Between Law and Morality." *Ethical Theory and Moral Practice* 3(1):9–26.

Cover, R. M. 1983. "The Supreme Court, 1982 Term – Foreword: Nomos and Narrative." *Harvard Law Review* 97:4–68.

Dingwall, R. 2006. "An Exercise in Fatuity: Research Governance and the Emasculation of HSR." *Journal of Health Services Research and Policy* 11(4):193–194.

Dingwall, R. 2008 "The Ethical Case Against Ethical Regulation in Humanities and Social Science Research." *21st Century Society* 3:1–12.

Douglas, M., and A. Wildavsky. 1982. *Risk and Culture: An Essay on the Selection of Technological and Environmental Dangers*. Berkeley: University of California Press.

Durkheim, É. 1984 (1893). *The Division of Labor in Society*. Translated by W.D. Halls. New York: Free Press.

Dyrbye, L. N., M. R. Thomas, A. J. Mechaber, A. Eaker, W. Harper, F. Stanford Massie, Jr., D. V. Power, and T. D. Shanafelt. 2007. "Medical Education Research and IRB Review: An Analysis and Comparison of the IRB Review Process at Six Institutions." *Academic Medicine* 82:654–660.

Ewick, P., and S. S. Silbey. 1998. *The Common Place of Law: Stories from Everyday Life*. Chicago, IL: University of Chicago Press.

Fish, S. 2009. "Think Again: Empathy and the Law." NYT blog, May 24, 2009. http://fish.blogs.nytimes.com/2009/05/24/empathy-and-the-law/.

Fisher, J. A. 2009. Medical Research for Hire: *The Political Economy of Pharmaceutical Clinical Trials*. New Brunswick, NJ: Rutgers University Press.

Fost, N. 1989. "Do the Right Thing: Samuel Linares and Defensive Law." *Law, Medicine, and Health Care* 17: 330–334.

Fox, R. C., and J. P. Swazey. 2008. *Observing Bioethics*. New York: Oxford University Press.

France, A. 1984. *The Red Lily*. Trans. Winifred Stephens. New York: Dodd, Mead.

Fuller, L. L. 1958. "Positivism and Fidelity to Law: A Reply to Professor Hart." *Harvard Law Review* 71(4):630–672.

Gaines, A. D., and E. T. Juengst. 2008. "Origin Myths in Bioethics: Constructing Sources, Motives and Reason in Bioethic(s)." *Culture, Medicine*, and Psychiatry 32:303–327.

Galanter, M. 1981. "Justice in Many Rooms: Courts, Private Ordering, and Indigenous Law." *Journal of Legal Pluralism and Unofficial Law* 19:1–47.

Gawande, A. 2007. "A Lifesaving Checklist." *New York Times*, December 30, 2007.

Goldman, G. M., K. M. Stratton, and M. D. Brown. 1989. "What Actually Happened: An Informed Review of the Linares Incident." *Law, Medicine, and Health Care* 17:298–307.

Gostin, L. 1989. "Editor's Introduction: Family Privacy and Persistent Vegetative State." *Law, Medicine, and Health Care* 17:295–297.

Gray, B. H., R. A. Cooke, A. S. Tannenbaum. 1978. "Research Involving Human Subjects." *Science* 201: 1094–1101.

Green, L. A., J. C. Lowery, C. P. Kowalski, and L. Wyszewianski. 2006. "Impact of Institutional Review Board Practice Variation on Observational Health Services Research." *Health Services Research* 41:214–230.

Griffiths, J. 1986. "What Is Legal Pluralism?" *Journal of Legal Pluralism and Unofficial Law* 24:1–55.

Griffiths, J. 2006. "The Idea of Sociology of Law and Its Relation to Law and to Sociology." *Current Legal Issues* 8:49–68.

Grodin, M. A. 1990. "The Nuremberg Code and Medical Research." *Hastings Center Report* 20(3):4.

Gunsalus, C. K. 2004. "The Nanny State Meets the Inner Lawyer: Overregulating While Underprotecting Human Participants in Research." *Ethics and Behavior* 14:369–382.

Halpern S. A. 2004. *Lesser Harms: The Morality of Risk in Medical Research.* Chicago: University of Chicago Press.

Halpern S. A. 2009. "Professional Autonomy and the Regulatory State: Social and Behavioral Sciences Confront Federal Human-Subjects Policies." Paper presented at Annual Meeting of the American Sociological Association, San Francisco.

Haltom, W., and M. McCann. 2004. Distorting the Law: Politics, Media, and the Litigation Crisis. Chicago: University of Chicago Press.

Hamburger, P. 2004. *"The New Censorship: Institutional Review Boards." Supreme Court Review 2004:271–354.*

Hamburger, P. 2007. "Getting Permission." *Northwestern University Law Review* 101:405–492.

Hammerschmidt, D. E., and M. A. Keane. 1992. "Institutional Review Board (IRB) Review Lacks Impact on the Readability of Consent Forms for Research." *American Journal of Medical Sciences* 304:348–351.

Hart, H. L. A. 1958. "Positivism and the Separation of Law and Morals." *Harvard Law Review* 71(4):593–629.

Healy, K. 2006. *Last Best Gifts: Altruism and the Market for Human Blood and Organs.* Chicago: University of Chicago Press.

Heimer, C. A. 1999. "Competing Institutions: Law, Medicine, and Family in Neonatal Intensive Care." *Law and Society Review* 33:17–66.

Heimer, C. A., and L. R. Staffen. 1998. *For the Sake of the Children: The Social Organization of Responsibility in the Hospital and the Home.* Chicago, IL: University of Chicago Press.

Heimer, C. A., and J. C. Petty. 2010. "Bureaucratic Ethics: IRBs and the Legal Regulation of Human Subjects Research." *Annual Review of Law and Social Science* 6. Forthcoming.

Heimer, C. A., J. C. Petty, and R. J. Culyba. 2005. "Risk and Rules: The 'Legalization' of Medicine." PP. 92–131 in *Organizational Encounters with Risk*, edited by B. Hutter, and M. Power. Cambridge, UK: Cambridge University Press.

Hiller, K. M., J. S. Haukoos, K. Heard, J. S. Tashkin, N. A. Paradis. 2005. "Impact of the Final Rule on the Rate of Clinical Cardiac Arrest Research in the United States." *Academic Emergency Medicine* 12:1091–1098.

Hitlin, S. 2008. *Moral Selves, Evil Selves: The Social Psychology of Conscience.* New York, NY: Palgrave Macmillan.

Johnson, T. S. 2008. "Qualitative Research in Question: A Narrative of Disciplinary Power With/in the IRB." *Qualitative Inquiry* 14:212–232.

Lempert, R. O., and J. Sanders. 1986. *An Invitation to Law and Social Science: Deserts, Disputes, and Distribution.* Philadelphia, PA: University of Pennsylvania Press.

Lederer, S. E. 1995. *Subjected to Science: Human Experimentation in America Before the Second World War.* Baltimore, MD: Johns Hopkins University Press.

Lepore, J. 2009. "The Politics of Death." *The New Yorker*, November 30:60–67.

Levine, R. J. 1988. *Ethics and Regulation of Clinical Research*, 2nd Ed. New Haven, CT: Yale University Press.

Lind, E. A., and T. R. Tyler. 1988. *The Social Psychology of Procedural Justice.* New York, NY: Springer.

Merry, S. E. 1988. "Legal Pluralism." *Law and Society Review* 22:869–896.

Merry, S. E. 1990. *Getting Justice and Getting Even: Legal Consciousness Among Working-Class Americans.* Chicago, IL: University of Chicago Press.

Meyer, J. W. 1983. "Centralization of Funding and Control in Educational Governance." PP. 179–198 in *Organizational Environments: Ritual and Rationality*, edited by J. W. Meyer, and W. R. Scott. Thousand Oaks, CA: Sage.

Michaels, R. 2009. "Global Legal Pluralism." *Annual Review of Law and Social Science* 5:243–262.

Mills, C. W. 1951. *White Collar: The American Middle Classes.* London: Oxford University Press.

Minow, M. 1991. *Making All the Difference: Inclusion, Exclusion, and American Law.* Ithaca, NY: Cornell University Press.

Murphy, K., T. R. Tyler, and A. Curtis. 2009. "Nurturing Regulatory Compliance: Is Procedural Justice Effective When People Question the Legitimacy of the Law?" *Regulation and Governance* 3:1–26.

National Bioethics Advisory Commission (NBAC). 2001. *Ethical and Policy Issues in Research Involving Human Participants, Vol. 1: Report and Recommendations of the National Bioethics Advisory Commission.* Bethesda, MD: National Bioethics Advisory Commission.

Office of the Inspector General (OIG), DHHS. 1998. *Institutional Review Boards: A Time for Reform.* OEI-1-97-00193. Washington, DC: DHHS.

OHRP (Office for Human Research Protections). 2008. OHRP Statement Regarding the New York Times Op-Ed Entitled "A Lifesaving Checklist." http://www.hhs.gov/ohrp/news/index.html. Viewed March 13, 2010.

Paasche-Orlow, M. K., H. A. Taylor, and F. L. Brancati. 2003. "Readability Standards for Informed-Consent Forms as Compared with Actual Readability." *New England Journal of Medicine* 348:721–726.

Pfeffer, J., and G. R. Salancik. 1978. *The External Control of Organizations: A Resource Dependence Perspective.* New York: Harper and Row.

Power, M. 1997. *The Audit Society: Rituals of Verification.* Oxford, UK: Oxford University Press.

Pronovost, P., D. Needham, S. Berenholtz, D. Sinopoli, H. Chu, S. Cosgrove, B. Sexton, R. Hyzy, R. Welsh, G. Roth, J. Bander, J. Kepros, and C. Goeschel. 2006. "An Intervention to Decrease Catheter-Related Bloodstream Infections in the ICU." *New England Journal of Medicine* 355:2725–2732.

Shweder, R. A. 2004. "Tuskegee Re-examined." http://www.spiked-online.com/Articles/0000000CA34A.htm.

Scott, W. R. 1994. "Law and Organizations." PP. 3–18 in *The Legalistic Organization,* edited by S. B. Sitkin, and R. J. Bies. Thousand Oaks, CA: Sage.

Scott, W. R., and G. F. Davis. 2007. *Organizations and Organizing: Rational, Natural, and Open System Perspectives.* Upper Saddle River, NJ: Pearson Prentice Hall.

Shamir, R. 1991. "Litigation as a Consummatory Action: The Instrumental Paradigm Reconsidered." *Studies in Law, Politics and Society* 11:41–67.

Sitkin, S. B., and R. J. Bies, eds. 1994. *The Legalistic Organization.* Thousand Oaks, CA: Sage.

Smith, C. 2003. *Moral, Believing Animals: Human Personhood and Culture.* New York: Oxford University Press.

Stinchcombe, A. L. 2001. *When Formality Works: Authority and Abstraction in Law and Organizations.* Chicago: University of Chicago Press.

Sutton, J., F. Dobbin, J. Meyer, and W. R. Scott. 1994. "Legalization of the Workplace." *American Journal of Sociology* 99:944–971.

Taylor, C. 1989. *Sources of the Self: The Making of the Modern Identity.* Cambridge, MA: Harvard University Press.

Titmuss, R. 1971. *The Gift Relationship: From Human Blood to Social Policy.* New York: Pantheon.

von Benda-Beckmann, F. 2002. "Who's Afraid of Legal Pluralism?" *Journal of Legal Pluralism and Unofficial Law* 47:37–82.

Waldholz, M. 2002. "African Crusaders Savor Wins in AIDS War but Need Funds." *Wall Street Journal* (Eastern edition). June 13, 2002:D6.

Zussman R. 1997. "Sociological Perspectives on Medical Ethics and Decision-Making." *Annual Review of Sociology* 23:171–189.

Zywicki, T. J. 2007. "Institutional Review Boards as Academic Bureaucracies: An Economic and Experiential Analysis." *Northwestern University Law Review* 101:861–895.

CHAPTER 11

Morality in Organizations

ROBERT JACKALL

This analytical account of morality in organizations is based on years of fieldwork studying key occupational and professional groups in a wide range of private and public bureaucracies.[1] The approach is descriptive, not normative. The essay asks: what rules guide the denizens of big organizations in their occupational lives and why?

The specific details of moralities always vary with the markets, industries, and functions of particular organizations. Outsiders usually catch fleeting and partial glimpses of these moralities only when they generate events that draw publicity. Thus, industrial corporate managers' decisions to close or relocate plants, or contest new occupational health and safety regulations, or market products despite scientific studies purporting to demonstrate, say, environmental risks always become regional and sometimes national news. A public morality play invariably follows with advocates condemning or defending managers' decisions, the rationales provided for them, and the moral frameworks that underpin them. Exactly similar scenarios play out when financial firms give big bonuses to executives even when they have run their firms aground; when the United Teachers Federation of New York City refuses to allow the firing of incompetent or sexually predatory school teachers and demands instead that the city's taxpayers sustain them at full salaries and benefits in "rubber rooms" where they do nothing (Brill 2009); when the Speaker of the House of Representatives uses military jets to ferry twenty-one members of Congress, along with some of their spouses and children, to Copenhagen for a climate summit at substantial costs to taxpayers while millions of Americans are unemployed and the national debt and federal budget deficits skyrocket; when police detectives trick criminal suspects into admissions of culpability thus violating publicly embraced notions of "fairness"; when intelligence agencies use water boarding to extract information

[1] This includes intensive fieldwork with: office workers in a large bank (Jackall 1978); corporate managers in several major corporations (Jackall 1988); whistleblowers in thirteen different organizations, both private and public (Jackall 2007); account executives, art directors, and copywriters in more than two dozen advertising agencies, as well as with public relations practitioners in a few large agencies (Jackall and Hirota 2000); uniformed police and police detectives in two big-city police departments (Jackall 1997, 2005); both state and federal prosecutors (Jackall 1997, 2005); faculty, staff, and administrators in big universities and small colleges; congressional staff; and federal counterterrorism officials. I draw as well on fieldwork with men and women in financial industries (Jackall 2009). In this essay, I focus on the higher echelons of big organizations because men and women in these strata decisively shape the ethos of their occupational worlds. I wish to thank Duffy Graham and Janice M. Hirota for their careful readings and critiques of this essay.

S. Hitlin, S. Vaisey (eds.), *Handbook of the Sociology of Morality*,
Handbooks of Sociology and Social Research, DOI 10.1007/978-1-4419-6896-8_11,
© Springer Science+Business Media, LLC 2010

when interrogating terrorists; or when the US Secretary of the Treasury and the Chairman of the House Ways & Means Committee are unmasked as tax scofflaws. Such peeks into normally opaque worlds provide great opportunities for bombastic punditry and sardonic humor, but they rarely get at the underlying structure of organizational morality. They fail to illuminate the rationality and logic of such choices within the ethos that dominates big organizations.

AUTHORITY AND MORALITY

Bosses determine the moral rules-in-use – the day-to-day occupational ethics that actually guide behavior – of subordinates in big organizations. Bosses set goals for their underlings and evaluate subordinates' efforts toward achieving these goals. Typically, there are no fixed standards for measuring work performance because everything depends on bosses' interpretations of subordinates' work. Thus, talent and hard work do not necessarily lead to organizational rewards. Goals are also changeable and are regularly reformulated. When bosses change goals, whether because of exigency, whim, or the shrewd exercise of self-interest, they devalue the previous work of their charges and start new rounds of probation for them. Further, especially in the corporate world, bosses themselves are changed with regularity due to organizational shakeups – the larger the corporation the more frequent the reorganizations. New bosses appoint men and women they trust to key positions and institute their own goals and their own criteria for judging underlings. Despite their external appearance of stolidity, big organizations are houses of cards, marked by a profound social psychological sense of contingency.

The exercise of authority in big organizations, always morally freighted, varies dramatically depending on organizations' purposes and functions and on the kind of people drawn to them. For instance, militaries are command organizations, top to bottom. Semimilitary units such as the police blend a command structure for civil-service ranks (typically sergeant, lieutenant, and captain) with a highly politicized hierarchy of upper ranks of inspectors and chiefs who serve entirely at the pleasure of a commissioner, who is usually appointed by an elected mayor. Corporations exhibit wide ranges of behavior in the exercise of authority from whip-snapping to chummy cajoling. Advertising agencies are governed by administrators who, in league with research and media professionals, interface with clients to discern clients' needs and, more important, their desires. These account executives and research/media allies try to harness the creativity of copywriters and art directors. The regular wars in ad agencies always pit the forces of business rationality against the expertise possessed by these "creatives," who actually produce the visual and verbal symbols that pervade our public culture. Bosses in organizations with many professional experts often rule by instituting forums that pass for decentralized self-government. Through these forums, bosses launch initiatives in response to needs articulated by different factions in the organization, establishing elaborate new committees to carry out those initiatives. Typically, those committees work long and hard to produce reports and recommendations. Bosses receive these with acclaim and appreciation, and then promptly move on to address new crises with yet new committees. The recommendations are put into a drawer or passed on to still other committees for consultation. Most recommendations soon become distant memories. The constant turmoil of committee work presents images of democratic and decentralized management. In fact, those images cloak bosses' centralized control.

Whatever style they employ, bosses always govern organizations for their own benefit and that of their key associates. They pack the hierarchies below them as well as boards of trustees nominally above them with associates who understand this fundamental principle of organizational governance. They frame action agendas and the parameters of legitimate discussions about them. They institute systems that separate performance and pay, as illustrated by executive salaries in good times or bad. They reward friends and punish those who oppose them. Over time, they come to believe that they deserve the good fortune that their organizational success has brought them.

THE BUREAUCRATIC ETHOS

The demons of bureaucracy shape everyday morality in big organizations. Consider some typical moral rules-in-use that emerge directly out of the hierarchical, compartmented, and segmented world of bureaucracy.

1. Bureaucracies' hierarchical structure binds superiors and subordinates in reciprocal fealty relationships. Subordinates must be loyal to their bosses. Therefore, they defer to their bosses in public; never go around their bosses; keep their bosses closely informed about anything that touches on their bosses' interests; and make sure that their bosses never are blindsided, because knowledge or its appearance is crucial to maintaining authority. Loyal subordinates allow their bosses to appropriate credit for their work and, if necessary, subordinates fall on their swords to protect bosses from authority-injuring blame for minor mistakes. In return, bosses have obligations to loyal subordinates. They run interference for these underlings with other bosses and they protect them, as much as possible, during the regular upheavals of organizational life. If all goes well, bosses take loyal subordinates along for the ride when they themselves are promoted.

2. In most US organizations, yesterday is ancient history. Despite constant upheavals, big organizations typically do not have reliable tracking systems to fix responsibility for decisions and actions. The boss of a sector receives the credit or blame for major success or disaster on his watch whether or not he had a hand in the triumph or failure. In the case of failure bosses try to escape responsibility by blaming others for catastrophes that occur on their own watch. The paradigm of the practice is in the political realm. One blames one's predecessors in office or, failing that, one's subordinates. Recent US political administrations have elevated the practice of blaming others to an art form. The success of this strategy depends on factors extraneous to actual decisions or performance in office, such as whether politicians are blessed with the celebrity star power that now passes for charisma.

3. Bureaucracies separate men and women from the consequences of their actions. Thus, managers need never meet workers now unemployed by decisions to move factories abroad; sales directors need never encounter people injured by the products their sales forces sell; New York or London investment bankers need not explain their wizardry, primary allegiance to self-interest, or sheer incompetence to Icelanders bankrupted by them. This disconnection between action and consequences fosters thinking in the short-term instead anticipating the long-run organizational/institutional results of

decisions. It also fosters thinking in abstractions, a habit of mind that facilitates rational/technical assessments of labour, capital, financing, and other factors of production, and is akin to the political pursuit of ideological goals without regard for their human costs.

4. The disconnection between action and consequences also leads to an ethos of rapid upward mobility in order to outrun one's mistakes. But promotion carries dangers as well. One can find oneself in the wrong place at the wrong time and being blamed for others' mistakes. The ideal, of course, is to rise quickly to a position where one has the power to blame others for one's own mistakes.

5. Bureaucracy also fosters the avoidance of responsibility. Shrewd and ambitious denizens of large organizations shun making important decisions until they absolutely have to be made. At that point, choices are invariably limited and, more often than not, the decision "makes itself." Even then, one still involves as many people as possible in the decision-making process to obscure responsibility in case things go south. Big organizations are vast systems of organized irresponsibility.

6. At the same time, the exigencies of law, regulation, and public expectations demand public rhetorics of upright moral probity and stewardship. Adeptness at inconsistency - the ability to think one thing and say another, to tailor talk for different audiences, to invent multiple explanations for acting on exigencies, to "walk back" public gaffes[2] - becomes an essential occupational virtue in big organizations. Only those men and women skilled at doublethink and doublespeak have the chance to burst out of the crowd and rise to the top.

7. To hone the skills of doublethink and doublespeak in up and coming personnel, big organizations regularly employ external interpretive experts adept at constructing fictive realities and concomitant vocabularies. These interpretive experts perform several functions: they school their charges in the use of euphemisms that cloud hard realities; they teach the use of fronts, the Potemkin Villages that disguise real interests; and, most importantly, they preach the art of symbolic reversal, the ability to turn one's opponents' arguments upside down. The ethos of interpretive experts has at its core several premises. These are: there is no such thing as "truth" even in a minimalist Aristotelian sense; everything is infinitely interpretable; and exigency always takes precedence, but must be cloaked with accounts - explanations, excuses, and justifications - suitable for placating different important audiences. This ethos comes to rule the top echelons of big organizations and pervade those circles' public communications, spoken and written, to both internal and external audiences.[3]

---

[2] "Walk back" is a neologism for denying or modifying what one or one's aides have stated in public. The British equivalent is "row back."

[3] Take, for example, the Department of Defense's report (2010) on the terrorist atrocity at Fort Hood that killed 13 people on 5th November 2009. The report does not even mention by name Major Nidal Malik Hasan, the sole suspect in the shooting, nor does it mention Hasan's increasingly aggressive public espousal of Islamist doctrine and rhetoric before the attack. Such sanitization marks most bureaucratic documents. In this regard, the mainstream press closely resembles government bureaucracies on many issues. For instance, one finds exactly one article in the *New York Times*, years after the event, and none at all in the *Washington Post* about the horrific rapes and murders of Channon Christian and Christopher Newsom in Knoxville, Tennessee [see the extensive reporting on this crime by Jamie Satterfield of the *Knoxville News Sentinel*], though similarly heinous crimes, with the race of victims and perpetrators reversed,

SELF-RATIONALIZATION

Corporations, nonprofit foundations, police departments, and congressional offices alike want as managers or top staff men and women who are smart, quick-witted, well-dressed, cool-under-pressure, ambitious team players willing to subordinate themselves to their bosses' judgments, capable of discerning "what has to be done" in particular situations, and adroit enough to avoid trouble or to extricate themselves from it quickly. They are also morally flexible, able to change direction in a hurry, and able and willing to live with the constant ambiguity that ever-shifting norms produce.

Many young people with these attributes and orientations gravitate to the big organizations that dominate modern economies and polities. These recruits find themselves in hierarchical frameworks with interlinked layers of men and women gradually bound to each other, at least provisionally, through personal and social ties, common work experiences, and political alliances. When these ambitious men and women realize that their fates are in others' hands, their resultant anxiety causes them to look up and look around. They turn toward their bosses, powerful cliques, and upwardly striving peers for cues on the public faces, interior attitudes, and habits of mind that will best position them for success in their worlds because only those who adopt this stance get ahead.

This is a voluntary process. Men and women after the main chance submit themselves to this regimen and internalize the ethos of their organizations because they want the power, money, and prestige that come with big organizational success. One looks for, recognizes, and internalizes the premiums stressed in a given organization or situation. Then one moulds one's public face, external behavior, and projection of attitudes, all to fit the expectations embedded in those premiums in the hopes of garnering the rewards promised.

Not everybody wants to or can do this. Some professionals' first loyalties are to the ethos of their professions, not that of big organizations. Whistleblowers, for example, typically invoke their adherence to professional, instead of organizational, ethics as explanations for their dissents. The committed denizens of big organizations usually condemn such rationales as evangelical nonsense irrelevant to real-world exigencies. Other men and women drop out of big organizational life entirely or accept fixed roles in organizations that do not require relentless subjection of themselves to others' expectations.

But there are always some people, including many professionals, who do respond to organizational premiums for self-rationalization and they make themselves into the men and women that their organizations desire and require. Such voluntary self-rationalization produces, frames, and paces the deepest internalization of organizational goals, creating relatively enclosed social worlds that cause people to bracket moralities they might adhere to in their homes, churches, or other social settings.[4] Occupational rules-in-use gain ascendancy over

---

are always widely reported. Compare these major newspapers' non-treatment of the Christian/Newsom rape-murders to their nearly obsessive coverage of the accusations against members of the Duke University men's lacrosse team, charges that proved to be wholly fabricated by the purported victim and pursued recklessly by a rogue district attorney. Newspaper editors, like government bureaucrats, see American society through certain templates. Facts that do not fit inside those frameworks are regularly ignored.

[4] Much more empirical research needs to be done on the bracketing of general moralities in order to conform to the rules of specific occupational milieux. In observing and interviewing professional criminals, for instance, one sees

more general ethical standards. Moral choices become inextricably tied to organizational fates. Organizational moralities are thus highly specific and situational.[5]

Those who persevere in the self-rationalization necessary for self-remaking and the internalization of specific and situational moral rules-in-use are highly self-conscious men and women who know how to guard their emotions and expressions of sentiment. They shield their selves from others. The demons of ambition, coupled with the need to display that ambition to others as signal or warning, make most organizational players into narcissists who see themselves as lead actors in a drama as they simultaneously watch that drama as lead critics from front-row seats. The boldest among them become shameless self-promoters who seek every opportunity to announce the coincidence of their own self-interest with that of bosses.

Advocacy groups, pundits, professors, and others frequently claim that some groups are endowed with ascribed personal qualities that enable them to transcend and transform the bureaucratic ethos described above. Many feminists, for instance, claim that women's cooperative natures foster a collaborative exercise of authority. To test this claim empirically, one need go no further than US colleges and universities, all now as thoroughly bureaucratized as corporations, to explore in depth the question of how female managers and professionals behave in organizations. Because women were largely excluded from the upper levels of corporations until fairly recently, they entered the academy in great numbers and became a powerful force there, especially in the humanities and social sciences and in various deans' offices. What does one find in the academy? Particularly apt examples are internal political struggles involving, say, gender or sexual orientation study programs or promotion of colleagues who specialize in these matters. In such cases, one readily observes the same patterns commentators on university settings have noted for over a century when men dominated the academy[6], that is, cronyism based on personal affinities and shared perspectives and the consequent abandonment of universalistic criteria for judging the work of colleagues or prospective hires. This includes the approbation of specious scholarship if it conforms to requisite "progressive" norms and mobilization of bloc voting to enforce one's group's will and destroy perceived enemies. It also means adeptness at inconsistency, particularly the use of moralistic rhetoric to keep opponents off balance and on the defensive; ceaseless claims on the resources of institutions for marginal programs that mirror one's own intellectual predilections; and, of course, the requisite ruthlessness necessary to triumph in organizational struggles.

---

the phenomenon in sharp terms. Armed robbers, drug dealers who use violence as a business tool, and drug-trade hit men are often good husbands, lovers, fathers, and friends. They talk about their work and the moral rules-in-use that govern it with objective dispassion, reflecting their view of its separate place in their life-worlds. For instance, Francisco Medina, known on New York City streets as Freddy Kreuger, pleaded guilty in the Southern District of New York federal court to 14 assassinations of drug-gang rivals. Medina, a *brujo* in the *santería* religion, calmly told the judge at his sentencing that he wanted it clearly understood that he had never killed an innocent person, that is, someone outside his line of business. (Jackall 1997:268)

[5] The business ethics industry, which has long historical antecedents in the preaching of many of the US Protestant sects, but only reached its fully institutionalized form in various centers, institutes, consulting firms, and business school curricula in the late 1980 s, still advocates variants of the Golden Rule, specifically the notion that "doing good" will lead to "doing well." Although corporate managers often publicly embrace this comforting doctrine, many deride it privately as irrelevant to their worlds because those who "do evil" often do quite well indeed.

[6] Among myriad books on the academy, see in particular: Veblen (1918) and Bailey (1977).

In another crucial institutional arena, black Americans, invoking the ideologies of multiculturalism, *diversity*, and change, have attained many political offices in the last 40 years. As it happens, the behavior of black politicians in office is indistinguishable from that of any other group of politicians regardless of race, color, or ethnicity. Their principal preoccupation becomes the retention of power, accomplished largely through the distribution of spoils to their confederates and potential allies.[7]

Morality in organizations does not depend on gender, race, or ethnicity. Instead, it turns on the extent to which men and women, driven by personal ambitions, subject themselves to the exigencies of their particular organizations. Such ambitious people are always alert to the precariousness of organizational life and they surround themselves with others who, they think, will support them, especially when things go awry. In the process, they recreate a world where morality is inseparable from the pursuit of one's own advantage.

REFERENCES

Bailey, F. G. 1977. *Morality and Expediency: The Folklore of Academic Politics.* Chicago: Aldine Publishing Company.

Brill, S. 2009. "The Rubber Room: The Battle over New York City's Worst Teachers." *The New Yorker*, August 31.

Department of Defense. 2010. *Protecting the Force: Lessons from Fort Hood.* Report of the DoD Independent Review. January. http://www.defense.gov/pubs/pdfs/DOD-ProtectingTheForce-Web_Security_HR_13jan10.pdf

Jackall, R. 1978. *Workers in a Labyrinth.* Montclair, NJ: Allenheld, Osmun & Co.

Jackall, R. 1988. *Moral Mazes: The World of Corporate Managers.* New York: Oxford University Press.

Jackall, R. 1997. *Wild Cowboys: Urban Marauders & the Forces of Order.* Cambridge: Harvard University Press.

Jackall, R., and J. M. Hirota. 2000. *Image Makers: Advertising, Public Relations, and the Ethos of Advocacy.* Chicago: University of Chicago Press.

Jackall, R. 2005. *Street Stories: The World of Police Detectives.* Cambridge: Harvard University Press.

Jackall, R. 2007. "Whistleblowing & Its Quandaries." *Georgetown Journal of Legal Ethics* XX(4):1122–1136.

Jackall, R. 2009. "Moral Mazes and the Great Recession." PP. 221–240 in *Moral Mazes: The World of Corporate Managers.* 20th Anniversary Edition. New York: Oxford University Press.

Veblen, T. 1918. *The Higher Learning in America.* New York: B. W. Buebsch.

---

[7] See, for instance, the history of the Harlem Political Club, known in New York City as Tammany Hall Uptown, for a paradigmatic case of how black Americans behave in municipal politics. At the national level, the workings of the Congressional Black Caucus provide rich materials for students of the relentless pursuit of racially-defined self-interests.

CHAPTER 12

Explaining Crime as Moral Actions

Per-Olof H. Wikström

> ...morality in human behavior and its direct import for criminal behavior [is] a subject that, strangely, has been relatively neglected by criminologists. (Tittle 2007, Review in *Contemporary Sociology* 36:5)

> If they are true to their calling, all criminologists have to be interested in morality (Bottoms 2002)

Morality is rarely the main topic in criminological theory and research. However, an analysis of what constitutes a crime and what moves people to engage in acts of crime suggests that questions of personal morality and the moral context in which people operate should play a central role in the explanation of acts of crime (Wikström 2006).

The basic arguments of this chapter are that (i) acts of crime are moral actions and therefore need to be analysed and explained as such and (ii) explaining acts of crime is not different from explaining breaches of moral rules more generally (the explanatory process is the same). A theory of crime causation should therefore be regarded as a special case of a more general theory of moral action. If we can explain moral action (why people follow and breach moral rules) we can also explain acts of crime (why people follow and breach moral rules defined in law).

Moreover, the realisation that acts of crime are fundamentally moral actions helps us to better understand the potential role of systemic factors (such as inequality, integration and segregation) and social change in crime causation by focusing our attention on the analysis of how these factors (as causes of the causes) may influence (i) the emergence, sustainability and changes of particular types of moral contexts and (ii) the social selection of kinds of people into kinds of moral contexts in which they develop and act.

I submit that analysing crime as moral action may help overcome some central analytical problems in current mainstream criminological theory and research. I will briefly discuss these shortcomings and then move on to present the foundations and content of a newly developed general theory of moral action and crime causation (Situational Action Theory) that aims to address these challenges.

S. Hitlin, S. Vaisey (eds.), *Handbook of the Sociology of Morality*,   **211**
Handbooks of Sociology and Social Research, DOI 10.1007/978-1-4419-6896-8_12,
© Springer Science+Business Media, LLC 2010

MAKING SENSE OF ALL THE CORRELATES

> ...it is difficult to see why anyone would be interested in statistical associations or correlations if the findings were not in some way relevant to the understanding of causative mechanisms (Rutter 2009)

Criminological research demonstrates a wide range of genetic, biological, psychological and social crime correlates (Ellis et al. 2009) including, for example, everything from a low resting heart rate to living in a socially disorganised area. In fact, "literally thousands of variables differentiate significantly between official offenders and nonoffenders or correlate significantly with self-reported offending" (Farrington 1992:256). This state of affairs has led some observers to ask whether "everything matters" (Matza 1964) and others to ask whether "anything matters" (Katz 1988). The main problem here is that most identified predictors (often referred to as risk factors) are likely to be only markers or symptoms and some, like sex and race, are clearly causally irrelevant, being attributes. To advance knowledge there is an obvious need for a theoretical framework that can help sort out the few causes from the many correlates and, among potentially causally relevant factors, the causes from the causes of the causes.

However, the large number of diverse theories on offer has not helped the situation. "The study of deviance and crime has traditionally been characterized by a multitude of seemingly unrelated and competitive theories" (Liska et al. 1989:1). Theory testing has not been able to solve this problem; "criminology has failed to make scientific progress in the past 20 years in the sense of falsifying some theories and accumulating verified knowledge in the context of other theories" (Bernard 1990:329). The situation has not become much better in the 20 years since these observations were published: "criminology risks being a field of study in which many ideas are developed and all are chosen – in which all theories have equal claim to legitimacy and in which only the most highly specialized scholars can separate the theoretical wheat from the chaff" (Cullen et al. 2008:2). How do we overcome this problem?

IDENTIFYING CAUSES AND PROVIDING EXPLANATIONS

> ...statistical correlation explains nothing; it is what cries for explanatory models (Bunge 2006)

I take it that the goal of a scientific theory is to make sense of reality and how it works by analytically identifying putative causes and providing plausible causal processes (causal explanations) that account for the phenomena (effect) under study and, on that basis, specify testable implications which can be subject to empirical examinations that, in turn, can help falsify or corroborate key propositions of the proposed theory and thereby put it to the test (see generally, Bunge 1999, 2006; Popper 2000).

I do not believe that in the current state of diversified criminological theorising more testing of existing theories per se is the remedy for advancing knowledge about the causes of crime (as such activities over the last 40 or so years have demonstrated). Nor do I believe that the advancement and utilisation of ever more sophisticated statistical techniques is the solution to the difficulty of distinguishing between correlates and causes. Such developments, which have clearly taken place within criminology (and in social and behavioural sciences more generally), are certainly helpful for the progress, particularly, of non experimental methods of theory testing, but not necessarily for the progress of theory. "Statistical techniques, no matter how powerful in revealing social regularities, cannot at the same time be used to crank out causal explanations of these regularities" (Goldthorpe 2000:19). The problem of identifying adequate causal explanations is primarily not an empirical but an *analytical* problem (on the general problem of causation and explanation (see von Wright 1971, Salmon 1998, Psillos 2002, Bunge 2004).

To advance knowledge on the causes of crime, there is a strong need to address some of the key analytical problems that characterise much of current mainstream criminological theorising. If we are successful in such a venture, it will provide more effective guidance for identifying among all the predictors (correlates) those empirical regularities that are potentially causally relevant and thus help concentrate future theory testing on the problem of corroborating or falsifying the role that causally relevant factors and their interactions play in crime causation.

ADDRESSING SOME COMMON ANALYTICAL PROBLEMS IN CRIMINOLOGICAL THEORISING

> No simple theory in the crime/deviance area... has proven to be more than minimally satisfactory in overall explanatory ability, in applicability to a wide range of deviance, or in empirical support for its tenets. All are plausible, yet they fail as general theories (Tittle 1995)

I submit that mainstream criminological theory generally (not all theories in all respects but all theories at least in some respects)[1] fail to fully address:

(i) what crime is (to clearly define what it is the theory aims to explain),
(ii) what it is that moves people to engage in acts of crime (to present an adequate action theory),
(iii) how personal and environmental factors interact in moving people to engage in acts of crime (to properly integrate key insights from personal and environmental explanatory approaches),
(iv) the role of broader social conditions and individual development (life histories) (to analyse their influence not as causes but as causes of the causes).

---

[1] Such as strain theory (e.g. Agnew 2005), anomie theory (e.g. Merton 1968), social bonding theory (e.g. Hirschi 1969), self-control theory (e.g. Gottfredson and Hirschi 1990), control-balance theory (Tittle 1995), power-control theory (Hagan 1988), social learning/differential association theory (e.g. Akers 2009, Sutherland et al. 1992), subcultural theory (e.g. Cohen 1955), labelling theory (e.g. Lemert 1967), reintegrative shaming theory (Braithwaite 1989), deterrence theory (Bentham 1970), social disorganisation/collective efficacy theory (e.g. Kornhauser 1978, Sampson 2006), routine activity theory (e.g. Cohen and Felson 1979) and institutional-anomie theory (Messner and Rosenfeld 2007). Again, I do not claim that all these theories fail on all four points raised but that they at least fail on some and, crucially, I do argue that to move criminological theory forward from its current deadlock of diverse and competing theories we need to effectively address in a comprehensive and integrative manner all four points, difficult as it may be.

Let me take a moment to elaborate somewhat on these points.

(i) *A cause has to be a cause of something.* Criminological theories rarely specify or clearly analyse what it is they aim to explain.[2] "Modern criminology pays little attention to the nature of crime" (Gottfredson and Hirschi 1990:15) and "there are ... questions about whether the dependent variable is the same in different theories" (Akers 1989:25). Why is this a problem? Without a clear understanding of what it is we propose to explain, it is difficult to unambiguously identify putative causes and suggest plausible causal processes that may produce the effect under study. Again, a cause has to be a cause of something (and a causal process has to explain something). Clearly defining what it is we want to explain (the problem at hand) helps us focus on what kinds of factors and processes may qualify as potential causes and explanations (and these will most certainly vary depending on how we define what it is we seek to explain).

Crimes are actions. However, crimes are not just any kind of action. What characterises acts of crime is that they are *actions that breach rules of conduct.* For example, when explaining sexual crimes we are not primarily interested in explaining why people engage in a particular sexual activity, but why they engage in such an activity when it is illegal to do so. When we look for causes and explanations of acts of crime we should look for causes and explanations of why people act in compliance with or in breach of rules of conduct (defined in law).

(ii) *A cause is something that produces something else.* To explain acts of crime we need to understand the processes (mechanisms) that produce the act. To do this we need an adequate theory of (moral) action that explicates how (the process by which) people are moved to act in one way or another. A major shortcoming of most criminological theories is that they lack a proper theory of action. "If criminological theories refer at all to theories of action they mostly make general references to the importance of choice without giving any more developed account of its role within the theory, typically alluding to self-interest, pleasure and pain, cost and benefits and similar grounds for action" (Wikström 2006:70).

Crimes are moral actions so what we need to explain acts of crime is a theory of moral action; an *action theory* that explains why and how people are moved to carry out acts in compliance with or in breach of rules of conduct. Such a theory helps us focus our attention on what kinds of personal and environmental factors may be causally relevant in the explanation of acts of crime (and thus help us distinguish causes from correlates which are merely markers or symptoms). Only factors that

---

[2] One illustrative, and not atypical, example is Felson's (2006:35) definition of crime as "any identifiable behavior that an appreciable number of governments has specifically prohibited and formally punished". This kind of definition does not give much guidance as to what a theory of crime causation aims to explain (because it does not tell us much about the nature of crime, only argues that crimes are behaviours that many governments prohibit and punish). Applying Felson's "definition" to the explanation of criminal acts by the situational model of his and Cohen's (1979) routine activity theory would read something like this: an identifiable behaviour that an appreciable number of governments has specifically prohibited and formally punished is caused by the convergence of a motivated offender and a suitable target, in the absence of a capable guardian. The latter (convergence of offender, target and lack of control) does not make much sense as an explanation of the former (behaviours prohibited and punished by many governments).

affect (help initiate, thwart or interrupt) processes that move people to engage in acts of crime are causally relevant factors in crime causation. To be a *causally relevant* factor means that if the factor is manipulated it will affect the outcome (in one way or another).

(iii) *Human action (including acts of crime) is an outcome of the causal interaction between personal and environmental factors.* Most criminological theory (and research) focuses either on the role of personal factors or the role of environmental factors in crime causation. Typically, theories (such as strain[3] and control theories[4]) aim to explain why some people engage more than others in committing acts of crime, or (such as social disorganisation/collective efficacy[5] and routine activity theories[6]) why certain places (or time periods) have higher rates of acts of crime than others. In other words, the focus is usually either on explaining crime as an outcome of (differential) crime propensity or as an outcome of criminogenic exposure. However, progressively more theories that focus on explaining individual differences in crime propensity acknowledge, for example, the role of differential opportunities to commit crime in crime causation (e.g. Gottfredson and Hirschi 1990) and, increasingly, theories that focus on environmental factors acknowledge the role of individual differences in crime causation (e.g. Felson 2002). Nevertheless, such accounts rarely provide any elaborate attempt to integrate individual and environmental factors in crime causation, for example, by detailing how (through what causal processes) their interaction is supposed to produce acts of crime. Few (if any) theories provide a situational model that explains *how* personal and environmental factors interact in crime causation.

The need to bring together key insights from different traditions of theory, particularly individually and environmentally oriented approaches, has long been acknowledged as a central problem of criminological theorising and research (e.g. Reiss 1986, Laufer and Adler 1989, Tonry et al. 1991, Farrington et al. 1993, Jensen and Akers 2003), although few (if any) successful attempts at such theoretical integration have been made (Wikström and Sampson 2006). Messner et al. (1989:18) point out that "many contemporary efforts that purport to pursue the goal of theoretical integration might better be described as attempts at prediction. Variables from two or more theories are included in the same prediction equation, but there is little concern with relating the concepts to one another". One key suggested reason for this is that "criminology lacks an accepted and general theoretical structure for guiding integrative inquiry into the causes of crime" (Wikström and Sampson 2006:1).

Acts of crime are an outcome of situational processes triggered by the interaction of causally relevant personal factors (propensity) and environmental factors

---

[3] E.g. Agnew (2005)

[4] E.g. Hirschi (1969), Gottfredson and Hirschi (1990, 2003)

[5] E.g. Kornhauser (1978), Sampson (2006)

[6] E.g. Cohen and Felson (1979)

(exposure). To explain acts of crime we therefore need a *situational* action theory which can integrate relevant insights from theory and research on personal and environmental factors in crime causation.

(iv) *There are causes and there are causes of the causes.* Most criminological theory fails to acknowledge the difference, or clearly distinguish, between causes and the causes of the causes in the explanation of acts of crime. When analysing the causes of action (such as acts of crime) we should, as discussed above, concentrate on understanding the situational causal processes initiated by the interplay between causally relevant factors of the person and the settings in which the person takes part. When we analyse the role of the causes of the causes (of action) we are concerned with, *in the first instance*, selection processes that place people in the particular settings, with particular moral contexts, in which they develop (e.g. acquire experiences, cognitive skills and moral values relevant to their crime propensity) and act (e.g. in response to criminogenic exposure) and, *in the second instance*, the processes by which particular kinds of settings, with particular moral contexts, emerge, are sustained and change. When analysing the role of selection processes a key question is how processes of social selection interact with the process of self-selection to place particular kinds of people in particular kinds of settings.

SITUATIONAL ACTION THEORY

Man is the source of his actions(Aristotle 1999[7])

Microsituational encounters are the ground zero of all social action and all sociological evidence (Collins 2000)

A main argument of this chapter so far has been that criminology lacks an adequate theory of (moral) action through which situational causal mechanisms can be addressed and levels of explanation can be integrated. *Situational Action Theory* (SAT) is a recently developed theory that aims to tackle this problem (e.g. Wikström 2004, 2005, 2006, 2010; Wikström and Treiber 2007, 2009a, b). The theory draws upon key insights from criminological theory and research, and theory and research from social and behavioural science more generally. It proposes to offer a comprehensive and integrative approach to the study of moral action and the causes of crime. More specifically:

(i) *SAT intends to be a general theory of moral action and the causes of crime.* It achieves this by focusing on explaining what all crimes, in all places, and at all times have in common, the *breach of a moral rule* (defined in law).

(ii) *SAT aims to offer an alternative to rational choice theory in the study of moral action and the causes of crime.* While the theory accepts that rationality and self-interest at times [see further point (iv) below] play a role in guiding human action, it reasons

---

[7] *Nicomachean Ethics*, book three.

that on a more fundamental level humans are *rule-guided actors* (and that the social order is essentially based on *shared moral rules*).

(iii) *SAT is developed to overcome the common (but unfruitful) divide between individual and environmental explanatory approaches to the causes of crime.* It accomplishes this by proposing a *situational mechanism* (a perception–choice process) that links the person and his or her environment to his or her actions. People engage in acts of crime because they (i) come to see such acts as viable *action alternatives* and (ii) *choose* (habitually or deliberately) to carry them out.

(iv) *SAT further aims to integrate behaviouristic and voluntaristic approaches to the explanation of crime.* It does so by recognising that human behaviour (including law-abidance and acts of crime) is predominantly caused by processes of either *habit* or *rational deliberation* (two different kinds of perception–choice processes).

(v) *SAT seeks to bridge macro and micro, and situational and developmental approaches in the study of crime.* It addresses this problem by stressing the need to carefully distinguish between *the causes* and *the causes of the causes* [8] in the analysis of crime causation, arguing that macro (structural, systemic) factors and (individual) developmental factors are best analysed as causes of the causes, while micro and situational factors are best analysed as causes.

CRIME AS MORAL ACTION

...the law is a rule of human conduct

The legal norm ... is merely one of the rules of conduct, of the same nature as all other rules of conduct (Ehrlich 2008)

Crimes are best analysed as moral action. Moral action is any action that is guided by (moral) rules about what it is right or wrong to do, or not do, in particular circumstances. Acts of crime are actions that breach moral rules defined in law. That is what all crimes, in all places, at all times, have in common. What defines acts of crime is thus not that they are particular types of actions but that they are *actions that breach rules of conduct* (defined in law). In principle, there is no difference between rules of conduct defined in law and rules of conduct more generally. To explain acts of crime is essentially to explain moral action. If we can explain moral action (why people follow and breach moral rules) we also have an explanation of acts of crime (why people follow and breach moral rules defined in law).

Analysing crime as moral action has the great advantage of being applicable to all kinds of crime, from shoplifting to major company fraud, from bar fights to mass shootings, from civil disobedience to roadside bombings, to mention just a few examples. What differs between types of crime is not the explanatory perception–choice process involved but its content (the

---

[8] The distinction between causes and causes of the causes is, of course, a simplification, because we can (in the form of causal chains) have causes of the causes of the causes, and so forth. Arguably when the aim is to explain action, however, the most important distinction analytically is between causes and the causes of the causes (not between, for example, "the causes of the causes" and "the causes of the causes of the causes").

particular moral rules relevant to the particular action, not the fact that the action is guided by moral rules).

The problem of finding a common explanation of (i.e. developing a general theory for) all the diverse acts that may constitute an act of crime [which has been raised, for example, by Wilson and Herrnstein (1985)] is thus overcome by focusing on the fact that crime is essentially a breach of a rule of conduct rather than the performance of any particular kind of act. When explaining acts of crime, the aim is not primarily to explain, for example, why people drive at 100 mph, smoke cannabis or demolish a building, but why they do so when it is against a rule of conduct (defined in law).

The fact that some acts are considered crimes in some jurisdictions and not in others, and that particular acts may be regarded as a crime at one point in time but not at another, does not cause a problem when analysing crime as moral action because the focus is on explaining the rule breaking, not the act in itself.[9] The question why certain acts are regarded as crimes at some times and places but not at other times and places is a different question from that why people follow or breach rules of conduct (defined in law).

In this context it is important to point out that one key reason why people may breach a moral rule (defined in law) is they may disagree with the rule (or do not care much for it). Sometimes breaching a moral rule (defined in law) may even be regarded by the person and others as a virtuous act (such as in some politically motivated crimes or gang-related violence). People may also breach rules because they are unaware of or do not fully understand the implications of a rule (e.g. due to ignorance, or age-related or otherwise limited mental capacities). Other examples include cases in which people breach a moral rule (they otherwise would not breach) because they are under duress (e.g. threatened with death if they do not comply).

Morality is a word with strong connotations. It is therefore important to stress that analysing acts of crime as moral actions does not (necessarily) imply any "moralistic" approach. SAT does not analyse morality in terms of any judgements about whether particular acts (or laws) are good or bad (virtuous or reprehensible) but only in terms of rules of conduct which guide people's action by specifying what it is right or wrong to do or not do in particular circumstances. However, the extent to which breaching particular moral rules is generally seen as reprehensible in a jurisdiction may, of course, be a factor influencing people's adherence to those rules. It may be easier to breach a moral rule few care strongly about than a rule that is likely to evoke strong negative emotions towards the person who breaches the rule.

What has been said so far should not be taken as a position of moral relativism, in terms of that any kind of moral rules are equally likely to emerge. Although there are some significant differences between societies and time periods in what acts are regarded as crimes, there also appears to be a significant overlap in the core of actions generally regarded as wrong and

---

[9] Gottfredson and Hirschi (1990:175) suggest another, but in my view less satisfactory, solution to this problem: "we must define crime such as that it includes at least the majority of acts defined as criminal in all societies" (compare Felson's definition – see footnote 2). The key question here is why the definition of crime only should include the majority and not all acts defined as criminal. In fact, Gottfredson and Hirschi's definition of crime as "acts of force or fraud undertaken in pursuit of self-interest" (ibid.:15) is rather a definition of *certain kinds of acts* (that may or may not be regarded as criminal – they talk about crime and analogous acts) *undertaken with a certain kind of motivation*, i.e. in pursuit of self-interest (see further Wikström and Treiber 2007).

criminalised (e.g. Newman 2008). For example, it appears that most societies in one way or another regulate ownership and the use of violence. It is plausible that the kinds of moral rules that emerge in a society are somehow related to *human nature* and the problem of creating *social order* in societies of varying degrees of development and complexity (on the general problem of social order, see Wrong 1994). But this is not a topic to be dealt with in this chapter.

THE SITUATIONAL MODEL

> …delinquent acts always depend on appropriate combinations of actor and situation.
> (Cohen and Short Jr. 1961)

Most people who walk past an unsupervised and unlocked car with the keys in the ignition do not see this as an opportunity to steal the car. However, some do, and of those who do, some will choose to actually go ahead and steal the car.

Most people who get annoyed or angry with another do not see beating that person up as a viable response. However, some do, and of those who do, some will choose to go ahead and batter the other person.

Most people who are unhappy with governments and their politics do not see blowing up government buildings or assassinating government representatives as an action alternative. However, some do, and of those who do, some will go ahead and blow up a government building or assassinate a public official.

Moral actions (such as acts of crime) are best analysed and explained as an outcome of situational processes. The key elements of the situational model of SAT are (i) person, (ii) setting, (iii) situation, and (iv) action (Table 12.1). The interaction between a person and a setting creates a situation (a perception of action alternatives and a process of choice) that results in an action (or inaction).[10] It is important to observe here that a *setting* is defined as

TABLE 12.1. Key Elements of the Situational Model

Element	Definition
Person	Body, biological and psychological make-up, experiences, agency (power to make things happen intentionally)
Setting	Part of the environment to which the individual is directly exposed and reacts; configuration of objects, persons and events accessible to the person through his or her senses (incl. any media present)
Situation	Perception of action alternatives and process of choice as the result of the person's interaction with a setting
Action	Bodily movements under the person's guidance

---

[10] On the surface, the situational model of SAT has some basic similarities with the situational model of Cohen and Felson's (1979) Routine Activity Theory (RAT). However, while SAT focuses on explaining *how* the intersection and interaction of people and settings (propensity and exposure) produces a causal process (a perception–choice process) that brings about acts of crime, RAT focuses on specifying the necessary conditions for a crime to occur (the convergence of a motivated offender, suitable target and lack of capable guardians) without really explaining *how* this convergence is supposed to cause a person to engage in an act of crime (for a more detailed comparison of these two theories, see Wikström et al. 2010).

the part of the environment a person can access with his or her senses and that a *situation* is defined as the perception–choice process that arises from the person–setting interaction.

People vary in their propensity to engage in acts of crime (and particular acts of crime). The concept of *crime propensity* refers to the personal factors that affect a person's likelihood of perceiving an act of crime as an action alternative and choosing to carry it out, in response to a particular setting. For example, person A has a higher crime propensity than person B if person A is more likely than person B to see an act of crime as an action alternative and choose to carry it out when they are in the *same setting*. This general reasoning is also applicable to analyses of specific kinds of crime, in which case we would talk about [*type of crime*] *propensity*, for example, shoplifting propensity or partner violence propensity.

Settings vary in the *criminogenic exposure* they provide, that is, in the degree to which their features promote acts of crime (or particular acts of crime) by influencing people's perception of action alternatives and process of choice. For example, setting A is more criminogenic than setting B if the *same person* is more likely to see an act of crime (a particular act of crime) as an action alternative and choose to carry it out when in setting A than when in setting B.

People differ in their propensity to engage in acts of crime and in their exposure to criminogenic settings. Specific combinations (interactions) of propensity and exposure are therefore likely to result in particular perception–choice processes (situations) that, in turn, will promote particular kinds of actions. The situational model's basic explanation of an act of crime can thus be summarised as

$$\mathbf{P} \times \mathbf{E} \rightarrow \mathbf{C}$$

where **P** stands for crime propensity, **E** for criminogenic exposure, $\rightarrow$ for the perception–choice process and **C** for an act of crime.

Situational Action Theory does not propose a simple additive model of propensity and exposure but that propensity and exposure *interact* to initiate a perception–choice process that

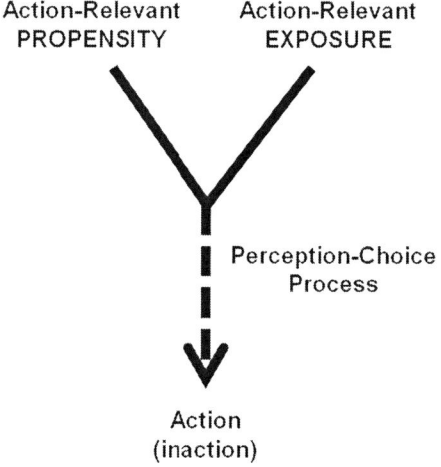

FIGURE 12.1. The propensity–exposure causal interaction illustrated.

encourages or discourages a person's crime involvement (as illustrated in Figure 12.1). Crime propensity is activated by criminogenic exposure and criminogenic exposure is made relevant by crime propensity. The general nature of this interaction is that the influence of exposure depends on a person's propensity: the importance of criminogenic exposure amplifies with increasing crime propensity (the nature of the interaction between propensity and exposure is developed in more detail in subsequent sections).

CAUSALLY RELEVANT PERSONAL AND ENVIRONMENTAL FACTORS

> When a normally constituted man tries to behave in a way repugnant to morality, he feels something that stops him just as clearly as when he tries to lift a weight too heavy for him. Durkheim (2002)

Not all individual characteristics and environmental features are relevant in the explanation of acts of crime. In fact, most are irrelevant (despite the fact that many of them are correlated with crime). Causally relevant factors in crime causation are *only* those factors that (directly or indirectly)[11] influence whether or not a person will perceive a breach of a moral rule (defined in law) as an action alternative, and those factors that influence the process of choice whether or not to act upon that alternative.

According to SAT, the main (directly) causally relevant personal factors that establish a person's *crime propensity* are his or her

  (i) morality (moral rules and moral emotions) and
  (ii) ability to exercise self-control,

while the key (directly) causally relevant environmental factors that affect the *criminogenic exposure* a setting provides are

  (iii) the moral rules of the setting, and
  (iv) their level of enforcement (through the process of deterrence).

Analysing crime as moral action naturally focuses on the roles of people's morality and the moral contexts in which they operate. What action alternatives (means) spring to mind to satisfy a particular motivation, and how these alternatives are evaluated, is largely dependent on the interplay between a person's morality (moral rules and related emotions) and the moral rules of the setting in which he or she takes part. Personal moral rules and the moral rules of a setting can either encourage or discourage acts of crime (the breach of moral rules defined in law).

With the exception of the meta-rule that one should abide by the rules of law (or more generally, should comply with rules and regulations), moral rules are best analysed in terms of their action relevance, meaning that particular moral rules are relevant in guiding particular types of actions (all moral rules are obviously not relevant for all kinds of actions in all kinds of circumstances). For example, when we analyse acts of violence, moral rules that guide and

---

[11] Directly as causes, and indirectly as the causes of the causes.

regulate the use of violence are relevant, and if we are analysing a specific form of violence, such as violence against a partner, moral rules that guide and regulate the use of that form of violence are particularly important. The concept of *action-relevant moral rules* in SAT refers to the moral rules (held by a person or that apply to a setting) that are relevant to a particular kind of action.

Moral rules vary in their strength. Strong moral rules naturally have greater importance in guiding a person's actions than those that are weak. A measure of the strength of a personal moral rule are the *moral emotions* attached to a breach of the rule (e.g. the potency of feelings of guilt and shame if one violates the rule),[12] and a measure of the strength of a moral rule that applies to a setting is the degree to which it is *shared* (cognitively and emotionally) by those taking part in the setting. If a person's relevant moral rules are strong and consistent with those that apply to the setting in which he or she takes part, it is likely that he or she will not see a breach of those rules as an action alternative.

The idea that moral rules have *causal powers* to influence action is far from new. One of the most well-known advocates of this position is Durkheim (2002:41): "moral rules are genuine forces, which confront our desires and needs, our appetites of all sorts, when they promise to become immoderate". However, while Durkheim appears mainly to see the role of morality in action as one of controlling (excessive) motivations, SAT maintains that the key role of moral rules is in their influence on what action alternatives (means) for satisfying a motivation a person sees *in the first place*.

According to SAT, moral rules causally affect action primarily by guiding what action alternatives a person perceives (and does *not* perceive) in response to a particular motivation. Together with controls (the ability to exercise self-control and deterrence) moral rules also influence how a person (when he or she deliberates) assesses the alternatives for action that come to mind.

To argue that propensity (based on a person's morality and ability to exercise self-control) and exposure (based on a setting's moral rules and their enforcement) are causally relevant factors in the explanation of acts of crime does not deny the role of agency in action; propensity and exposure are the *input* into the perception–choice process within which people exercise agency. To say that propensity and exposure are causally relevant means that changes in propensity and exposure (through their impact on the perception–choice process) will lead to changes in action.

THE SITUATIONAL PROCESS

> It is the self-monitored following of rules and plans that we believe to be the social science analogue of the working of generative causal mechanisms in the process which produce the non-random patterns studied by natural scientists (Harré and Secord 1972)

---

[12] Guilt refers to a person feeling bad about his/her actions; shame refers to a person feeling bad about his/her actions in front of others. For example, a person may not feel much guilt for shoplifting, but may feel shame if his or her parents were made aware of the shoplifting (on moral emotions generally, see Tangney and Fischer 1995).

> There is now abundant evidence for the existence of two types of processing in human reasoning, decision-making, and social cognition – one type fast, automatic, effortless, and non-conscious, the other slow, controlled, effortful, and conscious (Evans and Frankish 2009)

Criminological theories often ignore the role of *agency* (i.e. a person's power to make things happen intentionally) or only pay lip-service to its importance without further detailing its nature and function within the theory. Many theories (at least implicitly) appear to operate under the assumption that human action is deterministic.

Situational Action Theory integrates behaviouristic (deterministic) and voluntaristic ("free will") forces in the explanation of moral action and crime. SAT asserts that *people exercise agency within the constraint of rule-guided choice*. Rule-guidance can primarily take the form of either deliberation or habit. *Habitual action* involves automatically applying experienced-based moral rules of conduct to a setting and its circumstances (the actor only perceives *one* causally effective alternative[13]), while *deliberation* involves taking moral rules of conduct into consideration when actively choosing between action alternatives (see further Wikström 2006). While it is likely that most actions are predominantly either habitual or deliberate in nature, it is also likely that many actions (especially in prolonged action sequences) may include aspects of habit and deliberation (for example, that the action-guidance can change from habitual to rational deliberative due to sudden unexpected or unfamiliar events).

What action alternatives a person perceives as a response to a particular motivation in the first place is fundamental to his or her subsequent actions. For example, if a person does not perceive an act of crime as an action alternative there will be no crime. In this case the process of choice is irrelevant; the person does not choose to not commit an act of crime, he or she just does not see an act of crime as an action alternative. However, if a person does perceive an act of crime as an action alternative, he or she may (or may not), depending on the circumstances, primarily breach a moral rule (defined in law) either out of habit, or as an outcome of a process of deliberation (as illustrated in Figure 12.2).

When people act habitually, they routinely apply *past* experiences to guide current action (*exercising moral habits*); when they act deliberately they try to anticipate *future* consequences of perceived action alternatives and choose the best course of action (*making moral judgements*). Moral habits form in response to repeated exposure to particular settings and circumstances and are activated when the same (or similar) kinds of settings and circumstances are encountered, while rational deliberation (moral judgements) tends to occur when a person takes part in unfamiliar settings or circumstances or encounters conflicting rule-guidance (see further, Wikström 2006). Circumstances that involve high levels of stress and strong emotions tend to promote habitual action (regardless of the actor's familiarity with the setting and its circumstances).

The central role of rule-guidance in the explanation of human behaviour has been convincingly argued by Harré and Secord (1972:15), who write: "in order to understand what people do, one must see their activities in terms of deliberate followings of rules". Although SAT is a very different theory from their role-rules model of human behaviour, it shares the core idea that rule-guidance is the key to understanding human action and explaining social patterns of human behaviour.

---

[13] Which may be the alternative to do nothing.

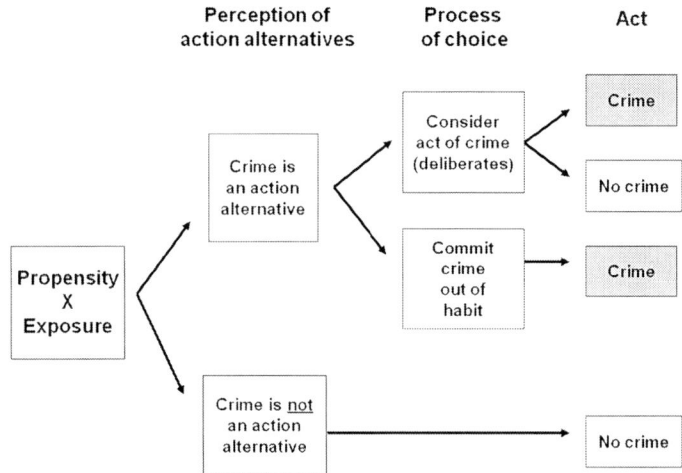

FIGURE 12.2. The steps of the perception–choice process in crime causation illustrated.

Harré and Secord (1972:93) specifically argue that it is *self-monitored* rule-guidance that is the generative mechanism of social patterns: "human actions are generated by the conscious self-monitoring of its performances in accordance with certain sets of rules". SAT, on the other hand, maintains that rule-guidance as a generative mechanism can take both the form of self-monitored (deliberate) and intuitive (habitual) rule-guidance and that the latter (habit) generally (without disregarding the significance of deliberation) may be the quantitatively more important source of the patterns in human action we observe. Harré and Secord (1972:9, italics in original) do acknowledge the role of habits, but argue, in contrast to SAT, that self-monitored behaviour are "the main factor in the production of specifically *social* behaviour". They rightly stress that for habit to develop it initially requires deliberate action ("it was initially learned through self-direction and self-monitoring"; ibid.:9), but this is not likely to change the fact that human actions largely are expressions of (acquired) habit since "most of our actions are not preceded by any conscious reasoning and deliberation" (Davidson 2004:107).[14]

While it is easy to argue that everyday human action is to a large extent driven by habit, the question remains as to what extent acts of crime (and breaches of common moral rules more generally) are impelled by habit. It is, for example, not difficult to imagine that persistent domestic violence is often habitual (automated) in nature or, more generally, that any kind of chronic offending includes important elements of moral habit. On the other hand, it is also not difficult to find examples of acts of crime that are likely to be an outcome of rational deliberation (based on moral judgement).

SAT thus purports that moral action and acts of crime are best analysed as outcomes of rule-guided choice, where the rule-guidance (as an outcome of the interplay between the moral rules of a person and a setting), depending on the circumstances (e.g., degree of familiarity

---

[14] Habit economises with effort. Just imagine if every action taken during a day was preceded by a process of rational deliberation; we would hardly accomplish anything.

and level of stress and emotions), may be predominantly habitual or deliberative in nature. But what about the role of motivation?

THE ROLE OF MOTIVATION

> The background is frequently cited, what people do being traced back to their childhood, to a strict or slack education, often to poverty, abuse, to bad parenting. Matters of that sort can't be ignored, but their bearing is indirect (Schick 1997)

One of the most popular explanations of why people engage in acts of crime, certainly in the public discourse, but also in some criminological theories is that "people are pressurised into crime by the negative emotions that result from strain" (Agnew 2005:23). In his general strain theory (GST), Agnew defines strain as "events or conditions that are disliked by individuals" (ibid.:4) and argue there are three major types of strains: "individuals may lose something they value (lose something good)", "individuals may be treated in an aversive or negative manner by others (receive something bad)" and "individuals may be unable to achieve their goals (fail to get something they want)" (ibid., p 4). Examples, according to Agnew (2009:116), of strains most likely to cause crime in Western societies include bad jobs, homelessness, parental rejection, child abuse, negative secondary school experiences, chronic unemployment, living in deprived communities, ethnic/race or gender discrimination. However, Agnew (2005) acknowledges (in a somewhat contradictory statement) that "while strains increase the likelihood of crime, most individuals do not respond to strains with crime" (ibid.:87) and attributes this to characteristics of "individuals and their environments" that affect "the ability to cope in a legal manner, the costs of criminal coping and the disposition for criminal coping" (ibid.:89). He goes on to specify what makes a person more likely to "cope with strains in a criminal manner", citing a list of such factors, including "poor coping skills and resources", "low levels of conventional social support", "low levels of social control", and "associat[ing] with criminal others and hold[ing] beliefs favorable to crime" (ibid.:103).[15]

Given that strains (events or conditions that are disliked by individuals), and even severe strains, mostly lead to responses other than acts of crime, experiencing strain is not a good explanation of why people commit crime (add to this the fact that people often commit crime for other reasons than experiencing negative emotions). By introducing coping mechanisms to explain why strain rarely leads to acts of crime, Agnew's theory (2005, 2009) tends to lose its initial focus on strain. It also suffers analytically because there is no detailed analysis and specification of how poor coping skills and resources turn negative emotions into acts of crime nor any conceptual integration of the various sources of criminal coping suggested: "a range of factors, then, are predicted to increase the likelihood that individuals will cope with their strains in a criminal manner" (Agnew 2005:103). In fact, the key "explanation" appears to turn into one of cumulative risk: "it may be best for researchers to consider individuals' overall standing on all of those factors that increase the likelihood of criminal coping. Individuals, in

---

[15] Some of these coping factors refer to key explanatory concepts in other prominent criminological theories such as social control (e.g. Hirschi 1969) and differential association theory (Sutherland et al. 1992).

particular, might be divided into several groups: those who possess all or most of the factors that increase the likelihood of criminal coping, those who possess some of the factors, and those who possess few or none. *Criminal coping should be most likely among those who possess all or most of the factors conducive to criminal coping*" (ibid.:104, *my emphasis*) .[16]

In the end, General Strain Theory becomes a theory of the role of *one* important kind of motivation for people to engage in acts of crime (there is no reason to believe that people only breach moral rules defined in law as a response to experiencing negative emotions), and GST's explanation of why people engage in acts of crime becomes that people (for various reasons) *lack the ability to cope with strain in a non-criminal way* rather than that strains per se pressurise them into committing crimes.

Situational Action Theory recognises the role of motivation (and agrees that negative emotions such as anger may be *one* common motive for why people engage in some kinds of acts of crime). However, it also maintain that people commit acts of crime for all sorts of reason (e.g. greed, thrills, envy, apathy, conviction, anger, lust, commitment, respect, revenge, security, boredom) and, crucially, that there are no particular kinds of motives (e.g. no particular kinds of desires, needs, wants, commitments) that always make people breach particular moral rules (or commit particular acts of crime).

According to SAT, *motivation* (defined as goal-directed attention) is a necessary but not sufficient cause of moral rule breaking and acts of crime: It is necessary because to act people first have to be motivated to do so, but it is not sufficient because no particular motivation (goal-directed attention) in itself always causes people to breach a moral rule (defined in law). People are *not* motivated to breach a rule of conduct but to attain a particular goal (where the perceived action alternatives to attain the goal may, or may not, involve breaching a rule of conduct). Even in cases in which people are motivated, for example, to breach a rule of conduct to protest against the rule, the goal is *rule change* rather than the breaking of a rule.

Goal-directed attention is part of the process that moves people to act. It has a general directional influence on *what kinds* of acts of moral rule breaking (and acts of crime) a person may (or may not) perceive and consider (for example, the action alternative of breaching a smoking ban is only likely to emerge for someone who is a smoker and therefore may desire to smoke). Motivation explains what kinds of things a person may want to do in a particular circumstance, but not whether he or she will breach a moral rule to satisfy a motivation (for example, a smoker may want to smoke, but to explain whether or not he or she is prepared to breach a smoking ban in order to smoke is a different question from explaining the urge to smoke).

Motivation is a situational concept arising from the interaction between the person and the setting. The two main classes of origins of motivation (goal-directed attention) in crime causation are temptation and provocation (see further Wikström 2006).

A *temptation* occurs when there is

  (i) a connection between a person's desires (wants, needs) and an opportunity to satisfy a desire (want, need) or
 (ii) an opportunity for a person to fulfil a commitment he or she has made.

---

[16] Agnew (2005) makes a similar argument as regards the effects of strains: "experiencing several strains at once is especially likely to generate negative emotions and tax the ability to cope in a legal manner".

A *provocation* occurs when

> (iii) a friction (an unwanted external interference) causes a person to feel anger or annoyance.[17]

While negative emotions clearly are part of what creates a provocation, the same does not hold for temptations and commitments that are more likely to be linked to positive emotions.

People perceive action alternatives in relation to motivations.[18] According to SAT, the crucial factor in the explanation of whether or not a particular motivation will involve an act of crime as an action alternative is the moral filter emerging from the interplay between a person's morality (moral rules and emotions) and the moral rules of the context in which he or she operates. The *moral filter* (defined as the moral rule-induced selective perception of action alternatives) circumscribes what actions are perceived as appropriate in response to a particular motivation (as illustrated in Figure 12.3): The action alternatives which some people perceive when they are tempted (or provoked) in a certain way may include an act of crime, but those which others perceive may not.

The moral filter is applied to motivations either habitually (through exercise of a moral habit) or as part of a rational deliberation (providing action alternatives for a moral judgement) depending on the familiarity of circumstances and congruence of rule-guidance in the setting in which the person takes part (as previously discussed).

However, even if a person is motivated (tempted or provoked) to act in a particular way, *and* a breach of a moral rule defined in law is perceived as an action alternative to satisfy the motivation (for example, he or she wants to have a particular CD *and* sees shoplifting as an

THE MORAL FILTER

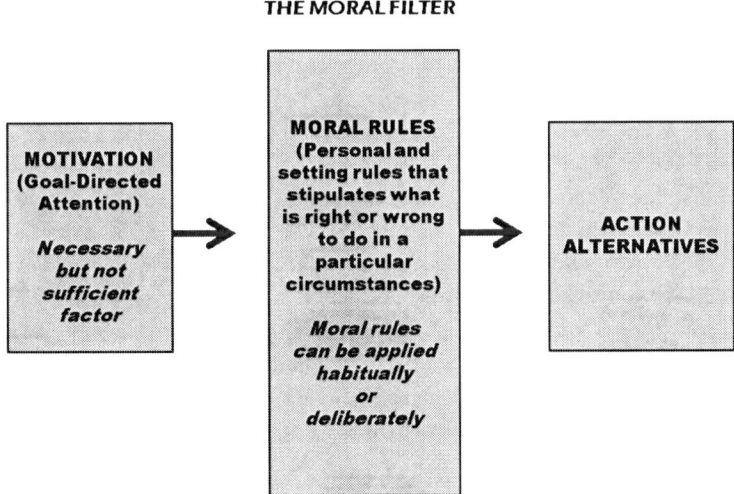

FIGURE 12.3. The role of the moral filter illustrated.

---

[17] Just as people vary in their desires and commitments, they also vary in their emotional sensitivity to particular frictions.

[18] On the relationship between motivation and action generally, see Heckhausen and Heckhausen (2008).

action alternative to get the CD) it is not certain that an act of crime will follow, because of the potential causal efficacy of controls.

THE ROLE OF CONTROLS

> Exercises of self-control oppose something in support of something else (Mele 2001)

> The critical importance of the criminal law as a threatening mechanism is restricted to those who must be threatened in order to secure their compliance. (Zimring and Hawkins 1968)

Control theory is currently one of the most, if not the most, popular theoretical perspectives in criminology (e.g. Briar and Piliavin 1965, Gottfredson and Hirchi 1990, Hirschi 1969, Reiss Jr. 1951). Its cornerstone is the assumption that people comply with the law (and moral norms more generally) because of (internal and external) controls. Hirschi defines control theory in relation to other main criminological theories (e.g. strain theory) by arguing that "the question 'Why do they do it?' is simply not the question the theory is designed to answer. The question is, 'Why don't we do it?' There is much evidence that we would if we dared" (1969:34).

However, if effective controls explain why we do not do it (what prevents the action), the lack of effective controls explains why we do it (what causes the action), when assuming that all people are equally motivated to do it ("we would if we dared"). As Hirschi (1969:16) himself states, "control theories assume that delinquent acts result when an individual's bond to society is weak or broken", that is, people do it (commit delinquent acts) when there is a lack of effective control (i.e. in this case, when they have weak or broken social bonds).[19] The key point Hirschi aims to argue is probably that control theory ignores (or finds irrelevant) the role of motivation[20] in the explanation of crime rather than that are different explanations of why we engage in or do not engage in crime.

Making the assumption that we all are (equally) motivated to commit (all) acts that breach moral rules defined in law ("we would if we dared") and that the sole thing that prevents us from breaching a rule of conduct (i.e. what differentiates those who do from those who do not) is the efficacy of (personal and social) controls, is not very plausible. For example, it is highly unlikely that the reason why most people refrain from having sex with toddlers, blowing up airplanes, breaking into their neighbours' houses or killing their spouses is the efficacy of controls (i.e. we would if we dared).[21]

If people lack motivation to engage in a particular action there is no need for (internal or external) controls to prevent them from engaging in that action (e.g. there is no need for intense police surveillance and threats of stiff penalties to make teetotallers refrain from drinking alcohol in places where alcohol use is banned). According to SAT, controls may *only* come

---

[19] Gottfredson and Hirschi (1990:111), in a later work specifically on self-control, argue that "people who do not develop strong self-control are more likely to commit criminal acts", that is, poor self-control explains why people commit crime (while strong self-control explains why people refrain from crime).

[20] Hirschi (2002 p. xvi) argues that "the view that crime is need-based or strongly motivated behavior has produced a series of concepts and hypothesis sharply at odds with the facts".

[21] This would certainly hold even if we allowed for (differential) opportunity.

into play (become causally relevant) when a person is motivated *and* sees an action that would breach a rule of conduct as an alternative to satisfy the motivation (otherwise there is nothing to control).

So, what is control? The concept of control is not always well defined in criminological theory and, therefore, often vague. In its most general account it appears to include any personal or social factors that (directly or indirectly) *influence* whether or not a person follows or breaches the moral norms and laws of society (control becomes synonymous with influence). The problem of conceptual ambiguity is not specific to criminological theories of social control but applies to the wider study of social control: "Even a cursory examination of the concept of social control will confront an apparently insurmountable problem: No definition of the term is agreed upon by sociologists" (Meier 1982:35). A similar observation was already made about 40 years earlier by Hollingshead (1941:219): "we have a widely used term almost devoid of clear conceptual content".

Two central themes in social control theory's explanation of why people comply with moral norms and laws are the importance of (i) the *internalisation of shared rules* (as a consequence of effective socialisation by key social institutions like the family and the school) and (ii) the *enforcement of shared rules* (through informal and formal monitoring, intervention and sanctions).

Reiss (1951:196), in his discussion of the role of personal and social controls in crime causation, argues that "delinquency may be defined as the behavior consequent to the failure of personal and social controls to produce behavior in conformity with the social system to which legal penalties are attached". He goes on to define personal control as "the ability of the individual to refrain from meeting needs in ways which conflict with the norms and rules of the community" and social control as "the ability of social groups or institutions to make norms or rules effective". For Reiss, acts that breach rules of conduct (defined in law) occur when a person has not properly internalised those rules and when the social group to which he or she belongs (e.g. the family, neighbourhood, or school) lacks the ability to enforce those rules: "the relative weakness of personal *and* social controls should account for. . . delinquent behavior" (ibid.:197, italics in original).

The relationship between internal and external controls and the mechanisms (causal processes) by which controls affect action are generally not well developed. Briar and Piliavin (1965:39) observe that "while social control theory can account for much delinquency, it, too, suffers limitations, since the nature of the processes by which social control is exercised and the sequential patterning of these processes have not been specified". They provide the example that "social control theories are ambiguous regarding the relationship between 'inner controls' and external (or social) controls". They suggest that a solution to this problem is to view "the central process of social control as 'commitments to conformity'", a term that, according to the authors, includes fear of punishment and personal and social consequences such as "to maintain a consistent self-image, to sustain valued relationships, and to preserve current and future statuses and activities". Briar and Piliavin (1965) thus appear to suggest that anticipation of negative consequences if violating a moral rule is the key component of control (what makes people comply) and that individual differences in commitment to conformity depends on factors such as "belief in God, affection for conventionally behaving peers, occupational aspirations, ties to parents, desire to perform well in school, and fear of material deprivations and punishments associated with arrest" (ibid.:41).

The ambiguity regarding the roles of internal and external controls and the nature of their relationship is glaringly illustrated by Hirschi's seminal involvement in the development of two different control theories: social bonds theory[22] (Hirchi 1969) and, with Gottfredson, self-control theory[23] (e.g., Gottfredson and Hirschi 1990, Hirschi and Gottfredson 1994). "They share important assumptions, but they are not the same theory, and should be judged on their own merits, as should some future theory that attempts to encompass them both" (Hirschi 2002:xiv).

Hirschi's (1969) social bonds theory stresses the significance of the strength of people's social bonds for their compliance with shared rules of conduct. "To violate a norm is ... to act contrary to the wishes and expectations of other people. If a person does not care about the wishes and expectations of other people – that is, if he is insensitive to the opinions of others – then he is to that extent not bound by the norms. He is free to deviate" (Hirschi 1969:18). According to Hirschi (1969:30–31) the social bond is a bond to key agents of socialisation (e.g. a parent) and social institutions (e.g. family and school). The elements of the bond (which all are assumed to be highly interrelated) include (i) *attachment*, which is important because "the essence of internalization of norms, conscience, or superego ... lies in the attachment of the individual to others" (ibid:18); (ii) *commitment*, which concerns people's investment in conventional society (education, job, etc.) and is important because it influences the costs of a person's deviance (e.g. risk of losing a job or relationship) – "few would deny that men on occasion obey rules simply from fear of the consequences. This rational component in conformity we label commitment" (ibid:20); (iii) *involvement* – "to the extent that he is engrossed in conventional activities, he cannot even think about deviant acts, let alone act out his inclinations" (ibid., p 22) and (iv) *belief* – "we assume ... that there is a *variation* in the extent to which people believe they should obey the rules of society, and, furthermore, that the less a person believes he should obey the rules, the more likely he is to violate them" (ibid., p 26, italics in original).

According to Hirschi (1969:30), belief is particularly related to attachment – "insofar as the child respects (loves and fears) his parents, and adults in general, he will accept their rules" – although he also argues that attachment has an independent influence on rule-following behaviour: "attachment may produce conformity even in the face of beliefs favorable to nonconformity", while belief ("in the obligatory character of rules") may continue to create conformity "even if the respect which brought it into being no longer exists". I think it is fair to argue that the concept of the social bond lacks somewhat in conceptual clarity and that the relationships between its suggested elements are not fully specified and, therefore, not properly analysed and integrated (see, e.g. LeBlanc and Caplan 1993).

Although it is one of the most popular and important theories in criminology, *self-control theory* is also currently one of the most discussed and criticised (e.g. Akers 1991, Geis 2000, Goode 2008, Wikström and Treiber 2007). While the problem addressed in social bonds theory (and social control theory more generally) is to explain what social environmental factors prevent people from acting "contrary to the wishes and expectations of other people", the problem addressed in self-control theory is to explain what *individual* factors, or factor, prevents people from committing "acts of force and fraud undertaken in the pursuit of self-interest"

---

[22] Generally referred to by Hirschi as "social control theory".

[23] Also referred to by the authors as "a general theory of crime"

(Gottfredson and Hirschi 1990:15).[24] The answer to the latter question is a person's ability to exercise self-control. In other words, people commit "acts of fraud and force undertaken in the pursuit of self-interest" because they have low self-control.

Gottfredson and Hirschi (1990) regard self-control as a stable individual trait (or a summary trait), established early in life, mostly as a consequence of ineffective early childhood training (ibid., e.g.:120 and 255),[25] and characterised by, for example, impulsivity, insensitivity, risk-taking and short-sightedness (ibid.:90–91), characteristics that prevent people from taking into account long-term consequences of their actions. They maintain that "people naturally pursue their own interests and unless socialized otherwise will use whatever means are available to them for such purposes" (Gottfredson and Hirschi 1990:117).

Self-control is defined as "the tendency to avoid acts whose long-term costs exceed their momentary advantages" (Hirschi and Gottfredson 1994:3) and in a later publication as "the tendency to consider the full range of potential costs of a particular action" (Hirschi 2004:543). Gottfredson and Hirschi (1990:111, italics added) claim that low self-control is "the *primary individual characteristic causing criminal behavior*" and that "self-control is the only *enduring personal characteristic* predictive of criminal (and related) behavior" and they go on to state that "*people who do not develop strong self-control are more likely to commit criminal acts*, whatever the other dimensions of their personality".

However, they also claim that "We *do not see self-control as the propensity to commit crime*, or as the motivating force underlying criminal acts. Rather, we see self-control as the barrier that stands between the actor and the obvious momentary benefits crime provides" (Hirschi and Gottfredson 1993:9, italics added). In a later publication they claim that "self-control is *the choice version of the causal concept of propensity*" (Hirschi and Gottfredson 2008:222, italics added), whatever that means. I believe that the use of concepts like traits, personal characteristics, propensity, self-control, barriers and choice, and their suggested relationships, needs to be made conceptually and analytically clearer to avoid unnecessary confusion and to bring out more explicitly the important insights self-control theory undoubtedly harbours.

According to Gottfredson and Hirschi, the *environment* (opportunity) plays a rather passive role in crime causation (although the social environment plays a central role in the (mostly) early development of a person's ability to exercise self-control). They talk about "the interaction of varying individual *predispositions* for delinquency and *logically possible opportunities*" (Gottfredson and Hirschi 2003:11, italics added). That is, opportunity may explain what kinds of crime a person can do (has the opportunity to commit), rather than whether or not he or she will engage in an act of crime (having the opportunity to do so). In other words, Gottfredson and Hirschi seem to argue that opportunity does not make the thief but that "the thief" (or person with low self-control) takes the opportunity to steal.

Just as in social bonds theory, *motivation* plays no role in self-control theory's explanation of crime (and analogous acts); "the theory requires that crime be understood without reference to motives or benefits" (Hirschi and Gottfredson 2008:221) and, therefore, "motives

---

[24] For a critique of the concept of crime in self-control theory see Wikström and Treiber (2007).

[25] Although Gottfredson and Hirschi (1990:105) acknowledge that "those not socialized sufficiently by the family may eventually learn self-control through the operation of other sanctioning systems and institution".

are irrelevant" (ibid.:222) .[26] I believe the argument that motivation lacks relevance is correct if this means that there are no specific motivations (motives) that necessarily cause (are sufficient to cause) a person to breach a rule of conduct (as previously discussed), but not if the claim is that motivation is unimportant in the explanation of the process that moves people to engage in particular actions, such as acts of crime. Again, irrespective of the efficacy of any controls, without an initial motivation to engage in an act that would breach a rule of conduct, such an act would not occur.[27] The problem is not whether motivation and/or controls are relevant in the explanation of crime, but rather what roles they play in crime causation.

Situational Action Theory acknowledge the significance of the role that internal and external controls play in the explanation of acts of crime (and moral action more generally). However, SAT argues that it is analytically important to differentiate between (i) moral rules[28] and (ii) controls (social control theory often tends to conflate the two) because their role in crime causation is different: *moral rules* affect what action alternatives a person perceives and how he or she assesses perceived action alternatives, while *controls* affect how a person chooses between action alternatives when at least one alternative involves a breach of a rule of conduct (in case of habitual action, where a person only sees one causally effective alternative, controls lack relevance because there is nothing to control).

Moreover, SAT maintains that it is analytically important to distinguish between (i) control as the *process* by which a person manages conflicting rule-guidance and (ii) controls as (a) the personal characteristics and (momentary) conditions that influence people's *ability* to act in accordance with their own moral rules (to exercise self-control) and (b) the environmental features that affect a setting's *ability* to make people comply with its moral rules (by creating deterrence, i.e. fear of consequences).

According to SAT, *control* is a situational process (and not, for example, a person's impulsivity or police presence in a setting), defined as *the cognitive process by which people manage conflicting rule-guidance when deliberating whether or not to act upon a particular motivation that involves a breach of a rule of conduct* (crucially, this implies that if there is no conflicting rule-guidance there is nothing to control and, hence, in these cases controls lack relevance for the action taken).

SAT asserts that the key personal characteristic that determines a person's general ability to exercise self-control is his or her executive capabilities (functions). Some conditions,

---

[26] They argue that all actions, including acts of crime, are undertaken in the pursuit of self-interest (a generalised motivation for action). However, as Popper (2000:xx) points out regarding the idea that "all human actions are egoistic, motivated by self-interest"; "this theory, with all its variants, is not falsifiable: no example of an altruistic action can refute the view that there was an egoistic motive hidden behind it".

[27] The role of motivations may be particular pertinent in the explanation of cases in which a crime or breach of a moral rule refers to an action in which few would be motivated to engage (such as incest). Generally, the more specific and less common a desire, commitment or friction is as a reason (motive) for engaging in an act that breaches a particular rule of conduct, the more important the part that the specific desire, commitment or friction will play in the explanation of that particular breach of a rule of conduct.

[28] When analysing the role of moral rules in crime causation, it is further important to clearly distinguish between (i) a person's moral rules as causes of his or her action and (ii) the factors that influence (as causes of the causes) the internalisation of a person's moral rules. The latter is important when explaining why people come to have certain crime propensities, while the former is important when explaining why a person acts in a particular way in response to a particular setting.

for example, alcohol and drug intoxication, high levels of stress and strong emotions, may momentarily lower this ability (see further Wikström and Treiber 2007). The key environmental aspects of a setting that determine its deterrent qualities are its (visible or otherwise known to the actor) levels of (formal and informal) monitoring, risk of intervention, and harshness of (social and legal) sanctions if a particular breach of a rule of conduct occurs (generally on the problem of deterrence, see Andenaes 1974, Zimring and Hawkins 1973).

Two key principles in Situational Action Theory that specify the role of moral rules and controls in crime causation are

(i)   The principle of moral correspondence
(ii) The principle of the conditional relevance of controls

The *principle of moral correspondence* states that if a person is motivated to do X and there is a correspondence between his or her personal moral rules and the moral rules of the setting, (i) he or she is *likely* to do X if the corresponding moral rules *encourage* [29] doing X, but (ii) *unlikely* to do X if the corresponding moral rules *discourage* doing X. In these two cases of moral correspondence (either encouraging or discouraging X), controls are irrelevant for whether or not X will occur. What controls control is adherence to personal and setting moral rules when there is a motivation to act in breach of either. If these rules are congruent in their action-guidance there is nothing to control (Figure 12.4).

The *principle of the conditional relevance of controls* applies in cases where a person is motivated to do X but there is a discrepancy between the guidance by the personal moral rules and those rules of conduct that apply in a particular setting. In such cases controls become causally relevant (Figure 12.4). The two ideal typical situations are (i) when a person's moral rules discourage doing X, but the moral rules dominant in the setting encourage doing X,

		Moral Rules of Setting (Exposure)	
		Encourage	*Discourage*
Personal Morality (Propensity)	*Encourage*	**Action Likely, Controls Irrelevant**	**Action Dependent on External Controls** (*Deterrence*)
	Discourage	**Action Dependent on Internal Controls** (*Ability to Exercise Self-Control*)	**Action Not Likely Controls Irrelevant**

FIGURE 12.4. What makes a particular moral action likely? The principles of moral correspondence and the conditional role of controls illustrated.

---

[29] Encouragement may in some instances include being neutral or indifferent to a particular breach of a moral rule. For example, if a person has a strong wish to smoke cannabis and the circumstance (setting) he or she takes part in is indifferent to such an action this may be enough to encourage him or her to go ahead with it.

in which case whether he or she will do X depends on his or her ability to exercise self-control (a typical example would be circumstances in which a person's *ability to exercise self-control* determines whether or not he can withstand "peer pressure" to breach a rule of conduct he himself holds) and (ii) when a person's moral rules encourage doing X, but the moral rules dominant in the setting discourage doing X, in which case whether he or she will do X depends on the *effectiveness of deterrence measures* in the setting (a typical example would be circumstances in which the level of perceived store security and threat of punishment if caught would determine whether or not a person would be put off from stealing something in a shop from which he considers stealing).

The relationship between motivation, moral rule-guidance (the moral filter) and controls in Situational Action Theory (Figure 12.5) can be summarised in the following manner:

(i) *motivation* (goal-directed attention) is a necessary precondition for (any) action

(ii) *moral rules* (the moral filter) determine what action alternatives a person perceives as means to satisfy the motivation (and, crucially, whether or not these alternatives involves a breach of a rule of conduct)

(iii) *controls* influence the process of choice among alternatives when (but only when) there is conflicting rule-guidance whether or not to act upon an action alternative that would breach a moral rule or law

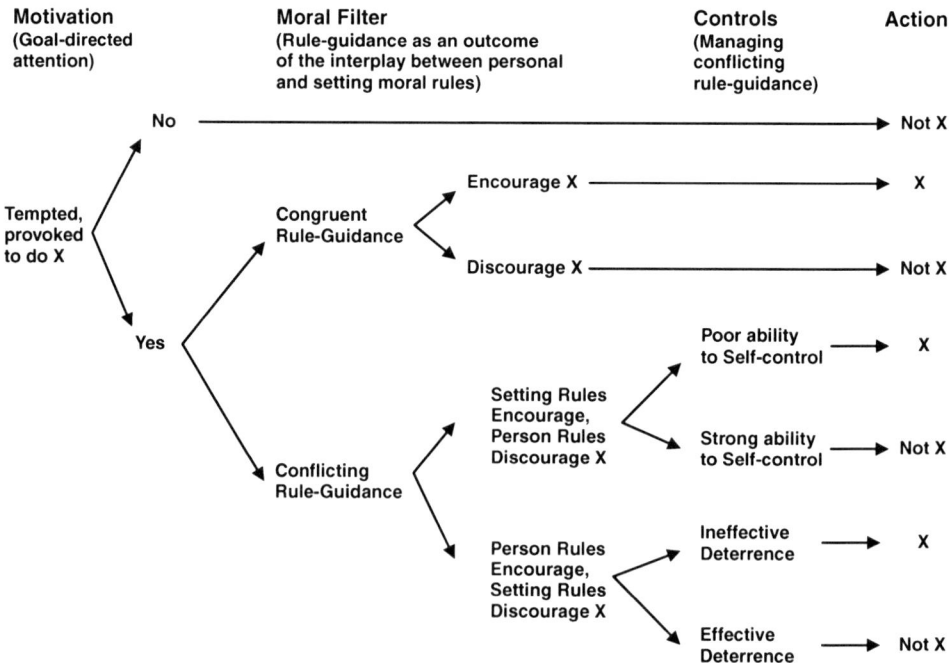

FIGURE 12.5. The roles of motivation, the moral filter and controls in the action process according to SAT illustrated.

ANALYSING THE CAUSES OF THE CAUSES OF MORAL ACTION AND CRIME

> Theories of action are ... of fundamental importance for explanatory sociological theories (Hedström 2005)
>
> What has been missing is a concept that directly links the community context to individual development and actions ... behavior-setting is a concept that may provide such a linkage' (Wikström and Sampson 2003)

Situational Action Theory makes a strong argument for the need to analyse and study *causes* of moral action and crime as *situational* rather than individual or collective. Kinds of actions are all about kinds of people in kinds of settings. This means that the core unit of analysis for action is *the person in the setting*, and the empirical investigation of causes of action, therefore, requires the development and utilisation of adequate methodologies that enable us to study *the person in the setting* (see Oberwittler and Wikström 2008, Wikström et al. 2010). However, this does not imply that the analysis and study of systemic factors and people's life histories are irrelevant; on the contrary. I will conclude this chapter with some general observations on the important role of such factors.

Systemic factors like inequality, segregation and poor social integration are *not* causes of crime, but may qualify as *causes of the causes* (of crime), and should therefore be analysed and studied as such. The same applies to aspects of people's life histories (e.g., their development of moral and cognitive skills and experiences of life events). Central questions that concern the causes of the causes (of crime) are

(i)   why people have different crime propensities (i.e. vary in their morality and ability to exercise self-control),

(ii)   why settings differ in their criminogenic features (i.e. in their moral rules and their enforcements) and, crucially,

(iii)   why certain kinds of people are exposed to certain kinds of settings.

A central argument of SAT is that to understand the role of systemic factors (such as segregation) and people's life histories (e.g. the role of specific life events) in crime causation, one needs to understand how these factors affect people's *exposur*e to particular settings in which they develop (e.g. their crime propensities) and act (e.g. respond to criminogenic influences).

A proper understanding of what factors move people to engage in acts of crime helps us focus our attention on what aspects of settings may influence the development of people's crime propensities or their decision to breach moral rules or laws.

When we are concerned with explaining the development and change in a person's *crime propensity* the main focus is naturally on understanding what aspects of settings are causally relevant influences on people's (i) *moral education* and (ii) development of *self-regulatory cognitive skills* (for particular developmental phases[30]).

---

[30] Environmental influences on the development of personal characteristics are likely to vary between developmental phases (for example, they are often much stronger in early compared to later phases of life).

When we are concerned with variation between settings (environments) in their crimino-genic influences, the prime focus is on factors that may explain (i) *why certain moral rules emerge* and (ii) *their level of enforcement* (through monitoring, intervention and threat of sanctions).

When we are concerned with what causes kinds of people's exposure to kinds of settings, it is all a question of selection processes. What kinds of settings people takes part in is far from random, an outcome of processes of (i) *social selection* (e.g. as a consequences of rules and resources that enable or constrain particular kinds of people's participation in particular kinds of settings) as related to systemic factors such as inequality and segregation and (ii) *self-selection* (e.g. based on a person's preferences and personal capital[31]), as related to a person's life history, within the broader environment in which he or she lives and operates.

REFERENCES

Agnew, R. 2005. *Pressured into Crime: An Overview of General Strain Theory.* Los Angeles, CA: Roxbury Publishing Company.

Agnew, R. 2009. "General Strain Theory: Current Status and Directions for Further Research." In *Taking Stock: The Status of Criminological Theory. Advances in Criminological Theory,* vol. 1, edited by F. Cullen. New Brunswick, NJ: Transaction Publishers.

Akers, R. L. 1989. "A Social Behaviorist's Perspective on Integration of Theories on Crime and Deviance." In *Theoretical Integration in the Study of Deviance and Crime: Problems and prospects,* edited by S. F. Messner, M. D. Krohn, and A. E. Liska. Albany: State University of New York Press.

Akers, R. L. 1991. "Self-Control as a General Theory of Crime." *Journal of Quantitative Criminology* 7:201–211.

Akers, R. L. 2009. *Social Learning and Social Structure. A General Theory of Crime and Deviance.* New Brunswick, NJ: Transaction Publishers.

Andenaes, J. (1974). *Punishment and Deterrence.* An Arbor: University of Michigan Press.

Aristotele. 1999. *Nicomachean Ethics,* translated by Martin Oswald. The Library of Liberal Arts, Upper Saddle River, NJ: Prentice Hall.

Bentham, J. 1970/1789. *An Introduction of the Principles of Morals and Legislation,* edited by H. L. A. Hart. London: Methuen.

Bernard, T. J. 1990. "Twenty Years of Testing Theories: What Have We Learned and Why?" *Journal of Research in Crime and Delinquency* 27:325–347.

Bottoms, A. E. 2002. "Morality, Crime, Compliance and Public policy." In *Ideology, Crime and Criminal Justice: A Symposium in Honour of Sir Leon Radzinowicz,* edited by A. E. Bottoms, and M. Tonry. Cullompton: Willan.

Briar, S., and I. Piliavin. 1965 "Delinquency, Situational Inducements, and the Commitment to Conformity." *Social Problems* 13:35–45.

Braithwaite, J. 1989. *Crime, Shame, and Reintegration.* Cambridge: Cambridge University Press.

Bunge, M. 1999. *The Sociology-Philosophy Connection.* New Brunswick, NJ: Transaction Publishers.

Bunge, M. 2004. "How Does it Work? The Search for Explanatory Mechanisms." *Philosophy of the Social Sciences* 34:182–210.

Bunge, M. 2006. *Chasing reality: Strife over Realism.* Toronto: University of Toronto Press.

Cohen, A. K. 1955. *Delinquent Boys: The Culture of the Gang.* New York: The Free Press.

Cohen, A. K., and J. F. Short Jr. 1961. "Juvenile delinquency." In *Contemporary Social Problems,* edited by R. K. Merton, and R. A. Nisbet. New York: Harcourt Brace & World.

Cohen, L. E., and M. Felson. 1979. "Social Change and Crime Rate Trends: A Routine Activity Approach." *American Sociological Review* 44:588–608.

Collins, R. 2000. Situational Stratification: A Micro-Macro Theory of Inequality. *Sociological Theory* 18:17–43.

---

[31] Human, financial and social capital that affect his or her agency (power to make particular things happen).

Cullen, F. T., J. P. Wright, and K. R. Blevins. 2008. *Taking Stock: The Status of Criminological Theory, Advances in Criminological Theory*, vol. 15. New Brunswick: Transaction Publishers.

Davidson, D. 2004. *Problems of Rationality*. Oxford: Clarendon Press.

Durkheim, E. 2002/1961. *Moral education*. Mineola, New York: Dover Publications.

Ehrlich, E. 2008/1936. *Fundamental Principles of the Sociology of Law*. New Brunswick, NJ: Transaction Publishers.

Ellis, L., K. Beaver, and J. Wright. 2009. *Handbook of Crime Correlates*. San Diego, CA: Academic Press.

Evans, J., and K. Frankish. 2009. *In Two Minds: Dual Processes and Beyond*. Oxford: Oxford University Press.

Farrington, D. P. 1992. "Explaining the Beginning, Progress and Ending of Antisocial Behavior from Birth to Adulthood." In *Facts, Frameworks, and Forecasts, Advances in Criminological Theory*, vol. 13, edited by J. McCord. New Brunswick, NJ: Transaction Publishers.

Farrington, D. P., R. J. Sampson, and P.-O. Wikström. 1993. *Integrating Individual and Ecological Aspects of Crime*. Stockholm: Fritzes.

Felson, M. 2002. *Crime and Everyday Life*, 3rd edition. Thousand Oaks: SAGE publications.

Felson, M. 2006. *Gime and Nature*. Thousand Oaks, CA: Sage Publications.

Frankish, K. 2009. "Systems and Levels: Dual-System Theories and the Personal-Subpersonal Distinction." In *In Two Minds: Dual Processes and Beyond*, edited by J. Evans, and K. Frankish. Oxford: Oxford University Press.

Geis, G. 2000. "On the Absence of Self-Control as the Basis for a General Theory of Crime: A Critique." *Theoretical Criminology* 4:410–419.

Goode, E. 2008. *Out of Control: Assessing the General Theory of Crime*. Stanford: Stanford University Press.

Goldthorpe, J. H. 2000. *On Sociology, Numbers, Narratives, and the Integration of Research and Theory*. Oxford: Oxford University Press.

Gottfredson, M. R., and T. Hirschi. 1990. *A General Theory of Crime*. Stanford, CA: Stanford University Press.

Gottfredson, M. R., and T. Hirschi. 2003. "Self-Control and Opportunity." In *Control Theories of Crime and Delinquency, Advances in Criminological Theory*, vol. 12, edited by C. L. Britt, and M. R. Gottfredson. New Brunswick, NJ: Transaction Publishers.

Hagan, J. 1988. *Structural Criminology*. Cambridge: Polity Press.

Harré, R., and P. F. Secord. 1972. *The Explanation of Social Behaviour*. Oxford: Basil Blackwell.

Hedström, P. 2005. *Dissecting the Social. On the Principles of Analytical Sociology*. Cambridge: Cambridge University Press.

Heckhausen, J., and H. Heckhausen. 2008. *Motivation and Action*. Cambridge: Cambridge University Press.

Hirschi, T. 1969. *Causes of Delinquency*. Berkeley: University of California Press.

Hirschi, T. 2002. "Introduction to the Transaction edition." In *Causes of Delinquency*, edited by T. Hirschi. New Brunswick: Transaction Publishers.

Hirschi, T. 2004. "Self-Control and Crime." In *Handbook of Self-Regulation: Research, Theory, and Applications*, edited by R. F. Baumeister, and K. D. Vohs. New York: The Guilford Press.

Hirschi, T., and Gottfredson, M. 1993. Commentary: Testing the General Theory of Crime. *Journal of Research in Crime and Delinquency* 30:47–54.

Hirschi, T., and M. R. Gottfredson. 1994. "The Generality of Deviance." In *The Generality of Deviance*, edited by T. Hirschi, and M. R. Gottfredson. New Brunswick, NJ: Transaction Publishers.

Hirschi, T., and M. R. Gottfredson. 2008. "Critiquing the Critics: The Authors Respond." In *Out of Control: Assessing the General Theory of Crime*, edited by E. Goode. Stanford: Stanford University Press.

Hollingshead, A. B. 1941. "The Concept of Social Control." *American Sociological Review* 6:217–224.

Jensen, G. F., and R. L. Akers. 2003. "Taking Social Learning Theory Global: Micro and Macro Transitions in Criminological Theory." In *Social Learning Theory and the Explanation of Crime, Advances in Criminological Theory*, vol. 11, edited by R. L. Akers, and G. F. Jensen. New Brunswick, NJ: Transaction Publishers.

Katz, J. 1988. *Seductions of Crime*. New York: Basic Books.

Kornhauser, R. R. 1978. *Social Sources of Delinquency*. Chicago: University of Chicago Press.

Laufer, W. S., and F. Adler. 1989. "Introduction: The Challenges of Advances in Criminological Theory." *Advances in Criminological Theory*, vol. 1, edited by W. S. Laufer, and F. Adler. New Brunswick: Transaction Publishers.

Leblanc, M., and A. Caplan. 1993. "Theoretical Formalization, A Necessity: The Example of Hirschi's Bonding Theory." PP. 239–343 in *New Directions in Criminological Theory, Advances in Criminological Theory*, vol. 4, edited by F. Adler, and W. S. Laufer. New Brunswick: Transaction Publishers.

Lemert, E. M. 1967. *Human Deviance, Social Problems and Social Control*. New York: Prentice-Hall.

Liska, A. E., M. D. Krohn, and S. F. Messner. 1989. "Strategies and Requisites for Theoretical Integration in the Study of Crime and Deviance." In *Theoretical Integration in the Study of Deviance and Crime: Problems and Prospects*, edited by S. F. Messner, M. D. Krohn, and A. E. Liska. Albany: State University of New York Press.

Matza, D. 1964. *Delinquency and Drift*. New York: John Wiley and Sons Inc.

Meier, R. F. 1982. "Perspectives on the Concept of Social Control." *Annual Review of Sociology* 8:35–55.

Mele, A. R. 2001. *Autonomous Agents: From Self-Control to Autonomy.* Oxford: Oxford University Press.

Merton, R. K. 1968. *Social Theory and Social Structure,* enlarged edition. New York: The Free Press.

Messner, S. F., M. D. Krohn, and A. E. Liska. 1989. *Theoretical Integration in the Study of Deviance and Crime: Problems and Prospects.* Albany: State University of New York Press.

Messner, S. F., and R. Rosenfeld. 2007. *Crime and the American Dream,* 4th edition. Belmont, CA: Thomson Wadsworth.

Newman, G. 2008. *Comparative Deviance: Perception and Law in Six Cultures.* New Brunswick, NJ: Transaction Publishers.

Oberwittler, D., and P.-O. H. Wikström. 2008. Why Small is Better. Advancing the Study of the Role of Behavioral Contexts in Crime Causation. In *Putting Crime in Its Place: Units of Analysis in Spatial Crime Research,* edtied by D. Weisburd, W. Bernasco, and G. Bruinsma. New York. Springer

Popper, K. 2000/1956. *Realism and the Aim of Science.* London: Routledge.

Psillos, S. 2002. *Causation and Explanation.* Montreal: McGill-Queen's University Press.

Reiss, A. J. Jr. 1951. "Delinquency as the Failure of Personal and Social Controls." *American Sociological Review* 16:196–207.

Reiss, A. J. Jr. 1986. "Why are Communities Important in Understanding Crime?" In *Communities and Crime: Crime and Justice: A Review of Research,* vol. 8, edited by A. J. Reiss, and M. Tonry. Chicago: University of Chicago Press.

Rutter, M. 2009. "Proceeding from Observed Correlation to Causal Inference." *Perspectives on Psychological Science* 2:377–395 (published online 2007).

Salmon, W. C. 1998. *Causality and Explanation.* Oxford: Oxford University Press.

Sampson, R. J. 2006. "Collective Efficacy Theory: Lessons Learned and Directions for Future Inquiry." In *Taking Stock: The Status of Criminological Theory, Advances in Criminological Theory,* vol. 15, edited by F. T. Cullen, J. P. Wright, and K. Blevins. New Brunswick: Transaction Publishers.

Schick, F. 1997. *Making Choices: A Recasting of Decision Theory.* Cambridge: Cambridge University Press.

Sutherland, E. H., D. R. Cressey, and D. F. Luckenbill. 1992. *Principles of Criminology,* 11th edition. Lanham: General Hall.

Tangney, J. P., and K. W. Fischer. 1995. *Self-Conscious Emotions: The Psychology of Shame, Guilt, Embarrassment, and Pride.* New York: The Guilford Press.

Tittle, C. R. 1995. *Control Balance: Toward a General Theory of Deviance.* Boulder, CO: Westview Press.

Tonry, M., L. E. Ohlin, and D. P. Farrington. 1991. *Human Development and Criminal Behavior.* New York: Springer.

Wikström, P.-O. H. 2004. "Crime as Alternative: Towards a Cross-Level Situational Action Theory of Crime Causation." PP. 1–37 in *Beyond Empiricism: Institutions and Intentions in the Study of Crime, Advances in Criminological Theory,* vol. 13, edited by J. McCord. New Brunswick, NJ: Transaction Publishers.

Wikström, P.-O. H. 2005. "The Social Origins of Pathways in Crime: Towards a Developmental Ecological Action Theory of Crime Involvement and Its Changes." In *Integrated Developmental and Life-Course Theories of Offending, Advances in Criminological Theory,* vol. 14, edited by D. P. Farrington. New Brunswick, NJ: Transaction Publishers.

Wikström, P.-O. H. 2006. "Individuals, Settings and Acts of Crime: Situational Mechanisms and the Explanation of Crime." In *The Explanation of Crime: Context, Mechanisms and Development,* edited by P.-O. H. Wikström, and R. J. Sampson. Cambridge: Cambridge University Press.

Wikström, P.-O. H. 2010. Situational Action Theory. In *Encyclopaedia of Criminological Theory,* edited by F. Cullen, and P. Wilcox. Beverly Hills: SAGE Publications.

Wikström, P.-O. H., and R. J. Sampson. 2003. "Social Mechanisms of Community Influences on Crime and Pathways in Criminality." In *Causes of Conduct Disorder and Juvenile Delinquency,* edited by B. B. Lahey, T. E. Moffitt, and A. Caspi. New York: Guilford Press.

Wikström, P.-O. H., and R. J. Sampson. 2006. "Introduction: Toward a Unified Approach to Crime and Its Explanation." In *The Explanation of Crime: Context, Mechanisms and Development,* edited by P.-O. H. Wikström, and R. J. Sampson. Cambridge: Cambridge University Press.

Wikström, P.-O. H., and K. Treiber. 2007. "The Role of Self-Control in Crime Causation: Beyond Gottfredson and Hirschi's General Theory of Crime." *European Journal of Criminology* 4:237–264.

Wikström, P.-O. H., and K. Treiber. 2009a. "What Drives Persistent Offending? The Neglected and Unexplored Role of the Social Environment." In *The Development of Persistent Offending,* edited by J. Savage. Oxford: Oxford University Press.

Wikström, P.-O. H., and K. Treiber. 2009b. "Violence as Situational Action." *International Journal of Conflict and Violence* 3:75–96.

Wikström, P.-O. H., V. Ceccato, B. Hardie, and K. Treiber. 2010. "Activity Fields and the Dynamics of Crime: Advancing Knowledge About the Role of the Environment in Crime Causation." *Journal of Quantitative Criminology* 26:55–87.

Wilson, J. Q., and R. J. Herrnstein. 1985. *Crime and Human nature*. New York: Touchstone Books.

Von Wright, G. H. 1971. *Explanation and Understanding*. London: Routledge & Kegan Paul.

Wrong, D. H. 1994. *The Problem of Order: What Unites and Divides Society*. New York: The Free Press.

Zimring, F. E., and G. J. Hawkins. 1968. "Deterrence and Marginal Groups." *Journal of Research in Crime and Delinquency* 5:100–114.

Zimring, F. E., and G. J. Hawkins. 1973. *Deterrence: The Legal Threat in Crime Control*. Chicago: University of Chicago Press.

CHAPTER 13

What Does God Require? Understanding Religious Context and Morality

Christopher D. Bader and Roger Finke

Morality is infused in many elements of culture and across many institutions, but here we explore the distinctive relationship between morality and religion. We recognize, of course, that religion is not necessarily unique in the behaviors it promotes or the morality it teaches. Indeed, the laws of secular states can influence the moral teachings of religious organizations and the religious organizations go to great lengths to have their morality adopted into legal code and enforced by the state. Likewise, we recognize that morality is not under the sole domain of religion. Virtually, all institutions and associations have codes of ethics or moral boundaries that help to distinguish right from wrong. Yet, despite the ubiquity of moral concerns and codes, we review research that identifies the distinctive contributions of religion when attempting to explain moral beliefs and behaviors.

We begin by briefly reviewing why religion is unique. Why does it hold a distinctive relationship with morality and what drives this relationship? In particular, we will draw attention to the belief in the supernatural and the demands the supernatural holds for those who believe. How does belief in a God or gods and in related institutions and codified teachings shape what is required for morality?

Next, we turn to the relationship between morality and religion. We will briefly explore how personal religiosity relates to attitudes about moral issues and related behaviors. We will focus upon two of the most active lines of related research, the relationship between religiosity and deviant/delinquent behavior, and the relationship between religiosity and sexual practices. Rather than merely highlighting how the religious beliefs or activities of individuals can shape their morality, we hope to draw attention to the religious context. How does religion contribute to the larger social order, and how do the group properties of religion shape beliefs and behaviors? Despite the attention lavished on this question by the field's founding theorists, the larger religious context is often missing in work that is more recent. A growing body of research has found that religious networks and religious context strongly influence when individuals will act on personal religious beliefs. Quite simply, we have to understand how religious context influences decision-making.

S. Hitlin, S. Vaisey (eds.), *Handbook of the Sociology of Morality*,
Handbooks of Sociology and Social Research, DOI 10.1007/978-1-4419-6896-8_13,
© Springer Science+Business Media, LLC 2010

We will then continue this line of thought by pulling back our focus to the level of nations. Building on the theory and data reviewed in the first two sections, and moving beyond the cultural context of local networks, we begin to outline a research agenda for understanding morality and religion using cross-national research. Finally, we will end with some general statements that summarize the current understanding of the relationship between religion and morality.

WHY RELIGION?

Any culture is filled with moral teachings on right and wrong and all institutions rely on moral codes to maintain order and cooperation, but religion is distinctive from most other forms. Perhaps most important, and certainly most distinctive, religion is based on belief in supernatural forces that have the power to act outside of time, space, and nature. Yet, social scientists have often shied away from talking about how belief in such powerful forces might influence behavior. Perhaps, there is a fear that to accept the real world impacts of religious beliefs is to accept the beliefs as real. Yet, social scientists should know better. W.I. Thomas and a long line of social psychologists have continually reminded us that when a believer defines something as real, it is real in its consequences (Thomas and Thomas 1928). Even when religious beliefs seem erroneous or outrageous to outsiders, we should expect them to motivate the actions of believers. Indeed, even though Durkheim and Marx were confident that belief in the gods would disappear, they recognized that until this happened religious belief would motivate social action.

Although, many forms of power and authority rely on a belief in a force greater than one, most religions are organized around a God or gods deemed to have power and authority over social action and institutions. In other words, believers view gods as an ultimate authority that can offer explanations that attempt to make human action and purpose intelligible.[1] The greater the gods' scope and power, the more demands they can make. Recent work has shown that belief in a God effectively predicts a variety of behaviors and attitudes when the God is viewed as interested in and judgmental of an individual's behavior (Greeley 1995, Stark 2001, Bader and Froese 2005, Froese and Bader 2007, 2008, Froese et al. 2008, Bader et al. 2010). The more powerful and responsive the God is perceived, the more the God can offer rewards of great value and punishment with high costs. The result is that monotheistic religions tend to place high demands on moral beliefs and behavior, while polytheistic religions give lesser attention to morality (Stark and Finke 2000, Stark 2001).

Over time, the demands of the god(s) are typically outlined in a systematic set of teachings, and in scores of less formal traditions that can vary widely from one religious group to the next. These formal guidelines are especially important when trying to understand the relationship between religion and morality because they offer ongoing assessments on where moral boundaries should be laid and they represent the wide variations

---

[1] This is most apparent in societies where there is a close link between church and state, such as some predominantly Islamic nations. But even in societies with a separation of church and state, the state is often justified as receiving authority from a god. The heated debate over removing "under God" from the U.S.A. pledge of allegiance offers one example.

that occur across religious groups. For example, Shari'a law was developed by Muslims to apply the Quran and the teachings of Muhammad to new and changing social situations. However, contrary to the views of many Westerners, there is no single version of Shari'a law and interpreting the law is far more fluid than many would expect. Currently, there are four major schools of Islamic law with many variations within each school (Dien 2004, Hallaq 2005).

These wide variations perhaps are even more pronounced in other monotheistic religions. The hundreds of Christian denominations and multiple Jewish sects within the USA alone display this variation in the morality taught and the manner in which adherents connect theology and morality. One of Weber's key insights was that teachings vary widely across Christian religions and that religion could shape social action just as the larger society shaped religion. Unlike Marx, Weber viewed the relationship between religious beliefs and economic action as reciprocal. Although, Weber's (1958) *Protestant Ethic* has been challenged, many other historical examples could be used to illustrate this reciprocal relationship. For example, the institution of slavery had a powerful impact on Christian churches, with some US denominations developing teachings to justify the institution (Ahlstrom 1975, Raboteau 1978). However, Christian teachings and institutions were also instrumental in abolishing slavery in Western Europe and the USA. Recent studies (Young 2002, Stark 2003) suggest that antislavery movements were guided by religious convictions and worked closely with religious institutions to mobilize support. Any discussion of religion and morality has to recognize the variation across religious groups and over time in what the gods require.

Religion is also a social phenomenon. At least since Durkheim, social scientists have recognized that religion, unlike magic, relies on the collective actions and beliefs of the group. The local congregational structure is especially important for the US Christianity, but virtually all monotheistic religions rely on collective beliefs and rituals for uniting the group. The collective qualities of religion not only contribute to how morality is defined, but they also help to explain how moral standards are enforced.

Of course, morality is not dependent on religion and religion is not confined to defining moral teachings. However, we would be naïve not to acknowledge that moral codes are often justified by religious teachings and those laying out the moral codes are often deified. Even the most secular states have failed to remove the divine as a source for justifying moral authority. Chairman Mao Zedong eliminated most vestiges of organized religion in China during the Cultural Revolution, and replaced the old ways with his own moral teachings but was unable to eliminate all belief in the divine. Ironically, the cult of Mao soon arose, granting him divine qualities and making him an object of prayer and confession (Zuo 1991). Mao's "personality cult" is only one of many that have arisen around strong dictators who laid out new moral codes. Even when the formal religious institutions are removed, many seek a higher power for justifying the moral code.

As we will review in the following sections, social networks are a key mechanism through which shared beliefs in higher powers influences moral behaviors. However, we will also find that influence of the religious context goes beyond immediate social networks. Unlike Durkheim, we do not assume a unified society with a shared collective conscience, but we do expect that religious cultures will vary across regions and these differences will be associated with variations in morality.

PERSONAL RELIGIOSITY AND MORAL ATTITUDES AND BEHAVIORS

Research has found the relationship between religiosity and attitudes on moral issues in the USA to be relatively straightforward. More religious people, as measured by frequency of church attendance, frequency of prayer, identification with a strict denomination, a literal interpretation of the Bible, and/or how religious a person considers him/herself to be, tend to hold more restrictive attitudes on moral issues. For example, religious beliefs are one of the strongest and most consistent predictors of attitudes about abortion in the USA (Jelen and Wilcox 2003). Religious beliefs are also one of the strongest predictors of the US attitudes towards and the tolerance of homosexuals (cf: Olson et al. 2006, Shulte and Battle 2004, Burdette et al. 2005, Froese et al. 2008) with conservative Protestants showing the lowest levels of acceptance (Ellison and Musick 1993, Reimer and Park 2001, Wilcox and Jelen 1990).

While the USA is often considered exceptionally religious compared to other industrialized nations, the relationship between religion and moral attitudes should not be assumed to be confined to the USA. Indeed, Smith (2003) argues that humans across cultures and across history are defined by a moral orientation that they often experience in spiritual or religious terms. Whether this is the case, religious beliefs have been found to be associated with conservative moral and political attitudes in other countries , such as Northern Ireland (Mitchell, et al. 2001, Taylor 1985), Israel (Kirschenbaum 1993), and Islamic regions in the Middle East and Central Asia (see Froese 2004, Marty and Appleby 1991, Adamczyk and Pitt 2009). There are also instances of religious movements aligning with liberal moral and political agendas (cf: Borowik 2002, Norris and Inglehart 2004, Moaddel 1996). However, the most common finding is that religiosity is associated with many restrictive moral attitudes.

Whereas, the relationship between religion and moral *attitudes* is relatively straightforward, the one between personal religiosity and *behavior* is far more complex. In some cases, there seems to be a clear connection. For example, scholars have devoted considerable attention to the relationship between personal religiosity and sexuality in the USA and have found a strong connection (cf: Adamczyk and Felson 2006, Brewster et al. 1998, Cochran and Beeghley 1991, Meier 2003, Regnerus 2003, Thornton and Camburn 1989). Religious teens tend to be older when having their first sexual encounter than secular teens (Cochran and Beeghley 1991, Meier 2003, Rostosky et al. 2004, Thornton and Camburn 1989). Moore and colleagues (1998) found that females who delay their first sexual experience tend to cite religious and moral reasons for their abstinence. As Adamczyk and Felson (2006:925) note: "[T]here is strong evidence that the relationship between religiosity and sexual debut is causal, although results are more robust for women than for men." Further, personal religiosity appears to limit the extent of sexual activity outside of marriage and the number of sexual partners (Jones et al. 2005, Davidson et al. 2004).

Unlike research on personal religiosity and sexual behaviors, initial studies on religion and deviant/delinquent behavior produced widely conflicting findings; disparate findings that ultimately led to new insights about the contextual effects of religion. In their often quoted "Hellfire and Delinquency" Hirschi and Stark (1969) used data from the Richmond Youth Study to examine the relationship between church attendance and delinquent behaviors amongst California youth. Surprisingly, Hirsch and Stark found that church attendance was not significantly related to delinquent or criminal behavior. In other words, kids who frequently attended church were no more or less likely than their non-attending peers to become involved in delinquency. Given criminology's traditional ambivalence towards the inclusion of religiosity measures in delinquency research, perhaps it is not surprising that Hirschi and Stark's findings were widely accepted.[2]

Yet, replications of Hirschi and Stark (1969) produced mixed results based on the region of the sample. Using a sample of teens from the Pacific Northwest, Burkett and White (1974) found that religious commitment reduced the probability of drug and alcohol use, but had no effect on other types of deviant behavior. Higgins and Albrecht (1977), however, found a strong, negative relationship between church attendance and delinquent behavior, using a sample of teenagers from Atlanta. Albrecht et al. (1977) also found a significant negative correlation between religiosity and delinquent behavior using a sample of Mormon youth living in Mormon wards in Idaho, Utah and Los Angeles, California.

In sum, early research on individual religiosity and delinquency found that the deterrent effects of religion appeared to depend upon where a sample was drawn. Studies conducted on the relatively irreligious West coast found that personal religiosity had little relationship to deviant behavior. However, samples drawn from more religious areas such as the South or Mormon wards in Utah found a significant deterrent effect. Coupled with the small group of macrolevel studies using ecological units of analysis that has consistently found that religion reduces most forms of social deviance (Stark et al. 1983, Bainbridge 1989, Stark and Bainbridge 1996, Ellison et al. 1997) it appears that the most convincing explanations for the relationship between religion and conservative morality must incorporate both macro- and micro-levels of explanation. Context matters.

THE IMPORTANCE OF CONTEXT

One of Durkheim's (1951) central propositions was that areas holding high levels of religious ritual (or social integration), will have lower rates of social deviance. Building on Durkheim's notion of "moral communities," Stark et al. (1982), Welch et al. (1991) proposed that individual religiosity deters delinquency, "but only in communities where the majority of people are actively religious" (Stark 1996:165). He argues that religion's ability to deter deviance relies on a context where religion "is accepted by the majority as a valid basis for action" (1996:164). Teens interpret societal norms in the context of their day-to-day interactions, he argues. A youth that experiences frequent interaction with religious people will learn that personal religiosity is a valid criterion for making decisions about behavior. Those surrounded by the irreligious will learn to use non-religious reasons or justifications for engaging in or avoiding certain behaviors. Hence, religion reduces delinquency for samples selected in highly religious Utah, but not in California. Stark's thesis is referred to as the "moral communities' hypothesis."

A key issue in testing the moral communities' hypothesis is how best to measure the strength of a religious context and, indeed, what qualifies as one. Stark et al.'s (1982) characterization of Seattle as a secular community, and Provo as a moral community, suggests cities or larger communities as the units of interest (see also Regnerus 2003). However, Stark

---

[2] After reviewing existing research on the relationship between religion and crime, Johnson and colleagues (2000:46) concluded, "[r]eligion is a large part of many people's lives, but it is not a large part of criminological research."

et al. (1982) and Regnerus (2003) also examine the religious character of schools, labeling them as secular or moral communities. Stark makes it clear that one cannot move too far from the individual when attempting to measure their religious context, for individuals experience membership in a moral community as part of their immediate surroundings or social setting: "[A] state is not a moral community" for the religious climates of states are too remote from the "everyday experience of individual boys" (Stark et al. 1982:15). In a similar vein, Evans et al. (1996) argue that many tests of the moral communities' hypothesis do not use sufficiently proximal measures of the religious context surrounding the individual.

Results do indeed vary depending upon the measure of religious context used. Regnerus (2003) found an interaction between religious homogeneity at the school and county level and personal religiosity in predicting delinquency. In other words, religious youth in more religious schools were less deviant than their non-religious counterparts, but the effect of personal religiosity was reduced in less religious settings. Stark et al. (1982) and Cochran and Akers (1989) both found significant effects of the religious character of a youth's school on his or her delinquency. On the other hand, Junger and Polder (1993) treated ethnic groups in the Netherlands as religious contexts, characterizing Moroccans and Turks as moral communities and the Dutch as a secular community. They found a significant, negative relationship between personal religiosity and deviant behavior, but this effect was not conditioned by the strength of the religious context surrounding the individual. Pearce and Haynie (2004) treated the family as a religious context, finding that the delinquency is related to religious disagreement in the family. If the youth was very either religious or the mother was not, or vice versa, the youth exhibited higher levels of delinquent behavior. In sum, research using schools, counties, and SMSAs, as the "community" suggests that it is not only the level of religious activity, but also the level of religious consensus or homogeneity that deters deviance (Ellison et al. 1997, Regnerus 2003). In addition, more research will determine whether the family can also operate as a supportive religious context for deterring delinquency.

When discussing the religion/deviance relationship, however, we must keep an exception in mind. A substantial body of research has found that the personal religiosity deters drug and alcohol use amongst youth regardless of the presence of a supportive religious context (cf. Burkett and White 1974, Cochran et al. 1988, Hadaway et al. 1984, Jensen and Erickson 1979, Perkins 1985). Religious youth appear less likely to use drugs and alcohol whether located in a religious or non-religious context.

Further complicating matters, more research has to be done to determine if religious context affects the relationship between personal religiosity and sexual behaviors. A recent line of research suggests that, like the findings for drug use, it may not. For example, in an examination of abortion decision-making, Adamczyk (2008) finds that identification with a conservative Protestant denomination was negatively related to the decision to have an abortion, but this effect was *not* dependent upon religious context. Conservative Protestant women were less likely to choose to have an abortion whether they lived in religious or non-religious areas. Further, using the religious composition of friendship networks, Adamczyk and Felson (2006) find that personal religiosity delays a youth's first sexual encounter as does the religiosity of his/her friends, but friend's religiosity does not condition the effect of personal religious convictions. In other words, having religious friends does not appear to increase the effect of one's personal religiosity in delaying the onset of sex.

Although, research on the moral communities hypothesis continues to grapple with measures of context, focusing upon local religious composition and immediate social networks, a recent body of work has moved up to the larger context of national differences. Using cross-national data, such research tries to understand how religion shapes the larger cultural context.

RELIGION AND MORALITY IN CROSS-CULTURAL CONTEXT

A core question for sociology is how does society shape personal beliefs and action? As just reviewed, most past research on religion and morality has looked at the effects of local social networks or institutions on the attitudes and actions of the individual; research questions that can easily be addressed with local or national surveys. However, the question also calls for attention to the larger society. How the larger cultural context does shapes personal beliefs and action? For the discipline's founders, this raised a series of questions about how religion contributes to the larger social order, and how the group properties of religion shape beliefs and behaviors. Weber's Protestant Ethic thesis and Durkheim's arguments on the integrative capacity of religion are perhaps the most familiar, but their discussions went far beyond these frequently cited propositions.

Virtually, all current sociological theories also point to identities, beliefs, and social structures that go beyond individuals and their local networks. Although, Durkheim's macrolevel arguments assuming a unified society with a shared collective conscience have faced sharp criticism (Pope 1976, Tilly 1981, Collins 1982), there is still the recognition of a collective identity (Alexander 1998), shared assumptions for exchanges (Coleman 1990) and a capital gained from knowing and understanding the culture (Bourdieu 1986). That is, there is a shared recognition that the larger context does matter. When applied to the religious national context, religious beliefs about morality are transmitted through social structures as well as cultural expectations.[3] In many religious nations, for example, religious messages about morality will be conveyed through public discourse, public institutions, legal codes, social norms, and family structures and gender roles.[4] Secular and religious people alike are exposed to this national religious context.

Because most quantitative research on morality relies on samples from a single nation, however, the influence of the larger cultural or national context receives little attention. Until recently, we have not had the data or the statistical methods necessary for sorting out the effects of personal religious beliefs and the contextual effects of the larger society. With the improving coverage of cross-national surveys and the use of Hierarchical Linear Modeling Techniques (HLM) some initial findings are beginning to emerge; findings that confirm the importance of the national religious context. Using fifteen nations from the 1991 International Social Survey Program (ISSP), studies have found that the people living in religious nations hold more orthodox religious beliefs (Kelley and De Graaf 1997) and that both individual and national religiosity influence personal moral attitudes (Scheepers et al. 2002). However,

---

[3] For a more detailed discussion on the importance of including both structural and cultural influences, see Rubinstein (2001) and Friedland (2001).

[4] Recent work by Moore and Vanneman (2003) illustrates the importance of religious context for shaping gender attitudes.

Jelen et al. (1993) find that the relationship between religion and morality can vary by the level of analysis. They report that at the individual-level, Catholics consistently hold negative attitudes toward legal abortion, but the contextual effects of Roman Catholicism run in the opposite direction.

The most convincing tests of the national religious context, however, have relied on many recent cross-national surveys with more nations. Using the WVS and the ISSP, Finke and Adamczyk (2008) find that both the religious context and the interaction between the religious context and the respondent's personal religious beliefs are strongly associated with attitudes on sexual morality even when multiple controls are entered. They also find that the influence of religion cannot be reduced to social ritual or social integration. The coefficients for religious importance were consistently stronger than those for religious ritual (e.g. worship attendance) and when alternative measures of social integration (e.g. migration) were added the coefficients for religiosity remained strong. Adamczyk and Pitt (2009) used HLM modeling to examine whether cultural orientation conditions the effects of personal religiosity on attitudes towards homosexuals across thirty-three nations. Drawing upon work by Inglehart and Baker (2000), Adamczyk and Pitt find that in nations characterized by a survival cultural orientation, religious prohibitions against homosexuality tend to be in line with secular norms and laws. Hence, in such nations personal religiosity will not have a strong effect on attitudes towards homosexuals. However, as nations' transition to a focus upon self-expression, secular norms about homosexuality will tend to liberalize, thereby providing religion a greater role in influencing attitudes towards homosexuals.

Despite such promising initial efforts to understand the relationship between morality and the national religious context, the existing work is still very limited. Much work remains and below we lay some initial groundwork for a future research agenda.

EXPANDING THE CROSS-NATIONAL RESEARCH AGENDA

The agenda for future cross-national research on religion and morality is boundless. Here, we will limit our attention to three areas. First, is the measurement of religion. Because the measures of religion used in predominantly Christian countries have little utility in a cross-cultural context, we have to rethink how we measure religion across multiple world religions (including atheism). Second, we have to be more attentive to how the religious context will be associated with different types of morality. In particular, we have to be attentive to the level of agreement between the morality promoted by religion and the morality sanctioned by the state. Third, we want to look at how the national context might have greater sway over some groups than others. Are some groups more effective in shunning the influence of the larger culture?

Perhaps, the greatest challenge for cross-cultural research on religion and morality is developing appropriate religion measures. Religious doctrines differ so dramatically, even within a single world religion, that common theological language and conceptions are often lacking as a point of comparison. Survey questions about the divinity of Jesus, the importance of spreading faith, how literally one takes the Bible, whether one has been "born again" and so on are often problematic for nations with a diverse Christian population and they are simply inappropriate for a majority non-Christian population. We propose that researchers avoid the ambiguities of beliefs, doctrines, or activities specific to one religion by focusing on an aspect of religion that is common to nearly all religions: conceptions of God.

Building on the work of Andrew Greeley, a series of articles (Bader and Froese 2005, Froese and Bader 2008, Froese et al. 2008, Froese and Bader 2010) have found two salient characteristics of God that affect social, moral and political attitudes. First, believing that God is actively engaged with the world is highly associated with attitudes and behaviors. When God is conceived of as a passive part of the cosmic order, believers pay little attention to how their moral behavior fit with "God's plan" (Stark 2001). As Simmel (1997:53) noted, "[a] deity that is subsumed into a unity with the whole of existence cannot possibly possess any power, because there would be no separate object to which He could apply such power." In contrast, a God who appears an active force in worldly events should influence the attitudes of believers on a whole host of topics. Second, God's "level of judgment" is also influential. For some, God is understood as a loving and endlessly forgiving deity while others posit a judgmental and punishing God. Andrew Greeley found that the Americans with more maternal and gracious conceptions of God will be more likely to vote Democrat (Greeley 1988), support "safe sex" education (Greeley 1991), support environmental protection (Greeley 1993), and oppose the death penalty (Greeley 1989:98). Overall, Greeley found significant bivariate correlations between viewing God as a mother, lover, or friend and more liberal policy opinions on specific issues.

Despite a paucity of cross-national measures for testing this new line of research, the initial results look promising. Froese and Bader (2008) found that images of God were strongly related to abortion attitudes and attitudes about sexual morality in seven Western industrial and postindustrial societies (Australia, France, Hungary, Ireland, New Zealand, Slovak Republic, the USA). Using the World Values Survey, Stark (2001) found that belief in the importance of a transcendental authority was significantly and negatively associated with attitudes toward smoking marijuana and stealing across Europe and in India, Turkey, and the USA; but the relationship did not hold in China or Japan. Following from his theoretical assumptions, Stark (2001b:624) concludes that self-reported importance of God had no effect on attitudes towards deviance in China and Japan because God is generally regarded as "unconcerned about morality, or as an impersonal essence" in these religious cultures. Therefore, the type of God imagined and not simply the idea of a transcendent authority was essential to how individuals understood social deviance.

A second item on the agenda is giving closer attention to the type of morality being studied. As mentioned earlier, despite holding unique properties, religion is not always distinctive in the behaviors promoted or the morality taught. Building on the work of a small group of studies from the USA (Burkett and White 1974, Tittle and Welch 1983, Hadaway et al. 1984), Finke and Adamczyk (2008) have argued that we should expect religious beliefs and the national religion context to be more influential when moral issues are not sanctioned by legal codes. They explain that all members of a nation are held accountable for actions violating legal codes, but personal beliefs and informal cultural expectations serve as the guide for morality not sanctioned by the state. As a result, when legal codes are absent and the morality in question is openly contested, the norms and sanctions of religion (and cultural norms more generally) should hold greater sway. In other words, when religious institutions and teachings stand alone in sanctioning a behavior, religion's influence should increase and when religion is one of many forces sanctioning a behavior, its effects should be reduced.

Based on this argument, the religious context should hold only a weak relationship with morality uniformly sanctioned by the state, such as stealing, but should have greater sway over contested morality, like sexual behaviors. As reviewed above, the initial cross-national studies have found that religion is associated with many conservative views of sexual morality, but many questions remain about the relationship religion holds with morality that is formally sanctioned by the state. Finke and Adamczyk's cross-national research found tentative support for the thesis that the relationship is diminished when morality is formally sanctioned by the state (i.e. multiple measures on cheating the government), but they also found that the line between moralities sanctioned by the state and those that are not is a faint one indeed. Although, cheating the government was uniformly sanctioned by the state and the heterosexual relations measured in the ISSP received few state sanctions, same-sex relations drew a varied response from the state. This suggests that it is not only whether the morality is sanctioned by the state that determines the influence of religion, but also the degree of morality in question is contested. Thus, future work should measure the extent to which legal codes are lenient, absent or even contradict the behaviors and beliefs proscribed by a religion.

A third issue that needs to be addressed is if the national religious context has greater influence on some than others do. To the extent that groups and individuals are more isolated from the national culture, we would expect the national religious context to have less influence. Small religious sects and communes offer one example of groups that attempt to isolate themselves from the dominant culture and develop their own religious culture. A long line of social theory has recognized the capacity of small religious sects to control the behavior of their members. Adam Smith wrote "in little religious sects . . . the morals of the common people have been almost always remarkably regular and orderly" (1776 [1976]:317). Likewise, Weber (Gerth and Mills 1946:316) and Troeltsch (1911:vol. I, p. 331) noted the small sects maintain high moral and religious standards. More recent work has shown how stringent membership demands and small fellowships allow religious groups to generate high levels of commitment to the group's teachings (Kelley 1972, Iannaccone 1994, Stark and Finke 2000, Olson and Perl 2001). Yet, the existing research has not tested the effects of the national context on the beliefs and actions of individuals.[5]

In short, the study of cross-national research on religion and morality is still in its infancy. Despite receiving extensive attention from early theorists, the relationship between the larger cultural/national context and the moral attitudes and behaviors of individuals is still poorly understood and seldom tested.

CONCLUSION

Thus, what do we know about the relationship between religion and morality? Based on a substantial body of research conducted in the USA, we offer the following summary statements.

---

[5] Moreover, religious groups are not the only ones to isolate themselves and to shun the demands of the larger culture. Groups can be isolated due to their physical location (e.g. remote rural areas or shunned urban areas) or their social location (e.g. age, social class, etc.) and many groups create a subculture in an effort to avoid the influence of the larger culture. For example, universities often become an isolated domain with its own cultural demands and recent immigrants create their own subcultures and communities to support elements of their homeland culture.

- Personal religiosity has a significant impact on *attitudes* regarding moral issues, with many religious people expressing more conservative/absolutist attitudes in most cases.
- With the exception of drug and alcohol use, there is evidence that the relationship between personal religiosity and *delinquent behavior* is conditioned by the religious context, as measured by the level of religious consensus or homogeneity at the school, county, SMSA and, perhaps, family level.
- The effect of personal religiosity on *sexual morality* does not appear to be conditioned by the level of religious consensus or homogeneity.

When we move into the global arena, however, the research is more limited and therefore the conclusions are far more tentative. Based on the limited body of work, we would offer the following statements.

- The moral attitudes of individuals are related to the national religious context, the individuals' religious beliefs, and the interaction between the two.
- Research suggests that this relationship might vary by the type of morality being studied and the degree to which that morality is sanctioned by the state.

We should caution, however, that the first statement is limited to moral attitudes (not behaviors) and the second statement has received little research attention.

In closing, we want to repeat our call for improving cross-national research on morality, in general, and on religion and morality more specifically. We suggest that the starting point is improving cross-national measures. In order to facilitate cross-cultural analyses, our measures of religion must be meaningful across multiple religious cultures and groups. For morality, the measures must include behaviors as well as attitudes and must include morality that varies to the degree it is prohibited by the state. Finally, we have to be aware of how the larger cultural context might influence some groups more than others. In the end, we want to know what individuals believe the gods require, if anything, and how social context shapes their willingness to live out these requirements.

BIBLIOGRAPHY

Adamczyk, A. 2009. "Selection or Socialization in the Link Between Friends Religiosity and First Sex." *Sociology of Religion* 60:5–27.

Adamczyk, A. 2008. "The Effects of Religious Contextual Norms, Structural Constraints, and Personal Religiosity on Abortion Decisions." *Social Science Research* 37: 657–672.

Adamczyk, A., and J. Felson. 2008. "Fetal Positions: Unraveling the Influence of Religion on Premarital Pregnancy Resolution." *Social Science Quarterly* 89:17–38.

Adamczyk, A., and J. Felson. 2006. "Friends' Religiosity and First Sex." *Social Science Research* 35:924–947.

Adamczyk, A., and C. Pitt. 2009. "Shaping Attitudes About Homosexuality: The Role of Religion and Cultural Context." *Social Science Research* 38:338–351.

Ahlstrom, S. E. 1975. *A Religious History of the American People*. Garden City, New York: Image Books.

Albrecht, S. L., B. A. Chadwick, and D. S. Alcorn. 1977. "Religiosity and Deviance: Application of the Attitude-Behavior Contingent Consistency Model." *Journal for the Scientific Study of Religion* 16:263–274.

Alexander, J. C. 1998. *Neo-Functionalism and After*. Oxford, UK: Blackwell.

Bader, C., S. Desmond, and B. Johnson. Forthcoming, 2010. "Divine Justice: How Images of God Impact Attitudes Toward Criminal Punishment." *Criminal Justice Review*.

Bader, C., and P. Froese. 2005. *"Images of God: The Effect of Personal Theologies on Moral Attitudes, Political Affiliation, and Religious Behavior."* Interdisciplinary Journal of Research on Religion *1, Article 11: v.*

Baier, C. J., and B. R. E. Wright. 2001. "'If You Love Me, Keep my Commandments': A Meta-Analysis of the Effect of Religion on Crime." *Journal of Research in Crime and Delinquency* 38:3–21.

Bainbridge, W. S. 1989. "The Religious Ecology of Deviance." *American Sociological Review* 54:288–295.

Brewster, K. L., E. C. Cooksey, D. K. Guilkey, and R. R. Rindfuss. 1998. "The Changing Impact of Religion on the Sexual and Contraceptive Behavior of Adolescent Women in the United States." *Journal of Marriage and the Family* 60(2):493–504.

Borowik, I. 2002. "The Roman Catholic Church in the Process of Democratic Transformation: The Case of Poland." *Social Compass* 49(2):239–252.

Bourdieu, P. 1986. "The Forms of Capital." In Handbook of Theory and Research for the Sociology of Education, edited by J. G. Richardson. New York: Greenwood Press.

Burdette, A. M., C. G. Ellison, T. D. Hill. 2005. "Conservative Protestantism and Tolerance Toward Homosexuals: An Examination of Potential Mechanisms." Sociological Inquiry 75:177–196.

Burkett, S. R., and M. White. 1974. "Hellfire and Delinquency: Another Look." *Journal for the Scientific Study of Religion* 13:455–462.

Cochran, J. K., and R. L. Akers. 1989. "Beyond Hellfire: An Exploration of the Variable Effects of Religiosity on Adolescent Marijuana and Alcohol Use." *Journal of Research in Crime and Delinquency* 26:198–225.

Cochran, J. K., and L. Beeghley. 1991. "The Influence of Religion on Attitudes Toward Nonmarital Sexuality: A Preliminary Assessment of Reference Group Theory." *Journal for the Scientific Study of Religion* 30:45–62.

Cochran, J. K., L. Beeghly, and E. Wilbur Bock. 1992. "The Influence of Religious Stability and Homogamy on the Relationship and Alcohol Use Among Protestants." *Journal for the Scientific Study of Religion* 31(4): 441–456.

Coleman, J. S. 1990. *Foundations of Social Theory.* Cambridge: The Belknap Press of Harvard University Press.

Collins, R. 1982. *Sociological Insight: An Introduction to Non-obvious Sociology.* New York: Oxford University Press.

Davidson, J. K., N. B. Moore, and K. M. Ullstrup. 2004. "Religiosity and Sexual Responsibility: Relationships of Choice." *American Journal of Health Behavior* 28:335–346.

Dien, M. I. 2004. *Islamic Law: From Historical Foundations to Contemporary Practice.* Notre Dame, Indiana: University of Notre Dame Press.

Durkheim, É. 1951. *Suicide.* New York: Free Press.

Ellison, C. G., J. A. Burr, and P. L. McCall. 1997. "Religious Homogeneity and Metropolitan Suicide Rates." *Social Forces* 76:273–299.

Ellison, C. G., and M. Musick. 1993. "Southern Intolerance: A Fundamentalist Effect?" *Social Forces* 72(2):379–398.

Evans, T. D., F. T. Cullen, V. S. Burton, Jr., R. G. Dunaway, G. L. Payne, and S. R. Kethineni. 1996. "Religion, Social Bonds, and Delinquency." *Deviant Behavior* 17:43–70.

Finke, R., and A. Adamczyk. 2008 "Cross-National Moral Beliefs: The Influence of National Religious Context." *The Sociological Quarterly* 49:617–652.

Friedland, R. 2001. "Religious Nationalism and the Problem of Collective Representation." *Annual Review of Sociology* 27:125–152.

Froese, P. 2004. "Forced Secularization in Soviet Russia: Why an Atheistic Monopoly Failed." *Journal for the Scientific Study of Religion* 43:1, 35–50.

Froese, P., and C. D. Bader. 2010. *America's Four Gods.* New York, NY: Oxford University Press.

Froese, P., and C. Bader. 2008. "Unraveling Religious Worldviews: The Relationship Between Images of God and Political Ideology in a Cross-cultural Analysis." *The Sociological Quarterly* 49:4: 689–718.

Froese, P., C. D. Bader, and B. Smith. 2008. "Political Tolerance and God's Wrath in the United States." *Sociology of Religion* 69(1):29–44.

Froese, P., and C. D. Bader. 2007. "God in America: Why Theology is not Simply the Concern of Philosophers." *Journal for the Scientific Study of Religion* 46(4):465–482.

Gerth, H. H., and C. Wright Mills, eds. 1946. *From Max Weber: Essays in Sociology.* New York: Oxford University Press.

Greeley, A. 1995. *Religion as Poetry.* New Brunswick, NJ: Transaction Publishers.

Greeley, A. M. 1993. "Religion and Attitudes toward the Environment." *Journal for the Scientific Study of Religion* 32:19–28.

Greeley, A. M. 1991. "Religion and Attitudes towards AIDS policy." *Sociology and Social Research* 75:126–132.

Greeley, A. M. 1989. *Religious Change in America.* Cambridge: Harvard University Press.

Greeley, A. M. 1988. "Evidence that a Maternal Image of God correlates with Liberal Politics." *Sociology and Social Research* 72:150–154.

Hadaway, C. K., K. W. Elifson, and D. M. Petersen. 1984. "Religious Involvement and Drug Use." *Journal for the Scientific Study of Religion* 23:109–128.

Hallaq, W. B. 2005. *The Origins and Evolution of Islamic Law.* Cambridge, United Kingdom: Cambridge University Press.

Higgins, P. C., and G. L. Albrecht. 1977. "Hellfire and Delinquency Revisited." *Social Forces* 55:952–958.

Hirschi, T., and R. Stark. 1969. "Hellfire and Delinquency." *Social Problems* 17:202–213.

Iannaccone, L. R. 1994. "Why Strict Churches are Strong." *American Journal of Sociology* 99(5):1180–1211.

Iannaccone, L. R. 1991. "The Consequences of Religious Market Regulation: Adam Smith and the Economics of Religion." *Rationality and Society* 3:156–177.

Inglehart, R., W. E. Baker. 2000. "Modernization, Cultural Change, and the Persistence of Traditional Values. *American Sociological Review* 65:19–51.

Jelen, T. G., and C. Wilcox. 2003. "Causes and Consequences of Public Attitudes Toward Abortion: A Review and Research Agenda." *Political Research Quarterly* 56:489–500.

Jelen, T. G., J. O'Donnell, and C. Wilcox. 1993. "A Contextual Analysis of Catholicism and Abortion Attitudes in Western Europe." *Sociology of Religion* 54:375–383

Jensen, G. F., and M. L. Erickson. 1979. "The Religious Factor and Delinquency: Another Look at the Hellfire Hypothesis." In *The Religious Dimension: New Directions in Quantitative Research,* edited by R. Wuthnow. New York: Academic Press.

Johnson, B. R., S. DeLi, D. Larson, and M. McCullough, 2000. "A Systematic Review of the Religiosity and Delinquency Literature. "*Journal of Research in Crime and Delinquency* 16:32–52.

Jones, R. K., J. E. Darroch, and S. Singh. 2005. "Religious Differentials in the Sexual and Reproductive Behaviors of Young Women in the United States." *Journal of Adolescent Health* 36:279–288.

Junger, M., and W. Polder. 1993. "Religiosity, Religious Climate, and Delinquency Among Ethnic Groups in the Netherlands." *British Journal of Criminology* 33:416–435.

Kelley, D. M. 1972. *Why Conservative Churches are Growing.* New York: Harper and Row.

Kelley, J., and N. D. De Graaf. 1997. "National Context, Parental Socialization, and Religious Belief: Results from 15 Nations." *American Sociological Review* 62:639–659.

Kirschenbaum, A. 1993. "Fundamentalism: A Jewish Traditional Perspective." In *Jewish Fundamentalism in Comparative Perspective,* edited by L. J. Silberstein. New York: NYU Press.

Marty, M., and R. S. Appleby. 1991. *Fundamentalism Observed.* Chicago: University of Chicago Press.

Meier, A. M., 2003. "Adolescents' Transition to First Intercourse, Religiosity and Attitudes about Sex." *Social Forces* 81:1031–1052.

Mitchell, P., B. O'Leary, and G. Evans. 2001. "Northern Ireland: Flanking Extremists Bite the Moderates and Emerge with their Clothes." *Parliamentary Affairs* 54(4):725–742.

Moaddel, M. 1996. "The Social Bases and Discursive Content on the rise of Islamic Fundamentalism." *Sociological Inquiry* 66: 330–355.

Moore, K. A., A. K. Driscoll, and L. D. Lindberg. 1998. *Statistical Portrait of Adolescent Sex, Contraception, and Childbearing.* Washington, DC: National Campaign to Prevent Teen Pregnancy.

Moore, L., and R. Vanneman. 2003. "Context Matters: Proportion Fundamentalists Effects on Gender Attitudes." *Social Forces* 82:115–140.

Norris, P., and R. Inglehart. 2004. *Sacred and Secular: Religion and Politics Worldwide.* Cambridge: Cambridge University Press.

Olson, D. V. A., and P. Perl. 2001. "Variations in Strictness and Religious Commitment Within and Among Five Denominations." *Journal for the Scientific Study of Religion* 40:757–764.

Olson, L. R., W. Cadge, J. T. Harrison. 2006. "Religion and Public Opinion about Same-Sex Marriage." *Social Science Quarterly* 87:340–360.

Pearce, L. D., and D. L. Haynie. 2004. "Intergenerational Religious Dynamics and Adolescent Delinquency." *Social Forces* 82 (4):1553–1572.

Perkins, H. W. 1985. "Religious Traditions, Parents, and Peers as Determinants of Alcohol and Drug Use Among College Students." *Review of Religious Research* 27(1):15–31.

Pope, W. 1976. *Durkheim's Suicide: A Classic Analyzed.* Chicago: The University of Chicago Press.

Raboteau, A. J. 1978. *Slave Religion: The "Invisible Institution" in the Antebellum South.* New York: Oxford University Press.

Regnerus, M. D. 2003. "Moral Communities and Adolescent Delinquency: Religious Contexts and Community Social Control." *Sociological Quarterly* 44:523–554.

Reimer, S., and J. Park. 2001. "Tolerant (In)civility? A Longitudinal Analysis of White Conservative Protestants' Willingness to Grant Civil Liberties." *Journal for the Scientific Study of Religion* 40:735–745.

Rostosky, S. S., B. L. Wilcox, M. L. C. Wright, B. A. Randall. 2004. The Impact of Religiosity on Adolescent Sexual Behavior: A Review of the Evidence. *Journal of Adolescent Research* 19:677–697.

Rubinstein, D. 2001. *Culture, Structure, and Agency: Toward a Truly Multidimensional Society.* Thousand Oaks, CA: Sage Press.

Scheepers, P., M. Te. Grotenhuis, and F. Van Der Slik. 2002. "Education, Religiosity and Moral Attitudes: Explaining Cross-National Effect Differences." *Sociology of Religion* 63:157–176.

Shulte, L., and J. Battle. 2004. "The Relative Importance of Ethnicity and Religion Predicting Attitudes Towards Gays and Lesbians." *Journal of Homosexuality* 2:127–142.

Simmel, G. 1997. "Religion and the Contradictions in Life." In *Essays on Religion.* Trans. by P. E. Hammond. London: Yale University Press.

Smith, A. 1776 [1976]. An Inquiry into the Nature and Causes of the Wealth of Nations, in *The Glasgow edition of the works and correspondence of Adam Smith*, vol. 2, edited by R. H. Campbell, A. S. Skinner, and W. B. Todd. Oxford: Oxford University Press.

Smith, A. 1981 (1776). *An Inquiry into the Nature and Causes of the Wealth of Nations*, 2 vols, Indianapolis: Liberty Fund.

Smith, C. 2003. *Moral, Believing Animals: Human Personhood and Culture.* New York: Oxford University Press.

Stark, R. 2003. *For the Glory of God: How Monotheism led to Reformations, Science, Witch-hunts, and the end of Slavery.* Princeton: Princeton University Press.

Stark, R. 2001. "Gods, Rituals, and the Moral Order." *Journal for the Scientific Study of Religion* 40:619–636.

Stark, R. 1996. "Religion as Context: Hellfire and Delinquency One More Time." *Sociology of Religion* 57:163–173.

Stark, R., and W. S. Bainbridge. 1996. *Religion, Deviance, and Social Control.* New York: Routledge.

Stark, R., W. S. Bainbridge, R. D. Crutchfield, D. Doyle, and R. Finke. 1983. "Crime and Delinquency in the Roaring Twenties." *Journal of Research in Crime and Delinquency* 20:4–23.

Stark, R., L. Kent, and D. P. Doyle. 1982. "The Ecology of a 'Lost' Relationship." *Journal for the Scientific Study of Religion* 19: 4–24.

Stark, R., and R. Finke. 2000. *Acts of Faith: Explaining the Human Side of Religion.* Berkeley, CA: University of California Press.

Taylor, D. 1985. "The Lord's Battle: Paisleyism in Northern Ireland." In *Religious Movements: Genesis, Exodus and Numbers,* edited by R. Stark. New York: Paragon House Publishers.

Thomas, W. I., and D. S. Thomas. 1928. *The Child in America.* New York: Alfred A. Knopf.

Thornton, A., and D. Camburn. 1989. "Religious Participation and Adolescent Sexual Behavior and Attitudes." *Journal of Marriage and the Family* 51:641–653.

Tilly, C. 1981. *As Sociology Meets History.* New York: Academic Press.

Tittle, C. R., and M. R. Welch. 1983. "Religiosity and Deviance: Toward a Contingency Theory of Constraining Effects." *Social Forces* 61: 653–671.

Troeltsch, E. 1931 (1911). *The Social Teaching of the Christian Churches,* 2 volumes. New York: Macmillan.

Weber, M. 1958 (1904). *The Protestant Ethic and the Spirit of Capitalism.* New York: Scribner's.

Welch, M. R., C. R. Tittle, and T. Petee. 1991. "Religion and Deviance among Adult Catholics: A Test of the 'Moral Communities' Hypothesis." *Journal for the Scientific Study of Religion* 30:159–172.

Wilcox, C., and T. Jelen. 1990. "Evangelicals and Political Tolerance." *American Politics Quarterly* 18:25–46.

Young, M. P. 2002. "Confessional Protest: The Religious Birth of U.S. National Social Movements." *American Sociological Review* 67:660–688.

Zuo, J. 1991. "Political Religion: The Case of the Cultural Revolution in China." *Sociological Analysis* 52:99–110.

CHAPTER 14

The Duality of American Moral Culture

Wayne Baker

In a lecture included in his *Essays, Lectures, and Orations* (1848), Ralph Waldo Emerson remarked on a universal pattern of alternation, "The two parties of which divide the state, the party of Conservatism and that of Innovation, are very old, and have disputed the possession of the world ever since it was made. This quarrel is the subject of civil history... The war rages not only in the battlefields, in national councils, and ecclesiastical synods, but agitates in every man's bosom with opposing advantages every hour. On rolls the whole world meantime, and now one, now the other gets the day and still the fight renews itself as if for the first time, under new names and hot personalities." The alternation of mutual opposites operates in political, cultural, and religious arenas (Baker 2005). Systems of mutual opposites – dualities – have been observed in cultures around the world (Maybury-Lewis and Almagor 1989) and have ancient roots (e.g., Jaspers 1953, Orrù 1987).

I explore the duality of American moral culture as follows. First, I define the two principles that constitute this moral dynamic: duality and alternation. I offer explanations of why duality occurs and what drives alternation. Second, I illustrate duality in seven domains in American society: moral visions, religion, family, politics, law, environment, and health-care (see Table 14.1 for an overview). I argue that the polar opposites in multiple domains cohere into two consistent sets or "radial categories." For example, absolutists (moral visions) tend to be conservatives (politics) who believe in an "originalist" interpretation of the US Constitution (law). Relativists (moral visions) tend to be liberals (politics) who believe in a "living Constitution" (law). When sets cohere, the dynamics of alternation involve synchronized shifts of these interconnected domains. I explore duality, coherence, and alternation by examining evidence of the American "culture war." Third, I argue that, while duality and alternation are not uniquely American, these principles animate moral dynamics in America in an exceptional way. I discuss the unique ideological foundation of the nation, which makes the alternation of mutual opposites central to the moral dynamics of American society.[1] Finally, I conclude with a summary of key points.

---

[1] This chapter expands and develops arguments first introduced in *America's Crisis of Values: Reality and Perception* (Baker 2005).

S. Hitlin, S. Vaisey (eds.), *Handbook of the Sociology of Morality*,
Handbooks of Sociology and Social Research, DOI 10.1007/978-1-4419-6896-8_14,
© Springer Science+Business Media, LLC 2010

TABLE 14.1. Dualities in Seven Domains

Domain	Examples of mutual opposites	Reference/source
1. Moral visions	Absolutists versus relativists	Hunter 1991; Baker 2005
2. Religion	Conservative christianity versus secularism	Greeley and Hout 2006; Conger 2009; Williams 2009
3. Family	Strict father versus nuturant parent	Lakoff 1996; 2004
4. Politics	Red versus blue states	Fiorina with Abrams and Pope 2006; Evans and Nunn 2006
5. Law	Originalism versus living constitution	Calabresi 2007
6. Environment	Dark versus bright greens	Hoffman 2009
7. Healthcare	Supporters versus opponents of public health insurance plan (public option)	Author's observations and commentary on www.OurValues.org

TWO PRINCIPLES

The world is a "big blooming buzzing confusion," wrote William James. We make it orderly and manageable by the convenient device of dividing aspects of it into categories. Categorization is fundamental to perception, cognition, language, social interaction, and so on. I propose that a special case of categorization – mutually opposed dual categories – is central to moral dynamics in America. I call this the duality principle. Of course, categorical systems with more than two categories exist; as I explain below, different categorical systems may be complementary rather than competing views of the world. Alternation – the shift back and forth between the two sides of a duality – is a fundamental dynamic of moral culture. One side of a duality may dominate at a given time, but eventually its dominance wanes and the other waxes, only to alternate again in the future. This is the alternation principle. The reasons for alternation are varied, but as I explain below, may be classified as internal (endogenous limitations or inconsistencies) or external forces (exogenous shocks or surprises).

DUALITY PRINCIPLE

Duality is defined as division into two interrelated and opposing categories. These binary categories may be expressed in dual social organization (e.g., moiety systems or two-party political systems) and/or as polarities of logic and experience (Needham 1980), social thought, ideologies, and social action. The Chinese concept of yin/yang is an example of an ancient duality that still informs thinking today. Similarly, the Latin American hot/cold duality is a pre-Hispanic worldview that continues to inform contemporary society. For example, native Mexican understanding of health and illness of humans and food plants continues to be shaped by hot/cold principles and their mutual interactions (Chevalier et al. 2002). These Chinese and Latin American dualities originate outside America, but Chinese Americans and Latinos would find American culture to be a hospitable environment for the reinforcement and expression of dualistic thinking.

Duality is widespread. As Maybury-Lewis (1989:1) noted his introduction to *The Attraction of Opposites: Thought and Society in the Dualistic Mode*, the organization of social thought and social institutions in patterns of opposites "... is reported from so many different parts of the world that it is clearly a kind of system that human beings keep inventing and living by, independently of each other." Similarly, Bell (1978:155) asked, "How did man [sic] come to think of two radically different, heterogeneous realms, the sacred and the profane? Nature itself is a unified continuum in a great chain of being, from the microcosm to the macrocosm. Only man has created dualities: of spirit and matter, nature and history, the sacred and the profane."

Where does dualistic thinking come from? In part, it may share the evolutionary advantage of categorization in general. For example, the human ability to rapidly categorize novel natural scenes to assess danger enhances survival (e.g., Li et al. 2002). Dualistic thinking in moral culture may be adaptive because it provides a quick way to assess complex and ambiguous moral situations. Some argue that categorization is common because humans are "cognitive misers" (Taylor 1981). If so, then dual categories offer the simplest and most efficient system of categorization. Overwhelmed by a barrage of information and social stimuli, people cope by taking cognitive short cuts, ignoring massive amounts of information and placing others in simple us-versus-them categories. Stereotyping is an example, where the "other" is categorized and perceived as an undifferentiated member of a group rather than a unique individual (e.g., Johnson and Fredrickson 2005). Of course, categorization "does not function in a social vacuum, in the minds of isolated, asocial perceivers; human cognition is not purely individual, private, asocial, unaffected by group memberships, social norms and values" (Turner 1999:28). Political actors, for example, manipulate the categorization process to achieve political and ideological domination, "reifying social categories and therefore denying alternative ways of social being" (Reicher and Hopkins 2001:383).

Dual models may stem from the polarities that are perceived in nature or as part of the human experience. "All cultures," writes Maybury-Lewis (1989:12), "note and deal with such oppositions as night-day (or darkness-light), male-female, sky-earth, life-death, and a host of others." Dual categories are often (if not always) simplifications of reality – divisions of infinite continua into binary categories. For instance, the night/day duality is an obvious simplification because the 24-h cycle is a continuous progression.

Maybury-Lewis, among others, offers a functionalist account of dualistic thinking, arguing that it provides the "harmonious interaction of contradictory principles" that helps to manage the inevitable conflicts that arise in the human experience (1989:13–14). Dualistic thinking "offers a solution to the problem of social order by holding out the promise of balancing contending forces in perpetual equilibrium" (Maybury-Lewis 1989:14). In a similar vein, dualistic models may offer resilience to a society because, as has been noted for other categorical systems (e.g., Mamadouh 1999:443), cultural diversity is less prone to surprise and better ability to accommodate shocks to the system compared with a single mode of thinking, ideology, or social organization.

Of course, dual models are not the only system of categorization. In some domains, multiple categories might be more appropriate and accurate than a dual model. However, dualistic thinking can coexist with other systems of categorization and need not be in competition with them. Consider, for example, group-grid theory, an influential approach to cultural analysis introduced by Mary Douglas and developed by her and many others (e.g., Douglas 1970, 1986, Douglas and Wildavsky 1982, Wildavsky 1986). The literature on group-grid theory and analysis is broad and deep (e.g., Mamadouh 1999) and here, I provide only a sketch to illustrate the compatibility of dual models and more complex categorizations.

In brief, the grid-group model is built from two dimensions of sociality: (1) degree of individual freedom or individuation (grid) and (2) degree of incorporation into a bounded group (group). Grid-group creates a two-dimensional space, which may be considered continuous or, more commonly, divided into four types or modalities (also called cultures, ways of life, or rationalities). Each type represents a different combination of social relations and cultural biases, from which "people derive a great many of their preferences, perceptions, opinions, values and norms" (Mamadouh 1999:387). Each of the four types goes by different names; common names are given here. Individualism or market refers to low group, low grid. Hierarchy or collectivism is the opposite type, referring to high group and high grid. State capitalism is an example. High grid, low group is fatalism or isolation; it combines binding prescriptions (high grid) with weak group incorporation. Low grid, high group is egalitarianism, sect, or enclave.

All four types are present in any society, but one or a combination of group and grid tends to dominate. Single cultures (i.e. one grid-group type) dominate some states; a combination of two cultures (i.e. two gird-group types) dominates others (Wildavsky 1986, Webber and Wildavsky 1986). American society is a "hybrid regime" in which two types – individualism and egalitarianism – jostle and compete (Wildavsky 1986:335, Webber and Wildavsky 1986:25). Different types in group-grid theory are antagonistic and adversarial; competition between types is always in a state of disequilibrium, with movements back and forth between them (Mamadouh 1999:397). In other words, the application of group-grid theory to American society suggests that moral culture revolves around a principal duality in the four-type model, and, possibly, that the movement between these two types corresponds to the alternation principle that animates moral dynamics in America. This does not imply that the grid-group model can be collapsed into one dimension; nor does it imply that a dual model trumps grid-group theory. Rather, it shows that binary and multicategory systems can be compatible, and, perhaps, even mutually reinforcing.

ALTERNATION PRINCIPLE

Alternation is the successive change from one state (or phase) to another state (or phase) and back again. Alternation in the political sphere is a clear example. In 1919, Henry Adams observed this alternating pattern: "A period of about twelve years measured the beat of the pendulum. After the declaration of independence, twelve years had been needed to create an efficient constitution; another twelve years of energy brought a reaction against the government then created; a third period of twelve years was ending in a sweep toward still greater energy; and already a child could calculate the result of a few more such returns" (p. 67). Similarly, historian Schlesinger (1949) argued that American politics alternates between conservatism and liberalism, an idea that his son developed with greater detail in *The Cycles of American History* (Schlesinger 1986). Huntington (1981) and Hirschman (1982) also propose cycle theories of American history and politics; Skowronek (1988) argues that presidential succession and leadership styles follow a cyclical pattern.

Alternation may occur for endogenous or exogenous causes or a combination of both (Baker 2005:112–134). An endogenous cause is the inherent imperfection of each side of a duality. Whatever its strengths, any version of "truth and reality" is inherently incomplete and inadequate; hence, it contains the seeds of its eventual replacement (Sorokin 1957:679–683). For example, Schlesinger, Jr. (1986) argued that political cycles stem from the inherent limitations of conservatism and liberalism. The limitations of one political ideology become more and more apparent over time, bringing about a shift to the other. Borrowing Hirschman's (1982) ideas of "private interests" and "public action," he notes that conservatism favors self-interest, free markets, and monetary gain (private interests) while liberalism promotes reform and regulation (public action). A period of liberalism follows a period of conservatism when the emphasis on private interests breeds too much corruption, scandal, inequality, and other social problems. "People grow bored with selfish motives and vistas," he says, "weary of materialism as the ultimate goal. The vacation from public responsibility replenishes the national energies and recharges the national batteries. People begin to seek meaning in life beyond themselves" (Schlesinger 1986:28–29). Eventually, however, they tire of reform, returning to a period of private concerns: "Worn out by the constant summons to battle, weary of ceaseless national activity, disillusioned by the results, [people] seek a new dispensation, an interlude of rest and recuperation" (Schlesinger 1986:28). Similarly, Huntington (1981) argues that an "ideals-versus-institutions gap" animates cyclical oscillations. When the gap between ideals and reality becomes intolerable, we initiate reform, regulation, and collective action to realign American institutions with American values.

Others locate the causes of political change in external events – economic depressions, wars, the business cycle, severe social problems, and disruptive technological developments. For example, the causes of "critical realignments" – "an abrupt, large and enduring form of change in prevailing electoral patterns...that is initiated by a critical election and results in a significantly different partisan balance in the electorate" (Nardulli 1995:11) – are typically considered to lie outside the political system "A different mix of political, moral, cultural, and economic forces" causes every critical realignment (Nardulli 1995:14). Similarly, Burnham (1970:10) argues that "abnormal stress in the socioeconomic system" causes such critical realignment. Others emphasize "severe stresses to the political system resulting from some cataclysmic event such as the Civil War or the Great Depression" (Abramowitz and Saunders 1998:635), or simply as "some exogenous 'shock' to the electoral system" (Beck 1979:130).

The "Great Awakenings" in America – periods of religious-political change – are driven by exogenous forces. A Great Awakening is a period of cultural revitalization that begin[s] in a general crisis of beliefs and values and extend[s] over a period of a generation or so, during which time a profound reorientation in beliefs and values takes place. Revivals alter the lives of individuals; awakenings alter the worldview of a whole people or culture" (McLoughlin 1978:xiii). These awakenings occur in unsettled times, when prevailing theology and wisdom no longer give "meaning and order to the lives of a people", due to "social, ecological, psychological, and economic changes" (McLoughlin 1978:xiii, 8; see, also, Fogel 2000).

Dualities in American Society

Dualities are found in many places. I describe seven examples, selected to illustrate the range of domains in which dualities occur. These descriptions are short due to space limitations. (Table 14.1 provides an overview of the seven domains. References in the text and in Table 14.1 provide supporting details). I note, however, that clear patterns of alternation are identifiable in most but not all domains. This may be due to a lack of empirical investigation of alternation; it may also be because some polarities do not alternate. Nonetheless, the dualities cohere, more or less, into two sets, and it is possible to discern patterns of alternation as the movement of these sets over time. After presenting the dualities, I discuss the alternation of two coherent sets of interconnected dualities.

SEVEN DUALITIES

1. Moral visions. Moral visions are worldviews about the location of moral authority and judgment: the "transcendental sphere" or the "mundane sphere" (Orrù 1987, Eisenstadt 1982, Jaspers 1953). For moral absolutists, the location is the transcendental sphere – usually thought to be God (or religion), but can also be in the realm of pure ideas (Plato) or even society itself (Durkheim). The transcendental sphere contains absolute, eternal, and universal laws that always apply to everyone. For moral relativists, moral authority and judgment reside in the individual or in the local social situation (Fletcher 1966). The individual decides what is right and wrong in any given situation. These dual moral visions have ancient roots (e.g., Jaspers 1953, Orrù 1987). The duality is expressed today in the idea of an American culture war' pitting moral absolutists against moral relativists (Baker 2005:64–109).

   I used a survey item from the World Values Surveys (WVS) to measure the extent to which Americans are divided along these lines (Baker 2005:78–85). The WVS asked respondents to pick between two statements. Moral absolutism is indicated by this statement : "There are absolutely clear guidelines about what is good and evil. These always apply to everyone, whatever the circumstances". Moral relativism is indicated by this statement: "There can never be absolutely clear guidelines about what is good and evil. What is good and evil depends entirely upon the circumstances at the time". The 2000 survey is the WVS of America that included this survey item. About half (49.2 %) of Americans agreed with the first statement, and about half (46.6 % agreed with the second. (About 4 % volunteered that neither of the statement was true.) Of course, an item with only two, mutually opposed response categories might be expected to yield (what appears to be) a polarized pattern. Therefore, in a national survey conducted in June 2009, I asked two questions about moral visions with 5-point Likert scales: (1) "What is right and wrong is up to each person to decide" and (2) "There can never be absolutely clear guidelines about what is right and wrong because it depends entirely on the circumstances at the time".[2] As shown in Figure 14.1, both items yielded a bimodal pattern consistent with the idea of polarized moral visions.[3] Most Americans agreed or disagreed with these statements; at most 12 % said "neither agree nor disagree."

---

[2] The national survey was a rider to the June 2009 Reuters/University of Michigan Survey of Consumers, based at the University of Michigan Institute for Social Research ($n = 500$).

[3] Figure 1 matches one of the hypothetical polarized distributions in Fiorina and Abrams (2008:566). This hypothetical distribution (Figure 2, top) shows a 7-point Likert scale, while Figure 1 here uses a 5-point Likert scale. Nonetheless, they are quite similar in shape. Is this conclusive evidence of polarization? As Fiorina and Abrams (2008:566) point out, the answer is open to interpretation. Advocates of the "polarization narrative" might say yes;

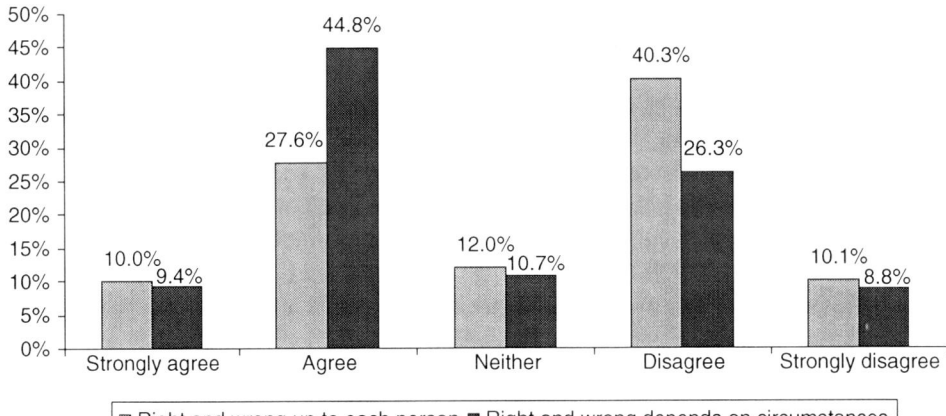

FIGURE 14.1. Percentage distributions of opinions about right and wrong.
Source: June 2009 Reuters/University of Michigan Survey of Consumers ($n = 500$, weighted) Item wording: (1) Right and wrong up to each person: "What is right and wrong is up to each person to decide." (2) Right and wrong depends on circumstances: "There can never be absolutely clear guidelines about what is right and wrong because it depends entirely on the circumstances at the time."

2. Religion. America remains one of the most religious (and religiously diverse) societies in the Western world. A prominent duality is the simplification of religious variation into Conservative Christians versus secular (non-religious) Americans. Greeley and Hout (2006) describe these mutual opposites in their introduction to *The Truth About Conservative Christians* (see, also, Smith 1998). On one side, "Conservative Christians defend the core values of both America and Christianity against the onslaughts of a secular and vulgar culture that will, if unchecked, undo both the nation and religion. Conservative Christians alone can be trusted to accomplish this, and in pursuing it, they become stronger". On the other side, Conservative Christians are viewed as a "dangerous juggernaut bent on undoing liberty, equality, and the fraternity of nations. Power-mad hypocrites, they mask hate with love, a judgmental streak with pieties, exclusion with appeals to inclusion, and monoculture in the name of diversity" (Greeley and Hout 2006:1). Of course, these stereotypes mask a wide range of diversity and agreement, as empirical studies have shown (e.g., Baker 2005, Davis and Robinson 1996, DiMaggio et al. 1996, Greeley and Hout 2006). But "[b]oth insiders and outsiders have an interest in exaggerating" (Greeley and Hout 2006:1). Williams (2009) argues, for example, that Conservative Christians have constructed secular elites as a "moral other," using this construction to boost political mobilization and strengthen collective identity. As noted above, reifying and simplifying categories is a strategy for achieving political and ideological domination (Reicher and Hopkins 2001).

---

other analysts might disagree because "lots of people consider themselves slightly conservative or slightly liberal, but the majority of respondents fall near the center of the scale."

3. Family. In *Moral Politics*, Lakoff (1996) argues that moral reasoning revolves around two opposed family models: "strict father" morality versus "nuturant parent" morality. This duality informs discourse about the domain of family per se. But, Lakoff argues, it informs thinking in almost all the other domains (see Table 14.1), such as national politics, where moral reasoning is based on "the common, unconscious, and automatic metaphor of the Nation-as-Family" (Lakoff 1996:13). The strict father model "a universal, absolute, strict set of rules specifying what it is right and what is wrong for all times, all cultures, and all stages of development" (p. 366). This model, as Lakoff (2004:7) summarizes in his political manual, derives from a set of assumptions: "The world is a dangerous place, and it always will be, because there is evil out there in the world. The world is also difficult because it is competitive. There will always be winners and losers. There is an absolute right and an absolute wrong. Children are born bad, in the sense that they just want to do what feels good, not what is right. There, they have to be made good. What is needed in this kind of a world is a strong, strict father who can: Protect the family in a dangerous world, support the family in the difficult world, and teach his children right from wrong".[4]

In contrast, the "nurturant parent" sees the world in a different way. This model "requires that one empathize with and be nurturant toward people with different values than one's own, including moral values. This means that one cannot maintain a strict good-evil dichotomy. To be able to see the world through other people's values and truly empathize with them means that you cannot see all people who have different moral values than yours as enemies to be demonized" (Lakoff 1996:127). The moral responsibility of the nurturant parent is "to teach your child to be a happy, fulfilled person who wants others to be happy and fulfilled" (Lakoff 2004:13). The goal is to raise children who will be "happy, empathic, able to take care of themselves, responsible, creative, communicative, and fair" (Lakoff 1996:11). Rewarding and punishing (the strict-father method) does not produce this type of child; only nurturance and empathy does – being cared for and respected, caring for and respecting others.

4. Politics. Nothing captures the duality in politics better than the maps of Red States versus Blue States from the 2000 and 2004 elections (The 2004 map is reproduced in Figure 14.2a). These images became darlings of the media and riveted public attention, portraying what looked like a geopolitically divided nation. An article in *The Atlantic Monthly* described the stereotypes of Red and Blue: "Red America is godly, moralistic, patriotic, predominantly white, masculine, less educated, and heavily rural and suburban; blue America is secular, relativistic, internationalist, multicultural, feminine, college educated and heavily urban and cosmopolitan. Reds vote for

---

[4] Lakoff (1996, 2004) argues that conservatives are better rhetoricians than liberals, better able to use strict-father reasoning to mobilize support and consolidate political and ideological power. In defense, he wrote the bestselling *Don't Think of an Elephant! Know Your Values and Frame the Debate* (2004). Called "the essential guide for Progressives," it tells liberals how to use the duality to promote their interests, turning the tables on the conservatives by employing their own rhetorical devices in reverse. Though Lakoff's theory of framing has fallen into disfavor as a useful political strategy, his insights as an analyst remain valid.

a. Original Red vs. Blue State map

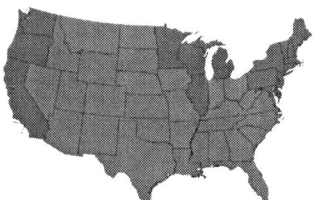

b. Cartogram taking population size into account

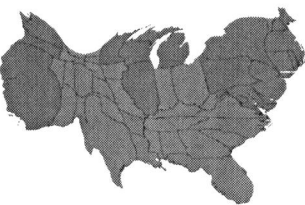

c. Map of county-level results, taking into account proportions of voters for
   Bush versus Kerry

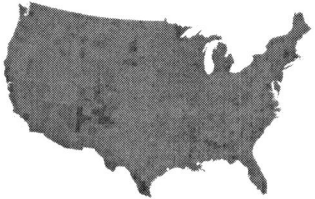

d. Cartogram of county-level results, taking voter proportions and population
   size into account

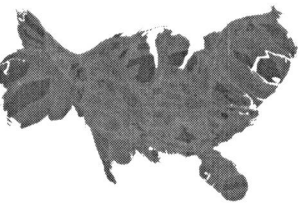

FIGURE 14.2. Maps and Cartograms of the 2004 Presidential Election: (a) Original red vs. blue state map, (b) Cartogram taking population size into account, (c) Map of county-level results, taking into account proportions of voters for Bush versus Kerry, (d) Cartogram of county-level results, taking voter proportions and population size into account. Source: Mark Newman's web site, University of Michigan < http://www-personal.umich.edu /~mejn/election/2004/>

guns and capital punishment and war in Iraq, blues for abortion rights and the environment. In red America, Saturday is for NASCAR and Sunday is for church. In blue America, Saturday is for the farmers' market (provided there are no actual farmers) and Sunday is for *The New York Times*" (Rauch 2005:102).

The Red/Blue map implies that the people with similar political ideologies and social attitudes cluster together, and that clustering is increasing over time. Increasing geopolitical clustering is theoretically possible (Baker and Faulkner 2009). However, whether "like-minded people cluster together. . .remains an open question" (Fiorina and Abrams 2008:563). Like all dualities, the red/blue duality contains important elements of truth, but it is a simplified version of reality. Empirically minded political scientists have expended effort debunking the myth of Red versus Blue States, showing that the differences are smaller than imagined; rather, citizens of Red and Blue States have a lot in common (e.g., Fiorina with Abrams and Pope 2006, Fiorina and Abrams 2008). Mark Newman, a physics professor at the University of Michigan, devised "cartograms" that redraw the Red/Blue maps to better represent geopolitical patterns. Figure 14.2b shows a cartogram of the USA (at the state level) that considers population. For example, New Mexico's acreage is much bigger than Florida's, but the Sunshine State is the 4th most populous state in the union and the Land of Enchantment is 36th. Hence, Florida is much bigger in the cartogram. Figure 14.2c shows a normal map at the county level, where counties are shades of red, blue, and purple to represent the proportions of Republican and Democratic supporters. This is superior to Figure 14.2a, but does not consider population. Finally, the cartogram in Figure 14.2d represents the most refined view, taking both proportions of voters and population size into account.

5. Law. A duality in law centers on how to use and interpret the US Constitution: "Originalism" versus the "living Constitution" (e.g., Calabresi 2007). Originalists like Judge Robert H. Bork and Associate Justice of the US Supreme Court Antonin Scalia argue that the meaning of the Constitution does not change over time. Judges should "interpret the [Constitution's] words according to the intentions of those who drafted, proposed, and ratified them" (Bork quoted in Calabresi 2007:14). Originalism is clearly connected to an absolutist moral vision. As Calabresi (2007:15) writes, "Many of us [originalists], myself included, believe in the existence of a divinely prescribed natural law".

Opponents of Originalism argue that the present-day meaning of the Constitution should not be determined by the "dead hand" of the long-ago Framers. Times change, and the interpretation of the Constitution should change with it. As Thomas Jefferson wrote, "I am not an advocate for frequent changes in laws and constitutions, but laws and institutions must go hand in hand with the progress of the human mind. As that becomes more developed, more enlightened, as new discoveries are made, new truths discovered and manners and opinions change, with the change of circumstances, institutions must advance also to keep pace with the times."

The duality was apparent in the 2009 confirmation hearings for Associate Justice of the US Supreme Court Sonia Sotomayor. Originalists saw her as a judicial advocate – someone who had and would take into account evolving norms, understandings, values, and ethics. Her ethnicity, gender, and humble roots figured in the debate, but the deep intent of questioning from conservative quarters was to reveal her as an advocate of the living Constitution. Obama coined the term "empathy" as a more palatable term for the living Constitution. In a news conference after Supreme Court Justice David Souter announced his retirement, Obama said, "I view that quality of empathy, of understanding and identifying with people's hopes and struggles, as an essential ingredient for arriving at just decisions and outcomes." Even the Framers, Obama wrote in 2006, argued about the meaning of the Constitution.

"Before the ink on the constitutional parchment was dry, arguments had erupted, not just about minor provisions, but about first principles. Not just between peripheral figures, but within the revolution's very core" (Obama 2008[2006]:108).

6. Environment. Debates about the environment (such as the reality of climate change) are rife with oppositions. These debates are often linked to different views of nature, as grid-group analysts have noted (e.g., Schwartz and Thompson 1990, Thompson et al. 1990). Though grid-group theory reveals four different views of nature,[5] there are also examples of dualities in debates about the environment. Consider, for example, a duality within the environmental movement. The shades of green are infinite, but environmentalists have constructed a duality that splits their ranks: "bright green" versus "dark green." "On the one extreme, the dark green groups— such as Greenpeace USA and Friends of the Earth—seek radical social change to solve environmental problems, most often by confronting the corporate sector," writes Hoffman (2009). "On the other extreme, the bright green groups - such as Conservation International and the Environmental Defense Fund - work within the market system, often in close collaboration with corporations, to solve environmental problems." The bright/dark duality appears to correspond with the grid-group duality I discussed above: bright greens in the individualism/market category (low grid, low group) and dark greens in the egalitarian category (low grid, high group). These also correspond to the views of nature associated with these grid-group types, "nature robust" versus "nature ephemeral," respectively (see footnote 5 for definitions).

The dark/bright division is widening, says Hoffman (2009), as each side criticizes and vilifies the other. The dark greens say the brights have been coopted by corporations, "helping them to greenwash their polluting activities." The bright greens say the dark greens are "out of touch radicals that only complicate the environmental agenda by resorting to extreme tactics like burning down chalets at Aspen or genetic engineering labs." However, the dark and bright greens need one another to accomplish their goals, says Hoffman. The dark greens "pull the tail of the political spectrum further in one direction, they shift the center of the debate and create a category of moderates." The moderate bright greens engage the powers-that-be, while the radical darks keep the tough issues on the table and help to set the agenda.

7. Healthcare. Healthcare reform was a big plank in the Democratic platform in the 2008 elections. Most Americans favor major reform. For example, in a July 2009 poll conducted by the Pew Research Center, 82 % favored forcing insurance companies to provide coverage to people with pre-existing medical conditions (Pew Research Center for People & the Press 2009). A large majority (66 %) supported the "individual mandate" requiring everyone to have insurance. Opinions about the "public option" were split, however – 55 % for, 45 % against (Pew described the public option as "a government health insurance plan to compete with private health insurance plans.") In 2009 and 2010, such healthcare reforms were fiercely debated, and the

---

[5] The four views of nature are (1) 'nature benign' (or 'nature robust'), corresponding to individualism (low grid, low group); (2) 'nature capricious', corresponding to isolation/fatalism (high grid, low group); (3) 'nature perverse' (or 'nature tolerant'), corresponding to hierarchy (high grid, high group); and, (4) 'nature ephemeral', corresponding to egalitarianism (low grid, high group) (e.g. Schwartz and Thompson 1990; Thompson, Ellis, and Wildavsky 1990).

legislative process polarized Congress along party lines. Democrats favored major reforms (though they were internally divided about some, like the public option). Republicans displayed military discipline in their unified and total opposition to anything the Democrats favored.

One duality in healthcare reform is the conflict between the two ideologies: individualism versus egalitarianism. These, as noted above, are the hostile and jostling "cultures" grid-group theorists say are central to American society (Wildavsky 1986:335, Webber and Wildavsky 1986:25). While individualism emphasizes self-reliance, independence, and freedom from governmental regulation, egalitarianism emphasizes equality of political, economic, social, and civil rights and opportunities for all. This duality is always present in moral debates, but it may be exacerbated for political and economic advantage. The extreme polarization of Congress along party lines appears to be an example, with each side vilifying the other and making compromise virtually impossible.

These seven dualities are just a few of the dualities that animate and structure moral debates. Each duality, like any system of categorization, is a simplification of reality. By moving down levels of observation, examining a domain in finer and finer detail, it is often easy to question the validity of a categorical system. For example, do the purple cartograms (Figure 14.2) mean that the Red/Blue duality is false? Are people simply ignorant or misinformed? Once they had the facts, would they drop the Red/Blue distinction? There are at least three answers. First, every duality (like any categorical system) is a myth that partially represents reality. An element of truth resides in each one. This truth (or factual accuracy) varies across time and space. For example, there are redder and bluer areas in the cartograms. Second, a duality represents two central tendencies. A duality is a set of complex categories, with many variations. However, the many variations are related to the two central tendencies. Despite complexity and variation, there are only two modalities. Third, a duality is a dominant way that people perceive and interpret the world. For example, people use the Red/Blue distinction as a way to think about and discuss ethical, political, social, and economic issues. To dismiss a duality as a misconception is to deny the reality of individual experience.[6]

Alternation of Domains as Sets

The alternation of mutual opposites is a common temporal pattern (Baker 2005). As discussed above, alternating patterns have been observed in political, economic, and social domains. Here, I make three claims: First, dualities are interconnected as "radial categories" (e.g., Lakoff

---

[6] Just as Lipset (1996:267) said with regards to the argument that the widespread perception of a moral crisis is simply the result of ignorance, panic, or media-flamed hyperbole: "The critics [of America] have exaggerated many of the problems in the quest to demonstrate decay. There is, however, no denying that the impression of a change in basic values exists, and to dismiss public perception [of crisis] as somehow wrong or misinformed is to deny the reality of individual experience."

1996). Second, the coherence of a related set of polarities is variable. Third, radial categories of moral domains alternate, rising and falling over time. These claims are testable. To the extent available data allow, I explore these claims by drawing on analyses of the "culture war" in America.

1. Dualities are radial categories. Building on Lakoff's (1996) work, I use the cognitive linguistic idea of "radial categories" to explain how domains are interconnected (Baker 2005:68–71). Radial categories "are the most common of human conceptual categories" (Lakoff 1996:7). They define both central tendencies and variations around these tendencies. The moral visions of absolutism versus relativism are the cores of two opposed radial categories; other domains revolve around them (Baker 2005). As illustrated in Figure 14.3, the spokes on the hub of absolutism include Conservative Christianity, Red State politics (conservatism), the strict father family model, originalism, and opposition to the public option in healthcare (worded in the affirmative in Figure 14.3 as support of private healthcare). The spokes on the hub of relativism include secular elites, Blue State politics (liberalism), the nurturant parent family model, living Constitution, and support of the public option in healthcare reform (I exclude the Bright/Dark Greens duality because it exists within the environmental movement, which, typically, is associated with liberal politics, secularism, and so forth. A broader duality – environmentalism versus non-environmentalism – fits the level of analysis represented in Figure 14.3).[7]

2. The coherence of a radial category is variable. Coherence is the extent to which the domains in a radial category are linked. The lengths of the spokes in Figure 14.3 represent how tightly domains are linked. For simplicity, the spokes are equal lengths in this figure, but in reality, the length of each spoke could be different, representing the strength of the connection of a polarity to a moral vision. Tight coherence means that the domains in a radial category are strongly linked; loose coherence means that they are weakly linked. It is possible that one radial category will be more or less coherent than the other will. For example, the debates and legislative struggles in 2009 and 2010 about healthcare reform (see domain 7) suggest that the coherence of the absolutist radial category was tighter than the coherence of the relativist radial category.

    The duality of American moral culture appears to be empirically valid when radial categories strongly cohere. Dualistic thinking seems to be less of a simplification and more of the "truth." Dualistic thinking appears to be incorrect and inaccurate when radical categories do not strongly cohere. There appears to be more complexity and variation than a dual model allows. Yet, the duality of American moral culture remains, even if it appears to recede at certain times and advance at others.

3. Radial categories alternate. One radial category of moral domains dominates for a time, only to be superseded by the other. Moral visions are the core of these radial categories. The duality of moral visions was created long ago (Jaspers 1953) and

---

[7] The Bright/Dark Greens duality suggests that alternation can occur at different levels. Moreover, two domains in the same radial category can be connected in patterns of alternation. For example, Conger (2009) argues that the relationship of Conservative Christianity and the Republican Party exhibits cycles of conflict and accommodation.

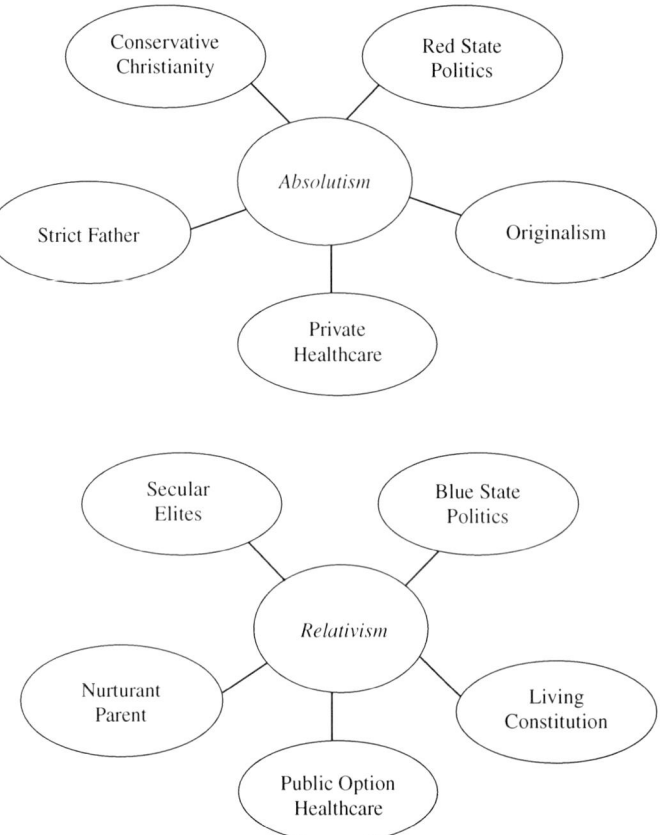

FIGURE 14.3. Illustration of dualities as radial categories.

has informed moral debates ever since (Orrù 1987). Recall, for example, Emerson's remarks quoted in the introduction to this chapter, as well as analyses of the Great Awakenings in America (Fogel 2000; McLoughlin 1978). These debates appear to be cyclical (Jaspers 1953, Orrù 1987). That is, moral visions alternate: one moral vision dominates for a time, only to be superseded by the other, and so on in a continual cyclical pattern. Building on this idea, I proposed a cyclical model of alternation (Baker 2005:147–156). Absolutism and relativism rise and fall over time, driven by endogenous and exogenous forces. The alternation of moral visions implies that their radial categories also alternate. The extent varies to which the domains of a radial category alternate with their moral vision. When radial categories tightly cohere, domains move in synchronicity with their moral visions; when they loosely cohere, domains move at different rates and appear to be less connected with their core moral vision.

Analyses of the American "culture war" provide an opportunity to explore these claims, at least to the extent that available data allow. Two claims underlie the culture war thesis (Baker 2005:66–85). First, the "polarization claim" argues that Americans are sharply divided into two moral camps based on absolutism/relativism duality. This duality is considered to be the overarching frame of the culture war (Hunter 1991). Second, the "linkage claim" argues that moral visions and the constellation of values and attitudes around them are tightly coupled. That is, people use their moral visions to derive their values and attitudes about a host of issues. "The polarization is most conspicuous in such hotly disputed issues as abortion, gay marriage, school vouchers, and prayers in public schools," writes Himmelfarb (2001:117–118). "But it has larger ramifications, affecting beliefs, attitudes, values, and practices on a host of subjects ranging from private morality to public policy, from popular culture to high culture, from crime to education, welfare, and the family." As defined above, coherence is the extent to which people actually hold consistent moral visions, values, and attitudes. Political activists and religious leaders always try to get their followers' beliefs to cohere as a way to consolidate political, economic, and ideological power. If the linkage claim is correct, then a radial category would closely cohere and polarization would extend from moral visions to religious values to social attitudes.

What limited data we have on moral visions suggest that they have become increasingly polarized over time (e.g., Baker 2005:78–80, 142–144). In 1981, Americans' views of moral authority were different from what they would be ten years later. In 1981, only 37 % of Americans chose the absolutist position in the World Values Survey; the majority (60 percent) chose the relativist position. By 1990, however, the proportions of relativists and absolutists were about the same (45 % versus 50 %, respectively). The roughly 50:50 split was reproduced in the 1995 and 2000 World Values Surveys.[8] This rising tide of absolutism occurred across all age cohorts, social classes, men and women, married and unmarried, and whites and non-whites. The bimodal distributions in Figure 14.1 indicate that polarized moral visions are still evident in 2009. Thus, the available survey data provide evidence of a clear duality of moral visions.

The coherence of radial categories is loose. Unlike moral visions, values and attitudes are not deeply polarized (Baker 2005, Davis and Robinson 1996, DiMaggio et al. 1996, Fiorina and Abrams 2008, Greeley and Hout 2006, Williams 1997). For example, God is more important in the lives of moral absolutists, compared to relativists. Absolutists are more likely than relativists to hold traditional values and to favor closer ties between church and state. Yet, absolutists and relativists have a lot in common (Baker 2005: Table 3.1). For example, 97 % of absolutists believe in the soul; 95 % of relativists do as well. About 95 % of absolutists believe in Heaven, compared to 80 % of relativists. The biggest difference concerns beliefs in Hell: 84 % of absolutists versus 65 % of relativists. Nonetheless, moral visions are significantly related to a host of religious, political, economic, and social values and attitudes (Baker 2005). In addition, the beliefs of some groups indeed have become more coherent over the last three decades, especially strong political partisans and wealthier and politically sophisticated voters (Baldassarri and Gelman 2008), suggesting that domains can move together with their core moral vision.

Despite evidence of weak coherence, the culture war debate continues (see exchanges in Hunter and Wolfe 2006). Hunter (2006), for example, says that we are looking in the wrong place when we look at what everyday Americans think and believe. Hunter (2006:20–21)

---

[8] The World Values Surveys were administered in the United States in 1981, 1995, 2000, and 2006. The 2006 survey did not include the item on moral visions.

argues that we should not view culture "as the norms and values residing in people's heads and hearts but rather as systems of symbols and other cultural artifacts, institutions that produce and promulgate those symbols, discourses that articulate and legitimate particular interests, and competing fields where culture is contested." Moreover, he says, "the heart of the culture war hypothesis was the contention that there had been a realignment in American public culture that had been and still is institutionalized chiefly through special interest organizations, denominations, political parties, foundations, competing media outlets, professional associations, and the elites whose ideals, interests, and actions give all these organizations direction and leadership." In other words, the culture war is more about elites and what they think and do, less about the masses and what they think and do.

There is no doubt that elites have become more polarized over time. Those who conclude that a deeply polarized America is a myth also conclude, based on empirical evidence, that elites are indeed polarized (e.g., Fiorina et al. 2006, Fiorina and Abrams 2008). In addition, as political parties have become more polarized, people have more clearly sorted along ideological lines (Baldassarri and Gelman 2008) Partisans have become "more closely associated with one or the other of the increasingly interconnected clusters" (Fiorina and Abrams 2008:577). Nonetheless, elite polarization has not translated into mass polarization. One reason, Fiorina (2006:86) says, is that elites are not as influential as they like to believe. It may also be that the ordinary Americans are not "cultural dopes," to use Garfinkel's felicitous phrase.

Continuing the debate about the culture war is essential for understanding the source and issue of value pluralism in society, as well as to maintain the health of democratic deliberation in the public sphere (Evan and Nunn 2005). The mass versus elite perspectives are not incompatible. The duality of moral visions may be expressed and promoted with greater force and clarity by elites, but the empirical evidence (Baker 2005) shows that moral visions do, indeed, inform the values and attitudes of the masses – just not as strongly. In other words, the radial categories of absolutism and relativism cohere more tightly for elites than they do for everyday Americans.

Though moral visions are only loosely connected to values and attitudes, we can expect the perception of crisis and conflict to be acute at a time when absolutism and relativism are held in equal measure (Baker 2005). At these times, disagreements between moral absolutists and relativists appear to be at their maximum, even though there are still wide areas of agreement in values and attitudes. In other words, the radial categories of absolutism and relativism appear to have moved farther apart. Elite discourse is especially shrill at these times. It feels as if the "harmonious interaction of contradictory principles" is in jeopardy, and "the promise of balancing contending forces in perpetual equilibrium" (Maybury-Lewis 1989:14) is hollow and false. If the data on the mass polarization of moral visions are indicators, it appears that we are in one of these periods (at the time of this writing). If historical patterns are repeated, the debate will subside, only to be renewed once again.

What is American about Dualistic Thinking?

Dualistic thinking is universal. It is not an American invention or monopoly. What is special about dualistic thinking in America? America is fertile soil for dualistic thinking – especially in moral domains – because of its unique ideological foundation (Baker 2005). The cultural adhesive of any nation-state is what Habermas (1998) calls the popular self-consciousness of belonging to a people. This self-consciousness forms "a relation of solidarity" between people (Habermas 1998:111). For almost all nations, this relation of solidarity stands on a common heritage, including common ancestry, religion, history, language, customs, traditions, and territory. This common heritage produces "the consciousness of belonging to "the same" people, and makes subjects into citizens of a single political community – into members who can feel responsible *for one another*. The nation of the *Volksgeist*, the unique spirit of the people – the first truly *modern* form of collective identity – provided the cultural basis for the constitutional state" (Habermas 1998:113).

America does not have this sort of "primordial substrate" (as Habermas calls it). America is not a "birthright" community (Lipset 1996). Rather, the popular self-consciousness of belonging to the same people rests on an ideological foundation – a shared (or thought to be shared) set of values and ideas (Baker 2005). This ideology-based relation of solidarity is America's "civil religion" (Habermas 1998), or what Ralph Waldo Emerson and Abraham Lincoln called America's "political religion" (Lipset 1996:18). Cultural citizenship is based on ideology: "Being an American. . .is an ideological commitment. It is not a matter of birth. Those who reject American values are un-American" (Lipset 1996:31).

In this context, disagreements become moral battles. As Lipset (1996:63) said, Americans "tend to view social and political dramas as morality plays, as battles between God and the Devil, so that compromise is virtually unthinkable." The well-known "splitting-projecting" dynamic operates with considerable force (Baker 2005:137–138). Each side "sees itself as good and its adversary as bad and uses this justification for being oppositional, applying logic such as 'only when they are eliminated will badness disappear.' Since each group takes the same position, the conflict escalates to the point where both are behaving self-righteously, wholeheartedly denying that the accusations of the opponent have *any* validity" (Smith and Berg 1988:77). This oppositional dynamic clearly operates in the domains considered here (Table 14.1).

Each side of a duality needs the other: absolutists and relativists, liberals and conservatives, strict fathers and nuturant parents, originalists and living Constitutionalists, and so on. Neither side truly wants to eliminate the other. As Smith and Berg (1988:79) note, "when A gets B to carry and express its displaced parts, A will be invested in remaining in the vicinity of B to obtain vicarious gratification as the disowned parts of itself are enacted and to maintain the strength of the subgroup that carries these disowned parts." For example, as Orrù (1987:156) puts it, absolutism and relativism "are dialectically related as parts of a common discourse."

Does the duality of American moral culture mean that there is no single truth, no single reality, for Americans themselves or for the sociologists, political scientists, philosophers, and humanists who study them? What Collins said about the fields of social science and the humanities applies here as well. "One way out of this conclusion [that there is no single reality, no truth] is the possibility that multiple realities and competing truths will turn out to be complementary. We may hope that the situation is that of the many blind men touching different parts of the same elephant; more appropriately, since that image is too static, we may hope that the competing factions of philosophers or sociologists are pursuing multiple paths of advance into the same wilderness. But is it also possible that this will not be the case; a unified map may never be filled in because the paths may never intersect" (Collins 1998:879).

CONCLUSION

I propose that two principles – duality and alternation – are central to the structure and dynamics of American moral culture. The division into mutually opposed categories (duality) is a simplification of reality. Like other systems of categorization, dualistic thinking may occur because people are "cognitive misers," because it confers evolutionary advantages, or because it is more resilient to shocks and surprises compared to a single mode. Dual categories in particular may come from the polarities that are perceived in nature or as part of the human experience. Dualistic thinking and dual social organization may be functional, providing a mechanism that harmonizes contradictions and solves the problem of social order by balancing oppositional forces. Dualistic thinking can be a tool to pursue political and ideological goals.

Dualities are ubiquitous. I presented dualities in seven domains in American society – moral visions, religion, family, politics, law, environment, and healthcare – to illustrate the diversity and range of duality. Like any categorical system, each duality is myth that is a partial representation of reality. Each contains elements of truth. A duality represents two central tendencies – two centers of gravity in moral discourse – even though the reality they represent is complex and variable. People use duality as a dominant way to perceive, frame, and interpret their experience.

Dualities form sets. These sets are radial categories, where spokes are domains and the hub is a moral vision. The coherence or consistency of each radial category varies over time and place. When a radial category tightly coheres, it appears to be a more accurate representation of reality than when it loosely coheres. Moral visions alternate over time, driven by internal (endogenous limitations or inconsistencies) or external forces (exogenous shocks or surprises). Alternation may coexist with long-term secular trends. When a radial category tightly coheres, domains move in synchronous pattern with their core moral vision. When a radical category loosely coheres, domains may move at different rates.

America is fertile ground for dualistic thinking. Disagreements escalate into moral battles between good and evil. Each side vilifies the other, each side denies the validity of the other, and compromise becomes remote. This oppositional dynamic is the theme of this chapter. Duality is not only an elite project, but also is a part of everyday moral culture.

Acknowledgment I thank David Mayer, Stephen Vaisey, and Christopher Winship for helpful comments on an earlier version of this chapter.

REFERENCES

Abramowitz, A., and K. Saunders. 1998. "Ideological Realignment in the U.S. Electorate." *Journal of Politics* 60: 634–652.

Adams, H. 1919. "The Rule of Phase Applied to History." *The Tendency of History*. NY: Macmillan.

Baker, W. 2005. *America's Crisis of Values: Reality and Perception*. Princeton, NJ: Princeton University Press.

Baker, W., and R. F. Faulkner. 2009. "Social Capital, Double Embeddedness, and Mechanisms of Stability and Change." *American Behavioral Scientist* 52:1531–1555.

Baldassarri, D., and A. Gelman. 2008. "Partisans Without Constraint: Political Polarization and Trends in American Public Opinion." *American Journal of Sociology* 114:408–446.

Bell, D. 1978. *The Cultural Contradictions of Capitalism*. NY: Basic.

Beck, P. A. 1979. "The Electoral Cycle and Patterns of American Politics." *British Journal of Politics* 9:129–156.

Burnham, W. D. 1970. *Critical Elections and the Mainsprings of American Politics*. NY: W. W. Norton Company.

Calabresi, S. G., ed. 2007. *Originalism: A Quarter-Century of Debate*. Regnery Publishing.

Chevalier, J. M., A. S. Bain, W. A. Bain, W. A. S. Bain. 2002. *The Hot and the Cold: Ills of Humans and Maize in Native Mexico*. Toronto: University of Toronto Press.

Collins, R. 1998. *The Sociology of Philosophies*. Cambridge, MA: Harvard University Press.

Conger, K. 2009. "Moral Values and Political Parties: Cycles of Conflict and Accommodation." PP. 280–304 in *Evangelicals and Democracy in America, Volume II: Religion and Politics*, edited by S. Brint, and J. R. Schroedel. NY: Russell Sage Foundation Press.

Davis, N. J., and R. V. Robinson. 1996. "Are the Rumors of War Exaggerated?." *American Journal of Sociology* 102:756–776.

DiMaggio, P., J. Evans, and B. Bryson. 1996. "Have Americans' Social Attitudes Become More Polarized?." *American Journal of Sociology* 102:690–755.

Douglas, M. 1970. *Natural Symbols, Explorations in Cosmology*. London: Barrie and Rockliff.

Douglas, M. 1986. *How Institutions Think*. Syracuse, NY: Syracuse University Press.

Douglas, M., and A. Wildavsky. 1982. *Risk and Culture: An Essay on the Selection of Technological and Environmental Dangers*. Berkeley, CA: University of California Press.

Eisenstadt, S. N. 1982. "The Axial Age." *European Journal of Sociology* 23:294–314.

Emerson, R. W. 1848. *Essays, Lectures, and Orations*. London: William S. Orr and Company.

Evans, J. H., and L. M. Nunn. 2006. "Geographic Polarization in Politics and Social Attitudes." Paper presented at the Annual Meetings of the American Sociological Association, Montreal, Quebec, Canada (August).

Fletcher, J. 1966. *Situation Ethics: The New Morality*. Louisville, KT: Westminster John Know Press.

Fiorina, M. 2006. "Further Reflections on the Culture War Thesis." PP. 83–89 in *Is There a Culture War? A Dialogue on Values and American Public Life*, edited by J. D. Hunter, and A. Wolfe. Pew Research Center. Washington, DC: Brookings Institution Press.

Fiorina, M., S. J. Abrams, and J. C. Pope. 2006 (second edition). *Culture War? The Myth of a Polarized America*. NY: Pearson Longman.

Fiorina, M., and S. J. Abrams. 2008. "Political Polarization in the American Public." *Annual Review of Political Science* 11:563–588.

Fogel, R. W. 2000. *The Fourth Great Awakening and the Future of Egalitarianism*. Chicago: University of Chicago Press.

Habermas, J. 1998. *The Inclusion of the Other*, edited by C. Cronin, and P. De Grieff. Cambridge, MA: MIT Press.

Himmelfarb, G. 2001 *One Nation, Two Cultures*. NY: Alfred A. Knopf.

Hirschman, A. O. 1982. *Shifting Involvements: Private Interests and Public Action*. Princeton, NJ: Princeton University Press.

Hunter, J. D. 1991. *Culture Wars: The Struggle to Define America*. NY: Basic.

Hunter, J. D. 2006. "The Enduring Culture War." PP. 10–40 in *Is There a Culture War? A Dialogue on Values and American Public Life*, edited by J. D. Hunter, and A. Wolfe. Pew Research Center. Washington, DC: Brookings Institution Press.

Hunter, J. D., and A. Wolfe. 2006. *Is There a Culture War? A Dialogue on Values and American Public Life*. Pew Research Center. Washington, D.C.: Brookings Institution Press.

Huntington, S. P. 1981. *American Politics: The Promise of Disharmony*. Cambridge, MA: Belknap/ Harvard University Press.

Jaspers, K. 1953. *The Origin of and Goal of History*, translated by Michael Bullock. London: Routledge & Kegan Paul.

Johnson, K., and B. L. Fredrickson. 2005. "We All Look the Same to Me: Positive Emotions Eliminate the Own-Race Bias in Face Recognition." *Psychological Science:* 16:875–881.

Hoffman, A. 2009. "Are you Green? ... Yes? But how 'Dark' or 'Bright' Green is that?" (April 27). "What are the crucial environmental issues—from bright to dark green?" (April 28). "In Praise of Dark Greens: Do we really want 'Green' to fade?" (April 30). Series on OurValues.org <http://www.OurValues.org> Accessed August 25, 2009.

Lipset, S. M. 1996. *American Exceptionalism*. NY: W. W. Norton.

Lakoff, G. 1996. *Moral Politics*. Chicago: University of Chicago Press.

Lakoff, G. 2004. *Don't Think of an Elephant! Know Your Values and Frame the Debate*. White River Junction, VT: Chelsea Green Publishing.

Li, F. F., R. VanRullen, C. Koch, and P. Perona. 2002. "Rapid Natural Scene Categorization in the Near Absence of Attention." PNAS (July 9):9596–9601.

Mamadouh, V. 1999. "Grid-Group Cultural Theory: An Introduction." *GeoJournal* 47:395–409.

Maybury-Lewis, D., and U. Almagor, eds. 1989. *The Attraction of Opposites: Thought and Society in the Dualistic Mode.* Ann Arbor, MI: The University of Michigan Press.

McLoughlin, W. G. 1978. *Revivals, Awakenings, and Reform.* Chicago: University of Chicago Press.

Nardulli, P. F. 1995. "The Concept of a Critical Realignment, Electoral Behavior, and Political Change." *American Political Science Review* 89:10–22.

Needham, R. 1980. *Reconnaissances.* Toronto: University of Toronto Press.

Obama, B. 2008 (2006). *The Audacity of Hope: Thoughts on Reclaiming the American Dream.* New York: Crown.

Orrù, M. 1987. *Anomie: History and Meanings.* Boston: Allen & Unwin.

Pew Research Center for People and the Press. 2009. "Mixed Views of Economic Policies and Health Care Reform Persist." (October 8). http://people-press.org/report/?pageid=1593 [accessed 10:38AM EST January 7, 2010].

Rauch, J. 2005. Bipolar Disorder. *The Atlantic Monthly*, January/February:102–110

Reicher, S., and N. Hopkins. 2001. "Psychology and the End of History: A Critique and a proposal for the Psychology of Social Categorisation." *Political Psychology* 22:383–407.

Schlesinger, A. 1949. *Paths to the Present.* NY: Macmillan.

Schlesinger, Jr., A. M. 1986. *The Cycles of American History.* Boston: Houghton Mifflin Company

Schwartz, M., and M. Thompson. 1990. *Divided We Stand: Redefining Politics, Technology and Social Choice.* New York: Harvester Wheatsheaf, Hemel Hempsted.

Skowronek, S. 1988. "Presidential Leadership in Political Time." PP. 115–119 in *The Presidency and the Political System,* second edition, edited by M. Nelson. Washington, DC: Congressional Quarterly Press.

Smith, C. 1998. *American Evangelicalism: Embattled and Thriving.* Chicago: University of Chicago Press.

Smith, K. K., and D. N. Berg. 1988. *Paradoxes of Group Life.* San Francisco, CA: Jossey-Bass.

Sorokin, P. 1957. *Social and Cultural Dynamics.* Boston: Porter Sargent Publisher.

Taylor, S. E. 1981. "The Interface of Cognitive and Social Psychology." In *Cognition, Social Behavior, and the Environment,* edited by J. H. Harvey. Hillsdale, NJ: Lawrence Erlbaum Associates.

Thompson, M., R. Ellis, and A. Wildavsky. 1990. *Cultural Theory.* Boulder, CO: Westview Press.

Turner, J. C. 1999. "Some Current Issues in Research on Social Identity and Self-Categorization Theories." PP. 6–34 in *Social Identity,* edited by N. Ellemers, R. Spears, and B. Doosje. New York: Wiley-Blackwell.

Webber, C., and A. Wildavsky. 1986. *A History of Taxation and Expenditure in the Western World.* NY: Simon and Schuster.

Wildavsky, A. 1986. *Budgeting: A Comparative Theory of Budgetary Processes.* Second, revised edition. New Brunswick, NJ: Transaction.

Williams, R. H., ed. 1997. *Cultural Wars in American Politics.* NY: Aldine de Gruyter.

Williams, R. H. 2009. "Politicized Evangelicalism and Secular Elites: Creating a Moral Other." PP. 143–178 in *Evangelicals and Democracy in America, Volume II: Religion and Politics,* edited by S. Brint, and J. R. Schroedel. NY: Russell Sage Foundation Press.

CHAPTER 15

Education and the Culture Wars

Morality and Conflict in American Schools

JEFFREY S. DILL AND JAMES DAVISON HUNTER

INTRODUCTION

The central claim of the culture war hypothesis is that there has been a fundamental realignment within American public culture that, in turn, has generated significant tension and conflict in the social order. These antagonisms have played out not just on the surface of social life (i.e. in its cultural politics) but at the deepest and most profound levels of meaning and moral order; not just at the level of partisan ideology but in its public symbols, its myths, its discourse and the institutional structures that generate and sustain public culture.

This realignment reflects a transformation of the longstanding divisions that have defined normative conflict through much of Western history. In the past, of course, the principal cultural divisions were religious and even theological in nature, dividing Christians and Jews; and dividing Protestants and Catholics. The new lines of tension and conflict are not so much religious in substance as they are religious in character - they take shape around conceptions of moral authority, the moral visions that emanate from them, and the public symbols and collective rituals that give expression to them. Animating one side of the new cultural divide is a sense of ultimate reality that is rooted in transcendent authority. Whether apprehended through the foundations of nature or religion or tradition, one can discern and articulate relatively fixed, even eternal, standards through which we can justly organize our personal and collective existence. Animating the other side of the cultural divide is a sense of ultimate reality that rejects the possibility of fixed standards outside of human experience, privileging instead that which we can apprehend through our senses in our personal experience. By these lights, what is real or what is good is not so much constant and enduring, but rather much more personal and these depend on the particularities of context.

The significance of this realignment along an axis of "orthodox" to "progressivist" impulses is seen in the way it cuts across the old divisions. This has created a historically unprecedented set of alliances among various traditionalists (for example, among evangelicals and fundamentalist Protestants, conservative Catholics, and Orthodox Jews) and among progressivists (as among liberal Protestants), that are played out, as we noted, in public policy disputes and in opposing nationalist rhetoric.

S. Hitlin, S. Vaisey (eds.), *Handbook of the Sociology of Morality*,
Handbooks of Sociology and Social Research, DOI 10.1007/978-1-4419-6896-8_15,

The dispositions, sensibilities, and assumptions as well as the ideas and ideals at the center of the dispute are articulated in innumerable ways with every conceivable nuance and shade of variation. So too among the citizens and institutions that give expression to these competing cultural systems, one can find nearly infinite variation. Yet, as these are filtered into the signs and symbols of public discourse and institutionalized within the structures of advocacy, they lose their complexity and nuance, and divide into sharply antagonistic positions.

In the language of Bourdieu, the fields of cultural conflict are the range of reality defining institutions at the center of American society, including the family, the arts, the media, popular culture, religion, law, party politics, and the state itself. This is because the end game of the conflict is the ability and power to define the terms by which public life is ordered and maintained: the nature of human life, liberty, justice, and community; cumulatively, the meaning of America.

Though these conflicts to define reality play out within and across many fields, education has had a central place.[1] This is certainly because schools influence and form the young. It is also because schools are one of the primary institutions for imparting shared understandings of collective identity and purpose. As Hunter argued in *Culture Wars*, "The education of the public at every level - from elementary school through college - is not a neutral process of imparting practical knowledge and technical skills. Above and beyond that, schools are the primary institutional means of reproducing community and national identity for succeeding generations of Americans" (1991:198). Put another way, schooling is one of the key institutional contexts through which a society tells itself a story about itself. In MacIntyre's (1984) apt phrase, the institution itself, in its parts and as a whole, provides an 'enacted narrative' within which are embedded a society's idealized understandings of itself and its most authentic members. The story is enacted again and again in multiple ways and levels, and in the process, selves are shaped, persons are formed and the social order is legitimated.

The very nature of modern pluralism makes conflict likely if not inevitable. Schools, then, are unavoidably places where competing conceptions of the good are contested. The inevitability of conflict is ensured by state mandated attendance as well as common curricula, standards of learning, and often common texts. The classic illustration of this conflict is the *kulturkampf* of late nineteenth century Germany, where Bismarck's efforts to force consensus among Catholics and Protestants led to a struggle over the control of the state's educational arm. As Clark and Kaiser (2003) note, Germany's educational battles were actually the norm, rather than the exception, of late nineteenth century Europe. Culture wars were a transnational phenomenon across the continent as emerging nation-states struggled over competing moral visions of the nation, usually played out in the context of schooling.

Similar disputes were unfolding in the USA between Catholics and Protestants. These were the great school wars, as Diane Ravitch fittingly named them (Ravitch 1974, Hunter 1991:Chapter 8). As Catholics immigrated into cities like Baltimore, Philadelphia, New York, and Boston intensified between the 1830 s and 1860 s, they discovered that despite its promise of religious freedom, America's schools were decidedly anti-Catholic. Horace Mann's 'common school' was conceived as the carrier of a particular vision of the moral character of the

---

[1] This observation is widely shared. See, for instance, Reich 2002; Reed 1997; Devine 1996; Green 1996; Gitlin 1995; Bernstein 1995; Jacoby 1994; Gates 1992; Bolton 1992.

nation, a forced consensus over what should unite "Americans" (Glenn 1988). The nonsectarian nature of the common school was in fact a rather particularized version of Anglo-Saxon Protestantism and elicited strong dissent from Catholics. The ensuing struggle led to the establishment of an alternative Catholic system that was consistent with their own moral sensibilities. At stake on this "battlefield of social change" (the sub-title to Ravitch's *The Great School Wars*) was the power and authority to define reality for the next generation.

The conflict over education in the USA continued through the early decades of the twentieth century. The journalist Walter Lippman, in 1928 Page-Barbour Lectures at the University of Virginia, discussed two prominent court cases involving controversies in schools (one in Dayton, Tennessee over Darwinism and the other in Chicago over nationalism in history textbooks):

> May I remind you, then, that the struggles for the control of the schools are among the bitterest political struggles which now divide the nations. Wherever there is a conflict of religious sects, you will find that the public schools are one of the chief bones of contention. It has been so in Canada for generations. It is so now in Mexico. In every country of Europe where there are national minorities, there is bitter dispute over the public schools. It is inevitable that it should be so. Wherever two or more groups within a state differ in religion, or in language and in nationality, the immediate concern of each group is to use the schools to preserve its own faith and tradition. For it is in the school that the child is drawn towards or drawn away from the religion and the patriotism of its parents (1993 [1928]:22–23).

In the modern world, then, schools always do more than offer the information and skills necessary for productive labor. The most dominant theoretical frameworks for research in the sociology of education tend to focus on how schooling serves economic and political interests. In our view, schools do more than just that. They are normative institutions engaged in forming persons and legitimating the social order.[2] As such, they are loci of contested ideas and symbols of collective self-understanding (Zimmerman 2002). This is no less true today though, as implied above, the conflict is no longer between different religious traditions and the institutions that carry them, but rather between competing moral visions rooted in very different epistemic assumptions.

RESEARCH ON EDUCATION AND THE CULTURE WARS

Since the early 1990s, there has been a significant body of research on cultural conflict in the sphere of education. While some of the work is not explicit about this connection, all of it

---

[2] Even the priority given to math and science skills—found in a half century of reforms beginning with the Sputnik "crisis" and the more recent No Child Left Behind Act—is far from normatively neutral. The explicit argument made in these reforms is that "STEM" (or instruction on "science, technology, engineering and math") will strengthen the national economy in the global market. And so it is that schools are forced to re-structure their educational strategies around new standards, by which instruction on some subjects like art or social studies is reduced in order to meet new requirements. The implicit normativity is found in the technical-rational and market assumptions about human purpose and social progress. Curiously, this largely functionalist (human capital) assumption remains even though there appears to be no association between number of engineers and scientists in the labor force and subsequent economic development (Ramirez and Lee 1995).

implicitly addresses some aspects of the conflict at the deeper levels we suggest here. Consider some of the main areas of conflict.

Curriculum

Educational curricula represent a key "front" in the culture war because they are the primary artifacts of socially legitimated knowledge (see Bernstein 1971, Young 1971, 2007; Brint 2006). As Apple and Christian-Smith have written, textbooks "participate in creating what a society has recognized as legitimate and truthful" (1991:4). As such, they provide frameworks through which knowledge, culture, belief, and morality are mediated as taken-for-granted reality. It is inevitable that conflicts over the curriculum involve contests over implied notions of social priority and distinction as well as failure and opprobrium.

As David Tyack argued, the "history wars" of the late twentieth century are simply "a late chapter in a long book" (Tyack 1999:922; see also Nash et al. 1997). Indeed, the contest over the telling of the past has existed for most of America's history (Lippman 1993 [1928], Zimmerman 2002). The acrimony has been especially sharp in the "southern histories" that first emerged in the mid-nineteenth century but persisted well into the twentieth (Moreau 2003). Southerners had their history and, on their account, their children were going to be fully socialized into the cultural ideals that represented *their* collective understandings, not those of the "northern aggressors." The social evils of slavery, Confederate massacres of black prisoners, and the heroics of black soldiers in the Civil war were noticeably absent from these texts, which instead constructed a narrative of the "mythology of the valiant White South and the Lost Cause" (Moreau 2003:90).

Catholics joined white Southerners in objecting to the dominance in this period of New England textbook writers. The Republican Party and its "emphasis on cultural homogeneity, political centralization, and social perfectionism" heavily influenced the writers of history textbooks during the late nineteenth century (Moreau 2003:92). Catholics countered Protestant nativism and anti-Catholic bias by publishing their own textbooks, highlighting the decisive roles Catholics played in formulating American ideals. Efforts by Catholics to tell their own version of American history, as Moreau points out, "infuriated many Protestants, who were, of course, trying to do the same thing" (2003:93).

Precisely these dynamics of the history textbook re-emerged in the latter decades of the twentieth century, beginning with Frances Fitzgerald's *America Revised* (1979). Although her narrative of unity to disunity in the patriotic voice of history textbooks was overly simplistic, and at times frankly incorrect (see Moreau 2003), her book was widely popular and struck a chord with many Americans who felt 'their' history was threatened. Fitzgerald argued that the political upheaval of the 1960s left an enduring mark on history texts that now told a significantly revised narrative of America's past:

> Poor Columbus! He is a minor character now, a walk-on in the middle of American history. Even those books that have not replaced his picture with a Mayan temple or an Iroquois mask do not credit him with discovering America…General Custer has given way to Chief Crazy Horse; General Eisenhower no longer liberates Europe single-handed; and, indeed, most generals, even to Washington and Lee, have faded away, as old soldiers do, giving place to social reformers such as William Lloyd Garrison and Jacob Riis (1979:8).

Fitzgerald's declension narrative "exaggerated a bygone serenity in the textbook-writing business" (Moreau 2003:3), and ignored evidence of prior conflicts, but it nonetheless served as a groundbreaking study and awakened the armies of cultural conflict for the history wars. In a review of Fitzgerald's book, Walter Karp noted:

> You cannot recount the past without making fundamental political judgments, and you cannot deliver those judgments in a classroom without impressing them deeply on the minds of future citizens. . .To teach American history to a great mass of American school children is to exercise genuine political power (1980:80).

America Revised, flawed as it may have been, captured these deeper realities about the teaching of history and sparked debate that has endured for decades.

These debates eventually led to a congressional commissioning of the National History Standards Project in 1992. Lynne Cheney, the Head of the National Endowment for the Humanities at the time of the commissioning, wrote a scathing article in the *Wall Street Journal* in October of 1994 titled "The End of History" roundly criticizing the standards as un-American. Her article opened with these provocative (and false, according to Nash et al. 1997) sentences: "Imagine an outline for the teaching of American history in which George Washington makes only a fleeting appearance and is never described as our first president. Or in which the foundings of the Sierra Club and the National Organization for Women are considered noteworthy events, but the first gathering of the U.S. Congress is not." Elsewhere Cheney argued that the progressive scholars who wrote the standards "paint a grim and gloomy picture of the American past, one that emphasizes failure and makes it seem that most of the faults of mankind have here found their most fertile ground" (1996). This led to a media firestorm and yet another front for the culture wars of the era (see Nash et al. 1997).

The debate focused on how much patriotic triumphalism should be included in "official" US history textbooks, how prominent lesser-known figures should be, and how much of the "grim and gloomy" side of American history should be included. Cheney argued that the history standards were overly "politically correct," for they mentioned Harriet Tubman more than Ulysses S. Grant and Robert E. Lee, made only fleeting references to George Washington and the US Constitution, gave too much attention to McCarthyism and the Ku Klux Klan, and made capitalism, and John D. Rockefeller specifically, look downright evil. For Cheney and her supporters, the standards were anti-Western, anti-American, anti-capitalist, anti-Christian, and at best a sordidly distorted narrative of America's great past. But to the authors and supporters of the History Standards, they represented an account of democratic progress and equality. While the strong reaction caught proponents of the standards off guard, they understood what was at stake: "It is not surprising that the political Right would open a history front in the culture wars. History, like politics, is about national identity" (Nash et al. 1997:7).

These ongoing debates have led several scholars to make vocal pleas for a "common cultural core" in American educational curriculum. Most prominent are Hirsh (1988, 1999) and Ravitch (2002), who each helped to found organizations dedicated to a "common core" in school curriculum. In a lead essay' in a *Daedulus* issue on education titled "Education after the Culture Wars," Ravitch wondered:

> "How, in a society as varied and rapidly changing as our own, can a common culture survive without a clear commitment to broadly shared standards for the teaching of literature and history? And absent any such shared culture, how can we communicate across

lines of race, religion, ethnicity, and social class in order to forge common purposes?"
(2002:6)

She was dismayed by what she saw as a hollowing out and "dumbing down" of school curriculum in the name of political correctness and multiculturalism. She was particularly bothered
by a "well-accepted principle in education publishing" that everything written before 1970
is racist and sexist, thus making most classic children's literature off limits for testing and
curriculum materials. The result, in Ravitch's opinion, is a curriculum void of any unifying
knowledge and steeped in mediocrity. In his contribution to the *Daedulus* issue, Hirsch agreed,
suggesting that schools have failed in their primary task. "A basic goal of public education in a
democracy," he argued, "is to integrate future citizens into a national community of discourse
based on common reference points and a common language, and in a general sense, common
values and common loyalties" (2002:30).

    But these calls for unity have themselves been contested. Progressive educational theo-
rists and scholars argued that the concerns of Ravitch and Hirsch were nostalgic and longed
for a common culture that is more a product of fictional 1950s television shows than any true
"American" identity. Joyce Appleby's response was illustrative: "The 'world we have lost' –
the one where young people's study of significant historical events and famous literary works
formed a core culture – exists more as an ideal than a verifiable reality" (2002:34). Similarly,
Deborah Meier suggested, "the old ethnocentric curriculum was not one whit more serious
or thoughtful than the multicultural curriculum often favored today" (2002:43). For those on
this side of the conflict, today's curriculum is reflective of the growing mosaic of freedom and
equality, accommodating more and more voices that the past has silenced – women, racial
minorities, and the poor and oppressed.

    And the conflict endures, not only at the national level, but also at the state and local level
too. When it comes to school curriculum, the stakes are high because both sides understand the
symbolic significance, not to mention the actual impact, of public education. The fundamental
questions behind the curriculum debates are in part about recognition and empowerment, most
specifically the extent to which minority voices should be heard and the voice of the majority
subdued or delegitimated. This very old conflict endures, as Jonathan Zimmerman has said,
"because schools remain the most important venue for teaching our kids who we are" (Quoted
in Simon 2009). As one respondent to the *Daedulus* issue flatly stated, "the United States is
no more beyond the culture wars than it is beyond tornadoes and hurricanes."

Multiculturalism

The disputes over various curricula represent one arena of conflict. Unrelated to the implicit
identity politics of the history texts are the means by which socio-cultural diversity is understood and managed pedagogically. The point of contention is, in a word, multiculturalism.

    Pluralism has been a central educational challenge for a long time. From its earliest days,
public education has been the primary field in which challenges and conflicts of diversity were
negotiated (Tyack 2003). It is not an overstatement to say that public schooling in the USA
has always been a project in the organization of difference. The common school of the mid-
nineteenth century (Kaestle 1983, Glenn 1988), the Americanization movement of the early
twentieth century (Olneck 1989, 1990, King 2000), intercultural education and cultural gifts

movements between the world wars (Kilpatrick 1947, Selig 2008) and multicultural education popular in recent decades were each strategic attempts to organize difference, to deal with cultural pluralism in an immigrant society (see also Tyack 1993). With each wave of expansion, conflicts arose as the claims of groups challenged the parameters of what should be taught. Through it all, the boundaries of identity and moral community have been challenged, negotiated, and re-negotiated. Multiculturalism - its ideals and the pedagogy itself - is only the most recent arena for these matters to be sorted through.

The details of the conflict over multiculturalism have been elaborated at considerable length elsewhere. (Reich 2002:Chapter 1, Ravitch 2000:Chapter 11, Fullinwider 1996:Chapter 1, Yamane 1996, Gitlin 1995, Bernstein 1995, Hunter 1993:Chapter 7). Our interest is simply to highlight the implicit normativity that animates competing interests. On the face of it, multiculturalism is simply a descriptive term for social diversity and a commitment to the mutual understanding of differences. But it also bears a moral burden. Multiculturalism attempts to address the central imperative of American democracy; the imperative of achieving unity through diversity. As William Galston put it, *e pluribus unum* is not "merely a geographical and institutional, but also a cultural and moral imperative" (1991:10). But *e pluribus unum* is also the central and enduring conundrum of American democracy. How much plurality? What kind of unity? On whose terms? Is the priority given to plurality or to unity? (Hunter 1991). While few if any on the political spectrum - Right to Left - deny the multiple goods implied in this ideal, the actual terms by which this conundrum is sorted out are opaque and contestable. Different versions reflect different interests.

The pedagogy of multiculturalism itself has its own problems, not the least of which is defining its terms.[3] On the surface, multicultural education is committed to celebrating and teaching about the variety of cultures represented in American society. Its curricular objective is to broaden students' horizon of knowledge and experience of that variety. Needless to say, as a tool for making sense of and negotiating difference, it represents a sharp departure from the strategies of the common school and Americanization movements, where assimilation into the American mainstream was the highest goal. By comparison, its critics see multiculturalism as an intellectual prop to tribalism (see discussions in Asante 1991, Asante and Ravitch 1991, or Gitlin 1995).

Debates about bilingual education, which were quite vigorous in the last decades of the twentieth century, reflect these larger concerns about assimilation, the heritage of cultural minorities, and the maintenance of group identities. The common use of the term, at least since the Bilingual Education Act in 1968, refers to separate education in the native language for those students not proficient in English. While linguists and educational theorists strongly supported this method of separate education for English language learners, popular dissent grew through the seventies and culminated in 1985 when William J. Bennett, then US Secretary of Education, called the Bilingual Education Act a "failed path, a bankrupt course" (see Crawford 1992:358). Bennett's words struck a nerve with growing support for 'Official English' policies. One disgruntled citizen, a grandson of Norwegian and Italian immigrants, captured the populist sentiment and claimed that bilingual education was "profoundly un-American and a menace to our national culture" (Quoted in Crawford 1991:13).

---

[3] The voluminous *Handbook of Research on Multicultural Education* (Banks 1995/2004) has no fewer than 11 sections (areas of research) and nearly 50 chapters.

Of course, beyond the populist distaste, there were debates about the empirical effects of separate bilingual education programmes, with critics arguing for more integrated approaches as an alternative (see Glenn and de Jong 1986, August and Hakuta 1997, Rossell 1999). Importantly, these questions and conflicts have been part of America's past, as an immigrant society, for centuries: from Benjamin Franklin's laments in 1753 of his Pennsylvania colony being overrun with German speakers (Crawford 1993:18) to the 1923 US Supreme Court case *Meyer v. Nebraska* overturning a law prohibiting a teacher in a Lutheran school from teaching in the German language, to recent court decisions upholding English only testing policies in California. The concerns in these conflicts always go deeper than mere educational policies. As James Crawford has noted, "Clearly, there is more at stake here than questions of educational effectiveness. Bilingual education is arousing passions about issues of political power and social status that are far removed from the classroom...It is not just a question of how we will run our schools, but of what kind of society we aspire to be: pluralist or conformist, humane or intolerant" (1991:12–13). This is precisely why the conflicts have proven so enduring.

Though the rhetoric in defense of minority group identities is strong, there are often unintended consequences. Olneck argued, for example, that some practices implicitly promote the traditional narrative of the dominant group: "Groups that have been historically oppressed, subordinated, and marginalized may be 'brought into' the main narrative by reconceptualizing their identities as being essentially the 'same as' those of dominant groups" (2001:344). Hunter (1993:Chapter 7) argued that for all of the emphasis on diversity, multiculturalism simultaneously, and altogether unintentionally, trivializes culture by defining it in terms of 'lifestyle choices', (tastes in food, clothing, social ritual, etc.) and thereby denies the more fundamental differences among cultures. What is more, multiculturalism relativizes culture by defining it in terms of its functionality, e.g. we may have different tastes in food but we all need to eat, we may have different mating practices, but all human beings need sexual intimacy, we may worship different gods but religion is a response to a universal human need. In short, the claims of culture are never taken seriously on their own terms and it this way, multiculturalism undermines the authority of cultural norms and cultural institutions, unwittingly teaching students that cultural differences really need not be taken seriously after all. In the name of celebrating difference, then, multiculturalism, in effect, denies the deepest differences. The real lesson to children is that the wide variety of cultures in the world and in our society are not so different after all.

Conflicts over multiculturalism are of course not limited to the USA. Immigration has dramatically increased the number of countries around the world that now think of themselves as multicultural. Many countries in Europe – long a bastion of the dominant Western majority - have significant conflicts over the rights and recognition of group identities as immigration steadily rises. These battlefronts have surfaced another vector - religion and secularism - in the multicultural education debates (see Asad 2006, Sniderman and Hagendoorn 2007).

Science, Religion, and Cosmology

As John Meyer suggests in his essay on the transcendent elements of schooling: "education contains and transmits knowledge of the rationalized and universal cosmos...and individual persons are empowered to act properly in this cosmos and can understand its lawful structure" (2000:209). On these terms, education is the transmission of a kind of cosmology that is, as we noted, religious in character if not in substance. Here too, there is abiding conflict.

In the summer of 1925, the small town of Dayton, Tennessee became the front line that would define the cosmological conflict between religious conservatives and progressives for a century. The Scopes Trial, challenging a Tennessee law forbidding the teaching of evolution in schools, has a much greater significance than a simple controversy in the Bible Belt over a local teacher's use of Darwinism in his classroom. It became a national affair due to major media attention and the involvement of two celebrity figures: the trial lawyer Clarence Darrow and the populist politician William Jennings Bryan. The clash symbolized the larger cultural struggles between science and faith, reason and revelation, religion and modernity that were deeply embedded in the public consciousness of America. The historian George Marsden framed the conflict as a cultural struggle: "The central theme was, inescapably, the clash of two worlds, the rural and the urban. . .Dayton surpassed all fiction in dramatizing the symbolic last stand of nineteenth-century America against the twentieth century" (1980:185). The controversy in Dayton became significant less for the facts of the case and than for the social and cultural transformations it symbolized: "Here, in the public arena, symbols were more effective than substance and 'evolution' became the chief symbol for a whole set of social changes that conservatives found ominous" (Marsden 1990:184).

The journalist Walter Lippman, who chronicled the trial in various newspaper editorials, wrote that it represented a "wide conflict between scholarship and popular faith, between freedom of thought and popular rule, which irritates American politics with deep discords" (1993[1928]:8). He also argued that the conflict had deeper roots that were fundamentally epistemological, 'that human reason and not divine revelation was the source of truth' and that a 'religion of revelation' was being replaced by a 'religion of rationalism' (1992[1928]:18–19). It was at this level - the sources of authority and knowledge - where the debate had its deeper, more intractable sources. as Lippman (1929) observed in *A Preface to Morals*,

> It is these supporting conceptions - the unconscious assumption that we are related to God as creatures to creator, as vassals to a king, as children to a father - that the acids of modernity have eaten away. The modern man's daily experience of modernity makes instinctively incredible to him these unconscious ideas which are at the core of the great traditional and popular religions (1929:52).

And though the acids of modernity were corroding former ways of knowing and being, the clash between reason and revelation was far from abated after the Scopes Trial. As historian Edward J. Larson points out, the 'summer for the gods' struck a nerve that would continue to be aggravated throughout the century: "[Darrow and Bryan] tapped into a cultural divide that deeply troubles American society. . .[and] has sporadically touched off maelstroms over the past eighty years - storms that sorely test America's national tradition of tolerance. If history offers a barometer for future events, it forecasts more heavy weather ahead" (2006: 278).

The symbolic significance of the Scopes Trial was on display again in the mid-1980s, when parents and other citizens of Mobile, Alabama sued the city's school board arguing that the textbooks were promoting the 'religion' of secular humanism in violation of the First Amendment's no-establishment clause (*Smith v. Board of School Commissioners of Mobile County* 1987). Though a local dispute, it attracted the attention and involvement of all the major national players in the culture war - the ACLU and People for the American Way on one side and Catholic and Evangelical groups on the other side. In this case, Christians were no longer defending their hegemony in the culture as they attempted roughly 60 years before in the Scopes Trial. Rather, at stake for the plaintiffs was the issue of fairness and balance of treatment for multiple worldviews, including the Christian worldview.

Parents and other citizens brought a lawsuit against the school board, alleging that the school system was teaching the tenets of an anti-religious religion called 'secular humanism'. The complainants asked that forty-four different elementary through high school level textbooks be removed from the curriculum. After an initial ruling in a federal district court in favor of the plaintiffs, the US Court of Appeals for the Eleventh Circuit ruled that as long as the school was motivated by a secular purpose, it did not matter whether the curriculum and texts shared ideas held by one or more religious groups. The Court found that the texts in question promoted important secular values (tolerance, self-respect, logical decision making) and thus the use of the textbooks neither unconstitutionally advanced a nontheistic religion nor inhibited theistic religions (see also Bates 1993 for an account of a similar local dispute in Hawkins County, Tennessee during the same year).

The latest chapter in the educational struggles between religion and science is the "Intelligent Design" controversy. Recent literature on this topic is expansive (Scott 2009, Humes 2008, Lebo 2008, Miller 2008, Slack 2008, Chapman 2007, Scott and Branch 2006, Forrest and Gross 2004). At the most popular level, the contemporary struggle between creationism and evolution is over religion's place in the public arena. The judge in the case in Dover, Pennsylvania - the most recent iteration of the Scopes Trial - called the bluff of parents and proponents of intelligent design who presented it as science when he definitively ruled that intelligent design amounts to religion, not science and thus has no place in the curriculum of a public school. But on a deeper level - just as it was in Dayton - the struggle is not really about science, or even religion in the public square per se, or about who is right or wrong, but rather legitimation of particular definitions of reality. This is evident even in some of the literature on the topic: two of the books listed above include the phrase "the battle for America's soul" in their subtitles (Humes 2008, Miller 2008) and another is titled *The Battle over the Meaning of Everything* (Slack 2008).

The struggle is over cosmologies – a hierarchy of values, abiding narratives, and unquestioned sources of authority. In a review essay, in *The New York Times* Book Review titled "When Cosmologies Collide", Shulevitz (2006) argues that the judge in the Dover case clearly made the right decision, but that the issue will not go away because evolution*ism* is a worldview that transcends the science of evolution. She explains evolution*ism* represents a cosmology just as much as creationism. The larger point here is how this debate illumines the ontological role education has on a cultural level: the institutionalized, cultural rules embedded within any educational system legitimate a particular cosmology. The issue is not about science, or the economy, or skills necessary for social improvement; the issue is an ontological one, legitimating a theory of reality.

Assessment

Although, it plays a much less prominent role in the public imagination for cultural conflict in education, the methods and principles behind assessment practices are often controversial. Decisions about how we judge educational quality and effectiveness, though simply pragmatic on the surface, mask deeply held assumptions about the purposes of education, the nature of human persons, and idealized visions of the future.

In the late 1980s and early 1990s, educators and politicians began to make a fundamental shift in how educational quality was measured; while previous evaluations were focused on "inputs" such as resources and services, newer thinking focused on "outputs" such as results, outcomes and effects. While logical on the surface, the change revealed deeper cultural differences that led to what one commentator called the "new school wars" (Manno 1995).

Almost all the interested parties agreed that outcomes mattered in assessing school quality; the source of the conflict emerged when Outcome-Based Education, as it had come to be known, took on a "transformational" quality that focused more on behaviors, attitudes and values students should develop rather than on cognitive and academic outcomes. The version of Outcome-Based Education that found its way into most state policies in the USA was highly focused on "behaviors that denote a positive social, emotional and physical well-being" (Spady 1988:69). Major controversies erupted over who decides the particulars of those behaviors and values. As one critic of Outcome-Based Education wrote:

> What sort of outcomes can a state reasonably require of every student in compulsory public schooling? Forcing parents to send their children to school is one thing. But for the state to declare that students cannot graduate from a government school they must attend unless they demonstrate values and attitudes the state prescribes – even when these values conflict with what those students and their families believe – raises the specter of Aldous Huxley's *Brave New World* (Manno 1995:723).

When school districts began prescribing outcomes in the realm of values and beliefs, they were implicitly making judgments about the kinds of people their students should become; these ontological assumptions became equated with "secular humanism," in the common parlance of the day, and sparked a firestorm of resistance from parents, usually religious conservatives.

One such battle played out in the early 1990 s in Gaston County, North Carolina (see Sargeant and West 1996). Religious conservatives in the district vociferously objected to the "secular values" they felt the new Outcome-Based Education program embodied. This case, though very much a small struggle in a local community, had all the hallmarks of the larger culture war. Cultural conflict is, more often than not, local rather than national. However, in this case, like in so many others, national advocacy organizations descended on the local community and took control of framing the conflict for the national media. This was a conflict between "teachers and preachers" in Sargeant and West's phrase, and although it was technically merely about methods for evaluating student learning, it reflected deeper struggles over the cultural and national values that should – or should not – be transmitted to children.

The language of "outcomes" eventually evolved into "accountability" and the landmark No Child Left Behind legislation of 2002 came to define what we deem valuable in assessing educational quality in the twenty-first century. The "high stakes" testing of No Child Left Behind - that is, schools must meet benchmarks or be closed - focuses on content knowledge and thus avoids some of the traps that caught Outcome-Based Education. But tests, standards, and accountability have proven no less controversial when carried out as policy. Initially passed with bi-partisan support (the late Ted Kennedy co-sponsored the bill), No Child Left Behind became a political symbol of the Bush Administration, often lumped together with other failed policies such as the Iraq war and the Patriot Act. This criticism was largely because while raising the expectations for schools, Bush failed to deliver federal resources, especially to districts with high populations of low-income students that stood to lose the most from "failure." No Child Left Behind, as a political symbol, became a battlefield for conservatives (accountability) and liberals (resources) to fight old wars. Lost in the middle of the debate were the unintended consequences of high stakes testing and the normative judgments it made about knowledge and human persons: only reading, math, and science (beginning in 2007) are tested. Subjects that are not tested lose out to those that are in the struggle for classroom time. As one critic stated, lamenting the loss of history teaching: "We are trying to help our children shape the next generation of democracy. And that will require that they know something of the generations that preceded them and give some thought to what will be required of them in the future" (Chenoweth 2002). Decisions about what to test reflect assumptions about the legitimation of certain forms of knowledge, the formation of certain kinds of people, and the nature of the society we hope to become (see footnote 2).

Sex Education

A final area of contestation is sex education. Sex education was invented at the dawn of the twentieth century, conceived as part of the larger social reform and public health initiatives of the Progressive Era (Moran 2000). In the first half of the century, sex education - largely warnings of venereal disease and tips on how to choose a compatible mate - enjoyed broad public support (Luker 2006). But all of this changed in the 1960 s, when the sexual revolution "questioned a whole set of assumptions about what were the right ways for men and women to relate to one another sexually, how sex was and should be related to maleness and femaleness, and how and where marriage and sex should coincide" (Luker 2006:7). In the second half of the twentieth century, and into the twenty-first, as Zimmerman noted, conflicts over sex education "touched upon the deepest religious and philosophical rifts in post-World War II America" (2002:189).

The battle lines in this debate fall as they do in others, between conservatives and progressives, but the nature of some of the positions has changed over time. Progressives argued consistently that ignorance about sexuality led to a host of negative social outcomes: teenage pregnancy, disease, abuse, and discrimination (especially towards homosexuality), while undermining possibilities for individual fulfillment and happiness. For much of the last five decades, conservatives argued that schools were no place for instruction on sexuality; rather, they argued, the home was the proper place for such morally charged discussion. For conservatives, sex education was another avenue through which "secular humanism" was eroding the moral fabric of the nation. In the words of one activist, sex education was "the major transmission belt" for "secular humanism...an aggressive atheism which denies God and shuns all moral absolutes" (quoted in Zimmerman 2002:209). The conservative argument has recently changed as they admit, implicitly at least, that sex can no longer be ignored in schools. They now advocate "abstinence only" sex education, as compared to "comprehensive" sex education advocated by progressives, which encourage young people to act responsibly in sexual relationships and include information about contraception and disease prevention (Luker 2006). Some comprehensive programs include discussion of a range of sexual practices and identities outside the heterosexual norm (Irvine 2002).

Battles over sex education have all the hallmarks of the abortion debates, the central conflict of the contemporary culture wars. Like the abortion debate, the battle plays out in the political arena and the struggle over the rhetorical use of language is primary. As the abortion sides played word games with "pro-life" and "pro-choice" and slogans like "choose life", so too the sex education sides seek to frame themselves with the right terminology (for instance, proponents of "comprehensive" sex education prefer to call it "abstinence based"). They use words to carefully vilify the enemy (in abortion debates: "murderers" and "pro-death activists" vs. "zealots" and "bigots"; in sex education debates: "pornographers" and "pedophiles" vs. "fundamentalists" and "extremists"). The two conflicts are also similar in the role national advocacy groups, such as Planned Parenthood or Focus on the Family, play in local conflicts; as one school board member said of a disruptive sex education opponent: "Somebody's giving him words" (quoted in Irvine 2002:3). (See Hunter 1993, Irvine 2002, and Luker 2006 for the similarities in the structure of these debates). The debates have only intensified in very recent years because of Bush Administration support of abstinence only programs. Some even argue that the terms of the conflict have spread internationally and represent a global movement to achieve the political goals of the Christian Right (Irvine 2002, Peppard 2008).

The conflict is much deeper, of course, than whether students in public schools should learn the proper way to use a condom. As Kristin Luker has said,

> Fights about sex are also fights about gender, about power and trust and hierarchy, about human nature, and not surprisingly, about what sex really is and what it means in human life. Even more deeply, fights about sex are fights about how we are to weigh our obligations to ourselves and others, issues that themselves are tied to our notion of what it means to be a man or a woman" (2006:7).

In other words, there is a particular anthropology at stake in these conflicts, and beyond that, a larger cultural order in which it makes sense and is taken for granted (or not). These conflicts are "far more than local school wars" as another commentator has said about programs discussing lesbian and gay identities, "they are battles not simply about homosexuality, but over which sexualities and which citizens are valued as legitimate" (Irvine 2002:167). In the end, battles over sex education reflect different moral visions for sexuality itself, and the sources of authority for those different approaches. This is why, for many in the debate, "values are more important than the facts" that could determine which program has empirical evidence of effectiveness (Luker 2006:31). The nature of how children are formed, and the ideal to which they should conform, are the heart of the conflict.

Toward a Sociology of Education, Culture, and Morality

The sociology of education has been dominated by a focus on stratification and inequality. In its course, the field has produced excellent quantitative work based upon sophisticated statistical modeling to explain how educational attainment situates individuals within the social class structure. Yet, as Mitchell Stevens has recently argued, "sociologists' penchant for quantification has tended to obscure the essentially cultural character of educational processes" (2008:98). In masking the cultural orientation of education, research often fails to reveal how school processes legitimate boundaries that constitute the negations and the affirmations of moral culture. When the study of education does turn to cultural sociology, it is mainly for theories of cultural and social reproduction (Bourdieu 1977). These explanations have helped to understand reproduction of structures of inequality via cultural capital or ideology transmitted through the educational system.

In the end, this cultural turn tends to serve neo-Marxist and neo-Weberian conceptualizations of conflict in education. Here, the end game is on the ways education - as ideology for neo-Marxists or credentialism for neo-Weberians - serves economic and political interests (Bowles and Gintis 1976, Collins 1971, 1979). In these perspectives, schools respond to the demands of certain status groups, socialize for particular interests and reproduce the inequalities of power and privilege in the social order. In the end, "culture" and "morality" really make sense only in relation to political economy which functions in relation to these.

These lines of inquiry have generated a vast amount of research that has illuminated our understanding of education and society. They do not, however, exhaust the possibilities of inquiry, either theoretically or empirically.

There are some promising signs, however, and some recent scholarship creates space for new thinking and different directions for research. Recent works by Brint et al (2001) and Arum (2003) point to the ways that schooling functions to socialize the young into different moral orders. Likewise, John Meyer's theoretical work (1977, 1986), drawing from both the Weberian and Durkheimian traditions, focuses attention on the ways the official structures of education legitimate the functioning of modern society. In his words, "formalized educational systems are, in fact, theories of socialization institutionalized as rules at the collective level" (1977:65). All of these efforts are both noteworthy and promising.

We would suggest, perhaps provocatively, yet further innovation in the direction of a neo-Durkheimian model of education and, in particular, conflict in education. What is distinctive about this approach is the way it takes culture and morality (e.g. its symbols, its normative claims, and the like) seriously on their own terms. It is nonreductive in that it does not assume that culture and morality are merely epiphenomenal to political economy. Rather, for all its natural and organic linkages to economic and political interest, culture and morality can be understood as relatively autonomous; that is, they possess their own energy, logic, structure, evolution, course of action, and so on.

A neo-Durkheimian model of conflict in education plays out on at least two levels. The first concerns conflict over particular moral issues obvious to everyone who reads a newspaper, including all the issues discussed here. The specific questions that animate the conflicts at this level - such as national histories, approaches to multicultural education, assessment strategies, sexuality, religion and science, etc. - though certainly enduring, will come and go and be used by competing communities to further the ends of solidarity, collective identity formation, legitimacy, and bids for cultural hegemony in addition to any political interests. The fields of conflict on such matters will continue to mainly play out locally in school boards, school districts, communities, and the like, but, from time to time, nationally through the work of special interest groups. Here also, highly emotive symbols are central to the cultural dynamics at work. The symbols of fairness, equality, toleration, the American identity, and the like, are the contested medium of educational content and purpose.

The second level of conflict operates at a more implicit level of normativity, what we call the deep structures of moral life by which social orders are constituted and through which humans make sense of their world (Hunter and Wolfe 2006). By this, we refer to the latent and typically unspoken frameworks of authority, teleology, anthropology, and narrativity that tend to define meaningful order and continuity in a culture. In education, these concerns play out in the implicit models and means by which persons are formed and the complex instrumentalities by which schools participate in the legitimation and reproduction of moral order in society. While the work of boundary creation and maintenance (in schools and elsewhere) is always implicitly about power, it is never *only* about the power to create or fortify social and economic inequalities. Within the normative frameworks of social life - and quite independent of the dynamics of political economy - are fundamental assumptions about the nature of the good (such as what constitutes a good person, benevolent action, common aspirational goods, ideals of well-being, etc.) that provide empowering motives and a range of possible alternatives for individual and collective action. These are constantly being challenged, resisted, negotiated, contested, and reinterpreted and schools are one of the most important institutional settings for this ongoing work. Yet, these dynamics are typically neglected in educational research.

The most obvious mistake, then, is in supposing that the deepest levels of formation and legitimation are measureable through either the variety of moral education programs on offer or the "hidden curriculum" that reinforces existing social inequality. Rather, our working assumption is that normativity, though largely tacit, permeates all aspects of education. Notions of the "good," whether the "good life" or the "good society," are not just one element of pedagogy but rather saturate all facets of the institution and the experience within them. Given the nature of pluralism in the late modern world, these tacit notions of the good will inevitably are evolving, changing and contested along the way. The outcome, needless to say, will be of profound consequence not only to the young who are formed in the care of these institutions, but also to the quality of civic life more broadly.

REFERENCES

Apple, M. W., and L. K. Christian-Smith, eds. 1991. *The Politics of the Textbook.* New York: Routledge.

Arum, R. 2003. *Judging School Discipline.* Cambridge: Harvard University Press.

Asad, T. 2006. "French secularism and the 'Islamic veil affair.'" *The Hedgehog Review* 8 (1&2): 93–106.

Asante, M. 1991. "The Afrocentric Idea in Education." *Journal of Negro Education* 60:170–180.

Asante, M., and D. Ravitch. 1991. "Multiculturalism: An Exchange," *American Scholar* 60:267–276.

August, D., and K. Hakuta, eds. 1997. *Improving Schooling for Language-Minority Children: A Research Agenda.* Washington, DC: National Research Council.

Banks, J. A., ed. and Cherry McGee Banks, associate ed. 1995. *Handbook of Research on Multicultural Education,* 2nd edition printed in 2004. New York: Macmillan.

Bates, S. 1993. *Battleground: One Mother's Crusade, the Religious Right, and the Struggle for Control of Our Classrooms.* New York: Poseidon Press.

Bernstein, B. 1971. "On the Classification of Framing of Educational Knowledge." PP. 47–69 in *Knowledge and Control: New Directions in the Sociology of Education,* edited by M. F. D. Young. London: Collier-Macmillan.

Bernstein, R. 1995. *Dictatorship of Virtue: How the Battle over Multiculturalism is Reshaping Our Schools, Our Country, and Our Lives.* New York: Knopf.

Bolton, R., ed. 1992. *Culture Wars.* New York: New Press.

Bourdieu, P. 1977. "Cultural Reproduction and Social Reproduction." PP. 487–516 in Power and Ideology in Education, edited by J. Karabel. New York: Oxford University Press.

Bowles, S., and H. Gintis. 1976. *Schooling in Capitalist America.* New York: Basic Books.

Brint, S. 2006. *Schools and Society.* Stanford, CA: Stanford University Press.

Brint, S., M. F. Contreras, and M. T. Matthewes. 2001. "Socialization Messages in Primary Schools: An Organizational Analysis." *Sociology of Education* 74:157–180.

Chapman, M. 2007. *40 Days and 40 Nights: Darwin, Intelligent Design, God, Oxycontin, and Other Oddities on Trial in Pennsylvania.* New York: HarperCollins.

Cheney, L. 1994. "The End of History" *Wall Street Journal* Editorial Page. October 20.

Cheney, L. 1996. "Politics in the Classroom is Nothing New" *Wall Street Journal* Editorial Page. January 3.

Clark, C., and W. Kaiser, eds. 2003. *Culture Wars: Secular-Catholic Conflict in Nineteenth-Century Europe.* New York: Cambridge University Press.

Collins, R. 1971. "Functional and Conflict Theories of Educational Stratification" *American Sociological Review* 36:1002–1019.

Collins, R. 1979. *The Credential Society.* New York: Academic Press.

Crawford, J. 1991. *Bilingual Education: History, Politics, Theory and Practice.* Los Angeles: Bilingual Educational Services, Inc.

Crawford, J., ed. 1992. *Language Loyalties.* Chicago: The University of Chicago Press.

Devine, P. 1996. *Human Diversity and the Culture Wars: A Philosophical Perspective on Contemporary Cultural Conflict.* Westport, CT: Praeger.

Fitzgerald, F. 1979. *America Revised: History Schoolbooks in the Twentieth Century.* Boston: Little, Brown and Company.

Forrest, B., and P. R. Gross. 2004. *Creationism's Trojan Horse: The Wedge of Intelligent Design.* New York: Oxford.

Fullinwider, R. K., ed. 1996. *Public Education in a Multicultural Society: Policy, Theory, Critique.* New York: Cambridge.

Galston, W. A. 1991. *Liberal Purposes: Goods, Virtues, and Diversity in the Liberal State.* New York: Cambridge University Press.

Gates, H. L. 1992. *Loose Canons: Notes on the Culture Wars.* New York: Oxford.

Gitlin, T. 1995. *The Twilight of Common Dreams: Why America Is Wracked by Culture Wars.* New York: Henry Holt.

Glenn, C. L. 1988. *The Myth of the Common School.* Amherst, MA: UMass Press.

Glenn, C. L. with E. J. de Jong. 1986. *Educating Immigrant Children: Schools and Language Minorities in Twelve Nations.* New York: Garland.

Hirsch, E. D. 1999. *The Schools We Need: And Why We Don't Have Them.* New York: Anchor.

Hirsch, E. D. 1988. *Cultural Literacy: What Every American Needs to Know.* New York: Vintage.

Hirsch, E. D. 2002. "Not to Worry?" *Daedalus* 131(3):30–32. Response to Ravitch.

Humes, E. 2008. *Monkey Girl: Evolution, Education, Religion, and the Battle for America's Soul.* New York: Harper Perennial.

Hunter, J. D. 1991. *Culture Wars.* New York: Basic Books.

Hunter, J. D. 1993. *Before the Shooting Begins.* New York: Free Press.

Hunter J. D., and A. Wolfe. 2006. *Is there a Culture War? A Dialogue on Values and American Public Life.* Washington, DC: Brookings.

Irvine, J. M. 2002. *Talk about Sex: The Battles over Sex Education in the United States.* Berkeley: University of California Press.

Jacoby, R. 1994. *Dogmatic Wisdom: How the Culture Wars Divert Education and Distract America.* New York: Doubleday.

Kaestle, C. F. 1983. *Pillars of the Republic: Common Schools and American Society 1780–1860.* New York: Hill and Wang

Karp, W. 1980. "Textbook America: The Teaching of History." *Harper's Magazine* (May), 80–88.

Kilpatrick, W. H., ed. 1947. *Intercultural Attitudes in the Making.* New York: Harper.

King, D. 2000. *Making Americans: Immigration, Race and the Origins of the Diverse Democracy.* Cambridge, MA: Harvard.

Larson, E. J. 2006. *Summer for the Gods: The Scopes Trial and America's Continuing Debate over Science and Religion.* New York: Basic Books.

Lebo, L. 2008. *The Devil in Dover: An Insider's Story of Dogma v. Darwin in Small-town America.* New York: New Press.

Lippmann, W. 1993 (1928). *American Inquisitors.* New Brunswick, NJ: Transaction Publishers.

Lippmann, W. 1929. *A Preface to Morals.* New York: Time Life Books.

Luker, K. 2006. *When Sex Goes to School: Warring Views on Sex—and Sex Education—Sine the Sixties.* New York: Norton.

MacIntyre, A. 1984. *After Virtue.* Notre Dame, IN: University of Notre Dame Press.

Marsden, G. M. 1980. *Fundamentalism and American Culture: the Shaping of Twentieth Century Evangelicalism: 1870–1925.* New York: Oxford.

Marsden, G. M. 1990. *Religion and American Culture.* New York: Harcourt Brace Jovanovich.

Meyer, John, W. 1977. "The Effects of Education as an Institution." *Sociology of Education* 83:55–77.

Meyer, John, W. 1986. "Types of Explanation in the Sociology of Education." in *Handbook of Theory and Research for the Sociology of Education,* edited by J. G. Richardson. New York: Greenwood Press.

Meyer, John, W. 2000. "Reflections on Education as Transcendence." PP. 206–222 in *Reconstructing the Common Good in Education: Coping with Intractable American Dilemmas,* edited by Larry and Dorthy Shipps Cuban. Stanford, CA: Stanford University Press.

Miller, K. R. 2008. *Only a Theory: Evolution and the Battle for America's Soul.* New York: Viking.

Moran, J. P. 2000. *Teaching Sex: the Sahping of Adolexcence in the 20th Century.* Cambridge: Harvard.

Moreau, J. 2003. *School Book Nation: Conflicts over American History Textbooks from the Civil War to the Present.* Ann Arbor: University of Michigan Press.

Nash, G. B., C. Crabtree, and R. E. Dunn. 1997. *History on Trial: Culture Wars and the Teaching of the Past.* New York: Knopf.

Olneck, M. 1989. "Americanization and the Education of Immigrants, 1900–1925: An Analysis of Symbolic Action," *American Journal of Education* 97: 398–423.

Olneck, M. 1990. "The Recurring Dream: Symbolism and Ideology in Intercultural and Multicultural Education." *American Journal of Education* 98(2): 147–174.

Olneck, M. 2001. "Re-naming, Re-imagining America: Multicultural Curriculum as Classification Struggle." *Pedagogy, Culture and Society* 9(3):333–354.

Peppard, J. 2008. "Culture Wars in South Australia: the Sex Education Debates" *Australian Journal of Social Issues* 43(3): 499–516.

Ramirez, F. O., and M. Lee 1995 "Education, Science and Development." PP 124–138 in *Social Changes and Educational Development: Mainland China, Taiwan, and Hong Kong,* edited by G. G. Postigione, and L. W. On. Hong Kong: University of Hong Kong, Center of Asian Studies.

Ravitch, D. 1974. *The Great School Wars: New York City, 1805–1973: A History of the Public Schools as Battlefield of Social Change.* New York: Basic Books.

Ravitch, D. 2002. "Education after the Culture Wars." *Daedalus* 131(3):5–21. With responses by H. Gardner, T. Sizer, E. D. Hirsch, Jr., J. Appleby, C. R. Stimpson, D. Meier, P. A. Graham, J. Mirel, R. Boyers, T. Bender, and A. Delbanco.

Reed, I. 1997. *MultiAmerica: Essays on Cultural Wars and Cultural Peace.* New York: Viking Books.

Reich, R. 2002. *Bridging Liberalism and Multiculturalism in American Education.* Chicago: University of Chicago Press.

Sargeant, K., and E. West. 1996. "Teachers and Preachers: The Battle over Public School Reform in Gaston County, North Carolina." PP 35–60 in *The American Culture Wars,* edited by J. L. Nolan, Jr. VA: University of Virginia Press. Charlottesville.

Scott, E. C. 2009. *Evolution vs. Creationism: An Introduction,* 2nd edition. Berkeley, CA: University of California Press.

Scott, E. C., and G. Branch. 2006. *Not in Our Classrooms: Why Intelligent Design is Wrong for Our Schools.* Boston: Beacon Press.

Selig, D. 2008. *Americans All: The Cultural Gifts Movement.* Cambridge, MA: Harvard University Press.

Shulevitz, J. 2006. "When Cosmologies Collide." In *The New York Times.* New York: Sunday Book Review.

Simon, S. 2009. "The Culture Wars' New Front: U.S. History Classes in Texas." *Wall Street Journal* A14. July 14 254(11).

Slack, G. 2008. *The Battle Over the Meaning of Everything: Evolution, Intelligent Design, and a School Board in Dover, PA.* San Francisco: Jossey-Bass.

Sniderman, P. M., and L. Hagendoorn. 2007. *When Ways of Life Collide: Multiculturalism and Its Discontents in the Netherlands.* Princeton, NJ: Princeton University Press.

Spady, W. G. 1988. "Organizing for Results: The Basis of Authentic Restructuring and Reform." *Educational Leadership* (October) 46(2):4–8.

Stevens, M. 2008. "Culture and Education." *The ANNALS of the American Academy of Political and Social Science* 619:97–113.

Tyack, D. 1993. "Constructing Difference: Historical Reflections on Schooling and Social Diversity." *Teachers College Record* 95(1):8–34.

Tyack, D.1999. "Monuments Between Covers: The Politics of Textbooks." *American Behavioral Scientist* 426: 922–932.

Tyack, D. 2003. *Seeking Common Ground: Public Schools in a Diverse Society.* Cambridge, MA: Harvard.

Yamane, D. 1996. "The Battle of the Books at Berkeley: In Search of the Culture Wars in Debates over Multiculturalism." PP 3–34 in *The American Culture Wars,* edited by J. L. Nolan, Jr. Charlottesville, VA: University of Virginia Press.

Young, M. 1971. *Knowledge and Control.* London: Collier Macmillan.

Young, M. 2007. *Bringing Knowledge Back In: From social constructivism to social realism in the sociology of education.* London: Routledge.

Zimmerman, J. 2002. *Whose America? Culture Wars in the Public Schools.* Cambridge, MA: Harvard.

CHAPTER 16

The Creation and Establishment of Moral Vocabularies

Why Moralizing and Moral Vocabularies Matter

BRIAN M. LOWE

Any social scientific inquiry of morality requires some examination of the *language* utilized by participants, onlookers, and agents of social control in the terms, phrases, and associations made or ignored. Hunter (1991) contends that many of the cultural conflicts of the United States during the 1990s were driven by the use of "code words" to communicate antagonistic meanings (such as those who characterized themselves as "pro-life" in opposition to "pro-choice" forces). The use of "coded words" is not limited to claimsmakers (Best 2007). Jamieson and Waldman (2003), for example, point out that some journalists describe a late-term abortion procedure as "intact dilatation and extraction" (favoring the medical normalcy of the medical procedure) while others describe the same procedure as "partial birth abortion" (favoring the anti-abortion stance that this practice is the murder of viable infants). Beyond posing a dilemma for journalistic objectivity, this debate infiltrated policy making, with 29 states banning "partial birth abortion" (Jamieson and Waldman 2003:xiv–xv).

The terms used to characterize a controversial subject, object, or practice and the moral language deployed is significant because it shapes the grounds of moral decision making. Stout (2006) argues, for example, that the American Civil War was initiated and accelerated in large part because of the moralistic rhetoric echoing from newspapers, pamphlets, and pulpits in both the North and South, which elevated the conflict to a quasi-religious phenomenon. Stout's work also shows that moralistic language *evolves*. The American Civil War began largely in the name of maintaining the Union and only subsequently did questions of the morality of the destruction of slavery enter into Northern rationales. Bronner (2008) cites a similar phenomenon amongst hunting enthusiasts, whose defense of hunting has recently adopted concepts such as "wildlife management" to defend their practice. Derber and Magrass (2008) cite how both the Roman and British empires defended their conquests and expansions in terms of supporting and maintaining "civilization." Code words, evolving meanings, collections of moral terms, resources, symbols and understandings – all placed here under the rubric of *moral vocabularies* – have been deployed to conceal or reframe and justify actions that are seemingly at odds with another, more established, moral vocabulary.

The above example suggests that any social scientific consideration of morality must consider at some analytical level the language or terminology used in public moral reasoning.

S. Hitlin, S. Vaisey (eds.), *Handbook of the Sociology of Morality*,
Handbooks of Sociology and Social Research, DOI 10.1007/978-1-4419-6896-8_16,
© Springer Science+Business Media, LLC 2010

Social scientists must consider how these terms and meanings are organized into some sort of coherent system or vocabulary, how these vocabularies allow those who rely on them to make sense of the world, how particular vocabularies intersect with other vocabularies, and how these factors evolve over time. What follows is, I argue, a promising approach to studying these questions in an inductive manner.

The moral vocabularies approach outlined here is intended to provide social science researchers with a way to organize and analyze the statements and activities of moral claims-makers that recognizes both the agency of claimsmakers and the material and social realities of the host society within which moral claims are made, challenged, and altered. In its simplest form, the moral vocabularies approach is a middle-range theoretical approach intended to identify, map, and organize the moral and/or ethical claims created and deployed by claims-makers (see Merton 1949). This approach attempts to identify "value-rational" (Weber 1978, 1992) vocabularies of motive, whereby actors engage in – or claim to engage in – activities "for their own sake" and then works to map these claims and their underlying assumptions in order to provide a more holistic perspective of the world view(s) from which they emanate. The moral vocabularies approach also seeks to grasp how moral and ethical claims intersect, mesh, or clash with the larger host societies and in what ways the particular moral vocabularies used by claimsmakers are informed by their perception of other complementary or competing moral vocabularies. As the name suggests, the moral vocabularies approach is also centrally concerned with identifying efforts at what Rozin (1997) termed "moralization": the process through which activities, practices, phenomena, objects and subjects acquire a moral standing that transcends personal preference or mere cultural convention. Moralization directly affects claimsmakers (who are attempting to alter the moral status of a specific object, practice, or phenomenon) and it also shapes the success of their efforts to "inject" at least a fragment of their moral vocabulary into the broader society. In this manner, the moral vocabularies approach may also be a useful tool for addressing some aspects of societal change. Though the term "vocabularies" suggests a focus on specific words, terms, phrases and other communicative devices, the larger directive of the moral vocabularies approach is to identify how a moral stance, once created and established, tends to produce and reinforce a specific form of moral logic for claimsmakers. Vocabularies make some actions highly desirable and possibly even mandatory for those subscribing or adhering to a specific moral vocabulary (in order both to maintain internal consistency and in-group legitimacy), while at the same time defining other actions as beyond consideration.

WHAT MORAL VOCABULARIES DO

While the universe of potential subjects for a sociological examination of morality is enormous – encompassing social movements, subcultures, religion, electoral politics, media and so on – most of these possible domains share four common traits which are considered through the moral vocabularies approach.

First, nearly all moral activity involves some sort of *claimsmaking*, citing some activity, phenomenon, practice or subject as being worthy of either condemnation or praise.

Second, the vehicle(s) for making these moral claims serve to create some sort of *solidarity or group membership* amongst those who subscribe to or circulate certain moral claims. For example, those who assert that nonhuman animals have "rights" are making both positive and negative claims regarding the treatment of animals and are also effectively proclaiming their identity as supporters of animal rights, even if they lack membership in a specific organization.

The presence of these claims within the larger society also possibly allows others to make such claims and not to be viewed as deviant.

Third, the claims, terms, and code words used by claimsmakers are likely to form a more organized pattern which becomes a *device for moral analysis*. A self-identified American conservative, for instance, may come to use a few claims from the conservative "toolkit" (see Swidler 1986), such as the desirability of "small government" to evaluate a variety of potential governmental programs and policies, thus attacking "big government" as inherently undesirable. Such behavior reinforces the conservative orientation by providing confirmatory evidence for the self-identity of the conservative.

Finally, if particular terms, code words, concepts, or other fragments of a moral vocabulary become disseminated into the wider host society, then such resources may *lead to a degree of social change*. For example, as tobacco control advocates succeeded in disseminating their claims that tobacco consumption caused lung cancer, heart disease and other "smoking related" conditions in the United States during the 1970s and 1980s, smoking rates began to decrease and more municipalities began to create "smoke free" spaces such as restaurants, offices and public buildings. Although the vast majority of the Americans who encountered, accepted, and internalized these claims did not join organizations like the American Lung Association, the tobacco control advocates' claims became increasingly normative, eventually displacing smoking as a socially acceptable practice.

In sum, the moral vocabulary approach offers an analytical strategy through which moralistic claims may be viewed as claims per se, as means to reinforce social solidarity among claimsmakers, as devices for individual and social reasoning, and as means for promoting social change in the broader, non-mobilized, society. It therefore provides a way to analyze how moral claims function among claimsmakers themselves as well as how these claims intersect with the larger social order.

AN INCOMPLETE PARADIGM: MEME THEORY

To highlight some of the advantages of the moral vocabulary approach, I contrast it with "meme theory," an already influential framework for explaining moral and cultural change. Richard Dawkins, who is generally considered to be the progenitor of meme theory, defines the "meme" as "...a unit of cultural transmission, or a unit of *imitation*...Examples of memes are tunes, ideas, catch-phrases, clothes, fashions, ways of making pots or building arches" (Dawkins 1976:206). Dawkins makes the analogy between memetic transmission and Darwinian natural selection, arguing that as genes "desire" to be reproduced so to memes "desire" to be replicated "...by leaping from brain to brain via...imitation" (Dawkins 1976:206). Dawkins (1982) later extended the analogy to evolutionary theory, arguing that those memes that are more successful in being replicated are those which encourage *fidelity* (each copy is largely like the original), *fecundity* (how many copies can a meme generate), and *longevity* (how long will a meme endure, especially as this relates to further replication) (Boyd and Richardson, in Aunger, editor 2000:155). Dawkins and other advocates of the memetic approach (Blackmore 1999, Brodie 2004) support the ontological assumption that human agency is irrelevant for understanding which memes are transmitted, contending that memetic transmission is a blind process analogous to genetic transmission.

Although the memetic perspective does appear to have some promise for theorizing the transmission of cultural meanings, it has several significant limitations. Dawkins (1982) has suggested that there may be some Lamarckian aspects to memetic transmission in addition to random mutations, thus rendering problematic his reliance on Darwinian analogies. Perhaps more significantly, the memetic approach discourages, and arguably rules out a priori, any consideration of the role of moral entrepreneurs in disseminating particular moral ideas into the wider society (see Becker 1963, Wagner-Pacifici and Schwartz 1991). In short, the memetic approach is effectively myopic in addressing how the strategies, opportunities, and resources of claimsmakers might contribute to the successful dissemination of part or all of a particular moral world view. Finally, the memetic approach does not address why some memes or moral resources appear to be at the core of a particular moral vocabulary or world view while others remain more optional or peripheral. For example, Madsen (1984) discusses the moral transformation of a Chinese village during and after the Cultural Revolution, noting that despite significant efforts to wipe out Neo-Confucian traditions, some beliefs and practices were retained (such as the importance of one's extended kinship network), whereas others (such as ancestor worship) were easily jettisoned (see also Lakoff 2002, Baker 2005). This observation of the apparent centrality of some moral resources and the relative vulnerability of others to being displaced are significant hurdles for the memetic approach.

Despite its limitations, more recent work that expands on the meme theory tradition is arguably quite helpful in explaining the dynamics of moral worldviews (see e.g., Balkin 1998 and the discussion below). Nonetheless, the strictly "Darwinian" approach taken by Dawkins, Blackmore and others is too reductionist and too blind to the roles of agents in promoting specific moral resources to provide an adequate explanation of the evolution of moral world views, vocabularies, or related phenomenon.

OVERVIEW OF MORAL VOCABULARIES AND THEIR COMPOSITION

Basic Features of Moral Vocabularies

A moral vocabulary may be defined as a form or ethos of moral reasoning which includes particular symbols, signs, code words, forms of argumentation and other moral resources (Lowe 2006). Moral vocabularies vary along a continuum between *expansionist* (making a variety of claims over multiple phenomena, objects, and/or practices) and discrete or *reductionist* (making a few, core claims). All moral vocabularies are comprised of moral resources, which serve as their building blocks. Moral resources vary widely in their forms and contents, but they all share qualities consistent with Geertz's definition of a symbol in their capacity to "...establish powerful, pervasive, and long-lasting moods and motivations" in persons (Geertz 1973:90). Moral resources also parallel Swidler's (1986) "tool kit" conception of culture in that moral resources both encourage and inhibit specific activities. Like Williams' (1995) discussion of "cultural resources," moral resources provide tactics and strategic goals; unlike cultural resources, moral resources carry an obligatory weight among those who are informed or constrained by a certain moral vocabulary.

All moral vocabularies share what Edelman termed meaning and information. Meaning "is associated with order – with a patterned cognitive structure that permits anticipation of future developments, so that perceptions and expectations are not surprising (Edelman 1971:32)." Like Berger and Luckmann's (1966) world view, established moral vocabularies offer cognitive consistency and "make sense" to adherents, allowing for (potentially) rapid evaluation of numerous events and phenomena and for sustaining collective emotional states across geographic and social distance. In other words, adherents to a given moral vocabulary are able to experience the same emotional states – such as outrage or fear – in initially reacting to the same event, despite lacking co-presence with each other or the event or phenomenon in question. Additionally, established moral vocabularies are characterized by creating *information*, data which are "ignored or not perceived" (Edelman 1971:32). Edelman's concept of information suggests that those within a given moral vocabulary will be more likely to ignore, downplay, or dismiss data seemingly at odds with the meaning of a given moral vocabulary: guns rights supporters will not address the apparently innocent victims of gun violence; supporters of free markets tend to ignore the state-supported conditions which have given rise to thriving markets, and so on. These characteristics of meaning and information are especially noteworthy in highly mediated societies, where the scale and scope of data provided through news and entertainment is relentless; a moral vocabulary acts as a "filter" allowing for adherents to economically sort data and data sources into categories of significance and insignificance.

A case in point is the 2004 American Presidential campaign and efforts to discredit Democratic Party presidential nominee Senator John Kerry of Massachusetts (see Manjoo 2008). A portion of the narrative surrounding Kerry's campaign was that he was a decorated Vietnam War veteran. As with all candidates (successful and otherwise), there is an attempt to transmute the candidate's biography into a compelling narrative in order to communicate specific messages to the electorate (Cornog 2004); in Kerry's case, his documented military service was perceived as especially significant because it both served to neutralize much of the case that Democratic candidates were lacking in the field of national security and to highlight the apparent hypocrisy of President Bush's and Vice President Cheney's use of the military while having avoided military combat themselves. Some conservatives were hostile to Kerry's narrative because of his well-documented opposition to American conduct of the Vietnam War following his military service. One form that this opposition took was through the formation of the Swift Boat Veterans for Truth, whose core membership claimed to have eyewitnesses that challenged the conduct that was cited in Navy documents as justification for awarding Kerry his military decorations. These claimsmakers initially brought their claims to conservative radio, Internet blogs, and other partisan media producers, through which their statements about exaggerated claims and falsification of records on Kerry's part were circulated largely uncritically. Eventually, some of these claims reached the "mainstream media" and were also circulated before much of the credibility of the Swift Boat Veterans was challenged. Manjoo argues that the Swift Boat Veterans strategy of undermining the very substance of Kerry's military record was undertaken in a milieu in which most journalists did not challenge the authenticity of Kerry's military record.

In "mapping" a moral vocabulary, it is centrally important to identify not only the specific moral resources but their meanings within a specific moral vocabulary. Weber (1947) made the case that simple observation was an insufficient methodology for identifying the meaning or motivation of a particular act: whether a man holding a gun is engaged in target practice or preparing for an anticipated but unlikely invasion is not discernable without understanding the perspective of the person involved (see also Alexander and Smith 1993). Likewise, a specific resource that is disseminated widely within the host society is associated with specific meanings, narratives, or images. For example, as Jacoby (1999) noted, the celebration of the 4th of July has been grounds for celebrating American independence from

British rule, as justification for succession from the United States by the Confederacy, and for African-Americans to emphasize the dissonance between espoused freedom and equality and the reality of slavery. The same historic event came to hold radically different (even antagonistic) meanings for different populations. The meanings of moral resources must be identified in relation to the population, subculture, social movement or other group being studied.

The Structure of Moral Vocabularies: Moral Resources and Relative Status

Moral resources, as the more basic units of moral vocabularies, may include (but are not limited to) beliefs and values, practices, symbols, historic events and/or persons which are historically and culturally rooted within the host society to some degree and are subject to forms of reevaluation. These moral resources allow for the communication of significance (what is of central concern), identification, appropriate tactics and goals, and even common perceptions of aesthetic qualities and criteria. Due to their assembled nature, moral vocabularies are inherently multi-vocal and are characterized by an internal status hierarchy of resources, which is reflected in the quantity of references made to these resources and in the ways claimsmakers subordinate other goals to these dominant resources.

Of course, because moral vocabularies are composed of a variety of resources, the relations between resources in a given context may not be entirely logically coherent (or even contradictory). Yet within a given moral vocabulary, certain moral resources will be central to shaping moral worldviews, making claims and encouraging or inhibiting activities. Jasper (1992) identifies a similar class of moral resource, which he calls "god terms" – ideas that "cannot be challenged or reduced to other ideas." The centrality of these moral resources can be analyzed using aspects of Milner's theory of status relations (1994). Milner contends that status is both relatively inexpansible (difficult to extend outwards) and inalienable (difficult to transfer). Therefore, given that all resources cannot be equally dominant and that the dominant character of certain resources is a function of its relationship to other resources , moral vocabularies should exhibit some degree of internal stability. For example, one of the key concerns of both the animal protectionists movements of the nineteenth century and the contemporary animal rights movement has been the centrality of compassion for animals. This dominant moral resource has encouraged a plethora of activities in both incarnations, including legislation defining and sanctioning animal cruelty, providing for the care of injured or abandoned animals, and the creation of "humane" education. While the centrality of compassion has remained constant within the historical animal protectionist movement and the contemporary animal rights movement, other moral resources have not. For example, the leadership of the animal protectionist movement was comprised of professing (Protestant) Christians which perceived animal protection as being one expression of their religious beliefs; conversely, the contemporary animal rights movement has been deeply informed by the writings of academic philosophers such as Singer (1975) and Regan (1983), who have argued for ethical considerations of animals without any reference to religious texts or authority. Moreover, while largely absent in the moralistic discourse of the animal protectionist movement, the significance of scientific evidence in both establishing the reality of animal suffering and therefore the imperative to curtail or prevent it, has become extensive.

The value of Milner's (1994) theory of status also sheds light on questions about which objects, subjects, and/or phenomena are attached to particular moral resources, both within the moral vocabulary and across the broader society. While a specific claim may be made in a universalistic fashion, attempts to attach this claim to a wide array of objects, subjects, and/or phenomena is likely to reveal that some objects of concern are more likely to elicit positive sanctions than others. In the case of the historical animal protectionist movement, claims regarding cruelty to animals were made primarily about livestock (those animals destined for slaughter for human consumption), labor animals (primarily horses), and companion animals (mostly dogs and cats). When Henry Bergh, one of the chief organizers and promoters of the American Society for the Prevention of Cruelty to Animals (ASPCA), attempted to extend newly enacted anti-cruelty statutes to pigeons hunted by a wealthy shooting club, both the courts and public opinion rebuked Bergh. Thereafter, the American animal protectionist movement limited its concerns to animals utilized for some economic purposes (consumption and transportation), the conditions of companion animals, and the promotion of "humane" ideals within the wider society (primarily through secondary education). In short, the dominant moral resource of compassion towards animals became tightly coupled with certain social categories of animals, suggesting a stable status hierarchy among animals and the relative inexpansibility of the "pool" of moral concern. It was only later, with the emergence of the contemporary animal rights movement, which other types of animals (such as primates) and practices (such as scientific and medical experimentation) become subject to moral approbation.

Moral Vocabularies, Discourse Formation, and Narratives: The Role of Metaphor Theory

However central moral entrepreneurship is to the creation and establishment of a moral vocabulary, moral entrepreneurship must be considered within the wider context of the host society. The condition(s) to which a moral entrepreneur is reacting, the moral resources that currently exist within the host society (either to be embraced, modified, or rejected), the existing status hierarchies within the host society, and the role(s) of the state and institutions relation to the moral vocabulary all inform to what degree the moral vocabulary will survive and spread or wither away. It bears repeating that, however much the moral vocabulary in question differs from the moral understandings of the wider society, all moral vocabularies are imprinted to some degree (at least initially) by the host society. Balkin's (1998) discussion of cultural software and bricolage are especially helpful in conceptualizing these matters. While utilizing concepts drawn from memetics, Balkin rejects the overtly decentered subject in favor of the interaction between cultural and ideological innovators (or moral entrepreneurs) and the wider context from which they draw upon in the creation of "cultural software": "…how tools of understanding are created through conceptual bricolage" (Balkin 1998:4). Metaphorically, the "cultural software of individuals in a culture is written and rewritten through acts of communication and understanding among individuals in a culture" (Balkin 1998:93). These interactions are deeply informed by Levi-Strauss's concept of bricolage, which emphasizes the recursive and cumulative nature of cultural and ideological production through the (re)use of previously existing cultural and ideological resources to create new meanings. The process of bricolage is cumulative (ideas, behaviors, practices, and so forth are retained in the cultural milieu), economical and recursive (certain core resources, ideas, or concepts may be utilized in multiple venues) and often involves unintended uses and consequences. In short, memes (moral resources) exist prior to the bricoleur/moral entrepreneur, who then utilizes them as both grounds on which to make moral claims and the tools with which to act on these claims in some fashion, drawing on the wider host society as a potential pool of these resources. Balkin's cultural software approach also suggests that, at least initially, that the bricoleur/moral entrepreneur will be channeled by existing cultural materials, especially regarding core or dominant understandings. A bricoleur/moral entrepreneur who is addressing some of these core resources may either be favored or challenged, even to the point of requiring geographic isolation for further cultural or moralistic innovation. Reynolds (2005) observes that John Brown was only able to freely experiment with abolitionist ideals of racial equality in North Elba, New York, an area well away from larger urban centers where even those sympathetic to ending slavery might have been unsettled by the sight of blacks and whites living and working together as equals. Like Edelman (1971), Balkin also suggests that filters may become established that favor the transmission of some concepts and hinder others. As a piece of "cultural software" the moral vocabulary is thus in a constant state of flux, influenced by the actions of the bricoleur/moral entrepreneur, the host society (including events and phenomena within it), and the emergence of new sources.

Metaphors and Moral Vocabularies: However reliant on societal resources or memes, the created moral vocabulary is both informed by the wider society and tends to become shaped into patterns which sustain the deployment of meanings across a wide range of substantive, and often apparently unrelated, issues. The structure of established moral vocabularies offer strong parallels with Lakoff's discussion of metaphors and cognition. Lakoff's "metaphor theory" (Lakoff and Johnson 1999) begins with the premise that much of human reasoning is influenced or channeled through and by metaphors that may not be obvious to actors: "A large proportion of our most commonplace thoughts make use of an extensive, but unconscious, system of metaphorical concepts, that is, concepts from a typically concrete realm of thought that are used to comprehend another, completely different domain. Such concepts are often reflected in everyday language, but their most dramatic effect comes in ordinary reasoning (Lakoff 1995:177)." Lakoff urges analytical attention be paid to how particular terms are deployed within the context of a broader moral vocabulary.

While language may offer a multitude of claims and resources, Lakoff argues that the metaphorical contours formed by claims and resources are much more limited. Lakoff argues that his approach "attempts to describe what people's actual unconscious worldviews are (Lakoff 2002:37)", in part through considering how "moral thinking" is imaginative and is dependent on the utilization of existing metaphors. Lakoff contends that there are roughly two dozen metaphors that collectively form "our metaphor system that is used to conceptualize morality (Lakoff 1995:178)", and within this metaphor system some metaphors are more dominant than others. One of the core metaphors within this system is the "moral accounting scheme" whereas the metaphor of accounting (such as debts owed) is used in conceptualizing both moral positions and the appropriate consequences for certain actions (Lakoff 1995:182–183). The great advantage of Lakoff's metaphorical analysis is that, despite citing universalistic metaphors (e.g., it is better to be "healthy" than to be "sick"), it deftly avoids over determination which often accompanies structural explanations through stressing the hierarchical emphasis within specific moral systems, allowing for explaining variations between moral systems.

Lakoff argues that, much like a moral vocabulary, metaphorical moral systems have dominant or core metaphors which dictate what matters are of ultimate concern and what types of societal structures and arrangements are desirable. As the priority of, and emphasis given to, different metaphors varies, so do the moral claims and objects of concern, making identical conduct moral and laudable in one system and immoral in another (Lakoff 2002:44): "What counts as a virtue or vice depends upon the moral schemes that one gives priority to (Lakoff 2002:88)."For example, Lakoff argues that many American conservatives interpret events and phenomena through "Moral Strength" which gives priority to internal moral strength and discipline and external strength through capabilities to deter aggression (or defend against it). This accounts for why Americans conservatives tend to favor strong police forces and militaries (because the world is threatening and may require force to answer the threat) and are hostile to social or economic policies which offer economic benefits or protections (because such needs, like lacking employment, are indicative of lacking self-discipline). Conversely, liberals are metaphorically informed by empathy and nurturance, meaning that liberals tend to favor policies and/or programs that are intended to either acknowledge the implicit disadvantage of certain groups or their vulnerabilities (such as animals, children, and the environment). Therefore, liberals favor policies advocating "protections" and also support initiatives of community and alliance building over unilateral actions (Lakoff 2002:109–117). Despite the seeming archetypical nature of these metaphorical systems, Lakoff also argues that there is a great deal of variation within these metaphors, which partially accounts for apparent ideological variation within groups of self-described conservatives and liberals. This variation is derived from "linear scales" along the "pragmatic-idealistic dimension" (in terms of priorities of results versus principles or practices) and in terms of "moral focus" (what particular domains or objects receive highest priority) (Lakoff 2002:285).

Both the metaphorical theory of Lakoff and the moral vocabularies approach emphasize that moral systems, once established, will come to embody certain patterns in which "selective fatalism" is likely to occur (in which some dangers are underemphasized) and certain causes more core or peripheral. However, Lakoff's approach is largely ahistorical (and American-centric), and does not address how certain moral systems have formed or evolved. For example, while many contemporary American evangelicals and fundamentalists are hostile to Darwinian natural selection, it would be difficult to explain how the initial American religious reaction to natural selection was couched in part because of the social Darwinism which was perpetuated in its name, whereas today this continued opposition to natural selection is also perpetuated by those who are hostile to market regulations and welfare benefits; effectively supporting the practices that were challenged by their evolution-opposing intellectual ancestors. The moral vocabularies approach, with its focus on moral claims and resources, is more readily able to address how some causes may remain core within a particular moral vocabulary (such as opposing the teaching of Darwinian natural selection) while measuring significant changes in others (such as favoring outcomes that were once opposed). While Lakoff's contribution to understanding how moral systems in general will develop patterns which favor internal consistency, it also suggests another significant means through which moral claims, understandings, and resources are shared and reinforced: through narratives.

MORAL VOCABULARIES AND MORAL ENTREPRENEURSHIP: COMMON STRATEGIES OF MORAL ENTREPRENEURSHIP

The creation, establishment, and maintenance of moral vocabularies cannot be explained without reference to the moral entrepreneurs who are actively promoting a particular network of moral resources linked to some claims and objects of concern. In this sense, the moral vocabularies perspective rejects a highly structuralist position of explaining the origins and perpetuation of specific moralistic perspectives which denies agency (for example, see Black 1981). As discussed previously, one of main flaws of the memetic approach is that it cannot account for the obvious roles of moral entrepreneurs and the commitment that various agents espouse towards certain core moral resources. However, the moral vocabularies approach does *not* claim that subjects possess overwhelming agency that allows them to shape the moral landscape (or even a portion of it) however they see fit. Rather, the creation of moral vocabularies is coupled to the dominant moral resources of the host society, the status of various moral claimsmakers, the roles of institutions and the state in embracing, challenging, and/or suppressing a particular moral vocabulary, as well as the presence or absence of other moral vocabularies within the same social space. Furthermore, "agency" can easily turn into "constraint"; as Weber (1978) argues in his discussion of charismatic authority, moral resources and claims which were once (somewhat) freely embraced later on constrain and compel moral entrepreneurship. Those who advocate pacifism, for instance, will lose legitimacy and status if they appear to only support pacifism in instances favoring specific actors.

Before considering how moral entrepreneurs impact and are impacted by societal trends and dynamics, it is useful to consider some of the common substantive areas towards which moral vocabularies are directed. While the types of moral claims made by moral entrepreneurs – and the associated moral resources upon which those claims are made – may cover a nearly infinite realm of substantive possibilities, the activities of moral entrepreneurs may be partially categorized regarding the units of analysis towards which their activities are based. These may include:

The body and its perceived needs. These may include security or protection (in promoting safety, the avoidance of contamination or the promotion of purity), the conditions under which the body may (or should) be exposed or concealed (and who or what may view what bodies), the conditions under which bodies may be kept or altered (such as conceptions of cruelty), and other matters of the extent or limitations of bodily autonomy. Such claims regarding how bodies may be treated are generally related to boundary maintenance (Lamont 2000), such as the importance of maintaining sexual propriety. Claims related to the body run along a continuum of the micro-sociological to placing the body in a more macro level environment; for example, in their documentary *The Education of Shelby Knox* (2005) filmmakers Rosenblatt and Lipshutz present the "abstinence only" sexual education curriculum within the Texas secondary educational through the microcosm of the Lubbock, Texas school district. The discussions of sexuality from the abstinence perspective is couched in terms of the importance of maintaining "purity" (not engaging in sexual intercourse or any other genital contact before marriage) and misrepresents the effectiveness of artificial contraceptives in preventing pregnancies and the transmission of sexually transmitted diseases to emphasize the centrality of the purity strategy in avoiding pregnancy and disease (see Douglas 1966). While the "abstinence only" strategy focused almost exclusively on the negative consequences of premarital sexuality to the body and emotions, other forms of emotional claims link individual practices to a wider moral agenda. For example, both animal rights and environmental activists stress the connections between dietary choices and wider societal trends (animal cruelty and environmental destruction), placing the uses of the body in a wider moral drama (see also Haidt and Graham's 2007 discussion of moral purity).

Organizations and their effectiveness. The proper roles or restraints of organizations are another common focus of moral entrepreneurship, such as the appropriate roles of government. As Becker (1963) notes in his discussion of rule-creating moral entrepreneurship, one of the central drives of moral entrepreneurs is to create at least one normative transformation, which virtually mandates either the creation of an independent organization or the assumption of some aspect(s) of the moral innovation(s) into an existing—often governmental—organization. For example, Morone (2003) argues that much of the federal governmental expansion into law enforcement, previously the purview of the local and state governments, was driven by moral panics and concerns about dangerous subversives and the need to control them. In fact organizational competence can become a moral resource; Stahl (2007) coined the term "militainment" to refer to the portrayal of the military (especially its technology) in both news media and popular culture as highly effective at completing its designated mission such that more nuanced and abstract questions about the political or ethical nature of the mission itself are diminished or downplayed. Questions of organizational effectiveness may also revolve around issues regarding the appropriate roles of specific organizations, essentially asking does a particular organization or its agents "belong" in a particular setting or context.

Distant suffering and managing social distance. Boltanski (1999) argues that modernity has been characterized by a "politics of pity" between those who are suffering and those who are not. This may also involve what Hannah Arendt termed a "spectacle of suffering," whereby the visibility of suffering is deployed by moral entrepreneurs in order to bring awareness and possible action on behalf of sufferers (Boltanski 1999:3). Distance may be measured both geographically (including physical distance and isolation) and socially (where those who are suffering may be physically close but socially distant). This is noteworthy in contemporary societies characterized by what Giddens (1984) terms "disembedding mechanisms," such as information technology, which greatly facilitates the communication of knowledge and narratives without the constraints of geographic distance. In the case of the geographic distance, Heller (2007) accompanies members of the Sea Shepherd organization as they attempt to prevent a Japanese whaling fleet from hunting whales in the Arctic Ocean. Both antagonists embrace international law as a dominant moral resource–the Japanese arguing that their whaling is legal and sanctioned by an ongoing scientific research agenda and Sea Shepherd arguing that international law protects the whales in question and that the ongoing scientific research is simply a deception to justify the hunting – but Sea Shepherd is also involved in actively documenting and reporting the activities of the whaling fleet to western nations, where whales are perceived as worthy objects of compassion. In short, while Sea Shepherd attempts to literally interfere with the controversial whaling practices, they simultaneously attempt to make the possibly sympathetic international public aware of the whaling in the hopes of bringing pressure to bear on the Japanese government. In the case of social distance, moral entrepreneurs may be involved in documenting or publicizing activities which occur geographically near a potentially sympathetic audience, but are socially distant or otherwise concealed. Upton Sinclair's *The Jungle* famously documented the working conditions under which mostly immigrant laborers worked in the Chicago slaughterhouses and Dorothea Lange and other members of the Farm Security Administration utilized photography to both document the conditions of poverty within the United States during the Great Depression as well as generate support for the New Deal programs intended to address this documented poverty (Durden 2006).

Unifying Perspectives: Some moral entrepreneurs are compelled to promote a coherent or seamless perspective (see Berger and Luckmann 1966) within which everything "makes sense" to those informed by that specific moral vocabulary. While this will be discussed more below, the significance here in terms of moral entrepreneurship is that the activities of these sorts of moral entrepreneurs may be driven as much to maintain the coherence of this perspective as they are to promote specific substantive issues. This may be significant for moral entrepreneur-ship, because it may allow for the creation of a concise, simple answer to apparently complex issues (Heath and Heath 2007). Libertarians, for instance, apply the metric "less government is better" as a moral resource to evaluate a wide variety of policies including law enforcement (especially in cases of searching for banned substances), welfare, and regulations of markets. The apparently simplicity and uniformity claimsmaking in a mediated environment, where conceptual space and time to build an argument may be limited, thereby offering a tactical advantage to moral entrepreneurs. Conversely, such an orientation may lead to ambivalence and confusion, when logical consistency contributes to apparently contradictory positions. In the case of libertarians, recent evidence suggests that many Americans favor reducing the "war on drugs" because of its expense, social costs, apparent failures, and intrusions (see Wolfe 1998, Baum 1997); American support for reducing governmental benefits to a wide range of citizens (such as publicly supported education), while consistent with the libertarian message, is much less popular. Likewise, the coalition of religious and cultural conservatives formed in the United States during the 1980s advocated what they termed "traditional family values." While invoking "family values" functioned well as a valence issue and served to weaken some criticism and erode tensions between Evangelicals and Roman Catholics, other critics noted that many of the policies promoted by moral entrepreneurs such as Pat Robertson and James Dobson, such as challenging the legitimacy of governmental programs like Aid to Families with Dependent Children or the passage of strengthened family leave programs, was actually antithetical to the interests of "real" families, and was in fact more indicative of the anti-public benefits stance of these social conservatives. In sum, what might appear as contradictory to outsiders in terms of espoused moral resources and undertaken activities may be a reflection of the need for moral entrepreneurs to maintain a unified perspective regarding a variety of substantive concerns.

Subjects and Moral Orientations: Recognizing the potential for vast degrees of varia-tion in both moral claims and the moral resources that these claims are made upon, Boltanski and Thevenot (1999) advocated ". . .a research strategy in the sociological field – as Michael Walzer has done in the philosophy of justice – that might enable us to escape having to choose between a formal universalism and. . .unlimited pluralism" (Boltanski and Thevenot 1999:364–365). Instead, they advocate "the possibility of a limited plurality of principles of equivalence. . ." in terms of core resources, claims and subjects within a given moral tradition. Like a moral vocabulary, Boltanski and Thevenot argue that even within somewhat defined moral parameters, morality is subject to interactions with both active subjects and a social milieu which resists simplistic categorization "in order to cope with uncertainty, rely on things, objects, devices which are used as stable referents. . ." (Boltanski and Thevenot 1999:367). Their primary devices are six "common worlds," based on classic political philosophy texts, which offer different central resources and key relationships. These include, for example, the "inspired" world that looks to an "external source," such as the divine and the "market" world, based on upholding rational self-interest between independent economic actors (Boltanski and Thevenot 1999:370–373). While Boltanski and Thevenot (1999) do not contend that there is an exhaustive catalog of "common worlds," they do argue that these are points of departure for initiating an analysis regarding disagreements of the "relative worth" of a claim, resource, or other contested object between "common worlds." In a parallel fashion, an analysis of moral entrepreneurship should address what categories of persons or activities within a moral vocabulary are core or essential, and how this impacts the activities of the moral entrepreneur in promoting what types of persons, objects, or activities as a paragon of that moral system. This suggests that however driven by the activities of moral entrepreneurs, moral vocabularies have their own internal dynamics which must also be considered.

MORAL VOCABULARIES EMERGING WITHIN THE HOST SOCIETY: MORAL ENTREPRENEURSHIP MEETS SOCIAL DYNAMICS

In addition to the internal morphology of moral vocabularies and the concern(s) toward which they are directed, the activities of moral entrepreneurs and the societal conditions in which these unfold must be considered. The memetic approach, in echoing Darwinian natural selection, necessarily downplays or ignores entirely the role(s) played by claimsmakers in intentionally promoting one or more specific moral resources, or even an entire moral vocabulary. Conversely, the moral vocabularies approach assumes that claimsmakers in some form – as individuals, small groups, informal networks, social movement organizations – are actively involved in promoting either specific moral resources or entire moral vocabularies within the host society and maintaining it amongst those that are already immersed within a particular moral vocabulary. While all moral entrepreneurs utilize at least some previously existing societal moral resources, how these are organized varies widely along a continuum between conservation of the existing order, alteration of one or more aspects of the existing moral landscape, and efforts intended to create more radical moral change. Some moral entrepreneurs may act in defense of the existing moral landscape, akin to Berger and Luckmann's (1966) "world maintenance" personnel, who act both to reinforce an existing socially constructed world view and to defend it from internal and external threats. More generally, moral entrepreneurs resemble Becker's (1963) conception of rule-creating moral entrepreneurs as those who embrace "...an absolute ethic; what he [or she] sees is truly and totally evil with no qualification...It is appropriate to think of reformers as crusaders because they typically believe that their mission is a holy one" (Becker 1963:148). Becker's conception of claimsmaking is especially helpful because it both suggests that their activities are not necessarily grounded in self-interest and that the activities of rule-creating moral entrepreneurs may be extended along several fronts (such as Progressive era reformers that supported women's suffrage and opposed child labor) (Gusfield 1986). Regardless of the support or opposition to prevailing societal conditions, he advancing of moral vocabularies necessarily involves the activation of moral resources, negotiating the advantages or burdens imposed by existing status hierarchies and narratives as vehicles for moral vocabularies.

Moral entrepreneurs necessarily must activate moral resources, attempt to overcome opposition (or simple obscurity), and embrace or resist societal trends. Activation of moral resources may include rhetorical invocation in public social performances (Eyerman, in Alexander et al. 2006), the creation of cultural artifacts which articulate the moral resource(s), and possibly use of state powers. For example, Morone (2003) argues that part of the growth of the federal government (especially the growth in federal governmental law enforcement) stems from the moral panics and moral crusades that both articulated and evoked anxieties over social disorder and potential subversives. The positive activation of moral resources may be accelerated by presence of high status moral entrepreneurs and/or sympathetic parties. For example, the early American animal protectionist movement was pushed towards social prominence through the active promotion by Henry Bergh, a member of the American upper class who was able to both have a public reading of his Declaration of the Rights of Animals at Clinton Hall in New York City (which was subsequently signed by several prominent New Yorkers, including newspaper editor Horace Greeley) and to have the ASPCA be chartered by New York state (in large part through the support of state assemblyman Ezra Cornell) (Shevelow 2008). More recently, many moral entrepreneurs within contemporary Western societies have attempted to utilize high status or prominent persons as vehicles for their messages, often regardless of relevant expertise in a given area. For example in 2007, Canadian singer and song-writer Sarah McLachlan participated in the creation of commercials for an animal shelter in Vancouver, British Columbia and subsequently on behalf of the American Society for the Prevention of Cruelty to Animals (ASPCA), which featured both her on-camera presence in asking for financial donations for these organizations and featuring her song "Angel" playing in the background as a prominent part of the commercial. According to Strom (2008), what has become known as "the Ad" in non-profit organizations has been a highly successful campaign: since 2007, the ASPCA has received 200,000 new donors and $30 million dollars in donations attributed to this commercial (Strom, December 25, 2008). This case is noteworthy because Ms. McLachlan does not provide any credentials or innovative evidence to bolster her claims about the significance of supporting the ASPCA and its mission; instead she simply invites viewers who feel some affinity for this cause and/or McLachlan's music to act in solidarity with her.

The role(s) of high status persons in promoting moral resources/and or a moral vocabulary is significant: persons or groups that are already high status may be able to elevate a specific moral resource, object of concern, and/or an entire moral vocabulary through their association with that resource, object, or moral vocabulary. This phenomenon is also noteworthy because of the finite arena of prominence for specific moral causes, objects of concern, or moral vocabularies, as has been noted in other regions of social life. Bob (2005) has argued that Nongovernmental organizations (NGOs) are necessarily involved in a competitive "global morality market" both in attempting to secure financial support but also to elevate or maintain the position of their cause in the public moral imagination. Likewise, Gusfield (1986) argues that status politics is characterized in part through elevation or degradation in status: "Victory...is the symbolic conferral of respect upon the norms of the victor and disrespect upon the norms of the vanquished" (Gusfield 1986:174). Similarly, moral entrepreneurs must be constantly attempting to elevate specific moral resources, objects of concern, and/or an entire moral vocabulary lest it be displaced by a rival or antithetical moral vocabulary.

Moral Vocabularies and Narratives: Any discussion of moral vocabularies without addressing the significance of narratives would be significantly deficient; one of the common units of analysis in the social scientific study of morality concerns how moral cases are made through stories, including legends and myths, personal anecdotes, rumors, and narratives made in speeches and in popular cultural expressions. Polletta's (2006) discussion of narratives is especially helpful here, including contemporary cultural ambivalence regarding stories. At once stories are "just stories," suggesting that their legitimacy in the face of other evidence is problematic; conversely, Polletta notes the variety of social environments in which stories are told – including courtrooms, political speeches, medical diagnoses, town hall and business meetings and social movements – indicating by weight of their presence that stories are significant in social life.

Polletta notes that narratives are also significant within the context of many moral entrepreneurial enterprises because stories reflect aspects of the structure of the larger organization from which moral entrepreneurship emerges. For example, the Student Nonviolent Coordinating Committee (SNCC), founded in 1960, began sit-ins. In 1961, the SNCC extended sit-ins to segregated restaurants, movie theatres, interstate bus lines. The SNCC had notable successes that inspired other civil rights organizations. The SNCC had been characterized by a decentralized organization and strong participatory democratic practices, which became popular within many other organizations by the end of the 1960s and beyond (in health clinics, newspapers, law firms, etc.). Despite apparent organizational successes, the SNCC eventually abandoned participatory democratic practices before its collapse at the end of the 1960s. Polletta's explanation hinges on metonymy (things representing other things); in this case, how "participatory democracy" became perceived as a concern only for privileged whites and not for serious civil rights activities. In sum, an apparently effective mode of organization was discarded because one of the core resources – participatory democracy – became antithetical to the wider moral vocabulary, despite its apparent utility in advancing movement goals (Polletta 2006).

Most sociologically relevant discussions of morality, outside of analyses of academic philosophers, necessarily involve the exchange, repetition, or challenges to meaningful narratives. In the case of moral vocabularies, accounts of how actors describe how they came to recognize a moral cause, the celebration of specific figures or events, how failures or resistance is explained all are of central concern. Consideration must be made of both specifics within these narratives (actors, events, outcomes), but also the more general patterns created. For example, sociologists have noted that narratives of fear often involve the source of danger as being external to the group (such as criminals or terrorists) (Glassner 1999, Altheide 2002, 2006), as in fears expressed about poisoned Halloween candy despite the lack of evidence of such activities, is a prime example. In the study of moral panics (Critcher 2003) targets of panics are often marginal or deviant groups who are perceived as threatening the social or symbolic order in some fashion (such as unwed mothers, whose childbearing outside of marriage may be perceived as a threat to familial life). Such moral panics may serve to reinforce the existing social order through emphasizing the hazards of deviation. Conversely, social movements that are advocates of an expansive moral vocabulary, such as the Animal Liberation Front, may engage in moral inversion (Lowe 2007) through which meanings and understandings within the host society are inverted, so that what is generally deviant becomes laudable and legal activities are cast as immoral. The ALF is a useful example of moral inversion because their strategy of "direct action" typically involves physical destruction of sites, equipment, or other forms of property used in what the ALF defines as animal abuse or cruelty; these actions are defined as "non-violent" by the ALF because these attacks (which have included arson) are not aimed at humans or nonhuman animals. These activities are defined as deviant and illegal in the larger host society, but in the moral vocabulary of the ALF these actions are undertaken to "liberate" or prevent animal cruelty and are morally praiseworthy. In *Free the Animals*, Newkirk (1992) provides an account of how a pseudonym "Valerie" transforms from law enforcement agent to ALF activist after witnessing animal suffering which was legally protected and sanctioned (e.g., laboratories) and becomes convinced that the legal structure is defending those engaged in immoral actions.

In analyzing moral vocabularies as coherent world views or systems of meaning, it is helpful to identify relevant themes, characters, metonymies or other phrases, and patterns of action that are identified as laudable or despicable. Viewing moral vocabularies in this manner helps to identify both how certain moral understandings are expressed and how they are perpetuated amongst adherents through repeating core narratives. For example, Phillips (2006) argues that one of the manners in which the coalition of petroleum-using constituents and conservative evangelicals and fundamentalists within the Republican Party from the 1990s onwards has been maintained is through couching actions which benefit petroleum interests in terms of "End Times" narratives expressed through such best-selling books as the *Left Behind* series (which provides a dramatic storyline that closely follows popular concepts of the "Rapture" and related events). Phillips goes so far as to argue that such beliefs, while not belabored publicly by Republican leaders, have been "…instead quietly promoted in clandestine meetings or loosely signaled by phrases and citations that reassure the attentive faithful" (Phillips 2006:96). Both the use of relevant "phrases and citations" and coterminous narrative patterns need to be identified and tracked.

Existing societal trends and moral vocabularies: Beyond direct promotion, moral entrepreneurs may also attempt to take advantage of societal trends, including selective fatalism, norm bandwagons, and norm cascades. Sunstein (1998) coined the term selective fatalism to connote the phenomena within a society how some sources of potential or real threats are given great (if not overblown) attention, whereas others are largely accepted as being "natural" or inevitable (see Goffman 1974, Glassner 1999). If a specific moral resource or object of concern – such as deaths caused by cigarette smoking – is largely uncontested, than it may prove far more difficult for moral entrepreneurs to actively promote concepts of tobacco control and smoking cessation (despite the strength of the empirical evidence). Conversely, in a milieu dominated by news coverage and popular cultural representations of criminal violence and/or terrorism, the promotion of "security" may be largely uncontested (despite the strength of empirical evidence) (Altheide 2002, 2006). *Norm bandwagons* "occur when the lowered cost of expressing new norms encourages an ever-increasing number of people to reject previously popular norms, to a 'tipping point'…small shifts lead to large ones, as people join the 'bandwagon'" (Sunstein 1996:912, 909). The utility of this concept is that it partially accounts for periods of moral innovation, when overall moral entrepreneurship may perceptibly accelerate, even if these efforts are substantively unrelated. Contrary to the "de-moralization of society" perspective advocated by Himmelfarb (1995) – that the moral hegemony of the British Victorian period has disintegrated and has left a vacuum only partially filled with personal preferences without societal or cultural bolstering – the concept of norm bandwagons suggests that host societies may be characterized by periods of significant moralization, although they may not result in an overarching moral hegemony. For example, following World War II, the United States witnessed the creation of several social movements – including the environmentalism, tobacco control, animal rights, and the organic food movements – which all shared the centrality of scientific evidence in making moral claims. Such bandwagons may also lead to *norm cascades*, which "occur when there are rapid shifts in norms" (Sunstein 1996:909). In other words, a norm cascade is indicated when public opinion shifts rapidly, for instance, when previously a tolerated phenomenon like drunk driving becomes rapidly stigmatized (see Rochon 1998:91). These transformations may be accompanied by a transformation of the meanings of common terms or ideological labels. Nunberg (2006), for instance notes that in the United States, the political label "liberal" was largely uncontested during the 1950s; but by the late 1970s, liberalism was already associated with "profligacy, spinelessness, malevolence, masochism, elitism, fantasy, anarchy, idealism, softness…" and on 14 August 1988 at the Republican National Convention President Ronald Reagan stated that "The masquerade is over. It's time to...say the dreaded L-word; to say the policies of our opposition are liberal, liberal, liberal" (Nunberg 2006:43). In sum, the hermeneutic metamorphosis of "liberal" from widely acclaimed political ideology to a pejorative term is also indicative of a norm cascade of a host of ideas and policies moving from near-universal acceptance to at best a controversial position. The significance of these concepts for the sociological analysis of a moral vocabulary is that not only must specific terms be tracked, but also their accompanying (and possibly evolving) meanings.

CONCLUSION

The moral vocabularies approach offers a strategy for organizing moral claims into a coherent topography for analysis while recognizing the potential for fluid evolution within a moral vocabulary. This approach seeks to strike a theoretical balance between recognizing the essential agency of moralistic activity (making claims, organizing actions related to moral claims, etc.), and the structured nature of morality, both in reaction to the wider host society and in how an established moral perspective serve to filter information and meaning which reinforces the existing moral orientation. Likewise, the moral vocabularies approach seeks to balance an understanding of discrete moral claims and the moral resources upon which they are made (akin to memes) as undergirding moral understandings, while also recognizing that moral vocabularies will eventually become patterned to some degree (like Lakoff's metaphors). The moral vocabularies approach is amenable to both micro or macro level research in fieldwork and/or discourse analysis, the study of social controversies and understanding which become attached to the controversies, and to the examination of mediated spectacles as vehicles for promoting ethical agendas (see Kellner 2003, Duncombe 2007).

While the moral vocabularies approach has drawn on other accounts of moral reasoning, through being grounded more in social science, there is more of a conceptual framework to examine how ideas are disseminated, challenged, repressed and communicated. As previously noted, the memetic approach relies on a Darwinistic approach to explaining moral and cultural change, effectively downplaying the roles of claimsmakers and/or the media utilized in claimsmaking. For example, an analysis of how a moral case was built for the 2003 invasion of Iraq would necessarily include how and why American news media were used by the George W. Bush administration to promote their case for war, without these claims receiving significant or sustained critiques or challenges (Rich 2006), such as the proposed invasion was part of a much longer trajectory of American petroleum-based policies (Phillips 2006) or the production of both pro and anti war spectacles (Duncombe 2007) in influencing public opinion. Without any means of discussing media and how media may act as a legitimating tool, the memetic approach would be largely unable to provide a useful account of the construction of the 2001–2003 case for war. Similarly, Lakoff's theoretical approach, while very helpful, is largely ahistorical and American centric, making historical analyses more problematic. For example, Kazin's (2006) account of William Jennings Bryan's opposition to the teaching of Darwinian natural selection in secondary schools is couched in terms of Bryan's fears that Darwinism would erode restraints on militarism (Kazin 2006:274–275). While skepticism and/or hostility towards Darwinian evolution has remained a mainstay of much of American conservative evangelical beliefs, these evangelicals do not appear to share Bryan's concerns about the United States using military force internationally (Phillips 2006). This significant transformation – challenging Darwinism because it might encourage military intervention to the largely uncritical support for military intervention – would be very difficult to chart in some fashion through Lakoff's metaphorical approach. Other processes, including the use of propaganda (O'Shaughnessy 2004) or agenda setting (McCombs 2004) that may impact perceptions of issues, subjects and causes would be difficult to discuss in terms of a metaphorical perspective.

This approach seeks to provide researchers with flexibility that allows for more scrutiny of data without making potentially problematic assumptions about the organization of moral claims into specific morphological compositions (like a "strict father" model). In sum, the moral vocabulary approach advocates an inductive analysis of the moral claims and resources that are made by a given group of claimsmakers along a continuum of core or central resources and more peripheral ones. These claims and resources also need to be coded in terms of how they are promoted (by what means) and to what objects/subjects of concern are they attached; for example, are claims made regarding animal cruelty universalistic or are they made towards specific social categories of animals (such as companion animals)? The question of whether a moral vocabulary is more expansionist (making claims which could impact a wide variety of substantive areas) or reductionist (making a few, core claims which are limited to a limited number of substantive subjects or activities). Attention should also be given to the types of subjects that are upheld for assessment (Boltanski and Thevenot 1999), such as those who are seen as worthy "victims," commendable heroes, and so on.

Once a rough outline of the moral vocabulary is established, that "map" should then be viewed in light of the host society in terms of the compatibility of moral resources and claims, the status hierarchy of objects of concern and state activities which may favor or challenge and any obvious expressions of selective fatalism that may inhibit or encourage claimsmaking. The moral vocabulary itself should also be viewed as a singular entity in terms of the narratives and forms of evidence (such as personal anecdotes, scientific evidence, religious experiences and so forth) which are widely accepted, limited in their acceptability, or openly scorned. The primary concern here is to understand what the moral vocabulary stresses and downplays. This approach will also allow for the historical analysis of moral vocabularies (such as what resources have risen or declined over time) and a comparative approach (such as the general structures of moral vocabularies as they emerge within social movements, nationalist movements, post-industrial states, and so on). This middle range theory may provide a platform for ongoing research in moral claimsmaking and their evolution.

BIBLIOGRAPHY

Alexander, J. C., and P. Smith. 1993. "The Discourse of American Civil Society: A New Proposal for Cultural Studies. *Theory and Society* April 22(2):151–207.

Altheide, D. L. 2002. *Creating Fear: News and the Construction of Crisis*. Hawthorne, New York: Aldine De Gruyter.

Altheide, D. L. 2006. *Terrorism and the Politics of Fear*. Lanham, Maryland: AltaMira Press.

Baker, W. E. 2005. *America's Crisis of Values: Reality and Perception*. Princeton, New Jersey: Princeton University Press.

Balkin, J. M. 1998. *Cultural Software: A Theory of Ideology*. New Haven: Yale University Press.

Baum, D. 1997. *Smoke and Mirrors: The War on Drugs and the Politics of Failure*. New York: Back Bay Books.

Becker, H. S. 1963. *Outsiders: Studies in the Sociology of Deviance*. New York: Free Press.

Berger, P., and T. Luckmann. 1966. *The Social Construction of Reality: A Treatise in the Sociology of Knowledge.* New York: Anchor Books.

Best, J. 2007. *Social Problems.* New York: W.W. Norton & Company.

Black, D. J. 1981. *The Manners and Customs of the Police.* New York: Academic Press.

Blackmore, S. 1999. *The Meme Machine.* Foreword by Richard Dawkins. New York: Oxford University Press.

Bob, C. 2005. *The Marketing of Rebellion: Insurgents, Media, and International Activism.* Cambridge: Cambridge University Press.

Boltanski, L. 1999. *Distant Suffering: Morality, Media and Politics.* Translated by Graham Burchell. Cambridge: Cambridge University Press.

Boltanski, L., and L. Thevenot. 1999. "The Sociology of Critical Capacity." *European Journal of Social Theory* 2(3):359–377.

Boyd, R., and P. J. Richerson. 2000. "Memes: Universal Acid or a Better Mouse Trap?" in *Darwinizing Culture: The Status of Memetics as a Science,* edited by R. Aunger with a foreword by D. Dennett. New York: Oxford University Press.

Brodie, R. 2004. *Virus of the Mind: The New Science of the Meme.* Second Edition. New York: Integral Press.

Bronner, S. J. 2008. *Killing Tradition: Inside Hunting and Animal Rights Controversies.* Lexington, Kentucky: The University Press of Kentucky.

Cornog, E. 2004. *The Power and the Story: How the Crafted Presidential Narrative Has Determined Political Success from George Washington to George W. Bush.* New York: Penguin Press.

Critcher, C. 2003. *Moral Panics and the Media.* Buckingham: Open University Press.

Dawkins, R. 1976. *The Selfish Gene.* Oxford: Oxford University Press.

Dawkins, R. 1982. *The Extended Phenotype.* Oxford University Press.

Derber, C. with Y. R. Magrass. 2008. *Morality Wars: How Empires, the Born-Again, and the Politically Correct Do Evil in the Name of Good.* Boulder: Paradigm Publishers.

Douglas, M. 1966. *Purity and Danger: An Analysis of Concepts of Pollution and Taboo.* New York: Praeger.

Duncombe, S. 2007. *Dream: Re-Imagining Progressive Politics in an Age of Fantasy.* New York: The New Press.

Durden, M. 2006. *Dorothea Lange.* London: Phaidon Press, Inc.

Edelman, M. 1971. *Politics as Symbolic Action: Mass Arousal and Quiescence.* Chicago: Markham Publishing Company.

Eyerman, R. 2006. "Performing opposition or, How Social Movements Move" in *Social Performance: Symbolic Action, Cultural Pragmatics, and Ritual,* edited by J. C. Alexander, B. Giesen, and J. L. Mast. Cambridge: Cambridge University Press.

Geertz, C.1973. *The Interpretations of Cultures.* New York: Basic Books.

Giddens, A. 1984. *The Constitution of Society: Outline of the Theory of Structuration.* Berkeley: University of California Press.

Glassner, B. 1999. *The Culture of Fear: Why Americans Are Afraid of the Wrong Things.* New York: Basic Books.

Goffman, E. 1974. *Frame Analysis: An Essay on the Organization of Experience.* New York: Harper & Row.

Gusfield, J. R. 1986. *Symbolic Crusade: Status Politics and the American Temperance Movement,* Second Edition. Urbana and Chicago: University of Illinois Press.

Haidt, J., and J. Graham. 2007. "When Morality Opposes Justice: Conservatives Have Moral Intuitions that Liberals May Not Recognize." *Social Justice Research* 20:98–116.

Heath, C., and D. Heath. 2007. *Made to Stick: Why Some Ideas Survive and Others Die.* New York: Random House.

Heller, P. 2007. *The Whale Warriors: The Battle at the Bottom of the World to Save the Planet's Largest Mammals.* New York: Free Press.

Himmelfarb, G. 1995. *The De-Moralization of Society: From Victorian Virtues to Modern Values.* New York: Alfred A. Knopf.

Hunter, J. D. 1991. *Culture Wars: The Struggle to Define America.* New York: Basic Books.

Jacoby, R. 1999. *The End of Utopia: Politics and Culture in an Age of Apathy.* New York: Basic Books.

Jamieson, K. H., and P. Waldman. 2003. *The Press Effect: Politicians, Journalists, and the Stories that Shape the Political World.* New York: Oxford University Press.

Jasper, J. M. 1992. "The Politics of Abstractions: Instrumental and Moralist Rhetorics in Public Debates". *Social Research* 59(2):315–344.

Kazin, M. 2006. *A Godly Hero: The Life of William Jennings Bryan.* New York: Alfred A. Knopf.

Kellner, D. 2003. *Media Spectacle.* New York: Routledge.

Lakoff, G., and M. Johnson. 1999. *Philosophy in the Flesh: The Embodied Mind and Its Challenges to Western Thought.* New York: Basic Books.

Lakoff, G. 1995. "Metaphor, Morality, and Politics, or, Why Conservatives Have Left Liberals in the Dust." *Social Research* 62(2):177–213.

Lakoff, G. 2002. *Moral Politics: How Liberals and Conservatives Think,* Second Edition. Chicago: The University of Chicago Press.

Lamont, M. 2000. *The Dignity of Working Men: Morality and the Boundaries of Race, Class, and Immigration.* New York: Russell Sage Foundation; Cambridge, Massachusetts: Harvard University Press.

Lowe, B. M. 2006. *Emerging Moral Vocabularies: The Creation and Establishment of New Forms of Moral and Ethical Meanings.* Lanham, Maryland: Lexington Books.

Lowe, B. M. 2007. "The Actions of the Animal Liberation Front as Social Performance. "*The Journal of Social and Ecological Boundaries*, 2 (2) Winter/Spring 2006–2007:85–118.

Madsen, R. 1984. *Morality and Power in a Chinese Village.* Berkeley: University of California Press.

Manjoo, F. 2008. *True Enough: Learning to Live in a Post-Fact Society.* New York: Wiley.

McCombs, M. E. 2004. *Setting the Agenda: Mass Media and Public Opinion.* Malden, Massachusetts: Blackwell Publishing.

Merton, R. K. 1949. *Social Theory and Social Structure.* New York. Free Press.

Milner, M., Jr. 1994. *Status and Sacredness: A General Theory of Status Relations and an Analysis of Indian Culture.* New York: Oxford University Press.

Morone, J. A. 2003. *Hellfire Nation: The Politics of Sin in American History.* New Haven: Yale University Press.

Newkirk, I. 1992. *Free the Animals! The Untold Story of the U.S. Animal Liberation Front and Its Founder, "Valerie".* Chicago: The Noble Press.

Nunberg, G. 2006. *Talking Right: How Conservatives Turned Liberalism Into a Tax-Raising, Latte-Drinking, Sushi-Eating, Volvo-Driving, New York Times-Reading, Body-Piercing, Hollywood-Loving, Left-Wing Freak Show.* New York: Public Affairs.

O'Shaughnessy, N. J. 2004. *Politics and Propaganda: Weapons of Mass Seduction.* Ann Arbor: University of Michigan Press.

Phillips, K. 2006. *American Theocracy: The Peril and Politics of Radical Religion, Oil, and Borrowed Money in the 21st Century.* New York: Viking.

Polletta, F. 2006. *It Was Like a Fever: Storytelling in Protest and Politics.* Chicago: The University of Chicago Press.

Regan, T. 1983. *The Case for Animal Rights.* Berkeley: The University of California Press.

Reynolds, D. S. 2005. *John Brown, Abolitionist: The Man Who Killed Slavery, Sparked the Civil War, and Seeded Civil Rights.* New York: Alfred A. Knopf.

Rich, F. 2006. *The Greatest Story Ever Sold: The Decline and Fall of Truth from 9/11 to Katrina.* New York: The Penguin Press.

Rochon, T. R. 1998. *Culture Moves: Ideas, Activism, and Changing Values.* Princeton, New Jersey: Princeton University Press.

Rosenblatt, R., and M. Lipschutz. 2005. *The Education of Shelby Knox.* Cine Qua Non/Incite Pictures.

Rozin, P. 1997. "Moralization". In *Morality and Health: Interdisciplinary Perspectives,* edited by A. M. Brandt, and P. Rozin. New York: Routledge.

Shevelow, K. 2008. *For the Love of Animals: The Rise of the Animal Protection Movement.* New York: Henry Holt and Company.

Singer, P. 1975. *Animal Liberation: A New Ethic for Our Treatment of Animals.* New York: New York Review of Books.

Stahl, R. 2007. *Militainment, Inc.: Militarism & Pop Culture.* Northampton: Media Education Foundation.

Stout, H. S. 2006. *Upon the Altar of the Nation: A Moral History of the American Civil War.* New York: Viking.

Strom, S. 25 December 2008, A20. "Ad Featuring Singer Proves Bonanza for the A.S.P.C.A." *New York Times.*

Sunstein, C. 1996. "Social Norms and Social Roles." *Columbia Law Review* 96(4):903–968.

Sunstein, C. 1998. "Selective Fatalism." *Journal of Legal Studies* 27:799–823.

Swidler, A. 1986. "Culture in Action: Symbols and Strategies." *American Sociological Review* 51:273–286.

Wagner-Pacifici, R., and B. Schwartz. 1991. "The Vietnam Veterans Memorial: Commemorating a Difficult Past." *The American Journal of Sociology* 97(2):376–420.

Weber, M. 1947. *The Theory of Social and Economic Organization.* Edited with an Introduction by Talcott Parsons.

Weber, M. 1978. *Economy and Society: An Outline of Interpretive Sociology,* edited by G. Roth, and C. Wittich. Berkeley: University of California Press.

Weber, M. 1992. *The Protestant Ethic and the Spirit of Capitalism.* Translated by Talcott Parsons, edited by A. Giddens. New York: Routledge.

Williams R. H. 1995. "Constructing the Public Good: Social Movements and Cultural Resources." *Social Problems* 42(1):124–144.

Wolfe, A. 1998. *One Nation After All: What Middle Class Americans Really Think About: God, Country, Family, Racism, Welfare, Immigration, Homosexuality, Work, the Right, the Left, and Each Other.* New York: Viking.

Part III
Morality in Action ("How Does It Work?")

CHAPTER 17

The Trouble with Invisible Men

How Reputational Concerns Motivate Generosity

ROBB WILLER, MATTHEW FEINBERG, KYLE IRWIN,
MICHAEL SCHULTZ, AND BRENT SIMPSON

INTRODUCTION

"I looked about me at the hillside, with children playing and girls watching them, and
tried to think of all the fantastic advantages an invisible man would have in the world."
- H.G. Wells, *The Invisible Man*

Typically portrayed as unrestrained, capricious, and immoral, literature and film have
traditionally turned a suspicious eye towards invisible men. For example, in *The Republic*,
Plato ([380 B.C.E.] 1955) describes a debate between his brother, Glaucon, and his mentor,
Socrates, on the nature of justice and human morality. Glaucon argues that just behavior of
humans is simply an artifact of their desire to avoid formal and informal punishment, making
his case via a thought experiment regarding what would happen should men possess rings that
could make them invisible. Glaucon argues that even those we perceive to be moral would
become evil if granted the power of invisibility: "There is no one, on this view, who is iron-
willed enough to maintain his morality... when he is able to take whatever he wants from the
market-stalls without fear of being discovered" ([380 B.C.E.] 1955).

Glaucon's message is the same as Wells': given freedom from both formal and informal sanctions, people will behave antisocially. Indeed, were the members of a whole society
somehow unable to monitor one another, the implication is that we would find ourselves in a
cruel, Hobbesian state of nature characterized by avarice and egoism. According to this line of
reasoning, the only thing sparing us from anarchy is our visibility, and thus, our reputational
accountability. These thought experiments relate to one of the most fundamental questions of
the social sciences, one that scholars have wrestled with for centuries: what are the roots of
human morality? What creates moral order? Do we limit ourselves, or do others? Are we good
because we are *good* or only good because we are *watched*?

Here, we focus on understanding the bases of one morally-charged domain of human
behavior: prosocial behavior. Prosocial behaviors are acts which benefit others, often at a cost
to the self. In the larger literature on morality, prosocial behaviors are examples of prescriptive

S. Hitlin, S. Vaisey (eds.), *Handbook of the Sociology of Morality*,
Handbooks of Sociology and Social Research, DOI 10.1007/978-1-4419-6896-8_17,
© Springer Science+Business Media, LLC 2010

and positive morality: benevolent actions that are socially valuable, but which groups typically do not expect of individuals (Janoff-Bulman et al. 2009). Understanding the mechanisms driving acts of generosity is important for social science because they are widely believed to be fundamental to the maintenance of social order (Comte [1851] 1973, Durkheim [1893] 1964, Sorokin 1954).[1] Though central to sociology, explaining prosocial behaviors is challenging, since individuals can benefit more by not helping others, instead pursuing their narrow self-interest.

Indeed, both lay people and many social scientists tend to assume that people are fundamentally selfish, driven primarily by pursuit of their own gain (Miller and Ratner 1998). Though the assumption that humans are by nature entirely selfish is untenable (Piliavin and Charng 1990, Dovidio et al. 2006), self-interest is without question, a tremendously significant motivator of behavior. The strength of self-interest motivates an important research question: what factors lead individuals to set aside narrow self-interest in favor of prosocial behaviors that are often costly to them?

Traditionally, social scientific research on prosocial behavior has focused on the role of either *material incentives* or *altruistic motives* in explaining prosocial behavior. These two classes of explanation follow very different logics. For example, in explaining routes to cooperation via material incentives, researchers have studied the role of material sanctions (Olson 1965, Yamagishi 1986) and the prospect of longer-term material benefit (Axelrod 1984) for behaving collectively. At the same time, other researchers have emphasized the role of having a "prosocial value orientation" (Liebrand 1986, Liebrand et al. 1986, van Lange 1999) or "altruistic personality" (Oliner and Oliner 1988) in explaining why people would sacrifice to help others.

Increasingly, researchers have also begun to focus on a third class of explanation for prosocial behavior based on *reputation*. A recent explosion of research across the social sciences has established a close link between prosociality and reputational standing. Substantial research from sociology (Willer 2009a, Simpson and Willer 2008), economics (Andreoni and Petrie 2004), biology (Milinski et al. 2002a, Zahavi and Zahavi 1997), psychology (Hardy and van Vugt 2006, Barclay 2004, Flynn et al. 2006), and anthropology (Chagnon 1988, Lemonnier 1996, Smith and Bird 2000, Price 2003) confirms the link between prosocial behavior and reputation. This research shows that generosity can lead to a diversity of social benefits, including respect, influence, cooperation, and trust. The logic is that, in light of the many reputational benefits due to those who behave generously, it is not surprising that prosocial behaviors are relatively common (Willer 2009b).

Research in this new and emerging literature is enormous, including contributions from the diverse fields noted above. In this chapter we review some promising strains of research in this domain, including the dynamics of reputational gain as a reward encouraging prosociality, how reputation systems are maintained in groups, and evolutionary models relating reputation and prosocial behavior. We begin our review by detailing research on the many reputational and reputationally mediated rewards for prosocial behavior, and then discuss theory and research causally linking these gains to individuals' decisions to behave prosocially. We

---

[1] Consistent with convention in the social sciences (Dovidio et al. 2006), we define "altruism" as the psychological *motivation* to increase another's welfare, even at a cost to self, while "generosity" and "prosocial behavior" refer to *actions* that benefit others.

also look at the role of reputational hierarchies based on status in structuring patterns of proso-cial behavior in groups. Because reputations are critical to the administration of sanctions, we discuss the dynamics of social and affective sanctions, informal bases of social control that are common in everyday life and effective in large part because individuals are deeply con-cerned about their reputations. Then, we briefly review the literature on information sharing in group's reputation systems, before concluding with a review of mathematical and computa-tional models highlighting the critical role reputation systems may have played in the evolution of prosocial behavior.

HOW PROSOCIAL BEHAVIOR LEADS TO REPUTATIONAL BENEFIT

Perhaps the aspect of reputations that people care the most about is their standing in terms of *status*. Different from being liked and more specific than having a "good reputation," status refers to an individual's relative standing in a group based on prestige, honor, and deference (Berger et al. 1972). Those who are higher status command more respect and wield more influence (Berger et al. 1977). Research in diverse settings, including highly controlled labo-ratory studies (Hardy and van Vugt 2006, Willer 2009a) as well as ethnographic field studies (Chagnon 1988, Patton 1996, Lemonnier 1996, Price 2003), shows that individuals who are more generous are viewed as higher status by fellow group members.

For example, the Status Theory of Collective Action (Willer 2009a, b) argues that costly contributions to group efforts earn individuals status gains because they signal that the indi-vidual is "group motivated" (Ridgeway 1982), a trait that is considered meritorious by group members. Willer (2009a) showed across a series of experimental studies that costly contri-butions to group efforts lead to improved status standing and greater interpersonal influence. Further, the effects of contributions on status standing were statistically mediated by the per-ceived group motivation of the contributor, confirming that contribution earns an individual status by signaling his/her underlying desire to benefit the group.

In addition to the status gains that result from prosocial behavior, generosity can tend to material benefits as well. For example, research from behavioral economics, social psy-chology, anthropology, and evolutionary biology on "indirect reciprocity" (Alexander 1987) proposes that prosocial behaviors are rewarded with, and motivated by, reputational benefits. Whereas, direct reciprocity approaches describe the tendency of individuals to directly return favors to others who have helped them in the past, indirect reciprocity occurs when an indi-vidual is rewarded for being generous to someone else in the past. Material and other rewards earned for one's generosity are mediated by reputation in the case of indirect reciprocity, and research suggests that individuals do pursue reputation for its own sake, and not only as a route to further material rewards (Huberman et al. 2004). A number of theories of indirect reci-procity have emerged in recent years, e.g. costly signaling (Zahavi 1995, Zahavi and Zahavi 1997, Smith and Bird 2000), image scoring (Nowak and Sigmund 1998), and image standing (Sugden 1986; Leimar and Hammerstein 2001, Panchanathan and Boyd 2004).[2]

---

[2] See Nowak (2006) for a review.

Taken together, research in this vein shows the magnitude and diversity of benefits due to individuals for developing a positive reputation: trust (Barclay 2004), respect (Hardy and van Vugt 2006, Willer 2009a), leadership positions (Milinski et al. 2002b), material gifts (Milinski et al. 2002a, Willer 2009a), access to profitable relationships (Barclay and Willer 2007), cooperation in diverse settings (Willer 2009a), social influence (Willer 2009a), and advancement in formal organizations (Flynn et al. 2006). The suggestion of this literature is that, in light of all these future rewards, it is not surprising that people give to groups and other individuals.

REPUTATIONAL BENEFITS ENCOURAGE PROSOCIAL BEHAVIOR

While the research reviewed above establishes a close connection between acts of generosity and the reputational benefits that are likely to follow, this does not necessarily imply that generosity is motivated by the pursuit of these reputational benefits. Indeed, research on human altruism has built a strong case that altruistic motivations are a real and significant cause of prosocial behavior (e.g., Batson 1991, Piliavin and Charng 1990). Still, researchers have also established that the pursuit of reputation serves as a complementary motive, also encouraging generous acts (Simpson and Willer 2008). This body of research has established two primary ways in which reputational gains motivate generosity: one based on instrumental, goal-directed behavior, the other based on learning.

First, prosocial behavior may often be driven by an instrumental pursuit of improved reputation. Several demonstrations show that people give more when greater reputational gain can be had (e.g. Milinski et al. 2002b, Semmann et al. 2004, Barclay 2004, Andreoni and Petrie 2004), and will even jockey to give more than one another, a phenomenon known as "competitive altruism" (Roberts 1998, Barclay and Willer 2007). Occupations that involve more prosocial aspects often pay at lower levels, suggesting that the prestige available to apparently generous employees serves as a "compensating differential" motivating their labor (Frank 2004). Research shows that even minimal cues that one's behavior is being watched – the presence of a pair of eyespots present in the individual's field of vision – can compel individuals to behave more prosocially (Haley and Fessler 2005). These authors further suggest that past demonstrations of apparent altruism in laboratory settings may simply reflect pursuit of reputational gain. Thus, at least some prosocial behavior is instrumentally motivated by the pursuit of future reputational rewards.

Another route from reputational rewards to prosocial behavior is more nuanced. Reputational rewards for past generous acts may increase the future rate of those acts through a learning mechanism, as any reward an individual values that regularly follows some action should tend to encourage higher rates of that action in the future. Following Macy's (1990; 1995) work on the role of reinforcement learning in collective action, Willer (2009a) proposed that receiving status for past contributions to group efforts could increase future giving by buttressing the contributor's underlying group motivation. In a sense, one's motivation to help the group is socially constructed, responding to others' feedback and signs of respect.

This claim was tested in an experimental study that manipulated status feedback to collective action contributors at high versus low levels (Willer 2009a, Study 4). Participants who received high status feedback tended to give more to the group in the future, an effect that was mediated by reported motivations to help the group. Contributors receiving high status feedback also identified with the group more and felt greater solidarity with its members.

STATUS AND THE ORGANIZATION OF COLLECTIVE ACTION

With few exceptions (e.g., Oliver et al. 1985, Oliver and Marwell 1988), the vast literature on collective action has assumed undifferentiated, homogenous actors facing a collective problem in the production of some public good. However, sociologists and social psychologists are in general agreement that undifferentiated groups are exceptional, if they exist at all. At least since Bales (1970), researchers have shown that a group that comes together to pursue a common goal quickly develops a status hierarchy. Once in place, this status hierarchy has powerful and lasting effects on group dynamics and group decisions. While prior work outlined above shows that differences in contributions to collective action produce status differences in groups, less is known about how existing status differences among group members affect collective action.

Simpson and Willer (2010) apply Status Characteristics Theory (Berger et al. 1972, 1977) in proposing ways in which status differences in groups help "organize" collective actions via three inter-related processes: a potential contributor's relative status affects *when* she gives to a collective action, *how much* she gives, and how much *others* give. These three processes deal, respectively, with the initiation of, contributions to, and continuation of collective action. Taken together, they suggest that status hierarchies help structure patterns of contribution to collective action. The result may lead groups with clear status hierarchies to successfully coordinate behavior, and thereby promote the efficient production of public goods.

Note that while sociologists have typically focused on the dysfunctions of status inequalities, Simpson and Willer argue that status hierarchies may also be functional for groups, providing "emergent" solutions to collective action problems. As a result, it is likely that status differentiated groups may produce larger public goods since these hierarchies encourage early and large contributions from high status members, whose contributions then influence higher subsequent contributions from lower status members.

For example, Kumru and Vesterlund (2008) randomly assigned participants to high or low status positions, based on an arbitrary scoring of a difficult quiz. After participants were informed of their own and others' status, they made decisions about how much of their private endowments to contribute in two-person, sequential decision public goods games. Thus, in addition to status information, participants also had full knowledge of each other's contributions. For instance, the second contributor made his or her contribution decision with full knowledge of the initial contribution amount. In half the groups, the high status participants were designated to make the first decision about how much of their private endowment to contribute; in the remaining half, the low status participant made the first decision.

If high status persons expect to have influence over those lower in status, we should observe higher contributions by high status first contributors than low status first contributors. In addition, if high status contributors accurately forecast the impact of their contributions on those lower in status, we should observe higher contributions by second movers when they are low status relative to first movers. This is precisely the pattern of results reported by Kumru and Vesterlund (2008). Most important, this pattern resulted in groups where high status members made their decisions first producing larger public goods than groups in which low status member made their decisions first.

This research shows how status standing affects initial contributions, and how early contributions by high status group members then influence subsequent contributions from low status members. However, in order for status hierarchies to fully organize solutions to

collective action problems those high in status need to take the lead by making initial contributions. Do status differences influence the sequencing of contributions, or do the beneficial
effects of status reviewed thus far require an additional mechanism, e.g. a monetary incentive, to motivate high status members to initiate collective action? If high status members take
the lead, following the results outlined above, they should contribute at high levels, and these
high contributions should influence those lower in status to contribute at similarly high levels.
This would mean that status hierarchies provide an endogenous solution to collective action
problems.

In a preliminary investigation of the hypothesis that status hierarchies lead those higher in
status to initiate collective action, Simpson and Willer (2009) assigned participants to high or
low status in three-person groups, where the two other group members were actually computer
simulated actors. The participants, all university undergraduates, were either given information
suggesting that the other group members were higher status (graduate students) or lower status
(high school students) relative to the participant. As expected, participants who were high in
status relative to others initiated collective action by contributing earlier then their lower status
counterparts. This finding suggests that collective action groups with extant status hierarchies
do not necessarily need an explicit mechanism to encourage high status members to initiate
collective action. Instead, the sequencing of contributions may occur as a direct consequence
of the status hierarchy.

THE POWER OF SOCIAL AND AFFECTIVE SANCTIONS

The above research establishes that reputational gains matter to people in part because they
promise both social and material benefits, and that these rewards compel people to behave
more prosocially. Another crucial way in which reputations matter and promote prosocial
behavior is their integral role in sanctioning systems. Indeed, information about people that is
conveyed through their reputations is a precondition for the effective functioning of sanctioning systems. While research on sanctioning has traditionally focused on the role of material
sanctions, recently this area has broadened to also study social and affective sanctions. It
is very likely that in informal groups, social and affective sanctions such as expressions of
approval or appreciation of prosocial acts on the one hand, or disapproval and disdain for antisocial acts on the other, are far more common in the course of everyday life than material fines
or rewards. Unlike material sanctions, social and affective sanctions are informally deployed
in the course of everyday interaction and may have several important advantages in compelling
prosocial behavior, relative to material sanctions.

Much research on sanctioning systems as ways to motivate prosocial behavior in groups
can be traced back to Olson's (1965) classic work on collective action. According to Olson,
material sanctions, side payments for contributions or fines for noncontribution to collective efforts, can be effective because they transform an individual's payoff structure to make
contribution in their individual self-interest. In this way, sanctioning systems help reduce or
eliminate the individual temptation to free-ride. Past research has demonstrated that material
sanctions are effective at encouraging greater generosity toward the group (Yamagishi 1986).
Further, individuals are willing to sanction others who fail to act generously, even when such
sanctioning is costly (Yamagishi 1986, Fehr and Gachter 2002). Importantly, individuals seem
to recognize the benefits of sanctioning systems: recent work by (Gurerk et al. 2006) shows

that, when given the option, individuals prefer a system allowing costly, material punishment to a system without sanctioning.

Findings from a new line of research, however, have led researchers to question the utility of formal, material sanctions for promoting the well-being of groups (e.g., Dreber et al. 2008, Fehr and Rockenbach 2003, Mulder et al. 2006, Nikiforakis 2008, Tenbrunsel and Messick 1999). For example, Mulder et al. (2006) find that the use of material sanctions undermines trust among group members because these systems "implicitly communicate that there is reason to doubt that group members will cooperate 'by themselves...'" (148). Further, contribution behavior in the presence of material sanctions leads individuals to attribute others' contributions to the threat of sanctions rather than to intrinsic motivation. Research has also demonstrated that material sanctions can undermine individuals' trustworthiness (Fehr and Rockenbach 2003) by creating antagonistic relations between group members. Finally, research shows that when material counter-punishment is allowed, cycles of retaliation emerge leading the use of material sanctions to decline, and with it cooperation (Nikiforakis 2008). In sum, systems using formal sanctions to deter free-riding can have deleterious side effects, including lower trust, trustworthiness, and cooperation.

Though often neglected in research, there is good reason to think that nonmaterial, social, and affective sanctions play at least as large a role as material sanctions in the maintenance of social order. Here, "social sanctions" refer to direct communications of disapproval, expressions of shame, and public embarrassment (Blau 1964, Masclet et al. 2003, Noussair and Tucker 2005). As such, social sanctions are penalties that "do not impose tangible costs on the offender, though they may decrease his or her utility" (Noussair and Tucker 2005). Social sanctions deter free-riding because individuals strongly desire social approval from others, and alter their behavior to avoid disapproval (Ellingsen and Johannesson 2008, Hollander 1990). Arguably, the use of social sanctions is more common than formal sanctions. While few individuals have the authority (or desire) to impose monetary fines on others, most group members can express disapproval or apply peer pressure when others behave selfishly.

Despite their apparent utility and ubiquity, only two published studies to date evaluate social versus material sanctions as deterrents to free-riding (Masclet et al. 2003, Noussair and Tucker 2005). In one study, Masclet et al. (2003) compare behavior in a public goods game across three conditions. In a monetary punishment, or formal sanctions condition, participants could reduce others' earnings at a cost. In a nonmonetary punishment (i.e., social sanctions) condition, participants could send "disapproval points" to others that were costless to both sender and receiver. In a control group, individuals were able to send neither monetary nor nonmonetary sanctions. Findings indicate that social sanctions significantly increase cooperation compared to groups with no punishment, though formal sanctions were slightly more effective at deterring free-riding. Yet, because of the monetary costs incurred through using formal sanctions (to both senders and receivers), overall earnings were similar in the two conditions.

Building on Masclet et al. (2003), Noussair and Tucker (2005) focus on the combination of formal and social sanctions for generating cooperative behavior. They find that, in a combined system, where participants can use either social or formal sanctions, contribution levels and payoffs are higher than when only one of the two types of sanctions are available. More precisely, the benefit of the combined system is that it is cheaper than a system using only formal sanctions, and more effective at increasing contributions than a system using only social sanctions.

This research suggests that social sanctions generate payoffs similar to formal sanctioning systems, and may be especially useful when used in conjunction with formal sanctions. However, it remains to be seen whether social sanctions, like formal sanctions, negatively affect group member perceptions and impede sustained cooperation. Future research should address whether social sanctions help sustain prosociality in groups without producing the negative side effects that result from material sanctioning systems.

Information Sharing and Reputation

Recent research has also begun to illuminate the role of reputational information sharing, or *gossip*, in the maintenance of basic social order. Gossip, defined here as communicating in a morally evaluative manner about others when they are not present, is usually perceived in a negative light. Yet, there is reason to believe that gossip plays an important and ubiquitous role in helping solve social dilemmas (Dunbar 2004, Sommerfeld, Krambeck, Semmann, and Milinski 2007, Wilson et al. 2000).

A major function of gossip is the spread of information about the character of others. Through gossip, individuals can keep tabs on other's behavior without being physically present. Moreover, gossip allows for the spread of evaluative information (i.e., reputation) about others (Dunbar 1996, 2004, Foster 2004), thus providing individuals a pretext with which to interact with others in their social network. Because of such information sharing, people's reputations often precede them. The spread of reputational information serves as a policing mechanism, helping social groups both deter and punish selfish behavior.

A significant body of research reviewed above shows that individuals forgo short-term material benefits in order to develop a good reputation. Individuals have good reason to do so. Having a tarnished reputation can hinder many of life's most important pursuits, such as developing successful trade relationships, forming friendships and social alliances, and being viewed as a viable romantic partner. It can also lead to ostracism from one's social group (Ouwerkerk et al. 2005, Spoor and Williams 2007, Williams 2007). Historically, when humans mainly existed in small, hunter-gatherer tribes, ostracism equated to a death sentence. However, even in present day, where mobility from one social group to another is more feasible, those ostracized suffer significant hardships in finding a new group and establishing themselves as an accepted member of that group. Without gossip, reputational information could not spread throughout a social network. As a result, there would be no reason for individuals to fear gaining a widespread negative reputation or to fear being ostracized from the group. At worst, individuals would develop a tarnished reputation only in the eyes of the person they defected on or cheated, and possibly observers of the transgression. The powerful reputational incentive to behave prosocially in social dilemma situations disappears.

Few experimental studies directly test the role of gossip in social dilemmas. The most relevant study examined gossip's influence in an indirect reciprocity game where paired participants decided to either keep a portion of an endowment for themselves or donate a larger portion of their endowment to their game partner (Sommerfeld et al. 2007). Some rounds involved receiving gossip about a partner's previous game behavior with other participants. Participants received this gossip about their current partners prior to playing the indirect reciprocity game with them, thus providing useful reputation information that could guide one's decisions about how to play. The results of this study revealed that gossip did influence game decisions. As expected, positive gossip about a player led to a higher likelihood that a partner would cooperate with them, and negative gossip led to a lower likelihood of cooperation. In this study, gossip was not examined as a deterrent – the experimental setup did not use the threat of being gossiped about as a means for influencing behavior. In a separate study, however, Piazza and Bering (2008) examined how threat of gossip associated with one's reputation could influence economic behavior. These researchers found that participants were more generous when they knew that their decisions in a distribution task would be relayed to an individual with whom they had gotten to know personally. Thus, even the possibility of having one's reputation tarnished for behaving selfishly seems to be enough to foster prosocial behavior. Although neither of these studies examined social dilemmas involving groups (rather than dyads), and neither specifically examined the influence gossip can have in policing free riders, the results do suggest that gossip can help solve social dilemmas by conveying reputational information and by fostering prosocial behavior. Furthermore, these studies coincide well with Enquist and Leimar's (1993) evolutionary modeling which found cooperation could be an evolutionary stable strategy only if gossip conveyed reputational information amongst the group. Without such gossip, however, free riders would take over the population, eliminating all cooperators.

But what motives underlie gossip? Although gossip has prosocial effects for recipients and groups, it also represents valuable information that is (typically) freely shared by individuals. A logical explanation would be that reputational information is reciprocally traded among allies (or friends) via gossip in the same way that other resources are exchanged (Trivers 1971). Another possibility is that gossiping may be a strategy for advertising one's own conformity to the social norms of the group (Baumeister et al. 2004). Such advertisement may help gossipers signal their underlying prosociality, communicating to others their trustworthiness. On the flip side, gossiping may also be a way of advertising that the gossiper is not someone who can be easily exploited. Through gossip, individuals may effectively communicate that they are part of a larger social network in which reputational information is readily diffused. Thus, any cheating would result in negative reputational information being broadcasted about the offender throughout the social network (Willer 2009b).

The proximal psychological motives driving gossip, however, remain largely unexamined. In the one experimental examination of the topic, Feinberg and Willer (2010) tested three potential reasons for gossip: (1) it relieves negative, and promotes positive, affect, (2) it punishes immoral and unjust behavior, and (3) it helps innocent others. In their first study, participants witnessed a social transgression during an economic game. Participants in the gossip condition were then able to send a short note to the next interaction partner of the transgressor. Participants' emotions were measured before and after sending the gossip note. Results showed that gossiping decreased negative emotion and increased positive emotion, relative to the control condition. Examination of the notes themselves showed that participants chose to gossip both to punish the transgressor as well as to help the future interaction partner. An analysis of the predictive value of these two motives suggested that the primary motive was to help rather than punish. In a second study, they added a third condition which involved gossiping to an uninvolved third party who would never interact with the target of the gossip. This condition was included to examine if the emotional benefits of gossip are only obtained when the information shared can potentially help someone. The results revealed that gossiping to a third party had similar, though muted, effects on positive and negative emotions. These results suggest that gossiping about transgressions in general both relieves negative and promotes positive emotions, though the effect is stronger when the recipient of the gossip will be helped by the information.

In both studies, the option to gossip was voluntary, yet more than 95% of participants chose to gossip even when there was no clear benefit for doing so. Self-reported motivations and content analyses of the actual gossip notes suggested that the primary motive behind gossiping was to help others. These findings raise the possibility that gossip, commonly considered antisocial and petty, is in fact an important form of prosocial behavior.

Formal Models of Reputation and the Evolution of Prosociality

Thus far, our review has focused on empirical research on the role of reputation as a proximal, situational cause of prosocial behavior. It is possible, however, that reputational dynamics can also help us understand the distal causation of prosocial behavior in humans via either biological or cultural evolution. The evolution of prosocial behaviors in humans is considered puzzling from the perspective of natural selection since individuals can presumably achieve greater fitness by not engaging in costly acts that benefit others. In recent years, mathematical and computational modeling in the social and biological sciences has increasingly questioned this reasoning, developing models of the evolution of prosocial behavior that emphasize the role of reputation and other informational mechanisms. These models consistently show that the evolution of human prosociality is far less puzzling if information on individuals' past behavior is widely available. Information on others' past levels of prosocial versus antisocial behavior encourages evolution of prosocial behavior by enabling, (1) assortative interactions among prosocial individuals that make prosociality a more profitable strategy and reduce the profits due to the narrowly self-interested, and (2) costly sanctions for antisocial behavior that reduce the fitness of this strategy.

Partner selection, which leads to biased assortative interactions among individuals with different levels of prosociality, is one mechanism that favors the evolutionary fitness of prosocial individuals. When relevant behavioral information is known, prosocial individuals can preferentially interact with other prosocial individuals, leaving antisocial individuals to disproportionately interact with one another (Orbell and Dawes 1993, Frank 1988, Macy and Skvoretz 1998). As a result of this biased assortment of interaction partners the benefits of prosociality will be disproportionately felt by other prosocials while the harms done by antisocial behavior fall disproportionately on the more antisocial. This pairing of similar individuals reduces the risk to prosocial individuals of being exploited by less cooperative others while reducing the rewards that antisocial individuals gain from more cooperative others. An individual's resulting fitness, in an evolutionary sense, will then be proportional to their prosociality. As a result, prosocials will, by cooperating with one another, become more numerous. Meanwhile, antisocials will compete with each other, becoming relatively less numerous and possibly extinct.

This "assortativity" can be induced through very simple preferential interaction mechanisms. In evolutionary models featuring unilateral giving, a preference to give to individuals with a good reputation over ones with a worse reputation makes prosocial behavior a more profitable strategy that is stable across generations in both static and dynamic networks (Takahashi 2000, Fu et al. 2008). Additionally, the positive effects of reputation-based partner selection on the amount of prosocial behavior in a population are robust to imperfect information. Axelrod et al. (2004) showed that in a population of agents with inheritable mutations, the existence of individual "tags" observable by others that signal prosocial inclinations combined with a preference for interacting with other similarly tagged agents was sufficient to produce stable pockets of prosocial agents and a trend towards increasing overall prosociality (c.f. Riolo et al. 2001). The levels of cooperation among tagged populations remained higher than among untagged populations even when the tag was a noisy indicator of prosociality, though this effect declined as the correlation between tag and prosocial behavior decreased.

Beyond simple preferential interaction, the costly sanctioning of uncooperative behavior (i.e., altruistic punishment), can further reduce the fitness of individuals who behave antisocially. In simulations featuring diverse populations of agents with varying propensities to cooperate and punish uncooperative others, the existence of high levels of cooperation is dependent on the presence of sufficient levels of punishment (Bowles and Gintis 2004, Fowler 2005, Eldakar and Wilson 2008). This punishment may take the form of "strong reciprocity," where cooperative agents also engage in punishment of noncooperation (Bowles and Gintis 2004, Boyd et al. 2003, Gintis 2003), or "hypocritical punishment," where uncooperative individuals punish other uncooperative individuals (Heckathorn 1989, Eldakar and Wilson 2008). Regardless of the form of punishment, when the proportion of punishers is sufficiently high, individuals who punish bear very little cost relative to those that do not (Boyd et al. 2003), minimizing the selection pressures that might otherwise undermine the evolution of sanctioning behavior.

Although sanctioning enables the development and persistence of cooperation in some circumstances, some studies question the real usefulness of altruistic punishment. Dreber et al. (2008) found that individuals that punish never outperform their opponents. Indeed, relative to their opponents, altruistic punishers usually perform worse. Sanctioning individuals only succeed through fostering consistently high levels of cooperation allowing both partners to reap high rewards. Less prosocial, nonsanctioning individuals may have lower overall levels of cooperation, but can outperform their partners, creating a relative fitness advantage. Recent research suggests that sanctioning may not be as necessary as proponents of strong reciprocity assert. In fact, altruistic punishment is necessary for only a small proportion of the conditions under which prosociality can evolve (Ohtsuki et al. 2009).

These studies complement empirical research linking reputation and prosociality. Even as researchers from diverse fields offer strong empirical demonstrations of the power of reputational concerns to ensure prosocial behavior in situations, models are increasingly emphasizing the causal role of reputation in the evolution of human prosocial behavior. These models show how reputation-based assortative interaction dynamics and sanctioning systems both are sufficient to favor prosociality in natural selection. It is also worth noting that these assumptions are also highly plausible, arguably much more plausible than the minimalist evolutionary models that make prosociality puzzling in the first place. As empirical research presented above demonstrates, it is sensible to assume that people would have at least minimal reputational information on one another, both from personal experience and reputational information sharing with others. Finally, although these models are typically presented as representing biological evolution – in which individuals possessing less fit strategies die off and those with more fit strategies proliferate – they could also be viewed as models of an individual or social learning dynamics – in which less profitable strategies are discarded in favor of ones that are more profitable.

CONCLUSION

We began this article by noting that portrayals of invisible men in literature and film invariably emphasize their immorality.[3] Invisible men are viewed as greedy and untrustworthy, not only unrestrained, but somehow also corrupted by their power. The suggestion is that individuals' antisocial urges are primerily regulated by image concerns. We behave morally, when we do, because we are watched. When we are watched, we become accountable, as our actions bring consequences for our reputations.

Here, we have reviewed several strains of research on the role of reputation in prosocial behavior. Our review establishes that individuals receive diverse social and material benefits for behaving prosocially. Further, these rewards for developing a "good" reputation influence decisions to behave prosocially, both as a reward individuals instrumentally seek, and as a positive reinforcement that leads individuals to learn to behave generously. We also discussed research indicating that status hierarchies, traditionally viewed as an antisocial basis of inequality, may actually increase group productivity by structuring patterns of contributions to collective efforts in functional ways.

Another function of reputation systems is the delivery of information critical to the maintenance of social and affective sanctioning systems. A recent line of research makes a related point: that reputational information (i.e. gossip) that is critical to the effectiveness of reputation systems is spontaneously diffused among individuals because of social and affective processes. Finally, a variety of mathematical and computational models asserts that reputational processes could have encouraged the evolution of prosociality via biological and/or cultural evolution.

Where past approaches to explaining prosocial behavior are broadly classifiable as either emphasizing sincere (altruism) or strategic (material incentives) motives, research on reputation blurs this distinction. While behaviors that are on face calculated efforts to better one's social standing (e.g., Barclay and Willer 2007) are classifiable as strategic, this is not the only way in which reputation may shape prosocial behavior. As reviewed above, some theory and research suggest that individuals may also be affected by reputational benefits via a learning process: once individuals contribute to groups they earn improved status, once this status is communicated to them via gestures of respect their motivation to help the group is increased and more costly contributions to group efforts follow (Willer 2009a). Thus, it may be that the role of reputational concerns in fostering prosocial behavior defies the classic distinction between altruism and strategic self-interest, shaping individuals' prosociality via both mechanisms.

Our review also discussed the relative impacts of social and material sanctions, an area that has gained some recent attention. Thus far the literature has focused on material sanctions, but the study of social and affective sanctions is promising both because these sanctions are likely more common in everyday life, and also because they bypass many of the negative by-products of material sanctioning systems. While material sanctions are typically more effective for guaranteeing pro-group behaviors because they transform individual self-interest (e.g., Olson 1965), their longer-term degradation of trust and prosocial motivation may

---

[3] Klosterman observes for example, that throughout his novel, Wells "seems maniacally preoccupied with illustrating how the invisible man was an asshole" (2009).

make them inappropriate applications. Future research should better establish the differences between these two classes of sanctions, and specifically investigate the interaction between the presence of different forms of sanctions and reputation systems in groups.

Research on reputational information sharing in groups is a neglected, but critical area. Until recently, it has been assumed that reputational information readily diffuses widely across group members. While this may be so, it is a fascinating phenomenon, amounting to a form of second-order altruism where individuals give away information of real, material value free of charge. Even more interesting is recent research showing that the underlying psychological motivations driving gossip (Feinberg and Willer 2010) may mirror those found to compel empathic helping (Batson 1991).

Finally, we have also discussed some mathematical and computational models in the area. Overwhelmingly, these models have focused on how reputational benefits may have aided in the biological evolution of human propensities for altruistic behavior. Far less studied, but likely promising, is how models of the cultural evolution of generosity might also profit from consideration of reputational dynamics. In addition, further modeling of reputational dynamics is necessary as social scientists strive for a more general understanding of the structure of status hierarchies within and across groups.

We also hope that future research investigates the interplay between altruistic motives and reputational concerns. Is it the case that individuals who appear altruistic are in fact simply pursuing some form of reputational gain? Should this literature linking reputation and prosocial behavior be read as offering an explanation for generosity that challenges the existence of altruism? Or, perhaps instead, more altruistic individuals are also less egoistic in their desires for reputational advancement? Perhaps it is egoists who behave prosocially (when they do) in an instrumental effort to better their reputations? While at least one article has begun investigation of this question, finding support for the notion that more altruistic individuals care less about reputational gain (Simpson and Willer 2008), more research is needed on this fundamental question.

In general, research on reputation must continue to grapple with the formulation of key concepts (Martin 2009). Where we have referred broadly to "reputation," it is very likely that people care about many dimensions of their reputation, and likely in different ways that vary across individuals. Reputation entails many aspects of how one is perceived, including how respected someone is, how generous they are seen to be, how well liked, how dominant. Social scientists have only begun to break apart these closely related concepts, but continuing to do so is critical not only to understand the dynamics of pro-community behaviors, but also the microsocial order more generally.

Acknowledgment Robb Willer and Brent Simpson wish to acknowledge support from the National Science Foundation (SES 0647169).

REFERENCES

Alexander, R. D. 1987. *The Biology of Moral Systems.* New York: De Gruyter.

Andreoni, J., and R. Petrie. 2004. "Public Goods Experiments without Confidentiality: A Glimpse into Fund-Raising." *Journal of Public Economics* 88:1605–1623.

Axelrod, R. 1984. *The Evolution of Cooperation.* New York: Basic Books.

Axelrod, R., R. A. Hammond, and A. Grafen. 2004. Altruism via kin-selection strategies that rely on arbitrary tags with which they coevolve. *Evolution* 58(8):1833–1838.

Bales, R. F. 1970. *Personality and Interpersonal Behavior*. New York: Holt, Rinehart, and Winston.

Barclay, P. 2004. "Trustworthiness and Competitive Altruism can Also Solve the 'Tragedy of the Commons.'" *Evolution and Human Behavior* 25:209–220.

Barclay, P., and R. Willer. 2007. "Partner Choice Creates Competitive Altruism in Humans." *Proceedings of the Royal Society B: Biological Sciences* 274:749–753.

Batson, C. D. 1991. *The Altruism Question: Towards a Social-Psychological Answer*. Hillsdale, NJ: Lawrence Erlbaum Associates.

Baumeister, R. F., Liqing Zhang, and Kathleen D. Vohs. 2004. "Gossip as Cultural Learning." *Review of General Psychology* 8:111–121.

Berger, J., B. P. Cohen, and M. Zelditch Jr. 1972. "Status Characteristics and Social Interaction." *American Sociological Review* 37:241–255.

Berger, J., M. Hamit Fisek, R. Z. Norman, and M. Zelditch, Jr. 1977. *Status Characteristics and Social Interaction: An Expectation States Approach*. Elsevier: New York.

Blau, P. M. 1964. *Exchange and Power in Social Life*. New York: John Wiley and Sons.

Bowels, S., and H. Gintis. 2004. "The Evolution of Strong Reciprocity: Cooperation in Heterogenous Populations." *Theoretical Population Biology* 65:17–28.

Boyd, R., H. Gintis, S. Bowles, and P. J. Richerson. 2003. "The Evolution of Altruistic Punishment." *Proceedings from the National Academy of Sciences* 100:3531–3535.

Chagnon, N. A. 1988. "Life Histories, Blood Revenge, and Warfare in a Tribal Population." *Science* 239:985–992.

Comte, A. 1973 (1851). *System of Positive Polity, Volume 1: Containing the General View of Positivism and Introductory Principles*. Translated by J. Henry Bridges. New York: Burt Franklin.

Dovidio, J. F., J. Allyn Piliavin, D. A. Schroeder, and L. A. Penner. 2006. *The Social Psychology of Prosocial Behavior*. Mahwah, NJ: Lawrence Ehrlbaum.

Dreber, A., D. G. Rand, D. Fundenberg, and M. A. Nowak. 2008. "Winners Don't Punish." *Nature* 452:348–351.

Dunbar, R. I. M. 1996. *Grooming, Gossip and the Evolution of Language*. Cambridge, MA: Harvard University Press.

Dunbar, R. I. M. 2004. "Gossip in Evolutionary Perspective." *Review of General Psychology* 8:100–110.

Durkheim, E. 1964 (1893). *The Division of Labor in Society*. New York: Free Press.

Eldakar, O. T., and D. S. Wilson. 2008. "Selfishness as Second-Order Altruism." *Proceedings of the National Academy of Sciences* 90(5):6982–6986.

Ellingsen, T., and M. Johannesson. 2008. "Anticipated Verbal Feedback Induces Altruistic Punishment." *Evolution and Human Behavior* 29:100–105.

Enquist, M., and O. Leimar. 1993. "The Evolution of Cooperation in Mobile Organisms." *Animal Behaviour* 45: 747–757.

Fehr, E., and S. Gachter. 2002. "Altruistic Punishment in Humans." *Nature* 415:137–140.

Fehr, E., and B. Rockenbach. 2003. "Detrimental Effects of Sanctions on Human Altruism." *Nature* 422:137–140.

Feinberg, M., and R. Willer. 2010. "The Good of Gossip? The Benefits of this Unlikely Prosocial Behavior." Unpublished manuscript. Department of Psychology. University of California, Berkeley.

Flynn, F. J., R. E. Reagans, E. T. Amanatullah, and D. R. Ames. 2006. "Helping One's Way to the Top: Self-Monitors Achieve Status by Helping Others and Knowing Who Helps Whom." *Journal of Personality and Social Psychology* 91:1123–1137.

Foster, E. K. 2004. "Research on Gossip: Taxonomy, Methods, and Future Directions." *Review of General Psychology* 8:78–99.

Fowler, J. H. 2005. "Altruistic Punishment and the Origin of Cooperation." *Proceedings of the National Academy of Sciences USA* 102: 7047–7049.

Frank, R. H. 1988. *Passions Within Reason: The Strategic Role of the Emotions*. New York: Norton.

Frank, R. H. 2004. *What Price the Moral High Ground?: Ethical Dilemmas in Competitive Environments*. Princeton, NJ: Princeton University Press.

Fu, F., C. Hauert, M. A. Nowak, and L. Wang. 2008. "Reputation-Based Partner Choice Promotes Cooperation in Social Networks." *Physical Review* E:78.

Gintis, H. 2003. "Solving the Puzzle of Prosociality." *Rationality and Society* 152:155–187.

Gurerk, O., B. Irlenbusch, B. Rockenbach. 2006. "The Competitive Advantage of Sanctioning Institutions." *Science* 312:108–111.

Haley, K. J., and D. M. T. Fessler. 2005. "Nobody's Watching? Subtle Cues Affect Generosity in an Anonymous Economic Game." *Evolution and Human Behavior* 26:245–256.

Hardy, C. L., and M. V. Vugt. 2006. "Nice Guys Finish First: The Nice Guys Finish First: The Competitive Altruism Hypothesis." *Personality and Social Psychological Bulletin* 32:1402–1413.

Heckathorn, D. D. 1989. "Collective Action and the Second-Order Free-Rider Problem.' *Rationality and Society* 1:78–100.

Hollander, H. 1990. "A Social Exchange Approach to Voluntary Cooperation." *American Economic Review* 80: 1157–1167.

Huberman, B. A., C. H. Loch, and A. Onculer. 2004. "Status as a Valued Resource." *Social Psychology Quarterly* 67(1):103–114.

Janoff-Bulman, R., S. Sheikh, and S. Hepp. 2009. "Proscriptive Versus Prescriptive Morality: Two Faces of Moral Regulation. *Journal of Personality and Social Psychology* 96:521–537.

Klosterman, C. 2009. *Eating the Dinosaur*. New York: Scribner.

Kumru, C. S., and L. Vesterlund. 2008. "The Effect of Status on Voluntary Contribution." *UNSW Australian School of Business Research Paper No. 2008 ECON 02.*

Leimar, O., and P. Hammerstein. 2001. "Evolution of Cooperation Through Indirect Reciprocity." *Proceedings of the Royal Society B* 268:745–753.

Lemonnier, P. 1996. "Food, Competition, and the Status of Food in New Guinea." PP. 219–234 in *Food and the Status Quest: An Interdisciplinary Perspective*, edited by P. Wiessner, and W. Schiefenhovel. New York: Berghahn.

Liebrand, W. B. G. 1986. "The Ubiquity of Social Values in Social Dilemmas." PP. 113–133 in *Experimental Studies of Social Dilemmas*, edited by H. Wilke, C. Rutte, and D. Messick. Frankfurt: Peter Lang Publishing Company.

Liebrand, W. B. G., H. A.M. Wilke, and F. J. M. Wolters. 1986. "Value Orientation and Conformity: A Study Using Three Types of Social Dilemma Games." *Journal of Conflict Resolution* 30:77–97.

Macy, M. W. 1990. "Learning Theory and the Logic of Critical Mass." *American Sociological Review* 55:809–826.

Macy, M. W. 1995. "PAVLOV and the Evolution of Cooperation: An Experimental Test." *Social Psychology Quarterly* 58:74–87.

Macy, M. W., and J. Skvoretz. 1998. "The Evolution of Trust and Cooperation Between Strangers: A Computational Model." *American Sociological Review* 635:638–660.

Martin, J. L. 2009. "Formation and Stabilization of Vertical Hierarchies among Adolescents: Towards a Quantitative Ethology of Dominance among Humans." *Social Psychology Quarterly* 72:241–264.

Masclet, D., C. Noussair, S. Tucker, and M.-C. Villeval. 2003. "Monetary and Nonmonetary Punishment in the Voluntary Contributions Mechanism." *American Economic Review* 93:366–380.

Milinski, M., D. Semmann, and H.-J. Krambeck. 2002a. "Reputation Helps Solve the 'Tragedy of the Commons.'" *Nature* 415:424–426.

Milinski, M., D. Semmann, and H.-J. Krambeck. 2002b. "Donors to Charity Gain in Both Indirect Reciprocity and Political Reputation." *Proceedings of the Royal Society of London* 269:881–883.

Miller, D. T., and R. Ratner. 1998. "The Disparity Between the Actual and Assumed Power of Self-Interest." *Journal of Personality and Social Psychology* 74:53–62.

Mulder, L. B., E. van Dijk, D. De Cremer, and H. A.M. Wilke. 2006. "Undermining Trust and Cooperation: The Paradox of Sanctioning Systems in Social Dilemmas." *Journal of Experimental Social Psychology* 42:147–162.

Nikiforakis, N. 2008. "Punishment and Counter-punishment in Public Goods Games: Can We Really Govern Ourselves?" *Journal of Public Economics* 92:91–112.

Noussair, C., and S. Tucker. 2005. "Combining Monetary and Social Sanctions to Promote Cooperation." *Economic Inquiry* 43:649–660.

Nowak, M., and K. Sigmund. 1998. "Evolution of Indirect Reciprocity Through Image Scoring." *Nature* 393: 573–577.

Nowak, M. A. 2006. *Evolutionary Dynamics: Exploring the Equations of Life.* Cambridge, MA: Harvard University Press.

Ohtsuki, H., Y. Iwasa, and M. A. Nowak. 2009. "Indirect Reciprocity Provides Only a Narrow Margin of Efficiency for Costly Punishment." *Nature* 457:79–82.

Oliner, S. P., and P. M. Oliner. 1988. *The Altruistic Personality: Rescuers of the Jews in Nazi-occupied Poland.* Free Press: New York.

Oliver, P. E., G. Marwell, and R. Teixeira. 1985. "A Theory of the Critical Mass. I. Interdependence, Group Heterogeneity, and the Production of Collective Action." *American Journal of Sociology* 91:522–556.

Oliver, P., and G. Marwell. 1988. "The Paradox of Group Size in Collective Action: A Theory of the Critical Mass. III." *American Sociological Review* 53:1–8.

Olson, M. 1965. *The Logic of Collective Action: Public Goods and the Theory of Groups.* Cambridge: Harvard.

Orbell, J. M., and R. M. Dawes. 1993. "Social Welfare, Cooperators' Advantage, and the Option of Not Playing the Game." *American Sociological Review* 58:787–800.

Ouwerkerk, J. W., N. L. Kerr, M. Gallucci, and P. A. M. Van Lange. 2005. "Avoiding the Social Death Penalty: Ostracism and Cooperation in Social Dilemmas." PP. 321–332 in *The Social Outcast: Ostracism, Social Exclusion, Rejection, and Bullying*, edited by K. D. Williams, J. P. Forgas, W. von Hippel. New York, NY: Psychology Press.

Panchanathan, K., and R. Boyd. 2004. "Indirect Reciprocity can Stabilize Cooperation without the Second-Order Free Rider Problem." *Nature* 432:499–502.

Patton, J. Q. 1996. *Thoughtful Warriors: Status, Warriorship, and Alliance in the Ecuadorian Amazon*. Dissertation: University of California at Santa Barbara.

Piazza, J., and J. M. Bering. 2008. "Concerns about Reputation Via Gossip Promote Generous Allocations in an Economic Game." *Evolution and Human Behavior* 29: 172–178.

Piliavin, J., and H.-W. Charng. 1990. "Altruism: A Review of Recent Theory and Research." *Annual Review of Sociology* 16:27–65.

Price, M. E. 2003. "Pro-Community Altruism and Social Status in a Shuar Village." *Human Nature* 14:191–208.

Ridgeway, C. L. 1982. "Status in Groups: The Importance of Motivation." *American Sociological Review* 47:76–88.

Riolo, R. L., M. D. Cohen, and R. Axelrod. 2001. "Evolution of Cooperation Without Reciprocity." *Nature* 414: 441–443.

Roberts, G. 1998. "Competitive Altruism: From Reciprocity to the Handicap Principle." *Proceedings of the Royal Society of London B*. 265:427–431.

Semmann, D., H.-J. Krambeck, and M. Milinski. 2004. "Strategic Investment in Reputation." *Behavioral Ecology and Sociobiology* 56:248–252.

Simpson, B., and R. Willer. 2008. "Altruism and Indirect Reciprocity: The Interaction of Person and Situation in Prosocial Behavior." *Social Psychology Quarterly* 71:37–52.

Simpson, B., and R. Willer. 2010. "Status and the Organization of Collective Action." Unpublished manuscript. Columbia, SC: University of South Carolina.

Smith, E. A., and R. A. Bliege Bird. 2000. "Turtle Hunting and Tombstone Opening: Public Generosity as Costly Signaling." *Evolution and Human Behavior* 21:245–261.

Sommerfield, R. D., H.-J. Krambeck, D. Semmann, and M. Milinski. 2007. "Gossip as an Alternative for Direct Observation in Games of Indirect Reciprocity." *Proceedings of the National Academy of Sciences* 104: 17435–17440.

Sorokin, P. A. 1954. *The Ways and Power of Love: Types, Factors, and Techniques of Moral Transformation*. Philadelphia: Templeton.

Spoor, J., and K. D. Williams. 2007. "The Evolution of an Ostracism Detection System." PP. 279–292 in *Evolution and the Social Mind: Evolutionary Psychology and Social Cognition*, edited by J. P. Forgas, M. G. Haselton, and W. von Hippel. New York: Psychology Press.

Sugden, R. 1986. *The Economics of Rights, Cooperation, and Welfare*. Blackwell: Oxford.

Takahashi, N. 2000. "The Emergence of Generalized Exchange". *American Journal of Sociology* 105(4):1105–1134

Tenbrunsel, A. E., and D. M. Messick. 1999. "Sanctioning Systems, Decision Frames, and Cooperation." *Administrative Science Quarterly* 44:684–707.

Trivers, R. 1971. "The Evolution of Reciprocal Altruism." *Quarterly Review of Biology* 46: 35–57.

Van Lange, P. A. M. 1999. "The Pursuit of Joint Outcomes and Equality in Outcomes: An Integrative Model of Social Value Orientation." *Journal of Personality and Social Psychology* 77:337–349.

Willer, R. 2009a. "Groups Reward Individual Sacrifice: The Status Solution to the Collective Action Problem." *American Sociological Review* 74:23–43.

Willer, R. 2009b. "A Status Theory of Collective Action." PP. 133–63 in A*dvances in Group Processes, Vol. 26*, edited by S. R. Thye, and E. J. Lawler. London: Emerald.

Williams, K. D. 2007. "Ostracism: The Kiss of Social Death." *Social and Personality Compass* 1: 236–247.

Wilson, D. S., C. Wilczynski, A. Wells, and L. Weiser. 2000. "Gossip and Other Aspects of Language as Group-level Adaptations." PP. 347–365 in *The Evolution of Cognition*, edited by C. Heyes, and L. Huber. Cambridge, MA: MIT Press.

Yamagishi, T. 1986. "The Provision of a Sanctioning System as a Public Good." *Journal of Personality and Social Psychology* 51:110–116.

Zahavi, A. 1995. "Altruism as a Handicap – The Limitations of Kin Selection and Reciprocity." *Journal of Avian Biology* 26:1–3.

Zahavi, A., and A. Zahavi. 1997. *The Handicap Principle: A Missing Piece of Darwin's Puzzle*. Oxford, England: Oxford University Press.

CHAPTER 18

The Justice/Morality Link

Implied, then Ignored, yet Inevitable

KAREN A. HEGTVEDT AND HEATHER
L. SCHEUERMAN

The study of justice has a long history in social psychology (see Colquitt et al. 2005, Tyler et al. 1997) and an even longer one in philosophy (see Solomon and Murphy 1990). Philosophical writings typically offer prescriptions for the just society whereas social psychological work examines people's subjective beliefs about what is just or fair (and what happens when those beliefs are violated). Conveyed by philosophers' prescriptions but largely – though not totally – missing in social psychological approaches and studies is the extent to which justice concerns constitute issues of morality. In the realms of ethics and moral philosophy, prescriptions for the just society detail what people ought to do when making distributions or decisions in order to reign in the pursuit of material self-interests or the exercise of unfettered power that may undermine society. Social psychological writing echoes these "oughts" when scholars argue that groups maximize collective rewards when they evolve systems for "equitably" apportioning rewards and costs among group members (Walster et al. 1978) or that "justice judgments ... are the 'grease' that allows groups to interact productively without conflict and social disintegration" (Tyler et al. 1997:7).

Few social psychologists who study justice would deny its roots in moral philosophy. Moreover, most would tout the importance of justice research because of its kinship with what makes society or people good – conducting themselves in a manner consistent with moral behavior. And yet explicit linkages to morality in general, let alone to the sociology of morality, are rare. Here we describe how the justice/morality link, long implied in justice research, was largely ignored in the hey-day of early distributive and procedural justice research only to emerge more recently with attention to the integration of approaches to justice (and in response to other developments in psychology and sociology). To do so, we begin with an overview of the meanings of morality and justice in order to show conceptual connections and the implication that the two are linked. Then we examine the evolution of work in the social psychology of justice in order to illustrate the suppression of the morality/justice link and its revitalization in the last 10 years. The revitalization includes theoretical and empirical work that contributes to an understanding of the implications of justice work for morality in society. Specifically, we review theoretical approaches that highlight the role of moral communities and morality in forming justice judgments. We also examine research on responses to injustice that involve moral emotions and observers who do not personally suffer an injustice. In effect,

S. Hitlin, S. Vaisey (eds.), *Handbook of the Sociology of Morality,*
Handbooks of Sociology and Social Research, DOI 10.1007/978-1-4419-6896-8_18,
© Springer Science+Business Media, LLC 2010

the latter pursue justice for others. We conclude with a discussion of when everyday justice assessments are questions of morality and when they ensure moral behavior.

THE *IMPLICIT* LINK: MEANINGS OF MORALITY AND JUSTICE

Given the number of volumes written separately on morality and on justice, this section provides, at best, only a circumscribed overview of the meanings of morality and of justice. The goal here is to identify conceptual commonalities and differences, noting the important overlap that makes discussions about justice within the realm of morality and the sociology of morality relevant. To achieve this end, we first briefly review philosophical approaches to morality and then demonstrate how justice – broadly defined – fits into these formulations. We conclude by offering social psychological conceptualizations of specific types of justice.

Philosophical Approaches to Morality and Justice

Common as well as philosophical definitions of morality typically refer to a system of moral conduct, based on moral principles. Such definitions beg the question, "What is moral?" In common usage, people are likely to conceive of morality in terms of right and wrong behavior or judgments of right and wrong. But what constitutes right and wrong?

The normative approach to morality (see Gert 2008) offers a response to this question. At the core of such an approach is the dictate to avoid and prevent harm to others. By doing so, an action constitutes what is "right." Dictates to prevent harm also extend to prohibit acts such as deception and breaking promises. Generally, the normative view of morality signifies a universal code of conduct accepted by "rational" persons and indicates that some behaviors certainly constitute immorality. Any act that violates moral dictates requires justification.

Additionally, some philosophers argue that a normative sense of morality also encourages charitable actions. Hobbes, in particular, emphasizes that morality promotes actions to ensure that people live together in peace and harmony (see Curly 1994, Gert 1991). Arguments of other scholars likewise entail positive social interactions and linkages as characteristic of morality. The sociologist Emile Durkheim ([1912]/1995) extends Hobbes's emphasis by arguing that morality constrains individuals' wants, ties people to each other, and in so doing builds society. Lakoff (1996) similarly asserts that "what is moral is what promotes experiential well-being in others" (p. 380). In effect, a universal moral code entails principles or laws (e.g., avoid and prevent harm; encourage others' well-being) that provide an explicit guide for behavior, and to which any individual action may be compared in order to determine its morality.

Gert (2008) distinguishes the descriptive approach to morality from the normative one. While both views include the dictate to avoid and prevent harm to others, the descriptive approach also stresses the relevance of other principles (e.g., sanctity, purity, accepting authority). Recognizing the possibility of differences in the number and importance of moral principles across social groups, the descriptive approach allows for variation in the content of moral codes, essentially relativistic definitions of what is moral. Moreover, a code of morality put forward by a particular group may or may not be accepted by an individual. Thus, a descriptive approach implies different, perhaps conflicting, moral content from group to group and possibly among individuals within a group. Nonetheless, moral standards are more than personal preferences because they imply an obligation to behave in a certain way (Hitlin 2008). Among the moral standards represented in the descriptive approach is justice.

Justice: Moral Standard and Social Psychological Concept

The work of Jonathan Haidt (2001, 2003, 2007) on the psychological foundations of morality explicitly draws attention to justice. Yet Haidt's approach to justice is fairly narrow, given the plethora of research in social psychology on justice. Here we introduce Haidt's approach and then highlight the correspondence between abstract characteristics of justice and facets of the philosophical approaches to morality.

Haidt (2007, Haidt and Graham 2007, Haidt and Joseph 2007) draws from the descriptive approach to morality to identify what he calls the five psychological foundations of morality: harm/care, fairness/reciprocity, ingroup/loyalty, authority/respect, and purity/sanctity. He argues that cultures or other social groups vary in terms of the extent to which they value or prioritize each foundation and their concomitant moral principles. As a consequence, differences arise in emotional reactions to issues pertinent to each foundation and to assessments of the morality of certain behaviors (see Haidt and Graham 2007). Haidt's formulation is consistent with the long-standing argument that the moral judgments of males and females stem from emphasis on different aspects of morality; for males, morality constitutes rule-based, justice concerns, whereas for females, morality focuses on issues of caring and prevention of harm (Gilligan 1982, Gilligan and Attanucci 1988, but see Jaffe and Hyde (2000) for a different interpretation).

Recognition that different social groups generate different views of morality resonates with a sociological approach that typically construes morality and moral judgments as socially determined constructs (see Abend 2008). Structural, cultural, and interactional factors are likely to affect moral judgments, feelings, and behaviors. And, according to Durkeim ([1912]/1995), the reverse is potentially true as well: the collective cognitive and, especially, emotional engagement of people with their social world (i.e., their "collective effervescence") provides a basis for morality in society (see Shilling and Mellor 1998). Haidt's work in psychology names fairness or justice as one of the key foundations of morality while philosophical approaches to morality stress ideas and processes echoed in social psychological theorizing about justice.

Haidt argues that justice and caring suggest that *morality is about protecting individuals* (Haidt and Graham 2007:100, emphasis in the original). Similarly, following Kohlberg's (1969) moral development approach, Turiel (1983) notes that the moral domain involves "prescriptive judgments of justice, rights, and welfare pertaining to how people ought to relate to each other," (p. 3), which echoes the works of philosophers (e.g., John Rawls) known for their work on justice (Turiel 2006). These psychological approaches, however, remain focused on individual-centered justice principles. Haidt and Graham (2007) attempt to bridge the individual-societal gulf by arguing that "when the moral domain is limited by definition to two foundations (harm/welfare/care, and justice/rights/fairness), then social justice is clearly the extension of morality out to the societal level…aim[ing] to maximize the welfare and rights of individuals" (p. 101). Although rudimentary, this psychologically oriented definition of social justice reflects basic abstract characteristics of justice discussed by social psychologists.

Although social psychological justice research often emphasizes individual deserving by linking a person to his or her outcomes (e.g., Lerner 1977, Feather 1999) or individual judgments of outcomes, procedures, and interaction, justice is really a collective phenomenon (see Hegtvedt and Johnson 2000). Justice focuses not simply on the situation of one person but on the situation of many (Hareli 1999). Such a focus extends the reach of justice beyond individual welfare to that of the group and raises questions about the responsibility of people and institutions toward others. On an abstract level, key characteristics of justice include (1) fostering social cooperation (Deutsch 1975, Reis 1986, Tyler and Blader 2000); (2) impartiality (Barry 1989, Leventhal et al. 1980, Rawls 1971); and (3) consensus (see Hegtvedt 2005).

Together, these characteristics ensure that what is fair for one person is likely to be viewed as fair for others as well. Emphasis on social cooperation corresponds to the Hobbesian normative morality dictate to encourage ways for people to live in peace and harmony. Impartiality requires decision makers to set aside their own interests and reinforces recognition of the consequences for others. And, consensus provides the basis for a particular principle or rule regarding a distribution of outcomes, a set of procedures, or the nature of interaction dynamics within a group to be viewed as normative.

Consideration of these features provides a basis for a more general definition of social justice than that offered by Haidt and Graham (2007). Social justice involves the distribution of resources, opportunities, and rights based on promoting human dignity and collective welfare while disallowing distributions, procedures, or treatments that are biased by the decision maker or recipients' gender, race, sexual orientation, religion, or social class (wealth). While issues of morality that arise in situations of social injustice are beyond the scope of this chapter, the interpersonal forms of justice discussed by social psychologists focus on distributions, decision-making procedures, and interactions that in the aggregate underlie social justice.

Social Psychological Types of Justice

In social psychology, a common, often implicit, definition of justice focuses on the congruency between an actual situation (e.g., outcome distribution, decision-making procedures, or interaction) and that expected based on a normative principle of justice (e.g., Greenberg and Cohen 1982, Hegtvedt and Markovsky 1995, Jasso 1980). This comparison parallels the process inherent in a normative approach to morality that involves comparing an individual action to the dictate to prevent and avoid harm to determine the morality of the behavior. Social psychologists typically examine three types of justice: distributive, procedural, and interactional.[1]

Descriptive rules providing the basis for *distributive justice* (i.e., fairness in distributions of outcomes) include equity, equality, or need (Deutsch 1975). As Leventhal et al. (1980)

---

[1] Organizational justice researchers also add a fourth type: informational justice, which pertains to the organizational context and the use of explanations for procedures and reasons for outcome distributions (see Colquitt et al. 2001). Informational justice includes principles such as timeliness of communication, selection of information, and so forth.

argue, which principle is normative often depends upon the situational goal. When the goal of the situation is to enhance productivity, people are likely to agree that equity or allocation of outcomes in proportion to contributions across individuals in the group constitutes the fair principle. When the situational goal is to enhance solidarity among group members or promote their welfare, then justice is served by the equality (equal outcomes) and needs (allocation of outcomes in proportion to needs of individuals) rules, respectively.

The set of rules constituting *procedural justice* (i.e., the fairness of decision-making procedures) includes (1) consistency of procedures across persons and time; (2) suppression of bias; (3) accuracy of information; (4) mechanisms to correct bad decisions; (5) representation of people affected by a decision; and (6) ethicality of standards (Leventhal et al. 1980). Suppression of bias captures the abstract element of impartiality that characterizes justice. And, research demonstrates that consistency and representation (or "voice") rules are more fundamental than other rules to assessing procedures as just (see Tyler et al. 1997).

Impartiality or neutrality also features as a central element of *interactional justice* (i.e., fairness in the interaction dynamics among group members or between authorities and subordinates) (Tyler and Lind 1992). Other interactional justice rules include demonstration of respect, trustworthiness, truthfulness, and justification (or provision of rationale) (Bies 2001). As normative rules governing distributions, decision-making procedures, and interaction dynamics, these rules dictate appropriate standards of conduct – or what is "right."

Many studies examine perceptions of and emotional and behavioral responses to violations of distributive, procedural, and interactional justice rules (see Cohen-Charash and Spector 2001, Colquitt et al. 2001, Greenberg and Colquitt 2005, Hegtvedt and Cook 2001, Tyler et al. 1997). The potency of cries of "It's not fair!" stems from the link between justice and morality, and their mutual link to people's affective responses (Folger 2001). Yet, despite the overlap between morality approaches and justice characteristics, issues of the immorality of the violation and the morality of responses remain largely unaddressed. With emphasis on reward maximization/cost minimization and instrumentality, early social psychological models of justice subverted the morality/justice linkage. Below we characterize traditions in social psychological justice research, revealing how they have tacitly ignored issues of morality until recently.

THE *IGNORED* LINK: EARLY SOCIAL PSYCHOLOGICAL APPROACHES TO JUSTICE PROCESSES

The first 25 years of justice research in social psychology focused on distributive justice issues. In the mid-1970s emphasis shifted to concerns with procedural justice. Ten years later, distinctions between procedural and interactional justice emerged. Current trends in justice research (see Colquitt et al. 2005) capture ways in which the types of justice may be integrated. Despite the different emphases over the years, research examines fundamental questions regarding how people perceive injustice and how they respond to the experience of injustice – emotionally, cognitively, and behaviorally (see Hegtvedt 2006).

Skitka, Bauman, and Mullen (2008) distinguish these research waves in terms of motivations underlying justice, i.e., assumptions of people as: economic actors (i.e., *homo economicus*) in distributive justice approaches and as social actors, embedded in social groups (i.e., *homo socialis*) in procedural and, to some extent, interactional justice perspectives. They

note, however, increasing emphasis on moral actors (i.e., *homo moralis*), which leads to refor-
mulating the ways of asking traditional questions about justice judgments. Folger (1998, 2001;
Folger et al. 2005) and Skitka (e.g., Skitka et al. 2005, 2008), in particular, explicitly attempt
to bridge the morality/justice gap.

Distributive Justice Research: The *Homo Economicus* Wave

Early theorizing in distributive justice (Adams 1965, Blau 1964, Homans 1974, Walster et al.
1978) reflected the perspective's roots in social exchange approaches to interaction. This foundation produced three key consequences. First, the exchange perspectives to distributive justice
cast individuals as rational utility maximizers who pursue their self-interest. Second, the give-
and-take characterizing exchange resulted in emphasis on equity or the proportionality of
outcomes to inputs across actors as the normative principle of justice. Walster et al. (1978),
however, give a nod to the justice/morality link when they suggest that people work together
to create rules that ensure the distribution of fair outcomes for a collectivity. Yet, with the
equity principle as given, most theorizing focused primarily on responses to inequity or the
objective inequality in the outcome/input ratio of one person compared to that of another. The
emphasis on equity, coupled with its ease of assessment, resulted in the third consequence: little theorizing focused on factors affecting and the processes involved in producing subjective
perceptions of injustice – an issue addressed by more recent formulations (described below)
that additionally consider the justice/morality link.

   In general, distributive justice perspectives presume that injustice (inequity) produces
distress, which is uncomfortable. Injustice may be both materially (in the case of unexpected
lower outcomes) and psychologically costly, thus stimulating actions to relieve the distress
and redress the injustice. While Adams (1965) addresses distress only in a global fashion,
Homans (1974) specifies that those disadvantaged by the inequity are likely to feel angry and
those advantaged by the inequity may feel guilt if their advantage is at the expense of another
person. Adams (1965) further specifies that people are likely to adopt the least costly means
to redress injustice. He offers several different strategies, which Walster et al. (1978) characterized as means to restore psychological equity (e.g., altering one's evaluation of inputs or
outcomes of self or others) or actual equity (e.g., increasing own outcomes or decreasing a
partner's outcomes to equalize ratios of outcomes to inputs). The emphasis on a rational calculus pervades the equity perspectives. Such rationality and concomitant emphasis on material
outcomes seem to outweigh and thereby suppress attention to the moral underpinnings of justice. Yet, as analyzed further below, emotional responses are a cornerstone to recent justice
and morality approaches.

   A challenge to equity theory came from researchers who argued that equity is only one
principle, among many, of distributive justice (e.g., Deutsch 1975, Leventhal 1976, Reis 1986).
These arguments shifted attention from responses to injustice to goals and factors affecting
the use of equity, equality, and need distribution principles. Leventhal et al. (1980) proposed a
model of allocation preferences, which assumes that individuals hold expectancies about how
a given distribution principle facilitates or interferes with a goal or goals (e.g., self-interest,
fairness, efficiency, obedience to authority) in the situation. An allocator's preference reflects
the importance of each relevant goal and the expectancy regarding the principle(s) that will
lead to goal attainment. Insofar as self-interest may drive some allocation decisions, the main

means to disentangle what is just from simply justified self-interest (Leventhal 1980) is to contrast the allocation preferences of first-party decision makers who share in the distribution of outcomes to third parties who are not outcome recipients. Regardless of the emphasis on first or third parties, Leventhal's model of decision making is certainly instrumental and generally fits with the "rational actor" approach of the exchange models, even if it does not explicitly involve outcome maximization and cost minimization calculations. Implicitly, however, employing a distribution principle that is most likely to achieve a stated goal is likely to minimize the potential for the decision maker to feel distress or worry and most likely to produce the desired outcome.

In general, the early distributive justice approaches hardly discuss the role of morality in justice processes. The emphasis on rational, economic motivations echoes both the social exchange and the emerging cognitive perspectives of the 1960s and 1970s. These motivations also underlie early work in procedural justice.

Procedural and Interactional Justice Research: The *Homo Socialis* Wave

Early work in procedural justice addresses a question that distributive justice perspectives ignored: What procedures do decision makers use in collecting information on contributions or needs or, more generally, in allocating outcomes to a circle of recipients? Two perspectives, one emphasizing economic motives and the other social motives, emerged to address this question. Concerns with the latter motivation also prompted consideration of not simply of fairness in decision-making procedures, but also between parties affected by any decision. Interactional justice emphasizes fairness in how one person treats another and provides a basis for moving beyond *homo socialis* to initial glimmerings of *homo moralis*. Here we briefly describe the procedural justice tradition and the emergence of interactional justice as a separate domain.

Leventhal and colleagues (1980) attempt to answer the question regarding the decision-making processes underlying distributions. As noted above, they identify key rules (e.g., consistency, suppression of bias, representation) governing fairness in decision-making procedures. Additionally, they extend their expectancy approach to procedural justice, arguing that people prefer procedural rules that fulfill the most important situational goals. While there are few tests of their essentially rational model, many studies examine the extent to which people perceived the various rules as fair (see Tyler et al. 1997). These studies often compare what came to be known as the two key procedural justice perspectives: the instrumental approach of Thibaut and Walker (1975), which emphasizes how procedures provide control over outcomes, and the group value model of Lind and Tyler (1988), which focuses on how procedures used by authorities signal to individuals their status in social groups.

Thibaut and Walker (1975) focused on the perceived fairness of two forms of dispute resolution. The adversarial approach, used in the US legal system, provides the judge with control over the outcome but not the process of presenting information relevant to the case. In contrast, the inquisitorial approach, used in many European legal systems, gives the judge control over both the outcome and the procedure. Research generally indicates that individuals perceive adversarial approaches as more fair. People value procedural control – procedural justice – because they perceive it to increase the likelihood of achieving distributive justice as well. In effect, control over procedures is instrumental to obtaining desired outcomes, even in the absence of control over outcomes. Such instrumentality may also imply the pursuit of self advantage. As a consequence, Thibaut and Walker's emphasis on the instrumentality of procedures may seem at odds with a justice/morality link. Yet, their belief that "...the major aims of the legal process is to resolve conflicts in such a way as to bind up the social fabric and encourage the continuation of productive exchange between individuals" (Thibaut and Walker 1975:67) hints at such a link. An understanding of what people perceive as fair in adjudicating disputes serves to prevent harm and promote social welfare.

Lind and Tyler (1988), however, challenge the instrumental value of procedural justice and instead emphasize its social value, which may seem more consistent with a justice/morality link. They cite studies (e.g., Lind et al. 1983, Tyler et al. 1985) that show individuals preferring fair procedures in general, regardless of the impact of those procedures on outcome distributions. This non-instrumental preference for fair procedures provides the foundation for the group value/relational approach to procedural justice (Lind and Tyler 1988; Tyler and Lind 1992). Stemming from social identity work (e.g., Tajfel and Turner 1986), this approach argues that people seek positive social identities and that the experience of fairness in procedures (as well as distributions and interaction) signals that they are valued members of a group. In addition, people want to belong to valuable groups; the pride they feel in response to the status of their group then bolsters the individual's own self worth. The group value model, thus, emphasizes the social meaning of justice as a basis for understanding one's own worth. The relational model of authority identifies key aspects of interpersonal treatment – respect, trustworthiness, and neutrality – that also communicate social information.[2] And, more recently, Tyler and Blader (2000, Blader and Tyler 2005) extend the group value formulation by indicating the consequences of procedural justice for social cooperation.

The emphasis on social value and cooperation in these procedural justice approaches underlies the metaphor *homo socialis*. Such imagery, moreover, evokes a more explicit justice/morality link. Concern focuses on groups and their individual members, suggesting consideration of the collectivity and its well being, consistent with some aspects of normative morality. Yet, the distinction between *homo socialis* and the *homo economicus* of the distributive justice models is somewhat illusory (Gillespie and Greenberg 2005, Hegtvedt 2006, van Prooijen 2008). Both models suggest that individuals seek to maximize their rewards – social rewards in the case of procedural justice and material rewards in the case of distributive justice. The extent to which a focus on oneself or on others (see Gillespie and Greenberg 2005) drives the pursuit of either or both reward types may clarify the justice/morality link. Although justice should be about a collectivity, most distributive and procedural justice studies examine the perceptions and responses of individuals in isolation from each other (see Hegtvedt 2005). Interactional justice brings the dynamic of the interacting group members to the forefront.

Research in interactional justice has sought to determine what people perceive as just in terms of the quality of interpersonal treatment in ongoing interaction – encounters between people, especially authorities and subordinates. These encounters may have nothing to do with a decision or resource allocation. Early studies (e.g., Bies and Moag 1986, Folger and

---

[2] Tyler and Lind (1992) suggest that procedural justice involves both a focus on decision-making rules and on interpersonal treatment. The relational model of authority highlights the latter with its emphasis on respect, trustworthiness, and neutrality. Others, however, suggest that the interpersonal element actually represents interactional justice (see Bies 2001; Cohen-Charash and Spector 2001; Colquitt et al. 2001). Except in specifically discussing Tyler and Lind's work, we consider the interpersonal aspect of procedural justice as part of interactional justice.

Bies 1989) identified a number of rules (e.g., respect, trust, truthfulness, justification) that characterize interactional justice. And later work clearly indicates that interactional justice is distinct from the structural elements of decision making covered by procedural justice (see Bies 2005).

Yet, because of its emergence in the context of procedural justice work, researchers adapt tenets of the group-value/relational models to suggest that people value interactional justice because it indicates their worth to the group and reinforces a positive social identity. And, to explain responses to interactional injustice, arguments parallel inequity premises about distress and motivation to relieve it through psychological or behavioral responses (e.g., Greenberg 1993, Brockner et al. 1994). A key category in studies of responses to interactional injustice involves "organizational citizenship behaviors," which include individual discretionary behaviors that, in the aggregate, promote the functioning of the organization.[3] Such behaviors, in effect, support the welfare of the group to which workers belong. For example, to the extent that subordinates do not perceive that their supervisor trusts them (i.e., interactional injustice exists) they are less likely to engage in organizational citizenship behaviors; conversely, the perception of trust enhances those behaviors (e.g., Aryee et al. 2002; Konovsky and Pugh 1994).

While interactional justice clearly draws attention to the social elements of a situation and to the potential for group welfare, like other justice processes, an assumption of rationality underlies interactional justice processes. Yet distinct from other approaches is the belief that the rationality may benefit the larger group as well as the individual. Thus, interactional justice begins to hint at the possibility that justice processes involve what Folger (1998) characterizes as a basic drive to respect human dignity or, in other words, to uphold moral virtues.

THE *INEVITABLE* LINK: THE *HOMO MORALIS* WAVE IN JUSTICE RESEARCH

A good portion of early social psychological work on procedural and interactional justice focused on determining what rules represent each type of justice, respectively. Then, like distributive justice work examining the conditions under which different distribution rules are considered fair, researchers began to investigate factors affecting the perceptions of procedural and interactional justice as well as responses to injustice. With emphasis on perceptions of justice per se, efforts in recent years have focused on circumscribing the "moral communities" to which the justice evaluations apply and to developing models that attempt to integrate distributive, procedural, and interactional justice processes (see Blader and Tyler 2005; Colquitt et al. 2005). In doing so, some of these models continue in the traditions of earlier, separate justice models, while others begin with the revolutionizing notion of *homo moralis*. Concomitant with the emergence of new theoretical approaches is empirical work addressing the experience of moral emotions in response to injustice and the responses of observers to others' injustice.

---

[3] At issue is the violation of rules such as respect or trust, although early studies place these rules under the procedural justice rubric and later studies under interactional justice.

Theorizing: Moral Communities and Integrated Models

Moral Communities. Preceding the emergence and evolution of integrative models that highlight *homo moralis*, Opotow (1990b) drew attention to the need to specify the scope of justice in the analysis of justice perceptions and associated reactions. Consistent with arguments in descriptive moral philosophy, Opotow (1990b) suggests that individuals "have beliefs about the sorts of beings that should be treated justly" and that "moral values, rules, and considerations of fairness apply only to those within this boundary for fairness" (p. 3). The boundaries for fairness, in effect, refer to a perceiver's moral community. Presumably, members of one's moral community are other people whose wellbeing matters to the perceiver. As a consequence, the perceiver is likely to act in a moral way toward those community members, sharing conceptions of justice and community resources, and potentially making sacrifices to promote a community member's wellbeing. An individual's moral community is particularly important in assessing the fairness of a distribution of valued outcomes to a group of recipients other than oneself (i.e., third party or observers' assessments, as discussed below).

While a moral community may promote certain types of distributions, procedures, or treatment as fair within its boundaries, it may also shun or even harm people outside of the community's boundaries. Opotow (1990b) describes the process of moral exclusion, which provides the basis for treating excluded individuals and groups as, at best, nonentities, and, at worst, expendable. As a consequence, moral exclusion provides a basis to justify unfairness, ill-treatment, or even harm to individuals or groups outside of a given moral community. Moral exclusion processes are inherent in "we–they" distinctions characterizing inter-group behavior. Historical examples of the consequences of moral exclusion abound, e.g., the internment of Japanese Americans during World War II (Nagata 1993) or the treatment of Black Americans during the Jim Crow era (Opotow 2008).

Although, in theory, the boundaries of any moral community may be somewhat fluid, as Opotow (1990a, 1995) notes, boundaries are likely to grow more rigid resulting in intensification of moral exclusion in times of conflict. Deterring moral exclusion requires expansion of the moral community and support for dissent or unconventional beliefs, especially from members within a given community (Opotow 1990a). The latter strategy implicitly highlights the potential importance of observers in securing justice beyond a bounded group. Moreover, hinted at in the categorization processes underlying moral exclusion, the potential to deter it may also lie in consideration of other types of information and focus on various (not just distributive) types of justice as well. Although largely independent of discussion of the scope of justice or of conflict situations, the integrative theories attempt to address how one type of justice influences evaluations of another type.

Integrated Models. Although how one type of justice affects another does not necessarily have any bearing on the justice/morality link, the evolution of these models demonstrates increasing consideration with issues of morality. The recent work of Folger (1998, 2001; Folger et al. 2005) and Skitka (Skitka et al. 2005, 2008) in particular highlight the role of morality.

General Integrative Models and Movement toward Morality Concerns. Fairness heuristic theory (Lind 2001, Van den Bos et al. 2001) and its related uncertainty management theory (see Van den Bos 2005, Van den Bos and Lind 2002) presume that people make justice judgments and evaluate the trustworthiness of authorities under conditions of uncertainty. As a consequence, they look for cues in the situation to direct their evaluations. These cues allow for mental shortcuts or heuristics to simplify fairness judgments, especially about the directives of authorities regarding resource allocations. These heuristic approaches combine types of justice by suggesting that information on one type may be used to assess another type. The "fair process effect" is the classic instantiation of these approaches: to the extent that an authority uses fair procedures, individuals are more likely to judge their outcomes as fair (in the absence of information on the outcomes of others) (Van den Bos et al. 1997). In effect, these models echo the "rationality" implicit in the instrumental and even group-value model discussed above.

Just as fairness heuristic theory depends upon individuals' cognitive assessments in the situation as a precursor to their fairness judgments, Folger (1986) introduces referential thinking and later counter-factual thinking (Folger and Cropanzano 1998, 2001) as a means for people to more thoroughly assess why procedures used to make distributions were unfair or why their outcomes fell short of those expected based on a distributive justice principle. The earlier referent cognition model suggests that people ask themselves "what might have been" in order to evaluate what actually happened. Importantly, Folger argues evaluations of injustice and feelings of resentment emerge when referent cognitions suggest that: (1) better outcomes could be imagined; (2) there is little hope for better outcomes; and (3) there is little justification for the level of received outcomes (see e.g., Folger and Martin 1986). Although inclusion of justification and its role in ameliorating felt injustice helps to understand justice perceptions, Folger (1993) recognized that justification does not distinguish causal responsibility from moral obligation.

To redress this issue, Folger and Cropanzano (1998, 2001) developed fairness theory, which conceptualizes cognitive assessments – even automatic ones – in terms of "if only" or counter-factual statements about the authority or perpetrator's behavior. Such statements figuratively "undo" an event by imagining it otherwise. The aim of fairness theory is to illustrate how perceivers come to attribute blame to an authority for an injustice. Blame is likely when individuals imagine that "if only had the authority acted otherwise" that they *would* have been better off, coupled with the belief that the authority *could* have and, importantly, *should* have acted otherwise. The "would" question implicitly taps into the comparison at the heart of justice evaluations between what was expected (based on a justice principle) and what actually occurred. The "could" question indicates the extent to which the authority might have had discretion in making the decision or distribution. And, the "should" question underlies concerns about moral obligation and ethical conduct principles. Although "fairness theory does not imply that people construe all behavior as calling for a moral judgment," (Folger et al. 2005:233), when individuals' analyses emphasize the "should" question, issues of morality are likely to arise. Moreover, responses to how an authority *should* have acted may trigger particular emotional responses, which inevitably link justice evaluations and morality.

Folger's Approach to Justice and Morality. With its emphasis on moral accountability, fairness theory fits with what Folger (1998, 2001; Folger et al. 2005) calls a deonic conceptual framework for understanding justice processes. Stemming from the Greek term *deon*, referring to that which is binding or obligatory, the framework emphasizes how injustice may trigger strong emotional responses and behaviors that are independent of individuals' self-interests with regard to either material or social rewards. The deonic perspective suggests that to the extent that an injustice involves a violation of a moral principle, the "transgressor" has placed himself or herself above others, pursuing self-interests without regard for others' welfare. When unfair conduct constitutes such ethical wrongdoing, people affected by the transgression as well as those who have observed it are likely to be upset. In effect, the injustice disrupts the fabric of the social group and spurs emotional responses.

Folger et al. (2005) argue that such consequences reflect the "evolved predispositions of humans as a species rather than the current self-interest of a given individual" (p. 220). In other words, when distributions, procedures, or interactions violate moral standards, they trigger automatic, "hardwired" emotional arousal and action in response to injustice. The emotions may take the form of "moral outrage" or deonic anger in response to an authority's failure to act in a manner consistent with moral accountability.[4] As described more fully below, deonic anger may characterize the response of people who observe the injustices suffered by others (e.g., Ellard and Skarlicki 2002; Turillo et al. 2002). Such emotional responses may lead to the suspension of rationally calculated behaviors and, consequently, involve acts of retribution for their own sake.

The moral virtues approach of Folger and his colleagues recognizes that not all instances of unfairness constitute moral violations. The approach ties justice to morality with its notion of moral accountability. Yet even in the absence of clear moral accountability, justice evaluations driven by material or relational concerns may take on moral connotations when individuals attempt to justify certain behaviors.

Skitka's Approach to Justice and Morality. Skitka and colleagues (Skitka et al. 2005, 2008) likewise recognize that justice and moral evaluations do not fully overlap. They contrast subjective individual preferences for what constitute fair distributions, procedures, or treatment with those defined by normative conventions (based on formal or informal group rules) and those shaped by moral convictions. The latter, in contrast to the two former approaches to justice evaluations, transcend situational contexts and imply that others should feel the same way about a given distribution, procedure, or treatment. As such, moral standards are universal and objective notions of right and wrong (Skitka et al. 2008). These moral beliefs influence individuals' conceptions of fairness regarding certain issues (Skitka 2002).

Skitka et al.'s (2008) integrated theory of moral conviction (ITMC) suggests that humans, as moral beings, have a predisposition to care about morality concerns above and beyond material self-interest (*homo economicus*) and the need to belong to a group (*homo socialis*). Three key ideas underlie ITMC: authority independence, moral certainty, and moral emotions. Emphasis on emotions resonates with Folger and other researchers' formulations as indicated by the review in the next section. In a series of specific studies, however, Skitka and her colleagues offer evidence regarding the extent to which people's fairness evaluations are independent of the dictates of authorities and situations eliciting responses based on moral certainty.

The ITMC proposes that moral motivation comes from within an individual rather than from the conventions of a group. Skitka et al. (2008) anchor this claim in research indicating that origins of right and wrong in humans may be relatively innate and that young children recognize moral wrongs, despite what their teachers or parents might indicate.[5] Their research supports

---

[4] Folger et al. (2005) label anger as "deonic" when it is in response to the violation of moral dictates and not simply a violation of individual interests.

[5] The ITMC's emphasis on moral emotions in the absence of significant deliberation is consistent with Haidt's (2001) social intuitionist model of morality, which suggests that emotions are sources or predictors of moral judgment. As

the "authority independence hypothesis," which predicts that individuals are more likely to reject and fail to comply with decisions made by legitimate authorities when they run counter to their moral convictions about policy issues (regarding, for example, physician-assisted suicide, capital murder cases, abortion) than when they depart from normative conventions (e.g., adherence to procedural justice rules) (Skitka 2006, Skitka and Houston 2001, Skitka and Mullen 2008). Results suggest that "perceived legitimacy and procedural fairness does not increase adults' willingness to accept authorities' decisions when those decisions are at odds with perceivers' personal moral convictions" (Skitka et al. 2008:11).

Indeed, various situations elicit evaluations of outcomes or procedures based on moral certainty. Although much research (noted above) suggests that people use procedural information to evaluate the likelihood of achieving their own desired level of outcomes or of ensuring their value to the group, in some situations people have moral certainty about what the outcomes should be, i.e., what authorities should deliver and how they should do so. Those moral convictions exist as a "litmus test" of the fairness and legitimacy of individuals or groups making outcome decisions. In evaluating people's reactions to public policy decisions, studies show that regardless of the presence of procedural fairness, individuals nonetheless experience injustice when a policy decision threatens their moral convictions (Skitka and Mullen 2002). People are more likely to perceive outcomes that match moral standards as fair and legitimate than outcomes that fail to match such standards, even if they involve procedural justice (Mullen and Nadler 2008, Mullen and Skitka 2006, Skitka and Houston 2001).

Studies examining the authority independence and litmus test hypotheses derived from the ITMC focus generally on policies regarding situations in which the perceivers may not be directly embedded or affected. As such, the individuals act as observers of injustices suffered by others. The work of Folger, Skitka, and their colleagues not only make explicit the long implied, yet too often ignored, link between justice and morality but also directs focus on two growing bodies of empirical work: emotional responses to injustice (especially those driven by moral convictions) and responses of observers.

Research Domains and Directions

Decades ago, Leventhal (1980) recognized how difficult it is to distinguish justice evaluations driven by self-interested motivations from those inspired by justice per se – concern for the welfare of others and upholding shared normative principles. Such an abstract notion of justice, as noted above, resonates with a moral sense of justice, but it remains difficult to assess empirically. Here we review two domains of studies that attempt to capture the implications of moral elements of justice. First, while emotional and other responses have characterized justice research since Adams (1965) offered his formulation of equity theory, more recently researchers have discerned specific moral emotions and the conditions eliciting them. And second, while some early work on allocation preferences differentiated the views of recipients (first parties) and non-recipients (third parties) of outcomes, only recently have many studies probed the role of third parties or observers of injustice, our second domain.

---

such, moral judgments result from autonomic and intuitive processes. The need to justify conclusions or persuade others (Haidt 2003) then prompts more controlled moral reasoning.

Moral Emotions and Responses to Injustice. The emotional responses specified by early distributive justice theorists and by procedural justice theorists stem from unfulfilled expectations about outcomes or procedures based on underlying concerns with personal material or social interests. A number of studies over the years have examined such responses (see Cropanzano et al. 2000, Hegtvedt 2006, Tyler et al. 1997). In justice situations, when expectations are met (either by upholding procedural or interactional principles or ensuring equitable outcomes) people feel happy or satisfied. In contrast, the failure to meet expectations and to be disadvantaged as a result meets with an array of outwardly focused, negative emotions such as anger, frustration, and resentment. Evidence with regard to unfairness that advantages the perceiver is mixed; the anticipated experience of guilt is usually weak, unless the advantage results from or produces someone else's disadvantage. These emotional responses to perceived injustice focus on consequences for the self or social norms, and are thus arguably distinct from those driven by moral convictions.

Specifically, moral emotions are (emphasis in original) "those emotions that are linked to the interests or welfare either of society as a whole or at least of persons other than the judge or agent" (Haidt 2003:853). Although sometimes sharing the same label as emotions identified in response to various types of injustice, emotions become moral when they occur as a reaction to conformity to or deviance from moral standards or codes, not simply normative violations (Haidt 2003, Hitlin 2008, Skoe et al. 2002,Turner and Stets 2006). Skitka et al. (2008) argue that moral emotions are stronger and more intense than those motivated by personal interests or normative conventions that characterize many justice approaches because they threaten core values. Haidt (2003) also notes that moral emotions imply a tendency toward pro-social action and represent the disinterest of the elicitors, such as successes, tragedies, and transgressions that do not directly affect the self. In effect, Haidt would contend that moral emotions must be "other" rather than self-focused and tied to moral convictions.[6] Yet as described above, an abstract conceptualization of justice involves promotion of social welfare and extends beyond individual self-interests. Perceptions of injustice that threaten the fabric of society beyond an individual's or group's specific interests thus potentially produce moral emotions, which in turn may inspire actions to restore justice and maintain moral codes.

To address the role of moral emotions in response to injustice, we first provide a brief overview of existing conceptualizations of such emotions, focusing largely on those that resonate with existing justice approaches. We then review research examining moral emotions in justice situations. We extend our analysis beyond social psychological justice work to include research on the purpose and consequences of stimulating feelings of shame in perpetrators of criminal acts as a means of redressing injustice suffered by others and at the same time re-integrating the perpetrator into the social group in order to uphold moral codes.

Moral Emotions. Haidt (2003) offers a typology of moral emotions in which he identifies conditions soliciting a type of emotion and behaviors that may follow from the experience of the emotion. His categories include: other-condemning (e.g., anger, disgust, contempt); self-conscious (e.g., shame, guilt, embarrassment); other-suffering (e.g., empathy, sympathy); and

---

[6] Although characterized by a focus on others, Haidt (2003) also recognizes that these emotions may provide indirect benefits to the self. The experience of moral emotions may lead to moral behavior that enhances the reputation of the actor and the likelihood that others will cooperate with him or her in the future (Haidt 2007).

other-praising (gratitude, awe, elevation). Justice studies examining moral emotions typically fall into the first two categories while other-suffering emotions may motivate observers to respond to another person's injustice.

"Other-condemning" emotions pertain to the actions and character of others who have violated important moral standards especially those pertaining to relationships (see also Hitlin 2008). Anger results when individuals perceive that their own or others' autonomy has been violated (Rozin et al. 1999) and occurs in response to unjustified affronts and blocked goals (Haidt 2003). Such violations indicate harm of some type – compromising or denying rights, freedoms, and choices or actual bodily or property injuries (Rozin et al. 1999) – which addresses the core of philosophical approaches to morality. Anger leads individuals to attack, humiliate, or get back at the perceived source of injustice or immorality, including making demands for compensation for victims (Haidt 2003). Capturing reactions to instances of extreme biases, prejudice, and other harmful social violations (Haidt 2003, Hitlin 2008), disgust propels people to avoid, expel, and cease contact with perpetrators of this emotion.

The experience of self-conscious emotions of shame and guilt in response to violations of personal and social standards provide a basis for upholding the social structure (Hitlin 2008). Shame results when a person acts in a manner inconsistent with his or her self-definition in the community and thus fails to meet expected standards of morality, aesthetics, or competence (Haidt 2003). Feelings of shame may be stigmatizing and thus lead to withdrawal from a community, or they may allow for renewed connections to the community (i.e., reintegrative shaming, as discussed below) (Hitlin 2008). Guilt generally stems from causing harm in specific interpersonal relationships (Haidt 2003, Hitlin 2008) and may prompt remorse and regret regarding such acts (Turner and Stets 2006). As a consequence, guilt may motivate people to make up for their behavior or to help a victim (Haidt 2003).

Although classified as other-suffering emotions, empathy and sympathy are akin to role-taking techniques that prompt the experience of emotion (Turner and Stets 2006). Typically, empathy occurs when an individual shares another person's emotional state whereas sympathy arises with the sharing of another's distress (Hitlin 2008). Experiencing empathy or sympathy – in effect sharing another's feelings – may prompt compassion about another's suffering and encourages comfort, or alleviate that suffering (Haidt 2003).[7]

While most other moral emotions focus on responses to types of harms, other-praising emotions signal responses to positive moral actions (Hitlin 2008). For example, people feel gratitude when they are the beneficiaries of intentional and voluntary good deeds performed by others (Haidt 2003). Such feelings, in turn, enhance trust and social cohesion by tying the giver to the receiver (Hitlin 2008, Turner and Stets 2006). In effect, other-praising emotions cement pro-social behavior that benefits a moral community.

Conceptualization of moral emotions highlights the importance of considering how a belief or behavior will impact not simply the self but others as well. Montada (1998) notes that justice is not purely related to individuals' self-focused interests. Consistent with arguments above, he suggests that justice may function as an "ought," independent of the rationality

---

[7] Turner and Stets (2006) note, however, that guilt, empathy, and sympathy may be used to maintain power over others and thus undermine the moral order.

of individuals and resulting in the experience of righteous anger or moral outrage, emotions strongly associated with moral violations.

Injustice and the Experience of Moral Emotions. Violation of moral standards (not simply personal expectations) underlying justice evaluations produces the experience of moral emotions. As noted above, Folger (1998, 2001; Folger et al. 2005) and Skitka (Skitka et al. 2008) anchor responses to injustice stemming from moral convictions to emotions, in particular anger or, in Folger's terms, "deonic" anger. The latter is akin to the moral outrage conceptualized by other researchers who likewise examine responses to injustice driven by violations of moral standards (e.g., Batson et al. 2007, Jost et al. 2008). In addition to anger, Montada and colleagues (Kals and Montada 1994, Montada 1998, Montada et al. 1986) provide some evidence on guilt as a moral response to injustice. And, others link the experience of moral emotions to self identities (Stets and Carter 2006) in justice situations.

Skitka and colleagues (2008) provide evidence of feelings of intense anger in response to justice situations involving threats to moral convictions regarding various policy issues. People are likely to experience anger in response to outcomes that conflict with moral beliefs and, as a consequence, rate the decisions that produced those outcomes as unfair (Mullen and Skitka 2006, Mullen and Nadler 2008). Even though people might remember procedural information, the activation of moral convictions decreases considerations of procedural justice when evaluating the resulting outcomes. In a related study, Bauman (2006) conceptualizes moral outrage as a combination or anger and disgust. He shows that moral outrage in response to a fictive university decision mediates the relationship between moral disagreement with the policy and intentions to protest or sever ties with particular groups, regardless of decision-making procedures. Such results imply that people may use more intuitive or emotional processes to infer justice. Given the results from this line of investigation, Skitka et al. (2008:21) claim that it appears that "people's emotions in response to morally relevant events have the potential to influence not just their fairness judgments, but also the process through which they arrive at their judgments." In effect, strongly felt moral emotions may prompt action without conscious deliberation of reasons for particular behaviors (Folger et al. 2005).

Jost et al. (2008) also focus on the evaluation of policies that have moral connotations. They examine how system justifying ideologies attenuate feelings of moral outrage thereby reducing support for policies that would redistribute resources to benefit the disadvantaged. Following the work of Montada et al. (1986), they define moral outrage as feelings of distress over injustice and inequality, measuring it with items such as: "I feel really angry when I learn about people who are suffering from injustice," "I believe that we should all work together to help those who are disadvantaged," "I think it's shameful that people allow injustice to occur," and the like. Also included is a measure of existential guilt (i.e., guilt over one's advantages or privileges). As expected, believing that the system of inequality is justified decreased both moral outrage and existential guilt. Moral outrage (but not existential guilt) positively affected support for redistribution and mediated the effects of system justifying ideology on redistribution. Such results demonstrate the power of moral outrage to affect support for policies clearly consistent with what might be considered just and morally right by enhancing the welfare of others.

Batson et al.'s (2007) work on moral outrage takes a relatively more explicit approach to the relationship between moral convictions and justice. On the theoretical level, they anchor moral outrage to violations of justice principles (equality, in particular) and explicitly distinguish it from personal anger (in response to having one's personal interests thwarted) and even empathetic anger (arising when the interests of a cared-for other are hindered). Presumably, personal and empathetic anger lead individuals to retaliate and to promote their own or others' interests; in contrast, moral outrage is likely to stimulate responses that reaffirm or re-establish the moral standard that was violated. Despite these arguments, experimental results in which subjects and others were treated unfairly produced only personal and empathetic anger. The "anger against humanity" implied by moral outrage may be difficult to tap into in the absence of a more specific target, such as the social policies examined in the research noted above.

While moral outrage is characteristically an emotion attributed to victims of injustice, existential guilt attempts to tap into the moral convictions of those who are advantaged by a social system. Although Jost et al. (2008) found no support for a relationship between existential guilt and redistribution policies, other work suggests that feelings of guilt emerge in response to unjustly disadvantaged victims; such feelings, moreover, inspire people to act in pro-social ways to benefit the disadvantaged (Montada 1998). In effect, those pro-social behaviors hold the potential to correct a moral wrong that has harmed individuals by reducing their resources. Research on pro-environmental commitments reinforces this idea by indicating that guilt (over one's own polluting behavior) motivates actions to ensure environmental justice (i.e., people living now and in the future have the right to enjoy the natural world) (Kals and Montada 1994). Violation of moral mandates regarding what is just in the distribution of natural resources across generations stimulates guilt and subsequent engagement in pro-environmental actions.

As implied above, emotions serve as signals of a disjuncture between a moral mandate or expectations based on justice principles and what actually occurs. The experience of emotions not only ties the individual to social structure and culture through self-awareness but also indicates feelings about oneself and one's identities (Turner and Stets 2006). Stets and Carter (2006) argue that negative moral emotions emerge when moral identities are inconsistent with behavior in response to moral dilemmas. They provide evidence that when people fail to live up to a moral identity of being caring and just, feelings of guilt and shame emerge. Being tied to the social structure through moral conceptions of the self, moreover, produces moral emotions when people perceive that allocations of status and prestige violate perceptions of fairness. In contrast to violations, confirming one's moral identity provides a basis for maintaining a favorable view of oneself as a moral and just person, which in turn influences subsequent justice judgments.

In a similar vein, Skitka (2002) offers a "value protection model" of justice reasoning. She argues that people are likely to judge as fair outcomes of decisions consistent with their moral convictions. When these convictions are threatened, in order to protect personal identities, individuals respond with moral emotions such as moral outrage that may be directed toward themselves or others who have led them to break their moral mandates. In addition, people will seek out ways to reaffirm themselves as good persons through acts of moral cleansing.

To the extent that injustice involves violations of moral convictions, individuals are likely to experience negative moral emotions, which may propel pro-social actions to restore a sense of justice or a positive moral identity. Importantly, the experience of moral emotions represents a connection between the individual and the welfare of a social group. In some instances, then, authorities can use the experience of negative moral emotions – especially shame – to reconnect individuals with the groups in which they are embedded and thereby promote future pro-social behaviors. As Hitlin (2008) notes, individuals are less likely to engage in anti-social or criminal behaviors if they understand those actions to be morally wrong and harmful to their community.

Reintegrative Shaming. In a broad sense, criminal behaviors violate justice principles. Destroying or stealing property inherently challenges notions of distributive justice and the intentional injury of a person is an extreme from of interactional injustice. One means of redressing injustices wrought by criminal behavior involves reintegrative shaming processes, which bring together issues of morality, justice, and emotions in order to curtail such behavior.

Specifically, reintegrative shaming incorporates condemnation of a criminal offence with the intent of invoking moral regret in the offender and subsequently motivating pro-social behavior through re-establishing ties with the community of law-abiding citizens (Hay 2001, Braithwaite 1989). The community instills guilt in the offender about how a particular act has done harm to others. Reintegrative shaming is most effective in reducing recidivism when there is consensus in the community regarding the immorality of the offense, the procedures involved in the shaming process are fair, and offenders meet with social approval when they acknowledge the wrongness of their past acts and make reparations for any harm that they have caused (Hay 2001, Tyler et al. 2007). These processes, in turn, may lead to the re-identification of positive aspects of the self and the desire to maintain links to significant others.

Botchkovar and Tittle (2005), however, caution that shaming may also lead to intense personal feelings of anger or embarrassment reflecting the offender's belief that his or her interests have been sacrificed or to the belief that criminal behaviors do not result in loss of respect from others. To eliminate these competing emotions and thus ensure the success of reintegrative shaming, it is imperative that the offender and community members share moral beliefs and standards.[8]

Summary. Moral emotions provide the impetus for individuals to enforce their moral beliefs and convictions (Kroll and Egan 2004) and provide the link between moral standards and moral behavior (Hitlin 2008). Like the emotions associated with (in)justice that influence subsequent behavior, moral emotions drive individuals to engage in actions that confirm their moral beliefs and their moral identities (Skitka 2002, Stets and Carter 2006). To date, most of the work linking morality, justice, and emotions pertains to other-condemning and self-conscious moral emotions. Feelings of anger and outrage, in particular, focus on evaluations of policies relevant to justice principles, but not on actual distributions, procedures, or treatments of groups. Reintegrative shaming processes are directed at an individual, but hold the promise of benefits for a community (i.e., reduction of crime and reinforcement of community-wide moral standards). While the studies reviewed above begin the process of investigating moral emotions in justice situations, a number of research questions remain.

First, as implied by Jost et al. (2008), what structural, cultural, and individual-level factors stimulate different moral emotions? Second, although scholars repeatedly state that moral emotions should evoke moral behaviors, how are behaviors associated with different moral emotions? Do feelings of shame or guilt result in different actions than behaviors inspired by anger or outrage? And, third, few studies investigate other-suffering or other-praising emotions. How might those emotions arise in justice situations? Much of the research on moral emotions and justice relies on responses to policies – in effect, perceivers are third parties.

---

[8] Shaming may be "disintegrative" when it stigmatizes and precludes affirmation of the offender's basic goodness of character and membership in the community. Under such circumstances, offenders fail to re-establish ties with the law-abiding community and instead seek out criminal subcultures (Braithwaite 1989, Hay 2001). Disintegrative shaming may also stimulate illicit and self-destructive behaviors (Tangney 1994, Ahmed and Braithwaite 2005).

Below we review in more detail how morality and justice intersect by examining research on how observers perceive and respond to justice for others. To some extent, their responses are indirectly influenced by implied other-suffering, role-taking techniques involving empathy.

Observers' Responses to Others' Injustice. Most of the work on the social psychology of justice has taken as its focus perceptions of and reactions to personal injustices and thus paid little attention to observers' responses to others' injustice. As noted above, with such a focus it is often difficult to discern whether self or social interests drive people's perceptions and responses. As a consequence, some early studies examining allocation preferences contrasted first and presumably impartial third parties' evaluations of "fair" distribution rules (Leventhal 1976). That research, however, was limited to discerning the conditions under which people designate equity, equality, and needs principles as fair. Little analysis of the moral underpinnings of such evaluations accompanied the studies. Currently two strains of work focus on how observers respond to the suffering of others.

The first pertains to work in the area of the justice motive or just world beliefs (Lerner 1975, 1977, 1980, 2003). Insofar as Lerner argues that people are intrinsically motivated to behave fairly, the perspective parallels more recent considerations of *homo moralis*. Moreover, empirical work examines third parties' reactions to others' disadvantage (see Hafer and Bégue 2005). Yet, in contrast to what a moral perspective would suggest, many studies show that the more intensely individuals believe in a just world, the more likely they are to discount the suffering of others. The second area of work focuses specifically on the role of third parties in evaluating and responding to others' injustices (see Skarlicki and Kulik 2005). While third parties should be impartial, what they witness may carry implications for their own situations in the future thereby compromising the extent to which their evaluations reflect moral concerns. Even though analysis of observers is an imperfect approach to understanding the justice/morality link, it provides insight to how this linkage might be examined in the future.

The Justice Motive and Just World Beliefs. Lerner (1977, 1980) suggests that individuals have a general desire for justice in social interactions (the justice motive) and thus want to believe that the world is just (just world beliefs). Together, the motive and beliefs translate into the expectation that people get what (outcomes or treatment) they deserve and deserve what they get. As such, distinct from our above formulation, justice is defined in terms of deserving. Yet, like our emphasis, Lerner (2003) contends that the justice motive is a source of motivation, independent from self-interests and often emotionally generated.[9]

To support this argument, he compares situations in which any injustice would have little impact to those in which injustice might have great impact. He draws on Bazerman et al. (1995) to show that in low impact situations individuals engaging in thoughtful decision-making (even if using cognitive heuristics to interpret information) are likely to justify maximizing their own outcomes rather than pursuing fairness. In contrast, to the extent that situations involve vivid, compelling injustices, i.e., high impact situations, they elicit automatic, intuitive responses – moral intuitions tied to strong emotions (Hafer 2000a, Lerner et al. 1998, Mikula et al. 1998). While the emotions may stimulate thoughtful moral judgments, they also fuel behaviors to

---

[9] Lerner (2003) attributes the empirical evidence suggesting that justice evaluations reflect normative expectations associated with rational self-interests to the nature of the methodology of those studies and an emphasis on first party evaluations.

redress injustice. In this way, Lerner's ideas parallel the effects outlined for the experience of moral emotions. And, while just world beliefs encourage helping injustice victims, other strategies also exist (Lerner 1980).

Ironically, especially given Lerner's (2003) strong commitment to highlighting the moral element of the justice motive, many studies show that the "belief in a just world" (BJW) may lead people to derogate victims of injustice, which, in effect, may cause harm (see Lerner 1980, Hafer and Bégue 2005). Innocent victims, who appear to have little responsibility for their negative outcomes, threaten individuals' beliefs in a just world by implying that a similar fate may befall them. As a consequence, people with a strong BJW may dissociate from and derogate injustice victims in order to protect themselves from a similar fate (Hafer 2000b; see also Hafer and Bégue 2005). In other words, BJW leads people to tolerate unjust treatment of others and conclude that those who experience injustice merit it (Olson and Hafer 2001). The same beliefs, additionally, provide a basis for making internal attributions for personal injustices, which in turn result in the experience of less anger and shame, leading to acquiescence with lower outcomes (Hafer and Correy 1999). Moreover, people who tend to tolerate personal deprivation are less likely to help others who experience injustice (Olson and Hafer 2001).

An alternative to derogation is responding directly to the perpetrator of another's injustice. Patterns emerging from correlational studies (e.g., Mohr and Luscri 1995; see Hafer and Bégue 2005) demonstrate that individuals holding strong just world beliefs are more likely to support punitive measures toward perpetrators in criminal justice cases. Another way to maintain belief in a just world in the face of others' suffering is by condemning the perpetrator (Ellard et al. 2002). By labeling the perpetrator as evil, observers recognize the injustice results from an anomaly in the way that the world usually works.

Other labels also reinforce just world beliefs. By labeling an injustice as senseless (Lodewijkx et al. 2001) or by relying upon a belief in ultimate justice – i.e., the notion that regardless of a current situational injustice, justice will prevail eventually (Maes 1998, Maes and Kals 2002) – people defend against threats to their just world beliefs. While helping victims and punishing perpetrators are means to rectify injustice, the labeling strategies do little to redress injustice. In comparison to derogating victims, however, they allow more consistency between maintaining a belief in the just world and the moral dictate of doing no harm.

Work in the tradition of just world beliefs highlights the justice motive in social groups and draws attention to how people attempt to maintain those beliefs and in doing so potentially redress the injustice of others. As Hafer and Bégue (2005) point out, however, much of the research has concentrated on BJW as an individual difference factor and, as a consequence, has deviated from the early emphasis on how the motive holds promise for ensuring justice in the collectivity. Of course, as noted above, the conceptualization of justice as deserving in the formulation is relatively narrow. In addition, the empirical focus on victims of assault or illness ignores the breadth of types of injustice that exist in groups. Thus, BJW studies essentially involve a limited form of injustice. In contrast, more recent work on third party responses to injustice attempts to examine responses to different forms of injustice.

Third-Party Justice Perceptions and Responses. In principle, observers' perceptions of and responses to others' injustice are likely to reflect more neutral interests than those of first parties. Third parties, by definition, are not recipients of the outcomes of a particular distribution, or the specific target of a decision-making procedure or treatment. Observers, however, are likely to make justice evaluations in a manner similar to that employed by individuals who personally suffer an injustice (Skarlicki and Kulik 2005). In other words, personal characteristics and motives coupled with situational factors shape the cognitive processes underlying third parties' perceptions of injustice and their subsequent emotional and behavioral responses to injustice suffered by another person.

Despite the similarity in the justice process for first and third parties, Skarlicki and Kulik (2005) note that the latter may possess different motives, access different types of information, and respond in different ways. Importantly, unlike a victim's personal response, the reactions of third parties may facilitate or constrain the development of unethical behavior, especially within an organization. With regard to observers, then, justice and morality may potentially be linked through underlying motives and the consequences of their reactions for the social group.

Insofar as observers are members of the social group to which a victim of injustice may belong, their shared identity as group members may contribute to observers' willingness to invoke fairness rules in order to assess the situation (e.g., Skarlicki et al. 1998). Additionally, that shared group membership may lead third parties to consider the implications of a distribution, procedure, or interaction pattern for their own personal or their group's wellbeing in the long run (see Hegtvedt et al. 2009). Although consideration of the implications for their own wellbeing suggests the economic or social motives described above, third parties without ties to the victim may grow upset owing to beliefs that harming others violates moral norms more generally, potentially threatens the moral community, and, consequently, should not be tolerated. As Folger's (2001) argument regarding deonic justice and Skitka's analysis of moral convictions (Skitka et al. 2008) suggest, third parties may be motivated to uphold moral principles disallowing harm and promoting human wellbeing.

Indeed, Turillo et al. (2002) provide evidence of such moral motivation. Their findings indicate that third parties would forego personal financial gain in order to punish someone who intended to act unfairly toward others. The intent to act unfairly, in effect, stimulates observers to act on behalf of an unfamiliar, intended victim. Feeling other-oriented moral emotions such as empathy and altruism may drive individuals to help others in need (Chapman et al. 1987, Hoffman 1982). Likewise, people are likely to feel compassion in response to others' experiences of suffering and feel angry and defiant when taking the role of an injustice victim (Aderman et al. 1974). In effect, role-taking enhances empathy for the victim. Situational conditions, however, may influence the level of empathy. Studies show that being close to injustice victims (Brockner and Greenberg 1990, Huo 2003), having personally experienced a mild form of the same type of injustice, or observing very severe injustice (Kray and Lind 2002) evoke more empathy and stronger responses in third parties.

Undoubtedly, the emotional responses of third parties may be less intense than those of people directly affected by an injustice. Yet, in addition to the work described above with regard to moral emotions, field studies of layoff survivors' responses to the experiences of layoff victims (e.g., Brockner et al. 1994) and experimental studies on observers' reactions to an authority who unfairly treats their peers (e.g., Hegtvedt et al. 2008) show that observers do respond emotionally to another's injustice. Situational circumstances, however, may enhance or diminish these emotional responses. For example, findings from Hegtvedt et al. (2008) indicate that procedural injustice clearly increases third parties' expression of feelings of anger, resentment, and frustration over a peer's unjust outcome but only when the decision-maker is legitimated. And, while these studies may reflect emotional responses of observers whose motives may be economic or social (and not moral per se), the emotions may spur behavioral reactions that have implications for ethical behavior within a social group.

Behavioral responses of observers may be stimulated by the self-interested desire to prevent future occurrences of injustice that may harm them or by moral concerns. Regardless of the underlying motivation, Skarlicki and Kulik (2005) note some particular characteristics of third-party responses. Although observers do not have direct control over the outcomes at issue, they are less constrained by fear of counter-retaliation from the transgressor and thus freer to act as agents for the injustice victim. In doing so, however, they may incur social costs, such as the irritation or wrath of a decision-maker, or secure social rewards like praise from colleagues, thanks from the injustice victim, or pride in upholding moral standards. Situational factors may shape the pursuit of justice for others. For instance, individuals are more likely to engage in pro-social behavior on behalf of others when they share a common in-group identity and when they have access to resources to pursue collective action (Beaton and Deveau 2005). Moreover, there is a greater likelihood of collective action to benefit unfairly treated others when the disparities between the in-group and out-group are small, rather than large and seemingly overwhelming (Kawakami and Dion 1993). And, observers are more likely to anticipate engaging in coalition formation to redress an outcome injustice suffered by a group member if the perpetrator used unfair procedures in making the distribution decision (Hegtvedt et al. 2009).

Together results from these studies provide indirect evidence for elements of Folger and Cropanzano's (1998, 2001) fairness theory: establishing an outcome as aversive to others, imagining an alternative process and outcome (e.g., enactment of fairer procedures by the person accountable for the outcome), and mustering the resources to make changes. In effect, observers might conclude that outcomes to others could have and should have been different – especially for victims within the observers' moral community. Third parties, however, may hesitate to act on behalf of an injustice victim if they identify with or recognize the legitimacy of the person or organization perpetrating the injustice (see Hegtvedt and Johnson 2000, Skarlicki and Kulik 2005).

Skarlicki and Kulik (2005) identify factors that facilitate attempts by third parties within organizations to take action to rectify injustices to others. They recognize that third parties may experience strong, moral emotions as described above and that moral outrage may even outweigh the costs associated with some actions. Even when observers engage in rational cost-benefit analysis, they may try to rectify others' injustice if they: recognize that the victim does not have the resources to help him or herself, believe that they have the knowledge and resources to help, occupy a power-advantaged position, can guard against their own vulnerability to mistreatment, and perceive that the organization's policy and climate are responsive to grievances and wrongdoing.[10] Skarlicki and Kulik (2005) describe a variety of consequences for the actions of third parties, emphasizing that successful redress of others' injustice reinforces moral codes of conduct. In contrast, they argue that failure to redress the injustice or, more generally, failure to act, can lead observers to question their own morality, ignore future instances of injustice, and contribute to the tolerance of injustice within the organization, creating a climate of unethical behavior. Thus while the motives of third parties may not stem

---

[10] Of course, theory and research on social movements (e.g., Diani and McAdam 2003, Davis et al. 2005, Poletta and Jasper 2001) may inform questions about how observers join forces to rectify others' injustice.

explicitly from moral concerns, their actions may have consequences for the morality of an enduring group.

Summary. At a very general level, research pertaining to both the justice motive and responses by third parties asks the question: when will observers "help" injustice victims? Although the approaches in each domain differ, both draw attention to individual character-istics, including beliefs and motivations, cognitive processes (such as labeling, attributions for the victim's outcomes and the perpetrator's behavior, self-defensive attributions, and cost/benefit analysis), and situational factors that shape justice perceptions and responses.

At the conceptual level, the notion of the justice motive clearly links justice concerns to issues of morality. Even though justice is defined in terms of deserving, behavior stimulated by the justice motive should protect the well-being of others. Unfortunately and especially when the related "belief in a just world" is treated as an individual difference factor, adherence to such beliefs may lead to derogation of injustice victims as a means for observers to protect themselves from evidence that the world is not just. As Lerner (2003) points out, however, what appears to be self-defensive analysis and retreat from helping injustice victims is more likely when the perceived injustices have low impact; in situations involving high impact, or vivid and extensive injustice, observers are more likely to experience moral emotions and act intuitively on the justice motive to lend help to others.

Much of the work on third-party responses to others' injustice similarly stresses the con-ditionalizing of those responses (see Skarlicki and Kulik 2005). A key consideration, often absent in BJW research owing to the emphasis on responses to assault or illness victims, is the extent to which third parties identify with group members who receive unfair outcomes or treatment within their organization. Theoretically, such identification enhances the empathy of observers. While such a consideration raises the possibility that assistance to injustice vic-tims stems not simply from justice or moral concerns but self-interested ones, what remains important is whether help is rendered to those suffering injustice. Whether observers attempt to redress others' injustice also clearly depends upon situational factors that facilitate or con-strain the likelihood of that help. Like research in BJW, extensive injustices are likely to evoke moral emotions and willingness to help, even at costs to the third parties themselves.

Although BJW research is extensive, as noted above, it is also limited. In contrast, work on observers' responses to others' injustice is a relatively new domain of investigation. The key theoretical question, "when will observers help?" implicitly involves empirical questions such as: What situational factors shape justice (not self-interested) motivations? What situa-tional factors facilitate interventions by third parties on behalf of injustice victims? Whether the impact of situational factors on responses to injustice depends upon observers' underlying motivations or upon the nature of the injustice (e.g., being the victim of an assault or ill-ness versus suffering explicit distributive, procedural, or interactional injustice) are additional avenues for research.

Likewise, a number of questions emerge as a basis for understanding the process linking motivations and/or situational factors to actual attempts to redress others' injustice. Of critical importance in fairness theory or in more specific theorizing about the effects of BJW or the influence of situational factors on third parties' responses are the attributions that observers make. Little research, however, explicitly measures these attributions. And, while empathy is proposed as a moral emotion stimulating third party involvement, the nature of empathy requires investigation. Is empathy an individual difference factor like BJW or is its emer-gence dependent on situational factors? A focus on observers' responses raises other questions about the dynamics among observers. Why are observers' perceptions of the injustice suffered by another similar or different? How do observers coalesce to redress others' injustice? As Skarlicki and Kulik (2005) would argue, what observers collectively determine may affect the extent to which an organization's climate is ethical and moral.

CONCLUSION

Although not always explicit, the link between justice and morality, as recent research suggests, is inevitable. Within social psychology, emphasis on the link was understandably ignored when research focused on personal instances of injustice, largely in organizational settings [though studies of justice in personal relationships also rarely addressed the link (see Lerner and Mikula 1994)]. Questions addressed perceptions of and responses to one's own injustice, often in the absence of information on how others in one's social group fared as well. Not only do such questions ignore the collective nature of justice, without consideration of "justice for all," issues of morality rarely arise.

As we argued in the first section of this chapter, an abstract conceptual understanding of justice as a collective phenomenon resonates readily with philosophical notions of morality that charge individuals and groups to "prevent harm" and to "promote wellbeing." Yet as both Folger (1998, 2001) and Skitka et al. (2008) point out, not all instances of unfairness constitute moral violations. Many experiences of injustice result from violations of preferences or normative conventions, i.e., violations of expectations based on economic or social motivations. As such, they lack an underlying moral motivation or consideration of what Folger labels "moral accountability," which directs attention to how a person *should* behave in order to ensure justice and thereby fulfill moral obligations to uphold principals that maintain the fabric of society. A focus on others seems to be a necessary, if not sufficient, condition to raise justice concerns to the level of moral analysis (see Gillespie and Greenberg 2005).

Yet that focus may hardly be conscious. As recent theorizing suggests, justice violations that evoke moral concerns may produce instantaneous emotions. Unlike traditional distributive justice approaches that presume that emotional responses follow justice evaluations, Folger's (1998, 2001) deonic approach [as well as Haidt's (2001) intuitionist model and Skitka et al.'s (2008) ITMC] suggests that experiencing moral emotions precedes evaluations. Empirical questions remain regarding the sequencing of emotions and evaluations and the extent to which underlying cognitive processes are automatic or controlled (see Fiske and Taylor 2008) in justice judgments in general, and more specifically with regard to moral issues.

Given the attention to trying to infer, shape, or assess moral motivations, there seems to be a presumption that moral motivations produce moral behavior, which strengthens the foundation of a social group (see Tangney et al. 2007). Yet rather than focus on underlying motives, researchers who seek to understand how justice processes foster moral behavior might focus instead on situational conditions alone, or in conjunction with individual characteristics, that increase awareness of the consequences of distributions, procedures, or treatment for others as well as oneself – regardless of underlying motivations. As Skarlicki and Kulik (2005) imply, the maintenance of an ethical climate in an organization depends on the actions of observers of injustice, not their motivations.

Of course, what constitutes the moral community of observers – the "others" whose injustice is focal – exists as an empirical question. In many circumstances, the question may not arise. When inter-group conflict occurs, however, different moral communities may inspire different definitions of what constitutes justice (see Hegtvedt 2005, Mikula and Wenzel 2000). As a consequence, moral communities may fuel conflict. Such dynamics are consistent with a descriptive approach to morality that allows greater structural and cultural variation in what is right. Conflict, however, may be ameliorated by a more normative moral approach – one that emphasizes the prevention of harm and the protection of human dignity.

Perceptions of unfairness permeate many encounters and decisions. Most of those instances reflect the violation of personal or social expectations – not the violation of moral principles. And most carry few implications for others. But when cries of injustice refer to the suffering of others – especially in systematic and enduring ways – the moral basis of justice can hardly be ignored. History is replete with examples of social changes (e.g., desegregation of schools in the United States; the end of apartheid in South Africa) that have occurred when justice and morality have coincided. Revitalization of the justice/morality link sets a broad agenda for future research that integrates motivational, cognitive, emotional, and behavioral processes.

Acknowledgments We would like to thank Steve Hitlin for his helpful feedback on this chapter. In addition, we are grateful to our colleagues Cathryn Johnson and Leslie Brody for their advice and encouragement.

REFERENCES

Abend, G. 2008. "Two Main Problems in the Sociology of Morality." *Theory and Society* 37:87–125.

Adams, J. S. 1965. "Inequity in Social Exchange." PP. 267–299 in *Advances in Experimental Social Psychology*, v. 2, edited by L. Berkowitz. New York: Academic Press.

Aderman, D., S. S. Brehm, and L. B. Katz. 1974. "The Just World Revisited." *Journal of Personality and Social Psychology* 29:342–347.

Ahmed, E., and J. Braithwaite. 2005. "Forgiveness, Shaming, Shame and Bullying." *The Australian and New Zealand Journal of Criminology* 38:298–323.

Aryee, S., P. S. Budhwar, and Z. X. Chen. 2002. "Trust as a Mediator of the Relationship between Organizational Justice and Work Outcomes: Test of a Social Exchange Model." *Journal of Organizational Behavior* 23:267–285.

Barry, B. 1989. *Theories of Justice*. Berkeley, CA: University of California Press.

Batson, C. Daniel, C. L. Kennedy, L. A. Nord, E. L. Stocks, D. A. Fleming, C. M. Marzette, D. A. Lishner, R. E. Hayes, L. M. Kolchinsky, and T. Zerger. 2007. "Anger at Unfairness: Is It Moral Outrage?" *European Journal of Social Psychology* 37:1272–1285.

Bauman, C. W. 2006. *Procedural and Moral Influences on Fairness Judgments and Group Rejection*. Unpublished doctoral dissertation, University of Illinois at Chicago.

Bazerman, M. H., S. B. White, and G. F. Lowenstein. 1995. "Perceptions of Fairness in Interpersonal and Individual Choice Situations." *Current Directions in Psychological Science* 4:39–42.

Beaton, A. M., and M. Deveau. 2005. "Helping the Less Fortunate: A Predictive Model of Collective Action." *Journal of Applied Social Psychology* 35:1609–1629.

Bies, R. J. 2001. "Interactional (In)justice: The Sacred and the Profane." PP. 89–118 in *Advances in Organizational Justice*, edited by J. Greenberg, and R. Cropanzano. Palo Alto, CA: Stanford University Press.

Bies, R. J. 2005. "Are Procedural Justice and Interactional Justice Conceptually Distinct?" PP. 85–112 in *Handbook of Organizational Justice*, edited by J. Greenberg, and J. A. Colquitt. NJ: Lawrence Erlbaum Associates, Inc.

Bies, R. J., and J. S. Moag. 1986. "Interactional Justice: Communication Criteria of Fairness." PP. 43–55 in *Research on Negotiations in Organizations*, edited by R. J. Lewicki, B. H. Sheppard, and M. H. Bazerman. Stamford, CT: JAI Press.

Blader, S. L., and T. R. Tyler. 2005. "Justice and Empathy: What Motivates People to Help Others?" PP. 226–250 in *The Justice Motive in Everyday Life*, edited by M. Ross and D. T. Miller. New York: Cambridge University Press.

Blau, P. M. 1964. *Exchange and Power in Social Life*. New York: John Wiley & Sons.

Botchkovar, E. V., and C. R. Tittle. 2005. "Crime, Shame and Reintegration in Russia." *Theoretical Criminology* 9:401–442.

Braithwaite, J. 1989. *Crime, Shame and Reintegration*. New York: Cambridge University Press.

Brockner, J., and J. Greenberg. 1990. "The Impact of Layoffs on Survivors: An Organizational Justice Perspective." PP. 45–75 in *Applied Social Psychology and Organizational Settings*, edited by J. S. Carroll. Hillsdale, NJ: Erlbaum.

Brockner, J., M. Konovsky, R. Cooper-Schneider, R. Folger, C. Martin, and R. J. Bies. 1994. "Interactive Effects of Procedural Justice and Outcome Negativity on Victims and Survivors of Job Loss." *Academy of Management Journal* 37:397–409.

Chapman, M., C. Zahn-Waxler, G. Cooperman, and R. J. Iannotti. 1987. "Empathy and Responsibility in the Motivation of Children's Helping." *Developmental Psychology* 23:140–145.

Cohen-Charash, Y., and P. E. Spector. 2001. "The Role of Justice in Organizations: A Meta-Analysis." *Organizational Behavior and Human Decision Processes* 86:278–321.

Colquitt, J. A., D. E. Conlon, M. J. Wesson, C. O. L. H. Porter, and K. Yee Ng. 2001. "Justice at the Millennium: A Meta-Analytic Review of 25 Years of Organizational Justice Research." *Journal of Applied Psychology* 86: 425–445.

Colquitt, J. A., J. Greenberg, and C. P. Zapata-Phelan. 2005. "What Is Organizational Justice? A Historical Overview." PP. 3–56 in *Handbook of Organizational Justice*, edited by J. Greenberg, and J. A. Colquitt. NJ: Lawrence Erlbaum Associates, Inc.

Cropanzano, R. S., H. M. Weiss, K. J. Suckow, and A. A. Grandey. 2000. "Doing Justice to Workplace Emotions." PP. 49–62 in *Emotions at Work*, edited by N. Ashkanasy, C. Hartel, and W. Zerbe. Westport, CT: Quorum Books.

Curly, E., ed.1994. *Hobbes Leviathan: With Selected Variants from the Latin Edition of 1668*. Indianapolis, IN: Hackett Publishing Company, Inc.

Davis, G., D. McAdam, W. Richard Scott, and M. N. Zald, eds. 2005. *Social Movements and Organizations.*New York: Cambridge University Press.

Diani, M., and D. McAdam, eds. 2003. *Social Movements and Social Networks*. Oxford, UK: Oxford University Press.

Deutsch, M. 1975. "Equity, Equality, and Need: What Determines Which Value Will Be Used as the Basis for Distributive Justice?" *Journal of Social Issues* 31:137–149.

Durkheim, E. 1995 (1912). *The Elementary Forms of the Religious Life*. New York: The Free Press.

Ellard, J. H., C. D. Miller, T. L. Baumle, and J. M. Olson. 2002. "Just World Processes in Demonizing." PP. 350–362 in *The Justice Motive in Everyday Life: Essays in Honor of Melvin Lerner*, edited by M. Ross. Cambridge: Cambridge University Press.

Ellard, J. H. and D. P. Skarlicki. 2002. "A Third-Party Observer's Reactions to Employee Mistreatment: Motivational and Cognitive Processes in Deservingness Assessments." PP. 133–158 in *Emerging Perspectives on Managing Organizational Justice*, vol. 2, *Research in Social Issues in Management*, edited by S. W. Gilliland, D. D. Steiner, and D. P. Skarlicki. Greenwich, CT: Information Age Publishing.

Feather, N. T. 1999. *Values, Achievement, and Justice: Studies in the Psychology of Deservingness*. New York: Kluwer Academic/Plenum Publishers.

Fiske, S. T., and S. E. Taylor. 2008. *Social Cognition: From Brains to Culture*. Columbus, OH: McGraw-Hill.

Folger, R. 1986. "A Referent Cognitions Theory of Relative Deprivation." PP. 33–55 in *Relative Deprivation and Social Comparison: The Ontario Symposium*, vol. 4, edited by J. M. Olson, C. P. Herman, and M. P Zanna. Hillsdale, NJ: Lawrence Erlbaum Associates.

Folger, R. 1993. "Reactions to Mistreatment at Work." PP. 161–183 in *Social Psychology in Organizations: Advances in Theory and Research*, edited by K. Murningham. Stanford, CA: Stanford University Press.

Folger, R. 1998. "Fairness as Moral Virtue." PP. 13–34 in *Managerial Ethics: Moral Management of People and Processes*, edited by M. Schminke. Mahwah, NJ: Erlbaum.

Folger, R. 2001. "Fairness as Deonance." PP. 3–33 in *Theoretical and Cultural Perspectives on Organizational Justice*, edited by S. Gilliland, D. Steiner, and D. Skarlicki. Greenwich, CT: Information Age Publishing.

Folger, R., and R. J. Bies. 1989. "Managerial Responsibilities and Procedural Justice." *Employee Responsibilities and Rights Journal* 2:72–90.

Folger, R., and R. Cropanzano. 1998. *Organizational Justice and Human Resource Mangement*. Beverly Hills, CA: Sage.

Folger, R., and R. Cropanzano. 2001. "Fairness Theory: Justice as Accountability." PP. 1–55 in *Advances in Organizational Justice*, edited by J. Greenberg, and R. Cropanzano. Stanford, CA: Stanford University Press.

Folger, R., R. Cropanzano, and B. Goldman. 2005. "What Is the Relationship Between Justice and Morality?" PP. 215–245 in *Handbook of Organizational Justice*, edited by J. Greenberg, and J. A. Colquitt. Mahwah, NJ: Lawrence Erlbaum Associates.

Folger, R., and C. Martin. 1986. "Relative Deprivation and Referent Cognitions: Distributive and Procedural Justice Effects." *Journal of Experimental Social Psychology* 22:531–546.

Gert, B., ed. 1991. *Man and Citizen*. Indianapolis, IN: Hackett Publishing Company.

Gert, B. 2008. "The Definition of Morality." *The Stanford Encyclopedia of Philosophy*, edited by E. N. Zalta. URL: http://plato.stanford.edu/archives/fall2008/entries/morality-definition/.

Gillespie, J. Z., and J. Greenberg. 2005. "Are the Goals of Organizational Justice Self-Interested?" PP. 179–213 in *Handbook of Organizational Justice*, edited by J. Greenberg and J. A. Colquitt. Mahwah, NJ: Lawrence Erlbaum Associates.

Gilligan, C. 1982. *In a Different Voice: Psychological Theory and Women's Development*. Cambridge, MA: Harvard University Press.

Gilligan, C., and J. Attanucci. 1988. "Two Moral Orientations: Gender Differences and Similarities." *Merrill-Palmer Quarterly* 34:223–237.

Greenberg, J. 1993. "Stealing in the Name of Justice: Informational and Interpersonal Moderators of Theft Reactions to Underpayment Inequity." *Organizational Behavior and Human Decision Processes* 54:81–103.

Greenberg, J., and R. L. Cohen. 1982. "The Justice Concept in Social Psychology." PP. 1–47 in *Equity and Justice in Social Behavior*, edited by J. Greenberg, and R. L. Cohen. New York: Academic Press.

Greenberg, J., and J. A. Colquitt, eds. 2005. *Handbook of Organizational Justice*. Mahwah, NJ: Lawrence Erlbaum Associates.

Hafer, C. L. 2000a. "Do Innocent Victims Threaten the Belief in a Just World? Evidence from a Modified Stroop Task." *Journal of Personality and Social Psychology* 79:165–173.

Hafer, C. L. 2000b. "Investment in Long-Term Goals and Commitment to Just Means Drive the Need to Believe in a Just World." *Personality and Social Psychology Bulletin* 28:1059–1073.

Hafer, C. L., and L. Bègue. 2005. "Experimental Research on Just-World Theory: Problems, Developments, and Future Challenges." *Psychological Bulletin* 131:128–167.

Hafer, C. L., and B. L. Correy. 1999. "Mediators of the Relation Between Beliefs in a Just World and Emotional Responses to Negative Outcomes." *Social Justice Research* 12:189–204.

Haidt, J. 2001. "The Emotional Dog and Its Rational Tail: A Social Intuitionist Approach to Moral Judgment." *Psychological Review* 108:814–834.

Haidt, J. 2003. "The Moral Emotions." PP. 852–870 in *Handbook of Affective Sciences*, edited by R. J. Davidson, K. R. Scherer, and H. H. Goldsmith. New York: Oxford University Press.

Haidt, J. 2007. "The New Synthesis in Moral Psychology." *Science* 316:998–1002.

Haidt, J., and J. Graham. 2007. "When Morality Opposes Justice: Conservatives Have Moral Intuitions that Liberals May Not Recognize." *Social Justice Research* 20:98–116.

Haidt, J., and C. Joseph. 2007. "The Moral Mind: How Five Sets of Innate Intuitions Guide the Development of Many Culture-Specific Virtues, and Perhaps Even Modules." PP. 367–398 in *The Innate Mind: Foundations and the Future*, vol. 3, edited by P. Carruthers, S. Laurence, and S. Stich. New York: Oxford University Press.

Hareli, S. 1999. "Justice and Deservingness Judgments: Refuting the Interchangeability Assumption. *New Ideas in Psychology* 17:183–193.

Hay, C. 2001. "An Exploratory Test of Braithwaite's Reintegrative Shaming Theory." *Journal of Research in Crime and Delinquency* 38:132–153.

Hegtvedt, K. A. 2005. "Doing Justice to the Group: Examining the Roles of the Group in Justice Research." *Annual Review of Sociology* 31:25–45.

Hegtvedt, K. A. 2006. "Justice Frameworks." PP. 46–69 in *Contemporary Social Psychological Theories*, edited by P. J. Burke. Stanford, CA: Stanford University Press.

Hegtvedt, K. A., and K. S. Cook. 2001. "Distributive Justice: Recent Theoretical Developments and Applications. PP. 93–132 in *Handbook of Justice Research in Law*, edited by J. Sanders and V. L. Hamilton. New York: Kluwer Academic/Plenum.

Hegtvedt, K., and C. Johnson. 2000. "Justice Beyond the Individual: A Future with Legitimation." *Social Psychology Quarterly* 63:298–311.

Hegtvedt, K. A., C. Johnson, and N. M. Ganem. 2008. "Expressing Emotional Responses to the Injustice of Others: It's Not Just What You Feel." PP. 203–226 in *Social Structure and Emotions*, edited by J. Clay-Warner, and D. Robinson. New York: Elsevier.

Hegtvedt, K., C. Johnson, N. M. Ganem, K. W. Waldron, and L. Brody. 2009. "When Will the Unaffected Seek Justice for Others?: Perceptions of and Responses to Another's Injustice." *Australian Journal of Psychology* 61:22–31.

Hegtvedt, K. A. and B. Markovsky. 1995. "Justice and Injustice." PP. 257–280 in *Sociological Perspectives on Social Psychology*, edited by K. S. Cook, G. A. Fine, and J. House. Boston: Allyn Bacon.

Hitlin, S. 2008. *Moral Selves, Evil Selves: The Social Psychology of Conscience*. New York: Palgrave-Macmillan.

Hoffman, M. L. 1982. "Development of Prosocial Motivation: Empathy and Guilt." PP. 281–313 in *The Development of Prosocial Behavior*, edited by N. Eisenberg. New York: Academic Press.

Homans, G. C. 1974. *Social Behavior: Its Elementary Forms*. New York: Harcourt Brace.

Huo, Y. J. 2003. "Procedural Justice and Social Regulation Across Group Boundaries: Does Subgroup Identity Undermine Relationship-Based Governance?" *Personality and Social Psychology Bulletin* 29:336–348.

Jaffe, S., and J. S. Hyde. 2000. "Gender Differences in Moral Orientation: A Meta-Analysis." *Psychological Bulletin* 126:703–726.

Jasso, G. 1980. "A New Theory of Distributive Justice." *American Sociological Review* 45:3–32.

Jost, J. T., C. J. Wakslak, and T. R. Tyler. 2008. "System Justification Theory and the Alleviation of Emotional Distress: Palliative Effects of Ideology in an Arbitrary Social Hierarchy and in Society." *Advances in Group Processes* 25:181–211.

Kals, E., and L. Montada. 1994. "Umweltschutz und die Verantwortung der Bürger." *Z. Sozialpsychol* 25:326–337.

Kawakami, K., and K. L. Dion. 1993. "The Impact of Salient Self-Identities on Relative Deprivation and Action Intentions." *European Journal of Social Psychology* 23:525–540.

Kohlberg, L. 1969. "Stage and Sequence: The Cognitive-Developmental Approach to Socialization." PP. 347–480 in *Handbook of Socialization Theory and Research*, edited by D. A. Goslin. Chicago: Rand McNally.

Konovsky, M. A., and S. D. Pugh. 1994. "Citizenship Behavior and Social Exchange." *Academy of Management Journal* 37:656–669.

Kray, L., and E. Allan Lind. 2002. "The Injustices of Others: Social Reports and the Integration of Others' Experiences in Organizational Justice Judgments." *Organizational and Human Decision Processes* 89:906–924.

Kroll, J., and E. Egan. 2004. "Psychiatry, Moral Worry, and Moral Emotions." *Journal of Psychiatric Practice* 10: 352–360.

Lakoff, G. 1996. *Moral Politics: What Conservatives Know That Liberals Don't*. Chicago: University of Chicago Press.

Lerner, M. J. 1975. "The Justice Motive in Social Behavior: Introduction." *Journal of Social Issues* 31:1–19.

Lerner, M. J. 1977. "The Justice Motive: Some Hypotheses as to Its Origins and Forms." *Journal of Personality* 45:1–52.

Lerner, M. J. 1980. *The Belief in a Just World: A Fundamental Delusion*. New York: Plenum Press.

Lerner, M. J. 2003. "The Justice Motive: Where Social Psychologists Found It, How They Lost It, and Why They May Not Find It Again." *Personality and Social Psychology Review* 7:388–399.

Lerner, J. S., J. H. Goldberg, and P. E. Tetlock. 1998. "Sober Second Thought: The Effects of Accountability, Anger, and Authoritarianism on Attributions of Responsibility." *Personality and Social Psychology Bulletin* 24:563–574.

Lerner, M. J., and G. Mikula. 1994. *Entitlement and the Affectational Bond: Justice in Close Relationships*. New York: Springer.

Leventhal, G. S. 1976. "The Distribution of Rewards and Resources in Groups and Organizations." PP. 91–131 in *Advances in Experimental Social Psychology*, volume 9, edited by L. Berkowitz, and W. Walster. New York: Academic Press.

Leventhal, G. S. 1980. "What Should Be Done with Equity Theory? New Approaches to the Study of Fairness in Social Relationships." PP. 27–55 in *Social Exchange*, edited by K. Gergen, M. Greenberg, and R. Willis. New York: Plenum.

Leventhal, G. S., J. Karuza Jr., and W. R. Fry. 1980. "Beyond Fairness: A Theory of Allocation Preferences." PP. 167–218 in *Justice and Social Interaction*, edited by G. Mikula. New York: Springer.

Lind, E. A. 2001. "Fairness Heuristic Theory: Justice Judgments as Pivotal Cognitions in Organizational Relations." PP. 56–88 in *Advances in Organizational Justice* edited by M. S. Greenberg, and R. Cropanzano. Stanford, CA: Stanford University Press.

Lind, E. A., and T. R. Tyler. 1988. *The Social Psychology of Procedural Justice*. New York: Plenum.

Lind, E. A., R. E. Lissak, and D. E. Conlon. 1983. "Decision Control and Process Control Effects on Procedural Fairness Judgments." *Journal of Applied Social Psychology* 4:338–350.

Lodewijkx, H. F. M., T. Wildschut, B. A. Nijstad, W. Savenije, and M. Smit. 2001. "In a Violent World a Just World Makes Sense: The Case of 'Senseless' Violence." *Social Justice Research* 14:79–94.

Maes, J. 1998. "Immanent Justice and Ultimate Justice: Two Ways off Believing in Justice." PP. 9–40 in *Responses to Victimizations and belief in a Just World*, edited by L. Montada, and M. J. Lerner. New York: Plenum.

Maes, J., and E. Kals. 2002. "Justice Beliefs in School: Distinguishing Ultimate and Immanent Justice." *Social Justice Research* 15:227–244.

Mikula, G., K. R. Scherer, and U. Athenstaedt. 1998. "The Role of Injustice in the Elicitation of Differential Emotional Reactions." *Personality and Social Psychology Bulletin* 24:769–783.

Mikula, G., and M. Wenzel. 2000. "Justice and Social Conflict." *International Journal* of *Psychology* 35:126–135.

Mohr, P. B., and G. Luscri. 1995. "Social Work Orientation and Just World Beliefs." *Journal of Social Psychology* 135:101–103.

Montada, L. 1998. "Justice: Just a Rational Choice?" *Social Justice Research* 11:81–101.

Montada, L., M. J. Schmitt, and C. Dalbert. 1986. "Thinking about Justice and Dealing with One's Own Privileges: A Study of Existential Guilt." PP. 125–143 in *Justice in Social Relations*, edited by H. W. Bierhoff, R. Cohen, and J. Greenberg. New York: Plenum Press.

Mullen, E., and J. Nadler. 2008. "Moral Spillovers: The Effect of Moral Violation on Deviant Behavior." *Journal of Experimental Social Psychology* 44:1239–1245.

Mullen, E., and L. J. Skitka. 2006. "Exploring the Psychological Underpinnings of the Moral Mandate Effect: Motivational Reasoning, Identification, or Affect?" *Journal of Personality and Social Psychology* 90: 629–643.

Nagata, D. K. 1993. *Legacy of Injustice: Exploring the Cross-Generational Impact of the Japanese American Internment.* New York: Plenum.

Olson, J. M., and C. Hafer. 2001. "Tolerance of Personal Deprivation." PP. 157–175 in the *Psychology of Legitimacy: Emerging Perspectives on Ideology, Justice, and Intergroup Relations*, edited by J. T. Jost, and B. Major. Cambridge: Cambridge University Press.

Opotow, S. 1990a. "Deterring Moral Exclusion." *Journal of Social Issues* 46:173–182.

Opotow, S. 1990b. "Moral Exclusion and Injustice: An Introduction." *Journal of Social Issues* 46:1–20.

Opotow, S. 1995. "Drawing the Line: Social Categorization, Moral Exclusion, and the Scope of Justice." PP. 347–369 in *Conflict, Cooperation, and Justice*, edited by B. B. Bunker, and J. Z. Rubin. San Francisco: Jossey-Bass.

Opotow, S. 2008. "Conflict and Justice after the American Civil War: Inclusion and Exclusion in the Reconstruction and Jim Crow Eras." *Advances in Group Processes* 25:55–85.

Polletta, F., and J. M. Jasper. 2001. "Collective Identity and Social Movements." *Annual Review of Sociology* 27: 283–305.

Rawls, J. 1971. *A Theory of Justice.* Cambridge, MA: Belknap Press of Harvard University Press.

Reis, H. T. 1986. "Levels of Interest in the Study of Interpersonal Justice." PP. 187–209 in *Justice in Social Relations*, edited by H. W. Bierhoff, R. L. Cohen, and J. Greenberg. New York: Plenum.

Rozin, P., L. Lowery, S. Imada, and J. Haidt. 1999. "The CAD Triad Hypothesis: A Mapping Between Three Moral Emotions (Contempt, Anger, Disgust) and Three Moral Codes (Community, Autonomy, Divinity)." *Journal of Personality and Social Psychology* 76:574–586.

Shilling, C., and P. A. Mellor. 1998. "Durkheim, Morality, and Modernity: Collective Effervescence, Homo Duplex and the Sources of Moral Action." *British Journal of Sociology* 49:193–209.

Skarlicki, D. P., J. Ellard, and B. Kelln. 1998. "Third-Party Perceptions of a Layoff: Procedural, Derogation, and Retributive Aspects of Justice." *Journal of Applied Psychology* 83:119–127.

Skarlicki, D. P., and C. T. Kulik. 2005. "Third-Party Reactions to Employee (Mis)treatment: A Justice Perspective." *Research in Organizational Behavior* 26:183–229.

Skitka, L. J., 2002. "Do the Means Always Justify the Ends, or Do the Ends Sometimes Justify the Means? A Value Protection Model of Justice Reasoning." *Personality and Social Psychology Bulletin* 28:588–597.

Skitka, L. J. 2006. "Legislating Morality: How Deep is the U.S. Supreme Court's Reservoir of Good Will?" Paper presented at the meeting of the International Society for Justice Research, Berlin, Germany.

Skitka, L. J., and E. Mullen. 2002. "The Dark Side of Moral Conviction." *Analyses of Social Issues and Public Policy* 2:35–41.

Skitka, L. J., and E. Mullen. 2008. "Moral Convictions Often Override Concerns about Procedural Fairness: A Reply to Napier and Tyler." *Social Justice Research* 21:529–546.

Skitka, L. J., C. W. Bauman, and E. Mullen. 2008. "Morality and Justice: An Expanded Theoretical Perspective and Empirical Review." *Advances in Group Processes* 25:1–27.

Skitka, L. J., C. W. Bauman, and E. G. Sargis. 2005. "Moral Conviction: Another Contributor to Attitude Strength or Something More?" *Journal of Personality and Social Psychology* 88:895–917.

Skitka, L. J., and D. A. Houston 2001. "When Due Process Is of No Consequence: Moral Mandates and Presumed Defendant Guilt or Innocence." *Social Justice Research* 14:305–326.

Skoe, E. E. A., N. Eisenberg, and A. Cumberland. 2002. "The Role of Reported Emotion in Real Life and Hypothetical Moral Dilemmas." *Personality and Social Psychology Bulletin* 28:962–973.

Solomon, R. C., and M. C. Murphy, eds. 1990. *What is Justice? Classic and Contemporary Readings.* New York: Oxford University Press.

Stets, J. E., and M. J. Carter. 2006. "The Moral Identity: A Principle Level Identity." PP. 293–316 in *Purpose, Meaning, and Action: Control Systems Theories in Sociology*, edited by K. McClelland, and T. J. Fararo. New York: Palgrave Macmillan.

Tajfel, H., and J. C. Turner. 1986. "The Social Identity Theory of Intergroup Behavior." PP. 7–24 in *Psychology of Intergroup Relations*, edited by S. Worchel, and W. G. Austin. Chicago: Nelson-Hall.

Tangney, J. P. 1994. "The Mixed Legacy of the Super-ego: Adaptive and Maladaptive Aspects of Shame and Guilt." PP. 1–28 in Empirical Perspectives on *Object Relations Theory*, edited by J. M. Masling, and R. F. Burnstein, Washington, DC: American Psychological Association.

Tangney, J. P., J. Stuewig, and D. J. Mashek. 2007. "Moral Emotions and Moral Behavior." *Annual Review of Psychology* 58:345–372.

Thibaut, J., and L. Walker. 1975. *Procedural Justice: A Psychological Analysis*. Hillsdale, NJ: Lawrence Erlbaum Associates.

Turiel, E. 1983. *The Development of Social Knowledge: Morality and Convention*. Cambridge, England: Cambridge University Press.

Turiel, E. 2006. "Thought, Emotions, and Social Interactional Processes in Moral Development." PP. 7–35 in *Handbook of Moral Development*, edited by M. Killen, and J. G. Smetana. Mahwah, NJ: Erlbaum.

Turillo, C. J., R. Folger, J. J. Lavelle, E. E. Umphress, and J. O. Gee. 2002. "Is Virtue Its Own Reward? Self-sacrificial Decisions for the Sake of Fairness." *Organizational Behavior and Human Decision Processes* 89:839–865.

Turner, J. H., and J. E. Stets. 2006. "Moral Emotions." PP. 544–566 in *Handbook of the Sociology of Emotions*, edited by J. E. Stets, and J. H. Turner. New York: Springer.

Tyler, T. R., and S. L. Blader. 2000. *Cooperation in Groups: Procedural Justice, Social Identity, and Behavioral Engagement*. Philadelphia, PA: Psychology Press.

Tyler, T. R., R. J. Boeckmann, H. J. Smith, and Y. J. Huo. 1997. *Social Justice in a Diverse Society*. Boulder, CO: Westview.

Tyler, T. R., and E. Allan Lind. 1992. "A Relational Model of Authority in Groups." *Advances in Experimental Social Psychology* 25:115–191.

Tyler, T. R., K. A. Rasinski, and N. Spodick. 1985. "Influence of Voice on Satisfaction with Leaders: Exploring the Meaning of Process Control." *Journal of Personality and Social Psychology* 48:72–81.

Tyler, T. R., L. Sherman, H. Strang, G. C. Barnes, and D. Woods. 2007. "Reintegrative Shaming, Procedural Justice, and Recidivism: The Engagement of Offenders' Psychological Mechanisms in the Canberra RISE Drinking-and-Driving Experiment." *Law and Society Review* 41:553–586.

Van den Bos, K. 2005. "What Is Responsible for the Fair Process Effect?" PP. 273–300 in *Handbook of Organizational Justice*, edited by J. Greenberg, and J. A. Colquitt. Mahwah, NJ: Lawrence Erlbaum Associates.

Van den Bos, K., and E. Allan Lind. 2002. "Uncertainty Management by Means of Fairness Judgments." *Advances in Experimental Social Psychology* 34:1–60.

Van den Bos, K., E. Allan Lind, R. Vermunt, and H. A. M. Wilke. 1997. "How Do I Judge My Outcome When I Do Not Know the Outcome of Others?" *Journal of Personality and Social Psycholog* 72:1034–1046.

Van den Bos, K., E. Allan Lind, and H. A. M. Wilke. 2001. "The Psychology of Procedural and Distributive Justice Viewed from the Perspective of Fairness Heuristic Theory." PP. 49–66 in *Justice in the Workplace*, edited by R. Cropanzano. Mahwah, NJ: Lawrence Erlbaum Associates.

Van Prooijen, J. W. 2008. "Egocentrism in Procedural Justice Effects." *Advances in Group Processes* 25:29–54.

Walster, E., G. W. Walster, and E. Berscheid. 1978. *Equity: Theory and Research*. Boston: Allyn & Bacon.

CHAPTER 19

Toward an Integrated Science of Morality

Linking Mind, Society and Culture

RENGIN FIRAT AND CHAD MICHAEL MCPHERSON

Morality has long been of interest to social scientists, yet over the last decade new tools have invigorated its scientific investigation. The most widely employed newly emergent tool is brain imaging technology employed within neuropsychological studies investigating the moral cognition and emotions. This chapter outlines broad themes from this research as a first step towards building an empirically-based and theoretically-informed bridge between moral psychology and sociologically derived understanding of culturally constructed moral schemas. With a few notable exceptions (e.g., DiMaggio, Haidt, Vaisey), researchers interested in morality focus on one or the other pole of the society–individual link. This can lead to theoretical blind spots, such as research focused on universally "hard-wired morality" that obscures differences in moral functioning shaped by social structure and culture. The way the human brain works is fundamentally social, "it is our nature to nurture and to be nurtured" (Wexler 2006:13). Among the animal species, human brain has the longest period of growth and development shaped by the environment. But the human brain is not only shaped by the environment, it also shapes the shared social world (Wexler 2006). At the same time, a sociology of morality becomes too insular if it fails to link so-called macro influences with current research on psychological functioning.

Fundamental challenges complicate any synthesis between sociological and neuropsychological research, primary among them are a lack of common language and common assumptions. Rather than seek to criticize scholars for failing to attend to the vast array of problems and challenges posed by others with whom they likely have minimal, if any contact, we instead hope to bring together literatures that typically talk past one another. Disciplinary boundaries render one field's central concerns – for example, sociological concerns with social structure, culture, interpersonal interaction and social context) – as "background noise" within another (like neurological psychology). We focus on introducing and potentially bridging concepts and findings, not methodologies. We do this in the service of motivating interdisciplinary research that properly includes sociological insights: how do we construct research that affords the investigation of human minds in relation to their social environment?

We suggest that the term 'person' offers a pivot for potential linkages, as it points to central concerns regarding members of a social community and not simply humans as biological

S. Hitlin, S. Vaisey (eds.), *Handbook of the Sociology of Morality*,
Handbooks of Sociology and Social Research, DOI 10.1007/978-1-4419-6896-8_19,

organisms (see also Smith 2003). As such, we spell out tools for linking "brain" with "society" in ways that differentiate our species as the "moral animal." The concept of the *moral schema* is the primary conceptual tool we propose here to serve the function of linking human mind and the environment. We develop the fledgling concept of moral schemas based on research from both the psychology of morality and sociology. The value of this construct lies in the nature of schemas, socially shaped individual mental cognitive/emotional constructs that highlight the social embeddedness of the human actor. Moral schemas highlight the reciprocal processes involving not only how individuals are embedded in the social system but also how the social system is embedded in the individual mind.

WHY AN INTEGRATED SCIENCE OF MORALITY?

Understanding of the human mind is essential for understanding human morality. Sociological approaches to morality would be improved with a nuanced understanding of the neuropsychology of morality. Studying the bodily and neural mechanisms evolved for social and moral behavior is essential if scholars are to investigate social phenomena such as stratification or social movements in relation to individual thought, especially if researchers intend to understand and explain how individual thought may create, perpetuate or justify these social phenomena (Howard and Renfrow 2003).

While research in neuroscience explicating morality is advancing rapidly, it is still at its infancy. As a result, there is still a limited focus on how morality depends on cultural and situational context (Moll et al. 2005). While researchers acknowledge the importance of culture, the methodologies in play within moral psychology rarely lend themselves to the study of cultural or structural differences. Experiments, for example the "trolley" problem so often utilized within this field, are conducted in artificial settings, and represent extreme situations that do not represent the everyday moral reasoning (Moll et al. 2005). Moreover, moral cognition involves emotions that are hard to capture in artificial settings (such as anger), and embedded in social environments that cannot be studied with fMRI machines (Casebeer and Churchland 2003).

As LeDoux (2002, 2003) puts it, nature and nurture are not different things from the point of view how the brain works, they are only different ways in which synapses are wired. So, if our minds and bodies are not dividing the world into "social" and "biological," why should researchers studying the complexity of human behavior be encapsulated by one, only to disregard the other? We propose a conceptual tool, the moral schema, as a step toward a more integrated science of morality. Moral schemas are cognitive schemas constructed through an internalization of the norms and values of the society and shaped by our use of cultural information in daily interactions. Our internalization of norms and values and use of culture, taken together, are associated with the appropriate emotions, behavior or body states, which are catalyzed by the subgroups (such as family, friend groups, or workplace) to which one belongs. Moral schemas emerge from the daily life experiences. Finally, as Turner (2000) reminds us, moral emotions (aspects of moral schemas) are likely products of evolutionary hard-wiring and thus biologically rooted. However, since experience in micro-groups (family or friends), relations in meso-groups (e.g., the company one works for), and understandings of macro-level structures (e.g., the society one lives in) are fluid and changing throughout life, moral schemas are also dynamic configurations. Our definition of moral schemas is anchored in moral psychological research, which we briefly summarize below.

A BRIEF PRIMER ON THE SOCIAL MIND

Human beings share most of their ability to conduct social behavior with other higher mammalians (Adolphs 2009, de Waal 2000). However, human cognition evolved socially and developed a moral capacity that builds and binds (Haidt et al. 2007, Hauser 2009) to aid not only in our struggle for existence but also for coexistence. So far none of the other mammalians have used social conduct to build (or destroy) civilizations transcending time and places, bringing people from different backgrounds, families, locations, even religions and ethnicities together as humans did (see Turner, this volume for a detailed discussion). We have come to understand that human morality does not solely depend on rational efforts and reasoning; morality is most profoundly an affective process. Research on the psychology of morality shows that the brain areas associated with moral cognition involves an axis tying prefrontal cortex, temporal regions and limbic structures (Adolphs 2009, Casebeer and Churchland 2003, Damasio 1994, Moll et al. 2002, 2003, 2005, 2007). This evidence suggests the operation of both a fast and automatic emotion process and a slow, conscious reasoning process as key mechanisms involved in moral cognition.

The limbic system is the primary brain area set in the inner border of the cortex that derives emotional information and guides behavior necessary for the survival of the species. It is common to all mammals, and receives inputs from the internal environment through visceroreceptive systems (MacLean 1990). The evolution of the limbic system characterized the evolutionary transition from reptilians to mammalians by leading to distinct mammalian social behavior including nursing and maternal care, audio-vocal communication among mother and the offspring, and play (MacLean 1990). Most limbic structures are subcortical regions including amygdala, hippocampus, hypothalamus and basal forebrain area. The only cortical region involved is cingulate cortex (Casebeer and Churchland 2003). While the amygdala has a key role in emotional memory and processing social signals of emotion, particularly fear (Adolphs et al. 1998, Dalgleish 2004, LeDoux 2000, Phelps and LeDoux 2005), the hippocampus is important for learning and memory, particularly long-term memory and declarative memory essential for making flexible representations based on relationships, combinations and conjunctions among stimuli (Squire 1992, Squire and Zolamorgan 1991). The hypothalamus is linked to the endocrine system and plays a key role in the reward network of the brain (Dalgleish 2004) and many metabolic functions including autonomic responses to stress (McEwen 2007), food intake (Schwartz et al. 2000), and circadian rhythms (Rusak and Zucker 1979).[1]

The limbic system is of vital importance for social behavior. For example, studies show that patients with bilateral amygdala damage fail to provide accurate social judgments on the

---

[1] The anterior cingulate cortex is involved in several important affective and cognitive tasks including but not limited to autonomic activity, conditioned emotional learning, internal emotional responses, motivation, motor activity and goal directed behavior (Bush et al. 2000, Devinsky et al. 1995), selective attention (Casebeer and Churchland 2003), and social cooperative action (Rilling et al. 2001).

basis of facial appearance, especially fearful facial expressions (Adolphs et al. 2005, Adolphs et al. 1998). Research on the moral emotions proposes that anterior and postero-superior temporal regions of hippocampus extract social perceptual and functional features from facial features, body posture, and gestures (Moll et al. 2005, 2007). Hypothalamus is related to anxiety (Simpson Jr. et al. 2001), viewing emotionally relevant stimuli (Lane et al. 1997) and emotional self-regulation (Beauregard et al. 2001, Davidson et al. 2000). Lesions in Anterior Cingulate Cortex can produce apathy, inattention, and emotional instability (Bush et al. 2000, Devinsky et al. 1995).

While limbic system is tuned with the internal environment, the neocortex, which is the evolutionarily later-developed outer layer surrounding limbic structures, is primarily oriented toward the external world by receiving auditory, visual and sensory inputs (MacLean 1990). The evolved development of this brain region allowed primates and humans above other primates to develop many cognitive skills including memory, and language. For example, the parietal and frontal regions of human neocortex are 5 to 9 times larger than other primates (Wexler 2006). The prefrontal cortex is known for its executive regulatory functions such as respiration, blood pressure, thermoregulation, and a variety of mental processes including decision making, emotions, attention and memory.

The limbic system is the brain region often suggested to be the emotional part of brain, and the prefrontal cortex is suggested to be the rational part providing conscious, planned, goal oriented behavior (see Massey 2002 for a more detailed discussion in relation to sociology). While the brain regions have functions independent of each other, overall maintenance of body homeostasis and survival and almost all the specific behavior or attitudes need an interdependent functioning of these regions. So, the so-called emotional and rational parts of brain function interdependently. The prefrontal cortex is reciprocally connected to sensory cortices and limbic structures (Casebeer and Churchland 2003), which also enables a reciprocal control and information system. Trembling of one's hands or voice when got anxious, or controlling one's facial expressions to hide certain emotions such as anger or happiness are two examples of this reciprocal interaction. The ventromedial area in the prefrontal cortex is the key region connected to limbic structures and emerges as one of the primary regions for social and moral knowledge regulating moral decisions and emotions (Adolphs 2009, Greene and Haidt 2002). Adults with damage to the ventromedial area fail to show autonomic responses to socially meaningful stimuli (Damasio et al. 1990). Lesion studies from patients with ventromedial damage who do poorly in tasks-related moral emotions and judgment also support the importance of this region in moral decisions (Damasio 1994). Ultimately, understanding how the "social" and the "moral" gets into the brain necessitates understanding the ways institutions and environments shape both levels of the human mind.

RESEARCH ON THE PSYCHOLOGY OF MORALITY

Current psychological approaches for the study of morality emerged as a critique to the rationalist perspective of the 1970s, pioneered by Lawrence Kohlberg's (1969, 1971) work on moral development. Famously building on Piaget's (1932/1965) theory of the developmental stages of cognition, Kohlberg's model focuses on how adult moral cognition progresses through developmental stages that may ultimately lead to the incorporation of universal moral principles. Rationalist approaches place conscious and rational moral reasoning as the cause of moral behavior.

This long-influential approach has been challenged by recent psychological and neurological models explicating human morality (see Damasio 1994, Greene 2007a, b, Haidt 2001, 2008, Hauser 2007, 2009, Moll et al. 2005, 2007). These newer models agree on the importance of emotions when investigating human morality; they diverge on their proposed mechanisms explaining the relationship between emotions, reasoning and moral judgments. Some models primarily focus on emotions, while others are more evenhanded in their emphasis on both reasoning and emotions as important for understanding moral judgments; yet others argue that judgments are the cause, not the result, of emotions and reasoning.

The initial challenge to the rationalist approach came from problems posed by empirical data. One of the early challenges was the "Somatic Marker Hypothesis" (Damasio 1994, Damasio et al. 1991), which proposed that individuals rely on bodily responses (somatic markers) to different possible options available for making decisions. These markers express themselves in emotions and affect our value-relevant decisions, in addition to higher reasoning. Instead of logically deducing appropriate decisions, Damasio suggests that our body "tells" us which options "feel" most appropriate, and these somatic markers are related to the ventromedial prefrontal cortex. Patients with damage to the ventromedial prefrontal cortex, the brain region involved in emotional regulation, show deficient moral, emotional, and judgmental responses (Damasio 1994, Damasio et al. 1991).

Haidt (2001, 2008) and Haidt et al. (1993, 2007) elaborate the role of emotions in human morality, developing his "Social Intuitionist Model" that stresses emotion-laden intuitions as the primary determinants of moral judgments. Haidt proposes the social intuitionist model as an alternative to the rationalist approach, focusing on how moral intuitions are fast, automatic, and affect-driven processes that guide moral conclusions. They "push" moral conclusions, related to somatic markers, but can be overridden by conscious post-hoc reasoning (Haidt 2001, Haidt et al. 2007). Haidt criticizes mainstream morality research for having a liberal-progress bias limiting morality to only harm and justice and undermining the role of groups and culture. His research shows that while Westerners focus more on harm and fairness, traditional societies rely on other domains tying individual to larger groups such as families, guilds or teams (Haidt et al. 1993). So, he suggests a research of morality including in-group, loyalty, authority, respect, and purity (Haidt et al. 2007).

Another model explaining moral cognition that comes from brain imaging studies using functional magnetic resonance imaging (fMRI) is called the "Event–Feature–Emotion Complex" (EFEC) (Moll et al. 2005, 2007). This model is different from the social intuitionist model as it argues that reasoning and emotions are both primary and precede moral judgment and behavior. The EFEC model relies on an earlier version called "Moral Sensitivity Hypothesis" (Moll et al. 2002, 2003). Moral sensitivity is automatic tagging of social events with moral values. When viewing morally stimulating pictures, brain areas associated with emotions are activated (such as medial orbitofrontal cortex). However, sometimes moral emotions fail to deal with moral situations, especially moral dilemmas, and a slower and conscious mechanism – moral reasoning – becomes decisive. One of the key contributions of this model is its emphasis on content specific cognitive processing that is related to moral emotions, values and long-term goals related to cultural context.

Greene's "Dual Process Theory" of moral judgment (Greene 2007a, b, Greene et al. 2001, 2004, 2008) also emphasizes the balance of emotions and reasoning as prior to moral judgments. This model focuses on two contrasting moral judgments: a) utilitarian judgments that approve harmful actions to maximize good actions and b) deontological judgments based on rights and duties. While deontological judgments (such as disapproval of killing someone to save greater number of people) are guided by rapid and automatic emotions, utilitarian judgments are driven by controlled cognition. A useful distinction proposed by this theory: personal versus impersonal moral judgments. While personal moral judgments (such as pushing someone in front of a trolley to save five other people) rely more on rapid, emotional responses implicating the limbic system, impersonal ones (such as diverting the trolley by hitting a switch so that it would turn to an alternative track where it will kill one person instead of five) rely on controlled cognitive processing (Greene et al. 2001).

These approaches all improve on the overly cognitive focus of moral psychology from decades past, focusing on moral judgment as the outcome. Another influential model suggests

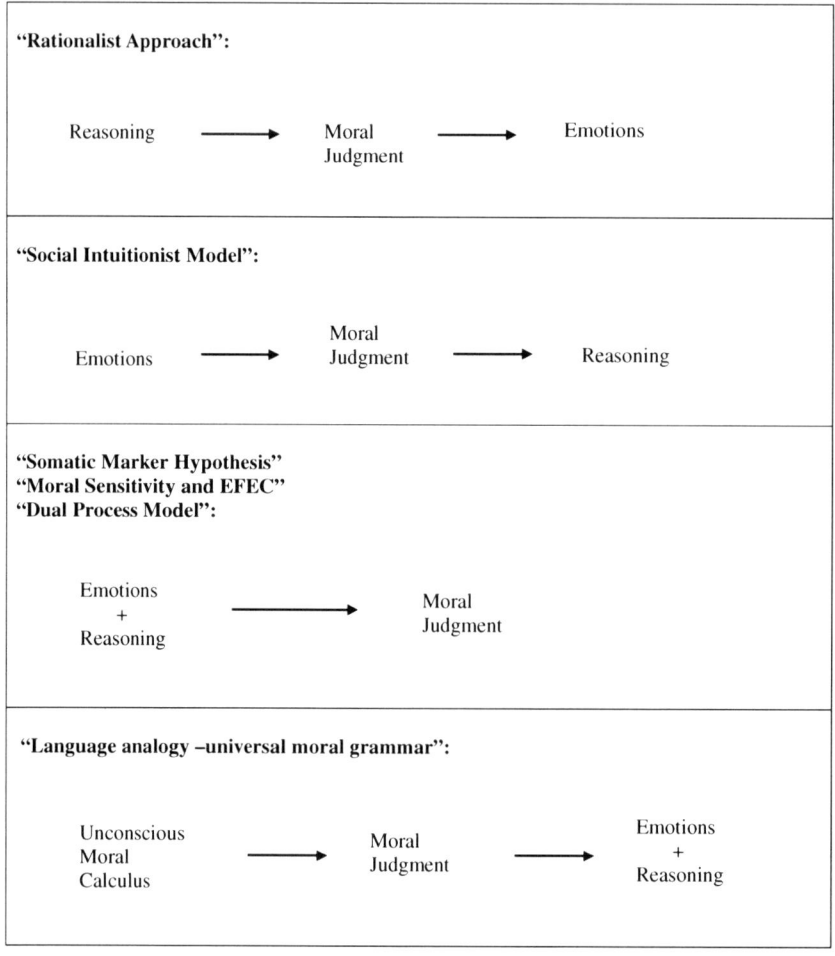

FIGURE 19.1.   Key theoretical perspectives on morality in psychology and cognitive neuroscience

both emotions and moral reasoning as a consequence – not a cause – of moral judgments (Hauser 2006, 2007, 2009, Hauser and Young 2008, Huebner et al. 2008). According to this model, human minds have evolved with a built-in universal moral grammar (moral principles) that unconsciously calculate the causes and consequences of actions leading to moral judgments that might or might not initiate emotions or reasoning. So, when an individual is faced with a moral situation he or she first analyses the situation fast and unconsciously to arrive at a moral judgment, and emotions or reasoning follow this moral judgment. This model uses a language analogy suggesting that, similar to the Chomsky's model for language acquisition, we have a "moral organ" built in with a universal moral grammar that unconsciously acquires moral knowledge and fast-processes information when we are faced with moral situations (Hauser 2006, 2007, Hauser and Young 2008) (Figure 19.1).

Our purpose is not to adjudicate between these models, but to highlight the various influential psychological approaches in the service of further incorporating sociological insights into the science of morality. Regardless of their relative focus, current models highlight the interplay between reasoning, emotion, and intuition in the human mind in the face of moral dilemmas. That all of these processes are shaped in social environments within wider patterned social and cultural structures, however, is less explicitly explored.

MORAL SCHEMAS: LINKING MIND, SOCIETY, AND CULTURE

Work on the moral mind pays too little attention to how culture and social structures become embedded in the mind. We offer moral schemas as a conceptual tool to link mind, society and culture. Individuals engage in daily social behavior by referencing their moral schemas, internalized knowledge about the appropriateness and inappropriateness of the expressions and behavior of oneself and others. Persons do not simply tacitly agree to these understandings; moral schemas reflect externally constructed guidelines coupled with understandings stored by people as they encounter their worlds.

Every human being has a capacity for a moral sense, just like the capacity of language (Hauser 2006, 2007), but like the varieties of languages in the world, this moral capacity is culturally and structurally shaped. Moral schemas are not simply constructed ends, rather they are processes being constructed and perpetually reconstituted with experience, in relationships with others, and through development over the life course. Moral schemas have two important components that bridge the structures of the human mind, discussed above: reasoning and emotions. Moral schemas are concentrically organized, from broadly applicable (and more general) to more specific and defined by rather concrete circumstances. Reasoning is a key part of morality; studies have shown that by reasoning people can override their initial judgments (Haidt 2001, Haidt et al. 2007) or think their ways through impersonal moral dilemmas (Greene et al. 2001). However, emotions or intuitions driven by emotions play an even more critical role in everyday morality by giving the initial and guiding pulse to the responses (Damasio 1994, Damasio et al. 1991, Haidt 2001, Haidt et al. 2007). Accordingly, conscious, deliberate reasoning is anchored in moral schemas in that individuals can reason through situations and circumstances that require action, referencing what the most appropriate behavior is or should be.

We draw upon Izard's (2007, 2009) definition of emotion schemas to anchor our notion of "moral schemas." Izard (2009) proposes that emotion schemas are essentially emotion–cognition-interacted constructions, ones that become enduring traits of personality (developed over time and specific to the person's lived experience) (Izard 2009). The determinants of a particular emotional feeling and what cognitive content is connected to an emotion schema varies by individual, learning, culture and nuanced personal conceptual processes (Izard 2009, 2007, Shweder 1994). What makes emotions moral is their capacity to enhance commitments to others, social structure and culture. People develop personally rooted moral schemas based upon unique lived experience, but their interaction and exposure to broader structural and cultural elements concretizes them, creating a shared language of moral emotional experience, as well shared elements of moral schemas themselves.

Moral schemas work through fast and automatic intuitions that guide social behavior. Moral emotions, for all intents and purposes, act as the glue of moral schemas. Emotions organize events, circumstances, experiences, more generally information, into schemas. At the same time, moral schemas may be aroused by the evocation of moral emotions. When it comes to referencing schemas, moral emotions are signals activating schemas' salience, intensity and content in people's everyday lives. Thus, habituated activity, the reoccurrence of similar events, relations and exchanges all reinforce moral schemas. Individuals can act also non-consciously or deliberatively to diffuse the impact and salience of transgressions against moral schemas in their minds. In some instances, particularly thought-provoking experiences and understandings (the unexpected) challenge the very fibers of a given moral schema, and moral emotions compel schematic reorganization. Psychologists have developed common terms such as defense-mechanisms, selective attention, reinterpretations (cognitive and emotional), distancing, repression and blame to reflect these processes.

Moral schemas do not begin within the individual, but are broadly constructed through cultural codes and inform the emotion states people are "supposed to" or "should" feel. When moral schemas are instantiated and accepted – often unconsciously – positive and reinforcing moral emotions are aroused. When the codes and moral schemas are violated, negative moral emotions (e.g., shame, guilt) are induced, thereby discouraging social transgressions and imprinting in individuals the need to act in accordance with moral cultural prescriptions. When schemas are called upon or adhered to, positive emotions (e.g., pride) resonate and validate the person. The intensity of moral emotional experience, and the individually and situation-defined circumstances that make different people respond to different moral emotions, shapes those moral schemas' present and future salience for individuals.

Let's think about a hypothetical example to aid our understanding of the moral schemas. Imagine a middle-aged man begging for money on the street. What are the mechanisms involved in a bystander's reaction? According to our proposal, the bystander's reactions will be guided by the emotions triggered by their internalized moral schemas, and with elapsed time this initial response may or may not be followed with reasoning and/or a change in the reaction. This basic process may be implicated in the moral psychological approaches discussed previously, but as sociologists we are concerned with a more elaborate picture that includes the social context. We propose that the type and intensity of the (moral) emotions activated will vary depending on the moral schemas shaped by cultural and structural factors (as well as our individual experiences with similar and dissimilar social referents). The moral schema of a stranger New York City might not trigger the same emotions as a stranger in Iowa City. A man in Iowa City might be more likely to feel sorrow and give money since he does not come across with as many people asking for money in the street as in the bigger cities. But a woman in either Iowa City or New York City might not be likely to give any money as their moral schemas arousing sorrow may be suppressed by fear of male strangers, regardless of the size of the city. These are just two sociological variables, the location of the event and the gender of the bystander, shaping moral schemas and resultant emotions and the reactions. Other factors influencing moral judgment (and potential actions) include age, ethnicity, social class, shared social groupings, number of people in the situation, mood, and previous individual experiences. The implication is quite clear: people are unique, but experience consistently high levels of moral schema overlap, both shaped by and drawn upon in interaction with broader culture and social structure.

We suggest that a large part of what it means to be a member of a social group or collective is to loosely internalize similar moral schemas that shape parallel emotive responses to social stimuli guide judgment, feeling, and action. This view mirrors Turner and Stets (2007) contention that the moral content of messages vary in evaluative intensity based upon the elements of culture in which they are carried. They suggest that the level at which these messages are shared and applied (society, community, corporate units, family, interactions), how abstract or specific they are, their embeddedness in ideologies, whether they are mandates or more general expectations, and their universality or situational character all shape the strength of moral content. We focused previously on the neural underpinnings of moral schemas. We now discuss how moral schemas are constructed through society.

THE SOCIAL CONSTRUCTION OF MORAL SCHEMAS: FROM CULTURAL TO MORAL SCHEMAS

The idea of routine, everyday moral schema construction and enactment relies heavily upon culturally available schemas – knowledge and emotion structures that represent objects or events and provide default assumptions about their characteristics and relationships. These culturally available schemas also instantiate the social structure which orders experience and which embeds moral understanding. For reasons of space, our focus will be simply to provide an introduction to the cultural construction of moral schemas.

We propose that moral schemas are partially drawn from more general cultural schemas that are shaped by structuralist carriers of culture (see Figure 19.2). Cultural schemas have been employed within sociology as generally cognitive constructs, though our discussion assumes schemas are also organized by emotions. We present a brief overview of cultural theories which disparately model culture's schematizing power, both emotionally and cognitively; then discuss how culture and structure transmits messages with emotional content; and finally elaborate our concept, the moral schemas, by coming back to our hypothetical example of encountering a street beggar. We draw upon these approaches setting the stage for future work that might model "outside-in" processes that explain the way societal moral codes become imprinted in the mind, and used by people.

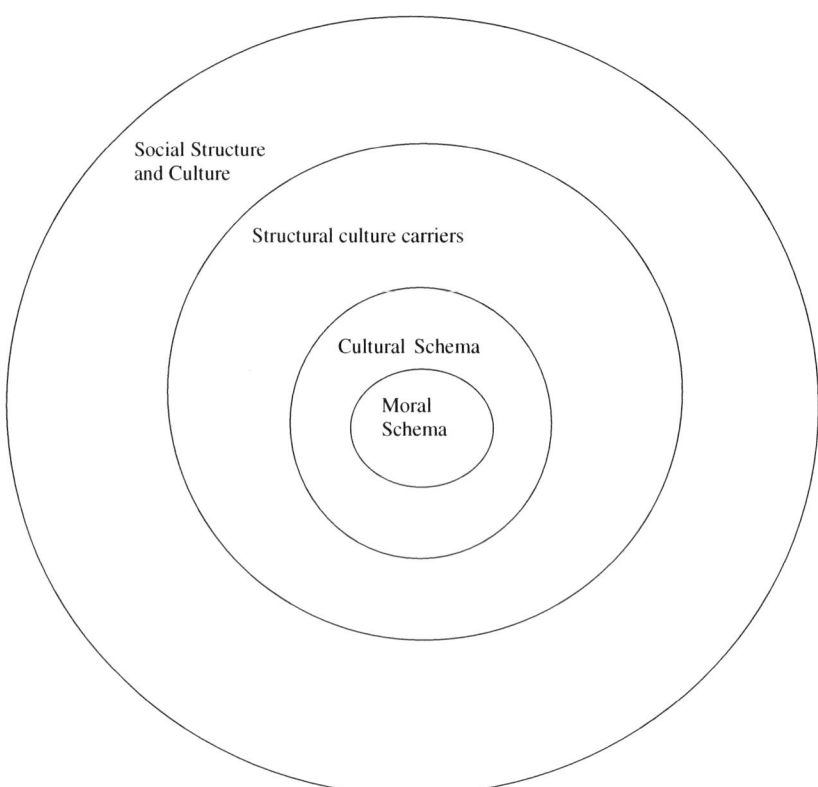

FIGURE 19.2. Social construction of moral schema

THEORIES OF STRUCTURE AND CULTURE

On Structure

We operationalize structure and culture first by drawing upon Sewell's (1992) essay. For Sewell (1992), "structures are in fact dual: how historical agents' thoughts, motivations, and intentions are constituted by the cultures and social institutions into which they are born, how these cultures and institutions are reproduced by the structurally shaped and constrained actions of those agents" (5). Put differently, social structures are sets of mutually sustaining schemas and resources that both empower and constrain social action. Social structures inherently tend to reproduce habituated social action. Thus, social structure provides a stable background for human activity. People venture through their day-to-day worlds with a minimum need to make straining decisions, freeing energy for new, difficult to categorize, encounters that seemingly fall outside-the-bounds of the expected interaction order[2].

---

[2] Warfield-Rawls (1987) suggests that it is the unexpected in basic interaction that makes up the moral (see her chapter, this volume).

Essentially, the background of habituated activity opens up a foreground for deliberation and innovation (Berger and Luckmann 1966).

Sewell (1992) indicates that resources "are read like texts, to recover the cultural schemas they instantiate" (13). Resources are what people use that's outside of their minds, both human and non-human, in the enactment of social structure. Schemas are the things people know: culture. The rules for how to use what you know are cultural schemas. Schemas, in Sewell's (1992) articulation, are similar to Douglas's (1986) notion of institutions; schemas are conventions, recipes, scenarios, principles, and habits grounded in something durable. Most often, schemas are instantiated without conscious effort. As social and cultural blueprints people are socialized to understand (or perpetually encounter in their lived worlds), by using schemas, people are in fact invoking and reaffirming social structure.

Conceptually, an explanation in terms of social structure is remiss without a consideration of two core sociological concepts: "status" and "power." Status positions are social differences, ordering the roles persons play and are expected to reproduce. Cultural codes can prescribe status positions, and different status positions are linked to distinct cultural codes. Power is a property of social relationships, and most fundamentally, emerges from others' dependence upon the focal actor. Power is the ability to induce people to act counter to their own desires (Emerson 1962). When power and distinction (status) are legitimized, they become embedded in social structure. Power and status afford some actors the ability to shape and more readily propagate cultural schemas (Hallett 2003). Lamont (1992) argues that power and position in class struggles provide some persons in advantageous positions with broader and more resonant cultural repertoires. Class distinctions are reproduced when persons put those cultural repertoires to use in moral discourses, producing boundaries of social distinction (Lamont 1992). Similarly, Bourdieu (1984) readily argued that socially reproduced positions provided differences in the capital people can employ in situations (e.g., Coleman 1988). As such, power and status differences also result in unequal access to reward structures and distributions of actual reward entailments (Cook 1977, Cook and Whitmeyer 1992, Cook et al. 1983).

Powerful, high status actors differentially command structurally advantageous positions, possess pre-existing resources others depend upon, thereby drawing the symbolic attention of others which allows them to define and shape cultural schemas at their disposal. As a result, some of the dominant elements of cultural understanding emerge from these powerful, high-status actors. Possessing this differential access to culture codes, powerful actors likely shape the elements of moral schemas that become shared by large groups. Violations of these codes induce moral emotional responses, thereby reinforcing dominant frameworks. Although there may be elements of universality in some form of abstract morality, in real life, people are embedded in structures and culture which shape moral understandings, understandings disproportionately informed by persons and groups of people in powerful and high-status positions.

On Culture

Culture shapes and justifies moral emotions both at the level of individual action, in which persons reconstitute, reconfigure and deploy cultural resources (Bourdieu 1990, Carley 1991, Sewell 1992, Swidler 1986), and at the supra-individual level (DiMaggio 1997, DiMaggio and Powell 1983, 1991, Friedland and Alford 1991, Meyer and Rowan 1977), in which scripts, schemas or logics dictate the moral attributes and approbation of culturally valued means and ends. Yet surprisingly, cultural sociology is quite fragmented on this point. We draw from Vaisey (2008), who recently argued that two dominant approaches in sociology posit different conclusions as to how culture matters. The key question which each perspective seeks to answer is this: how do persons perceive, come to acquire, process and draw upon culture experienced in everyday life? As Vaisey suggests, the first perspective best captures the Parsonian interpretation of Weber's value-rational action, which he terms the "Socratic model." Relating things to the moral, this once dominant perspective in sociology suggests that people develop ideas and beliefs (necessarily culture-specific) that are morally charged. These morally-charged beliefs are often dichotomies, whether bright lights or bright lines (Hitlin 2008), that define "shoulds" and "should nots." Internalized through experience, interaction, and as a result of socialization processes, these beliefs and values inform, and sometimes compel, people to act in certain ways.[3]

In contrast to the Socratic model, Vaisey (2008) suggests that the contemporary approach to culture views it as something used by persons to construct meaning from – to justify their experience and understanding of – the world. Structures are "situations, social networks and institutions" (Vaisey 2008:605; e.g., Sewell 1992); the routes by which shared understandings are transmitted and reproduced, providing access and constraint in terms of available cultural codes. This "newer school," implicates culture as tools used in reasoning, sense-making of experience, used to justify our worldviews and action. As Holland (1997) and Kondo (1990) suggest, culture becomes a tool in the referential construction of selves. This "newer school" is represented by Swidler's (1986) culture-as-toolkit model, Boltanski and Thevenot's (2006) macro-logics of justification, Sewell's (1992) scripts and schemas, DiMaggio's (1997) synthesis on the relation between culture and cognition and Peterson's (1976, 1979) production culture (e.g., Peterson and Anand 2004). Rather than view culture as directly shaping persons' decisions to act, this process is "inside-moving-out" in which persons draw upon cultural tools to strategize, rationalize, or less deliberately explain how they feel and act (Kaufman 2004). Structural constraints limit the available scripts and schemas people are exposed to, and thus able to draw upon. Very few institutional entrepreneurs possess the social skill (Fligstein 1987, 1997, 2001), symbolic power (Hallett 2003), and access (Sewell 1992) to a broader variety of resources necessary to justify action or creatively construct and contour meaning "outside the box."

Vaisey's (2008) larger argument is that cultural sociologists seem to be entrenched in one or the other camp, while he proposes unification through the construction of a third, all-encompassing framework. We are not convinced that Vaisey entirely achieves this goal, but we certainly agree that both cultural approaches are useful. Acting when we bump into the beggar on the street – assuming we do not avoid them and cross the street altogether – depends upon not only the moral schemas that culture instantiates through socialization and internalization, but also upon the culturally available moral schemas used to justify what we just did. In either

---

[3] We do not advocate for an approach that perilously constructs an over-socialized perspective of persons. Wrong's (1961) point is quite clear, and just, and socialization is but a reduced-form construct explaining how social information is acquired and retained.

case, conceptualizing how culture matters so far does little to address the paradoxical treatments of this literature in relation to our argument, and more importantly, in application to the work of moral psychologists and neuroscientists.

The grand theories of culture and structure fail to make explicit the connection between structure and emotions. Working within the oversimplified emotion/cognition framework we use to map out this chapter, cultural theories take two different perspectives on their relation. The first perspective indicates that moral commitments through emotions and emotional processes are the seeds of structural and cultural production and instantiation [emotions → moral commitments → structure and culture] (Turner 2000). The second perspective specifies structure and culture to be filled with moral codes, and that these codes, by being prescriptive, general and translated by powerful social actors or widely taken-for-granted as truth, arouse emotions and encode experiences with emotional categories of feeling (e.g., Turner and Stets 2007) [structure and culture → moral codes + powerful actors → emotional categories of feeling encoded in experiences]. A successful bridging, we suggest, must be based on psychodynamic and neural processes that implicate moral systems. As an attempt to bridge the social "outside" world with the individual "inside," we focus on intermediary agents of structure and culture that carry the outside to inside and vice versa by constructing cultural and moral schemas.

CULTURE CARRIERS AND SCHEMA TRANSMITTERS

Attempting to explain how groups or categories of people come to think, feel, and act in a similar manner cannot be understood without accounting for the structure of social relations among concrete entities that constitute the boundaries of groups (and their thinking, feeling and acting) in the first place (Emirbayer and Goodwin 1994; Wellman 1983). As we have noted, DiMaggio (1997) suggests that individuals experience culture as disparate bits of information and structures organize this information. The carriers of culture – institutions, networks and social movements – diffuse, activate and differentially select available schema that persons come to internalize and/or readily draw upon. Essentially, social structures, and the circumstances people find themselves in, activate schemas and scripts. Culture is a complex of rule-like structures put into use by people (Martin 1992, Tilly 1992, Swidler 1986), often in a strategic and deliberative manner (Swidler 1986, Bourdieu 1990, Sewell 1992).

Three main culture carriers are institutions, networks and social movements. Social institutions order reality and its taken-for-granted character (Berger and Luckmann 1966) and congeal in highly generalized macro-forms, such as institutions of "family," "religion," or "polity" (Friedland and Alford 1991, Jepperson 1991). Institutions also manifest in patterned relations and perpetually encountered abstractions, specific to place, organization, and relationships in time and space (DiMaggio and Powell 1991). These institutions develop internal logics and governance structures that are highly abstract but can be applied to concrete organizations and groups (Douglas 1986, Rao et al. 2003, Sewell 1992). Institutions are conventions perceived as external to people and social construction (Douglas 1986), proffering ways to define activity, sort things, create order and as a basis from which to coordinate activities (Biggart and Beamish 2003, Friedland and Alford 1991).

Culture is also transmitted through networks and social movements. Networks are groups of actors (people or organizations) engaged in reciprocal patterns of communication and exchange (Powell 1990). Networks are the interlocks and interactions of complex and defined social relationships (Boorman and White 1976). Social movements are motors of institution building (Rao et al. 2003, 2000). Rao et al. (2003) specifies that movements act as structures for change, transmitting and proliferating cultural codes (McAdam 1995, Rao et al. 2000). Movements are organized in different ways, from well-constructed and governed forms to informal and decentralized (Melucci 1996). Culture at each of these levels is transmitted, reproduced, and instantiated through everyday social interactions (Collins 1981). Collins (1981; e.g., Kemper and Collins 1990) suggest that that rituals in interaction are so emotionally valenced that they compel, micro-foundationally, patterns of shared and repeatable activity that create macro-structures (such as institutions, movements, and network patterns).

CULTURAL BINARIES AS CULTURE CARRIERS

Culture is coded in equally powerful positive and negative messages that provide generalized proscriptions. People both use these guides to shape decisions and actions, and to evaluate behavior as ad-hoc reasons for action's contingencies. In this perspective, no universal objective culture exists; but people do share an internal "common cultural typification" that oftentimes manifests in social life through similarities in individual action (Alexander and Smith 1993, Alexander 1988).

Like Vaisey (2008), Alexander and Smith (1993) are critical of cultural studies that seem to either focus on a structure-centered or individual-centered approach to culture and how it matters for people. According to Alexander and Smith, culture is "a structure composed of symbolic sets. Symbols (or signs) that have a generalized status and provide categories for understanding the elements of social, individual and organic life" (1993:156). Cultural systems are composed of several cultural structures (not to be confused with social structures), including (1) narratives (or cultural stories); (2) social conglomerations of symbols, the meanings of which only emerge through their relations to other symbols (or "signifiers"), in which "the cultural life of society can be visualized as a web of intertwining sets of binary relations" (1993:157); (3) sign sets organized into discourses (e.g. Bergmann 1998, Drew 1998, Maynard 1998). Discourses [or as others have termed, schemas or scripts (Sewell 1992) or logics of action (Friedland and Alford 1991, Jackall 1988)] "not only communicate information, structuring reality in a cognitive way, but also perform a forceful evaluative task" (Alexander and Smith 1993:157). Cultural binaries are organized into discourses and provide cognitive truth and understanding for experience.[4] We build on this by suggesting that such cultural binaries are emotively charged, and emerge as, culturally organized and morally tagged with strong emotional qualities. The notion of culture as a flood of binaries that are emotionally charged provides a useful linkage to research on the mind.[5]

---

[4] In Alexander and Smith's (1993) terms, binaries are dualistically organized: good versus bad, right versus wrong, clean versus dirty. We suggest that the world is a far more complex place. This approach does not reflect gradations of evaluation.

[5] Interested parties might look to New Institutionalism in organizational sociology, which has long investigated culture as shaping and directing lines of action (see Powell and DiMaggio 1991, Friedland and Alford 1991 for theoretic orientation; Thornton and William 1999, Haveman and Rao 1997, Rao et al. 2003). More recently, new institutional

Alexander and Smith's (1993) argument regarding cultural binaries has significant appeal. The ideas can be likened to Hunter's (1991) "culture wars" hypothesis (e.g., Wuthnow 1996). "Culture war" arguments suppose that two dominant worldviews – the orthodox and progressive – overarch social debates and shape the dominant discourses in moral issues (at least in the Western world – see Dill and Hunter, this volume; also Baker, this volume). Evans (1997) finds limited support for the "culture wars" theory suggesting that dominant orthodox and progressive worldviews are filtered by social groups – the groups to which one belongs – in how people frame issues and come to have emotionally resonant beliefs about issues. There may be no duality in guiding cultural worldviews, but individual issues, persons, actions and beliefs have a tendency to be structured as opposing duals via cultural messages and through relationships with others.

Emotionally charged binaries provide labels which evaluate the right or wrong, clean or dirty (and possibly shameful), inclusive or exclusive aspects of encountered circumstances, events and experiences. To Alexander and Smith (1993), the codes and anti-codes of culture, at the level of actors, social relationships and institutions, morally regulate social life, providing forums which classify the right and wrong sides of social crises and circumstantial problems, and promote cooperative understanding (though not without competition, division and conflict). Thus, competence, acceptance, membership, and reward structures are all tied to the adherence to proscriptive elements of cultural codes (Alexander and Smith 1993), transmitted through their sometimes moral and always emotive character. It is because these codes are generalized and conceptual, rather than finely detailed, that they are available and transmutable across localities and historical contexts.

GENERAL CULTURAL SCHEMAS

How is it that people embedded in families, in friendship groups, in formal and informal organizations, communities, regions, and societies come to largely think, feel and act in morally similar ways? Structures of relations instantiate, perpetuate, reaffirm and transmit the moral elements of culture. DiMaggio (1997) suggests that people use mental structures to perceive, process and retrieve information transmitted through relations; people use memory processes to store cultural messages. Categorization occurs through the classification of messages into generalized schema, and research evidences the cross-cultural variation in the content of messages and also in their coding or categorizing through cognitive processes (processes themselves more universally applicable). Such mental categorizing makes cultural information more easily stored and readily available for retrieval. People might be universally hardwired to classify and code information, and might even have universal moral grammars (see Hauser's work), but the context in which culture is classified varies as much as does the cultural information itself, based on people's embeddedness in and exposure to different relations.

---

scholarship has loosened the constraints of theory, acknowledging discursive processes between culture and interpretation by organizational actors. Persons filter, construct and strategically utilize this cultural information to direct action and pursue interests (see Hallett 2003, Hallett and Ventresca 2006a, b, Binder 2007, Hallett 2010).

Cultural schemas are related to emotions in two ways. First, cultural schemas are laden with emotional content. Emotions are basic to our communication structures and understanding our worlds (and in relation to other people). Second, schemas, apart from their content, have emotional qualities. Because schemas are durable, shared and order social life without conscious deliberation, our complex human social world partially depends upon their existence and reproduction. Their quality of being shared, ordered, and transposable itself has an emotive quality, a quality of fundamental sociality that is entirely moral (see Maynard and Turowetz, this volume). Culture has a stabilizing capability, creating order and rules through socialization (a classic cultural stance taken by early functionalist sociologists). Aptly described, culture acts as "the software of the mind" (Hofstede 1991), and this definitional or programming function of culture emotively drives our use and reproduction of it.

Culture's schematizing qualities can be referenced in Lamont and colleagues' work on symbolic boundaries (Lamont 2000, 2001, Lamont and Fournier 1992, Lamont and Molnar 2002; see Lamont, this volume). Symbolic boundaries are the schematic distinctions made by actors, categorizing objects, people and practices (Lamont and Molnar 2002). Boundaries are relational (Emirbayer 1997), and as Lamont (2000, 2001) has argued, individuals and groups struggle over these definitions and "compete in the production, diffusion, and institutionalization of alternative systems and principles of classification" (Lamont and Molnar 2002:168). Symbolic boundaries separate people, and in making group distinctions, generate feelings of similarity and dissimilarity. Boundaries facilitate status acquisition and produce resource differentials between people and groups. When symbolic boundaries, and the differences they define, become objectified or institutionalized, they congeal into identifiable patterns of social boundaries linked to inequality and stratification (Lamont 2000, Lamont and Fournier 1992; see also Sayer, this volume).

Symbolic boundaries produce emotional evaluations of favorable in-group and unfavorable out-group biases (Tajfel and Turner 1985). These differential evaluations of groups (to which one belongs or does not belong) occur because people draw upon their moral schemas to evaluate people (Lamont 1992). As Lamont and Molnar (2002) indicate, symbolic boundaries are tools that can be used to "enforce, maintain, normalize, or rationalize social boundaries as exemplified by the use of cultural markers," but so too they can be employed to challenge existing frameworks (186). Boundaries are measuring sticks for inclusion and exclusion, and shape the differential distribution of concepts (schemas) that are available (e.g. Bourdieu 1984). The emotive quality of symbolic boundaries is communicated and reinforced through relationships. Boundary adherence and violation is both subject to others' attention and emotive reactions, but also to the internalized meanings and emotions in moral schemas (which house boundary messages).

REVISITING MORAL SCHEMAS: THE CASE OF THE STREET BEGGAR

Persons are shaped by the loose and sometimes disparate pieces of information gathered and experienced in their cultural environment (encoded and transmitted by social structures). This cultural information shapes perceptions, beliefs, values, and action. Further, cultural information is emotionally charged. Too, as DiMaggio (1997), Swidler (1986), and Tilly (1992) suggest, people draw upon these cultural elements, such as macro-logics of justification (Boltanski and Thevenot 2006, Friedland and Alford 1991), to explain their perspectives and action, because they are taken-for-granted as valid and true. These supposedly opposing perspectives seem mutually constitutive, both necessary to understand how culture operates. Select elements of culture congeal into general cultural schemas from which we draw moral schemas.

Moral schemas are informed by cultural schemas, and are the emotionally valenced rules that act as constraints on behavior. As transmitters of culture, social structure filters these moral schemas through emotion-laden processes. Whether via individual interactions, negotiation and exchange between groups, or through more general networks, movements and institutions, reinforcing and discouraging mechanisms act to induce and reward certain thoughts, feelings and behaviors, and discourage and punish others. Moral schemas are guided by the feeling, attitude and value rules that are imposed upon situations and used to make sense of those situations. Moral schemas act as proscriptions and prescriptions of a pro-social kind. Moral schemas are the recipes for thinking and feeling – experiencing – the world in relation to other persons. Moral schemas trigger emotions fast and automatically and push people in the direction of certain behaviors, yet these emotions can be overridden (as suggested by the social intuitionist theory) with conscious thinking. Thus, moral schemas can be manipulated with deliberative efforts. Although persons can manipulate schemas, moral schemas are generally more divisive than broader cultural schemas, providing less opportunity for reconstitution in terms that violate relational or pro-social motives. Just as cultural schemas are inherently in-group biased and tools for favorable categorization of one's shared group memberships, so too do moral schemas emerge with understandings that are preferential to "we-ness": the groups of which we are a part.

In interaction, and in intimate relations, people enact and reinforce – through emotional language, body states, and gestures – the emotional aspects of moral schemas (as informed by culture codes). In organizations or groups, relationships of belongingness and identity permit action that fits the general moral schemas shared by the group. Expressing and acting in accordance with group expectations is met with acceptance, reinforced through acknowledged belongingness, and moral emotional validation by others. Further, in groups, like in more macro-structures of networks, movements and institutions, resources (material, financial, cognitive, ideological, relational, emotional energies, etc.) are rewarded to those who adhere to shared moral schemas. Their shared nature and quality unifies people, groups and larger communities, and their enactment resonates in formal and informal exchange.

Let us return to our hypothetical example. In the case of the street beggar, the evocation of moral emotion significantly dictates the moral schema used to construct action. In turn, the product of that action (how we respond to the beggar and what happens when we do respond) influences the contours of that moral schema for the future (albeit elements are unlikely to change significantly unless the circumstance is particularly resonant). Although our moral schemas remain rather consistent in content, they are dynamic processes shaped over time. Moral emotional qualities both act as precursors to their activation (like as signals for some form of "giving" moral schema), and moral emotions are products of a persons' response to schemas that are imaged in the mind. What moral emotions are produced depends upon how the person self-constructs their actual adherence to or use of that schema derived from cultural knowledge. The process underlying moral schemas, the centrality of emotions, is fundamentally intertwined with the self. Moral emotions contained in moral schemas do increase commitments to others, but do so by directing people to adhere to the culturally-defined codes in the first place.

Moral schemas non-consciously influence how a given person will respond and act. The moral schema invoked depends upon a person's past experiences combined with the immediacy of larger, salient events, situational definitions of embedded interactional groups, and larger cultural codes. Macro-culturally, "giving" or "helping" might be shaped by such things as the economic conditions of the moment (such as a recession or depression), and the prominence of world events (e.g., catastrophic natural disasters that advance the cause of aid and donation). Moral schemas might be shaped by the perceptibility of local conditions, issues of poverty, knowledge about the homeless population and programs of assistance, as well as how others have responded to such circumstances. Encountering the beggar, the focal actor draws upon the schematic character of the experience to make sense of it, including accordant somatically marked emotional reactions. How then the person responds to moral schema activation (and how the situation unfolds when they do act) can reinforce the schema's quality and content, or may reorder the salience of the schema and emotions in similar circumstances.

This incorporates elements of both the Socratic approach to culture, insofar as common moral principles in the United States have dueling elements of helping the less fortunate versus a notion of self-sufficiency. It also draws on the 'newer school' of cultural analysis that suggests people draw upon cultural ideas as a justification for their action, to create shared understanding of the situation, to reaffirm one's selfhood or authenticate one's distinct self in relation to others. From the cultural "newer school," encountering the street beggar, a person might respond in any number of ways. Using variant's of potential cultural responses ranging from ignoring the beggar to buying him food, the person draws upon moralized elements of culture to justify or explain their actions (and their making-sense of the situation). We highlight how both cultural approaches are embedded with moral schemas and relevant emotions, hinted at in Vaisey's (2008) model, but well-established within moral psychology.

LIMITATIONS OF A NECESSARILY BROAD OVERVIEW

Certainly this chapter introduces broad theoretical overviews of how culture is used – how culture matters – without explicitly covering all elements of the culture-emotion link. First, our overview of culture neglects to integrate some concrete research introduced by sociologists interested in the relation of culture (and structure) to emotions. This is intentional, insofar as we attempt to begin linking literatures and fields of inquiry by focusing on theory and concepts at abstract levels. Given the lack of consensus within this rapidly growing sociological subfield, measuring culture in action is extremely difficult. Discussing culture, most abstractly, affords ongoing dialogue about its most useful measurement and how it can be integrated by scholars in moral psychology and neuroscience.

Second, both sociological and psychological audiences would notice that our general theoretical approach fails to do justice to either literatures' approach to understanding human emotions. We see each of the frameworks discussed as providing sources of information to ground the linkage between society and the moral mind. We suggest that our readers reference a number of works we see as exemplars of the sociology of emotions: Kemper (1990); Smith-Lovin (1995); Turner and Stets (2005, 2006). We believe elements of the cultural and structural argument pertaining to the moral mind are latently evidenced in each of these perspectives. Turner and Stets (2006) argue there are five sociological approaches to understanding emotions: dramaturgical theories, symbolic interactionist theories, interaction rituals, power and status theories, and exchange theories. They suggest that sociology still lacks understanding of the structural and cultural conditions producing and enlivening moral emotional processes. Our contention, guiding future research, is that moral schemas seem to be both causes and consequences for the processes discussed in each of these literatures.[6]

CONCLUSION

The mind is central to moral understanding and action. Neuropsychologically rooted models advance perspectives on morality that contradict notions of people as rational calculators of their moral experience and action, a bleak and unrealistic model of human action. Instead, they've introduced new visions of the lived moral experience, ones in which people seem to make quick-responding assessments of their experiences, and do so in manner that might expose the significant common responses and actions people demonstrate with others in their lived social worlds.

But as the human mind is important, so are elements of shared social structure and culture. As sociologists, studying human morality that "builds and binds" from the perspective of psychology and neuroscience, we have discovered that most of the current research overlooks the social context in which this morality is formed and maintained. However, the emergent portrayal of people's socially moral worlds found in this hotbed of psychology and neuroscience is also quite amenable to structural and cultural sociology for a number of reasons. First, by focusing on emotions, memory and lived experience, researchers fundamentally explicate ways that social structure does exactly what sociologists argue it to do: provide structure to and in people's lives, experiences and behaviors, in this case morally. Second, by focusing on brain processes that enable moral capacity, and recognizing that these brain processes themselves are informed by a person's experiences, and the emotions and cognitions attached to those experiences, sociology can rightfully contribute ideas regarding "the embeddedness in culture" and 'belongingness of groups' as shaping the input and output of those brain processes (thereby also shaping moral capacity, understanding and action). Finally, underlying these neuropsychological research programs is an understanding that people make decisions to act (or simply act) based upon a number of socially constructed, referentially oriented, and taken-for-granted "things."

Real life moral situations don't always present themselves as opportunities to ponder life's big questions. People rarely pause to construct cost/benefit analyses of the consequences

---

[6] Only suggestively, and guided by Turner and Stets (2006): dramaturgical theories are rooted in capturing how culture acts to define which emotions should be both experienced and expressed in a given situation (e.g., Goffman 1959, 1967, Hochschild 1983, Scheff 1988). Symbolic interactionist theories are rooted in understanding the relation of the self and identity to emotions through interaction. The self and identity are embedded in, constructed and reproduced through interaction (e.g., Mead 1934, Burke 1991, McCall and Simmons 1978, Stryker 1980, Turner 2002). Power and status theories generally connote the effects of status processes and power dynamics in the evocation of emotions or emotional states (Kemper and Collins 1990, Bianchi 2004, Ridgeway and Johnson 1990, Ridgeway 1994). Finally, exchange theories focus on exchange processes between actors (necessary acts in social life), in which exchange can be conceptualized in a bevy of manners. Importantly, each of these theories of exchange examines how exchange processes evoke or construct emotions and feeling states (e.g. Lawler 2001, Molm 1997, Cook and Emerson 1978, Kollack 1994, Lawler and Yoon 1998).

of acting. Everyday life requires rapid responses, and in order for people to divide their energies and attention between the ever-widening stimuli for which they are surrounded, to reduce to cognitive and emotional load, people follow rule structures, socially accepted ideas and attuned notions of "what to do," "how to think and feel," "how to act." In line with these propositions, we suggest a conceptual tool: the moral schema. Key to our arguments is the construction of moral schemas through cultural schemas. Accordingly, experiences, relationships, and socialization processes all shape a person's cultural schemas through structuralist culture carriers and emotionally-charged reinforcing culture binaries. People draw upon their moral schemas, in part comprised of cultural schemas (the "hows," "whys," and "shoulds" steeped with moral emotional overtones), to explain and justify their worldview and action. By drawing upon these moral schemas, persons both reinforce their own perspectives, but also reproduce, micro-foundationally, the roots of culture in its shared and macro-constitutional forms. The emotional qualities of moral schemas are as readily understood and transmitted as are the messages themselves (albeit most often unconsciously, without drawn out deliberation).

We have attempted to explicate some underlying social and cultural ideas as they pertain to biological mechanisms by focusing on moral schemas. What motivates our attempt is our belief in an integrated science of morality. We argue that to broaden our understanding of human morality, we have to pursue an integrated science that embraces the construction of "the moral" through a reciprocal interaction between society and mind. It is time that sociology comes forward to share their contribution to what makes the moral truly pro-social, that is, the social world as providing and shaping representations in the mind.

REFERENCES

Adolphs, R., F. Gosselin, T. W. Buchanan, D. Tranel, P. Schyns, and A. R. Damasio. 2005. "A mechanism for impaired fear recognition after amygdala damage." *Nature* 433:68–72.

Adolphs, R., D. Tranel, and A. R. Damasio. 1998. "The Human Amygdala in Social Judgment". *Nature* 393:470–474.

Adolphs, R. 2009. "The Social Brain: Neural Basis of Social Knowledge". *Annual Review of Psychology* 60: 693–716.

Alexander, J., eds. 1988. *Durkheimian Sociology: Cultural Studies.* Cambridge: Cambridge University Press.

Alexander, J., and P. Smith. 1993. "The Discourse of American Civil Society: A New Proposal for Cultural Studies". *Theory and Society* 22(2):151–207.

Beauregard, M., J. Lévesque, and P. Bourgouin. 2001. "Neural correlates of conscious self-regulation of emotion". *Journal of Neuroscience* 21(18):1–6.

Berger, P., and T. Luckmann. 1966. *The Social Construction of Reality.* New York: Doubleday.

Bergmann, J. R. 1998. "Introduction: Morality in Discourse". *Research on Language and Social Interaction* 31(3&4):279–294.

Bianchi, A. 2004. "Rejecting Others' Influence: Negative Sentiment and Status in Task Groups". *Sociological Perspectives* 47:339–355.

Biggart, N. W., and T. D. Beamish. 2003. "The Economic Sociology of Conventions: Habit, Custom, Practice, and Routine in Market Order". *Annual Review of Sociology* 29: 443–464.

Binder, A. 2007. "For Love and Money: Organizations' Creative Responses to Multiple Environmental Logics". *Theoretical Sociology* 36: 547–571.

Boltanski, L., and L. Thevenot. 2006. *On Justification: Economies of Worth*, translated by Catherine Porter. Princeton: Princeton University Press.

Boorman, S. A., and H. White. 1976. "Social Structure from Multiple Networks: II. Role Structures". *American Journal of Sociology* 81: 1384–1446.

Bourdieu, P. 1984. *Distinction: A Social Critique of the Judgment of Taste,* translated by R. Nice. Cambridge, MA: Harvard University Press.

Bourdieu, P. 1990 (1980). "Structure, Habitus, Practices". PP. 52–65 in *The Logic of Practice*. Stanford: Stanford University Press.

Burke, P. 1991. "Identity Processes and Social Stress". *American Sociological Review* 56: 836–849.

Bush G., P. Luu, and M. I. Posner. 2000. "Cognitive and Emotional Influences in Anterior Cingulate Cortex". *Trends in Cognitive Sciences* 4(6): 215–222.

Carley, K. 1991. "A Theory of Group Stability". *American Sociological Review* 56: 331–354.

Casebeer, W. D., and P. S. Churchland. 2003. "The Neural Mechanisms of Moral Cognition: A Multiple-Aspect Approach to Moral Judgment and Decision-Making". *Biology and Philosophy* 18: 169–194.

Coleman, J. 1988. "Social Capital in the Creation of Human Capital". *The American Journal of Sociology* 94: S95–S120.

Collins, R. 1981. "On the Microfoundations of Macrosociology". *American Journal of* Sociology 86: 984–1014.

Cook, K. 1977. "Exchange and Power in Networks of Interorganizational Relations". *The Sociological Quarterly* 18: 62–82.

Cook, K., and R. Emerson. 1978. "Power, Equity and Commitment in Exchange Networks". *American Sociological Review* 43: 721–739.

Cook, Karen, Richard Emerson, Mary Gillmore, and Toshio Yamagishi. 1983. "The Distribution of Power in Exchange Networks: Theory and Experimental Results". *American Journal of Sociology* 89(2): 275–305.

Cook, K., and J. Whitmeyer. 1992. "Two Approaches to Social Structure: Exchange Theory and Network Analysis". *Annual Review of Sociology* 18: 109–127.

Dalgleish, T. 2004. "The Emotional Brain". *Nature Reviews Neuroscience* 5: 582–589.

Damasio, A. R. 1994. *Descartes' Error: Emotion, Reason, and the Human Brain.* New York: Avon Books.

Damasio, A. R., D. Tranel, and H. Damasio. 1990. "Individuals with sociopathic behavior caused by frontal damage fail to respond autonomically to social stimuli." *Behavioural Brain Research* 41: 81–90.

Damasio, A. R., D. Tranel, and H. Damasio. 1991. "Somatic markers and the guidance of behaviour: theory and preliminary testing." PP. 217–229 in *Frontal Lobe Function and Dysfunction,* edited by H. S. Levin, H. M. Eisenberg and A. L. Benton. New York: Oxford University Press.

Davidson, R., K. M. Putnam, and C. L. Larson. 2000. "Dysfunction in the Neural Circuitry of Emotion Regulation: A Possible Prelude to Violence". *Science* 289: 591–594.

DiMaggio, P. 1997. "Culture and Cognition". *Annual Review of Sociology* 23: 263–287.

DiMaggio, P. J., and W. Powell. 1983. "The Iron Cage Revisited: Institutional Isomorphism and Collective Rationality in Organizational Fields." *American Sociological Review* 48: 147–160.

DiMaggio, P. J., and W. Powell. 1991. "Introduction to the new institutionalism." PP. 1–38 in *The New Institutionalism in Organizational Analysis,* edited by W. Powell and P. J. DiMaggio. Chicago: University of Chicago Press.

Douglas, M. 1986. *How Institutions Think.* Syracuse, NY: Syracuse University Press.

Drew, P. 1998. "Complaints About Transgressions and Misconduct". *Research on Language and Social Interaction* 31(3&4): 295–325.

Emerson, R. 1962. "Power-Dependence Relations". *American Sociological Review* 27(1): 31–41.

Emirbayer, M. 1997. "Manifesto for a Relational Sociology". *American Journal of Sociology* 103(2): 281–318.

Emirbayer, M., and J. Goodwin. 1994. "Network Analysis, Culture, and the Problem of Agency". *American Journal of Sociology* 99(6):1411–1454.

Evans, J. 1997. "Worldviews or Social Groups as the Source of Moral Value Attitudes: Implications for the Culture Wars Thesis". *Sociological Forum* 12(3):371–404.

Fligstein, N. 1987. "The Intraorganizational Power Struggle: Rise of Finance Personnel to Top Leadership in Large Corporations, 1919–1979." *American Sociological Review* 52: 44–58.

Fligstein, N. 1997. "Social Skill and Institutional Theory". *The American Behavioral Scientist* 40: 397–405.

Fligstein, N. 2001. "Social Skill and the Theory of Fields". *Sociological Theory* 19(2): 105–125.

Friedland, R., and R. Alford. 1991. "Bringing Society Back In: Symbols, Practices, and Institutional Contradictions". PP. 232–263 in *The New Institutionalism in Organizational Analysis,* edited by W. Powell, and P. DiMaggio. Chicago: The University of Chicago Press.

Goffman, E. 1959. *The Presentation of Self in Everyday Life.* Garden City, NY: Doubleday.

Goffman, E. 1967. *Interaction Ritual: Essays on Face-to-Face Behavior.* Garden City, NY: Anchor Books.

Greene, J. D. 2007a. "The Secret Joke of Kant's Soul". PP. 59–66 in *Moral Psychology,* Vol. 3, edited by W. Sinnott-Armstrong. Cambridge, MA: MIT Press.

Greene, J. D. 2007b. "Why are VMPFC Patients More Utilitarian? A Dual-Process Theory of Moral Judgment Explains". *Trends in Cognitive Sciences* 11(8):322–323.

Greene, J. D., R. B. Sommerville, L. E. Nystrom, J. M. Darley, and J. D. Cohen. 2001. "An fMRI Investigation of Emotional Engagement in Moral Judgment." *Science* 293: 2105–2108.

Greene, J. D., and J. Haidt. 2002. "How (and Where) Does Moral Judgment Work?" *Trends in Cognitive Sciences* 6(12): 517–523.

Greene, J. D., L. E. Nystrom, A. D. Engell, J. M. Darley, and J. D. Cohen. 2004. "The Neural Bases of Cognitive Conflict and Control in Moral Judgment". *Neuron* 44(2):389–400.

Greene, J. D., S. Morelli, K. Lowenberg, L. Nystrom, and J. Cohen. 2008. "Cognitive Load Selectively Interferes with Utilitarian Moral Judgment". *Cognition* 107(3): 1144–1154.

Haidt, J. 2001. "The Emotional Dog and Its Rational Tail: A Social Intuitionist Approach to Moral Judgment." *Psychological Review* 108: 814–834.

Haidt, J. 2008. "Morality". *Perspectives on Psychological Science* 3(1): 65–72.

Haidt, J., S. H. Koller, and M. G. Dias. 1993. "Affect, Culture, and Morality, or Is It Wrong to Eat Your Dog?" *Journal of Personality and Social Psychology* 65(4): 613–628.

Haidt, J. et al. 2007. "The New Synthesis in Moral Psychology". *Science* 316: 998–1002.

Hallett, T. 2003. "Symbolic Power and Organizational Culture." *Sociological Theory* 21: 128–149.

Hallett, T., and M. Ventresca. 2006a. "Inhabited Institutions: Social Interactions and Organizational Forms in Gouldner's *Patterns of Industrial Bureaucracy*". *Theoretical Sociology* 35: 213–236.

Hallett, T., and M. Ventresca. 2006b. "How Institutions Form: Loose Coupling as Mechanism in Gouldner's *Patterns of Industrial Bureaucracy*". *American Behavioral Scientist* 49(7): 908–924.

Hallett, T. 2010 (in press). "The Myth Incarnate: Institutional Recoupling and Turmoil in an Urban Elementary School". Obtained with Permission from Author via email Correspondence in August 2008.

Hauser, M. D. 2006. *Moral Minds: The Nature of Right and Wrong.* New York: HarperCollins Publishers.

Hauser, M. D. 2007. "What's fair? The Unconscious Calculus of Our Moral Faculty". *Empathy and Fairness* 278: 41–55.

Hauser, M. D. 2009. "The Possibility of Impossible Cultures". *Nature* 460: 190–196.

Hauser, M. D., and L. Young. 2008. Modules, Minds and Morality. In *Hormones and Social Behavior.* Verlag, Berlin, Heidelberg: Springer.

Haveman, H., and H. Rao. 1997. "Structuring a Theory of Moral Sentiments: Institutional and Organizational Coevolution in the Early Thrift Industry". *American Journal of Sociology* 102: 1606–1651.

Hitlin, S. 2008. *Moral Selves, Evil Selves: The Social Psychology of Conscience.* New York: Palgrave MacMillan.

Hochschild, A. 1983. *The Managed Heart: The Commercialization of Human Feeling.* Berkeley: University of California Press.

Hofstede, G. 1991. *Cultures and Organizations: Software of the Mind.* London: McGraw-Hill Book Company.

Holland, D. 1997. "Selves and Cultured: As Told By An Anthropologist Who Lacks a Soul". PP. 160–190 in *Self and Identity: Fundamental Issues*, edited by R. Ashmore, and L. Jussim. New York: Oxford University Press.

Howard, J., and D. Renfrow. 2003. "Social Cognition". PP. 259–281 in *Handbook of Social Psychology*, edited by J. Delamater. New York: Kluwer Academic/Plenum Publishers.

Huebner, B., S. Dwyer, and M. D. Hauser. 2008. "The Role of Emotion in Moral Psychology". *Trends in Cognitive Sciences* 13(1): 1–6.

Hunter, J. 1991. *Culture Wars: The Struggle to Define America.* New York: Basic Books.

Izard, C. 2007. "Basic Emotions, Natural Kinds, Emotion Schemas, and a New Paradigm". *Personality and Psychological Science* 2: 260–280.

Izard, C. 2009. "Emotion Theory and Research: Highlights, Unanswered Questions, and Emerging Issues". *Annual Review of Psychology* 60: 1–25.

Jackall, R. 1988. *Moral Mazes: The World of Corporate Managers.* New York: Oxford University Press.

Jepperson, R. 1991. "Institutions, Institutional Effects, and Institutionalism". PP. 143–163 in *The New Institutionalism in Organizational Analysis*, edited by W. Powell, and P. DiMaggio. Chicago: The University of Chicago Press.

Kaufman, J. 2004. "Endogenous Explanations in the Sociology of Culture". *Annual Review of Sociology* 30: 335–357.

Kemper, T., ed. 1990. *Research Agendas in the Sociology of Emotions.* Albany, NY: State University of New York Press.

Kemper, T., and R. Collins. 1990. "Dimensions of Microinteraction". *American Sociological Review* 96: 32–68.

Kohlberg, L. 1969. "Stage and Sequence: The Cognitive-Developmental Approach to Socialization". In *Handbook of Socialization Theory and Research*, edited by D. A. Goslin. Chicago: Rand McNally.

Kohlberg, L. 1971. "From is to Ought: How to Commit the Naturalistic Fallacy and Get Away with It in the Study of Moral Development". PP. 151–235 in *Cognitive Developmental Epistemology*, edited by T. Mischel. New York: Academic Press.

Kollack, P. 1994. "The Emergence of Exchange Structures: An Experimental Study of Uncertainty, Commitment, and Trust". *The American Journal of Sociology* 100(2): 313–345.

Kondo, D. 1990. *Crafting Selves: Power, Gender, and Discourses of Identity in a Japanese Workplace.* Chicago: University of Chicago Press.

Lamont, M. 1992. *Money, Morals, and Manners: The Culture of the French and the American Upper-Middle Class.* Chicago: University of Chicago Press.

Lamont, M. 2000. *The Dignity of Working Men: Morality and the Boundaries of Race, Class and Immigration.* Cambridge, MA: Harvard University Press.

Lamont, M. 2001. "Culture and Identity". PP. 171–185 in *Handbook of Sociological Theory*, edited by J. Turner. New York: Kluwer Academics/Plenum.

Lamont, M., and M. Fournier, eds. 1992. *Cultivating Differences: Symbolic Boundaries and the Making of Inequality*. Chicago: University of Chicago Press.

Lamont, M., and V. Molnar. 2002. "The Study of Boundaries in the Social Sciences". *Annual Review of Sociology* 28: 167–195.

Lane, R. D., E. M. Reiman, M. M. Bradley, P. J. Lang, G. L. Ahern, R. J. Davidsona, and G. E. Schwartz. 1997. "Neuroanatomical Correlates Of Pleasant and Unpleasant Emotion." *Neuropsychologia* 35(11): 1437–1444.

Lawler, E. 2001. "An Affect Theory of Social Exchange". *American Journal of Sociology* 107: 321–352.

Lawler, E., and J. Yoon. 1998. "Network Structure and Emotion in Exchange Relations". *American Sociological Review* 63: 871–894.

LeDoux, J E. 2000. "Emotion Circuits in the Brain". *Annual Review of Neuroscience* 23: 155–184.

LeDoux, J. E. 2002. *Synaptic Self-How Our Brains Become Who We Are*. New York: Viking.

LeDoux, J. E. 2003. "The Self: Clues from the Brain". *Annals of the New York Academy of Sciences* 1001: 295–304.

MacLean, P. D. 1990. *The Triune Brain in Evolution: Role in Paleocerebral Functions*. New York: Plenum Press.

Martin, J. 1992. *Cultures in Organizations: Three Perspectives*. Oxford: Oxford University Press.

Massey, D. 2002. "A Brief History of Human Society: The Origin and Role of Emotion in Social Life: 2001 Presidential Address". *American Sociological Review* 67(1): 1–29.

Maynard, D. 1998. "Praising Versus Blaming the Messenger: Moral Issues in Deliveries of Good and Bad News". *Research on Language and Social Interaction* 31(3&4): 359–395.

McAdam, D. 1995. Doug McAdam, "`Initiator' and `Spinoff' Movements: Diffusion Processes in Protest Cycles." In *Repertoires and Cycles of Collective Action*, edited by M. Traugott. Durham, North Carolina: Duke University.

McCall, G., and J. L. Simmons. 1978. *Identities and Interactions*. New York: Free Press.

McEwen, B. S. 2007. "Physiology and Neurobiology of Stress and Adaptation: Central Role of the Brain". *Physiological Review* 87: 873–904.

Mead, G. H. 1934. *Mind, Self and Society*. Chicago: University of Chicago Press.

Melucci, A. 1996. *Challenging Codes*. Cambridge: Cambridge University Press.

Meyer, J., and B. Rowan. 1977. "Institutionalized Organizations: Formal Structure as Myth and Ceremony". *American Journal of Sociology* 83: 333–363.

Moll, J., R. de Oliviera-Souza, P. J. Eslinger, I. E. Bramati, J. Mourao-Miranda, P. Angelo Andreiuolo, and L. Pessoa. 2002. "The Neural Correlates of Moral Sensitivity: A Functional Magnetic Resonance Imaging Investigation of Basic and Moral Emotions". *The Journal of Neuroscience* 22(7): 2730–2736.

Moll, J., R. de Oliviera-Souza, and P. J. Eslinger. 2003. "Morals and the Human Brain: A Working Model". *Neuroreport* 14: 299–305.

Moll, J., R. Zahn, R. de Oliviera-Souza, F. Krueger, and J. Grafman. 2005. "The Neural Basis of Human Moral Cognition". *Nature Reviews Neuroscience* 6: 799–809.

Moll, J., R. de Oliviera-Souza, G. J. Garrido, I. E. Bramati, E. M. A. Caparelli-Daquer, M. L. M. F. Pavia, R. Zahn, and J. Grafman. 2007. "The Self as a Moral Agent: Linking the Neural Bases of Social Agency and Moral Sensitivity". *Social Neuroscience* 2(3–4): 336–352.

Molm, L. 1997. *Coercive Power in Exchange*. Cambridge, UK: Cambridge University Press.

Peterson, R. 1976. "The Production of Culture: A Prolegomenon". PP. 7–22 in *The Production of Culture*, edited by R. A. Peterson. Beverly Hills, CA: Sage.

Peterson, R. 1979. "Revitalizing the Culture Concept". *Annual Review of Sociology* 5: 137–166.

Peterson, R., and N. Anand. 2004. "The Production of Culture Perspective". *Annual Review of Sociology* 30: 311–334.

Phelps, E. A., and J. E. LeDoux. 2005. "Contributions of the amygdala to emotion processing: from animal models to human behavior." *Neuron* 48:175–187.

Piaget, J. 1965. *The Moral Judgment of the Child*. New York: Free Press. (Original work published in 1932).

Powell, W. 1990. "Neither Market Nor Hierarchy: Network Forms of Organization". PP. 295–336 in *Research in Organizational Behavior*, vol. 12, edited by B. Staw and L. L. Cummings. Greenwich, CT: JAI Press Inc.

Powell, W., and P. J. DiMaggio. 1991. *The New Institutionalism In Organizational Analysis*. Chicago: University of Chicago Press.

Rao, H., P. Monin, and R. Durand. 2003. "Institutional Change in ToqueVille: Nouvelle Cuisine as an Identity Movement in French Gastronomy". *American Journal of Sociology* 108: 795–843.

Rao, H., C. Morrill, and M. N. Zald. 2000. "Power Plays: How Social Movements and Collective Action Create New Organizational Forms". *Research in Organizational Behavior* 22: 237–281.

Rawls, A. W. 1987. "The Interaction Order Sui Generis: Goffman's Contribution to Social Theory". *Sociological Theory* 5(2): 136–149.

Ridgeway, C. 1994. "Affect". PP. 205–230 in *Group Processes: Sociological Analyses*, edited by M. Foschi, and E. Lawler. Chicago: Nelson-Hall.

Ridgeway, C., and C. Johnson. 1990. "What is the Relationship Between Socioemotional Behavior and Status in Task Groups?" *American Journal of Sociology* 95: 1189–1212.

Rilling, J. K., D. A. Gutmana, T. R. Zeha, G. Pagnonia, G. S. Bernsa, and D. Clinton. 2001. "A Neural Basis for Social Cooperation". *Neuron* 35: 395–405.

Rusak B., and I. Zucker. 1979. "Neural Regulation of Circadian-Rhythms". *Physiological Reviews* 59(3): 449–526.

Scheff, T. 1988. "Shame and Conformity: The Deference-Emotion System". *American Sociological Review* 53: 395–406.

Schwartz, M. W., S. C. Woods, D. Porte, Jr, R. J. Seeley, and D. G. Baskin. 2000. "Central Nervous System Control of Food Intake". *Nature* 404: 661–671.

Shweder, R. 1994. ""You're Not Sick, You're Just in Love": An Attributional Theory of Motivation and Emotion". PP. 32–44 in *The Nature of Emotion: Fundamental Questions*, edited by P. Ekman, and R. Davidson. New York: Oxford University Press.

Sewell, W. 1992. "A Theory of Structure: Duality, Agency, and Transformation". *The American Journal of Sociology* 98: 1–29.

Simpson Jr. J. R., W. C. Drevets, A. Z. Snyder, D. A. Gusnard, and M. E. Raichle. 2001. "Emotion-induced Changes in Human Medial Prefrontal Cortex: II. During Anticipatory Anxiety". *Proceedings of the National Academy of Sciences of the United States of America* 98(2): 688–693.

Smith, C. 2003. *Moral, Believing Animals: Human Personhood and Culture*. Oxford: Oxford University Press.

Smith-Lovin, L. 1995. "The Sociology of Affect and Emotion". PP. 118–148 in *Sociological Perspectives on Social Psychology*, edited by K. Cook, G. A. Fine, and J. House. Boston: Allyn & Bacon.

Squire, L. 1992. "Memory and the Hippocampus – A Synthesis from Findings with Rats, Monkeys, and Humans". *Psychological Review* 99(2): 195–231.

Squire, L., and S. Zolamorgan. 1991. "The Medial Temporal-Lobe Memory System". *Science* 253(5026): 1380–1386.

Stryker, S. 1980. *Symbolic Interactionism: A Social Structural Version*. Caldwell, NJ: The Blackburn Press.

Swidler, A. 1986. "Culture in Action: Symbols and Strategies". *American Sociological Review* 51: 273–286.

Tajfel, H., and J. Turner. 1985. "The Social Identity Theory of Intergroup Behavior". PP. 7–24 in *Psychology of Intergroup Relations*, edited by S. Worchel, and W. Austin. Chicago: Nelson-Hall.

Thornton, P. H., and O. William. 1999. "Institutional Logics and the Historical Contingency of Power in Organizations: Executive Succession in the Higher Education Publishing Industry, 1958–1990." *American Journal of Sociology* 105:801–843.

Tilly, C. 1992. "How to Detect, Describe, and Explain Repertoires of Contention". *Working Paper No. 150*. Center for the Study of Social Change. New School For Social Research.

Turner, J. 2000. *On the Origins of Human Emotions: A Sociological Inquiry into the Evolution of Human Affects*. Stanford: Stanford University Press.

Turner, J. 2002. *Face-to-Face: Toward a Sociological Theory of Interpersonal Behavior*. Stanford: Stanford University Press.

Turner, J., and J. Stets. 2005. *The Sociology of Emotions*. New York: Cambridge University Press.

Turner, J., and J. Stets. 2006. "Sociological Theories of Human Emotions". *Annual Review of Sociology* 32: 25–52.

Turner, J., and J. Stets. 2007. "Moral Emotions". PP. 544–566 in *Handbook of the Sociology of Emotions*, edited by J. Turner, and J. Stets. New York: Springer.

Vaisey, S. 2008. "Socrates, Skinner, and Aristotle: Three Ways of Thinking About Culture in Action". *Sociological Forum* 23(3): 603–613.

Wellman, B. 1983. "Network Analysis: Some Basic Principles". PP. 155–200 in *Sociological Theory 1983*, edited by R. Collins. San Francisco: Jossey-Bass.

Wexler, B. E. 2006. *Brain and Culture: Neurobiology, Ideology, Social Change*. Cambridge: MIT Press.

Wrong, D. H. 1961. "The Oversocialized Conception of Man in Modern Sociology." *American Sociological Review* 26: 183–193.

Wuthnow, R. 1996. "The Restructuring of American Religion: Further Evidence." *Sociological Inquiry* 66: 303–329.

CHAPTER 20

The Social Psychology of the Moral Identity

Jan E. Stets

For some time, psychologists have been studying the relationship between moral reasoning and moral behavior. A growing body of research insists that a moral identity rather than moral reasoning is crucial to understanding moral functioning. However, despite the interest in moral identity, there is no general theory that helps us understand this identity, or more generally, the moral self. In this chapter, I discuss the well-established control systems approach of identity theory to show how different aspects of the moral self: one's moral identity, moral behavior, and moral emotions are linked in a logical and coherent way. I conceptualize social actors as self-regulating moral entities whose goal is to verify their moral identities. When moral identity verification does not ensue, moral emotions arise and motivate individuals to behave differently in order to produce outcomes that will better accomplish moral identity verification. I also discuss how we can theoretically understand the moral identity given the various other identities individuals claim.

In sociological social psychology, we have typically taken a neutral stance to studying the self. When we say that individuals have a self, it means that they have the ability to take themselves as an object, take account of themselves and plan accordingly and manipulate and control themselves in order to bring about future states (Stets and Burke 2003). The hallmark of selfhood is reflexivity; humans formulate and reflect, and this process is ongoing. In studying how people formulate standards and goals, and how they manipulate and control themselves to achieve particular end-states, we have neglected to examine how people orient themselves to the "good" (Taylor 1989). We know that persons rank some issues as important and more valuable than others (Inglehart and Baker 2000, Schwartz 2006), but researchers have not developed a theory of the self that takes into account individuals as having goals that reflect what is moral.

Psychologists have been more attentive than sociologists to human moral functioning beginning with the moral stage tradition of Piaget (1965 [1932]), and later, Kohlberg (1981).[1] In the Kohlbergian tradition, moral judgment progresses developmentally through three general levels of morality. In level 1, moral reasoning involves doing the right thing to avoid

---

[1] Since then, alternative approaches that have been offered (e.g., Damon 1984, Rest et al. 1999).

S. Hitlin, S. Vaisey (eds.), *Handbook of the Sociology of Morality*,
Handbooks of Sociology and Social Research, DOI 10.1007/978-1-4419-6896-8_20,
© Springer Science+Business Media, LLC 2010

punishment. In level 2, moral reasoning entails adhering to particular behaviors because they are agreed upon by a group or society. In level 3, moral judgments are based on the application of universal moral principles such as justice and rights. Overall, individuals at higher levels of moral development are more likely to engage in more consistent and responsible moral behavior than individuals at lower stages of moral development because the moral principles that are employed are more abstract and stable.

Despite this influential theory of moral development, empirical research has not found a strong relationship between more advanced moral development and moral behavior, suggesting that factors other than moral reasoning influence moral action (Blasi 1980). For Blasi, the missing link between moral judgment and moral action is the moral self. Specifically, one's moral identity is crucial to understanding moral functioning (Blasi 1984). For Blasi, what provides the impetus to act morally is fidelity to the moral self rather than fidelity to moral principles.

For roughly two decades, Blasi advanced the role of the self and identity in moral functioning, thereby expanding the Kohlbergian tradition. Since then, other psychologists have been developing the role of the self and identity in morality using a social-cognitive approach (Aquino and Freeman 2009, Aquino et al. 2009, Lapsley and Narvaez 2004a). I will summarize the dominant psychological approaches to moral identity before offering a sociological approach. The sociological approach fills an important gap in psychological work on moral identity by providing a conceptual framework that links different aspects of the self into a coherent theoretical structure. For example, psychologists typically emphasize the cognitive aspects of the self that serve as the basis for moral behavior while neglecting the emotional aspects of the self. Blasi (1999), for instance, maintains that any moral action should be intentional and based on moral reasoning. While he acknowledges that moral emotions such as guilt may emerge from immoral behavior, these moral emotions are not well-integrated into his model. Recently, some psychologists (Haidt 2001, Hardy 2006, Hoffman 2000, Prinz 2004) and neuroscientists (Greene et al. 2001, Koenigs et al. 2007) have been studying the relationship between moral judgments, moral behavior, and moral emotions. However, we still need a clear theory that links the cognitive, behavioral, and emotional dimensions of the moral self in a coherent manner.

A sociological theory that offers a logical way of linking the various dimensions of the self into a moral self is the control systems approach of identity theory (Burke and Stets 2009). This is a well-established theory that has been supported by a systematic program of research for the past 30 years. A guiding assumption in identity theory is that humans actively engage in goal-directed action that is always under their evaluation as they interact with the environment. Goal accomplishment involves people controlling their perceptions in the environment so that their perceptions (that is, how they see themselves and how others see them in situations) are kept near their internal identity standards. This is identity verification. When individuals are *unable* to control perceptions (of who they are in situations) at the level of their internal identity standard, they will experience negative arousal. In turn, the negative arousal will motivate them to behave differently in their environment in order to produce perceptual outcomes that result in a better match with their internal identity standard. When I apply the control systems approach of identity theory to the moral self in this chapter, we will see the cognitive dimension of the moral self: the control of perceptions to match internal, moral identity standard meanings, the behavioral dimension of the moral self: moral action in the service of moral identity standard meanings, and the emotional dimension of the moral self: the experience of moral emotions in response to behavior and cognitive moral meanings.

To begin to illustrate the theory, let us take a simple example. Suppose Mary sees herself as kind and caring. Kind and caring would be the meanings that comprise her moral identity standard. For Mary, goal accomplishment involves her obtaining feedback from others in situations that she is kind and caring. For example, if Mary sits and listens to her friend, Jane, talk about the recent breakup of her marriage, at some point Jane may exclaim "You are such a kind person to sit and listen to me, Mary!" Upon Mary hearing this, she perceives that this evaluation of her is consistent with her identity standard meanings. Her moral identity has been verified in the situation. However, if Mary spends her time with Jane talking about herself rather than listening to Jane, she may hear Jane remark, "Mary, it's unkind of you to be dominating the discussion and not allowing me to share my marital problems." Upon hearing this, Mary will perceive this evaluation as inconsistent with her identity standard meanings. In response, Mary will likely experience negative emotions such as guilt or shame. These negative feelings will motivate her to behave differently in the situation, perhaps spend less time talking about herself and more time listening to Jane with the hope that Jane will evaluate Mary as kind after all. More generally, the goal is for Mary to obtain feedback from others in situations in which the meanings of this feedback are consistent with the meanings in her identity standard.

The identity process that I will discuss in this chapter is general and applies to individuals when they take on *person* identities, *role* identities, and *social* identities. I will just be focusing on the moral identity which is a *person* identity. Person identities involve individuals claiming distinctive meanings about themselves that often are not shared with others; identity verification of these distinctive meanings produces feelings of authenticity. There are also role identities which entail embracing the meanings associated with particular roles in society such as student, friend, or spouse; identity verification in roles leads to feelings of competence. Additionally, there are social identities which comprise the meanings that individuals claim while in a group such as a church, community organization, or local country club; verification of one's identity in groups activates a sense of belongingness and self-worth. In identity theory, person, role, and social identities are subject to the same self-regulatory process. Individuals regulate the meanings of their identity, these meanings are maintained through the perceptual control process that is the basis of identity verification, and negative arousal will be felt when identity verification is not obtained. This self-regulatory process will be discussed in some detail in this chapter as it applies to the moral self. Let me begin by discussing how we might conceptualize (the) moral person identity.

CONCEPTUALIZING (THE) MORAL IDENTITY

Let me first define morality. Broadly speaking, morality is the "evaluative cultural codes that specify what is right or wrong, good or bad, acceptable or unacceptable" in a society (Turner and Stets 2006:544). As Turner and Stets have argued, as one proceeds from the macro level to the micro level, moral codes decrease somewhat in the intensity of their evaluative content along the good/bad dimension. At the broadest level are *values* which are highest in evaluative content, are context-free, and shared by most in a society. In western societies, these values include personal control, individualism, and competitiveness. When values are translated into moral codes for broad institutions, they become *ideologies*. For example, in western societies, the value of control is translated in the family into the belief that parents have the right to control their children. At the level of institutions, *norms* emerge. Norms also emerge in face-to-face interactions. Compared to values and ideologies, norms are not as heavily laden with evaluative content as to what is good/bad or right/wrong, but they do carry expectations of appropriate behavior. These expectations vary as to how much they comprise the principle of what is good/bad or right/wrong thus making some behavior both moral and normative, other behavior distinctively moral, and still other behavior distinctively normative. I will have more to say about this later. Finally, at the level of the person, we can think of individuals internalizing meanings as to who they are along the good–bad dimension. This is one's moral identity.

Surprisingly, psychologists and sociologists conceptualize the moral identity in different ways. It is important to discuss this difference because it is premised on historically dissimilar views of the self. In general, many psychologists maintain that having a *moral identity* means that being moral is at the core of the self. It is the essence of who one is. Alternatively, many sociologists assert that claiming a moral identity does not mean it is central to the self. Rather, *the moral identity* simply identifies one among a host of identities that an individual may claim. Psychologists and sociologists do share this view: (the) moral identity offers a self-view or set of self-meanings that can guide one's perceptions and behavior within and across situations.

I will first outline the different ways that (the) moral identity has been conceptualized in each discipline. Then, I will discuss two dominant models that have been used in psychology to understand moral identity: the self model and social-cognitive model. Following this, I will present an identity theory approach to explaining the moral identity that I think significantly advances current thinking.

Psychology

For psychologists, an *identity* is the center or essence of one's being; it is one's "essential self" (Blasi 1984, 1993). Individuals will vary on what personal characteristics or traits they claim as essential to themselves. Some may claim competitiveness or kindness or friendliness as core to themselves. Whatever they claim as essential, this identity orders their life, provides purpose, and influences their lifelong projects. When individuals identify being moral persons as core to themselves, they have a *moral identity*.[2] Blasi (1984) recognized that different moral aspects may characterize the moral identity of different individuals. For example, some may see care as essential to their moral identity while others may see justice as central. Despite this variation within and across individuals, he insisted that when moral notions are central, it inspires moral action. Others share this view (Aquino and Freeman 2009, Aquino et al. 2009, Aquino and Reed 2002, Hardy 2006, Reed and Aquino 2003, Reed et al. 2007). Because the moral identity is at the center of the self, it is experienced as the real me, the authentic self, the deepest principle that guides the self.

---

[2] Blasi (2004) claimed that a mature identity is a moral identity.

The above view conceptualizes identity as a unitary construct. Whatever identity persons claim, it represents who they are at the deepest level. If identity is understood in this way, then correspondingly, the self will be seen in a similar way. This is particularly evident in the writings of Blasi who is considered one of the seminal thinkers on moral identity (Lapsley and Narvaez 2004a). Rather than seeing the self (as sociologists would) as an entity that is multifaceted and differentiated given the many characteristics that individuals may identify as uniquely descriptive of themselves, the various roles they take on in society, and the different groups that they may belong to, Blasi saw this view as fragmenting the self into multiple domains that did not provide any coherence to the self.

To make sense of the self, Blasi (1988, 1993; Blasi and Glodis 1995) maintained that we must return to an important aspect of Erikson's (1968) work on identity, that is, the *experience* that individuals have as to who they are at a deep level. For Blasi, rather than focusing on Erikson's idea of a *crisis* where individuals are asked the question, "Who am I?," and they respond by describing themselves in ways based on their group memberships or role occupancies [what Blasi (1995) identified as "external matters"], researchers need to study identity phenomenologically. We need to investigate the self "as subject" or "as knower." Here, the focus is on individuals as they know themselves to be, as they experience themselves as agents and the source of their intentional actions, and as they come to know themselves as a unique, yet unified entity. The unity of the self is revealed in individuals finding a principle by which to order their past, present, and future and form a coherent biography. Discovering this coherence or organizing framework means that while persons may identify traits and characteristics that describe themselves, they organize these characteristics into an internal hierarchy as to what is central or peripheral, important or unimportant. What is central forms one's core or essential self (Blasi 2004).

Sociology

In sociology, the self is often conceptualized not in unitary terms with respect to individuals having a core self. Instead, the self is conceptualized as differentiated, complex, yet organized (Stets and Burke 2003). This is because the context within which the self is shaped and develops is society, and society is differentiated, complex, yet organized (Stryker [1980] 2002). When the self is viewed in this way, a number of different views about the self may be invoked within and across situations because of the different groups they are members of and the various roles they assume in society. These groups and roles ask particular commitments of individuals, and correspondingly, certain identities that are to be acted upon over others. The fact that individuals have a variety of self-views as to who they are given their various commitments does not divorce them from their immediate experiences as some claim (Blasi 2004, Blasi and Glodis 1995). These different commitments and allegiances are meaningful and real to individuals and influence how they act in situations. They form the "essential self" at the time, although the content of the essential self may change as the commitments to groups and roles change in the situation. In general, sociologists take seriously James' (1890) idea that there are as many selves as there are different groups to which the self responds and different positions that one holds in society.

If individuals have multiple selves, it follows that they have multiple identities. An *identity* is the set of *meanings* that persons attribute to themselves as a person (person identity), role holder (role identity), or group member (social identity) and these meanings guide how they behave. [3] For example, the student role identity may contain the meaning of being "academic," and we should find that the person holding this student identity meaning will regularly attend class, take notes, pass exams, and finish courses (Burke and Reitzes 1981). Alternatively, the student identity may contain the meaning of being "social" rather than being "academic," thus we would expect this person to spend time socializing with friends and attending parties rather than going to class and doing well in courses. At the same time, the person claiming the student identity also may claim the friend identity, fraternity or sorority identity, basketball or soccer identity, son or daughter identity, a moral identity, and so forth.

Multiple identities may not be activated at the same time in a situation, but if they are, three scenarios may occur (Burke and Stets 2009). Multiple identities may share meanings so that the activation of one identity invokes another identity with the result that the identities are supporting each other. For example, the moral identity may hold meanings in common with the friend identity such as being "caring" such that when a situation arises where a friend wants to drive home drunk, the response of driving the friend home facilitates being a friend and a moral person. Alternatively, multiple identities may be in conflict with one another because the meanings of one identity oppose the meanings of another identity. For example, the meaning of "care" in the moral identity may conflict with the meaning of "negligence" in the delinquent identity. Finally, the meanings of identities may simply be irrelevant to one another as when the meaning of "care" in the moral identity is irrelevant to the meaning of being "clever" and "creative" in the identity of author.

In identity theory in sociology, multiple identities are reflected in the notion of identity salience. More salient identities are those identities that are ranked higher in people's internal rank ordering of all the identities that they claim. And, more salient identities are more likely to operate across situations. As we will see, identity *salience* is similar to identity *centrality* in psychology in which a more important identity is activated across situations. The difference is that identity centrality does not incorporate the idea that individuals are simultaneously holding other identities. Recently, psychologists have begun to discuss the idea that multiple identities exist, and they have used the term identity salience to describe the process by which situational factors make salient or activate some identities over others in situations. However, we will see that identity salience in psychology emphasizes the role of the situation in determining what identity becomes salient while identity salience in sociology maintains that salience is internally derived rather than derived from the situation.

PSYCHOLOGICAL MODELS OF MORAL IDENTITY

The Self-Model

As mentioned above, Blasi advanced a phenomenological approach to self and identity. From this perspective, identity is understood from the perspective of the self "as subject" where the different aspects of the self are integrated, experienced in intentional action, and individuals

---

[3] As we will see later, these meanings are contained in the identity standard.

find a principle that orders their past, present, and future and that forms their core self – their identity. If the organizing principle is in moral terms, then one has a moral identity. Therefore, moral knowledge is not the motivational force that influences moral behavior as Kohlberg theorizes. Rather, it is moral knowledge as it is integrated into the self and becomes essential to who one is (as a moral identity) that is important in influencing moral behavior. Thus, the cognitive foundation of morality is retained, but it is incorporated into the self to more adequately account for moral functioning.

In Blasi's self model (1983), moral judgments more reliably predict moral behavior if they are filtered through *responsibility* based on moral identity and acted upon on the basis of *self-consistency*. Responsibility is the feeling that one is compelled to act on what is good or right. One sees that it is necessary to carry out the action. There is an obligation to behave morally. What is important about responsibility is that the self is directly implicated in the action. Self-consistency is congruity of judgment and action not based on beliefs or knowing what is good but based on aligning one's actions to one's own sense of self as a moral being. It is acting consistently with what is core to the structure of the self. It is engaging in moral action because it fits with one's self-definition.

Because the self has multiple needs that may conflict with carrying out moral actions that are consistent with one's essential self, Blasi pointed out that the self needs to be equipped to ward off these conflicts. Conflicts can occur at any stage of the decision-making process: in interpreting a situation as morally potent, in assessing whether it is one's responsibility to act, and in evaluating whether one has provided the proper response. In the latter case, emotions such as guilt may emerge if there is inconsistency between what one does and what one feels is his responsibility to do.

Following Blasi's lead, Aquino and his colleagues empirically studied the centrality notion of moral identity which they referred to as moral identity's *self-importance* (Aquino and Reed 2002). They developed a two-dimensional scale of moral identity's self-importance comprised of *internalization* and *symbolization*. Internalization refers to whether individuals identify moral characteristics as representing their inner self. Symbolization is the degree to which individuals represent moral identity through moral action in situations. More generally, these two dimensions examine the degree to which individuals' self-conceptions are privately (internalization) and publicly (symbolization) organized around moral qualities.[4]

While the centrality of moral identity helps advance our understanding of how moral cognition influences moral action given that moral knowledge gets integrated into the self structure and serves as its own motivating factor for moral behavior, even the centrality of moral identity does not always lead to moral behavior (Hardy and Carlo 2005). Additionally, not all moral behavior is intentional and deliberate as Blasi assumed. Some moral action is more automatic, and a model is needed that takes this automaticity into account (Hardy and Carlo 2005). Researchers have begun to examine how situational factors interact with self factors to influence moral behavior, and how moral behavior is more or less deliberative.

---

[4] Studies using the centrality measure of moral identity find that those high in moral identity are more likely than those low on moral identity to perceive and behave more benevolently to out-group members (Reed and Aquino 2003), and they are less likely to use moral disengagement maneuvers that facilitate people supporting war-related activities (Aquino et al. 2006).

For example, Cervone (2004) has developed the Knowledge-and-Appraisal Personality Architecture (KAPA) Model in which consistency in behavior across situations is a function of: (1) self-schemas (internal knowledge structures or mental representations as to how people see themselves) and (2) beliefs about social situations and the expectations of behavior. While the first feature takes into account relatively enduring elements of self-knowledge, the second capitalizes on dynamic processes involving the construction of meaning in a situation regarding expectations of behavior. The two coalesce to produce behavior in a situation that is consistent with individuals' mental representations of themselves at the time. As applied to moral identity, if individuals have a self-schema that is moral, moral behavior will emerge in a situation only if the situation is interpreted as carrying moral expectations of behavior.

A more prominent approach is the social-cognitive model that brings together elements of: (1) schemas that make particular encoding of one's surroundings (such as encoding the world in moral terms) more available in memory for use in situations and (2) situational cues that temporarily activate or deactivate self-schemas such as the moral self-schema (Aquino and Freeman 2009, Aquino et al. 2009, Lapsley and Narvaez 2004b). In this way, a central moral identity will be more readily accessible for use across situations, but it may be deactivated if the situation cues another self-schema.

The Social-Cognitive Model

The social-cognitive model is grounded in the social-cognitive approach (Howard and Renfrow 2003). An assumption in this approach is that humans have cognitive limits in their processing of information, thus they develop systems of categorization. One system is schemas. These are abstract, yet organized knowledge structures about any stimulus whether it is visual, auditory, olfactory and so forth that get stored in memory and are available for retrieval when information needs to be processed in situations. Schemas are one's "theory" about the content and operations of stimuli. Individuals develop various organized knowledge structures about different schemas such as self-schemas (information about one's self), person schemas (information about particular people), role schemas (expectations associated with particular roles), and event schemas (expectations about everyday events). Tied to schemas are goals to be achieved and behaviors that meet those goals.

The more that a schema is used or retrieved from memory and invoked in a situation, the more accessible it becomes in the future for activation. Accessible schemas will have a ready-made, available way of processing information in a situation and corresponding behavioral routines associated with those schemas.[5] Finally, while the accessibility of particular schemas varies from person to person, schema activation is not completely dependent upon the person. It may also be influenced by the situation. Some situations "cue" or "bring to the foreground" some schemas over others (Lapsley and Narvaez 2004b).

Aquino and his associates recently applied a social-cognitive model to moral identity (Aquino and Freeman 2009, Aquino et al. 2009). While in earlier work they referred to moral

---

[5] This is where unconscious and automatic cognitive processing is evident in the social-cognitive model compared to intentional or deliberate action in the self model.

identity's centrality in terms of self-importance, in later work, they indicate that when moral identity is very central or very important to the self, it should be activated more strongly and more often than other self-schemas, thereby making it chronically accessible. Therefore, moral identity's centrality or self-importance is equated with the chronic accessibility of the moral self-schema. Individuals vary on the chronic accessibility of the moral self-schema, but whatever its level, it is conceptualized as operating in a fairly stable manner across situations.

A further extension that Aquino and his colleagues make from earlier thinking is the idea that though moral identity may be more accessible than other self-schemas, situational cues may activate or deactivate it. Therefore, they introduce moral identity *salience* to refer to the temporary activation of moral identity in consciousness in a situation; it is brought to the fore by situational factors. When temporary moral identity salience *and* moral identity centrality (chronic accessibility) are high, they become readily available in the *working self-concept* for processing of information in situations. The working self-concept consists of one's subset of self-views that are currently "at play" in a situation either because they have been activated in a recent situation and they stay "turned on" in the current situation, they have been elicited by the current situation, or they form one's core self-view (Markus and Kunda 1986).[6] Thus, the working self-concept is made up of core self-views as well as tentative self-views.

Aquino and his colleagues recognize that individuals have multiple identities but that only a few can be held at any given time in their working self-concept. They maintain that when multiple identities conflict within the working self-concept, for example, there is temporary activation of both moral identity and a self-interested identity in consciousness, thus making each *salient*, it can create psychological tension. Whichever identity is "cued" or "primed" in the situation will be the identity most likely to have an influence in the situation. For example, if the self-interested identity is cued in the situation, its salience will influence behavior. Moral identity salience is essentially deactivated in the working self-concept. Further, this has implications for moral identity centrality – one's core self-view. Moral identity centrality will be temporarily reduced in accessibility in the working self-concept, serving to reduce the psychological tension between the activated self-interested identity and deactivated moral identity in the situation. Here we get a glimpse as to the role of distress or negative emotions. Identity theory will have more to say about this. In general, the above processes have been supported in empirical studies (Aquino and Freeman 2009, Aquino et al. 2009).

If situational factors temporarily activate an identity such as a self-interested identity that may not be core to the self (such as moral identity), how can a central, accessible identity be enduring and stable and operate across situations? Aquino and his associates (Aquino et al. 2009) maintain that if individuals regularly encounter situations where the self-interested identity is activated and reinforced, over time this could reduce the accessibility of moral identity and induce situational variability in the person's commitment to moral action. Thus, the accumulation of experiences that challenges the relevance of moral action may threaten one's core self-view: one's moral identity. Alternatively, experiences that reinforce the relevance of moral behavior will enhance the accessibility of moral identity.

---

[6] The working self-concept is very similar to the idea, in identity theory, of our *self-image* or *working copy* (Burke 1980). This is the self-view that we bring into situations and that is subject to constant change and revision based on situational influences in contrast to our idealized views of who we are that are relatively unchanging.

The self model and the social-cognitive model address moral identity in slightly different ways. The self model focuses on the unity of the self, the phenomenological experience of identity for individuals, intentional action, and the important role of self-consistency. In contrast, the social-cognitive model takes into account persons' multiple self-conceptions, how these self-conceptions are activated in situations, and the automaticity of self-conceptions given chronic accessibility and the associated behaviors that provide a ready-made response in situations. While some have argued that the social-cognitive approach does not assume a self-consistency motive because: (1) people can change their self-views and goals and (2) consistency with one's essential self may be a preoccupation with only Western individuals (Cervone and Tripathi 2009), Aquino and his colleagues (2009) indicate that one premise in their social-cognitive model is that moral identity is a powerful source of moral motivation because people generally desire to maintain self-consistency. Self-consistency is an important assumption in identity theory as well, but we will see that identity theory offers a more comprehensive theoretical explanation for the existence and maintenance of the moral self. This is because it links identity, behavior, and emotions in a way that psychologists have not been able to do.

IDENTITY THEORY

Identity theory in sociology (Burke and Stets 2009) offers several advances over the self model and the social-cognitive model. First, rather than emphasizing the "self as subject" in the self model (given the phenomenological orientation) or conceptualizing the "self as object" in the social-cognitive model (given the multiple self-conceptions view), identity theory assumes that individuals are both "subjects" and "objects" within and across situations. Individuals act on the basis of their identity standard meanings (self as "subject"), and they evaluate the meaning of their actions and monitor these meanings so that they are consistent with their own self-meanings (self as "object"). Thus, identity theory reveals a self that is both an "I" (an agent) and a "Me" (an object of reflection) in situations.

Second, identity theory allows for a multiple self-conception view of the self like the social-cognitive model, and it also assumes a self-consistency motive as initially proposed in the self model. The assumption in identity theory is that individuals control perceptions to maintain their self-meanings in their identity standard. However, the self-meanings in their standard are always changing though at a very slow rate (Burke and Stets 2009). The change is not noticeable except over long periods of time ranging from weeks to months to even years. The identity verification motive serves the purpose of *resisting* identity change. Because of this resistance, there is stability. But, resisting change is not the same as sustaining no change. The change will simply occur very slowly, although there are some exceptions to this slowness rule as when one experiences brainwashing.

Third, like the social-cognitive model, identity theory focuses on situational meanings that influence how one behaves in a situation. In fact, identity theorists are beginning to investigate how "cueing" some identities over other identities in a situation influences behavior (Carter 2010). However, identity theorists also study another important situational influence: the meanings others "give off" in the situation including the expectations others have as to how one should behave. This feedback can facilitate or impede identity verification for the self.

Finally, emotions are incorporated into identity theory in a way that they are not in the self model or social-cognitive model. In both Blasi and Aquino's writings, we get a hint as to how negative emotions may emerge when individuals behave in ways that are contrary to their core self or central identity, but the role of emotions is never fully developed. Identity theory fills this gap. The theory links the cognitive, behavioral, and emotional aspects of the self in a logical way. Let me first discuss how any identity operates.

Identity Operations

The control systems approach of identity theory addresses the internal dynamics that operate within the self when a person claims an identity such as the moral identity. In the control systems approach, when an identity is activated in a situation, the meanings that define the identity serve as the standard for individuals and a feedback loop is established as shown in Figure 20.1 (Burke and Stets 2009). This loop has five components: (1) the identity standard (the self-meanings of an identity), (2) output (meaningful behavior) to the situation, (3) perceptual input of meanings from the situation including how one sees oneself (self-appraisals) as well as the meaningful feedback one obtains from others (reflected appraisals), (4) a process that compares the perceptual input with the identity standard (the comparator), and (5) emotions that immediately result from the comparison process and that increase the gain (negative emotions) or decrease the gain (positive emotions) for the self-directed system. Let me apply each of the feedback loop components to the moral self..

IDENTITY STANDARD: The moral identity is the identity standard in Figure 20.1. This identity standard contains the *meanings* that are associated with being moral. In earlier research, I have discussed and operationalized two underlying meaning dimensions of the moral identity: a justice and rights meaning dimension and a care and relationship orientation dimension (Stets and Carter 2006, Stets et al. 2008). This is consistent with earlier discussions in the literature regarding the basis of morality (Gilligan 1982, Kohlberg 1981). However, there is no clear agreement either among philosophers or psychologists as to the meaning of morality. For example, some philosophers would argue that rather than understanding morality as an instance of an individual applying the principle of justice or care, morality should be understood as a community activity in which community members come to a consensus as to how to resolve moral problems that they encounter, thus reaching a "common morality" (Walzer 1983). Alternatively, psychologists have postulated other dimensions of morality than justice or care. For example, some have identified three moral codes that exist cross-culturally: autonomy, community, and divinity (Shweder et al. 1997), while others have expanded this to investigate five moral foundations: harm/care, fairness/reciprocity, ingroup/loyalty, authority/respect, and purity/sanctity (Graham et al. 2009, Haidt and Graham 2007).

Focusing on justice and care emphasizes the idea that the fundamental unit of moral value is the individual. Individuals' autonomy and welfare are to be protected. However, the group is another fundamental source of moral value as revealed in such moral concerns as community, loyalty, respect for others, and sacredness. The emphasis is on interdependence, cohesiveness, attachment to groups and beyond. In this way, while the moral dimensions of justice and care highlight an *individualizing* approach to morality that may characterize Western countries, it

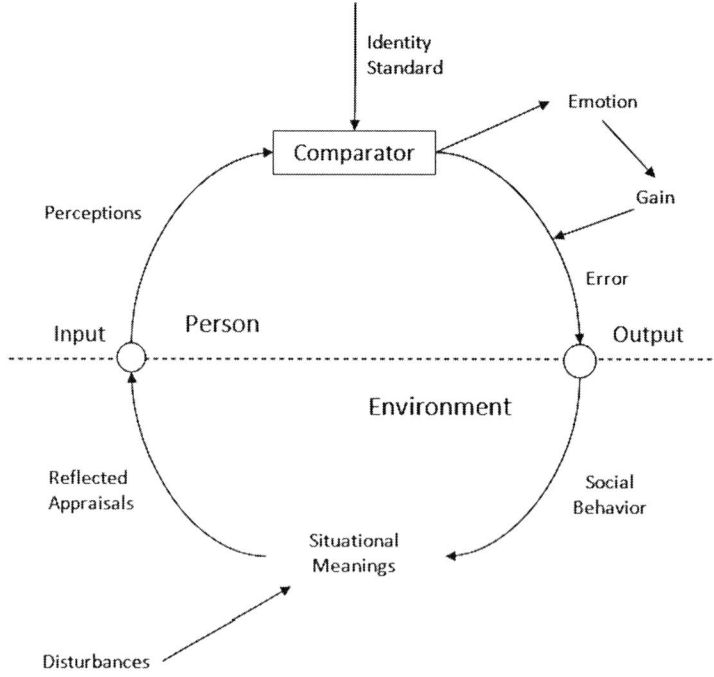

Model 1. Identity Control

FIGURE 20.1. Identity control.

omits a *binding* approach to morality that may describe many non-Western countries (Haidt 2008).[7] The meanings for any identity can vary from society to society given the culture, and within a society, from group to group.

In identity theory, whatever the meanings that comprise the identity standard, once they are activated in a situation, the feedback loop is set in motion. Identity activation means that people are attempting to *verify* an identity at that moment. As I will discuss later, individuals vary in terms of whether their moral identity will be activated in a situation depending upon the salience of the moral identity in their overall rank ordering of salience of all the other identities they claim.

Output: When the moral identity is activated in a situation, it influences moral behavior. This is the output in Figure 20.1. Moral behavior is different from normative or conventional behavior. While normative behavior consists of socially agreed upon practices, moral behavior

---

[7] Individuals may have individualizing *and* binding elements within their moral meaning structure thus "speaking two or more moral dialects" (Wong 2009:103). Thus not all meanings are internally and logically consistent. Rather than thinking they lead to contradictions and psychological tension, Wong indicates that they may simply reflect moral complexity that may result in novel behaviors.

is consensually based conduct that is imbued with the expectation to do what is right or good (Turner and Stets 2006). As mentioned earlier, while some behavior may be viewed as both moral and normative, other behavior may be characteristically moral or characteristically normative. For example, when police officers dress themselves in a blue uniform, this behavior is based on custom. It has very little moral content and may be seen as distinctively normative conduct. When a police officer comes to the aid of someone being physically attacked, this response is moral ("one helps another") as well as normative (protecting a citizen is part of a police officer's job). Behavior that signals stronger moral content would occur if a citizen intervened to protect someone who was being physically attacked. We do not expect a citizen to intervene, but when the person does, we attribute their actions as morally good. While it is hard to find a norm that does not carry at least some moral content, not all normative behavior is moral. For example, conforming to a group's normative expectations of participating in a lynch mob is immoral. Alternatively, non-conforming behavior such as reporting a wrongdoing in a corporation is moral. Thus, social consensus alone does not determine moral behavior. One needs to also determine whether the principles of what is right or good also are guiding the behavior. Once moral behavior is enacted in the situation, the meanings that it "gives off" serve as the basis for a response in the situation.

Input: When moral behavior is enacted, there are two responses. One response is individuals' own perceptions as to the meanings that their behavior implies. These are *self-appraisals*. The other response is others' responses to the meanings of individuals' behavior in situations. These are *reflected appraisals*. Both sets of appraisals, which together are perceptions' of self-relevant meanings in situations, serve as the input in Figure 20.1 although most theory and research in identity theory has been on reflected appraisals. Self-appraisals involve actors comparing the meanings of their behavior with the meanings stored in their identity standard. Reflected appraisals are actors' perceptions of how they *think* others perceive them in the situation given the identity that they are portraying. These perceptions may be based on the behavior of others in the form of their overt actions or in the form of expressions that they "give off," or it may be a combination of the two. For example, a person may see herself as being rather just and kind (meanings in her moral identity standard). In a situation, she may enact behaviors that are consistent with these meanings such as treating another fairly and being supportive and thoughtful. Others in the situation may react to her behavior verbally and nonverbally, which tells her that she is seen as behaving in a relatively fair and caring manner. Her observations of her own behavior may also lead her to evaluate her behavior as typifying that she is fair and caring.

Comparator: The perceptions of the meanings of one's own and others' reactions are being continuously fed into the comparator in Figure 20.1. The comparator compares the input perceptions of meanings relevant to an identity with the meanings stored in the identity standard. It produces an "error signal," which is the difference between the input meanings and standard meanings. The identity standard meanings are the "ruler" for measuring input perceptions. In thinking about this numerically, if the identity standard is set at 7 (on a scale of 0–10) for being caring, and the person is acting "7" in terms of being caring in the situation, there is a perfect match between input and identity standard meanings. In identity terms, this is *identity verification*. The perceived meanings in the situation correspond to the meanings in the identity standard, and the person is verifying that she is the person her identity standard indicates.

As a consequence of identity verification, the person will feel good. The goal of being caring has been met. Alternatively, if the person is acting a "3" in terms of being caring in the situation, there is a mismatch or non-correspondence between input meanings and identity standard meanings. What results is *identity non-verification* and the person will feel bad.

Emotion: In Figure 20.1, emotion signals the degree of correspondence between input meanings and identity standard meanings. Continuous identity verification produces positive emotion such as happiness and identity non-verification produces negative emotion such as sadness. Negative emotions will create a greater force, pressure, or drive to reduce the non-correspondence between input and identity standard meanings. In Figure 20.1, this greater force or pressure is the "loop gain" (Powers 1973). When identity non-verification occurs, negative feelings increase gain and drive the system in a stronger manner to counteract the disturbance. Behaviorally, this translates into a person working harder to resolve the discrepancy, doing whatever it takes to facilitate congruity.[8] Alternatively, positive feelings reduce gain and push the system less forcefully.

In the above example, if the person were to act "3" rather than "7" in terms of being caring in the situation, the negative emotion that emerges will increase gain in the system, thereby driving the self to work harder to resolve the discrepancy. Thus, the person may take the time to help others often and with increased intensity so that the perceptual input meanings more closely match the internal standard meanings. However, if the person were to behave as a "10" in terms of care, there is still a mismatch. The difference is that the input meanings are exceeding the identity standard meanings rather than falling short of them. In identity theory, this still produces negative emotion because the goal has not been met. In response, the person might work hard at becoming less thoughtful or caring since current perceptions reveal excessive caring.

For the moral identity, it is important to examine emotions that are not simply negative or positive but that are moral emotions. Much attention has been given to studying the moral emotions of guilt and shame (Scheff 1988, 2000, Tangney et al. 2007). Guilt and shame are *self-critical* emotions in that individuals become an object to their own actions and they evaluate their behavior in light of their standards or goals (Lewis 2008). To the extent that actors feel responsible for failing to live up to their standards or goals, they will feel guilt or shame. Shame is an intense feeling experienced for the violation of a moral standard in which the "whole self" is seen as responsible. Persons reflect upon themselves as "horrible agents." They feel small, worthless, and otherwise in disfavor with others and want to hide, escape, or strike back. In contrast, guilt concerns a particular behavior individuals have committed. Rather than seeing the global self in negative terms, guilt leads persons to see that they "did a bad thing" while generally not devaluing the whole self. Thus, guilt is less painful, leading people to experience emotions such as remorse and regret and motivating them to confess, apologize, and repair the wrongdoing.

---

[8] As we will see a little later, identity theorists earlier labeled this "effort" commitment, with greater effort reflecting greater commitment to an identity and reduced effort reflecting less commitment to an identity (Burke and Reitzes 1991).

There are other moral emotions that are *other-critical* such as contempt, anger, and disgust (Rozin et al. 1999). These emotions are associated with the moral codes of community, autonomy, and divinity, respectively, that have been identified cross-culturally (Shweder et al. 1997). Contempt reflects negative evaluating others and feeling morally superior in comparison to others. It thus violates notions of community. Anger is often expressed when another is thought to be responsible for blocking one's goals. Therefore, anger is associated with the violation of the moral code of autonomy. Disgust is the emotional reaction that is triggered when people degrade themselves or strip others of their dignity. It violates the moral code of purity or sanctity.

While moral emotions might be expanded to include *other-suffering* emotions such as sympathy and empathy, *other-praising* emotions such as gratitude and elevation (Haidt 2003), and a range of other emotions by combining primary emotions (Turner and Stets 2006), what is most important is identifying the underlying theoretical process that produce these moral emotions. In identity theory, identity non-verification influences negative feelings. Recently, it has been suggested that the process by which individuals make an internal or external attribution to identity non-verification in a situation may influence the specific emotional responses that are felt (Stets and Burke 2005). For example, the self-critical emotion of shame may emerge for those individuals who blame themselves (an internal attribution) for not being able to verify their moral identity. Thus, people who hold the moral identity standard of fairness but then get caught not paying their full taxes because they omit reporting additional income in their Turbo Tax program would feel shame. They are the source of the identity discrepancy and are responsible for the disruption in the verification of their moral identity. Alternatively, if the tax error is the result of tax accountants being negligent in their calculations, then individuals would feel anger because the other in the situation is the source of their identity discrepancy (an external attribution).

The attribution process may also influence the different moral emotions that people may experience when taking into account each other's status position in the social structure in situations (Stets and Burke 2005). For instance, for two people (A and B), A can have higher status than B, equal status with B, or lower status than B. If A is responsible for not being able to verify his moral identity in a situation (an internal attribution), he may be more likely to feel shame if this occurs in the presence of a higher status B. If it occurs in the presence of an equal status other, embarrassment may be felt, and if it occurs in the presence of a lower status other, mild discomfort may be experienced. If another is the source of not being able to verify one's identity, hostility may be felt if the other is of lower status and anxiety may be experienced if the other is of higher status. In general, the role of attributions in advancing our understanding on the relationship between the identity verification or non-verification of the moral identity and moral emotions needs empirical testing. The power that the attribution process may have is in identifying which particular moral emotion emerges in specific contexts.

Summary: Overall, the identity process as outlined in Figure 20.1 traces identity meanings from the environment where the meanings are perceived, to the comparator where they are compared with the identity standard meanings. If there is a discrepancy in the two meanings, negative emotion is felt, and behavior is altered or outputs are modified to the social situation so that new perceptions are input to the comparator as the cycle continues. Thus, the identity system has the goal of matching situational inputs to internal standards. Persons act to control perceptions to keep them at or near the standard and to verify their identities.

The above process is continuous and ongoing. The cycle is never ending. Perceptions of meaning are continuously coming into the comparator and meaningful behavior is continuously output to the environment. Action does not stop while perception occurs and perception does not stop while action is occurs. For example, if an individual sees his moral identity to involve being a "just" person, he will constantly monitor his environment and perceive indications regarding the degree to which he is just. He will observe his own behavior in the environment and others will observe his behavior as well. In combination, these perceptions will be fed into the comparator, but neither the input nor the identity standard alone predicts the behavior that will follow. Rather, it is the relationship between input meanings and identity standard meanings that predicts behavior. This is because the behavior is a direct function of the differences that are detected by the comparator.

Some may argue that the identity verification process is reductionist; that the meaning of all action is reduced to whether it is consistent with identity standard meanings. We need to keep in mind that the operation of any one identity occurs within an overall hierarchy of identities which I will discuss next. Depending on the basis of the identity (a person, role, or group identity), and whether multiple identities are activated in a situation will influence how the identity process unfolds in a situation. Further, the meanings that emerge for an identity standard or set of identity standards come, in part, from culture. As cultural meanings change from society to society or over time, so do the individuals' identity standards that form the basis of action.

Multiple Identities

As I indicated earlier, sociologists follow James' (1890) idea that we have as many "selves" as we have others with whom we interact. The idea of multiple selves has changed somewhat since James' writing, and we now talk about people have multiple identities rather than selves, but the idea is the same. We take on many identities over the course of our life and in any one situation, multiple identities may be activated. At issue is how the moral identity fits with the various other identities individuals may hold. There are two ways to conceptualize this relationship. The first is in terms of the rank ordering of identities given all of the identities that individuals may claim, with more salient identities ranked higher relative to lower ranked identities. The second is in terms of the hierarchy of identities given the perceptual control system. Let me discuss each.

Identity Salience: The activation of the moral identity in a situation is influenced by how *salient* the moral identity is given the ranking of salience of all other identities that an individual may claim (Stryker [1980] 2002). Identity salience is the readiness to act out an identity across situations. If the moral identity ranks high in relative salience, then it will be activated across situations generally prior to other lower salient identities. High salience is influenced by a strong commitment to an identity. Strong commitment is having: (1) a large number of persons who are tied to one on the basis of the identity and (2) deep ties with these persons (Stryker and Serpe 1982, 1994). Strong commitment also reveals itself in greater motivational force to respond to non-verifying meanings in a situation by working hard to move the self from a non-verifying state to a verifying state (Burke and Stets 2009).

When the moral identity is salient and activated in a situation, it becomes a filter or lens that directs attention to controlling moral meanings in the situation. Individuals become sensitive to cues that indicate expectations of good or bad, proper or improper behavior. This is similar to the idea in the social-cognitive model of individuals have a moral self-schema that organizes issues of right and wrong in a situation and that guides morally appropriate behavior. The schema becomes accessible for processing in the situation. For example, when the moral identity is more salient, a party situation in which one must decide whether a friend should drive home drunk will be interpreted as morally potent and steer the individual to drive the friend home.

The above assumes that the situation introduced moral meanings and encouraged a moral response. The situation may not bring about moral expectations if, for example, peers encourage a person to continue having a good time and ignore the drunk friend who is about to leave. Another identity such as the sociable identity (Stets and Cast 2007) may get activated over the moral identity. If there is present at the party a moral exemplar (Walker and Frimer 2007, 2009; Walker and Hennig 2004), it may remind the person that this is an instance in which moral action is expected, thereby activating the moral identity. In this way, situational expectations can facilitate or impede the expression of a salient moral identity depending upon whether the meanings that are "given off" in the situation complement or contradict the salient identity meanings. This is similar to Aquino and his associates recent ideas (Aquino et al. 2009), but what identity theory adds is the idea that the activation or deactivation of a salient identity arises because of a correspondence or lack on correspondence in *meanings*.

The meaning of identity salience among sociologists is slightly different than identity centrality or self-importance that psychologists use to refer to moral identity. Centrality or self-importance assumes that individuals are aware of what identity is most important to them. In identity salience, people may not be aware of how salient an identity is compared to the other identities they may claim, but frequently invoked behaviors and the meanings these behaviors imply may inform people as to what identities are ranked higher for them (Stryker and Serpe 1994). Despite these differences, centrality and salience are very similar concepts. Both are a more enduring (rather than fleeting) source of behavior. Once an identity is salient or central, it influences the choices people make in the long-run compared to the short-term.[9] Additionally, both salience and centrality provide an image of one's internal self-views as rank ordered, with some more paramount than others. Indeed, Blasi (1984) discussed an image of the self as ordered in terms of a hierarchy of characteristics in which some aspects of the self were more central while others were more peripheral. Those that were more central comprised the core self. In identity theory, a more salient identity does not invoke the image of a core self. Rather, salience reflects current commitments to particular meanings that an identity implies and acting in a manner that attempts to verify those meanings.

However, a salient moral identity as conceptualized in identity theory is not the same as moral identity salience in the social-cognitive model (Aquino and Freeman 2009, Aquino et al. 2009). In the social-cognitive model, moral identity salience is influenced by situational factors that "cue" or call forth a specific identity given situational expectations. In identity theory, a salient moral identity is influenced by people's commitments to certain identities. In this way it is internally driven (rooted in the self) rather than externally determined (by the expectations of

---

[9] Future research will want to disentangle the causal ordering between identity centrality and salience, that is, whether an identity that is important influences which identity gets invoked or whether an identity that gets invoked influences which identity becomes important.

a situation). Further, there is the assumption in identity theory that when an identity is salient, individuals may *seek out* situations where the identity can be played out (Stryker [1980] 2002). Put another way, individuals create a self-verifying context in which they routinely receive a steady supply of self-verifying feedback from others on their salient identity (Burke and Stets 2009). In this way, rather than the situation having an influence as to what identity emerges, it is the other way around. Individuals often self-select themselves into particular situations in which the probability of obtaining support for their salient identity is high.

For example, if a person is driving on the highway and witnesses another on the side of the road with a flat tire needing help, rather than the situation activating the moral identity of a caring, helpful person, it is the fact that the person has a salient moral identity which encourages the moral response of helping. It is not uncommon to find people who do not help in such a situation, suggesting that situational expectations are not always influential. On the other hand, even an individual with a salient moral identity may not stop to help if some other identity demands greater attention as when a husband is driving his wife to the hospital because she is in labor. Indeed, multiple identities that individuals claim may conflict with each other in a situation. The fact that one witnesses another needing help on the side of the road does help in steering behavior toward helping. However, if the person had not witnessed this event, the individual likely would have found some other event that warranted acting in a caring and helpful manner. As mentioned earlier, when the moral identity is salient in a situation, it becomes a filter that directs attention to controlling moral meanings in the situation that are consistent with the identity standard meanings. Thus, while situational factors are sufficient in the activation of a moral identity, they are not necessary.

The above is not to suggest that situational factors never influence which identity gets activated in a situation. Rather, it is a matter of how much this happens. People may find themselves in situations in which they routinely are unsuccessful in verifying a salient identity because the expectations in the situation solicit an alternative identity that will produce successful outcomes. Alternatively, they may receive non-verifying feedback from others in the situation on the identity they are enacting. In either case, strong negative feelings will emerge over time, and correspondingly, reduce commitment and salience of the identity (Stryker 2004). This is similar to Aquino and his colleague's discussion on how a central identity may be reduced in accessibility over time (Aquino et al. 2009).

Perceptual Control System of Identity Hierarchy: As I mentioned initially in this chapter, in identity theory, there are three bases of identities: person, role, and identities (Burke and Stets 2009). As earlier mentioned, a person identity is the meanings that individuals apply to themselves as unique persons. This may include meanings of being controlling (Stets and Burke 1994) or meanings of being moral (Stets and Carter 2006, Stets et al. 2008). The verification of person identities activates a sense of authenticity.

A role identity is the meanings individuals apply to themselves while in a role. Individuals are socialized into the cultural meanings of such roles as professor, student, parent, spouse, worker, friend, and so forth. Every role identity has a corresponding counter-role identity, for example, the parent identity has the counter-identity of child, and the employer has the corresponding counter-identity of employee. There are different perceptions and actions between role identities that are negotiated and coordinated in interaction. Verification of role identities activates a sense of efficacy or competence.

A social identity is based on individuals' identification with the meanings of a particular group. Having a particular social identity means seeing things from the group's perspective and behaving as they do; there is uniformity in thought and action. Examples of social identities include membership into particular political parties, religious organizations, professional and voluntary organizations, one's family, peer group, and so forth. Having a social identity as a group member verified activates a sense of belongingness and raises self-worth.

From the above, we see that individuals may claim the person identity of being moral, but they may also claim the role identity of parent, and social identity of Parent–Teacher Association member. How does the moral identity function given the other identities that individuals claim? Central to identity theory is the idea that there is a hierarchical perceptual control system in which identities are located. This hierarchical system is composed of an interlocking set of individual control systems at multiple levels such as that which is depicted in Figure 20.2 (Powers 1973, Tsushima and Burke 1999).

One of the highest levels in the hierarchical control system is the "principle level" which influences and is influenced by the level just below it, the lower-order "program level" of control. The program-level monitors the perceived accomplishment of concrete goals in situations such as helping someone on the side of the road, returning a lost wallet to its owner, or driving a friend who had been drinking home. The principle level provides the standards for program-level control. These standards are general and include one's beliefs and morals (Powers 1973, Robertson and Powers 1990, Stets and Carter 2006). They guide the selection and implementation of program activities. While program-level standards represent activities in specific situations, principle-level standards represent more abstract goals and meanings

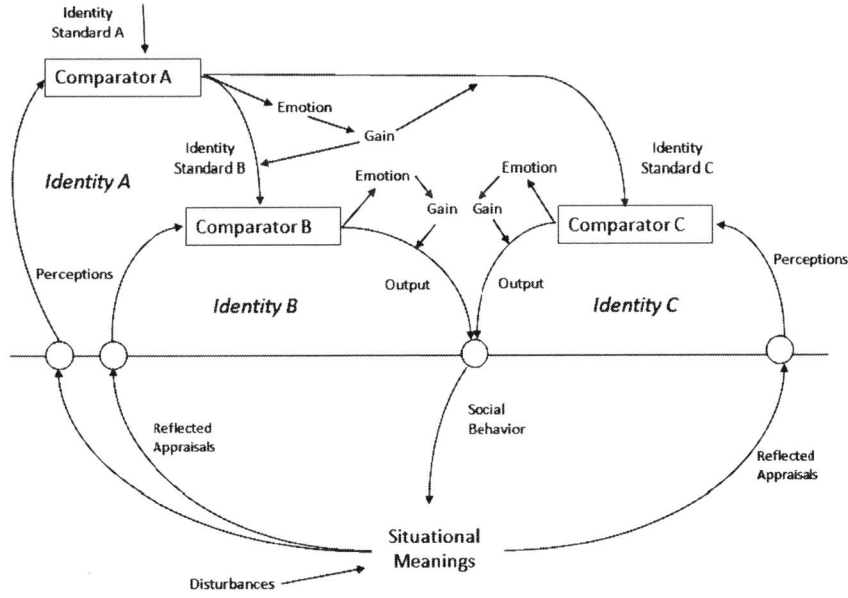

Model 2. Hierarchy of Identity Control

FIGURE 20.2. Hierarchy of identity control.

that operate across situations and that serve as the basis of different activities in different situations.

Person, role and social identities are at the principle level in the hierarchical perceptual control system. They are the *meanings* that serve as standards for program-level activity. However, the principle level is also hierarchically arranged with person identities such as the moral identity that carries abstract meanings about morality that apply to many concrete situations. In this way, these meanings operate like a "master" identity influencing the selection of role and social identities (Burke 2004, Stets and Carter 2006) as well as other person identities that may not be as general and abstract as morality such as being sociable or controlling (Stets and Burke 1994, Stets and Cast 2007).

In Figure 20.2, Identity A might represent the moral identity. Identity B and Identity C may be a role and social identity, respectively. Notice that the output of the higher Identity A is the standard of the lower Identity B and Identity C. To be clear, the higher Identity A does not control the behaviors/output of Identity B and Identity C. It does not tell Identities B and C how to obtain verification. Rather Identity A only controls the standards or goals of B and C. It only identifies what meanings need to be verified. It is the task of the lower identities (B and C) to match the self-meanings in the situations with the meanings held in the identity standard, and those meanings are set by Identity A. In this way, what the lower identities actually do depends upon the goals set by the higher identity. Since the higher identity in some sense controls the lower identities, they cannot be in conflict. Instead, the lower identities are the servant of the higher identity.

For example, the moral person identity might involve meanings of care, kindness, and compassion. In turn, individuals may be more likely to choose roles that also carry these meanings such as the role of parent, priest, or nurse. Social groups that encompass these roles would include a family, a parish, and a hospital staff. Thus, individuals work to select or enact only those role identities and social identities which are compatible in meaning with the meanings found in the more general and abstract person identity of being moral.

At issue is how the hierarchical perceptual control system of identities relates to an individual's rank ordering of salient identities I just discussed. It is likely that individuals vary in terms of how attentive they are to the abstract moral meanings that infiltrate the many identities they claim. To the extent that they are attentive to these general moral meanings, those identities that are imbued with stronger moral meanings will be more salient in their overall ranking. For example, the parent identity may be more salient than the role identity of a computer scientist or gardener. What makes some individuals more attentive to abstract moral meanings than others?

It may be that some individuals are more likely to be exposed to particular social contexts and individuals that facilitate the transmission of moral meanings in situations. Good parenting is likely important. For example, research reveals that adolescents are more likely to internalize moral values when their parents are involved in their lives, encourage a strong sense of agency, and provide structure such as clear expectations (Hardy et al. 2008). Further, high parental involvement as in frequent parent-adolescent joint activities influences moral action in the form of voluntary participation in community service (Hart et al. 1999). The educational system also can encourage community service as well as provide an atmosphere that fosters moral values such as justice and virtue (Atkins et al. 2004). And, religious participation which promotes reflection on moral issues and provides the opportunity to explore moral action such as charitable work (Hart and Atkins 2004). Even neighborhoods can encourage moral sensitivity with those living in affluent neighborhoods exposed to rich networks of organizations that have moral goals such as nonprofit civic organizations and social action groups (Hart and Matsuba 2009). Taken together, we see that the internalization of moral values is likely shaped by exposure to social contexts and actors that are resource rich.

More generally, researchers need to more closely theorize and empirically examine the roots of multiple identity configurations. For example, we might consider testing the idea that identity meanings that are closer to one another in semantic space will be the more likely to be combined such that what ties multiple identities together within the self is a common system of meaning such as moral meanings.

CONCLUSION

Identity theory in sociology provides an important contribution to the social psychology of the moral identity beyond current psychological models. It offers an underlying theoretical process that recognizes central aspects of the moral self that are intimately related including the cognitive, behavioral, and emotional dimensions. An assumption in identity theory is that the person is multifaceted and complex, and because of this, the person has many identities. The various identities that individuals maintain can be seen across the different situations they navigate in and out of that carry different expectations and different social networks of others who react to them. The fact that persons have various identities does not mean that they do not have self-meanings that characterize their deeper, true self. Indeed, this is what we label person identities in identity theory. Person identities facilitate the expression of one's authentic self. Individuals can have multiple person identities that characterize their authentic self. The question becomes when moral self-meanings that are part of the authentic self such as being "kind," "just," or "respectful" can be expressed. This raises the issue about how we can understand individuals who have a strong moral identity but yet do not behave morally in all situations. Sociologically, I think it is an issue of understanding the intersection of agency and social structure and the meanings that are to be controlled in the situation. Let me explain.

Agency is individual actions that are oriented to and guided by the self-meanings in people's identity standard. The actions involved in agency are *intentional* in that there is a commitment to verify the self-meanings in person's identity standards. The actions are also *monitored* in that individuals reflect upon progress toward identity verification. And, the actions are *regulated* in that it is individuals who make the choices that execute the actions. For agency to be effective, actors must be adaptive, managing disturbances in the environment in order verify their identities. These are all assumptions in identity theory.

However, agency occurs within the context of social structure. While the social structure can provide resources and opportunities for agency, it may also impose constraints. It is this intersection that may enlighten us as to the relationship between the moral identity and moral action. If agency involves individuals seeking to verify self-meanings, if these meanings are consistent with the meanings to be accomplished in situations, the meanings become reinforcing not only for individuals, but also the situations and the structures within which the situations are embedded. If the meanings are in opposition to situational meanings, interactions become disrupted and destabilize existing situations and the structures within which they are embedded. Thus, for example, if one has the goal of being "caring," "fair," "loyal," or "divine," but a situation carries meanings of "self-interest" or "selfishness," unless one is willing and has the skills to counteract these situational meanings, the person may succumb to them. Yielding to situational meanings may be even more likely when others in the situation reinforce these meanings. This is when an alternative identity gets activated in the situation that is consistent with the situational meanings such as being self-interested.

Considering the influence of situations and the broader social structure makes us aware that our outcomes are not completely orchestrated by our own or even others' actions. Social structural arrangements can persist according to their own principles and intrude into situations, and they can constrain the actions of individuals. Indeed, every situation has an implicit status hierarchy, a distribution of resources, a set of norms that shape and guide interaction and so forth, and this may constrain what individuals can accomplish.

Good social psychological work on the moral identity is research which goes back and forth between the agency of individuals and the situations and larger social structure in which their actions take place. Such work shows how situations and social structures are the accomplishment of individuals, but it also reveals how people are always acting within the structures they create. It is individuals who are producing actions to verify their own identities, the patterns of which constitute social structure. But, social structural forces also act back on their creators guiding and limiting what individuals can do. This dynamic, reciprocal process needs to be better understood and applied to understanding the moral self.

In conclusion, identity theory is an approach that can deepen our understanding of the moral self. If we begin with the assumption that the self is a self-regulating moral entity, then we can see how this self-regulation is facilitated or impeded given social structural opportunities or constraints that individuals experience. Additionally, we can explore how the complexity of the self and the multiple identities that individuals claim interact with these opportunities or constraints serving to create identity clarity or confusion. In short, these and other ideas serve to illustrate how identity theory is a rich theory that can advance our understanding of who we are as moral persons.

REFERENCES

Aquino, K., and D. Freeman. 2009. "Moral Identity in Business Situations: A Social-Cognitive Framework for Understanding Moral Functioning." PP. 375–395 in *Personality, Identity, and Character: Explorations in Moral Psychology*, edited by D. Narvaez, and D. K. Lapsley. New York: Cambridge University Press.

Aquino, K., D. Freeman, A. II Reed, and V. K. G. Lim. 2009. "Testing a Social-Cognitive Model of Moral Behavior: The Interactive Influence of Situations and Moral Identity Centrality." *Journal of Personality and Social Psychology* 97: 123–141.

Aquino, K., and A. II Reed. 2002. "The Self-Importance of Moral Identity." *Journal of Personality and Social Psychology* 83: 1423–1440.

Aquino, K., A. II Reed, S. Thau, and D. Freeman. 2006. "A Grotesque and Dark Beauty: How Moral Identity and Mechanisms of Moral Disengagement Influence Cognitive and Emotional Reactions to War." *Journal of Experimental Social Psychology* 43: 385–392.

Atkins, R., D. Hart, and T. M. Donnelly. 2004. "Moral Identity Development and School Attachment." PP. 65–82 in *Moral Development, Self, and Identity*, edited by D. K. Lapsley, and D. Narvaez. Mahwah, New Jersey: Lawrence Erlbaum.

Blasi, A. 1980. "Bridging Moral Cognition and Moral Action: A Critical Review of the Literature." *Psychological Bulletin* 88: 1–45.

Blasi, A. 1983. "Moral Cognition and Moral Action: A Theoretical Perspective." *Developmental Review* 3: 178–210.

Blasi, A. 1984. "Moral Identity: Its Role in Moral Functioning." PP. 128–139 in *Morality, Moral Behavior, and Moral Development*, edited by W. M. Kurtines, and J. L. Gewirtz. New York: Wiley.

Blasi, A. 1988. "Identity and the Development of the Self." PP. 226–242 in *Self, Ego, and Identity: Integrative Approaches*, edited by D. K. Lapsley, and F. C. Power. New York: Springer.

Blasi, A. 1993. "The Development of Identity: Some Implications for Moral Functioning." PP. 99–122 in *The Moral Self*, edited by G. G. Noam, and T. E. Wren. Cambridge, MA: The MIT Press.

Blasi, A. 1995. "Moral Understanding and the Moral Personality: The Process of Moral Integration." PP. 229–253 in *Moral Development: An Introduction*, edited by W. M. Kurtines, and J. L. Gewirtz. Needham Heights, MA: Allyn and Bacon.

Blasi, A. 1999. "Emotions and Moral Motivation." *Journal for the Theory of Social Behaviour* 29: 1–19.

Blasi, A. 2004. "Neither Personality nor Cognition: An Alternative Approach to the Nature of the Self." PP. 3–25 in *Changing Conceptions of Psychological Life*, edited by C. Lightfoot, C. Lalonde, and M. Chandler. Mahwah, NJ: Erlbaum.

Blasi, A., and K. Glodis. 1995. "The Development of Identity: A Critical Analysis from the Perspective of the Self as Subject." *Developmental Review* 15: 404–433.

Burke, P. J. 1980. "The Self: Measurement Implications from a Symbolic Interactionist Perspective." *Social Psychology Quarterly* 43: 18–29.

Burke, P. J. 2004. "Identities and Social Structure: The 2003 Cooley-Mead Award Address." *Social Psychology Quarterly* 67: 5–15.

Burke, P. J., and D. C. Reitzes. 1981. "The Link between Identity and Role Performance." *Social Psychology Quarterly* 44: 83–92.

Burke, P. J., and D. C. Reitzes. 1991. "An Identity Theory Approach to Commitment." *Social Psychology Quarterly* 54: 239–251.

Burke, P. J., and J. E. Stets. 2009. *Identity Theory*. New York: Oxford University Press.

Carter, M. J. 2010. "Dissertation Thesis: Examining the Social Context in Identity Theory." Sociology, University of California, Riverside.

Cervone, D. 2004. "The Architecture of Personality." *Psychological Review* 111: 183–204.

Cervone, D., and R. Tripathi. 2009. "The Moral Functioning of the Person as a Whole: On Moral Psychology and Personality Science." PP. 30–51 in *Personality, Identity, and Character: Explorations in Moral Psychology*, edited by D. Narvaez, and D. K. Lapsley. New York: Cambridge University Press.

Damon, W. 1984. "Self-Understanding and Moral Development from Childhood to Adolescence." PP. 109–127 in *Morality, Moral Behavior, and Moral Development*, edited by W. M. Kurtines, and J. L. Gewirtz. New York: Wiley.

Erikson, E. H. 1968. *Identity: Youth and Crisis*. New York: Norton.

Gilligan, C. 1982. *In a Different Voice: Psychological Theory and Women's Development*. Cambridge, MA: Harvard University Press.

Graham, J., J. Haidt, and B. A. Nosek. 2009. "Liberals and Conservatives Rely on Different Sets of Moral Foundations." *Journal of Personality and Social Psychology* 96: 1029–1046.

Greene, J. D., R. Brian Sommerville, L. E. Nystrom, J. M. Darley, and J. D. Cohen. 2001. "An fMRI Investigation of Emotional Engagement in Moral Judgment." *Science* 293: 2105–2108.

Haidt, J. 2001. "The Emotional Dog and Its Rational Tail: A Social Intuitionist Approach to Moral Judgment." *Psychological Review* 108: 814–834.

Haidt, J. 2003. "The Moral Emotions." PP. 852–870 in *Handbook of Affective Sciences*, edited by R. J. Davidson, K. R. Scherer, and H. H. Goldsmith. New York: Oxford University Press.

Haidt, J. 2008. "Morality." *Perspectives on Psychological Science* 3: 65–72.

Haidt, J., and J. Graham. 2007. "When Morality Opposes Justice: Conservatives have Moral Intuitions that Liberals may not Recognize." *Social Justice Research* 20: 98–116.

Hardy, S. A. 2006. "Identity, Reasoning, and Emotion: An Empirical Comparison of Three Sources of Moral Motivation." *Motivation and Emotions* 30: 207–215.

Hardy, S. A., and G. Carlo. 2005. "Identity as a Source of Moral Motivation." *Human Development* 48: 232–256.

Hardy, S. A., L. M. Padilla-Walker, and G. Carlo. 2008. "Parenting Dimensions and Adolescents' Internalization of Moral Values." *Journal of Moral Education* 37: 205–223.

Hart, D., and R. Atkins. 2004. "Religious Participation and the Development of Moral Identity in Adolescence." PP. 157–172 in *Nurturing Morality*, edited by T. A. Thorkildsen, and H. J. Walberg. New York: Kluwer Academic/Plenum.

Hart, D., R. Atkins, and D. Ford. 1999. "Family Influences on the Formation of Moral Identity in Adolescence: Longitudinal Analyses." *Journal of Moral Education* 28: 375–386.

Hart, D., and M. Kyle Matsuba. 2009. "Urban Neighborhoods as Contexts for Moral Identity Development." PP. 214–231 in *Personality, Identity, and Character: Explorations in Moral Psychology*, edited by D. Narvaez, and D. K. Lapsley. New York: Cambridge University Press.

Hoffman, M. L. 2000. *Empathy and Moral Development: Implications for Caring and Justice*. New York, NY: Cambridge University Press.

Howard, J. A., and D. G. Renfrow. 2003. "Social Cognition." PP. 259–281 in *Handbook of Social Psychology*, edited by J. DeLamater. New York: Kluwer Academic/Plenum.

Inglehart, R., and W. E. Baker. 2000. "Modernization, Cultural Change, and the Persistence of Traditional Values." *American Sociological Review* 65: 19–51.

James, W. 1890. *Principles of Psychology*. New York: Holt Rinehart and Winston.

Koenigs, M., L. Young, R. Adolphs, D. Tranel, F. Cushman, M. Hauser, and A. Damasio. 2007. "Damage to the Prefrontal Cortex Increases Utilitarian Moral Judgements." *Nature* 446: 908–911.

Kohlberg, L. 1981. *The Philosophy of Moral Development*. San Francisco: Harper and Row.

Lapsley, D. K., and D. Narvaez. 2004a. *Moral Development, Self, and Identity*. Mahwah, NJ: Lawrence Erlbaum.

Lapsley, D. K., and D. Narvaez. 2004b. "A Social-Cognitive Approach to the Moral Personality." PP. 189–212 in *Moral Development, Self, and Identity*, edited by D. K. Lapsley, and D. Narvaez. Mahwah, NJ: Lawrence Erlbaum.

Lewis, M. 2008. "Self-Conscious Emotions: Embarrassment, Pride, Shame, and Guilt." PP. 742–756 in *Handbook of Emotions*, edited by M. Lewis, J. M. Haviland-Jones, and L. F. Barrett. New York: Guilford.

Markus, H., and Z. Kunda. 1986. "Stability and Malleability of the Self-Concept." *Journal of Personality and Social Psychology* 51: 858–866.

Piaget, J. 1965 (1932). *The Moral Judgment of the Child*. New York: Free Press.

Powers, W. T. 1973. *Behavior: The Control of Perception*. Chicago: Aldine Publishing.

Prinz, J. J. 2004. *Gut Reactions: A Perceptual Theory of Emotion*. New York: Oxford University Press.

Reed, A. II, and K. F. Aquino. 2003. "Moral Identity and the Expanding Circle of Moral Regard Toward Out-Groups." *Journal of Personality and Social Psychology* 84: 1270–1286.

Reed, A. II, K. Aquino, and E. Levy. 2007. "Moral Identity and Judgments of Charitable Behaviors." *Journal of Marketing* 71: 178–193.

Rest, J. R., D. Narvaez, M. J. Bebeau, and S. J. Thoma. 1999. *Postconventional Moral Thinking: A Neo-Kohlbergian Approach*. Mahwah, NJ: Lawrence Erlbaum.

Robertson, R. J., and W. T. Powers. 1990. *Introduction to Modern Psychology: The Control-Theory View*. Gravel Switch, Ky.: Control Systems Group.

Rozin, P., L. Lowery, S. Imada, and J. Haidt. 1999. "The CAD Triad Hypothesis: A Mapping Between Three Moral Emotions (Contempt, Anger, Disgust) and Three Moral Codes (Community, Autonomy, Divinity)." *Journal of Personality and Social Psychology* 76: 574–586.

Scheff, T. J. 1988. "Shame and Conformity: The Deference-Emotion System." *American Sociological Review* 53: 395–406.

Scheff, T. J. 2000. "Shame and the Social Bond: A Sociological Theory." *Sociological Theory* 18: 84–99.

Schwartz, S. H. 2006. "A Theory of Cultural Value Orientations: Explication and Applications." *Comparative Sociology* 5: 137–182.

Shweder, R. A., N. C. Much, M. Mahapatra, and L. Park. 1997. "The Big "Three" of Morality (Autonomy, Community, and Divinity), and the Big "Three" Explanations of Suffering." PP. 119–169 in *Morality and Health*, edited by A. Brandt, and P. Rozin. New York: Routledge.

Stets, J. E., and P. J. Burke. 1994. "Inconsistent Self-Views in the Control Identity Model." *Social Science Research* 23: 236–262.

Stets, J. E., and P. J. Burke. 2003. "A Sociological Approach to Self and Identity." PP. 128–152 in *Handbook of Self and Identity*, edited by M. Leary, and J. Tangney. New York: Guilford.

Stets, J. E., and P. J. Burke. 2005. "New Directions in Identity Control Theory." *Advances in Group Processes* 22: 43–64.

Stets, J. E., and M. J. Carter. 2006. "The Moral Identity: A Principle Level Identity." PP. 293–316 in *Purpose, Meaning, and Action: Control Systems Theories in Sociology*, edited by K. McClelland, and T. J. Fararo. New York: Palgrave MacMillan.

Stets, J. E., M. J. Carter, M. M. Harrod, C. Cerven, and S. Abrutyn. 2008. "The Moral Identity, Status, Moral Emotions, and the Normative Order." PP. 227–251 in *Social Structure and Emotion*, edited by J. Clay-Warner, and D. T. Robinson. San Diego: Elsevier.

Stets, J. E., and A. D. Cast. 2007. "Resources and Identity Verification from an Identity Theory Perspective." *Sociological Perspectives* 50: 517–543.

Stryker, S. 2004. "Integrating Emotion into Identity Theory." *Advances in Group Processes* 21: 1–23.

Stryker, S.2002 (1980). *Symbolic Interactionism: A Social Structural Version.* Caldwell, NJ: Blackburn Press.

Stryker, S., and R. T. Serpe. 1982. "Commitment, Identity Salience, and Role Behavior: A Theory and Research Example." PP. 199–218 in *Personality, Roles, and Social Behavior*, edited by W. Ickes, and E. S. Knowles. New York: Springer.

Stryker, S., and R. T. Serpe. 1994. "Identity Salience and Psychological Centrality: Equivalent, Overlapping, Or Complementary Concepts?" *Social Psychology Quarterly* 57: 16–35.

Tangney, J. P., J. Stuewig, and D. J. Mashek. 2007. "Moral Emotions and Moral Behavior." *Annual Review of Psychology* 58: 345–372.

Taylor, C. 1989. *Sources of the Self.* Cambridge: Harvard University Press.

Tsushima, T., and P. J. Burke. 1999. "Levels, Agency, and Control in the Parent Identity." *Social Psychology Quarterly* 62: 173–189.

Turner, J. H., and J. E. Stets. 2006. "Moral Emotions." PP. 544–566 in *Handbook of the Sociology of Emotions*, edited by J. E. Stets, and J. H. Turner. New York: Springer.

Walker, L. J., and J. A. Frimer. 2007. "Moral Personality of Brave and Caring Exemplars." *Journal of Personality and Social Psychology* 93: 845–860.

Walker, L. J., and J. A. Frimer. 2009. "Moral Personality Exemplified." PP. 232–255 in *Personality, Identity, and Character: Explorations in Moral Psychology*, edited by D. Narvaez, and D. K. Lapsley. New York: Cambridge University Press.

Walker, L. J., and K. H. Hennig. 2004. "Differing Conceptions of Moral Exemplarity: Just, Brave, and Caring." *Journal of Personality and Social Psychology* 86: 629–647.

Walzer, M. 1983. *Spheres of Justice.* New York: Basic Books.

Wong, D. D. 2009. "Cultural Pluralism and Moral Identity." PP. 79–105 in *Personality, Identity, and Character: Explorations in Moral Psychology*, edited by D. Narvaez, and D. K. Lapsley. New York: Cambridge.

CHAPTER 21

Morality and Mind-Body Connections

Gabriel Ignatow

INTRODUCTION

The renewal of sociological interest in morality, the breadth and depth of which is evinced by the contributions to this volume, has been characterized by an openness to concepts and findings from psychology and cognitive neuroscience that is unusual for sociology. Research from psychology and cognitive neuroscience has informed sociological reflection on how social forces interact with the mind and body in the construction of "moral selves" (Hitlin 2008, Joas 2000:174) and collective moral orders (Wuthnow 1987, Smith 2003). Prominent examples of this sociological incorporation of psychological concepts include Scheff's use of both psychoanalytic theory and modern psychology to argue that sociologists ought to incorporate emotions – shame in particular – into the heart of sociological theory (Scheff 1997a, 2000, 2003) and research (1997b). Turner (2000) cites a wide variety of research from evolutionary biology, evolutionary psychology, neurology and other fields to argue that the human capacity for language developed from early humans' ability to use a wide array of emotions, and those moral codes are, like language, based on emotions. While evolution does not directly favor some moral codes over others, Turner argues that it gave early humans "the neurological ability to construct moral codes and to feel emotionally their power" (p. 52; also, for more recent psychologically informed sociological studies of morality, see Vaisey 2009, Hitlin 2003, 2007, 2008, Ignatow 2009a, b).

Despite the prominence of ideas from psychology and cognitive science in some sociological research on morality, overall, sociological familiarity with these fields is still very limited. Partly as a consequence, sociologists who study morality (defined in terms of morally-relevant beliefs, values, and behaviors) have often tacitly, rather than critically and reflexively, incorporated a wide variety of models of mind-body connections into their research. The purpose of this chapter is to try to unpack and explore at least a few of these models. I propose

Gabriel Ignatow is an assistant professor in the Department of Sociology at the University of North Texas. His research interests are mainly in the areas of cultural sociology and issues related to globalization, and he can be reached virtually at ignatow.blogspot.com

S. Hitlin, S. Vaisey (eds.), *Handbook of the Sociology of Morality*, Handbooks of Sociology and Social Research, DOI 10.1007/978-1-4419-6896-8_21,

that sociologists who have studied morality have employed three main conceptions of the connections between mind and body. These are *cognitivism, intuitionism,* and *holism*. These three categories are heavily influenced by developments in cognitive science and psychology that have unfolded over the past half century, and because these models of mind-body connections are each supported by one or more established research programs from psychology or cognitive science, they can all be robustly defended on psychological grounds. While they have each contributed to innovative, influential sociological research, I will argue that mind-body holism is the most psychologically realistic model, and the one that points to the most promising path for future research on moral beliefs, discourses, and behavior.

Mind-body connections are extremely complex, and because of this complexity it can be argued that sociologists who study lay morality are justified in selecting theoretical models from a fairly large conceptual toolkit. However, as the sociology of morality develops further, scholars may benefit from not only being receptive to a variety of models of psychological functioning, but also from engaging in more critical analysis of the models of mind-body connections that are implied in their preferred theoretical frameworks. Thus, in this chapter I attempt to develop a set of conceptual categories useful for analyzing these connections sociologically. In developing these categories, I discuss research programs that, to one degree or another, exemplify each. I do not claim that this review is exhaustive, and the categories developed here may ultimately be found to be far from ideal. Yet, it is my hope that this chapter can provide a refreshed map of the current psychological and sociological theoretical terrain, a map that can inform critical reflection on the psychological models implied by sociological theories. In so doing it may contribute to the development of sociological research that is better formulated to contribute to cross-disciplinary debates on the nature of morality (see Hitlin and Vaisey's contribution to this volume).

COGNITIVISM

The first and one of the most prominent models of mind-body connections in sociological studies of morality can be referred to as *cognitivism*. The term cognitivism is used here in basically the same way it is used in psychology and cognitive science: it refers to the idea that cognition consists of discrete, internal concepts whose dynamics can be modeled in terms of formal rules and algorithms that are universally valid. Put another way, cognitivist research models thought in terms of computer-like information processing. It presumes a Cartesian dualism between mind and body, and trains its sights mainly on the mind at the expense of the body. For contemporary sociology, the psychological basis of cognitivism is provided by the "cognitive revolution" of the 1960s and 1970s and the disciplines that formed in its wake, among them cognitive science, cognitive psychology, and cognitive social psychology. Among sociologists who study morality, it is possible to identify three broadly cognitivist, partly overlapping analytical orientations: *individual, social,* and *cultural cognitivism*.

Individual Cognitivism

Anthony Giddens' analysis of the moral cosmology of late modernity is an exemplar of an individualist cognitivist sociology of morality. For Giddens, modernity has no collective moral order in Durkheim's sense. Rather, the self develops "under conditions of substantial moral deprivation"; self-development is set against a "backdrop of moral impoverishment" (Giddens 1991:169). Modern societies face an "evaporation of morality" (1991:143) in which moral outlooks are no longer integrated into day-to-day practices. Tradition is dispensed with, and claims to moral authority are viewed with suspicion. Wherein traditional societies share sacred traditions that have a "'binding' normative character" (1991:145), the morality that exists in modern societies is dependent upon *individuals'* capacity for thought and justification of *personal* choices.

Thus for Giddens, the wellspring of modern morality is the reflexive individual *thinker*. While Giddens does not neglect emotions or the body in his account, he argues that guilt and other binding moral emotions only perform socially crucial functions in "traditional" societies: "The characteristic movement of modernity, on the level of individual experience, is away from guilt" (1991:155). Instead, for Giddens modern people are *"essentially* minds" who "tend only to be shaped by their sensual bodily responses *after* a breakdown in their reflexive attempts to understand or engage with the world" (Shilling and Mellor 1998:200). The rational, reflexive modern person inhabits self-referential symbolic systems that are not primarily informed by morally guiding emotions.

Giddens' modernist views share their psychological presuppositions with the psychologist Lawrence Kohlberg's cognitive-developmental framework for the analysis of morality (for useful discussions of Giddens and Kohlberg, see Bryant and Jary 1997:73, Johnson 1990:123). As Giddens argues that societies *evolve*, in one way or another (Giddens 1986:Chapter 5), from social systems based on shared sentiments and traditions to systems based on self-referential symbolic communication and reflexive thought, Kohlberg, following Piaget (1999), argued that the individual develops through six universal stages of moral reasoning (Kohlberg 1969, 1971). The most rudimentary stage is based on an orientation to obedience and punishment; the most advanced, on reasoning from universal principles. Moral development over the life course proceeds through this "stage hierarchy" in a step-wise, invariant sequence, regardless of cross-cultural variation in moral norms and beliefs. As for Giddens, for Kohlberg emotions are secondary to self-conscious rational thought, becoming more so as a person's moral reasoning develops from one stage to the next.

Contemporary social psychology research on justice and fairness shares a cognitivist orientation with Giddens and Kohlberg, but abandons Kohlberg's stage hierarchy framework. Instead, researchers in this area have turned their attention to differences in the cognitive functioning of adults with different moral and political orientations. American social psychologists in particular have focused on differences between political liberals and conservatives (e.g., Jost et al. 2003). As with Giddens and Kohlberg, though, here emotions do not play much of a role. The motivations that drive social judgments are conceived as mainly cognitive in nature: while political conservatives are argued to be driven by a "need for cognitive closure" (Jost et al. 2003), liberals are more motivated by curiosity and their greater "openness to experience" (Carney et al. 2008; cf. Greenberg and Jonas 2003, de Zavala and Van Bergh 2007). Moral emotions such as shame, guilt, and anger are treated mainly as reinforcing differences in the development of cognitive orientations (i.e. closed- versus open-mindedness) during childhood socialization. However, for adults emotions are secondary: it is differences in cognitive orientations, even in cognitive abilities (Jost et al. 2003:353), that are thought to give rise to different moral/political orientations.

Social Cognitivism

Habermas has more closely allied his thought with the cognitive developmental psychology of Piaget and Kohlberg than has Giddens (see Habermas 1979:Chapter 2, Giddens 1987:247). In a chapter on moral development and ego identity, Habermas argued that analytic ego psychology, and drew on Piaget to claim that cognitive developmental psychology and symbolic interactionist theory had converged on several basic conceptions, including the idea that the formative processes of subjects capable of speaking and acting runs through a series of increasingly complex stages of development (Habermas 1979:4).

Habermas argued that the developmental direction of this formative process is in the direction of increasing *autonomy*, defined as "the independence that the ego acquires through successful problemsolving [*sic*], and through growing capabilities for problemsolving [*sic*]" (74). In his analysis of "moral consciousness," Habermas considered "only the cognitive side, the ability to make moral judgments" (78). However, while he borrowed much of his conceptual apparatus from cognitive developmental moral theory, Habermas fused Piaget and Kohlberg's ideas with Parsonian sociology. Skeptical of the moral autonomy posited by cognitive developmentalism, he seeks to reformulate Kohlberg's stages of moral development within a "general action-theoretic framework" that incorporates ideas of communications structures, systems of norms, situational elements, behavioral expectations, and role behavior.

Some recent strands of social psychology justice research resemble Habermas's approach to moral development in their fusion of cognitive and social theory. Hegtvedt, for instance, argues that groups play multiple roles in justice phenomena: as "a collective standard, a structure in which evaluations occur, a source of identity, and a context of interaction" (2005:25; see also Hegtvedt's contribution to this volume). In this social psychological approach, as in Habermas's formulations, emotions and the body are treated as secondary, as guided by cognitive frameworks rather than as constitutive elements of moral cosmologies.

Cultural Cognitivism

A third cognitivist approach to morality treats group culture, rather than innate mental processes or small-group dynamics, as the main source of the cognitive models that inform moral judgments and actions. Sociological practice theorists such as Lamont, Boltanski, and Thévenot conceive of culture as a group's "toolkit" (Swidler 1986) or "repertoire" (Boltanski and Thévenot 2001) of cultural resources with which individuals are able to respond in a flexible manner to changing social realities. Here again, emotions play little if any role. Rather, moral judgments and actions are seen as being shaped mainly by a person's position in society, because it is social position that determines access to particular cultural repertoires. These repertoires provide ideational resources that enable people to interpret their life situations and to justify their decisions and actions on moral grounds (for more detailed treatments, see Ignatow 2009a:109, Silber 2003, Vaisey 2009).

Some Advantages and Disadvantages of Cognitivism

In the interest of brevity, I will not delve too deep into the critical literatures on Giddens, Kohlberg, justice researchers, or repertoire theorists. It is striking though that several concerns have been raised repeatedly from different quarters about many of these authors and research programs. First, several cognitivist theoretical frameworks have been argued to provide only one-dimensional accounts of human *motivation* (e.g. on Giddens, see Johnson 1990:116; on repertoire theory, see Smith 2003). Second, there is the related criticism that the role of *emotion* is truncated in these theories (on Giddens, see Shilling and Mellor 1998; on Kohlberg, see Haidt and Joseph 2008; on justice research, see Haidt and Graham 2007). Finally, there are questions of the *cross-gender* (on Kohlberg and Piaget, see Gilligan 1982) and *cross-cultural validity* of many of these theories (Cortese 1990). Despite these concerns, though, few would deny that cognitivist theoretical frameworks have generated valuable concepts, categories, and methods for sociological analysis of morality – for studying moral worldviews comparatively, in small group situations, and over the life course. However, cognitivist approaches like these lately find themselves challenged, in social theory (see Joas 2000), cognitive science (Barsalou 1999), psychology (Haidt 2002), and other fields by theoretical frameworks in which emotions and intuitions receive top billing.

INTUITIONISM

> "[The moral sentiments] are so rooted in our constitution and temper, that without entirely confounding the human mind by disease and madness, 'tis impossible to extirpate and destroy them... Nature must furnish the materials, and give us some notion of moral distinctions." (Hume 2003:337)

Intuitionist sociology can be seen as one strand of the "turn to the body" in sociology (see Turner 2008, Cregan 2006). Distinct from the sociology *of* the body as such, intuitionism prioritizes the body and emotions over abstract mental operations (Shilling and Mellor 1998). Intuitionist theory's philosophical precursors include Hume, Nietzsche, Scheler, and the American pragmatists James and Dewey (see Joas 2000). The psychological basis for sociological intuitionism includes psychoanalytic theory as well as contemporary intuitionist psychology (Haidt 2002). Among intuitionist sociologists, of which there are relatively few, there is a theoretical division between inverted Kantians such as Zygmunt Bauman. They argue for a moral universalism based on individuals' intuitive moral capacities, and those sociologists, most famously Pierre Bourdieu, who argue that social divisions shape our intuitions as much as they do our more abstract and reflexive thoughts (see Sayer 2005 and in this volume).

Individual Intuitionism

Bauman argues, not unlike Giddens, that modernity is an amoral, rationalizing system. However, for Bauman, the moral consequences of modernity are more dire than they are for Giddens: modernity gives rise to anonymous, dehumanizing violence, as in the Holocaust, because of the ability of bureaucratic institutions to operate irrespective of people's innate empathetic emotional responses to others (Bauman 1989). Modernity invented "a way in which cruel things could be done by non-cruel people" by removing them from face-to-face confrontations with each other and with the human consequences of their actions (Bauman 1995:195, 198). Bauman argues that, although it is crushed by modernity, the "primeval" human condition is one of interpersonal empathy, of "being *for* the other" (1993:13, 35).

Intuitionist theoretical frameworks developed in recent years by psychologists of moral-ity have generally been more culturally relativist than is Bauman's approach. Haidt (2002) likens moral decision-making to a rider on an elephant, in which the rider represents ratio-nal deliberative mental processes, the elephant intuitions. Haidt argues, contra Kohlberg, that when mature, well-adjusted adults make moral judgments, the emotional component of those judgments generally occurs earlier and with greater force than does the component of princi-pled reasoning. Hence, people can be quite easily "morally dumbfounded": in experimental situations, they quickly and harshly judge the morality of acts they find *physically* repulsive. However, they are often unable to offer coherent principled *reasons* for their moral condem-nations. While intuitions often precede inferences (Zajonc 1980), intuitions are not universal but are rather culturally variable, at least insofar as different cultures make use of different emotional capacities, such as shame, disgust, anger, and empathy, for different social purposes (see e.g., Haidt and Joseph 2008).

Social Intuitionism

With his concept of the *habitus*, Pierre Bourdieu developed a sophisticated theoretical analysis of the interactions between social structures, culture, and the body. For Bourdieu, the *habitus* comprises a large number of bodily phenomena, including the actor's posture and bearing, demeanor, accent, eating conventions, and aesthetic preferences (Bourdieu 1984:466). The *habitus* also comprises cognitive schemas, which Bourdieu conceives as independent of, and often *directed by*, these bodily phenomena. Bourdieu thus claimed that "practical belief" is more a "state of the body" than of the mind (1990:68–69), and that

> every social order systematically takes advantage of the disposition of the body and language to function as depositories of deferred thoughts that can be triggered off at a distance in space and time by the simple effect of re-placing the body in an overall posture which recalls the associated thoughts and feelings, in one of the inductive states of the body which, as actors know, give rise to states of mind (Bourdieu 1990:69).

Thus the *habitus* is society's imprint on the individual's body, a storehouse of intuitions which allow individuals to "just know," without extended deliberation, that some actions, objects, social groups, and individuals are superior or inferior to others.

Advantages and Disadvantages of Intuitionism

Sociological and psychological intuitionist theories bring to the fore essential experiential dimensions of morality. They are in many ways more psychologically realistic than are ratio-nalist cognitivist theories, and offer more powerful, and in many cases more culturally sensitive and less ideologically driven accounts of the multiplicity of moral worldviews. However, like cognitivism, sociological intuitionism can stumble over questions of the universality of the social and psychological phenomena that are its central focus. The question of the universality of emotion is a complex, empirical question (see Levy 1984, Haidt and Keltner 1999) that is generally glossed over in sociological accounts. For example, neither Bauman nor Scheff provide convincing accounts of why, respectively, empathy ought to be treated as a "primal and primary 'brute fact'" (Bauman 1993:35) or shame as the "premier social emotion" (Scheff 2000:84). Because sociological intuitionists generally refrain from critical engagement with the psychological literature on emotional universality and cultural particularity, their arguments can appear determinist: a given intuition is treated as central and determinative of the individual's ideas and opinions, her social relations and social outcomes [see Probyn (2004) on Bourdieu; Shilling and Mellor (1998) on Bauman; Hauser (2006) on Haidt]. A potentially less problematic approach would be to treat intuitions as consequential, but as but one element in tightly interconnected networks of bodily and sociocultural inputs that shape moral judgments and actions.

MIND-BODY HOLISM

Mind-body holism is, strictly speaking, an oxymoron, and it may be the case that strongly holistic ways of understanding mind-body relations present a view of reality that is "badly handicapped for appealing to the 'common sense'" of Westerners (Whorf 1941:210). However, it may be a useful oxymoron nonetheless insofar as it suggests a super-tight integration of mind and body. In this vein, both DiMaggio (2002) and Vaisey (2009) have challenged Cartesian dualist tendencies in contemporary sociology. DiMaggio argues that sociologists interested in how social contexts influence cognition ought to model cognition in terms of either "hot" or "cool" cognition, i.e., in terms of thought that is either "passionate" and "emotional," or else "detached." Vaisey (2009) argues for a "dual process" model of culture in action. Integrating intuitionist psychology and Bourdieu with both sociological value theory (Hitlin and Piliavin 2004) and practice theory (Swidler 1986), Vaisey argues that it is psychologically realistic to conceptualize culture as operating at two levels, or in terms of two processes. These processes include a system of intuitions that is "fast, automatic, and largely unconscious", and a cognitive system that is "slow, deliberate, and largely conscious" (1683). While the hot-and-automatic versus cool-and-deliberate distinctions drawn by DiMaggio and Vaisey may be more psychologically realistic than strictly cognitivist or intuitionist accounts, I suggest that neither cognitivist nor intuitionist models, nor DiMaggio's hybrid model or Vaisey's dualist model, are entirely satisfactory. As we will see, none of these models is quite in accord with an emerging consensus in psychology and cognitive science that cognition is *always* an embodied phenomenon (Ignatow 2007). I will suggest that it is both possible and desirable to treat the mind and body in an even more holistic manner than do Dimaggio and Vaisey. Psychology and cognitive science can show us the way, and there are already some sociological studies of morality, and some social theory (e.g., Joas 2000), that is more thoroughly holistic in its concepts and methods.

"Rawlsian" Morality and Embodied Cognitivism

The evolutionary psychologist and biologist Hauser (2006) argues that morality is the product of a "moral instinct" that has evolved to "generate rapid judgments about what is morally right and wrong" (xvii). Hauser draws on the philosophical writings of John Rawls to argue that morality is instinctual but not entirely innate, because it operates *through* a "grammar of action" provided by culture, and by a "culture's specific moral norms" (xviii). Hauser contrasts his holistic approach to morality with "Kantian" approaches like Kohlberg's (Hauser 2006:14–17) that presume that individuals deliver moral judgments based on conscious reasoning from relevant principles, and with "Humean" approaches such as Haidt's (Hauser 2006:23–29, 52–53) in which moral judgments are based on precognitive intuitions. In Hauser's more holistic Rawlsian approach (pp. 42–54), the human capacity for morality emerges much as does the capacity for languge:

> In the same way that grammaticality judgments emerge from a universal grammar of principles and parameters, the Rawlsian creature's ethicality judgments would emerge from a universal moral grammar, replete with shared principles and *culturally switchable parameters* (p. 43; emphases added).

> Our shared emotional code generates a shared moral code. Cultural variation emerges because individual cultures teach particular moral variants that, through education and other factors, *fuse with emotions*. Once fused, responses to moral transgressions are fast and unreflective, fueled by unconscious emotions (p. 44; emphases added).

Hauser argues that cultural practices and beliefs are *fused* with emotions during childhood socialization. These fusions, stored in long-term memory, are the neural foundations of life-long moral orientations.

A related argument for the inseparability of mind and body in moral judgments and actions comes out of the "turn to the body" in cognitive science (see Clark 1999). Recently developed theories of "embodied cognition" argue that cognition includes not only abstract mental representations, but also perceptual content (Barsalou 1999). Perceptual inputs (such as for touch, taste, smell, hearing, and vision) are recorded by systems of neurons in sensory-motor regions of the brain, and this perceptual information is then used in categorization, judgment, and perception of new events. Perceptions, sensations, and bodily and emotional states are disassociated from mental representations only later, in a secondary process of abstraction.

Theories of embodied cognition are supported by studies showing tight connections between the body and the processing of social information. For example, in a series of experiments by Williams and Bargh (2008), experimenters asked participants to hold a cup of hot or cold coffee temporarily before having them fill out trait assessments of a random person. Holding a cup that was hot led participants to rate the person as warmer as and friendlier than did holding a cup that was cold. Zhong and Leonardelli (2008) found that recalling an experience of being socially excluded actually felt cold to people, and led to lower estimated room temperature than did recalling an experience of being included in a group. A subsequent experiment directly induced social exclusion through an online virtual interaction and found that being excluded led participants to report greater desirability for warm foods and drinks (Williams et al. 2000). In another set of experiments, Zhong and Liljenquist (2006) found that how people think about moral concepts influences how they perceive physical cleanliness. People not only describe moral transgressions using terms related to physical cleanliness (e.g. he has a *clean* record), but also they experience the need to physically cleanse after recalling past misdeeds (see also Schubert 2005, Bargh et al. 1996, Strack et al. 1988, Stepper and Strack 1993, Wells and Petty 1980).

For sociologists, both Hauser's Rawlsian arguments and research on embodied cognition suggest that it may be beneficial to try to analyze moral judgments more holistically than has generally been the case, as it is psychologically unrealistic to treat either their cognitive or emotional components as *sui generis* phenomena. The rest of this section considers some ways this can be accomplished.

Three Sociological Holisms

An early argument for holistic sociological analysis is found in Marcel Mauss's 1930s lectures to psychologists (Mauss 1979[1935]). Mauss argued for a sociology of "psychophysiological" complexes, of "physio-psycho-sociological assemblages of series of actions." He wanted both sociologists and psychologists to study the "whole man" (*l'homme totale*) rather than the stylized being depicted in Cartesian social science – including in much of Durkheim and Mauss's own "neo-Kantian" earlier work (Joas 2000:64–65). Mauss's arguments fell mostly on deaf ears, and many of the Durkheim-trained sociologists who would likely have been Mauss's most receptive audience had perished decades earlier in the Great War. In recent years, however, the sociological scene has taken something of a Maussian turn (Ignatow 2010), and three holistic sociological approaches have emerged, or perhaps reemerged, that are of particular relevance to the sociology of morality. We can refer to these as *civilizational holism*, *ethnographic holism*, and *embodied cognitivism*.

Civilizational holism. One way to analyze morality holistically is via macro-comparative "civilizational" sociology (Arjomand and Tiryakian 2004) and comparative values analysis (see Baker, this volume). Both research traditions take inspiration from Weber's *Protestant Ethic*, and analyze morality in terms of the cultural *systems* in which it is embedded and the values that, in Parsonian fashion, are thought to generate the binding structures of cultural systems. In analyzing morality from on high, social science's traditional Cartesian dualism is defocused; analysts are free to investigate values and mores without much concern for meso-level or micro-psychological processes such as internalization, intergenerational transmission, cultural change, or intracivilizational variation. Like civilizational sociology, contemporary cross-cultural psychology employs a culture-as-system understanding of culture as cultural wholes comprised of folkways, language, religion, customs, rituals, and social roles. For example, in an influential series of studies, the psychologists Cohen et al. (1996) have argued that a "culture of honor," in which personal affronts are met with violent retribution, is a characteristic feature of the American south. This honor culture is claimed to be based on the social patterns of pre-industrial herding society, but to still shape the cognitions, emotions, behaviors, and physiological reactions of southern white males. Cohen et al.'s arguments are based on a series of experiments on white male college students who had grown up in either the North or South. Students in the experiments were bumped into and insulted by a fellow student before realizing the experiment had begun. While the northerners were relatively unaffected by the insult, southerners were more likely to think their masculine reputation was threatened, more upset, more primed for aggression, and more likely to engage in aggressive and dominant behavior. The authors also suggest that "southern institutions" such as relatively loose gun control laws and unrestrictive self-defense statutes (Cohen 1996) perpetuate this culture. Thus, the Southern culture of honor can be profitably analyzed as though it were a cultural whole, a moral system comprising beliefs, values, perceptual schemas, scripted emotional reactions, and institutions.

Ethnographic holism. A second way of analyzing morality holistically is through ethnographic analysis that is attuned to mind-body connections. Several recent studies stand out for their explicitly holistic approaches to the ethnographic investigation of moral practices.

The first is Winchester's (2008) study of the Muslim "moral habitus." Through his ethnography of and interviews with adult Muslim converts in Missouri, Winchester shows how embodied religious practices such as ritual prayer, fasting, and covering effected a "qualitative reorganization of the social actor's embodied relationship with everyday space and time," and produced within converts the moral dispositions associated with being a "good Muslim" (1755). He argues that religious practices are not *guided by* moral attitudes and dispositions, but rather, "embodied practices and moral subjectivities operate through a *relational and mutually constitutive process* that unfolds over time" (1754–1755; italics added).

Pagis's ethnographic study of "embodied self-reflexivity" (2009) is based on ethnographic observations and interviews of Vipassana Buddhist meditation practitioners in Israel and the USA. She argues that "hyper-awareness of the body is at the base of meditation," and that in meditation, "self-knowledge is anchored in the observation of bodily sensations" (p. 265). She emphasizes the "reflexive capacity of the body" (p. 274) and argues against the "linguistic monopoly" (p. 266) that has become axiomatic in sociological studies of the self that view the body as a completely symbolic abstract entity made up of "internal conversations" (Archer 2007). Contra Giddens and other theorists of the modern self, she discusses self-reflexivity not only as a form of intellectualization, but as an embodied process "based predominantly on feeling the body, in which the relation with oneself unfolds through a corporeal medium by way of practices that increase awareness of sensations, such as meditation, yoga, and dance" (p. 266).

Embodied cognitivism. Two recent studies that come out of the cognitive sociology tradition of Cicourel (1974), Zerubavel (1999), Cerulo (2002), and DiMaggio (1997, 2002) provide a third way of studying morality holistically and sociologically. Danna Lynch's 2009 study of the work practices of home-based employees is not about morality per se, but it is an example of a holistic approach to cognitive sociology. Based on interviews with twenty home-based employees in the New York metropolitan area, Lynch argues that these workers used several micro-psychological practices to interact productively with familiar objects in their surroundings. One of these practices is "emotional alignment," the "affective component" of role-identification processes, which draw workers' attention to specific object meanings that are congruent with their emotions. Lynch finds that

> the role identity-object interpretation-affect link is so strong that if the proper mood cannot be mustered, respondents may negotiate a different meaning that better matches their emotional state...Through processes of emotional alignment, home-based employees...evaluate the meanings of objects according to their emotional state rather than through a goal-oriented schema or a data-driven experiential routine (p. 94)

For these home-based workers, emotional alignment that allows for productive work involves the "fusion of emotion, perception, sensation, and subjective experience" (p. 94) in the establishment of objects' meanings.

A second recent study with intellectual roots in American cognitive sociology is my own 2009 study of the discourses of secular and religious Internet overeaters support groups. In this study, I argue for a revision of Bourdieu's *habitus* concept that treats cognition as fully embodied, and analyze posts by members of Internet-based overeaters' support groups based on this revised conceptualization. My method is neither ethnographic nor based on interviews. Rather, I argue for a structural cultural analysis (Mohr 1998) that identifies cultural schemas and theorizes their interactions with social structures and institutions. Based on an analysis of the unique abstract language and embodied metaphors used by members of religious and secular overeaters' support groups, I found that the religious group used far more "cleanliness" metaphors, and members who made frequent use of such metaphors remained with the group longer and posted more messages. This effect was not found for either group's abstract language, or for the secular group's embodied metaphors. From these findings, I argued for a strong discursive influence on social bonding, an influence that is most clearly seen when culture is operationalized in terms of embodied cognitive schemas that operate within both the individual's *habitus* and a group's discourse.

Survey methods, priming, and framing. The research discussed above shows that it is possible to use archival, ethnographic, interview, and content analytic methods in support of holistic arguments about morality. It may be possible and fruitful to try to use survey methods as well, and two literatures provide guidance for doing so: political science studies of "framing effects" (Druckman 2001, 2004), and psychology studies of "priming" (Bargh and Chartrand 2000). While political scientists (with psychologists and game theorists) have shown that different but logically equivalent phrases in survey items can cause individuals to alter their preferences by casting the same information in a positive or negative light, psychologists have shown that "priming" respondents by having them read vignettes, look at pictures, or complete word scrambles can alter their preferences as well. Both framing and priming activate cognitive schemas through which subsequent information is interpreted. However, if cognitive schemas are conceptualized holistically, it becomes possible to look for unintuitive but theoretically important mind-body connections. For example, based on Inbar et al.'s (2008) finding that political conservatives are more disgust-sensitive than liberals, we can hypothesize that priming disgust emotions will alter the moral preferences and judgments of political conservatives more than those of liberals. Blair-Loy's studies of "gendered cultural models of work and family life" (2001; also see her contribution to this volume) provide another opportunity to try out framing and priming techniques. Blair-Loy is critical of strict cognitivist approaches to gender ideologies that leave out emotional and normative components of gender. Rather, she uses the term "devotion" to capture the depth of commitment people have to certain ways of understanding and living gender roles. If gendered cultural models work the way Blair-Loy claims they do, it ought to be possible to prime these models in such a way as to alter people's moral judgments and preferences related to gender. Cultural models of work and family life would be expected to play a mediating role in psychological priming effects, such that people who have more lived experience (see Bourdieu 1990) with a particular model will be more susceptible to primes associated with that model, while conflicting models should delay the processing of new information and formation of new moral judgments (Druckman and Nelson 2003). Sociological use of priming methods in survey research on respondents of different ages and social categories, and with different life experiences, may allow us to discover when and how cultural models of gender, as well as models that inform social and political preferences of all kinds, develop over the life course and across social space.

CONCLUSIONS

The empirical studies discussed in this chapter reveal some of the complexity of mind-body connections, and the value of being able to employ multiple conceptions of these connections in sociological studies of morality. However, in my view at least, holistic analysis of morality is an especially promising direction for future research. Holistic sociologies of morality already have various methods of analysis at their disposal, including interviews and ethnography, content analysis, and framing and priming methods. In addition, they can draw from many sources of inspiration and ideas, including the American pragmatist philosophical tradition (Joas 2000); Mauss's lectures on mental and social phenomena (Mauss 1979[1935]); cognitive science theories of embodied cognition (Ignatow 2007, 2009a); and research on the psychology and biology of morality (Hauser 2006). With these methods and intellectual resources at their disposal, sociologists appear well positioned to contribute to interdisciplinary debates on morality, debates in which the line between mind and body is increasingly blurred.

REFERENCES

Archer, M. S. 2007. *Structure, Agency, and the Internal Conversation*. New York: Cambridge University Press.

Arjomand, S., and E. Tiryakian. 2004. *Rethinking Civilizational Analysis*. London: Sage.

Bargh, J A., and T. L. Chartrand. 2000. "The Mind in the Middle: A Practical Guide to Priming and Automaticity Research." In *Handbook of Research Methods in Social and Personality Psychology*, edited by H. T. Reis, and C. M. Judd. New York: Cambridge University Press.

Bargh, J. A., C., M., and L. Burrows. 1996. "Automaticity of Social Behavior: Direct Effects of Trait Construct and Stereotype Activation on Action. *Journal of Personality and Social Psychology* 71:230–244.

Barsalou, L. W. 1999. "Perceptual Symbol Systems." *Behavioral and Brain Sciences* 22:577–609.

Bauman, Z. 1989. *Modernity and the Holocaust*. Ithaca, NY: Cornell University Press.

Bauman, Z. 1993. *Postmodern Ethics*. Cambridge, MA: Basil Blackwell.

Bauman, Z. 1995. *Life in Fragments, Essays in Postmodern Morality*. Cambridge: Polity.

Blair-Loy, M. 2001. "Cultural Constructions of Family Schemas: The Case of Women Finance Executives." *Gender and Society* 15(5):687–709.

Boltanski, L., and L. Thévenot. 2001. "The Sociology of Critical Capacity." *European Journal of Social Theory* 2(3):359–377.

Bourdieu, P. 1984. *Distinction*. Cambridge, MA: Harvard University Press.

Bourdieu, P. 1990. *The Logic of Practice*. Cambridge, UK: Polity.

Bryant, C., and D. Jary. 1997 *Anthony Giddens: Critical Assessments*. New York: Routledge.

Carney, D. R. D., J. T. Jost, and S. D. Gosling. 2008. "The Secret Lives of Liberals and Conservatives: Personality Profiles, Interaction Styles, and the Things They Leave Behind." *Political Psychology* 29:807–840.

Cerulo, K., ed. 2002. *Culture in Mind: Toward a Sociology of Culture and Cognition*. New York: Routledge.

Cicourel, A. V. 1974. *Cognitive Sociology: Language and Meaning in Social Interaction*. New York: Free Press.

Clark, A. 1999. "An Embodied Cognitive Science?" *Trends in Cognitive Sciences* 3(9):345–351.

Cohen, D. 1996. "Law, Social Policy, and Violence: The Impact of Regional Cultures." *Journal of Personality and Social Psychology* 70:961–978.

Cohen, D., R. E. Nisbett,, B. F. Bowdle, and N. Schwarz. 1996. "Insult, Aggression, and the Southern Culture of Honor: An Experimental Ethnography." *Journal of Personality and Social Psychology* 70(5):945–960.

Cortese, A. 1990. *Ethnic Ethics: The Restructuring of Moral Theory*. Albany: State University of New York Press.

Cregan, K. 2006. *The Sociology of the Body*. London: Sage.

Danna Lynch, K. 2009. "Objects, Meanings, and Role Identities: The Practices that Establish Association in the Case of Home-Based Employment." *Sociological Forum* 24(1):76–103.

De Zavala, A. G., and A. Van Bergh. 2007. "Need for Cognitive Closure and Conservative Political Beliefs: Differential Mediation by Personal Worldviews." *Political Psychology* 28(5):587–608.

DiMaggio, P. 1997. "Culture and Cognition." *Annual Review of Sociology* 23:263–287.

DiMaggio, P. 2002. "Why Cognitive (and Cultural) Sociology Needs Cognitive Psychology." PP. 274–281 in *Culture in Mind: Toward a Sociology of Culture and Cognition*, edited by K. Cerulo. New York: Routledge.

Druckman, J. N. 2001. "The Implications of Framing Effects for Citizen Competence." *Political Behavior* 23(3): 225–256.

Druckman, J. N. 2004. "Political Preference Formation: Competition, Deliberation, and the (Ir)relevance of Framing Effects." *American Political Science Review* 98(4):671–686.

Druckman, J. N., and K. R. Nelson. 2003. "Framing and Deliberation: How Citizens' Conversations Limit Elite Influence." *American Journal of Political Science* 47(4):729–745.

Giddens, A. 1986. *The Constitution of Society*. Berkeley, CA: University of California Press.

Giddens, A. 1987. *Social Theory and Modern Sociology*. Stanford, CA: Stanford University Press.

Giddens, A. 1991. *Modernity and Self-Identity*. Stanford, CA: Stanford University Press.

Gilligan, C. 1982. *In a Different Voice*. Cambridge, MA: Harvard University Press.

Greenberg, J., and E. Jonas. 2003. "Psychological Motives and Political Orientation—The Left, the Right, and the Rigid: Comment on Jost et al. (2003)." *Psychological Bulletin* 129(3):376–382.

Habermas, J. 1979. *Communication and the Evolution of Society*. Trans. Thomas McCarthy. Boston: Beacon Press.

Haidt, J. 2002. "Dialogue Between my Head and my Heart: Affective Influences on Moral Judgment." *Psychological Inquiry* 13:54–56.

Haidt, J., and J. Graham. 2007. "When Morality Opposes Justice: Conservatives Have Moral Intuitions that Liberals may not Recognize." *Social Justice Research* 20 (1):98–116.

Haidt, J, and C. Joseph. 2008. "The Moral Mind: How Five Sets of Innate Intuitions Guide the Development of Many Culture-Specific Virtues, and Perhaps Even Modules." PP. 367–392 *The Innate Mind, Vol. 3*, P. Carruthers, S. Lawrence, and S. Stich. Oxford, UK: Oxford University Press.

Haidt, J., and D. Keltner. 1999. "Culture and Emotion: Multiple Methods Find New Faces and a Gradient of Recognition." *Cognition and Emotion* 13:225–266.

Hauser, M. 2006. *Moral Minds: The Nature of Right and Wrong*. New York: HarperCollins.

Hegtvedt, K. A. 2005. "Doing Justice to the Group: Examining the Roles of the Group in Justice Research." *Annual Review of Sociology* 31:25–45.

Hitlin, S. 2003. "Values as the Core of Personal Identity: Drawing Links Between Two Theoriesof the Self." *Social Psychology Quarterly* 66 (2):118–137.

Hitlin, S. 2007. "Doing Good, Feeling Good: Values and The Self's Moral Center." *Journal of Positive Psychology* 2 (4):249–259.

Hitlin, S. 2008. *Moral Selves, Evil Selves: The Social Psychology of Conscience*. New York: Palgrave-Macmillan.

Hitlin, S., and A. Piliavin. 2004. "Values: Reviving a Dormant Concept." *Annual Review of Sociology* 30:359–393.

Hume, D. 2003 (1739–1740). *A Treatise of Human Nature*. Mineola, NY: Dover Publications.

Ignatow, G. 2007. "Theories of Embodied Knowledge: New Directions for Cultural and Cognitive Sociology?" *Journal for the Theory of Social Behavior* 37(2):1–21.

Ignatow, G. 2009a. "Why the Sociology of Morality Needs Bourdieu's *Habitus*." *Sociological Inquiry* 79 (1):98–114.

Ignatow, G. 2009b. "Culture and Embodied Cognition: Moral Discourses in Internet Support Groups for Overeaters." *Social Forces* 88(2):643–669.

Ignatow, G. 2010. "Mauss's Lectures to Psychologists: The Case for Holistic Sociology, Then and Now." Unpublished manuscript, Department of Sociology, University of North Texas.

Inbar, Y., D. A. Pizarro, and P. Bloom. 2008. "Conservatives are More Easily Disgusted than Liberals." *Cognition and Emotion* 23 (4):714–725.

Joas, H. 2000. *The Genesis of Values*. Chicago: University of Chicago Press.

Johnson, D. P. 1990. "Security Versus Autonomy Motivation in Anthony Giddens' Concept of Agency." *Journal for the Theory of Social Behaviour* 20 (2):111–130.

Jost, J. T., J. Glaser, A. W. Kruglanski, and F. Sulloway. 2003. "Political Conservatism as Motivated Social Cognition." *Psychological Bulletin* 129:339–375.

Kohlberg, L. 1969. "Stage and Sequence: The Cognitive-Developmental Approach to Socialization." In *The Handbook of Socialization Theory and Research*, edited by D. A. Goslin. Chicago: Rand McNally.

Kohlberg, L. 1971. *From Is to Ought: How to Commit the Naturalistic Fallacy and Get Away with It in the Study of Moral Development*. New York: Academic Press.

Levy, R. 1984. "The Emotions in Comparative Perspective." PP. 397–412, in *Approaches to Emotion*, edited by K. R. Scherer, and P. Ekman . Hillsdale, NJ: Erlbaum.

Mauss, M. 1979 (1935). *Sociology and Psychology: Essays*. Translated by Ben Brewster.

Mohr, J. 1998. "Measuring Meaning Structures." *Annual Review of Sociology* 24:345–370.

Piaget, J. 1999 (1932). *The Moral Judgment of the Child*. Abingdon, UK: Routledge.

Probyn, E. 2004. "Shame in the Habitus." *The Sociological Review* 52 (2):224–248.

Sayer, A. 2005. *The Moral Significance of Class*. Cambridge: Cambridge University Press.

Scheff, T. J. 2003. "Shame in Self and Society." *Symbolic Interaction* 26 (2):239–262.

Scheff, T. J. 2000. "Shame and the Social Bond: A Sociological Theory." *Sociological Theory* 18 (1):84–99.

Scheff, T. J. 1997a. *Emotions and the Social Bond: Part/Whole Analysis*. Cambridge, UK: Cambridge University Press.

Scheff, T. J. 1997b. *Bloody Revenge: Nationalism, War, and Emotion*. Boulder, CO: Westview.

Schubert, T. W. 2005. "Your Highness: Vertical Positions As Perceptual Symbols of Power." *Journal of Personality and Social Psychology* 89:1–21.

Shilling, C., and P. A. Mellor 1998. "Durkheim, Morality and Modernity: Collective Effervescence, Homo Duplex and the Sources of Moral Action." *British Journal of Sociology*. 49(2):193–209.

Silber, I. 2003. "Pragmatic Sociology as Cultural Sociology: Beyond Repertoire Theory?" *European Journal of Social Theory* 6 (4):427–449.

Smith, C. 2003. *Moral, Believing Animals: Human Personhood and Culture*. Oxford: Oxford University Press.

Stepper, S., and F. Strack. 1993. "Proprioceptive Determinants of Emotional and Nonemotional Feelings." *Journal of Personality and Social Psychology*. 64:211.

Strack, F., L. Martin, and S. Stepper. 1988. "Inhibiting and Facilitating Conditions of the Human Smile: A Nonobtrusive Test of the Facial Feedback Hypothesis." *Journal of Personality and Social Psychology* 54:768–777.

Swidler, A. 1986. "Culture in Action: Symbols and Strategies." *American Sociological Review* 51 (2):273–28.

Turner, B. S. 2008. *The Body & Society: Explorations in Social Theory*. London: Sage.

Turner, J. H. 2000. *On the Origins of Human Emotion*. Stanford, CA: Stanford University Press.

Vaisey, S. 2009. "Motivation and Justification: A Dual-Process Model of Culture in Action." *American Journal of Sociology* 114:1675–1715.

Wells, G., and R. Petty. 1980. "The Effects of Overt Head Movement on Persuasion: Compatibility and Incompatibility of Responses." *Basic and Applied Social Psychology*. 1:219–230.

Whorf, B. L. 1941. "The Relation of Habitual Thought and Behavior to Language." PP. 75–93 in *Language, Culture, and Personality: Essays in Memory of Edward Sapir*, edited by L. Spier. Menasha, Wis.: Sapir Memorial Publication Fund.

Williams, L. E., and J. A. Bargh. 2008. "Keeping One's Distance: The Influence of Spatial Distance Cues on Affect and Evaluation." *Psychological Science* 19(3):302–308.

Williams, L. E., and J. A. Bargh, 2008. "Temperature to Temperament: Warm Objects Alter Personality Impressions." Unpublished manuscript. New Haven, CT: Yale University,.

Williams, K. D., C. K. T. Cheung, and W. Choi. 2000. Cyberostracism: Effects of Being Ignored Over the Internet. *Journal of Personality and Social Psychology* 79:748–762.

Winchester, D. 2008. "Embodying the Faith: Religious Practice and the Making of a Muslim Moral Habitus." *Social Forces* 86(4):1753.

Wuthnow, R. 1987. *Meaning and Moral Order: Explorations in Cultural Analysis*. Berkeley, CA: University of California Press.

Zajonc, R. B. 1980. "Feeling and Thinking: Preferences Need No Inferences." *American Psychologist* 35:151–175.

Zerubavel, E. 1999. *Social Mindscapes: An Invitation to Cognitive Sociology*. Cambridge, MA: Harvard University Press.

Zhong, C.-B., and G. J. Leonardelli. 2008. "Cold and Lonely: Does Social Exclusion Literally Feel Cold?" *Psychological Science* 19 (9):838–842.

Zhong, C.-B., and K. Liljenquist. 2006. "Washing Away Your Sins: Threatened Morality and Physical Cleansing." *Science* 313:1451–1452.

CHAPTER 22

Moral Power

JAL MEHTA AND CHRISTOPHER WINSHIP

INTRODUCTION

Despite their many differences, when Barack Obama speaks about the Muslim world, his words are remarkably similar to those of his predecessor, George W. Bush. Compare the September 2006 speech President Bush gave to the UN with the June 2009 Cairo speech of President Obama. Both presidents talked about the importance of human rights, self-determination, and democracy in Muslim nations; both said that America will respect the history and traditions of the Muslim world; both argued that America is not at war with Islam; both called on Muslim moderates to join America in denouncing the perpetrators of the September 11th attacks. The reaction to the two men from the Muslim community, however, could not be more different: shoe throwing hatred for President Bush, and, at least as of June 2009, healthy respect for President Obama.[1]

The difference in the way that the two presidents have been received by the Muslim world, we argue, lies not in what these men have said, but in how they are perceived. As a product of their past actions, their biographies, and the narratives that they have crafted for themselves they have entirely different moral status and standing, or what we call *moral power*, in their relationship to the Muslim world. As a result, their words are interpreted quite differently. This difference in moral power is critical for understanding not only how they are perceived, but also is one of the resources they have available to persuade and affect the actions of others.[2]

---

[1] Michael Crowley, "Just Like Bush," June 4, 2009, *The New Republic*. Accessed online at: http://www.tnr.com/politics/story.html?id=770a874d-9279-4cda-b0e4-2fd0533b07b6.

[2] There is some overlap with what Joseph Nye has called *soft power*, but *moral power* is a distinct concept. Nye (2004: x) defines soft power as "the ability to get what you want through attraction rather than coercion or payments." Nye, a foreign relations scholar whose interest is in the power of nations, argues that the "soft power of a country rests primarily on three resources: its culture. . ., its political values. . ., and its foreign policies" (Nye 2004: 11). The more outsiders are attracted to America on those various dimensions, argues Nye, the greater the nation's soft power. Moral power is thus a more specific concept than soft power: soft power refers to the range of attributes that might attract another to do one's bidding; moral power is focused on the degree to which one's moral status and standing affect one's ability to sway others. Moral power can contribute to soft power, but soft power need not rest on a moral basis. As Nye (2004: 17) writes, "Much of American soft power has been produced by Hollywood, Harvard, Microsoft, and Michael Jordan."

S. Hitlin, S. Vaisey (eds.), *Handbook of the Sociology of Morality*,
Handbooks of Sociology and Social Research, DOI 10.1007/978-1-4419-6896-8_22,
© Springer Science+Business Media, LLC 2010

To claim the importance of moral power is not to discount more traditional forms of power such as economic or military power. Rather it is to say that there are frequently situations where other forms of power are not dispositive, and moral power is one critical resource in these situations. In these cases, there is often an important but uncommitted middle; moral power is critical to persuading that middle that a particular interpretation of a situation is the correct one, which in turn affects which positions that middle will adopt.[3] Put another way, moral power is important when there is moral ambiguity and the ability to persuade those on the fence as to what is moral is critical. This is frequently the case in politics, but can also be true in other spheres of life. In situations such as these, moral claims about what is right or just and/or what is best for the common good are often made to influence people to support one position or another. A classic example to which we will return is the Civil Rights movement and the passage of federal civil rights legislation during the 1960s. It is difficult to argue that the power of blacks and black leaders as understood in its traditional sense was the key factor in pushing through this legislation. Rather, it was, at least in part, the moral arguments made by Martin Luther King and others that were critical. Furthermore, it was not just the arguments that King and other clergy made, but their moral status and standing as ministers that was influential.

Morality and power are often taken to be opposites, with morality grounded in altruism and a commitment to the common good, and power located in self-interest. Our contention is that moral power, seemingly an oxymoron, is actually a widely present and important factor in social and political life. Our aim is to introduce and situate the concept, offer a theory of how moral power is generated and what role it plays, and give examples that illustrate its importance.

Moral power is the degree to which an actor, by virtue of his or her perceived moral stature, is able to persuade others to adopt a particular belief or take a particular course of action. While there has been some writing about the importance of *moral claims* and *narratives* (Jasper 1997, Polletta 2006, Ganz 2008), it is our argument that it is not only the perceived morality of the claims, as argued by Boltanski and Thévenot (2006), but also the *moral power* of the specific *actor* making the claim that is important in determining the outcome.[4] Thus, the quite different reception of Bush's and Obama's comments in the Muslim world.

The importance of moral power as a form of influence is exemplified in the widespread debate about the extent to which the US behavior in foreign affairs is consistent with the moral claims that it espouses. One common view is that although the United States preaches the virtues of democracy, its practices violate that claim in important ways (e.g. by engaging in torture or supporting authoritarian or dictatorial leaders). The issue here is not whether the USA has the economic or political muscle to convince other countries to take particular actions, but rather whether it has the ability to persuade other countries that particular actions are morally justified given the perceived moral inconsistencies of its own behavior.

---

[3] There are some similarities here to Fligstein's (2001) notion of social skill, in that both ideas are about creating cooperation among actors. However, social skill seems to be more highly rooted in understanding, shaping, and responding to the needs and preferences of other actors, while moral power is more about how actors' moral status affects their abilities to get others to follow their lead.

[4] An actor could be an individual, organization, or corporate actors more generally.

Below we develop the outlines of a theory of moral power. Specifically, we argue that moral power is a function of whether one is perceived as *morally well-intentioned*, *morally capable*, and whether one has *moral standing* to speak to an issue. With respect to *intentions*, the issue is whether an actor is perceived to be promoting a particular position out of concern with what is morally right or good, as opposed to being driven by self-interest or other motivations, and, relatedly, whether that actor is perceived to be trustworthy. In terms of *capability*, the question is whether an individual is seen to be both generally wise and knowledgeable in forming moral judgments and appropriately informed about the specific issue at hand. *Moral standing* refers to the degree to which the actor is understood to be a member of the relevant moral community.

In the next section of the chapter, we place our argument in the context of previous theoretical work. We start by discussing the antipathy between power and morality as concepts in traditional sociological writings. We then discuss the relationship between our use of the concepts of power and morality and how they have been used by others. Next, we develop our analytic model and define our key terms. We then present several extended examples drawn from our own work to illustrate the impact of moral power: Winship's work on the partnership that arose between the Boston Police Department and a group of black inner-city ministers known as the Ten Point Coalition, and Mehta's work on the federal education program No Child Left Behind. We conclude the chapter by discussing the potential importance of moral power as a concept for future research.

THEORETICAL CONTEXT

Our interest in moral power is also part of the larger project, shared by other contributors to this volume, of reviving interest in the sociology of morality. Morality was a central concern of the discipline's founding fathers, particularly Durkheim and Weber, but it has fallen largely off the agenda in the past four decades. A full accounting of this decline is beyond the scope of this chapter, but one central strand has been the rejection of Talcott Parsons' notion of a unifying moral or normative code that holds society together. This neo-Durkheimian notion was virulently attacked by conflict theorists such as Dahrendorf and others, who argued that such a claim ignored important differences in power, and aimed to legitimize a functionalist view of society that was rapidly being eclipsed by the events of the 1960s. In subsequent years, the Parsonsian view has also come under attack for assuming too much homogeneity across the population in its notions of morality and too much coherence in individuals' views of morality (Alexander 1987).

If Parsons' notion of morality mistakenly overlooked issues of power, subsequent theorists of power have made a similar error in overlooking morality. Post-Parsonian sociology is right to see society as made up of individuals, organizations, institutions and logics rather than overarching functional norms. However, as some more culturally-inclined scholars have recognized,[5] the presence of conflict does not necessarily imply that actors are acting out of narrow self-interest or that the only resources that actors possess are material ones. While

---

[5] See Adams, Clemens, and Orloff (2005).

power can be a function of role or of social status, power can also be derived from the perceived moral weight of the actors involved.[6] Our view of moral power thus tries to avoid both dangers, seeing society as pluralistic rather than unified, but accepting that moral claims and the moral power of the actors who make them are an important part of how social and political decisions are made.

In a sense, our work harkens back to the classic sociology of Weber, who was similarly interested in both power and morality, before those concepts came to be seen as antithetical. Weber's (1968, 1946) notion of charismatic authority has some parallels to our view of moral power: they are both about a form of power that is not traditional or rational-legal, but rather dependent in part upon the qualities of the leader. We also share Weber's sense that power is relational. Thus, a particular individual may have particular power with respect to some individuals, but not others. For example, arguments about the evils of gay marriage by an evangelical minister may be persuasive to other evangelicals, but be seen as irrelevant by atheists.

At the same time, moral power is not the same as charismatic authority. According to Weber, charisma "will be applied to a certain quality of an individual personality by virtue of which he is considered extraordinary and treated as endowed with supernatural, superhuman, or at least specifically exceptional power or qualities. These are such as are not accessible to the ordinary person, but are regarded as of divine origins or as exemplary" (1968: 241). While charismatic authority can generate moral power, moral power can also adhere to people who are not conventionally charismatic or extraordinary, and it is potentially much more widespread than charismatic authority. Parents, for example, frequently use moral power in trying to establish the justice of their rules. Teach for America founder Wendy Kopp is a good example of someone who is frequently described as more "discipline" than "dynamism" and "has never been a charismatic public speaker," but who is able to use the moral clarity of her cause to advance the mission of her organization.[7] Thus while leaders like Martin Luther King or Gandhi can rightly be seen as examples of both charismatic authority and moral power, moral power can also exist in the absence of charisma, and is thus a much more common feature of social life.[8]

In terms of Lukes' (2005) famous typology of the three dimensions of power, moral power is most closely related to his third dimension.[9] Summarizing crudely, Lukes' first dimension of power is the ability of an actor to directly determine the outcome where there are competing recognized alternative outcomes; his second dimension is the ability of an actor to define the agenda, that is, what alternatives are publicly recognized and debated; his third dimension is the extent to which an actor is able to influence and change what others see as desirable. To the degree that people want what is morality right, moral power is about changing wants, Lukes' third dimension of power.

---

[6] This chapter is intended to investigate moral power; it is not intended to an exhaustively catalogue different types of power. See Lukes (2005) for one such attempt.

[7] Jodi Wilgoren, "Wendy Kopp, The Leader of Teach for America," *New York Times,* November 12, 2000.

[8] We also offer a more specific account of the sources of moral power than Weber does of the sources of charismatic authority; see the next section on components of moral power.

[9] Presumably moral power could also matter at the level of the first or second dimension of power; actors who are perceived to have moral power can also have influence on how debates are decided or what is on the agenda.

Moral power is particularly salient when a moral conflict is less about general principles than the appropriate interpretation of those principles in particular contexts (Boltanski and Thévenot 2006). Abortion is a good example: the lines of disagreement are less about the values each side seeks to uphold (many on both sides of the debate are for "choice" and for "life" as general principles), but rather whether abortion should be seen as a case of "life" or one of woman's "choice." Thus, deploying moral power is often less about changing others' principles, and more often about convincing them the right way to understand the world.[10]

COMPONENTS OF MORAL POWER

We see moral power as a function of whether one is perceived to *morally well-intentioned*, *morally capable*, and whether one has *moral standing* to speak to an issue. We argue that all three are needed for an actor to have moral power.

To be perceived as *morally well-intentioned* is to be seen by others as consistently acting in accordance with moral principles. This often takes the form of an actor who is seen as motivated by concern for the common good rather than out of self- or group-interest (Boltanski and Thévenot 2006). The classic example is Martin Luther King, whose argument for civil rights for all was seen by many as grounded in universal moral principles, not because it solely and narrowly advanced the interests of African-Americans. At the same time, it may be the case that moral worthiness is demonstrated by defending the in-group rather than expanding it to include morally compromised members outside of the group. Torturing alleged terrorists to prevent future plots, for example, can be seen as morally admirable or morally bankrupt depending upon the standards of the surrounding community. Hence we emphasize *perceived* moral intentions because we see moral power as it operates in the world as socially constructed, not as an *a priori* philosophical attribute.

However, moral intentions are not enough to achieve moral power; moral power is also a function of *moral capability*. Moral capability is the ability to effectively diagnose and act in a moral situation. It is akin (with a particular emphasis on what is moral) to what Aristotle called *phronesis* or practical wisdom, defined as the knowledge gained through experience of how to act (morally) in particular situations. The key attribute here is the relationship between the particular and the general; to be morally capable means to be able to make persuasively the moral judgments about particular cases with reference to broader moral principles. If the situation sits within a set of governing institutional norms (i.e. a bioethical dilemma, or one within a religious faith), to be morally capable will additionally require technical knowledge of the domain, and the ability to effectively assess the particulars of the situation within the broader governing principles of the domain.[11] Moral capability provides an important complement to moral intentionality. For example, if one is well-intentioned, but is unable to recognize when one is being swindled or taken advantage of by a malevolent actor, then one is not perceived

---

[10] We also assume that people's sense of morality may be affected explicitly or implicitly. For example, Martin Luther King was able to persuade many that blacks should have the same political rights as whites. This would be *explicit* influence. A prominent, charitable member of a community might influence others to be charitable simply by example. This would be *implicit* influence.

[11] See Abbott (1988) on the importance of diagnosis as key to skilled practice within a domain.

by others to be an effective moral guide. Since moral power is in part about the ability to per-suasively define what is moral, having the capability to effectively make such distinctions is an important part of this equation.

A third essential component of moral power is *moral standing*. Moral standing is whether an actor is perceived to be part of the moral interpretive community that is relevant to the question at hand. Moral philosophers are an example of a group that is morally capable and well-intentioned but has little moral standing with respect to many questions of social and political life. Moral standing can come within a rational-legal structure if the structure is perceived as legitimate (i.e. judges). Alternatively, it can emerge through a kind of open juris-dictional claims-making (as advocates often do in politics). This means that moral standing can sometimes derive at least in part from one's role, while at other times it may be more informally negotiated.

Much of politics is about who has moral standing with respect to an issue: issues that sit at the intersection of race and other social problems are potent examples of the fights over who has moral standing in the dispute between different claims. Another example is euthana-sia: the debate over who should decide (medical professionals? family members? ethicists? society writ large?) is in part a question of who has appropriate moral standing in the matter. Extremely powerful and skilled moral actors are often able to claim membership in multiple moral communities. To return to the Martin Luther King example, the civil rights leader was part of at least three such communities: the black community, the Christian community, and the American community, and his standing within each of them effectively allowed him to broaden the reach of his moral power and mobilize multiple moral communities.

It should be clear from the preceding discussion that we view moral power as something which is both highly relational and socially constructed. There is no 'view from nowhere' when it comes to moral power—there are only actions which are seen as moral or not by a relevant community, which in turn then allows the actor to utilize (or not) moral power with reference to that community. As such, there is a strong "performative" (to use Jeffrey Alexander's term) dimension to moral power. Whether an individual has moral power is a function of whether their performance in relation to others is successful, which requires that it be perceived as "authentic" (Alexander 2004). Here, we argue that perceived intentions, capa-bility, and moral standing are the essential ingredients for initially achieving moral power. Over time, moral power can become a kind of social fact—once an actor's moral power is widely seen as legitimate, it then becomes a resource, which that actor can use as new situations arise.[12]

A THEORY OF MORAL POWER

Figure 22.1 presents a theory of moral power. At the core of our argument is the claim that moral power is a result of a cultural/symbolic process, that is socially constructed, where the enactment and perception of moral standing, intentions, and capability coheres into a "suc-cessful performance." Our theory of how moral power works is similar to Jeffrey Alexander's

---

[12] We discuss this further in the section below on uses of moral power.

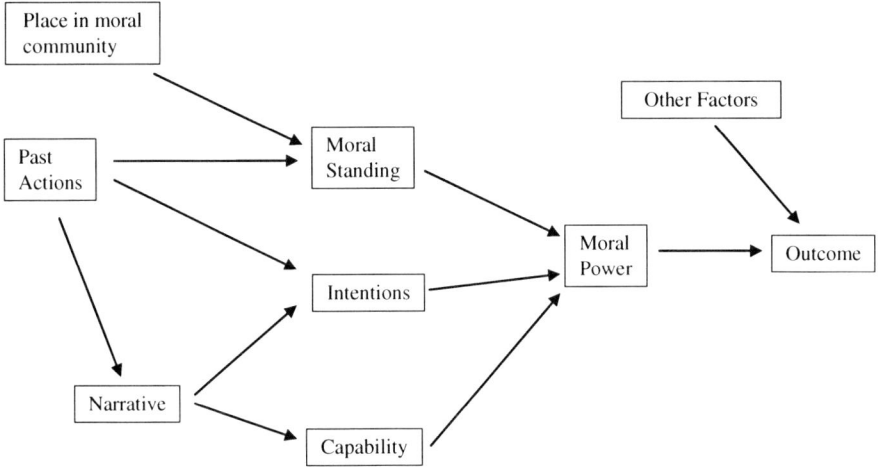

FIGURE 22.1. A theory of moral power.

view of how social "performances" work more generally, and so we draw upon some of his thinking here. For Alexander, the understanding of a situation is the result of the cultural performances of the individuals involved and how the "audience" experiences and understands that performance. A key issue for Alexander is the necessary conditions for a performance to be persuasive and thus successful. He argues that the critical component of success is that the performance be seen as authentic. To quote Alexander: "a strategy's success depends on belief in the validity of the cultural contents of the strategist's symbolic communication and on accepting the authenticity and even the sincerity of another's strategic intentions" (2004: 528).

Note that while the language of "strategy" and "performance" seem to imply that moral power is something which is contrived, we do not mean to suggest that that is necessarily so. It may be that the most convincing and sustainable way to establish moral power is simply to consistently act in a way that is broadly seen as morally right (e.g. Gandhi). However, given that moral power is ultimately relational, and that it is the perception of the surrounding community that matters, it is also the case that some actors will seek to achieve moral power by intentionally creating a narrative of their moral worthiness and concealing their immoral actions.

Our argument is that moral standing, intentionality and capability are the needed ingredients for an actor to be seen as morally "authentic" and thus achieve and maintain moral power. A failure in any one of these components is likely to lead to a performance being seen as invalid, and thus result in the loss of moral power. As such, moral power is fragile. If it is discovered that an actor's intentions are based in self-interest, the actor's arguments lose their persuasive power. Similarly, if the actor is thought to be morally incapable, no one is likely to give credence to the arguments the actor makes. If she is perceived to be outside the relevant moral community, her opinions are easily ignored.

Because moral power is fragile, it is easily attacked. Political actors as well as others are frequently accused of ill intentions. As such, ad hominem attacks can actually be very powerful, because of their potential to undermine an actor's moral intentions, and hence their moral power. Similarly, an actor's arguments may be dismissed if the actor is perceived as not having the appropriate knowledge, that is, not having moral capability.

The fragility of moral power is socially important because it requires and constrains specific behavior on the part of actors. This is closely related to Merton's notion of a self-fulfilling prophecy (Merton 1968). A perception of what is true causes individuals to act in a way consistent with that perception, with the result that it becomes true. To the extent that others would like to deny someone moral power, an individual must be sure that they are perceived as well intentioned, capable and having moral standing in the community if they want to retain their moral power, or, in some cases, their power more generally. An obvious recent case is John Edwards. Edwards built much of his presidential candidacy on a moral basis as an advocate for the poor and disenfranchised, but the revelation of his affair, illegitimate child, and cover-up, eliminated his ability to make moral claims and presumably finished his career as a politician. Edwards' situation is an interesting contrast to Francois Mitterand, former President of France, who had many extramarital affairs, with one mistress even attending his funeral with their daughter. Context matters in terms of what types of behavior can undermine moral power.

There is also the question of the relationship between moral power and other forms of power. Are actors who have high degrees of financial, social, military, political, or organizational power more or less likely to possess moral power? This is ultimately an empirical question worthy of further research. Clearly there are extreme examples on both sides: leaders who possessed tremendous political, financial, or military power but whose actions robbed them of any chance at moral power (i.e. genocidal dictators, rapacious Wall Street executives), as well as actors who built upon other forms of power to enhance or exhibit moral power (i.e., major philanthropists). In the first case, the problem is people may well believe that "power corrupts." In the second case, power in the traditional sense may provide individuals with the resources to promote their moral power. This may be in the form of money, access to the media or more influential social networks (Alexander 2004).

There may also be spillover effects, whereby actors' high status in one domain makes them more credible in another. From the perspective of moral power, one way to interpret the Milgram (1974) electric shock experiments is that the social and professional authority of the experimenters led the subjects to trust their moral judgment as well. (Again, this points to the perception-based nature of moral power; clearly what the experimenters were asking the subjects to do was to act immorally, but one way to read what happened is that they were able to persuade the subjects to do so because of their social, professional, and moral authority.) Conversely, Akerlof (1983) has made the argument that high moral status can result in high social status. In particular, he argues that Quakers have been particularly socially and economically successful because they are perceived to be of high moral character by others and thus trustworthy. This is an area that would benefit from further research.

EXTENDED EXAMPLES

Black Ministers and the Boston Miracle

In a series of articles, one of us, Winship (and co-authors), has described how during the 1990s, a group of inner-city black clergy know as the Ten Point Coalition developed a partnership that successfully dealt with the problem of youth violence and homicide in Boston. Although the story of how this partnership came about is its own story, for the purposes of this chapter our interest is in illustrating how the partnership worked.

At the height of the partnership, the Boston police and black ministers conducted "gang forums" as part of a program called Operation Cease-Fire. The purpose of the forums was to let individuals know that they needed to stop their gang activities (gang-banging), and that if they did, they would get help. To quote Berrien et al. (2000: 275), paraphrasing the ministers:

> "You have a choice. Stop your gang-banging and we will help you—help you get back in
> school or get a job, help you deal with your family, your girlfriend; help you straighten
> out your life. Continue to gang-bang and we will work as hard as we can with the police
> to see that you are put in jail. Both for your own good, and the good of community.
> As long as you are gang-banging you are a danger to yourself and to others. What I
> ultimately want to avoid more than anything is presiding over your funeral."

The moral content of this message is obvious: as a minister, I care about you and your well-being, but as a minister, I also require you to act in a way that is consistent with your own and the community's best interest.

For the purposes of this chapter, the Ten Point story is interesting for two reasons. First, the ministers provided what Berrien et al. (2000) called an "umbrella of legitimacy" for the police. Specifically, people in the community believed that the ministers had full knowledge of what the police were doing to curb youth violence and that the ministers would loudly and publicly speak out if they thought that police activity was illegitimate.[13] This had two consequences. First, as one high-ranking police official said, it allowed the police to intervene more aggressively to deal with youth violence than they might have otherwise. Second, however, before intervening, the police would confer with the ministers to make sure that they thought that what the police were going to do was appropriate. Thus, in a direct way, as discussed generally above, the desire of the police to be seen as legitimate and maintain their moral power constrained their behavior and caused them to act in ways that were moral, at least as defined by the ministers. In addition, the fact that this moral power was dependent on the ministers' support and community understanding of the relationship between the ministers and police illustrates both the perceptual and relational dimensions of moral power.

The second reason the Ten Point story is of interest here is the nature of the moral power of the ministers themselves. The legitimacy of their partnership with the police was often questioned by local black politicians and other clergy. Their status as members of the clergy gave them a degree of moral power, but not enough to thwart criticism and establish the nature of their intentions, their capability, or appropriate moral standing. Having "walked the walk" is clearly important as a means both of signaling one's moral intentions and of establishing oneself as an important member of the relevant moral community. The fact that the ministers had chosen to live and work in some of Boston's most dangerous neighborhoods and that one of them had decided to give up a career as a doctor provided the needed evidence that their actions were motivated by the good of the black community as a whole, not personal self-interest. Their ability to defuse potential gang violence and negotiate favorable outcomes for youth charged with crimes provided evidence of their considerable moral capability. The fact

---

[13] At that point the Ten Point ministers participated in a study of racial profiling being carried out by a Northeastern University faculty member that was highly critical of police behavior (Berrien et al. 2000).

that they lived where they worked, as well as the fact that one of the ministers had been a gang member in his youth established their moral standing in the community.

As briefly discussed above, access to the media can be an important resource in creating moral power. In the Boston example, *The Boston Globe* played a critical role in the creation of a narrative, often called "The Boston Miracle" wherein it was claimed that the fact that the Boston Police Department and the Ten Point ministers were working together explained an 80% drop in Boston's homicide rate over the 1990s. The Ten Point ministers were acutely aware of the importance of the media; often publishing op-ed pieces, making themselves available for interviews, and offering pithy phrases to explain particular situations.

The black inner-city ministers in Boston enjoyed considerable moral power within Boston's black community (Berrien et al. 2000). Many individuals, however, particularly Boston's black politicians, were unhappy with their influence. As a result, the black ministers' behavior was constantly under scrutiny, most importantly in Boston's black newspaper, *The Bay State Banner*. Claims that the ministers' behavior was guided by self-interest and/or not in line with the interests of Boston's black community were used against them and, if they had been persuasive, their influence most certainly would have been undermined. Given this constant scrutiny, the Ten Point ministers were under constant pressure to act in a way consistent with their image.

No Child Left Behind

The research of the other one of us, Mehta, on educational politics provides a second extended illustration of the role and impact of moral power. In January of 2002, the United States signed into law the No Child Left Behind Act (NCLB). The act declared that all children would be proficient in reading and math by 2014. Students would be tested annually in grades 3–8, and schools that failed to show the expected rate of improvement ("adequate yearly progress" or AYP) would face an escalating series of consequences, culminating in the closure of schools and the replacement of staff. Whether this legislation was a good idea or whether it has been efficacious in achieving its goals is not our concern here. What is interesting from our perspective is that it came into being in the first place, as it owes its existence in part to the impact of moral power.

NCLB represented a significant and unexpected departure from previous American educational politics. For more than two centuries, American education was resolutely localized by international standards, with local districts having primary responsibility for schools. This began to change somewhat with the passage of the Elementary and Secondary Education Act in 1965, which for the first time granted the federal government some formal responsibility for the role of schools, but still the federal contribution to schooling remained at less than 10%, and most powers remained devolved to districts and states. NCLB represented an unprecedented expansion of the federal role in American education. That this change happened under a Republican president was even more surprising, given longstanding conservative opposition to a federal role in education.

Existing theories did little to predict this change. Institutional accounts emphasize the ways in which long entrenched patterns of federalism are expected to be inertial and constrain the opportunities for change. (They explain well why the system stayed so localized for so long.) Interest group accounts are also particularly unsuited for explaining these changes, because by widespread consensus one of the strongest interest groups in American education politics are the teachers unions, which have long resisted efforts to introduce accountability and testing in American education.[14]

In other work, Mehta has argued that the key reason for this set of changes was the emergence of a paradigm that linked together the nation's economic and educational futures. This new paradigm legitimized a greater state and federal role, and also created urgency around the reform. It generated business support, was friendly to both liberal Democrats seeking equal opportunity and conservative Republicans seeking more skilled workers, and thus generated bipartisan political support.

So how does moral power come into this story? That the aims of the act—to close gaps between more- and less-advantaged children—were broadly seen as a moral imperative strengthened the hand of proponents and weakened the hand of opponents. This was particularly true of the materially powerful teachers unions, who were largely undermined by their lack of moral power. Discussions with legislators, including Democratic legislators, revealed that the unions were viewed as compromised moral actors. The unions were perceived as being more invested in the self-interest of their members than in improving the school system, which undermined the legitimacy of their arguments against NCLB. This compromised moral status was derived from their previous positions. To take just one example, union opposition to districts' ability to fire what districts regarded as incompetent teachers was seen as the unions favoring the interests of their members over the broader social goal of increasing opportunity for poor students. These specific positions crystallized into a broader narrative of teachers unions being opponents of almost any type of "reform," which, in a political climate that was demanding reform, left them on the losing side of the debate.[15]

An interesting counterpoint to the unions was a small liberal think tank called the Education Trust. The Ed Trust, with fewer than 50 employees, no national base of support, and relatively few dollars, was a critical player in NCLB, according to detailed work on the creation of the Act. The Ed Trust was a proponent of NCLB, and they made a simple moral case: schools, particularly urban schools, have failed our students, and we need to hold them accountable until they improve. The Ed Trust had everything the unions lacked in terms of moral power: their past actions indicated that they were deeply committed to the cause, as the organization was staffed by a number of former civil rights actors; they had capability, in that they produced a number of reports detailing the failings of the current system; they were viewed as largely impartial, meaning that their numbers were seen as trustworthy; and their overall narrative successfully positioned them as a fair-minded group, with strong social scientific skill, that was deeply committed to expanding opportunity for all children, particularly poor children. The strength of their moral power, in other words, largely outweighed what they lacked in material power, and they became integral players in the development of the legislation.

This example also illustrates the possibility of a kind of *moral surrogacy*, whereby the moral power of one actor is used to enhance the position of another. In this case, the support of the Ed Trust and another longstanding civil rights organization, the Citizens Commission

---

[14] This was particularly true of the National Education Association, and less true of the American Federation of Teachers. The NEA is the larger and more powerful of the two unions. See Mehta (2006) for details.

[15] See Mehta (2006) for details.

on Civil Rights, were used to buttress the moral credibility of the legislation. When centrists and Democrats were accused by union members and other critics of the legislation of being complicit in a right-wing scheme to scapegoat schools as failures and pave the road for privatization, they would point to the support of these civil rights groups as a way of defusing the criticism and signaling the moral importance of the issue.

USES OF MORAL POWER

Moral power is like the other forms of capital: it is a resource, which allows actors to do things that they would not be able to do without it. Just like actors can differ in their level of financial capital, or human capital, or even social capital, they can differ in their level of moral power, which affects what they can do and what options they have at their disposal. Unlike financial or political capital, one does not deplete moral power by "spending it"; effective moral leadership enhances one's moral power for the future.

Moral power is important for everyone from parents to leaders of organizations to heads of state. Parents of adolescents today need to rely almost entirely on their persuasive powers, and the ability to make well-intentioned and morally capable judgments are the keys to getting their children to accede to their wishes. Organizational leaders often have some form of coercive or top-down power, but in more collaborative or less hierarchical organizations, moral power can be a means to overcome collective action dilemmas and motivate one's charges to action. Inconsistencies between what one is asking from others and what one is willing to do oneself erode moral power, as when clergy drive Cadillacs or university presidents' pay themselves extravagantly while raising tuition or freezing faculty salaries. Similarly, when world leaders gather and make requests to one another to amend treaties or contribute troops or humanitarian aid, how they are viewed morally by their contemporaries is often a critical factor in the success of these efforts.

Like other sources of power, the importance of moral power is in its ability to convince other actors to do something or to allow something to be done. However, moral power does more than this. As David Beetham has argued in his book *The Legitimation of Power*, legitimation of authority is created by the expressed consensual behavior of individuals who obey that authority whether they in fact believe in the legitimacy of that authority or whether in any principled sense that authority is legitimate. For example, although George W. Bush's election in 2000 was initially contested, the fact that the media covered his inauguration as they had past inaugurations in part legitimated his election. In a similar way, when individuals act in consent with the moral power of an actor, they cause both that actor and the actions he advocates to be seen as moral. To return to Martin Luther King, King not only convinced the majority of Americans that blacks deserved equal rights, but also that this was morally correct and thus established himself as a moral leader. As Tom Tyler has argued in *Why People Obey the Law* (Tyler 2006) persuading people to do something because it is right is a far more effective form of influence than outright coercion, which is often costly to carry out. Thus, democracy has proved a more viable form of government in many situations than authoritarian totalitarianism as its stability is to a large degree a function of people's belief in its legitimacy.

CONCLUSION

Moral power is a centrally important factor in social life which has not been given its proper due. We suggest in this chapter that outcomes are not just determined by standard structural factors (the economic and social resources of various actors and the relationships between them), but by the relative ability of different actors to persuade and influence others by asserting the correctness of particular moral positions. Differences in the moral power of various actors in their relationships with others are an important and at times key determinant of various outcomes. We have found moral power to be a useful concept in our own work in explaining everything from school policy to presidential politics to the relationship between cops and ministers. Our hope is that other researchers will find the concept of moral power similarly useful in explaining a variety of outcomes.

Acknowledgments We would like to thank Gabriel Abend, Wayne Baker, Nicola Beisel, Neil Gross, Steven Hitlin, Jennifer Hochschild, Steven Lukes, Jane Mansbridge, Brian Steensland, attendees of the Inquiries in the Sociology of Morality session at the International Institute of Sociology World Congress in Budapest. And also the participants at the Harvard Culture and Social Analysis workshop and the National Science Foundation Conference on the Sociology of Morality for their helpful comments and suggestions.

BIBLIOGRAPHY

Abbott, A. 1988. *The System of Professions: An Essay on the Division of Expert Labor.* Chicago: University of Chicago Press.

Adams, J., E. S. Clemens, and A. S. Orloff. 2005. *Remaking Modernity: Politics, History, and Sociology*. Durham: Duke University Press.

Akerlof, G. 1983. "Loyalty Filters." *American Economic Review* 73(1):54–63.

Alexander, J. 2004. "Cultural Pragmatics: Social Performance between Ritual and Strategy." *Sociological Theory*, 22(4):527–537.

Alexander, J. 1987. *Twenty Lectures: Sociological Theory Since World War II*. New York: Columbia University Press.

Arum, R. 2003. *Judging School Discipline: The Crisis of Moral Authority*. Cambridge: Harvard University Press.

Beetham, D. 1991. *The Legitimation of Power*. Atlantic Highlands, NJ: Humanities Press International.

Berrien, J., O. McRoberts, and C. Winship. 2000. "Religion and the Boston Miracle: The Effect of Black Ministry on Youth Violence." In *Who Will Provide?*, edited by M. J. Bane, B. Coffin, and R. Thieman. Boulder: Westview Press.

Boltanski, L., and L. Thevenot. 2006. *On Justification: Economies of Worth*. Princeton: Princeton University Press.

Cialdini, R., and M. Trost. 1988. "Social Influence: Social Norms, Conformity, and Compliance." PP. 151–192 in *The Handbook of Social Psychology*, edited by D. Gilbert, S. Fiske, and G. Lindzey. Boston: McGraw Hill.

DiMaggio, P. 1997. "Culture and Cognition." *Annual Review of Sociology* 23:263–287.

Fligstein, N. 2001. "Social Skill and the Theory of Fields." *Sociological Theory* 19(2):105–125.

Ganz, M. 2008. "What is Public Narrative?" Working paper, Harvard Kennedy School.

Jasper, J. 1997. *The Art of Moral Protest: Culture, Biography and Creativity in Social Movements*. Chicago: University of Chicago Press.

Lukes, S. 2005. *Power: A Radical View*, 2nd ed. New York: Palgrave.

Mehta, J. 2006. "The Transformation of American Educational Policy, 1980–2001: Ideas and the Rise of Accountability Politics." Ph.D. Dissertation, Department of Sociology, Harvard University.

Merton, R. K. 1968. *Social Theory and Social Structure*. New York: Free Press.

Milgram, S. 1974. *Obedience to Authority*. New York: Harper Row.

Nye, J. 2004. *Soft Power: The Means to Success in World Politics.* New York: Public Affairs.

Polletta, F. 2006. *It Was Like a Fever: Storytelling in Protest and Politics.* Chicago: University of Chicago Press.

Tyler, T. 2006. *Why People Obey the Law,* 2nd ed. Princeton: Princeton University Press.

Weber, M. 1946. *From Max Weber,* editor and translator H. H. Gerth, and C. Wright Mills. New York: Oxford University Press.

Weber, M. 1968. *Economy and Society.* Berkeley: University of California Press.

CHAPTER 23

Moral Dimensions of the Work–Family Nexus

Mary Blair-Loy

In recent decades, transformations in family and work life in the USA have led to widespread feelings of conflict between these two domains. This essay argues that the massive scholarly literature on work-family conflict has largely ignored the moral dimensions of this issue. The literature is hamstrung by a model of human action that is simultaneously too individualistically strategic and too universally passive. I label these dominant assumptions in the work-family literature "narrow rational action" and "structural determinism."

I then draw on a largely separate research stream that has analyzed the institutions of the family and the workplace as the site of moral meanings.[1] I show how the workplace and the family are sites of moral prescriptions, experienced as externally binding and subjectively compelling. I show how adopting a moral lens from this research could help the work-family literature transcend some theoretical limitations and solve some empirical puzzles. I encourage a model of human action that more fully recognizes ideological constraint: institutions define morally potent ends that motivate action. This model also recognizes more creativity, by which people use moral understandings to justify work-family situations and to interpret them as meaningful and honorable.

This approach adds to our understanding of gender. People often act in accordance with gendered identities, which are imbued with moral obligations and constrained by institutions that evaluate women and men differently. Finally, I raise questions about how the work-family nexus articulates with axes of social inequality and broader ideologies of individualism.

WORK AND FAMILY LIFE IN THE USA

In the last 40 years, family and work life in the USA have been transformed by rising numbers of employed mothers and single parent families. In 1965, 45% of mothers of children under age 18 were employed; by 2000 that figure had risen to 78% (Bianchi and Raley 2005:26).[2] By

---

[1] The literature reviews are illustrative rather than exhaustive.

[2] Other studies report that 71% of mothers of children under age 18 participated in the US labor force 2007, up from 47% in 1975 (Bureau of Labor Statistics 2009b, Galinsky et al. 2009:4). Statistics on labor force participation of

S. Hitlin, S. Vaisey (eds.), *Handbook of the Sociology of Morality*,
Handbooks of Sociology and Social Research, DOI 10.1007/978-1-4419-6896-8_23,
© Springer Science+Business Media, LLC 2010

2009, less than one fifth of US families were of the breadwinner father–homemaker mother variety and women held 49.9% of the nation's non-farm jobs.[3]

Women's lives have changed more dramatically than men's have during this period, yet aspects of family and work life have become more challenging for both genders. As home-makers are disappearing, an aging population means that Americans face increasing elder care responsibilities (Neal and Hammer 2007). At the same time, work has become more intensely demanding for some and more insecure and precarious for others (Jacobs and Gerson 2004).[4]

A burgeoning scholarly literature has examined the problem of experiencing work-family conflict, a worker's perception that "the demands of work and family roles are incompatible in some respect so that participation in one role is more difficult because of participation in the other role" (Voydanoff 2004:399). Studies suggest that over a third to more than half of the US workers are afflicted by the sense of work-family conflict, while similar numbers feel overworked (Jacobs and Gerson 2004, Reynolds 2003) and always rushed (Bianchi and Raley 2005). Over half of employed parents feel that they spend too little time with their children (Milkie et al. 2004).

Work-family scholarship has been enormously fruitful.[5] However, it has generally been hamstrung by two dominant assumptions which, in turn, grant people too little and too much agency with respect to broader cultural and social structures. These assumptions posit human beings as peculiarly dispassionate and morally neutral as we confront structural constraints and weigh costs and benefits of different options.

I use the shorthand label "structural determinism" to describe the first assumption: structural work and family conditions have near-universal effects on all US workers with broadly similar demographic characteristics. For example, studies have documented that structural factors such as long work hours, work pressures, a lack of schedule control, parenthood, and especially motherhood aggravate the sense of work to family conflict by specified amounts.[6] However, this research has overlooked whether variation in the experience of work-family conflict among people in similar social locations could be based on their capacity to subjectively construct different meanings out of similar constraints.

Hitlin's broader critique of a missing analysis of morality in contemporary sociology argues that as "the discipline has become more and more focused on structural forces that shape individuals, less and less attention has been paid to the possibility that people make choices" (Hitlin 2008:16). In the case of the work-family literature, it is true that studies have

---

mothers vary depending on which universes of people are used, question wording, and reference period (Cohen and Bianchi 1999).

[3] Of all married couple families in 2008, the husband was the sole breadwinner in 19.5% and the wife was sole breadwinner in 6.9% (Bureau of Labor Statistics 2009a, c). As of November 2009, women held an all-time high percentage of (seasonally adjusted) nonfarm payroll jobs: 49.9% (author's calculation from Bureau of Labor Statistics [2009d, e]). Most of the layoffs in the current recession have affected men (Rampell 2009).

[4] The minimal level of national and corporate support for working families in the USA compared to other industrialized nations makes the work-family nexus here particularly problematic. For a review of international cultural models of work and family, see Blair-Loy and Frenkel (2005).

[5] For reviews, see Perry-Jenkins et al. (2000), Kossek (2005), Kelly et al. (2008), Bianchi and Milkie (2010).

[6] See e.g., Jacobs and Gerson (2004), Voydanoff (1995, 2004), Galinsky et al. (1996), Schnittker (2007), Bianchi et al. (2006), Fredriksen-Goldsen and Scharlach (2001), Wharton and Blair-Loy (2006).

produced increasingly sophisticated analyses of structural conditions aggravating felt work-family conflict. Yet in contrast to Hitlin's complaint, the problem is not that the literature has ignored choices. Rather, it is the literature's assumptions about the nature of human choice.

This observation leads to the second assumption, which I label "narrow rational action." Individuals consciously strategize, negotiate, cope with, and make rational trade-offs among workplace and family obligations.[7] People are presumed to make choices, but the choices all end up being similar kinds of intentional strategies that maximize some kind of self-interest. Much of this literature implicitly or automatically assumes that the populations under study are engaging in this kind of rational action. A more thoughtful and explicit version of rational action is in Becker and Moen's (1999) analysis of how couples deploy conscious and reflexive strategies to "scale back" at work after children are born.

The dominant assumptions of the work-family literature are used as shorthands for conducting much social scientific research. They can be useful and valid in certain circumstances. However, they miss much of what happens in social life.

Some studies have complicated the structural determinism assumption. However, the analyses generally retain the second assumption of narrow rational action and simply complicate the terrain that people negotiate. For example, some scholars note rising societal expectations for more concentrated effort at work and for higher parenting standards at home (Jacobs and Gerson 2004:81–82). Some add mediating or moderating effects to linear models (e.g., Gareis and Barnett 2002). Other research emphasizes the enriching or positive effects of work on family and family on work.[8] For instance, Bakker and Geurts (2004) find that the individual experience of feeling totally engrossed in one's work mediates the effect of autonomy on the positive effects of work on family life. Bakker and Geurts (2004:346) summarize the broader literature on the positive effects of work-family enrichment as follows: "Several scholars have argued that workers may also benefit from combining work and family, and that *these benefits may outweigh the costs*" (emphasis added).

Thompson and Bunderson (2001) conceptualize workers as assigning different meanings to different workplace experiences, which in turn shape the effects of work time on work-family conflict. They argue that time at work is less predictive of work to family conflict when that time is "identity affirming" rather than "identity discrepant." While their focus on meaning making is welcome, this research simply adds more tools (e.g., pursue work that is very engrossing and identity affirming) to the toolkits of rationally strategizing, individual workers making trade-offs between workplace and family obligations.

These dominant assumptions in the work-family literature render the institutions of work and family as peculiarly amoral or perhaps morally neutral. This characterization is at odds with rich studies of the historical development of the Western nuclear family and capitalist work organizations. These institutions are defined by moral prescriptions, which can at times motivate action, justify action, and organize and activate emotions that make certain actions

---

[7] See, e.g., Becker and Moen (1999), Gareis and Barnett (2000), Mennino and Brayfield (2002), Ammons and Edgell (2007), Jacobs and Gerson (2004:80).

[8] Scholars use terms such as positive spillover (Grzywacz and Marks 2000), enrichment (Greenhaus and Powell 2006, Rothbard 2001), facilitation (Voydanoff 2004), and positive interference (Bakker and Geurts 2004) from work to family life and from family life to the workplace.

seem like the right or moral thing to do. When institutions proclaim contradictory mandates, they create moral dilemmas for their members.

THE FAMILY AND WORKPLACE AS SITES OF MORAL MEANINGS

This section will briefly summarize the "separate spheres" literature on the development of the Western family. I also briefly discuss Weber's insights into the devotion to work as a calling, which defines work as an end in itself. The moral definitions of these historical institutions still resonate today, but the moral dilemmas have changed. The section will then address how these moral definitions continue to resonate in an era in which most adults are breadwinners and few families have the luxury of a full-time caregiver.

The contemporary Western family has its cultural roots in a middle class "separate spheres" ideology of the 18th and 19th centuries. This separate spheres ideology began forming when production began shifting from family farms to factories, and when distinctions appeared between men's wage labor in the public sphere and women's domestic work in the private sphere (Cott 1977). The separate spheres ideology conceptualized the division of labor as a gendered division of *moral* labor that socially sanctioned conduct as right or wrong (Gerson 2002). Women were seen as uniquely called to be full-time defenders of a pious, private family life, protected from the competitive marketplace. At this time, the cultural understanding emerged of children as sacred and fragile, deserving of a mother's protective, devoted care (Aries 1962, Zelizer 1985).

Although women from working class and minority and immigrant backgrounds have always been likely to work for wages (Weiner 1985), moral prescriptions about American family life are generally defined by the white middle classes (Garey 1999). This cultural ideology of female caregiver and male breadwinner fit the in reality of family life fairly well in the 1950s, when three-fifths of American families had a male breadwinner and female full-time homemaker (Skolnick 1991). Today, less than 20% of families fit the separate spheres template. Yet, aspects of this ideology continue to provide moral definitions of the institution of the family and moral expectations of family members.

Hays (1996:148) describes the "ideology of intensive motherhood," which prescribes a mother's "child-centered, expert-guided, emotionally absorbing, labor-intensive, and financially expensive" care for a child she considers sacred. This ideology is part of the "family devotion schema" (Blair-Loy 2003), which promises financial support and an intimately rewarding emotional life for women who spend most of their adult lives intensively caring for loving provider-husbands and vulnerable, sacred children. This schema specifies consecrated relationships that are laden with expectations of trust, obligation, care, and mutual dependence. Family devotion is defined as a moral end in itself, which provides both a motivation for and a justification of many women's behavior. Even when women are employed full-time, many sacrifice sleep, leisure, and professional advancement to live up to the ideology of intensive motherhood when they are not working (Blair-Loy 2003, Garey 1999).

Gerson's (2002, 2009) study of young adults (mean age 24) imagining their future lives is one of the very few work-family studies to explicitly analyze the work-family nexus as presenting moral dilemmas. As such, it is an important step forward. Yet since her interviews ask young adults to talk in the abstract about hypothetical family ties, future goals and fallback positions, she too falls back on assumptions about intentional, rational decision-making. Gerson (2002) conceptualizes her respondents as "crafting moral strategies" (p. 14), to negotiate potential career and family trajectories. Her term "moral strategies" under-estimates the externally binding aspects of moral mandates that help define institutions and shape our responses in taken-for-granted, deeply legitimated ways. To complement this analysis of young people's largely hypothetical strategic choices, it is useful to foreground the morally defined institutions and trajectories that constrain the array of options from which to choose.

Gerson's (2002) young adults view the work world as a site of autonomy, independence, and personal freedom, whereas Hays' (1996) mothers see it as competitive and ruthless. However, both studies emphasize work as lacking the lacking the qualities of commitment to others and care giving that characterize family life. In contrast, other studies of work conceptualize work as potentially a site of moral obligations, intense relationships, and opportunities for broader service.

Weber (1976) argued that 17th century Puritan idea of work as a methodical and ascetic calling profoundly shaped the early character of the USA. This calling was viewed as one's divinely ordained life purpose or vocation. One's calling entails the moral duty to use God's gifts in ways that are ascetically virtuous, socially useful, and demonstrate God's grace now and in the hereafter (1976:161). Weber contended that economic success and secular Enlightenment ideas gradually eroded the religious foundation of the calling. Yet he maintained that professional work such as science (broadly conceived) continued to offer secular vocations. Although he ([1946] 1981) cautioned that occupations such as science should not explicitly determine the social ends of action, he nonetheless implied that personal dedication to one's work could be an end in itself, worthy of service with integrity. "For nothing is worthy of man as man unless he can pursue it with passionate devotion" (Weber [1946] 1981:135). Akin to a great artist, a great scientist has never "done anything but serve his work and only his work" (Weber [1946] 1981:137).

Jackall (1988) maintains that even the secularized version of Weber's vocation was eroded by the development of centralized bureaucracies, in which workers are at the mercy of their boss's whim and the vagaries of the market (pp. 9, 192). Jackall argues that for managers in the late 20th century bureaucratic work organizations "actual organizational moralities are contextual, situational, highly specific, and most often, unarticulated" (p. 6). In contrast, other research finds that work continues to be defined by coherent moral expectations, which imbue jobs with meaning. Blair-Loy and others find that some workplaces are shaped by prescriptive ideologies about work devotion, while studies by Heimer and by Dodson reveal how people use workplace relations in complex ways to develop a sense of moral responsibility for others.

Blair-Loy (2003) found that the US corporations are defined in part by a cultural model that assumes elite employees will manifest undivided "devotion to work," including long hours, organizational commitment, career dedication, and a minimization of family caregiving. The work devotion schema is institutionalized in organizational "practices of evaluation, compensation, and advancement," and "has become semi-autonomous from purely economic considerations and acquired its own normative impact" (Blair-Loy 2003:21). Like other rhetorics of normative control throughout American history (Barley and Kunda 1992), the schema of work devotion shapes assumptions and identities.

This schema may currently be more firmly entrenched in the USA than elsewhere (Wharton and Blair-Loy 2002, 2006).Others have described similar cultural structures as the "career mystique" (Moen and Roehling 2005), "overtime culture" (Fried 1998), and as "ideal worker norms" (Williams 2000). Hochschild (1997) argues that employees of a corporation she studied are both "architects and prisoners" of the norm that "time spent on the job is an indicator of commitment" (p. 19).

In the USA, the work devotion schema has several dimensions, each of which may be more or less embraced by different employees. These include an adrenaline high" from challenges and relationships that work provides, the cognitive acceptance of the legitimacy or intractability of work demands, a moral and emotional identification with one's employer or profession, inspiration and transcendence of personal limitations from the larger projects. This schema offers an implicit contract between the worker and the firm, assuring the worker that her sacrifices of time, talent, and energy will be honored (as signaled by high incomes, autonomy, exciting work, professional respect, and membership in an elite corps). Work devotion is both a cause and consequence of professional success (Blair-Loy 2003). In at least one firm, the work devotion mandate may be expected of – and embraced by – some hourly workers as well (Wharton et al. 2008).

The US workers have a range of responses to these cultural structures. Hochschild (1997) found that in one large US company, many workers had no desire to cut down on work hours, ignored company policies that would allow them to do so, and preferred time at work over time at home. In a large survey of one company, Blair-Loy (2003) found that about half of the executive women she interviewed remain enthusiastic adherents of work devotion, taking for granted its demands and relishing their moral and emotional commitment to their employer and career. Yet half of the sample had become disenchanted with work devotion and slogged through their days with quiet exhaustion and resentment, fearful of the career consequences of open skepticism. Yet whether these elite workers "ultimately believe in it or renounce it, they never regard it with indifference" (Blair-Loy 2003:Chapter 2).

Similarly, executive men simultaneously embrace and feel coerced into the mandate of work devotion. Material self-interest plays only a limited role in motivating executive men's long hours. Although they believe that the business world has its share of "sharks and villains," many executive men generally frame their own work commitment as a service to clients and society. Some men use this schema to shore up their own legitimacy and to motivate or compel their employees. At the same time, many are also personally captivated by it. Not only do they deploy it, they are held by it. (Blair-Loy 2010). The work devotion schema elevates the social and personal meaning of professional goals, and, in its purest form, defines work as an end in itself (Weber [1946] 1981).

Studies by Heimer and Dodson shed more light on how morality is constructed by organizations and institutions. They consider the work-family nexus from a different angle. How does the workplace engender a sense of moral responsibility to others? How do those in middle-class helping professions deal with the family challenges of those they serve? Heimer's research (Heimer 2010; Heimer and Staffen 1998) shows how neo-natal intensive care units are characterized by social arrangements that construct critically ill babies' essential humanity and produce a sense of moral responsibility, competence, and agency among parents for taking care of their ill infants. In this study, responsibility for vulnerable others is organized and enforced as part and parcel of the organization of professional work.

Dodson (2009) study reveals how some middle-class supervisors adopt responsibility for the well-being of their low-wage subordinates in ways that resist and subvert official workplace rules, even at personal risk. Some retail and food service supervisors discussed the moral dilemma between fulfilling business norms of regarding subordinates as cogs "to get the job done" and getting to know them as people, who get paid too little to support their families. A big box retail manager first gave Dodson a supervisory ethics account of enforcing rules and keeping a professional distance from employees. She then admitted her trespass by mixing up the prom dress inventory, which allowed her to slip an extra dress to an employee, who could not afford one for her daughter. Dodson also interviews restaurant managers who quietly inflate lower-income workers' hours in order to augment paychecks and who serve their children without cost when they come to the restaurant after school. Dodson's (2009) workers' "transgressions were discussed as acts of conscience and finally acts of solidarity. And they mark … how people will step out of a culture of utter self-interest, the market culture, and then intentionally turn against it."

In sum, the workplace is a potent site of moral expectations, identities, emotions, and contradictions. Organizations construct moral agents that are simultaneously pressed on by social structures and empowered to act: neonatal intensive care unit staff construct mothers as fatefully enjoined to shoulder an extra burden of care for "special" babies yet also able to develop the professional expertise to do so (Heimer and Staffen 1998). The workplace also creates moral dilemmas. Supervisors interact daily with hard working, low paid workers desperately trying to make ends meet, but helping them would violate organizational and occupational rules and possibly break the law (Dodson 2009). Elite workers feel ennobled by work they love, which simultaneously drains their time from cherished family relationships (Blair-Loy 2003, 2010).

The work-family literature's dominant assumptions of structural determinism and narrow rational action posit human behavior that is not only amoral but also acultural. Moral expectations are components of culture, and this essay sheds light on how culture shapes action. Many adults spend the lion's share of their time and energy within workplace or family settings. These institutions are defined by cultural schemas that provide (sometimes contradictory) justifications and motivations for moral action. In addition, the workplace and family evoke and organize unconscious emotions, such as devotion, sacrifice, and competition. Experiences of the work–family nexus can never be captured by the simplistic language of cost-benefit tradeoffs.[9]

BACK TO THE WORK-FAMILY LITERATURE: THEORETICAL BLINDSPOTS AND EMPIRICAL PUZZLES

This essay began by describing two dominant assumptions in the mainstream of work-family literature: structural determinism and narrow rational action. These assumptions are adequate for certain circumstances and have allowed scholars to document a great deal. However, they

---

[9] My argument is consistent with Vaisey's (2008a, b) discussion of how people's moral judgments and actions are shaped by schemas made compelling by conscious reasoning and by unconscious intuitions and emotions. I have long argued that certain types of cultural elements (e.g., schemas of devotion) within institutions define ends that motivate action (Blair-Loy 2003). I also recognize that people use culture to justify or make sense of externally defined ends (Swidler 2001). Like Swidler (2001, 2008), I emphasize that cultural schemas – whether consciously recognized or unconsciously experienced – are organized and evoked by patterned interactions and obligations within particular institutions.

fail to take into account the morally prescriptive definitions of the workplace and the family as institutions, and they ignore moral subjectivities and emotions of workers and family members. These omissions have led to some empirical puzzles.

Gender and Work-Family Actions

Cost-benefit calculating actors in a heterosexual marriage in these uncertain economic times might rationally plan to maximize the couple's earning potential and to minimize the threat to family income of a job loss. It could make good financial sense for each partner to focus on their careers and to hire some childcare. If paid child care were to be unaffordable relative to the household income or if "benefit" were defined more broadly to include a preference for having children spend more time in a parent's care, then the cost-benefit calculation would be revised such that the partner with less long-term earning potential would cut back at work in order to give more time to the children and household (cf. Becker 1981).

So if work-family decisions are truly freely chosen to maximize an individual or couple's utility, why do women's "trade-offs" differ systematically from men's? A study of dual-career couples in upstate New York found that wives were twice as likely as husbands to "scale back" at work (Becker and Moen 1999). Nationally, mothers are six times more likely than fathers (30% vs. 5%) to be out of the labor market and six times more likely to work part-time (18% vs. 3%).[10]

The common answer – that the couples rationally protect the higher earning male partner's job – is insufficient. Seventy-nine percent of married or partnered couples were dual-earners in 2008, and the women contributed an average of 44% of the family income. In one out of four dual-earner couples, the wife out-earns the husband by at least 10% that year (Galinsky et al. 2009:9). However, the long-term gender gap in earnings is much larger: over a 15-year period, women (aged 26 to 59) earn only about 38% of what comparably aged men earn (Hartmann and Rose 2004). Mothers' decisions over the family life course to reduce hours or leave the labor force come at a huge financial cost to themselves and their families (Crittenden 2001, Jacobs and Gerson 2004:111, 115). Even in the case of extremely high earning MBAs, women but not men are likely to cut back on work hours or leave the labor force after childbearing (Bertrand et al. 2009, Stone 2007). This gender difference is simply not well explained by the dominant assumption of conscious, reflexive, rational action.

A moral analysis brings into focus the ways in which the family devotion schema and the ideology of intensive motherhood are still the default normative definitions of women's obligations within institution of the family. At the same time, the work devotion schema continues to define the ideal worker as one who can give primary allegiance to the employer organization (Blair-Loy 2003). Mothers are viewed at work as less competent and less committed than women without children (Correll et al. 2007) or then men. These normative expectations help pull women into family care giving (alongside their jobs) and push them out of full-throttled careers. The moral definitions of work and family shape institutional demands and

---

[10] Author's calculations from Table 5 in BLS (Bureau of Labor Statistics 2009a).

invade people's preconscious expectations in ways not captured by the work-family literature's language of individual "trade-offs" and "strategies."

Nonetheless, mothers have strikingly increased their representation in the labor force since the 1960s. Given lengthening work days for many employees (Jacobs and Gerson 2004), we would expect that a "trade-off" mothers make to work for pay would necessarily entail spending less time with children. The puzzle is that when Bianchi and colleagues actually measured time use, they find that maternal time with children in 2000 has stayed at the same level it was in 1970, an average of about 48 hours a week (Bianchi and Raley 2005:33)! This puzzle makes sense if viewed through the moral lens of the family devotion and intensive mothering. These ideologies define children as needing and deserving a mother's time. They also define a good mother as one who provides that time, regardless of the cost to careers, civic engagement, and personal care (Bianchi and Raley 2005:34).[11]

Consequences of Moral Schemas for Work-Family Conflict

Much research suggests that ideal worker norms exacerbate the sense of work to family conflict by stigmatizing workers who wish to spend more time with family or who use officially available family–friendly organizational policies to manage their family obligations (Blair-Loy and Wharton 2002, 2004a, 2004b, Glass 2004, Hochschild 1997, Jacobs and Gerson 2004, Williams 2000). Prescriptions for work devotion can be particularly draconian for lower-income workers. Many of the workers in Dodson's (2009) study are in jobs that do not provide stability, autonomy, family accommodation, or even a living wage. Because wages are so low, they often juggle multiple jobs. Given these conditions, often the only recourse for mothers who need to spend time caring for children is to serially quit or to be fired. Employers define them as lacking work ethic and personal responsibility. The stigma of failing to conform to ideal worker norms is also extended to a denigration of their parenthood abilities and personal character (Dodson 2009).

The effects of work devotion on the lives of professionals are complex. Using a national sample, Schieman et al. (2009) challenge the common view that high status workers are using work-related resources to reduce their work-family conflict. They find that normative expectations of work devotion, embraced by high status workers, lead these workers to blur the boundaries between work and family (by taking work home, for example). This permeability between work and family increases work-family conflict.

However, another study found that work devotion could help reduce work-family conflict. In a quantitative study of women in science, technology, and related fields, Blair-Loy and Cech (2009) found that the individual embrace of the work devotion schema significantly reduces the

---

[11] The data suggest possibly increasing normative expectations for involved fathering. Average fathers' time with children increased from 26 hours a week in 1970 to 33 hours in 2000, although fathers were far more likely to spend this time helping their spouse, while wives were more likely to care for their children solo (Bianchi and Raley 2005:34). According to 2008 National Survey of the Changing Workforce data, mothers' time with children continued at the same levels through 2008. In 2008, the average young mother and young father (under age 29) spent more time with children under age 13 compared to the same-gender parent over age 30 (Galinsky et al. 2009:15).

sense of work-family overload-imbalance. The ideological frame of work devotion counteracts the toll of structural conditions like long hours and work pressures.

However, the power of work devotion to buffer the sense of overload-imbalance is curtailed for the science professionals with young and school aged children. Blair-Loy and Cech speculate that these women must also reckon with moral definitions of their responsibilities as mothers that compete with organizational dedication. The cost of time that intense careers rob from children defined as fragile and sacred may be culturally defined as too high for many mothers in the sample, leading to feelings of overload-imbalance even for those who embrace work devotion. The embrace of the work devotion schema seems to regain its power for women with older and adult children (Blair-Loy and Cech 2009).

Incorporating a moral analysis would help the work-family literature develop a better framework for understanding gender differences in work and family behavior, which are not well explained by narrow rational action assumptions. Action is influenced by gendered identities, imbued with moral obligation, and constrained by gendered institutions, which evaluate women and men differently. I encourage a model of human action that acknowledges more ideological constraint: personal beliefs are structured by moral commitments, often gendered, which are enforced by institutions. This model should also more fully recognize creativity, by which people make their work-family situations meaningful.

The Work–Family Nexus and Inequality

This section briefly presents five vexing issues connecting the work-family nexus to broader axes of social inequality. We need to pay more attention to variation by race/ethnicity and social class and to relationships between researchers and their subjects. I hope that future research focusing on these topics takes moral meanings into account.

First, an understudied area is how the moral definitions of work and family vary by race/ethnicity and social class. Moral definitions of the workplace, the family, and gendered obligations are inflected by particular cultures based on nationality, race/ethnicity, and religion. These definitions evolve further as people face new structural circumstances as a result of exclusion, immigration, and new economic challenges and opportunities (Espiritu 1997, 2000, Hondagneu-Sotelo and Avila 1997). For example, compared to white women, African American women's biographies and mothering ideologies have historically been more likely to include being a strong breadwinner and self-sufficient role model for their children (Collins 1987, 2001). Within-race class differences are important as well. One study of white, employed mothers found that middle-class women generally regarded motherhood as a personal achievement after attaining adulthood, while working-class women regarded it as the means for establishing one's adulthood (McMahon 1995).

The second point is that ideologies that are powerfully institutionalized in workplaces may similarly affect workers from diverse backgrounds. For example, the pressures of a legal career compel women attorneys intent on advancement to delay or avoid motherhood, whether they are white (Hagan and Kay 1995, Hull and Nelson 2000), or African American (Blair-Loy and DeHart 2003). In a large financial services firm, organizational expectations of work devotion seem to affect hourly workers as well as managers (Wharton et al. 2008). Gerson's (2009) study of a nationally representative sample of young adults does not show social class or race differences in young adults' ideal life trajectories or fall-back positions as they envision their futures. We need more research investigating similarity and variation in moral definitions of work and family by race/ethnicity and social class.

The third point is that much work-family scholarship may be smuggling a middle-class bias into analyses. Conventional measures of work-family conflict may be overlooking aspects of the work-family nexus that are most pressing groups. In new research, Edgell et al. (2009) go beyond these measures to ask about job insufficiency and disruption. In a nationally representative sample, they find that African Americans, Latinos (compared to whites), and those with lower incomes (compared to those with higher incomes) are more likely to experience work as insufficient to provide for their families and to experience family needs as disrupting their job histories. Similarly, Dodson (2009) argues that standard measures of flexibility that previous research associates with reduced work-family conflict – including worker's control over the number of work hours, work schedules, time off, and work location, time off and breaks – are simply irrelevant to many lower-income workers. Employers often will not guarantee stability – including a set schedule or number of hours – let alone flexible arrangements for the worker's benefit.

Fourth, the dominant assumption that people strategically and intentionally weigh the costs and benefits of different options may be even more inaccurate for working class and poor workers than for middle and upper-class workers. While all people can exercise a certain degree of agency, workers with less power and autonomy at work and fewer resources at home may have fewer benefits to weigh and fewer options to consider. The "choice" about whether to "scale back" at work may not be a choice at all, if there is no other stable breadwinner in the family, if the job is precarious, or if paid child care is simply unaffordable.

Finally, I ask whether analysts rational individual model of action is an insufficiently critical reflection of middle class workers' accounts of their action. Workers' own discussions of strategic decision making may be evidence of the constraints of another construct of moral ideologies in the USA: individual achievement by expressive selves (cf. Charles and Bradley 2009). It is remarkable how supposedly conscious and reflexive strategies around work and family consistently reproduce the gender order. Much more so than men, women "scale back" at work after children are born, at great financial cost to themselves and their families. Much more so than men, employed women sacrifice career advancement and sleep in order to maintain high levels of time with children. Middle-class women's accounts of these kinds of decisions are replete with a soft feminist, "soft essentialist" (Messner 2009) rhetoric of personal choice that serves to make meaningful their own conscription into reproducing an unequal society.

CONCLUSION

The dominant assumptions of much work-family literature simultaneously grant individuals too much and too little agency. One assumption (narrow rational action) posits individuals as strategically negotiating work and family obligations in line with the personal preferences they hold. In contrast, a moral analysis of work and family emphasizes how people are often *held by* their personal beliefs, which are structured by and resonate with socially imposed moral commitments. The second assumption (structural determinism) in much of the literature posits workers as being affected in near universal ways by structural forces largely beyond their control. In contrast, a moral analysis sees workers as meaningfully responding to structural conditions, ideologies, and dilemmas in ways that make their work and family actions comprehensible and honorable.

Moral prescriptions, experienced as externally binding and subjectively compelling, have defined the institutions of work and family and our participation in them as women and men, as workers and nurturers. This moral valence creates obligations but also offers relationships that make life worth living.

Acknowledgment I thank Steve Hitlin for valuable comments and Timothy Bolin for helpful research assistance with the references.

REFERENCES

Ammons, S. K., and P. Edgell. 2007. "Religious Influences on Work-Family Trade-Offs." *Journal of Family Issues* 28:794–826.

Aries, P. 1962. *Centuries of Childhood: A Social History of Family Life.* New York: Vintage Books.

Bakker, A. B., and S. A. E. Geurts. 2004. "Toward a Dual-Proess Model of Work-Home Inteference." *Work and Occupations* 31:345–366.

Barley, S. R., and G. Kunda. 1992. "Design and Devotion: Surges of Rational and Normative Ideologies of Control in Managerial Discourse." *Administrative Science Quarterly* 37:363–399.

Becker, G. S. 1981. *A Treatise on the Family.* Cambridge: Harvard University Press.

Becker, P. E., and P. Moen. 1999. "Scaling Back: Dual-Earner Couples Work-Family Strategies." *Journal of Marriage and the Family* 61:995–1007.

Bertrand, M., C. Goldin, and L. F. Katz. 2009. "Dynamics of the Gender Gap for Young Professionals in the Corporate and Financial Sectors." Cambridge, MA: National Bureau of Economic Research.

Bianchi, S. M., and S. B. Raley. 2005. "Time Allocation in Families." PP. 21–42 in *Work, Family, Health, and Well-Being,* edited by S. M. Bianchi, L. M. Casper, and R. B. King. Mahwah, New Jersey: Lawrence Erlbaum Associates.

Bianchi, S. M., and M. A. Milkie. 2010. "Work and Family Research in the First Decade of the 21st Century." *Journal of Marriage and the Family* 72:705–725.

Bianchi, S. M., J. P. Robinson, and M. A. Milkie. 2006. *Changing Rhythms of American Family Life.* New York: Russell Sage.

Blair-Loy, M. 2003. *Competing Devotions: Career and Family Among Women Financial Executives.* Cambridge, MA: Harvard University Press.

Blair-Loy, M., and M. Frenkel. 2005. "Societal Cultural Models of Work and Family: An International Perspective." In *Work-Family Encyclopedia,* edited by M. Pitt-Catsouphes and P. Raskin. Chestnut Hill, MA: Sloan Work and Family Research Network at Boston College. http://wfnetwork.bc.edu/encyclopedia_template.php?id=1960

Blair-Loy, M. 2010. "The Power and the Glory: Work Devotion and Masculinity among Executive Men." Unpublished ms., Department of Sociology, University of California, San Diego.

Blair-Loy, M., and G. DeHart. 2003. "Family and Career Trajectories among African American Female Attorneys." *Journal of Family Issues* 24:908–933.

Blair-Loy, M., and A. Wharton. 2004a. "Organizational Commitment and Constraints on Work-Family Policy Use: Corporate Flexibity Policies in a Global Firm." *Sociological Perspectives* 47:243–267.

Blair-Loy, M., and A. S. Wharton. 2004b. "Mothers in Finance: Surviving and Thriving." *Annals of the American Academy of Political and Social Science* 596:151–171.

Blair-Loy, M., and A. S. Wharton. 2002. "Employee's Use of Work-Family Policies and the Workplace Social Context." *Social Force* 80:813–846.

Blair-Loy, M., and E. Cech. 2009. "Demands and Devotion: Work-Family Overload-Imbalance among Women in Science and Technology Industries.": Department of Sociology, University of California, San Diego.

Bureau of Labor Statistics. 2009a. *"Employment Characteristics of Families in 2008."* edited by Bureau of Labor Statistics. Retrieved August 3, 2010. (http://www.bls.gov/news.release/archives/famee_05272009.pdf).

Bureau of Labor Statistics. 2009b. "*Labor Force Participation of Mothers with Infants in 2008: The Editor's Desk.*" Retrieved August 3, 2009. (http://www.bls.gov/opub/ted/2009/may/wk4/art04.htm).

Bureau of Labor Statistics. 2009c. "*Employment and Married-Couple Families in 2008: The Editor's Desk.*" Retrieved August 3, 2010. (http://www.bls.gov/opub/ted/2009/may/wk4/art03.htm).

Bureau of Labor Statistics. 2009d. "*Table B-3: Employees on Nonfarm Payrolls by Major Industry Sector and Selected Industry Detail, Seasonally Adjusted.*" Retrieved August 3, 2010. (ftp://ftp.bls.gov/pub/suppl/empsit.ceseeb3.txt).

Bureau of Labor Statistics. 2009e. "*Table B-4: Women Employees on Nonfarm Payrolls by Major Industry Sector and Selected Industry Detail, Seasonally Adjusted.*" Retrieved August 3, 2010. (ftp://ftp.bls.gov/pub/suppl/empsit.ceseeb4.txt).

Charles, M., and K. Bradley. 2009. "Indulging Our Gendered Selves? Sex Segregation by Field of Study in 44 Countries." *American Journal of Sociology* 114:924–976.

Cohen, P., and S. M. Bianchi. 1999. "Marriage, Children and Women's Employment: What do We Know?" *Monthly Labor Review* 122:22–30.

Collins, P. H. 1987. "The Maternal Role: The Meaning of Motherhood in Black Culture." *Sage: A Scholarly Journal on Black Women* 4:3–10.

Collins, P. H. 2001. *Black Feminist Thought: Knowledge, Consciousness, and the Politics of Empowerment.* New York: Routledge.

Correll, S. J., Stephen Benard, and In Paik. 2007. "Getting a Job: Is There a Motherhood Penalty?" *American Journal of Sociology* 112:1297–1338.

Cott, N. 1977. *The Bonds of Motherhood: "Women's Sphere" in New England, 1780–1835.* New Haven: Yale University Press.

Crittenden, A. 2001. *The Price of Motherhood.* NY: Henry Holt and Company.

Dodson, L. 2009. *The Moral Underground : How Oridnary Americans Subvert an Unfair Economy* New York: The New Press.

Edgell, P., S. K. Ammons, and E. Dahlin. 2009. "Work and Family: How Race and Religion Shape Experiences of Sufficiency and Stability." In *Presentation to the Inequalities Workshop.* Department of Sociology, UC San Diego.

Espiritu, Y. L. 1997. "All Men Are Not Created Equal: Asian Men in U.S. History." PP. 35–44 in *In Men's Lives*, edited by M. S. Kimmel, and M. A. Messner. Boston: Allyn and Bacon.

Espiritu, Y. L. 2000. "We Don't Sleep Around Like White Girls Do: Family, Culture, and Gender in Filipina American Lives." *Signs* 26:415–440.

Fredriksen-Goldsen, K. I., and A. E. Scharlach. 2001. *Families and Work: New Directions in the Twenty-first Century.* New York: Oxford University Press.

Fried, M. 1998. *Taking Time: Parental Leave Policy and Corprorate Culture.* Philadelphia: Temple University Press.

Galinsky, E., K. Aumann, and J. T. Bond. 2009. "2008 National Study of the Changing Workforce : Times are Changing: Gender and Generation at Work and at Home." Families and Work Institute.

Galinsky, E., J. T. Bond, and D. E. Friedman. 1996. "The Role of Employers in Addressing the Needs of Employed Parents." *Journal of Social Issues* 52: 111–136.

Gareis, K. C., and R. C. Barnett. 2000. "Reduced Hours Employment: The Relationship Between the Difficulty of Trade-Offs and the Quality of Life." *Work and Occupations* 27:168–187.

Gareis, K. C., and R. C. Barnett. 2002. "Under What Conditions Do Long Work Hours Affect Psychological Distress?" *Work and Occupations* 29:483–497.

Garey, A. 1999. *Weaving Work and Motherhood.* Philadelphia: Temple University Press.

Gerson, K. 2002. "Moral Dilemmas, Moral Strategies, the Transformation of Gender: Lessons From Two Generations of Work/Family Change." *Gender and Society* 16:8–28.

Gerson, K. 2009. *The Unfinished Revolution: How a New Generation is Reshaping Family, Work, and Gender in America.* New York and Oxford: Oxford University Press.

Glass, J. L. 2004. "Blessing or Curse? Family Responsive Policies and Mother's Wage Growth over Time." *Work and Occupations* 31:367–394.

Greenhaus, J. H., and G. N. Powell. 2006. "When Work and Family are Allies: A Theory of Work-Family Enrichment." *Academy of Management Review* 31:72–92.

Grzywacz, J. G., and N. F. Marks. 2000. "Reconceptualizing the Work-Family Interface: An Ecological Perspective on the Correlates of Positive and Negative Spillover Between Work and Family." *Journal of Occupational Health Psychology* 5:11–126.

Hagan, J., and F. Kay. 1995. *Gender in Practice.* Oxford: Oxford University Press.

Hartmann, H., and S. J. Rose. 2004. "Still a Man's Labor Market: The Long-Term Earnings Gap." Institute for Women's Policy Research, Washington DC.

Hays, S. 1996. *The Cultural Contradictions of Motherhood.* New Haven and London: Yale University Press.

Heimer, C. 2010. "Legal Systems and Moral Codes." in *Final Report on Morality Workshop*, edited by S. Hitlin and J. Stets. Arlington, VA: National Science Foundation. In press.

Heimer, C. A., and L. R. Staffen. 1998. *For the Sake of the Children: The Social Organization of Responsibility in the Hospital and the Home* Chicago: University of Chicago Press.

Hitlin, S. 2008. *Moral Selves, Evil Selves, Social Psychology of Conscience.* New York: Palgrave-Macmillan.

Hochschild, A. 1997. *The Time Bind: When Work Becomes Home and Home Becomes Work.* New York: Metropolitan Books.

Hondagneu-Sotelo, P., and E. Avila 1997. "I'm Here, But I'm There": The Meanings of Latina Transnational Motherhood." *Gender and Society* 11:548–571.

Hull, K. E., and R. L. Nelson. 2000. "Assimilation, Choice, or Constraint? Testing Careers of Gender Difference in the Careers of Lawyers." *Social Forces* 79:229–264.

Jackall, R. 1988. *Moral Mazes: The World of Corporate Managers.* New York, Oxford: Oxford University Press.

Jacobs, J. A., and K. Gerson. 2004. *The Time Divide: Work, Family, and Gender Inequality.* Cambridge, MA: Harvard University Press.

Kelly, E. L., E. E. Kossek, L. B. Hammer, M. Durham, J. Bray, K. Chermack, L. A. Murphy, and D. Kaskubar. 2008. "Getting There from Here: Research on the Effects of Work-Family Initiatives on Work-Family Conflict and Business Outcomes." *Academy of Management Annals* 2:305–349.

Kossek, E. E. 2005. "Workplace Policies and Practices to Support Work and Families." In *Work, Family, Health and Well-Being*, edited by S. M. Bianchi, L. M. Casper, and R. B. King. Mahwah, NJ: Lawrence Erlbaum.

McMahon, H. 1995. *Engendering Motherhood: Identity and Transformation in Women's Lives.* New York: The Guilford Press.

Mennino, S. F., and A. Brayfield. 2002. "Job-family Trade-offs: The Multidimensional Effects of Gender." *Work and Occupations* 29:226–256.

Messner, M. A. 2009. *It's All for the Kids: Gender, Families, and Youth Sports.* Berkeley and Los Angeles: University of California Press.

Milkie, M. A., M. J. Mattingly, K. M. Nomaguchi, S. M. Bianchi, and J. P. Robinson. 2004. "The Time Squeeze: Parental Statuses and Feelings About Time With Children." *Journal of Marriage and Family* 66 739–761.

Moen, P., and P. Roehling. 2005. *The Career Mystique: Cracks in the American Dream.* Lanham, MD: Rowman and Littlefield Publishers.

Neal, M. B., and L. B. Hammer. 2007. *Working Couples Caring for Children and Aging Parents: Effects on Work and Well Being.* Malwah, NJ: Lawrence Erlbaum Press.

Perry-Jenkins, M., R. L. Repetti, and A. C. Crouter. (2000). "Work and Family in the 1990s." *Journal of Marriage and the Family* 62:981–998.

Rampell, C. 2009. " As Layoffs Surge, Women May Pass Men in Job Force." In *New York Times.*

Reynolds, J. 2003. "You Can't Always Get the Hours You Want: Mismatches between Actual and Preferred Work Hours in the U.S." *Social Forces* 81:1171–1199.

Rothbard, N. P. 2001. "Enriching or Depleting? The Dynamics of Engagement in Work and Family Roles." *Administrative Science Quarterly* 46:655–684.

Schieman, S., P. Glavin, and M. A. Milkie. 2009. "When Work Interferes with Life: Work-Nonwork Interference and the Influence of Work-Related Demands and Resources." *American Sociological Review* 74:966–988.

Schnittker, J. 2007. "Working More and Feeling Better: Women's Health, Employment, and Family Life, 1974–2004."*American Sociological Review* 72:221–238.

Skolnick, A. 1991. *Embattled Paradise: The American Family in an Age of Uncertainty.* New York: Basic Books.

Stone, P. 2007. *Opting Out? Why Women Really Quit Careers and Head Home.* Berkeley and Los Angeles: University of California Press.

Swidler, A. 2001. *Talk of Love: How Culture Matters.* Chicago and London: University of Chicago Press.

Swidler, A. 2008. "Comment on Stephen Vaisey's 'socrates, Skinner, and Aristotle: Three Ways of Thinking About Culture in Action'." *Sociological Forum 2008* 23:614–618.

Thompson, J. A., and J. Stuart Bunderson. 2001. "Work-Nonwork Conflict and the Phenomenology of Time." *Work and Occupations* 28:17–39.

Vaisey, S. 2008a. "Reply to Ann Swidler." *Sociological Forum 2008* 23:619–622.

Vaisey, S. 2008b. "Socrates, Skinner, and Aristotle: Three Ways of Thinking About Culture in Action." *Sociological Forum 2008* 23:603–613.

Voydanoff, P. 1995. "Work Role Characteristics, Family Structure Demands, and Work/Family Conflict." PP. 51–61 in *The Work and Family Interface: Toward a Contextual Effects Perspective*, edited by G. B. J. Pittman. Minneapolis: National Council on Family Relations.

Voydanoff, P. 2004. "The Effects of Work Demands and Resources on Work-to-Family Conflict and Facilitation." *Journal of Marriage and the Family* 66:398–412.

Weber, M. 1976. *The Protestant Ethic and the Spirit of Capitalism.* Translated by T. Parsons. New York: Charles Scribner's Sons.

Weber, M. 1981 (1946). "Science as a Vocation." In *From Max Weber: Essays in Sociology,* edited by H. H. Gerth, and C. W. Mills. New York: Oxford University Press.

Weiner, L. Y. 1985. *From Working Girl to Working Mother: The Female Labor Force in the United States, 1820–1980.* Chapel Hill: University of North Carolina Press.

Wharton, A. S., S. Chivers, and M. Blair-Loy. 2008. "Use of Formal and Informal Work-Family Policies on the Digital Assembly Line." *Work and Occupations* 35:327–350.

Wharton, A. S., and M. Blair-Loy. 2002. "The 'Overtime Culture' in a Global Corporation: A Cross National Study of Finance Professional's Interest in Working Part-time." *Work and Occupations* 29:32–63.

Wharton, A. S., and M. Blair-Loy. 2006. "Long Work Hours and Family Life: A Cross National Study of Employees' Concerns." *Journal of Family Issues* 27:415–436.

Williams, J. 2000. *Unbending Gender: Why Family and Work Conflict and What to Do about It.* Oxford and New York: Oxford University Press.

Zelizer, V. A. 1985. *Pricing the Priceless Child.* New York: Basic.

CHAPTER 24

Moral Classification and Social Policy

BRIAN STEENSLAND

INTRODUCTION

Classification is fundamental to social life. Corporations classify people on the basis of age, productivity, and criminal background. Organized religions monitor the boundaries between orthodox and heterodox belief. Voluntary associations reinforce codes of desirable and undesirable behavior. From examples like these, it is clear that classificatory systems often have a moral dimension. Their categories refer not only to vertical distinctions, but also to normative hierarchies. These moral categories constitute the basis of social life and, in part, create the very realities to which they apply.

One powerful source of classification is the government, and one of its chief tools of classification is social policy. Through social policy, the state allocates rights and resources based on adherence to normative models of citizenship. In doing, so, social policy both reflects and creates patterns of moral classification. Policymakers are themselves members of society who are influenced by common understandings about desirable behavior, the definition of needs, and the degree of similarity between groups. Thus, social policy may codify moral distinctions that are already widely shared in society. Yet, classification is also contentious. There are typically competing classification schemes vying for dominance. Any given scheme may advance the material interests and moral commitments of some groups over others. This means that the moral distinctions embedded in social policy are as much the result of politics and power struggles as they are a reflection of societal consensus. In either case, the state's decisions to classify are highly consequential for citizens, shaping outcomes ranging from collective identities to economic life chances.

Scholars recognize the moral distinctions embedded in social policy. Yet, in empirical research, the connections between morality and policymaking are drawn too infrequently. After discussing the connections between social categories, inequality, and the state, this chapter will outline how social policy both responds to and produces moral categories in society. The examples are drawn primarily from the policies that constitute the welfare state, which taken together provide many of the social rights of citizenship. Three types of morally laden social categories—those based on work, race, and gender—are the basis for much

S. Hitlin, S. Vaisey (eds.), *Handbook of the Sociology of Morality*,
Handbooks of Sociology and Social Research, DOI 10.1007/978-1-4419-6896-8_24,
© Springer Science+Business Media, LLC 2010

of the sorting that occurs within the welfare state because they often shape perceptions of "deservingness." I discuss each in turn and conclude with an overview of my own work on moral classification and its influence on American anti-poverty policy during the 1960s and 1970s. As a growing body of research now shows, moral categories have played a much more instrumental role in American social policy development than previously acknowledged.

CATEGORIES AND INEQUALITY

Sociologists have been thinking about the origins and consequences of moral categories since the birth of the discipline in the early twentieth-century. In *The Elementary Forms of Religious Life*, Emile Durkheim posited that categories serve as the basis for all human knowledge: "They are like the solid frames that confine thought" (Durkheim 1995:9). What made this a sociological insight was his contention that mental categories are patterned on the structure of the social world. Durkheim further argued that the origin of *all* social categorization was found in the religious distinction between the sacred and the profane. A well-integrated community required ways of distinguishing between the moral and the immoral, and it was the mutual regard for the sacred that gave a group its moral cohesion.

   This Durkheimian approach to categories continues to be influential in the discipline (see Zerubavel 1991). Among its most prominent practitioners, Douglas (1966) contends that the distinction between the "pure" and "impure" still structures much of contemporary social life, playing both an instrumental and symbolic role. People deploy moral codes to influence behavior and to express their views of the social order. Moral categories further form the basis of social hierarchies and the distribution of power. One of the chief strategies people use to guard moral boundaries is the mobilization of "pollution beliefs": ideas about the impure contaminating the pure. One prominent example from US history is the "one-drop rule," which legally codified a binary classification between blacks and whites, rather than defining racial classification along a continuum (Davis 1991). Douglas sums up the role of moral categories and symbolic pollution in this way: "The whole universe is harnessed to men's attempts to force one another into good citizenship. Thus we find that certain moral values are upheld and certain social rules defined by beliefs in dangerous contagion. . .it is not difficult to see how pollution beliefs can be used in a dialog of claims and counter-claims to status" (Douglas 1966:3).

   A number of scholars have taken up the idea that categories serve as the basis for systems of hierarchy. Some downplay the moral dimension of social categories, largely seeing morality as a by-product of power struggles. Others place moral categories at the conceptual center of their analyses. Tilly (1998) puts social categories at the center of his analysis of "durable inequality." He argues that binary pairs—such as black/white or male/female—do much of the "organizational work" in maintaining inequality. One mechanism through which this takes place is opportunity hoarding. Bounded social networks that are homogenous along a binary dimension monopolize valued resources. These binary categories serve as the foundation for social closure. Once in place, categorical systems of inequality get reproduced through two additional mechanisms—emulation, where established patterns of action diffuse throughout society; and adaptation, in which the behavioral responses to categorical inequality, among both dominant and subordinate groups, further consolidate existing patterns of inequality. On the basis of this type of analysis, Tilly urges scholars to shift from individual-level to categorical ways of thinking about the processes that generate inequality.

Douglas Massey directly takes up this call. In *Categorically Unequal* (2007), Massey draws upon Tilly's conceptual framework to elucidate the workings of the American stratification system. He also fleshes out the role played by categories in a number of ways. For instance, while Tilly largely assumed binary thinking among individuals, Massey delves into studies of social cognition to provide substantial empirical support for the argument that humans are cognitively biased to think in categorical terms. This categorical bias is one reason that stratification is so challenging to overcome. Cognitive categories congeal into stereotypes that powerful groups then promulgate to maintain social distinctions. These distinctions serve as the basis for in-group/out-group boundary formation that results in spatial and social segregation, which in turn leads to differential access to resources. Using the concepts of opportunity hoarding and exploitation, Massey shows how this chain of processes functions along some of the major categorical fault lines in modern America, including race, class, gender, and immigrant status.

Neither Tilly nor Massey places the moral nature of social categories at the heart of their analyses, though they both recognize it in passing. In contrast, Lamont's (2000) study of working class men in the USA and France shows that moral boundaries are firmly ensconced in their mental worlds. These moral boundaries combine with race- and citizen-based categories to powerfully impact social differentiation in both countries. In the US, for instance, working-class whites draw moral (not economic) distinctions between themselves and upper-middle-class whites and working-class blacks. White workers criticize the white professional class for lacking personal integrity. They criticize black workers for lacking discipline and the work ethic. While these are moral distinctions, it is also clear that moral boundaries and racial differences are closely intertwined among both blacks and whites. Lamont provides evidence that traditional morality and adherence to the work ethic are the main criteria that white workers use to elevate themselves above blacks. These moral distinctions serve as the building blocks for symbolic racism, though as Lamont notes, members of the white working class would contend that their views of blacks are not based on racial animosity but upon concern for traditional American values.

Taken together, the work sketched out here represents three distinct views of the role categories play in generating and maintaining inequality. Tilly emphasizes the material interests at the foundation of categorical inequality, Massey recognizes the importance of the material but also emphasizes the central role played by mental categories, and Lamont shows that the boundaries that separate social classes and racial groups have a strong moral component. This diversity of viewpoints reflects broader differences over the conceptual status of moral categories. Do they independently shape patterns of inequality or are they better viewed as a consequence of it? Disagreement over this question turns out to play a significant role in explaining how—and the extent to which—moral categories are incorporated into the literature on the state and social policy.

MORAL CATEGORIES: HOW AUTONOMOUS?

Most policy scholars attribute little causal weight to moral classification in their explanatory accounts of social policy. This reflects a widely held view that cultural patterns are an epiphenomenal reflection of the more obdurate features of social life—labor market dynamics, network relations, organizational structures, power differentials, and so forth (Goldberg

2007). From this vantage point, moral categories are a consequence, not a cause. The theoretical foundations for this position are found in a particular reading of Karl Marx's statements on class conflict and ideology.

Marxian views of culture are typically rooted in the proposition that society's material base determines its ideational superstructure. Yet, as Williams (2005) argues, it would be better to begin from a different Marxian proposition, namely that social being determines social consciousness. The latter implies a flux in social relations and cultural formations rather than two fixed entities in a spatial relationship. Better still would be to unpack the meaning of "determine," since Marx's usage of the term was specifically in response to, and in parallel with, the claims of Hegelian idealism. Williams argues that a more fruitful reading of Marx would recognize a number of important qualifications. The most important concern the elasticity of the temporal relationship between the material and ideal, the internal complexity of whatever is considered to be "material," and the many mediating processes that link social relations and social consciousness in only indirect ways. Recognizing these qualifications would correct the tendency, still prominent in much 21st-century cultural theorizing, to view social structure and culture as homologous systems operating in a one-to-one correspondence. The simplistic base-superstructure formulation is one reason that moral categories are often seen more as consequence than as cause in the social policy scholarship.

Representative is Tilly's own version of this perspective. He would almost certainly recognize the moral boundaries that Lamont documents, but argue that their sources lay in competition for resources and that their independent influence on inequality is minimal. He asserts that "social scientists dealing with such durable forms of inequality must hack through dense ideological growth to reach structural roots"; he also posits that "beliefs and practices shift together under the pressure of collective experience" (Tilly 1998:15, 102).

A different conceptual approach to categories—one that seeks to turn the materialist formulation on its head—is advanced by Jeff Alexander and his collaborators (Alexander 2003, Alexander and Smith 1993). It draws on hermeneutics and French structuralism to argue that binary categories constitute the infrastructure of social life. These categories are normative at their root—sacred/profane, democratic/undemocratic, good/evil. They provide the basic cultural grammar that makes social life meaningful. Alexander positions his framework in direct opposition both to Marxian reflection theory and to what he calls "weak" versions of cultural analysis that, in his view, too easily reduce moral codes to their instrumental uses and material sources. Instead, cultural structures should be seen as having their own internal logic and autonomous influence, even when combined in explanatory accounts with factors such as resource-laden actors and constraining institutions.

Lamont makes a related point when comparing the mental maps of working-class men in the USA and France. She finds that American men draw different types of moral boundaries than their French counterparts. This difference obtains despite the fact that her respondents in both countries occupy similar structural locations—as defined by labor market position, proximate social networks, and the characteristics of their respective communities. She attributes the differences she observes in boundary work to the cultural scripts readily available to members of each nation. She summarizes by saying that groups who "find themselves in relatively similar structural positions can draw very different [moral] lines precisely because their environment and/or subculture exposed them to different sets of cultural tools" (Lamont 2000:7).

While the differences between neo-Marxian approaches and Alexander's "strong program" for cultural analysis can seem stark, a perspective based on the concept of "relative autonomy" strikes a middle ground. It addresses some of the blindspots of both perspectives. Elements of culture are considered relatively autonomous when they exert social influence in ways that are independent of the social conditions from which they originate (Kane 1991). An example can be seen in Glaeser's (2000) analysis of the cultural boundaries drawn between East and West Berlin. While these cultural distinctions clearly had roots in patterns of lived reality during the Cold War, they far outlasted the city's reunification. More broadly speaking, a variety of factors—such as the "sunk costs" of social cognition, emotional investment in social identities, or the absence of new cultural content to replace the old—can be invoked to explain why social structure may change without attendant changes in cultural structures. Recognizing the prospect of relative autonomy overcomes problems of stark reductionism in materialist accounts. It also helps to recognize the simplistic assumption of one-to-one correspondence between social relations and social consciousness, the reality of complex mediating linkages between the two, and the fact that material resources can be "read" in multiple ways based on different schemas (Sewell 1992). Thinking about relative (as opposed to absolute) autonomy also tempers overly deterministic cultural accounts, since such accounts pay little attention to the material roots of moral categories or the shifting relationships between categories (the *signifiers*) and their contents (the *signified*).

These different views of culture help account for the various ways in which moral categories are incorporated into the literature on social policy development. If culture is epiphenomenal, then moral categories reflect patterns of social provision and merit only secondary interest. If culture is autonomous, then moral categories warrant mapping but their influence on social policy is typically presumed rather than documented. If culture is treated as relatively autonomous, then moral categories can be seen as potentially shaping *or* reflecting patterns of social provision, in which case the analytic objective shifts to examining the factors, mechanisms, and conditions potentially at play in both processes. This often involves tracing causal sequences during pivotal movements in policymaking.

MORAL CLASSIFICATION AND SOCIAL POLICY

To Govern is to Classify

The act of governing requires classification, and the state's official categories become woven into the fabric of social life in myriad ways. Categories group together previously distinct entities, define common interests among disparate groups, create systems of incentives and sanctions, and prescribe appropriate lines of action (Starr 1992, Stone 1997). In these ways, government classification also influences collective mentalities. State categories become "impersonal cognitive commitments" from which it is difficult to recover "preconceptual innocence" (Starr 1992:272). These categories are difficult to "unthink." Because they are backed by the force of government, they create strong incentives for cognitive accommodation by citizens. As Mary Douglas asks, "How can we possibly think of ourselves in society except by using the classifications established in our institutions?" (Douglas 1986:99).

The welfare state provides an example *par excellence*, especially when it comes to the matter of social inequality. It is common to assume that the welfare state is designed to reduce levels of social inequality and to ameliorate the material consequences of poverty. Yet as Gøsta Esping-Andersen convincingly argues, "the welfare state is not just a mechanism that intervenes in, and possibly corrects, the structure of inequality; it is, in its own right, a system of stratification. It is an active force in the ordering of social relations" (Esping-Andersen 1990:23). There is a strong moral component to these social relations. Welfare states create and reinforce moral hierarchies (Handler and Hasenfeld 1991). Means-tested public assistance is designed to stigmatize or punish recipients who are not meeting society's moral expectations. This is explicit among supporters of "paternalistic" policy measures (e.g., Mead 1986). Particularly through the allocation of stigma and citizenship rights, the welfare state prescribes appropriate moral behavior and creates classes of individuals who are deemed as falling short. Three social categories that have been central to social policy development are those based on work, gender, and race.

Work and Deservingness

Marshall (1950) developed the notion that central to the welfare state is the idea of social citizenship, which includes both rights and obligations. Chief among these rights is economic security in the face of circumstances such as old age, sickness, permanent disability, or unemployment. To the extent that work effort is not requisite for the full rights of citizenship, scholars say that labor has been "de-commodified," since economic security does not rely on labor market participation. Countries vary in the extent to which their social policies decommodify labor. According to a prominent typology of welfare states, the "social democratic" countries of Scandinavia are the most de-commodifying and the "liberal" welfare states of the English-speaking West are the least so. The "conservative" welfare states of the Mediterranean region are located in the middle (Esping-Andersen 1990).

By most accounts, the US decommodifies labor the least out of all Western industrial democracies. This is reflected in the sharp normative distinction drawn between the deserving and undeserving poor (Handler and Hasenfeld 1991, Mohr 1994). The "deserving" are those who are not expected to work based on factors such as their age, gender, family status, or physical limitations. Individuals in this "deserving" category typically receive relatively generous benefits from the government. The "undeserving" poor, on the other hand, are expected to work and consequently receive limited, if any, government benefits. These moral categories are also apparent in the two-tier structure of American social policy as a whole. Since the birth of the modern welfare state during the New Deal era, scholars have generally recognized the distinction between *social insurance* programs (such as Old-Age Insurance, or "social security") that are contributory and relatively generous, and *public assistance* programs (such as Temporary Assistance for Needy Families, or "welfare") that are means- or work-tested and stigmatizing.

Most countries have some elements of this deserving-undeserving distinction embedded in their systems of social provision, but in the USA, the stigmatized status of the "undeserving" is particularly potent and the proportion of the poor who fall into this category is comparatively large. Historians trace the rise of categories of deservingness to the spread of wage labor that attended the growth of industrial capitalism and the move from close-knit communities to urban metropolises (Katz 1986). By the late 1800s, this moral distinction was firmly established in American culture. Business owners clearly benefit from a moral system in which the able-bodied, non-working poor receive only stigmatizing and limited public assistance. This helps maintain a ready supply of cheap labor. Even into the mid-twentieth-century, scholars have found strong correlations between the influence of business interests and the stigma attached to the receipt of government social provision (Krinsky 2007, Reese 2005). This bolsters the view that a primary goal of American welfare policy is not to alleviate poverty, but to regulate the labor market (Piven and Cloward 1993). Yet, the prevalence of these categories cannot be reduced to the machinations of the business class alone. Many working-class people draw these same moral distinctions. Other factors are also required to explain the influence of these categories. Prime candidates include the legacy of the Protestant ethic, the expansive size of the charitable sector, the absence of a programmatic socialist party, and a culture wedded to rugged individualism.

While the deserving-undeserving distinction has deep roots in American culture, the populations who fall into each category have changed over time. This is why it is important to focus not only on the existence of moral categories—as analyses oriented by structural hermeneutics may be wont to do—but on their internal composition. Understanding the factors that have led to changes over time reveal the complex ways in which categories of deservingness based on work are entangled with other classification schemes. Two of particular importance are gender and race.

Gender

One of the concepts that has traditionally oriented the scholarship of welfare states is de-commodification. More recently, feminist scholars have sought to reorient studies of the welfare state by using the notion of autonomy, by which they mean the freedom of women (and men) to "make choices about reproduction, family, and work, and the resources to act on one's choices" (O'Connor et al. 1999:35). One of the contributions of this scholarship is to highlight that government social provision is not only entangled with work-based categories of deservingness but also rooted in moral assumptions concerning gender roles, family formation, and sexuality. Men have historically been held accountable to the work ethic, while women have also been held to the "family ethic" (Abramovitz 1988).

Social categories based on gender have been integrated into policy studies in different ways. For example, Suzanne Mettler and Linda Gordon both examine gender and the creation of the modern welfare state. They agree that the New Deal institutionalized gender differences in citizenship rights. Yet the differences in their causal accounts reflect the broader division between materialistic and cultural accounts of the link between moral categories and social policy.

Mettler (1998) examines a number of New Deal policy domains—including old-age insurance, old-age assistance, employment insurance, and Aid to Dependent Children—and argues that labor market dynamics and federalism were the two chief factors that resulted in a welfare state bifurcated along gender lines. More generous entitlement programs excluded individuals with inconsistent labor market participation and many low-wage occupations (e.g., domestic, restaurant, or agricultural work). These criteria disproportionately excluded women from coverage in the more generous programs, leaving them to rely on stigmatizing, means-tested programs that offered stingier benefits. Pressure for means-tested programs to be administered by state governments, as opposed to the federal government, led to further changes in coverage that disproportionately weakened social protections for women.

In contrast, Gordon's (1994) account emphasizes the influential role played by normative gender expectations. She recognizes the factors that Mettler documents, especially how leaving key decisions about administration and eligibility to the states could lead to discrimination against minority and immigrant women. Yet she also provides abundant evidence that normative conceptions of the gendered division of labor—especially concerning women's role as mothers—shaped social policy at many stages of development. Within the government, these gender norms became programmatically reinforced where one might least expect it—in federal agencies run by female policy experts who themselves to did not conform to the gendered expectations of the era.

The evolution of social programs since the New Deal reveals that while social classification according to gender expectations has been a constant, the groups sorted into particular categories, along with the stigma associated with them, have shifted. Since World War Two, there has been an increasing emphasis placed on women's labor market participation as a requirement for government benefits. One important change occurred in 1967, when Congress passed legislation that included work requirements for mothers who received public assistance. This was in marked contrast with policy priorities during the Progressive era, which sought to structure incentives to keep women in the private sphere of household labor and child rearing. As gender roles regarding work shifted, so too did categories of social provision based upon them. Along with changes in work, expectations for women came changes in the level of stigma associated with receipt of welfare benefits. Studies suggest that increasing stigmatization was partially race-based, since it was associated with the rising number of households headed by unmarried black mothers on the welfare rolls. The original Assistance to Dependent Children program had originally been intended for widowed white mothers (Reese 2005).

Race

The fact that views of welfare policy changed as the proportion of black recipients grew larger signals that racial categories have been as central to American social policy formation as those based on normative gender expectations. In fact, a number of scholars have argued that race-neutral social policies really do not exist (Brown 1999, Lieberman 1998). Many important race-laden policy decisions, like those based on gender norms, were institutionalized during the New Deal. Whether racial animus was a key motivating factor in the racial classification that occurred is a matter of debate, but there is wide agreement about one general outcome of the New Deal legislation. Economic security was far more readily available to whites than to blacks.

New Deal policies sorted Americans by class, largely by differentiating populations on the basis of occupation and work status. As Robert Lieberman shows, "in so doing, they also sorted Americans by race; in keeping with the prevailing racial norms of the 1930s, and the institutional structure of American politics, welfare discriminated by design" (Lieberman 1998:5). Racism was pervasive in the South, and while southern policymakers were central to the design of New Deal social programs, but one need not invoke overt racism to account for institutionalized racial discrimination. As Lieberman argues, this discrimination resulted from racially structured power relations rooted in class conflict, party coalitions, and the design of political institutions.

Other scholars have pushed farther on the argument that race-stratified social programs need not have explicitly racist motivations at their core. Davies and Derthick (1997) contend that considerations about states' rights and administrative concerns were the main factors that ended up excluding blacks from the most generous social programs. Pointing to similar legislative patterns in Canada and Great Britain, where racial factors were not at play, they argue that racism need not be invoked to explain patterns of coverage and inclusion. Brown (1999) contends that blacks' disadvantaged position within the American welfare state has stemmed from a combination of employment discrimination and fiscal constraints. Discrimination against blacks in the labor market was the condition that allowed occupation-based categories in the New Deal to take on their racial consequences. Race-based occupational discrimination effects work status, and because work status is a key element of social citizenship, it becomes a primary sorting device in the programmatic structure of social policy. Fiscal conservatism further reinforced this structure, since targeted (as opposed to universal) programs are less expensive, and those with stigmatized populations such as racial minorities are less prone to expansionary pressures. Over time, as some programs began to take on a strong racial cast in the 1960s, political leaders—even liberal ones—found it difficult to increase funding for programs perceived as mainly benefiting blacks. This was all the more difficult for programs, such as public assistance, that were administered at the local level. Giving state administrators control over social provision has long worked to unevenly distribute benefits according to race.

Other accounts place considerably more causal emphasis on the moral categories associated with race. Gilens (1999) examines the sociological roots of opposition to welfare spending since the 1970s. His analysis of survey data suggests that Americans do not oppose welfare spending due to their self-interest or individualistic values. Rather, their opposition rests on their perceptions of the poor. Two views in particular are central. First, Americans do not think that most welfare recipients are truly needy. The public believes that most of the poor could work and support themselves. Second, Americans tend to think that blacks lack a commitment to the work ethic. Moreover, they overestimate the percentage of welfare recipients who are black. Taken together, the general public equates welfare recipients with undeserving blacks. Gilens' survey analysis begs a number of questions, such as why Americans consider blacks as lacking the proper work ethic. He cites studies of stereotyping and in-group boundary work similar to those discussed in Massey's book and further grounds these conceptions in the history of slavery and Reconstuction. However, Gilens also conducts an innovative study of media portrayals of poverty since the 1960s. He finds that blacks are overrepresented in the photographs and film footage that accompany media stories about poverty. He further shows convincing evidence that blacks are especially overrepresented in negative portrayals of poverty rather than sympathetic ones, in which whites are much more prominent. This evidence suggests that media coverage reinforces racial stereotypes and bolsters whites' views of the undeservingness of blacks.

The entanglement of race with categories of deservingness, especially since the 1960s, has been paralleled by the entanglement of race with concerns about reproduction and sexual morality. This has been clearest in the case of debates over Assistance to Families with

Dependent Children (AFDC), the program commonly referred to as "welfare."[1] With the passage of legislation in 1939 that allowed widows to gain access to old-age insurance, AFDC began to serve larger numbers of unwed mothers and racial minorities (Reese 2005). This set the stage for the backlash against welfare that began in the 1960s. Policymakers and politicians became concerned that the welfare system provided incentives for out-of-wedlock childbirth. This aligned with contemporaneous concerns about sexual promiscuity and family disintegration within the black community. In one of the era's most infamous illustrations of this view, a senator referred to black welfare recipients as "a bunch of brood mares" (Reese 2005:119).

THE INFLUENCE OF MORAL CATEGORIES: A CASE STUDY

While scholars have widely recognized the existence of cultural categories of deservingness as a facet of the American welfare state, they have seldom systematically incorporated the influence of moral categories into their explanatory models. Theda Skocpol, for instance, observed that the "institutional and cultural oppositions between the morally 'deserving' and the less deserving run like fault lines through the entire history of American social provision (1992:149). Yet this comment remained confined to the narrative middle of her book, with no discussion of the influence of these moral categories in her theoretical framework. This reflects the widespread assumption, discussed above, that moral classification is best seen as an outcome of government policy rather than as a causal influence.[2]

Yet the impact of moral categories on policy development is demonstrable. Perhaps nowhere is this influence more apparent than in the struggle over guaranteed income policies during the 1960s and 1970s (Steensland 2008). These proposals represented the boldest attempt to transform the foundation of the American welfare system because they sought to base the provision of government benefits on economic need rather than work status. The proposals' advocates viewed poverty in economic terms, not in behavioral or moral terms. Therefore, guaranteed income proposals mixed "deserving" and "undeserving" groups in the same government program. Need alone became the basis of deservingness. The disabled and the elderly would receive the same benefits in the same program as unmarried mothers and underemployed but able-bodied men. Perhaps surprisingly from today's vantage point, one of these proposals—President Nixon's Family Assistance Plan—nearly passed into law in the early 1970s. President Carter proposed similar legislation during his first year in office. Because these proposals challenged the existing categorical logic of the American welfare state, the political dynamics they generated threw the influence of categories of deservingness on policymaking into sharp relief.

One clear factor in the failure of guaranteed income proposals was the influence of categorical thinking. As Starr argued, there are cognitive "sunk costs" that accompany the cognitive accommodation to official categories, and social provision in the USA has a long

---

[1] In 1962, the Assistance to Dependent Children program was renamed Assistance to Families with Dependent Children.

[2] Two notable exceptions are Skrentny (2006) and Goldberg (2007).

history of categorical differentiation based on deservingness. These categories created a template through which people understood Nixon's Family Assistance Plan, even though it was anti-categorical in nature. Strikingly, even some proponents of Nixon's legislation used analogies and arguments that unintentionally bolstered the very normative categories that they sought to override. Therefore, a number of Nixon's policy experts devoted considerable energy to explaining that Nixon's plan was a new type of social provision founded on different moral assumptions. Yet their explanations consistently encountered cultural obstacles based on categories of deservingness.

Beyond the cognitive level, the language that Nixon and others used to describe the plan was categorical, even though the policy itself was not. In his public statements about his plan, Nixon drew sharp binary distinctions between the "work ethic" and the "welfare ethic," and between the "welfare rolls" and the "payrolls," even though the substance of his plan created a continuum between government assistance and work. Nixon used this language to sell his plan to the public, since he knew it resonated with a strong public desire to be "tough on welfare." However, the effects of this rhetoric were counterproductive. For instance, groups who would have clearly benefited economically from his plan, such as the working poor who would have received income supplements, never rallied behind it because they did not consider themselves to be "welfare" recipients and did not want to be considered as such in the future. Nixon's plan was, after all, a "welfare" program.

This misapprehension points to a significant feature of the debates over guaranteed income plans: the prevalence of symbolic pollution. Recall that Mary Douglas posited that the moral hierarchies created by categorical distinctions become threatened if these distinctions break down. This weakening leads to "pollution beliefs" about the impure contaminating the pure. Because Nixon's plan treated the "undeserving" and "deserving" poor in the same way and placed them in the same program, pollution beliefs proliferated. Nixon's new plan was universally referred to as a "welfare" plan and its costs were considered "welfare costs," even though the bulk of the plan's spending went to "deserving" populations. Labeling the program "welfare" invoked all the heated imagery of the era's racial unrest and violence. Importantly, this symbolic pollution also shaped perceptions of economic interests in the calmer confines of the nation's business organizations, such as the US Chamber of Commerce. Because Nixon's plan placed the working poor and non-working poor in the same "welfare" program, the business leaders at the chamber were deeply concerned that the stigma of receiving "welfare" would harm the work ethic of those already fully employed in the labor force. Business opposition on these moral grounds is striking, considering that Nixon's plan improved business owners' bottom line. It socialized the costs of low-wage labor by providing a government income supplement to the working poor. Yet, entrenched moral categories, and the threat posed by their dissolution, shaped business owners' views of their interests.

Beyond the influence of moral categories based on the work ethic, the struggle over guaranteed income policy reveals the mutual entanglement of categories based on work, race, and gender. As Gilens and others have argued, welfare politics became strongly racialized during the 1960s. By the early 1970s, despite the fact that blacks were neither the majority of the poor population, nor the majority of people receiving public assistance, "welfare" and race had become largely synonymous in the public mind. One place where this influence was clear was in the attempt to place AFDC recipients and the working poor in the same program, since the latter were white by a large majority. The working poor—especially the white ethnics of the Northeast—actively distanced themselves from any government benefit that could be conceived as "welfare" (Rieder 1985). This dynamic was very similar to the race-laden moral differentiation that Lamont observed three decades later among working-class whites.

During this period, rates of female labor market participation were conspicuously rising, so efforts to provide poor women with the option of staying home with their children rather than entering the workforce were increasingly difficult to make. Why, some legislators asked, should poor mothers be able to stay home when many married, working-class mothers felt compelled to work in order to make ends meet? Notably, this argument ran at odds with another historic objective of welfare reform: keeping mothers at home so they could properly socialize their children. Further complicating this debate was the view that many welfare recipients were sexually promiscuous. Some policymakers did not want to be seen as rewarding immoral behavior by supporting Nixon's plan.

The clearest consequences of the gender-based nature of moral categories of deserving-ness can be seen in the 1970s. Results from a long-running series of government experiments on the behavioral effects of receiving guaranteed income benefits became public. The exper-iments showed that receiving a guaranteed income did not harm the work ethic nearly as much as critics had expected. Moreover, it appeared that the ten percent reduction in work effort that the studies did find was used for job searching rather than loafing. Yet, the results also showed that if married women had the economic safety net of a guaranteed minimum income, they were considerably more likely to leave their husbands or seek divorce. Feminists argued for viewing this in a positive light, since it might mean that women no longer felt compelled to remain in unhappy, and possibly abusive, relationships out of economic neces-sity. They could have economic security on their own. This is precisely the type of autonomy that feminist scholars have placed at the center of many recent policy studies. However, crit-ics of guaranteed income policies held these women to the standards of the "family ethic," not the work ethic, and coming at a moment when concerns about family breakdown were running high, the experiments' results were a devastating blow to guaranteed income policy's prospects.

One final lesson from this policy episode shows the impact of moral classification on new government classification. Proponents of guaranteed income legislation challenged the dominant classification scheme based on the work ethic and promoted a new schema based on economic need. This was rooted in a view that all the poor were morally deserving of govern-ment assistance. The counter-reaction to this movement was fierce because opponents realized that this new schema threatened the ideological foundation of the existing welfare regime. In response, congressional conservatives created two new anti-poverty policies that provided ben-efits only to the "deserving" populations contained in the Nixon legislation, thereby isolating the "undeserving" groups in the existing AFDC-based system. Supplemental Security Income provided a guaranteed annual income for the aged, blind, and disabled and the Earned Income Tax Credit provided income supplements for the working poor without the stigma of "welfare." In Tilly's terms, these new social programs did much of the "organizational work" in sustaining patterns of durable inequality. However, in contrast to Tilly's materialism, the moral templates of deservingness held by advocates for these programs were a central influence of the creation of this legislation, not an epiphenomenal by-product. These programs were explicitly cre-ated to institutionally reinforce the moral boundaries between the deserving and undeserving poor.

CONCLUSION

Social policy has moral origins and consequences. Moral categories serve as the normative infrastructure of contemporary welfare states, and government welfare policies create and reinforce moral distinctions between groups of people and types of behavior. These distinctions are important for understanding patterns of social inequality. Moral commitments can spur the use of social policy to alleviate inequalities between groups that are viewed as unjust. Moral commitments can also result in social policies that, intentionally or not, reinforce moral distinctions based on both ascribed and behavioral characteristics.

The majority of research on social policy development exhibits little recognition of the links between social provision and the moral order. Of the minority of work that does, most looks at the consequences of social policy for categorical inequalities. Far less work systematically examines the influence of moral distinctions on policy development. This relative neglect is a consequence of both theoretical and methodological factors. At the theoretical level, research on social provision is not well grounded in analytic approaches that acknowledge the potential influence of moral categories and commitments. Particularly in historically-oriented research on policy development, an analytic perspective based on the relative autonomy of culture is a productive step. At the methodological level, policy scholars would benefit from closer attention to the language of policy debates. This does not mean credulously focusing only on the *text* of public political statements, since policymakers and legislators often use moral rhetoric to cloak more crass interests. Rather it means focusing more on the *subtext* and *context* of language—written both for public and private consumption—to look for implicit assumptions, shared schemas, normative commitments, and perceptions of moral constraints.

Finally, a more morally-attuned genre of policy scholarship should still recognize the centrality of conflict to policymaking. Some conflicts involve the types of economic and political stakes that are the bread and butter of mainstream policymaking scholarship. In addition, culturally informed policy scholarship needs to be attentive to the connections between the pursuit of material interests and the moral discourse this pursuit generates. Yet, at the same time, policy scholars need to recognize that debates over social policy are just as centrally about status-based conflicts over appropriate lifestyle, the rights of social citizenship, and competing visions of the moral order.

REFERENCES

Abramovitz, M. 1988. *Regulating the Lives of Women: Social Welfare Policy from Colonial Times to the Present.* Boston, MA: South End Press.

Alexander, J. C. 2003. *The Meanings of Social Life: A Cultural Sociology.* New York, NY: Oxford University Press.

Alexander, J. C., and P. Smith. 1993. "The Discourse of American Civil Society: A New Proposal for Cultural Studies." *Theory and Society* 22:151–207.

Brown, M. K. 1999. *Race, Money, and the American Welfare State.* Ithaca, NY: Cornell University Press.

Davies, G., and M. Derthick. 1997. "Race and Social Welfare Policy: The Social Security Act of 1935." *Political Science Quarterly* 112:217–235.

Davis, F. J. 1991. *Who Is Black? One Nation's Definition.* University Park, PA: Pennsylvania State University Press.

Douglas, M. 1966. *Purity and Danger: An Analysis of the Concepts of Pollution and Taboo.* New York, NY: Routledge.

Douglas, M. 1986. *How Institutions Think.* Syracuse, NY: Syracuse University Press.

Durkheim, E. 1995. *The Elementary Forms of Religious Life.* New York, NY: Free Press.

Esping-Andersen, G. 1990. *The Three Worlds of Welfare Capitalism*. Princeton, NJ: Princeton University Press.

Gilens, M. 1999. *Why Americans Hate Welfare: Race, Media, and the Politics of Antipoverty Policy*. Chicago, IL: University of Chicago Press.

Glaeser, A. 2000. *Divided in Unity: Identity, Germany, and the Berlin Police*. Chicago, IL: University of Chicago Press.

Goldberg, C. A. 2007. *Citizens and Paupers: Relief, Rights, and Race, from the Freedmen's Bureau to Workfare*. Chicago, IL: University of Chicago Press.

Gordon, L. 1994. *Pitied But Not Entitled: Single Mothers and the History of Welfare, 1890–1935*. Cambridge, MA: Harvard University Press.

Handler, J. F., and Y. Hasenfeld. 1991. *The Moral Construction of Poverty: Welfare Reform in America*. Newbury Park, CA: Sage Publications.

Kane, A. 1991. "Cultural Analysis in Historical Sociology: The Analytic and Concrete Forms of the Autonomy of Culture." *Sociological Theory* 9:53–69.

Katz, M. B. 1986. *In the Shadow of the Poorhouse: A Social History of Welfare in America*. New York, NY: Basic Books.

Krinsky, J. 2007. *Free Labor: Workfare and the Contested Language of Neoliberalism*. Chicago, IL: University of Chicago Press.

Lamont, M. 2000. *The Dignity of Working Men: Morality and the Boundaries of Race, Class, and Immigration*. New York, NY and Cambridge, MA: Harvard University Press and Russell Sage Foundation.

Lieberman, R. C. 1998. *Shifting the Color Line: Race and the American Welfare State*. Cambridge, MA: Harvard University Press.

Marshall, T. H. 1950. *Citizenship and Social Class*. Cambridge, UK: Cambridge University Press.

Massey, D. S. 2007. *Categorical Inequality: The American Stratification System*. New York, NY: Russell Sage Foundation.

Mead, L. 1986. *Beyond Entitlement: The Social Obligations of Citizenship*. New York, NY: Free Press.

Mettler, S. 1998. *Dividing Citizens: Gender and Federalism in New Deal Public Policy*. Ithaca, NY: Cornell University Press.

Mohr, J. W. 1994. "Soldiers, Mothers, Tramps, and Others: Discourse Roles in the 1907 New York City Charity Directory." *Poetics* 22:327–357.

O'Connor, J. S., A. S. Orloff, and S. Shaver. 1999. *States, Markets, Families: Gender, Liberalism and Social Policy in Australia, Canada, Great Britain and the United States*. New York, NY: Cambridge University Press.

Piven, F. F., and R. A. Cloward. 1993 (1971). *Regulating the Poor: The Functions of Public Welfare*. New York, NY: Vintage.

Reese, E. 2005. *Backlash against Welfare Mothers: Past and Present*. Berkeley and Los Angeles, CA: University of California Press.

Rieder, J. 1985. *Canarsie: The Jews and Italians of Brooklyn Against Liberalism*. Cambridge, MA: Harvard University Press.

Sewell, W. H., Jr. 1992. "A Theory of Structure: Duality, Agency, and Transformation." *American Journal of Sociology* 98:1–29.

Skocpol, T. 1992. *Protecting Soldiers and Mothers: The Political Origins of Social Policy in the United States*. Cambridge, MA: Harvard University Press.

Skrentny, J. D. 2006. "Policy-Elite Perceptions and Social Movement Success: Understanding Variations in Group Inclusion in Affirmative Action." *American Journal of Sociology* 111:1762–1815.

Starr, P. 1992. "Social Categories and Claims in the Liberal State." *Social Research* 50:263–295.

Steensland, B. 2008. *The Failed Welfare Revolution: America's Struggle over Guaranteed Income Policy*. Princeton, NJ: Princeton University Press.

Stone, D. 1997. *Policy Paradox: The Art of Political Decision Making*. New York, NY: W. W. Norton.

Tilly, C. 1998. *Durable Inequality*. Berkeley and Los Angeles, CA: University of California Press.

Williams, R. 2005. "Base and Superstructure in Marxist Cultural Theory." PP. 31–49 in *Culture and Materialism: Selected Essays*. New York, NY: Verso.

Zerubavel, E. 1991. *The Fine Line: Making Distinctions in Everyday Life*. Chicago, IL: University of Chicago Press.

CHAPTER 25

The Moral Construction of Risk

Leslie T. Roth

Late in 2009, hackers gained access to hundreds of emails between climate scientists at the University of East Anglia Climate Research Unit in an attempt to discredit the science behind global warming. Global warming skeptics claimed that these emails indicate scientists' efforts to manipulate data to exaggerate the risks of global warming. Relatedly, 260 protesters were arrested in violent protests at the United Nations conference on climate change in Copenhagen while advocating climate justice for developing nations. While many disagree on the reality of the risk, some argue that the price-tag of fixing the problem will cause greater suffering in the developing world as money earmarked to fight global warming is not spent on disease eradication and development (Lumborg 2007). The debate has come to resemble Pascal's wager. How should we act as individuals and a society when faced with a risk that is difficult to measure, but where the stakes are so high? The controversy over global warming—its reality, the risk assessments associated with it, and what, if anything, should be done—provides a case study into the close relationship between morality and risk.

Abend (2008) defines the sociology of morality as "the sociological investigation of the nature, causes, and consequences of people's ideas about the good and the right" (p. 87). These ideas about the good and the right are often dependent on what people know to be true. Increasingly, what people know to be true, good, right, healthy or dangerous is communicated through the language of risk. The development of sociology of morality calls for engagement with what Max Weber considered the world of facts and the world of values, which he saw as distinct. We can facilitate our understanding of the relationship between these two worlds through empirical investigations of the intersections between morality and risk. The concept of risk tends to exist between notions of fact and value, but it is a concept with a growing research literature and one that is relevant to social and individual notions of morality. This chapter presents a survey of sociological research at the intersection of morality and risk, highlighting moral discourses that provide a backdrop for the discipline's understanding of risk. I attempt to answer two questions: (a) Where do morality and notions of risk intersect? and (b) How can exploring diverse perspectives on the reality of risk help us recognize and understand varieties of moral discourse? The first part of this chapter defines risk and presents a brief overview of three sociological perspectives that differ in their assumptions about what constitutes risk. In the second part, I provide a typology that associates each risk perspective with corresponding moral projects. In the third part of the chapter, following the typology, I examine literature from each risk perspective that emphasizes the connections between morality and risk, allowing us

S. Hitlin, S. Vaisey (eds.), *Handbook of the Sociology of Morality*,
Handbooks of Sociology and Social Research, DOI 10.1007/978-1-4419-6896-8_25,
© Springer Science+Business Media, LLC 2010

to see how varying attitudes toward the reality of risk lead to a focus on particular aspects of morality.

DEFINITIONS OF RISK

Scholars have had difficulty agreeing on a definition of risk. Garland (2003:50) distinguishes risks from dangers by defining them as "estimates of the likely impact of dangers." Whereas danger manifests as "the potential for harm that inheres in a thing, a person, or a situation" (ibid:50), risk measures how likely and to what extent that potential for harm is to be realized. This implies a concept of "risk [as] a rationality" (Dean 1999:184), specifically a measurable, calculative rationality (Ewald 1991). Likewise, it implies an understanding of "danger" as ontologically given. In this view, a risk assessment is merely an estimate of an objectively existent potential for harm. Yet, Garland (2003:51) is careful to note that the concept of danger is useful primarily in a relational sense as "dangers are *dangers for someone*...nothing is dangerous as such, not even floods or lightning" (italics original).

Because of this close relationship between the concepts of risk and danger, others question whether we can conceptually separate risk from danger, arguing that estimates and mathematical likelihood of an occurrence are rarely what we mean when we speak colloquially of risk: "the word *risk* now means danger; *high risk* means a lot of danger" (Douglas 1992:24, emphasis in original). Even when mathematical probabilities *are* what we mean, the difficulty of categorizing a danger as such without first engaging in a risk assessment leads some to conclude that risks and dangers are both "cultural products" (Fox 1999:22). Risk provides a frame for organizing the dangers in our lives, quantifying the uncertain, and making predictions about the future.

THE "REALITY" OF RISK

The question remains: how real are the risks we identify? Much of the difficulty in coming to a consensus definition of risk lies in different understandings of the ontological basis of risk. How we answer this question directly informs research questions about the social function of risk and how notions of what is risky have changed over time. Lupton (1999a, b) and Fox (1999) propose a tripartite division of risk sociology into realist, weak constructionist, and strong constructionist perspectives based on underlying differences concerning the ontology of risk. Because this consideration of risk has important implications for researchers' engagement with morality, I will provide a brief description of each perspective.

Soft Realism: Some Risks Are Real

I identify those who take a realist position on risk as 'risk society' theorists, after Ulrich Beck's work of the same name. These theorists argue that many of the risks individuals—and humanity as a whole—face in Modernity are real and fundamentally different from risks in previous eras. Beck (1992) argues that the proliferation of risks in modern society indicates a shift from a society focused on industrial production to a society focused on risk minimization. Humanity should be concerned about risks because, "in advanced modernity the social production of wealth is systematically accompanied by the social production of risks" (ibid:19). The technology that we create to solve one problem creates a whole host of others so that "in the risk society individuals are waiting for the latest technological development to catch up with the negative consequences of the previous innovation" (Denney 2005:30). The risk society is forced to cope with hazards that threaten humanity globally (nuclear war, pollution, ecological disaster, etc.), the precise risk of which is impossible to calculate scientifically. Individuals must come to terms with these threats even though they, as individuals, can do little to minimize them. At the same time, the proliferation of mass media stokes the anxiety that increased risk awareness brings (Giddens 1991; see also Wilkinson 2001 for in-depth discussion of anxiety in a risk society).

The entire process of risk production is placed against a backdrop such that "new risks [are] part and parcel of modernization itself" (Zinn 2008:22) and spring from both the technological and the social realm. While modernization may bring risk of ecological collapse, it also threatens the social in the form of changing gender and work relations. As structural conditions of modernization support women's move into the workforce, more traditional members of society see a threat to the institution of the family. This reflexive modernization "means self-confrontation with the effects of risk society that cannot be dealt with and assimilated in the system of industrial society—as measured by the latter's institutionalized standards" (Beck 1994:6).

In the Modern era, individuals' lives will not match institutionalized norms; they must construct their own biographies with no institutionalized reference point. Science itself faces constant revisions that leave individuals adrift and uncertain, in a state of ontological anxiety and existential dread (Giddens 1991). Science is supposed to have the answers; yet, to lay individuals, scientists seem in a perpetual state of disagreement about the important risks of our time—from the likely impact of global warming to whether and how often women should receive mammogram screenings for breast cancer. This allows science to "become part of social conflicts itself...[since] it is no longer science alone which determines the validity of knowledge" (Zinn 2008:28–29). With the onset of the risk society, knowledge production institutions are in a double bind: unable to offer the certainty they provided in industrial society, they are simultaneously responsible for the production of even more risks. The individualization endemic to modernity is a defense mechanism, "a default outcome of a *failure* of expert systems to manage risks" (Van Loon 2002:32). [1]

Strong Constructionism

Strong constructionist perspectives tend to view risk as a proxy for moral discourse. At the root of this perspective is a deep skepticism of the value neutrality of instrumental rationality.

---

[1] More recently, Beck (1999) has softened his stance on the realism of risks, incorporating a form of weak constructionism into the risk society thesis and acknowledging the permanent state of tension between risk and its perception (Zinn 2008:25).

Weber (1949) claimed that science is fundamentally incapable of answering the important moral questions of what we should do or how we should live—as Hume might put it, one can't derive an 'ought' from an 'is.' The strong constructionists, on the other hand, might argue that behind the 'is' lies an implicit 'ought.' In this perspective, it is not only risk assessments that are implicated morally, but also the statistical techniques that generate those risk assessments. For example, Hacking (1990) argues that in the nineteenth century, statistical techniques replaced the concept of 'human nature' with that of the 'normal,' thus redefining deviance as failure to adhere to a statistical norm. Where weak constructionism may accept the ontological reality of some hazards, strong forms of constructionism challenge this position going as far as to argue that "risk perceptions fabricate hazards...it is only in the analysis of *risks* that the *hazard* comes into existence: if the risk is assessed as zero or close to zero, the inert object would remain just that..." (Fox 1999:19–20).

Governance plays an important role in strong constructionist theorizing about morality and risk. Foucault introduced the concept of governmentality as a corrective to the lack of agency in his earlier theorizing about discipline. It consists of techniques that States, social institutions, and individuals can utilize to various ends. He divided these techniques into

> technologies of power, which determine the conduct of Individuals and submit them to certain ends or domination... [in addition] technologies of the self, which permit individuals to Effect by their own means, or with the help of others... operations on their own bodies and souls, thoughts, conduct, and way of being, so as to transform themselves in order to Attain a certain state of happiness, purity, wisdom, perfection, or immortality (Foucault 2003:146)

Drawing on the Foucauldian concept of "governmentality," risk can be viewed as "a technique; a way of governing conduct of individuals, collectivities, and populations" (Dean 1999). This standpoint implicates risk in a regime of social control that occurs as an outcome—whether intended or not—of institutional and individual use of risk rationality: "governmentality focuses attention on the diverse ways in which we may govern the conduct of others and ourselves" (O'Malley 2008:54).

Weak Constructionism

Though 'risk society' theorists focus on the production of new objective risks in modernity, 'weak constructionist' theorists focus instead on the ways certain risks and not others become culturally salient, the influence of institutional structure on risk perception, and the symbolic narratives that accompany risk discourses. Cultural anthropologist Mary Douglas identified taboos concerning dirt, cleanliness, and hybrids of all types as serving a boundary-policing function (Douglas 2002). Whether certain foods or practices reflected a preoccupation with a "real" risk is irrelevant; Douglas is concerned with how threats to purity are threats to the very community itself. In particular, organizational culture creates a lens through which risks are sorted: some are deemed worthy of attention, others disregarded (Douglas 1992). This perspective has the advantage of providing a structural alternative to realist theories that situate risk perception within individuals, as social context influences perceptions of risks and the response to dangers posed by risk (Douglas 1985). Because "risk serves a particular function within the community at a particular time [. . .] risk cannot be isolated from the moral, aesthetic and political foundations of a community" (Denney 2005:24).

Scientific risk assessments often aid in social control of particular groups by labeling them as particularly implicated with respect to risk. This may mean that they are "at risk from" some hazard and require the paternalistic protection of the State: "thus, well-labeled, natural vulnerabilities point to certain classes of people as likely victims; their state of being 'at risk' justifies bringing them under social control" (Douglas 1985:57) in the eyes of the State. On the other hand, they may pose a "risk to" another group or population and be subject to social controls accordingly. This does not mean, however, that there is no objective element of risk. Hazards—the underlying dangers—may be real, but risk, Douglas argues, is the spotlight that focuses on different hazards in turn. Weak constructionism asks to what end and for what purpose do groups choose to focus on a particular hazard in a given time and location. Because "hazards are natural [and] risks are cultural" (Fox 1999:17), culturally salient risks may or may not be genuine. What is important is how organizations, associations, and cultures differ in their perception of various risks and in their likely response to them.

MORAL PROJECTS

Most sociological understandings of the relationship between morality and risk recognize that "identification of a threat or danger, and of adverse consequences, is based on judgments about 'goodness' and 'badness' and distinctions between right and wrong" (Ericson and Doyle 2003a:2). Links can be drawn between each of the risk perspectives discussed above and a particular moral project (see Table 25.1). A 'moral project,' suggests implicit aspects of morality within each perspective that provide a means of linking different moral dimensions to risk. The concept of responsibility, for example, enables both strong constructionists and realists to theorize intersections between morality and risk. While moral projects are not mutually exclusive—for instance, strong constructionists sometimes talk about risk creating moral boundaries—the table represents a general schema that implicates morality in different ontological risk positions.

Individualized and Social Responsibility

The 'risk society' perspective permits an examination of individualized and social responsibility within the framework of modernization. Unlike the strong constructionist perspective, which analyzes creation of new norms of responsibility, Beck's primary engagement with responsibility is in terms of justice. Beck prescribes social responsibility, in particular,

TABLE 25.1. Moral Projects of Three Risk Perspectives

Risk perspective	Moral project
Risk society (soft realism)	Individualized responsibility; social responsibility
Strong constructionist/foucauldian	Responsibilization; self-regulation of risk
Weak constructionist/cultural-symbolic	Boundary construction/"othering"

for coping with the challenges of a risk society. This sets his approach in contrast to the two-constructionist perspectives, which are largely descriptive with respect to morality. Considering Beck's subject matter, the topic of climate change is particularly apropos to a discussion of his work. Risk society-based research questions about the climate change debate might include: How do media and other risk communication institutions encourage or discourage social responsibility for the risks of climate change? What role did discourses of organized irresponsibility play in the negotiations between rich and poor countries at Copenhagen? How have climate change challengers used sub-politics to get their voices heard while facing increasing opposition?

Beck (1992) and Giddens (1991) are somewhat at odds on whether risk becomes a proxy for morality in the risk society or replaces it altogether. Giddens (1991) argues that in high modernity, morality has evaporated, "for moral principles run counter to the concept of risk and to the mobilizing of dynamics of control" (p. 145). Because Giddens envisions morality providing social cohesion and guidance to traditionally organized societies, he associates it with a form of social organization that is disappearing in the face of reflexive modernization. Beck, on the other hand, contradicts this view of morality's relation to risk: "Determinations of risk thus oddly straddle the distinction between objective and value dimensions. They do not assert moral standards openly, but in the form of a quantitative, theoretical and causal implicit morality [sic]…Statements on risk are the moral statements of scientized society" (Beck 1992:176).[2]

On its own, risk society's engagement with morality often has a prescriptive quality. Humanity faces challenges in the form of globalization and individualization—the result of processes of reflexive modernization. The simultaneous emergence of globalized hazards and the process of individualization—i.e. "the disembedding and…re-embedding of industrial society ways of life by new ones, in which the individuals must produce, stage and cobble together their biographies themselves" (Beck 1994:13)—creates a political action problem. Individuals must find ways to cope with collective threats to humanity while contending with traditional institutions that may not be up to the task. The issues of accountability and justice that inevitably arise in the risk society force counterpoised ethical narratives of individualized and social responsibility to emerge. The structural changes accompanying modernization contribute to the development of individualized responsibility; at the same time, agentic responses to the threat of ecological catastrophe may help create a new politics of social responsibility. The process of individualization itself does not result in "atomization, isolation, loneliness, the end of all kinds of society, or unconnectedness" (ibid:13), but rather a fully institutionalized individualism (Zinn 2008) that is interwoven into the labor market, welfare state, family, and medicine. The individual is still implicated in a multiplicity of institutions, but in a new way that elides the import of structural changes even as those self-same changes affect the individual in a more pronounced way. Individualized responsibility comes about in two ways.

---

[2] In highlighting risk assessments as proxies for moral discourse, Beck opens the door to more constructivist approaches to studying the risk society. Consequently, some research shows willingness to position the risk society as an umbrella under which cultural and discursive interpretations of risk can operate. Even so, scholars who wish to explore moral dimensions of risk while preserving the risk society narrative must borrow heavily from sociocultural or postmodernist paradigms to bridge the gap between risk society's grand narrative and the lived embodied experience of risk by diverse individuals (Tulloch and Lupton 2003).

First, old dividing lines like gender and social class become less salient in the risk society. The individual has new responsibility for choices that he/she would once have had structured for him/her. Second, as risk society constantly produces new risks, societal definitions of what it means to be a prudent person shift. As an example, with the advent of gene technology, the concept of health—and along with it, what it means to be responsible for that health—will expand, creating new opportunities for individuals to show themselves conscientious and responsible (Beck-Gernsheim 2000).

Lash (1994) identifies the ethical component of risk society theory in Beck's concept of "organized irresponsibility"—a situation where "the coalition of business firms, policy-makers and experts who create the dangers of contemporary society then construct a set of discourses of disavowal of such responsibility" (p. 201). The ethical project of the risk society becomes how to ensure responsibility in the face of the failure of industrial society's institutions to cope with risk society threats and the organized irresponsibility they engender. Beck (2000) remains optimistic, holding out hope that more responsive democracy—through sub-politics, social movements and the like—will act as a remedy to self-destructive technocracy: "*the door of the iron cage of modernity is opening up*. . .there is a utopia built into risk society and risk society theory—the utopia of a *responsible* modernity. . ."(p. 222 emphasis original).

Beck's risk society theory has few advantages for a sociology of morality, but some serious drawbacks. Beck has articulated a theory that recognizes risk as unavoidable in modernity. Whether the risks are real or not, there is mass awareness of risks due to media, the scientific establishment, and other risk communication networks; risks—and fear of them—have become more salient in the lives of the everyday citizen (Furedi 2002). At the same time, the limitations of this perspective come through in Beck's preference for a grand narrative approach to risk that minimizes cultural differences in risk perceptions (Lash 2000) along with the importance of ascribed characteristics in risk selection (Tulloch and Lupton 2003). As it stands, his realist stance towards risk leads him to a prescriptive—rather than analytical—engagement with morality. As a result, Beck fails to empirically investigate social responsibility with respect to risk; rather, he advocates it as a solution for making risks—temporarily—more manageable.

Strong Constructionism: Responsibilization and Self-Regulation

The strong constructionist perspective enables researchers to investigate how risk techniques generate new norms, and how individuals adapt their behavior to conform to these norms. In particular, it provides insight into how risk techniques contribute to an evolving concept of responsibility. To return to the example at the beginning of this chapter, a strong constructionist perspective on global warming suggests several broad research questions: Has statistical climate modeling changed the way individuals conceptualize the environment and their relationship to it? If so, how have understandings of the climate 'at risk' helped to define a concept of moral conduct towards the environment? How does adoption of neo-liberal philosophies on risk shape individuals' understanding of themselves as moral actors with respect to the environment? To answer these questions, a strong constructionist might use a genealogical approach that traces historical changes in both the scientific and nonprofessional's conception of nature to display the concurrent evolution of notions of responsibility to the environment.

Strong constructionists blend the concepts of morality and risk in ways useful for research into the sociology of morality; but there are also serious drawbacks to adopting this perspective. The main benefit comes from an analytical standpoint that locates norm-production and the creation of deviance in techniques or procedures rather than in goal-oriented actors. It enables researchers to examine how the moral ideals of society can be created and expanded, not through the heavy-handed designs of church leaders, a ruling class, or political parties; but, more subtly, through the very mechanisms that produce our understandings of risk. At the same time, however, this perspective proves a double-edged sword for the sociologist of morality as the radical constructionism that provides a novel way of understanding risk tends toward an impoverished appreciation of morality.

Strong constructionism assumes that individuals are morally responsible for managing risk; the ways subjects do this involves self-construction as moral actors. This emphasis tends to take two forms. Governmentality perspectives focus on how various social institutions produce norms of responsibility through the use of quantitative expert techniques. 'Everyday life' perspectives, on the other hand, show that experts are not the sole disseminators of moralized risk discourse; street signs, administrative regulations, and the like encourage responsibility as well. Governmentality perspectives view the current neo-liberal paradigm as enabling social institutions to enforce certain moralities through proxies of efficiency, choice, and responsibility (O'Malley 1996, 2008, Hunt 2003). They see Western society in particular as increasingly judging moral worthiness—not on the basis of avoiding sin per se or adherence to religious law—but, instead, by an individual's acceptance and self-maintenance of risk governance. It is incumbent upon individuals to inform themselves and make rational decisions about risks. Ericson et al. (2000) note the five dimensions of neo-liberalism that support this outcome, including (1) a minimal State that (2) emphasizes the free market and (3) encourages risk-taking, while stressing the importance of (4) individual responsibility and the duty to accept (5) inequality as an outcome of poor risk-management strategies or choices on the part of individuals.[3] Governmentality theorists argue that insurance risk is a useful technique to encourage the responsibility and ethical self-governance that is of particular importance to the neo-liberal political paradigm. While an individual benefits through the security provided by holding insurance, actuarial logic also has governing effects on behavior, constituting certain activities as relatively safe and discouraging others as risky and deviant. In this way, insurance can act as a soft form of social control on policyholders—insurers discourage irresponsibility through higher rates or ejection from the insurance pool rather than through incarceration or other traditional means of State sanctioning:

- ...The net effect is that much of the work of governing is displaced
- from political systems where legislation is debated to administrative

---

[3] There is a direct link here between 'responsibilization' and the work of Max Weber (1958), who conceived of responsibility as a duty to a calling, the fulfillment of which became "the highest form which the moral activity of the individual could assume" (p. 80). While religion may have been the engine for Protestant acceptance of the responsibility ethic, rationalization stripped away the religion leaving only the ethic—"The Puritan wanted to work in a calling; we are forced to do so" (p. 181). This ethic is enshrined within the political philosophy of neo-liberalism. No longer is "the unequal distribution of the goods of this world...a special dispensation of Divine Providence" (p. 177); instead, it is the result of individuals' poor risk-management practices. God may be out of the picture, but responsibility remains through the instrumental rationality of risk techniques.

- ones where regulations are issued by insurer fiat. . .By using
- actuarial techniques to predict and compensate for accidents and
- other statistically deviant behavior, insurers reduce the social costs
- of non-normative behavior. By facilitating adaptation to risk,
- actuarial techniques make the punishment, control, or reshaping of
- abnormal or unacceptable behavior less necessary (Heimer 2003:284–285).[4]

While acknowledging the positive outcomes of the development of actuarial risk, strong constructionists argue for a view of insurance as a technique of governmentality because it is "the practice of a type of rationality potentially capable of transforming the life of individuals and that of a population" (Ewald 1991:2000), a true biopolitics (Foucault 1984a). In some measure, insurance gains its status as a governmental technique through the individual accepting the calculative logic involved in the imposition of a small burden in order to relieve the possibility of a larger, future burden:

- Insurance is a moral technology. To calculate a risk is to master time,
- to discipline the future. . .Above all, it means. . .transforming one's
- relationships with nature, the world and God so that, even in misfortune,
- one retains responsibility for one's affairs by possessing the means to
- repair its effects (Ewald 1991:207).

To accept responsibility means to accept a form of moral governance that makes it incumbent upon the individual to sacrifice resources of his/her own in order to transfer the monetary burden of accident, sickness, or happenstance to the collective social body. Not to participate in insuring against potential misfortune when it is possible to do so and when most fellow citizens are insured becomes a moral failing, a failure of responsibility.

The rejection of those deemed uninsurable by the actuarial tables can be laid at the feet of pure statistics; insurance logic would seem to deny discrimination on the basis of a moral standard. Yet, "in assessing who are 'normal people' for inclusion in an insurance risk pool, and who should be de-selected and unpooled, insurance technologies create morally based social distinctions, hierarchies, and exclusions" (Ericson and Doyle 2003b:319). Moreover, the exclusion of bad drivers from the insurance pool (or their inclusion at astronomical rates) is understood within the neo-liberal paradigm as the result of the irresponsibility of the drivers themselves, and not the result of the norm-production of insurance logic. "Through such techniques as the exclusion of the immoral and the surveillance of the behavior of those allowed into the insurance pool" (Baker 2000:566), responsible risk-takers are rewarded through inclusion in the collective and partially protected against the future irresponsibility of their fellows.

States, institutions, and others encourage the acceptance of responsibility through many channels, and can govern through other means than the rationalizing techniques of actuarial

---

[4] Examining insurance this way requires that the researcher look at the outcomes of actuarial risk production and not necessarily the goals of particular insurance providers. Insurers certainly do not set out to become enforcers of public morality. At the same time both insurers and the State benefit from these governance techniques through reduced economic and social costs.

tables. Hunt (2003) argues that risk discourses are not moralized solely through expert techniques utilizing specialized forms of knowledge. Everyday life provides myriad opportunities to moralize risk discourses. Some scholars using the governmentality perspective for its analytics of risk (Moore and Valverde 2000, Hunt 2003) critique it for too narrowly defining techniques of governance, suggesting instead that hybrids of morality narratives and scientific data may work together to entwine morality discourses with risk discourses. This enables both expert and lay understandings of risk to co-exist without privileging the one over the other. Theoretically, "the most striking feature of the hybridization of morals and risks is the creation of an apparently benign form of moralization in which the boundary between objective hazards and normative judgments becomes blurred" (Hunt 2003:167). Moore and Valverde (2000) found the risk discourse surrounding so-called 'date-rape drugs,' to be "a hybrid space of governance, in which not always exaggerated medical and social information about risks circulates alongside many other bits of texts, from feminist advice on sexual assault to lurid tales of sexual risk" (p. 522). In this case, scientific risk discourses intertwine with moral narratives of gendered responsibility. Another example focuses on how the medical establishment sees pregnant women as a clinical risk; this differs from an actuarial risk in that the medical techniques used to govern them "implement population based calculations, forming risk groups by applying risk categories to the bodies of persons who are then placed under continuing surveillance or treatment" (Weir 1996:382). On one hand, compliance with these surveillance measures—keeping pre-natal appointments, submitting to ultrasounds and other procedures—identifies the mother-to-be as a moral subject, likely to prove a fit parent. At the same time, doctors warn women that the medical procedures themselves may place the fetus at risk—forcing pregnant women to engage in cost-benefit analysis as "a woman may now be held personally accountable for her baby's disability if she decides not to undergo the tests" (Lupton 1999b:69). In this damned-if-you-do, damned-if-you-don't situation, "any possible outcome can be seen as a consequence of [a pregnant woman's] decision" (Samerski 2007:68). Ultimately, individuals must weigh options on their own; in keeping with the neoliberal paradigm, it is no longer acceptable to be merely a passive recipient of expert advice (Lupton 1999b).

The two main problems with this perspective for a sociology of morality center on agency and resistance and how the perspective defines morality. The relationship between morality and risk is a close one, but perhaps not as close as governmentality theorists might have it. A view where risk techniques are the agents of norm creation—where morality is implicit in the methods—can lead to a 'technique determinism' that ignores the role of institutional actors, politicians, and others in norm creation [see Heimer (2003)]. Because of this, the potential for resistance is undertheorized. Just how effective are these risk techniques at governing behavior? Who is more or less likely to be successfully governed? What are some of the ways people may constitute themselves morally as counter to these technique-created norms?

Finally, because unlike risk, morality itself is not clearly defined, strong constructionist accounts focus on the connections between risk and morality in terms of harm, safety, and the responsibility to avoid harmful or dangerous outcomes. The Foucauldian world of morality is presented as "a world of disenchantment, with no hint of the sacred. . ." (Miller 2002:63). A more comprehensive approach that takes account of the role of emotion in generating moral discourse might find other aspects of morality—for example, reciprocity, hierarchy, and purity (Haidt and Joseph 2004)—implicated in risk discourse.

Boundary Construction and "Othering"

The cultural-symbolic perspective highlights the role of boundary construction and 'Othering' for the maintenance of community solidarity. The creation of a community of any sort requires some means of demarcating who is part of the in-group and who is excluded. These borders may be more or less permeable depending on the organizational culture of the group, but maintenance of group solidarity requires the policing of symbolic boundaries between 'us' and 'them.' Groups, organizations, and individuals will often frame moral discourses about outsiders in terms of risk in order to maintain group purity and avoid pollution by 'Others.' Returning once again to the global warming debate, several research questions in the cultural-symbolic vein suggest themselves: Does the organizational culture of climate change activists affect the type of moral discourse employed against climate change challengers? How do climate change challengers use moral discourse to portray climate change activists as risks to the social collective? What cultural codes and narratives do activists and their challengers draw upon to frame the risks of global warming—or lack thereof—in moral terms?

Cultural-symbolic perspectives have their genesis in the writings of Durkheim, who influenced Mary Douglas's work on boundary construction through his conception of social solidarity as the wellspring of moral life. Cultural narratives and codes provide frameworks of meaning that individuals, groups, and nations refer back to when engaged in moral boundary work. These frameworks often divide objects, people, or practices into binary categories of 'sacred' or 'profane' (Alexander 2003), reflecting Douglas's (2002) understanding of purity as an aspect of morality necessary to community cohesion. Issues of purity become particularly salient when a community is attempting to define itself against an outside group. Anything that weakens a group boundary is likely to be coded as 'risky,' a threat to group purity. Likewise, societies are likely to code anything that cannot be easily classified, or that slips between categories, as 'risky.' Threats to purity thus become threats to the social order.

Pregnant women pose a particular challenge to the community. Lupton (1999b) observes the 'grotesque' aspect of the pregnant body that makes its prior penetration visible and creates an uncomfortable slippage between self and other. The permeable borders of the pregnant body may lead to extreme attempts to control it, as it proves difficult to classify and thus a pollution threat to the collective social body (Douglas 2002, Hacking 2003). Naturally, some pregnant bodies are seen as more of a threat to the collective than others are. Media portrayals have presented women of color as a larger threat by depicting them as unable to regulate their behavior so as not to bring harm to their fetuses. For these women, judges often deemed the informal 'advice and admonitions' mentioned in the previous section insufficient and, instead, sentenced them to incarceration until they delivered their babies. Racialization, itself, can be seen as "a strategy of boundary maintenance, and risk signifies the dangers of boundary violations" (Van Loon 2002). When risk is racialized, sorting processes can occur making it more likely for minority women to come under state surveillance. White women—by virtue of their skin color and use of private hospitals—bypassed the medical-moral surveillance net consisting of urine tests and hospital social workers. Moralized risk discourses about the effects of cocaine on babies and their future burden on the nation coded poor black women as irresponsible, reckless, and in need of supervision, helping to construct and maintain boundaries around race and class.

Moral discourses also combine with risk discourse to preserve the boundaries of the nation-state. Much like the pregnant body, the discursive border—and often the physical border—around the nation-body is permeable and governments and citizens often desire to tightly control what is allowed in. Alexander (2003) argues that the discourse of American civil society maps actors, relationships, and institutions onto a binary discursive structure consisting of a democratic and counter democratic code. Acceptance into the civil society means a discursive association with elements of the democratic code, which requires that individuals portray themselves as rational, autonomous, and controlled; that they engage in relationships that are open, trusting, and straightforward; and that equality, rule of law, and inclusion characterize the institutions they create. Groups desiring inclusion in civil society must align themselves discursively with the positive qualities of the American democratic code that democratic actors, relationships, and institutions exemplify. American atheists are one example of a group marginalized in this way. Edgell et al. (2006) observed that intervie-wees "used the atheist as a symbolic figure to represent their fears about trends in American life—increasing criminality, rampant self-interest, an unaccountable elite—that they believe undermine trust and a common sense of purpose" (p. 228).

Anxieties over community purity frequently manifest themselves in other moral terms. Nations that pride themselves on their commitment to fairness and justice must sometimes defend their symbolic boundaries from challengers who invoke these moral dimensions, as Mackey (1999) found in her study of the fight in Australia over aboriginal land rights. She notes, "Debates about danger, risk, and native title. . .articulate deep-seated and long-contested conflicts about the history, present and future of the nation, and the kinds of normative values the nation should hold" (p. 112). In these debates, aborigines—by demanding land rights—challenged the Australian state's public commitment to equality and justice for all people. The Australian state pushed back, "Otherizing" the aborigines by rejecting their values as important to the future of the nation. Instead, by "constructing the nation and the nation-building project as 'at risk' and 'endangered' by Aboriginal people" (p. 127), the Australian government was able to assure the continuance of policies that create structural inequalities and privilege the white majority.

Moral discourses that re-inscribe symbolic national boundaries can influence a nation's willingness to expose itself to a particular level of risk. Hacking (2003) argues that Canada's universal health insurance system serves a symbolic purpose, allowing Canadians to retain a clear sense of national identity—and superiority—with respect to the USA due to their shoul-dering of this burden for the common good. In this case, an understanding of a risk shared among fellow citizens for the sake of greater security creates such a sense of national solidar-ity that for the USA to devise a universal care system could threaten the way Canadians see themselves as a nation (p.35). Similarly, Hacking argues that legalized handgun possession in the USA will continue perpetually because handguns, despite any empirical risk or danger they might pose "are symbols of purity, of origin, of identity, of what preserves the border against transgression at all costs" (p. 40).

Benefits of the cultural-symbolic perspective include a soft constructionism that pro-vides greater latitude for research questions, recognition of the role emotion plays in morality, and opportunities for investigation into varieties of moral discourse. The weak constructionist viewpoint on risk allows for studies that privilege the role of risk perception in maintaining community cohesion. This focus highlights structure in the selection of risks that individuals, groups, or institutions emphasize without negating the agency of the perceiver. Agnosticism with respect to risk takes the focus off of whether a risk is real or not; enabling comparative studies on boundary construction that seek to answer why groups focus on particular threats in certain historical contexts. More importantly, the cultural-symbolic perspective accentuates a direct link between morality and risk in the role that emotions play in both. Durkheim (2008) coined the term 'collective effervescence' to describe the raw outpouring of emotion associated with group religious experiences that reinforce the bonds of the community. Clearly, social solidarity is not produced in an emotional vacuum.[5] Because of this, we should not see boundary construction and "Othering" as rational activities undertaken by disinterested actors; rather, they are moral projects that involve extensive emotional engagement. There is support for this focus on emotions in the research of some cognitive psychologists who have stressed the importance of emotions in moral judgments. Haidt (2003) isolates a set of 'other-condemning emotions'—contempt, anger, and disgust— which he associates with a boundary-maintenance function. An attempt to elicit these emotions usually accompanies efforts to "otherize" groups, nations, or individuals. Border policing is an end; often groups do not address the concept of borders or purity directly in their discourse. Instead, as Mackey (1999) shows, they may use emotional language that calls into question the fairness or commitment to justice of other parties. In other cases like the 'crack baby' panic, legislators, judges, and the media use discourses of harm, responsibility and burden to justify heavier monitoring of poor, urban black women that help maintain their marginalization. Ultimately, social life provides many discursive options for moralizing risk. The limitations of the cultural-symbolic perspective stem from its various treatments of the relationship between social structure and culture.[6] Nevertheless, a weak constructionist/cultural-symbolic perspective on risk offers the most maneuverability for scholars interested in the intersections of morality and risk, while an appreciation of the affective dimension enriches our understanding of morality.

CONCLUSION: MORAL DIMENSIONS OF DISCOURSES ABOUT RISK

This chapter highlighted the benefits and limitations of three perspectives on risk ontology for a sociological understanding of morality. Ultimately, the most useful approach is what I term the 'weak constructionist/cultural-symbolic' orientation. First, weak constructionism's agnosticism about risk ontology allows researchers to sidestep the question of which risks are real. This broadens the possible intersections between morality and risk. A realist stance tends to shift the focus from morality as a phenomenon to be investigated with respect to a particular risk onto prescriptive remedies for coping with the risk itself, turning what could be a sociological examination of morality into something more closely resembling public policy.

---

[5] Alexander (2003) notes the absence of this affective element in the Foucauldian emphasis on technique, which he criticizes as reducing discourse to "dry modes of technical communication" (p. 20). Certainly, the affective dimension plays a large role in the dissemination of risk discourse, which can stoke fear and anxiety in a population (Furedi 2002).

[6] Alexander and Smith (1996) critique Douglas and Wildavsky's (1982) approach for a cultural determinism that aligns culture too closely with social structure. By conflating institutional culture with organizational structure, their analysis of environmentalism's appeal to the masses not involved with formalized environmental groups falls short. However, radically unhooking culture from social structure (see Alexander 2003) creates problems of its own in terms of how the symbol-sets and narratives that constitute culture are created.

Likewise, a strong constructionist stance on risk also causes problems, leading to theorizations of norm-creating techniques that fail to account for the importance of actors and values in creating shared understandings of morality. Second, the cultural-symbolic approach foregrounds the role of emotions in moral attitudes and processes of risk selection. This is in contrast to the primacy of rationalized governance techniques in the strong constructionist perspective, and the rationality of the actor who makes cognitive judgments about risks in the realist perspective. Third, the cultural-symbolic approaches provide the broadest appreciation of different dimensions of morality and how they may contribute to boundary maintenance. Whereas governmentality and risk society theories examine morality in terms of responsibility, harm, and—for risk society theory—justice, the cultural-symbolic perspective incorporates an additional focus on purity. Cultural-symbolic perspectives have a final advantage in the way they can easily combine with the other two perspectives to theorize purity and self-governance (Lupton 1999b) and grant a more cultural understanding of the risk society (Lash 2000, Tulloch and Lupton 2003).

Morality and risk intersect at boundaries and borders of all kinds, in techniques of governance, and in the discourse of cultural narratives and codes. There is still a great need for further research into these intersections and new ones. This chapter—and indeed, much research—explore morality in the context of risk avoidance. How might morality intersect differently with risk when individuals, groups, or nations embrace risk? How do moral discourses differ? Finally, the concept of risk incorporates an element of uncertainty. A given danger may or may not manifest. How can we incorporate an understanding of uncertainty into sociological investigations of morality? Future cultural-symbolic research on morality and risk should attempt a sociological theorization of moral uncertainty that can take us beyond binaries of good/evil and sacred/profane.

REFERENCES

Abend, G. 2008. "Two Main Problems in the Sociology of Morality." *Theory and Society* 37(2):87–125.
Alexander, J. 2003. *The Meanings of Social Life: A Cultural Sociology.* New York: Oxford University Press.
Alexander, J., and P. Smith. 1996. "Social Science and Salvation: Risk Society as Mythic Discourse." *Zeitschrift fur Soziologie* Aug:251–262.
Baker, T. 2000. "Insuring Morality." *Economy and Society* 29 (4):559–577.
Beck, U. 1992. *Risk Society: Towards a New Modernity.* London: Sage Publications.
Beck, U. 1994. "The Reinvention of Politics: Towards a Theory of Reflexive Modernization." In *Reflexive Modernization: Politics, Tradition and Aesthetics in the Modern Social Order,* edited by U. Beck, A. Giddens, and S. Lash. Stanford, CA: Stanford University Press.
Beck, U. 1999. *World Risk Society.* Malden, MA: Polity.
Beck, U. 2000. "Risk Society Revisited: Theory, Politics and Research Programmes." PP. 211–229 in *The Risk Society and Beyond: Critical Issues for Social Theory,* edited by B. Adam, U. Beck, and J. Van Loon. London: Sage Publications.
Beck-Gernsheim, E. 2000. "Health and Responsibility: From Social Change to Technological Change and Vice Versa." PP. 122–135 in *The Risk Society and Beyond: Critical Issues for Social Theory,* edited by B. Adam, U. Beck, and J. Van Loon. London: Sage Publications.
Dean, M. 1999. *Governmentality: Power and Rule in Modern Society.* London: Sage Publications.
Denney, D. 2005. *Risk and Society.* London: Sage Publications.
Douglas, M. 1985. *Risk Acceptability According to the Social Sciences.* New York: Russell Sage Foundation.
Douglas, M. 1992. *Risk and Blame.* London: Routledge.
Douglas, M. 2002. *Purity and Danger.* New York: Routledge.

Douglas, M., and A. Wildavsky. 1982. *Risk and Culture: An Essay on the Selection of Environmental and Technical Dangers*. Berkeley, CA: University of California Press.

Durkheim, E. 2008. *The Elementary Forms of the Religious Life*. New York: Oxford University Press.

Edgell, P., J. Gerteis, and D. Hartmann. 2006. "Atheists as 'Other:' Moral Boundaries and Cultural Membership in American Society." *American Sociological Review* 71 (2):211–234.

Ericson, R., D. Barry, and A. Doyle. 2000. "The Moral Hazards of Neo-Liberalism: Lessons From the Private Insurance Industry." *Economy and Society* 29(4):532–558.

Ericson, R. V., and A. Doyle. 2003a. "Risk and Morality." PP. 1–11 in *Risk and Morality*, edited by R. Ericson, and A. Doyle. Buffalo: University of Toronto Press.

Ericson, R. V., and A. Doyle. 2003b. "The Moral Risks of Private Justice: The Case of Insurance Fraud." PP. 317–364 in *Risk and Morality*, edited by R. Ericson, and A. Doyle. Buffalo: University of Toronto Press.

Ewald, F. 1991. "Insurance and Risk." PP. 197–210 in *The Foucault Effect: Studies in Governmentality*, edited by G. Burchell, C. Gordon, and P. Miller. Chicago: University of Chicago Press.

Foucault, M. 1984a. "Right of Death and Power over Life." in *The Foucault Reader*, edited by P. Rabinow. New York: Pantheon Books.

Foucault, M. 2003. "Technologies of the Self." PP. 145–169 in *The Essential Foucault: Selections from the Essential Works of Foucault 1954–1984*, edited by P. Rabinow, and N. Rose. New York: The New Press.

Fox, N. 1999. "Postmodern Reflections on 'Risk,' 'Hazards,' and Life Choices." PP. 12–33 in *Risk and Sociocultural Theory: New Directions and Perspectives*, edited by D. Lupton. New York: Cambridge University Press.

Furedi, F. 2002. *Culture of Fear: Risk-taking and the Morality of Low Expectations*. New York: Continuum.

Garland, D. 2003. "The Rise of Risk." PP. 48–86 in *Risk and Morality*, edited by R. Ericson, and A. Doyle. Buffalo: University of Toronto Press.

Giddens, A. 1991. *Modernity and Self-Identity: Self and Society in the Late Modern Age*. Stanford, CA: Stanford University Press.

Hacking, I. 1990. *The Taming of Chance*. New York: Cambridge University Press.

Hacking, I. 2003. "Risk and Dirt." PP. 22–47 in *Risk and Morality*, edited by R. Ericson, and A. Doyle. Buffalo: University of Toronto Press.

Haidt, J. 2003. "The Moral Emotions." PP. 852–870 in *Handbook of Affective Sciences*, edited by R. J. Davidson, K. R. Scherer, and H. H. Goldsmith New York: Oxford University Press.

Haidt, J., and C. Joseph. 2004. "Intuitive Ethics: How Innately Prepared Intuitions Generate Culturally Variable Virtues." *Daedalus*: 55–66, Special issue on human nature.

Heimer, C. 2003. "Insurers as Moral Actors." PP. 284–316 in *Risk and Morality*, edited by R. Ericson, and A. Doyle. Buffalo: University of Toronto Press.

Hunt, A. 2003. "Risk and Moralization in Everyday Life." PP. 165–192 in *Risk and Morality*, edited by R. Ericson, and A. Doyle. Buffalo: University of Toronto Press.

Lash, S. 1994. "Expert Systems or Situated Interpretation? Culture and Institutions in Disorganized Capitalism." In *Reflexive Modernization: Politics, Tradition and Aesthetics in the Modern Social Order*, edited by U. Beck, A. Giddens, and S. Lash. Stanford, CA: Stanford University Press.

Lash, S. 2000. "Risk Culture." PP. 47–62 in *The Risk Society and Beyond: Critical Issues for Social Theory*, edited by B. Adam, U. Beck, and J. Van Loon. London: Sage Publications.

Lumborg, B. 2007. *Cool It: The Skeptical Environmentalist's Guide to Global Warming*. New York: Knopf.

Lupton, D. 1999a. *Risk*. New York: Routledge.

Lupton, D. 1999b. "Risk and the Ontology of Pregnant Embodiment." PP. 59–85 in *Risk and Sociocultural Theory: New Directions and Perspectives*, edited by D. Lupton. New York: Cambridge University Press.

Mackey, E. 1999. "Constructing an Endangered Nation: Risk, Race and Rationality in Australia's Native Title Debate." PP. 108–130 in *Risk and Sociocultural Theory: New Directions and Perspectives*, edited by D. Lupton. New York: Cambridge University Press.

Miller, W. W. 2002. "Morality and Ethics." PP. 55–68 in *Durkheim Today*, edited by W. S. F. Pickering. New York: Berghahn Books.

Moore, D., and M. Valverde. 2000. "Maidens at Risk: 'Date-Rape Drugs' and the Formation of Hybrid Risk Knowledges." *Economy and Society* 29(4):514–531.

O'Malley, P. 1996. "Risk and Responsibility." PP. 189–208 in *Foucault and Political Reason: Liberalism, Neo-Liberalism, and the Rationalities of Government*, edited by A. Barry, T. Osborne, and N. Rose. London: University College of London Press.

O'Malley, P. 2008. "Governmentality and Risk." In *Social Theories of Risk and Uncertainty: An Introduction*, edited by J. O. Zinn. Malden, MA: Blackwell.

Samerski, S. 2007. "The 'Decision Trap:' How Genetic Counselling Transforms Pregnant Women into Managers of Foetal Risk Profiles." PP. 55–74 in *Gendered Risks*, edited by K. Hannah-Moffat, and P. O'Malley. New York: Routledge.

Tulloch, J., and D. Lupton. 2003. *Risk and Everyday Life*. London: Sage Publications.

Van Loon, J. 2002. *Risk and Technological Culture: Towards a Sociology of Virulence*. New York: Routledge.

Weber, M. 1949. "Science as a Vocation" in *From Max Weber: Essays in Sociology*, edited by H. H. Gerth, and C. W. Mills. New York: Oxford University Press.

Weber, M. 1958. *The Protestant Ethic and the Spirit of Capitalism*. New York: Charles Scribner's Sons.

Weir, L. 1996. "Recent Developments in the Government of Pregnancy." *Economy and Society* 25 (3):372–392.

Wilkinson, I. 2001. *Anxiety in a Risk Society*. New York: Routledge.

Zinn, J. O. 2008. "Risk Society and Reflexive Modernization." In *Social Theories of Risk and Uncertainty: An Introduction*, edited by J. O. Zinn. Malden, MA: Blackwell.

CHAPTER 26

Moral Discourse in Economic Contexts

Rebekah P. Massengill and Amy Reynolds

The relationship between morals and markets has been a central question within sociology from the discipline's very beginnings. Weber's (1958) famous argument about the Protestant ethic, for example, asserts that moral ideals have material outcomes, and views the market system in part as an institutional outcome of a particular religious ideology. Throughout history, key moments of ideological change rarely occur without market restructuring. As Wuthnow (1989) argued in *Communities of Discourse*, major turning points in human history (specifically, the Reformation, the Enlightenment, and Marxist Socialism in Germany) shared the common feature of a restructuring market ideology, in that these periods of "exceptional cultural fervor" (559) reoriented the way market structures shaped (and were shaped by) society. In our own present history, recent financial crises and growing concerns over globalization have also prompted questions about the ethical sustainability of free market capitalism itself – further emphasizing the timeliness of sociologists' inquiries into the ways that individuals and institutions enact morality in their market accounts and behavior, along with the ways that moral ideals are captured in the rules and scripts found in market institutions.

Within the academy, sociologists have also begun to pay renewed attention to the moral dimensions of economic behavior. Fourcade and Healy's (2007) recent work exemplifies this interest in how moral contexts shape different evaluations of the market, its mechanisms, and its influences upon individuals and society. Economic sociology is particularly well-positioned to inform the emerging subfield of the sociology of morality because by its very definition, economic sociology represents an examination of the ways in which culture – including contextual definitions of what is right and wrong, desirable or undesirable – influences market transactions, both in the structure of market exchanges and the meanings that actors ascribe to them. Accordingly, we view economic sociology as one of the richest subfields in our discipline where concerns about morality garner increasing attention, even as many of these concerns remain at the margins of the subfield (Fourcade 2007).

In this chapter, we consider morality as expressed in economic contexts in three primary ways – the significance of moral discourse in constructing one's identity in relation to the workplace, in framing economic decisions and boundary crossings within the market, and in articulating the shared norms that undergird the larger structures and institutions of market systems. In the first two cases, we focus primarily on the language and narratives of individuals, while the third shifts our attention to the moral discourse produced by organizations and larger

S. Hitlin, S. Vaisey (eds.), *Handbook of the Sociology of Morality*,
Handbooks of Sociology and Social Research, DOI 10.1007/978-1-4419-6896-8_26,
© Springer Science+Business Media, LLC 2010

collectivities. Regardless of this distinction, our focus remains *moral discourse about market activities*, and thus we consider the larger significance of discourse analysis in understanding the ways in which morality "works" in society writ large. The analysis of discourse has long been central to cultural sociology because it offers a valuable tool for investigating the ways in which culture both informs and constrains the moral judgments that individuals (and indeed whole societies) bring to bear on different aspects of economic activity. Focusing on the ways that individuals and groups use moral language to describe market phenomena offers a unique perspective into both the larger cultural framework that informs economic exchange, as well as the strategic ways that individuals use those cultural resources to create moral order in market contexts.

Although a robust literature examines discourse about a host of morally contested social issues – such as abortion, school curricula, bioethics, and welfare (see for example Luker 1984, Binder 2002, Evans 2002, Steensland 2008) – analyses of similar discourse surrounding markets appears curiously underdeveloped by comparison. The terms in which both individuals and groups openly discuss moral dilemmas proves a critical measure of both the explicit reasons social actors give for their moral positions, while also hinting at some of the unconscious motivations for their behaviors. We distinguish moral discourse from moralistic discourse, which Jasper (1992) characterizes as occurring in settings in which actors invoke reference to the divine or to higher moral principles; we propose to consider moral discourse slightly differently and more expansively. For the purposes of this review in particular, we follow closely the definition offered by Wuthnow, which highlights "modes of reasoning and talking that define things as legitimate" according to a set of ideals and values about the way things ought to be (1996:52). Thus, we define moral discourse as language that proscribes conceptions of worth and value to particular people and activities based on an appeal to a larger conception of the good. We resist the temptation to view moral discourse as a strictly instrumental activity (e.g., a way to strengthen one's position relative to another's) but instead entertain the possibility that moral discourse actually speaks to more deeply held values, or commonly shared moral precepts in any given society. At the same time, we also acknowledge that both individuals and institutions can use morally-charged rhetoric to mask existing inequalities and expressions of power – evaluating the influence and function of this discourse remains an important focus in future research.

MORAL DISCOURSE

Language represents a critical means by which human beings contest different evaluations of the good – both in widely shared conventions and individual, contextualized applications of them. As Boltanski and Thevenot (1999, 2006) argue, collective conventions suggest strategies of justification that individuals may use strategically to ground their arguments in larger, shared conceptions of worth. Accordingly, we argue that examining moral discourse is a particularly important means of identifying both larger moral worldviews and codes, as well as suggesting important avenues for exploring how the culture "out there" (for example, the symbol systems, public talk and moral ideals that animate the social world) becomes the culture within – in other words, the moral schema and worldviews that take up residence in the minds of individuals themselves. Explicitly examining moral ideals as they are tied to market institutions reminds us that social norms are not "free floating bits of behavioral expectations governing self and others" but are rather "tied to larger moral orders in relation to which they make sense and carry influence" (Smith 2003:19–20). In like manner, Robin Wagner-Pacifici has elegantly defined discourse analysis as that which probes the relationships between "systems of symbolic representation (most notably speech) and the organizations and institutions of the social world through which such symbol systems flow" (1994:5). Given the market's preeminent role in structuring human relationships, ordering exchange, creating inequality, and fostering cross cultural interaction (to name only a few of its functions!), examining moral discourse in economic contexts promises an important contribution to the larger enterprise of creating a sociology of morality that takes seriously the relationship between institutions, social structures, and symbolic normative codes.

Discourse is particularly useful because it arguably embodies both levels of cognition that are presumed to be at work in human beings and their language: the "deep frames" or schemata that govern automatic cognition and moral beliefs about right and wrong, as well as more strategic, deliberative work that implies intentional negotiation (see DiMaggio 1997, Lakoff 2006, Vaisey 2009)[1]. Public talk is therefore significant because it not only potentially represents an imprint of the moral worldviews of a collection of individuals, but also because it becomes a reified creation that in turn structures and orders internal thought. Such a conception, while resonating with the work of cognitive science, also recalls older work in the sociology of knowledge that emphasizes this dialectic between individual and society (e.g., Berger and Luckman 1966). As sociologists work to reconcile the findings of cultural and cognitive sociology with those from the behavioral sciences (see Vaisey 2009 and DiMaggio 1997 for reviews), discourse analysis helps to illumine the contours of the collective moral order as it is reproduced in individuals. As Christian Smith has astutely observed, "precisely because human actors are constituted, developed, propelled, and guided by the social institutions in which their lives are embedded, the moral orders animating social institutions also find imperfectly corresponding expression *within* human actors – in the assumptions, ideas, values, beliefs, volitions, emotions, and so on of human subjectivity, conscience, consciousness, and self-consciousness" (2003:26–27). Moral discourse between individuals and the societies in which they are embedded are never entirely separate. We view language as a key link in this dialectic process between the individual and society – a premise we will return to at the conclusion of this chapter.

In the pages that follow, we explore what individuals, groups, and indeed whole societies say about one particular social institution: the marketplace. Following Friedland and Alford (1991), we argue that these three levels are in constant relationship with one another, and thus the discourse of each level is shaped in part by the others. Even though explicit analyses of

---

[1] The methodological range of economic and cultural sociologists attests to the importance of multiple levels of inquiry, ranging from the discourse of collective enterprises to the cognitive workings of individual social actors. We believe it is important to distinguish between the "levels of morality" described through these various means, and to articulate the unique value of these different approaches. Intentionally worded surveys can measure unconscious moral constructs (Vaisey 2009) interviews can illustrate "accounts" prepared for public display and evaluation (Wuthnow 1996), and legal norms and other collectively-produced public statements illustrate the commonly shared moral beliefs of any given society (e.g. Abend 2008). All of these approaches offer important findings about moral reasoning, including the ideas and strategies embraced by individuals (as evidenced by interviews), the shared moral schema that underlie their activities and attitudes (as in multivariable analysis), as well as the larger social constructs that speak to shared, even taken for granted moral norms (e.g. legal codes).

moral discourse in market contexts are rare, we argue in this chapter that a substantial body of empirical research can be understood in this light. By focusing on the prescriptive dimensions of what individuals and groups actually say about market activities, the beginnings of a field come into sharper focus. In particular, many qualitative or mixed-method studies can be properly understood as discursive investigations, as the actual language that actors use represents the central empirical corpus for the researchers' investigations. Thus, although many of the authors discussed in the subsequent pages might not necessarily identify themselves as scholars of moral discourse, their work suggests the beginnings of a field that represents a promising avenue for research both in economic sociology and in the sociology of morality more broadly.

We proceed by first discussing literature that considers the language of individuals in a variety of market settings. In particular, we focus on discourse that legitimates key aspects of individuals' identities in relation to the labor market and the workplace. A key finding in this body of work concerns the role of discourse in constructing symbolic boundaries between different categories of people depending on their relationships with different aspects of the labor market. In the second section, we consider the significance of discourse in categorizing economic transactions and legitimizing boundary transgressions – such as introducing previously "sacred" goods (such as human reproductive material) into the marketplace. In the chapter's final section, we consider the discourse of larger organizations and institutions, including public discourse about the market and capitalism. In the process, we explore how studies of moral economic discourse inform our knowledge about the different ways and means by which individuals interact with larger cultural systems: both those that are explicit, such as the legal order, as well as more implicit, such as ideas about barter and other forms of exchange. In this overview, we describe some of the ways in which economic sociology speaks to this relationship, including our own work on moral discourse about contentious economic issues, including debates over Wal-Mart and international trade policy.

MORAL DISCOURSE AT WORK

Most people spend a significant amount of time in interaction with formal market systems, such as the labor market and formal systems of exchange. Given the central role of the market in all aspects of social life, some scholars go so far as to question the very distinction between market and non-market settings (Fourcade and Healy 2007). Accordingly, market systems imbue many aspects of social life with moral order, particularly through the creation of moral boundaries and systems of categorization (Fourcade and Healy 2007). Just as larger processes of political deliberation draw discursive boundaries between the deserving and undeserving poor (e.g., Steensland 2008); other studies suggest that individuals practice this same kind of boundary work in their own interactions with market institutions, particularly the formal labor market.

Moral Boundaries and the Labor Market

Although Wuthnow (1996) finds that people often justify their work and financial decisions with economistic logic, respondents also use moral discourse to infuse their position in the economic order with a deeper meaning. In particular, people invoke such discourse in concert with their work-based experiences in order to construct a system of moral categorization. For instance, studies of the urban poor suggest that marginalized social groups create categorical distinctions [e.g., between "decent" and "street" (Anderson 1999)] that use individuals' relationships with different aspects of the labor market as a key mechanism for identifying moral boundaries. Accordingly, immigrants judge native-born blacks as "lazy" for their perceived underperformance in the labor market (Mahler 1995, Waters 1999) and even workers on the outer fringes of the formal labor market voice support for the American Dream and its accompanying ethic of individual effort as a source of moral worth (see, for example, Newman 1999, Young 2004, Wilson 1996).

This same body of qualitative work also considers the discontinuity between folk theories of "making it" and the reality of racial discrimination, deindustrialization, and residential segregation. Thus, Wilson (1996) notes that poor urban blacks verbally endorse the moral code of formal labor market activity even though they are not able to live up to it. In a similar vein, MacLeod (1995) finds that some of the black low-income youths he studies not only endorse the American Dream, but are slow to blame structural constraints (or the faulty Dream itself) when their hopeful aspirations are not met. Here, individuals' moral discourse affirms a larger code even as those who espouse it violate its precepts.

Other research shows that even those heavily involved in illegitimate activities still articulate a high regard for the classic pathways to mobility. Drug dealers, for example, explain that they must partake in illegal activity because avenues of formal labor organization are not available to them. As one of Wilson's respondents explains, "Me myself I have sold marijuana, I'm not a drug pusher, [. . .] I'm trying to keep bread on the table – I have two babies" (1996:58). Likewise, one of MacLeod's respondents – who initially sold crack to make ends meet – talks idealistically about getting out of the business: "I really don't wanna sell drugs to people . . . I don't wanna try to make people do bad. . . I don't wanna try to down no one or nothing. It's the only way I can make a living right now" (MacLeod 1995:210). Such discourse illustrates what Smith (2003) observes about moral codes writ large: shared morals may be identified by the extent of the rationalization offered by those who fail to embody them. Even when admitting to illegal activity, these respondents explain that they would like to make an honest living, but structural factors make this goal unattainable. In this case, the discourse serves at least two functions: it lends credence to the shared ethos of the American Dream (which may or may not be attainable in reality) and it justifies the speaker's departure from these norms. Thus, language is a place where speakers both submit to the power of a shared (and to some extent, hegemonic) ideology, but also challenge it with their own experiences.

Accordingly, most scholars of urban poverty take care to show how their poor urban respondents actually endorse the ideals of hard work and self-reliance; even as the media often presents them as intentionally defying these norms (see also Newman 1999, Young 2004). Dohan (2003) reaches similar conclusions in his study of two communities of Mexican immigrants, both of which must pursue illegal activity in order to achieve financial survival (undocumented work in one case and hustling in the other). Here, respondents' language suggests coherence around a larger moral code that judges it acceptable to break the law when institutional constraints make compliance impossible – even as they sanction each other for the particular illegal strategies chosen by each group (Dohan 2003). In such cases, moral discourse suggests boundaries between in groups and out groups (largely dualistic, as in "hard working migrants" and "law breaking residents") while also holding out a hypothetical ideal –

the self reliant, law abiding worker – that may not be an empirical reality. Thus, language becomes both a means of empowerment (i.e. "my group's survival strategies are morally superior") even as it permits and encourages factions among these dominated groups, who use categories to create distinctions between themselves and other groups who are similarly disadvantaged.

The urban poor are not unique in their affirmation of the labor market despite their alienation. For example, they have much in common with the poor, rural whites analyzed by Sherman (2009) along with the displaced middle class workers profiled by Newman (1988). Downwardly mobile managers also verbally affirm a market ideal that celebrates individual virtue and effort, and thus their experience of downsizing leads to feelings of shame and low self-worth. If market success means moral success, being laid off equal's moral failure. At the same time, displaced factory workers interviewed by Newman in the same study tend to fault larger groups – derelict managers, ethnic minorities – for their factory's downfall and their ensuing job loss. Comparing these two groups in Newman's study thus suggests that a key difference concerns each group's level of confidence in larger institutions: The more closely allied a group is to the legitimating institution of the labor market (as is the case with well educated white managers), the more their discourse of dislocation blames individualizing factors (one's age, interpersonal presentation, or moral worth) for their failure. This suggests the larger significance of the workplace as a site where such moral ideologies take shape, and where individuals learn to internalize and employ such moral rhetoric – in some cases, to their own detriment.

Moral Logics and Workplace Bureaucracy

Accordingly, classic studies of corporate bureaucracy, such as Robert Jackall's *Moral Mazes* (1988) and Rosabeth Moss Kanter's *Men and Women of the Corporation* (1977), reveal some of the ways that organizational membership shapes the moral worldviews of white-collar workers. Jackall, for example, concludes that the main morality present within the corporation is situational: managers are trained by the workplace code to do first what is best for the company (and thus what is often best for one's career) with little regard for the moral rectitude of the resultant outcome. In similar fashion, Kanter famously concluded that "organizations make their workers into who they are" (1977: 263), such that people without organizational power (e.g., women in positions of token recognition) acted in ways that majority groups had come to associate with gendered roles and negative stereotypes. Thus, the larger corporate system (and its distorted sex ratios) ultimately created an ideology that served to legitimize gender inequality as a perceived "natural" outcome of women's particular abilities and preferences.

The evolving corporate workplace – and its increasingly visible "family friendly" policies – creates new moral dilemmas for a different generation of corporate workers who seek to adjudicate between ideologies of work and moral codes regarding care of the family. Analyzing interviews with workers at the family friendly "Amerco", Hochschild (1997) similarly finds that workers of both sexes describe their difficulties (and frequently articulate internal emotional conflict) in making use of the organization's formal paternal leave policies. At the same time, parents who decline such opportunities experience less conflict and offer explanations for their behavior that emphasize workplace commitment and productivity (see Wuthnow 1996 for a similar finding). The internalization of such larger ideologies regarding the workplace (such as those that circumvent the explicit codes surrounding things like paternal leave) represents the ultimate triumph of bureaucracy: workplace-based scripts become the default language that respondents use to explain any deeper significance of their employment (Wuthnow 1996). As Wuthnow (1996) notes, the predictable language of the workplace makes it well placed to fill the gaps that emerge when individuals find themselves unsure of how to negotiate competing commitments, such as those between work and family. With constant reinforcement from settings of formal institutionalization, workers are quick to rely upon the moral discourses of hard work or commitment to one's job and career development when they are asked to consider their work as a place of moral significance.

Accordingly, some of the most interesting studies of economic discourse address the conflicts that occur when the moral code from one sphere (or institutional logic, e.g. Friedland and Alford 1991) conflicts with that of another. For example, Blair-Loy (2003; see also contribution in this volume) documents this tension among elite women professionals who try to carve out part-time positions that allow them to fulfill aspects of both the schemas of work and family devotion. These respondents report myriad problems in attempting to challenge the devotion to work schema as it is practiced in work organizations; one respondent reasoned that her clear devotion to her family (as evidenced by her "mommy track" hours) implicitly challenged her male coworkers' devotion to work: "My pushing the system implies that they have a choice as well. Their sacrifices are suddenly not prescribed to the same extent" (Blair-Loy 2003:105). In most cases, however, the merging of schemas remains an uneasy one: part time workers face ghettoization in the workplace (because they do not fully consent to its moral code of full submission to work) and they also encounter difficulty in being accepted in networks of stay at home mothers (Blair-Loy 2003). Living between two worlds, defying both moral schemas, proves a socially and cognitively difficult task.

Interestingly, Newman (1988) finds something similar in her study of displaced male managers – those who are married and carry family responsibilities (particularly the role of the breadwinner/provider) report more depression and feelings of inadequacy than the homosexual mangers she studied by comparison. She reasons that this spirit of dejection is less common among homosexuals because their social networks were more varied and they did not face the same breadwinner pressures as their married managerial counterparts. Although studying very different groups – highly successful women and downwardly mobile men – both Newman and Blair-Loy point to the difficulties that arise when the moral logics at work in the spheres of work and family do not easily coexist. It is difficult to determine the degree to which respondents use moral language instrumentally (e.g. reference larger ideals that justify the decisions they have already made) or are nudged by these larger moral codes towards certain decisions (e.g. leaving the workplace to be a caregiver for one's children). Moreover, these two outcomes may not be mutually exclusive; regardless, a common finding is that individuals seek coherence between their own moral schemas and those of others in their social network; in like manner, changing schemas requires finding other, likeminded companions who can validate one's evolving moral development (see Blair-Loy 2003:140).

CATEGORIZING ECONOMIC TRANSACTIONS

Not only does moral categorization help people to navigate their identity in relation to the workplace, but moral boundaries also define the appropriate transactions within the market, largely defined by the relationships between actors. For example, Zelizer's (2005) investigation of legal disputes and codes surrounding intimate financial transactions reveals how the nature of participants' relationships dictate whether or not they believe it is morally appropriate for money to change hands – married couples do not pay each other for the same sexual services offered by prostitutes, for example. Similarly, poor single mothers may demand that boyfriends "pay to stay" – e.g., by contributing money for food or diapers – even though they would not consider themselves prostitutes (Edin and Lien 1997, see also Zelizer 2005). Categorizing a worthy boyfriend as one who contributes to the household makes the difference between cohabitation and prostitution a clear moral boundary. Thus, the nature of relationships often determines what is allowed, or not allowed, to transpire between actors.

Narratives constitute a key means by which individuals construct such moral boundaries, and can provide meaning for spending decisions, especially those that may initially seem lacking in significance. Zelizer's (1994) work on pin money and women's financial decisions, for example, highlights how women mentally categorize money for different purposes. While women decide that money from a working spouse may only be spent on necessary (and morally valuable) products such as food or shelter, they also categorize money made through 'extra' work as a morally permissible source of spending for luxury items. Similarly, Miller's (1998) study of mundane shopping experiences (such as buying groceries) argues that shoppers construct moral meaning through their discussions of everyday shopping. Precisely because shoppers (who are mostly women) focus the bulk of their shopping on the needs of others, Miller observes that most shoppers allow themselves to purchase a morally sanctioned "treat" for their own enjoyment. The purchase is a "treat" because it is not a necessity; the purchase is moral because shoppers believe they have earned it through their hard work in caring for others. This allows shoppers to rationalize the frivolous acquisition even though it violates the conventions of thrift that shape most other purchases (Miller 1998).

The Household Economy

In addition to the meanings embedded in consumption decisions, gift activity also constitutes a significant part of actors' market transactions, particularly when money and goods change hands among family members—such as gift exchanges between husbands and wives, or children and parents. Family members rarely describe such transfers as payments, even when parties exchange goods and services. Much of Zelizer's work protests the idea that the family exists apart from economic life, arguing instead that exchanges among kin reveal the negotiated, economic nature of relationships – some of which are considered morally acceptable by actors, while others are not. While she notes the role of social relationships in determining the type of exchanges (see, for example, Zelizer 1994), she has also argued that the terminology describing such economic activity is similarly important. For example, in discussing California policies that propose to provide family care-givers with money for their actions, she notes that plans to "reimburse" families for care expenses are typically considered more acceptable than those that propose to "pay" people to care for a loved one (Zelizer 2005).

Discourse also reveals the tensions involved in intimate transactions. In her interviews with home child-care providers, Nelson (1990) discusses how her respondents describe the moral dilemmas that come with being paid to provide love for a child. Charging too much for those services can make the care appear less valuable or authentic – for example, one mother recounts that "It's more than a job for Nancy and she gives quality care; it's a warmth thing." (Nelson 1990:68). Here, care that is "warm" and desired is juxtaposed with care that is perceived as solely profit-driven. On the flipside of the relationship, providers themselves talk about how valuable, in monetary terms, the care they provide should be to parents – one provider asks, "How can she be so cheap with me?" (Nelson 1990:61) regarding a mother who does not pay the provider what she considers a fair wage. The two parties in this relationship make different moral evaluations of the money exchanged and its significance for the children's care.

Legitimizing Moral Disruptions

While the examples mentioned above highlight the way that moral discourse provides meaning and context to transactions within traditional (and non-traditional) markets, at times discourse also plays a crucial role in legitimating transactions that might otherwise be seen as illegitimate by the actors involved. Actors use discursive work to redefine and recategorize the transaction taking place. The narrative behind an item (or the narrative behind its exchange) may be essential for constructing the transaction as morally permissible, especially when individuals see such transactions as potentially blurring established moral boundaries.

In her analysis of the sale of reproductive material, for example, Almeling (2007) notes the important discursive work required to legitimate women's sale of their eggs. Because genetic material is not typically considered an economic commodity, agencies speak instead of the process as one of "donation" – even though donors are financially compensated for their contribution. Healy's (2004, 2006) work on organ donation similarly describes how such donations become legitimated. While donors do not trade for monetary gain, the very act of donating one's organs can be seen as an inappropriate use of one's body, crossing the boundaries of the sacred and the more secular realm (e.g., Douglas 1966). Were organ transfers defined as market transactions, recipients and families of deceased individuals would have participated in organ donation at lower rates: Healy (2004) thus finds that the organ procurement organizations worked to morally justify such organ transfers through their language, for example, in the stories publicized to bring attention to organ donation. Zelizer's (1979) work on the life insurance industry also reveals how the industry itself had to argue that life was not being bought and sold before life insurance gained any legitimacy (and was able to succeed as a business).

In a similar vein, studies of families provide a window into the discourse people use to legitimate transactions that blur traditional hierarchical gender relationships. This is particularly evident in the context of female migration, which challenges traditional patriarchy. Gamburd (2004) discusses the loss of dignity that many men face when their wives become the new breadwinners. While she and others (Bittman et al. 2003) have discussed some of the behavioral changes employed by both partners to cope with this new hierarchy, she also notes the public discourse often associated with such a change in position. In the small Sri Lankan town that Gamburd studies, women are often described in public talk (by men and women alike) as driven by profit and sexual appetite. Thus, women who want to earn money are viewed as suspect, and they must offer competing accounts for their migration desires and decisions.

This discourse of legitimation among women in the workforce has been noted by other scholars. One of the most interesting findings from Hochschild's (1990) study of two-career couples concerns the discourse of traditional couples whose household work she finds surprisingly egalitarian in actual practice. Here, both partners frame their equal domestic labor as an ironic expression of traditional gender stereotypes: e.g., the husband must help in the kitchen because the wife is a bit inept. Similarly, Nelson (1990) finds that among home day-care providers, both the women and their husbands often talk about childcare provision as domestic work that exalts traditional mothering, unlike the work of a "real job". Ammerman (1987) finds a comparable dynamic at work among a conservative Christian community, where women were often employed, but described their roles in largely traditional terms that espoused the non-working role of the mother. Here, as in other places, the discursive work invoked to legitimize the disruption in the social order suggests that a larger moral code has been transgressed in the eyes of the individual herself.

DISCOURSE, INSTITUTIONS, AND LARGER MARKET PROCESSES

In this final section, we turn from an examination of the ways that individuals use scripts to provide meaning and legitimation to their behaviors in the market, toward the discourse of organizations (which are often echoed by individuals) that both legitimates and challenges the current economic market structure. These tasks require deliberate culture work, and empirical research on these subjects relies heavily on scholars who are either traditionally involved in studies of social movements or in the sociology of culture and religion. Wuthnow's work (1987, 1989) has been instrumental in understanding how ideologies become institutionalized – and subsequently, an important part of the public discourse. The selection process among ideologies, and the institutionalization that must occur to establish them, highlights the energy and deliberative processes required for ideologies to not only be created, but to become part of a public discourse that is eventually reproduced in individuals.

Fourcade and Healy (2007) observe that while economists are typically presumed morally neutral in their research, the structures and practices embodied in current market systems are increasingly considered morally saturated. Wuthnow's (1989) study of capitalism throughout history has also suggested that a variety of cultural themes were articulated over time and connected to capitalism's vitality: theems such as individualism, rationalization, pluralism, discretion, and virtue. Accordingly, Best (2005) suggests that even those promoting a purely technical view of free-market systems, increasing amounts of moral arguments to address the international political economy, particularly concerning capitalism. Although it is hard to assess whether such moral language is providing legitimation or motivation for the practices of capitalism, what is clear is that moral claims receive increasing attention by agents championing the current system.

Organizational expenditures are similarly a subject of cultural legitimation and construction. Here, one can think about the discourse surrounding studies of corporate social responsibility, and the growing need for organizations to present a publicly acceptable narrative as part of their identity. Palazzo and Scherer (2006) describe the social legitimacy that businesses often gain in affirming key social norms, and argue those corporations' moral legitimacy results from public discourse and discussion. That is, moral actions alone do not create moral legitimacy: rather, it is the acknowledgement in the public sphere that a business is a moral actor that grants them moral legitimacy. These authors argue that in an era of increasing globalization, as concerns are voiced over widening economic gaps and the greed of the corporation, moral legitimacy becomes more important to the success of business actors, and as such, a "core source of societal acceptance" (78).

Legitimating moral discourse also receives attention from those studying larger social collectivities or religious groups and other moral communities. For example, Emerson and Smith (2000) examine the particular moral community of evangelicals in the USA and note how individualistic religious values translate into individualistic understandings about the market. In other words, those whose religious worldviews often center on individual relationships reflect those same values in their discourse about the market, which affirms individual agency and personal responsibility for one's own life. Likewise, in considering some of the impediments to community organizing, Wood (2002) shows how discourse focusing on individuals and their need for personal salvation can ultimately hinder some churches from participating in a movement whose discourse hinges on saving the community. Hart's (1994) work is perhaps most useful in this regard, as he explores people's use of religious ideas in their arguments about the economy. While he also draws attention to individualism and communitarianism (e.g., voluntarism and univeralism), he additionally highlights the importance of a "this-worldly" and "other-worldly" divide, which he argues is significant in shaping people's ideas about the moral economic order. Such values influence one's understanding about the ultimate goal of the market, as well as the role of the market in relationship to spiritual and non-earthly affairs. Discourses centered on redeeming the market, or living a good life within the market, can promote radically different economic behaviors, just as a focus on individual freedom has different consequences for individual action than a focus on equality of outcomes.

Within the field of economic sociology in particular, our own work speaks to the significance and richness of discourse analysis as a means of exploring moral values as they are expressed in public and shared among social groups. Massengill's analysis of the language of pro- and anti-Wal-Mart organizations uncovers key differences among each body of actors, in that pro-Wal-Mart speakers place the family at the center of their discourse, while those who are critical of the giant and controversial retailer frame their arguments with reference to the central category of the citizen. Prioritizing different categories of individuals reflects each groups' different conclusions about the merits and detriments of the discount superstore: focusing on families highlights the moral virtue of thrift, while Wal-Mart's detractors focus on the ways in which Wal-Mart threatens the rights of groups of citizens – in particular, women and African-Americans who have allegedly been disadvantaged by Wal-Mart's employment practices. This analysis thus points to moral strategies and ways of reasoning that may prove useful for further analysis of the motivating moral schema that may be present among individuals.

Nations have long been regarded in the academic literature as a source of shared moral values that enter the repertoires of actors. Anderson (1983) has discussed the importance of the nation state as a community, in part due to the shared understandings and ways of thinking about the state among its members. While not about economic contexts per se, Ferree (2003)'s work on the feminist movement demonstrates how economically relevant concepts – those of individual rights, for example - are utilized differently in social movements in different national contexts. The concept of individual rights, for example, has more resonance in the USA and is accordingly reflected in discourse over feminism. Understandings about what is moral in the economic realm are influenced in part by national values; an emphasis on individualism or the community, even when unspoken, underlie market constructions. In her cross-national comparison of religious organizations involved in political discourse on the economy, Reynolds shows how national values on human rights have led actors in Canada to concentrate on market outcomes in analyzing the market, while a focus on rationalism in the USA, by contrast, has made the mechanisms of markets a source of moral discussion.

WHERE SHOULD WE GO?

As suggested by this volume, the sociology of morality is at once experiencing resurgence while also developing anew as an area of interest for sociology. In considering the significance of moral discourse to this larger enterprise, we view this avenue of investigation as critical for a number of reasons, and conclude by suggesting several ways that this body of work could be further developed. First, discursive analyses shed light on the larger social context of moral reasoning that both shapes individuals' moods and motivations while also evidencing the conscious cultural work that human beings engage in to justify their decisions. Viewed in this way, discourse is a symbolic representation of what human beings believe to be desirable and acceptable in the larger context of a society's moral order. Alongside the question of motivation in cultural sociology – e.g. does what people *say* really explain what they *do* (Vaisey 2009) – discourse analysis can help to shed light on the larger social order that shapes cognitive schemas (e.g. Berger and Luckman 1966, Smith 2003) and thus, potentially their motivations as well. Discourse, particularly interviews and narratives, need not always be unconnected to action [or invoked retrospectively to explain one's actions (Vaisey 2009)], as demonstrated by analyses that argue that individuals either seek action that affirms their internal schemas (as elicited through their language) or create new schemas that accord with their decisions (e.g., Blair-Loy 2003, Wuthnow 1996).

Accordingly, discourse analysis demands close attention to the ways in which language is tied to concrete social locations and institutions (Wagner-Pacifici 1994) – something that Walder (2009) describes as currently lacking from the social movements enterprise in sociology.[2] This invites renewed attention to the significance of motivations as they are rooted in distinct social structures, such as families, workplaces, social classes, ethnic enclaves, and so on (Walder 2009; for a related discussion see also Smith 2003). Following from Wuthnow's (1989, 1994) attention to the way that organizations are central to producing moral ideologies, Reynolds' work looks at the moral discourse on the economy produced by religious actors, with attention to structural factors that impact political discourse. While she finds that the religious values of organizational actors are central in their political critiques, her work also suggests that a group's institutional strength in relation to the state and the strength of transnational networks influence the moral perspectives of actors regarding the economy.

Not only do organizations exist as actors who participate in moral discourse, but organizations also affect the discourse of individuals within those organizations. An important question

---

[2] The significance of "framing" analyses, for example could be significantly enhanced via careful attention to the ways in which different social groups are more likely to produce certain interpretations as well as find particular frames more resonant and compelling (Walder 2009).

for future research thus becomes how organizations and social contexts shape the modes of moral reasoning that are eventually articulated by individuals. Research investigating narratives and identity accordingly emphasize that one's institutional identity is an important part of the discourse employed by individuals as they make sense of their lives (Ammerman 2003, Somers 1994). Moral discourse describing how individuals conceive of and experience their place in the economic realm is certainly closely tied to those institutions – such as race, class, education, and gender – which influence both their experiences and understandings of market processes.

Accordingly, gender deserves special attention in economic contexts. As some have argued, economic discourse itself is thoroughly gendered; Bielby and Bielby (2003) have noted that even the economic categorization of effort and work by economists and others often starts with gendered assumptions about the commitment of mothers and fathers to their work. Zelizer's (2005) work on relationships within the household also reveals the way that gender matters as people make sense of economic transactions. We argue that more work should explicitly explore how gender pervades most all economic discourse, especially when actors may not specifically realize the gendered nature of their actions and language.

A related issue concerns discourse as it is tied to specific agents and audiences – specifically, who is producing the discourse and for whom it is being produced. In much of the literature we review here, the causal connections between language and actors' social positions remains somewhat unspecified – e.g. corporate workers espouse the moral language of the workplace, but the causal direction of this relationship cannot be fully determined. To be sure, Marxist notions of false consciousness persist, and much of this work notes that those with less economic power (such as poor urban youth) do tend to espouse beliefs that support the very market systems that may well disadvantage them (such as a belief in the American Dream and the power of individual effort). At the same time, we also note many studies of individual narratives that show how people use language instrumentally, particularly to justify their actions or decisions as economically moral. Such questions of agency and cultural production may matter less in qualitative studies analyzing interviews and narratives among individuals, but these issues should be central to analyses of social movement discourse and the public language of organizations and institutional actors (see also Walder 2009). This raises the question of moral power (see Mehta and Winship, this volume) and how that power is variable depending on social context, history, and group style (Eliasoph and Lichterman 2003). Such questions are ultimately important in understanding the distinction between discourse that is motivating, legitimating, or foundational (e.g., Jasper 1992). Discourse meant to rally those to a social movement may make far more instrumental use of moral terminology than the inner proceedings of a small church trying to act ethically in a particular local context – in some cases, organizational actors use moral language instrumentally to justify a particular economic position, while other situations prompt individuals and small groups to develop a language that accounts for their present reality.

In light of the power struggles that exist between competing groups and moral interests, we suggest further research that investigates the conflicts that occur when moral logics from one sphere conflict with those of another (e.g., Boltanski and Thevenot 1999, 2006). As Boltanski and Thevenot note, "it is precisely because persons, unlike things, can exist in a plurality of worlds that they always have the possibility of denouncing a situation as unjust" (1999:373). How do people negotiate, make peace, create hybrids, or ignore moral codes when social context requires them to engage in strategic negotiation? Accordingly, some key questions for the future concern the ability of other "moral logics" to counter the market-based scripts that many of our colleagues find dominant in workers' reasoning about workplace, and indeed many family issues as well (e.g., Wuthnow 1996, Newman 1999, Blair-Loy 2003, Hochschild 1997, Kanter 1977, Jackall 1988). Massengill's work on the moral rhetoric of anti-Wal-Mart activists suggests that one avenue for critiquing market processes actually involves using familial concepts and ways of reasoning, such as locating economic suffering in the experience of family disruption rather than the wrongdoing of distant corporations (see Boltanski and Thevenot 1999, 2006). Doing so not only activates personal and emotional points of connection among unconverted activists (Jackall and Hirota 2000), but also critiques the "greedy institution" of the market (Coser 1974; see also Blair-Loy 2003:19) by prioritizing the demands of another.

We also urge greater attention to questions about the settings in which moral discourse is most salient, and conversely the settings in which it fails to convince. Related to the questions of audience, institutional location, and moral power posed earlier, we note that just because moral perspectives animate decision-making or attitudes in one area does not necessarily mean that this influence will be transferable to other areas as well. Martin (2002), for example, has found in his analysis of communes that leaders in one area (for example, the religious realm) may not exercise authority in the decisions people make in the economic or political realm.

This leads us to conclude with some final observations about why discourse matters. In understanding the sociology of morality – and particularly as it is enacted in market settings – we argue that a variety of methodological approaches are useful, ranging from quantitative analysis of individual level variables to the analysis of moral discourse about economic issues. Yet one might make the objection that "talk is cheap" (as the saying goes), and sometimes talk is just that – talk. Social scientists cannot escape the burden of explaining why social phenomena really matter for action and for our understanding of societal processes more broadly. At a most basic level, we suggest that closer examination of moral discourse provides important findings about the larger structure of moral worldviews that characterize different social groups within society, and how those moral logics are anchored to specific places, groups, and institutions. Discourse can also create concrete, symbolic images that make it easier for people to imagine certain outcomes or decisions as morally acceptable (Gusfield 1981, see also Abend 2008), as the studies of the significance of survey question wording regarding abortion have made clear (e.g., Adamek 1994). Even discourse that seems to only create a symbolic order that bears little relationship to concrete reality should not be dismissed as inconsequential. As Wagner-Pacifici observes, "even here, the discourse is doing something – masquerading, fictionalizing the real actions of those in power" (1994:7). Analyzing moral discourse, then, points to some of the patterns of thought – both conscious and unconscious – that characterize society *sui generis*, and thus provides important findings for researchers examining the complex interplay between moral norms and social actors. Particularly in market settings – a sphere that many worry has become too powerful in both theory and practice – moral discourse imagines both ideas and strategies for challenging the existing social order, and thus represents a valuable tool for sociologists who are interested in understanding the complex workings of power, inequality, and resistance in modern society.

Acknowledgments The authors wish to thank Stephen Vaisey for his useful comments on an earlier version of this chapter.

REFERENCES

Abend, G. 2008. "Two Main Problems in the Sociology of Morality." *Theory and Society* 37: 87–125.

Adamek, R. J. 1994. "A Review: Public Opinion and Roe V. Wade: Measurement Difficulties." *The Public Opinion Quarterly* 58: 409–418.

Almeling, R. 2007. "Selling Genes, Selling Gender: Egg Agencies, Sperm Banks, and the Medical Market in Genetic Material." *American Sociological Review* 72: 319–340.

Ammerman, N. T. 1987. *Bible Believers: Fundamentalists in the Modern World.* New Brunswick: Rutgers University Press.

Ammerman, N. T. 2003. "Religious Identities and Religious Institutions." PP. 207–224 in *Handbook of the Sociology of Religion,* edited by M. Dillon. Cambridge: Cambridge University Press.

Anderson, B. 1983. *Imagined Communities: Reflections on the Origin and Spread of Nationalism.* London: Verso.

Anderson, E. 1999. *Code of the Street: Decency, Violence, and the Moral Life of the Inner City.* New York: W.W Norton.

Berger, P. L., and T. Luckmann. 1966. *The Social Construction of Reality : A Treatise in the Sociology of Knowledge.* Garden City, NY: Doubleday.

Best, J. 2005. *The Limits of Transparency: Ambiguity and the History of International Finance.* Ithaca: Cornel University Press.

Bielby, D. D., and W. T. Bielby. 2003. "Telling Stories about Gender and Effort: Social Science Narratives About Who Works Hard for the Money." PP. 193–217 *The New Economic Sociology: Developments in an Emerging Field,* edited by M. Guillen, R. Collins, P. England, and M. Meyer. New York: Russell Sage Foundation.

Binder, A. J. 2002. *Contentious Curricula: Afrocentrism and Creationism in American Public Schools.* Princeton: Princeton University Press.

Bittman, M., P. England, L. Sayer, N. Folbre, and G. Matheson. 2003. "When Does Gender Trump Money? Bargaining and Time in Household Work." *American Journal of Sociology* 109:186–214.

Blair-Loy, M. 2003. *Competing Devotions: Career and Family Among Women Executives.* Cambridge: Harvard University Press.

Boltanski, L., and L. Thevenot. 1999. "The Sociology of Critical Capacity." *European Journal of Social Theory* 2:359–377.

Boltanski, L., and L. Thevenot. 2006. *On Justification: Economies of Worth.* C. Porter, Translator. Princeton: Princeton University Press.

Coser, L. A. 1974. *Greedy Institutions; Patterns of Undivided Commitment.* New York: Free Press.

DiMaggio, P. 1997. "Culture and Cognition." *Annual Review of Sociology* 23:263–287.

Dohan, D. 2003. *The Price of Poverty: Money, Work, and Culture in the Mexican American Barrio.* Berkeley: University of California Press.

Douglas, M. 1966. *Purity and Danger: An Analysis of Concepts of Pollution and Taboo.* London: Routledge and K. Paul.

Edin, K., and L. Lein. 1997. *Making Ends Meet: How Single Mothers Survive Welfare and Low-Wage Work.* New York: Russell Sage Foundation.

Eliasoph, N., and P. Lichterman. 2003. "Culture in Interaction." *American Journal of Sociology* 108:735–794.

Emerson, M., and C. Smith. 2000. *Divided by Faith.* New York, Oxford University Press.

Evans, J. H. 2002. *Playing God?: Human Genetic Engineering and the Rationalization of Public Bioethical Debate.* Chicago: University of Chicago Press.

Ferree, M. M. 2003. "Resonance and Radicalism: Feminist Framing in the Abortion Debate in the United States and Germany." *American Journal of Sociology* 109:304–344.

Fourcade, M. 2007. "Theories of Markets and Theories of Society." *American Behavioral Scientist* 50:1015–1034.

Fourcade, M., and K. Healy. 2007. "Moral Views of Market Society." *Annual Review of Sociology* 33:285–311.

Friedland, R., and R. Alford. 1991. Bringing Society Back in: Symbols, Practices, and Institutional Contradictions. PP. 223–262 in *The New Institutionalism in Organizational Analysis,* edited by W. Powell, and P. DiMaggio. Chicago: University of Chicago Press.

Gamburd, M. 2004. "Breadwinner No More" PP. 190–206 in*Global Woman: Nannies, Maids, and Sex Workers in the New Economy,* edited by B. Ehrenreich, and A. R Hochschild. New York. Metropolitan Books.

Gusfield, J. R. 1981. *The Culture of Public Problems: Drinking-Driving and the Symbolic Order.* Chicago: University of Chicago Press.

Hart, S. 1994. *What Does the Lord Require? How American Christians Think About Economic Justice.* New York: Oxford University Press.

Healy, K. 2004. Sacred Markets and Secular Ritual in the Organ Transplant Industry. PP. 336–359 in *Sociology of the Economy,* edited by F. Dobbin. New York: Russell Sage.

Healy, K. 2006. *Last Best Gifts: Altruism and the Market for Human Blood and Organs.* Chicago: University of Chicago Press.

Hochschild, A. R. 1997. *The Time Bind : When Work Becomes Home and Home Becomes Work.* New York: Metropolitan Books.

Hochschild, A. R. 1990. *The Second Shift.* New York: Avon Books.

Jackall, R. 1988. *Moral Mazes: The World of Corporate Managers.* New York: Oxford University Press.

Jackall, R., and J. M. Hirota. 2000. *Image Makers: Advertising, Public Relations, and the Ethos of Advocacy.* Chicago: University of Chicago Press.

Jasper, J. 1992. "The Politics of Abstractions: Instrumental and Moralist Rhetorics in Public Debate." *Social Research* 59:315–344.

Kanter, R. M. 1977. *Men and Women of the Corporation.* New York: Basic Books.

Lakoff, G. 2006. *Thinking Points: Communicating OUR AMERICAN VALUES and Vision : A Progressive's Handbook.* New York: Farrar Straus and Giroux.

Luker, K. 1984. *Abortion and the Politics of Motherhood.* Berkeley: University of California Press.

MacLeod, J. 1995. *Ain't No Makin' It : Aspirations and Attainment in a Low-Income Neighborhood.* Boulder, Westview Press.

Mahler, S. J. 1995. *American Dreaming: Immigrant Life on the Margins.* Princeton: Princeton University Press.

Martin, J. L. 2002. "Power, Authority, and the Constraint of Belief Systems." *American Journal of Sociology* 107: 861–904.

Miller, D. 1998. *A Theory of Shopping.* Cambridge: Polity Press.

Nelson, M. K. 1990. *Negotiated Care : The Experience of Family Day Care Providers.* Philadelphia: Temple University Press.

Newman, K. 1988. *Falling from Grace: The Experience of Downward Mobility in the American Middle Class.* New York and London, Free Press and Collier Macmillan.

Newman, K. 1999. *No Shame in My Game : The Working Poor in the Inner City.* New York, Knopf and the Russell Sage Foundation.

Palazzo, G., and A. Scherer. 2006. "Corporate Legitimacy as Deliberation: A Communicative Framework." *Journal of Business Ethics* 66:71–88.

Sherman, J. 2009. *Those Who Work, Those Who Don't: Poverty , Morality, and Family in Rural America.* Minneapolis: University of Minnesota Press.

Smith, C. 2003. *Moral, Believing Animals: Human Personhood and Culture.* Oxford and New York: Oxford University Press.

Somers, M. R. 1994. "The Narrative Construction of Identity: A Relational and Network Approach." *Theory and Society* 23:605–649.

Steensland, B. 2008. *The Failed Welfare Revolution: America's Struggle Over Guaranteed Income Policy.* Princeton, Princeton University Press.

Vaisey, S. 2009. "Motivation and Justification: A Dual-Process Model of Culture in Action." *American Journal of Sociology* 114:1675–1715.

Wagner-Pacifici, R. E. 1994. *Discourse and Destruction: The City of Philadelphia Versus MOVE.* Chicago: University of Chicago Press.

Walder, A. 2009. "Political Sociology and Social Movements." *Annual Review of* Sociology 35:393–412.

Waters, M. C. 1999. *Black Identities : West Indian Immigrant Dreams and American Realities.* New York and Cambridge: Russell Sage Foundation and Harvard University Press.

Weber, M. 1958. *The Protestant Ethic and the Spirit of Capitalism.* New York: Scribner.

Wilson, W. J. 1996. *When Work Disappears: The World of the New Urban Poor.* New York, NY, Alfred A. Knopf: Distributed by Random House Inc.

Wood, R. 2002. *Faith in Action: Religion, Race, and Democratic Organizing in America.* Chicago: University of Chicago Press.

Wuthnow, R. 1987. *Meaning and Moral Order: Explorations in Cultural Analysis.* Berkeley: University of California Press.

Wuthnow, R. 1989. *Communities of Discourse: Ideology and Social Structure in the Reformation, the Enlightenment, and European socialism.* Cambridge: Harvard University Press.

Wuthnow, R. 1994. *Producing the Sacred: An Essay on Public Religion.* Urbana: University of Illinois Press.

Wuthnow, R. 1996. *Poor Richard's principle: Recovering the American Dream Through the Moral Dimension of Work, Business, and Money.* Princeton: Princeton University Press.

Young, A. A. 2004. *The Minds of Marginalized Black Men: Making Sense of Mobility, Opportunity, and Future Life Chances*. Princeton: Princeton University Press.

Zelizer, V. A. 1979. *Morals and Markets: the Development of Life Insurance in the United States*. New York: Columbia University Press.

Zelizer, V. A. 1994. *The Social Meaning of Money*. New York: BasicBooks.

Zelizer, V. A. 2005. *The Purchase of Intimacy*. Princeton: Princeton University Press.

CHAPTER 27

Morality in the Social Interactional and Discursive World of Everyday Life

Jason J. Turowetz and Douglas W. Maynard

INTRODUCTION

Recent advances in neurobiology, brain imaging, and evolutionary psychology have generated much debate and discussion about the nature of moral cognition. At the center of these crosscutting dialogues is a protean self whose moral sensibilities are being (re)-specified in terms of synaptic junctions (Le Doux 2002), evolved dispositions (De Waal 1995, Pinker 2008), and the exigencies of psychosocial environments (Zimbardo 2007). These various lines of research, though enlightening and provocative, are linked together by a common thread, namely, their conception of moral cognition as something that happens primarily in the cognitive space of people's heads. "Social cognition" is the name that social psychologists give to this perspective, which regards moral reasoning as occurring outside of, prior to, or alongside social interaction. This, in turn, points to a conception of mind that Ryle (1949:32) memorably dubbed, "the ghost in the machine." Mind and body are partitioned into two separate entities, with the former thinking, planning, desiring – in a word, having thoughts, and the latter executing, or doing, them. This dualistic position invites the inference that actions are caused by internal states of mind, leading to questions about where the causal mechanisms are located and how they operate.

The present essay examines scholarship in two closely related traditions, ethnomethodology (EM) and conversation analysis (CA), that take a markedly different approach to matters of moral cognition. Rather than locating morality or cognition more generally in people's heads, these lines of inquiry treat moral reasoning as a property of the embodied interactional practices by which members of society engage. A situation has intrinsic moral significance through the concerted actions by which its character is established, negotiated, and elaborated (Drew 1998). The EM/CA approach does not demand an outright rejection of cognitivist conceptions of morality, much less a commitment to any variant of behaviorism. It does, however, recommend an agnostic stance on the existence of a "mind" that has thoughts, moral or otherwise,

S. Hitlin, S. Vaisey (eds.), *Handbook of the Sociology of Morality*,
Handbooks of Sociology and Social Research, DOI 10.1007/978-1-4419-6896-8_27,
© Springer Science+Business Media, LLC 2010

and proposes to treat cognition as a phase or component of action, instead of its precursor (Maynard 2006:106, Heritage 1990–1991). In this respect, EM and CA display affinities with the progenitors of pragmatism (Mead 1934, Dewey 1896) and its contemporary revivalists (cf. Joas 1985, 1996, Emirbayer and Maynard, *forthcoming*), along with certain strains of phenomenology (Merleau-Ponty 1962), and ordinary language philosophy (Wittgenstein 1953, 1965, Anscombe 1957).

If the moral status of an action or matter is not given in advance it is, however, constituted through the understandings and orientations parties display, or can be taken to display, to one another in an interactional setting. Morality *in* interaction is to be distinguished from the morality *of* interaction, and concerns the rights and obligations accorded people by dint of their membership in the interaction order of society (Bergmann 1998, Maynard 1998, Goffman 1983) and adheres to what Schutz (1962) and Garfinkel (1967) call the attitude of daily life. The attitude of daily life involves a coproduction of features of social life through taken-for-granted, seen-but-unnoticed practices and methods which achieve the very intelligibility of our daily lives. We certify others and ourselves as competent, morally accountable members of society by selectively attending to unremarkable gestalts as assembled through our practices, by means of which we also produce the apparent naturalness of the social order. Deviations from this natural universe have a visceral effect on us, and occasion efforts to repair a breakdown of shared understandings. Further, this orientation, or "natural attitude" to a shared life-world (Schutz 1962:7–8) is something that members actively display for one another by artfully bringing their actions into line with social norms and rules, and rationalizing failure to do so through an appeal to behavioral accounts that others see as reasonable in light of local circumstances.

The moral order *of* interaction – what Bergmann (1998) calls "protomorality" – is the deep set of mutual assumptions and orientations by which members fashion moral claims and consequences at the surface level in talk and social interaction. Although these assumptions about what is normal and natural can be analyzed in the abstract (as in theoretical discussions regarding the attitude of daily life), their concrete manifestations are inseparable from the way they undergird the sequential, turn-by-turn contexts occasioned in and through speech and practical action. When we turn from the deep moral order *of* interaction to moral order *in* action, we find that people engage in practices to justify, impugn, excuse, praise, exemplify, exculpate, and otherwise account for and perform a wide variety principled actions.

The *collaborative* aspect of practices warrants remarking, as CA proposes that the moral sense of an utterance is fashioned as much by recipients as speakers. Consider a mundane instance in which A says to B, "He promised to take me to the movies and never called. He always does this." This utterance is designed as a complaint about some third party who broke a promise; further, the speaker, using the extreme case descriptor "always" (Pomerantz 1986) formulates this indiscretion as part of a pattern that ramifies to the offender's character. Whether this utterance actually gets *realized* as a complaint, however, depends on the way its recipient deals with it. Though B could treat it as a complaint by, for instance, aligning with the speaker (i.e., "that's awful"), B could just as easily orient to it as "just" news, using a receipt ("oh, really") that tends to discourage elaboration (Maynard 2003:Chapter 4; cf. Heritage 1984b). In the latter case, a complaint sequence is avoided in favor of a news delivery sequence, and one that foreshortens further topical talk. This move not only has consequences for the exchange at hand, but also the nature of the relationship between the parties that person-A projects in treating B as someone to whom s/he can complain about third-party transgressions (Drew 1998:Fn. 8). Extreme case formulations (Pomerantz 1986), complaining (Jefferson 1984), news-delivery-receipts (Maynard 2003), and morally implicative character-izations of third-party transgressors (Drew 1998) are so many generic devices and tools that members draw on to shape, and manage, issues of morality in a local exchange.

The present chapter will provide an overview of ethnomethodological and conversation analytic findings about the patterned, orderly ways in which people use such devices to accom-plish moral ends. We begin with a review of ethnomethodological studies that delineate how members constitute the social order as a moral order of everyday life (Garfinkel 1967). We then proceed to examine the closely related discipline of conversation analysis through a review of work on moral talk in institutional and non-institutional (everyday) settings. After explicating what we currently know about situated action, speech, and morality, we will then sketch pos-sible directions for future research, with a focus on the kinds of knowledge that would repay inquiry.

EARLY ETHNOMETHODOLOGY

The insight that the social order is a moral one is worked out in research conducted by eth-nomethodologists, conversation analysts, and cognate inquiries. As this body of research has been ably reviewed elsewhere (cf. Mehan and Wood 1975, Heritage 1984a, b, Maynard and Clayman 2003), we confine ourselves here to a succinct overview of some canonical texts concerned with the accomplishment of gender, the use of rules or codes as putative sources of orderly social relations, and the orientation of social actors to an obdurate world of everyday life.

Garfinkel (1967) famously documents the experiences of an inter-sexed person named "Agnes" as she attempts to procure a sex-change operation. Because she was born a male, Agnes had to learn how to be a female by observing and emulating the practices that "natural" women take for granted. As a practical methodologist, Agnes highlights how being female is an achievement, a "doing," rather than a natural fact. Being a woman entails engaging in the methodical practices through which members constitute themselves as female, and deviations from this line of activity arouse suspicion, consternation, and indignation. The force of the natural attitude toward womanhood is exhibited in Agnes's insistence that she really is, in essence, a female and that it was only through a cruel twist of fate that she wound up with male genitals. Agnes further exhibits her orientation to the naturalness of womanhood by roundly condemning cross-dressers, homosexuals, and other gender outlaws who engage in willful acts of deviance. In contrast to them, she is naturally female and has only to correct the mistake that encumbered her with male physiology.

Agnes's efforts to "pass" for female do much more than illustrate the contingent nature of gender identity. They also train a lens on the deep sense of *moral entitlement* that permeates the natural attitude. Regarding herself as someone who really is, in actual fact, female, Agnes feels entitled both to an operation and to be treated by others as a woman. She can only claim this prerogative, though, if she orients to others' entitlement to interact with a woman in their dealings. Any slip-ups would eviscerate her claim to participate rightfully in the collaborative give-and-take behind which female identity is taken for granted in everyday life. In other words, Agnes' efforts to pass are the very means by which she sustains a deep moral sense of self as well as surface prerogatives attached to her gendered self.

The case of Agnes reveals how the natural attitude is produced in and through the orderly, concerted actions of society's members. It also provides an example of how people actively bring their conduct into alignment with rules and norms, rather than passively internalizing them. Agnes does not simply orient to rules of social etiquette, but more or less skillfully uses them to design her actions in noticeably feminine ways.

In early ethnomethodology, the dynamic interplay of rules and practical action is poignantly expounded in Weider (1974) and Bittner (1967a, b). In *Language and Social Reality: The Case of Telling the Convict Code*, Weider (1974) offers an analysis of the day-to-day routines that he observed in a halfway house known for being progressive in its encouragement of cooperative, transparent relationships among staff and house-members. This agenda was consistently frustrated by the rules and norms of a convict code, which house-members used as an informal means of regulating the conduct of fellow borders. However, the code was less a formal set of rules than an interpretive device that could be deployed to perform any number of actions, from justifying one's own conduct to impugning that of another. In other words, rather than being a set of guidelines, boarders and staff invoked the code selectively as a resource for explaining why members behaved as they did. Participants did not passively follow rules, but actively used them to make their own behavior, and that of others, intelligible. In line with Wittgenstein (1965), Weider finds that an orientation to rules does not cause behavior. Instead, rules provide members with resources that they can use to fashion moral claims by ascribing motives to themselves and one another, motives that facilitate other actions such as avoiding friendly talk or "doing distance," giving good advice or sanctioning, justifying aberrant behavior, and the like.

Bittner (1967a) shows how police, like the convicts in the preceding example, make flexible use of laws to maintain the peace on skid row. Their orientation is to practical efficacy in the estimation of peers and community members, rather than strict enforcement of legal statutes per se. In fact, rigid application of legal statutes is considered poor craftsmanship, as it suggests that policemen lack the ability to size up a situation and handle it in a way that maintains social order. For example, in dealing with emergencies concerning mentally ill persons, police refuse to make *ad hoc* diagnoses of targets, preferring to orient to the situation as officers whose primary job is to ensure that persons do not pose a threat to themselves or others (Bittner 1967b). Bringing people to the hospital is a last resort that police go with when they have no other recourse, such as accompanying the individual to a safe place with persons who can watch over them. The extent of a person's illness, then, is not the primary basis for how they are dealt with as a practical matter. The law is used flexibly, and a strict interpretation of its letter is subordinate to practical tasks like keeping the peace.

We have distinguished between the deep morality of everyday life and surface morality concerned with its normative features. What a woman is entitled to do is a surface matter, while the claim of femaleness or womanhood is a deep assertion about one's self. How members use a code – whether in a halfway house, on the streets, or elsewhere – is a surface matter that enables sense-making and normative conduct, while the sense of the code's obdurate reality operates at a deeper level. The natural attitude presumes, at the deeper level, the existence of an objective world that exists apart from subjective perceptions of it. In his analysis of the mundane reasoning practices through which this shared sense of a real world known in common is enacted and sustained, Pollner (1987) delineates a set of "idealizations" to which actors continuously adhere. These include (a) object determinacy, which assumes that the parts and aspects of a given scene are partial elements of a larger totality, (b) object coherency, or the assumption that these pieces will come together in an intelligible whole that respects the constraint of (c) non-contradictoriness, such that the pieces are congruent with one another and the overall whole of which they are parts (Pollner 1987:Chapter 2). As constitutive preconditions for the existence of an objective world, these idealizations are perpetually hidden from the actors who employ them. Idealizations only become perceptible to actors when they are made problematic by a "crisis" of mundane reason, which occurs when contradictory accounts of a real-world event emerge. When this happens, mundane reason provides a solution, such as finding fault with the objectivity or perception of one or more participants in the crisis, so that the sense of an external and objectively knowable world is preserved (cf. Maynard and Clayman 1991).

CONVERSATION ANALYSIS

Conversation analysis derives from various sources, of which ethnomethodology is a prominent one. CA shares EM's commitment to distilling the practices through which the features of everyday and institutional life are achieved. In addition, however, conversation analysts look for robust, systematic patterns in data that can be generalized across local contexts (Maynard and Clayman 2003). In coupling careful examination of individual cases with cross-case comparisons of given phenomena, such as greetings or requests, conversation analysts ground generalizations about local phenomena in extensive collections of empirical records of interactional data. The devices used to produce these phenomena are at one and the same time context-independent, in that they transcend the exigencies of local interaction, and context-sensitive, such that they are adapted to the peculiarities of situated engagements (Sacks et al. 1974).

   CA's naturalistic observational method provides for detailed examination of the orderly, collaborative actions through which social phenomena are realized. As a largely unmotivated, bottom-up mode of inquiry, conversation analysis makes no *a priori* assumptions about which phenomena are worth studying, or what embodied details of talk-in-interaction contribute to their production (Sacks 1972). However, CA also embraces what Clayman and Gill (2004) refer to as "beginning with a vernacular action," such as making a request or doing an interview. In either case, analysts meticulously sort through raw and transcribed data with a view to specifying the patterned, sequential organization of talk-in-interaction, and the various social actions these sequences routinely accomplish. In the following paragraphs, we adumbrate the key features of conversation analysis as they relate to the subject matter of this chapter and volume.[1]

Moral Phenomena in Everyday Life

The very machinery through which conversational interaction occurs has normative features and implications (Heritage 1984a). Co-present conversationalists perform linguistic and

---

[1] For more detailed, in-depth treatments of conversation analysis, see Clayman and Gill (2004), Maynard (2003:Chapter 3), Hutchby and Wooffitt (1998), Sidnell (2010), Heritage (1984a:Chapter 8), and ten Have (1999).

paralinguistic actions by means of a turn-taking system (Sacks et al. 1974). This turn taking system, which orders and organizes both general and more restricted forms of speech
exchange, has a number of properties to which participants consistently orient: one person
speaks at a time, inter-turn gaps and interruptions are kept to a minimum, and parties are
expected to display an appreciation and understanding of immediately prior utterances by
attending to the actions they perform. A pervasive way of structuring utterances, which project
a limited range of conditionally relevant next actions, is through adjacency pairs. An adjacency
pair is a sequence of two adjacent utterances, ordered into first and second pair parts, where the
first is designed to elicit a particular type of response from the second (Schegloff and Sacks
1973). Common examples of adjacency pairs include question-answer, greeting-reciprocal,
and invitation-acceptance/declination. Production of a first pair part carries with it the expectation that an appropriate second is forthcoming. As such, both speakers and recipients treat
situations in which a projected response is absent, or observably insufficient, as specifically
accountable. Inadequate or absent accounts can be taken to constitute normative breaches and,
in this way, become the basis for morally implicative, indeed often negative, attributions. Thus,
an unreturned greeting may be interpreted as a snub, an unanswered question as being evasive.
By the same token, in cases where recipients provide acceptable reasons for their behavior,
accounts may furnish grounds for exculpation, forgiveness, and so forth.

Close examination of adjacency pair sequences has shown that first part utterances tend
to systematically "prefer" some second parts to others. For example, an invitation prefers an
acceptance as its second part and disprefers a rejection (Atkinson and Drew 1979) and an
assessment prefers agreement over disagreement (Pomerantz 1984). Preferencing also affects
first pair parts or initiating actions. For example, offers are preferred over requests, such that
speakers often approach a requesting action in ways that elicit an offer, and only make an
explicit request when such is not provided. It should be emphasized that preference does not
refer to a cognitive state in the minds of actors. A preferred second pair part is one that is
offered with minimal delay and few turn components. A preferred answer to the invitation,
"would you like to get a drink?" is often a simple and immediate "yes," or an acceptance token
coupled with a minimal turn constructional unit, like "yeah + sure." In contrast, dispreferred
second pair parts display markers including delays, prefaces, deferral of the response over
multiple turns, and accounts or explanations.

As constitutive elements of everyday interaction, turn taking, adjacency pairs, and preference structures shape, and are reflexively shaped by, numerous morally relevant activities. We
turn now to a consideration of three types of morally inflected action which pervade ordinary
social conduct. In a section following discussion of the three types, we explore systematic
ways in which these practices are adapted to institutional environments.

Agreeing and Disagreeing as Moral Phenomena

A particularly fecund, and consequential, site for the examination of morality in discourse
is that of making and handling assessments. Assessments are delicate objects in that they
provisionally commit the assessor to a particular stance on objects, persons, or events in the
social world, and place the recipient in the position of aligning with, disaffiliating from, or
bypassing the evaluative utterance. Further, assessment sequences involve epistemic displays

whereby participants claim their rights to make these assessments (Heritage 2002, Heritage and Raymond 2005).

In a now classic investigation, Pomerantz (1984) shows how recipients of assessments produce second-position responses. Disagreements in second position are typically of the form "Agree + Disagree," such that recipients voice weak, or qualified, agreement tokens before explicitly disagreeing with an initial assessment. One common way of prefacing disagreement is with contrastive conjunctions like, "that's true, but. . ." where the "but" clause does the work of parsing the turn into separate components. As Lerner (1996) notes, this parsing allows for projection of disagreement, so that the first speaker can intervene with a preemptive completion that provides for agreement after all. Consider the following example, in which Ron is asking his daughter, Cathy, why she would not get married if she found someone with whom she was compatible:

(Lerner 1996 :312) [Normalized Transcript; R=Ron, C=Cathy]

1) R: What would be good is to sit down here and tell-
2)   you tell me what is wrong if you find, like your
3)   mother says someone that you-
4) C: Nothing if you're sure,
5) R: Well honey (0.5 second's silence) in this world
6)   really truly,
7) C: you can't be sure   ← [anticipatory completion]
8) R: No, you really can't   ← [agreement]

In his utterance on line 5, Ron projects disagreement with Cathy by combining a "well" preface with an incipient account. Anticipating that the second part of his compound turn will be of the canonical form [preface + disagreement], Cathy interjects a candidate completion (line 7). Her candidate provides a rendition with which Ron can agree (line 8). In this way, Cathy's preemptive completion converts what would have been a dispreferred action (Ron disagreeing) into a preferred one (Ron agreeing).[2]

In addition to methods for converting incipient disagreement into agreement, speakers can gauge the likelihood of recipient disagreement before offering an assessment. One pervasive device for doing this is a perspective display sequence, which involves eliciting the position of a relevant other on some referent before venturing one's own (Maynard 1989). In its most basic form, the sequence has three components: opinion-query [first speaker], response-perspective display [second speaker], and assessment-report [first speaker, third position]:

(Maynard 1989 :92) [Normalized Transcript; square brackets indicate overlapping talk]

1) Rich: You like that sos- sosh class?
2)   (0.6 second's silence)
3) Mark: Yeah I dig it d'[you?]
4) Rich: [Yeah] it's pretty good.

---

[2] There are some actions where agreement is the *dis*preferred response. This can be seen in phenomena like self-deprecation, when proper receipt entails disagreeing with the initial assessment (Pomerantz 1984).

In this example, we see Rich eliciting Mark's assessment of a sociology class they are both (line 1) taking before offering his own assessment on line 4. When Mark offers a positive assessment of the class, Rich produces an affiliative evaluation in third position. Rich's second assessment, which comes in overlap with the tag question ("do you?") at the end of Mark's turn, "maximizes" agreement by minimizing the gap between assessments and explicitly agreeing with the previous utterance (Maynard 1989:92, Pomerantz 1984:64, Sacks 1987). Had Mark expressed a negative opinion on line 3, Rich could have contracted the sequence into two parts by moving to another topic. Alternatively, had Mark's answer been equivocal, Rich could have expanded the sequence by encouraging him to elaborate before venturing his own opinion.

As we noted earlier, alongside the matter of agreement per se, there are also the terms on which it occurs, and what these imply about the relationship between conversants. Assessments in first position imply that the first speaker has evaluative priority by dint of her proposing the initial assessment. However, second speakers can assert epistemic independence, which implies that their knowledge of the referent and, by extension, their assessment, is independent of the first speaker's. In the next example, Ilene suggests that one of Norman's dogs is starting to breed at a comparatively young age. After he informs her that the dog is a year old, Ilene evaluates the animal with respect to another of Norman's dogs, Trixie:

(Heritage and Raymond 2005 :26): [Normalized Transcript: I=Ilene, N=Norman]

```
 1) I: No well she's still a bit young though isn't she [I me]an
 2) N:                                                  [she ]
 3) I: uh[-
 4) N:    [She was a year last week.
 5) I: Ah yes. Oh well any time now [then.]
 6) N:                             [Uh  ] [m
 7) I:                                    [Yes
 8) N: But she['s
 9) I:         [Cuz Trixie started so early [didn't sh[e,      ←
10) N:                                     [Oh    [yes.   ←
11) I: Yeah
```

With a tag question positioned after her first assessment at line 9, Ilene displays a kind of downgrades epistemic stance. Heritage (1984b, 2002) has shown that an "oh"-preface is a systematic way for speakers to signal independent access to an object, and on line 10, Norman's oh-preface embodies a recollection of his own experience, on which he grounds his confirmation token, "yes." By formulating his assessment as independent of Ilene's, Norman asserts primary rights to assess his dogs (Heritage and Raymond 2005:26). Tag-questions and oh-prefacing both represent procedures speakers use to negotiate epistemic rights to assess in interaction (Heritage 2002, Heritage and Raymond 2005).

Blame Negotiation

Insofar as agreeing and disagreeing with assessments involve preference structures, devices for reconciling potential perspectival discrepancies and methods for asserting epistemic access and rights, assessment sequences are replete with moral overtones and implications. A more intuitively palpable feature of everyday moral conduct is blame negotiation. As with agreement and disagreement, conversation analysts have used a combination of naturalistic observation and detailed analysis of talk-in-interaction to discern a set of systematic, robust patterns in this domain of social conduct.

The allocation of blame is a thoroughly collaborative achievement. It involves ascribing responsibility for an event, or series of events, to a particular person or group. The work of ascription is tightly interwoven with that of description, for the materials used to formulate an account of blameworthy behavior, along with the motives, intentions, and markers of deliberateness that are enlisted to explain it, are forged in the reports people offer about the incident(s) under scrutiny. It follows that if we are to understand how blame negotiation occurs in real time, we need to examine the practices through which reports and descriptions are woven into morally consequential stories.

The basic sequence in which blame ascription develops has two parts (Pomerantz 1978). In the first, someone announces an "unhappy incident." The announcement routinely assumes the form of a stark, unelaborated "object-action" story fragment, such as "the car is broken." Noteworthy about this utterance, aside from its sparseness, is its lack of an actor-agent putatively involved in the event. This announcement occasions the second part of the sequence, in which a recipient may transform the lexical content of the statement from "object-action" to "subject–action–object," thereby attributing blame to an actor (Pomerantz 1978:119). The following example is illustrative of a more general pattern:

(Pomerantz 1978 :117)

1) A: It blew up   ←[unelaborated report]
2) R: Didju really?
3)   ((Brief pause))
4) R: Whadju do to it?   ←[attribution of responsibility]

As this example suggests, unelaborated reports of unhappy incidents routinely meet with immediate attributions of responsibility by co-participants.

If the default pattern in a blame sequence is "announcement-blaming," tailoring a report so as to avoid being blamed requires a measure of artfulness. Deliverers of bad news use a number of procedures to deflect, forestall, or obviate attributions of responsibility to themselves (Maynard 1998, 2003, Chapter 7). When announcing bad news, speakers regularly elide mention of their own agency, but do detail the background circumstances and setting of the event(s) so as to tacitly propose that they, along with the news recipient, are victims of situational factors. Recipients cooperate in this enterprise by attending to the unfortunate character of the situation. In the following excerpt, Charlie (C) is informing Ilene (I) that a planned trip to Syracuse and, consequently, her ride, is to be cancelled:

[Trip to Syracuse, Normalized Transcript]

1) C: I spoke to the gir- I spoke to Karen
2)   (0.4 second's silence)
3) C: And um it was really bad because she decided of   ←
4)   all weekends for this one to go away   ←
           .
           .
           .
5) C: Y'know I really don't have a place to stay   ←
6) I: .hh Oh

    7) (0.2 second's silence)
    8) I: so you're not gonna go up this weekend?
    9) (0.2 second's silence)
    10) C: Nuh I don't think so

Note that, in delivering his report, Charlie simultaneously accounts for why he and, by extension, Ilene, can't go to Syracuse ("I don't have a place to stay") and assigns blame to a third
party, "Karen" (*cf.* Maynard 1998 for a more detailed treatment of this example; *see also*
Drew 1984). In general, if and when bearers of bad tidings do assume responsibility for an
outcome, it is *after* the news has been delivered in an idiom which foregrounds situational
exigencies. We find an opposite pattern where the news in question is good, with deliverers
and recipients working to foreground the teller's personal agency (Maynard 1998, Pomerantz
1978).

It is not only in cases where blame for an outcome is a directly relevant action that speakers orient to inferences about responsibility that can be drawn from their reports. In rejecting
an invitation, for instance, people routinely assert an inability to do something, rather than
an unwillingness to do it (Drew 1984). Thus, objective, external circumstances beyond the
control of the invitee are commonly invoked to decline an invitation without explicitly stating
"no" or using another item of rejection. In reporting circumstances, the invitee is only officially responsible for conveying some bit of news to a co-participant; it is left to the inviter to
formulate the upshot of this description that the invitation is to be rejected (Drew 1984:137).
And by being the one to overtly formulate the other's report as a rejection, as Ilene does in
the preceding example (lines 25–27), the inviter comes to share in the responsibility for its
production (Drew 1984:130). As these cases suggest, morality, in the form of issues surrounding responsibility, comes to the fore in discourse when bad news, rejection of invitations, and
other everyday actions are underway. The pragmatic features of moral reasoning, then, are
deeply woven into the fabric of ordinary activities, rather than being independent or outside
of them.

Making and Managing Complaints

A third domain of ordinary moral conduct to which conversation analysts have turned their
attention is making and managing complaints. Complaints are dispreferred relative to apologies or other actions that preempt an actual complaint. Complaining is a particularly delicate
practice because every complaint can itself be complained about – that is, because every
complaint is accountable, the complainant runs the risk of being discredited and perceived
as a "complainer" should she be unable to provide sound reasons for her grievance (Sacks
1992:634–638). For this reason, complainants work to furnish, in the articulation of their
reports, persuasive grounds in support of their claims. As with blaming, these reports are
not neutral, but selectively keyed to particular dimensions of the situations they elaborate. Put
succinctly, "Complaints are constitutive features of the troubles they report" (Drew and Holt
1988:399).

In the next example, Leslie calls Robbie to discuss school and classroom decorum
because they are familiar with the same class of children at a local school. Robbie is their

regular teacher and Leslie has been a substitute. Robbie, although being the call recipient, initiates first topic by suggesting she was "thinking" about Leslie "today," and by launching a complaining utterance about the "lotta' children" in her class. As the conversation continues, she produces a further series of complaints about the staff, a particular teacher, the children as a group, and several individual children. Leslie shares and sympathizes with these complaints, although not completely. At a point well into the conversation, and just after talking about one child who "really worries" Robbie, the following takes place:

[Holt 5/88-1-5:11; Normalized Transcript; descriptions of audible sounds are in double parentheses]

1) R: Well and the other thing I was disgusted b- I'm sorry
2)   you're getting'n earful of this you couldn't have phoned
3)   at a better time heh he[h
4) L: [Oh that's alright,
5) R: Well the other thing I've found very strange is
6)   there weren't any dictionaries in the classroom
7) L: ((breathes [in))
8) R: [<u>Not</u> actua[l
9) L: [No children's di- eh well not many
10)   children's dictionarys, hh
11) R: Well, they have those little booklety things

Robbie, at line 1, starts to produce yet another complaint, stops, and apologizes, also suggesting (lines 2–3) that the timing of Leslie's call was propitious for herself. Leslie (line 4) accepts the apology and grants absolution (Robinson 2004), whereupon Robbie then continues with the complaint, although it is now slightly mitigated ("disgusted," line 1 becomes "very strange," line 5). As Schegloff (2005:465) has observed, apologies like Robbie's in lines 1–2 indicate an understanding that some piece of prior conduct can be complainable even though there has been no criticism of it. In this case, by taking the initiative to apologize, Robbie pre-empts possible protesting from Leslie about Robbie's complaining, and it permits the production of another in the series of complaining actions on her own part. The regularity with which participants may do such pre-empting of complaints is one indication of their dispreferred and morally suspect status in conversation.

As an accountable reporting of others' conduct, a complaint does implicit and explicit moral work. The implicit work suffuses one's own actions as innocent in relation to the situation at issue, as complainants routinely make efforts to portray themselves as unfortunate victims. The explicit moral work entails finding fault with others by formulating a normative standard that they have transgressed. Reports of these transgressions regularly contain expressions of moral indignation, which constitute bids for sympathetic affiliation from the complaint's recipient. Expressing indignation, often by means of reports about how the violation in question made one feel, is especially salient in cases where a sympathetic hearer cannot be taken for granted. Drew (1998) identifies a set of procedures by which complainants convey indignation through reconstructed versions of target events. First, speakers describe the background circumstances that led to the impropriety. Second, in so doing, they emphasize the deliberateness of the other's conduct. One way of doing this is with overdetermined descriptions of this conduct. For example, rather than say, "he drove the car," a complainant might assert, "<u>he took the car</u> and drove" (Drew 1998:318–319). The words "he took the car" do not add semantically to the utterance, though they do highlight the deliberate nature of the action. Third, complainants strengthen their claims by reporting what the other said, which has the effect of animating the offender's behavior in suggestive ways. For instance, in her complaint about a third party who insinuated she was cheap, Lesley animates the offensive features of his behavior through a combination of prosodic inflection and direct quotation: "he came up t'me n' he said Oh hhello Lesley, still trying to buy something f'nothing," (Drew 1998:319–320; underlines indicate prosodic emphasis).

Complainants tend to make use of "extreme case formulations" (Pomerantz 1986). These are maximal descriptors such as, "*completely* innocent," "out *all* day," and "it *always/never* happens" that strongly propose some moral violation in the face of potentially non-sympathetic recipients. And, when listeners do not offer expressions of sympathy at junctures where they have been made relevant, complainants recurrently use idioms, as when, speaking of hotel services, someone states, "the whole thing's gone to pot." These figurative expressions succeed generating displays of alignment and affiliation from co-participants. These displays, in turn, can close the topic on a note of mutuality and facilitate transition to a new one (Drew and Holt 1988:411, Sacks 1992).

MORAL PHENOMENA IN INSTITUTIONAL SETTINGS

In the interest of brevity, we focus on two areas in which a great deal of conversation analytic work has been conducted. Law and medicine are, in many ways, prototypical of the professions, and have long been topics of sociological interest. Conversation analysis begins from the ground up by looking at how members' practices systematically constitute and reproduce institutional contexts. Further, because they use findings from ordinary conversations as a baseline for comparison, they are able to see how generic devices for producing social actions are modified in organizational environments and adapted to the attainment of institutional aims.

MEDICINE

In this section, we examine three thematic facets of doctor-patient interaction: the doing and management of patient requests, formulating diagnoses, and clinically assessing patient competence in the form of cognitive testing. As our review will show, each of these phenomena is an interactional achievement produced through the concerted actions of doctor and patient.

Patient Requests

Making requests of doctors can be a morally delicate proposition for patients. This is especially so where the request concerns procedures, objects, and assessments over which the doctor has authority and discretion. Because contemporary medicine rests on an asymmetric relationship between doctor and patient (Parsons 1951) in which the former has primary access to a specialized body of knowledge and techniques, a patient's request can seem presumptuous or inapposite, intruding on and challenging the physician's medical expertise (Heath 1992,

Stivers 2002a, Gill 1998). The problems of epistemic entitlement pervading ordinary conversation are thus magnified in the medical environment, where rights to know and evaluate are institutionalized in distinct roles. In this context, requests are not *just* requests. Instead, they can be taken to indirectly propose something about the doctor-patient relationship that may contribute to or threaten its integrity. For this reason, patients work to formulate and perform requests in more or less subtle and tacit ways. Physicians display sensitivity to these practices in how they attend or *dis*attend to projected requests.

Gill (2005) closely documents a case involving a "tug of war" between a patient who wants a diagnostic test and a doctor who appears reluctant to affirm her request. Throughout, the patient applies increasing pressure by means of tactics used to request without officially or overtly requesting, while the physician persistently denies without officially or overtly denying. The interaction unfolds through multiple phases. We briefly review these here, as they provide propitious examples of the varied procedures available to doctor and patient for doing and managing requests.

The patient begins by launching a pre-request sequence,[3] requesting information about a particular blood test in a way that implies a candidate diagnosis without challenging the doctor's expertise or giving her outright grounds for refusal. Further, she cites another physician's actions to legitimate her query. Proposing candidate diagnoses and referencing second opinions are resources patients routinely use to advocate for treatment (Stivers 2002a, b; *see below*). The patient also phrases her inquiry with "yes-no interrogatives" (Raymond 2003) that, in projecting a narrow range of conditionally relevant responses, restrict her recipient's scope of available actions. Nevertheless, the doctor responds by treating the patient's interrogatives as asking for information, rather than requesting treatment. The patient then upgrades her inquiry, citing her previous doctor's concern about the symptoms she is reporting. When the physician simply provides further information about the test, the patient "praises the predecessor" (Maynard 1998), her previous doctor, noting how his ordering the test had assuaged her anxiety. This praise simultaneously proposes a model for how her current doctor should behave and *tacitly criticizes* the latter. Finally, the doctor consents to the test but masks the act of giving into the patient by formulating her decision as a reasoned response to the woman's medical history. The doctor thereby manages to preserve her professional autonomy and accommodate the patient at the same time.

It might be said that the asymmetry in doctor–patient interaction is tinged with morality at every juncture. Laypersons (patients) are extremely cautious in demanding anything of the expert or professional (doctor), who must artfully grant or deny underground requests through practices that preserve the integrity of their institutionally based authority. This pattern can also be seen in Stivers' (2002a, b, 2006) findings about how parents subtly pressure pediatric doctors to prescribe antibiotics for their children, and how physicians deal with this pressure. If a doctor recommends a non-antibiotic treatment, or no treatment, parents can apply subtle pressure for a prescription by citing positive past experiences with the drug and/or implicitly

---

[3] A pre-sequence is preliminary to an action sequence, and projects the kind of act that will be performed (i.e., invitation, question, request, and so forth). Pre-sequences can be a means of avoiding dispreferred responses, since recipients can address, and signal their orientation to, the projected action before it is actually executed. As we noted earlier, requests are *dispreferred* relative to offers, and the pre-request sequence often works to elicit a preemptive offer (Schegloff 2007:90–91).

or explicitly proposing a candidate diagnosis for which the standard treatment is antibiotics. Doctors display recognition of these pressures when they acquiesce to tacit demands (for example, by changing their treatment recommendation), ignore or resist them, or work to persuade patients to accept non-antibiotic treatments. Doctors pursue acceptance by detailing diagnostic findings, offering additional recommendations, and ending turns with tag questions such as "okay?," which strongly invite alignment (Stivers 2006:288).[4]

The moral implications of an official request are different from those of a covert one, as the latter can be ignored or avoided without such actions occupying the surface of the talk, while the former must be accountably managed. As such, the interactional practices of doctor and patient recurrently are occupied with shaping moral features in the discourse of the medical encounter.

Diagnosis and Accountability

Patients ordinarily do not participate in the diagnostic process. Physicians appear to encourage this disposition by volunteering only scant information about the particulars of the diagnosis. What little information they do provide is by way of explaining the prescription being handed out (Byrne and Long 1976). The passive attitude and demeanor patients typically display when receiving a diagnosis has been interpreted as reflecting the asymmetric structure of the doctor-patient relationship. Some see in it the domination of lifeworld concerns by a biomedical model of healthcare (Mishler 1984).

In his conversation analytic examination of the diagnostic phase of the medical interview, Heath (1992) delineates the practices that actively reproduce an interactional asymmetry between doctor and patient. Specifically, patients often handle the delivery of a diagnosis with silence or a downward-intoned token like "er" or "yeh," which has the effect of encouraging a transition to the next (treatment) phase of the consultation. This is so despite the regular provision by doctors of a post-delivery slot in which patients can make inquiries if they so choose. Heath (1992:241–242) reports that patients only make use of this slot when doctors display uncertainty, present a finding that contrasts with the patient's candidate diagnosis, or phrase the diagnosis in the form of a question, which makes an answer relevant as its second pair part. Patients may also be responsive when faced with negative findings about their complaint. In these instances, they typically produce accounts to justify having sought medical attention in the first place (Heath 1992:256). Patients work to present themselves as reasonable, knowledgeable monitors of their health (Halkowski 2006, Heath 1992:263–264) and their conditions as "doctorable" (Heritage and Robinson 2006:58), or fully warranting intervention.

Examining the diagnostic process in light of the medical consultation as a whole, Perakyla (2006) expands on Heath's findings, suggesting that the design of a diagnostic statement is highly sensitive to the sequential environment of its production. When doctors plainly assert

---

[4] Consider also how adult patients present candidate diagnoses of their illnesses for the doctor to confirm or disconfirm (Gill 1998, Gill and Maynard 2006). When offered to occasion an evaluation of their adequacy, explanations are regularly designed in a markedly cautious, equivocal way. The delicate character of explanations soliciting assessments stems in part from their status as covert ways of self-diagnosis, which attain the status of soliciting the doctor's confirmation or disconfirmation in and through the collaborative work of doctor and patient.

a diagnosis without articulating its grounds, they do so in a context where these grounds are concretely present for, and transparent to, the patient. For example, when a diagnostic statement is placed immediately after examination, its evidentiary basis is palpable to both participants. In situations where examination and diagnosis are temporally separated from one another, or when the diagnostic formulation is marked by uncertainty or otherwise opaque to the patient, doctors make an effort to justify their claims. Also accountable are discrepancies between a patient's candidate diagnosis and a physician's findings (*cf.* also Heath 1992). As uncertainty and discrepant perspectives pose a threat to doctors' epistemic authority (Perakyla 1998:112–114), they commonly explicate the evidence, whether disconfirming a candidate diagnosis, supporting an equivocal one, or reasserting a diagnosis that is questioned by the patient. Questioning most often occurs when the seriousness of a condition or complaint is in dispute. Under these circumstances, patients may challenge doctors using many of the procedures we have discussed, expressing skepticism about a diagnosis in ways that preserve the practitioner–patient asymmetry (Perakyla 2006:241).

In an investigation that returns to the deep issues regarding the morality of discourse, Maynard (2004) elaborates on Perakyla's inquiry by showing how surface practices for delivering diagnosis also grow out of considerations rooted in the interaction order upon which the institutional context of the medical encounter is built. By regularly citing the evidence for a diagnosis prior to the delicate act of predicating it as an attribute of the person, doctors display an orientation to achieving intersubjective agreement, which is a problem for participants in any setting, institutional or otherwise (Maynard 2004:70–71).[5] From this standpoint, medical authority can be seen to derive from the interactional structures of everyday life and the moral dimensions they embody (Maynard 1991). Taken together, Heath (1992), Perakyla (1998, 2006), and Maynard (1991, 2003, 2004) show how both patients *and* doctors orient to the moral accountability of their utterances in medical interactions. Newsworthy events involving health tear at the fabric of the lifeworld, and, depending on how they are handled, can even create a sense of anomie or disorientation that precipitates a noetic crisis (Maynard 1998). For this reason, disclosure is a matter of great moral delicacy.

In our discussion of blame work, we saw the importance of negotiating responsibility for, and tempering, a news announcement. One way to temper the news is to enlist one's coparticipant in its realization. This can be done by employing a perspective display sequence where, as mentioned earlier, deliverers invite recipients to tell their version of an event or condition, and follow with a clinical version in such a way as to confirm the recipient's perspective while affirming that of the clinic. By co-implicating recipients in the articulation of bad news, that is, clinicians can effect a measure of perspective convergence and diffuse responsibility for news content and management across parties (Maynard 2003:Chapter 6). A feature of the

---

[5] Related to the pervasive issue in medicine regarding evidence, another critical aspect of designing diagnostic delivery is how to handle is how to handle bad, uncertain, and good news (Maynard 2003:Chapter 2). In ordinary conversation, people routinely work to expose good news and shroud bad, and this happens in the clinic as well. Uncertain news, when evidence is not present for certain conditions but symptoms continue, tends to be handled like bad news – it is regularly foreshadowed, downplayed, delivered hesitatingly, and so forth (Maynard 2003, Maynard and Frankel 2006). Specifically, when a diagnosis is ruled out, the patient can be anxious about what else could be causing the symptoms, leaving "symptom residue" or unexplained discomfort or pain, which may lead to another kind of noetic crisis, anomie (Maynard and Frankel 2006:278), or ontological insecurity (Giddens 1984) that physicians handle through practices associated with delivering bad news.

perspective display sequence is how a doctor may co-implicate a patient in developing a diagnosis by detailing the evidence in a syllogistic idiom (Gill and Maynard 1995). Having once
stated the premises for a stigmatizing or disfavored diagnosis without explicitly articulating
it, the doctor invites the recipient to draw a conclusion. This procedure not only facilitates
delicate disclosure and patient participation in the diagnostic process, but also provides for
physician accountability.

Evaluating Competence

So far, we have considered competence as something that patients, in presenting symptoms,
and doctors, in evaluating them, actively display for one another. Much of time, the competence of both parties is taken for granted. Doctors operate on the pretext that patients are
knowledgeable monitors of their health, and only question this presumption when some aspect
of the interaction becomes problematic. In other words, the presumption of competence is only
overtly broached under exceptional circumstances. We turn now to a situation – cognitive testing – where the entire interaction between practitioner and patient is structured around the
assessment of competence. Cognitive tests are standardized instruments, scored and ranked
against a relevant subset of the general population, that are designed to elicit, code, and evaluate demonstrations of competence. In clinical settings, tests of cognitive ability are combined
with other instruments to formulate psychological profiles and diagnoses that, in turn, are used
to place individuals in morally and practically relevant (for schools, the workplace, etc.) membership categories (Sacks 1992) – i.e., having autism spectrum disorder, mental retardation,
learning disabilities, attention deficit disorder, and the like.

   Conversation analysts explore the interactional processes through which tests are used
to translate local, situated performances into objective, reportable measures of ability. In so
doing, they have opened the black box (Latour 1987) where raw data are sorted and converted
into standardized indices. By investigating clinical judgment in situ and "on the ground," so
to speak, CA exposes the reasoning practices involved in doing assessments that can have
profound social, educational, and occupational consequences for the examinee (Cicourel et al.
1974, Mehan et al. 1986). We concentrate here on assessments of children suspected of having
learning disabilities.

   A standard cognitive battery consists of subtests that measure ability in one or more
domains. These tests are combined into an index that reflects aptitude in the relevant area(s). In
line with psychometric presumptions about intelligence, the scoring of test questions, such as
those on the Brigance Inventory of Early Development, reflects a bias toward answers that are
theoretical, generic, and abstract, rather than concrete, particular, or grounded in lived experience (Maynard 2005:512–514, Marlaire and Maynard 1990). Put succinctly, such exams often
demand "disembedded thought" (Donaldson 1978). Drawing selectively on the natural language competencies that individuals possess and are required to display in everyday life, they
may privilege one kind of performance above others, while eliding the more primordial, practical forms of intelligence (Levinson 1995) that are required to do the exam in the first place.
Conversation analysis, however, cannot "unmask" (Mannheim 1952) some hidden function
these tests serve. Rather, the point is to understand the interactional processes whereby professionals generate their results, making relevant the available morally tinged diagnoses, labels,

and categories for situating children and others in particular programs, treatment regimens, and other social placements.

LAW

In legal proceedings, the disposition of a case depends on the relative weight of the evidence that disputants provide. If parties are credible, their deposition or courtroom testimony is more likely to be believed, and positively weighted, than if not. Questions of credibility are especially prominent in Anglo-American trial courts, where most of the evidence fact-finders receive is through witness testimony. The matter of credibility is tightly interwoven with a party's character, and the moral implications that can be drawn from it. In trial settings, overt mentions of character are generally prohibited or kept to a strict minimum, lest they unduly prejudice jurors. Nonetheless, attorneys and witnesses work together or at cross-purposes to project character attributes that either impeach or bolster witness credibility. These covert claims about character are meant to invite specific inferences from a jury, which functions as a silent audience to which participant's arguments are addressed (Atkinson and Drew 1979, Drew 1992, Maynard and Manzo 1993). In less formal contexts, such as plea bargaining, where restrictions around direct claimsmaking are relaxed, participants routinely mobilize character descriptions to support and negotiate their positions (Maynard 1984). In this section, we review and synthesize conversation analytic research on character and credibility in legal settings. We begin with a look at the informal negotiations of plea bargaining, followed by an examination of the formal organization of criminal trials.

Plea Bargaining

In the American judicial system, approximately ninety percent of criminal cases are resolved before they go to trial. As the primary vehicle for affecting these resolutions, plea bargaining forms the backbone of the criminal justice system. The interactional practices used to negotiate case dispositions thus provide a perspicuous object of investigation. Maynard (1984) examines how district attorneys (DA) and public defenders (PD) formulate morally implicative characterizations of defendants during plea-bargaining to achieve local goals. The meaning of a defendant attribute like age, sex, or race has no intrinsic moral significance. Instead, its moral sense is determined by the way it is fitted to descriptions used to justify, excuse, rationalize, impeach, or otherwise construe and constitute conduct.

Maynard identifies two classes of descriptors applied to defendants (1984:136–137). The first employ membership categorization devices (Sacks 1992) that propose the defendant is a certain type of person by virtue of her membership in a category, such as "elderly woman" or "someone very poor." These categories have moral resonance, and DA's and PD's work to link person-references with descriptions of an event that make a defense seem plausible or implausible, acceptable or unacceptable. The reasonableness of a defense depends, in large part, on whether it *fits with*, or is accountably applicable to, the *kind of person* by whom it is proffered. For example, it is more acceptable for a "poor person" to steal "an item of necessity" than for a "young woman" to pilfer soap because, "she was in too much of a hurry to pay for it" (Maynard 1984:124–125). As these contrasting cases suggest, descriptions of people and events play a constitutive role in formulating and challenging a defense.

The second class of descriptors includes assessment items such as "honest," or "sketchy," and subjective opinions about a defendant, such as "I think he's telling the truth." The two modes of description can be combined to formulate implicit claims about a defendant's character, as when a public defender remarks about his client, "Mister Larson is a highly educated young economist at the college, he's teaching out there" (Maynard 1984:137). In this instance, the assessment terms "educated" and "young" are coupled with a categorical description, "economist at the college" and an associated activity, "teaching," to present a picture of someone who is a respectable professional. The adverb "highly" proposes that he is better educated, and perhaps more competent and reasonable, than the average member of society, while the addition of a place locator, "at the college" projects something about his social status and relation to a legitimizing institution. Finally, the adjective "young," intimates that he has his whole career ahead of him, which would make the disposition of the present case consequential for his future. Of course, these are only interpretive possibilities; analytically it matters how the district attorney and judge hear and deal with these descriptions in their responses, matters that, for reasons of space, we do not discuss here. However, we suggest that the descriptions of the defense attorney are related to ones (discussed earlier) that participants use to negotiate blame and make complaints in ordinary conversation. These descriptions are related to issues of responsibility, rights, obligations, and other morally-tinged issues to which participants display an orientation when talking about persons in legal circumstances.

Criminal Trials

Anglo-American judicial systems are built on an adversarial logic, which holds that the most equitable and accurate way to arrive at the true facts of a case is to have rival parties contest one another's version of events. The majority of evidence is presented through direct witness testimony, with cross-examination affording each party a chance to confront and challenge the other's claims. Being conscious of attempts to discredit them, witnesses design their testimony in ways that preempt challenges or mitigate and neutralize them once they are made. Given its centrality in criminal trials, conversation analysts have devoted considerable attention to delineating the concerted actions that constitute cross-examination sequences (Atkinson and Drew 1979, Drew 1992, Hobbs 2002, Komter 1997). Our focus is on how accusations are designed, recognized, and managed (Atkinson and Drew 1979), and the tactics lawyers and witnesses may use to tacitly make, and deny, insinuations about the latter's character and motives (Drew 1992). Accusations regularly follow a three-part sequence (Atkinson and Drew 1979:184–185):

   (I)   Accusation/complaint
   (II) Defense/admission
   (III) Rejection/acceptance

When the accused produces a defense or denial in second position, the accuser's third turn prefers rejections to acceptances, which is to say that accepting a proffered defense is markedly dispreferred. In ordinary conversation, this makes good sense, as an acceptance could occasion a counter-complaint (Drew 1998, Atkinson and Drew 1979:186). In their study of cross-examination sequences from an Irish tribunal on police misconduct, Atkinson and Drew (1979) show how witnesses orient to the expectation that their defenses will be rejected, and the concomitant probability that they will lead to overt challenges. Witnesses work preemptively to address a projected accusation that they failed to act appropriately. Answers to questions that project blame allocation commonly find the witness explicitly noticing, and accounting for, his failure to act in an expected way. In the Irish tribunal, this meant handling a blame-implicative description by re-characterizing events so as to minimize their seriousness, shift blame to other parties, and mitigate and qualify the particulars of the attorney's version.

By contrast, when an accusation is not headed off and gets produced, witness replies are formatted as "rebuttal + account." In the Irish case, rebuttals dissented from the proposal that an officer could or should have taken action and emphasized situational constraints on their ability to act (Atkinson and Drew 1979:166). Overall, in the Irish tribunal hearing, preemptive exculpatory details and rebuttals + accounts are the two main defense strategies witnesses employ. Appearing at different points in an accusation sequence, they provide witnesses with resources for managing blame-allocations. In an environment controlled by interrogators, such resources are crucial for dealing with the tacit moral claims cross-examiners make about witness's character and credibility. Since character and credibility are enacted for the court in and through the interactional work of witness and attorney, this work is a core site of moral contestation in trial settings.

A further example of this contestation can be found in Drew's (1992) analysis of the cross-examination of an alleged victim's witness testimony during a rape trial. At issue in this exchange is whether the victim knew the defendant was "interested in her," which would support his claim that the intercourse was consensual. Both attorney and witness fashion descriptions that implicitly propose contrasting versions of the relationship and, by extension, the nature of the offense. These descriptions gloss the event as a whole in conflicting ways (1992:492–493). Take, for example, the question, "Well yuh had some uh fairly lengthy conversations with the defendant uh did'n you?" (Drew 1992:479). First, apropos of its design, the question is a yes/no interrogative that, as we noted earlier, works to restrict the relevant next actions an interlocutor can accountably perform (Raymond 2003). Further, it is polarized to prefer an affirmative response and, as a yes/no question, nothing more.[6] Finally, the question's content implies an overall schematic, or gloss, of the event consistent with the argument that the witness knew the defendant was interested in her and did not try to dissuade him. In her response, "Well we were all talkin'" the witness characteristically withholds a type-conforming response (i.e., yes/no) and provides an alternative gloss, inconsistent with the attorney's but fitting with her own narrative. Without overtly correcting the attorney's version, then, she manages to propose a candidate replacement of her own. Other instances of disputed descriptors concern the place where she and the defendant were "all talking," which the attorney calls a "bar" and the witness, a "club," and its characterization as "a place where girls and fellas meet," to which the witness replies, "People go there" (Drew 1984:489). Besides indexing competing glosses, the two sets of descriptors project different accounts of the *kind of person* the witness is and, as such, her moral probity and believability.

---

[6] The polarity of an interrogative refers to the kind of response it prefers in an interactional sense. Positively polarized questions work to elicit affirmative replies, while negative ones do the opposite (Raymond 2003, Heritage et al. 2007).

A powerful technique for impugning a witness's character and credibility is the "contrast device" (Drew 1992) which trades on the fact that courtroom interaction operates with a restricted speech exchange system (Sacks et al. 1974, Atkinson and Drew 1979) in which speaker roles and prerogatives are pre-allocated and communication follows a question–answer format. Specifically, a cross-examiner may elicit conflicting facts from a witness, and then bring them together in a formulation that highlights the discrepancy. Then, instead of allowing the witness to account for the discrepancy, the attorney will leave it as an unsolved puzzle for fact-finders (judge and/or jury members) to ponder. Specifically, in Drew's (1992:510) study, an attorney positions the witness's insistence that she and the defendant had nothing more than a casual relationship with the fact that he kissed her goodnight but not allowing response to each detail individually. This practice of juxtaposing contrasting details is especially effective because if the witness has no response, it is an absence that in itself is discrediting. Here, the surface norms whereby courtroom testimony is conducted legitimately entails a violation of the deep structure of ordinary interaction where, even as a witness is faced with an intractable dilemma, responses are incumbent to produce.

CONCLUDING REMARKS

In this chapter, we brought together some instances (but by no means all) of ethnomethodological and conversation analytic research related to moral phenomena in everyday and institutional settings. This literature, as well as cognate bodies of scholarship in the areas of discursive psychology (Edwards and Potter 1992, Potter and Wethrell 1987) and linguistic anthropology (Ochs and Kremer-Sadlik 2007, Brown and Levinson 1987), locates morality in the observable, reportable conduct of social actors. We distinguished the deep morality *of* everyday life, or what Bergmann (1998) calls protomorality, from the surface morality of rules, norms, rights, and obligations that protomorality undergirds. In all, moral reasoning is something we actively and accountably display for one another in our interactional engagements. The ontological status of morality as a *specifically social* phenomenon is coextensive with its collaborative realizations, exhibited in discourse both in ordinary conduct and the institutions that draw upon it.

Although their respective domains of inquiry differ, ethnomethodology and conversation analysis have the potential to engage in a fruitful dialogue with empirical social psychology, in both its sociological and psychological varieties (House 1977) and including the wide area known as social cognition. Because ethnomethodology and conversation analysis re-specify cognitive concepts in terms of recurrent social actions, they provide for a disciplined, naturalistic examination of "cognition in the wild" (Livingston 2008, Sacks 1992). A naturalistic approach to social-psychological phenomena can thus challenge, modify, and ultimately complement findings and generalizations based on survey research and experimentation. As an example of one such re-specification, consider Maynard's (2003:Chapter 7) analysis of the asymmetric delivery and uptake of good and bad news, which resonates strongly with what psychologists call the *actor–observer attribution bias* (Heider 1958). Just as people tend to ascribe their successes to personal traits and shortcomings to situational circumstances (and vice versa with respect to other persons), so too do we find deliverers and recipients of news collaboratively working to foreground the agency of those telling good news and shifting blame to third-parties or external circumstances in the case of bad news. This phenomenon, along with others ranging from rejecting invitations (Drew 1984) to allocating responsibility (Pomerantz 1978, Atkinson and Drew 1979) and detailing complaints (Drew 1998) follows the same logic as the cognate notion of attribution bias in social psychology, but is specified as a feature of the interaction order that is made available for natural observation and analysis.[7]

Re-specifying psychological concepts in an interactional idiom also holds the potential for more fine-grained, detailed coding schemes that can be used in large-N quantitative studies (Maynard and Schaeffer 2006, Heritage and Maynard 2006). It will also aid in experimental design, allowing researchers to explore how interactional phenomena are modified under a range of controlled conditions. An example is provided in Heritage et al. (2007). The authors divided a sample of twenty physicians and 224 patients into three groups in order to test whether the format of a question designed to elicit patient concerns has an effect on the number of concerns presented. The two treatment questions "Is there anything else you want to address in the visit today?" and "Is there something else you want to address in the visit today?" were distinguished by one word that reversed their polarity. Where the word "any" is negatively marked and prefers a negative response, "some" is biased toward a positive one.[8] Combining experimental with pre and post-survey data, the authors found that, relative to the control group, the positively marked query elicited 78% of unmet concerns, while the negatively marked one had no significant effect (Heritage et al. 2007:1431–1432). If, as we noted previously, the doctor–patient relationship is tinged with morality at every juncture, research combining a focus on talk-in-interaction with more traditional research methods, such as experimental manipulation, can provide us with more expansive insight into the specific interactional practices that shape medical encounters and their outcomes.

Finally, following Schegloff (2003) and Maynard (2006), we suggest that the programs of neurobiological and social-interactional research can proceed in parallel with one another. In re-specifying cognition and its moral components in discursive and interactional terms, ethnomethodology and conversation analysis can engage in a productive dialogue with both social psychology and the natural sciences in ways that address how different processes that distinct domains of study address are ordered intrinsically, organized through everyday practices, and, possibly, interrelated.

REFERENCES

Anscombe, E. 1957. *Intention*. Oxford: Basil Blackwell.
Atkinson, J. M., and P. Drew. 1979. *Order in Court: The Organization of Verbal Interaction in Judicial Settings*. London: Macmillan.
Bergmann, J. 1998. "Introduction: Morality in Discourse." *Language and Society* 31:279–294.
Bittner, E. 1967a. "The Police on Skid-Row: A Study of Peacekeeping." *American Sociological Review* 32:699–715.
Bittner, E. 1967b. "Police Discretion in the Apprehension of Mentally Ill Persons." *Social Problems* 14: 278–292.

---

[7] For an extended treatment of attribution theory as a discursive, interactional phenomenon, along with a poignant critique of more traditional conceptualizations, see Edwards and Potter (1993).

[8] "Any" is negatively polarized because it generally appears in negative declarative sentences: compare "I haven't got any" with "I've got any." By the same logic, "some" is positively polarized, as in "I've got some" as opposed to, "I haven't got some" (Heritage et al. 2007:1430, Horn 1978).

Brown, P., and S. C. Levinson. 1987. *Politeness: Some Universals in Language Usage*. Cambridge: Cambridge University Press.

Byrne, P., and B. Long. 1976. *Doctors Talking to Patients: A Study of the Verbal Behaviors of Doctors in the Consultation*. London, England: HMSO.

Cicourel, A. V., K. H. Jennings, S. H. M. Jennings, K. C. W. Leiter, R. Mackay, H. Mehan, and D. Roth. 1974. *Language Use and School Performance*. New York: Academic Press.

Clayman, S. E., and V. T. Gill. 2004. "Conversation Analysis." PP. 589–607 in *Handbook of Data Analysis*, edited by M. Hardy, and A. Bryman. Thousand Oaks, CA: Sage Publications.

De Waal, F. 1995. *Our Inner Ape: A Leading Primatologist Explains Why We Are Who We Are*. New York, NY: Penguin Books.

Dewey, J. 1896. "The Reflex Arc Concept in Psychology." *Psychological Review* 4:357–370.

Donaldson, M. 1978. *Children's Minds*. London: Croom Helm.

Drew, P. 1984. "Speakers' Reportings in Invitation Sequences." PP. 152–164 in *Structures of Social Acton: Studies in Conversation Analysis*, edited byJ. M. Atkinson, and J. Heritage. Cambridge: Cambridge University Press.

Drew, P. 1992. "Contested Evidence in a Courtroom Cross-Examination: The Case of a Trial for Rape." PP. 470–520 in *Talk at Work: Social Interaction in Institutional Settings*, edited by P. Drew, and J. Heritage. Cambridge: Cambridge University Press.

Drew, P. 1998. "Complaints about Transgressions and Misconduct." *Research on Language and Social Interaction* 31:295–325.

Drew, P., and E. Holt. 1988. "Complainable Matters: The Use of Idiomatic Expressions in Making Complaints." *Social Problems* 35:398–417.

Edwards, D., and J. Potter. 1992. *"Discursive Psychology."* London: Sage.

Edwards, D., and J. Potter. 1993. "Language and Causation: A Discursive Action Model of Description and Attribution." *Psychological Review* 100:23–41.

Edwards, D., and J. Potter. 1992. CÉ*Discursive Psychology*.DÉ London: Sage.

Emirbayer, M and D.W. Maynard (in press). CÉ*Pragmatism and Ethnomethodology*DÉ in Qualitative Sociology.

Garfinkel, H. 1967. *Studies in Ethnomethodology*. Englewood Cliffs, NJ: Prentice-Hall.

Giddens, A. 1984. *The Constitution of Society: Outline of the Theory of Structuration*. CA: University of California Press.

Gill, V. T. 1998. "Doing Attributions in Medical Interaction: Patients' Explanations for Illnesses and Doctors' Responses." *Social Psychology Quarterly* 61:342–360.

Gill, V. T. 2005. "Patient 'Demand' for Medical Interventions: Exerting Pressure for an Offer in a Primary Care Clinic Visit." *Research on Language and Social Interaction* 38:451–479.

Gill, V. T., and D. W. Maynard. 1995. "On 'Labeling' in Actual Interaction: Delivering and Receiving Diagnoses of Developmental Disabilities." *Social Problems* 42:11–37.

Gill, V. T., and D. W. Maynard. 2006. "Explanations for Health Problems and Physicians' Responsiveness in the Medical Interview." PP. 115–150 in *Communication in Medical Care: Communication between Primary Care Physicians and Patients*, edited by J. Heritage, and D. W. Maynard. Cambridge: Cambridge University Press.

Goffman, E. 1983. "The Interaction Order." *American Sociological Review* 48:1–17.

Halkowski, T. 2006. "Realizing the Illness: Patients' Narratives of Symptom Discovery." PP. 86–114 in *Communication in Medical Care: Communication between Primary Care Physicians and Patients*, edited by J. Heritage, and D. W. Maynard. Cambridge: Cambridge University Press.

Heath, C. 1992. "Diagnosis and Assessment in the Medical Consultation." PP. 235–267 in *Talk at Work: Social Interaction in Institutional Settings*, edited by P. Drew, and J. Heritage. Cambridge: Cambridge University Press.

Heider, F. 1958. The *Psychology of Interpersonal Relations*. Hillsdale, NJ: Lawrence Erlbaum Associates.

Heritage, J. 1984a. *Garfinkel and Ethnomethodology*. New York: Polity Press.

Heritage, J. 1984b. "A Change of State Token and Aspects of Its Sequential Placement." PP. 299–345 in *Structures of Social Action: Studies in Conversation Analysis*, J. Maxwell Atkinson, and J. Heritage. Cambridge: Cambridge University Press.

Heritage, J. 1990–1991. "Intention, Meaning and Strategy: Observations on Constraints on Interaction Analysis." *Research on Language and Social Interaction* 24:311–332.

Heritage, J. 2002. "Oh-prefaced responses to assessments: a method of modifying agreement/disagreement." PP. 196–224 in *The Language of Turn and Sequence*, edited by C. Ford, B. Fox, and S. Thompson. New York, Oxford University Press.

Heritage, J., and G. Raymond. 2005. "The Terms of Agreement: Indexing Epistemic Authority and Subordination in Assessment Sequences." *Social Psychology Quarterly* 68:15–38.

Heritage, J., and D. W. Maynard. (2006)."Introduction: Analyzing Interaction between Doctors and Patients in Primary Care Encounters." PP. 1–21 in *Communication in Medical Care: Communication between Primary Care Physicians and Patients*, edited by J. Heritage ,and D. W. Maynard. Cambridge: Cambridge University Press.

Heritage, J., and J. Robinson. (2006). "Accounting for the Visit: Giving Reasons for Seeking Medical Care." PP. 48–85 in *Communication in Medical Care: Communication between Primary Care Physicians and Patients*, J. Heritage, and D. W. Maynard. Cambridge: Cambridge University Press.

Heritage, J., J. Robinson, M. Elliott, M. Beckett, and M. Wilkes. 2007. "Reducing Patients' Unmet Concerns in Primary Care: The Difference One Word Can Make." *Journal of General Internal Medicine* 22: 1429–1433.

Hobbs, P. 2002. "Tipping the Scales of Justice: Deconstructing an Expert's Testimony on Cross-Examination." *International Journal for the Semiotics of Law* 15:411–424.

Horn, L. 1978. "Some Aspects of Negation." PP. 127–207 in *Universals of Human Language*, edied by J. H. Greenberg. Stanford, CA: Stanford University Press.

House, J. S. 1977. "The Three Faces of Social Psychology." *Sociometry* 40:161–177.

Hutchby, I., and R. Wooffitt. 1998. *Conversation Analysis: Principles, Practices, and Applications*. Malden, MA: Blackwell Publishers.

Jefferson, G. 1984. "On the Organization of Laughter in Talk about Troubles." PP. 346–369 in *Structures of Social Action: Studies in Conversation Analysis*, edited by J. Maxwell Atkinson, and J. Heritage. Cambridge: Cambridge University Press.

Joas, H. 1985. *"G.H. Mead: A Contemporary Reexamination of His Thought."* Cambridge: Polity Press.

Joas, H. 1996. *The Creativity of Action*. Chicago: University of Chicago Press.

Komter, M. L. 1997. "Remorse, Redress, and Reform: Blame-Taking in the Courtroom." PP. 239–264 in *Law in Action: Ethnomethodological and Conversation Analytic Approaches to Law*, edited by M. Travers, and J. F. Manzo (eds.). Aldershot, UK: Ashgate Publishing.

Latour, B. 1987. *Science in Action: How to Follow Scientists and Engineers Through Society*. Cambridge, MA: Harvard University Press.

Le Doux, J. 2002. *The Synaptic Self: How Our Brains Becomes Who We Are*. New York, NY: Penguin Books.

Lerner, G. 1996. "Finding 'Face' in the Preference Structures of Talk-in-Interaction." *Social Psychology Quarterly* 59:303–321.

Levinson, S. 1995. "Interactional Biases in Human Thinking." PP. 221–260 in *Social Intelligence and Interaction: Expressions and Implications of the Social Bias in Human Intelligence*, edited by E. Goody. Cambridge: Cambridge University Press.

Livingston, E. 2008. *Ethnographies of Reason*. Burlington, VT: Ashgate Publishing Company.

Marlaire, C. L., and D. W. Maynard. 1990. "Standardized Testing as an Interactional Phenomenon." *Sociology of Education* 63:83–101.

Maynard, D. W. 1984. *Inside Plea Bargaining: The Language of Negotiation*. New York: Plenum Press.

Maynard, D. W. 1989. "Perspective-Display Sequences in Ordinary Talk." *Western Journal of Speech Communication* 53: 91–113.

Maynard, D. W. 1991. "Interaction and Asymmetry in Clinical Discourse." *American Journal of Sociology* 97: 448–495.

Maynard, D. W. 1998. "Praising vs. Blaming the Messenger: Moral Issues in Deliveries of Good and Bad News." *Research on Language and Social Interaction* 31: 359–395.

Maynard, D. W. 2003. *Bad News, Good News: Conversational Order in Everyday Talk and Clinical Settings*. Chicago: University of Chicago Press.

Maynard, D. W. 2004. "On Predicating the Diagnosis as an Attribute of a Person." *Discourse Studies* 6:53–76.

Maynard, D. W. 2005. "Social Actions, Gestalts, and Designations of Disability: Lessons from and about Autism." *Social Problems* 52:499–524.

Maynard, D. W. 2006. "Cognition on the Ground." *Discourse Studies* 8:105–115.

Maynard, D. W., and S. E. Clayman. 1991. "The Diversity of Ethnomethodology." *Annual Review of Sociology* 17:385–417.

Maynard, D. W., and J. Manzo. 1993. "On the Sociology of Justice: Theoretical Notes from an Actual Jury Deliberation." *Sociological Theory* 11:171–193.

Maynard, D. W., and S. E. Clayman. 2003. "Ethnomethodology and Conversation Analysis." PP. 173–202 in *Handbook of Symbolic Interactionism*, edited by L. Reynolds, and N. Herman-Kinney. Walnut Creek, CA: Altamira Press.

Maynard, D. W., and R. M. Frankel. 2006. "On the Edge of Rationality in Primary Care Medicine: Bad News, Good News, and Uncertainty." PP. 248–278 in *Communication in Medical Care: Communication Between Primary Care Physicians and Patients*, edited by Heritage and Maynard. Cambridge: Cambridge University Press.

Maynard, D. W., and N.-C. Schaeffer. 2006. Standardization-in-Interaction: The Survey Interview. PP. 9–27 in *Talk and Interaction in Social Research Methods*, edited by P. Drew, G. Raymond, and D. Weinberg (eds.). London: Sage Publications.

Mannheim, K. 1952. *Essays on the Sociology of Knowledge*. London: Routledge and Kegan Paul.

Mead, G. H. 1934. *Mind, Self, and Society*. Chicago: University of Chicago Press.

Mehan, H., and H. Wood (1975). *The Reality of Ethnomethodology*. New York: John Wiley.

Mehan, H., A. Hertweck, and J. Meihls. 1986. *Handicapping the Handicapped: Educational Decision Making in Students' Careers*. Stanford, CA: Stanford University Press.

Merleau-Ponty, M. 1962. *Phenomenology of Perception*. London: Routledge and Kegan Paul.

Mishler, E. G. 1984. *The Discourse of Medicine*. Norwood, NJ: Ablex.

Ochs, E., and T. Kremer-Sadlik. 2007. "Morality as Family Practice." *Discourse and Society* 18:5–10.

Parsons, T. 1951. *The Social System*. New York: Free Press.

Perakyla, A. 1998. "Authority and Accountability: The Delivery of Diagnosis in Primary Healthcare." *Social Psychology Quarterly* 61:301–320.

Perakyla, A. 2006. "Communicating and Responding to the Diagnosis." PP. 214–247 in *Communication in Medical Care: Communication between Primary Care Physicians and Patients*, edited by Heritage and Maynard (eds.). Cambridge: Cambridge University Press.

Pinker, S. 2008. "The Moral Instinct." *The New York Times Magazine*, January 13: pp. 32–37, 52–58.

Pollner, M. 1987. *Mundane Reason: Reality in Everyday and Sociological Discourse*. Cambridge: Cambridge University Press.

Pomerantz, A. 1978. "Attributions of Responsibility: Blamings." *Sociology* 12:115–121.

Pomerantz, A. 1984. "Agreeing and Disagreeing with Assessments: Some Features of Preferred/Dispreferred Turn Shapes." PP. 57–101 in *Structures of Social Action: Studies in Conversation Analysis*, edited by J. Maxwell Atkinson, and J. Heritage. Cambridge: Cambridge University Press.

Pomerantz, A. 1986. "Extreme Case Formulations: A Way of Legitimizing Claims." *Human Studies* 9: 219–229.

Potter, J., and M. Wethrell. 1987. *Discourse and Social Psychology: Beyond Attitudes and Behavior*. London: Sage Publications.

Raymond, G. 2003. "Grammar and Social Organization: Yes/No Interrogatives and the Structure of Responding." *American Sociological Review* 68:939–967.

Robinson, J. D. 2004. "The Sequential Organization of 'Explicit' Apologies in Naturally Occurring English." *Research on Language and Social Interaction* 37:291–330.

Ryle, G. 1949. *The Concept of Mind*. New York: Barnes and Noble.

Sacks, H. 1972. "An Initial Investigation of the Usability of Conversational Data for Doing Sociology." PP. 31–74 in *Studies in Social Interaction*, edited by D. Sudnow New York: Free Press.

Sacks, H. 1987. "On the Preferences for Agreement and Contiguity in Sequences in Conversation." PP. 54–69 in *Talk and Social Organization*, edited by G. Button, and J. R. E. Lee (eds.). Clevedon, England: Multilingual Matters.

Sacks, H. 1992. *Lectures on Conversation (Vol.1: Fall 1964-Spring 1968)*. Oxford: Blackwell.

Sacks, H, E. A. Schegloff, and G. Jefferson (1974). "A Simplest Systematics for the Organization of Turn-Taking in Conversation." *Language* 50:696–735.

Schegloff, E. A. 2003. "Conversation Analysis and 'Communication Disorders.'" in *Conversation and Brain Damage*, edidted by C. Goodwin (ed.). New York: Oxford University Press.

Schegloff, E. A. 2005. "On Complainability." *Social Problems* 52: 449–476.

Schegloff, E. A. 2007. *Sequence Organization in Interaction: A Primer in Conversation Analysis*. Cambridge: Cambridge University Press.

Schegloff, E. A., and H.Sacks. 1973. "Opening Up Closings." *Semiotica* 8:289–327.

Schutz, A. 1962. *Collected Papers I: The Problem of Social Reality*. The Hague: Martinus Nijhoff.

Sidnell, J. 2010. *Conversation Analysis: An Introduction*. NJ: Wiley-Blackwell.

Stivers, T. 2002a. "Participating in decisions about treatment: Overt parent pressure for antibiotic medication in pediatric encounters." *Social Science and Medicine* 54:1111–1130.

Stivers, T. 2002b. "'Symptoms only' and 'Candidate Diagnoses': Presenting the Problem in Pediatric Encounters." *Health Communication* 14: 299–338.

Stivers, T. 2006. "The Interactional Process of Reaching a Treatment Decision in Acute Medical Encounters." PP. 279–312 in *Communication in Medical Care: Interactions Between Primary Care Physicians and Patients*, edited by J. Heritage, and D. W. Maynard. Cambridge: Cambridge University Press.

ten Have, P. 1999. *Doing Conversation Analysis*. London: Sage Publications.

Weider, L. 1974. *Language and Social Reality*. The Hague: Mouton.

Wittgenstein, L. 1953. *Philosophical Investigations*. New York: Macmillan.

Wittgenstein, L. 1965. *The Blue and Brown Books*. New York: Harper Perennial.

Zimbardo, P. 2007. *The Lucifer Effect: Understanding How Good People Turn Evil*. New York: Random House.

Part IV
Future Directions for Sociological Science

CHAPTER 28

Morality, Modernity, and World Society

SABINE FRERICHS AND RICHARD MÜNCH

WORLD SOCIETY AND THE MORAL BRAIN

The overarching aim of this volume is to re-establish and further develop the "sociology of morality." To us, this seems to be a two-pronged initiative that is directed both to the sociological discipline and to the subject-matter of morality. The overall project thus comprises a "*sociology* of morality" as well as a "sociology of *morality*." While the former (*sociology* of morality) is driven by internal, sociological developments, the latter (sociology of *morality*) draws on external, cross-disciplinary developments. We will address both aspects in turn.

As regards the *sociology* of morality, we can roughly distinguish between three phases of development: In the first phase, the founding fathers of the discipline were naturally engaged in sociology as a "science of morality," namely Durkheim who explicitly used this term (Durkheim 1986). In the second phase, functionalist sociology – notably in the style of Talcott Parsons – further emphasized, or rather overstated, society's moral consensus. As a reaction, critical sociology, in the third phase, did away with morality as an analytical concept (Stivers 1996). Hence, for a while, the sociology of morality had lost its credit – and thus its attractiveness for scholars and students. However, with the present re-launch of the sociology of morality, we have obviously entered a fourth phase. In this perspective, the "new" sociology of morality, which is documented in this handbook, aims to fill the void created by the internal dynamics, fashions and frictions of the sociological discipline.

As regards the sociology of *morality*, we can witness a growing interest in the subject also outside the boundaries of sociology, especially on part of the behavioral and neurosciences. (Sinnott-Armstrong 2008a, b, c) In simple terms, natural sciences, social sciences and humanistic sciences nowadays compete in how to explain (*erklären*), understand (*verstehen*) and act on morality. This has not always been the case: Traditionally, explorations into the subject of morality rather fell into the domain of the humanistic and social sciences. The humanities (comprising philosophy and religion, languages and literature, and, for that matter, also law and history) provided expertise in moral reflection and moral education alongside the classic humanistic ideal. The social sciences (such as sociology, politics and economics, psychology

S. Hitlin, S. Vaisey (eds.), *Handbook of the Sociology of Morality*,
Handbooks of Sociology and Social Research, DOI 10.1007/978-1-4419-6896-8_28,
© Springer Science+Business Media, LLC 2010

and pedagogy) focused on morality as a social fact, that is, an empirical and practical phenomenon which can be analyzed from the outside (observer's perspective) and/or from the inside (participant's perspective). However, today, morality also ranks high on the agenda of the natural sciences which get a lot of public attention for their new – or not so new – findings. Occasionally, these results directly threaten the moral ideas and realities that the humanistic and social sciences have established about (modern) society. In this respect, the sciences of man seem, once again, subject to "colonization" by the sciences of nature.

As part of the "future directions" section of this volume, our chapter needs to be responsive to the challenges related both to the internal (intra-disciplinary) and external (inter-disciplinary) dimensions of this ongoing project. Our twofold aim is thus to contribute both to the *sociology* of morality and to the sociology of *morality*. Again, we will briefly elaborate on each point.

On the one hand, we would like to put forward a genuine sociological perspective which draws both on the works of the classics and on more contemporary approaches. This brings us back to Durkheimian and Parsonian lines of argument that consider morality as a constitutive and not just derivative factor in the making of society. At the same time, it takes us forward to timely questions about the moral texture of today's "world society" – a globalized society that shares, in spite of its extensions, certain cultural scripts and characteristics (Heintz et al. 2005).

On the other hand, we want to engage in a cross-disciplinary dialogue on the moral foundations (and contingencies) of human nature and human society which acknowledges the state-of-the-art in the different fields of science. We have thus to consider also other than sociological approaches to the problem at hand. This means, not least, steering between the high ideals of a free will and moral agency as they are fostered by the liberal arts, and the deterministic or functionalist models of behavioral scientists that scrutinize the mechanisms of the "moral brain" (Loye 2002, Moll et al. 2005, Tancredi 2005, Verplaetse et al. 2009).

While the general intention of this chapter thus resonates well with the envisaged renewal of the sociology of morality, our more specific goal is not on the object-level but on the meta-level; it does not concern the ontological dimension of the problem (connected with the question of "what?") but the epistemological dimension (connected with the question of "how?"). In other terms, not only do we have to know *what* morality is as a social phenomenon and as a scientific object; we also need to learn more about *how* morality is constructed, first of all. Our focus is thus on the moral constructions that are made by modern society, in general, and modern science, in particular, and that generate "discursive truths" about morality. Hence, we want to shed light on the self-reflection of society in the form of moral discourses, namely "scientized" discourses about morality.

These discursive self-reflections nowadays encompass the talk of "world society" as well as the talk of "moral brains." With these terms, the discussants reach out for the biggest possible as well as for the smallest possible sociological entities: While the world society is, presumably, the most encompassing society one can ever imagine, moral brains are probably the most reduced form of speaking about individuals. To be sure, a sociology of morality that delves into the moral nature of the world society is much different from a sociology of morality that starts from the moral realities that are engraved in individual brains. Nevertheless, both discourses are – somewhat fashionable – expressions of how contemporary society reflects and reconstructs itself in the "science of morality." In the eyes of a sociologist, they may therefore be considered as interlinked.

This is not without consequence for a sociology of morality that aims to encompass both object- and meta-levels. In fact, one could claim that in order to live up to both its intra- and inter-disciplinary ambitions, the sociology of morality has to consider all possible levels of analysis: from the bottom of the "moral brain" to the top of "world society" plus the meta-level which elucidates the cognitive and normative backgrounds of any objective statement. A true multi-level approach would therefore not only include the micro- and macro levels but also the neuro- and meta levels of morality as a social phenomenon. These "extensions" can be illustrated in the following way:

Whereas microsociology typically focuses on individuals, their action and interaction, interests and identities, macrosociology addresses collectivities, their emergence and effects, structure and culture. Both levels – the micro level and the macro level – are as important for the sociology of morality as for sociology in general. Accordingly, they are dealt with extensively in the various chapters of this book. Yet, morality research also has to go below the level of individuals and beyond the level of collectivities – which are, of course, themselves morally constructed entities. To illustrate, we can build on the dichotomy of material and immaterial needs (or motives) of human beings.

On the one hand, individuals are nothing without their bodies: Human life originates from a physical, or rather biological, substrate. In order to understand the "material cause" of the individual mind, we can therefore learn more from neurobiology – and "neurosociology": a sociology that is aware of its neuro-foundations (Franks and Smith 1999, Hari and Kujala 2009, Deutschbein and Frerichs 2010) – than from (micro) sociology alone. Such a move from the micro- to the neuro level is typically found in approaches that are anyway characterized by a focus on the individual ("methodological individualism") and, hence, used to thinking in physiological entities of the human body and its organic systems, which are then addressed as "persons."

On the other hand, collectivities are nothing without the ideas that bind them together: Human society strives, in this sense, for metaphysical self-reflection and self-transcendence. The "final cause" of social life is thus, last but not least, expressed in religions and philosophies that codify and glorify the "collective conscience" (Durkheim 1984). The different cultural belief systems are an important sociological object: They are considered as "social facts" and can thus be analyzed without "value-judgments." Nevertheless, sociology is itself part of a cultural belief system that emphasizes the modern ideals of science and enlightenment. In other words, it is inevitably "value-related" (Weber 2004). Again, a move from the macro- to the meta level is most likely in approaches that are already familiar with thinking in abstract ideational entities, such as "imagined communities" (Anderson 1991).

All in all, a comprehensive multi-level approach to the sociology of morality would thus include (or, at least, be aware of) four different levels of analysis: three object levels – neuro, micro, and macro – and a meta level.

SCIENTIFIC DISCOURSES ABOUT MORALITY

In the following, we will use the "moral brain" and the "world society" as reminders of the full range (from the bottom to the top) of the "new" sociology of morality as it is envisaged here. This chapter focuses, not least, on the "missing" link between these moral entities which are, at first sight, diametrically opposed to each other. As we already indicated above, this link is rather to be found on the meta-level than on the object-level of morality research. Hence, there is no single theory that claims that world society emerges from or can be reduced to moral brains. Rather, these notions have engendered distinct scientific discourses that are interlinked only by the fact that they have become popular self-reflections of one and the same society. In order to understand how these moral constructions interact, we have thus to turn to the level of scientific discourses.

In the following, we will first briefly characterize the most relevant discourses on morality inside and outside the scientific field. In a very simplified, "ideal-typical" manner (Weber 2004), morality discourses can thus be depicted as centering around four major themes that can be arranged two by two: eschatology and evolution (divinity vs. profanity), on the one hand, and embeddedness and enlightenment (community vs. autonomy), on the other hand. Instead of "the 'big three' of morality" (Shweder et al. 1997) we can thus refer to the "big four."

If we exclude eschatological reflections about the afterworld and their implications for this world from what is considered modern, secular science, only three major perspectives are left for academic discussion, namely theories of moral evolution, embeddedness, and enlightenment. However, the transcendental or teleological dimension of morality re-enters scientific analysis not only as a (positive) content but also as a (negative) condition of rational discourse: A "science of morality" does not only analyze moral behavior and beliefs out there in the field but is itself inherently a moral endeavor – albeit one which is not inspired by religious ideas but merely follows human reason (which is considered more down-to-earth).

Taken as first-order observations, the "rationalized" discourses on evolution, embeddedness and enlightenment that are dominating science clearly differ with respect to the type of moral order they address (such as natural order, customary order, and rational order, to use Aristotelian terms) and the time span they cover (roughly $\pm 10^4$, 10^3, and 10^2 years). The first discourse attributes the evolution of "sentient and sapient" human beings to universal laws of nature. The second discourse focuses on "traditional societies" that are embedded and entrenched in mores and customs and can be considered the historical norm. The third discourse emphasizes the rationalized forms of order in a "modern society" that has gone through the Age of Enlightenment.

However, this does not mean that there are three different moralities at work in society. Nor would representatives of the three discourses simply "agree to disagree." It is not that they are just talking about different things. Instead, they put forward alternative explanations of what morality is in practice. In fact, on the object-level, the various orders overlap and their time lines converge. Each of the discourses has an idea about how to explain morality in the here and now – drawing either on human evolution, traditional embeddedness or modern enlightenment. Hence, a second-order observer interested in the "simultaneity of the non-simultaneous" can focus on how the different morality discourses not only coexist and complement each other but also how they compete in today's scientific field. This is the position we are taking in this chapter.

In order to elaborate on the sociological meta-level of contemporary discourses on morality, we start from the assumption that modern science and modern society are mutually constitutive: Science analyzes and reflects social realities (reflexivity of society in science) as much as scientific theories pervade and perform society (performativity of science in society). However, modern science constructs and reconstructs not only modernity but also the history of society (from traditional to modern societies) and the development of mankind (as a peculiar social species). In the modern *Wissenschaftsgesellschaft* – a society that reflects itself in the mode of science – both structure and semantics have thus become rationalized and "scientized". (Latour 1987, Foucault 2002, Drori et al. 2003)

Against this background, we can assume that the relative weight of different scientific discourses and arguments also gives insights into what rationalities and moralities are predominant in contemporary society. In this regard, evolution, embeddedness, and enlightenment discourses would indicate the respective roles of nature, custom and reason in (re-)constructing the moral order. In other terms, they demonstrate the "cultural significance" (Weber 2004) of socio-biological, cultural anthropological, and social philosophical "rationalizations" of who we are, what we believe, and how we act.

Again, it has to be noted that the pre-modern ethics of divinity has largely been replaced by atheistic or agnostic ethics of profanity in modern (rationalized) society. However, the full list of moral resources available to human beings "on the top of history" would include profanity as well as divinity, community as well as autonomy, that is, naturalist and super-naturalist (i.e., religious), collectivist and individualist forms of ethics. The four ideal types of moral discourses are summarized in Table 28.1.

Turning to the sociology of morality as a subfield of sociology, we can draw on the distinction between micro- and macrosociological approaches that focus either on the morality of individuals or collectives. However, surprisingly or not, questions of "collective moral order" and "individual moral action" are often conceived through the lens of religion and, thus, the sociology of religion. Hence, one might wonder if the ethics of divinity is, in the eyes of sociologists, still paramount in explaining contemporary morality.

To be sure, religion has never disappeared as a source of morality. Nevertheless, in modern society, it is neither the only one nor the most typical one. Moreover, by equating morality with religion, we underestimate the simultaneity of the "secularization of the sacred" and the "sacralization of the secular" (in Durkheimian terms, cf. Gephart 1993:321–418): Accordingly, the process of modernization entailed not only a loss of religious authority but also the relocation of authority from religious to secular institutions. Endowed with a charismatic, quasi-religious aura, the latter have thus themselves become moral authorities.

In this sense, supernatural ethics (divinity) has been absorbed both by collectivist ethics (community) and individualist ethics (autonomy). Ultimately, not even the "scientized" ethics of naturalism (profanity) seems to be free from moral appeals to a higher – yet completely natural – order of things. In order to specify today's moral order, we would thus need approaches that are not confined to religious patterns but also suitable to bring out the distinctive characteristics of secularized forms of morality, such as the rational "cult" of science (Drori et al. 2003). However, whereas there is much research on religious moralities (both on the level of moral communities and the level of moral agency), the constitutive morality of modern society and modern selves seems largely left to exegetical work on the sociological classics.

TABLE **28.1. Four Ideal Types of Moral Discourses**

Moral discourse	"The big four"	Notion of order	Idea of ethics	Scientific focus
Eschatology	Divinity	Divine order	Religious	Theology, religious dogmatics
Enlightenment	Autonomy	Rational order	Individualist	Social philosophy, humanities
Embeddedness	Community	Customary order	Collectivist	Cultural anthropology, social sciences
Evolution	Profanity	Natural order	Naturalist	Socio-biology, natural sciences

Talking about the morality of world society entails the risk of falling into the "old" Parsonian trap. Talcott Parsons' name is commonly associated with the idea that societies are unified by a moral consensus (Parsons 1967). This notion has been unanimously rejected by his critics – materialists and constructionists alike – and seems even more dubious when moving from the national to the global level. Consequently, the "new" (post-Parsonian) sociology of morality tries to avoid overstretched claims of this kind. Yet, the current focus on middle-range approaches has its own shortcomings, namely a lack of insights into what happens on the macro level of societies that have, in many respects, become interdependent ("globalization"). Nevertheless, studies at an intermediate level are important in order to understand how individuals and groups act and interact in the name of morality – even more so under modern conditions of functional differentiation, rationalization, and individualization.

Apart from that, two orientations within the "new" sociology of morality are particularly important to our project: On the one hand, there is considerable work on or below the micro level that conceives moral actors less in the perspective of embeddedness (in a moral community) or enlightenment (through moral education) but rather in the perspective of human evolution. The focus then turns to the "natural" predisposition of human brains – or, more generally, human beings – for moral behavior (Joyce 2006, Krebs 2008, Turner and Maryanski 2008). On the other hand, there is also increasing work on the meta level of the sociology of morality, namely critical and (so-called) deconstructionist studies of how "scientized" moral discourses produce moral realities – not least how they rationalize, normalize, and thereby justify the political economy that "runs" society (Fourcade and Healy 2007, Sum and Jessop forthcoming).

GLOBALIZATION, GOVERNANCE, AND GOVERNMENTALITY

The sociology of morality envisaged and exemplified in this chapter is premised on the idea of world society. Hence, we claim that "socio-logy" – the scientific study of society – cannot be confined to national societies anymore but also has to acknowledge the emerging (or already established) realities of a "global(ized)" society. Technically, world society can be conceived as the all-encompassing social system that arises from the links and interdependencies between all other social systems, territorial as well as functional ones. At the same time, the (rather) new condition of "globality" also feeds back into social action at any of the subordinate levels of society. (Luhmann 1997:145–171, Münch 1998, Krücken and Drori 2009)

Re-framing contemporary sociology as the study of world society does not mean, though, that global interdependencies have to be at the centre of every single piece of research. Nevertheless, a field as broad and as central as the sociology of morality would not be complete without elaborating on the global dimension of moral action, integration and order. This is even more important when we consider world society itself a moral entity with increasing cultural significance, as it is done in this chapter.

A simple demonstration of how world society works can be given with the slogan "Think globally – act locally" which has become popular in the environmental movement but is also applied elsewhere. It contains a call for action that rests on the assumption that global ideas and values can (and should) be realized through concerted action at the local level. In the same way, world society relies on the global diffusion of normative scripts which are adapted and enacted in local practices all over the world. It is thus a moral fact established as much from above (theory) as from below (practice).

Whereas the term world society is still a good marker for sociological talk (and thus sounds somewhat esoteric to outsiders), the idea of "globalization" is not bound to any academic discipline and is widely used in political and public discourse. Globalization denotes both a process and an outcome and can be observed in many dimensions – from the economic and political to the ecological, cultural and social (Held et al. 1999). Since these dimensions are substantially interlinked, globalization also points to a *problématique globale* that becomes manifest in recurrent clashes and crises with worldwide repercussions. Still, there is also hope for a better management of global interdependencies: if not in the form of a fantastic world government then possibly through reflexive mechanisms and flexible policies of "global governance."

A proper sociological term for globalization is "global integration" which resonates with the classic idea of societal integration (Münch 1998, 2001). Under these premises, globalization research can easily be linked to a wide range of integration theories: theories of systems integration (focusing on the interplay of different social spheres or systems) as well as theories of social integration (focusing on mutual exchange and agreement among actors) (Lockwood 1964). Global integration can thus be conceived in terms of systems and/or actors. Moreover, it can be analyzed from the outside (focusing on its structure, or material basis) as well as from the inside (focusing on its semantics, or acquired meaning). In this sense, the concept of world society forms part of a comprehensive heuristic for sociological theory-building "in the global age" (Albrow 1996).

While the notions of world society and global integration thus give a sociological twist to the (otherwise rather ambiguous) globalization debate, they can also be related to "governance" and "governmentality" discourses. Both governance and governmentality are derivations of the verb "to govern" and stand for alternative ways of thinking and theorizing about institutions of government and the state. To be sure, just as there is no world society which would anyhow match the institutional density – or "thickness" – of established national societies, there is no world government that would anyhow come near to the material and ideational power of modern nation states. However, just as we can observe certain phenomena of societal integration on the transnational level, there are also structures and semantics of governance that clearly go beyond the nation state.

In fact, much globalization research deals with the transformations of the (nation) state and the emergence of "new" forms of governance that are less hierarchical and more negotiable than classic forms of government and, importantly, that also extend into the transnational dimension. Ongoing debates on "European governance" or "global governance" thus address the (perceived and performed) shift from government to governance, and from national to transnational forms of politics. (Pierre 2004, Benz 2004, Leibfried and Zürn 2005, Frerichs 2008) At the same time, today's globalized political economy is increasingly discussed in terms of "governmentality." This somewhat enigmatic concept refers to the political rationalities behind modern forms of government – or governance, for that matter (Bröckling et al. 2000, Foucault 2007, 2008). These include moral templates of individuals as well as collectives, of what is true and what is right in a polity.

WORLD SOCIETY AND THE CULT OF THE INDIVIDUAL

Whereas our chapter thus presumes the moral relevance of an abstract collectivity called world society, we are ultimately interested in the morality of the individual, or, more precisely, in the individual as a moral projection of world society. Since collective consciousness and individual consciousness are mutually constitutive, the morality of world society is reflected in the morality of the individual – and vice versa. (Frerichs and Münch 2009) In other terms, the globalized morality is, at the same time, a highly individualized one.

Again, we do not conceptualize world society – and the global consciousness it engenders – in terms of religion, here. However, we take the aforementioned idea seriously that processes of secularization (of the sacred) and sacralization (of the secular) are closely intertwined. Modernization, hence, does not imply that all notions of sanctity are lost and appeals to a "higher order" have become obsolete. Instead, moral authority is transferred from traditional, religious institutions to worldly institutions with a "nimbus" of modernity and rationality. The ideas and values embodied in secularized institutions may thus appear just as sacrosanct as the world views cultivated in religious settings.

At the same time, by developing strong notions of universality and individuality, the occidental religions also paved the way for Western modernity. Already on this side of the equation, authority has thus been relocated, if only schematically, from god to church (or other religious organizations), and from church to individuals, namely "individual souls" (Meyer and Jepperson 2000:101). On the other side of the equation, secular social spheres, such as the law, the economy, and science, have not only severed their links to religion but themselves developed globalized and individualized moralities.

Our focus is thus the global "cult of the individual" (Durkheim 1961, 1973) which draws less on religious sources than on the rationalizations of modernity itself. In this chapter, we will particularly focus on the rationalities of the law, the economy, and science, since these spheres also play a central role in today's "world polity." The latter term includes, in the present context, world society as a site of government, governance, and governmentalities. In the following, we will first briefly outline how legal, economic, and scientific globalization contributes to the cult of the individual, and after that further elaborate our argument in separate sections on the three social spheres.

As regards the law, the double logic of secularization and sacralization seems most obvious: Law replaces – and imitates to some extent – religion in implementing a higher moral order in concrete social settings. It can thus be considered a secular (or civil) form of religion. In contrast to other social spheres, such as the economy or science, law mainly fulfills integrative functions for society as a whole. In other words, the social bonds that form the basis of reciprocity and redistribution in modern societies are largely supported through legal means. In this sense, legal communities do not have to rely on primordial bonds anymore but can also include more abstract forms of "solidarity among strangers".

However, with respect to the spatial dimension of societies, law's role remains ambiguous: On the one hand, it seems that integration through law is much easier to achieve in a self-contained national society than in a world society without borders. In fact, the classic idea of the rule of law is closely related to the historical form of the nation state. On the other hand, law can also be understood as a moral resource – and even a driving force – of the world society. Eventually, legal rationalization, or the legalization of modern moralities, triggers itself processes of globalization and individualization, as it is demonstrated in contemporary claims for universal human rights and global citizenship.

While law thus illustrates best the rationalization of religious moralities (that is the relocation of authority from god and church to law and state), economy and science transform these legal rationalities again in substantial ways. As regards the economy, the continuities –

or rather discontinuities – between religious moralities and economic rationalities come to the fore. Unlike the law, the economy is usually seen not in line but in contrast with any meaningful notion of morality. In fact, moral considerations seem largely suspended within the economic sphere: At least in the liberal ideal-type of the market economy, allocation takes, by definition, priority over redistribution; economic efficiency hence precedes social justice. In this perspective, markets actually appear as a-moral settings. Consequently, economics is considered a "secular religion" only in a critical or cynical sense (e.g., Bourdieu 1996).

Nevertheless, it is misleading to juxtapose markets and morals, in the first place, since the very distinction already presupposes that both spheres can indeed be separated. In this sense, the vision of a market society rests itself on moral presuppositions. It, therefore, seems necessary also to scrutinize the above rationalizations of markets (and other economic institutions) as "moral-free zones." The question then turns to how markets have, first of all, become "disembedded" from society at large and disconnected from other social spheres. Only in such a moral setting, the fiction of an isolated "economic man" could come true.

In considering economics as the main rationale behind disembedded modern economies, we have already entered the field of science. In fact, the model of *homo oeconomicus* – and its worldwide diffusion – is but an example of how science pushes towards a rationalized global culture. As functional subsystems, economy and science thus share a general openness towards social relations and exchange across national borders. With respect to society as a whole, they are specialized on functions of innovation and adaptation, in contrast to the functions of stability and integration which seem to characterize the law.

However, just as globalized markets cannot be taken for granted but depend on national economies opening up their borders, "universal" science has itself national roots. This seems somewhat counter-intuitive inasmuch as the argumentative core of scientific theories is concerned (where explicit "value judgments" are avoided) but looks much more plausible as regards the implicit "value relatedness" of science as a social practice (Weber 2004). These hidden value commitments are likely to vary with time and space, and thus we can not only expect differences between the various national cultures but also discrepancies between national and global cultures of science. For obvious reasons, this concerns cultural sciences more than natural sciences; however, the idea of "science as culture" implies cultural contingencies not only for the former but also for the latter.

As in the legal and economic spheres, the modern rationalities embodied in science thus work towards the globalization and individualization of moral bonds once tied to the nation. World society is, last but not least, a "society of science" (*Wissensgesellschaft*) that furthers "scientized" forms of governance and self-governance. A core feature of the global cult of science is the proliferation of rational actors, both in theory and in practice. Whilst the capacity to act is typically attributed to individuals or well-organized collectives, we can also count in rationalized "actants" other than or below human beings, including the human brain. (Meyer and Jepperson 2000, Latour 1987, Reichertz and Zaboura 2006) With its rationalized worldview, modern science stands in sharp contrast to religious belief systems. Nevertheless, it is endowed with a similar moral authority.

To conclude, the relationship of morality and modernity is clearly shaped by law, economy, and science. Moreover, all three spheres contribute effectively to the global cult of the individual. In the following sections, we will, therefore, further elaborate on and also illustrate the rationalities inherent in these fields, namely the concurrent logics of globalization and individualization. While we will address each of these fields in turn, we will also come

TABLE 28.2. Moral Discourses in World Society

Moral discourse	Human condition	Social sphere	Basic conflict	Governable self
Eschatology	Interaction with god	Religion	Afterworld vs. this world	Creature of god, individual soul
Enlightenment	Freedom of the mind	Law	Legal reason vs. political will	Legal person, individual rights
Embeddedness	Interaction with others	Economy	Economic efficiency vs. social justice	Economic man, individual interests
Evolution	Necessities of the body	Science	Natural restraints vs. cultural contingencies	Cerebral subject, individual brain

back to issues of enlightenment, embeddedness, and evolution, that is, the three main themes of contemporary morality discourses identified above (again, if eschatological reflections are excluded).

In fact, in modern society, the human condition is likewise interpreted in terms of the necessities of the body, the interaction with others, and the freedom of the mind, thus alluding to physical, social and mental aspects of human existence (not to mention "interaction with god," that is, the religious dimension of life). Overall, these aspects play a different role in the rationalizations of the world offered by law, economy, and science, or, more precisely, by the "theories of reflection" that are developed in the respective functional systems (Luhmann 1997).

Not surprisingly, these meta-theories also deal – more or less explicitly – with moral visions and tensions inherent in the different spheres. In the case of the law, morality is largely defined in terms of rational enlightenment but also subject to a trade-off between legal reason and political will. As regards the economy, morality is prominently framed in terms of social (dis)embeddedness and discussed whenever conflicts between economic efficiency and social justice arise. In science, morality can be reconstructed in terms of the human evolution, with all its ambiguities between natural restraints and cultural contingencies. These features are summarized in Table 28.2.

NOMOS: WORLD SOCIETY AND THE LAW

Sociology has established itself as a "science of order" that focuses on the normative order that makes up society. However, it is also a "science of disorder" inasmuch as it is concerned with social change and crisis, that is, periods of relative normlessness, or anomie (Repplinger 1999). In a way, sociology and jurisprudence thus share a certain preoccupation with society's normative order (*nomos*) – if it is codified or not. Not surprisingly then, their interests converge in matters of legal sociology, in general, and criminology, in particular. At the same time, the sociology of crime is an important subfield of morality research. In order to test our understanding of the rationalized world society and its inherent cult of the individual, we can thus apply it to questions of anomic crime. By anomic crime, we mean delinquency that results from a conflict between cultural inclusion (promising individual achievement) and structural exclusion (perpetuating individual underachievement), or the combined effects of an individual failure to conform to cultural values and an institutional failure to integrate potential under-achievers. While our approach draws on the leading works of classic and institutional anomie theory (Durkheim 1952, 1984, Merton 1938, 1968, Rosenfeld 2006), it adds world society as a source of global cultural convergence and attributes structural discrepancies mainly to different types of national regimes. Based on an empirical study with 20 OECD countries, we argue that anomic crime (e.g., robberies) is increasingly to be understood as a consequence of the mismatch between global values and individual means, mediated – for better or worth – by national policies. Namely the integration capacities of conservative (family-based) and social-democratic (state-based) regimes, less so those of liberal (market-based) regimes, seem to be challenged by a parallel progression of globalism and individualism. (Frerichs et al. 2008)

If we turn from crime as a (negative) indicator of moral disintegration to law as a (positive) indicator of moral integration, the question becomes how to conceive of "integration through law beyond the nation state" (Frerichs 2008). Again, one can start from the idea that law has inherited its moral authority and integrative capacities from religion: If "god's reign" was to be achieved through some form of world religion, the modern world polity presumes a universal system of law; at the same time, the sanctity of "individual souls" has taken the form of inviolable human rights. Institutions of governance and self-governance have thus become secularized and legalized. As regards the national rule of law, the sociology of world society offers two complementary perspectives: On the one hand, modern nation states and national legal systems can be considered as global forms, that is, as projections of world society. In this top-down perspective, modern nation states are not primordial entities that establish, by themselves, an international legal order (as in the classic realist view); rather they are social constructs that are endowed with legal and political authority – or sovereignty – through global cultural scripts (Krücken and Drori 2009). On the other hand, if the national rule of law is per se considered a global form, the question remains how to make sense of legal globalization, that is, the development of distinctly transnational or supranational forms of integration through law. In order not to fall back into the "methodological nationalism" of state-centered bottom-up perspectives that do not take into account the emergent qualities of world society (Beck 1997), one would thus have to argue that national polities only fulfill mediating functions between global governance and individual self-governance in the name (and rationality) of the law.

The legal dimension of world society can be explored through the lenses of a wide range of sociological theories – provided that they do not reify the concept of the nation state but are prepared to put it in its broader historical and social context. Four examples of how to address questions of supra- and transnational legal integration from a sociological point of view can be given with systems theory (following Niklas Luhmann and Gunther Teubner), discourse theory (following Jürgen Habermas and Christian Joerges), structural functionalism (following Talcott Parsons and Richard Münch), and regulation and field theory (following Pierre Bourdieu and Bob Jessop). These theories differ in how much emphasis is put on social integration through law, that is, integration among individuals and groups, and systems integration through law, that is, integration between different social spheres. While systems theory and regulation/field theory are mostly interested in the objective rationality and the functional interplay of different social spheres (observer's perspective), discourse theory and structural functionalism also address the subjective morality of actors, meaningful interaction and community building (participant's perspective). At the same time, the approaches also differ in their analytical preference for either consensus or conflict paradigms of social order, with structural functionalism and systems theory leaning to the former and discourse theory and regulation/field theory tending to the latter (Frerichs 2008). Nevertheless, all these theories point to the contingency of the nation state as a "conclusive" form of legal and social order. With the project of modernity entering the global age, national biases have thus lost much of their structural viability and semantic plausibility, not least in the law. This is exemplified by the increasing role of the principle of non-discrimination in the European Community of Law.

Our eclectic – or rather, encompassing – approach to world society builds on the idea that structure and semantics co-evolve in the (ongoing) modernization process and also interact in bringing about more globalized and, at the same time, more individualized modes of integration. If law is situated at the intersection of objective forces and subjective meanings, we can take account of the structures as well as the semantics of law and legal solidarity. In other words, law mediates between the political-economic realities and the socio-cultural ideas of order that are at work in modern society. To the same effect, legal philosophers and sociologists have drawn a distinction between law's *ratio* (reason) and law's *voluntas* (will), that is, between the moral principles and values internal to law and the political purposes and functions external to law (Tuori 2007). Our point is here that world society as a structural reality "out there" (from an observer's point of view) also affects the ideas about right and wrong we develop "in here" (from a participant's point of view). This is relevant, not least, for present notions of constitutions and citizens: Even though constitutional discourse can mainly be considered a semantic exercise on normative – that is, ultimately, counter-factual – grounds, we have to bear in mind the selective pressures that are de facto exerted by forceful developments in the political and economic spheres. These include enabling as well as restrictive factors that, nowadays, seem to push towards more functional and more transnational constitutions. At the same time, the "postnational constellation" (Habermas 2001) also entails a new understanding of citizenship: In times of more abstract (in scale) and more specific (in scope) constitutions, the entitlements that are connected with citizenship will also be more inclusive and, at the same time, more restricted. (Münch 2008a, b)

OIKOS: WORLD SOCIETY AND THE ECONOMY

In the legal dimension, world society's cult of the individual is thus expressed in claims for universal human rights and global citizenship (with reflections also on national and European constitutions). However, the re-definition of legal solidarity in transnational contexts is not merely an artifact of an ever more expansive constitutional discourse but also based on material changes in the international division of labor. This is, basically, a Durkheimian argument which can be elaborated as follows: Schematically, there are two types of solidarity, a traditional form ("mechanical solidarity") that rests on the principle of segmentary differentiation, and a modern form ("organic solidarity") that builds on the principle of functional differentiation. In this respect, modernization consists in a move from relatively self-contained social units – with strong bonds within and weak bonds in-between – to highly specialized and, at the same time, highly interdependent entities. Nonetheless, even modern societies do not fully rely on functional differentiation but have their own relics of segmentary differentiation, namely in the form of the nation state. While the globalized division of labor generally facilitates "inclusive" forms of solidarity alongside transnational networks of production and exchange, the modern welfare state still relies on "exclusive" forms of solidarity within national borders. Ideally, we can thus distinguish between three stages of the economy and three related stages of solidarity: The traditional household economy is mostly based on mechanical forms of solidarity; the modern national economy combines high intra-border and low cross-border exchange with "nationally contained" forms of organic solidarity; and today's integrated world economy brings about new transnational forms of network solidarity. (Münch and Büttner 2006, Münch and Frerichs 2008)

Whereas the economy used to be a matter of the private household (*oikos*) in the old – and ancient – days, in modern times, it has become an affair of the state: The political economy is run by the state; nation states organize national economies. Know-how is provided by the science of economics which started out as a state-related and "statistical" discipline. However, today, economic wisdom is less about the political side of the economy than about the universal laws of the market (Foucault 2007, 2008). In this sense, economics can also be understood as a scientific rationalization, or theory of reflection, of the global economic system. In the perspective of the sociology of knowledge, market order and moral order are closely intertwined. In world society, we thus have to explore the specific morality of a globalized market society. To this end, we can draw both on classical and contemporary approaches developed within and between economics and sociology. A recent collection of "moral views of market society" (Fourcade and Healy 2007) distinguishes the perspectives of "civilizing markets," "destructive markets," "feeble markets," and "moralized markets." These four views can be specified and interrelated as follows: The idea that market freedoms also further a free and virtuous society is part of the "liberal dream" of classical and neoclassical economists. Their strongest critics, typically with a Marxist background, consider market society as a "commodified nightmare" instead where market values undermine all other social values. In both perspectives, the moral order thus reflects, for better or for worse, the laws of the market. But one can also reverse the argument: A given social order can act both as "shackles and blessings" on economic activities. Economies are then ultimately embedded in social rationalities. But, again, also the opposite is true: In times of a rising "economism," societies are also embedded in – that is, pervaded by – economic rationalities (Frerichs and Münch 2009).

This brief overview helps us to turn from the level of first-order observations, or "realities," to the meta-level of second-order observations, or "rationalities." Starting from the notion of "markets as scientific and moral projects" (the fourth of the above perspectives), we can therefore distinguish between three competing discourses about markets and morality (indicated by the other three perspectives). On the one hand (arguing from market to morals), market society can thus either be seen as a positive civilizational model or as a dangerous capitalist threat for society and its moral substance. On the other hand (arguing from morals to markets), a pre-existing moral order may either integrate and subordinate the market sphere, as in the classic notion of social embeddedness, or it may itself anticipate and absorb the logic of the market, as in the contrary notion of economic embeddedness (Polanyi 1957, Callon 1998, Frerichs 2010a, b). After all, market society has to be understood as an encompassing social project: Even if it appears as an artifact of economic thinking, it is not a moral projection of economists alone, nor is it just an unintended consequence of the rationalization of the economic sphere. Rather, the basic ideas and institutions of market society – namely the economic freedoms – have a moral backing in society at large. In our reading of world society (and its inherent rationalities), the emphasis is thus on the moral foundations of market society as a modern form of order that allows for high degrees of globalism and individualism. This semantic construction fits well with the structural realities of a globalized economy that fundamentally changes the social frame of reference of economic efficiency and legal solidarity. In particular, society's cognitive embeddedness in the world market entails a shift from national to transnational levels of governance.

While legal and economic sphere are analytically and logically distinct, they are, nevertheless, empirically and pragmatically intertwined. The structural coupling of these two spheres can be interpreted in terms of the economic constitution that makes up market society. In the broadest sense, this concept includes structural as well as semantic, formal as well as material aspects of the interplay of economic and legal order, of *oikos* and *nomos*. In the global age, the economic order takes more and more transnational forms, that is, national economic constitutions gradually merge into regional (e.g., European) and global economic constitutions (Frerichs 2008, 2009). Since the economic system can be considered a paradigm case of functional differentiation and global integration, economic realities and rationalities have become somewhat predominant on the level of world society. This implies that the construction of legitimate actors – namely states, organizations and individuals – in universalized scripts of action will largely be based on notions of rational as well as rightful economic actors. The paradigmatic shift from the national to the transnational level can hence be illustrated with substantial changes in the respective role descriptions for governments, corporations and consumers in the context of economic globalization. These substantial re-definitions include a transition from Keynesian welfare states to Schumpeterian workfare regimes, a move from formalistic structures of corporatism to flexible network structures, and a conversion of passive consumers into active producers. Altogether, the globalized market society is thus maintained and enacted by entrepreneurial selves who maximize their human capital and whose notions of solidarity and justice are, therefore, much aligned with economic principles of efficiency and fairness. (Jessop and Sum 2006, Opitz 2004, Bröckling 2007, Streeck 2009).

PHYSIS: WORLD SOCIETY AND SCIENCE

At the outset, we called for a sociology of morality that would pay specific attention to the meta level of scientific discourses. Accordingly, world society can be defined as a *Wissenschaftsgesellschaft* in which the moral order has become highly rationalized and scientized. Hence, science plays a central role in deconstructing and reconstructing morality. Having dealt with legal and economic rationalities in the preceding sections, we can thus finally turn to the scientific field. Sure enough, scientific knowledge is also part of the rationalization of legal and economic practices and has, to this extent, already been touched on above. In fact, the scientific field, as we understand it here, covers all fields of science, namely humanistic sciences, natural sciences, and social sciences. Morally speaking, it spans from noble ideals of enlightenment and the freedom of the mind (as they are cultivated in the humanities) to functionalist notions of human evolution and the necessities of the body (as they are cultivated in the natural sciences) and also includes – somewhere in between – the embeddedness (or disembeddedness) talk of social scientists who are specialized in man's interaction with others. While legal theory can be taken as a representative of the former (humanities), economic theory stands for the latter (social sciences). Our main focus here is, however, in the natural sciences and, more specifically, in evolutionist perspectives on human morality. In particular – if only pars pro toto – we thereby want to point to recent studies and debates on the "moral brain."

World society has been characterized as furthering a cognitive rather than a normative style of expectations (Luhmann 1975). On the global level, the flexibility of rules thus plays a – relatively – bigger role than their stability. According to that, expectations are rather adjusted to actual behavior than behavior to idealized expectations; the prospective attitude of learning (on the basis of factual outcomes) is valued more than the retrospective attitude of being right (considering the norms at stake). The move from more hierarchical forms of traditional government to more heterarchical – and often transnational – forms of network governance points in the same direction. In fact, so-called new forms of governance are characterized by a higher emphasis on exploratory settings, practical experience and external expertise than on the authoritative enforcement of preset rules and standards. However, the shift from national government to transnational governance is also accompanied by a change in the "value relations" underlying science: These turn away from the specificities of national cultures towards the commonalities of world culture. This cultural change obviously concerns the sciences of man more than the sciences of nature since national ideas and regimes affect meaningful action more than metabolic behavior. Nonetheless, the line between culture and nature remains difficult to draw. In the end, a move from the cultural to the natural and from the national to the global pole of science cannot be explained without a sociological theory of the scientific field. When we refer to the scientization of world society, we therefore imply the imposition of an ever more "universal" model of science that is borrowed from the natural sciences but also affects the ways humanistic and social sciences are understood, both in theory and in practice.

The new emphasis on a unified model of science is, not least, demonstrated by the university reforms that are currently undertaken in many countries in order to adapt research and teaching to international standards of "excellence." These activities are supported by another globalized form: that of independent expertise the results of which are condensed in evaluation reports and popularized through ranking lists. In world society, excellence and expertise are thus largely defined outside the national context; at the same time, external monitoring systems transform, and often replace, mechanisms of professional self-regulation (Münch 2007, 2009). While the universalization of scientific knowledge and expertise helps to overcome the specific bonds and biases of more localized forms of knowledge production, it also modifies – namely decontextualizes – the relationship between scientific truth and moral values. The global integration of science (in its broadest sense) thus comes along with a disintegration of epistemic communities as ethical communities that build on a particular value consensus, including national university systems and academic professions. Within the scientific field, the gradual transition from a national to a global mode of science becomes manifest in a series of changes and crises which, apparently, affect the humanistic and historical sciences more than the natural and behavioral sciences. This overall shift in the "morality of science" also concerns the predominant positions and dispositions within the legal discipline (as a corollary of the legal system) and the economic discipline (as a corollary of the economic system): Context-sensitive scholarship based on specific legal cultures or economic regimes tends to lose out against general theories with a universal ambit.

The scientization of world society is based on the principle of functional differentiation. The functional autonomy and global expansion of different social subsystems – including legal and economic systems – is rationalized (and thus legitimated) by theories of reflection that typically claim to be "sciences" of the subject-matter at hand. Again, we can assume that structure and semantics are mutually constitutive and that, accordingly, also social spheres and scientific discourses co-evolve. In the preceding sections, we argued that processes of transnational integration further both globalism and individualism while they weaken national moralities. Similar developments can now also be observed in the scientific field. On the one hand, the globalization of science seems to strengthen the natural science model: Since it can ignore cultural differences and contingencies, it is clearly the more universalist one. In this sense, human behavior becomes "naturalized". On the other hand, science reflects and also reinforces the global cult of the individual: While "methodological nationalism" naturally loses ground in a globalized system of science, "methodological individualism" seems to become even stronger. In other words, the preferred model of man is a liberal one. However, the definition of individual freedom and actorhood is no longer left to the liberal arts; rather it is re-constructed through the lenses of the social and natural sciences. By drawing an imaginary line from individual rights to individual interests and individual brains, we can, therefore, illustrate how "liberal" jurisprudence gets linked to economics and "liberal" economics to neuroscience. In fact, we see a certain reductionism at work that brings the legal order (*nomos*) closer to the economic order (*oikos*) and the economic order closer to the natural order (*physis*). Hence, the "free self" is replaced with the "moral brain" as the ultimate moral entity (Frerichs and Deutschbein 2009).

THE HUMAN CONDITION IN THE GLOBAL AGE

To conclude our tour d'horizon of the moral underpinnings of today's world society, we want to come back to the notions of governance and governmentality introduced above. In the center of what has been aptly termed "neo-liberalism" (and is also referred to as "neo-liberal governance" or "neo-liberal governmentality") (Gertenbach 2007, Lee Mudge 2008) is the governable self which is not only a subject of governance but also a subject of self-governance. In other terms, in the modern world polity, the cult of the individual takes the form of governance through self-governance. This implies that the individual subject also internalizes itself the criteria of good and effective governance that are otherwise employed by external authorities, such as the nation state or global experts. Insider and outsider perspectives are thus blended into each other. At the same time, the notions of world society, global governance and global governmentalities also suggest to think of "globalized" individuals. While the global cultural scripts generally favor rational actors, this "rationality" requires further definition. Arguably, in a world of science, the rationality of actors is contingent on the rationality of the models that guide their action. Any scientific model of action would thus also lend itself to "rationalize" action. Rational action can be conceived and analyzed both from the perspective of an observer who tries to explain actual behavior "from the outside" or from the perspective of a participant who tries to interpret its intended meaning "from the inside." Accordingly, it can refer to moral behavior that is externally defined and objectively shown as well as to moral reasons that are internally constructed and subjectively perceived.

Sociologically speaking, the law comes closest to the philosophical and humanistic pole of the rational schemes of action that are available to the modern individual. At this end, the capacity to act morally is typically attributed to the "mind" which is supposed to be free and independent. In this sense, law builds on strong notions of moral agency. The rationalizations offered by the life sciences are, in contrast, connected to the "body" and its responses to certain (positive or negative) stimuli. Moral action is then, first of all, a re-action of organic systems on which also psychic and social systems ultimately rely. Accordingly, neuroscientists start with the moral capacity of the brain rather than with the individual or the society. We are thus at the naturalist and empiricist pole of rational action schemes. The social sciences navigate between these two poles and are, at the same time, most exposed to socio-technological and socio-practical concerns – namely questions of governance and self-governance. In this perspective, moral action is a matter of social inter-action, reciprocity and exchange; the individual is not conceptualized through the body or the mind, but through its relations with others. At the same time, one can distinguish between self- and other-centered, "egoistic" and "altruistic" moralities within the social sciences. Whereas economics typically starts from *ego* as a prototype of social action, sociology is rather based on *alter* (Hartfiel 1968). Our main point is here, that these different models of action are perfect alternatives only in a theoretical sense. In social practice, they are often combined and integrated in a (more or less) encompassing "rationalization" program referred to above as governmentality – the governmental rationality of world society. The rationalities of law, economics and neuroscience are then streamlined according to the *Zeitgeist* of neo-liberalism.

In a nutshell, today's world polity thus consists in the hegemony of universalized notions of science, law and the economy. While economic and legal spheres have long been scientized, their theories of reflection have not always followed universalist ambitions. Instead, the historical schools of economics and jurisprudence supported relatively provincial models of law and economics that allowed for – and even cultivated – national or professional idiosyncrasies. However, in the global age, these traditional approaches have lost their credits, and legal and economic theories have themselves become driving forces of the globalization of rights and freedoms, markets and constitutions. Since the law and the economy are structurally coupled, patterns of economic organization also translate into forms of legal solidarity (and vice versa). Accordingly, a transnational division of labor furthers moral bonds between individuals all over the world, irrespective of their nationalities. Nonetheless, compared to national societies, the normative cohesion of the globalized market society remains rather weak. Global citizens are, hence, first of all, market citizens. In this respect, law's morality is adjusted to the logic of the market – it becomes "economized". While many liberal economists still perceive the market economy as a realm of freedom, their models rather insinuate a realm of necessities. In fact, the free play of market forces can be understood as a "state of culture" – a cultural achievement, so to speak – which imitates the "state of nature", namely the principle of natural selection. In cognitive terms, the enlightenment paradigm is thus subordinated to the evolution paradigm. Not surprisingly then, economics is strongly attracted by the behavioral and neurosciences that scrutinize the empirical basis of individual decisions – thus moving from micro- to neuro-foundations (Weber and Dawes 2005, Camerer et al. 2005). In this way, economic rationalities become "naturalized."

In this chapter, we addressed three types of order – the legal order (*nomos*), the economic order (*oikos*), and the natural order (*physis*) – that are constitutive for the modern world polity. By modern world polity, we referred not to a utopian *cosmo-polis* as a distant moral vision but to the moral order that is already established through the globalized systems of law, the economy and science. While we emphasized that the sociology of morality has to go beyond religious moralities, the metaphysical dimension is also present in modern societies. In fact, the modernization process can be portrayed as a dialectic of secularization and sacralization. References to a higher order are thus not only found in traditional settings that are shaped by religious world-views but also in modern constellations that draw on moral scripts of freedom and justice – and try to perpetuate themselves through some sort of constitution building. On the collective level, authority – the capacity to govern – has thus been relocated from god to the church, from the church to the sovereign and the territorial state, and from the state to the functional systems of law, economy and science. On the individual level, the same process has generated respective entities of self-governance: first, "immortal souls" as addressees of god and the church, then "mere subjects" as addressees of the sovereign and the state, and, finally, a whole bunch of "rational actors" as addresses of the law, the economy, and science. While world-society's neo-liberal constitution thus rests on the rationalities of functional systems that strive for a universal rule of law, an integrated world market, and a unified model of science, the human condition is ultimately defined through the cult of the legal, the economic, and the cerebral subject, or *homo juridicus, homo oeconomicus*, and *homo cerebralis* (Supiot 2007, Kirchgässner 1991, Hagner 1997).

REFERENCES

Albrow. M. 1996. *The Global Age: State and Society Beyond Modernity*. Cambridge: Polity Press.

Anderson, B. 1991. *Imagined Communities: Reflections on the Origin and Spread of Nationalism*. London: Verso.

Beck, U. 1997. *Was ist Globalisierung? Irrtümer des Globalismus, Antworten auf Globalisierung*. Frankfurt/M.: Suhrkamp.

Benz, A., ed. 2004. *Governance – Regieren in komplexen Regelsystemen: Eine Einführung*. Wiesbaden: VS.

Bourdieu, P. 1996. "Warnung vor dem Modell Tietmeyer: Europa darf sich den neoliberalen Theorien des Bundesbankpräsidenten nicht unterwerfen." *DIE ZEIT*, November 1. Retrieved 15 January, 2010 (http://pdf.zeit.de/1996/45/Warnung_vor_dem_Modell_Tietmeyer.pdf).

Bröckling, U. 2007. *Das unternehmerische Selbst: Soziologie einer Subjektivierungsform*. Frankfurt/M.: Suhrkamp.

Bröckling, U., S. Krasmann, and T. Lemke, eds. 2000. *Gouvernementalität der Gegenwart: Studien zur Ökonomisierung des Sozialen*. Frankfurt/M.: Suhrkamp.

Callon, M. 1998. "Introduction: The Embeddedness of Economic Markets in Economics." PP. 1–57 in *The Laws of the Markets*, edited by M. Callon. Oxford: Blackwell.

Camerer, C. F., G. Loewenstein, and D. Prelec. 2005. "Neuroeconomics: How Neuroscience Can Inform Economics." *Journal of Economic Literature* 43(1): 9–64.

Deutschbein, O., S. Frerichs, 2010. "*Homo neurooeconomicus* und *homo neurosociologicus*. Das Ich zwischen Natur und Kultur." PP. 186–201 in *Gefährliche Menschenbilder: Biowissenschaften, Gesellschaft und Kriminalität*, edited by L. Böllinger, M. Jasch, S. Krasmann, A. Pilgram, C. Prittwitz, H. Reinke, and D. Rzepka. Baden-Baden: Nomos.

Drori, G. S., J. W. Meyer, F. O. Ramirez, and E. Schofer. 2003. *Science in the Modern World Polity: Institutionalization and Globalization*. Stanford, CA: Stanford University Press.

Durkheim, É. 1952. *Suicide: A Study in Sociology*. London: Routledge and Kegan.

Durkheim, É. 1961. *Moral Education: A Study in the Theory and Application of the Sociology of Education*. New York: Free Press.

Durkheim, É. 1973. "Individualism and the Intellectuals." PP. 43–57 in *On Morality and Society*, edited by R. N. Bellah. Chicago, IL: University of Chicago Press.

Durkheim, É. 1984. *The Division of Labour in Society*. Basingstoke: Macmillan.

Durkheim É. 1986. "The Positive Science of Morality in Germany." *Economy and Society* 15(3):346–354.

Foucault, M. 2002. *The Order Of Things: An Archaeology of the Human Sciences*. London: Routledge.

Foucault, M. 2007. *Security, Territory, Population: Lectures at the Collège de France 1977–1978*. Basingstoke: Palgrave Macmillan.

Foucault, M. 2008. *The Birth of Biopolitics: Lectures at the Collège de France, 1978–1979*. Basingstoke: Palgrave Macmillan.

Fourcade, M., and K. Healy. 2007. "Moral Views of Market Society." *Annual Review of Sociology* 33(1): 285–311.

Franks, D. D., and T. S. Smith, eds. 1999. *Mind, Brain, and Society: Toward a Neurosociology*. Stamford, CT: Jai Press.

Frerichs, S. 2008. *Judicial Governance in der europäischen Rechtsgemeinschaft: Integration durch Recht jenseits des Staates*. Baden-Baden: Nomos.

Frerichs, S. 2009. "The Legal Constitution of Market Society: Probing the Economic Sociology of Law." *Economic Sociology – European Electronic Newsletter* 10(3):20–25.

Frerichs, S. 2010a (forthcoming). "Re-embedding Neo-liberal Constitutionalism: A Polanyian Case for the Economic Sociology of Law." In *Karl Polanyi, Globalisation and the Potential of Law in Transnational Markets*, edited by C. Joerges, and J. Falke. Oxford: Hart Publishing.

Frerichs, S. 2010b (forthcoming). "Zur transnationalen Verfassung der Marktgesellschaft: Perspektiven einer Wirtschaftssoziologie des Rechts." In *Unsichere Zeiten: Herausforderungen gesellschaftlicher Transformationen. Verhandlungen des 34. Kongresses der Deutschen Gesellschaft für Soziologie in Jena 2008*, edited by H.-G. Soeffner. Wiesbaden: VS.

Frerichs, S., and O. Deutschbein. 2009. "Law Goes Neuro: Wie kommt das Recht ins Hirn?" PP. 69–84 in *Citizen by proxy und Individualrechte: Über das Rechtssubjekt und seine Stellvertreter*, edited by R. Kreissl. Münster: LIT-Verlag.

Frerichs, S., and R. Münch. 2009. "Was die Weltgesellschaft im Innersten zusammenhält: Kult des Individuums und Moralisierung des Marktes." PP. 37–62 in *Was hält die Gesellschaft zusammen? Jahrbuch für Christliche Sozialwissenschaften 50*, edited by Karl Gabriel. Münster: Aschendorff.

Frerichs, S., R. Münch, and M. Sander. 2008. "Anomic Crime in Post-Welfarist Societies: Cult of the Individual, Integration Patterns, and Delinquency." *International Journal of Conflict and Violence* 2(2):194–214.

Gephart, W. 1993. *Gesellschaftstheorie und Recht: Das Recht im soziologischen Diskurs der Moderne*. Frankfurt/M.: Suhrkamp.

Gertenbach, L. 2007. *Die Kultivierung des Marktes: Foucault und die Gouvernementalität des Neoliberalismus*. Berlin: Parodos.

Habermas, J. 2001. *The Postnational Constellation: Political Essays*. Cambridge, MA: MIT Press.

Hagner, M. 1997. *Homo cerebralis: Der Wandel vom Seelenorgan zum Gehirn*. Berlin: Berlin Verlag.

Hari, R., and M. V. Kujala. 2009. "Brain Basis of Human Social Interaction: From Concepts to Brain Imaging." *Physiological Reviews* 89(2):453–479.

Hartfiel, G. 1968. *Wirtschaftliche und soziale Rationalität: Untersuchungen zum Menschenbild in Ökonomie und Soziologie*. Stuttgart: Enke.

Heintz, B., R. Münch, and H. Tyrell, eds. 2005. *Weltgesellschaft: Theoretische Zugänge und empirische Problemlagen*. Sonderheft der Zeitschrift für Soziologie. Stuttgart: Lucius & Lucius.

Held, D., A. McGrew, D. Goldblatt, and J. Perraton. 1999. *Global Transformations: Politics, Economics and Culture*. Cambridge: Polity Press.

Jessop, B., and N.-L. Sum. 2006. *Beyond the Regulation Approach: Putting Capitalist Economies in their Place*. Cheltenham: Edward Elgar.

Joyce, R. 2006. *The Evolution of Morality*. Cambridge, MA: MIT Press.

Kirchgässner, G. 1991. *Homo Oeconomicus: Das ökonomische Modell individuellen Verhaltens und seine Anwendungen in den Wirtschafts- und Sozialwissenschaften*. Tübingen: Mohr.

Krebs, D. L. 2008. "Morality: An Evolutionary Account." *Perspectives on Psychological Science* 3(3):149–172.

Krücken, G., and G. S. Drori, eds. 2009. *World Society: The Writings of John W. Meyer*. Oxford: Oxford University Press.

Latour, B. 1987. *Science in Action: How to Follow Scientists and Engineers through Society*. Cambridge, MA: Harvard University Press.

Lee Mudge, S. 2008. "What is Neo-liberalism?" *Socio-Economic Review* 6(4):703–731.

Leibfried, S., and M. Zürn, eds. 2005. *Transformations of the State?* Cambridge: Cambridge University Press.

Lockwood, D. 1964. "Social Integration and Systems Integration." PP. 244–257 in *Explorations in Social Change*, edited by G. K. Zollschan, and W. Hirsch. Boston, MA: Houghton Mifflin.

Loye, D. 2002. "The Moral Brain." *Brain and Mind* 3(1) 133–150.

Luhmann, N. 1975. "Die Weltgesellschaft." PP. 51–71 in *Soziologische Aufklärung 2*, by Niklas Luhmann. Opladen: Westdeutscher Verlag.

Luhmann, N. 1997. *Die Gesellschaft der Gesellschaft*. Frankfurt/M.: Suhrkamp.

Merton, R. K. 1938. "Social Structure and Anomie." *American Sociological Review* 3(5):672–682.

Merton, R. K. 1968. *Social Theory and Social Structure*. New York: Free Press.

Meyer, J. W., and R. L. Jepperson. 2000. "The 'Actors' of Modern Society: The Cultural Construction of Social Agency." *Sociological Theory* 18(1):100–120.

Moll, J., R. Zahn, R. de Oliveira-Souza, F. Krueger, and J. Grafman. 2005. The Neural Basis of Human Moral Cognition. *Nature Reviews/Neuroscience* 6(10): 799–809.

Münch, R. 1998. *Globale Dynamik, lokale Lebenswelten: Der schwierige Weg in die Weltgesellschaft*. Frankfurt/M.: Suhrkamp.

Münch, R. 2001. *Offene Räume: Soziale Integration diesseits und jenseits des Nationalstaats*. Frankfurt/M.: Suhrkamp.

Münch, R. 2007. *Die akademische Elite: Zur sozialen Konstruktion wissenschaftlicher Exzellenz*. Frankfurt/M.: Suhrkamp.

Münch, R. 2008a. "Constructing a European Society by Jurisdiction." *European Law Journal* 14(5) 519–541.

Münch, R. 2008b. *Die Konstruktion der europäischen Gesellschaft: Zur Dialektik von transnationaler Integration und nationaler Desintegration*. Frankfurt/M.: Campus.

Münch, R. 2009. *Globale Eliten, lokale Autoritäten: Bildung und Wissenschaft unter dem Regime von PISA, McKinsey & Co*. Frankfurt/M.: Suhrkamp.

Münch, R., and S. Büttner. 2006. "Die europäische Teilung der Arbeit: Was können wir von Emile Durkheim lernen?" PP. 65–107 in *Die Europäisierung sozialer Ungleichheit: Zur transnationalen Klassen- und Sozialstrukturanalyse*, edited by M. Heidenreich. Frankfurt/M.: Campus.

Münch, R., and S. Frerichs. "Markt und Moral: Transnationale Arbeitsteilung und Netzwerksolidarität." PP. 394–410 in *Handbuch der Wirtschaftssoziologie*, edited by A. Maurer. Wiesbaden: VS.

Opitz, S. 2004. *Gouvernementalität im Postfordismus: Macht, Wissen und Techniken des Selbst im Feld unternehmerischer Rationalität*. Hamburg: Argument.

Parsons, T. 1967. *The Structure of Social Action: A Study in Social Theory with Special Reference to a Group of Recent European Writers*. New York, NY: Free Press.

Pierre, J., ed. 2004. *Debating Governance*. Oxford: Oxford University Press.

Polanyi, K. 1957. *The Great Transformation*. Boston: Beacon Press.

Reichertz, J., and N. Zaboura, eds. 2006. *Akteur Gehirn – Oder das vermeintliche Ende des handelnden Subjekts: Eine Kontroverse*. Wiesbaden: VS.

Repplinger, R. 1999. *Auguste Comte und die Entstehung der Soziologie aus dem Geist der Krise*. Frankfurt/M.: Campus.

Rosenfeld, R, ed. 2006. *Crime and Social Institutions*. Aldershot: Ashgate.

Shweder, R. A., N. C. Much. 1997. Manamohan Mahapatra, and Lawrence Park. 1997. "The 'Big Three' of Morality (Autonomy, Community, Divinity) and the 'Big Three' Explanations of Suffering." PP. 119–169 in *Morality and Health*, edited by A. Brandt, and P. Rozin. New York, NY: Routledge.

Sinnott-Armstrong, W., ed. 2008a. *Moral Psychology, Volume 1: The Evolution of Morality*. Cambridge, MA: MIT Press.

Sinnott-Armstrong, W., ed. 2008b. *Moral Psychology, Volume 2: The Cognitive Science of Morality*. Cambridge, MA: MIT Press.

Sinnott-Armstrong, W., ed. 2008c. *Moral Psychology, Volume 3: The Neuroscience of Morality*. Cambridge, MA: MIT Press.

Stivers, R. 1996. "Towards a Sociology of Morality." *International Journal of Sociology and Social Policy*: 16(1/2): 1–14.

Streeck, W. 2009. *Re-Forming Capitalism: Institutional Change in the German Political Economy*. Oxford: Oxford University Press.

Sum, N.-L., and B. Jessop. (forthcoming). *Towards A Cultural Political Economy*. Cheltenham: Edward Elgar.

Supiot, A. 2007. *Homo Juridicus: On the Anthropological Function of Law*. London: Verso.

Tancredi, L. R. 2005. *Hardwired Behavior: What Neuroscience Reveals About Morality*. New York, NY: Cambridge University Press.

Tuori, K. 2007. *Oikeuden ratio ja voluntas*. Helsinki: WSOY [English version forthcoming].

Turner, J. H., and A. Maryanski. 2008. "Explaining Socio-Cultural Evolution: The Limitations of Evolutionary Theory from Biology." *Sociologica – Italian Journal of Sociology on line* 2(3):1–23.

Verplaetse, J., J. de Schrijver, S. Vanneste, and J. Braeckman, eds. 2009. *The Moral Brain: Essays on the Evolutionary and Neuroscientific Aspects of Morality*. Berlin: Springer.

Weber, M. 2004. "The 'Objectivity' of Knowledge in Social Science and Social Policy." PP. 359–404 in *The Essential Weber: A Reader*, edited by Sam Whimster. London: Routledge.

Weber, R., and R. Dawes. 2005. "Behavioral Economics." PP. 90–108 in *The Handbook of Economic Sociology*, edited by N. J. Smelser, and R. Swedberg. Princeton, NJ: Princeton University Press.

CHAPTER 29

The Social Construction
of Morality?

STEVEN LUKES

"It is a pity that talk of the moral sentiments has fallen out of favor"
(Strawson 2008:35)

"Morality" and "morals" were central topics among sociologists at the turn of the last century but did not survive as a field of attention or inquiry. There were, of course, fields of study devoted to "norms" and "values," to "deviance" and "reciprocity" and, more specifically, there have been notable and influential studies of moral education, moral crusades and moral panics, but the notion that "morality" names a field of inquiry to which sociological ideas and techniques relate disappeared. The "sociology of knowledge" survived but the "sociology of morality" did not.

Indeed, the only discipline where "morality" and "moral" have remained central is, of course, moral philosophy. Moral philosophers have been, so to speak, the academic guardians of "morality." For the philosopher, I venture to suggest, sociology's withdrawal is not a matter for regret, since the very idea of sociology of a morality might seem to make what looks like an unacceptable assumption. This is the idea that the very category of the "moral" (and thus, within morality what counts as moral as opposed to immoral) is, as they say, a "social construction": that it is socially shaped and will vary from one historical period and one social context to another, so that there are (to use an opaque phrase that will, I hope, become somewhat less so) *multiple moralities*, of which our own is only one among others (talk of "moralities" is as unfamiliar to moral philosophers as talk of "knowledges" is to epistemologists).

Moral philosophers are, with few (and thus striking) exceptions committed to the enterprise of finding the best account of moral thinking or reasoning. They seek to justify and criticize the judgments we make when faced with moral issues. They debate with one another, at different levels, about the question: what is the right way to reach correct or objective or the best-justified moral judgments? How, they ask, is one to decide moral questions? They may give complex or indecisive or multiple or skeptical or despairing answers, but that is their question. From this standpoint, the assumption indicated cannot be entertained. For if it were to be upheld, "morality" would cease to be the name of a stable and unified field: what is to count as "moral" (and thus, I repeat, what is "moral" and what is "immoral") would be seen as varying indefinitely from context to context and subject to empirical inquiry. In this chapter, I shall examine that assumption: namely, the assumption that both the content and the scope of morality vary indefinitely across different societies and contexts? Is there, in short, a convincing way for us to identify "morality" as a field for sociological inquiry and research that

S. Hitlin, S. Vaisey (eds.), *Handbook of the Sociology of Morality*,
Handbooks of Sociology and Social Research, DOI 10.1007/978-1-4419-6896-8_29,
© Springer Science+Business Media, LLC 2010

does not express and endorse our own moral outlook and thereby prejudge the limits of moral diversity?

The English word "morality" has a range of meanings and is used in different contexts. We can distinguish two broad ranges of usage: high and low. Talk of morality is central to the reflections of certain kinds of intellectuals, notably philosophers, theologians, clergymen and educators; but there is also a second, everyday "lay" or "folk" conception, or range of conceptions, of morality which overlap but do not coincide with the various versions of the first. In addition, then there are the natural and social scientists, coming from various disciplines, who seek to analyze and explain moral judgments and behavior (and is it obvious that morality is appropriate as an analytical or *scientific* category?) What is clear is that what "morality" denotes is subject to endless contestation.

Consider first the philosophers. G.J. Warnock starts from the Humean idea of "limited sympathies." He thinks that "the general object" of morality is to cultivate good dispositions, or moral virtues, and provide moral principles that will counteract these "limited sympathies" and their potentially most damaging effects. It is, he suggests, "the proper business of morality, and the general object of moral evaluation, to expand our sympathies, or, better, to reduce the liability to damage inherent in their natural tendency to be narrowly restricted." (Warnock 1971:26) A Kantian view of morality, on the other hand, focuses on the Moral Law and the idea that a good person is exclusively motivated by the duties or obligations it imposes, indeed, in Bernard Williams's phrase it tries "to make everything into obligations." (Williams 1985:180). On this view, morality involves self-denying values imposing law-like obligations and is pervaded by the language of rights and duties, commands, guilt and blame. Contrast both these pictures with the predominant utilitarianism in the English-speaking countries in recent times, with its consequentialist focus on calculating, measuring, aggregating and maximizing pleasures or preference-satisfaction or welfare or on minimizing suffering, and with the revival of virtue ethics, with its roots in Aristotle, focusing on the conditions of human flourishing or the enabling of human capabilities or the cultivation of character. In addition, what about the scope and distribution of moral concern? Do moral judgments or rules apply to all and to all equally? For Kurt Baier adopting "the moral point of view" means acting on "rules which are meant for everybody" and which are "for the good of everyone alike" (Baier 1958:208), and yet, as Brian Leiter reminds us, Nietzsche clearly repudiates this "egalitarian premise of all contemporary moral and political theory—the premise, in one form or another, of the equal worth and dignity of each person." (Leiter 2008:290).

These few examples are enough to suggest, not only the contestedness of the concept of morality among philosophers, but also the peculiarity of that contest. For to practice moral philosophy is to assume that it is a contest that can be won–that arguing and theorizing can in principle achieve its resolution. And yet, although the last hundred years of philosophical reasoning and debate have indeed hugely clarified the issues, they have brought us no nearer to such resolution. Nietzsche offered an interesting diagnosis of the reason why:

> It is precisely because moral philosophers knew the facts of morality only somewhat vaguely in an arbitrary extract or chance abridgement, as morality of their environment, their class, their church, the spirit of their times, their climate and zone of the earth, for instance—it was precisely because they were so ill-informed and not even very inquisitive about other peoples, ages and former times, that they did not so much as catch sight of the real problems of morality—for these come into view only if we compare *many* moralities (Nietzsche 1990:186)

Anthropologists, on the contrary, are engaged in doing just that. Traditionally they favored a far more capacious and relativizing approach than the philosophers did. Their professional concern was with what I have called the "low" sense of morality, with morality as viewed by its practitioners—with morality as *mores*. Thus William Graham Sumner wrote that "immoral never means anything but contrary to the mores of the time and place" (Sumner 1960:355) and Ruth Benedict wrote that "morality. . .is a convenient term for socially approved habits." (Benedict 1956:73).

However, this is clearly a thoroughly inadequate approach, since we want to know both how locals distinguish moral from non-moral customs and habits (as they typically do) and how to do so ourselves. Here, more recent anthropologists, though they have provided some clues, have not helped much. For, as James Laidlaw has observed, despite "some individually brilliant discussions of morality by anthropologists" and the fact that some "of the greatest ethnographies are dominated by the explication of moral concepts and reasoning," we do not have an account of what makes such concepts and reasoning moral, for "there is no anthropology of ethics" and "no connected history we can tell ourselves about the study of morality in anthropology, as we do for a range of topics such as kinship, the economy, the state, or the body" (Laidlaw 2002:312, 311).

Should we, then, look to the psychologists for help? For in recent times, they have been exploring the question of which traits and capacities are universal (perhaps because innate) and which are subject to cultural variation. In addition, here morality has been a central concern generating a range of interesting and conflicting hypotheses. Eliot Turiel and his colleagues (see Turiel 1983, 2002) have sought to show that children from a very early age are able to distinguish between the domains of the moral and the conventional. Children, they claim, can distinguish between, and react differently to, moral and conventional norms. In particular, they distinguish between rules prohibiting injury, theft, or promise breaking, on the one hand, and rules prohibiting inappropriate dress, bad manners or talking in class, on the other. Moral transgressions, they propose, are more serious, usually involve harming victims, and are independent of the say-so of authorities, and involve rules that are general in scope and are justified by appeal to harm, justice and rights. Conventional transgressions, by contrast, are less serious, and the rules are dependent on the dictates of particular authorities, local in scope, and not justified by reference to harm, justice, or rights. They conclude that their subjects, when questioned about transgressions of rules of both types, judged this distinction between domains as both psychologically real and important. The idea is that these are seen as distinct conceptual domains to which different responses are appropriate because compliance is justified by different kinds of reasons. Furthermore, they claim that their conclusions are supported by evidence that this basic division is drawn from toddlers to adults across cultures, classes, and economic classes.

Yet, this claim of universally recognized domains has met with severe and broadly convincing criticism. Apart from the citing of contrary evidence, the central objections are several. First, consider seriousness. Some seemingly conventional breaches can be desperately serious. Jon Elster recounts the story of a young officer in pre-Revolutionary France, wealthy but not noble, who, having tried to gatecrash a party at Versailles, was driven to suicide by the ridicule with which he was greeted (Elster 2007:364). Conversely, actions plainly accepted as immoral, such as corruption and white-collar crime, are often treated with little concern and even indifference. Second, as for harm, justice and rights, seemingly conventional practices, such as scarification, can be harmful, while violations of prevailing morality, such as consensual gay sex, harm no one and invade no-one's rights. Third, as for authority-independence, consider the story of Abraham and Isaac and the fact that Jews and Moslems, for instance, view dietary laws as moral because commanded by God. Conversely, most conventional rules are followed irrespective of the dictates of any particular authority. In short, the suggested critieria do not succeed in mapping a difference between kinds of norms as they function in social life. Moreover, it often happens that conventions appear to have a moral aspect (if you fail to observe a conventional norm of politeness, say, you show disrespect and breaking traffic regulations can put others in danger). In general, as Jesse Prinz observes, the "very same act can count as a moral violation or as a conventional violation depending on how it is described." (Prinz 2008:386).

Perhaps, then, we should endorse Prinz's suggestion that the moral/conventional distinction is not a distinction between kinds of rules but should rather be understood as distinguishing "dimensions of rules that we *regard* as moral, and dimensions of rules that we *regard* as merely conventional." (Prinz 2008:386). (Here "we" refers, presumably, to the psychologists and the locals, to both observers and observed). What, then, distinguishes the moral way of regarding rules from the conventional way? Prinz's answer is that "the moral dimensions of rules are psychologically grounded in moral sentiments." More specifically he proposes that "any dimension of a rule enforced by emotions of self-blame and other blame and directed at third parties qualifies as a moral rule." (Prinz 2008:386). *Mature* moral judgments, he suggests, "are enforced by meta-emotions. If you do something wrong and don't feel guilty, I will be angry at you for your conduct and for your lack of remorse." In sum, to "have a moral attitude towards φ-ing," he writes, "one must have a moral sentiment that disposes one to feel a self-directed emotion of blame for φ-ing, and an emotion of other directed blame when someone else φs" (Prinz 2008:369) (So, for example, when "we say that it is "morally wrong" to disrespect others, we express our belief that we would blame someone for disrespecting others"). Then, significantly, Prinz comments that "the disposition for blaming people for behaving in some way may itself be a culturally inculcated value." In addition, notice that the very claim that morality is grounded in moral sentiments is controversial. Rationalists, such as Kantians, who ground morality in the ability to form and act on judgments of what ought to do, will not agree. Nor may those psychologists whose hypothesis is that moral judgments arise out of innately given pre-rationalized intuitions (see Haidt and Joseph 2004) or grounded in an inuititive and unconscious moral grammar (see Hauser 2006). In addition, among those who do agree, Prinz's proposal is only one among others, and yet, as I shall argue, it is along the right lines.

What I have so far sought to show is that there is wide, persistent and seemingly irresoluble disagreement over the criteria for applying the concept of "morality," over what lies within the scope of moral appraisals and judgments and what does not. Philosophers disagree not only about the best or appropriate way to reach and justify moral judgments but also over what moral judgments are: over how to define what morality is. Anthropologists and psychologists are similarly non-convergent. Indeed, it would seem that differing answers to this question are inextricably tied to different moral outlooks: that how one conceives of "morality" reveals and expresses one's own morality: that is, one's first-order moral judgments, values, and principles.

However, this is not the only sense in which morality may be thought of as multiple. For, as Charles Taylor has observed, "one of the big illusions shared by moral philosophers is the belief that there is a single consistent domain of the 'moral', that there is one set of considerations, or mode of calculation, which determines what we ought 'morally' to do". (Taylor 1985:233). As I shall now argue, it is by no means obvious that "morality" names a unified object or field.

Is there any reason to think that the moral domain is unified by a distinctive set of common concerns?[1] The anthropologist Richard Shweder and his colleagues have proposed the hypothesis, based on fieldwork in India, that there are in all cultures three broad domains of moral discourse –three "culturally coexisting discourses of morality" –namely, "the ethics of autonomy," "the ethics of community" and "the ethics of divinity." Their idea is that, within the Hindu social order, these foster different types of "goods," each indispensable and all enhancing human dignity and self-esteem; and that, in general, cultures "differ in the degree to which one or another of the ethics and corresponding moral 'goods' predominate in the development of social practices and in the elaboration of a moral ideology" (Shweder et al 1997:140–142).

With similar implications but in a different idiom, the psychologists Jonathan Haidt and Craig Joseph have proposed that one should think of morality as *modular*. Their focus is on moral intuitions —"fast and automatic responses to specific environmental triggers" that they conceive as "primitive and innate, or at least innately prepared" in the human evolutionary past and as undergirding "the moral systems that cultures develop, including their understandings of virtues and character." (Haidt and Joseph 2004:60, 61, 56). They suggest that there are four such modules that correspond to distinct stimuli: namely, suffering, hierarchy, reciprocity/fairness, and purity. (In addition, they add a possible fifth "ingroup module" with the associated emotion of loyalty). They think of such intuitions as distinct "pattern-recognition systems" that "often launch moral emotions" and generate distinct complexes of what are seen as virtues in different cultures. In addition, elsewhere, Haidt has suggested that distinct emotions are elicited by distinct kinds of immorality. In general, write Haidt and Joseph, morality is "innate (as a small set of modules) and socially constructed (as sets of interlocking virtues)." (Haidt and Joseph 2004:64). Morality, on such views, in short, is composed of non-unified, distinct elements that, in combination, yield different social moralities.

Should we, then, think of morality as "socially constructed" and what would that thought precisely amount to? Here we can find help from Ian Hacking's checklist (Hacking 1999) of the three component ideas that the notion of "social construction" comprises: namely, (1) *contingency*: the thought that what is claimed to be socially constructed could have been quite otherwise—so that, for example, there could have been an equally successful physics in no sense equivalent to existing physics; (2) *nominalism*: the thought that our categories and classifications are not fixed by the nature of things or the structure of the world but by our linguistic conventions; and (3) *externalism*: the thought that we believe what we do, not because of the reasons that appear to justify what we believe, but because of factors such as the influence of the powerful or of social interests or of institutional imperatives or of social networks.

Beginning with the last, it is clear that, just as (3) lies at the origin of "the sociology of knowledge," so, comparably, it sets out part of what must be the agenda of a sociology of morality: namely, the role of the powerful and dominant interests, and alongside them moral entrepreneurs, within social institutions and networks, in drawing moral boundaries, imposing

---

[1] For this section, I am indebted to Walter Sinnot-Armstrong, whose contribution to the 2009 conference on the sociology of morality (Sinnot-Armstrong 2009) I found both stimulating and instructive.

moral standards, inculcating moral ideologies and defining moral virtues. Clearly, it embraces a vast array of existing sociological works, both historical and contemporary, that examine the extent of and limits to such influence, from studies of the respectable poor and of forms of patriarchy to contemporary studies of evangelical Christianity or the teaching of ethics in business schools, and also the various reformist and conflict-reducing uses of "moral power," as discussed in this volume by Jal Mehta and Chistopher Winship. Seeing such work and future such studies through this lens helps focus attention on the social actors and social determinants that, to a greater or lesser extent, influence what I have called low conceptions of morality.

However, it also, of course, helps focus attention on the manifold ways in which individuals and groups escape and resist such influences. Huckleberry Finn was acting morally when he resisted his "duty" to turn in Jim the slave, as were those who rescued and protected Jews during the Holocaust and there was a "moral life" within the concentration camps (see Todorov 1996). Thus, for instance, a moral sociology in this vein would attend to moral codes generated within counter-cultural and deviant subcultures but also, to what James Scott calls the "arts of resistance" (see Dodson 2009). Scott, who focuses on domination in highly stratified societies and institutions, suggests that there are two kinds of evidence of such resistance. On the one hand, there are the "hidden transcripts" –generated in secluded settings, behind the scenes in the victims' "life apart in the slave quarters, the village, the household, and in religious and ritual life," in "a social space in which offstage dissent to the official transcript of power relations may be voiced," in forms such as "linguistic disguises, ritual codes, taverns, fairs, the "hush arbors of slave religion" and consisting in "hopes of a returning prophet, ritual aggression via witchcraft, celebration of bandit heroes and resistance martyrs." (Scott 1990:85. xi). On the other hand, there are the open but disguised expressions of ideological insubordination that can be decoded by interpreting "the rumors, gossip, folktales, songs, gestures, jokes and theater of the powerless as vehicles by which, among other things, they insinuate a critique of power while hiding behind anonymity or behind innocuous understandings of their conduct." (Scott 1990:xiii).

(1) and (2), however, raise a different kind of question: namely, whether there are limits to what can be constructed in the name of morality. Specifically, can we adduce reasons based on "natural" facts—facts about human nature and about how human beings interact socially–for fixing boundaries around what is to count as morality, within which variation occurs, thereby setting an agenda for the sociology of morality? Is there a prospect of identifying a distinctive, trans-human way in which people interact and relate to one another which will satisfy the following three demands: (1) that it is compatible with most commonly accepted meanings of "morality" and "moral"; (2) that it is compatible with the main alternative philosophical theories of morality; and (3) that it allows for wide variation in empirical realizations in the form of moral judgments, behavior, codes and practices?

The philosopher P. F. Strawson made two suggestions that, I believe, offer, in combination, a promising way of answering this question. In the first place, Strawson wrote that

> certain human interests are so fundamental and general that they must be universally acknowledged in some form and to some degree in any conceivable moral community.

Allowing for the possible diversity of moral systems and the possible diversity of demands within a system, Strawson wrote, the recognition of certain general virtues and obligations will be a logically or humanly necessary feature of almost any conceivable moral system: these will include the abstract virtue of justice, some form of mutual aid and to mutual abstention from injury and, in some form and in some degree, the virtue of honesty. (Strawson 1970:111)[2]

In a later, justly famous, and influential essay, Strawon developed a further idea that significantly advances this "naturalistic" approach: namely the claim that there is a range of distinctive "reactive attitudes" that "have common roots in our human nature and our membership of human communities." (Strawson 2008:29) These "participant reactive attitudes are essentially natural human reactions to the good or ill will or indifference of others towards us as displayed in their attitudes and actions" (25): they reveal "how much we actually mind, how much it matters to us, whether the actions of other people—and particularly of some other people—reflect attitudes towards us of goodwill, affection or esteem, on the one hand or contempt, indifference, or malevolence on the other." (22) As evidence, Strawson cites the difference it makes to us whether or not we see an injury we incur as resulting from the actions of an agent or agents for which he or they were *responsible* (and there is a range of different reasons why they might not be). Strawson's suggestion is made in the context of discussing freewill and determinism—a discussion into which we will not enter. Here the key point to notice is his claim that "our natural human commitment" to these "ordinary interpersonal attitudes" is "part of the general framework of human life." (28) His idea, in short, is that human beings "naturally" engage in the practice of holding one another responsible for benefits and injuries and in doing so display a range of "attitudes" that respond to what they perceive as good or ill will or indifference of others; and that these attitudes express an engaged "first-person" perspective of participants in the practice.

Which are these "reactive attitudes" – these "non-detached attitudes or reactions of people directly involved in transactions with each other"? Strawson first offers a few examples: "attitudes and reactions of offended parties and beneficiaries," such things as "gratitude, resentment, forgiveness, love, and hurt feelings," (21) observing that they arise in "ordinary interpersonal relationships, ranging from the most intimate to the most casual." (23) But then he develops a typology of three kinds of such attitudes: (1) personal attitudes, such as resentment, which react directly to ill will or indifference of others to ourselves; (2) "sympathetic or vicarious" attitudes. These are "impersonal or disinterested or generalized analogues" of the first kind. These

> rest on, and reflect, exactly the same expectation or demand in a generalized form. . .for the manifestation of goodwill and regard, on the part of others, not simply towards oneself, but towards all those on whose behalf moral indignation may be felt, i.e., as we now think, towards all men. (29)

And, just as (1) concerns demands on others for oneself and (2) concerns demands on others for others, there are (3) "self-reactive attitudes" associated with "demands on oneself for others": notably "feeling bound or obliged (the 'sense of obligation'); feeling compunction; feeling guilty or remorseful or at least responsible; and the more complicated phenomenon of shame." (29)

---

[2] This suggestion is reminiscent of H. L. A Hart's 'minimum content' of Natural Law (Hart 1994:192–193)

Strawson himself suggested that we should speak specifically of the second category as "moral," arguing that it is "the impersonal or vicarious character of the attitude" that entitles it to this qualification. But I suggest that we discard this suggestion (seeing this view of morality as morality in its narrower sense) and (seeking a broader sense) focus rather on the indicated practice, as such: on his claim to have identified a "general framework of attitudes" that we are "given with the fact of human society." (35), a "complicated web of attitudes and feelings which form an essential part of the moral life as we know it." By attending to this range of attitudes, we can "recover from the facts as we know them a sense of what we mean, i.e. of all we mean, when, speaking the language of morals, we speak of desert, responsibility, guilt, condemnation, and justice." (34)

What does "the moral life" thus understood exclude? Significantly, Strawson refers to what he calls the "objective attitude," which he sees as "profoundly opposed" to the "involvement or participation in a human relationship" that these attitudes share. To adopt the objective attitude to another human being

> is to see him, perhaps, as an object of social policy; as a subject for what, in a wide range of senses, might be called treatment; as something certainly to be taken account, perhaps precautionary, account of; to be managed or handled or cured or trained; perhaps simply avoided. . ... (24–25)

Adopting the objective attitude, writes Strawson, is "a consequence of our viewing the agent as incapacitated in some or all respects for ordinary interpersonal relationships." (26)

There are several gains in viewing morality in this broad way. First, it offers, as a sociological agenda, a way of identifying and investigating multiple moralities as species of a common genus, exemplifying varying ways in which these attitudes are manifested in different cultural and social contexts, in which some attitudes may be more or less predominant and others even absent. Indeed, one can view the "reactive attitudes" as constituting a trans-human repertoire, an arc of possibilities from which different moralities draw, emphasizing some and de-emphasizing others, sometimes to the point of suppression or exclusion. It also enables one to see where the "objective attitude" is at work—sometimes in ways that do not involve the suspension of ordinary reactive attitudes (as when inflicting punishment or treating, say, the mentally ill) but sometimes in ways that do (as when, say, racism involves social exclusion). In this way, the approach offers a kind of "bridgehead" into the understanding of alien moral worlds, about which one can ask what are the distinctive grounds within them for experiencing and exhibiting moral sentiments, and the limits to doing so.

One may, of course, wonder whether at least some of these reactive attitudes, so described, are not themselves culturally specific rather than natural to humans. Strawson himself commented on the "increased historical and anthropological awareness of the great variety of forms which these human attitudes may take at different times and in different cultures" and declared that one should therefore be

> chary of claiming as essential features of the concept of morality in general, forms of these attitudes which may have a local and temporary prominence. No doubt to some extent my own descriptions of human attitudes have reflected local and temporary features of our own culture.

But, he concluded,

> an awareness of variety of forms should not prevent us from acknowledging also that in
> the absence of any forms of these attitudes it is doubtful that we should have anything
> that we could find intelligible as a system of human relationships, as human society.
> (36)

Which leads me to a further advantage of this account of a distinctively human framework or web of reactive attitudes. For it offers, I suggest, the most helpful and comprehensive way of conceiving of human uniqueness in the active current debates about morality in animals. Thus Frans de Waal has asked the (rhetorically intended) question: "What is different about the way we *act* that makes us, and not any other species, moral beings?" (de Waal 1996:111). De Waal stresses "the continuity between human social instincts and those of our closes relatives, the monkeys and the apes" (de Waal et al. 2009:37) and, in general, "the profound similarities between human and animal behavior (e.g, maternal care, sexual behavior, power seeking)." (65). He has advocated anthropomorphism – "the description of animal behavior in human, hence intentionalistic terms" (de Waal et al. 2009:63) – as a strategy for the description of animal behavior, not as a projection of "human emotions and intentions onto animals without justification, explication or investigation" (64) but with the scientist's goal of arriving at "testable ideas and replicable observations" (63). Specifically, he has focused on empathy, "targeted helping" (also found among dolphins and elephants), reciprocal altruism and (he claims) fairness among monkeys and even gratitude among chimpanzees. Needless to say, much of this is highly controversial, not only among animal scientists, but also among philosophers.

Thus the Kantian Christine Korsgaard robustly asserts that what is key is "the ability to be motivated by an ought." (Korsgaard 2009:117). The non-human animal, she claims, has "purposes...given to him by his affective states," whereas

> the capacity for normative self-government and the deeper level of intentional control
> that goes with it is probably unique to human beings. And it is in the proper use of this
> capacity—the ability to form and act on judgments of what we ought to do—that the
> essence of morality lies, not in altruism or the pursuit of the greater good. (116)

And she observes that for Adam Smith too the impartial spectator (the "man in the breast") is at work judging the propriety of our feelings and motives—when, that is, it is "proper" for us to experience them–and thus enhancing our capacity to be motivated by thoughts of what we ought to do and ought to be like. And Philip Kitcher too, while noticing that de Waal's argument relies on "the sentimentalist tradition in ethical theory" in suggesting that the animals in question display sympathy or altruism, observes that this is not yet morality: that what is needed is "a capacity for normative guidance and self-control." For sympathy, even when enlarged, is not enough. For without a device such as the impartial spectator, there are only "limited and idiosyncratic sympathies, types of psychological altruism that may be necessary if moral responses are to develop...but fall a long way short of morality" –not least because "altruistic dispositions are too weak, often of the wrong kinds, and because conflicting altruistic impulses need adjudication." (Kitcher 2009:133,134).

My suggestion is that Strawson's scheme of reactive attitudes offers a really helpful way of identifying moral dispositions by showing that device at work, engaged in determining when one or another such attitude is "proper" and thus when and how to respond to others' attitudes towards us, when to hold whom responsible for injuries, and how to distinguish attitudes of "goodwill, affection or esteem, on the one hand or contempt, indifference, or malevolence on the other." In this way, it provides an effective way of discriminating (given all the evidence) which concepts appear applicable uniquely to humans (such as "resentment," "indignation," "guilt," and "shame"). It also enables us to distinguish between *different* ways of understanding those concepts that appear applicable across the human/non-human divide, such as empathy, sympathy, and the like. Such concepts can be given, so to speak, a "thinner" or a "thicker" interpretation. Thus, "sympathy" among apes and chimpanzees is not only, as Kitcher has argued, "limited and idiosyncratic" in intensity, range, extent and skill, but crucially lacks an adjudication device, leaving them "vulnerable to whichever impulse happens to be dominant at a particular moment." (Kitcher 2009:136). And it is questionable, for instance, whether the grooming service performed by chimpanzees for those individuals who previously shared food with them registers, as de Waal suggests, "a psychological mechanism known in humans as 'gratitude'"—namely, a feeling of thankfulness in appreciation of the kindness, or perceived goodwill, of another.

I have sought to show in what way it is plausible to see morality as socially constructed and in what way it is not. Both "high" and "low" or folk conceptions of what is moral (and thus moral and immoral) conduct are remarkably divergent across time and space. This "diversity of morals" is a traditional, long-forgotten but recoverable part of the agenda of sociology and social anthropology (see Ginsberg 1956, Snare 1980). The idea of "social construction" can help focus attention on the role of dominant elites and moral entrepreneurs in shaping and ssustaining moral codes, and in encouraging reforms and resolving conflicts, and on investigating the limits to their moral power.

But what is the diversity of morals a diversity of? Is the very idea of what is moral "socially constructed" in the sense that there are just different answers, or is there a common object of inquiry and research such that different moralities can be seen as distinct species of a common genus? I have argued that Strawson's notion of "reactive attitudes" provides a positive answer and thus presents a viable agenda for the sociology of morality. These attitudes can be seen as forming a repertoire of moral sentiments that are realized in strikingly different ways in different social contexts. The repertoire itself is not socially constructed but a "natural" part of "the general framework of human life"; its various social, culturally conditioned realizations are widely diverse and sometimes deeply conflicting and incompatible. What is the role of honor, pride, respect, guilt, sympathy, or compassion, resentment, remorse, gratitude, forgiveness, love, shame, disgust and so on in motivating behavior of differently situated individuals in different social and institutional settings? What, for instance, are the historical origins and social bases of different configurations of these sentiments and their corresponding virtues and vices? How, for example, did hierarchical notions of honor become transformed into egalitarian notions of respect, with a corresponding democratization of the notion of "dignity" (see Waldron 2007)? And under what conditions do the limits of moral concern contract and expand?

Recognition of the diversity of moralities is thus compatible with, indeed requires, a coherent account of what morality is. But (I should add, without elaborating the argument here[3]) to recognize such diversity is not to acquiesce in an attitude of moral relativism. Such recognition is from an observer's perspective and the relativist makes the illegitimate inference

---

[3] For the elaboration of the argument, see Lukes 2008.

that one can transfer one's observations into the first-person perspective of a moral agent, a participant in the practice of morality.

I conclude with a final example: the case of the Nazis. From the end of the Second World War until today, the Nazis have represented for countless moral philosophers the epitome of radical evil—the paradigm of what is beyond the moral domain. On the approach recommended here, we should rather inquire both into the extraordinary success of the Nazi leaders in securing not only compliance but enthusiasm on such a large scale; and into the moral attitudes of the various kinds of Nazi perpetrators, investigating how, when and on what basis they experienced and exhibited resentment, gratitude, forgiveness, regret, indignation, guilt, pride and shame, and so on[4]. We should also inquire into the limits of their morality, where the participant, reactive attitudes are replaced by the most extreme form of the "objective attitude" in which other human beings are treated as beyond the human pale.[5]

BIBLIOGRAPHY

Baier, K. 1958. *The Moral Point of View.* Ithaca, NY: Cornell University Press.

Benedict, R. 1956 (1934). "Anthropology and the Abnormal." *Journal of General Psychology,*101 reprinted in *Personal Character and General Milieu* edited by Douglas Haring. Syracuse: Syracuse University Press.

de Waal, F. 1996. *Good Natured. The Origins of Right and Wrong in Humans and Other Animals.* Cambridge, Mass.: Harvard University Press.

de Waal, F. et al. 2009. *Primates and Philosophers : How Morality Evolved.* The Tanner Lecture edited and introduced by S. Macedo, and J. Ober. Princeton: Princeton University Press.

Dodson, L. 2009. *The Moral Underground: How Ordinary Americans Subvert an Unfair Economy.* New York: New Press.

Elster, J. 2007. *Explaining Social Behavior: More Nuts and Bolts for the Social Sciences.* Cambridge: Cambridge University Press.

Ginsberg, M. 1956 (1953) "On the Diversity of Morals," *Royal Anthropological Institute Journal,* lxxxiii (1953) 117–135 republished in *On the Diversity of Morals.* London: Heinemann.

Hacking, I. 1999. *The Social Construction of What?*Cambridge, Mass.: Harvard University Press.

Haidt, J., and C. Joseph. 2004. "Intuitive Ethics: how innately prepared intuitions generate culturally variable virtues." *Daedalus,* Fall 55–66.

Hart, H. L. A. 1994 (1961). *The Concept of Law.* Oxford: The Clarendon Press.

Hauser, M. 2006. *Moral Minds: How Nature Designed Our Universal Sense of Right and Wrong.* New York: HarperCollins.

Kitcher, P. 2009 "Ethics and Evolution: *How To Get from Here to There*". PP. 120–139 in De Waal 2009.

Korsgaard, C. 2009. "Morality and the Distinctiveness of Human Action." PP. 98–119 in De Waal 2009.

Laidlaw, J. 2002. "For an Anthropology of Ethics." *Journal of the Royal Anthropological Institute* (N.S.) 8:311–332.

Leiter, B. 2008. "Against Convergent Moral Realism: The Respective Roles of Philosphical Argument and Empirical Evidence." PP. 333–337 in *Moral Psychology.* Vol. 2: *The Cognitive Science of Morality: Intuition and Diversity* edited by Walter Sinnot-Armstrong. Cambridge, MA: MIT Press.

Lukes, S. 2008. *Moral Relativism.* New York: Picador and London: Profile Books.

Nichols, S. 2004. *Sentimental Rules: On the Natural Foundations Of Moral Judgment.* Oxford: Oxford University Press.

Nietzsche, F. 1990 (1888). *Beyond Good and Evil,* edited by M. Tanner. Harmondsworth: Penguin.

---

[4] I am grateful to David Velliman for letting me read a yet unpublished paper by Herlinde Pauer-Studer and himself entitled 'Distortions of Normativity,' which explores this latter question.

[5] I am much indebted to Adam Wilkins for his sharp and insightful comments on an earlier draft of this chapter.

Prinz, J. 2008. "Is Morality Innate?" in *Moral Psychology.* Vol. 1: *The Evolution of Morality: Adaptations and Innateness,* edited by W. Sinnot-Armstrong. Cambridge, Mass.: MIT Press.

Scott, J. C. 1990. *Domination and the Arts of Resistance: Hidden Transcripts.* New Haven: Yale University Press.

Shweder, R., N. C. Much, M. Mahapatra, and L. Park. 1997. "The 'Big Three' of Morality (Autonomy, Community, Divinity) and the 'Big Three' Explanations of Suffering.' PP. 119–169 in *Morality and Health* edited by A. Brandt, and P. Rozan. New York: Routledge.

Sinnot-Armstrong, W. 2009 "Are Moral Judgments Unified? Paper Presented to the workshop understanding morality: Developing Interdisciplinary perspectives." June 15–16 2009. National Science Foundation, Arlington, Virginia.

Snare, F. E. 1980. "The Diversity of Morals." *Mind* 89(355), July:353–369.

Strawson, P. F. 1970 (1961). "Social Morality and Individual Ideal." *Philosophy* 36(136): January 1961 1–17 reprinted in Wallace and Walker 1970

Strawson, P. F. 2008 (1962). "Freedom and Resentment" Originally Published in *Proceedings of the British Academy,*48 (1962), 187–211 most recently reprinted in *Free Will and Reactive Attitudes: Perspectives on P. F. Strawson's "Freedom and Resentment."* edited by Michael McKenna and Paul Russell. Farnham: Ashgate, 2008.

Sumner, W. G. 1960 (1906) *Folkways.* New York: Mentor Books.

Taylor, C. 1985. *Philosophical Papers.* Vol. 2: *Philosophy and the Human Sciences.* Cambridge: Cambridge University Press.

Todorov, T. 1996. *Facing the Extrme: Moral Life in the Concentration Camps.* New York: Metropolitan Books.

Turiel, E. 1983. *The Development of Social Knowledge: Morality and Convention.* Cambridge: Cambridge University Press.

Turiel, E. 2002. *The Culture of Morality: Social Development, Context and Conflict.* Cambridge: Cambridge University Press.

Waldron, J. 2007. "Dignity and Rank" *Archives européennes de sociologie (European Journal of Sociology)* 48(2): 201–237.

Wallace, G., and A. D. M. Walker 1970. *The Definition of Morality.* London: Methuen.

Warnock, G. J. 1971. *The Object of Morality.* London: Methuen.

Williams, B. 1985. *Ethics and the Limits of Philosophy.* London: Fontana.

CHAPTER 30

What's New and What's Old about the New Sociology of Morality

GABRIEL ABEND

OLD-NEW SOCIOLOGY OF MORALITY[1]

Question: What's "the science which, of all the sciences which have yet opened upon men, is, perhaps, the least cultivated, the least definite, the least ascertained in itself, and the most difficult in its application"? Answer: "[T]he science of Morals." So claimed Harriet Martineau (1838:3) in her book *How to Observe Morals and Manners*, some 170 years ago. Yet, however little cultivated the "science of Morals" might have been in the 1830s, it surely made major strides in the late nineteenth and early twentieth centuries.

In 1869 two important works appeared: Irish historian W. E. H. Lecky's two-volume *History of European Morals* ([1869]1884) and French philosopher Charles Renouvier's two-volume *Science de la morale* ([1869]2002). In France the science of morality would soon start to gather momentum. Durkheim's version—variously called *science de la morale, science des faits moraux,* or *physique des moeurs* – developed over the course of 30 years: from his article "La science positive de la morale en Allemagne" (1887) to the introduction to his unfinished treatise *La Morale* (1917). Equally influential was Lucien Lévy-Bruhl (1903) book, *La Morale et la science des moeurs,* which only two years later was already available in English as *Ethics and Moral Science.* As Dominique Parodi observed, there was at the time much excitement around the sociology of morality: "people don't grow tired of discussing the connections between *la morale* and sociology; and it is the same problem that fills most contemporary publications" (quoted in Merllié 2004:426; my translation[2]). Or, as Bayet (1905:1) put it, "[t]he idea that *la morale,* for a long time religious or metaphysical, must henceforth rest on science,

---

[1] For comments on an earlier draft I'd like to thank Howard Benson, Carol Heimer, Steven Hiltin, Steven Lukes, Mildred Schwartz, and Christopher Winship.

[2] I use existing English translations wherever possible; all others are my own. The translations of "*la morale*" and "*science de la morale*" aren't straightforward. In his "Preface to the Translation" of *Division of Labor*, George Simpson (1933:x) writes: "I have often translated 'la morale' as *ethics,* although sometimes as *morality.* I do not think Durkheim made any sharp distinction between them." But Simpson doesn't say what *he* means by them, nor in

S. Hitlin, S. Vaisey (eds.), *Handbook of the Sociology of Morality,*
Handbooks of Sociology and Social Research, DOI 10.1007/978-1-4419-6896-8_30,

is today very widespread" (see also Bayet 1925, Belot 1921, Bouglé 1922, Fauconnet 1920, Gurvitch 1937, Leroux 1930).

In Germany, the first edition of Wilhelm Wundt's *Ethik* appeared in 1886, which advocated a scientific approach to morality. Wundt proposed an investigation into the "facts" and "laws" of moral life. A few years later, Georg Simmel published in two volumes *Einleitung in die Moralwissenschaft* (1891–1892), i.e., an introduction to the science of morality. Simmel, too, argued for a descriptive science, which he opposed to philosophers' prescriptive aims (respectively, *beschreibende Ethik* and *vorschreibende Sittenlehre*). Durkheim was much influenced by this German tradition, as evidenced by his discussion of Wundt's thought in the above-mentioned article "La science positive de la morale en Allemagne" (Hall 1993, Isambert 1990:130–131).

In light of the impact of evolutionary theories on social thought in general in the late nineteenth century, it's not surprising that it had an impact, too, on the study of morality (see, e.g., Dewey 1898, Huxley 1893, Spencer 1879, Stephen 1882, Tufts 1912). Among others, here one may cite Sutherland's two volumes *Origin and Growth of the Moral Instinct* (1898) and L. T. Hobhouse's two volumes *Morals in Evolution* (1906). Of special sociological interest is Edward Westermarck's two-volume, 1,500-page *Origin and Development of the Moral Ideas* (1906–1908). Far from a theoretical or methodological manifesto, it empirically addressed some basic sociology-of-morality questions: "Why do moral ideas in general differ so greatly? And, on the other hand, why is there in many cases such a wide agreement? Nay, why are there any moral ideas at all?" (1906:1). Durkheim's ([1907]1979) criticisms notwithstanding, Westermarck's work remains an impressive early attempt to utilize a wide array of empirical data to answer questions about morality.

In 2010, more than 100 years later, the present *Handbook of the Sociology of Morality* is being published in the United States. This handbook reflects the fact that the sociology of morality has become a legitimate subfield of sociological research in this country. In turn, it is likely to further strengthen the subfield's legitimacy. There were many earlier calls for a sociology of morality. For example, in 1970 Maria Ossowska made a "plea for a sociology of morality" (1970:27–29). In 1973 Steven Lukes lamented that "the sociology of morality is the great void in contemporary social science" (1973:432). In 1991 Craig Calhoun lamented that "[f]or the most part, sociologists have not carried forward Durkheim's task of creating a sociology of morality" (1991:232). But we had to wait until the beginning of the twenty-first century for a self-aware intellectual social movement to emerge (see Frickel and Gross 2005). Today no eyebrows are raised when "sociology of morality" is used as an attributive noun – e.g., someone may teach a sociology-of-morality class or write a sociology-of-morality paper. Naturally, institutionalization lags a bit behind, but some small steps have already been taken.

In short, a sociology of morality has come about. However, we've seen that this isn't the first time that a sociology of morality comes about. It seems apposite to ask, then, what's new

---

which cases he uses which. Durkheim's introduction to *La Morale* is titled "Introduction to Morality" in one collection of essays (translation by Mark Traugott), and "Introduction to Ethics" in another (translation by H.L. Sutcliffe) (Durkheim [1920]1978, [1920]1979). Remarkably, Durkheim begins this piece precisely by discussing two senses of "*la morale.*" In my translations I leave the word "*morale*" in French. [Cf. Sutcliffe (1979:viii): "As is the custom amongst translators of Durkheim, certain words for which there is no precise and unambiguous English equivalent have been left in the original" (see also Fields 2005:174–175.]

and what's old about this new sociology of morality. What might it learn from earlier sociologies of morality? What empirical, theoretical, methodological, and epistemological gaps need to be filled? What wheels needn't be reinvented?

In the second section of the chapter I discuss three old issues: (a) whether morality can and should be scientifically investigated and how this scientific investigation might differ from academic moral philosophy, popular moralizing, and normative arguments in general; (b) whether and how morals vary across time and place; and (c) whether and how social factors can causally explain these variations. I spell out these three points using the writings of Martineau, Lévy-Bruhl, and Durkheim. In the third section of the chapter I discuss two new challenges for the new sociology of morality: (a) the implications of moral realism and (b) the implications of moral neuroscience. While I can only sketch these implications and I don't try to actually address the challenges that they pose, I do explain why they should be attended to. Finally, in the fourth section, I very briefly consider the future of the new sociology of morality: what's next and what unique contributions it can make.

WHAT'S OLD

Science

The sociology of morality intends to develop a social-scientific understanding of morality, in the same sense that the sociologies of religion, literature, and science intend to develop social-scientific understandings of religion, literature, and science. Sociologists of morality should be able to obtain a special kind of knowledge, different from common sense knowledge, inaccessible to the layperson, obtained using methods that the layperson doesn't master, and so on.

As early as 1838 Harriet Martineau argued that there was a science of morals, which required a special expertise and special methods, much like geology, architecture, botany, or statistics.[3] Martineau (1838:2) imagines a traveler who goes abroad and observes people's morals and manners:

> If, on his return from the Mediterranean, the unprepared traveller was questioned about the geology of Corsica, or the public buildings of Palermo, he would reply, "Oh, I can tell you nothing about that—I never studied geology; I know nothing about architecture." But few, or none, make the same avowal about the morals and manners of a nation. Every man seems to imagine that he can understand men at a glance; he supposes that it is enough to be among them to know what they are doing; he thinks that eyes, ears, and memory are enough for morals, though they would not qualify him for botanical or statistical observation; he pronounces confidently upon the merits and social condition of the nations among whom he has travelled; no misgiving ever prompts him to say, "I can give you little general information about the people I have been seeing; I have not studied the principles of morals; I am no judge of national manners."

---

[3] On Martineau's (arguably neglected) methodological treatise, *How to Observe Morals and Manners*, see: Hill (1989), Hoecker-Drysdale (1992:50–53), Lengermann and Niebrugge (2001).

For his part, Lévy-Bruhl's ambition in *La Morale et la science des moeurs* is to establish the epistemological foundations of the science of morality, understood as a sociological science. After arguing against "theoretical ethics," he argues for a science whose object is "ethical rules, obligations, laws, and whatever generally is contained in the conscience":

> Since a science cannot be normative as well as theoretical, no theoretical science of ethics exists or can exist in the traditional sense of the words. Is scientific research in respect to ethics impossible? On the contrary, the rational distinction between the theoretical and practical points of view permits us to define the object of that research. While the confused conception of a "theoretical ethics" is destined to disappear, another conception, clear and positive, begins to be formed. It consists in the consideration of ethical rules, obligations, laws, and whatever generally is contained in the conscience, as a given reality, as a unity of facts; in short, as an object of science that must be studied in the same spirit and by the same method as other social facts. (Lévy-Bruhl [1903]1905:11)

As is usual when new disciplines emerge, the infancy cliché is quickly taken advantage of. That is, the cliché that a new discipline is "still" in its "infancy," as an explanation of its meager yields up to that point. Usually, the comparison to physics' infancy comes next: "In classical antiquity … 'physical science' offered characteristics remarkably like those which the 'science of ethics' presents now." Thus, Lévy-Bruhl assures us that we don't need to worry: the science of morality isn't abnormal; there are phases all sciences must go through; as a young discipline it can "profit by the experience of its elder sister [physics]"; its maturity is "unfortunately still very distant"; but it will eventually yield great returns; and so on (pp. 48, 87, 123, see also pp. 169–170; see also Bayet 1905:5, 34–35, 52).

For it to count as a scientific discipline, the science of morality ought to be objective, and it ought to be concerned with what is, not with what ought to be. To Lévy-Bruhl, "[e]thical reality" "must be regarded … with the same objectivity as physical reality":

> The main point is that ethical reality shall henceforth be incorporated in nature, that is, that ethical facts shall be placed with social facts, and that social facts in general shall be conceived as an object of scientific research, by the same right and the same method as the other phenomena of nature. [. . .] Henceforward speculative effort will no longer consist in determining "what ought to be," that is, in prescribing. It will, as in every science, bear on a given objective reality, that is, on ethical facts, and on other social facts inseparable from them (Lévy-Bruhl [1903]1905:200, 26)

This passage sounds quite Durkheimian. Indeed, earlier on in the book Lévy-Bruhl has a foot-note acknowledging his debt to *The Rules of Sociological Method* as follows: "We are in entire agreement with the spirit of that work, and are glad to acknowledge here what we owe to its author" (p. 11; see also p. 96). Even though Lévy-Bruhl was never one of Durkheim's devo-tees, *La Morale et la science des moeurs* is his most Durkheimian book (Horton 1993, Merllié 2004:420, Pickering 1979:8). In turn, Durkheim positively reviewed Lévy-Bruhl's book in *L'Année sociologique* and linked it to his own efforts: "In this work Lévy-Bruhl offers the reader an uncommonly skilful dialectical analysis of the idea which underlies all my work in this sphere, namely, that a positive science of moral facts does exist, and that it is upon such a science that the practical speculations of moralists must be based" (Durkheim [1904]1979:29).

Durkheim's idea of a positive science of moral facts, which "underlies all [his] work in this sphere," originates in his early article on the German "positive science of morality." There he noted that "the science of morality [*science de la morale*] is only in the process of being born.":

> Ethics [*la morale*] is not an applied or derived science, but an autonomous one. It has its own object which it ought to study as the [physicist] studies physical facts or as the biologist studies biological facts, and employing the same methods. Its facts are mores, customs, legal prescriptions, and economic phenomena insofar as they become the subject of legal dispositions. It observes, analyzes, and compares these facts, progressively elevating itself toward discovery of the laws which explain them. [. . .] Moral facts. . . are related to all other social facts, but are not identical with these. Ethics is not a derivate or a corollary of sociology, but a social science beside and in the midst of the others ([1887]1993:134, 127).

These points that Durkheim made in 1887 would recur in his later work: there are moral facts that are analogous to natural facts; there is a special social science of moral facts; and this science should discover the laws that explain those facts. For example, in 1906 Durkheim delivered a paper at the Société française de philosophie, " The Determination of Morals Facts." According to Lukes (1973:412), this is "the clearest formulation of his conceptual scheme, which he saw as the theoretical framework for his sociology of morality." The point about the special science of morality came out most clearly in the discussion that followed his presentation, where he calls it a "branch of sociology":

> The science of which I speak is not general sociology, and I am not trying to say that research into social structures and political and economic systems will produce deductions as to the moral system. The only science that will furnish methods of approaching these judgments on moral matters is the special science of moral facts. In order to understand morality we must proceed from the moral data of the present and the past. Certainly this science of moral facts is, I am convinced, a sociological science, but it is a very particular branch of sociology (Durkheim [1906]1974:71–72).

Durkheim argues that morality can be the object of scientific investigation. Moreover, he distinguishes this project from the attempt to deduce morality from science. As he says in the preface to the first edition of *The Division of Labor in Society*:

> This book is above all an attempt to treat the facts of moral life according to the methods of the positive sciences. [. . .] We do not wish to deduce morality from science, but to constitute the science of morality [*science de la morale*], which is very different. Moral facts are phenomena like any others. They consist of rules for action that are recognisable by certain distinctive characteristics. It should thus be possible to observe, describe and classify them, as well as to seek out the laws that explain them (Durkheim [1893]1984:xxv).

Attempts to deduce morality from science are a recurrent feature of Western ethical thought, and are as common in our days as they were in Durkheim's. Let me then elaborate on his distinction. (This distinction could be objected to in more than one way, but I circumvent these possible objections here.) First, there's the project of turning ethics or moral philosophy into a science, in the sense that answers to substantive moral questions are to be arrived at using scientific methods. Or, more conservatively, they are to be arrived at reasoning from or drawing on scientific facts. While the latter is a weak condition and hence it applies to many very diverse authors and arguments, they share the aim of doing normative ethics. As Spencer

(1879:v) writes in *The Data of Ethics*, "my ultimate purpose … has been that of finding for the principles of right and wrong in conduct at large, a scientific basis" (see also Sidgwick 1880; Spencer 1881).

Second, there's the project of scientifically observing, describing, classifying, and explaining morality. This is what sociologists of morality typically believe to be in the business of: they use scientific methods not to answer moral questions, but to account for people's answers to moral questions. Some sociologists – including notably Durkheim and Lévy-Bruhl themselves – believe that their empirical researches may have practical implications or applications of some sort, or even that they may lead in some way to normative conclusions. A very tricky question, though, is of just what sort and in just which way. For example: what a "rational moral art" might be, or how to move from moral science to moral art (Bayet 1905; Lévy-Bruhl [1903]1905; Small 1905:662–665, 1910:214–243; cf. Isambert 1990: 142–144; Pharo 2004; Turner 1993; Watts Miller 1996). In any case, presumably these sociologists still believe that their primary aims and the primary questions they set out to address aren't normative or practical ones.

However, it's more often the case that sociologists say that they are *only* interested in the scientific description and explanation of morality, not in making value judgments or normative arguments. To give just one illustration, Robert Jackall's book about the morality of corporate managers "treats ethics and morality sociologically":

> As they are popularly used, of course, the notions of morality and ethics have a decidedly prescriptive, indeed moralistic, flavor. They are often rooted in religious doctrines or vague cultural remnants of religious beliefs, like the admonition to follow the Golden Rule. However, this book treats ethics and morality sociologically, that is, as empirical, objective realities to be investigated. Therefore, in using the terms morality and ethics, I do not refer to any specific or given, much less absolute, system of norms and underlying beliefs. Moreover, I imply no judgment about the actions I describe from some fixed, absolute ethical or moral stance, as the terms are often used in popular discourse, sometimes even by corporate managers themselves (Jackall 1988:4).

In "Two Main Problems in the Sociology of Morality" (Abend 2008) I argue that this sort of position represents the current orthodoxy in the sociology of morality. I presume this is roughly the view of most of the contributors to this *Handbook of the Sociology of Morality*, too.

Variation

That different people and different peoples have different morals is a simple and uncontroversial observation. It's an old one, too. For example, a staple of undergraduate ethics courses and textbooks is Herodotus's story in the third book of his *Histories* about the Persian king Darius, the Greeks, and the Callatiae. This is how classics scholar Rosalind Thomas (2006:69) tells it:

> [I]n a well-known passage, Herodotus claims that Darius asked some assembled Greeks how they treated the corpses of their parents. Upon learning that the Greeks burned them, he asked some Indians, who said they ate theirs; each group is horrified at the others' habits, and Herodotus takes this to show that all people adhere to their own customs: 'And I think Pindar was correct to say that *nomos* is king of all' (3.38.4).

One of the starting points of the sociology of morality – old and new – is the observation that morality varies a lot across time, place, and a host of social variables. Some people eat the corpses of their parents and think that burning them would be morally abominable, while some other people burn the corpses of their parents and think that eating them would be morally abominable. Some people are pro-life, some people are pro-choice. Some people hold that property is theft, some people hold that the estate tax is theft. The sociologist's job is to describe and explain these moral variations.

What (if anything) follows from these simple and uncontroversial observations is a complex and controversial question (see, e.g., Lukes 2008; Moody-Adams 1997; Rachels 2001). Does the fact of moral variation lend support to metaethical skepticism – that is, the view that "values are not objective, are not part of the fabric of the world," right and wrong are invented, or something along these lines (Mackie 1977:15)? Does the fact of moral variation contradict moral nativism – that is, the argument that morality is innate or hard wired or something along these lines (see, e.g., Joyce 2006a, 2006b; Prinz 2007, 2008) [4]?

Here the sociology of morality, much like cultural anthropology, has a long tradition of: (1) rejecting moral nativism and the concept of universal human nature and (2) drawing metaethically skeptical conclusions from its empirical investigations. For instance, in *Modernity and the Holocaust* Zygmunt Bauman (1989:176) maintains that "the dominant sociological theory avers" a "programmatic relativism" – a fact that Bauman bemoans. One more-or-less recent example is Goode and Ben-Yehuda's "relativist" or "subjectively problematic" approach to morality:

> To the adherent of the relativist or subjectively problematic approach, no quality of absolute evil lurks immanently or inherently in adultery, homicide, human sacrifice, pornography, or abortion. What is crucial is how the behavior is defined, judged, and evaluated in a particular context. What counts is these varying definitions and evaluations; it is they and they alone that determine the status of an act with respect to morality and immorality. [...] [I]n the abstract, how do we know that adultery is immoral, killing is evil, abortion is murder? According to whose perspective? What measurable criteria will allow us to establish these positions? (Goode and Ben-Yehuda 1994:68).

As I've pointed out elsewhere (Abend 2008), the sociology of morality has often been seduced by arguments of the following form:

(1) *A* believes *p*.
(2) *B* believes *q*.

Therefore,

(3.1) neither *p* nor *q* are correct, valid, true, better than the other, etc.; and
(3.2) neither *p* nor *q* can be correct, valid, true, better than the other, etc.

---

[4] One can't really speak of the moral nativism thesis, since there are many dissimilar moral nativism theses. Joyce (2006b:257–258) tries to clarify what the "innateness of morality" means as follows: "I suggest that what people generally mean when they debate the 'innateness of morality' is whether morality (under some specification) can be given an adaptive explanation in genetic terms: whether the present-day existence of the trait is to be explained by reference to a genotype having granted ancestors reproductive advantage, rather than by reference to psychological processes of acquisition."

For example, according to many people Hitler was an evil man, but some other people (e.g., his many followers in the 1930s and 1940s) disagree. Therefore, it can't be established whether Hitler was an evil man or not; that's just a matter of opinion or taste. Unfortunately, this is a clear *non sequitur*. On the other hand, while nothing follows logically from moral disagreement in and of itself, it can be argued that persistent moral disagreement among well-meaning and well-informed people increases the plausibility of metaethical skepticism (Mackie 1977). Still, there are many issues about which persistent disagreements among well-meaning and well-informed people don't suggest the conclusion that it's just a matter of opinion or taste – including much of philosophy, social science, and even natural science!

Unlike much contemporary sociology of morality, Martineau's and Lévy-Bruhl's arguments about these issues are multifaceted, and thus difficult to pigeonhole. Consider Lévy-Bruhl's argument about "ethical progress":

> That our ethics should not be "absolute" at least in its essential rules is, in its [the conscience's] eyes, an "immoral" idea. That conviction is revealed for instance in the manner in which ethical progress is ordinarily represented. It is to be imagined that men will recognize their duties more and more, will become more and more attached to them, will more and more prefer the consciousness of having accomplished them to any other satisfaction; that they will become, in short, more wise and more virtuous. But it is not imagined that the duties themselves will change and be transformed, although reflection and history show that as a matter of fact they are not immutable. Every society obeys the imperious need of regarding rules on which it instinctively believes its stability and existence to depend as absolute (Lévy-Bruhl [1903]1905:205; see also pp. 230–231).

Thus, the sociology of morality's third-personal perspective debunks the first-personal experience of morality as absolute and eternal. In contrast to people "[i]n feudal society or in Chinese society," Lévy-Bruhl asks, "how can we refuse to extend universal relativity to ethics?" (p. 119). Further, he harshly criticizes moral philosophy's "postulate" that "human nature is always identical with itself at all times and in all places" (p. 53). Sociological research, he thought, proves it wrong.

> [O]ur presumed knowledge of "human nature" in general, from the moral and mental point of view, is destined to give place to an entirely different psychology. It will be based on the patient, minute, methodical analysis of the customs and institutions in which the feelings and thoughts are objectified in the various human societies now existing, or in societies the existence of which has left traces that we can interpret. Sociology has only just begun to undertake that analysis, and has already obtained some positive results. It shows, by contrast, how artificial and poor is the idea of "man" with which psychology and theoretical ethics have hitherto been contented. (p. 65)

In this passage Lévy-Bruhl uses scare quotes around "human nature." Similarly, he uses them elsewhere in the book around "ethical truth" (p. 173), "immoral" (pp. 190, 205), and the like. As usual, the implication seems to be that, although people speak of "human nature," "ethical truth," and so on, in reality there are no such things. However, while he rejects the concept of human nature, he still maintains that sociology and psychology will eventually reveal "the unity of the mental structure in the human species."

> It will manifest itself by the striking analogy of complicated mental processes produced in different portions of humanity without apparent communication between them: the same formation of myths, the same beliefs in spirits, the same magical practices, the

same organizations of the family and the tribe. But if that unity is confirmed it will nevertheless remain different from that which is admitted a priori by the postulate we have criticized. (pp. 65–66; see also pp. 221–222)

Moreover, Lévy-Bruhl categorically rejects skepticism. Specifically, he takes up the objection that from his arguments "ethical scepticism must result almost of necessity, for it is clear that in a different civilization, different obligations would be imposed on consciences with an authority and a legality equal to those which in our eyes belong to our duties." The objector thus protests: "not only do you not offer us a rule of action, but so far as it depends on you, you destroy what we had" (p. 212). Lévy-Bruhl's response to this objector is as follows:

> There is no reason that because our ethics is relative it should at once lose its value. We are not obliged to choose between the two alternatives: our ethics either has an absolute character or it loses all authority. The proof that an intermediate position is possible, and not paradoxical, is that all empirical systems of ethics (and they are numerous enough both in ancient and modern times!) obtain their places without thereby compromising the validity of their precepts. As relativity of knowledge may be admitted without depriving human knowledge of all logical value, so to admit the relativity of ethics, or rather of ethical systems, does not *ipso facto* deprive them of all authority and legality. But the authority and the legality themselves become relative and that is what we intended to state. (p. 213). [5]

For her part, Martineau (1838:22) argues against a "universal Moral Sense" by appealing to empirical observations such as the following:

> A person who takes for granted that there is an universal Moral Sense among men, as unchanging as he who bestowed it, cannot reasonably explain how it was that those men were once esteemed the most virtuous who killed the most enemies in battle, while now it is considered far more noble to save life than to destroy it. They cannot but wonder how it was that it was once thought a great shame to live in misery, and an honor to commit suicide; while now the wisest and best men think exactly the reverse. And, with regard to the present age, it must puzzle men who suppose that all ought to think alike on moral subjects, that there are parts of the world where mothers believe it a duty to drown their children, and that eastern potentates openly deride the king of England for having only one wife instead of one hundred.

In this paragraph, Martineau might come across as rehearsing the traditional argument: there's moral variation, hence there's no universal moral sense. However, like Lévy-Bruhl's, Martineau's stance is complex, because she does recognize certain moral universals:

> Knowing that some influences act upon the minds of all people in all countries, he [the traveller] looks everywhere for certain feelings of right and wrong which are as sure to be in all men's minds as if they were born with them. For instance, to torment another without any reason, real or imaginary, is considered wrong all over the world. In the same manner to make others happy is universally considered right. (p. 23)

---

[5] It's beside the point for the purposes of this chapter whether this argument is sound. But I do think that Lévy-Bruhl is sometimes in trouble, especially when he argues that "experience itself testifies against that objection" (p. 214), and uses the expressions "ethical objective reality" and "objective" in an ambiguous fashion (e.g., pp. 214–215).

Indeed, Martineau believes that "[t]here is the same human heart everywhere" (p. 42). [6] Nonetheless, the important point here is that these "feelings of right and wrong" aren't innate. Instead, they "begin very early; and this is the reason why they are supposed to be born with men." One piece of evidence for this claim is that "they are few and imperfect in childhood, and, in the case of those who are strongly exercised in morals, they go on enlarging and strengthening and refining through life" (p. 23).

Finally, Martineau argues that moral difference isn't vice, but it *is* "ignorance and barbarism":

> His [the traveller's] own moral education having been a more elevated and advanced one than that of some of the people he contemplates, he cannot but feel sorrow and disgust at various things that he witnesses; but it is ignorance and barbarism that he mourns, and not vice.

She gives several examples: "the Arab or American Indian offer[s] daughter or wife to the stranger, as a part of the hospitality which is, in the host's mind, the first of duties," "the Ashantee offers a human sacrifice," "the Hindoo exposes his sick parent in the Ganges," "the Georgian planter buys and sells slaves," etc. But these things, "acted upon by the ignorant and deluded, they are very different from the wickedness, perpetrated against better knowledge, if the supposition of a universal, infallible Moral Sense were true" (pp. 24–26). This argument makes her views even more difficult to label, because ignorance, barbarism, and delusion imply a purportedly objective judgment of worth – even if not moral worth, as vice and wickedness would.

Explanation

If morality isn't innate and universal, one should explain where it comes from and what accounts for moral variation. According to Martineau (1838:23), "all fair evidence and just reflexion [sic]" should suggest the conclusion that

> …every man's feelings of right and wrong, instead of being born with him, grow up in him from the influences to which he is subjected. We see that in other cases,— with regard to science, to art, and to the appearances of nature,—feelings grow out of knowledge and experience; and there is every evidence that it is so with regard to morals.

Right and wrong aren't "born with [man]," but determined by "the influences to which he is subjected." In other words, "every prevalent virtue or vice is the result of the particular circumstances amidst which the society exists"; the result of "gigantic general influences" (pp. 27, 40).

---

[6] Behind these claims lies Martineau's metaphysics, which at the time of her writing *How to Observe Morals and Manners* still had room for "Providence" and "[man's] Creator": "The general influences under which universal ideas and feelings of right and wrong are formed, are dispensed by the Providence under which all are educated. That man should be happy is so evidently the intention of his Creator, the contrivances to that end are so multitudinous and so striking, that the perception of the aim may be called universal" (p. 25; cf. Hoecker-Drysdale 1992:26).

What are these "circumstances" and "influences"? Martineau illustrates her causal argument using two cases: "the Feudal System" and US society [whose morals she had recently discussed at great length in *Society in America* (Martineau 1837).] She identifies several relevant independent variables – my phrase, of course – at both the individual and societal levels. For instance, in the feudal system case they include class, gender, occupation, cultural variables such as prevalent ideas about the past, nature of people's pastimes, nature of people's dwellings, the dummy variable "coarse furniture," and so on. And then she analyzes the effects of these variables on the dependent variable, "morals," as well as some interaction effects (pp. 31–34).[7] Throughout the book, she considers many other independent variables and their causal effects. For example: "the extent of the commerce" (p. 158), life expectancy (p. 166), population density (p. 189), racial composition of a population (p. 211), and so on.

Martineau's data are sometimes dubious – e.g., substandard historical and anthropological evidence (or, to be more considerate, as good as it could be back then), variables about which statistically representative data weren't available, etc. Plus, her main aim was methodological anyway. But what's remarkable is that the logic of her 1838 sociology of morality is exactly the logic of most 2010 sociology of morality. Present-day scholars often set out to find out what factors account for moral rules, ideas, beliefs, institutions, practices, etc.; what social independent variables account for the variance of moral dependent variables. They might ask, for instance, why people in a particular society or social group have a particular institution (say, slavery, or corporate social responsibility indexes), or a prevalent conviction/value/feeling (say, that slavery is an unjust institution, or that business has moral obligations to society) rather than another.

This logic is systematically laid out by Maria Ossowska (1970:28) in her discussion of "moral phenomena as dependent variables" (see also Brandt 1954:1–14). Ossowska "review[s] the different factors which at various times have been considered influential on the moral life of societies." She then considers numerous "factors" or "determinants", including "economic determinants," "political factors," "the role of industrialization," "the role of the past," "the role of social stratification," "the division of labor," "demographic factors," among others social variables (she also considers a non-social one, "the role of the physical environment," basically the climate).

Much like their predecessors, present-day sociologists of morality are often after causal arguments. Unlike their predecessors, however, they tend to make probabilistic rather than deterministic causal arguments. For example, Martineau uses the modal verb "must" to establish a relationship between the social conditions and the morals of a "district" or "country." She asks, deterministically: "what *must* be the morals of such a district as this? and [sic], it may be added, of the whole country of which it forms a part?" Indeed, she says that the effects of "the state of society" are "inevitable" (pp. 32, 34; emphasis added). Moreover, she speaks of the *laws* of the science of morality – "the laws under which feelings of right and wrong grow up in all men" (p. 21) – as Durkheim would many years later.

No less deterministic is Lévy-Bruhl. He ([1903]1905:158) argues that "ethical feelings and practices" are "bound up with other concomitant series of social phenomena." His list

---

[7] For example, she argues that, given the nature of the feudal system, "[t]he clergy will be politic, subservient, studious, or indolent, kind-hearted, effeminate, with a strong tendency to spiritual pride, and love of spiritual dominion. It will be surprising, too, if they are not driven into infidelity by the credulity of their pupils" (p. 33).

of independent variables includes "religious beliefs," "economic and political conditions," "intellectual acquisitions," "climatic and geographical conditions," and "the past of that society." And he goes on to claim that "[s]ince the ethical feelings of a given society rigorously depend on its collective ideas, beliefs and customs, they are at every moment what those ideas, customs and beliefs (present and past) exact that they shall be" (p. 189). In other words:

> The past of a certain people, its religions, sciences and arts, its relations with neighbouring peoples, its general economic condition being given, its ethics is determined by the mass of facts of which it is the outcome. A more or less harmonious system—but only one system—of ethical rules wholly defined, corresponds to a wholly defined social condition. It is in that sense that Greek ethics differs from modern ethics and Chinese ethics from European ethics. (p. 115)

Lévy-Bruhl, too, believed that there are "laws" that govern the "social objective reality" (e.g., p. 19). Furthermore, the sociology of morality should use comparative and historical methods to discover these laws (e.g., pp. 100–102, 142–144; see also Fauconnet 1920:18–23). Indeed, he anticipated contemporary discussions about the role of history in comparative-historical sociology. [8]

WHAT'S NEW

In the previous section I discussed three old issues concerning the sociological investigation of morality, which Martineau, Lévy-Bruhl, and Durkheim wrote about. In this section I discuss two new challenges for the new sociology of morality. These challenges stem from recent developments in moral philosophy and in moral neuroscience.

Moral Reality and Truth

The old sociology of morality did consider what (if any) metaethical conclusions followed from the fact of moral variation. But the new sociology of morality has to grapple with the recent metaethical literature on moral reality and truth, which presents the problem in a different and much more sophisticated manner. Once upon a time, one could confidently assert that facts and values were two different kinds of things; that "fact and value are totally disjoint realms, that the dichotomy 'statement of fact *or* value judgment' is an absolute one" (Putnam 1981:127; emphasis in original). According to this dichotomy, facts are the realm of objectivity; statements of fact are truth-apt. In contrast, values are the realm of subjectivity; value judgments aren't truth-apt. For example, the sentence, "The speed of light is 299,792,458

---

[8] For example, he writes: "There are then sciences which ought to play an indispensable part in 'ethical physics,' analogous (I do not say entirely similar) to that of mathematics in physics properly so called. They are the historical sciences. [...] If we understand, as we should, by historical sciences, not only the political, diplomatic and military history of nations, but also the history of languages, arts, technology, religions, law, customs, civilization, and institutions, those are the oldest and most fruitful in results of the sciences studied by 'social nature'; indeed, failing them, the effort to establish sociological laws would be vain. The comparative method, indispensable to reach such laws, is only applicable thanks to the results of the historical sciences" (p. 100).

meters per second" is capable of being objectively true or false. But the sentence, "It's wrong to torture a child for the sake of it" is a subjective value judgment, which is not capable of being objectively true or false, correct or incorrect, valid or invalid.

This dichotomy was very useful for many institutions (and, incidentally, it facilitated the establishment of a science of society). However, its foundations have turned out to be wobbly to say the least (see, e.g., Putnam 2002). On the one hand, we've grown much less confident in the objectivity of facts and in the truth-aptness of statements of fact. More specifically, several realizations have made us question our epistemic capabilities and possibilities, including – but not limited to – our realizing that: (a) the scientific knowledge we have hasn't been obtained in the way scientific methods textbooks and teachers prescribe; (b) perception and evidence are theory-laden; and (c) theories can only be tested holistically. [9] More generally, we've grudgingly accepted that, our being humans and not gods, we can't possibly attain a "view from nowhere" (Nagel 1986) or "viewpoint of no one in particular" (Fine 1998) – in science, in ethics, in politics, in art, or anywhere else.

On the other hand, we've grown much less confident in the subjectivity of values and in the non-truth-aptness of value judgments, especially moral ones. Many philosophers have taken issue with the argument that moral judgments are just like subjective preferences, matters of opinion, judgments of taste, etc. That is, the argument according to which my conviction that slavery is unjust is basically analogous to my conviction that Circe Maia's poetry is beautiful, my preference for soccer over tennis, or my loving sweet potatoes but disliking tomatoes. Thus, much like there's no arguing about tastes, there's no fact of the matter as to whether slavery is unjust. It's my subjective opinion against yours; "thy blood or mine," in economist Lionel Robbins's words (quoted in Putnam 2002:54).

Now, this argument has been objected to on many grounds. But a particularly relevant one for this chapter is as follows: To be sure, we'll never get an objective, final, irrefutable, corroboration that slavery is unjust. But we'll never get an objective, final, irrefutable corroboration of a scientific theory either! That sort of standpoint is not available to us. Moreover, ethics and science have dissimilar objects, so why subject the former to the standards of proof and validity of the latter? If we accepted that these standards should be specific to morality – that moral and practical reasoning constitute an autonomous domain, as Scanlon (2009) has recently put it – we could show that slavery is indeed an unjust institution and Hitler was indeed a wicked person (see also Putnam 2004). If so, anyone who said, "Hitler was a good person," would be making a mistake, just like anyone who said, "In 1988 the President of Uruguay was Yubert Lemos."

It's the job of metaethicists to deal with these problems. Why would a sociologist of morality need to pay attention to them at all? There are two main reasons. First, suppose it turned out that moral statements – e.g., "Slavery is unjust" – are capable of truth, objectivity, validity, correctness, or something like that. Then, one could argue that the purported fact that slavery is unjust should play a role in a sociologist's explanation of why a lot of people believe that slavery is unjust. Similarly, one could argue that the purported fact that Barack Obama is the President of the United States should play a role in the explanation of why a lot of

---

[9] In order to test theory *T* one needs many auxiliary theories, including the theories embedded in one's measurement instruments and methodological techniques. But then one is not testing theory *T* alone, but *T and* the auxiliary theories as a whole (cf. Duhem [1906]1991, Quine 1953).

people believe that he is. (One might use counterfactual conditionals to argue for this, e.g., "If Barack Obama hadn't won the 2008 election, it wouldn't be the case that today a lot of people believe that he is the President of the United States.") The expression I use, "to play a role," is purposefully ambiguous, because just what role is a knotty problem, too. In any case, the basic idea here is that the world impinges on people's beliefs about it, even if, obviously, this impingement is mediated by many other social factors. [10] According to this line of reasoning, the sociology of morality should add moral truth to its explanatory equation.

In an earlier paper I argued that the sociology of morality should not add moral truth to its explanatory equation (Abend 2008). My argument then was based on pragmatically agnostic grounds – what a sociologist should do in view of: (a) her not knowing whether there are moral truths or not at all; and (b) assuming that there are, her often not knowing *what* they are. However, more recently I've started to have some doubts about this argument. I'm not convinced anymore that if there were moral truths, then the sociologist's explanation would *always* or *necessarily* need to use them. Nor am I clear on how to determine in which kind of cases it would, if in any (cf. Harman and Thomson 1996, Loeb 2005, Sturgeon 1998, Thomson 1998).

In any event, the philosophical problem of moral truth encroaches on the sociology of morality in a second way. Consider the sociology of the Holocaust, which poses significant challenges to a sociological account of morality (Alexander 2002, Bauman 1989). Let's imagine a sociologist named Jones who sets out to sociologically explain why the Nazis believed what they believed. Suppose Jones decides to assume, for the purposes of her scientific endeavor, that there are no moral truths. That is, she assumes that the Nazis didn't do anything objectively wrong, they didn't have any evil beliefs, Hitler wasn't a moral monster, etc. That's just the socially and culturally determined view that she, as someone born in a particular place at a particular time, happens to hold. Hence, she may act on it in her life, but it has no room in her science. Thus, Jones writes her book impartially and symmetrically. She's very careful never to imply that the Nazis believed and did horrendous things; they just had unusual preferences or tastes. And she tells a story about the social factors that explain their beliefs, just like she would have explained why some people believe that jazz is awesome and reggae is awful.

How well would Jones's story fare as a sociological explanation? An objector would argue that it's impossible to really understand the Nazi worldview, ideology, or belief system – its rise, success, causes, consequences, etc. – if one doesn't understand that it *was* a wicked one, perhaps the most wicked that has ever existed. According to this objection, the most fruitful or instructive research questions are not, "Why did the Nazis believe *p*?," or "How did they come to believe *p*?" Rather, they are, "Why did the Nazis believe such morally terrible things

---

[10] For instance, Sturgeon (1988:245–246) proposes this counterfactual: "I do not believe that Hitler would have done all he did if he had not been morally depraved, nor, on the assumption that he was not depraved, can I think of any plausible alternative explanation for his doing those things. Nor is it plausible that we would all have believed he was morally depraved even if he hadn't been." See the extensive debate in metaethics about "moral explanations," kicked off by Harman (1977). The question is analogous to the question of symmetry and impartiality in the sociology of science (Bloor 1991). What's the difference, if any, between a sociological explanation of purported truths (e.g., some people's belief that the Earth is an oblate spheroid that revolves around the sun) and a sociological explanation of purported falsehoods (e.g., some people's belief that the Earth is a flat disk floating in an ocean or supported by a giant tortoise)? For an analogous question in the sociology of religion, see Berger (1967) and Porpora (2006).

as p?," "How could they possibly come to believe p?," "What were they blinded or misled by?," and so on. Therefore, someone devoid of moral understanding – a skeptic, a Martian, or a psychopath – might gather and master many empirical facts about the Nazi worldview, its genealogy, its supporters, the statistical predictors of NSDAP party affiliation, etc. But she wouldn't be able to fully understand the Nazi worldview as an empirical phenomenon. Its astonishing wickedness needs to be grasped not only by the moralist, the moral philosopher, the teacher, the judge, and indeed any responsible citizen, but by the empirical scientist as well. [11]

I won't take sides on this last issue here, because that would require an extensive analysis. My goal has been less ambitious. I've just tried to show that the problems of moral truth, reality, and explanation can't be quickly dismissed with a wave of the hand. While ultimately philosophical, they may have important sociological implications. Perhaps the sociologist who wishes to attain a complete explanation and full understanding of moral views, practices, and institutions can't reasonably bracket and ignore their content and/or their worth.

The Moral Brain

According to Randolph Nesse (2009:201), "[t]rying to understand morality has been a central human preoccupation for as far back as human history extends, and for very good reasons."

> So, for several thousands of years, philosophers have tried to find general moral principles. [...] Thousands of books chronicle the human quest for moral knowledge. Now, in a mere eye blink of history, the scene has changed. Completely new kinds of knowledge are being brought to bear. Neuroscience is investigating the brain mechanisms involved in moral decisions, moral actions, and responding to moral and immoral actions by self and others. Evolutionary biology is investigating why those brain mechanisms exist, how they give a selective advantage, and why there is genetic variation that influences moral tendencies. This is an exciting time for those of us curious about morality.

This is an exciting time indeed. Moral neuroscience or the neuroscience of morality is, as Walter Sinnott-Armstrong (2008:xiii) observes, a "mere baby." As all mere babies in the history of science, it comes equipped with an account about its novelty, how it supersedes earlier approaches, why it constitutes a major step forward, and so on. [12] Furthermore, as all babies, this one "is growing fast" (ibid.).

First, the amount of moral neuroscience research is growing fast. According to the editors of a recent book, *The Moral Brain*, "[a] stream of papers queues in the mailboxes of

---

[11] Admittedly, the skeptic would retort that the Nazis weren't really wicked. That's just some people's opinion. Hitler's opinion was that they were morally admirable folks. Recall, however, that Jones is assuming that the Nazis weren't really wicked as far as her scientific endeavor is concerned. Outside the office and the classroom, she does think they were. (This is obviously not an argument against the skeptic, though.)

[12] Moral neuroscience's account about itself relies on another common trope in the history of science: a subject or set of issues traditionally studied by philosophers strikes lucky and starts to be studied by scientists instead, gets promoted to scientific status, we obtain reliable empirical data instead of mere speculation, etc. Here's another example: "Debates on the moral nature of man have occupied the center of discussions among theologians, philosophers, and layman for millennia. Only recently have we been able to delve empirically into the neural organization of moral behavior" (Moll et al. 2003:299; see also Prehn and Heekeren 2009:129).

the editorial boards of high-ranking journals like *Science, Nature, Neuron,* and *NeuroImage.* Between 2000 and 2008, around a hundred papers on the moral brain appeared." As they put it, "[i]nvestigating the moral brain is hot" (Verplaetse et al. 2009:8, 20). Second, the amount of attention given to moral neuroscience research is growing fast, most notably by the media and funding agencies. People seem very excited to hear that there's a "link between morality and [the] brain's wiring" (*Wall Street Journal* 2007).

So, why is the moral brain so hot? What are the objectives and accomplishments of moral neuroscience? A review of its theoretical and empirical substance is beyond the scope of this short subsection. But probably Nesse's summary, just quoted above, is accurate: "Neuroscience is investigating the brain mechanisms involved in moral decisions, moral actions, and responding to moral and immoral actions by self and others." More generally, Moll and his colleagues identify one of the core tenets of the field: "converging lines of evidence from evolutionary biology, neuroscience and experimental psychology have shown that morality is grounded in the brain" (Moll et al. 2003:299).

Neuroscientists' job, then, is to figure out how exactly morality is "grounded in the brain." The most common methodological strategy has been to scan people's brains while they are presented with and try to respond to moral questions or dilemmas, or are presented with stimuli that are somehow related to morality (e.g., an image or a text), or something along these lines. (While brain scanners aren't presently portable, the same methodological strategy would apply, in principle, to moral action – e.g., a subject's actually helping a stranger on the street who appears to be in despair, as opposed to her saying that she would, or that one should.) Then, the neuroscientist typically considers what areas of her subjects' brains were "implicated" in making the judgment or decision (or "activated," "recruited," etc.). One main question here is how brain activation patterns are correlated with different kinds of stimuli and tasks and responses – e.g., whether a subject, presented with a moral dilemma, made a deontological or a utilitarian moral judgment. A second main line of research focuses on people with brain damage in areas that are hypothesized to be in some way involved in or to have to do with moral judgment. To give but one example of this work, a recent paper in *Nature* argues that "damage to the prefrontal cortex increases utilitarian moral judgements [sic]" (Koenigs et al. 2007).

How do these recent trends in the neuroscience of morality affect the sociology of morality? On a practical level, they threaten to make the sociology of morality irrelevant – and not only in the eyes of society at large, public opinion, and the polity, but also in the eyes of the scientific community, universities, and funding agencies. For instance, if the journals *Science* and *Nature* are a reliable indicator of what we think of as our best, most important, state-of-the-art scientific knowledge, then the current experts on morality are neuroscientists, psychologists, biologists, and primatologists. Surely not sociologists of morality.

On an epistemic level, the key problem is how to connect the arguments and theories of the neuroscience of morality and those of the sociology of morality. More specifically, can there be a neat division of academic labor, whereby both fields do their part, which can be integrated into a coherent body of scientific knowledge about morality? According to the standard view of science, this is how scientific progress and growth ought to work. And, incidentally, it would serve the practical interests of sociologists to participate in – and to be seen as participating in – a joint quest with neuroscientists for a new science of morality. (I sidestep the questions of whether sociologists should want this to happen, all things considered, and if so what kind of joint, "interdisciplinary" quest they should want to participate in – see Pippin 2009.)

Is this sort of integration feasible, then? Let's consider an example. Several psychologists, neuroscientists, and philosophers have argued that emotions help predict moral judgment and behavior. If one could reduce all emotions to objective brain states (which is, however, a very contentious matter), then these would be predictive of moral judgment and behavior. Whether or not this is possible, what does seem clear is that the manipulation of a person's emotions – e.g., making her experience disgust (Wheatley and Haidt 2005) – has an effect on her moral judgments.

RESPONSE A: BEST PREDICTORS. Sociologist *A* agrees with the psychological claim about the causal effects of emotions. However, she still argues that, overall, the best predictors of moral judgment and behavior are to be found among people's social attributes. For instance, their socioeconomic status, education, age, religion and religiosity, community participation, networks, and the like. That's why projects like the World Values Survey have been so influential. What's important for my analysis, though, is that these two perspectives aren't at all inconsistent. Given a particular case, outcome, or data set, one can investigate how neuroscience, psychology, and sociology contribute to the explanation: which variable wins the race, which effects aren't significant, which interactions are significant, etc. It so happens that investigations of this kind aren't very common – e.g., statistical models that integrate neuroscientific, psychological, and sociological data. But they could be (for a pre-neuroscience example, see Haidt et al. 1993; on a similar question regarding genetic and social data, see Alford et al. 2005, Freese 2008, Olson et al. 2001).

RESPONSE B: LEVEL OF ANALYSIS. Sociologist *B* makes a different kind of argument. She claims that a satisfactory scientific understanding of morality requires an understanding of some phenomena that *in principle* can't be captured by individual-level measurements – neither by brain scans, nor by large-scale surveys, nor by in-depth interviews. Take variation in blood and organ donation rates in different countries and states. As Kieran Healy (2006:2) shows, here an individual-level explanation of altruism fails: "to understand this world of goods we must get away form the character and motives of individual donors and look instead to the cultural contexts and organizational mechanisms that provide people with reasons and opportunities to give." Take responsibility. Carol Heimer and Lisa Staffen (1998:31) show that to explain responsibility one needs to attend to how "social control systems induce people to take responsibility by shaping incentive systems, setting standards, and shaping our sense of the social world we inhabit." Note that not only sociologists make this kind of argument. One of the conclusions of Henrich and colleagues' (2005:795, 809) study of game behavior in 15 small-scale societies is that "group-level differences in economic organization and the structure of social interactions explain a substantial portion of the behavioral variation across societies." By contrast, "[w]ith a few group-specific exceptions, nothing [they] measured about individuals other than their group membership (society, village, camp, or other subgroup membership) predicted experimental behavior." Similarly, situationist psychologists' predictions aren't based on individual-level facts, but on facts about the "situation." For example, whether subjects are standing outside a bakery that smells delicious (see, e.g., Ross and Nisbett 1991).

Sociologist *B*'s claims are consistent with the claim that there's a correlation between a particular person's action – that is, her body's moving in a particular way, so as to donate blood, or give some money to a homeless person on the street – and the objective states in which her brain is at that time. But the point remains that cultural and organizational variables are needed to explain and predict the incidence of altruism in a group or society. Individual motives, values, and brain states aren't. Furthermore, besides scientific understanding, there's the question of the practical and policy significance of research about morality. In order for it to have one at all, organizational and cultural factors must be understood and eventually manipulated. How neuroscience data and theories can help address societies' moral problems is not obvious — at least, an argument to this effect is needed.

This discrepancy between neuroscience and sociology can be stated in more general terms. Neuroscience's approach is individualistic. I'm not referring here to the intricate philosophical problem of psychological individualism (Fodor 1980; Wilson 1995, 2004). Instead, I'm making the simple methodological point that neuroscientists try to understand morality by looking at people's brains, one at a time. While experimental conditions are obviously different from natural settings – and this applies to all experimental research – the former might still get at the essence or core of human morality.

By contrast, a key sociological idea is that, as Durkheim ([1895]1982:129) puts it, "society is not the mere sum of individuals, but the system formed by their association represents a specific reality which has its own characteristics." To be sure, there's considerable disagreement about this matter within sociology. Still, that social reality, social facts, and social groups are *sui generis* is arguably what justifies the existence of sociology as a distinct discipline (as opposed to a subfield of psychology that uses larger, statistically representative samples of individuals). At a minimum, sociology's ontology contains such things as culture and institutions, rules and networks, which have independent effects, permit certain social things and preclude certain others, and so on.

RESPONSE C: THICK MORALITY. As described thus far, this level-of-analysis discrepancy doesn't imply that the sociology and the neuroscience of morality are logically inconsistent or contradictory. For certain purposes, the best policy is to examine individuals' brains, one at a time, and then add up the data. For certain other purposes, the best policy is to examine individuals' utterances and actions, one at a time, and then add up the data. For yet other purposes, the best policy is to examine social- or group-level phenomena and processes, such as organizational configurations and the cultural availability and legitimacy of reasons and accounts. But none of these lines of research questions the truth or validity, much less the coherence or intelligibility, of the others. They just make claims as to where it's fruitful and where it's fruitless to look for answers to particular research questions. While it's not clear how to integrate these findings and theories, at least one might say that they focus on different aspects of morality, or bring to light different things that are worth knowing about morality.

Yet, sociologist C may press the following objection against the neuroscience of morality's individualism. Much of morality *presupposes* a host of social- or group-level facts. They don't merely shape morality in various ways; they are its conditions of possibility or intelligibility. To clarify what this means, let's compare morality to (a traditional view of) the primary emotions. It's been often argued that the latter are independent of language, society, and culture. Take fear. You see a predator approaching, and automatically your heartbeat increases, you secrete epinephrine and norepinephrine, etc. No doubt, there are "cultural differences in how emotions are expressed and interpreted" (Turner and Stets 2005:11). But fear *itself*, the natural kind, has nothing to do with these expressions and interpretations. As for language, "fear" is the string of sounds that English speakers happen to use to refer to the experience. Nothing more. The primary emotions are universal and have universal brain correlates. [13]

Consider now the moral judgments, "He's a materialistic person," or "That's a humane attitude." First, judgments about materialism or humanness presuppose certain social, economic, institutional, and cultural facts. The argument here is not that these facts have causal effects on moral judgment – e.g., given a concept of materialism or humanness, different people and groups apply the predicates "is materialistic" or "is humane" differently. Rather, the argument is that if those facts didn't obtain, judgments about materialism or humanness would have no sense. They would be downright unintelligible. Second, judgments about materialism or humanness can't be decomposed into two: a description of a kind of person or action, and a good or bad evaluation of it, on top of the description, as it were. That is, the judgment can't be recast as: "performing that kind of action or being that kind of person is bad, wrong, or ought not to be done." This is because the description has the evaluation built into it (Putnam 1990, 1992, 2002). Such is the nature of "thick ethical concepts" – e.g., integrity, piety, cruelty, rudeness, exploitation, and fanaticism – in contradistinction to "thin ethical concepts" – e.g., right and wrong, good and bad (Williams 1985). Because of these two reasons, thick morality constitutes a serious obstacle to the most ambitious goals of moral neuroscience. For it's unclear what exactly we could learn about it by looking at brain correlates of judgments – what would these data mean? It's also dubious that thick morality can be meaningfully said to be hard-wired, the way the primary emotions are said to. What is more, there are problems for intercultural research, because not all societies, past and present, have had the same thick concepts.

A moral neuroscientist may respond that she concerns herself with thin moral concepts only: right and wrong, "acceptable," "permissible," "appropriate," "okay," etc. But this raises two difficulties. On the one hand, it seems that, under any reasonable definition, morality comprises both thick and thin. If this is so, then research about thin morality doesn't license conclusions about morality *tout court*. On the other hand, some people would argue that thin moral concepts have social-level presuppositions as well. The issue here would be whether thin moral concepts are more like the primary emotions or more like thick moral concepts.

I won't try to address these questions here. Nor will I try to argue for or against sociologist *C*'s objection. Is the intelligibility of neuroscience data, findings, and theories contingent on a particular set of cultural and institutional facts? If one considers thick rather than thin morality, what do brain activation data tell us, exactly? As in the previous subsection, my goal has been more modest. I've simply suggested some challenges to the integration of sociological and neuroscientific knowledge about morality, which can be neither ignored nor easily dismissed.

WHAT'S NEXT

I've argued that the sociology of morality is an old project. Martineau, Durkheim, and Lévy-Bruhl, each in their own way, proposed a science that could describe and explain moral variation. In France, the sociology of morality eventually became a well-established field, led

---

[13] I'm not interested in evaluating these arguments here, but they are far from unproblematic – see, e.g., Barrett (2006), Barrett et al. (2007), Lindquist et al. (2006), Lindquist and Barrett (2008).

by Durkheim's students and especially under Georges Gurvitch's leadership. After Gurvitch's death, the "sociologie de la vie morale" was rechristened "sociologie de l'éthique" at the Centre de Sociologie de l'Éthique, directed by François-André Isambert and subsequently by Paul Ladrière (Bateman-Novaes et al. 2000, Gurvitch 1960, Isambert et al. 1978, Ladrière 2001, Pharo 2004:147–153). [14] In the United States, by contrast, the sociology of morality never really took off until now.

In this conclusion I wish to very briefly discuss some tasks that lie ahead for this new sociology of morality that is presently taking off. While several disciplines can contribute to our understanding of morality, what *unique* contributions can sociologists make drawing on their substantive knowledge and methodological strengths? The following are six issues that, I think, sociologists are uniquely qualified to address:

(1) Organizations, organizational arrangements, and social networks: their effects on moral actions, views, and society-level outcomes.

(2) Moral reasons and accounts. Sometimes people must give reasons and accounts to others – neighbors, employers, spouses, customers, and even random strangers they interact with. Sometimes people give reasons to themselves. Psychologists such as Haidt (2001) have shown that sometimes these reasons and accounts don't explain individuals' judgments (and presumably behavior) at all. But some *other* times they very likely do. Moreover, they no doubt help explain moral outcomes at the collective level: small groups, big groups, and whole societies. Now, given a particular social and cultural context, some reasons and accounts are more legitimate and better regarded than others. Indeed, there's much variation across time and place in the reasons and accounts that are available at all (that is, what counts as a reason, what can occur to people, etc.). Sociologists should identify them and find out what their effects are.

(3) Historical sociology of thick moral concepts (cf. Hacking 2002; Somers 1995). I've argued that morality has thin and thick elements. As examples of thick concepts I mentioned materialism, integrity, piety, cruelty, humanness, rudeness, exploitation, and fanaticism. But there are hundreds of others, and not all societies and cultures share all of them. Thus, a historical sociologist may want to ask how particular thick concepts – as well as the practices and institutions based on them – came about in particular places and times. To what degree do they overlap across societies and cultures? What practical difference do they make?

(4) Methodology: better samples. Experimental researchers tend to use small samples of subjects, and for the most part of US undergraduates at research universities (cf. Henrich et al. 2004). While their practical reasons for doing so are understandable, one still needs large, representative samples to control for confounding factors and reliably generalize to populations.

(5) Methodology: real-life moral actions, views, institutions, and practices. Because of its very nature, morality is inherently tied to practice. While experimental and survey

---

[14] In 1995 the center became the Centre de Recherche Sens, Éthique et Société and the new director Patrick Pharo. The next directors were Simone Bateman and currently Edwige Rude-Antoine. Morality has also been a central theme for Luc Boltanski, Laurent Thévenot, and their Groupe de Sociologie Politique et Morale.

research are surely valuable, for some purposes natural-setting and participant observation are unavoidable. Data exclusively on what people say they would do won't
do. Nor will data exclusively on what they say one ought to do.

(6) Finally, the sociology of morality can provide an empirical account of people's moral
life. Much research on morality implicitly reduces it to discrete instances of judgment or decision. The problem is typically set up as follows. There is one person,
who has certain attributes – things like 14 years of formal education, damage to
the prefrontal cortex, being a 20-year-old woman, or having just been grossed out.
That's time t_0. Then comes the stimulus at t_1. And then this person makes a choice
at t_2 – say, cooperate or defect, utter the words "that's acceptable" or "that's inappropriate," press one or another button, and so on. This methodological setup may
be useful for certain purposes, but it does load the theoretical dice. To begin with,
some essential moral issues are thereby left out of the picture – for example, what
would it be for my life to go well, what kind of person I ought to be, and what I
find morally admirable, saintly, or heroic (supererogatory as opposed to permissible
and obligatory). More generally, there seems to be much more to a moral life than a
series of discrete judgments or decisions made in reaction to stimuli. Sociological
methods and the sociological perspective are well suited to avoid this kind of
reductionism.

REFERENCES

Abend, G. 2008. "Two Main Problems in the Sociology of Morality." *Theory and Society* 37(2):87–125.
Alexander, J. C. 2002. "On the Social Construction of Moral Universals: The 'Holocaust' from Mass Murder to
   Trauma Drama." *European Journal of Social Theory* 5(1):5–86.
Alford, J., C. Funk, and J. R. Hibbing. 2005. "Are Political Orientations Genetically Transmitted?" *American Political
   Science Review* 99(2):153–167.
Barrett, L. F. 2006. "Are emotions natural kinds?" *Perspectives on Psychological Science* 1:28–58.
Barrett, L. F., K. Lindquist, and M. Gendron. 2007. "Language as a context for emotion perception." *Trends in
   Cognitive Sciences* 11:327–332.
Bateman-Novaes, S., R. Ogien, and P. Pharo, eds. 2000. *Raison pratique et sociologie de l'éthique*. Paris: CNRS.
Bauman, Z. 1989. *Modernity and the Holocaust*. Ithaca: Cornell University Press.
Bayet, A. 1905. *La morale scientifique*. Paris: F. Alcan.
Bayet, A. 1925. *La science des faits moraux*. Paris: F. Alcan.
Belot, G. 1921 (1907). *Études de morale positive*. 2 volumes. Paris: F. Alcan.
Berger, P. L. 1967. *The Sacred Canopy: Elements of a Sociological Theory of Religion*. Garden City: Doubleday.
Bloor, D. 1991 (1976). *Knowledge and Social Imagery*. 2nd ed. Chicago: University of Chicago Press.
Bouglé, C. C. A. 1922. *Leçons de sociologie sur l'évolution des valeurs*. Paris: A. Colin.
Brandt, R. 1954. *Hopi Ethics: A Theoretical Analysis*. Chicago: University of Chicago Press.
Calhoun, C. 1991. "Morality, Identity, and Historical Explanation: Charles Taylor on the Sources of the Self."
   Sociological Theory 9(2):232–263.
Dewey, J. 1898. "Evolution and Ethics." *The Monist* 8(3):321–341.
Duhem, P. M. M. 1991 (1906). *The Aim and Structure of Physical Theory*. Translated by Philip P. Wiener. Princeton:
   Princeton University Press.
Durkheim, É. 1975 (1887). "La Science positive de la morale en Allemagne" PP. 267–343 in *Textes. 1. Éléments d'une
   théorie sociale,* edited by V. Karady. Paris: Éditions de Minuit.
Durkheim, É. 1993 (1887). *Ethics and the Sociology of Morals*. Translated with an introduction by Robert T. Hall.
   Buffalo: Prometheus Books.
Durkheim, É. 1984 (1893). *The Division of Labor in Society*. Translated by W. D. Halls. With an Introduction by
   Lewis A. Coser. New York: Free Press.

Durkheim, É. 1982 (1895). *The Rules of Sociological Method and Selected Texts on Sociology and its Method.* Edited with an introduction by Steven Lukes. Translated by W. D. Halls. New York: Free Press.

Durkheim, É. 1979 (1904). "Review 'Lévy-Bruhl, *La Morale et la science des moeurs*, Alcan, Paris, 1903'." PP. 29–33 in *Durkheim: Essays on Morals and Education.* Translated by H. L. Sutcliffe, edited by W. S. F. Pickering. London: Routledge & Kegan Paul.

Durkheim, É. 1979 (1907). "Review 'Westermarck, *The Origin and Development of the Moral Ideas*, vol. I, London, 1906'." PP. 40–51 in *Durkheim: Essays on Morals and Education.* Translated by H. L. Sutcliffe, edited by W. S. F. Pickering. London: Routledge & Kegan Paul.

Durkheim, É. 1979 (1920). "Introduction to ethics." PP. 79–96 in *Durkheim: Essays on Morals and Education.* Translated by H. L. Sutcliffe, edited by W. S. F. Pickering. London: Routledge & Kegan Paul.

Durkheim, É. 1978 (1920). "Introduction to Morality." PP. 191–202 in *Emile Durkheim on Institutional Analysis.* Edited, Translated and with an Introduction by Mark Traugott. Chicago: The University of Chicago Press.

Durkheim, É. [1906]1974. "Replies to Objections." PP. 63–79 in Durkheim, É. 1974. *Sociology and Philosophy.* Translated by D. F. Pocock. With an Introduction by J. G. Peristiany. New York: Free Press.

Fauconnet, P. 1920. *La responsabilité; étude de sociologie.* Paris: F. Alcan.

Fields, K. E. 2005. "What Difference Does Translation Make? *Les Formes élémentaires de la vie religieuse* in French and English." PP. 160–180 in *The Cambridge Companion to Durkheim*, edited by J. C. Alexander, and P. Smith. Cambridge: Cambridge University Press.

Fine, A. 1998. "The Viewpoint of No-One in Particular." *Proceedings and Addresses of the American Philosophical Association* 72(2):9–20.

Fodor, J. 1980. "Methodological Solipsism Considered as a Research Strategy in Cognitive Science." *Behavioral and Brain Sciences* 3:63–73.

Freese, J. 2008. "Genetics and the Social Science Explanation of Individual Outcomes." *American Journal of Sociology* 114:S1–S35.

Frickel, S., and N. Gross. 2005. "A General Theory of Scientific/Intellectual Movements." *American Sociological Review* 70(2):204–232.

Goode, E., and N. Ben-Yehuda. 1994. *Moral Panics: The Social Construction of Deviance.* Oxford; Cambridge: Blackwell.

Gurvitch, G. 1937. *Morale théorique et science des moeurs.* Paris: Presses Universitaires de France.

Gurvitch, G. 1960. "Sociologie de la Vie Morale." PP. 137–172 in *Traité de sociologie* (tome second), edited by G. Gurvitch. Paris: Presses Universitaires de France.

Hacking 2002. *Historical Ontology.* Cambridge: Harvard University Press.

Haidt, J. 2001. "The Emotional Dog and Its Rational Tail: A Social Intuitionist Approach to Moral Judgment." *Psychological Review* 108(4):814–834.

Haidt, J, S. H. Koller, and M. G. Dias. 1993. "Affect, Culture, and Morality, or is It Wrong to Eat Your Dog?" *Journal of Personality and Social Psychology* 65(4):613–628.

Hall, R. T. 1993. "Introduction." PP. 11–53 in Durkheim, Émile. [1887] 1993. *Ethics and the Sociology of Morals.* Buffalo: Prometheus Books.

Harman, G. 1977. *The Nature of Morality: An Introduction to Ethics.* New York: Oxford University Press.

Harman, G., and J. J. Thomson. 1996. *Moral Relativism and Moral Objectivity.* Cambridge: Blackwell.

Healy, K. 2006. *Last Best Gifts: Altruism and the Market for Human Blood and Organs.* Chicago: University of Chicago Press.

Heimer, C. A., and L. R. Staffen. 1998. *For the Sake of the Children: The Social Organization of Responsibility in the Hospital and the Home.* Chicago: University of Chicago Press.

Henrich, J., R. Boyd, S. Bowles, C. Camerer, E. Fehr, and H. Gintis, eds. 2004. *Foundations of Human Sociality: Economic Experiments and Ethnographic Evidence from Fifteen Small-Scale Societies.* Oxford: Oxford University Press.

Henrich, J., R. Boyd, S. Bowles, C. Camerer, E. Fehr, H. Gintis, R. McElreath, M. Alvard, A. Barr, J. Ensminger, N. Smith Henrich, K. Hill, F. Gil-White, M. Gurven, F. W. Marlowe, J. Q. Patton, and D. Tracer. 2005. "'Economic Man' in Cross-Cultural Perspective: Behavioral Experiments in 15 Small-Scale Societies." *Behavioral and Brain Sciences* 28:795–855.

Hill, M. R. 1989. "Introduction to the Transaction Edition: Empiricism and Reason in Harriet Martineau's Sociology." PP. xv–lx in: Martineau, Harriet. [1838] 1989. *How to Observe Morals and Manners.* New Burnswick and Oxford: Transaction Publishers.

Hobhouse, L. T. 1906. *Morals in Evolution: A Study in Comparative Ethics.* London: Chapman and Hall.

Hoecker-Drysdale, S. 1992. *Harriet Martineau: First Woman Sociologist.* Oxford and New York: Berg.

Horton, R. 1993. "Lévy-Bruhl, Durkheim and the Scientific Revolution." PP. 63–104 in *Patterns of Thought in Africa and the West: Essays on Magic, Religion and Science.* Cambridge: Cambridge University Press.

Huxley, T. H. 1893. *Evolution and Ethics, Delivered in the Sheldonian Theatre, May 18, 1893.* London; New York: Macmillan & Co.

Isambert, F.-A. 1990. "Durkheim: une science de la morale pour une morale laïque." *Archives des Sciences Sociales des Religions* 69(1):129–146.

Isambert, F.-A., P. Ladrière, and J.-P. Terrenoire. 1978. "Pour une sociologie de l'éthique." *Revue Française de Sociologie* 19(3):323–339.

Jackall, R. 1988. *Moral Mazes: The World of Corporate Managers.* New York: Oxford University Press.

Joyce, R. 2006a. *The Evolution of Morality.* Cambridge: MIT Press.

Joyce, R. 2006b "Is Human Morality Innate?" PP. 257–279 in *The Innate Mind, Volume 2: Culture and Cognition,* edited by P. Carruthers, S. Laurence, and S. Stich. New York: Oxford University Press.

Koenigs, M., L. Young, R. Adolphs, D. Tranel, F. Cushman, M. Hauser, and A. Damasio. 2007. "Damage to the Prefrontal Cortex Increases Utilitarian Moral Judgements." *Nature* 446(7138):908–911.

Ladrière, P. 2001. *Pour une sociologie de l'éthique.* Paris: Presses Universitaires de France.

Lecky, W. E. H. 1884 (1869). *History of European Morals from Augustus to Charlemagne.* In Two Volumes. 6th ed. London: Longmans, Green, and co.

Lengermann, P. M., and J. Niebrugge. 2001. "The Meaning of 'Things': Theory and Method in Harriet Martineau's *How to Observe Morals and Manners* (1838) and Émile Durkheim's *The Rules of Sociological Method* (1895)." PP. 75–97 in: *Harriet Martineau: Theoretical and Methodological Perspectives,* edited by M. R. Hill, and S. Hoecker-Drysdale. New York and London: Routledge.

Leroux, E. 1930. "Ethical Thought in France Since the War." *International Journal of Ethics* 40(2):145–178.

Lévy-Bruhl, L. 1905 (1903). *Ethics and Moral Science.* Translated by Elizabeth Lee. London: Archibald Constable & Co.

Lindquist, K., L. F. Barrett,, E. Bliss-Moreau, and J. A. Russell. 2006. "Language and the perception of emotion." *Emotion* 6:125–138.

Lindquist, K., and L. F. Barrett. 2008. "Constructing emotion: The experience of fear as a conceptual act." *Psychological Science* 19:898–903.

Loeb, D. 2005. "Moral Explanations of Moral Beliefs." *Philosophy and Phenomenological Research* LXX(1): 193–208.

Lukes, S. 1973. *Émile Durkheim, His Life and Work: A Historical and Critical Study.* London: Allen Lane.

Lukes, S. 2008. *Moral Relativism.* London: Profile Books.

Mackie, J. L. 1977. *Ethics: Inventing Right and Wrong.* Harmondsworth, New York: Penguin.

Martineau, H. 1837. *Society in America. In Three Volumes.* London: Saunders and Otley.

Martineau, H. 1838. *How to Observe. Morals and Manners.* London: Charles Knight and Co.

Merllié, D. 2004. "La sociologie de la morale est-elle soluble dans la philosophie ? La réception de *La morale et la science des moeurs.*" *Revue Française de Sociologie* 45(3):415–440.

Moll, J., R. de Oliveira-Souza, and P. J. Eslinger. 2003. "Morals and the Human Brain: A Working Model." *NeuroReport* 14(3):299–305.

Moody-Adams, M. M. 1997. *Fieldwork in Familiar Places: Morality, Culture, and Philosophy.* Cambridge: Harvard University Press.

Nagel, T. 1986. *The View from Nowhere.* New York: Oxford University Press.

Nesse, R. 2009. "How Can Evolution and Neuroscience Help Us Understand Moral Capacities? PP. 201–209 in *The Moral Brain: Essays on the Evolutionary and Neuroscientific Aspects of Morality,* edited by J. Verplaetse, J. De Schrijver, S. Vanneste, and J. Braeckman. Dordrecht: Springer.

Olson, J. M., P. A. Vernon, J. Aitken Harris, and K. L. Jang. 2001. "The Heritability of Attitudes: A Study of Twins." *Journal of Personality and Social Psychology* 80(6):845–860.

Ossowska, M. 1970. *Social Determinants of Moral Ideas.* Philadelphia: University of Pennsylvania Press.

Pharo, P. 2004. *Morale et sociologie: le sens et les valeurs entre nature et culture.* Paris: Gallimard.

Pickering, W. S. F. 1979. "Introduction." PP. 3–28 in Durkheim, Émile. 1979. *Essays on Morals and Education.* Translated by H. L. Sutcliffe, edited by W. S. F. Pickering. London: Routledge & Kegan Paul.

Pippin, R. B. 2009. "Natural and Normative." *Daedalus* Summer 2009:35–43.

Porpora, D. V. 2006. "Methodological Atheism, Methodological Agnosticism, and Religious Experience." *Journal for the Theory of Social Behaviour* 36(1):57–75.

Prehn, K., and H. R. Heekeren. 2009. "Moral Judgment and the Brain: A Functional Approach to the Question of Emotion and Cognition in Moral Judgment Integrating Psychology, Neuroscience and Evolutionary Biology." PP. 129–154 in *The Moral Brain: Essays on the Evolutionary and Neuroscientific Aspects of Morality,* edited by J. Verplaetse, J. De Schrijver, S. Vanneste, and J. Braeckman. Dordrecht: Springer.

Prinz, J. 2007. *The Emotional Construction of Morals.* Oxford and New York: Oxford University Press.

Prinz, J. 2008. "Is Morality Innate?" PP. 367–406 in *Moral Psychology, Volume 1: The Evolution of Morality: Adaptations and Innateness*, edited by W. Sinnott-Armstrong. Cambridge: MIT Press.

Putnam, H. 1981. *Reason, Truth, and History*. Cambridge; New York: Cambridge University Press.

Putnam, H. 1990. "Objectivity and the Science/Ethics Distinction." PP. 163–178 in *Realism with a human face*. Cambridge: Harvard University Press.

Putnam, H. 1992. "Bernard Williams and the Absolute Conception of the World." PP. 80–107 in *Renewing philosophy*. Cambridge: Harvard University Press.

Putnam, H. 2002. *The Collapse of the Fact/Value Dichotomy and Other Essays*. Cambridge: Harvard University Press.

Putnam, H. 2004. *Ethics Without Ontology*. Cambridge: Harvard University Press.

Quine, W. V. O. 1953. "Two Dogmas of Empiricism." PP. 20–46 in *From a Logical Point of View*. Cambridge: Harvard University Press.

Rachels, J. 2001. "The Challenge of Cultural Relativism." PP. 53–65 in *Moral Relativism: A Reader*, edited by P. K. Moser, and T. L. Carson. New York: Oxford University Press.

Renouvier, C. 2002 (1869). *Science de la morale*. 2 vols. Paris: Fayard.

Ross, L., and R. E. Nisbett, 1991. *The Person and the Situation: Perspectives of Social Psychology*. New York: McGraw-Hill.

Scanlon, T. M. 2009. *Being Realistic About Reasons*. 2009 Locke Lectures. Oxford University.

Sidgwick, H. 1880. "Mr. Spencer's Ethical System." *Mind* 5(18):216–226.

Simmel, G. 1989–1991 (1891–1892). *Einleitung in die Moralwissenschaft: Eine Kritik der ethischen Grundbegriffe*. Frankfurt am Main: Suhrkamp.

Simpson, G. 1933. "Preface to the Translation." PP. vii–xi in: Durkheim, Émile. [1893] 1933. *The Division of Labor in Society*. Translated by George Simpson. Glencoe: Free Press.

Sinnott-Armstrong, W. 2008. "Introduction." PP. xiii–xix in *Moral Psychology, Volume 3: The Neuroscience of Morality: Emotion, Brain Disorders, and Development*. Cambridge: MIT Press.

Small, A. W. 1905. *General Sociology: An Exposition of the Main Development in Sociological Theory from Spencer to Ratzenhofer*. Chicago: University of Chicago Press.

Small, A. W. 1910. *The Meaning of Social Science*. Chicago: The University of Chicago Press.

Somers, M. R. 1995. "What's Political or Cultural about Political Culture and the Public Sphere? Toward an Historical Sociology of Concept Formation." *Sociological Theory* 13(2):113–144.

Spencer, H. 1879. *The Data of Ethics*. New York: D. Appleton and company.

Spencer, H. 1881. "Replies to Criticisms on the Data of Ethics." *Mind* 6(21):82–98.

Stephen, L. 1882. *The Science of Ethics*. New York: G. P. Putnam's sons.

Sturgeon, N. 1988 (1984). "Moral Explanations." PP. 229–255 in *Essays on Moral Realism*, edited by G. Sayre-McCord. Ithaca and London: Cornell University Press.

Sturgeon, N. 1998. "Thomson Against Moral Explanations." *Philosophy and Phenomenological Research* 58(1): 199–206.

Sutcliffe, H. L. 1979. "The Translations." P. viii in *Durkheim: Essays on Morals and Education*. Translated by H. L. Sutcliffe, edited by W. S. F. Pickering. London: Routledge & Kegan Paul.

Sutherland, A. 1898. *The Origin and Growth of the Moral Instinct*. London: Longmans, Green, and Co.

Thomas, R. 2006. "The Intellectual Milieu of Herodotus." PP. 60–75 in *The Cambridge Companion to Herodotus*, edited by C. Dewald, and J. Marincola. Cambridge: Cambridge University Press.

Thomson, J. J. 1998. "Reply to Critics." *Philosophy and Phenomenological Research* 58(1):215–222.

Tufts, J. H. 1912. "Recent Discussions of Moral Evolution." *Harvard Theological Review* 5(2):155–179.

Turner, J. H., and J. E. Stets. 2005. *The Sociology of Emotions*. Cambridge; New York: Cambridge University Press.

Turner, S. P. 1993. "Introduction: Reconnecting the Sociologist to the Moralist." PP. 1–22 in *Émile Durkheim: Sociologist and Moralist*, edited by S. P. Turner. London: Routledge.

Verplaetse, J., J. Braeckman, and J. De Schrijver. 2009. "Introduction." PP. 1–43 in *The Moral Brain: Essays on the Evolutionary and Neuroscientific Aspects of Morality*, edited by J. Verplaetse, J. De Schrijver, S. Vanneste, and J. Braeckman. Dordrecht: Springer.

Wall Street Journal. 2007. "Scientists Draw Link Between Morality and Brain's Wiring." May 11, 2007, p. B1.

Watts Miller, W. 1996. *Durkheim, Morals and Modernity*. London: UCL Press.

Wheatley, T., and J. Haidt. 2005. "Hypnotically Induced Disgust Makes Moral Judgments More Severe." *Psychological Science* 16:780–784.

Williams, B. 1985. *Ethics and the Limits of Philosophy*. Cambridge: Harvard University Press.

Wilson, R. A. 1995. *Cartesian Psychology and Physical Minds: Individualism and the Sciences of the Mind*. Cambridge: Cambridge University Press.

Wilson, R. A. 2004. *Boundaries of the Mind: The Individual in the Fragile Sciences*. Cambridge; New York: Cambridge University Press.

Wundt, W. 1886. *Ethik: Eine Untersuchung der Thatsachen und Gesetze des sittlichen Lebens*. Stuttgart: Verlag von Ferdinand Enke.

Subject Index

S. Hitlin, S. Vaisey (eds.), *Handbook of the Sociology of Morality*,
Handbooks of Sociology and Social Research, DOI 10.1007/978-1-4419-6896-8,
© Springer Science+Business Media, LLC 2010

Lightning Source UK Ltd.
Milton Keynes UK
UKOW012315071212

203348UK00002B/14/P